W9-BZG-859

WITHDRAWN FROM
MACALESTER COLLEGE
LIBRARY

World Philosophers
and
Their Works

World Philosophers and Their Works

Volume II

Freud, Sigmund — Oakeshott, Michael

EDITOR
John K. Roth
Claremont McKenna College

MANAGING EDITOR
Christina J. Moose

PROJECT EDITOR
Rowena Wildin

SALEM PRESS, INC.
Pasadena, California   Hackensack, New Jersey

Managing Editor: Christina J. Moose   *Project Editor:* Rowena Wildin
Research Supervisor: Jeffry Jensen   *Research Assistant:* Jun Ohnuki
Acquisitions Editor: Mark Rehn   *Production Editor:* Cynthia Beres
Photograph Editor: Karrie Hyatt

Copyright © 2000, by Salem Press, Inc.
All rights in this book are reserved. No part of this work may be used or reproduced in any manner whatsoever or transmitted in any form or by any means, electronic or mechanical, including photocopy, recording, or any information storage and retrieval system, without written permission from the copyright owners except in the case of brief quotations embodied in critical articles and reviews. For information, address the publisher, Salem Press, Inc., P.O. Box 50062, Pasadena, California 91115.

Some of the essays in this work, which have been updated, originally appeared in the following Salem Press sets: *World Philosophy: Essay-Reviews of 225 Major Works, Great Lives from History: Ancient and Medieval Series, Great Lives from History: Renaissance to 1900 Series, Great Lives from History: Twentieth Century Series, Great Lives from History: British and Commonwealth Series, Great Lives from History: American Women Series, Critical Survey of Literary Theory.*

Library of Congress Cataloging-in-Publication Data
World philosophers and their works / editor, John K. Roth.
   p. cm.
   Includes bibliographical references and indexes.
   ISBN 0-89356-878-3 (set) — ISBN 0-89356-879-1 (v. 1) — ISBN 0-89356-880-5 (v. 2) — ISBN 0-89356-881-3 (v. 3)
   1. Philosophers — Biography — Encyclopedias. I. Roth, John K.
B104.W67 2000
109—dc21   99-055143

First printing

PRINTED IN THE UNITED STATES OF AMERICA

Contents

Volume II

Contents

Sigmund Freud

Freud was the founder of psychoanalysis and as such has had a tremendous impact on contemporary thought and popular culture by baring the irrational and subconscious roots of much human action.

Principal philosophical works: *Die Traumdeutung*, 1900 (*The Interpretation of Dreams*, 1913); *Zur Psychopathologie des Alltagslebens*, 1904 (*The Psychopathology of Everyday Life*, 1914); *Drei Abhandlungen zur Sexualtheorie*, 1905 (*Three Essays on the Theory of Sexuality*, 1910); *Der Witz und seine Beziehung zum Unbewussten*, 1905 (*Wit and Its Relation to the Unconscious*, 1905); *Eine Kindheitserinnerung des Leonardo da Vinci*, 1910 (*Leonardo da Vinci: A Psychosexual Study of an Infantile Reminiscence*, 1916); *Totem und Tabu*, 1913 (*Totem and Taboo*, 1918); *Vorlesungen zur Einführung in die Psychoanalyse*, 1917 (*A General Introduction to Psychoanalysis*, 1920); *Jenseits des Lustprinzips*, 1920 (*Beyond the Pleasure Principle*, 1922); *Massenpsychologie und Ich-Analyse*, 1921 (*Group Psychology and the Analysis of the Ego*, 1922); *Das Ich und das Es*, 1923 (*The Ego and the Id*, 1926); *Hemmung, Symptom, und Angst*, 1926 (*Inhibitions, Symptoms, and Anxiety*, 1936); *Die Frage der Laienanalyse*, 1926 (*The Question of Lay Analysis*, 1947); *Die Zukunft einer Illusion*, 1927 (*The Future of an Illusion*, 1926); *Das Unbehagen in der Kultur*, 1930 (*Civilization and Its Discontents*, 1930); *Der Mann Moses und die monotheistische Religion*, 1938 (*Moses and Monotheism*, 1939); *Abriss der Psychoanalyse*, 1940 (*An Outline of Psychoanalysis*, 1949)

Born: May 6, 1856; Freiberg, Moravia, Austrian Empire (now Příbor, Czech Republic)
Died: September 23, 1939; London, England

Early Life

Sigmund Freud was born on May 6, 1856, in Freiberg, a small Moravian town within the Austrian Empire. The infant, who was named Sigismund Schlomo, was the son of a somewhat ineffectual and rather poor, nonreligious Jewish wool merchant, Jacob Freud, and his young and energetic third wife, Amalia Nathansohn. Young Freud had two half brothers, who were older than his mother, and a nephew, simultaneously his best friend and archrival, who was his senior by a year. Freud's later recall of his ambivalent feelings toward these relationships within his family served as the basis for the discovery and elaboration of many of his psychoanalytic theories.

In 1860, Freud's family, after a brief stay in Leipzig, settled in Leopoldstadt, the old Jewish section of Vienna. There, the family's poverty was exacerbated by the birth of seven children between 1857 and 1866. Such hardships in Vienna, in contrast to romantic memories of Freiberg, left in Freud an ambivalence toward the city, which he loved but in which he never felt comfortable. The period of liberal ascendancy in Vienna, which accompanied his youth and early adulthood, was both a stimulation and an encouragement. Despite the family's relative poverty, Freud, always the favorite of whom great things were expected, was pampered. By the time Freud entered the University of Vienna in 1873 to study medicine, his family's fortunes had improved.

Freud began his university studies shortly after a stock market crash. In the wave of anti-Semitism that followed the collapse, Freud, although intensely antireligious, became acutely aware of his own Jewishness, an experience that prompted the development of a critical independence. Freud was drawn to medicine as a means of channeling his insatiable curiosity and love of nature along more empirical and less

Sigmund Freud. *(Library of Congress)*

speculative lines. The normal five-year course was extended by Freud's broad curiosity and fascination for research, and he did not receive his degree until 1881. Among the most influential of his professors was the physiologist Ernst Brücke, a positivist who aspired to a complete understanding of humankind through scientific investigation.

Freud spent another year in Brücke's laboratory before taking a junior position at Vienna's General Hospital to gain the clinical experience necessary for a medical practice. The compelling reason for Freud's beginning his practical career was the twenty-one-year-old daughter of a prominent Hamburg Jewish family, Martha Bernays, whom he met in April, 1882, and to whom he became engaged in June. In October, 1885, Freud went to Paris for several months to study under Jean-Martin Charcot at the Salpêtrière Clinic. Freud was strongly influenced by the personality and skill of Charcot, who indicated the

psychological rather than organic origins of hysteria and demonstrated the therapeutic value of hypnosis. It was Charcot who nudged Freud down the path, which had already attracted him, to psychology. A particular legacy of Charcot was a dedication to theory rooted in observable facts.

Life's Work

In April, 1886, Freud, having returned to Vienna, established his private medical practice and, in September, married Bernays. The first of six children was born in October, 1887. Dissatisfied with the results of hypnosis in the treatment of his neurotic patients and influenced by his friend and mentor Josef Breuer, Freud turned to the "talking cure" as a means of evoking a catharsis in his patients. In 1895, Freud and Breuer published *Studien über Hysterie* (*Studies in Hysteria*, 1936), the founding statement of psychoanalysis, in which they described their success with this technique.

Freud's professional and personal relationship with Breuer was ruptured, as were those with a number of subsequent associates, because of theoretical and personal differences. By the mid-1890's, Freud was convinced that problems in sexual development were the dominant factor in neuroses. He particularly emphasized the importance of infantile sexuality and what he called the Oedipus complex. Although he rejected his earlier belief that neuroses were rooted in the sexual abuse of children, Freud unflinchingly stressed the role that early sexual desires, repressed into the unconscious, play in the formation of the personality. He developed the technique of analyzing dreams to extract these childhood memories from the unconscious mind.

In 1897, Freud undertook a pioneering analysis of himself, using dream analysis. His closest intellectual associate during this period was the German physician Wilhelm Fliess. Freud used Fliess as a sounding board for his ideas and for emotional support while developing his revolutionary ideas. As their friendship was approaching its end, Freud published the results of his self-analysis and theory on dreams. *The Interpretation of Dreams*, published in 1900, was Freud's most significant work. In it, Freud demonstrated that dreams serve as a window to the unconscious, and by interpreting dreams, the unconscious determinants of behavior could be understood and addressed. His exposition of the notion of infantile sexuality and its impact on the personality was published as *Three Essays on the Theory of Sexuality* in 1905. In this work, Freud used the term "Oedipus complex" for the "nuclear complex" of all neuroses, which he had described in *The Interpretation of Dreams*. The Oedipus complex, which Freud believed all humans experienced, consisted of deep love for one parent and a feeling of hatred for the other.

Freud's ideas met with much resistance. He had long desired the largely honorary appointment as extraordinary professor at the University of Vienna but was denied it because of anti-Semitism and opposition to his theories. Through the intervention of a prominent former patient, however, he overcame the political obstacles. He received the prestigious appointment in 1902 and as a consequence was able to spread his ideas through uncompensated but well-received Saturday lectures at the university.

That same year, Freud organized a small weekly discussion group, which developed into the Vienna Psychoanalytical Association. It promoted the development and spread of psychoanalytic theory, and in 1908, it spawned the International Psychoanalytical Association. Both groups, however, were eventually focal points for theoretical and personal divergence and animosity. There was a bitter split in 1911 between Freud and Alfred Adler over Adler's emphasis on environmental determinism and biologically inherited psychological traits. This split foreshadowed an even more bitter divergence in 1914 between Freud and his heir apparent, Carl Gustav Jung, over Jung's doubts concerning the primacy of sexual factors in psychological disorders and Jung's mystical and religious proclivities.

Freud was constantly engaged in elaborating and expressing his theories. His writings explored the broad-ranging impact of the unconscious, from its manifestations in everyday life in such works as *The Psychopathology of Everyday Life* and *Wit and Its Relation to the Unconscious*, to the development and expression of culture in such works as *Leonardo da Vinci: A Psychosexual Study of an Infantile Reminiscence* and *Totem and Taboo*.

After World War I, his application of psychoanalytic theory to social life continued and was accompanied by the elaboration of his theory of personality and its components: the id, or unconscious, the seat of sexual and aggressive instincts, striving for self-satisfaction and release; the ego, or reason, which controlled the drives of the id; and the superego, or conscience, which sought to subject the id completely to its ideals. During this period, Freud also emphasized the importance of the aggressive drive in human behavior. The instinct for self-preservation and creation, the libido, was in counterposition to a death drive, which sought expression through self-destruction or outward hatred and aggression. His principal works during this period were *Beyond the Pleasure Principle*; *Group Psychology and the Analysis of the Ego*; *The Ego and the Id*; *Inhibitions, Symptoms, and Anxiety*; *The Future of an Illusion*; *Civilization and Its Discontents*; and *Moses and Monotheism*.

In June, 1938, Freud and his family, through the intervention of influential foreigners, were allowed to leave Austria, which had been annexed by Nazi Germany in March of that year. The alert and still-productive eighty-two-year-old Freud, who was dying from the cancer which, despite thirty-three operations, had been developing since 1923, was permitted to trade house arrest for exile in England, where he died on September 23, 1939.

Influence

The psychoanalytic treatment developed by Freud sought to expose memories and emotions that the individual, in an effort to protect the self, had buried in the unconscious. In order to allow the patient to come to terms with the repressed material, it was to be bared with the aid of a therapist employing dream analysis and free association, the uninhibited eliciting of images, emotions, and memories.

Some critics have taken Freud to task for overemphasizing the role of sex in the development of the personality and for giving to subconscious forces a degree of determination that overrides the ability of the individual to act freely. Freud's ideas, however, have had an impact that transcends the discipline of psychology. There is wide acceptance of his notions of the role of the unconscious in motivating human behavior, the importance of childhood experiences in forming the adult personality, and the function of defense mechanisms.

Bernard A. Cook

Civilization and Its Discontents

Type of philosophy: Ethics, philosophical psychology, social philosophy
First published: Das Unbehagen in der Kultur, 1930 (English translation, 1930)
Principal ideas advanced:

◇ Civilization mandates the socialization of instinctive tendencies and confers many benefits in controlling natural dangers.

◇ Psychoanalysis suggests, however, that we pay a considerable psychological price for such benefits.

◇ The inborn sexual instinct that leads to the formation of social bonds is inevitably frustrated in being constrained to adult monogamous relationships.

◇ Aggression is instinctive in origin and a derivative of a human propensity toward destruction, or the "death instinct"; its rawer forms must be even more rigidly suppressed by civilized societies than the sexual instinct.

◇ These instinctually based desires can be expressed only in muted, indirect forms that are never completely satisfying and result in chronic frustration.

◇ Our unhappiness and malaise are compounded by the tensions of controlling these instincts as demanded by civilized society.

◇ Among the more oppressive controls are those from our own consciences; conscience afflicts each of us with unconscious guilt that irrationally punishes us for misdeeds and even misthoughts.

◇ Civilization provides us with many defenses to sublimate and disguise this condition.

◇ None of these defenses, even the illusions of religion, are completely successful in securing optimal pleasure; all leave the aggressive instinct perpetually simmering within the unconscious, threatening a destructive release.

Civilization and Its Discontents is a work of social commentary by the physician-psychotherapist who founded psychoanalysis, Sigmund Freud. The early twentieth century when Freud first introduced psychoanalysis was a time of profound optimism. Thought was influenced by several strands of philosophy that assumed progress. Still popular nineteenth century utilitarian philosophers believed that individuals could rationally seek pleasure and avoid pain, and influential social critics such as Jean-Jacques Rousseau and Karl Marx viewed humans as corrupted by evil social conditions but fundamentally virtuous. Obvious nineteenth century progress in scientifically based technology contributed to the optimism. By the turn of the century, social thought was dominated by a smug conviction that rational science would soon unlock the keys to existence itself.

Freud's social views, based on the dreams and fantasies of his troubled patients, stood in stark contrast to this optimism. Human beings, to Freud, from earliest childhood were dominated by unconscious conflicts surrounding the sexual instinct. By 1930 when *Civilization and Its Discontents* appeared, Freud's views had evolved to consider human nature as equally obsessed by another powerful instinct, destructive aggression. Not since the writings of English philosopher Thomas Hobbes in 1651 had such a bleak picture of humankind been presented. Hobbes had described the human condition as a "war of every man against every man" and felt humans needed strong controls imposed from without by a powerful ruler. Freud viewed the main checks on this human potential for destructive aggression to lie within, a tyrannical conscience imposing its burden of irrational guilt. Freud saw these controls as precariously balanced. At any time, this destructive aggression could be unleashed on humankind. As the economic depression of the 1930's deepened and German Nazi Adolf Hitler emerged the dominant leader of all Europe, Freud spent his last years with the conviction this pessimism was not misplaced.

Civilization as a Control
Civilization, which mandates the socialization of human instincts, confers many benefits in controlling realistic dangers. It also exacts a price

in the suppression of intrinsic human nature.

Threats to life arise from the random destructiveness of natural events, the feebleness of our bodies, and maladjustments in human relationships. The technology of civilized society has vastly diminished these threats. It has extended human sensory capacities through microscopes and telescopes, enabled people to travel vast distances at high speeds through motorized vehicles, tamed floods through dams and controlled water channels, and extended the expected length of life. Through technology, people have become a sort of "prosthetic God." Social organization also has evolved. The arbitrary will of the strongest individual, imposed in primitive times, becomes tempered by the will of the majority of a civilized community. Beauty, order, and cleanliness approach much higher standards in civilized societies. Regulations prescribe how tasks are to be accomplished with monotonous precision. Time becomes available for higher mental activities such as philosophical and religious concerns. Genuine progress in tackling physical threats to existence is undeniable.

These benefits have been purchased, however, at a considerable cost in diminishing the potential for human happiness. A major task of civilized social organization is that of controlling human instincts of sex and aggression lest they manifest themselves in murder, rape, and incest. The very foundations of civilization rest on the suppression and redirection of such desires. These desires are powerful and persistent. The task of controlling and channeling them is a difficult and painful one.

Sex and Aggression

Eros, or love, is a troublesome instinct. Sexual love is the glue that binds intimate relationships, but it must be rigorously controlled. The course of individual development from early childhood involves a sequence of suppressions and displacements of various forms of the sexual instinct. The toddler, for example, takes an "anal erotic" interest in the excretory function. This must yield to a conflicting disdain for dirt and excrement. The preschool child's love for the parent of the opposite sex assumes a sexual component. Such "incestuous desires" must be suppressed and stricken from memory. Reemerging

genital sexual desires during adolescence become the basis for emotional ties to a loved sex-object and the formation of a new family. Each advance toward more mature sexual expressions involves the conflict of renouncing less mature erotic urges. Few adult individuals, indeed, find all their sexual interests flowing neatly into the prescribed channels. The cultural demand for a single monogamous relationship based on a permanent bond between one man and one woman seldom permits total sexual fulfillment. Inhibited and frustrated sexuality and persistent disruptions by the residues of immature erotic desires form the common lot of humankind.

Civilized society demands displacements of erotic love even more distant from instinct-based objects. The risks of concentrating all one's emotional involvements on a single individual who could be lost by unfaithfulness or death encourages most adults to expend some of their affection on a broader circle of friends in less erotically charged relationships, in "aim-inhibited love." Civilization depends on such emotional ties to broader communities. The pleasure such ties can give is much weaker and more muted than the pleasures of erotic fulfillment. Mentors implore us to observe such unrealistic injunctions for aim-inhibited love as the Christian admonition to "love thy neighbor as thyself." A serious attempt to observe such an admonition would spread an individual's love impossibly thin. It would, moreover, disadvantage those vulnerable people who in observing this admonition fail to react to enemies with appropriate assertiveness.

Civilization demands even more rigid controls on aggression than on sex. Aggression is instinctive in its origin, built into human nature. Although earlier viewed in psychoanalysis as a derivative of self-preservation motives, aggression is more aptly treated as an intrinsic derivative of the unconscious desire of organisms to "return to the inorganic state," a death instinct. Aggression is everywhere and exists regardless of the way a particular society is organized. The Marxist view of aggression as a mere side-effect of the ownership of private property is most assuredly wrong. Aggression is expressed in young children before they have any concept of property. Differences in talents and status would still spawn aggressive competition even if private property were abolished. Even the most brutal forms of aggression can be rationalized as virtuous acts. The most savage acts of crusading Christians were considered to have a high moral purpose. Remarkably similar competing groups search for small differences and build hatreds on these differences. Although sublimated aggression sometimes inspires the competitive uses of talent, this instinct more commonly has destructive consequences.

Guilt and Other Responses

Compounding the anxiety and malaise of the civilized condition is guilt. Guilt originates in the social anxiety experienced by transgressing children who anticipate punishment and rejection by their seemingly omnipotent, protecting parents. Such anxious guilt experienced after forbidden deeds or even thoughts becomes automatic and "internalized" as a part of one's own personality in the conscience or "superego." The superego, a residue of parental values, is oppressive, absolute, punitive, and irrational. The pain of guilt may be experienced after perfectly sensible acts that violate taboos that remain from resisting the unconscious impulses of early childhood. Guilt may be felt as a consequence of impulse-driven thoughts and fantasies never carried out or even expressed in words. An irony of nature is that the people most moral in actions are those who most inhibit impulses and who most torture themselves with guilt. The people of Israel in biblical times, for example, whose priestly religion prescribes "overly strict commandments," were obsessively condemned by their prophets for "sinfulness." Guilt continuously inhibits the capacity for spontaneous joy among civilized human beings.

The defenses of everyday life help but a little. One can withdraw from emotional involvements with others and thereby protect oneself against the wounds of social rejection. One can attempt a quiet happiness from the mastery of internal needs as recommended by the percepts of Eastern religions. One can sublimate passions by the creation of artistic beauty or by the solution of scientific riddles. One can temporarily lose oneself in erotic love. One can release pent-up instincts and accept the anguish that follows such short-lived pleasures. One can seek escape through intoxicating substances that dull pain.

One common solution to the stresses of life is an involvement with the various illusions provided by religion. Such illusions are particularly convincing because they are supported by social consensus. In the earlier stages of childhood, the helpless infant longs for the powerful and supportive father in whose hands he or she feels safe. The believer faces the dangers of the world by transferring this infantile fantasy of the powerful father to an image of God. For the religious person, the purpose of life is defined and the frustrations and injustices of life are compensated in the hereafter. An "oceanic feeling" of spiritual union with the universe reported by religious people involves a psychological retreat to the period of earliest infancy before any distinction is made between oneself and the surrounding world. Freud regarded most such religious experiences as "patently infantile" escapes from reality.

Unfulfilled but incessant sexual passions, simmering anger, the self-flagellations of conscience, and the cruelties of nature and bodily decay are the lot of civilized human beings. Neither love, drink, madness, enjoyment of beauty, involvement in work, nor the consolations of religion provide a permanent escape from this fate. Whether civilization will endure is still an open question.

Impact and Subsequent Views

Because Freud's work fit the temper of the bleak times, it proved astonishingly popular and the first edition quickly sold out. In subsequent years, various schools of thought within psychology and psychoanalysis have each in their own way softened the gloomy thesis of this work. Psychoanalysts of the next generation gave renewed emphasis on the part of personality Freud called the ego. The ego is the reasoning part of personality that makes sense out of the world and adjusts instinctive demands realistically. Not only did the newer generation of psychoanalysts hold that the ego was stronger than maintained by Freud, but they held that this ego had its own motives for developing and expressing the individual's own talents. To the ego psychoanalysts, instincts became less threatening after they were molded by the human capacity to reason.

An important movement within post-1950 psychology was even more antagonistic to

Freud's pessimistic thesis. This movement, called humanistic psychology, was identified with the psychotherapeutic method of Carl Rogers. To Rogers, the vital and often hidden part of the human personality is its built-in potential for growth. Each of us is born with possibilities for creative achievement and love that can be thwarted only if we are kept from actualizing ourselves. Our nature is basically good. Humanistic psychology represented a full-circle return to Rousseau's thesis of the noble human corrupted by an ignoble society.

Freudian views seem to many current psychologists too gloomy an interpretation of the human condition, and certainly too simplistic in view of what is now known about bodily chemistry and its effect on the brain and human emotions. Yet few would consider Freud's views entirely wrong, and they retain their import for philosophy. If spontaneously expressed impulses of the real self are not always depraved, neither are they always virtuous. Many psychologists have dealt with criminals who seem to feel quite good about themselves after perpetrating spontaneous acts of great brutality. All humans some of the time and some humans most of the time have a darker side than is acknowledged by the humanists. *Civilization and Its Discontents*, which acts as a counterbalance to the pre-Freudian optimism of Rousseau and the post-Freudian optimism of humanistic psychology, remains among the most widely read of Freud's books.

Thomas E. DeWolfe

Additional Reading

Clark, Ronald W. *Freud: The Man and the Cause, a Biography*. New York: Random House, 1980. This is a very readable biography, which is especially good in its treatment of Sigmund Freud's private life.

Fromm, Erich. *Greatness and Limitations of Freud's Thought*. New York: Harper & Row, 1980. This is a critique of Freud by a dissenting psychoanalyst. Fromm believed that Freud exaggerated the role of sex in determining human behavior and that Freud's concept of love was narrow and self-serving.

Gay, Peter. *Freud: A Life for Our Time*. New York: W. W. Norton, 1988. Gay is a historian of distinguished reputation. In this artfully written and exhaustively researched biography, he employs the psychohistorical technique to shed additional light on Freud's personality, his relations with his associates, and his career as the creator and propagator of psychoanalysis.

Grubrich-Simitis, Ilse. *Back to Freud's Texts: Making Silent Documents Speak*. Translated by Philip Slotkin. New Haven, Conn.: Yale University Press, 1996. This important contribution to the study of Freud offers understanding of the man as a writer as well as insight into Freud's creative process. The text details the history of Freud's German-language publications and examines key works.

Rosenzweig, Saul. *Freud, Jung, and Hall the King Maker: The Historical Expedition to America*. St. Louis, Mo.: Rana House, 1993. Rosenzweig describes Freud's only visit to the United States in 1909. The 1909 expedition was important because it introduced Americans to the theory and development of psychoanalysis and allowed Freud to interact with Carl Gustav Jung, and G. Stanley Hall, the organizer of the visit. Text includes completed correspondence between Freud and Hall.

Bernard A. Cook, updated by Lisa A. Wroble

Hans-Georg Gadamer

Gadamer framed a position that became known as philosophical hermeneutics, which stresses meaning and truth in a text and examines the relationship between the text's tradition and its interpreter.

Principal philosophical works: Platos dialektische Ethik, 1931 (*Plato's Dialectical Ethics,* 1991); *Plato und die Dichter,* 1934 (*Plato and the Poets,* 1976); *Volk und Geschichte im Denken Herders,* 1942; *Wahrheit und Methode: Grundzüge einer philosophischen Hermeneutik,* 1960 (*Truth and Method,* 1975); *Kleine Schriften I-IV,* 1967-1977; *Hegels Dialektik: Fünf hermeneutische Studien,* 1971 (*Hegel's Dialectic: Five Hermeneutical Studies,* 1976); *Philosophical Hermeneutics,* 1976; *Vernunft im Zeitalter der Wissenschaft: Aufsätze,* 1976 (*Reason in the Age of Science,* 1981); *Poetica,* 1977; *Die Aktualität des Schönen,* 1977 (*The Relevance of the Beautiful,* 1986); *Philosophische Lehrjahre,* 1977 (*Philosophical Apprenticeships,* 1985); *Die Idee des Guten zwischen Plato und Aristotle,* 1978 (*The Idea of the Good in Platonic-Aristotelian Philosophy,* 1986); *Plato: Texte zur Ideenlehre,* 1978; *Dialogue and Dialectic: Eight Hermeneutical Studies on Plato,* 1980; *Heideggers Wege,* 1983 (*Heidegger's Ways,* 1994); *Gesammelte Werke,* 1985; *Die Univerität Heidelberg und die Geburt der modernen Wissenschaft,* 1987; *Das Erbe Europas: Beiträge,* 1989; *Gedicht und Gespräch: Essays,* 1990; *Hans-Georg Gadamer on Education, Poetry, and History: Applied Hermeneutics,* 1992; *Über die Verborgenheit der Gesundheit: Aufsätze und Vorträge,* 1993; *Literature and Philosophy in Dialogue: Essays in Germany Literary Theory,* 1994.

Born: February 11, 1900; Marburg, Germany

Early Life

Hans-Georg Gadamer was born on February 11, 1900, in Marburg, Germany, home of the neo-Kantian philosophers Hermann Cohen and Paul Natorp. His father, Johann Gadamer, was a professor of pharmaceutical chemistry at the local university. A bashful and immature young man, Gadamer began to study philosophy in 1918, against his father's wishes. At Marburg University, he studied philosophy, German literature, art history, and classical philology.

Life's Work

After writing a doctoral thesis under Natorp in 1922, Gadamer became interested in the work of philosopher Martin Heidegger, who taught in Marburg from 1923 to 1927 and by whose personality and work Gadamer was spellbound. In 1928, he wrote his thesis for Heidegger on Greek philosopher Plato's dialectical ethics.

Gadamer taught at Marburg University from 1923 to 1938, first as an assistant and then, from 1928, as a *privatdocent,* but, under the rising power of Adolf Hitler's Nazism, he was denied a full professorship. Finally, he was given the professorship in 1937 and received an offer from the University of Leipzig a year later. He stayed in Leipzig until 1948. In 1946, Gadamer was appointed rector of the university and worked for its reconstruction after World War II, but he decided to leave Leipzig after becoming disillusioned by the interference of the East German Communist Party, which was seizing power in the Russian-occupied East German sector.

After a brief stint at the University of Frankfurt (from 1948 to 1949), Gadamer became Karl Jasper's successor as chair of the philosophy department at the University of Heidelberg, where he worked until his retirement in 1968. It was during his Heidelberg years that Gadamer completed *Truth and Method.* After retiring, he remained active in the scholarly world by participating in and presiding over various learned societies, writing, and teaching at Boston College, a task that Gadamer regarded as "like a second youth." Among the many awards that Gadamer received are the Grand Federal Cross of Merit and Star and honorary doctorates from universities in Ottawa and Washington, D.C.

Gadamer's primary legacy is philosophical hermeneutics, which analyzes the problems that arise when a reader tries to understand a text. The main questions with which Gadamer is concerned could be formulated as follows: How can one understand tradition as it is provided in texts? Is there such a thing as a truth that goes beyond the truth the "exact" sciences offer? How do the answers to these questions affect humanity's understanding of itself?

The sciences, in Gadamer's view, only provide an explanation (*Erklärung*) of the world, not an understanding (*Verständnis*—an opposition first used by philosopher Wilhelm Dilthey). Gadamer writes in *Truth and Method* that it is his intention "to seek that experience of truth that transcends the sphere of the control of scientific method wherever it is to be found and to inquire into its legitimacy."

Gadamer wants to overcome the hubris of the natural sciences, which for him is the hubris of modern times—namely, that an objective, clear truth that is apparent to everyone can be assured by scientific methodology. His evaluation of the sciences does not acknowledge that a critique of the unquestioned obviousness of scientific methodology and its results was opened up in the 1920's from within the sciences, and that since then every responsible scientist would admit that the scientific perspective is only one out of many possible outlooks. Gadamer attempts to hold up the notion that meaning and understanding— and ultimately truth—can be found only in the process of communication (*Verständigung*), either between individuals or, more important for hermeneutics, between a text and its reader. One of his strongest arguments is that each person is part of a tradition (and Gadamer means the philosophical tradition of the West) that is responsible for values and prejudices (*Vorurteile*) and therefore influences one's understanding of texts and of the world in general.

In order to understand Gadamer's position, one must consider the tradition of which Gadamer himself is a part: Platonic philosophy and the principles of hermeneutics, from Friedrich Schleiermacher and Georg Wilhelm Friedrich Hegel to Martin Heidegger. Scholarship on Plato up to the 1920's had been mainly concerned with revealing a systematic philosophy in Plato's dialogues, which were seen as containing a hidden truth be**neath** the Socratic method of dialogical questioning and answering. The scholars of that period took Plato's ironic approach as a disguise for this truth. For this philosophical school, Aristotle's ethical writings were the first major step toward an "empirical," "objective" way of thinking.

Gadamer believes, on the contrary, that Plato's dialogues constitute the paradigmatic hermeneutical attitude in which a human being seeks to understand the world, and that truth lies in the Platonic model itself. It must be stressed that Gadamer, rooted in this Platonic background and unlike his philosophical opponent Jacques Derrida, believes firmly in a truth that is present in the texts of the human tradition. Gadamer does not take part in "the great project of hermeneutic trouble-making," instigated by philosophers Friedrich Nietzsche and Søren Kierkegaard. He assumes that texts speak to their readers in a meaningful way about meaningful matters and that each reader has only to obey the hermeneutic rules of understanding in order to engage in a fruitful dialogue with these texts.

Yet what exactly is hermeneutics, and in which way does Gadamer further its theory and practice? The word "hermeneutics" was derived from the Greek god Hermes, who served as messenger for the other gods. Until the nineteenth century, hermeneutics was defined as the art of understanding and interpreting texts. In the Middle Ages, the preferred text for hermeneutic exercises was the Bible, and the hermeneut's task was to restore the Bible's original contents and intentions, thus reestablishing its normative authority for the pious reader. Hermeneutics basically dealt with erasing the uncertainties, inconsistencies, and ambiguities of a text. Understanding a text was understanding its contents, an apparently unproblematic venture.

With the advent of secular rationalism in the seventeenth century, a variety of texts were explicated. Because rationalistic thinking holds that what can be said can be said clearly, all unexplainable ambiguities in a given text had to be a result of its author's inability to make himself or herself understood.

Hermeneutics' leap into modernity took place in the nineteenth century, with the arrival of both the Romantic and the historicist movements. The Romantic philosopher Schleiermacher was the first to stress an author's individual creativity and the problems this poses for the interpreter. For Schleiermacher, a text does not necessarily reveal an everlasting truth; instead, it is simply a particular utterance of a particular author at a particular time. In order to understand fully the author's intention, the hermeneut has to reconstruct the historical circumstances of the author's period and to delve into this period. A text's meaning is not at all self-evident but has to be explored in the content of its historical conditions. Schleiermacher's concept remained the hermeneutic model well into the twentieth century and was elaborated by philosopher Wilhelm Dilthey.

Gadamer, in *Truth and Method*, made Schleiermacher's concept a subject of criticism from a hermeneutic standpoint. For Gadamer, the reconstruction of a certain historical moment is "a pointless undertaking in view of the historicity of our being." He claims that, instead, one must follow Hegel's ideas. For Hegel, historicity is overcome by the self-revelation of the absolute spirit in history, because—according to Gadamer—Hegel posits "the most extreme counterposition to the self-forgetfulness of historical consciousness." Truth is not merely revealed in history; it is experienced as a higher knowledge beyond history. Gadamer's foremost goal is to attain this knowledge.

By adopting Hegel's principle, Gadamer was able to offer a solution to one of the main problems of all hermeneutic efforts since Schleiermacher: the hermeneutic circle. Romantic and historicist hermeneutics had always pointed out that the parts of a literary work (sentences, paragraphs, chapters, and so on) can be understood only in the context of the whole work. Yet this notion clearly rests on circular reasoning: The interpreter is supposed to understand the whole of a text if he wants to understand its parts, but the understanding of the whole is precisely what he wants to gain by the interpretation of the parts. The problems that the hermeneutic circle necessarily poses are exacerbated by the prejudices of the interpreter, for which his historical situation

is responsible. The role of these prejudices becomes larger when the hermeneut tries to understand a text that was written under completely different historical conditions.

Like Heidegger and the phenomenological philosopher Edmund Husserl, Gadamer perceives the hermeneutic circle and the prejudices of the interpreter as positive forces. The importance of Heidegger's philosophy is based on his insight into the historicity of human life, a historicity that is ruled by "a past [the human being] did not create and a future over which it has no control." Historicity, which Heidegger called "thrownness in the world," cannot be escaped, not even by the exact sciences that derive their claim of objectivity from the denial of this historicity. It is to Gadamer's credit to have placed the historicity of understanding at the center of his hermeneutics as the condition for any understanding. With his theory, the humanities again emerges as the field in which humankind tries to define itself.

To understand history and to learn from it no longer means to bury it under historistic falsifications, but to claim and presuppose the truth, which can be found in history and in the human tradition. Still, the truth in history must be considered with the truth the historian or the interpreter of literature knows already, leading to a higher truth. Gadamer calls this process the "fusion of horizons" of the interpreter and of the author of the text in question.

For Gadamer, the privileged experience of truth is the experience of art, an experience that exceeds any truth methodological or epistemological knowledge can provide: "That truth is experienced through a work of art that we cannot attain in any other way constitutes the philosophic importance of art. . . . The experience of art issues the most pressing challenge to the scientific consciousness to acknowledge its own limits."

In adherence to this concept, Gadamer commences *Truth and Method* with a systematic critique of idealistic aesthetics, which had placed the experience of art within the subject and had understood itself, in the tradition of Immanuel Kant, as a science of art "that would produce the truth *about* art but could not acknowledge the truth of art." It is this truth of art, as a means in the process of understanding humanity, with which Gadamer is concerned.

The proper mode of being in which one can experience the truth of art is the mode of play. Yet, unlike Kant or Friedrich Schiller, Gadamer does not see play as a subjective activity opposed to the objective attitude of science; he sees it as a mode in which one can "lose" oneself in a literary text, thus allowing the text to "speak" about its truth (an "objectivistic" enterprise in Gadamer's opinion). When "we speak of play, this refers neither to the attitude nor even to the state of mind of the creator or of those enjoying art, nor to the freedom of a subjectivity expressed in play, but to the mode of being of the work of art itself."

After criticizing both traditional aesthetics and hermeneutics and claiming as fundamental for understanding the search for and acceptance of truth in art and literature, Gadamer widens his view by stressing the importance of the medium in which truth, as Gadamer conceives it, reveals itself: language. He reduces his standpoint to the simple Heideggerian statement: "Being that can be understood is language." To interpret a text and to understand it means always to "translate" it from one language into another, from the one of the original text into the one of the interpreter, a proceeding, which, as shown, ultimately leads to the "fusion of horizons."

By rooting the hermeneutic process in the dialogical situation of language, Gadamer returns to the beginnings of his own development: Truth lies in the dialogues of Plato and in all the texts of the human tradition. Being a philosophical hermeneut means to take part in a dialogue with this tradition and to listen to its truth.

Influence
Gadamer's contribution to philosophy is the concept of "philosophical hermeneutics," which has been adopted and applied by numerous scholars. His influence peaked after the publication of his most important work, *Truth and Method*. Philosophical hermeneutics and the stress on meaning and truth in a text, as opposed to the epistemological knowledge of the natural sciences, are often compared to Jacques Derrida's method of deconstruction, which runs counter to hermeneutics. Deconstructionists rejected the theory of hermeneutics as the last bastion of "the metaphysics

of presence." In the 1970's and 1980's, Gadamer's work became a major force in literary criticism in the United States. Almost all Gadamer's writings are available in English translation, and many secondary studies on philosophical hermeneutics have been written by American scholars.

Michael Büsges

Truth and Method

Type of philosophy: Epistemology, metaphysics
First published: Wahrheit und Methode: Grundzüge einer philosophischen Hermeneutik, 1960 (English translation, 1975)
Principal ideas advanced:
◇ Hermeneutics is the study of how understanding is possible, and understanding is the essential mode of human being.
◇ Human consciousness is always historically situated; therefore, all understanding is relative to the present historical perspective, and there is no method of understanding that can elude this relativity.
◇ Human understanding is trapped within a linguistic tradition; the object of study in the human sciences is the linguistically constituted world.
◇ The truth of the human sciences cannot be arrived at methodologically as it is in the natural sciences; hence, the human sciences cannot employ the objective standards of knowledge used in the natural sciences.
◇ The proper goal of the human sciences is to investigate the relation of humans to the world and raise the level of reflection on historical traditions.

Hans-Georg Gadamer's *Truth and Method* remains the premier work in the hermeneutic philosophy of the twentieth century. Following in the footsteps of philosophers Friedrich Nietzsche, Edmund Husserl, and Martin Heidegger, Gadamer acknowledges the possibility of true or authentic experience but criticizes the methods of modern science and philosophy that seek to translate those experiences into universal norms. From Nietzsche, Gadamer takes the notion that all human understanding includes a perspective. Gadamer adopts Husserl's discovery that all experience occurs within a given horizon that gives the experience context and meaning. From Heidegger, Gadamer learns that the essence of human being is understanding and that this understanding is constituted in language. Gadamer's conclusion, the Linguistic Turn, holds that people's experience of the world is trapped in language and that they have no direct, nonlinguistic access to the real world. Without direct access to the real world, the human sciences become a study of language.

Gadamer's clear formulation of the Linguistic Turn and his open recognition of the relativity of human understanding pave the way for the postmodern philosophers of the 1960's and 1970's. The postmodernists argue that the Linguistic Turn undermines all philosophical positions, and therefore, they must abandon the notion of truth altogether. However, Gadamer was committed to finding the truth of human understanding. He derives his conclusions from an exhaustive analysis of the history of hermeneutics that involves questioning the truth of aesthetic experience, the truth of understanding in the human sciences, and the linguistic boundaries of understanding. However, understanding itself remains the central issue, and Gadamer's goal is to distinguish and thereby free the truth of human understanding from the methodologies of the natural sciences, which, he believes, dominate twentieth century thinking.

Although Gadamer claims that *Truth and Method* is intended as a study into how human understanding is possible and not as a methodological guide for the human sciences, he begins by pointing out that developing the human sciences along the model of the natural sciences has failed to serve the purpose of these sciences. Gadamer defines that purpose as the effort to understand how specific peoples, cultural objects, or institutions have come to be what they are. He distinguishes this purpose from the purpose of the natural sciences, which he describes as the effort to confirm and extend experiences in order to predict future experiences. The challenge then for the human sciences, and hermeneutics in general, is to understand the world as it truly is, not in order to control it.

Art and Understanding

Gadamer begins his investigation of understanding with the development of the theory of aesthetic judgment. The question raised in the history of aesthetic theory asks, "How does one experience the truth of an art object?" What is it that works of art signify? Does understanding art require understanding the historical context of the work or the artist's intentions? Here Gadamer makes the somewhat controversial assumption that there is a true experience of art, and he concludes that art presents itself.

To illustrate artistic self-presentation, Gadamer points out the possibility of aesthetic differentiation, the capacity to experience works of art outside their original context and function. Through aesthetic differentiation, the work becomes visible as a pure work of art, abstracted from all other significance. This abstracted experience allows the work to exist on its own. Because of the independence of the work of art, the aesthetic experience is not disappointed by any more genuine experience of reality. Seeing an apple, vase, and table does not decrease our appreciation of a still-life painting. Similarly, no scientific discovery can discredit our aesthetic experience. Hence, the truth of a work of art is located in neither another time nor another object. Art signifies itself, and we experience it as art when that experience is integrated into our own time and place in history.

Sciences and Texts

Having revealed the true experience of art, Gadamer then questions the truth of the human sciences. Like the question of art, the truth of the human sciences involves understanding what historical texts signify. To uncover this truth, Gadamer carefully investigates the central figures in hermeneutics, including the Enlightenment period thinkers, the Romantic thinkers, the historical thinkers, and the phenomenological thinkers.

The Enlightenment technique for interpretation involved an effort to reveal the original meaning of texts, which was thought to have become alien or inaccessible. The texts that most concerned Enlightenment thinkers, the Bible and ancient Greek and Roman texts, were translated from foreign languages into the Latin of the Middle Ages. For Enlightenment thinkers such as Martin

Luther, the literal meaning of the text is the original meaning. However, Scripture, which is not univocally intelligible from beginning to end, required a more sophisticated interpretive technique in order to achieve a consistent understanding of the text. Therefore, Luther and other Enlightenment thinkers adopted a technique from classical rhetoric that called for understanding the details of the text from the overall aim of the text. In this way, Enlightenment hermeneutics relied on the historical assumption that Scripture (and other texts) presented a unified purpose.

Under pressure to produce results that were equal in rigor to those in the natural sciences, the subsequent Romantic and historical thinkers offered revised methods of interpretation that focused historical research on deciphering texts, so as to neutralize the distance between the reader and the historical event. Consequently, the object of research in history became the text, which allowed researchers to study history in the same way a natural scientist studies objects. Gadamer points out that these efforts failed because the knowledge of the human sciences is different from the knowledge of the natural sciences. Even these improved interpretive methods functioned on the scientific notion that experience is self-evident, failing to recognize how history influences the way people experience and interpret the world.

It was the phenomenological approach that revealed the historical character of experience. In an effort to get to the "things themselves," Husserl proposed to investigate the subjective modes of experience, to understand what it is that the individual experiences in perception. For Gadamer, Husserl's most interesting discovery was the realization that all experience is given within the context of a horizon. The horizon provides a context such that all experience is understood in terms of the whole of experience. The horizon is defined by the historical tradition of which one is a part, and it prejudices the way one understands the past, present, and future. Gadamer accepts this notion of the horizon and the prejudices associated with it, but Husserl still hopes to provide a method for getting at the "things themselves," and in this regard, he failed to free himself from the standards of the natural sciences.

It was Husserl's student, Heidegger, who realized that understanding is not a mode of behavior; understanding is the character of human existence. People are temporal beings, beings that contemplate the past, present, and future. When Husserl showed that all understanding occurs out of a historical tradition, and that this tradition is continuously transformed by human understanding, it became clear to Heidegger that all understanding is self-understanding. If the historical tradition in which one lives defines the way one lives in the world and one's understanding of that world, and the way one understands the world in turn alters the historical tradition in which one lives, then all understanding is about ourselves—the way we live in the world and understand it. For Gadamer, this was the ultimate discovery in hermeneutics, for it was this discovery that finally made sense of the human sciences. With the recognition that all human understanding is a historically conditioned self-understanding, the human sciences could finally shrug off the objective, ahistorical viewpoint sought in the natural sciences. There is no objective, ahistorical standpoint for interpreting and understanding history.

Gadamer's analysis of art and the human sciences revealed that understanding is always personal and determined by the tradition of which one is a part. The tradition provides a way of looking at the world, which prejudices all standards of evaluation, making all interpretations relative to the tradition in which they occur. Gadamer is aware of the contradiction that relativism involves: To claim that it is unconditionally true that all interpretations are conditional is itself a contradiction. Gadamer makes the controversial claim that this contradiction only applies to objective assertions about particular things. While one cannot claim that Euclidian geometry proves that Euclidian geometry is false, what one says about oneself is not an objective assertion about a particular being, but a subjective assertion about human beings whose self-understanding is self-defining. Hence, the contradiction is irrelevant.

The Linguistic Turn

Having shown that understanding in the human sciences remains trapped within a historical tradition, Gadamer then argues that that tradition is sustained by language. This position, called the Linguistic Turn, holds that the human experience of the world is completely mediated by language. To have an orientation toward the world requires us to maintain a certain freedom from the world so that we can represent the world to ourselves. Language provides the distance between the world and ourselves that allows us the freedom to communicate that world to other people. We are not trapped in the world of objects because language allows us to see and question that world. However, we are trapped in language. Our orientation toward the world is mediated by language, and the understanding we reach with other people always presupposes a shared linguistic perspective. Hence, the Linguistic Turn leads Gadamer to the position of linguistic idealism; we can understand neither the world nor ourselves except within the confines of our linguistic tradition.

Given this characterization of human understanding, Gadamer offers a description of the human sciences and a recommendation for improving understanding. Rather than to eliminate the prejudice of tradition, as per the natural sciences, the goal of the human sciences is to rehabilitate prejudice. Gadamer describes this rehabilitation as developing an "openness" to investigate the validity of the tradition. In this open investigation, the interpreter can neither follow the tradition blindly nor get outside the tradition in order to understand it in its entirety. Gadamer describes this as an investigation from within. This openness cannot be sustained methodologically because the methodology itself (as a product of its own tradition) would be subject to continual rehabilitation. Hence, the purpose of the human sciences is to raise the level of reflection on tradition itself.

Truth and Method was widely influential for philosophy and the human sciences in the 1960's and 1970's. Gadamer's work transformed hermeneutics from a discipline associated with the interpretation of ancient texts into a study of human nature itself. This transformation showed that the truth of the human sciences could not be derived methodologically. It forced researchers in the human sciences to reconcile the objective claims of their work with the linguistic tradition in which they work. Gadamer's linguistic ideals may also be seen as the last stage in modern philosophy, a philosophical position committed to the discovery of universal truth. Although Gadamer abandoned the notion of objective, ahistorical truth, he proposed a definition of human understanding that he believed to be universally true.

The postmodern philosophers of the 1970's and 1980's radicalized Gadamer's linguistic idealism and suggested that once we have acknowledged that language mediates between the subject (individual) and the world, then all we can ever know is language. Hence, we must abandon all beliefs about the subject, the world, and the notion of truth, which connected human understanding to the world. As radical as *Truth and Method* was in 1965, postmodernism has declared an end of philosophy and moved the debate over the proper subject for philosophy and the human sciences beyond Gadamer's linguistic idealism. Postmodernism declares that the proper object of study for the human sciences is language, and that the proper purpose is to identify institutions of power used for human oppression. However, Gadamer's study of hermeneutics may ultimately offer a rational middle ground for the human sciences that acknowledges the historical character of human understanding without abandoning the notion of truth.

Jack Simmons

Additional Reading

Hahn, Lewis Edwin, ed. *The Philosophy of Hans-Georg Gadamer*. Library of Living Philosophers, vol. 24. Chicago: Open Court Press, 1996. The series in which this volume appears is designed to create a context in which great living philosophers can respond to critical essays on their works. This volume contains twenty-nine essays by leading experts on a variety of aspects of Hans-Georg Gadamer's works and his individual responses. Of particular interest to the general reader is the accompanying sixty-page philosophical autobiography, "Reflections on My Philosophical Journey." The work also contains an excellent, comprehensive bibliography of Gadamer's works.

Palmer, Richard. *Hermeneutics*. Evanston, Ill.: Northwestern University Press, 1969. This book was instrumental in introducing hermeneutics to an American audience. The clarity of Palmer's presentation makes this volume an excellent starting point for someone wanting to understand the basic elements of Gadamer's theory of interpretation.

Risser, James. *Hermeneutics and the Voice of the Other: Re-reading Gadamer's Philosophical Hermeneutics.* Albany: State University of New York Press, 1991. In this volume, Risser develops an insightful assessment of the single project reflected in the complexity of Gadamer's thought: making sense of the act of understanding. This book will be most helpful to those readers who have already been introduced to Gadamer's philosophy.

Smith, P. Christopher. *Hermeneutics and Human Finitude: Toward a Theory of Ethical Understanding.* New York: Fordham University Press, 1991. Taking the philosophical thought of Gadamer on art and the interpretation of texts as a foundation, Smith carefully develops its implications for understanding what ethical knowledge consists of, concluding that ethical choices are best made by interpreting the voice of tradition.

Warnke, Georgia. *Gadamer: Hermeneutics, Tradition and Reason.* Stanford, Calif.: Stanford University Press, 1987. A lucid study of how three important themes in Gadamer's writings—art, history, and philosophy—are interrelated. Sympathetic to and yet critical of Gadamer's views, Warnke argues that the key to understanding Gadamer is to see him as steering a middle course between endorsing the Enlightenment's project of clarifying the rationality of our beliefs and accepting the view that this project is misguided.

Weinsheimer, Joel. *Gadamer's Hermeneutics: A Reading of "Truth and Method."* New Haven, Conn.: Yale University Press, 1985. One of the translators of Gadamer's *Truth and Method*, Weinsheimer presents a well-written, in-depth analysis of Gadamer's most significant work. This volume is a helpful guide for the general reader and scholar alike.

Wright, Kathleen, ed. *Festivals of Interpretation: Essays on Hans-Georg Gadamer's Work.* Albany: State University of New York Press, 1990. A collection of essays by some of the most renowned European and North American scholars of Gadamer, intended to celebrate the necessity of interpretation by examining a wide range of topics considered in Gadamer's work, including the relation of hermeneutics to ethics and justice, the application of hermeneutical interpretation to the law, and the relation of poetry to politics. Readers with little or no familiarity with Gadamer's work may still find this book rewarding.

Michael Büsges, updated by Diane P. Michelfelder

Mohandas K. Gandhi

Gandhi, as one of the main figures of the Indian independence movement, pioneered the use of nonviolent protest. The strategies and tactics he employed have been adapted by many groups struggling to achieve justice, including the Civil Rights movement in the United States. Gandhi also worked to reform traditional Indian society, speaking out for women's rights and for the group known as the untouchables.

Principal philosophical works: Hind Swaraj, 1909 (*Swaraj in One Year,* 1921; best known as *Indian Home Rule*); *Dakshina Afrikana Satyagrahano itihasa,* serialized 1924-1925, published in 2 volumes 1924-1925 (*Satyagraha in South Africa,* 1928); *Satyana prayogo, athava, Atmakatha,* serialized 1925-1929, published in 2 volumes 1927-1929 (*An Autobiography: The Story of My Experiments with Truth,* serialized 1925-1929, published in 2 volumes, 1927-1929); *Collected Works,* 1958-1994.

Born: October 2, 1869; Porbandar, India
Died: January 30, 1948; New Delhi, India

Early Life

Mohandas Karamchand Gandhi was the fourth child of the prime minister of the tiny city-state of Porbandar, about halfway between the major cities of Bombay and Karachi. Gandhi received the normal education for a boy of his family's position. His family married him at age thirteen to a girl from another locally important family; Kasturba remained his wife until her death in 1944. After the death of Gandhi's father in 1885, the family decided that Gandhi should go to Great Britain and study law, with the hope that he might enter the civil service of local Indian princes.

Gandhi left for Great Britain in 1888. He did not study very hard and apparently spent much of his time trying to maintain a strict vegetarian diet (the start of a lifetime interest in diet) and studying comparative religion, including his first serious research into his own Hindu culture.

Gandhi returned to India in 1891 to open a legal practice. For a variety of reasons, especially Gandhi's own shyness and diffidence, the practice was a failure, first in his native region and then in Bombay. In 1893, a case required him to go to South Africa. He ended up staying, making only a few short trips back to India and Great Britain, until 1914.

On the train from the port to Pretoria that first evening, Gandhi was literally kicked off for trying to sit in the first-class compartment when a white passenger objected to his presence. This event catalyzed Gandhi's energies. A week later, overcoming his shyness, he began speaking at meetings, and then started organizing his own. At first, his goal was to protect Indian workers and traders in South Africa and then to expand their rights. Because there were Indians from all over the Indian Empire working together in South Africa, news of Gandhi's work was sent back throughout the subcontinent. When he left in 1914, Gandhi was already one of the best-known Indians alive.

Life's Work

When Gandhi returned to India to stay, he found himself already being proclaimed a *mahatma,* a term in the Hindu religion meaning "great soul"; some went even further, believing him to be a reincarnation of Vishnu. More practically, Gandhi became one of the leaders of the Indian independence movement. From the 1920's through the early 1930's, he was the movement's leading planner, and throughout the interwar period, he served as a bridge between rival religious factions, the various Hindu castes, the growing Westernized upper-middle class, and the masses working in the fields.

While in South Africa, Gandhi had developed his philosophy of nonviolent protest, which he called *satyagraha*, truth-force or soul-force. In India, he brought that vision to fruition. At times he organized a section of the country to hold a general work stoppage or bring the entire Indian Empire to a halt as he fasted for an end to the terrible conditions of the so-called untouchables, rioting, or other problems besetting the country as a whole. In short, Gandhi evolved from an important political and cultural leader to the conscience of the Indian Empire and all of its people.

It was Gandhi's belief that *satyagraha* was the only way to win independence from Britain honorably, for if a free India was born in violence, it might never recover. Therefore, Gandhi had to spend much time establishing and then maintaining as strict a control over his own people as was possible in order to win independence from the British. Preventing fighting among Indians was important because the British could use the internal quarrels of the various Indian groups as an excuse to keep ultimate power in their own hands, no matter what reforms they might offer. Therefore, as the 1930's ended, the independence movement had not really come much closer to its goal after two decades of struggle. Gandhi had staged impressive demonstrations (such as the march to protest the salt tax in March and April of 1930), started numerous publications, written scores of articles, unified the various factions, and won concessions from the British after some bloody riots and reprisals, but India was not independent.

Gandhi also had trouble keeping control of day-to-day events, in part because of the sheer scope of the unrest affecting the huge subcontinent, but also because of the amount of time he spent in prison. Between 1922 and 1944, Gandhi spent nearly six years (2,089 days) in jail, mostly during the 1930's and in the latter part of World War II.

World War II would prove decisive for the fate of India. While Gandhi and his followers preferred the British and the Americans to the Nazis and Japanese, for the most part, they refused to cooperate with the Allies unless India was given its independence. Gandhi and many of his closest followers spent most of the war in custody. Mohammad Ali Jinnah, the leader of the Moslem League and a former follower of Gandhi, used the war to make the Moslem League independent of Gandhi and the Indian National Congress (the umbrella organization for most of the pro-independence organizations). By backing the Allies when most Indian groups refused, Jinnah was setting the stage to proclaim a separate Muslim state whenever India was granted independence.

When World War II was over, the Labour Party under Clement Attlee came to power in Great Britain. One of its goals was to establish the Indian Empire as an independent dominion within the British Commonwealth. The divisions that Gandhi had managed to unite within the Indian independence movement came forward as the

Mohandas K. Gandhi. *(Library of Congress)*

probability of independence came closer. Gandhi was committed to a united India, but the Muslims, the rulers of most of Northern India before the British came but an overall minority, were inspired by Jinnah to seek a separate country for those areas with a Muslim majority. Although the British offered a plan for a confederated India that might have satisfied Muslim demands while maintaining a united Indian government, few of the Indian leaders on either side, including Gandhi, were willing to trust the British plan in 1946. The result was an India divided on religious lines, India and Pakistan becoming independent dominions in 1947.

When a divided India became inevitable, Gandhi basically kept silent on the plan, devoting the rest of his life to quelling the religious unrest that welled up in 1947 and 1948, as Muslims and non-Muslims (many of them unwillingly) left their homes and made their way to areas where they would be in the majority. Hundreds of thousands of people died from violence, disease, and malnutrition during the riots and forced marches and in the relocation camps. Gandhi made his way to some of the worst scenes of conflict, pleading, arguing, and fasting to bring the violence to an end. Although he nearly died from the fasting and was often threatened by mobs, he was finally able to bring the worst of the violence to an end by the beginning of 1948. Religious and ethnic tensions remained, but there was, in general, peace between Hindus, Sikhs, Muslims, and the other groups.

On January 30, 1948, Nathuram Godse, a thirty-five-year-old high-caste Hindu newspaper editor and a refugee from Muslim violence, bowed in respect before Gandhi, who was on his way to a prayer meeting, and shot him three times, killing him almost instantly. This was the only way Godse and his fellow conspirators could deal with Gandhi's message of peace for all Indians.

Influence

Gandhi was not fully successful in his work in South Africa. When he left, Indians were treated as second-class citizens and looked down on by the whites who controlled the country. They were, however, treated as citizens with some rights, a vast improvement over the system that had been slowly taking hold since the late 1880's, which was tantamount to slavery. More important, Gandhi had found his life's work and had won respect for himself and his ideals of nonviolence.

Gandhi also failed in much of what he tried to accomplish for India. While he was able to modify the caste system and many of the social taboos that went with it, they were still in effect in much of the country as the twentieth century drew to a close. Although he succeeded in freeing India from British rule, the Indian Empire was split between India and Pakistan (as Pakistan itself was later split between Pakistan and Bangladesh), and religious and class strife is still rampant throughout the former Indian Empire. The small, self-sufficient, self-governing villages that Gandhi hoped would be the center of Indian cultural and political life remain largely a dream in an India troubled by chronic poverty and political unrest. Gandhi nevertheless succeeded in giving the people of the subcontinent an example of the best their culture had to offer, in promoting an ideal that they—and people throughout the world—could strive to achieve.

Terrance L. Lewis

An Autobiography

The Story of My Experiments with Truth

Type of philosophy: Ethics, Indian philosophy, social philosophy

First published: Satyana prayogo, athava, Atmakatha, serialized 1925-1929, published in 2 volumes 1927-1929 (English translation, serialized 1925-1929, published in two volumes 1927-1929)

Principal ideas advanced:

◇ Religion, in the broadest sense, is self-realization or knowledge of the self and therefore is part of philosophy.

◇ God can be realized only through service, and that service should have as its goal a desire for self-realization.

◇ *Brahmacharya* (self-restraint) and *ahimsa* (nonviolence) are ways of protecting body, mind, and soul.

◇ The idea of renunciation sets a moral example and promotes equability (*samabhava*).

◊ *Satyagraha* is an attribute of *ahimsa*, for truth-force must have as its basis a renunciation of violence.

◊ Service without humility is selfishness; God can never be realized by one who is not pure of heart and free of passions.

In India, Mohandas K. Gandhi's autobiography is seen as a Western preoccupation because autobiography writing is done by those in the West, not in the East. However, the work is a candid and humble account that illuminates the moral and spiritual side of an extraordinary leader. Gandhi's book is solidly rooted in a historical context that spans forty years of his life in the India of the 1870's to the 1920's, without, however, being bound by such specificity. This is because it is not a simple chronicle but a quest for ways of attaining Absolute Truth. Interweaving details of his life, historical and political incidents, and his personal philosophy of conduct, Gandhi is able to present different planes of experience. Gandhi exploits his eclectic reading—the Bhagavad Gita, the Qur'an, the Bible, works by Sir Edwin Arnold, John Ruskin, Leo Tolstoy, and the Theosophists—in order to develop his own approach to solving social, political, and moral problems, particularly those issuing from imperial colonialism, the Indian caste system, and humanity's own disposition toward corruption. However, Gandhi's tone is never pompous, aggressive, or rigid. The story of his life is narrated dispassionately, for he wants to appeal to youth as well as to adults.

In the introduction, Gandhi acknowledges that the true purpose of his autobiography is self-realization in order to attain moksha (freedom from birth and death), the Hindu version of salvation. Accordingly, although he chronicles his social and political ventures, he tends to view them in spiritual or moral terms that are subjective but absolutely correct, for, as he asserts, he would not base actions on his beliefs if these were not convincingly justified to himself.

The Search for Absolute Truth

His quest for Absolute Truth begins with personal truth, for even as a teenager, he submitted himself to an examination of conscience, a scrupulous self-critique that refused to sanction any frenzied novelty of custom or direction in life—such as the eating of meat or imitations of Western practices. The crux of part 1 is Gandhi's attraction to ideas of *brahmacharya* (self-restraint) and *ahimsa* (nonviolence) as ways of eradicating the canker of Untruth.

Gandhi's philosophy is essentially religious, not in a dogmatic sense but rather in that it is a system of thought based on the idea of self-realization or knowledge of the self. His reading of the Ramayana (the story of Rama) and the Bhagavad Gita evokes his religious fervor, but his early exposure to all branches of Hinduism and its sister religions (primarily Jainism and Buddhism) as well as to Christianity, Islam, and Zorastrianism (through his father's Parsi friends) gives him a grounding in tolerance. He sees that all religions are paths to God or the Absolute Truth, but when he reads the Manusmriti (laws of Manu, a Hindu lawgiver), he is impressed by its view that morality is the basis of things and that truth is the substance of morality.

Self-Control and Early Influences

Gandhi's early dietary habits, shyness, and vocal reticence are initial indications of his disposition toward general restraint in thought, feeling, and conduct. These forms of self-control became preliminary modes of the renunciation he later practiced, and they are consistent with the Theosophical philosophy with which he came into contact in England, especially through Annie Besant's *Why I Became a Theosophist* (1890), Sir Edwin Arnold's *The Light of Asia* (1879), and Madame Blavatsky's *Key to Theosophy* (1889). Like the Bhagavad Gita (which Gandhi regarded as his supreme guide to conduct), Theosophy advocates a denial or at least a discipline of the senses so that immoderate desire may be curbed, and with it, reckless passion. Renunciation, then, became the highest form of religion for him, a view for which he found support even in Thomas Carlyle's *On Heroes, Hero-Worship, and the Heroic in History* (1841), where the greatest hero is the prophet who, in addition to greatness and bravery, exemplifies austere living. Part 1 ends with an assertion of those acts—such as supplication, worship, and prayer—that are ways of cleansing the heart of passions.

In part 2, Gandhi acknowledges three modern

figures who made a deep impression on his life. One is the poet Raychand, or Rajchandra, the son-in-law of a family friend and a man of great character who possesses wide knowledge of the scriptures and a burning passion for self-realization. Though Raychand's moral earnestness appeals to Gandhi, who regards him as a refuge in times of spiritual crises, Gandhi declines to accept him as his guru. (Gandhi's belief in a guru is an offshoot of Hindu philosophy, according to which spiritual realization is impossible without true knowledge, and true knowledge impossible without a guru.)

The second modern figure of import to Gandhi is Leo Tolstoy, whose books on religion and moral action prompt Gandhi to increasingly realize the infinite possibilities of universal love. The third figure is John Ruskin, but Gandhi holds back from explaining his significance until later in the *Autobiography*.

Service and Sacrifice

The aim of self-realization is given paramount importance as Gandhi undertakes a comparative study of religions. He comes to believe that God, like self-realization, can be reached only through service. In part 3, this deep-rooted yearning to be of service to his community, nation, and fellow humans inspires Gandhi upon his next return to South Africa, where he continues to perform humanitarian work. He sees a need to take the vow of *brahmacharya* once he is influenced by Raychand's question: Which is more prized, the devotion of a servant or that of a wife to her husband? Plagued by guilt over his own immoderate sexual lust and weak will in marriage, Gandhi practices celibacy to diminish desire. Once desire is gone, it becomes clear that a vow of renunciation is the natural or inevitable fruit. Therefore, in 1906, Gandhi takes the vow—to which his wife has no objection—though he has trouble making the final resolve.

In *brahmacharya* lies the protection of the body, mind, and soul. It is not simply a process of hard penance but a matter of consolation and joy. Because *brahmacharya* means the control of the senses in thought, word, and deed, fasting is as necessary as proper diet, though fasting does not stop temptation.

Part 4 is imbued with a quickened spirit of sacrifice. He dedicates himself to struggling with Indian settlers for rights in the Transvaal, but the spirit of self-sacrifice is tempered by the desire to create something for the future. Though Gandhi conditions himself, his family, and his disciples to a philosophy of self-reliance, he uses ideas from Theosophy to promote the idea of brotherhood. Ironically, it is the questions of curious theosophical friends that impel Gandhi to turn to Hinduism for answers. It is from Hinduism that he cultivates notions of *aparigraha* (nonpossession) and *samabhava* (equability); subsequently events in South Africa and India provide him with a motive to develop and nurture his idea of *satyagraha* (truth-force or soul-force) as an attribute of *ahimsa* (nonviolence). *Satyagraha* is used to effect practical compromises among disputants in the home, in the workplace, and in politics without demeaning the very idea of compromise by implying that one party lost something that the other party has gained.

Influenced by English art critic and writer John Ruskin's *Unto This Last* (1860), a critique of the economic world of nineteenth century England in the form of articles about the dignity of labor and the good of the individual being contained in the common good, Gandhi makes his final vow of *brahmacharya*. This vow of self-purification is his preliminary to *satyagraha*, which, in turn, is based on a renunciation of passion and appetite. According to Hindu belief, self-realization is possible only in the fourth stage of life (that of the *sannyasa*), but Gandhi thinks that those who defer preparation for this stage until old age will inherit only a second and pitiable childhood.

His philosophy is a comprehensive one, in which all beliefs are linked and the whole amounts to a unified system of conduct based on the implicit idea of the unity of all life. As the error of an individual can affect all others in a society, it is necessary for every individual to attempt to free himself from error.

Part 5 is filled with examples of Gandhi's dedication to *satyagraha* on various scales and in many forms. His gentle but decisive approach wins over many disputants who realize that the doctrine is informed by consideration of and love for fellow humans. The true *satyagrahi* is self-effacing in humility and purity of heart, and such an individual is on the way to *moksha* (salvation).

Tenets for a Way of Life

An Autobiography is generally considered to be a major work, not so much because it is by a world figure from the East but as it shows the genesis of Gandhi's personal philosophical tenets for a way of life and conduct with social, political, and spiritual significance. Although the philosophy is rooted in Hinduism, it is not doctrinaire or authoritative. Its strands intertwine around the concept of self-realization.

Gandhi was, of course, no academic philosopher or priest, but an individual who, though brought up on traditional Hindu practices, chose to select whatever ideas were useful to him for his self-development and in public service. Every time he came across a new idea, he tested it, and if it was valuable, he integrated it into his way of life. Though his speculations are rooted in the Bhagavad Gita, the Sanskrit poem that argues the law of love, they issue out of a deep aspiration for true knowledge and pure action that could lead to freedom from worldly attachments and passions.

Gandhi's book exerted enormous influence for generations, not only in India but in the West as well. Although it is sometimes read for its historical context, it is chiefly consulted for its moral argument, which uses personal examples for illustration. In some sense, there are few novel beliefs in the work, for most of its ideas, including those about renunciation, self-control, and nonviolence, can be traced to ancient sources. However, the idea of *satyagraha* as a vehicle for domestic, social, political, and moral reform is indubitably Gandhi's own creation. The work forges connections between interpersonal relations and national affairs as well as between social change and moral evolution. Gandhi's autobiography is perused by many who seek insights that can be applied to their own lives.

Keith Garebian

Additional Reading

Chadha, Yogesh. *Gandhi: A Life.* New York: John Wiley & Sons, 1998. Retelling the story of Mohandas K. Gandhi's life, Chadha captures the essence of the man—a political powerhouse of unshakeable faith who used nonviolence to rattle the branches of the great British Empire. This balanced, objective account of the life and influence of Gandhi separates the man from the myth, documenting key events in his intellectual, spiritual, and political development.

Easwaran, Eknath, and Michael N. Nagler. *Gandhi, the Man: The Story of His Transformation.* Tomales, Calif.: Nilgiri Press, 1997. This very accessible text follows the spiritual development of one of the most influential men of the twentieth century. It focuses primarily on the influence of the Bhagavad Gita on Gandhi's life.

Gandhi, Mohandas K. *All Men Are Brothers: Life and Thoughts of Mahatma Gandhi as Told in His Own Words.* Paris: United Nations Educational, Scientific, and Cultural Organization, 1958. This selection of Gandhi's writings and speeches covers topics in politics, economics, education, and religion.

_____. *Gandhi's Letters to a Disciple.* London: Victor Gollancz, 1950. Madaleine Slade, known as Mira, the daughter of a British admiral, became one of Gandhi's most famous disciples in the early 1920's. In effect, Mira became a spiritual daughter of Gandhi, whom she called *bapu* (father), like most of the common people in India. When she and Gandhi were separated, usually when Gandhi was traveling or in prison, they would exchange letters. The letters rarely touch on the major political and social battles of the times; instead, they focus on everyday events in the lives of the people surrounding Gandhi.

Huttenback, Robert A. *Gandhi in South Africa.* Ithaca, N.Y.: Cornell University Press, 1971. This is a detailed monograph on Gandhi's years in South Africa. Huttenback traces the origins of the problems Gandhi faced and details the solutions for which Gandhi worked.

Iyer, Raghavan. *The Moral and Political Thought of Mahatma Gandhi.* New York: Oxford University Press, 1973. In this highly detailed work, Raghavan explores the conceptual foundations of Gandhi's religious, moral, and political ideologies and their interconnections. He is also interested in showing how much deeper Gandhi's philosophy was than the applications of most of his followers (especially his political followers) might suggest.

Terrance L. Lewis, updated by Lisa A. Wroble

Alan Gewirth

Drawing his inspiration from Immanuel Kant, Gewirth attempted to provide a rational basis for a universal system of morality.

Principal philosophical works: Marsilius of Padua and Medieval Political Philosophy, 1951; The Defensor Pacis, 1956; Moral Rationality, 1972; Reason and Morality, 1978; Human Rights: Essays on Justification and Applications, 1982; The Community of Rights, 1996; Self-Fulfillment, 1998.

Born: November 28, 1912; Union City, New Jersey

Early Life

Alan Gewirth was born in Union City, New Jersey, on November 28, 1912, the son of Hyman and Rose Lees Gewirth. He attended Columbia University in New York, where he was elected to Phi Beta Kappa. After being awarded the degree of Bachelor of Arts with honors in philosophy in 1934, Gewirth began his postgraduate work at Cornell University, where from 1936 to 1937 he was a Sage fellow in philosophy. In 1937, he left Cornell for the University of Chicago. There he was a research assistant and also taught, meanwhile continuing to work on his doctorate. During this period, Gewirth was also producing scholarly articles. In 1941, two of his essays appeared in scholarly journals, "Experience and the Non-Mathematical in the Cartesian Method" in the *Journal of the History of Ideas*, and "The Cartesian Circle" in the *Philosophical Review*. Gewirth's continuing interest in the French philosopher René Descartes was also evident when a third article, entitled "Clearness and Distinctness in Descartes," was published in *Philosophy* in 1943.

However, Gewirth's academic career was interrupted when the United States entered World War II. In 1942, he became an officer in the United States Army. By the time he was discharged in 1946, he had risen to the rank of captain.

Gewirth lost no time in resuming his academic work. He returned to Columbia University as a Rockefeller Foundation fellow and completed the requirements for his doctorate in philosophy, receiving his doctorate in 1947. Gewirth's outstanding work at Columbia was recognized the following year when he was presented with the prestigious Woodbridge Prize.

Meanwhile, Gewirth had returned to Chicago, which became his permanent home. In 1947, he became a member of the University of Chicago faculty and began rising through the ranks. Thereafter, he left the university for a significant length of time only when his duties as a visiting professor at another major institution made it necessary for him to do so.

Although Gewirth was still interested in epistemology, or the theory of knowledge, and especially in Descartes's emphasis on the primacy of reason, he had also done extensive research on an important medieval Italian political theorist, Marsilius of Padua. In *Defensor Pacis*, published anonymously in 1324, Marsilius of Padua argued that the Church should have no authority over the state and suggested that the secular power should rest in the hands of the citizenry and their elected representatives. Marsilius and his ideas were the subject of Gewirth's first published volume, *Marsilius of Padua and Medieval Political Philosophy*, which went through four editions in fifteen years, an impressive record for a first book by a scholar who was just beginning to establish his reputation. In 1956, Gewirth published a translation of *Defensor Pacis*, along with an introduction and appendices. This standard translation also went into several reprints.

Gewirth's work on Marsilius of Padua marked the end of his apprenticeship, establishing him as both a painstaking scholar and a first-class analytical thinker. Gewirth now proceeded to make some important changes in his personal life. On March 18, 1956, he married Marcella Tilton, to whom his most famous work, *Reason and Morality*, would be dedicated. Their family would eventually consist of five children, James, Susan, Andrew Alan, Daniel Tilton, and Letitia Rose.

Life's Work

Gewirth's status as an authority on Marsilius of Padua and his work remained unchallenged over the decades that followed. He was the author of the entry on Marsilius of Padua in the *Encyclopedia of Philosophy* (1967) and of the essay on the *Defensor Pacis* in Scribner's *Dictionary of the Middle Ages* (1984). In 1980, Gewirth lectured on Marsilius at the University of Padua in Italy. Gewirth's research into Marsilius's era was also the basis for his lengthy essay "Philosophy and Political Thought in the Fourteenth Century," published in *The Forward Movement of the Fourteenth Century* (1961), edited by F. L. Utley. However, Gewirth also had two articles published in *Journal of Philosophy* that dealt with Descartes and his philosophy, Cartesianism, "The Cartesian Circle Reconsidered" (1970) and "Descartes: Two Disputed Questions" (1971).

Even though the two philosophers who so fascinated Gewirth were separated in time by three centuries, both of them believed that humans should rely on their own reason, rather than external authority, to guide them in choosing between courses of action. Marsilius rejected the idea that God spoke through popes and kings; he believed that the people had it in their power to ascertain the truth through the use of their own reason. Descartes, too, exalted reason, and though he was careful to exempt matters of faith from his system, in fact it left no room for Catholic dogma or for the Christian faith. Gewirth, too, thought that there should be some basis for the decisions human beings make, either as individuals or through their social and political institutions; but like Marsilius and Descartes, he had decided that reason was the only power on which humanity could depend.

The comprehensive nature of Gewirth's investigations had already been indicated in 1949, when one essay in which he discussed politics and psychiatry, and another in which he considered "The Psychological Approach to Politics,"

appeared in the journal *Ethics*. In 1954, *Philosophy of Science* published not only his article "Subjectivism and Objectivism in the Social Sciences" but also another one, in which Gewirth sought the answer to the more basic question, "Can Men Change Laws of Social Science?" From 1956 on, the titles of most of Gewirth's publications contained words such as "ethics," "morality," "moral," or "justice," suggesting his concentration on ethical issues, whether they involved a single individual or the state. The application of ethics to institutions is the subject of his essay "Political Justice," which was included in a collection he coauthored, *Social Justice* (1962). It is hardly surprising that he also produced an edited volume entitled *Political Philosophy* (1965).

However, in the 1960's and the 1970's, Gewirth was not merely analyzing the way ethics applied to human institutions; more basically, he was attempting to construct a system on which ethical decisions could be based. Thus an essay in a 1964 *Philosophical Review* was called "The Generalization Principle"; one in a 1967 *Philosophical Quarterly*, "Categorial Consistency in Ethics"; and still another, published in a 1971 *Review of Metaphysics*, "The Normative Structure of Action." Included in the published *Proceedings and Addresses of the American Philosophical Association* (1974) was Gewirth's "The 'Is-Ought' Problem Resolved." That same year, he wrote the entry on "Ethics" for the *Encyclopedia Britannica*.

Gewirth's stature in the academic community at this time is evident in his visiting professorships, at Harvard in 1957, at the University of Michigan in 1959-1960, at The Johns Hopkins University in 1966-1967, and at Indiana University in South Bend in 1972. He was also a Cooper Foundation lecturer at Swarthmore College in 1961, a Niebuhr lecturer at Elmhurst College in 1969, and a Lindley lecturer at the University of Kansas in 1972. His Lindley lecture, "Moral Rationality," was published the same year as a book. In 1975, Gewirth delivered a Perspectives lecture at the University of Notre Dame and a Mellon Foundation lecture at Marquette University. Among Gewirth's other honors during this period were his election to the presidency of the American Philosophical Association in 1973-1974 and his selection by the National Endowment for the Humanities as a senior fellow (1974-1975) and also as a John Simon Guggenheim Memorial Foundation fellow (1975-1976). Gewirth's own university recognized his achievements by naming him the Edward Carson Waller Distinguished Service Professor of Philosophy, beginning in 1975.

By now, Gewirth was in his sixties. He had been a member of the University of Chicago faculty for almost thirty years, had published important works in several different areas, and had won more than his share of honors. However, he did not rest on his laurels. In 1978, he published the work for which he would be best known. In *Reason and Morality*, Gewirth presented what he believed was a valid, strictly rational foundation for ethics. For this publication, the University of Chicago Press awarded him the Gordon Laing Prize in 1980. In 1982, a related volume was published, *Human Rights: Essays on Justification and Applications*.

During the 1980's, Gewirth spoke at various universities in the United States, including Wheaton College in Illinois, Westminster College, Wabash College, the University of California at Riverside, the University of Rochester, and St. Louis University. In 1981, he was the Hannah Arendt Memorial lecturer at the New School for Social Research in New York City. His lectures outside the United States, in addition to that presented at Padua in 1980, included the Bar-Hillel lecture at Tel Aviv University in Israel in 1987; an appearance at the World Congress of Philosophy in Brighton, England, in 1988; the Fabri lecture at the University of Tübingen, the Federal Republic of Germany, in 1989; and still another lecture that same year at the Twelfth Interamerican Congress of Philosophy in Buenos Aires.

In 1996, the University of Chicago Press published the long-awaited sequel to *Reason and Morality*. In *The Community of Rights*, Gewirth applies the abstract moral principles outlined in the earlier work to specific issues, balancing property rights against individual rights, for example, and insisting that government should be supportive, rather than oppressive, enabling citizens to acquire an education and to find employment, even assuring them a minimum income. This work was followed in 1998 by *Self-Fulfillment*, in which Gewirth used the principles outlined in *Reason and Morality* to examine various forms of self-fulfillment and

their effects both on individuals and on society.

It has been pointed out that the second half of the twentieth century was characterized by increasing skepticism. Rejecting the idea of a supernatural power to guide and sustain them, more and more people found themselves adrift, lacking any basis on which they could make everyday decisions or formulate social, political, and economic policies. This pervasive skepticism led philosophers and literary critics alike to spend their time analyzing language rather than dealing with moral issues, ignoring the outcries against widespread offenses against human rights, denials of legal and social justice, and violations of the natural environment. Becoming convinced that what his era needed, above all else, was a solid moral system, Gewirth set about to construct one. Influenced by Marsilius, Descartes, and, most important, by the eighteenth century philosopher Immanuel Kant, Gewirth based the system he constructed on a profound faith in reason. However, while Kant's "categorical imperative" placed the emphasis on duties, Gewirth chose to think of fundamental principles in terms of "rights."

Although Gewirth was not the first philosopher to suggest a new look at Kant's theories or to argue for a "practical reason" approach to ethics, he has been one of the most influential. *Reason and Morality* is cited in every essay on the "neo-Kantians" or on practical reasoning, and both it and Gewirth's later works are often mentioned in discussions of such concrete issues as property rights, civil liberties, capitalistic structures, and taxation. It seems obvious that Gewirth's influence, both as a neo-Kantian theorist, who defended the worth of reason in a skeptical age, and as a citizen, who believed that social, economic, and moral issues could be sensibly approached through the practical application of his system, will not soon decline, but will continue to be felt for years to come.

Rosemary M. Canfield Reisman

Reason and Morality

Type of philosophy: Ethics
First published: 1978

Principal ideas advanced:

◇ Though the task of justifying a universal moral system is difficult, there is a critical need for such a system.

◇ Reason, applied to action, is the means by which such a system can be justified.

◇ All action must be defined as both voluntary and purposive.

◇ The search for justification must begin with human beings, or agents, rather than with abstractions.

◇ Every agent claims two rights, well-being and freedom, the latter being necessary for the pursuit of well-being.

◇ Because all agents have the right to well-being and freedom, these rights provide the basis for a universal moral system.

◇ According to this system, or the "Principle of Generic Consistency," everyone's actions should be based on the assumption that everyone else has identical generic rights.

Reason and Morality is a work in the rationalist tradition. Deriving from the emphasis on reason in Greek philosophy, rationalism had a profound effect on the early humanists, most of whom sought to reconcile reason and faith. However, in the seventeenth century, with the development of scientific thought, reason began to be seen as replacing religion as a foundation for life. Although philosophers such as René Descartes insisted that reason and faith were meant to govern different areas of human existence, ultimately rationalism became an opponent of religious institutions and of faith itself. At the very least, there was an effort to eliminate religious bigotry and intolerance, which the French writer Voltaire labeled "infamy." For many, however, the supernatural was seen simply as a falsehood, probably perpetrated by the hierarchy whose power depended on popular belief.

In his *Kritik der reinen Vernunft* (1781; *The Critique of Pure Reason*, 1838), Kant ruled out traditional metaphysics as the source of truth and constructed a moral system on the basis of reason. However, succeeding philosophers extended their skepticism to reason itself, doubting that anything in this world or outside it was a certainty. From this posture came such vague popular declarations as "everything's relative" and

often a resulting inability to make decisions based on ethical principles. Alan Gewirth and the other neo-Kantians, then, are in one sense conservative, in that they seek to reclaim the earlier belief in reason so as to establish a basis for moral choices. However, Gewirth is not merely Kant's disciple. His arguments, the moral system he develops, and his practical applications are all highly original.

Justification

As Gewirth explains in the preface, one of the most important questions philosophers attempt to answer is whether justification can be found for a system of morality. Without such a system, one cannot battle evil in oneself or in others because there is no way to label anything as evil. Realizing the critical need for a means of justifying a set of moral principles that are universally applicable, Gewirth set out to find it. The result is this book.

Reason and Morality is divided into five sections. In the first, entitled "The Problem of Justification," the author explores the issue. After commenting on the conflicts that can arise from competing moral rules, Gewirth identifies the primary questions of moral philosophy as, first, why should one be moral; second, what other interests should one consider in making decisions; and finally, what other interests can be identified as *good* enough to affect one's decisions.

Gewirth then proceeds to systematic analysis, using a method that he will continue to use throughout the book. After stating a question for which he obviously has formulated an answer, he outlines the objections that opponents to his point of view would raise, answers them, and proceeds to the next question. Thus he argues that a moral system is necessary in order to provide some consistency in people's lives and that it must have some basis, so that people can be protected against those who might be consistent but are evil.

Gewirth's next question is about the possibility of justifying such a principle. After demonstrating that neither deductive nor inductive methods can accomplish such a feat, Gewirth asserts that the answer he seeks can be found by applying reason to action, looking at what human beings will themselves to do. While admitting that both reason and action are morally neutral, Gewirth nevertheless asserts that they can provide the answer he seeks. However, he insists on some limitations as to what is implied by the word "action." First, it must not be the result of either coercion or ignorance; it must issue from a voluntary choice. Second, it must not be the result of a whim; it must have a specific purpose. After briefly explaining his "dialectically necessary method," Gewirth asserts that this method, applied to action, will result in everyone's accepting a single "supreme principle of morality."

What Is Good
In the second section of *Reason and Morality*, Gewirth explores "The Normative Structure of Action." Although any individual's view of what is "good" can vary from time to time, Gewirth explains, as human beings, we always seek gains, rather than losses; we work for whatever will ensure our well-being, at least in the long run; we pursue what we value. Moreover, not only do human beings claim well-being as a right, but they also assert a second right, the freedom to work toward that well-being. As the author points out, if everyone believes that he or she has those two rights and also admits that all other human beings have the same rights, then the basis for a universal moral system has been established.

Before he can proceed with his argument, however, Gewirth must deal with the fact that there is an almost infinite number of variables in life, both differences between individuals and differences between one set of circumstances and another. Gewirth proceeds to outline the ways that philosophers have tried to deal with the fact of variability, which range from accepting it as inevitable to attempting to accommodate it, while still arguing for universal principles. As is his habit, Gewirth looks for an answer not to abstractions but to the concrete and to "agents," or human beings. Although one cannot include children too young to vote in the category of voters, for example, because all of those of a certain age will be able to vote at the same future time, clearly they participate in the general category of voters. Obviously, then, one can be a "prospective purposive agent." The point is that,

upon close examination, variables may be only superficial.

The Principle of Generic Consistency
In the third section, Gewirth asserts the core of his argument, the "Principle of Generic Consistency," or the PGC. Reminding his readers that he has established freedom and well-being as "necessary goods" for everyone, and that because action is impossible without freedom and well-being, it is only logical that every human being, or "agent," will claim both freedom and well-being as rights. Moreover, every rational agent will realize that the only way one can exercise one's rights is to allow others to do so as well. In other words, the agent's self-interest will motivate him or her to make sure that others have the freedom to work for their own well-being. Thus Gewirth moves from "is" to "ought," and to what he identifies as the supreme principle of morality, or the Principle of Generic Consistency, defined as follows: *"Act in accord with the generic rights of your recipients as well as of yourself."* The PGC is strikingly similar to the Golden Rule, which commands Christians to treat others as they would wish to be treated, and to Kant's categorical imperative, which directs human beings to proceed with an action only when the rule governing it could be elevated into a universal law.

Having stated his PGC, Gewirth proceeds to detail the logical argument that led eventually to his assertion of the PGC, to defend it as being both a formal and a material necessity, and to discuss questions he anticipates being raised, such as the relationships between analytic truth and morality and between motivation and rationality. At the end of this section, Gewirth comments that he has now accomplished the main purpose of his book: to show how one can move logically from the concept of generic moral action to a universal principle of morality.

The last two sections of *Reason and Morality* suggest and analyze direct and indirect applications of the PGC. For example, consistent with his interest in political philosophy and his concern about social justice is Gewirth's formulation of what he terms an "Equality of Generic Rights." He considers such practical matters as the difference between providing equal opportunity and basic needs and working to reduce everyone to the same level; ensuring justice and providing for self-defense; the duty to rescue, which the author demonstrates is not as simple as it might seem; and rights as they apply to losing and gaining goods. Section 4 concludes with a thoughtful discussion of the implications of the PGC as to what limits should be set on individual freedom. Sensibly, Gewirth concludes that one person's freedom should be limited only when it is "needed to prevent or remedy interferences with other persons' necessary conditions of action."

In the final section of his book, Gewirth applies the PGC to social rules and institutions. Having explored the various possibilities of social and political structures, he concludes by describing what he sees as the state that best fulfills the moral rule he has established. Gewirth rejects the libertarian ideal, which would preserve the status quo, assuming that the wealthy had acquired their worldly goods in a just and legal manner; similarly, he rejects the egalitarian ideal, which would redistribute wealth so as to benefit the poorest members of society. Noting that these extremes violate claims to well-being and to freedom, Gewirth suggests instead a democratic and "supportive state," which, as he explains, is consistent with the PGC.

There follows a closely reasoned defense of the PGC against anticipated objections, in which Gewirth argues that his system is complete—in other words, that it can be used to determine right and wrong in every situation and for every individual, and, moreover, that it is consistent and, therefore, can be used to resolve what are perceived as conflicts between duties. In "Some Concluding Reflections," the author sums up the process by which he arrived at his supreme moral principle and reiterates the statement of faith on which *Reason and Morality* and the PGC are based: that the human reason is the only certain guide to truth.

Criticism and Impact

Several years before *Reason and Morality* was published, articles attacking the ideas that Gewirth was advancing in essays and in lectures were already appearing in scholarly journals. Once the completed work was in print, not only was it widely reviewed but it also was the subject of an amazing number of articles, in which all the elements of Gewirth's argument were examined and what the authors saw as logical flaws were pointed out. Often Gewirth was provided with an opportunity to respond to his critics, as he did to E. J. Bond in a four-essay series published in 1980 by *Metaphilosophy* and called a "Symposium on Reason and Morality." Gewirth's system, as it was described in *Reason and Morality*, was also discussed in *Gewirth's Ethical Rationalism: Critical Essays with a Reply by Alan Gewirth*, a collection edited by Edward Regis, Jr. (1984). This book and similar publications indicate how much time other scholars were spending on the study of Gewirth's ideas during the years immediately after publication of *Reason and Morality*.

Thirteen years after *Reason and Morality* appeared, it was still the subject of heated debate. In a massive work entitled *The Dialectical Necessity of Morality: An Analysis and Defense of Alan Gewirth's Argument to the Principle of Generic Consistency* (1991), Deryck Beyleveld cited dozens of comments by Gewirth's opponents, classified their attacks on Gewirth's system into sixty-six "objections," and devoted almost three hundred pages to stating and refuting their arguments. In the reviews of Gewirth's subsequent books, *Reason and Morality* is almost invariably mentioned. Thus in *Theological Studies* (September, 1997), Stephen J. Pope begins his review of *The Community of Rights* (1996) by describing it as "a sequel to Gewirth's magisterial volume *Reason and Morality*," which is then summarized.

Even though scholars cannot agree as to whether Gewirth succeeded in arriving at a supreme principle of morality and though it will be some years before the full impact of the work can be assessed, *Reason and Morality* has certainly attained the status of a classic and its author, that of a philosopher of major importance.

Rosemary M. Canfield Reisman

Additional Reading

Allen, Paul. *Proof of Moral Obligation in Twentieth-Century Philosophy*. New York: Peter Lang, 1988. A monograph exploring the question of whether moral obligation itself can be proven. After analyzing several writers' attempts to demonstrate such a principle, Allen utilizes Gewirth's ideas in developing what he believes is irrefutable proof of moral obligation.

An interesting publication, not least as a revelation of Gewirth's importance as an influence on later writers.

Beyleveld, Deryck. *The Dialectical Necessity of Morality: An Analysis and Defense of Alan Gewirth's Argument to the Principle of Generic Consistency.* Chicago: University of Chicago Press, 1991. A formal analysis of the argument Gewirth presented in *Reason and Morality* is followed by the systematic refutation of every objection that has been raised. Most students will find the detailed discussion, with its sixty-six divisions, somewhat daunting. Gewirth's foreword is useful, as are Beyleveld's summary and his brief identification of "key issues." Copious notes and a good bibliography. Indexed both by author and by subject.

Bond, E. J., and Alan Gewirth. "Symposium on Reason and Morality." *Metaphilosophy* 11 (January, 1980): 36-53. In "Gewirth on Reason and Morality," Bond briefly summarizes and questions Gewirth's point of view. In the extensive "Comments on Bond's Article" that follow, Gewirth accuses Bond of failing to understand his arguments. In his "Reply to Gewirth," Bond again points out what he believes are flaws in Gewirth's reasoning. The final article in this revealing "symposium" is contained in the next issue of the journal, in Gewirth's "Reason and Morality: Rejoinder to E. J. Bond," *Metaphilosophy* 11 (April, 1980): 138-142.

Brandt, Richard B., ed. *Social Justice.* Englewood Cliffs, N.J.: Prentice-Hall, 1962. Consists of five essays on what the editor argues is a neglected subject, the issue of what is "just" and what is "unjust." All are based on Cooper Foundation lectures delivered at Swarthmore College in spring, 1961. Includes Alan Gewirth's "Political Justice." Though identified in the preface as a student of "historic political philosophers," presumably because of his research on Marsilius, Gewirth does not base his essay on history but proposes a system based on abstract principles, as he was later to do in *Reason and Morality.*

Boylan, Michael, ed. *Gewirth: Critical Essays on Action, Rationality, and Community.* Lanham, Md.: Rowman & Littlefield, 1999. An important collection of essays that address Gewirth's political and ethical philosophies.

Regis, Edward, ed. *Gewirth's Ethical Rationalism: Critical Essays with a Reply by Alan Gewirth.* Chicago: University of Chicago Press, 1984. Contains an incisive introduction by the editor, twelve essays, and Gewirth's lengthy response, in which each section is preceded by the name or names of the authors to whom he is responding. Includes a list of Gewirth's writings through 1984 and a useful index. The essays are not easy reading; however, because they represent all of the major responses to Gewirth's ethical system and also include his response, the volume is considered essential for any student of Gewirth and his thought.

Rosemary M. Canfield Reisman

Gongsun Long

Gongsun Long left the largest corpus of the Chinese School of Names. He produced paradoxical conclusions that followed from the examination of references of words.

Principal philosophical works: Gongsun Longzi, early third century B.C.E. (*The Works of Kung-sun Lung-tzu,* 1952; best known as *Gongsun Longzi*)

Born: c. 320 B.C.E.; Chao (now Shanxi), China
Died: c. 250 B.C.E.; China

Early Life

In traditional Chinese sources, Gongsun Long's date of birth is given as 380 B.C.E., but subsequent scholarship indicates he was probably born about sixty years later. Gongsun Long was a native of the state of Chao (now Shanxi). He was an entertainer at the court of the Lord of Bin Yuan and amused and confounded his audience with logical paradoxes and arguments rather than with magic tricks or physical dexterity.

Legend has it that Gongsun Long produced his most notable work, "The White Horse Dialogue," to convince a customs official that he should not be prevented from transporting his horse across the border. The dialogue is a record of a conversation that Gongsun Long had with Gong Zhuan. Several anecdotes are preserved about debates between the two concerning various outlandish or paradoxical claims. This suggests that Gongsun Long was less serious in intent than some other members of the School of Names (a group of Chinese sophists), including Hui Shi, who may have been producing paradoxes in the service of a metaphysics of the unity of all things in one entity and a morality of concern for everyone. Ironically, Hui Shi's more serious work survives only in fragments, while Gongsun Long's essays are preserved in extensive form. Hui Shi's paradoxes, some of which resemble the Greek philosopher Zeno's paradoxes, have been given a geographical and political interpretation. In contrast, Gongsun Long's

paradoxes have no relevance whatsoever to political, moral, or practical issues and therefore are unusual in Chinese philosophy. This lack of practical political relevance led Gongsun Long's work to be ignored during most of Chinese history, although interest in the School of Names revived during later periods.

Life's Work

The original version of *Gongsun Longzi,* written in the early third century B.C.E., had fourteen chapters. By the Tang Dynasty (618-907), the extant version contained only six chapters, five consisting of essays and one of biographical material. The essays, attributed to Gongsun Long, are "The White Horse Dialogue," "Pointings and Things," "The Hard and the White," "Understanding Change," and "On Names and Actuality."

One Western commentator likened the views in "The Hard and the White" to those of the German idealists of the nineteenth century in that the essay discusses the conditioning of the senses by the mind. Part of the argument involves the fact that "white" is recognized by sight and "hard" is recognized by touch, but sight cannot determine hard and touch cannot determine white. Furthermore, the mind must process and combine the sensations to form whole objects. Some Western scholars have suggested that "The Hard and the White" is a later forgery because it involves the Buddhist theory of knowledge that developed in China centuries after Gongsun Long's life. However, many Chinese scholars consider the treatise authentic. The early Chinese philosopher Mencius refers to this idea in passing, so essays on the subject are assumed to have existed during this time. If the essay on hard and white dates from this early period, it would be the first mention of the theory of knowledge in Chinese philosophy. However, if the essay dates from six centuries later, when the Buddhist theory of knowledge was well known in China, then it is of much less significance.

"Pointings and Things" develops puzzles of reference. Gongsun Long states that one cannot point to a pointing, nor can one point to the universe as a whole. Similarly, Ludwig Wittgenstein, in his "Logisch-philosophische Abhandlung" (1921; best known by the bilingual German and English edition title of *Tractatus Logico-Philosophicus*, 1922, 1961), posited that one cannot see one's own eye and that the world as a limited whole is the "mystical" and is beyond the sort of reference that can pick out facts. The Chinese philosopher's idea also resembles German philosopher Immanuel Kant's notion that the universe as a whole and the knowing subject are not objects in the way that bounded, delimited things are. Gongsun Long's essay also implicitly distinguishes reference to an object from reference to a referring expression or meaning. To attempt to refer to the whole universe would also refer to the referring expression or pointing itself. However, if the referring expression or pointing must be separate from the object, then this is impossible.

The paradox that opens "Understanding Change" appears to depend on the Chinese way of writing the number two with two parallel horizontal strokes. It can be claimed that the stroke on the bottom is not two and the stroke on the top is not two, yet together they are two. This passage is generally agreed to be an authentic piece of the sophistry or argumentation prevalent during the Warring States period (475-221 B.C.E.), although the rest of the chapter is most likely a later forgery based on misunderstood borrowings from Mohist logic developed by followers of the fifth century B.C.E. philosopher Mozi.

"The White Horse Dialogue" is the most famous, puzzling, and controversial of Gongsun Long's essays. His claim that a white horse is not a horse puzzled many in his own day. Zhuangzi, in the *Zhuangzi* (c. 300 B.C.E., *The Divine Classic of Nan-hua*, 1881; also known as *The Complete Works of Chuang Tzu*, 1968; commonly known as *Zhuangzi*, 1991), refers to this argument and suggests Gongsun Long ought to have pointed to a nonhorse rather than a horse to make his point. Fung Yu-lan, the greatest Chinese historian of philosophy, claimed that Gongsun Long had discovered the theory of forms (as Plato had in ancient Greece). What he meant is that Gongsun Long had conceived of the existence of qualities (such as whiteness) that existed independently and separately from individual white objects. "The White Horse Dialogue" shows that the quality of "horseness" is not the same as a particular horse. "The Hard and the White" shows the separateness of the forms from the qualities of "hard" and "white," even though form and quality may be unified in particular objects such as stones. Some experts believe that Gongsun Long was showing the paradoxicality or undesirability of such forms separate from particular objects, but this seems doubtful, given that no one else in Chinese philosophy held such a doctrine, and therefore, there was no need to refute the position.

During the late twentieth century, classical Chinese scholar Chad Hansen developed a radically new interpretation of Gongsun Long's essay. Hansen suggested that classical Chinese nouns were mass nouns. (Mass nouns, less common in English than countable nouns, are nouns that cannot be counted or quantified without using a measure—for example, a cup of *coffee*, a bucket of *water*, a bushel of *sand*.) Because classical Chinese nouns do not take definite and indefinite articles ("the" and "a" in English) and do not distinguish between singular and plural ("man" in Chinese can mean either one man or all of humanity), Hansen said they functioned as mass nouns. He stated that the appropriate theory of objects in a mass-noun language is the relation not between an individual and a quality or a class (which motivates Plato's forms and other abstract notions in Western philosophy) but between a part and the whole that contains it. He argues that "whiteness" is part of a white horse but not of a nonwhite horse, and "horseness," or horse-shape (as distinct from color, weight, or other qualities), is part of a white horse. Therefore, the dialogue can be interpreted as playing on the ambiguity between "horse" as the entire animal with all its qualities and "horse" as horse-shape. Gongsun Long shifts between these two meanings of "horse."

Christoph Harbsmeier, a leading late twentieth century Western expert on classical Chinese, criticized Hansen's claims. He noted that investigations into classical Chinese grammar in the 1970's found distinctions between mass and count nouns, which would seem to negate Hansen's theory. He also objected to what he saw as mereology, a formal apparatus invented by Polish logicians to deal with part-whole relations. However, other scholars have pointed out that the details of this apparatus need not have been known to the ancient Chinese any more than were the details of their formal grammar. This apparatus is merely a modern technical formalization of the notions of part and whole. Harbsmeier believes that "The White Horse Dialogue" is not as coherent as logically sophisticated twentieth century commentators attempt to make it. In the wake of Harbsmeier's comments, scholar A. C. Graham, originally an ardent supporter of Hansen's theories, tempered his enthusiasm somewhat but still thought that it was useful to think of the ancient Chinese as treating the world as a continuous whole that can be broken into parts for various purposes rather than as something that is built up out of substances and atoms.

Influence

The six-chapter version of Gongsun Long's work existed at least as early as 672 C.E. and possibly during the Sui Dynasty (581-618). At least some, if not all, of the essays contained in that version, date back to the early fourth century B.C.E. Graham has argued that "Names and Actualities," "The Hard and the White," and the possibly spurious later part of "Understanding Change" contain passages borrowed from the Mohist logicians that were largely misunderstood by the compilers and forgers and combined with much-later Buddhist epistemology. The work of the School of Names died out with the rise of the Chinese empire in the Qin Dynasty (221-207 B.C.E.). The school's work was thought to be a useless pastime not helpful in political rule.

Once Buddhism became widespread in China, there was some revival of interest in philosophy, and the Buddhists introduced logical doctrines. Interest in the logicians or sophists developed again during the Six Dynasties (220-589) period, perhaps sparked by the "neo-Daoist" interest in clever conversation and in the dark and mysterious. Daoist commentaries were written on Gongsun Long, and the best old edition of the work is the one found in the Daoist canon. Interest declined again when the influence of Buddhism and Daoism was displaced by that of neo-Confucianism. However, in the nineteenth and twentieth centuries, the introduction of Western science and logical formalization in China sparked new study of Gongsun Long. The 1975 Hansen thesis concerning mass terms spawned discussion concerning the linguistic basis of the work of Gongsun Long among analytical philosophers studying Chinese thought.

Val Dusek

Gongsun Longzi

Type of philosophy: Chinese philosophy, epistemology, logic, metaphysics
First transcribed: Gongsun Longzi, early third century B.C.E. (*The Works of Kung-sun Lung-tzu,* 1952; best known as *Gongsun Longzi*)
Principal ideas advanced:
◇ Universals, the properties common to many individual things, must be considered as distinct from individuals.
◇ Thus, a white horse is not a horse, for the universal "horse" cannot be specified by color.
◇ A hard and a white stone must be two entities, for hardness is perceptible to touch, while whiteness is perceptible only to vision.
◇ Names refer to universals; thus, to confuse names is to confuse the natures of things, and such confusion is a cause of social disorder.
◇ Because universals are known only through particulars, which consist of universals, everything in the universe is really a universal, and yet nothing in the universe is really a universal as such.
◇ Only particulars change.

Much of ancient Chinese thought is characterized by its practical orientation. The early Chinese thinkers seem to have been preoccupied with the devising of political and social formulas to meet practical and pressing problems of their time; they gave little attention to pure abstraction. However, the six chapters that remain of *Gongsun Longzi* (originally a fourteen-chapter work) are almost exclusively devoted to metaphysics and logic.

Gongsun Long had one of the few bisyllabic Chinese family names—Gongsun. A leader of the School of Names, he was a court entertainer who amused his audience with his outstanding oratorical and argumentative skills. His opponents, whose works provide a vague outline of Gongsun Long's life, accused him of artfully using words merely to win arguments, never to convince people completely. However, Gongsun Long's own book shows that he was not arguing for argument's sake but was driven by a zeal to "rectify the names" in quite the same manner as was Confucius. At least one ruler valued Gongsun Long's views enough to give him an important government appointment, and the philosopher spent most of his life around different princes to whom he offered his advice on how to govern. His personal political fortunes waxed and waned in proportion to the confidence he could win from his patrons.

The primary concern of the School of Names was an investigation into the "names of things," or into what lies behind a name. In *Gongsun Longzi*, Gongsun Long quite succinctly presents a summary of the problems that he and his fellows treated with tireless persistence. All these problems seem to center on the key question of the distinction between the universal and the particular, between the abstract idea as the essence of things and the concrete things themselves as objects of sense-perception.

The White Horse Discourse

Gongsun Long is best known for "The White Horse Dialogue," one of the six chapters in his book. He is said to have admitted that this discourse constitutes the core of his philosophy. The argument starts with Gongsun Long's premise that "A white horse is not a horse."

Gongsun Long "proves" his thesis in several ways. To begin with, "horse" can be any kind of horse because it is a universal concept of horse. This term does not exclude any color, unlike the description "white horse," which fits only a particular kind of horse. Hence, the two names are not equal. Additionally, the term "horse" excludes the concept of "all colors"; that is, the essence of horse (horseness) has nothing to do with color. Because horseness cannot be equal to horseness plus whiteness, a white horse is not a horse.

By the same token, a white horse is not "white" either. The abstract concept of whiteness does not involve any object that is white. Whiteness has nothing to do with "making anything white." However, the "white" of a white horse is inseparably involved in the concrete object of a white horse; therefore, whiteness plus horseness cannot be the same as whiteness alone.

The moment the reader grasps that Gongsun Long is merely trying to expound on the existence of "universals" as independent entities, the famous white horse discourse presents no difficulty to understand. With the same understanding, the reader will also be able to appreciate Gongsun Long's position in another of his celebrated discourses, the argument on "The Hard and the White."

Hardness and Whiteness

A hard and white stone is actually two entities, according to Gongsun Long. He argues that hardness is perceptible to touch while whiteness is perceptible only to sight. Because the tactile and visual senses are separate, there must be two entities—a white stone and a hard stone—in a hard and white stone. In this argument, Gongsun Long made the distinction between these entities on an epistemological basis. If only that which is perceived through the senses constitutes an entity, then the abstraction "stoneness" does not exist. Stoneness must be perceived either through whiteness or hardness.

Gongsun Long, however, always went back to his basic distinction between a concrete thing considered as an object of sense perception and a universal concept conceived in the mind without the aid of any sense data. When his opponents countered his argument by saying that because both hardness and whiteness can be perceived only through the existence of a stone, the three entities are actually inseparable and one, Gongsun Long's answer was to repeat the reasoning he used in his discourse on the white horse: Neither whiteness nor hardness as such depends on its attachment to any concrete object in order to exist. They exist as "independent universals." (It may be argued that if Gongsun Long had wished to be thoroughly consistent, he should have insisted that a hard and white stone is actually three separate entities.)

To prove further that whiteness as a universal exists independently, Gongsun Long argued that if there were no independent whiteness as such, no concrete thing could be made white by being joined with something called "white." Therefore, there must be a "general whiteness"—which is the term used for the essence of "whiteness" as a universal.

Universals and Particulars

These discourses illustrate the views on reality and existence that Gongsun Long sums up in his theory of name, reference, and things discussed in the chapter "On Names and Actuality." A thing is a concrete object. It has actuality and holds a position in the universe. Heaven, earth, and the myriad objects are all things. This is to say that Gongsun Long's "thing" is but a concrete particular.

A name is commonly understood as "pointing at" a concrete particular or at a concrete actuality. However, according to Gongsun Long in the chapter "Pointings and Things," a name "refers" to a universal idea. Thus, the reference of a name is a universal, not a particular. The term used by Gongsun Long for "reference" is *zhi*, which literally means "to point at" and has been translated by some as "designation." However, he stresses the common confusion of a reference (universal) with a thing (particular). In this chapter, Gongsun Long was trying to show that a thing commonly goes under a name, but what a name truly refers to is not that thing alone but a universal concept of that thing. Hence, he took pains to argue about the misnaming of concrete things. The last point is part of the common intellectual tradition shared by Gongsun Long and many other thinkers of his time, including the Confucians. All those who included this point in their philosophical systems emphasized the moral significance of "calling a thing by its correct name." Their common belief was that a confusion of

names is the direct cause of social disorder; when names are confused, people no longer know what to live by.

Gongsun Long made it absolutely clear that concrete things exist with or without names; hence, names and their references (universals) also exist quite separate from concrete particulars. If so, how is a universal (*zhi*, or reference) ever perceived? Gongsun Long emphasized the point that universals cannot be perceived through the senses unless they are joined with concrete particulars. In a lengthy and rather involved argument, Gongsun Long attempted to explain that every particular consists of a number of universals and that no universal is perceived except through its "universal-particular" (*zhi wu*) combination or through its manifestation in a particular. Hence, it may be said that all things in the universe are, in essence, universals, and yet nothing in the universe is really a universal as such. This argument amounts to an exposition on the existence of particulars and the subsistence of universals in space and time. As an illustration, Gongsun Long pointed out that although an ox and a horse do not add up to either two oxen or two horses, they do make "two" things. The universal of number subsists in the two entirely different particulars—ox and horse. People cannot perceive number as such, for what they do perceive is an ox or a horse, which is a "universal-particular." This, in brief, is Gongsun Long's tour de force known as the theory of *zhi wu*, or universal-particular. The last illustration appears in "Understanding Change," a chapter devoted to a discussion on change. In regarding every particular as only a particular combination of manifested universals, Gongsun Long recognized the distinction of one species of things from another. Furthermore, he even hinted at his acceptance of the distinction between genus and species. Consequently, he carried the above illustration further by declaring that there is a closer comparison between ox and horse than between ox and fowl.

If the particular consists of many manifested universals, and if universals do not change, what then does change? Gongsun Long's explanation in "Understanding Change" is that change occurs only in the particular. The universal "right" does not change, but anything that is placed to the right can be "changed" to the left. Or, the universal "right" remains constant, but its manifestation can appear in different combinations, such as "right hand," "right leg," or "right side."

The admission that particulars change led Gongsun Long to offer a theory of change. What is offered, however, verges on an elaboration of the "five elements" school of thought in ancient China. This school, having found its sources in the photo-philosophical and sometimes superstitious ideas of China's high antiquity, maintained a system of cyclical change, mutual destruction, and begetting of the five "basic elements" (agents or forces: water, fire, wood, metal, earth) as an explanation of life and existence. These elements were further matched to social and political institutions. Therefore, when Gongsun Long asserts that wood should not be allowed to overcome metal, lest green displace white and the subjects usurp the prerogatives of the prime minister, he is simply borrowing a page from the "five elements" school to explain the need for a fixed order in society in accordance with the natural order in the universe. Any violation of this order would bring disaster, and to confuse the proper designations of this order would be an inexcusable act of "disorderly naming."

However, much as Gongsun Long was concerned with the right use of names, there is something incongruous about attaching a "five elements" argument to the discourse on change that still centers around the distinction between universals and particulars. His argument is quite complete and consistent without bringing in the semimetaphysical system of the five elements, and the latter really has nothing to do with Gongsun Long's central thesis. This incongruity has caused many scholars to conclude that this portion of "Understanding Change" may be spurious.

An interesting theory about similarity and difference has been attributed to Gongsun Long by other Chinese writers from about the same period, although it does not appear in *Gongsun Longzi*. Although the question of attribution has not been settled conclusively, the theory does fit the philosopher's central thesis. The theory holds that all things are, in one sense, different and, in another sense, the same. A number of schools of thought in ancient China have provided explanations of this statement. Gongsun Long and his disciples, however, explained the theory with their universal-particular dualism: Because everything is but a manifestation of universals, and the latter do not change, then all things are really the same. Hence, a white horse and a yellow horse are the same because both are horse; even ox and fowl are the same because both are universal-particulars. On the other hand, every particular is different from another, so no two horses are really completely alike.

The Paradoxes

Gongsun Long owes his popular recognition to a number of paradoxical statements that are recorded in the works of other Chinese writers. None of them is preserved in *Gongsun Longzi*, but all have become favorite subjects of discussion throughout the past two millennia. "A white horse is not a horse" is itself a paradox, and Gongsun Long used it as a vehicle for his major argument. Some of the better-known paradoxes follow: A fowl has three legs; fire is not hot; things never come to an end; the shadow of a flying bird never moves; and an orphan calf never had a mother.

All these paradoxes can be supported if one accepts Gongsun Long's two main arguments: the metaphysical distinction between the universal and the particular and the epistemological distinction between one sense perception and another. All can be explained, to a large extent, by following the same pattern of argument observed in his white horse dialogue. The universal "leg" and the two actual legs of a chicken make three legs. Fire and hot are two universals that are not to be equated; also, because fire is perceived through the eyes and "hot" is learned through touch, they are not the same thing and the copula "is" cannot be applied. Things as containers of universals may change their appearances but never their essences; consequently, they are never exhausted. The shadow of a flying bird moves only as a particular, but the universal of shadow neither moves nor stands still because it is not in time or space. This paradox has also been explained in the fashion of the Greek philosopher Zeno with the observation that because at any infinitesimally short instant, the shadow must be standing still, it never really moves. The orphan calf, as a universal, has had no mother. Furthermore, a calf does not become orphaned until its mother dies; hence, the moment the term "orphan calf" becomes meaningful, the mother of the calf no longer exists.

Throughout the years, numerous attempts were made to interpret these paradoxes in various ways, and with every attempt, interest in the School of Names was revived. While some of the attempted explanations are transparently trivial, others do relate themselves to fundamental problems in logic and epistemology.

Gongsun Long and His Critics

Much of the difficulty in understanding Gongsun Long stems from the fact that Chinese is an uninflected language. Particularly in archaic Chinese, it is impossible to distinguish "white" from "whiteness." The few prepositional words that exist can tolerate a large variety of interpretations, and depending on its position in the sentence, every word can function as a verb. Bearing these features in mind, the reader can readily imagine the abstruse language in which Gongsun Long tried to make clear his ideas about universals and particulars. The modern reader is not the only victim. Some of Gongsun Long's contemporaries objected to his arguments on the ground that they did not "convince" the heart; however, they admitted that they could not outwit Gongsun Long with words. They paid full respect to Gongsun Long's sophistry.

The mere fact that the members of the School of Names made it their principal concern to argue in abstraction has won for them a permanent position among ancient Chinese thinkers. Gongsun Long's interest in the proper use of names is directly related to the didactic and moralistic Confucian doctrine of rectification of names, but the moralistic element is almost completely submerged in his metaphysical system. The lack of the moralistic element is why the orthodox Confucians belittled the contribution of the School of Names, describing the latter's efforts as mere plays on words. It is possible that Gongsun Long and his group actually expounded a fully developed system that failed to survive because of powerful opposition by Confucians. Whatever the case, only a few pages of his works remain, and annotation and commentary on his works are sparse. Contempt for abstract argument as "empty words" has been a persistent trend in Chinese intellectual tradition, and as a result, *Gongsun Longzi* has not received a great deal of critical attention.

Kai-yu Hsu, updated by John K. Roth

Additional Reading

Allinson, Robert E., ed. *Understanding the Chinese Mind*. Oxford: Oxford University Press, 1989. Contains an article by Christoph Harbsmeier, a leading grammarian of classical Chinese, that criticizes Hansen's mass nouns hypothesis.

Chan, Wing-tsit. *A Source Book in Chinese Philosophy*. Princeton, N.J.: Princeton University Press, 1963. This comprehensive anthology, with bibliography and glossary, contains a translation of part of *Gongsun Longzi*. Although Chan regards the logicians as having had no influence on Chinese thought, the selections are useful.

Fung Yu-Lan. *A History of Chinese Philosophy*. Translated by Dirk Bodde. Princeton, N.J.: Princeton University Press, 1952-1953. Perhaps the most authoritative survey of the complete history of Chinese philosophy. The discussion of Gongsun Long treats him as having discovered the Platonic world of forms.

_____. *A Short History of Chinese Philosophy*. Translated by Dirk Bodde. New York: Macmillan, 1948. A brief but good introduction to Chinese philosophy.

Graham, A. C. *Disputers of the Dao: Philosophical Argument in Ancient China*. La Salle, Ill.: Open Court, 1989. This is a thorough introduction to ancient Chinese philosophy that makes comparisons to traditional and twentieth century Western philosophy, both analytical and deconstructionist. Graham explains the white horse dialogue using a dialogue concerning a sword and blade and gives considerably qualified defense of the mass noun idea.

_____. *Studies in Chinese Philosophy and Philosophical Literature*. Albany: State University of New York Press, 1990. Contains three studies on the white horse dialogue, including a textual study on the dating and composition. An earlier study interprets the white horse discourse in terms of class and number, and a later study treats it in terms of part and whole. Graham is considered the one of the best translators of Chinese in the second half of the twentieth century.

Hansen, Chad. *A Daoist Theory of Chinese Thought*. New York: Oxford University Press, 1992. This is a comprehensive history of ancient Chinese philosophy, with Daoist sympathies to counter the Confucian accounts of Wing-tsit Chan and other Chinese scholars. It contains a revised version of the mass noun interpretation of Gongsun Long.

_____. *Language and Logic in Ancient China*. Ann Arbor: University of Michigan Press, 1983. The original version of the author's mass noun hypothesis.

Harbsmeier, Christoph. *Language and Logic*. Vol. 7, part 1 of *Science and Civilization in China*, edited by Joseph Needham. Cambridge, England: Cambridge University Press, 1997. In the concluding volume of this monumental study of China, Harbsmeier presents a survey of Chinese grammar and gives his interpretation of Gongsun Long.

Val Dusek

Nelson Goodman

Goodman's wide range of interests in the philosophy of art, language, and science has yielded influential studies of logic, epistemology, metaphysics, and symbolic systems, particularly in the realm of aesthetics.

Principal philosophical works: *The Structure of Appearance*, 1951; *Fact, Fiction, and Forecast*, 1954; *Languages of Art: An Approach to a Theory of Symbols*, 1968; *Problems and Projects*, 1972; *Ways of Worldmaking*, 1978; *Of Mind and Other Matters*, 1984; *Reconceptions in Philosophy and Other Arts and Sciences*, 1988 (with Catherine Z. Elgin); *A Study of Qualities*, 1990.

Born: August 7, 1906; Somerville, Massachusetts

Early Life

Henry Nelson Goodman was born in Somerville, Massachusetts, on August 7, 1906, to Henry Lewis Goodman and Sarah Elizabeth (Woodbury) Goodman. He attended Harvard University in neighboring Cambridge and received a bachelor of science degree, magna cum laude, in 1928. From 1929 to 1942, he supported himself as part owner and operator of Goodman-Walker, an art dealership and gallery in Boston, while working on his doctoral degree at Harvard, which he completed in 1941. Goodman served in the U.S. Army from 1942 to 1945 as a psychologist and psychiatric assistant in a rehabilitation and training center and married artist Katharine Hosmer Sturgis in 1944. After a year as an instructor of philosophy at Tufts College in Medford, Massachusetts (1945-1946), Goodman was awarded a Guggenheim Fellowship (1946-1947) to support his work on his first book. He taught philosophy at the University of Pennsylvania in Philadelphia from 1946 to 1964. Goodman was a visiting lecturer at Harvard University in 1951 and also served as the vice president of the Association for Symbolic Logic from 1950 to 1953.

Life's Work

Goodman's first book, *The Structure of Appearance*, developed out of his 1940 doctoral dissertation (eventually published as *A Study of Qualities* in 1990). In this foundational work, he applies the techniques of modern symbolic logic to the construction of a logical system that addresses a range of philosophical problems in the analysis of phenomena. Although much of the book is difficult for any reader not thoroughly grounded in the methodology of symbolic logic, it does introduce, at least implicitly, a number of important positions developed in Goodman's later and more generally accessible works. These positions include *nominalism*, and the refusal to countenance universals or any entities other than individuals; *relativism*, the conviction that there is no unique system of reasoning that people ought to use but that various systems can be equally valid in different cases; *cognitivism*, a perspective that emphasizes the cognitive functions of emotional response; and *constructivism*, the view that both everyday and scientific knowledge are at least in part made by laypersons and scientists rather than strictly determined by the external facts of the world.

A series of special lectures at the University of London given by Goodman in 1953 formed the bulk of his second book, *Fact, Fiction, and Forecast*, which quickly became one of the most widely read and heatedly debated works of modern philosophy. Through commonplace examples and everyday language, Goodman, building on the foundational analyses of Scottish philosopher David Hume, demonstrates that scientific induction, the classical method of generalizing from experience and observation, has no formal logical validity. The most famous illustration of his argument, which he calls "the new riddle of induction," revolves around his coinage of the term "grue," which applies to all things examined before a given future time and found to be green or not so examined and blue. Thus, one can say "all emeralds are green" and "all emeralds are grue" with equal logical validity; either label is justified and confirmed by the history of scientific observation. Although no one (including Goodman) believes that emeralds examined in the future will be grue rather than green, the reasons for believing that green is right and grue wrong rest largely on pragmatic factors such as habit and convenience (what Goodman calls the history, or "entrenchment," of the terms and categories used) rather than exclusively on logic or empirical data. Even the most entrenched hypothesis can, of course, be violated, and nothing in Goodman's model precludes innovation and change.

Although it is sometimes claimed that such relativism means that all hypotheses are equally valid or invalid and implies a nihilistic rejection of reason as a guide to belief, Goodman's version of relativism stipulates that the validity of rules and systems can be evaluated. Goodman argues that rules and particular inferences are justified by being brought into agreement with each other; a rule is amended if it yields an inference we are unwilling to accept, and an inference is rejected if it violates a rule we are unwilling to amend. Over the course of time, this process of mutual adjustment produces what some philosophers have labeled a "reflective equilibrium" that produces not absolute truth—an impossibility in Goodman's view—but rather a set of serviceable approximations that fit different circumstances. His simple but elegant "riddle" has proven remarkably resistant to more traditional solutions, and the resultant destabilization of the logical basis of most rational thinking has had profound implications not only for philosophy but also for psychology and the sciences.

The enormous stir created by *Fact, Fiction, and Forecast* firmly established Goodman's reputation, and a number of prestigious invitations and appointments followed, including a stint as a visiting lecturer at Princeton University (1958), the presentation of the Alfred North Whitehead Lecture at Harvard University (1962) and the John Locke Lectures at Oxford University (1962), a year as a visiting research fellow at the Center for Cognitive Studies at Harvard (1962-1963, further evidence of Goodman's continuing interest in psychology), and the presentation of the Whiton Lecture at Cornell University (1965). His academic employment went through a comparably vertiginous cycle: Goodman left the University of Pennsylvania in 1964 to become the Harry Austryn Wolfson Professor of Philosophy at Brandeis University, then left Brandeis in 1967 to be a research associate in education at Harvard, where he founded and directed Project Zero, a research program in arts education, from 1969 to 1974 at the Graduate School of Education. In 1967, Goodman was elected president of the Eastern Division of the American Philosophical Association. In 1968, he was named the Meriwether Distinguished Visiting Professor at C. W. Post College, delivered the Eisenberg Lecture at Michigan State University, and, finally, became professor of philosophy at Harvard (1968-1977), bringing his academic career and personal life full circle with a return to his alma mater and to his birthplace.

The John Locke Lectures he delivered at Oxford eventually became the core of his third book, *Languages of Art: An Approach to a Theory of Symbols*, a study of symbol systems and their functioning in psychology, linguistics, science, technology, visual arts, music, literature, and dance—among other fields. Goodman ranges well beyond the usual parameters of aesthetics in his consideration of the symbol, a term he uses to cover not only letters, words, and texts but also such nonverbal systems as musical notation, pictures, diagrams, maps, and models. Goodman argues that aesthetic experience is dynamic rather than static, an active form of cognitive experience with understanding as its dominant goal rather than a passive, predominantly emotional experience with appreciation and evaluation as its goals. From this perspective, aesthetics becomes an integral part of metaphysics and epistemology. In addition, focusing on the cognitive aspects of aesthetics opens the way to a closer alignment of the arts and the sciences, a direction he would pursue in subsequent books. Goodman also offers a threefold revision of the concept of reference, the ways in which art relates to reality:

first, in stressing the importance of considering not only denotation but also exemplification as constituting reference (and thus providing a basis for considering that abstract art, though nonrepresentational, is nevertheless referential); second, in arguing that metaphorical reference is just as real as literal reference, and, by extension, that metaphorical truth is real truth; third, that reference may be indirect and complex rather than direct, and that these indirect references (especially in the study of literature) may be more important than the direct ones.

In 1972, Goodman, in collaboration with his wife, the artist Katharine Sturgis, choreographer Martha Gray, and composer John C. Adams, created, directed, and produced a multimedia dance performance entitled "Hockey Seen: A Nightmare in Three Periods and Sudden Death," which provided, in addition to an aesthetic experience, nonverbal illustrations of the major kinds of reference (denotation, exemplification, expression) described in Goodman's work. That same year, he published his fourth book, *Problems and Projects*, which gathers a number of essays, most previously published, on a variety of topics. Some are occasional pieces and others are aimed at clarifying points made in his earlier books or at replying to criticism of those books. While breaking little new ground, the collection frequently provides valuable introductions to and summaries of ideas developed at length elsewhere.

As had been the case with *Fact, Fiction, and Forecast* and *Languages of Art*, an invitation to deliver a series of lectures, this time the first Immanuel Kant Lectures at Stanford University, provided the impetus for Goodman's fifth book, *Ways of Worldmaking*. In this work, Goodman most fully argues the provocative thesis—implicit throughout his earlier books—that people make their worlds through the construction of symbol systems rather than through the direct perception of a single given reality. Within this framework, he synthesizes and summarizes many of the major themes of his earlier works and pursues a number of the implications of the principles of constructivism and relativism made in these works.

Of Mind and Other Matters, Goodman's sixth book, gathers together a decade's worth of papers published separately in journals and collec-

tions, most of them aimed at updating various aspects of his other books or at responding to reviews and criticism. Like the similar *Problems and Projects, Of Mind and Other Matters* may be read as a book of recapitulation and consolidation rather than as a distinct new stage in Goodman's work. The book also contains the revised text of a television interview conducted in Brussels in August, 1980, by Frans Boenders and Mia Gosselin, in which Goodman offers illuminating commentary on several of his major theses.

Goodman coauthored his seventh and final major book, *Reconceptions in Philosophy and Other Arts and Sciences*, with Catherine Z. Elgin, Goodman's primary interpreter and literary executrix. The book usefully summarizes much familiar Goodman territory, offering refinements of and adjustments to his ideas and providing provocative new illustrations of such key concepts as the relation between knowing and making and the nature of artistic representation and variation. Among the more significant of the "reconceptions" is Goodman and Elgin's replacement of the discussion of truth and acceptability offered in *Ways of Worldmaking* with a new formulation in which the concept of "knowledge," traditionally tied to truth, belief, and substantiation, gives way to an approach centered on the notion of "understanding," which recognizes that statements may be understood regardless of their truth or believability and that much human communication and art is neither true nor false yet clearly comprises key elements in human cognitive activity. "Understanding" is a broader and more inclusive label for the cognitive faculty than is "knowledge," just as rightness is broader than truth and provisional adoption broader than certainty. The authors also continue Goodman's career-long practice of extending his earlier ideas to new fields, including, for example, a chapter on architecture, "How Buildings Mean." In 1990, Goodman's 1940 dissertation was published in book form as *A Study of Qualities*. Goodman's papers have been gathered in the Harvard University Archives.

Influence

Goodman's pioneering books and his more than one hundred published articles have earned him recognition and have been translated into French,

German, Italian, Japanese, Portuguese, and Spanish. His wide range of interests—aesthetics, epistemology, metaphysics, philosophy of education, psychology, and science—is unparalleled among major American philosophers. One of the few modern philosophers who is also a fine prose stylist, Goodman has attracted an extraordinarily large audience of nonspecialists with his humor, concision, and reliance on nontechnical everyday language and commonsense examples, running most of his books through several editions. His accessible style and broad range of interests have helped extend his influence well outside the ranks of his academic discipline, and Goodman is just as likely to be discussed by literary critics, psychologists, and educational theorists as by professional philosophers.

William Nelles

Ways of Worldmaking

Type of philosophy: Aesthetics, epistemology, metaphysics
First published: 1978
Principal ideas advanced:

◊ There is no neutral or objective description or version of the world that can be regarded as *the* true version.

◊ There are only multiple versions of reality and hence multiple worlds, and these are made, not simply found.

◊ Not all versions make worlds, only right ones, which fit past practice and observation and promote further understanding; truth of statements and rightness of descriptions are primarily matters of this fitting and promoting.

◊ The boundary between art and science is not sharp but fluid and porous, and it cannot be based on distinctions between emotion and reason or between fiction and fact. Properly conceived, science is one of the humanities.

◊ The arts must be taken no less seriously than the sciences as modes of discovery, creation, and enlargement of knowledge and the general advancement of understanding.

◊ The question to be asked by aesthetics is not "What is a work of art?" or "What is good

art?" but "When is an object a work of art?" That is, under what circumstances does an object function as an aesthetic symbol?

In his first book, *The Structure of Appearance* (1951), Nelson Goodman puts forward his conviction that there can be no one right way of describing the world, remarking in the introduction that equally correct systems of logical philosophy may be founded on different bases and constructed in different ways. In *Ways of Worldmaking*, he develops in a less technical and formal manner the thesis that there are multiple worlds, constructed differently according to the categories used by a given observer, and examines the implications of this radical relativism for philosophical discourse as well as for what would traditionally have been considered purely objective discourses, including experimental psychology and scientific theory. Even the most careful observation necessarily entails a creative ignoring of some features and highlighting of others (the whole truth could never be manageably formulated or addressed), and even the most constrained scientific hypothesis inherently demands inductive generalization beyond the observed data. Thus art and science are better imagined as overlapping segments of a continuum rather than rigidly distinguished on such bases as fictionality versus factuality. This does not, however, mean that anything goes. Goodman offers a relativism with restraints that enables him to chart a course between nihilism and absolutism.

As Goodman notes, *Ways of Worldmaking* does not run a straight course from beginning to end but instead presents a series of variations on recurrent themes, working through the same topics from different approaches or applying a particular approach to different topics rather than pursuing consecutive steps in an argument. The central focus of the book is Goodman's fullest and most accessible exposition of his controversial model of "a radical relativism under rigorous restraints, that eventuates in something akin to irrealism." Goodman's irrealism does not hold everything or even anything to be unreal but finds that worlds and versions of worlds are inextricably melted into each other. Goodman is interested in exploring the ways in which it is profitable to talk about many worlds rather than one, and his chosen path of investigation is by means of an analytic study of the types and functions of symbols and symbol systems. His model can best be discussed by his own preferred methodology: the use of concrete examples.

Truth and Rightness

One of the key illustrations in *Ways of Worldmaking*, returned to at several points throughout the book, is taken from astronomy. Consider the statements "The earth rotates clockwise" and "The earth rotates counterclockwise." Both of these conflicting statements are equally true from different points of view, depending on whether one imagines looking at Earth from the South or the North Pole. Consider then these two equally conflicting statements: "The earth rotates, while the sun is motionless," and "The earth is motionless, while the sun revolves around it." Although one might reconcile these statements by arguing that they amount to "The spatial relationships between the earth and the sun vary with time according to formula *f*," Goodman notes that this fifth and final statement—the only one of the series that might be considered technically "true" by an astronomer—is entirely compatible with not only both the third and fourth "false" statements but also with the statement that the earth rotates for a time and then stops while the sun moves around it. The true statement is essentially useless for most purposes, including the astronomer's. One is severely handicapped if rather than saying whether or how an object moves, one is restricted to describing changes in relative position. Scientists can no more limit themselves to neutral statements such as the fifth one than can creative artists or people in everyday situations. People, in effect, move or stop the earth by the way they conceive its motion, and frames of reference dictate the contexts within which statements such as the third and fourth are, if not true, "right" and provide perfectly reliable descriptions. Within the appropriate system, statements such as "The earth is at rest" and "The earth dances the role of Petrouchka" are also true and meaningful and offer equally right versions of Earth's motion. Furthermore, people can readily accept all these statements, and many others, by shifting their own cognitive framework back and forth.

Goodman argues accordingly that there is no such thing as *the* way the world moves but rather many ways in which it moves and that many descriptions of how it moves are equally true. These frameworks are most profitably analyzed as a recognition of different worlds or different true versions of the world (which, for Goodman, amounts to the same thing) and that truth is only one of many considerations in choosing among different versions. Some truths are too trivial or too complex to be guides for behavior or applicable only to a different world version than the one in question. As Goodman remarks, an astronomer who miscalculates the position of a planet probably has a wrong fact under a right framework; when a guard, ordered to shoot any prisoner who moves, immediately shoots them all because they were moving rapidly around the earth's axis and the sun, one may conclude that the guard probably has a right fact under a wrong framework. However, the astronomer and the guard seem to be using the same framework. Right approximations frequently have more relevance, utility, and coherence than the truth does. Therefore, knowing cannot be exclusively or even primarily a matter of determining what is true. Even for a physicist, light may be thought of as waves or as particles, depending on a number of criteria besides truth. Goodman accordingly argues that truth is best considered as primarily a matter of fit with practice, subject to continual revision on the basis of further practice. Although pure truth may be an unattainable absolute, the long-term acceptability of a version may be taken as a sufficient condition of rightness.

Style, Art, and Perception

Other chapters in *Ways of Worldmaking* consider a variety of more specific topics. "The Status of Style," for example, approaches the problem of defining style in literature (and, by extension, the other arts) by first breaking down the three prevalent dichotomies of form and content, emotion and cognition, and the internal and external, according to which style was an aspect of form, internal to a work, and expressed emotion. Goodman demonstrates that style is also a matter of content, with components external to the work that express cognitive properties. He further shows that style is something not only possessed by or expressed in a work but also exemplified by it, just as a tailor's sample swatch exemplifies a fabric by standing as a sample of it. Having thus broadened the definition of style, Goodman proceeds to severely limit it by confining it only to those features of the symbolic functioning of a work that are characteristic of author, period, place, or school—in short, only aspects of how and what a work symbolizes. Exactly which aspects these are, according to Goodman, can be determined only within a specific framework by a given critic and depend upon the critic's purposes and sensitivity, as well as on the power of a genuinely new work, to alter a viewer's sensibility and create a new sensitivity in its own critics. As with versions of worlds, of course, there can be multiple right versions of art objects. In the related chapter "When Is Art?" Goodman extends this analysis to make the characteristically relativist point that there are also multiple versions of what is or is not an art object: An object may symbolize different things at different times and nothing at other times, thus making the key problem for aesthetics the consideration of how a work functions in a given time and place—what it *does*, rather than what it *is* in any timeless or absolute sense.

In an unusual step for a philosopher, Goodman also includes a chapter outlining "A Puzzle About Perception," in which he discusses psychological laboratory research on motion perception. Studies show that when a light is flashed very briefly, then followed by a second flash a short distance away, most subjects report seeing a single spot actually move from the first position to the second rather than seeing two distinct spots flashed successively. Goodman argues that the facts concerning such "apparent" motion are just as important as those concerning "real" motion, and that "apparent" and "real" here are insidiously prejudicial labels for facts of different kinds. In Goodman's interpretation, this data suggests another way in which the processes of worldmaking occur at all levels, including the production of "facts" about the physical world by the mechanisms of human visual perception.

Goodman's Engaging Hybrid

Goodman's lucid, engaging prose style and consistently perspicuous examples, together with his wide range of concerns, have earned him a readership well beyond the boundaries of academic philosophy. Like all his books, *Ways of Worldmaking* has been read with profit and considerable pleasure by nonspecialists and by readers who do not accept some (or any) of his philosophical premises or conclusions but simply see his work as a collection of creative and challenging ideas presented with remarkable clarity and even humor (the book's name index, by way of illustration, runs from "Allen, Woody" to "Wittgenstein, Ludwig"—with Goodman characteristically approving the comedian's position and rejecting the philosopher's).

Goodman's highly original hybrid, a radical relativism that operates only within rigorous restraints, has offered one way out of the classic dichotomy between nihilism and absolutism. Unlike most other contemporary versions of epistemic relativism, Goodman's model stresses the role of reconstruction over that of deconstruction and insists upon people's ability to adjudicate competently among the claims of competing systems and to determine appropriate standards of rightness for given contexts. The admission that there are many right systems does not collapse the distinction between right and wrong but instead makes the careful investigation of that distinction all the more important. One *Ways of Worldmaking* reviewer remarked that, "Insofar as it deals with art, it struck me as standing in relation to classical aesthetics as relativity theory does to classical physics." Goodman's suggestion that understanding rather than knowledge is the key cognitive state to be theorized and that art and science both aim at the same cognitive goals has similarly revolutionary implications for literary theory, psychology, and the sciences that are only beginning to be explored.

William Nelles

Additional Reading

Elgin, Catherine Z., ed. *The Philosophy of Nelson Goodman: Selected Essays.* 4 vols. New York: Garland, 1997. Each volume contains both the general introduction to the series and an introduction to the concerns of the individual volume, all written by Elgin, Goodman's literary executrix and major interpreter. The first volume examines nominalism, constructivism, and relativism; the second, Goodman's riddle of induction; the third, his philosophy of art; and the fourth, his theory of symbols. Elgin has gathered several dozen valuable critical responses to Goodman's work as well as some of his responses.

_____. *With Reference to Reference*. Indianapolis, Ind.: Hackett, 1983. Elaborates and extends Goodman's theories of reference and the symbol.

Hausman, Alan, and Fred Wilson. *Carnap and Goodman: Two Formalists*. Iowa City: University of Iowa Press, 1967. Hausman's monograph, "Goodman's Ontology," analyzes the ontological position developed in *The Structure of Appearance* with a view to offering a Platonistic alternative to Goodman's nominalism.

The Journal of Aesthetic Education 25, no. 1 (Spring, 1991). This special issue contains mostly papers originally presented at a 1990 conference at the University of California, Santa Barbara, on Goodman's work, especially *Ways of Worldmaking*. Includes Sigrid Berka's valuable and comprehensive "An International Bibliography of Works by and Selected Works About Nelson Goodman."

Rudner, Richard, and Israel Scheffler, eds. *Logic and Art: Essays in Honor of Nelson Goodman*. Indianapolis, Ind.: Bobbs-Merrill, 1972. A mixed assortment of essays addressing aspects of Goodman's earlier works.

Schwartz, Robert. "I'm Going to Make You a Star." In *Studies in Existentialism*. Vol. 11 in *Midwest Studies in Philosophy*. Minneapolis: University of Minnesota Press, 1986. A clear and accessible explication of Goodman's notion of the conceptual construction of multiple worlds by one of his former research assistants.

_____. "The Power of Pictures." *Journal of Philosophy* 82, no. 12 (December, 1985): 711-20. Expands an example from the visual arts (Pablo Picasso's portrait of Gertrude Stein, briefly discussed in Goodman's *Languages of Art*) by explaining Goodman's provocative claim that works of art not only reflect the world but also play an important role in making it.

Siegel, Harvey. "Goodmanian Relativism." *The Monist* 67, no. 3 (July, 1984): 359-75. Presents a brief history of the development of Goodman's radical relativism, affording special attention to *Ways of Worldmaking*.

Stalker, D. *Grue: The New Riddle of Induction*. La Salle, Ill.: Open Court, 1994. A collection of essays discussing Goodman's "new riddle of induction." Contains an annotated bibliography.

William Nelles

Antonio Gramsci

Gramsci, an active Italian revolutionary, was one of the first European communists to establish the theoretical foundations for a Western Marxism free of reliance on the Soviet Union. Imprisoned by Italy's Fascist dictator Benito Mussolini, he developed a new method of social analysis with his writings on culture and hegemony.

Principal philosophical works: Lettere dal carcere, 1947, rev. ed. 1965 (Letters from Prison, 1973); Il materialismo storico e la filosofia di Benedetto Croce, 1948; Quaderni del carcere, 1948-1951 (6 volumes), 1975 (4-volume critical edition; partial translation, Selections from the Prison Notebooks of Antonio Gramsci, 1971; complete translation, Prison Notebooks, 1992-1996); Gli intellettuali e l'organizzazione della cultura, 1949; Note sul Machiavelli, sulla politica, e sullo stato moderno, 1949; Letterature e vita nazionale, 1950; Passato e presente, 1951; The Modern Prince and Other Writings, 1959; Antonio Gramsci: Selections from His Political Writings, 1910-1920, 1977; Selections from Cultural Writings, 1985.

Born: January 23, 1891; Ales, Sardinia, Italy
Died: April 27, 1937; Rome, Italy

Early Life

Antonio Gramsci was born in Ales, a small agricultural village in Sardinia, on January 23, 1891. His family lived modestly, supported by a father who was a clerk in the Italian state bureaucracy. The family moved frequently between several villages during much of Gramsci's youth. At the age of four, Gramsci severely injured his spine; he remained a hunchback and suffered from poor health for the rest of his life.

Gramsci was a gifted student and an avid reader even as a young boy. He was graduated from elementary school early, at age ten. In 1908, he left home to attend secondary school, studying languages in Cagliari, the capital city of Sardinia. In 1911, he won a scholarship to study at the University of Turin. It was in Turin that Gramsci developed as an intellectual and political figure. He abandoned linguistics for the study of society and philosophy. Interested in the social questions of a new, industrial society, particularly those of a mass working class, Gramsci entered the youth movement of the Italian Socialist Party in 1914. Soon after Italy's entry into World War I in 1915, Gramsci withdrew from the university, convinced that the moment had ar-

rived to change and not merely to study society.

Gramsci displayed a remarkable talent for writing and contributed articles to the Socialist press throughout the war years. From Italy, Gramsci praised Vladimir Ilich Lenin prior to the Bolshevik Revolution and even more strongly afterward. Gramsci himself never ceased to struggle with the question of how to make a revolution in Italy. He supported the formation of workers' councils and in 1919 helped launch a new Socialist newspaper, *Ordine nuovo* (new order), which promoted these councils and rapidly became the most influential paper in the Turin area. In January, 1921, Gramsci formed the Communist Party of Italy and adopted a revolutionary program for Italy.

From 1921 to 1922, Gramsci suffered from poor health, depression, and even a nervous breakdown. In 1922, while in Russia, he met Giulia Schucht; they married shortly afterward and had two sons. Gramsci was in Vienna when he was elected as a deputy to the Italian Parliament in 1924. He took advantage of his parliamentary immunity from arrest to return to Fascist Italy in May, where he became an outspoken opponent of dictator Benito Mussolini. In November, 1926, Gramsci was arrested by the Fascists and charged with six counts of treason. The prosecutor noted that the state had to "prevent this brain from functioning for twenty years." Gramsci began his prison sentence near Bari. He would remain in jail for a decade, until his death in 1937.

Life's Work

It was during his prison years that Gramsci produced his most important work—a series of notebooks entitled *Prison Notebooks*. He wrote these volumes under the most difficult of conditions, with little, if any, access to primary sources or secondary literature. The scrutiny of prison censors forced Gramsci to adopt an elliptical writing style and to employ code words (for example "philosophy of praxis" instead of the more direct "Marxism") in order to have his works pass outside the prison walls. The result is a collection of writings that is incomplete and often ambiguous. Nevertheless, *Prison Notebooks* stands as one of the most important revisions of social and political theory in the twentieth century.

The principal question that Gramsci set himself during the prison years was how best to explain the failure of Communism in Italy immediately after World War I. Marxists maintained that revolution would first take place in the most advanced capitalist societies. Italy certainly did not fit that description, but neither did Russia—both countries were economically and socially backward, and Gramsci, with firsthand experience of peasant Sardinia, had already written extensively on the "Southern Question" before incarceration. Why had Bolshevism triumphed in Russia—the "East" in Gramsci's prison code—and not elsewhere? The search for an answer led Gramsci to the first of many important insights: his assertion that there was more to revolution than the mere seizure of the state. Gramsci began to explore the question of power in modern societies in a new fashion.

Power, Gramsci maintained, needed to be considered under two, related aspects: coercion and consent. The coercive element of power lay in the direct control over society that the state exercised through its political institutions—police, army, and legislature. According to Gramsci, coercion was the primary form of power in less advanced societies, where control was maintained directly by a repressive state. Czarist Russia was the best European example of a coercive state, and Lenin's tactic of a frontal assault (Gramsci's "war

of maneuver") was the correct strategy in such conditions.

In Western Europe, however, the issue of power was more complex. Alongside the state and its coercive strength lay the power derived from the citizens' recognition of the state's right to rule. This was "consent," and, according to Gramsci, this kind of power was even more important in the West than pure coercion. Consent, though, was not spontaneous; rather, it was taught by the many institutions—schools, church, family, and others—of what Gramsci termed "civil" or "private" society. All of these institutions passed along certain ideas, reinforced a way of thinking, and instilled a set of values, thereby creating a dominant culture that tended to reinforce the state and confer legitimacy on its rule.

For Gramsci, culture then played an important social role in educating consent; its conservative function lay in restricting one's ability to view critically the present and imagine (and act on) a vision of a substantially different future. The label Gramsci gave to this phenomenon was "hegemony": the power of a dominant way of thinking to reinforce the social status quo. The concept of hegemony and its origins in civil society was Gramsci's greatest theoretical contribution.

If revolution had failed in Italy (and elsewhere in the West) after World War I, Gramsci believed it was the result of a failure to understand the power of culture and the strength of consent. Gramsci also took up the issue of how to counter the hegemony of contemporary bourgeois culture over consciousness and action. He noted the need to substitute for the Eastern "war of maneuver" a different tactic for social change in the West, what he termed the "war of position."

Two ideas were central to Gramsci's thinking on Western revolution. The first was the creation of a separate awareness that would act as a counterconsciousness to the dominant strains of thought in bourgeois society. Gramsci called for the articulation of a working-class culture with its own ideas and ethos that would gradually spread and acquire hegemony in certain areas of society. This undertaking would be the work of individuals who could apply their intelligence and organizational abilities to questions of culture. The revolutionary character of their work would be guaranteed only when these individu-

Antonio Gramsci.

als came from the working class itself and not from traditional intellectual elites. Gramsci gave the term "organic intellectuals" to these people, who—very much like himself—had working-class origins and turned their energies to the articulation of an alternative consciousness and culture. Therefore, organic intellectuals, fighting for ideas and culture, would play a key role in the revolutions in the West.

Gramsci's second idea for the "war of position" was the creation of a new kind of political party, which he called the "Modern Prince." Drawing inspiration from political philosopher Niccolò Machiavelli, Gramsci declared that the complexity of modern societies required that revolution become the business of an organized group and not a single ruler. Hence, in the twentieth century, the Modern Prince must be the political party. In his writings on the revolutionary political party, Gramsci openly accepted the distinction between "leaders" and "led." His Modern Prince was a reformulation of Karl Marx's Communist Party as the "vanguard of the proletariat"—a revolutionary elite acting to inspire

and direct a potentially revolutionary population. Though the goal of the Modern Prince was the elimination of the difference between "leaders" and "led," there is little in Gramsci's writings on politics to show how he proposed to avoid a concentration of power in the hands of his "organic intellectuals." Indeed, Gramsci remained too enthusiastic a supporter of Lenin to consider critically Russian events after the November Revolution; later, he was too isolated in prison (and his Italian comrades often misrepresented events in the Soviet Union) to be aware of developments in Stalinist Russia in the 1930's.

Ill health plagued Gramsci throughout the years of his incarceration. By 1935, his physical condition had deteriorated so greatly that Fascist officials transferred Gramsci to a private clinic in Rome. A year and a half later, in April, 1937, Gramsci died. The *Prison Notebooks* found their way through clandestine channels from Fascist Italy to Moscow, where they were kept until after World War II. It took nearly thirty years until a complete, definitive edition was published in 1975.

Influence

Gramsci's contribution to European communism was a significant one. In his analysis of East and West, the state and civil society, and coercion versus consent, Gramsci provided the foundations for a Western Marxism substantially different from that of the Soviet Union. His focus on culture, hegemony, and ideology allowed contemporary Marxists to emphasize the role of consciousness in the process of changing societies. Gramsci's work thereby aided in the rediscovery of an earlier, humanist Marxism that had been lost between evolutionary socialism, Fascism, and Stalinism.

Gramsci's greatest influence, however, lies outside strictly political circles. His writings on hegemony and culture have influenced virtually every other field of study of human society. Gramsci inaugurated the tendency to view culture not as an abstract body of knowledge, beliefs, or habits but as a social construction. Society's institutions are now understood as contributors to the creation of well-articulated worldviews, with profound effects on human consciousness and action. Scholars influenced by Gramsci's terms and analysis may be found in all branches of the humanities: anthropology, history, linguistics, political science, religious studies, sociology, and the study of ideas. Few other thinkers have worked under such difficult conditions; fewer still have made as significant a contribution to such a wide range of disciplines.

David Travis

Prison Notebooks

Type of philosophy: Ethics, political philosophy, social philosophy

First published: Quaderni del carcere, 1948-1951 (6 volumes), 1975 (4-volume critical edition; partial translation, *Selections from the Prison Notebooks of Antonio Gramsci*, 1971; complete translation, *Prison Notebooks*, 1992-1996)

Principal ideas advanced:

◇ The distinction between social and political leaders and those led must be eliminated.

◇ A new vision of politics should be oriented toward those previously on the social margins rather than toward the already powerful and privileged.

◇ Leftist politics should develop the democratic impulses of Marxism, while underplaying the sense of historical inevitability in Marxism.

◇ When analyzing social struggle, Marxism has concentrated too much on economic factors and the role of state power and not enough on ideological factors and the role of civil society.

◇ All reflective human activity is political and all thinking humans are intellectuals in an important sense.

◇ A successful revolution—one able to realize a classless, radically democratic society—must prefigure its vision in the means used to achieve its aims.

In 1924, Antonio Gramsci was elected as a Communist deputy in the Italian Parliament. Despite enjoying parliamentary immunity, he was arrested on November 8, 1926, under orders of the Fascist head of state, Benito Mussolini. Convicted of political subversion after a perfunctory trial, Gramsci was incarcerated until a few days before he suffered a massive cerebral hem-

orrhage that caused his death on April 27, 1937.

In January, 1929, Gramsci gained permission to write in his cell. He used large, lined exercise books to chronicle his observations about historical events and his readings. Over the next six years, Gramsci wrote almost three thousand pages, which eventually became the *Prison Notebooks*.

Each page Gramsci wrote was subject to censorship by the prison warden. Thus, Gramsci's task was to advance a program to energize socially disenfranchised people while evading the gaze of prison censors. His writings were not detached searches for abstract truths but contributions to concrete political struggle.

After World War II, Gramsci's literary executors published selections of the *Prison Notebooks* organized around themes such as "The *Risorgimento*" and "Literature and the National Life." Numerous other editions of selections followed. It was not until 1975, however, that the *Prison Notebooks* were published, under the editorship of Valentino Gerratana, in their entirety and in chronological order.

The *Prison Notebooks* must be understood in context. First, Gramsci intended to sketch a new vision of politics empowering those hitherto on the margins of power and privilege. Second, although a committed Communist, Gramsci nevertheless cast a critical eye toward the excesses of fundamental Marxist theory and Soviet practice. Third, he avoided freezing his political thoughts in fixed doctrines or philosophical systems. Instead, he self-consciously wrote in fragments that invited future development. Fourth, the work was written under censorship, so the precise meanings of many of Gramsci's fragments are inherently controversial. Fifth, his readings while in prison were limited and he was frustrated by his inability to consult all available sources. Sixth, Gramsci evaluated his work concretely—Would it contribute to the political struggle against the dominant social order?—although he understood that prison life isolated him from the people on the margins who must translate his theory into political action. Gramsci did not take himself to be imposing abstract ideas on social reality. His work has value only if the ideas arise from social reality and help realize a politics of inclusion.

The *Prison Notebooks* show the influence of the philosophical idealism of Benedetto Croce.

Gramsci criticized Croce for contributing to the defense of mainstream liberal-capitalist politics and for defining national character in terms of an intellectual elite. Nevertheless, Gramsci also saw Croce as a promoter of intellectual reform who rejected religion, scientific dogmas, philosophical system building, and irrational myths. Moreover, Gramsci appreciated Croce's concise, clear literary style and historicism, which he took to be prime reasons for Croce's growing influence in Europe. Gramsci also deepened his understanding that all human activity is political through his reading and analysis of Croce's writings.

Ideological Hegemony

Gramsci aspired to loosen Marxism's scientific and material inclinations and reinstate the importance of cultural and ideological change. He was inspired by Marxism's democratic impulses and by the need to translate ideas into political action. Earlier Marxist thinkers insisted that the working class was an inherently revolutionary force, that capitalism's collapse was inevitable, and that the manner of collapse was predictable. Gramsci rejected these convictions. Instead, he believed that liberal-capitalist regimes were able to transform and reproduce themselves despite their persistent economic contradictions. They did this, according to Gramsci, by establishing ideological hegemony.

An ideological hegemony consists of values, cultural attitudes, beliefs, social norms, and legal structures that thoroughly saturate civil society. Whereas earlier Marxist theorists stressed the role of the state and the way economic forces molded dominant ideas, Gramsci emphasized the active role ideas play in class struggle and denied that a single cause, such as economics, could explain all social development.

Major social institutions—the state, legal systems, schools, workplaces, churches, families, media—transmit the dominant ideas and the practices they support. A nation's popular consciousness is thus transformed. The most solid ideological hegemonies receive general acceptance and come to be viewed as natural, appropriate, perhaps even inevitable. In this manner, the ruling ideas become so deeply embedded in social relations that they are internalized by citizens as common sense. An ideological hegemony conceals the sources of its ideas and practices—particular power relations and specific historical circumstances—and presents itself as ahistorical truth.

Social Change and Revolution

For Gramsci, the state mobilizes both force and consent. As a forum of ideological and political dispute and a major medium through which the dominant classes lure popular consent, the state plays a major role in solidifying ideological hegemony. However, instead of relying mainly on the dominant Marxist analyses of economic base-ideological superstructure and state power, Gramsci introduces the notions of *historical bloc* and *ensemble of relations*. A historical bloc is formed by popular groups built around a common ideology that challenges the dominant set of ideas. Economic, social, and ideological forces combine to change social conditions. Social forces intrude on existing class domination, and coalitions are formed to shift the ensemble of relations, the totality of social relations in historical context, to a new social order. Although he did not ignore the important role of economics in social change, Gramsci refused to view all cultural and ideological reality as caused only by economic factors.

Gramsci contrasted passive revolution with popular political struggle. Conducted mainly through state agency, passive revolutions respond to perceived crisis by changing the economic structure from above. In contrast, popular political struggle requires the active participation of the masses. Popular political struggle requires a crisis of authority. Revolution must undermine the spiritual power of the ruling classes by penetrating the false appearances tied to the dominant order and by creating a new set of beliefs, cultural attitudes, and social relations. A counter-hegemony must challenge and augur the collapse of the old authority patterns.

At early stages of revolt, one can expect mass apathy, cynicism, and confusion as the gap between the promises and the performances of the dominant order widens. Next, one can expect overt, political forms of class struggle: the spread of antiauthoritarian norms, the development of new social relations, antiestablishment subcultures, new language codes, and emerging ways of life. State repression and force may follow. Such a response may serve to quell rebellion if the underlying counterhegemony is weak or to ennoble the rebels by drawing new supporters if the counterhegemony is strong. Successful revolution requires the unsettling of the old ensemble of relations and the transformation of civil society, which prefigures a new state system built on nonauthoritarian foundations. The revolutionary process will involve lengthy transition periods and much unpredictability. Such revolutionary strategies constitute a war of position in which the civil society of a developed nation is the object of attack. In contrast, in primitive societies, Gramsci advised wars of movement in which the state is the object of frontal attack.

What will energize a revolution? Marxists were divided between two answers: spontaneity and vanguardism. Advocates of the spontaneity theory held that the working class would rise up to overthrow the state once capitalism could no longer mask its economic contradictions. A time would come when capitalism could no longer efficiently make use of developing technology. Economic conditions would be so bleak that workers would no longer be mystified by the ideological superstructure and they would solidify into a revolutionary class. In contrast, advocates of vanguardism were less likely to view workers as an inherently revolutionary class. They stressed the role of the communist party in actively promoting and organizing political struggle.

Although Gramsci at various times was drawn to each of these models, his considered judgment was that each was fatally flawed. His relentless commitment to political inclusion undermined vanguardism by an elite force, and his equally strong conviction about the revolutionary role of ideas unsettled spontaneity theory. Instead, he advanced the notion of organic intellectuals.

Organic Intellectuals

Gramsci viewed traditional intellectuals such as writers, artists, philosophers, and the clergy as an independent social class typically divorced from social action. He emphasized how all human action is inherently political and how all reflective humans are intellectuals. He viewed working-class intellectualism as part of everyday life. Gramsci was convinced that there exists a general historical process that tends continually to unify the entire human race. Once he combined his inclusive vision of politics, his conviction that history tended to extend high culture, and his belief that all human action is political, his notion of organic intellectuals followed. The underclasses must generate their own intellectual base, revolutionary consciousness, and political theories from self-activity. The solution to lagging revolutionary consciousness among workers is not a vanguard elite who seek to impose a rebellious spirit externally. Nor is the solution blind insistence that communist revolution is inevitable and working-class consciousness will arise on cue at the appropriate historical moment. The solution is for workers to become revolutionaries through activity in the workplace, in the home, and in civil life generally. Decades before contemporary feminism, Gramsci insisted that the personal is political. Again, Gramsci highlights the importance of extending democracy through ideas that translate to social activity. The revolutionary party must be a mass party rooted in everyday existence. It must be an agent of social change that coordinates historical forces already in motion. Most important, it cannot be a force of external imposition if it is to prefigure a classless, radically democratic social order.

An Alternative to Marxism

Gramsci presents a clear alternative to the historical materialism of Karl Marx, the vanguardism and state centralism of Vladimir Ilich Lenin, the spontaneity theory of Rosa Luxemburg, and the social democracy of Eduard Bernstein. He underscored the democratic impulses in Marxism: the need for workers to nurture and express their own critical consciousness; the importance of liberating oneself from the constraints of false necessities; the practical advantage of viewing revolution as a series of human, active political events; and the role of consent in both sustaining and unsettling dominant political arrangements. Gramsci distanced himself from the scientism of Marxism. His historical bloc and ensemble of relations analysis alters the economic base and ideological superstructure model; he did not believe in the historical inevitability or clear predictability of communist revolution; and he viewed history as indeterminate.

Perhaps more than any other Marxist thinker, Gramsci understood that political ends are prefigured in the means used to achieve them. If the goal is a classless, sharply democratic society that absorbs the functions of the modern state, then revolutionary activity must itself assume that form. Rather than advancing a universal model of communism, as did Joseph Stalin, Gramsci counseled popular movements that paid careful attention to existing national character and differences in historical circumstances. Because he understood theoretical activity as a changing, dialectical part of mass struggle, he was sensitive to novel ideas, ambiguity, unevenness, and indeterminacy. His own work reflects little dogmatism and a robust sense of the inherent contestability of political strategies and ideas.

Gramsci has had great influence, particularly in Italy, among leftist thinkers who are suspicious of the scientism of early Marxism, the tyrannical excesses of the Soviet model of communism, and the doctrinal posture of Communist parties generally. Perhaps it is not merely a coincidence that for decades Communists in Italy, inspired largely by Gramsci, have gained consistent political influence through parliamentary means. A dispute will remain, however, whether this shows that political activity inspired by Gramsci's work is easily coopted by liberal-capitalist regimes or whether we are witnessing the building of a counterhegemonic force capable of eventually unsettling the dominant ensemble of relations in Europe.

Raymond Angelo Belliotti

Additional Reading

Adamson, Walter L. *Hegemony and Revolution: A Study of Antonio Gramsci's Political and Cultural Theory*. Berkeley: University of California Press, 1980. Traces the formation of Gramsci's thought within the context of Western Marxism and the political and intellectual horizons of his time.

Bellamy, Richard, and Darrow Schecter. *Gramsci and the Italian State*. Manchester, England: Manchester University Press, 1993. Emphasizes the political ramifications of Gramsci's writings, focusing on the specific historical context of Gramsci's role in contemporary political debates in Italy. Includes a biographical outline.

Cammett, John M. *Antonio Gramsci and the Origins of Italian Communism*. Stanford, Calif.: Stanford University Press, 1967. One of the best books on Gramsci, this is the text that introduced his work to an English audience. Cammett treats Gramsci's life up to his arrest in great detail and concludes with a general overview of the principal concerns in *Prison Notebooks*.

Clark, Martin. *Antonio Gramsci and the Revolution That Failed*. New Haven, Conn.: Yale University Press, 1977. This book's concerns are the postwar revolutionary years, the rise of workers' councils, and the period of factory occupation. It highlights Gramsci's role and the theoretical insights developed between 1919 and 1920.

Coben, Diana. *Radical Heroes: Gramsci, Freire, and the Politics of Adult Education*. New York: Garland, 1998. A look at the political aspects of adult education and socialism.

Femia, Joseph. *Gramsci's Political Thought*. Oxford: Clarendon Press, 1981. One of the most thorough discussions of Gramsci's work, which develops in some detail his ideas on hegemony, organic intellectuals, and the role of the modern political party. Femia also indicates the areas in which Gramsci has had a strong influence on the thinking of contemporary Italian communists.

Martin, James. *Gramsci's Political Analysis: A Critical Introduction*. New York: St. Martin's Press, 1998. An important dissection of Gramsci's political thought and his contribution to political science.

Sassoon, Anne Showstack, ed. *Approaches to Gramsci*. London: Writers and Readers, 1982. A collection of essays by leading scholars from many different disciplines on Gramsci, his life and work, his commitment to revolution, and the cultural applications of his theories.

Williams, Gwyn A. *Proletarian Order: Antonio Gramsci, Factory Councils, and the Origins of Italian Communism, 1911-1921*. London: Pluto Press, 1975. The best English-language treatment of the formative years in Gramsci's political development, 1915-1920. Williams locates the stimulus to Gramsci's later thinking in the revolutionary two years in Turin that followed World War I.

David Travis, updated by William Nelles

The Great Learning

Originally entitled *Da Xue* (c. end of first century B.C.E.; English translation, 1861), *The Great Learning* is one of the Four Books of Confucianism, the philosophy's primary texts. Though neglected for more than a millennium after its initial composition, it has served since the twelfth century as a primer to Confucian thought.

Authorship and Context

Tradition attributes *The Great Learning* to Zengzi (b. 505 B.C.E.), one of the most influential of Confucius's original seventy-seven disciples. Zengzi is frequently quoted in Confucius's *Lunyu* (late sixth or early fifth century B.C.E.; *Analects*, 1861), usually in clarification of the master's statements. Although the *Analects* portrays Zengzi as the ultimate figure of Confucian orthodoxy, some critics have accused him of overemphasizing the concept of filial piety—in effect transforming Confucius's scattered admonitions on the subject into a fundamental principle of the Confucian creed.

Zengzi's preeminence among the master's disciples is illustrated by the number of anecdotes relating to him in the *Analects*. Most notable is an incident in which Confucius once puzzled his disciples with a complicated exposition of his philosophy: Zengzi explained—to the master's evident delight—that his principles were ultimately based on *yi* (righteousness) and *ren* (benevolence). After Confucius's death, Zengzi perpetuated the school that the master had founded. This assumption of authority is underscored by the structure of the *Analects* itself; in the latter chapters, Zengzi appears more frequently, particularly in an extended anecdote relating to his steadfast virtue in the face of a near-fatal illness. In a consummate display of filial piety, the stricken Zengzi asked his disciples to note his still healthy hands and feet, proudly explaining that he had maintained them in the condition in which he had received them from his parents. Mencius's *Mengzi* (early third century B.C.E.; *The Works of Mencius*, 1861; commonly known as *Mengzi*) makes Zengzi's role as Confucius's ideological heir even more explicit. It is recorded there that after the death of Confucius, some of his disciples initially devoted themselves to one of their peers simply because he physically resembled the master—until Zengzi reminded them that the master's virtue, not his appearance, was the proper object of their veneration.

Although Confucian orthodoxy has exalted Zengzi himself to the level of a sage, his ultimate importance to the creed lies in his position as transitional figure between Confucius and Mencius. Tradition credits Zengzi with having been the teacher of Zi Si (483-402 B.C.E.), Confucius's grandson and the reputed master of Mencius (c. 372-289 B.C.E.). Although the years in which they lived, according to modern scholarship, would seem to rule out an actual personal connection between Zi Si and Mencius, they are linked by a similar interpretation of the Confucian tradition. Zi Si is credited with the authorship of *Zhong Yong* (fifth to fourth century B.C.E.; *The Doctrine of the Mean*, 1861), another of the Four Books that, like *The Great Learning*, shifts the focus of Confucianism away from a unquestioning reverence for antiquity toward an inquiry-centered rational humanism. Some scholars have suggested that Zi Si composed *The Great Learning* as well—perhaps serving in the role of amanuensis for his master Zengzi.

Mencius, the so-called Second Sage of Confucianism, is regarded as having formalized the peripatetic insights of Confucius into a systematic philosophy. Significantly, Zengzi makes frequent appearances in *Mengzi*, perhaps in an attempt by its author to establish a canonical line between himself and the master. Zengzi often acts as the voice of Mencius as the Second Sage identifies rational self-examination as the core of Confucius's philosophy.

Most scholars are willing to give Zengzi or his disciple Zi Si credit for authoring some of *The Great Learning*, particularly the simpler anecdotal sections reminiscent of the *Analects*. The simplicity and repetitive nature of some sections suggest that parts of the work may have been chanted by Zengzi and his disciples, a practice common in the semiliterate China of the fifth century B.C.E. Perhaps the best example of this is the famous sorites, or extended syllogism, that summarizes the work:

> The ancients who wished to illustrate virtue throughout the kingdom, first ordered well their own States. Wishing to order well their States, they first regulated their families. Wishing to regulate their families, they first cultivated their persons. Wishing to cultivate their persons, they first rectified their hearts. Wishing to rectify their hearts, they first sought to be sincere in their thoughts. Wishing to be sincere in their thoughts, they first extended to the utmost their knowledge. Such extension of knowledge lay in the investigation of things.

However, other sections exhibit a literary sophistication well beyond the era in which Zengzi and Zi Si flourished. The complex structure of *The Great Learning*'s introductory chapter suggests a literary rather than an oral audience and presumes a familiarity with the *lun* (essay) form that in the fourth century B.C.E. had begun to supplant the *jing* (anecdotal) form as the primary means of philosophic discourse. Certain phrases, too, point to later date of composition—or at least to later interpolations within an older text. For instance, the term *zhong guo* (literally, middle kingdom) as a designation for the collection of Chinese states is common in the work and does not seem to have been much in use before the fourth century B.C.E.

The subject matter of the book also points to the Warring States period (475-221 B.C.E.), characterized by social and philosophic upheaval. In this respect, it is tempting to view *The Great Learning*, so preoccupied with maintaining social hierarchy, as a call to the traditional Chinese val-

ues that had fallen into disrepute in this unstable era. Scholar E. R. Hughes speculates, quite convincingly, that the work may have been a response to the materialistic philosophy of the *fa jia*, or Legalist, school. Legalism had risen to prominence in the Warring States period, offering a philosophic rationalization for the hegemony of petty warlords seeking to extend their power within the shell of the Zhou Dynasty (1122-221 B.C.E.). For instance, the Legalists argued that the ruler's word was law *(fa)* and advocated the ruler's use of absolute power for the greater material good of his subjects. In contrast, *The Great Learning* posits a bond of reciprocity between ruler and ruled based on the Confucian principle of *ren*, or benevolence.

The twentieth century scholar Fung Yu-Lan is willing to push the date of the text as late as the third century B.C.E., locating in it numerous echoes of the work of Xunzi (c. 313-after 238 B.C.E.). Whether the final version of the text was a product of the fourth or third centuries, it clearly seems to have developed over time, perhaps building upon either an oral or a written text established by Zengzi or his disciples centuries before. One interesting theory, proposed by Hughes, places the origin of the text in the late third century B.C.E. He suggests that it may have been composed in one of the smaller, more vulnerable states such as Qi, or even Confucius's native state of Lu, both of which had clung to their Confucian heritage in the face of external threats; the text's familiarity with leisure sports such as archery and its emphasis on governance certainly support the notion that it was originally intended for an elite audience.

According to tradition, *The Great Learning* was originally a chapter in the *Li Ji* (sixth to fifth century B.C.E.; *Book of Rites*, 1885), a ritual manual and one of the Five Classics purportedly edited by Confucius. However, this ascription is difficult to authenticate because the *Book of Rites*, originally written on bamboo slips, fell into considerable disarray during the Warring States period. An increasingly rationalistic Confucianism, faced with competition from popular philosophies such as Daoism, Mohism, and Legalism, seemed willing to dissociate itself from the type of archaic ritual prescribed in the *Book of Rites*. The work barely survived the Qin regime's burning of the books in 213 B.C.E.; however, during the restoration of learning in the Han Dynasty (207 B.C.E.-220 C.E.), Ma Yong attempted to assemble a text of the *Book of Rites* using the surviving, and often misarranged, bamboo slips. Ma Yong's edition included *The Great Learning*, though it remains unclear whether the work was originally part of the *Book of Rites* edited by Confucius or a later addition. Nevertheless Ma Yong's *The Great Learning* served as the standard edition for more than a millennium.

The fragmentary nature of the text and its continued inclusion in the increasingly marginalized *Book of Rites* prevented the work from reaching a wide audience until the book was rediscovered by Zhu Xi (1130-1200), the father of the neo-Confucian movement during the Song Dynasty (960-1279). Zhu Xi lifted the text from relative obscurity and ordained it one of the Four Books, including it in such austere company as the *Analects, Mengzi,* and *The Doctrine of the Mean.* Zhu Xi's edition remains the standard, even though he took various liberties with the Ma Yong text. Although he reassembled the chapters and interpolated lengthy commentaries to fill gaps, perhaps his most significant revision concerns a single word in the text. In Ma Yong's edition, the ruler is exhorted to "love" the people; however, Zhu Xi, following the scholar Cheng Yi, changed "love" to "renovate" or "make new," reconfiguring the regent's role from that of patriarchal benefactor to active agent of change. With very little basis in the text itself, Zhu Xi also arbitrarily divided the work into sections: a short introductory statement that he attributed to Confucius himself and a lengthy subsequent commentary attributed to Zengzi. Zhu Xi also interpreted the title *The Great Learning*, which literally translates "great learning," in the more narrow sense of "higher education," implying that the work was an introductory textbook to Confucianism rather than a philosophical treatise best understood within the context of the *Book of Rites.* This narrow reading of the title became institutionalized in 1313 when *The Great Learning* and the rest of the Four Books became the subject matter of the state's civil service examinations.

Zhu Xi's edition of the Four Books with interpolated commentary made him the undisputed father of the neo-Confucian movement and ac-

corded him the status of sage, subordinate only to Confucius and Mencius. However, by the Ching Dynasty (1644-1912), Confucian scholars began to question Zhu Xi's editing practice, preferring the older variants assembled during the Han Dynasty. Most notably, scholars attacked the commentary that Zhu Xi had interpolated into the text of *The Great Learning.* Ironically, however, the Ching scholars retained the text as one of the preeminent books of Confucianism. Even as they adopted modern, more scientific techniques of textual analysis, they seemed unable to propose a definitive version of the text to supplant Zhu Xi's. Of course, part of their problem lay in the fragmentary nature of the Ma Yong and other Han Dynasty variants of the texts from which they worked. In a broader sense, however, their revisionary work was undermined by the very respect for tradition (even when questionable) implicit in Confucianism.

In twentieth century China, waning interest in the Confucian tradition—spurred by the open hostility of the Communist movement—contributed to the stagnation of editorial efforts to create a standardized text. Though Chinese interest in Confucianism renewed at the end of the century with a state subsidy for Confucian research, Zhu Xi's text remains the dominant, if not universally accepted, version of *The Great Learning.* This lack of a standard edition is mirrored in the lack of a standard English translation. Significantly, the two most obvious contenders—James Legge's formal 1861 text and Wing-tsit Chan's spirited 1963 translation—both rely on Zhu Xi's text while stating their reservations.

Luke A. Powers

Overview

Type of philosophy: Chinese philosophy, ethics, political philosophy
Compiled: Da Xue (c. end of first century B.C.E.; English translation, 1861)
Principal ideas advanced:
◇ The purpose of *The Great Learning* is to teach humanity to know the great virtue, to love the people, and to pursue the highest good.

◇ To make the great virtue prevail and to bring peace to the world, people must first cultivate themselves; only then can they cultivate the family, the state, and the world.

◇ To cultivate oneself, one must rectify the heart, but that involves making thoughts sincere, and that in turn involves extending knowledge by the investigation of things.

◇ The pursuit of knowledge is to continue until humankind achieves moral excellence.

◇ The investigation of things is an intuitive comprehension of the essence of things.

◇ There are three principles of the art of government: Rulers should cultivate their own moral stature; they should make use of wise and moral people; and they must esteem what is right above what is profitable.

Among the dozen or so great books that have exercised a significant influence on the Chinese mind since ancient times is the *Li Ji* (sixth to fifth century B.C.E.; *Book of Rites*, 1885), said to have been compiled originally by Confucius himself. In the first century B.C.E., Ta Dai (elder Dai) and his cousin Xiao Dai (younger Dai) revised the chapters in the *Book of Rites*. Most of the chapters in the work deal with the various types of rites—from the arrangement of the most important imperial shrine to the funeral of a plain citizen—and their philosophical import. A few of these chapters, however, treat fundamental philosophical problems not at all connected with any ritual.

One of these chapters is *The Great Learning*, which was removed from the *Book of Rites*, annotated, and installed as one of the Four Books, the most important Confucian classics, in the twelfth century by Zhu Xi. The other three classics included in the Four Books are Confucius's *Lunyu* (late sixth or early fifth century B.C.E.; *Analects*, 1861), *Mengzi* (early third century B.C.E.; *The Works of Mencius*, 1861; commonly known as *Mengzi*), and *Zhong Yong* (fifth to fourth century B.C.E.; *The Doctrine of the Mean*, 1861). The last work is also a chapter of the *Book of Rites*. After Zhu Xi, four books became the primers given to every young student, as well as the principal texts on which the candidates for civil service were examined. The ideas in these books as interpreted by Zhu Xi constituted a durable intellectual orthodoxy that curtailed effectively the Buddhist influence on the Chinese mind and maintained a dominance in Chinese thought until modern times.

The Pursuit of Virtue

It is not difficult to see why this short work, which until the late twentieth century every student learned by heart, was used as a basic guide to people's self-cultivation. Within its ten short chapters, the author outlines a complete theory on how to realize the Confucian ideal of life. He describes the process of making human beings worthy of their name out of an existence in ignorance. He teaches people how to attain the ideal goal of a person, which is self-perfection, in order to prepare themselves for the supreme task of bringing peace and order to the world.

The opening paragraph puts forth the gist of *The Great Learning*: to teach a man (at that time, almost always a man and not a woman) to know the great virtue, to love the people, and to pursue the highest good as his ultimate goal. Immediately after this statement, the reader is told that pursuing the highest good to perfect oneself individually is actually the first step, in which one proceeds to influence all people with one's personal virtue until the principle of great virtue is understood and accepted by all. When this condition obtains, a utopian state will exist on earth.

The author explains in greater detail the process of making the great virtue prevail. One must first cultivate oneself to perfection, then put one's own house in order, then bring the same harmonious order to the state, and finally extend the same influence to all corners of the world so that there will be universal peace and prosperity. For achieving this perfection, the author urges each individual to "rectify his heart [mind]." However, this cannot be done unless one traces this process back to its very beginning in the following order: make one's thoughts sincere, extend one's knowledge, and investigate things. The last is, therefore, the real beginning of people's self-cultivation.

The Meaning of Investigation

Two problems emerge. One is a linguistic question on the order of the last two steps. The original language could mean either "to obtain knowledge is for the purpose of understanding things," or "investigating things in order to extend knowledge." The other problem involves the exact meaning of the phrase, "investigation of things." The text does not explain further, and two diametrically opposed schools of thought center their arguments on this phrase.

The school headed by Zhu Xi (whose annotations have become orthodox) believes in a dualism of principle and matter. Because each being contains its own principle, people's minds can comprehend the universe only after they have investigated all the principles of all things. Chapter 5 of *The Great Learning*, according to Zhu Xi, deals with this question. However, as the entire chapter is lost except for two fragmentary phrases, Zhu Xi's annotation becomes the only authoritative conjecture. Zhu Xi says that students must start from the principles of limited things already known to them and "search exhaustively for all the principles of all things." After a lengthy period of such concentration, students would "suddenly penetrate" the universal principle and then their knowledge would become complete. Zhu Xi's opponents tend to entertain a monistic view and regard the universal principle as indivisible. They therefore see no value in investigating the outside world but urge people to search within their own minds for an understanding of the universal principle.

Without going into details about this debate that lasted for centuries, it seems reasonable and acceptable to arrive at an understanding of this problem on the basis of several other key ideas in *The Great Learning*. One of these ideas is the notion of "the end" of the process of pursuing knowledge.

The Pursuit of Knowledge

It has been noted that the end of this process is stated in the opening paragraph as "the highest good." To know the end of this process is important because without knowing where to stop, people would go on searching for knowledge, drifting and getting confused, and being led astray by their contact with and involvement in the outside world. Consequently, they would never attain the "complete knowledge." Thus, the pursuit of knowledge continues until the attainment of extreme moral excellence. *The Great*

Learning does not urge people to keep on accumulating objective facts and data which, as the author of this work rightly hints, are endless and confusing.

Also, the beginning paragraph contains some elaboration on the importance of "knowing where to stop." To know where to stop, it is said, precedes the fixation of the object of pursuit. Having fixed the object of pursuit, people can achieve the peace of mind (or quiescence, or calm) that is a necessary condition for deliberation. Without deliberation, no knowledge can be obtained. Thus, without knowing where to stop in the process of pursuing knowledge, there can be no possibility that people will ever acquire knowledge.

The next key idea is the notion of "root and branches." This is not merely a notion of a fixed order of things—for the root precedes the branches—it is a recognition of the distinction between the principal and the adjunct, or between the essence and its extension. The overriding principle upheld in *The Great Learning* is that people must distinguish the root from the branches when they approach anything, acquisition of knowledge being no exception. To know a thing is to know its essence, and the person who has learned of the essence of things possesses "complete knowledge." The author of this work considers knowledge of the distinction between the essence and the outward features of things to be the work's central theme. The underlying assumption is that knowledge of phenomena is not true knowledge.

A third key idea lies in the term "peace of mind" or "quiescence." The attainment of quiescence is necessary to acquiring knowledge. This state of mind is directly linked to the theory of "rectifying the heart [mind]." The author stresses the importance of maintaining an undisturbed mind, free from anger, anxiety, sorrow, and even the feeling of fond attachment. Only after one has succeeded in ridding one's mind of all prejudices that ordinary people erroneously call knowledge can one expect to reach true or complete knowledge. A rectified mind is a mind immune to emotional influences. Such a mind comes close to the "empty mind" of the Daoists, whose approach to knowledge is intuitive rather than investigative.

Sincerity

The author demands that a person "make his thought sincere" in order to rectify the mind. Sincere thought means thought of concentration. The thought of a distracted mind cannot be sincere. When applied to the practical level of understanding, the author here is advising people to keep their minds on the object when they seek knowledge of it. Metaphysically, the author seems to assume that knowledge can be attained only by maintaining an ever-present mind, which is still an intuitive approach to knowledge.

Another application of the idea of "making one's thought sincere" is the author's injunction that an ideal person would be careful about action and speech even, and especially, when that individual is alone. When alone, an individual must consider himself or herself "watched by ten eyes and pointed at by ten fingers." As a moral admonition, the author urges people to behave according to one moral standard by which they could face the world as well as themselves. However, as an elaboration of the notion of sincerity, the author here advocates a unity of being. A person's mind and behavior are one; his or her inner thought and outer expression cannot contradict each other because anyone "knowing" the individual could see the inner self, which no amount of pretension can hide. The underlying assumption here is that there is a unity of reality. The moment one perceives even a fraction of what is real and essential, one has perceived the whole.

A Political Application

Examining the foregoing key ideas together, it is apparent that what the author means by "investigation of things" is, basically, an intuitive comprehension of the essence of things, which lies beyond deceptive appearances. In order to arrive at such intuitive comprehensions, one must prepare one's mind for the task by "emptying one's mind" of all biases and by ensuring undivided concentration. Having grasped the essence of things, one stops any further pursuit of knowledge because one's knowledge is already complete and because one has reached the highest good, which is also supreme moral excellence. The wise, in other words, is also the morally good. The author applies the whole theory to politics and develops a theory of the exemplar.

The final goal of self-cultivation being the maintenance of a peaceful and prosperous world, the author never loses sight of the application of his principles to politics. Each of the ten chapters develops one step in the process from "investigation of things" to "bringing peace to the world." The last chapter, dealing with the art of government, occupies half of *The Great Learning*.

The Art of Governing

Three principles of the art of government are discussed in this work. The first is that people of themselves will do exactly what the ruler does. People will follow their ruler as long as the latter is "sincere"; that is to say, as long as the ruler keeps his or her words and deeds in agreement and consistent. In the remote past, some rulers were said to have been benevolent and other kings violent, but the people followed them equally until the sovereign proved himself to be inconsistent in that he demanded his subjects to be moral while he himself exhibited no moral scruples. People always imitate their leaders. This premise is parallel to Mozi's teaching in the *Mozi* (fifth century B.C.E.; *The Ethnical and Political Works of Motse*, 1929; also known as *Mo Tzu: Basic Writings*, 1963; commonly known as *Mozi*). Therefore, if rulers set an example, they will function as the yardstick against which the conduct of their people will be measured. *The Great Learning* cites a number of historical cases to prove that the taste and value standards of a nation change along with what the royal court upholds. The Confucian doctrine of rule by moral magnetism thus finds another exponent in the author of this work. Rulers seeking the best way to run a state are always asked to examine their own conduct and to cultivate their own moral stature.

The second principle is to be able to recognize and make use of wise and moral people. From the sovereign down to the village chief, if the head can use good people as assistants and expel the bad elements from positions of influence, the state will be well governed. In this effort, the ruler must be "sincere"; he or she must not seek the good and capable merely because they are useful but because the ruler "likes them more than he can say." The ruler must be genuinely fond of these people and hate those who cannot practice the same principle. A minister who is jealous of others of the same caliber must be removed and exiled to the "land of the barbarians and never allowed to return."

The third principle is the esteem of what is right above what is materially profitable. The ideas of righteousness and profit were made the basis for the political philosophy of Mencius, and *The Great Learning* reaffirms the same principle by instructing the ruler to value moral excellence above material gain. A moral ruler attracts people and commands their respect. When people flock around the ruler, his or her domain extends. As the domain extends, the wealth of the nation grows, and the king has no need to be concerned with any insufficiency of material supplies. It is not that *The Great Learning* disregards the solvency of a state. Rather, it stresses the importance of "accumulating wealth in the right way."

Such a morally magnetic ruler is one who appears in the eyes of his people under a paternal halo. *The Great Learning* metaphorically calls this ruler a "people's parent" and advises him or her to "like what the people like and hate what the people hate." What is unclear about the last statement is how it can be reconciled with the exemplar theory that sees the people as "followers" and not as the ones to make decisions. If the ruler is to observe only what the people want, then how is the ruler to function as an exemplar?

The answer seems to lie in the confusion about a basic understanding of human nature that disturbed the philosophical world of ancient China and was not clarified even within the Confucian orthodoxy. Confucius himself was silent on this point, and his sayings merely suggest faith in the teachability of humankind. According to Confucius, people can and need to be cultivated toward the good. Mencius, the second standard-bearer of Confucianism, insisted on the innate goodness of human nature, but he also acknowledged the need for self-cultivation. Xunzi, the third great Confucian philosopher whose doctrines are said to have influenced *The Great Learning* more than those of the two earlier philosophers, held a diametrically opposed view. He said that people have undesirable propensities that, if uncurbed, will inevitably lead them to evil.

On the question as to what the ruler should do for the people, *The Great Learning* reflects all three views in different passages. When it says that people follow only examples above them, the book accepts Xunzi's views. When it advises the ruler to love what the people love, the book takes Mencius's theory. However, in most instances, the book appears to stay with Confucius himself in holding that people can be taught to follow the good, so that the responsibility of the ruler is teaching by demonstration, using himself or herself as an example. Consequently, the cycle appears to be as follows: At first, people are ignorant and seek only to meet their basic needs, which are neither good nor bad. They follow the good example of a ruler and cultivate their moral senses until the atmosphere (moral customs) of the nation becomes good. When they have attained this moral discipline, they know, generally, what is good and what is bad. Hence the ruler loves what the people love and hates what the people hate.

The influence of the key ideas in this book, however underdeveloped and ill-defined they may be in the original text, can hardly be exaggerated. After Zhu Xi extracted the work from the *Book of Rites*, the ideas it contained became a force in molding the ideology of China for hundreds of years. Self-cultivation, explained exactly in Zhu Xi's terms, was upheld by all orthodox educators up to the very end of the nineteenth century. Self-education, explained with some variation, remained a living idea among the Marxist and the rightist Chinese theorists at the end of the twentieth century. An authoritative pamphlet written by the Chinese Communist leader Liu Shaoqi (elected chairman of the People's Republic of China in 1959) instructs the youth of the nation to "set their thoughts sincere" and "watch over their behavior when alone" in order to become good communists. The whole "cadre" theory in the Marxist frame, urging the good and capable to set themselves up as exemplars, is so congenial with the exemplar theory in *The Great Learning* that it won the nation overnight without encountering any resistance.

Kai-yu Hsu

Additional Reading

Chan, Wing-tsit, ed. *Chu Hsi and Neo-Confucianism.* Honolulu: University of Hawaii Press, 1986. A collection of essays that examine the editor of the Four Books and his founding role in the neo-Confucian movement.

_____. *A Source Book in Chinese Philosophy.* Princeton, N.J.: Princeton University Press, 1963. This anthology includes Chan's excellent translation of and commentary on *The Great Learning.*

Fang, T. H. *The Chinese View of Life: The Philosophy of Comprehensive Harmony.* Taipei: Linking, 1981. This work posits a historical trend in Chinese philosophy toward achieving consensus rather than accentuating difference between the Confucian and other schools of thought.

Fingarette, H. *Confucius: The Secular as Sacred.* New York: Harper & Row, 1972. This standard critical biography of Confucius explores the nuances of his philosophy by analyzing his relationships with various disciples such as Zengzi.

Fung Yu-lan. *A History of Chinese Philosophy.* Vol. 1. Translated by Derek Bodde. Princeton, N.J.: Princeton University Press, 1952. This standard history of Chinese philosophy (originally published in Chinese in 1913) includes a lengthy discussion of *The Great Learning*, in which the author explores the influence of the Warring States period Confucian philosopher Xunzi on the work.

Hall, D. L., and Roger Ames. *Thinking Through Confucius.* Albany: State University of New York, 1987. A general study of Confucian philosophy that focuses on the differences between Chinese and Western ideologies.

Hughes, E. R. *"The Great Learning" and the Mean-In-Action.* New York: E. P. Dutton, 1943. Includes an urbane and highly readable English translation with a detailed introductory essay on the authorship and date of *The Great Learning.* Among Hughes's many interesting theories regarding the text is his hypothesis that it may have been a reaction to the materialist philosophy of Shang Yang.

Legge, James. *The Confucian Analects, The Great Learning, and The Doctrine of the Mean.* Hong Kong: J. Legge, 1861. Reprint. Vol. 1. Oxford: Clarendon Press, 1893. Contains a good, if dated, translation of *The Great Learning* based on the Zhu Xi edition. Although his Christian missionary bias often colors his work, Legge's detailed introduction provides a good overview of the critical controversies regarding the text.

Lin Yutang. *The Wisdom of Confucius.* New York: Illustrated Modern Library, 1943. A good general introduction to Confucianism, this amply annotated text includes a highly accessible translation of *The Great Learning.*

Schwartz, Benjamin I. *The World of Thought in Ancient China.* Cambridge, Mass.: Harvard University Press, 1985. This intellectual history of pre-Han China discusses *The Great Learning* both as a political document preoccupied with the reunification of China during the Warring States period and as a philosophical text best understood within the context of Mencian Confucianism.

Tu Wei-ming. *Humanity and Self-Cultivation.* Berkeley, Calif.: Asian Studies Press, 1979. An excellent analysis that uses *The Great Learning*'s concept of self-examination as one of the fundamental principles of Confucianism.

Luke A. Powers

Jürgen Habermas

An important member of the Frankfurt School for Social Research, Habermas is best known for his attempts to articulate a comprehensive and emancipatory theory of language, communication, and the evolution of society within an ethical framework.

Principal philosophical works: *Strukturwandel der Öffentlichkeit*, 1962 (*The Structural Transformation of the Public Sphere*, 1989); *Theorie und Praxis: Sozialphilosophische Studien*, 1963, 4th ed. 1973 (*Theory and Practice*, 1973); *Erkenntnis und Interesse*, 1968 (*Knowledge and Human Interests*, 1971); *Zur Logik der Sozialwissenschaften*, 1970 (*On the Logic of the Social Sciences*, 1988); *Legitimationsprobleme im Spätkapitalismus*, 1973 (*Legitimation Crisis*, 1975); *Zur Rekonstruktion des historischen Materialismus*, 1976 (*Communication and the Evolution of Society*, 1979); *Theorie des kommunikativen Handelns*, 1981 (2 volumes; *The Theory of Communicative Action*, 1984-1987, 2 volumes); *Moralbewußtsein und kommunikatives Handeln*, 1983 (*Moral Consciousness and Communicative Action*, 1990); *Der philosophische Diskurs der Moderne*, 1985 (*The Philosophical Discourse of Modernity*, 1987); *Kleine politische Schriften*, 1985-1987 (*The New Conservatism: Cultural Criticism and the Historians' Debate*, 1989); *Nachmetaphysisches Denken*, 1988 (*Postmetaphysical Thinking*, 1992); *Faktizität und Geltung*, 1992 (*Between Facts and Norms*, 1996).

Born: June 18, 1929; Dusseldorf, Germany

Early Life

Jürgen Habermas, the son of Ernst Habermas and Greta Kottgen Habermas, grew up in Gummersbach, Germany, where his father was the head of the bureau of industry and trade. His parents supported neither the Nazis nor the opposition, but Habermas was, for a time, a member of Adolf Hitler's youth group. His attitude toward Nazism changed when, at age fifteen, he listened to reports of the Nuremburg trials and saw documentaries about life in the German concentration camps. These experiences shattered his sense of normality and raised his level of political consciousness.

After graduating from high school in 1949, Habermas studied philosophy, history, psychology, German literature, and economics at the Universities of Göttingen, Zurich, and Bonn. At this time, he was struck by the fact that World War II had not affected the thinking of his professors and had not caused them to reflect critically on the philosophical views they held and taught. Their indifference to self-reflective criticism gen-erated his interest in and enthusiasm for critical theory. He received his doctorate from the University of Bonn after completing his dissertation on the Absolute and history in the work of German philosopher Friedrich Schelling. He married Ute Wesselhöft in 1955 and fathered three children.

Habermas's burgeoning interest in critical theory brought him to the Frankfurt School for Social Research, where he served as a research assistant for philosopher Theodor Adorno from 1955 to 1959. After this initial association, Habermas became a professor of philosophy at the University of Heidelberg, a position he held until 1964, when he became a professor of philosophy and sociology at the University of Frankfurt. In 1971, he took over the directorship of the Max Planck Institute in Starnberg.

Life's Work

The critical theorists of the Frankfurt School advocated three tenets that became influential in Habermas's work. They wanted to see society move in the direction of the rational and to see it free itself from unnecessary domination. They understood reason or rationality in terms of progressive self-consciousness and saw the apparent unconscious acceptance of technological rationality as inimical to human concerns. They also advocated a unity of theory and practice. Although the school grounded its work in Marxist thought, Habermas did not accept all of Karl Marx's teachings. Habermas was also strongly influenced by hermeneutics, which sees understanding arising out of a dialogue between text and interpreter. He was likewise influenced by the psychoanalytical psychology of Sigmund Freud. Psychology's paradigm of an individual trying to access the unconscious gave Habermas an analogy for critical theory's attempt to uncover, through language, the ideologies that work toward domination within society. Another positive influence on Habermas was the philosophy of language as detailed by philosophers Ludwig Wittgenstein, J. L. Austin, and John Searle, especially the last two's formulation of the speech act. A negative influence to which Habermas frequently reacted was positivism, which tended to separate the knower from the object studied so that it could be examined objectively.

Cumulatively, these influences induced Habermas to recast the study of society as a study of communication. His work falls into four major stages. The first stage consists of his examination of the universal aspects of reason embedded in language. The second stage involves an exploration of the nature of human knowledge. The third stage is his work with explicating communicative action, the possibilities for a rational society arising from the use of language in interaction with others. The final stage deals more explicitly with critical theory, an exploration of the ways that communication is enhanced or confined by social institutions and structural parameters. In each of these stages, Habermas remains interested in the way language usage affects society's capacity for rationality and how systemic distortion of language use impedes the realization of rationality.

In 1963, Habermas published *Theory and Practice*. In this book and related writings, he develops his theory of universal pragmatics, uncovering what he held were the universal aspects of language use and the types of rationality connected with them. Habermas argues that every speech act has a dual content: a propositional one that makes factual sense and an illocutionary one that leads to performance. He then concerns himself with three different types of speech acts and the validity claims arising from them. *Constative* speech acts assert facts, have propositional content, and make a truth claim. *Regulative* speech acts, such as commands, prohibitions, and promises, govern the relations between speaker and hearer, have an interpersonal relationship content, and pose a claim of rightness or appropriateness. *Avowals* are speech acts that disclose the speaker's intention, feelings, or wishes. Avowals raise the validity claim of sincerity.

Each type of validity claim is based on a different type of rationality, and when a validity claim is challenged by the hearer, resolution must be pursued differently. If sincerity claims are challenged, participants must engage in further communicative action. When truth or appropriateness claims are leveled, participants must move to the level of discourse, a level of performance where one seeks to share the grounds of cognitive utterances. In the discourse mode, nothing is taken for granted and usual assumptions are suspended. Although resolution is sought on the discourse level when either truth or appropriateness claims are leveled, Habermas makes a distinction between the two cases. When truth is questioned, theoretic discourse must ensue. When appropriateness is questioned, speakers engage in practical discourse. However, beyond these lies another level of discourse: metatheoretical discourse in which the basic conceptual framework that grounds arguments is questioned. Beyond this level of discourse lies metaethical discourse in which participants argue about how knowledge is conceptualized and about the criteria used to determine what counts as knowledge

In 1968, Habermas published *Knowledge and Human Interests*. In this work, he argues that all human beings have three basic orientations or interests: work, interaction, and power. By work, he means what one does to provide for material existence. It demands a basic way of knowing that allows one to exert control over nature. This approach, in modern society, has culminated in the use within the empirical, analytical sciences of instrumental rationality, a form of rationality used to achieve a goal. Because humans are social beings, they must interact functionally and symbolically and strive for mutual understanding with others in order to survive. Such interaction requires practical reasoning and, as a way of knowing, has been systematized in the hermeneutical sciences. Finally, humans must also deal with domination or power. Although power is unavoidable in social groups, unnecessary power results from distorted communication or ideologies embedded so deeply in society that they remain outside consciousness. Members of society make these ideologies conscious by employing critical rationality, which has been formalized in the science of critical theory. To Habermas, these three domains penetrate one another, and any one-dimensional approach to understanding the world is, therefore, inadequate. Furthermore, it is by examining the interaction of these domains of work, language, and power in modern society that trouble spots and emergent crises can be discerned.

Habermas's work with speech acts and levels of discourse constitutes fundamental building blocks in subsequent writings, especially *The Theory of Communicative Action*. To Habermas, communicative action occurs when at least two competent speakers seek to reach an understanding about an action situation (a teleogical action, or action taken to achieve a goal) in order to coordinate their actions. He also discusses three domains of activity. The first is the *external* or *objective world*. The validity claim is truth, the correspondence between the external world and statements made about it. The second domain is that of *social interaction*, where speech acts are directed toward the conforming of behavior to shared norms or values and where the validity claim is rightness. The final domain is the *subjective world* to which each person has exclusive or privileged access. The communicative act here is presentational or dramaturgical and allows for free and selective self-expression. Sincerity is the validity claim characteristic of this domain. The domain of communicative action incorporates and transcends these domains as speakers and hearers refer simultaneously to things in the objective, social, and subjective realms in order to arrive at a mutually shared understanding of a situation.

Habermas also discusses the concept of the "lifeworld," the general storehouse of knowl-edge, traditions, and customs that form the background consensus of everyday life and get passed on unconsciously from one generation to the next. However, Habermas also claims that societies consist of systems, the structural features of life that are governed not by the medium of language as in the lifeworld but by nonlinguistic media, especially the media of money and power.

Habermas contends that it is necessary to make the assumptions of the lifeworld problematic by raising them to the conscious level so members of a society can act rationally and make informed decisions. This is particularly necessary in modern times when the systematic forces at work in society—institutions, rules, bureaucracies, economics—exert greater influence than language. The systematic side of life has proven stronger than the lifeworld and "colonized" it, with two major results: First, members of a culture are less likely to be in agreement about the basic assumptions of the lifeworld. Second, there is less need for achieving consensus because disagreements can be settled by recourse to laws and established structures of power.

Habermas also argues that modern societies are more rational than traditional societies because consensus has been replaced by critical thought and evaluation. He holds, however, that modern societies have not achieved emancipation—the desired outcome of critical theory. For him, an emancipated society is not one in which the lifeworld is subjected to the demands of maintaining systems but rather one in which the mechanics of the system accommodate the needs of the individuals. He points to environmental and women's liberation movements as demanding an end to the colonization of the lifeworld and a return to the correct balance between lifeworld and system.

Influence

The influence of Habermas, long a dominant intellectual figure in his native Germany, extended outside his native land through visiting professorships at various universities in the United States, the translation and dissemination of his works in English and other languages, and his great eagerness to engage in intellectual debate. The breadth of his intellectual inquiries and his ability to synthesize knowledge from a wide variety of disciplines made him a key figure with influence in almost every area of the humanities and social sciences.

Habermas's major contribution to philosophy and sociology lies in the way he recasts critical theory. He diverts attention from the analysis of concrete social and political situations and details the changing structure of consciousness in modern societies. Ironically, Habermas makes it clear that modernity embodies an almost intractable paradox. Increasing differentiation between the objective, social, and subjective worlds and between the lifeworld and systems has forced greater critical reflection and rationalization and provided more processes for communicative action. Differentiation has also allowed the colonization or technocratization of the lifeworld and a subsequent devaluation of communicative action as a means of meeting human needs.

Christine R. Catron

The Theory of Communicative Action

Type of philosophy: Ethics, social philosophy
First published: Theorie des kommunikativen Handelns, 1981, 2 volumes (English translation, 1984-1987, 2 volumes)
Principal ideas advanced:

◇ Many of the premises of modern philosophy find their origin in René Descartes's model of a solitary thinker deriving proof of his or her existence from the ability to reason logically.

◇ This paradigm has constrained subsequent philosophers and social theorists to think in terms of subjective and individualist reason or rationality and confined their works to the "philosophy of consciousness."

◇ This philosophical paradigm is inadequate; therefore, a theory that has as its object collective or consensual validity rather then "truth" must be developed.

◇ Society has two levels: a "lifeworld," or the depository of mutually shared convictions that shape a culture, and the complex economic and political systems that instrumentally coordinate human activities; these systems make the objective to reach successful outcomes rather than to arrive at meaning.

◇ In earlier times, the convictions in the "lifeworld" were simply accepted, but in modern societies, many of these convictions have become problematic, and societies must create processes for raising and criticizing validity claims in order to reach mutual understandings.

◇ Advanced capitalism has "colonized" the lifeworld and instrumentalized spheres of activity that were formerly part of the communicative structure of the lifeworld; subsequently, society has experienced pathologies and individuals have experienced a loss of both freedom and meaning.

◇ The lifeworld needs to be decolonized by expanding areas in which action is coordinated by communicatively achieved agreement.

Jürgen Habermas is perhaps the most renowned member of the second generation of the Frankfurt School for Social Research. Like other members of the school, Habermas was strongly influenced by the work of philosophers Karl Marx and George Wilhelm Friedrich Hegel. Habermas, however, rejects the pessimism of Theodor Adorno and Max Horkheimer, earlier members of the Frankfurt School. Instead, he conceives of his life's project as an attempt to formulate a critical theory of society with the practical intention of helping individuals emancipate themselves from various forms of domination. To develop a critical theory of society, Habermas's first concern was to develop systematically its philosophical underpinnings. In the early 1970's, he began to formulate elements of a theory of language, communication, and the evolution of society, intending to build up a framework for his larger view of emancipatory action. Early in his career he had argued that the system, especially the economy, dominated the whole of society at the expense of the "lifeworld," the immediate milieu of the individual. He also held that science in the capitalist era was being turned against human beings and impoverishing their cultural lives because of its emphasis on instrumental reason. His thinking about these issues culminated in the two volumes of *The Theory of Communicative Action*.

The Theory

Habermas begins *The Theory of Communicative Action* by distinguishing between instrumental rationality, or reason geared toward self-maintenance and adaptation to a contingent environment, and communicative rationality, through which people reach agreement on the validity of proposed assertions. He then argues for the authenticity of collective validity as a rational means of understanding reality.

This concept is a key one because Habermas claims that most Western societies promote a distorted understanding of rationality fixated only on instrumental aspects. Using the work of Swiss psychologist Jean Piaget on learning as an evolving structure of consciousness, Habermas claims that an individual learns to differentiate between the objective world, the social world, and the self. These three aspects of reality form three different contexts in which individuals can come to collective agreement. Agreement on an assertion about the objective world constitutes agreement about a fact and depends on cognitive instrumental rationality. Agreement about the justification of a way of ordering social life constitutes a norm in the evaluative domain and depends on ethical rationality. Agreement regarding the authenticity of a subject making an assertion about his or her own condition constitutes agreement rationally reached in the expressive domain. Thus an assertion must be accepted on all three levels. It must be true, it must be right in the existing normative context, and it must manifest the intention of the speaker.

The consensus a society reaches rationally on all three levels composes the "lifeworld" of the individuals who compose that society. In equating communicative action with consensually agreed upon validity, Habermas argues that all three aspects of meaning come into play. In attempting to come to an understanding with one another, participants share in a cultural tradition that they both use and renew. In doing so, they also strengthen the integration of the group and internalize its values. Structurally, the lifeworld consists of three interpenetrating entities: the culture, the society, and the individual. Communicative action, with its mutual understanding, coordination of action, and formation of personal identity, strengthens all three components and is crucial to the healthy functioning of the lifeworld.

Rationality

Habermas realizes that he must demonstrate that his model has universal validity without falling back on the guarantees of past philosophical traditions. In pursuit of this goal in the remainder of the work, he explains the sociological approaches to a theory of how rationality functions in society. He points out the conceptual strategies, assumptions, and lines of argument for these approaches and lays out the various problems encountered. He then demonstrates how these problems can be solved by the application of his threefold approach to rationality in his theory of communicative action.

Habermas then begins this indirect process of proof by arguing that previous approaches to interpretive sociology that did conceive of society as a lifeworld, whether that term or a synonym was used, were one-sided, emphasizing only one of the structural components of the lifeworld. They all exhibit, therefore, an impoverished and incomplete notion of rationality. To account for this lack, Habermas recapitulates the evolution of modern society, relying heavily on the work of German sociologist Max Weber. In his work with world religions, Weber found that religions that developed a dualism between God and the world came to emphasize the ethical aspect of rationality and stressed adhesion to norms. Such a worldview tended to reject the world and objectify it. In dealing with the rise of capitalism and the Protestant ethic, Weber claimed that the Protestant vision of an ordered hardworking life as the path to salvation was washed away under capitalism in favor of an instrumental attitude toward work that enshrined an instrumental rationality. Weber, in dealing with the evolution of law and legal institutions, claimed that in the modern era, the validity of law based on traditional consensus has been replaced by reliance on rational consensus, a kind of belief in the legality of enacted laws.

Habermas believes that Weber's work still has much to offer, but it is fundamentally flawed. He sees Weber's model as an atomistic one, a model of action for individual actors but lacking any process for coordinating actions through which interpersonal relations come about. Therefore, Weber's model can be assessed only under the aspect of purposive rationality, where actions are coordinated solely for the purpose of individual success, not for reaching understanding. After a lengthy discussion of speech act theory, Habermas launches his topology of communicative action to complement the instrumental action and rationality he found in other theories: conversation (cognitive), normatively regulated (evaluative), and dramaturgical (expressive).

Habermas also argues that while society is relying more and more on instrumental rationality, the reservoir of traditional knowledge that a society accepts as unproblematic has been shrinking; therefore, communicative action is even more necessary for the vital preservation of the lifeworld. Habermas see that the "uncoupling" of communicative action from the processes of reaching understanding has resulted in coordinating actions through nonlinguistic media such as money and power. As he sees it, increasingly actions are set loose from an integration provided by value consensus and become governed by purposive or instrumental rationality to the denigration of the lifeworld.

Habermas then turns to the work of earlier members of the Frankfurt School, Theodor Adorno and Max Horkheimer, who set the foundations for a critical view of society to explain how capitalism simultaneously heightens the forces of production and immobilizes the forces of subjective resistance. He argues that their work floundered because they operated within the paradigm of a philosophy of consciousness. He insists on a paradigm centered not on the relation of a solitary actor to an objective world but on the intersubjectivity of actors relating simultaneously to something in the objective world, something in the common social world, and something in one another's subjective world. Habermas sees such a shift in the work of philosophers George Mead and Émile Durkheim, which he discusses in detail.

From Mead, Habermas stressed the notion that as human beings mature and interact with one another on a symbolic level, authority no longer rests on sanctions but on moral as well as cognitive perceptions of collective good. From Durkheim's study of the evolution of law from its origins in belief in the sacred to modern legal institutions, Habermas saw a transition from accepting the binding force of moral agreement founded in traditional values to moral agreement binding because of the generality of underlying interest achieved through communicative action. Habermas called this process the linguistification of the sacred.

Lifeworld and System
From Durkheim, Habermas also gleaned another significant insight, one he would later develop through the work of philosopher Talcott Parsons: the need to see society differentiated into both lifeworld and system. He takes up the question as to how the lifeworld is limited and changed by the structural transformation of society as a whole. He argues that communicative action, as a simultaneous process of mutual understanding, coordination of action, and socialization, renews cultural knowledge, strengthens social integration, and enhances the formation of personal identity. He also argues that social integration is different from system integration. System integration, he insists, more and more occurs in ways that have been "delinguistified": ways that operate mainly through the media of money and power, media independent of the lifeworld. Habermas then turns to Parsons and his work with integrating systems theory with a theory of society.

However, whereas Parsons started with individuals and then added an intersubjective concept of order, Habermas's theory begins with and is centered in a cultural system with intersubjective values shared from the start. He likewise disagrees with Parsons's contention that the formation of consensus can be replaced by delinguistified media. The lifeworld can expand technologies of communication but cannot itself be technicized.

The Tasks of Critical Theory
In the last section of his book, Habermas revisits the work of Weber and Marx, pointing out their main weaknesses and, in these weaknesses, finding verification for his own departures from their thinking in his theory of communicative action. Finally, Habermas turns to the future tasks of critical theory. Primarily its role is to uncover

paradoxical situations in which systems steered by media such as money (economic systems) and power (government bureaucracies) turn around and threaten the values or even the communicative infrastructure of the lifeworld. He sees these paradoxes covered over by mass consumption and client-bureaucrat relations that tend to create pacification in the sphere of social labor and neutralization in political decision making. Most profoundly, Habermas breaks away from the philosophy of history on which the earlier critical theories he examined relied but which he claims is no longer tenable. Instead, he argues a critical theory of society has to be open to self-criticism.

Habermas's *The Theory of Communicative Action* and his other works generated much discussion and debate among practitioners of various disciplines. The breadth of his knowledge of classical and contemporary thinkers, the variety of issues he addresses, and his own willingness to rethink his theories in the light of criticism have often helped scholars refine their thinking and see their disciplines in a new light. Despite the praise showered on his work, two areas remain problematic for many scholars, especially American scholars. The first area is his antipositivist stance and his insistence on methodological dualism, that is, his contention that the methods of the social sciences and natural science are distinct. The second position often attacked is his support of modernist ideas and his belief in rational consensus at a time when postmodernists argue over the possibility or even the desirability of a final consensus. Yet, in spite of these detractions, Habermas's project of analyzing society in both breadth and depth, from historical and philosophical perspectives in order to emancipate it fully, continues to challenge and excite readers.

Christine R. Catron

Additional Reading

Berstein, J. M. *Recovering Ethical Life: Jürgen Habermas and the Future of Critical Theory*. New York: Routledge, 1995. The author places Jürgen Habermas's work in the context of critical theory as a whole—past, present, and future. He also focuses on the evolution of Habermas's thinking on communicative action. Sympathetic as this study is, Berstein contends that Habermas contributes to the very problems of ethical dislocation and meaninglessness that he is trying to diagnose and remedy.

Braaten, Jane. *Habermas's Critical Theory of Society*. Albany: State University of New York Press, 1991. The author explains Habermas's theory of rationality, which she sees as the core of his social theory and method. She also examines his philosophy of social theory, which offers a preliminary outline of and method for a theory of societal rationalization. She assess his critical theory by looking at three applications in the United States.

Chambers, Simone. *Reasonable Democracy: Jürgen Habermas and the Politics of Discourse*. Ithaca, N.Y.: Cornell University Press, 1996. This book highlights Habermas's contributions to political science and discuss Habermas's view of the social aspects of democracy.

Deflem, Mathieu, ed. *Habermas, Modernity, and Law*. Thousand Oaks, Calif.: Sage Publications, 1996. A riveting overview of Habermas's work, with chapters ranging from human rights to law. Extremely helpful to professionals and students studying legal, political, or social theory.

Foss, Sonja K., Karen A. Foss, and Robert Trapp. *Contemporary Perspectives on Rhetoric*. Prospect Heights, Ill.: Waveland Press, 1985. The chapter of this book that focuses on Habermas summarizes his contribution to the field of rhetoric. The book also offers a chapter on Stephen Toulmin, whose work Habermas claimed influenced his.

Held, David. *Introduction to Critical Theory: Horkheimer to Habermas*. Berkeley: University of California Press, 1980. Although this book was written before publication of many of Habermas's works, it is helpful in providing a detailed picture of the evolution of critical theory in the Frankfurt School and Habermas's continuities and discontinuities with it.

McCarthy, Thomas A. *The Critical Theory of Jürgen Habermas*. Cambridge, Mass.: MIT Press, 1982. After translating several of Habermas's works into English, the author realized that many misreadings of Habermas arose because so few of his works were available in English. This book provides a systematic and comprehensive overview of Habermas's thought by explicating, interpreting, connecting, and systematizing Habermas's works.

Rehg, William. *Insight and Solidarity: A Study in the Discourse Ethics of Jürgen Habermas*. Berkeley: University of California Press, 1994. The author examines Habermas's most important writings on moral theory. This book will be of interest to all who are concerned with moral, social, political, or legal theory.

White, Stephen K., ed. *The Cambridge Companion to Habermas*. Cambridge, England: Cambridge University Press, 1995. The author presents a collection of essays that contextualize Habermas's ideas within European political, philosophical, and sociological thought and that critique various aspects of his work, especially from feminist and postmodernist positions.

Christine R. Catron

Alexander Hamilton

Born: January 11, 1755; Nevis, British West Indies
Died: July 12, 1804; New York, New York

James Madison

Born: March 16, 1751; Port Conway, Virginia
Died: June 28, 1736; Montpelier, Orange County, Virginia

John Jay

Born: December 12, 1745; New York, New York
Died: May 17, 1829; Bedford, New York

Hamilton, Madison, and Jay all made significant contributions to the United States' public life before 1820. Together they wrote *The Federalist* to market the 1787 Constitution during the bitter ratification struggle.

Principal philosophical work: *The Federalist*, 1787-1788 (serial); 1788 (book in 2 volumes; also known as *The Federalist Papers*)

Early Life

James Madison and John Jay were born into established positions in the American colonial aristocracy, Madison in Virginia and Jay in New York. In contrast, Alexander Hamilton was born an illegitimate child on the island of Nevis in the British West Indies and migrated to the American colonies in 1772. He worked hard to attain the social status Jay and Madison enjoyed from birth. Perhaps because of his background, Hamilton was a risk taker throughout his life. Although he died a member of the Episcopal Church, he had periods of religious skepticism unknown to Jay and Madison. Although Jay and Madison were loyal, devoted husbands, Hamilton's insecurity led him into sex scandals.

Both Hamilton and Jay were lawyers who graduated from King's College in New York City, which later became Columbia University. Madison, a graduate of Princeton University, did not pursue specialized professional training because his chronic ill health led him to expect an early death. However, Madison was exceptionally learned in history, religion, and political theory by the time he left Princeton.

Life's Work: Hamilton

Hamilton served as a lieutenant colonel on George Washington's staff from 1777 to 1781 during the Revolutionary War and married Elizabeth Schuyler Hamilton in 1780. As a practicing attorney, he was an able and vigorous advocate who quickly attained success in difficult cases and secured the respect of his peers. Hamilton was particularly successful in *Rutgers v. Waddington*, a 1784 case that enabled him to defend a policy of lenient treatment for former Tories (colonists sympathetic to the British during the Revolutionary War) and that helped establish the doctrine of judicial review.

A master of the art of rhetoric, Hamilton planned the scope of *The Federalist* and wrote more essays than Madison and Jay combined, although scholars have differed as to which essays were written by Hamilton and which by Madison. He was well positioned for success as President Washington's secretary of the treasury from 1789 to 1795, and his economic platform of a national bank, creditor rights, payment of state debts accumulated during the Revolution, and friendly relations with Great Britain helped create a sound economic footing for the United States. Statesman Thomas Jefferson opposed Hamilton's economic principles, and Jefferson's political party, the Democratic Republicans, sought and eventually gained the political power held by Hamilton and the Federalist Party. Despite their disagreements, in 1800 Hamilton backed Jefferson over Aaron Burr in his bid for the presidency. Burr became Hamilton's bitter enemy, and he shot Hamilton in a fatal duel in 1804.

Life's Work: Madison

At the Constitutional Convention in 1787, Madison, who had been elected to the Continental Congress in 1779, backed the Virginia plan, favored by the larger states, to create a three-branch federal government. The plan provided for a national executive who would serve seven years and enjoy veto power, a congress, and a federal court. Madison's contributions earned him the title of "Father of the Constitution," and his comprehensive notes on the business of the convention have proved invaluable to historians.

During the ratification struggle that followed the Constitutional Convention, Madison contributed only slightly fewer essays to *The Federalist* than did Hamilton. Although these two men developed significant ideological differences that make their later works easily distinguishable, historians still debate the authorship of some essays in *The Federalist* because Hamilton, Madison, and Jay all wrote under the pseudonym Publius. Madison was elected to the House of Representatives in 1789. He served as President Jefferson's secretary of state from 1801 to 1808 and became the fourth president, serving from 1809 to 1817.

Ill health undermined Madison's self-confidence, as did his rejection as a suitor by the pretty Catherine Floyd. In his forties, Madison married the vivacious widow Dolly Payne Todd, who helped him increase his self-confidence. However, from his youth to his old age, Madison was a dedicated public servant who advocated the Virginia Bill of Rights, the U.S. Bill of Rights, and the

James Madison. *(Library of Congress)*

gradual abolition of slavery through the work of the American Colonization Society. Like his mentor Jefferson, Madison worked to secure the separation of church and state and protect religious minorities.

Life's Work: Jay

Less well known than either Hamilton or Madison, Jay contributed only five essays to *The Federalist* because of ill health. Despite his prestige as a former president of the Continental Congress, New York chief justice, and secretary of state under the Articles of Confederation, Jay was unable to get elected as a delegate to the Constitutional Convention because of the strong anti-Federalist views of New York governor George Clinton, who even begrudged Hamilton a convention role and did not want the national government strengthened. However, Jay was a delegate to the New York ratifying convention at Poughkeepsie, and he played a key role in getting the convention to ratify the Constitution by a close vote after forty grueling days. President John Adams regarded Jay as the critical factor in obtaining New York's somewhat grudging ratification.

Despite the limited number of essays Jay wrote, his contribution to *The Federalist* was valuable. Jay was the only author of *The Federalist* to have traveled abroad. Jay's foreign policy expertise allowed him to explain why the passage of the Constitution was needed for the United States to gain respect overseas. In addition, he made a convincing case that if they were not united effectively, the states would war among themselves.

After the ratification of the Constitution, Jay served as the first chief justice of the United States under appointment by President Washington from 1789 to 1795. Jay's Supreme Court service included circuit court riding in New York and New England. In 1794, Jay left the bench to travel to London and to negotiate Jay's Treaty with Great Britain. In 1795, Jay resigned from the Supreme Court and paved the way for John Marshall's Supreme Court career when he refused to accept reappointment to the court by President Adams in 1800. Between 1795 and 1801, Jay served as governor of New York.

Jay's remaining years were spent in retirement at his Bedford, New York, estate. These years were saddened by the death of his wife, Sally Livingston Jay, in 1802. He actively opposed the War of 1812 despite recognizing its constitutional legitimacy, and he became increasingly convinced that slavery was a serious threat to the survival of the Union.

Influence

The authors of *The Federalist*, who used the pseudonym Publius, based on Greek biographer Plutarch's account of the Roman politician Publius Valerius Publicola, provided a critical exposition of the Constitution immediately after it was written in eighty-five essays originally published serially in a newspaper and later in book form. *The Federalist* played a crucial role in the struggle to ratify the Constitution, especially in the vital swing state of New York, and it provided a good argument that the governance problems that the United States experienced under the Articles of Confederation were too severe to be remedied by patchwork alterations by 1787. Although the more limited Annapolis Convention of 1786 had only recommended revisions to the articles after examining the political situation, propertied, informed individuals sought more drastic change. Therefore, in 1787, a Constitutional Convention was called in Philadelphia with the stated goal of salvaging the Articles of Confederation, and it produced an entirely new document, creating a strong central government and allowing it to act directly on individuals, which the Confederation government never had the authority to do.

Both Hamilton and Madison, convention delegates, defended a work they had participated in writing from charges of usurpation of power. For more than two centuries, *The Federalist* has commanded respect as an outstanding work of U.S. political theory and been cited by lawyers seeking to interpret the Constitution.

Susan A. Stussy

The Federalist

Type of philosophy: Ethics, political philosophy
First published: 1787-1788 (serial); 1788 (book; also known as *The Federalist Papers*)

Principal ideas advanced:

◇ The Articles of Confederation cannot meet the needs of the newly independent United States in 1787 for respect abroad and stability at home.

◇ The Articles of Confederation are too deficient to be changed by the process of amendment, and a new governing document is needed; reform of the Articles of Confederation was recommended by the Annapolis Convention of 1786, and the Constitutional Convention in Philadelphia justifiably exceeded its mandate.

◇ The federal union might dissolve if the central government is not significantly strengthened, and the dissolution of the union could lead to warfare between competing states.

◇ The federal government needs authority to act directly on individuals.

◇ The size of the United States is not too large for the creation of a republican form of government; the Constitution proposed a workable federal republic in which the states would retain some, if not all, of the characteristics of sovereignty.

◇ Power should be separated among the three branches of the federal government: executive, legislative, and judicial.

Alexander Hamilton, an influential New York lawyer and convention delegate, conceived *The Federalist* as a series of newspaper essays to defend the work of the Constitutional Convention that met in Philadelphia in 1787. He recruited James Madison, a notable Virginia delegate to the Convention, and John Jay, a respected diplomat and former New York jurist, as coauthors. All three men believed that New York's ratification of the Constitution was crucial in setting up an effective central government, and *The Federalist* was designed first to influence events in New York and then to make a nationwide impression. The impact of *The Federalist* helped make New York the eleventh state to ratify the new Constitution on July 26, 1788.

The first essay, written by Hamilton and outlining the projected plans for a series of articles defending the Constitution, appeared on October 27, 1787. The series concluded with the eighty-fifth essay, which was published on August 16, 1788. The first thirty-six essays were collected in

March, 1788, and a volume containing essays thirty-seven to eighty-five appeared later that year. All three authors used the pseudonym Publius. The ratification of the Constitution was not seen as a foregone conclusion in 1787-1788 because many respected Americans became anti-Federalists out of fear of an overly strong federal government, and *The Federalist* was an effective propaganda piece that helped sway public opinion during a crucial period.

Despite multiple authorship, *The Federalist* retained an impressive degree of internal unity. More than two hundred years later, *The Federalist* is still considered one of the United States' best contributions to world political philosophy, and conservative contemporary lawyers tend to cite it to defend their constitutional interpretations.

In the first essay, Hamilton described the scope of *The Federalist*. He stated that later essays would examine the usefulness of the Union, the inadequacy of the Articles of Confederation to preserve the Union, and the necessity of an "energetic," or strong, central government. The work would also attempt to prove that the proposed federal Constitution did not violate republican ideals and was analogous to existing state constitutions and that the adoption of the Constitution would preserve liberty, property, and existing forms of government. Most contemporary and later observers have agreed that *The Federalist* was a credible attempt to achieve these goals by men learned in history, law, political theory, and philosophy as these disciplines were understood in late eighteenth century terms by British Americans nurtured on the traditions of classical antiquity. The authors were pragmatic optimists who were well aware of human failings but optimistic that the American people could create a government worthy of emulation by others.

The Value of the Union

In the second essay, Jay set out to prove the value of the newly independent states remaining united, which had not been questioned until just before the writing of *The Federalist*. He argued that Americans logically constituted one people by ancestry, religion, manners, and customs as well as the possession of common governmental principles, and Americans had worked together to secure their independence in the recent Revolutionary War against Great Britain. He also stressed that the American people had recognized the importance of remaining united in the most difficult periods of the Revolutionary War conflict. In addition, Jay declared that the dissolution of the Union would end America's greatness.

Having established or attempted to establish the value of the Union, *The Federalist* turned to the flaws of the Articles of Confederation for the effective conduct of foreign policy. In the third essay, Jay used his foreign policy expertise to show that weak states were not treated with respect by other countries. Jay gave the historical example of French king Louis XIV's humiliation of Genoan representatives in 1685 at a time when he would not have dared to inflict similar humiliation on representatives from England or Spain. In addition, Jay declared that moderation and reason were more likely to prevail in the national government, which could attract higher caliber individuals to positions of authority. Thus, Jay held that a strong central government would be less likely to go to war than the weaker state governments, and that the national government could conduct necessary wars more effectively than state governments.

In essay 6, Hamilton provided an even stronger defense of a strong Union. Where Jay had concentrated on foreign policy, the more domestically oriented Hamilton warned that the absence of a strong Union was bound to produce dangerous internal conflicts between states. Additionally, in essay 7, Hamilton argued that an America lacking unity would be more likely than an America with a strong federal union to get involved in European politics and wars.

An "Energetic," Republican Government

Because the authors of *The Federalist* saw the Articles of Confederation government as too weak to deal effectively with foreign powers and to maintain the public credit, they sought an "energetic" national government with strong powers to deal with foreign nations and manage the economy as well as a judiciary to secure sound administration of the laws on the federal level. In essay 22, Hamilton stressed that a viable national government needed the power to regulate commerce, raise armed forces, and allow the larger and more

populous states to have more input in national decisions than smaller states such as Rhode Island.

In addition to an "energetic" government, the authors of *The Federalist* sought a government that embodied the republican ideals of the Revolution in a workable and potentially lasting governmental structure. Madison, who elaborated on his fear of factions in essay 10, stressed that republicanism as embodied in the proposed Constitution provided a remedy for the instability that had historically hobbled democratic governments. He believed that the people would be better governed by their representatives than by attempting to govern themselves directly, and that a republic could provide good government to a larger territory and a greater number of citizens than a democracy could accommodate. At the conclusion of essay 10, Madison stated his views:

> In the extent and proper structure of the Union, therefore, we behold a republican remedy for the diseases most incident to republican government. And according to the degree of pleasure and pride we feel in being republicans ought to be our zeal in cherishing and supporting the charter of federalists.

Because they wished to preserve the republican ideals of their generation, the authors of *The Federalist* thoroughly familiarized themselves with both the strengths and the weaknesses of existing state constitutions. Throughout these essays, the authors referred to state constitutions in order to justify features of the proposed constitution. For example, in essay 81, Hamilton justified separating judicial and legislative powers by reference to the constitutions of New Hampshire, Massachusetts, Pennsylvania, Delaware, Maryland, Virginia, North Carolina, South Carolina, and Georgia. British tradition did not separate judicial and legislative powers, but these constitutions provided significant validation to the independent judiciary envisioned in the proposed Constitution.

Showing that the proposed federal constitution was comparable to existing state constitutions helped the authors of *The Federalist* buttress their contention that the proposed federal Constitution would preserve important concepts such as the sacred nature of citizens' rights to life, liberty, and property. In essay 84, Hamilton confronted fears that the adoption of the Constitution would help erode the jury trial rights long cherished by the English and their American descendants. Hamilton noted that the Constitution established the right to trial by jury in criminal cases, and he compared this guarantee to the state constitution of Connecticut, which did not establish the right to trial by jury in either criminal or civil cases.

Separation of Powers

In addition to treating the topics listed by Hamilton in the initial essay of *The Federalist*, the coauthors discussed other topics such as the separation of powers at considerable length. Because they shared the view of most of their contemporaries that the concentration of powers led to abuses and admired the work of the French philosopher Montesquieu, the collaborators dwelt at some length on the checks and balances that the Constitution provided to limit overreaching by the executive, judicial, and legislative departments.

Having removed themselves from the reach of King George III, the framers of the Constitution did not want to have a de facto kingship in the form of a strong executive. Thus they gave the president veto power over legislative acts, but they did not make that veto power absolute, allowing a determined legislative branch to override a presidential veto.

In essays 67-77, Hamilton treated presidential powers at length. Hamilton, who was often said to have monarchist leanings, wanted to strengthen the executive branch of the federal government in order to prevent legislative encroachment on the necessary prerogatives of the presidency. For this reason, as he explained in essay 70, Hamilton considered a plural executive unworkable. In essay 75, Hamilton defended his view that the House of Representatives was too numerous a body to make treaties with foreign powers and that the president should negotiate treaties to be ratified later by the Senate. Summarizing his view of the presidency in essay 77, Hamilton contended that the need to stand for reelection every four years and the legislature's power to impeach placed reasonable limits on presidential abuse of power.

In addition to defending the necessity of a strong presidential office, *The Federalist* argued for a strong and independent judiciary to place effective restraints on the actions of the executive and legislative branches. In essays 78-83, Hamilton employed his experience as an attorney and political figure to justify the need for a strong and independent judiciary. For Hamilton, the judiciary was by nature the weakest branch of government, and it performed the invaluable function of limiting the impact of popular passions on governmental decision making because the judges could act without fear of losing their positions. He believed that the Constitution should be more important than future legislative statutes, and in essay 78, he provided a compelling defense of the need for judicial review.

Before discussing the proposed functions of the executive and judicial branches of the proposed federal government, *The Federalist* discussed the organization and powers of the envisioned two-chamber legislative branch at length with special emphasis on the powers of the Senate. The writers viewed the legislature as potentially the most powerful branch of the new federal government, and they wanted to assure readers that the creation of a Senate and a House of Representatives to share legislative duties provided for a legislature that reflected popular views while allowing citizens at least some time to think through issues before making potentially irreversible decisions. Turning from domestic to foreign policy, in essay 64, Jay used his background as a seasoned diplomat to defend the Senate's participation in the treaty-making process along with the president of the United States.

Short-Term and Long-Term Effects

In the short term, *The Federalist* helped convince New York to become the eleventh state to ratify the Constitution. These collected essays were also read by pro-Constitution Federalists throughout the country, and the worried anti-Federalists resisting the ratification of the Constitution did not produce an equivalent document.

In the long term, *The Federalist* continues to influence American concepts of government and law more than two centuries later. The authors were not perfect prophets; the anti-Federalists were not impressed with Hamilton's contention in essay 84 that a bill of rights was not needed, and the Bill of Rights was adopted in 1790. In 1951, the Twenty-Second Amendment, which limited the president's eligibility for reelection, was adopted because after Franklin D. Roosevelt's prolonged tenure, the case Hamilton made for the indefinite eligibility of the president for reelection no longer seemed valid. Although the authors of *The Federalist* failed to predict all future needs, they believed that most of their work would endure while recognizing that future generations would need to alter the form of government they established.

Susan A. Stussy

Additional Reading

Adair, Douglass. *Fame and the Founding Fathers: Essays*. Edited by Trevor Colbourn. Indianapolis, Ind.: Liberty Fund, 1998. An important series of essays, worthy of a thorough reading.

Blackmun, Harry A. "John Jay and *The Federalist Papers*." *Pace Law Review* (Spring, 1988): 237-248. Blackmun presented this speech at the Peter Jay family home on the occasion of the bicentennial of *The Federalist*. He discussed John Jay's contributions to *The Federalist* and the flaws in the 1787 Constitution's treatment of African Americans, American Indians, and women.

Carey, George W. *"The Federalist": Design for a Constitutional Republic*. Urbana: University of Illinois Press, 1994. An examination of *The Federalist*.

Epstein, David F. *The Political Theory of The Federalist*. Chicago: University of Chicago Press, 1984. Epstein holds that the authors of *The Federalist* envisioned a new government that could accommodate both its most and its least pretentious citizens as well as make use of factions. Epstein devotes a chapter to essay 10, in which James Madison treated factions and also shows how the partisanship of the people, spirited election contests, and the exclusion of citizens in the aggregate help create a workable framework for republican government.

Furtwangler, Albert. *The Authority of Publius: A Reading of "The Federalist Papers."* Ithaca, N.Y.: Cornell University Press, 1984. Furtwangler's work provides a more critical and less reverential approach to the analysis of *The Federalist*. The author sees *The Federalist* as a piece of high-quality journalism that should be studied not with uncritical reverence but with an examination of the contradictions between different essays.

Millican, Edward. *One United People: The Federalist Papers and the National Idea*. Lexington: University Press of Kentucky, 1990. Millican's text stresses nationalism as the key factor motivating the authors of *The Federalist*. He connects Alexander Hamilton's support of a strong, centralized government with the views of Franklin D. Roosevelt and New Deal liberals. Millican contends that both the political left and the political right fell short of Publius's sound brand of nationalism in the 1980's.

White, Morton. *Philosophy, "The Federalist," and the Constitution*. New York: Oxford University Press, 1987. White analyzes the philosophical assumptions that guided Hamilton, Madison, and Jay in their writings as Publius. White finds that Publius was both a pragmatist and an ideologist who was sometimes troubled by conflicting beliefs such as the need to retain slavery in order to preserve the Union in the context of the realities of 1787. In conclusion, White holds that *The Federalist* was a philosophical hybrid of "Lockean rationalism" in morals and "Humeian empiricism" in politics.

Wills, Garry. *Explaining America: "The Federalist."* Garden City, N.Y.: Doubleday, 1981. Wills, a convert from *National Review* conservatism to moderate liberalism, offers a unique perspective on the ideology of *The Federalist*. He illustrates Scottish philosopher David Hume's influence on Hamilton and Madison as authors of *The Federalist*.

Susan A. Stussy

Han Feizi

Combining the philosophies of the Daoist, Confucian, Mohist, and especially Legalist (*fa*) traditions, Han Feizi synthesized and articulated better than any of his predecessors the complex set of philosophical and practical ideas about government known as Legalism. He advocated promulgation of law to punish criminals severely and to reward good citizens, irrespective of relationship or rank.

Principal philosophical works: *Han Feizi*, latter half of third century B.C.E. (*The Complete Works of Han Fei Tzu: A Classic of Chinese Legalism*, 1939-1959, 2 volumes; commonly known as *Han Feizi*)

Born: 280 B.C.E.; the state of Han, China
Died: 233 B.C.E.; the state of Qin, China

Early Life

Han Feizi was born into a high-ranking aristocratic family in the state of Han in central China in 280 B.C.E. and lived in the late Warring States period (475-221 B.C.E.). According to *Shi-ji* (first century B.C.E.; *Records of the Grand Historian of China*, 1960; rev. ed. 1993) by the historian Sima Qian, Han Feizi, being a habitual stutterer, was unable to deliver fluent speeches but was very smart. He thought and wrote very well. Han Feizi studied under the Confucian philosopher Xunzi. His fellow student Li Si later became the prime minister to the First Emperor of the Qin Dynasty (221-207 B.C.E.). Though his teacher was a Confucian master, Han Feizi was more interested in the arts of *fa* (law), *shi* (power), and *shu* (statecraft) than Confucius's *li* (rituals, rites, proprieties) and *yi* (righteousness or proper character).

Han Feizi made many attempts to volunteer his advice to the king of Han, but the king did not put his advice into practice. Han Feizi became incensed with the king, whom he felt was not capable of listening to good advice or of reforming the state of Han. He instead concentrated his time and energy on writing both to express his views on government and to vent his personal frustrations. Most of his works were composed in this period. Later, when the state of Qin was going to attack the state of Han, the king of Han finally sent Han Feizi as a goodwill envoy to Qin. This was the first time and the last time he was used by a ruler.

Han Feizi's works were known in Qin, and the king of Qin had read his essays "Solitary Indignation" and "Five Vermin." The king was very impressed by Han Feizi's thoughts and admired him greatly. Han Feizi suggested that the king of Qin unite with the state of Han to attack the state of Zhao; however, the king of Qin did not listen to this suggestion. Han Feizi stayed in the state of Qin, hoping the king would employ him after his mission was finished. The king of Qin did like him and showed interest in employing him. However, before the king gained confidence in him and took him into service, his prime minister, Li Si, who was envious of Han Feizi's talents and afraid that Han Feizi might replace him, slandered him before the king by challenging Han Feizi's loyalty. The king of Qin instructed officials to pass sentence on Han Feizi. Later, Li Si sent people to give poison to Han Feizi and ordered him to commit suicide. Han Feizi wanted to plead his innocence before the throne but was barred from seeing the king. Later, the king of Qin realized his mistake and instructed his people to pardon the philosopher, but Han Feizi had already died.

Life's Work

Han Feizi wrote fifty-five essays, mostly on subjects related to government and the legal system.

His works were collected after his death under the title *Han Feizi*. Most of the essays are short and concise. His basic thoughts are presented in twelve essays: "The Way of the Ruler," "On Having Standards," "The Two Handles," "Wielding Power," "The Eight Villainies," "The Ten Faults," "The Difficulties of Persuasion," "The Difficulty of Bian Hei," "Guarding Against the Interior," "Facing the South," "The Five Vermin," and "Eminence in Learning: A Critical Estimate of Confucians and Mohists."

Han Feizi lived during the great chaos known as the Warring States period (475-221 B.C.E.), which resulted from the collapse of the old feudal order toward the end of the Zhou Dynasty (1122-221 B.C.E.). Wars among the states were constantly being fought as each state sought ways to strengthen its own power and maintain social order. Because Han Feizi was the only member of the nobility among the important early Chinese philosophers such as Confucius, Mozi, and Xunzi, he seemed more responsible to his native state and more interested in searching for new ways to run a country and rule citizens. This turbulent period provided him a great opportunity to observe political chaos and changing societies so that he could compare the situations of his time with those of history. These observations and comparisons helped him form his philosophy and thoughts on the practical political affairs of government. His concept of the art of rulership, perhaps his greatest contribution to ancient Chinese philosophy, consists of three essential elements: *fa* (law), *shi* (power), and *shu* (statecraft). Even though these three elements were put forward individually by his Legalist predecessors, it was Han Feizi who first realized them equally important for good government and combined them.

Han Feizi studied the philosophy of Confucius but did not follow Confucian learning. Unlike Confucius, who believed that human beings are naturally good and can achieve self-perfection, Han Feizi believed that the great majority of people are self-interested. Because of their self-interested nature, people have the tendency to commit crimes. When the idea of committing crimes does not trouble them mentally, they do so. Therefore, stern punishment should be introduced to prevent crimes. When punishments are severe, people dare not transgress, and therefore, there will be no punishments. Thus, criminal law should be made and put into practice. According to Han Feizi's criminal theory, norms must be standardized in writing, criminals should be convicted according to evidence, and punishments should match the crimes committed. Han Feizi was strongly against practicing mercy when criminal punishments were carried out because he believed mercifulness would cripple the legal system and eventually promote crimes.

In Han Feizi's view, the promulgation of clear laws (*fa*) and the establishment of severe punishments (*xing*) save the masses of people from disorder, get rid of calamities in the world, ensure that the strong do not override the weak and the majority do not oppress the minority, and permit the aged to live out their years and the young and orphaned to attain maturity. He also believed that the border regions would not be invaded, that ruler and minister would have mutual regard for each other, that father and son would mutually support each other, and that none of the calamities of death, destruction, bonds, and captivity would occur.

Han Feizi argued that a government, if it is to be strong, must destroy factionalism and privilege. Therefore, it is imperative for a government to publicize its laws to all, and everyone—except the ruler (king)—should be equal before the law regardless of his or her ranking. This was a very important contribution to Chinese legal history. Before Han Feizi, by custom and according to principle, criminal punishment was not applied to members of the nobility, high-ranking officials, or anyone above these officials. Han Feizi did not believe a government based on *li* (the rituals of Confucian principles) could improve individual behavior because *li* is unwritten, particularistic, and subject to arbitrary interpretation. He believed that law is the basis of stable government because, being fixed and known to all, law provides an exact instrument with which to regulate individual conduct.

Han Feizi also thought that, to be effective, law needs strong political power, the second essential element for good government. In his view, everyone should respect the ruler's sovereignty and put the country's interest first. This awe-inspiring political power should be wielded by the ruler alone and cannot be shared by ministers and the nobility. In order to hold on to this absolute power, the ruler should retain sole control of rewards and punishments. The system of enfeoffment, in which the king invests in the nobility by giving them hereditary titles, territories, and slaves, should be put to an end. Ministers and members of the nobility should be stripped of special privileges and be equally subject to the law as ordinary citizens. Furthermore, ministers and members of the nobility should not be given power to reward and punish people and should merely act as the agents of the sovereign in enforcing the law. Otherwise, they will be able to abuse their power for personal gain.

Shu (statecraft, policies, methods, rulership, or arts of governing) is Han Feizi's third essential element for good government. In his view, the officials and the people at large may be guided and kept in line by laws, but the ruler, who is the author of law and outside and above it, must master the arts of governing and apply them effectively to wield authority and control the population. First, the governing power needs to be centralized. Second, to break the power of the old aristocracy, the ruler should select people from the lower ranks of society according to their abilities but not their social status and promote them to administrative posts. Third, the ruler cannot run the day-to-day operation of government but must rely on the bureaucracy. However, as the concerns of government get more complex, the bureaucracy constantly expands and becomes far-reaching for the ruler. Therefore, the ruler should know how to manipulate the officials to make certain they are doing their work efficiently. To do so, the ruler should keep a certain distance from the officials and live in secret in the palace in order to create an air of mystery. The ruler should also become emotionless and never show delight and anger before the officials.

Influence

The influence of Han Feizi's thoughts on Chinese political science is far greater than on Chinese philosophy because his Legalism addressed political policies for rulers. Han Feizi took no interest in ordinary individuals or their lives except to the extent that they affect the interests of the ruling class. Unlike Confucius and Mozi, Han Feizi made no attempt to prescribe moral values and how human beings could improve their morality to make for a better society. In addition, Han Feizi's idea of stern criminal punishment has influenced all the Chinese dynasties and governments after the Qin Dynasty and is reflected in the modern-day Chinese criminal justice system.

Although the king of Han did not appreciate Han Feizi's political ideas, the king of Qin, the enemy and eventual destroyer of the Han, put them into practice by encouraging agriculture and warfare, disciplining his people with stern laws, and conducting the state's foreign affairs with cold-blooded cynicism. In 221 B.C.E., Qin completed his conquest of the other states and united China under a central government. Under the influence of Han Feizi's idea that all private teachings except for Legalism should be banned in order to keep people under the line of law, the first emperor of Qin had thousands of Confucian scholars buried alive and their books burned. The Qin Dynasty lasted only fourteen years and was overthrown by rebellion. Most Chinese historians have blamed its downfall on its harsh and ruthless treatment of people and criticized Han Feizi and other Legalist philosophers for their lack of mercy. Maybe for this reason, Han Feizi's Legalism has never entered into the mainstream of Chinese philosophy. However, because of the practical aspects of Han Feizi's teachings, many rulers throughout Chinese history have tried to apply his political philosophy in a diluted form.

Mao Zedong, the first chairman of the People's Republic of China, thought very highly of Han Feizi. He spent much time studying the philosopher's writings and became a master of applying Han Feizi's political philosophy to manage personnel. Mao publically proclaimed that he favored Legalism over Confucianism. Following Han Feizi's teaching, Mao lived a mysterious life and never trusted any of his ministers, even those he handpicked. Because of his suspicions, Mao started several political campaigns, including the Great Cultural Revolution and the Ideological Campaign Against Confucianism in the early 1970's, to bring down ministers whom he suspected to be his political opponents.

Wei Luo

Han Feizi

Type of philosophy: Chinese philosophy, ethics, philosophy of law, political philosophy

First transcribed: Han Feizi, latter half of third century B.C.E. (*The Complete Works of Han Fei Tzu: A Classic of Chinese Legalism,* 1939-1959, 2 volumes; commonly known as *Han Feizi*)

Principal ideas advanced:

◇ Nothing interests people except material profit.

◇ Laws are necessary; one who obeys the law is good, and one who disobeys the law is bad.

◇ Nothing is more important than having a prosperous state with strong armies; to make the realization of this goal possible, the ruler should use the promise of reward and the threat of punishment as instruments for the control of selfish citizens.

◇ To make government successful and to achieve a uniformity of standards, actualities must be made to conform with names; the behavior of citizens should match the descriptions prescribed by the law-giving rulers.

◇ If laws are made according to *dao,* the Way of nature, the state can rule itself.

◇ The five termites of the state are the political advisers, the scholars, the merchants, the artisans, and the knights-errant.

All early Chinese philosophical schools were concerned with political problems, and their systems were more in the nature of political formulas than they were pure metaphysical speculations. Even so, it is still startling to read a work such as *Han Feizi* in which ethics is totally absent and morality is completely ignored. The Legalists (*fa jia,* or the advocates of rule by law) of ancient China were unique in their undisguised Machiavellian attitudes toward political realities.

The steadily deteriorating political and social situation that existed during the Warring States period (475-221 B.C.E.) must have contributed to a hardening realism in the intellectual climate of the time, but this climate alone did not give rise to the Legalist school. Han Feizi, to whom this book is attributed, studied with the great Confucian master Xunzi. From his teacher, Han Feizi acquired one basic concept about human nature that was to serve as the bedrock of the Legalists' theories.

The Necessity for Law

Xunzi distinguished himself by challenging Mencius's idealistic view of human nature. According to Xunzi, human nature is like the young craboak tree: Without restraining influence, the tree will grow crooked. Although Xunzi never lost sight of a moralistic ideal in advocating the need for education, his disciple Han Feizi carried this view one step further to assert that nothing interests people except material profit. The hired hand works hard only because of a promised reward, says Han Feizi, and even parents do not raise their children for love but for their own future security. If this is not the case, asks Han Feizi, then why do people value their baby boys so much that they drown their baby girls? (Presumably this practice was still observed in Han Feizi's time.)

Han Feizi did not deny that there were ancient sages, a common belief shared by most people in China at that time. However, he believed that good people are the exception rather than the rule. Furthermore, those who are good by nature are of little value to an orderly society and a prosperous state. If a ruler relies upon the few good people to run the country, Han Feizi argues, it would be like the archer who counts on the few naturally straight branches with which to make arrows. The archer would not have many arrows to shoot. A few good people do not make an orderly society—for orderliness to exist, everyone must observe the interests of society. Therefore, the only thing that counts is a set of laws. The person who obeys the law is good. This is the only necessary standard of good and bad or right and wrong.

Environment offers an explanation for the existence of the Sage Kings in China's golden past. In high antiquity, material supplies were abundant and people few. No one needed to steal for a living. However, as the population grew and the land became more crowded, the struggle for existence made manifest the true nature of humankind, which is profit-centered and selfish. Therefore, although in the golden past, as the Confucians explain in their teachings, a moral life was possible, the same material conditions no longer exist. Han Feizi applied this theory to explain the behavior of the legendary kings who abdicated their thrones without regret. Legend says that the Sage Kings worked harder than the common peasant and enjoyed less comfort, so why should they have regrets about giving up their "burdens"? However, times had changed, and the throne had become a coveted position that bestowed comfort, power, glory, and material rewards on its holder. It is small wonder, says Han Feizi, that people all aspire to be a ruler.

In many chapters and through various analogies, Han Feizi attempts to prove his theory of economic determinism. He cites the relative value of water on high mountains and near the river shore to show that generosity with water is conditioned by the amount of its supply. He tells the story of a disobedient son—incorrigible in spite of all the affection his parents showered on him and chastened only when imprisoned—to prove that there is no reliable "moral sense" in human nature. As evidence of the ignorance of the masses, he recounts the predicaments of several ancient sages whose benevolence was met with popular resentment. Han Feizi's distrust in the ability of the people to govern themselves is absolute.

The Art of Rulership
The only available documentary evidence shows that Han Feizi wrote *Han Feizi* as a result of his inability to win a position of direct influence on the ruler of his state, the state of Han. If this is true, it is understandable why the book reveals a constant emphasis on the art of government and a persistent belief in the value of a prosperous state with strong armies. Toward these goals, Han Feizi constructed his philosophy. Because he saw material gain as the only governing force in human nature and could find no proof anywhere of humanity's intelligence, he logically turned to reward and punishment to induce people to do what should be done. Punishment and reward, what Han Feizi calls the ruler's "two helms," allow the sovereign to rule successfully. In order to enable the common people to know clearly what will bring pleasure and what pain, a set of specific rules is essential. These rules are laws.

Like the carpenter's compass and square, the laws must be fixed and rigid, and their enforcement constant and consistent. The ruler must not follow the Confucian advice to respect the opinions of the learned. To do so would undermine the authority of the law and cause confusion. The ruler paying much attention to the advice of the wise not only will destroy the smooth functioning of a government but also may endanger his personal position because his subjects may strive to become cunning so that they can either deceive or even replace the ruler. There must be only one authority and one standard, and that standard rests with the ruler alone. With legal codes as their books and law-enforcement officers as their teachers, the people need nothing else to keep them well behaved.

Names and Actuality
The Legalists' punishment-reward theory closely parallels the views of Mozi, which were common knowledge in Han Feizi's time. However, the real inspiration of Han Feizi's belief in law is to be found in the common concern over the confusion of names. Confucius urged a rectification of names to restore a proper social hierarchy and reestablish desirable social relationships. The members of the School of Names, including Gongsun Long, examine names to dramatize certain problems in human knowledge. Han Feizi also demanded a "search for actuality through examination of its name." Han Feizi wanted a uniformity of standards, and the only way to achieve it, as he saw it, depended on an exact correspondence between names and actualities. If the meaning of a name is not clear, then its actuality must be investigated to clarify the name. If the name is unknown, then its actuality must be searched out to arrive at a proper appellation.

The important and interesting aspect of this theory is that Han Feizi did not urge any adjustment of names to match actualities. On the contrary, in Han Feizi's philosophy the names provide the norm, and it is the actuality that must be adjusted to match the names. Therefore, Han Feizi insisted that the ruler hold the name in his hand and that his subjects adjust their behaviors in order to conform to the name. Then and only then could a uniformity of standards be achieved and government be made successful. This idea concerning the use of names represents the extreme of the evolution of the theory on rectification of names. It is, as it has worked out, not a "search for actuality through an examination of its name," but rather a "demand that actuality conform with its name."

Once the names are fixed in the form of laws controlled by the ruler, these laws must be enforced so strictly that no deviation from them, for better or worse, is tolerated. Han Feizi does not hesitate to advise punishment of anyone whose claims or promises are not borne out exactly by subsequent performance. Even if a person does more and better than promised, the individual must be punished, because the harm that person does by corrupting the exact correspondence between name and actuality more than offsets the excess service rendered or the excess goods produced. To Han Feizi, a "small loyalty" (partial fulfillment of one's promise) is detrimental to the "great loyalty" (exact fulfillment of one's promise).

The Ruler's Lofty Position

A philosopher named Shenxiu, who lived shortly before Han Feizi, has expounded the principle of force that comes from one's position. Han Feizi quotes Shenxiu and gives the latter support. According to Shenxiu, a rock acquires its smashing force only when it falls from an altitude. Depending on where an object is located, it may have greater or less power. Han Feizi elaborates on this theory and acknowledges that dragons without clouds to float them would be as miserable as earthworms. He advises rulers to make best use of their lofty position, for their position is the rulers' sole source of power. Even an ancient Sage King would have been totally disabled if his orders had not been obeyed. Therefore, Han Feizi urges rulers to maintain their lofty, august position by remaining aloof from their subjects, including the top-ranking ministers. The wise sovereign rules by merely demonstrating "awe-inspiring majesty," without which the ruler would be a fish out of water and could do nothing.

Han Feizi recognized the possibility of abuse of power in the hands of undeserving rulers, but he argued for the need of a position of power in order for anyone to rule. A good chariot can travel far even when handled by a mediocre driver, and with a good driver, it can perform miracles. However, if the chariot is rickety, even the best of drivers cannot make it perform well. Han Feizi preferred to gamble on the greater odds against having many bad rulers who abuse power.

The theory of the ruler's position is one of the important aspects of statecraft that Han Feizi discusses in great detail. By maintaining a lofty position, the ruler of a state can command obedience and ensure internal order. With order comes the opportunity to build the strength and wealth of the state for the ultimate purpose of becoming the leader (*ba*) of all the states. This was the political ideal pursued by all the rulers of the states at that time. A collapsed old feudal order left the field wide open and resulted in a power struggle. Each state sought political supremacy to rule over the entire territory of China. Therefore, Han Feizi presents lengthy arguments on how to maneuver interstate politics in order to acquire the status of a ruling state. He examines many historical events involving the success or failure of a ruler and comments on the causes. Invariably, he finds these historical cases supporting his political philosophy.

Rule Through Nonactivity

Legalism and Confucianism are curiously similar regarding one concept. The Confucians believed that the best king rules by moral magnetism: If a ruler's moral virtues are perfect, his subjects and neighboring states will of themselves recognize him as their leader. Han Feizi believed in rule by the magic of power: If the king's majesty is awe-inspiring, his subjects will obey without further ado. When the laws are complete, the people will know what to do without the need for the ruler to make any move.

This is an extension of the Daoist idea of nonactivity. Two chapters in the *Han Feizi* are devoted to an explication of the *Dao De Jing*. In giving his views on the *Dao De Jing*, Han Feizi makes it clear that he subscribes to the idea of *dao* as nature's Way. There is a proper way for everything, for its existence and function. "Things have their appropriateness and materials have their right use," and because the ruler who learns of *dao* knows how to put everything in its proper place and to assign it its proper function, there is nothing left to be done. What a ruler has to do is to set up laws according to the Way; then the state will go on to rule itself. The king ultimately will rule by not ruling.

Laws backed by the ruler's infinite authority and enforced through the ruler's instruments, the ministers, will free the ruler from any personal concern. Han Feizi here completes his idea of a perfect rule through nonactivity, for if every part of this political mechanism functions as it should, the ruler really does not have to be concerned with government. Han Feizi cites a number of historical cases in which a king indulged in comfort and yet his kingdom lasted; the philosopher attributes this result to the good laws set up by the king. Although Han Feizi stresses the importance of the king's vigilance over the welfare of his state, the suggestion that the state can rule itself while the king enjoys life must have had a great appeal to many rulers.

"Termites" of the State

The sole criterion for judgment of right and wrong or good and bad in Legalism is whether something contributes to the prosperity of the state and to the strength of its armies. The law, therefore, also determines reward and punishment in accordance with this very principle, which is an application of Mozi's utilitarianism. The ruler recognizes the "merit" of subjects in relation to their actual material contribution to the state. Against this yardstick, the Confucians are useless and meritless because their principles of human-heartedness and rules of propriety concern only the individual's life. Encouragement given to the study of literature, praise of knight-errantry, and indulgence in idle theoretical discussions are all, in Han Feizi's opinion, irrelevant to the good of the state. To uphold any one of these would pose another standard in competition with the standard of utility to the state.

The "five termites of the state" are classified by Han Feizi on this very basis. They are the traveling political advisers (a trade that flourished only during times such as the Warring States period), the scholars, the merchants, the artisans, and the knights-errant. The first two groups use their glib tongues to confuse the rulers and undermine the laws. The merchants and artisans speculate and produce goods of no real utility but deceive the people in order to realize undeserved increment in the process. The knights-errant take laws in their own hands in defiance of governmental authority. If these people are not discouraged, says Han Feizi, nobody will be willing to sweat in the fields (to produce grains) and to bleed on horseback (to fight for the state). Han Feizi values only the farmers and the soldiers; this is another parallel between Mozi and the Legalists.

The Ruler of Qin and Han Feizi

The harshness of Han Feizi's realism appealed to power-hungry rulers of the states embroiled in a bloody political struggle; it also impressed a seasoned Legalist such as Han Feizi himself. The authority of the ruler, in Han Feizi's own theory, had to be so absolute and infinite that to approach the ruler with any kind of advice was a dangerous undertaking at best. Chapters 3 and 12 express the frustration of the philosopher whose speech impediment (stuttering) made the eloquence of his arguments anything but apparent.

As chapter 11 makes amply clear, the Legalist's career was a precarious one. Han Feizi's theories made him extremely unpopular among the other courtiers, and he constantly risked "official execution or secret assassination." Han Feizi's own life bore tragic witness to these observations. According to the biography written by the Han Dynasty (207 B.C.E.-220 C.E.) historian Sima Qian, Han Feizi's works became known to the ruler of the state of Qin, who harbored ruthless political ambitions. The treatises caught the fancy of this aggressive ruler, and he sought Han Feizi's services so desperately that he ordered a siege of the state of Han by Qin soldiers. The defeated ruler of Han surrendered Han Feizi. However, the irony of history found its agent in a man named Li Si, who studied under Xunzi with Han Feizi and also was a Legalist, although somewhat inferior to Han Feizi in his intellectual achievement. At this juncture, Li Si had been advising the ruler of Qin for some time already. Fearing that the arrival of Han Feizi in the Qin court would spell his political death, Li Si slandered Han in front of the Qin ruler and forged an order to demand Han Feizi's suicide. Han Feizi drank the poison and died before serving in the court of Qin.

Han Feizi died, but the school of political thought that went under his name lived on and found a powerful exponent in the ruler of Qin. Aided by the scheming Li Si and having adopted a number of Legalist measures, the state of Qin became a "prosperous state with strong armies" and conquered the whole of China in 221 B.C.E., establishing the first truly unified empire in Chinese history. Even the Daoist element in Han Feizi's system seemed to have been absorbed by the Qin ruler, who became the first Chinese emperor. He set up severe laws, burned the Confucian theoretical books, and buried "useless" scholars. Then, when he felt that his empire was being governed quite smoothly and efficiently, he turned to a search for drugs of longevity and material enjoyment, trusting his country to rule by nonactivity.

Kai-yu Hsu, updated by John K. Roth

Additional Reading

Graham, A. C. *Disputers of the Tao: Philosophical Argument in Ancient China*. La Salle, Ill.: Open Court, 1989. A well-informed and thorough discussion of Legalist philosophy, including that of Han Feizi.

Han Feizi. *Han Fei Tzu: Basic Writings*. Translated by Burton Watson. New York: Columbia University Press, 1964. This translation of twelve books of Han Feizi's works by a Western scholar in Chinese and Japanese studies provides another perspective on Han Feizi's works. The translator includes a preface and a helpful introduction that places the philosopher in relation to Chinese history and thought.

MacCormack, Geoffrey. *The Spirit of Traditional Chinese Law*. Athens: University of Georgia Press, 1996. This book devotes a section to a discussion of the teachings of the Legalist school, including Han Feizi's view of rule by law.

Tong, Shuye. "A Study of Han Fei's Thought." *Chinese Studies in Philosophy* 14, no. 61 (Winter, 1982-1983). This article uses the Maoist theory of classes to analyze the sources of Han Feizi's philosophy and to study his methodology. The author also discusses Han Feizi's political thinking and his theory of human nature and ethical views.

Wang, Hsiao-Po, and Leo S. Chang. *The Philosophical Foundations of Han Fei's Political Theory*. Honolulu: University of Hawaii Press, 1986. This book reconsiders the role of Legalism in Chinese philosophical and political history. The authors challenge the traditional Chinese historians' view, which treats the thought of Han Feizi as a philosophical and political anomaly, and hold that Han Heizi fits within traditional Chinese thought, despite his utilitarian approach. The authors also conclude that Han Feizi's Legalist thinking has exerted a greater influence on the Chinese governmental system than traditionally believed, even affecting contemporary governing structures and policies.

Wei Luo

H. L. A. Hart

Combining the approaches of postwar linguistic philosophy and British analytical jurisprudence, Hart revived the field of philosophy of law, making distinctive and notable contributions to such issues as the nature of law, the relationships between law and morality, punishment and responsibility, and the concept of rights.

Principal philosophical works: *Causation in the Law*, 1959, 2d ed. 1985 (with Tony Honoré); *The Concept of Law*, 1961, 2d ed. 1994; *Law, Liberty, and Morality*, 1963; *Punishment and Responsibility*, 1968; *Essays on Bentham*, 1982; *Essays in Jurisprudence and Philosophy*, 1983.

Born: July 18, 1907; Harrogate, England
Died: December 19, 1992; Oxford, England

Early Life

Herbert Lionel Adolphus Hart was the third son of Simeon Hart and Rose Hart. His father was a wool merchant of German Jewish extraction. Hart was educated at Chettenham College and Bradford Grammar School, then went to New College, Oxford University, where he studied the classics, ancient history, and philosophy. H. W. B. Joseph, a well-known logician, was Hart's tutor there. Joseph later observed that Hart, among his many students, was a rare individual who combined exceptional philosophical acumen with solid judgment and good sense. Although offered a teaching post in philosophy at Oxford, Hart instead chose to study law. He was called to the bar in 1932 and served as a Chancery barrister from 1932 to 1940. During the war years, he served as a civil service member in the War Office, doing military intelligence work. In 1945, he was invited to become a fellow and tutor in philosophy at Oxford. He accepted the position and became one of the leading teachers of philosophy at that institution. Hart was increasingly influenced by his colleagues in philosophy, Gilbert Ryle, Stuart Hampshire, and especially J. L. Austin, all of whom were central figures in what was called linguistic philosophy, or ordinary language philosophy. Hart was elected to the chair of jurisprudence at Oxford when it was vacated in 1952.

Life's Work

In his inaugural lecture as professor of jurisprudence, "Definition and Theory in Jurisprudence," Hart employed the methods of linguistic philosophy to address certain traditional issues in the law. The philosophical approach emphasized that human language had a great diversity and complexity of uses and that meaningful forms of human discourse were many and varied. Hart sought to apply this insight to the study of a number of jurisprudential concepts. Legal theorists, in seeking to define, per genus and species, terms such as "right" and "corporation," had been led into obscure and unenlightening theories. Hart suggested that it would be more fruitful not to pursue such traditional definitions, which involve inquiring into what such terms "stood for," and instead to examine the conditions under which statements using these terms are regarded as true. Such careful attention to language remained characteristic of Hart's work; however, his approach was not confined to narrow linguistic analysis but extended to substantive theories and normative issues in philosophy and jurisprudence. Still, he remained committed to the methodological value of careful attention to language, expressed in J. L. Austin's remark that we can use "a sharpened awareness of words to sharpen our perception of the phenomena."

Hart's rising reputation attracted the attention of Harvard Law School professor Lon Fuller, who invited Hart to spend a term at Harvard in 1956.

Hart delivered the Holmes Lecture, under the title "Positivism and the Separation of Law and Morals," which was later published in the *Harvard Law Review* along with a lengthy reply by Fuller. The Hart-Fuller debate—in particular, Hart's vigorous defense of legal positivism—attracted widespread interest. Legal positivism was a doctrine advocated by the famous nineteenth century utilitarians, Jeremy Bentham and John Austin.

The core of the doctrine, in Hart's view, was the denial of any necessary connection between law and morality. Hart agreed with Bentham and Austin that it is better to maintain a distinction between the issues of what the law is and what the law ought to be, both for understanding and for making moral criticism of the law. Hart criticized traditional natural law theory, which grounded positive law in higher law or natural law and insisted that unjust or evil laws were not genuine laws. In contrast, the main tenets of legal positivism, according to Hart, consisted of two claims:

> First, in the absence of an expressed constitutional or legal provision, it could not follow from the mere fact that a rule violated standards of morality that it was not a rule of law; and, conversely, it could not follow from the mere fact that a rule was morally desirable that it was a rule of law.

Fuller, while praising the clarity and acuity of Hart's discussion, developed a lengthy critique, sharply challenging the implication of legal positivism that law was morally neutral. Law was a purposive human institution, Fuller maintained, and as such it constituted a morally good order, worthy of respect and fidelity of those subject to it. The most heated exchange concerned the example of Nazi Germany, with discussion of the claim that the legal positivist leanings of most members of the German legal profession may have fostered a subservient attitude to the Nazi regime and its corruption of legal processes. There was also attention given to the problematic cases faced by postwar German courts involving wartime activities of German civilians that were "lawful" under some questionable Nazi statutes.

Hart incorporated many of the ideas and arguments of these early essays into his most famous work, *The Concept of Law*. In this work, he de-

fended a sophisticated form of legal positivism, elaborated an analysis of law as a union of primary and secondary rules, and offered sustained criticisms of competing theories of law, including natural law theory, American legal realism, and John Austin's command theory of law. Austin claimed to have found the "key to the science of jurisprudence" in the idea of a command or order backed up by credible threats. This provided a simple, clear, and seemingly compelling model of what the law really is. Hart subjected Austin's theory to a withering attack, noting its inability to account plausibly for many of the familiar and characteristic aspects of laws and legal rules in mature legal systems, such as those enabling people to make wills and empowering courts to adjudicate disputes.

From the late 1950's through the mid-1960's, Hart was engaged in a debate with a prominent British jurist, Sir Patrick Devlin. In his Maccabean Lecture in Jurisprudence delivered to the British Academy called "The Enforcement of Morals," Devlin took issue with the Wolfenden Committee Report. The committee had recommended repeal of the law criminalizing homosexual practices, even among consenting adults in private. Devlin objected to the committee's basis for its recommendation, namely, that such conduct was part of "a realm of private morality and immorality which is, in brief and crude terms, not the law's business." Devlin argued that "the suppression of vice is as much the law's business as the suppression of subversive activities." Hart criticized Devlin's views on this matter and in particular Devlin's comparison of vice with subversive activities, initially in an article "Immorality and Treason" published in the *Listener*. In the Harry Camp Lectures delivered at Stanford University, Hart presented a more elaborate critique of legal moralism, the principle endorsed by Devlin, which states that a society has a right to enforce its moral code legally. These lectures were published in 1963 in a short book called *Law, Liberty, and Morality*. Scholars and jurists on both sides of the Atlantic joined the Hart-Devlin debate about the proper role of criminal law and the limits of individual liberty. Devlin, who became a member of the House of Lords, was prompted to develop his views more fully, publishing them in *The Enforcement of Morals* in 1965.

Hart's reputation as one of the leading philosophers of law in the English-speaking world was enhanced by his work on other issues besides the nature of law and the relationship of law and morality. Hart, along with Tony Honoré, his colleague at Oxford, published a detailed study of causation in their 1959 book *Causation in the Law*. They contended that the law used the conception of causation rooted in ordinary life and in everyday speech, distinguishing the cause of an event from other necessary conditions according to complex but discernible criteria. Hart and Honoré sought to defend the ordinary conception of causation and its use in the law from legal theorists who derided the use of causal language by the courts as a smokescreen for normative or policy judgments made by judges.

Hart also had a keen interest in philosophical questions surrounding responsibility and punishment in criminal law. A number of papers and lectures on these themes were assembled in the book *Punishment and Responsibility*. Hart provided a careful treatment of concepts related to legal responsibility, including intention, negligence, excuse, and *mens rea* (criminal intent). He affirmed the importance of the values of individual liberty and fair opportunity in legal policies and practices; as Hart observed, "Human society is a society of persons; and persons do not view themselves or each other as so many bodies moving in ways which are sometimes harmful and have to be prevented or altered. Instead persons interpret each others' movements as manifestations and choices." The first essay in the volume, on criminal punishment, sought to reconcile the competing philosophical theories of punishment, utilitarian and retributive, by pointing out that the justification of punishment is, in fact, a complex set of questions, with different aims and different values at stake.

Hart resigned the chair of jurisprudence at Oxford in 1968 and became a research fellow at University College. One of his major projects was participating in the editing of Bentham's papers. In 1973, he became the principal of Brasenose College, serving in that position until 1978, when he returned to University College to resume scholarly research. During this period, Hart continued to publish important and well-received articles in moral philosophy and philosophy of law. He developed a distinctive theory of rights, defending a "will" or "choice" theory that held that conferring a right is recognizing the primacy of some individual's choice over others with respect to some matter. For example, if one has a right to refuse medical treatment, then the choice of receiving or not receiving medical treatment is up to the individual; it is one's choice that determines whether one receives or does not receive treatment. Hart also undertook to review his theory of law, revising it in places and defending and clarifying it in others. He began writing a response to the many critics of his views in *The Concept of Law*, particularly those of the American legal philosopher Ronald Dworkin. Dworkin's early writings were a critical analysis of Hart's theory of law, and on the basis of this work, Dworkin had been selected to succeed Hart in the chair of jurisprudence at Oxford. A second edition of *The Concept of Law*, with a new postscript, was published in 1994. The new edition contains unfinished drafts composed by Hart and edited by Joseph Raz and Penelope Bulloch.

Hart died in 1992 and was survived by Jennifer Williams Hart, his wife of fifty-one years, as well as one daughter and three sons.

Influence

Hart is widely credited for the revival of jurisprudence and philosophy of law in the post-World War II era. Dworkin once stated that after becoming professor of jurisprudence at Oxford in 1952, Hart dominated and transformed legal theory, a feat that Dworkin attributed to Hart's lucid mind and to his command of moral philosophy. *The Concept of Law* is considered a classic in the field, and even those who are unconvinced by its main theses, including Dworkin, feel compelled to address the issues raised by Hart in the terms in which he framed them.

Hart's work, while primarily dealing with the philosophy of law, affected a number of other areas, including social and political philosophy and ethics. His treatment of issues was always clear and illuminating, providing a fresh and incisive perspective on issues. For example, his 1955 paper "Are There Any Natural Rights?" is still regarded as a seminal study of rights, even though Hart himself later rejected its main argument as mistaken. Hart was evenhanded and fair, intellectually honest, and generous and gracious in acknowledging the merit in the work of those he criticized and those who criticized his work.

Hart's philosophical outlook was broadly liberal, recognizing a plurality of moral values and principles. In this respect, he was very much akin in intellectual spirit to his close friend and Oxford colleague, Isaiah Berlin. Hart was very much impressed with and influenced by the British utilitarian tradition, but he insisted on the need to bring into play other types of moral concerns and principles, such as justice, fairness, and respect for individual rights.

Mario Morelli

The Concept of Law

Type of philosophy: Epistemology, ethics, philosophy of law
First published: 1961; 2d ed., 1994
Principal ideas advanced:

◇ The best way to understand law is in terms of the concept of rules, particularly as the union of primary and secondary rules.

◇ John Austin's classic command theory is too simple and reductionist to be an adequate theory of law.

◇ Law as a social phenomenon is best understood from an internal perspective, taking into account the viewpoint of those who look to the law as setting a standard of conduct.

◇ There is no necessary connection between law and morality, but it is reasonable to expect a considerable overlap between a society's moral code and its legal code.

◇ Legal rules have an area of indeterminacy of application because they contain open-textured general terms.

H. L. A. Hart's *The Concept of Law* is a systematic treatment of central issues in legal philosophy and jurisprudence that enlivens these areas of inquiry with fresh perspectives and new ideas. Hart suggests that the work may be viewed in a number of ways. From the lawyer's perspective, it can be regarded as an essay in analytical jurisprudence, that is, an effort to provide a general

analysis of law and major legal concepts. Philosophically, Hart employs the method and style sometimes called linguistic analysis, with close attention to the definitions of and distinctions among key terms and expressions. Further, the work constitutes an essay in descriptive sociology in the sense that its task is to elucidate law as a social phenomenon. One of Hart's major theses is that law is best understood as a method of social control related to, but distinct from, coercion and morality. Other traditional theories of law failed to pay sufficient attention to the differences, assimilating law too closely to coercion (command theories) or to morality (natural law theories).

The Command Theory of Law

Hart begins the substantive portion of the book with an extended critique of nineteenth century jurist John Austin's command theory of law. Austin sought to analyze law in terms of the behavioral elements of commands, habits, and obedience. Law is the command of the superior (sovereign) to those who have acquired a habit of obedience (subjects). Commands are expressions of a wish that others do or refrain from some action, accompanied by a threat of sanctions for noncompliance. The sovereign is a person or group who issues commands that are obeyed and who does not habitually obey another person. This model of law as orders backed by threats, despite its power, fails to capture some salient and familiar features of modern legal systems and cannot provide a sound basis for understanding central legal notions such as authority and obligation.

Hart presents several objections to Austin's model. First, Austin's account is at variance with the content of laws found in developed legal systems. Many laws do not impose duties and are not enforced by sanctions but instead confer powers on individuals and groups. Examples include legal rules defining how to make a valid will or contract. Second, the plausible idea that the lawmaker may be bound by laws is absent in the command theory. Laws, unlike most commands, possess a general character, applying to legislators and ordinary citizens alike. Third, in many legal systems, customs come to have the force of law through legal recognition by courts.

Austin sought to explain this by means of the implausible supposition that the sovereign's silence constitutes a tacit command.

In addition to these criticisms, Hart offers a more fundamental challenge to Austin's command theory, calling into question the very existence in any modern legal system of a sovereign in Austin's sense. Hart points out that the quasi-psychological notion of a habit of obedience fails to account for the continuity of law over time and the persistence of the legal order upon the change from one sovereign to a successor. The relationship suggested by the idea of a habit of obedience is both too simple and too personal to fully accommodate the idea of a legal authority entitled to make law. Additionally, lawmaking authority in a modern state has legal limitations: Legal rules, often in constitutions, stipulate disabilities or limits on legislative authority. The division of powers between the federal government and the states and the guarantee of individual rights against the government in the U.S. Constitution provide clear examples.

The Idea of a Rule

After diagnosing the problems with the command theory, Hart proposes a "fresh start," one giving a prominent role to the idea of a rule. He begins by making several distinctions. The first is between primary and secondary rules, invoked earlier in his attack on the command theory. He puts this idea to constructive use, with the claim that law is best understood as a union of primary and secondary rules. It is possible, Hart grants, to imagine a small, stable society that is a regime of only primary rules (rules imposing duties on the community's members). However, for most human societies, such an arrangement would be highly inefficient. Among its defects would be uncertainty about what the rules are and how they apply, the inability to adjust to changing situations because of the static character of such rules, and the difficulties of enforcing such rules without mechanisms and procedures to detect and deal with violations. Hart argues that secondary rules (rules about primary rules) are needed to remedy these defects. They include a rule of recognition (to identify authoritatively primary rules), rules of change (to specify how to enact new rules and to repeal or modify old ones), and

rules of adjudication (to establish procedures and to authorize individuals and agencies to ascertain violations of primary rules and to provide enforcement mechanisms). Although Hart characterizes the addition of these secondary rules to a regime of primary rules as a change from the prelegal to the legal, his point is conceptual rather than historical.

Another distinction emphasized by Hart is between "being obliged" and "being under an obligation." The command theory, focusing on the coercive aspects of law, misleadingly portrays an obligation imposed by a legal rule as if it were identical to being obliged by a threat of force. In this account, legal authority is really no different from the armed person forcing individuals to hand over their money. Missing from this picture is the point of being under an obligation: Rules imposing obligations set standards of conduct and justify the imposition of coercive sanctions for breaches. The command theory's reductionist view of obligations collapses being obligated under rules into being obliged by threat of force.

One of Hart's aims is to provide a general descriptive account of law as a rule-governed social phenomenon. To understand rule-governed behavior, the distinction between internal and external aspects of rules must be recognized. Earlier theorists, such as Austin and the American jurist Oliver Wendell Holmes, failed to make this distinction, neglecting the internal aspect of rules. Holmes advanced the famous claim that law can be seen as a prediction of what the courts will do. This view seeks to explain law from a purely external perspective, that of the outside observer who notices behavioral regularities but misses the normative aspect of rules. An outside observer, oblivious to the internal aspect of rules, may record that many motorists stop at red lights. Although such "observed regularities" may have some predictive value in forecasting future behavior, the external viewpoint cannot provide a proper understanding of the complex role of rules in social life and the character of rule-governed behavior. People stop at red lights because there is a rule to that effect, and they criticize those who run red lights for violating the traffic rule. This distinction is important methodologically for understanding law and other rule-governed practices in human society.

Although Hart insists that the normative character of law must be recognized, this should not lead to a conflation of law and morality. In *The Concept of Law*, Hart reiterates his commitment to legal positivism with its separation of law and morality. For a positivist, an unjust or immoral law may still be a valid rule in a legal system. For Hart, it would depend on that legal system's rule of recognition, the master rule used to identify valid laws that is embedded in the practice of the society's legal officials. The Fugitive Slave Laws, though unjust, were valid laws in nineteenth century America because they were enacted and upheld by the relevant legal authorities, namely, Congress, the president, and the courts. Hart sticks to the position he took in his 1950's debate with Harvard University's Lon Fuller that positivism's separation of law and morality has decided theoretical and practical advantages over the natural law theorist's view that an unjust law is not a genuine law. Hart does, however, make several concessions, embracing a "minimal version" of natural law according to which (assuming survival as an aim) it is "naturally" necessary for any viable human society to enforce certain rules of conduct. Furthermore, he admits that there is a close connection between rule by law and formal justice (the precept of treating like cases alike and different cases differently). Laws have general application, which precludes some forms of arbitrary treatment (although Hart hastens to add that laws may still be substantively unjust and legal systems evil and oppressive).

The Role of Judges

A final major issue considered in *The Concept of Law* concerns the nature of adjudication. Hart attempts to steer a middle course between the formalism or "mechanical jurisprudence" often associated with British judicial practice and the "rule skepticism" defended by American legal realists in the 1920's and 1930's. The former sees the role of judges as finding relevant legal rules and strictly applying them to particular cases. Hart agrees with the legal realists that such a view of judicial practice is misleading, for legal rules are seldom applied in such a mechanical way nor can they be, because they are framed in general terms that are vague and "open textured." Hart cites as an example the term "vehi-

cle" in an ordinance prohibiting vehicles from a public park. This rule may be readily interpreted as banning cars and trucks, but it is not clear whether it excludes tricycles and skateboards. Judges must employ discretion in applying rules to such indeterminate or hard cases. Hart thinks that legal realists who regard judges as unbound by rules ("rule skeptics") overlook how rules guide judges in clear cases. In the hard cases, Hart submits that judges do appeal to factors such as legislative purpose, consistency, and even equity and other moral and political principles. He concedes that in some hard cases, the law is so indeterminate and the other guiding factors so uncertain that judges in fact make law rather than find it.

This view of adjudication developed by Hart has been a source of continuing controversy. Legal philosopher Ronald Dworkin, Hart's foremost critic in this regard, charges that the positivist view, which bases validity on the "pedigree" of rules, is seriously deficient. It neglects the role of principles and policies in judicial decision making. Dworkin regards the positivist attempt to sharply separate law and morality as a misrepresentation of judicial practice. Judicial discretion is constrained by rules, principles, and policies as well as the requirement that the body of law be coherent. Dworkin holds that there is always some definite "right answer" or correct decision in any legal dispute, one that best fits or represents the law's integrity. Hart, in the postscript to the second edition of *The Concept of Law*, singles this out as the most important point of disagreement between Dworkin's view of adjudication and his own. Hart acknowledges that he overemphasized the role of rules in his early work, but he reiterates his belief that his theory of law and adjudication can accommodate a more extensive place for principles and policies. Hart remains steadfast in defending much of his theory of law as originally presented, suggesting that many critics, including Dworkin, fail to appreciate the character of his study of law as a general, descriptive, analytic one.

The Concept of Law remains a landmark in philosophy of law and legal theory. Its many theses, analyses, and arguments contain significant insights about the law, a point acknowledged by even its most vigorous critics. In addition to making notable contributions to the treatment of substantive issues in legal philosophy, the work links philosophical method with legal theory and legal philosophy with other areas of philosophy such as ethics, political philosophy, philosophy of mind, and philosophy of language. Hart's penetrating account of rules and rule-governed behavior marks a worthwhile contribution to the study of law and other related forms of social phenomena, particularly in its illustration of the way in which careful attention to ordinary thought and language can reveal the rich complexity of such behavior. His criticism of the command theory, natural law theory, and the predictive theory of law reveal fatal flaws in such theories, so much so that it is difficult to imagine their resurrection as plausible and illuminating theories of the nature of law.

Mario Morelli

Additional Reading

Bayles, Michael. *Hart's Legal Philosophy*. Dordrecht, Netherlands: Kluwer Academic Publishers, 1992. This careful and thorough analysis of H. L. A. Hart's legal philosophy places Hart's contributions in a wider context. The author is sympathetic to most of Hart's positions, defending them against various criticisms.

Boos, Eric J. *Perspectives in Jurispurdence: An Analysis of H. L. A. Hart's Legal Theory*. New York: Peter Lang, 1998. This book examines the perpetual controversy between legal positivism and natural law and explores Hart's approach to the link between law and morality.

Devlin, Patrick. *The Enforcement of Morals*. London: Oxford University Press, 1965. This collection of Patrick Devlin's papers and lectures contains a well-developed defense of legal moralism and an interesting appraisal of the complex role of criminal law.

Dworkin, Ronald. *Law's Empire*. Cambridge, Mass.: Belknap Press, 1986. This work is the most comprehensive and systematic development of Dworkin's views about the nature of law and adjudication. He continues his critique of Hart and legal positivism, and emphasizes the importance of interpretation in trying to understand law and adjudication.

_____. *Taking Rights Seriously*. Cambridge, Mass.: Harvard University Press, 1978. Dworkin's first book consists of previously published major articles, emphasizing the theme of the importance of individual rights. It also includes several papers, starting with the "The Model of Rules," in which he develops a series of criticisms of Hart's legal positivism.

Fuller, Lon. "Positivism and Fidelity to Law: A Reply to Professor Hart." *Harvard Law Review* 71(1957):630-672. Harvard law professor Lon Fuller published his reply to Hart's Holmes Lecture in the same volume of the *Harvard Law Review* that contained the printed version of Hart's lecture. Together they form the celebrated Hart-Fuller debate, referred to by one commentator as "perhaps the most interesting and illuminating exchange of views on basic issues of legal theory to appear in English in this century."

Hacker, B. M. S., and J. Raz, eds. *Law, Morality, and Society*. Oxford: Clarendon Press, 1977. This excellent collection of original articles was published in honor of Hart on the occasion of his seventieth birthday. The essays all examine either Hart's work or issues in philosophy of law that Hart discussed.

MacCormick, D. Neil. *H. L. A. Hart*. Stanford, Calif.: Stanford University Press, 1981. This remains the best available single study of Hart's legal philosophy. The author is generally sympathetic to Hart's views on the nature of law but sharply disagrees with other aspects of Hart's theory such as the nature of legal rights.

Martin, Michael. *The Legal Philosophy of H. L. A. Hart*. Philadelphia, Pa.: Temple University Press, 1987. This critical appraisal of Hart's legal philosophy examines the development of Hart's views and Hart's celebrated debates with Dworkin, Fuller, and Devlin.

Mario Morelli

Charles Hartshorne

Hartshorne advanced the idea of process theology, which held that process or change was the basic characteristic of all beings, including God. This concept had a major influence on American Protestant theology.

Principal philosophical works: *The Philosophy and Psychology of Sensation*, 1934; *Beyond Humanism: Essays in the New Philosophy of Nature*, 1937; *Man's Vision of God, and the Logic of Theism*, 1941; *The Divine Relativity: A Social Conception of God*, 1948; *Reality as Social Process: Studies in Metaphysics and Religion*, 1953; *The Logic of Perfection, and Other Essays in Neoclassical Metaphysics*, 1962; *Anselm's Discovery: A Re-examination of the Ontological Proof for God's Existence*, 1965; *A Natural Theology for Our Time*, 1967; *Creative Synthesis and Philosophic Method*, 1970; *Born to Sing: An Interpretation and World Survey of Bird Song*, 1973; *Aquinas to Whitehead: Seven Centuries of Metaphysics of Religion*, 1976; *Whitehead's View of Reality*, 1981; *Insights and Oversights of Great Thinkers: An Evaluation of Western Philosophy*, 1983; *Omnipotence and Other Theological Mistakes*, 1984; *Creativity in American Philosophy*, 1984; *Wisdom as Moderation: A Philosophy of the Middle Way*, 1987; *The Darkness and the Light: A Philosopher Reflects upon His Fortunate Career and Those Who Made It Possible*, 1990; *The Zero Fallacy and Other Essays in Neoclassical Philosophy*, 1997.

Born: June 5, 1897; Kittanning, Pennsylvania

Early Life

Charles Hartshorne's father was an Episcopal clergyman, and his mother was the daughter of an Episcopal clergyman. Hartshorne began his college education at the Pennsylvania Quaker college Haverford, from which his father had graduated, spent 1917-1919 in the U.S. Army, and then went to Harvard. At Harvard, he studied with R. B. Perry, W. E. Hocking, and C. I. Lewis and wrote a dissertation on "the unity of all things in God." He spent 1923-1925 as a postdoctoral student in Europe, where he attended lectures by Edmund Husserl and Martin Heidegger, then became a Harvard instructor and research fellow during the years 1925-1928. He taught at the University of Chicago from 1928 to 1955, where he was a colleague of Rudolf Carnap and Richard McKeon. He was part of the faculty of Emory University in Atlanta from 1955 to 1962 and the University of Texas in Austin from 1962 to his retirement in 1978. He continued lecturing and writing after his retirement and was the subject of a volume in the Library of Living Philosophers, the prestigious series founded by Paul Arthur Schilpp.

Life's Work

Influenced most by the logician and metaphysician Alfred North Whitehead, as well as by Gottfried Wilhelm Leibniz and Charles Sanders Peirce, Hartshorne developed his own variety of process philosophy. In this complex and wide-ranging system, the theory of reality is a version of idealism that is similar to many Buddhist traditions in its fundamental metaphysical stance. It posits momentary entities as the ultimate constituents of the world. However, Hartshorne's view is unlike Buddhism because Hartshorne claims that the existence of God is a logical necessity.

Under mind-body dualism, minds are self-conscious beings and bodies are spatially extended beings. No thing can be both essentially self-conscious (as are minds) and essentially non-self-conscious (as are bodies). Minds and bodies interact. Under materialism, however, there are

Charles Hartshorne. *(Center for Process Studies)*

spatially extended things and no other kind of things. Minds are simply capacities of more complicated physical organisms. No issue of interaction arises.

Hartshorne partly reverses materialism. A materialist holds that every mental state is identical to a physical state. For Hartshorne, however, what are commonly called material states are mental states, or at least like them. A materialist also holds that many material states are not identical to any mental states at all; a large number of states are not mental in any sense or to any degree, which rules out, the materialist holds, any chance of reducing matter to mind.

Hartshorne rejected the idea that many material states cannot plausibly be thought of as mental rests because of his views concerning the fundamental constituents of the world. The basic or

simple entities, he holds, are active items; anything inert is composite. These active basic entities are not perceptible as simple things because no simple item can be sensed; only composites are perceptible in the sense of being observed by sight, taste, touch, hearing, or smelling. Hartshorne holds that to be active is to be mental, to some degree and in some manner. Simple active entities are experiences or like experiences. Only in the case of our experiences are individual entities available to observation—to introspection, not sense perception.

Typically, mind-body dualists and materialists agree that however many kinds of items there are, the items there are kinds *of* are substances. A substance possesses qualities but is not itself a quality; it can, and typically does, endure through time and remains the same despite change of its non-essential qualities. Trees and persons are substances. Hartshorne denies that there are any substances; what appear to be substances are merely collections of simple active entities. His view, then, is not dualism or materialism, but idealism. It is not like Bishop George Berkeley's idealism, for which (roughly) to exist is to be either a mind or a thought in a mind. It is an idealism for which to exist is either to be a simple item that is somehow and to some degree an experience or feeling, or to be a composite of such simple items. Minds for Hartshorne do not *have* but *are composed of* ideas.

According to Hartshorne, then, the ultimate constituents of reality are momentary concrete events, each being to some degree an experience. He holds that there are no positive properties that can be ascribed to material events that cannot be properly ascribed to mental events, and his view is idealistic rather than materialist or dualistic. His form of idealism, however, is one for which conscious and self-conscious beings are conceived of as made up of momentary experiences. In his process theory of reality, processes are composed of one momentary event after another. In a substance theory of reality, an event is simply an enduring substance coming to have a property it did not previously have or losing a property it possessed; there can be no events and hence no processes without there being something to which the event occurs or something that endures through the process. Events or processes that occur to nothing do not occur at all. A substance philosopher will argue that Hartshornian events, processes, or concrete occasions are momentary bearers of properties; they differ from substances only in their lack of endurance through time.

Another central feature of Hartshorne's metaphysic is his rejection of determinism. He understands every simple or basic entity to be active in a sense that entails its being creative and interprets its being creative to mean its being in some sense free. The notion of creativity is best understood in contrast to standard views of causality that hold that whatever comes into existence has a cause and that a cause of something is a set of necessary and sufficient conditions for the existence of that thing. Hartshorne holds that the only necessary and sufficient condition for some item X is simply X itself; while the conditions that precede something constrain what can occur, they do not require that exactly the thing that occurs come into existence. Any set of conditions in which some thing X comes to be are conditions in which something else, Y, might have come to be—*actually* might have, under exactly the same conditions. Determinists will object that in this view, everything that occurs is a chance occurrence. Hartshorne responds that "chance is the negative side of what Peirce called *spontaneity*, others call *freedom*." Those who accept libertarian freedom hold that free human actions lack necessary and sufficient determining conditions; Hartshorne holds that every event lacks necessary and sufficient conditions.

Hartshorne's view of freedom requires a rejection of the traditional doctrines of divine omnipotence and omniscience. His view, rejected by most of those who accept the doctrine that God is omnipotent, is that God's being omnipotent entails lack of power and libertarianly free uses thereof on the part of created persons. He also holds that if God is omniscient and therefore knows the future, the future is hence determined, a view controversial among those who hold that God is omniscient. Hartshorne holds that unless something has already occurred, no one can know that its occurrence is something that will be

part of the history of the world. Thus in Hartshorne's view, God's knowledge grows moment by moment, as does God's mind generally, for God is viewed as affected and enriched by all that occurs. The theological core of process thought is its doctrine of God, which is developed in sharp contrast to classical Christian doctrine.

Hartshorne holds that either it is logically impossible that God exists or it is logically necessary that God exists and that the former is false and the latter is true. However, while it is logically necessary that there is a God, it is not logically necessary, so to speak, that a particular God exists. The world might have been different, and if it had been different, because the world affects God (it is properly thought of as God's body), God would then have been different. Hence there is a necessary, timeless aspect of God and a contingent, temporal aspect of God. Relative to God's necessary, timeless aspect, God is unsurpassable; relative to God's contingent, temporal aspect, God is surpassable only by God.

Hartshorne denies that the existence of evil is evidence of God's existence. Evil occurs given freedom. Freedom is present where there is creativity, and it is logically impossible that there be a world whose constituents are not creative; to exist at all is to be active and have the power to be creative and to be free. Thus it is logically impossible that there be a world without evil. Further, he claims that "the *risks* of freedom are justified by the *opportunities* freedom makes possible."

It is controversial whether one can give a coherent and defensible account of persons, personal identity, choice, responsibility, and memory within the type of metaphysic that Hartshorne favors. This dispute is cross-cultural, occurring (for example) among Cartesians and Humeans in a European context and between Jains and Buddhists in an Indian context. The issue is whether the free choices that Hartshorne prizes can really be processes that are themselves made up of momentary processes and are a person's choices only in the sense that they take place in a context of other momentary processes.

The relevant issues are moral as well as metaphysical. Hartshorne offers the view that later stages of oneself—which will be composed of momentary states that occur later in the series of states to which one belongs and that are numerically as distinct from the states that now compose oneself as are any states that now compose someone else—are as much objects of one's altruism as are the states of others. There can be no such thing as self-interest relating to one's future states. Correspondingly, however, if nothing that is not a composite lasts more than a moment, all joy as well as all pain lasts for only nanoseconds. If there are no enduring things, then whatever value resides in beings is lost. Historically, ethics based on respect for people have been associated with belief in enduring persons—with self-conscious substances—and utilitarianism has been associated with the idea of momentary states being the locus of genuine worth. It is not at all clear that this linkage is not conceptual as well as historical, and if it is, a process thinker such as Hartshorne is not entitled to appeal to an ethic based on respect for people.

Influence

Hartshorne developed an influential theory of process theology in which God is constantly growing and affected by other beings. His views were in part developed as an alternative to classical theology, which holds that God is eternal (timeless), immutable (incapable of change), and not capable of being affected by anything. Although Hartshorne's theory did not make deep inroads into American philosophy, it had a greater impact on American Protestant theology, though in this field, too, it was a minority view, competing with both traditional orthodoxy and views in which God is conceived as a temporal being capable of suffering but also as an enduring substance not composed of momentary elements.

Keith E. Yandell

The Divine Relativity

A Social Conception of God

Type of philosophy: Metaphysics, philosophical theology, philosophy of religion
First published: 1948

Principal ideas advanced:

◇ Processes are the basic sort of entity; whatever else there is, including God, is made of processes.

◇ The traditional notion of God as immutable, uncaused, independent, and absolute is self-contradictory; the notion of a deity who is changeable, caused, dependent, and relative is not worthy of worship.

◇ If it is logically possible that God exists, then it is logically necessary that God exists.

◇ God's being omniscient is externally related to the world, but God's omniscience having the content that it does is internally related to the world.

◇ God's knowledge is always growing.

In *The Divine Relativity*, Charles Hartshorne's concern is with the question "What can most reasonably be meant by the religious word *God*?" He thinks that classical theism—the monotheism developed and defended by such philosophers and theologians such as Saint Augustine, Saint Thomas Aquinas, Moses Maimonides, and Avicenna, and influenced significantly by Plato, Aristotle, and Plotinus—is as much Greek as Jewish, Christian, or Islamic. He also regards classical theism as an incorrect restatement of the central religious concepts—particularly the concept of God—as philosophical categories, and he endeavors to show that his assessment is correct.

His concern is also to offer a restatement of the central monotheistic concepts, one cast in process philosophy rather than substance philosophy terms. A substance is something that has properties, is not itself a property, endures through time, and retains its identity over time, despite change of its nonessential properties. A process, for a substance philosophy, is simply a matter of a substance gaining a property it lacked or losing a property it had. For Hartshorne, there are processes, but not substances; he takes a process (not, of course, as defined by substance philosophy) to be the basic sort of entity, of which everything else, God included, is made. He takes his restatement to be a significant move toward making philosophical theism accord well with contemporary natural science, theology, and philosophy.

Notions of God

In Hartshorne's view, God has an abstract absolute essence or immutable character but is also "surrelative," or supremely relative. Just as the concrete includes and exceeds the abstract, so the changeable (the relative) includes and exceeds the absolute. God, Hartshorne says, is constituted of social relationships. The purpose of *The Divine Relativity* is to explain and defend these neoclassical and puzzling notions.

Hartshorne claims that the traditional notion of God as immutable, uncaused, independent, and absolute is self-contradictory and that the notion of a deity who is changeable, caused, dependent, and relative is not worthy of worship. He proposes a medium between these extremes, a concept of God that he takes to be logically consistent and that he believes describes a being who is worthy of worship—a notion of a God who has two aspects. Hartshorne believes that if it is logically possible that God exists, then it is logically necessary that God exists. From this, it follows that if one establishes that there is a concept of God that is logically consistent, one has established half of an ontological proof that God exists.

One central element in Hartshorne's view is the distinction between internal and external relations. For convenience, assume that the number two is a necessarily existing abstract object. If one comes to know that the number two is even, this knowledge does not make the number two change. If knowing is a relationship between the knower and what is known—for example, between the self and the number two—then it is an *external* relationship. If one sits on a soft chair, the chair becomes indented in a way in which it previously was not; in this instance, the chair is changed (it is indented) and the sitter has changed (he or she is now seated) and so the relationship is *internal*—both items are different as a result of having become related. The relationship between the knower and the number two is strictly internal to the knower (who is more knowledgeable than previously) but external to two (which is unchanged by having become better known by someone).

Saint Thomas Aquinas held that typically in cases of knowledge, the knower is internally related to the known (is changed in at least the sense of being more knowledgeable than before) and the known is externally related to the knower (is not itself altered by its having become known). The great exception, Thomas contends, is God and the objects of God's knowledge. The objects of God's knowledge exist because they are caused by their knower, and God is not changed by knowing them.

Hartshorne argues as follows. First, God knows all truths, including such logically contingent (could-have-been-false) propositions as "There are humans." Because what God knows is true and "There are humans" might have been false—there might not have been any humans—what God knows is internally related to the contingent fact that there are humans. The same of course applies to everything that God knows to exist provided that they might not have existed—every apple, table, and grain of sand, for example. God's knowledge is internally related to everything that exists contingently. Second, it is a necessary truth that if God exists, God is omniscient. "God's being omniscient" does not vary in worlds in which God exists, but because what distinguishes one world from another is what exists in those worlds, what God knows to exist differs from world to world. Therefore, the content of divine omniscience varies from world to world.

Hartshorne infers from these two points that God has two distinct aspects: *being omniscient,* which is an abstract, world-invariant aspect, and *having the particular knowledge God has, the particular content that God knows because our world rather than some other world exists.* God's being omniscient is externally related to the world (where *the world* is everything that exists besides God) but God's omniscience, having the content that it does, is internally related to the world.

It is not clear that Hartshorne's argument succeeds. It is a necessary truth that the number two is even and a contingent truth that two is the number of hands that were part of Plato's body. Two is even in every possible world but two is not the number of Plato's hands in every possible world. There are, for example, possible worlds so unfortunate as not to contain Plato (were one of them to exist, Plato would not). It does not follow that there are two aspects of the number two, one corresponding to (or being) two's absolute essence and another corresponding to (or being) two's being the number of hands Plato had.

A Perfect Being

Hartshorne also offers this argument: A perfect being will either contain within itself all imperfect beings or it will not. If it does not, then there is something more perfect than it is, namely the whole composed of the perfect being plus all the imperfect beings that exist. This whole is more perfect than the perfect being because it contains all the things that exist, or all the reality there is, whereas the most perfect being does not. If the perfect being does contain all imperfect beings, then there is a possible whole that would be more perfect than it. The reason for this is as follows: For any collection X of imperfect beings, there is a collection X^* of imperfect beings that is better than X. Because every collection of imperfect beings can be surpassed by another, it is logically impossible that there be a best possible collection of imperfect beings; any such collection is surpassable by another, which in turn is itself surpassable. Therefore, the whole composed of the perfect and all imperfect beings is not itself unsurpassable in perfection. The perfect being would be unsurpassable in perfection. Therefore, the whole composed of the perfect being and all imperfect beings is not perfect. Whether the perfect being does or does not include all imperfect beings, it is not the perfect being. Here, Hartshorne argues, is a dilemma that process theology escapes.

In this argument, two criteria for perfection seem to be used. One considers a being to be perfect if it has all the desirable properties in the highest possible degree. This, at any rate, is what the classical tradition being criticized meant by *perfect being*. The other criterion considers a being perfect if it contains everything that exists. Historically, the French philosopher René Descartes's idea of a perfect being was one who met the first criterion, and Baruch Spinoza's idea of a perfect being was one who met the second. However, it is not clear that satisfying both criteria is anything that any defensible notion of perfection will require, and the dilemma can be escaped by simply denying that satisfying the second criterion is a legitimate part of the notion of a perfect being.

Hartshorne's way of dealing with the dilemma is to ascribe to God both a surpassable and an unsurpassable aspect. God's abstract nature (what is true of God in all possible worlds) is unsurpassable in principle. God's concrete omniscience, for example, includes as part of its content those contingent propositions that are true in the actual world. Further, in Hartshorne's view, future-tense propositions lack truth value; they are neither true nor false until the time comes to which they are tensed. For example, "A woman will be elected president of the United States in the year 2020" is tensed to the year 2020. Thus God's knowledge any time before the year 2020 will not contain knowledge that a woman will be elected president of the United States in 2020, even if a woman will be elected then. According to Hartshorne, God's knowledge is always growing. At no time is God's knowledge surpassed (no one else knows, at any given time, everything true at that time), but it is surpassable (God will know more tomorrow than God knows today). It is, of course, controversial that future-tense propositions lack truth value; for example, it seems a necessary truth that "Either some eclipse will darken London tomorrow or not," and if it is true, then one of its elements, "Some eclipse will darken London tomorrow" and "No eclipse will darken London tomorrow," is true and one is false.

In addition to these abstract arguments, Hartshorne makes abstract considerations, one of which concerns divine love. His claim is that if it is true that God loves Susan, then the relation *being loved by God* cannot be a relation that is external to God. It must include something in God that might not have been there, some divinely internal state directed toward Susan that favors Susan's well-being and that might not have existed because Susan might not have existed. Such a state, Hartshorne contends, is contingent (it is a state that God might not have been in) and affective (it involves feeling as well as knowing).

Hartshorne's neoclassical or process monotheism is sometimes called pantheism, but it is not strictly pantheistic (it does hold that all things are contained in God but denies that God is identical to the collection of all things) or standardly monotheistic (it does not distinguish sharply between God and creation). Its main theistic competitors are classical monotheism and what might be called *new classical monotheism*. Classical theism, Hartshorne's target of critique in *The Divine Relativity*, holds that God is eternal (atemporal, possessed of no temporal properties) as well as immutable, omniscient, omnipotent, and existentially independent of all else. New classical theism holds that God is temporal. It adds that God is immutable in the sense that God cannot lose any essential properties; losing any essential property would involve cessation of existence and God's existence is not dependent on the existence or activity of anything else. New classical theism agrees with neoclassical theism that God can be affected (be in relations to created persons that are internal to both God and created persons) and have emotions. New classical theists tend to continue to take God to be a substance, not a series of processes, and to reject the idea that viewing God as having a necessary and a contingent aspect is the best, or even a coherent, way of regarding God as temporal (everlasting rather than eternal, existing at all moments rather than existing but existing at no moment). Readers of *The Divine Relativity* should keep two questions in mind: (1) Are the alleged contradictions in classical monotheism real or merely alleged? (2) If they are real, is neoclassical theism a better way of avoiding them than is new classical theism?

Keith E. Yandell

Additional Reading

Bainger, David. *Divine Power in Process Theism.* Albany: State University of New York Press, 1988. A critique of process thought, especially regarding its notion of divine omniscience.

Cobb, John, and David Ray Griffin. *Process Theology: An Introductory Exposition.* Philadelphia: Westminster, 1976. An explanation of process theology by two of its leading proponents.

Dombrowski, Daniel A. *Analytic Theism, Hartshorne, and the Concept of God.* Albany: State University of New York Press, 1996. An important look at Hartshorne's contribution to theism.

Hahn, Lewis, ed. *The Philosophy of Charles Hartshorne.* La Salle, Ill: Open Court, 1991. Twenty-nine essays on Hartshorne's philosophy with his replies and his intellectual biography.

Pailin, David A. *God and the Processes of Reality.* London: Routledge, 1989. A presentation and defense of Hartshorne's views.

Pittenger, Norman. *Process Thought and Christian Faith.* New York: Macmillan, 1968. An introduction to the thought of Hartshorne, Alfred North Whitehead, and Pierre Teilhard de Chardin.

Swinburne, Richard. *The Coherence of Theism.* Oxford: Oxford University Press, 1979. A defense of a view that is close to classical theism, much closer at any rate than is process theology.

Towne, Edgar A. *Two Types of New Theism: Knowledge of God in the Thought of Paul Tillich and Charles Hartshorne.* New York: Peter Lang, 1997. A detailed examination into the thought of Hartshorne and Tillich.

Wierenga, Edward. *The Nature of God.* Ithaca, N.Y.: Cornell University Press, 1989. An excellent discussion of the divine attributes that defends an essentially classical standpoint.

Keith E. Yandell

Georg Wilhelm Friedrich Hegel

Hegel developed many philosophical theories that influenced the social sciences, anthropology, sociology, psychology, history, and political theory. He believed that the mind is the ultimate reality and that philosophy can restore humanity to a state of harmony.

Principal philosophical works: *Differenz des Fichte'schen und Schelling'schen Systems der Philosophie*, 1801 (*The Difference Between Fichte's and Schelling's Philosophy*, 1977); *Die Phänomenologie des Geistes*, 1807 (*The Phenomenology of Spirit*, 1868; also known as *The Phenomenology of Mind*, 1910); *Wissenschaft der Logik*, 1812-1816 (*Science of Logic*, 1929); *Encyklopädie der philosophischen Wissenschaften im Grundrisse*, 1817 (*Encyclopedia of Philosophy*, 1959, includes *Die Logik* [*The Logic of Hegel*], *Naturphilosophie* [*Philosophy of Nature*], and *Die Philosophie des Geistes* [*Philosophy of Mind*]); *Grundlinien der Philosophie des Rechts*, 1821 (*The Philosophy of Right*, 1855); *Vorlesungen über die Philosophie der Geschichte*, 1837 (*Lectures on the Philosophy of History*, 1852-1861).

Born: August 27, 1770; Stuttgart, Württemberg (now in Germany)

Died: November 14, 1831; Berlin, Prussia (now in Germany)

Early Life

Georg Wilhelm Friedrich Hegel was born into a Protestant middle-class family in Stuttgart, the eldest of three children. His father was a minor civil servant for the Duchy of Württemberg, and his family had roots in Austria. To escape persecution by the Austrian Catholics in the sixteenth century, his ancestors settled among the Lutheran Protestants of the German territories, which consisted of more than three hundred free cities, duchies, and states loosely united under the rule of Francis I of Austria. Though little is known about his mother, all accounts describe her as having been highly intelligent and unusually educated for a woman of that time.

Hegel received the conventional schooling for his social class, entering German primary school in 1773, Latin school in 1775, and the Stuttgart *Gymnasium illustre* in 1780. Upon graduating from the *Gymnasium* (equivalent to high school) in 1788, he entered the famous seminary at the University of Tübingen to study philosophy and theology in preparation for the Protestant ministry. As a student, Hegel became friends with Friedrich Hölderlin, a Romantic poet, and Friedrich Wilhelm Joseph Schelling. He shared the top floor of the dormitory with Schelling, who became famous before Hegel as an idealist philosopher. In 1790, Hegel received a master's degree in philosophy.

After passing his theological examinations at Tübingen in 1793, Hegel began many years of struggle to earn his living and establish himself as a philosopher. Instead of entering the ministry, he began working as a house tutor for a wealthy family in Bern, Switzerland. In 1797, he became a tutor in Frankfurt, continuing throughout this time to read, think, and write about philosophical questions, usually along radical lines. For example, he considered Jesus inferior to Socrates as a teacher of ethics, and he considered orthodox religion, because of its reliance on external authority, an obstacle in restoring humankind to a life of harmony. Although Hegel always retained some of his skepticism toward orthodox religion, he later in life considered himself a Lutheran Christian. In 1798, he began to write on the philosophy of history and on the spirit of Christianity, major themes in his philosophical system. Upon his father's death in 1799, Hegel received a modest inheritance and was able to stop tutoring and join his friend Schelling at the University of Jena, in the state of Weimar.

Life's Work

Hegel's life's work as a teacher and philosopher began at Jena. From 1801 to 1807, Hegel taught as an unsalaried lecturer at the University of Jena, his first university position as a philosopher, for which he was paid by the students who attended class. While in Jena, Hegel cooperated with Schelling in editing the *Kritisches Journal der Philosophie*. He also published *The Difference Between Fichte's and Schelling's Philosophy*. During this time, Hegel began to lecture on metaphysics, logic, and natural law. In 1805, he was promoted to *ausserordentlicher Professor* (distinguished professor) on the recommendation of the German Romantic poet Johann Wolfgang von Goethe. Hegel was very prolific, yet beginning in 1802, he announced each year a significant forthcoming book to his publisher without producing it.

These were momentous times. In 1789, just after Hegel's nineteenth birthday, the fall of the Bastille announced the French Revolution across Europe; in 1806, after putting an end to the thousand-year Austrian Empire, Napoleon I crushed the Prussian armies at the Battle of Jena. On October 13, 1806, Napoleon victoriously entered the walled city of Jena, an event that Hegel described to a friend as follows:

> I saw the Emperor—that world-soul—riding out to reconnoiter the city; it is truly a wonderful sensation to see such an individual, concentrated here on a single point, astride a single horse, yet reaching across the world and ruling it.

October 13, 1806, was also the day that Hegel finished his book, long promised to his publisher, and sent the manuscript amid the confusion of war. The book was his early masterpiece, *The Phenomenology of Spirit*. On October 20, the French

army plundered Hegel's house, and his teaching position at the University of Jena came to an end. Hegel left for Bamberg in Bavaria, where he spent a year working as a newspaper editor. He then became headmaster and philosophy teacher at the *Gymnasium* in Nuremberg, where he worked successfully from 1808 until 1816.

The Phenomenology of Spirit, which exemplifies the young Hegel, was strongly influenced by German Romanticism. This movement provided a new and more complete way of perceiving the world and was developed by German philosophers and artists such as Schelling and Friedrich Hölderlin. German Romanticism stood in opposition to French rationalism and British empiricism, the two major philosophies of the seventeenth and eighteenth centuries, dominated by reason and immediate sensory experience, respectively. German Romanticism had been influenced by the German philosopher Immanuel Kant, whose theory of knowledge synthesized

Georg Wilhelm Friedrich Hegel. *(Library of Congress)*

rational and empirical elements. Kant argued that the laws of science, rather than being the source of rationality, were dependent on the human mind and its pure concepts, or categories, such as cause and effect. Kant believed that it is the mind that gives its laws to nature, and not the reverse.

Hegel's philosophical system expands upon this philosophy, in which reality depends on the rational mind for its perception. Hegel's absolute idealism unites the totality of all concepts in the Absolute Mind or Spirit, which he also referred to as the ultimate reality, or God. Hegel's metaphysics thus takes from German Romanticism the "inward path" to truth; the notion of nature as Spirit, or the immanence of God within the universe; the quest for the totality of experience, both empirical and rational; and the desire for infinity.

Hegel argued that reality belongs to an absolute mind or a totality of conceptual truth, and that it consists of a rational structure characterized by a unity-amid-diversity. The purpose of metaphysics is to reveal the truth of this unified diversity. To this end, Hegel developed his highly influential theory of dialectic, a process involving three concepts: the thesis, the antithesis, and the synthesis. This dialectical process provides a way of transcending oppositions to a higher level of truth. Hegel argued that the dialectical triad, as the rhythm of reality, underlies all human knowledge and experience. Moreover, he defined the absolute mind as being the totality of concepts in a dialectical process. Yet Hegel believed that contradictions are never entirely overcome. Rather, the dialectic is both the essence of reality and the method for comprehending reality, which is always a unity-amid-diversity. Hegel's notion of conceptual truth, being immanent within the world, is timebound rather than transcendental, despite his ambiguous reference to the absolute mind as God. Hegel's dialectic thus differs from that of Plato, which gives rise to timeless forms.

On the basis of his dialectic, Hegel begins *The Phenomenology of Spirit* by introducing his theory that the history of philosophy is a biography of the human spirit in its development over the course of centuries. The relationship between successive philosophies is one not of conflict but of organic growth and development. Hegel describes philosophy as a living and growing organism like the world itself. Each philosophy corresponds to the stage of a plant: the bud, the blossom, and the fruit. In addition to organicism, Hegel developed the metaphor of historicism, which holds that the understanding of any aspect of life is derived through its history, its evolution, and not through its static condition in the present. Hegel ends *The Phenomenology of Spirit* by arguing that the Age of Reason and philosophy must supersede the age of religious consciousness. He also argued that history evolves toward a specific goal, a state of freedom, and that the purpose of history is the unfolding of the truth of reason.

During the time Hegel taught in Nuremberg, he published *Science of Logic* and *Encyclopedia of Philosophy*. Hegel regarded the latter as having a dialectical structure, with the opposites of thought and nature united in mind and society, and ultimately in the self-referential act of philosophical self-consciousness. In 1811, Hegel married Maria von Tucher of Nuremberg, and in 1816, his nine-year-old illegitimate son, Ludwig, joined the household. Also in 1816, Hegel became a professor at the University of Heidelberg, and in 1817 for the first time taught aesthetics. By this time, his reputation was so well established that the Prussian minister of education invited him to accept the prestigious chair of philosophy at the University of Berlin, where Hegel taught from 1818 until his death during a cholera epidemic in 1831.

During this final period, the climax of his career, Hegel lectured for the first time on the philosophy of religion and the philosophy of history. He published one of the great works of genius of Western culture, *The Philosophy of Right*, which exemplifies the mature or late Hegel in contrast to the early Hegel seen in *The Phenomenology of Spirit*. Hegel argued in his moral philosophy that ethics, like the individual, has its source, course, and ultimate fulfillment in the nation-state, particularly the state of Germany. The nation-state is a manifestation of God, which Hegel defines not as a personal God but rather as the Absolute. This totality of truth manifests itself in stages to each of the key nations of history, culminating in Germany.

During the 1820's, Hegel toured Belgium and

the Netherlands and also traveled to Vienna and Prague. In 1824, he interceded with the Prussian government to free his friend Victor Cousin, a French liberal philosopher. Hegel was not an eloquent lecturer, but after his death, a group of his students collated their lecture notes and published an edition of his works in eighteen volumes (1832-1840). Hegel's writing is notoriously difficult, both stylistically and conceptually.

Influence

Hegel's idealist philosophy has been criticized for elevating the reality of concepts over the material aspects of reality, such as economics, environment, technology, and natural resources. Moreover, there seems to be a contradiction in Hegel's notion of the Absolute, in his definition of God as being externalized or existing in human consciousness. Finally, Hegel's philosophy of history has been criticized for masking a hidden defense for German nationalism, an aversion for democracy and individualism, and a fear of revolutionary change.

Nevertheless, Hegel has contributed many profound concepts to Western philosophy: the dialectical nature of thought, organicism and historicism, the concept of culture, the theory of ethics, and the theory of humanity's need for wholeness, in terms of both consciousness and social unification. Hegel believed that there are three important dialectical stages in ethical life responsible for social unity: the family (thesis), its antithesis in civil society, and their synthesis in the developed national state. As the French philosopher Maurice Merleau-Ponty said, "All the great philosophical ideas of the past century, the philosophies of [Karl] Marx, [Friedrich] Nietzsche, existentialism and psycho-analysis had their beginning in Hegel."

Although he supported Christianity, Hegel placed philosophy above religion. He believed that religion and art are different ways of understanding the absolute idea, but that philosophy is a better way because it allows one to comprehend the absolute conceptually, not in religious symbols, and thereby subsumes both religion and art. For Hegel, ethical ideals, such as the ideals of freedom, originate in the spiritual life of a society.

William S. Haney II

The Phenomenology of Spirit

Type of philosophy: Epistemology, metaphysics, philosophy of history
First published: Die Phänomenologie des Geistes, 1807 (English translation, 1868; also known as *The Phenomenology of Mind,* 1910)
Principal ideas advanced:
◇ As the science of appearances, phenomenology is distinct from metaphysics, which is the science of being.
◇ Phenomenology of spirit observes and describes the forms of unreal consciousness and the necessity that causes consciousness to advance from one form to another.
◇ Knowledge of the dialectical structure of reality makes possible the scientific study of the forms in which consciousness appears.
◇ In its evolution, mind has passed through three moments: consciousness of the sensible world, consciousness of itself and of other selves, and consciousness of the identity of the self and the sensible world.

While Napoleon was defeating the Prussians outside the walls of Jena, Georg Wilhelm Friedrich Hegel was completing his *The Phenomenology of Spirit*. Napoleon's victory signified for Hegel the triumph throughout Europe of enlightened self-rule and marked the beginning of a new social era; and in the preface to *The Phenomenology of Spirit*, he drew a parallel between Napoleon's achievement and his own. "It is not difficult to see that our epoch is a birth-time and a period of transition," he wrote. "The spirit of man has broken with the old order of things and with the old ways of thinking." Changes leading up to the present had, he said, been quantitative, like the growth of a child in the womb, but recent events had marked a qualitative change such as happens when the child draws its first breath.

When Hegel made this optimistic assessment of his own achievement, he was thinking not merely of the book in hand but of the system of knowledge for which he was later to become famous and which, even then, he was expounding in university lectures. *The Phenomenology of Spirit* was to introduce the system to the public. Originally he had planned to include the work in the first volume of his *Wissenschaft der Logik* (1812-1816; *Science of Logic*, 1929), but the project outgrew the limits of an introduction and was published as a separate work.

Metaphysics

Like philosophers Johann Gottlieb Fichte and Friedrich Wilhelm Joseph Schelling, Hegel was a metaphysician in the tradition that stemmed from the Greek philosopher Parmenides. The problem of philosophy in the broadest sense had to do with the identity of being and knowing. Admitting that the way of mortals is mere seeming, each of the three in his own way was trying to expound the way of truth. For Fichte, the Absolute (ultimate reality, the Kantian thing-in-itself) is the self that produces the phenomenal world and then overcomes it. For Schelling, the Absolute is the common source of the self and the world. Both men held that the task of philosophy is to lead the finite mind to the level of immediacy at which the difference between knowledge and being disappears in vision. Hegel thought that both men went too far in their attempts to abolish diversity. In his opinion, an intuition that leaves all difference behind is ignorance rather than knowledge. He said, rather unkindly, that Schelling's Absolute is "the night in which all cows are black." He agreed that knowledge demands immediacy but he denied that the distinctions present in human consciousness are incompatible with the unity demanded of knowledge, it being sufficient that the logic of thought and the logic of being are the same. In short, when one thinks dialectically, one thinks truly. This, as is often pointed out, was also Aristotle's solution to the Parmenidean problem. According to Aristotle, divine mind—mind fully actualized—" thinks itself, and its thinking is a thinking of thinking."

An obvious difference between Aristotle and Hegel is that for the latter, the divine mind is immanent in the world process. Hegel expresses this by saying that Substance and Subject are one. Spirit, which is Hegel's Absolute, is said to be "the inner being of the world." It exists in itself (*an sich*) as Substance, but it also exists for itself (*für sich*) as Subject. "This means, it must be presented to itself as an object, but at the same time straightway annul and transcend this objective

form; it must be its own object in which it finds itself reflected." The process Hegel describes as a circle that has its end for its beginning. What he means is that when the movement begins, Spirit is one, and when it ends, it is again one, while in between, it is divided and tormented by the need to end the division. From Hegel's point of view, the circular movement was not in vain. In the beginning, Spirit was potentially everything but actually nothing. Only by means of the processes known as nature and history does Spirit attain to actuality.

Phenomenology

All of this is metaphysics. Like Parmenides, Hegel, when he speaks of Absolute Spirit, views the world not as it *appears* to mortals but as it is *known* by the gods. Metaphysics, the science of reality, is not phenomenology, which is the science of appearances. In *The Phenomenology of Spirit*, Hegel, without abandoning the standpoint of one who knows, observes and describes the opinions of finite spirits in their multiplicity and contrariety. It is like history, says Hegel, in that it includes the sum of human experience, both individual and communal; but, whereas history views these experiences "in the form of contingency," phenomenology views them "from the side of their intellectually comprehended organization." Most of the book is a far cry from metaphysics; and if one finds some parts indigestible, the explanation is usually that Hegel is alluding to things one has never encountered in one's reading. Incidentally, the German word *Geist*, unlike the English words "mind" and "spirit," covers the whole range of human concerns. Psychology, history, philology, sociology, theology, ethics, and aesthetics, each of which Hegel manages to illuminate, are all referred to in German as *Geisteswissenschaften*, or "sciences" of *Geist*.

The Phenomenology of Spirit, therefore, is the story of humankind. It is concerned directly with finite spirits and only indirectly with the Absolute, which must be thought of as hidden behind these appearances. Nevertheless, in order to understand the layout of the book, one needs to keep in mind what Hegel says in the preface about the movement of the Absolute realizing itself in a threefold process: first, positing itself as a living and moving being, in constant change from one state to its opposite; second, negating the object and becoming subject, thereby splitting up what was single and turning the factors against each other; and third, negating this diversity and reinstating self-identity. This final movement, Hegel reminds us, is a new immediacy, not the immediacy with which the process began:

> It is the process of its own becoming, the circle which presupposes its end as its purpose and has its end for the beginning; it becomes concrete and actual only by being carried out, and by the end it involves.

In *The Phenomenology of Spirit*, the three movements are designated not from the standpoint of Absolute Spirit but from the standpoint of humanity. Part A, "Consciousness," is concerned with humanity's attempts to achieve certainty through knowledge of the sensible world. Part B, "Self-Consciousness," deals with humanity as doer rather than as knower, but it is mainly concerned with the self-image to which humanity's action leads. Part C, not titled in Hegel's outline, exhibits the stage in which humans sees themselves reflected in the external world. Hegel explains that these three moments are abstractions arrived at by analysis; he does not intend anyone to think that the dialectic that he traces in the development of consciousness was anterior to that which he traces in the development of selfhood. On the other hand, because what is meaningful in history comes from humanity's efforts to attain self-knowledge, the great moments in history may be seen as illustrative of this triadic movement. Thus, the extroverted mind of pre-Socratic Greece serves to illustrate the first stage; the introverted mind of late antiquity and the Middle Ages, the second; and the boisterous, self-assertive mind of modern humans, the third. The plan was simple, but the execution is complicated by Hegel's tendency to loop back into the past to give a fuller exhibition of the dialectic.

Consciousness and Self-Consciousness

Part A, "Consciousness," is an essay in epistemology. Specifically it is a critical history of humanity's attempt to base knowledge on sensation. Although it seems probable that Hegel first envisaged the problem as it appeared to Plato in *Theaetētos* (middle period dialogue, 388-368 B.C.E.;

Theaetetus, 1804), his exposition makes full use of the light shed on it by modern empiricism. In three chapters, Hegel traces humanity's attempt to find certainty through knowledge, first on the level of sensation, then on the level of perception, and finally on the level of scientific understanding. Sensations are indeed immediate, but they cease to be such the moment one makes them objects of knowledge. The object of perception, of which common sense is so sure, turns out to be a collection of properties. The chemical or physical force in terms of which humanity tries to explain these properties turns out to be unknowable and has to be abandoned in favor of descriptive laws, which, although satisfactory from a practical standpoint, are unsatisfactory to consciousness bent on knowledge. In the end, consciousness learns that the sensible world is like a curtain behind which an unknown inner world "affirms itself as a divided and distinguished inner reality," namely, self-consciousness. However, says Hegel, to understand this "requires us to fetch a wider compass."

In part B, "Self-Consciousness," Hegel makes a new start. The wider compass means taking account of humanity's animal condition. Life, says Hegel, is an overcoming. The animal does not contemplate the sensible world but consumes it. Self-consciousness dawns when humanity's appetites turn into desires. Unlike appetites, desire is universal. What one desires is the idea of overcoming. One is not content to consume what one needs: One destroys for the sake of proving that one is an overcomer; however, not satisfied with proving it to oneself, one needs to prove it to others. Thus, says Hegel, self-consciousness is a double movement. In order to be certain that one is a self, one needs to be recognized as such by other selves.

Hegel works through the dialectic of self-consciousness in a famous section titled "Lordship and Bondage." It is by killing a rival in life-and-death combat that primitive humanity attains to selfhood. If the rival lacks mettle and cries out to be spared, the double movement is still accomplished: The rival survives not as a self but as a slave who exists only to serve the lord's desires. The slave, however, although lacking an independent existence at first, learns to value himself as a worker and, through the skills that he acquires, gradually wins the recognition of his master. In the end, the master, who wanted nothing more than to be independent, finds himself dependent on his slave.

Much has been made, by German philosopher Friedrich Nietzsche and others, of the two types of consciousness, that of the master and that of the slave. For Hegel, however, this section is scarcely more than an introduction to the one that follows, entitled "The Freedom of Self-Consciousness." Failure of consciousness to find independence in the mutual relation between the two selves leads to the negation of the double movement. "In *thinking* I am free, because I am not in another but remain simply and solely in touch with myself." This bold attempt to recover immediacy Hegel illustrates by reference to the subjective philosophies of late antiquity, when culture was universal and life was burdensome to master and slave alike. In Stoicism, thought affirmed itself indifferent to all the conditions of individual existence, declaring its universality. In skepticism, individuality reasserted itself in the giddy whole of its disorder. In Christianity, the attempt was made to combine the universality of the former with the facticity of the latter, giving rise to the consciously divided self that Hegel calls "the unhappy consciousness." Devotion, ceremony, asceticism, mysticism, and obedience are viewed by Hegel as means of overcoming this rift, but the healing remains a mere "beyond." Meanwhile "there has arisen the idea of Reason, of the certainty that consciousness is, in its particularity, inherently and essentially absolute." Thus, humanity enters the last stage of its pilgrimage.

Reason, Spirit, and Religion

Part C, left untitled by Hegel, is the synthesis of consciousness and self-consciousness; but the synthesis, insofar as it falls within the compass of *The Phenomenology of Spirit*, is incomplete. This incompleteness must be kept in mind when considering the titles that Hegel gave to the three subdivisions of part C. They are Reason, Spirit, and Religion. The titles are part of the passing show, banners around which modern people are accustomed to rally.

Reason, as understood in this major division, is the reason of newly awakened modern human-

ity. In contrast to the ascetic soul of the Middle Ages, modern humans are blessed with sublime self-confidence, certain of their vocation to pull down the rickety structures of the past and to build new ones on the foundation of reason. Hegel discusses the rise of science, humanity's pursuit of pleasure, and the doctrine of natural law. This section is memorable mainly for the comical situations into which people's zeal and good intentions get them. Disregarding their objective nature, they plunge into life, only to find themselves mastered by fates beyond their control. Retreating somewhat, they take refuge in "the law of the heart," which the cruel world refuses to understand. Or, as a "knight of virtue," they engage in sham fights with the world. All this appeal to immediacy, Hegel says, is "consciousness gone crazy, . . . its reality being immediately unreality." A delusory objectivity is achieved in the third section of this division when the individual undertakes to find meaning in life by devoting himself to some worthy cause. Hegel's title for this section, "The Spiritual Zoo, or Humbug!" indicates that high-mindedness has its low side.

The excessive claims made for reason provoked reactions, known historically as pietism, illuminism, and Romanticism. These are all dealt with in the section "Spirit," which represents people looking for the truth within themselves. The fact that Hegel loops back in time in order to draw a contrast between the conscientiousness of the Greek heroine Antigone and that of the "beautiful soul" cherished and cultivated by German Romantics somewhat obscures the dialectical movement. In this section, Hegel examines court life in France under the *ancien régime*, which, for him, was a brilliantly orchestrated variation on the old theme of self-alienation. To be recognized as a self, one had to sacrifice oneself to society by fighting, working, or talking. Almost everybody who was anybody chose the third way. The prerevolutionary salon made Paris appealing to outsiders such as philosopher David Hume, but to insiders it was a snake pit. Hegel points out that the revolt against the meanness and duplicity of the existing order was two-pronged: religious and philosophical. Wilhelm Bossuet exemplifies one party, Voltaire the other. However, the difference, Hegel tries to show, was superficial. Both parties were otherworldly, taking flight to the Absolute, whether it was called the Trinity or the Supreme Being. The philosophical party was to triumph as the party of Enlightenment. It lacked cohesion, however, and splintered into political sects that stoked the fires of revolution and, in their pursuit of absolute freedom, were consumed in the Terror.

Morality

Absolute freedom is undoubtedly what every self demands. However, the lesson Hegel draws from the Enlightenment is that the individual cannot claim to be absolute: The truth that is in one must be in everyone else as well. This was the new morality that was then enjoying great success in Romantic circles. Morality has the task of harmonizing thought and inclination. It recovers the wholeness known to the ancient Greeks but it does not do so by means of custom but by means of the voice of conscience, the moral reason present in every person.

This section of *The Phenomenology of Spirit* is important chiefly for its criticism of deontological ethics. Universal law raised above all the contingency and duty divorced from all advantage made obvious targets for Hegel's satire. Far from harmonizing the soul, morality gives rise to dissemblance. The beautiful soul is divine in conception—the "self transparent to itself" is similar to Hegel's definition of the Absolute. Unfortunately, reality did not match the concept, as one must recognize when one judges one's fellows, but also occasionally when one judges oneself. On such occasions, conscientious people want to confess their faults and ask forgiveness, and this can be rewarding, except when the individual is hard-hearted and "refuses to let his inner nature go forth." Here, as Hegel points out, morality anticipates religion.

Religion

Hitherto, consciousness has conceived of itself alternately as object and subject, as individual and social. At each level, Spirit has taken into itself more of the content of human experience, although it continues to mistake each new experience for the whole toward which it aspires. This wholeness Hegel finds in "Revealed Religion," by which he means Christianity. However, once

again he loops back in time and, in the final section, presents an entire phenomenology of religion.

Religion had been of major concern to Hegel from the time when, as a theological student, he had found difficulty reconciling biblical revelation with Greek *paideia*. His survey traces religion through three stages: the cosmological stage represented by Persia and Egypt, the anthropological stage represented by classical Greece, and the revelational stage represented by Christianity. The first stage removed the divine too far from humanity, and the second brought it too close (for example in classic comedy), leaving it for the gospel of the incarnation of God's Son to find the proper distance. For Hegel, the doctrine of the Trinity—one God revealed to humanity simultaneously as being, as being-for-itself, and as the self knowing itself in the other—comes as close as religion can possibly come to Absolute Knowledge. However, in religion, self-consciousness is not fully conceptualized. The self does not yet know itself directly but only as appearance.

"The last embodiment of Spirit," Hegel explains in a brief concluding chapter, "is Absolute Knowledge. It is Spirit knowing itself in the shape of Spirit." Consciousness, which in religion is not perfectly one with its content, is here "at home with itself." Although the particular self is "immediately sublated" to the universal self, however, it is not absorbed into it, for the latter also is consciousness; that is to say, "It is the process of superseding itself." However, that leaves phenomenology and places the reader on the threshold of Hegel's system.

Jean Faurot

Science of Logic

Type of philosophy: Logic, metaphysics
First published: Wissenschaft der Logik, 1812-1816 (English translation, 1929)
Principal ideas advanced:
◊ What is real is rational, and what is rational is real.
◊ Logic, which is a systematic creative process, has three stages: the abstract stage, the dia-

lectical stage, and the speculative stage.

◊ In the abstract stage, terms of thought are considered separately; in the dialectical stage, one realizes that for something to exist it must be not separate but in relation to others; and in the speculative stage, one understands the unity of opposites in their opposition.

◊ There are three subdivisions of logic—the Doctrine of Being, the Doctrine of Essence, and the Doctrine of Idea—by which being is known not only for itself and for another, but in-and-for itself.

Hegel's philosophy is in the idealist tradition that evolved in Germany in the late eighteenth and the nineteenth centuries. Immanuel Kant and the post-Kantians felt that the empirical philosophy of David Hume, with its skeptical consequences, was inadequate; that mind through intuition, understanding, and reason could discover the grounds of experience either in an a priori categorical structure or in experience itself, if that experience were looked upon as primarily rational. Kant took the first alternative and argued that although events in themselves are unknowable (thus, keeping an element of Humean skepticism), as phenomena that one perceives, they are constructed according to the categories of the understanding and the forms of intuition. As such, they have their intelligible basis in mind, although there is an empirical content given from the external world. Hegel believed that the categories and forms are as much a part of reality as anything else, that the dichotomy between mind and its objects is a false one, and, hence, that reality is as rational as thought itself. He expressed this view in his famous statement, "What is real (actual) is rational; what is rational is real (actual)."

How is thought to express the nature of reality? Philosophy from Hume through Kant (and earlier) held that the agreement of thought with reality is the criterion of truth. However, Hegel claimed that thought alone brings to light the nature of things; this is the true sense of thought and reality being in agreement.

Like all idealists, Hegel maintained that because reality is known by means of ideas, and because the only thing that can agree with an idea is something like an idea, reality must be mindlike. In seeking to know the nature of things via reflection, the individual concentrates upon the universal character of things. However, thought so directed loses its individual character, for in proceeding in this way, a person reflects as any other individual would who was in pursuit of the truth. Reflective thought thus loses its subjective aspect and becomes objective; thought and reality become one.

The Three Stages of Logic

Hegel held that thought expresses itself in triads, each of which usually has its own triadic structure, a structure that often has a triadic structure of its own. Thus, logic has three stages; its subdivisions are three, and each of these has a triadic structure. It is interesting that Hegel apparently did not use the expression "thesis-antithesis-synthesis," which has been correctly used to characterize his position. At any rate, the emphasis upon the development of thought in terms of a point of view, its negation, and the reconciliation of the two is reminiscent of the dialectical procedure of Socrates and Plato. Hegel, keenly aware of this resemblance, used the term "dialectical" for his own philosophy.

Hegel uses the word "logic" in somewhat the same sense that Saint John spoke of "logos." That is, the word refers to a systematic creative process rather than to an analysis of language and argument. For him, there are three stages of logic: the abstract stage, or that of the understanding; the dialectical stage, or that of negative reason; and the speculative stage, or that of positive reason.

In the *abstract* stage, every term or product of thought appears separate and distinct from the others. The understanding believes that they exist on their own account. What Hegel is saying is that on reflection, the individual initially considers the elements of his thought—that is, whatever he is reflecting upon—as taken from the context of experience (or abstracted) and as having an existence of their own independent of anything else. This stage in thinking occurs throughout the history of thought, so that in each stage of philosophical development, people begin by abstraction. Thus the first stage has its own abstract beginning, but the stage itself, when compared to the next stage, will be seen as abstract.

As an illustration, consider the philosophical view called "empiricism." In the abstract stage of empiricism, only the immediately given, that which is presented here and now, has ultimate reality. These data, usually called "impressions," turn out to be bare "givens" devoid of relations and predicates and hidden in a skeptical mist, yet held to be separate and distinct and existing on their own account. However, the empiricist seems to pass from this "reality" about which he can say nothing, to his ideas about which he says everything that he can say. However, his ideas belong to a different level of knowledge; memory and reflection are involved, and thus the empiricist passes from the stage of abstraction to that of dialectic wherein mediate thought is now the subject matter.

The *dialectical* stage is one in which the understanding views the elements in their separate and distinct capacity and as such recognizes that no more can be said of them. (In Hume's work, this stage can be seen in his denial of necessary connection in experience and in his skepticism regarding reason and the senses.) There is a "positive" side to dialectic, however, in its indication that whatever is finite, when seen as separate and distinct and as free from all relations to others, ceases to exist. To be one without others is impossible. Existence involves a relationship between at least two entities.

The last stage of logic is the *speculative*, in which reason is wholly positive. For Hegel, the contradictory character of certain metaphysical principles is finally reconciled. In the concept of causation, it is argued that for every effect there must be a cause and that every cause is an effect for which there is yet a cause. This concept is such that the notion of a first cause is untenable, since it too would have to have a cause. However, since causation that has no limits leaves any system of philosophy incomplete, such a concept is repugnant to reason. The same sort of analysis may be made with regard to time as a sequence of events that can have neither a beginning nor an end but still must have both. These paradoxical philosophical problems that Hegel argued had not been solved are reconciled by speculative reason, which apprehends the unity of the categories in their very opposition.

The Three Doctrines

As noted earlier, the subdivision of logic also has three parts. These are the Doctrine of Being, the Doctrine of Essence, and the Doctrine of Notion or Idea. It should also be pointed out that in these doctrines, Hegel intended the sort of development mentioned earlier; that is, implicit in the exposition of each is to be found the grounds for the next. Although each may be taken as a doctrine in itself, each would then be an abstraction (another instance of the first stage of logic) and hence untrue as well as incomplete.

In the Doctrine of Being, we are faced with an analysis of the given in its immediacy. In the history of philosophy, there have been innumerable ideas concerning the nature of Being advanced by philosophers claiming to have identified the basic ontological stuff. The One of Parmenides, Aristotle's primary substance, and Hume's impressions are all candidates wearing the label of "Being." Under this doctrine, Hegel analyzes the full meaning and consequences of the immediately given and indicates wherein he thinks it false.

The Doctrine of Essence takes up where the failure of Being as a satisfactory philosophical doctrine occurs. If the immediate nature of things cannot reveal their essential characteristics to thought, if the search for them forces one to mediate knowledge—that is, to look for intervening features, to wonder how the given came to be as it is—then one can no longer consider the given in itself, but only in its relation to an other. (The other need not be an entity in addition to the immediately given; it may simply be the recognition that the given has limits, a recognition that Hegel believed takes one beyond the immediate.) It is here that the Doctrine of Essence enters, for in order for the essential features of a thing to be known by thought, it must be seen in its relations to an other. The Doctrine of Essence, however, is concerned in itself with an exclusive analysis of the mediate; hence it, too, is incomplete.

The Doctrine of Notion or Idea is that in which the inadequacy of the previous two is reconciled. Being must be known not only for itself and for an other, but in-and-for itself. ("For an other" need not imply a second given; it might indicate the limits of the given, its finiteness, and hence refer to itself. In its immediacy nothing can be said about Being.) However, when seen in this way, Being is understood as a Notion or Idea, and the truth of the given is grasped by reason.

Being

In discussing the Doctrine of Being, Hegel attempted to accomplish two things: to present the totality of Being and to abolish the immediacy of Being. There are three grades to Being that are necessary to this discussion of it: quality, quantity, and measure. These grades are concerned not only with the history of philosophic thought but also with the evolution of thought itself.

In the bare beginnings of thought is, as it were, an indeterminate something from which something determinate is to come; Hegel calls this bare beginning "Being." This impression of which there is not yet an idea cannot be talked about. It is taken as a here-now; in order to talk about it, think about it, predicate anything of it, one would have to take it out of the here-now and make of it something determinate, but as something determinate, it would have a quality. A bare datum is without distinction, without time, and to say of it that it is here in a specified way is already to take it out of the immediate and determinate it.

The bare beginnings then pass to a stage in which the given is qualified, is made something; it is saved from not being anything. That it is something and not others, that it has a distinct character which differentiates it from others, subjects it to change and alteration. No longer indeterminable (Being itself) or nothing (not-Being), it stands between the two in the world of becoming.

Perhaps Hegel's discussion will be easier to follow if a philosophical illustration is considered. Impressions may be regarded as similar to indeterminable Being. Impressions are sensations below the level of consciousness, about which one can say nothing because of their fragmentary, fleeting nature; they are gone before they can be talked about. Consciousness arises concomitantly with the birth of ideas. From the fleeting impressions, mind selects and holds for observation—determines, as it were—one of these, and thus ideas are born. In the analysis of ideas, mind finds qualities, time, cause, change. So for Hegel, Being is quality—that determining characteristic without which the given would cease to be.

One observes that a determinate entity is what it is independently of any increase or decrease of its quantity, since a qualitative characteristic defines it. Quantity is both discrete and continuous, for it rests upon a unit construction that is exclusive and that is equalized. Numbers, for instance, fulfill this requirement and may be used to determine both discrete and continuous magnitudes. Yet quantity itself cannot be considered as an absolute notion, for as an object is decreased or diminished, eventually a quantitative difference will make a qualitative one.

Generally, Hegel views change of quantity in terms of absolutes; that is, he conceives of increase or decrease to the infinitely large or infinitesimally small, the one approaches the entire universe, the absolute; the other approaches nothing, not-Being. A house may be a house no matter how large or small; but "no matter how" must be taken relatively; a house cannot be nothing or everything. Hegel considers this an instance of the dialectical at work in quantity, making it what it is not; that is, quality.

Thus, one arrives at the third grade of Being, a quantified quality, or measure. In measure, one attains the knowledge that everything is not immediate, but relative or mediate. For everything has its measure, its proper qualitative and quantitative range, as it were, beyond which it cannot remain the same. To know the proper measure of a thing, of Being, is to know its Essence.

Hegel thus accomplished what he set out to do; that is, he presented the totality of Being by analyzing its three grades, quality, quantity, and measure, and he abolished the immediacy of Being by showing that its Essence, whatever makes it what it is, rests not on its immediately given appearance, but on its measure, which is a mediate or relative concept demanding that the given be seen in terms of an other. This analysis depended not on mere perception of the immediately given, but rather on reflective thought. Thought and its object are progressing together. Being is the immediate appearance of reality; through reflection the philosopher has proceeded to the mediate aspect of reality, its Essence. Neither Being nor Essence is more real than the other; reflective thought has gone from one to the other to give us a greater insight into reality.

Essence

In the Doctrine of Essence, there are three grades: identity, diversity, and ground. An analysis of a thing is such that it is conditioned by, and conditions, something else. In order to be determinate, not only are the boundaries of the thing needed, so that it can be defined as a finite object, but in its very definition it is distinguished from what it is not. Thus, not only is it related to itself in terms of its identity, but also it is related to others in terms of its difference.

Hegel's argument is reminiscent of Plato's analysis of the One and the Many in the *Parmenidēs* (middle period dialogue, 388-368 B.C.E.; *Parmenides*, 1793). Plato showed that the paradox of the One—that it is and yet that it is not—can be resolved if the concepts of identity, difference, and other than are introduced. The One is (identical with itself) and the One is not (others); that is, the One is other than or different from. Hegel's work contains a similar (although in many ways different) analysis. In order to understand the essence of a thing, one must grasp the apparently contradictory characteristics of identity and diversity in some sort of unity. Unity is found in the concept of the ground. In order for a thing to be, that is, to exist, there must be more than its self-identity, for self-identity, when not contrasted with what the self is now, would once more lead to an indeterminate, abstract Being. On the other hand, there must be more than the mediating relations that indicate that there are others than the self. That is, one cannot concentrate only on what the self is not. In the concept of a ground, Hegel finds the proper meaning of Essence, for the thing is seen in its inward relations (its self-identity) *and* in its relations to an other also; but this is the concept of the ground.

Notion

The final subdivision in Hegel's logic is that of the Doctrine of Notion or Idea. (Hegel uses the German *Begriff*, a term that, replete with difficulty, has the conflicting shades of meaning alluded to earlier and, as it were, all present at the same time.) The three grades of this doctrine are universal, particular, and individual.

Having presented two aspects of reality, its immediate and mediate appearance, its Being and its Essence, Hegel was ready to consider reality in its totality. The movement from Being to and through Essence is a dialectical process involving reflection, a process by which the nature of the given is revealed. The Doctrine of Idea emphasizes that the only way in which one can discover the nature of a thing is to proceed through this kind of process. Hegel points out in the Doctrine of Idea that in the process of development, the thing is revealed to reflective thought in the aforementioned grades. In its bare beginnings as immediate Being, it is an indeterminate, undefinable thing-in-itself, the very *Ding an Sich* of which Kant spoke. It is an undeveloped universal. From the immediately given, one proceeds to a consideration of the thing as a differentiated something. (Hegel refers to this as the particularizing phase of development.) Finally, in reflecting upon the further development of the thing into a Being that is both immediate and mediate, identical and different, universal and particular, the individual is realized. However, to see the individual as it is, it must be understood in terms of its process from undifferentiated universal to differentiated particular to individual. If the parts are to be understood, we must understand the process as a whole. Thus, for Hegel, the process of knowledge and that which is known, Being, ultimately are one. Reality and rationality are interchangeable.

Theodore Waldman

Lectures on the Philosophy of History

Type of philosophy: Philosophy of history, metaphysics
First published: Vorlesungen über die Philosophie der Geschichte, 1837 (English translation, 1852-1861)
Principal ideas advanced:
◇ Spirit is freedom and self-consciousness acting to realize their own potentiality.
◇ The real is the rational, and the rational is the real; idea or reason is the formative principle of all reality.
◇ The goal of history is the liberation of Spirit from its confinement in nature in order that Spirit might be reunited with its essence as idea.

◇ The Spirit could not realize its reunion with idea were it not for the force of will, as derived from human passions.

◇ The individual as individual is unimportant; only the historically decisive actor, the hero, makes a significant difference in history; but whether an individual be a conventional citizen, a courageous person, a hero, or a victim, that person is nothing but the Spirit's instrument.

◇ The embodiment of the Spirit's freedom is the state; the state is the concrete unity of freedom and passion.

History is understood by Georg Wilhelm Friedrich Hegel as the movement of Spirit toward the attainment of self-consciousness. To comprehend world history as the progress of the consciousness of Spirit it is necessary to arrive at a conceptual grasp of the three constitutive elements that structure historical movement: the idea of Spirit, the means of actualization, and the state as the final and perfect embodiment of Spirit.

Spirit

Hegel begins his discussion with a formulation of the abstract characteristics of the idea of Spirit. The peculiar quality of Spirit is grasped when it is seen in contrast with its opposite—matter. The essence of matter is gravity, which means that it has its center outside itself and thus is dependent upon a central point toward which it tends. The essence of Spirit is freedom, which designates a self-contained existence.

Another characteristic of Spirit is self-consciousness. It is of the essence of Spirit to know itself or be conscious of itself. The self-contained existence of Spirit as freedom is thus self-consciousness. In the phenomenon of self-consciousness, two modes must be distinguished—the fact *that I know* and *what I know*. There is the self that is conscious, and there is also the self of which the self is conscious. Insofar as in self-consciousness the self is conscious of itself, these two modes are merged into a unity. The self has itself within itself. Self-consciousness is a unity, but it is a unity that expresses a reduplication. I can know myself, I can love myself, and I can hate myself. Spirit as freedom is self-reflexive or self-reduplicative. As it is the nature of Spirit to know

itself, so also it is the nature of Spirit to actualize itself. Spirit forever drives beyond that which it is *potentially* to make itself what it can become *actually*. Spirit yearns for actualization. "The very essence of Spirit is activity; it realizes its potentiality—makes itself its own deed, its own work—and thus it becomes an object to itself; contemplates itself as an objective existence."

Reason and Reality

Hegel's definition of Spirit must be understood in its context of a rational philosophy that proclaims an identification of reason and reality. In the Hegelian system, the laws of logic are at the same time the laws of being. This undergirding principle of Hegel's philosophy was first formulated in *Die Phänomenologie des Geistes* (1807; *The Phenomenology of Spirit*, 1868; also known as *The Phenomenology of Mind*, 1910), and he expressed it thus: The real is the rational and the rational is the real. This principle also governs his interpretation of history. In *Lectures on the Philosophy of History*, he writes:

> The only Thought which Philosophy brings with it to the contemplation of History, is the simple conception of *Reason*; that Reason is the Sovereign of the World; that the history of the world, therefore, presents us with a rational process. . . . That this "idea" or "Reason" is the *True*, the *Eternal*, the absolutely *powerful* essence; that it reveals itself in the World, and that in that World nothing else is revealed but this and its honor and glory—is the thesis which, as we have said, has been proved in Philosophy, and is here regarded as demonstrated.

Idea or reason thus constitutes the primary formative principle in Hegel's philosophical system. This idea expresses itself first in nature but also in Spirit. The triadic unity of idea, nature, and Spirit thus defines the whole of Hegel's system. Expressed in terms of his dialectical logic, idea is the thesis, nature the antithesis, and Spirit the synthesis. Nature exhibits the emergence of the idea in space; Spirit exhibits the actualization of the idea in time and history. The primary category for nature is space. The primary category for Spirit is time. Through the workings of Spirit, the idea is wrested from its localization in space and becomes temporized and historicized. Both nature and Spirit are subject to a development under the impetus of the idea, but the development in nature is that of a quiet and subdued unfolding, whereas Spirit expresses a dynamic self-realization in which conflict and alienation are integral movements.

> Thus Spirit is at war with itself; it has to overcome itself as its most formidable obstacle. That development which in the sphere of Nature is a peaceful growth, is in that of Spirit, a severe, a mighty conflict with itself. What Spirit really strives for is the realization of its ideal being; but in doing so, it hides that goal from its own vision, and is proud and well satisfied in this alienation from it.

Spirit is alienated from the idea in its subjugation or bondage to nature, but in the process of self-realization through which it attains self-consciousness, Spirit becomes sovereign over nature, subordinates nature to its purposes, and thus drives to a reconciliation of itself with the idea. It is in the historical consciousness of the Hebrew people that Hegel finds the first liberation of Spirit from nature. In the Hebrew doctrine of creation, Nature is understood as a creature and a servant, and Spirit appears as the creator and the master.

The aim or goal of history is the actualization of Spirit as freedom, wresting itself from its confinement in nature, and seeking reunion with itself as idea. This aim or goal defines at the same time God's purpose for the world. Hegel's philosophy of history thus takes on the function of a theodicy—a justification of the ways of God. God's providential activity in the world is the self-realization of Spirit. Hegel converts the truths of philosophical categories and seeks to establish a conceptual justification for the suffering and sacrifices that occur in the course of world history.

> Itself is its own object of attainment, and the sole aim of Spirit. This result it is, at which the process of the World's History has been continually aiming; and to which the sacrifices that have ever and anon been laid on the vast altar of the earth, throughout the long lapse of ages, have been offered. This is the only aim that sees itself realized and fulfilled; the only

pole of repose amid the ceaseless change of events and conditions, and the sole efficient principle that pervades them. This final aim is God's purpose with the world; but God is the absolutely perfect Being, and can, therefore, will nothing other than himself—his own Will. The Nature of His Will—that is, His Nature itself—is what we here call the idea of Freedom; translating the language of Religion into that of Thought.

Human Passions

The second constitutive element of the world-historical process is that of the means of actualization. The idea of Spirit, as the aim or goal of history as such, is merely general and abstract. It resides in thought as a potentiality that has not yet passed over into existence, so a second element, actualization, must be introduced. The source of power that drives Spirit from its potential being into actuality is will. Hegel defines will as "the activity of man in the widest sense." In this definition, he seeks to keep the ranges of meaning sufficiently broad so as to include people's needs, instincts, inclinations, and passions. "We may affirm absolutely," Hegel says, "that *nothing great in the World* has been accomplished without *passion*." Two elements are thus disclosed as essential for an understanding of history. One is the idea of Spirit; the other is the complex of human passions. Hegel speaks of the former as the warp and of the latter as the woof of the cloth of universal history. The concrete union of these two provides the third and final element of world history—freedom embodied in the state. The means or material of history is thus the passions and interests of people, used by Spirit for the attainment of its end.

Individuals, activated by their inclinations and passions, constitute the power plant for the world-historical process. However, these individuals are, in the final analysis, sacrificed for the end or goal of history. History is the slaughter bench at which the happiness and welfare of each individual is sacrificed. The individual constitutes but a moment in the vast general sweep of world history and remains historically unimportant. "The particular is for the most part of too trifling value as compared with the general: individuals are sacrificed and abandoned. The idea pays the penalty of determinate existence and of corruptibility, not from itself, but from the passions of individuals." Spirit uses people's passions to attain its final self-consciousness. It sets the passions to work for itself. This integration of human passions with the aim of Spirit is accomplished through the "cunning of Reason." The cunning of reason weaves together all the expressions of passion and makes them contributory to the final goal.

The Four Types of Individuals

The passions that are put to work by the cunning of reason arise from the wills of particular individuals, as they play their diverse roles and carry out their various functions. These particular individuals are classified by Hegel into four distinct, yet interrelated, historical categories: the citizen, the person, the hero, and the victim.

The *citizen* is subject to what Hegel calls customary morality. The determinant of action for the citizen is the will of society, the will of a nation-state, or the will of a religious institution. The citizen has not yet apprehended his or her subjective existence and consequently has no consciousness of freedom—neither personal nor universal.

The *person* is the individual who can transcend the morality of his or her particular society and act on the basis of a morality grounded in subjectivity. It is in the person that subjective freedom makes its appearance. The morality of the person is not subordinate. It is determined by a personal consciousness of freedom. The person exhibits an implicit awareness of the idea as Spirit, and thus drives beyond the static customary morality of the citizen. Hegel finds in Socrates the example par excellence of the person who has been liberated from the confining morality of the citizen. "Though Socrates himself continued to perform his duties as a citizen, it was not the actual State and its religion, but the world of Thought that was his true home."

However, it is only the *hero* who is the "world-historical individual." The hero is the historically decisive actor. Like all other people, he or she is motivated by private gain and interest, but the hero's actions express at the same time an attunement with the will of the World-Spirit. The hero's own will incorporates the larger issues of world

history. The heroes of history are practical and political people. They are neither philosophers nor artists. They have no theoretical understanding of the idea that they are unfolding. However, they have insight into what is timely and needed as well as courage to act decisively on the basis of their convictions. They know what their age demands, and they commit themselves to its challenge. Caesar, Alexander the Great, and Napoleon were such men. They responded to the requirements of their times and shaped the history of the world through their decisive actions. After seeing Napoleon ride through the streets of Jena, Hegel retired to his study and wrote: "Today I saw the World-Spirit riding on horseback." Napoleon was an instrument, used by the cunning of reason, in the actualization of the self-consciousness of freedom. To become heroes or world-historical individuals, these people had to sacrifice personal happiness.

> If we go on to cast a look at the fate of these World-Historical persons, whose vocation it was to be agents of the World-Spirit—we shall find it to have been no happy one. They attained no calm enjoyment; their whole life was labor and trouble; their whole nature was nought else but their master-passion. When their object is attained they fall off like empty hulls from the kernel. They die early, like Alexander; are murdered, like Caesar; are transported to St. Helena, like Napoleon.

The *victim*, the fourth category, moves solely in the realm of private desires and inclinations. He or she has no interest in and offers no contribution to the customary morality of the citizen, nor to the subjective morality of the person, nor to the march of universal freedom exhibited by the hero. The victim is abandoned to his private situation. His or her goal is private success and happiness. Hegel has few good words for this type of individual. Obviously, the victim cannot become historically decisive. In a sense, history moves on without the victim, but in another sense, the victim remains part of the historical pattern insofar as the cunning of reason must use all the material that passion provides. In the final analysis, Spirit makes use of the hero and victim alike. There is a real sense in which both the hero and the victim are "victims." The victim is a "victim" of the hero and the age; the hero in turn is a "victim" of the World-Spirit. From all this emerges the implicatory principle of Hegel's philosophy of history that the individual *as* individual is unimportant. As philosopher Søren Kierkegaard, the chief of all critics of Hegel, later demonstrated, the existential significance of the individual is sacrificed to the universal and the general. A frank admission of this disregard for individuality is expressed when Hegel writes:

> The History of the World might, on principle, entirely ignore the circle within which morality and the so much talked of distinction between the moral and the politic lies—not only in abstaining from judgments, for the principles involved, and the necessary reference of the deeds in question to those principles, are a sufficient judgment of them—but in leaving Individuals quite out of view and unmentioned.

The State

The third constitutive element of world history is the state. The aim or goal of history is Spirit as freedom; the means of actualization are the passions of humankind; the embodiment or fulfillment of this freedom is found in the state. The state, as understood by Hegel, is the concrete unity of universal, objective freedom and particular, subjective passion. Thus the state synthesizes freedom and passion, the universal and the particular, the objective and the subjective. In the state, universal freedom becomes concretized and is given substance. The freedom of subjective passion is mere arbitrariness and caprice. The actualized freedom of universal history, on the other hand, is *organized* liberty, or freedom structured by a state.

In the final analysis, the entities that are under consideration in Hegel's philosophy of history are "peoples" or cultural totalities. The state rather than the individual embodies universal freedom. The state does not exist for its subjects—it exists for its own sake. It is its own end. The subjects of a state are means toward its end. It is important not to confuse Hegel's definition of the state with an individual bureaucratic political organization. Such a political organization—British monarchism, French constitutional-

ism, American democracy—may express the will of a state, but the two are not identical. The state, for Hegel, designates a cultural complex that integrates the art, religion, politics, and technology of a people into a unified self-consciousness. The Third Reich of Adolf Hitler, for example, according to the Hegelian philosophy, must be understood as a ghastly distortion of the true meaning of a state. Nazism constituted a pseudostate—a state without cultural content. The state, for Hegel, becomes the foundation for any organization—political or otherwise. The state is responsible for all cultural activities. The implication of this is the subordination of personal morality, personal religion, and political self-determination to a corporate or group substance. This group substance or state, insofar as it provides the foundation for all of humanity's temporal activities, is understood as an expression of God's purpose for the world. The state is thus defined to be the divine idea as it exists on earth. There is no room for personal religion and personal morality in Hegel's system. The individual as individual stands outside morality and outside history itself. Only as a moment in the march of universal freedom, embodied in the state, does the individual become significant. The state or the culture, rather than the individual, is, for Hegel, the bearer of history.

Philosophy of History

In formulating his philosophy of history, Hegel traces the development of the consciousness of freedom as it moves from Eastern to Western civilization. History travels from East to West. Asian civilization is the childhood of history. Greek civilization marks the period of adolescence. In Roman civilization, history develops to adulthood. Germanic civilization appears as the fourth phase of world history—old age. The Asians had acknowledged only *one* person as free—the despot. Insofar as the freedom of the despot expressed itself in the recklessness of passion, it must be accounted as mere caprice; hence, in Asian civilization, freedom, properly understood, does not yet exist. In Greece and Rome, the consciousness of freedom manifested itself in the acknowledgment that *some* people are free. Slavery, with its restriction of freedom, was an accepted institution in both Greece and Rome. It is not until the Germanic nations that it is acknowledged that *all* people are free. Germanic civilization, under the influence of Christianity, attained the consciousness of universal freedom.

Among the peoples of China and India, who compose Asian civilization for Hegel, only the first glimmerings of a historical consciousness exist; history as such does not begin until the rise of the Persians. In China and India, the idea remains bound to nature. The peculiar determinants of Spirit are lacking. In China, morality is equated with legislative enactments, individuals are stripped of personality, and the will and the passions of the emperor constitute the highest authority. The emperor as the supreme head of political affairs is also at the same time the chief priest of religion. Religion is thus subordinated to the despotism of a particular bureaucratic organization. Such an organization, according to Hegel, is the very negation of a historical state as a cultural unit.

The civilization of India exhibits a similar bondage to nature. This is expressed particularly in the institution of the caste system. The individual does not choose a particular position for the self but receives it from nature. Nature is the governing power. Thus, in Asian civilization, the universal idea emerges in nature, but it does not drive beyond itself to the self-consciousness of Spirit.

The Persians are the first historical peoples. Historical consciousness is expressed in their use of light as a symbol for the good (*Ormuzd*). Light provides the condition for the exercise of choice, and it is precisely choice, action, and deeds that constitute the stuff of history. Historical states are what their deeds are. The Persians understood history as a struggle between good and evil, in which the actors were confronted with the inescapability of choice. There is a deficiency, however, in the historical consciousness of the Persians. They failed to grasp the higher unity in which the antithesis of good and evil is synthesized. Judaism, which took its rise in the same general geographical and cultural milieu, provides a further advance in the progressive development of the consciousness of freedom. In Judaism, Spirit is liberated from nature and is purified. Both the individual and Israel as a nation come to a consciousness of themselves as

distinct from nature. Jehovah, as the quintessence of Spirit, is understood as the lord of nature. Nature is subordinated to the role of creature. Spirit is acknowledged as the Creator.

> The idea of Light has at this stage advanced to that of "Jehovah"—the *purely One*. This forms the point of separation between the East and the West: Spirit descends into the depths of its own being and recognizes the abstract fundamental principle as the spiritual. Nature—which in the East is the primary and fundamental existence—is now depressed to the condition of a mere creature; Spirit now occupies the first place. God is known as the creator of all human beings, as he is of all nature, and as absolute causality generally.

Judaism thus marks the transition from East to West. Spirit is acknowledged in its separation from nature, but neither Spirit nor nature is yet fully comprehended.

In Greek civilization, another advance becomes apparent. Greece, as part of the adolescent period of the historical process, introduces the principle of subjective freedom or individuality. This principle is expressed both in the personal or subjective morality of Socrates (as contrasted with the customary morality of society) and in the rise of Athenian democracy. As despotism was the peculiar characteristic of the political life of Asia, so democracy is the peculiar characteristic of the political life of Greece. Spirit becomes introspective and posits itself as particular existence, but it posits itself precisely as the ideal and thus suggests the possible triumph over particularity through a comprehension of universality itself.

However, the universals of Greek thought are fixed and static essences; hence they are still fettered by the limitations of nature. They still remain dependent upon external conditions. Therefore, the new direction projected by the consciousness of the Greek spirit still retains natural elements. A concrete expression of this principle is the continued practice of slavery, which grants freedom to some but not to all. In Rome, in which history attains its adulthood, an advance is made from democracy to aristocracy. The institutions of the people are united in the person of the emperor. In the will of the emperor, the principle of subjectivity, enunciated in Greek thought, gains unlimited realization. The will of the emperor becomes supreme. However, insofar as subjectivity is universalized and objectivized at the expense of the claims of art, religion, and morality, the state that emerges in Roman civilization is still an inferior state, lacking in cultural content.

The state, understood as the concrete embodiment of subjective and objective freedom, comes to its full realization in the German spirit. The German spirit, like the Greek, apprehended the principle of subjectivity, but unlike the Greek, it became the bearer of the Christian ideal and thus universalized the principle to mean that *all* people are free. The Greek and Roman spirit still kept some people (the slaves) in chains. People's individual interests and passions thus find their fulfillment only in the German spirit. This fulfillment is the unification of the objective idea of freedom, as the aim of history, with the particular and subjective passions of humankind, in the concrete embodiment of a cultural whole. Subjective freedom, without objective order, is mere caprice—expressed either in the will of a despot or emperor, or in the chaos of anarchy. Thus, subjective freedom cannot be realized until it finds its place within a structured whole—the state:

> This is the point which consciousness has attained, and these are the principal phases of that form in which the principle of Freedom has realized itself;—for the History of the World is nothing but the development of the idea of Freedom. However, Objective Freedom—the laws of *real* Freedom—demand the subjugation of the mere contingent Will—for this is in its nature formal. If the Objective is in itself Rational, human insight and conviction must correspond with the Reason which it embodies, and then we have the other essential element—Subjective Freedom—also realized.

Calvin O. Schrag

Additional Reading

Butler, Clark. *G. W. F. Hegel*. Boston: Twayne, 1977. A comprehensive study of Georg Wilhelm Friedrich Hegel that aims not to be merely about Hegel but to communicate the essence of Hegelian philosophy to a wider public by being accessible but not oversimplistic. Approaches Hegel from the cultural standpoint of the present. Contains an annotated bibliography and a chronology of Hegel's life.

Christensen, Darrell E., ed. *Hegel and the Philosophy of Religion: The Wofford Symposium*. The Hague: Martinus Nijhoff, 1970. A collection of essays presented at the first conference of the Hegel Society of America, which analyzes many aspects of Hegel's philosophy of religion. Considers Hegel's historical context by discussing the philosophies of Immanuel Kant, Friedrich Nietzsche, and Karl Marx.

Gillespie, Michael Allen. *Hegel, Heidegger, and the Ground of History*. Chicago: University of Chicago Press, 1984. Compares and contrasts Hegel's philosophy of history with that of Martin Heidegger, a twentieth century German philosopher who sought an alternative to Hegel and who eventually supported Nazi ideology under Adolf Hitler. Reveals the role of Hegel in shaping modern philosophies of history.

Hondt, Jacques. *Hegel in His Time*. Translated by John Burbridge, with Nelson Roland and Judith Levasseur. Lewiston, N.Y.: Broadview Press, 1988. Translator's introduction discusses the author's perception of Hegel. Translator's notes also very helpful. Covers Hegel's life, the political setting of his time, and Hegel's attack on that setting. Examines the use of Hegel's philosophy of history by Karl Marx and Friedrich Engels.

Kainz, Howard P. *G. W. Hegel*. New York: Twayne, 1996. Excellent overview of Hegel's philosophical system. Includes an autobiographical sketch written by Hegel at age thirty-four. Discusses philosophical influences on Hegel as a student. Has a brief chronology of Hegel's life. Very readable and attempts to define terms as Hegel used them.

Kojeve, Alexandre. *Introduction to the Reading of Hegel: Lectures on Phenomenology*. Edited by A. Bloom, translated by J. H. Nichols. New York: Basic Books, 1969. The author was instrumental in reviving Hegel's philosophy, especially on phenomenology of Spirit. Clearly written; appropriate for beginning students on Hegel.

Lauer, Quentin. *Hegel's Idea of Philosophy*. 2d ed. New York: Fordham University Press, 1983. Discusses the works of Hegel and his place as a philosopher. Includes the full text and a good analysis of Hegel's *Lectures on the History of Philosophy* (given first at Jena in 1805-1806).

Lavine, T. Z. *From Socrates to Sartre: The Philosophic Quest*. New York: Bantam Books, 1984. A survey of six Western philosophers, including Hegel. An easily read review of Hegel's life and work. Highlights Hegel's influence on Karl Marx.

Plant, Raymond. *Hegel*. New York: Routledge, 1999. An excellent biographical introduction to the thoughts of the philosopher, clearly presented and requiring no special background. Bibliography.

Rosen, Michael. *Hegel's Dialectic and Its Criticism*. Cambridge, England: Cambridge University Press, 1982. Emphasizes Hegel's dialectic method of seeking truth. Discusses the difficulty in understanding many of Hegel's ambiguous phrases.

Singer, Peter. *Hegel*. New York: Oxford University Press, 1983. A ninety-page pamphlet in the Past Masters series. A broad overview of Hegel's ideas and major works. Very clearly written.

William S. Haney II, updated by Glenn L. Swygart

Martin Heidegger

From within the Continental tradition of philosophy known as existentialism, Heidegger strove to free philosophy from what he claimed were its millennia-old metaphysical shackles. Using complex and arcane terminology, he investigated the confrontation of the human being with Being itself and cleared a way for the answer to the question of why there is something rather than nothing.

Principal philosophical works: *Sein und Zeit*, 1927 (*Being and Time*, 1962); *Vom Wesen des Grundes*, 1929 (*The Essence of Reasons*, 1969); *Was ist Metaphysik?*, 1929 ("What Is Metaphysics?," 1949); *Kant und das Problem der Metaphysik*, 1929 (*Kant and the Problem of Metaphysics*, 1962); *Die Selbstbehauptung der deutschen Universität* (1934; *The Self-Assertion of the German University*, 1985); *Platons Lehre von der Wahrheit. Mit einem Brief über den "Humanismus,"* 1947 (*Plato's Doctrine of Truth and "Letter on Humanism,"* in *Philosophy in the Twentieth Century*, 1962); *Existence and Being*, 1949; *Holzwege*, 1950 ("The Origin of the Work of Art," in *Poetry, Language, and Thought*, 1971); *Einführung in die Metaphysik*, 1953 (*An Introduction to Metaphysics*, 1959); *Was heißt Denken?*, 1954 (*What Is Called Thinking?*, 1969); *Vorträge und Aufsätze*, 1954 (3 volumes); *Was ist das—die Philosophie?*, 1956 (*What Is Philosophy?*, 1958); *Zur Seinfrage*, 1956 (*The Question of Being*, 1958); *Der Satz vom Grund*, 1957 (*The Principle of Ground*, 1974); *Identität und Differenz*, 1957 (*Identity and Difference*, 1969); *Gelassenheit*, 1959 (*Discourse on Thinking*, 1966); *Unterwegs zur Sprache*, 1959 (*On the Way to Language*, 1971); *Nietzsche*, 1961 (2 volumes; English translation, 1979-1984, 4 volumes); *Die Frage nach dem Ding*, 1962 (*What Is a Thing?*, 1967); *Wegmarken*, 1967; *Zur Sache des Denkens*, 1969 (*On Time and Being*, 1972); *Poetry, Language, Thought*, 1971; *Early Greek Thinking*, 1975; *The Question Concerning Technology and Other Essays*, 1976; *The Piety of Thinking*, 1976; "Nur noch ein Gott kann uns retten," 1976 ("Only a God Can Save Us," 1976); *Martin Heidegger: Basic Writings*, 1977.

Born: September 26, 1889; Messkirch, Germany
Died: May 26, 1976; Messkirch, West Germany

Early Life

Martin Heidegger was the son of Friedrich Heidegger, a Catholic sexton at Messkirch, a small village in the Black Forest region of southwestern Germany, and Johanna (Kempf) Heidegger. Martin, the elder of the couple's two sons, attended public school in Messkirch and then entered the *Gymnasium* at Constance, with an intention to study for the Jesuit priesthood. In 1909, after three years of study at the *Gymnasium* at Freiburg, he entered the University of Freiburg. Unable to pursue the priesthood because of poor health, he was drawn toward a lifelong devotion to philosophy through his study of Christian the-ology and medieval philosophy after courses in physics and mathematics.

Heidegger's doctoral dissertation in 1913, *Die Lehre vom Urteil im Psychologismus* (the doctrine of judgment in psychologism), published the next year, took issue with the kind of simplistic reductionism that would collapse speculative philosophy into mere psychology. Heidegger acknowledged the influence of Edmund Husserl, the father of phenomenology, who called for the critical examination of the phenomena of consciousness on their own terms. Heidegger continued his studies even after the outbreak of World War I in 1914, his poor health leading to a quick discharge from military service.

By 1916, a second book-length work, on the doctrine of categories of the medieval Scholastic

Martin Heidegger. *(AP/Wide World Photos)*

philosopher John Duns Scotus, enabled Heidegger to teach philosophy at Freiburg as a privatdocent (an unsalaried lecturer paid out of students' fees). Elfriede Petri became Heidegger's wife in 1917; the couple had two sons, Jörg and Hermann.

In 1916, Husserl went to Freiburg, and by 1920, Heidegger had become his assistant, though Heidegger began to be uncomfortable with the kind of analysis of the "things" of consciousness promoted by Husserl. Heidegger believed that the ancient Greeks, especially the pre-Socratics, had had an experience of Being itself, that is, the "isness" of all things—something Husserl's epistemology (or theory of knowledge) merely obscured.

From 1923 until 1928, when he returned to Freiburg to succeed Husserl in the chair of philosophy, Heidegger taught as an associate professor at Marburg, where he was exposed to influences to which he would owe much in the shaping of his ontology (or theory of being). A new friendship with the theologian Rudolf Bultmann introduced Heidegger to the work of another theological writer, Karl Barth. That opened the way to a study of Martin Luther and existentialist Søren Kierkegaard. It was at Marburg that Heidegger published the first volume of his masterpiece, *Being and Time*.

Life's Work

Being and Time was Heidegger's attempt to start philosophy over again, to return to the pre-Socratic insights into Being lost with the advent of the rationalistic metaphysics of Plato. Heidegger was convinced that the pre-Socratics—true "thinkers" such as Parmenides and Heraclitus of Ephesus—had stood astonished before the presence of Being: that which was manifested in all the actually existing beings of the universe. For Heidegger, authentic human being was an openness to exactly this same astonishment, obscured by centuries of forgetfulness of Being, of neglect of the most important question: Why is there something rather than nothing? By an extraordinary etymological analysis of the pre-Socratics, Heidegger detected evidence of this primordial awareness of Being. Heraclitus said "One is all" (*panta ta onta*), and for Heidegger, this was precisely the insight that "all being is in Being."

The questioning of Being is Heidegger's task in *Being and Time*. This questioning is what gives humanity to people, who as human beings are "beings-in-the-world" (*In-der-Welt-Sein*), finite creatures bounded by death. Time and Being are inextricably linked, contrary to Western metaphysical thought, which had attempted to ground its theories in some notion of the eternal. Human being (Heidegger's *Dasein*) is open to its "throwness" into the world with no reference except to that of "no-thing-ness," or death. Yet

Dasein often fails to respond to its being-in-the-world and instead, says Heidegger, becomes an alienated "they," mass humanity, with the incessant chatter of words drowning out the speech through which Being expresses itself. *Dasein* does not listen. Only with the experience of an existential angst, or dread—the realization that one's being-in-the-world is an open question—can the voice of Being be heard once again.

There is no easy way to achieve authenticity in one's human being, for one's very existence means being-with-others and a falling away from true self-possession. Yet the uncanny feeling of homelessness in the world, elicited by one's angst, serves to shatter complacency and allow the human being to see that his or her authenticity must come in the caring for Being, in the answering to Being. This insight allows Heidegger to commend, in his later writings, those who care for the earth by working with it, and to condemn the technological rapacity of both the Soviet Union and the United States. *Dasein* is a being-toward-death, and this future inevitability must mark how humanity perceives its past as well as its present. It must be the same for whole peoples: History is a working out or working with the destiny that will come to all. It is here that *Being and Time* abruptly ends.

Despite the book's convoluted German coinages and abstract analysis, Heidegger's fame grew. Returning to Freiburg in 1928, he replaced Husserl at the elder philosopher's retirement; Heidegger's inaugural address, published in 1929 as *Was ist Metaphysik?*, represents, in the estimation of some scholars, a *Kehre* (or turning) from the thought expressed in his magnum opus. He sought not to repudiate his central insights into Being but to deemphasize the anthropocentrism of his work, in which the truth of Being "uncovers" itself through *Dasein*; the truth comes not by way of the human being but by language itself.

On May 27, 1933, Heidegger gave another inaugural address, this time as the newly elected rector of the university. Entitled *Die Selbstbehauptung der deutschen Universität* (1934; *The Self-Assertion of the German University*, 1985), it affirmed the autonomy of the university (in the face of National Socialist pressure, as Heidegger later maintained) and the *Führerprinzip* by which

Heidegger would take control of the school, bypassing its senate. In the speech, Heidegger glorified the historical mission of the German people, though he was not clear on the exact nature of that mission. Regardless, the rector must guide students and teachers alike into the "spiritual mission of the *Volk*," the destiny of the German people. Elsewhere, Heidegger was not so ambiguous; on November 3, 1933, he told students that "the Führer alone is the present and future German reality and its law."

Heidegger had joined the Nazi Party, reluctantly or not, but he apparently never resigned. He did resign the rectorate in 1934, disillusioned with the grand promise of National Socialism—not with the "inner truth and greatness of the National Socialist movement" but with the "works that are being peddled about nowadays as the philosophy of National Socialism." Heidegger had appeared at official Nazi functions wearing National Socialist insignia and as rector had secretly denounced several colleagues and students as having unsuitable philosophy. In November, 1944, with the end of the war approaching, Heidegger ended his lectures at the university; the next year, the Freiburg denazification committee issued its report on Heidegger, charging him with holding significant Nazi office, with introducing the *Führerprinzip*, and with inciting students against certain professors. Heidegger's health broke in 1946, and he spent three weeks at a sanatorium. The denazification hearings dragged on into 1949, when Heidegger was declared a Nazi "fellow traveler" and forbidden to teach until 1951; subsequently, he participated in periodic university seminars and continued to speak elsewhere, especially in France.

During the war years, Heidegger had taught several courses on Friedrich Wilhelm Nietzsche, who had also called for the death of Western metaphysics; yet Heidegger contended that Nietzsche's "will to power" was merely the culmination of Western metaphysical nihilism and not its overcoming. Power was a manifestation of all that was wrong in European civilization—the need to exert human will over the forces of nature, to bend and shape nature into human design. The conception of truth, that of a correspondence between statements and states of affairs, encouraged this imposition of humankind's will upon the world, shaping it to "correspond" with what humanity's power willed. Heidegger returned to the early Greeks for his understanding of truth. Humankind does not pursue truth; truth pursues humankind and opens itself up to humanity. *Dasein* must be open to the truth; humankind must be a mediator, not a calculator. The survival of civilization depended on it.

In his "Letter on Humanism," Heidegger disdained any affinity with French existentialist Jean-Paul Sartre, though Sartre himself was much influenced by Heidegger. Sartre's form of humanism, like all humanisms, recast humankind's relation only to other beings, not to Being itself; Sartre's dictum that existence precedes essence was still a metaphysical construct. Such "language under the dominance of the modern metaphysics of subjectivity . . . still denies us its essence: that it is the house of the truth of Being." In *Being and Time*, Heidegger had spoken of the resoluteness to choose authenticity in order to encounter Being; now he said that the guardianship of Being lay in language, and in the greatest poets of the language. True thinking was an openness to Being as it disclosed itself to and in humanity. Humanity was the trustee, or shepherd, of Being; humanity must possess an active readiness to receive the disclosure. Great art, especially poetry, brought Being to humankind in a way that no metaphysical construct, concerned as it is with beings, could do. Great art was no mere imitation of something eternal; it housed Being, as all human creations should. Technology, said Heidegger, alienated humankind from nature, and in turn nature alienated humankind from Being.

Heidegger was enamored of the countryside, turning down opportunities in the 1930's of a professorship in Berlin to remain near the Black Forest and his ski hut above Todtnauberg near Freiburg. In his later years, the stocky Heidegger, with piercing eyes, mustache, and thinning hair, often affected the garb of a Swabian peasant for his ascetic and contemplative life.

Influence

Heidegger exerted a profound influence on the development of existentialism, especially through Sartre. Additionally, his reflections on language and the way in which it disclosed the truth of Being were central to the French deconstruction movement, notably to Jacques Derrida. Theologians such as Bultmann were deeply influenced by Heidegger's ambiguous depiction of humanity's fallenness "into the world." The hermeneutic movement, associated with former student Hans-Georg Gadamer, built on Heidegger's work in textual criticism; psychoanalysis, especially the schools of existentialist therapy and phenomenological psychology, also benefited from Heidegger. In philosophy, the Marxists warmed to Heidegger's critique of technology, and Ludwig Wittgenstein's analysis of language showed some affinity with that of Heidegger.

Heidegger's thought has been praised as offering a revolutionary way back to Being and has been excoriated as obscurantist and almost meaningless, based on fanciful etymological interpretations. Above all, in the years since his death both friends and foes of Heidegger have wrestled with the fact that, whatever the quality of his thought, he was also a Nazi. Some have seen an organic connection between Heidegger's thought and National Socialism in Heidegger's sense of German destiny and narrow nationalism; others have excused him as one among many who were caught up in Hitlerism. Most vexing of all was Heidegger's determined silence about the Holocaust; despite his critique of the perversions of technology, he refused to make any public statement about the death camps. Heidegger's lifelong questioning of Being would endure to challenge future philosophers; some of the "answers" he chose to endorse would endure as a warning.

Dan Barnett

Being and Time

Type of philosophy: Existentialism, metaphysics
First published: Sein und Zeit, 1927 (English translation, 1962)
Principal ideas advanced:
◇ The world, existentially and phenomenologically understood, is a region of human concern; each person is a being-in-the-world in that by participation and involvement, the

world becomes constitutive of a person's being.

◇ A person has being in an environment; that person's world is a world he or she shares with others.

◇ Human beings are creatures of concerns. In relation to environment, their concerns are practical; in relation to the communal world, their concerns are personal.

◇ The three fundamental features of human beings are factuality (they are already involved in the world), existentiality (they are both project and possibility, that which has been but also that which can become), and fallenness (they have the tendency to become a mere presence in the world, failing to make the most of their possibilities because of gossip, curiosity, and ambiguity).

◇ Through anxiety, human beings encounter nothingness and become aware of their finitude and the necessity of death; but through resolution, human beings, who move from past to future through the present, appraise themselves, choose with the whole of their being, and thereby achieve authentic existence.

The primary philosophical problem for Martin Heidegger is the problem of Being. His major philosophical treatise, *Being and Time*, constitutes an attempt at a formulation of the basic questions and forms of analysis that are to lead to a clarification of the meaning and structures of Being. The form of analysis that peculiarly characterizes *Being and Time* is what Heidegger calls *Daseinsanalytik* (analysis of human being). This form of analysis is adopted because it is believed that humankind is the portal to the deeper levels of reality and that only through a disciplined analysis and description of human being can the path be opened for an apprehension of Being itself.

Phenomenological Ontology

In his analysis and description of human being or presence (*Dasein*), Heidegger makes use of the phenomenological method. Philosophy thus becomes "phenomenological ontology." The ontological content of philosophy is Being, and the method that is used to clarify and explicate the meaning of Being is phenomenology. Heidegger was a student of the philosopher Edmund

Husserl and, at least in part, took over Husserl's transcendental phenomenology and its program of a return "to the data themselves." Adherence to this formula, argues Heidegger, will preclude abstract constructions and formulations, sterile concepts, and the adoption of pseudoquestions that tend to conceal the phenomena or the data rather than reveal them. In the use of the phenomenological method Heidegger seeks to get back to the data of immediate experience and to describe these data as they "show themselves" in their primitive disclosure.

The word "phenomenon" has a Greek etymological root *phainomenon*, derived from the Greek verb *phainesthai*, which means "that which shows itself or that which reveals itself." The original Greek meaning of *logos*, the second constitutive etymological element in the word "phenomenology," is discourse, which "opens to sight" or "lets something be seen." Thus, phenomenology, properly understood as the "logos of the phenomenon," is the disciplined attempt to open to sight that which shows itself and to let it be seen as it is. In using the phenomenological method, one must therefore discard all preconceived logical and epistemological constructions and seek to examine and describe the phenomena as they show themselves.

The application of the phenomenological method in the analysis of human being, or *Dasein*, discloses first of all the foundational experience of being-in-the-world. People emerge in a world of going concerns and initially discover themselves in their engagement and involvement in practical and personal projects. Heidegger's phenomenological and existentialist concept of the world should not be confused with any objective conceptualization of the world as a substance or an abstract continuum of points. It is Heidegger's persistent argument that René Descartes's conceptualization of the world as a *res extensa* (material substance) entailed a phenomenological falsification of the world as a datum of immediate experience. The world is not an extended substance or an objective spatial container into which people are placed. The world, existentially understood, is a field or region of human concern that is never disclosed independent of this concern. There is no world without humanity.

Thus, to say that humanity's being is a being-in-the-world is to describe human reality in terms of a self-world correlation that underlies all concrete participation and engagement. Humanity is *in* the world in the sense of being *in* a profession, being *in* the army, being *in* politics, being *in* love, and the like. The relationship between human beings and the world is not that of a coinherence of substances or objects, but rather the relationship of existential participation and involvement. *Dasein* is in the world in the sense of "being preoccupied, producing, ordering, fostering, applying, sacrificing, undertaking, following through, inquiring, questioning, observing, talking over, or agreeing." The phenomenon of "being-in" denotes the intimacy and familiarity of "being-with" as distinct from the objective spatial proximity of "being-besides."

As the phenomenon of world is falsified when understood as a substance or objectivized entity, so also human being or *Dasein* is distorted when interpreted as a substantial self or a self-identical subject. Again, the error of Descartes's isolation of the thinking substance (*res cogitans*) is disclosed, and the spurious character of the epistemological quandaries that such a view entails is made apparent. The human being is not an isolated epistemological subject who first apprehends his or her own existence and then seeks proof for an objective external world. In his or her primordial experience, the human being already has his or her world given in his or her immediate concerns and preoccupations. The world is constitutive of his or her being. It is in this way that Heidegger's phenomenology undercuts the subject-object dichotomy, bequeathed by the Cartesian tradition to contemporary epistemological theory, and liberates the self from its lonely, worldless isolation.

A phenomenological description of our being-in-the-world shows that the world is structurally differentiated into various regions or existential modalities. There is the region of the *Umwelt* (environment), initially disclosed through the utensils that *Dasein* uses in practical concerns. My world is disclosed in one of its modifications as an instrumental world in which utensils are accessible for the realization of my various undertakings. The German word *Zuhandensein*, which can be translated as "at-handness," designates

this accessibility of utensils that constitutes an integral part of my world. Utensils are "at hand" for one's use and application. However, my *Umwelt* is also disclosed in the mode of *Vorhandensein* ("on-handness"). This modality lacks the existential proximity of at-handness and is epistemologically secondary and derivative. Heidegger's favorite illustration of these two modifications of the *Umwelt* is his example of the hammer and the act of hammering. In our primitive experience of our world, the hammer is an instrument with which we hammer. The hammer is revealed as a utensil or instrument through the act of hammering. On this level of experience, knowledge and action, or understanding and doing, are in an inseparable unity. Action is already a form of knowledge, and knowledge involves action. One can, however, objectivize one's environmental world and view one's hammer as a physical object in abstraction from its instrumental value. When a hammer becomes a mere object or thing, we can speak of it only as being "on hand" as contrasted with being "at hand." The hammer in the mode of on-handness becomes the object of a theoretical, scientific construction and is defined in terms of the qualities of weight, composition, size, and shape that constitute it as a material substance. When we say that the hammer *as utensil* is heavy, we mean that it will render more difficult the act of hammering. When we say the hammer *as object* is heavy, we mean that it has such and such a scientifically determined weight. The mode of at-handness is thus our existentially primitive mode—the mode through which *Dasein* first encounters the world in practical concerns. The world as "on hand" is a later construction.

Humanity's being-in-the-world thus includes a relatedness to an environmental region—in the mode either of at-handness or of on-handness. However, humanity's environment does not exhaust the world. Coupled with humanity's relatedness to an environmental region is humanity's relatedness to a communal region. The *Dasein*-world correlation encompasses a *Mitwelt* as well as an *Umwelt*. Our world is a world that we share with others. Human being is essentially communal ("Dasein ist wesenhaft Mitsein"). The communality of human being is a pervasive phenomenon that shows itself in our experience of aloneness as assuredly as in our experience of being-with-others. Aloneness is itself a deficient mode of being-with. We experience aloneness only as a privation of an original communal relatedness. Thus *Dasein* possesses an indelible communal character. In society and in solitude, human beings are structurally communal creatures. Now, for the most part, human beings exist in the unauthentic communal mode of the "anonymous one." To exist in the mode of the anonymous one is to exist in one's communal world in such a way that one's unique selfness is depersonalized and reduced to the status of an on-hand being. In short, the human being transforms itself and another self into an object or a thing, thus depriving both of their unique existential freedom that alone makes authentic communication possible.

The movements of the *Mitwelt* are conceptualized in terms of the categories and relations that obtain in the *Umwelt*, and the human being becomes a tool or utensil that can be used by another, or a mere object or thing. The anonymous one, thus depersonalized, moves in the realm of the customs, habits, and conventions of everyday life, succumbing to what Heidegger calls the everydayness of existence. The human being simply takes on the mechanical habits, the established customs, and the accepted conventions of everyday life. The anonymous one is further characterized by an "averageness," in which the average becomes the measure of a person's potentialities and the final standard for his or her creativity. That person lives by a spurious "golden mean" in which social behavior is calculated on the basis of socially binding "laws of averages," which leads to a leveling process in which all superiority is flattened and all originality trivialized. Publicity is another existential quality of the anonymous one. That person "opens" himself or herself to the public, conforms to its demands and opinions, accepts its standards, and thus retreats from personal commitment and responsible decision. *Das Man* is the term Heidegger uses to designate that leveled and reduced self that thinks what the public thinks, feels what the public feels, and does what the public does.

In the various projects of his being-in-the-world, *Dasein* is disclosed to himself as a creature of care or concern. His existential relation to his environmental world is a relation of practical concern, and his relation to his communal world is one of personal concern. The human being's engagement or involvement in practical and personal projects discloses *Dasein* as that being whose movements are peculiarly characterized by the existential quality of concern. Concern is the ground determinant of the being of *Dasein*. Concern permeates every modality of his being-in-the-world. Heidegger finds it to be significant that this existential self-understanding of human being as concern was already expressed in an old Latin myth attributed to Gaius Julius Hyginus, the compiler of Greek mythology:

As Concern was going across a river she saw some clay. Thoughtfully she took a piece of it and began to form it. As she was contemplating that which she had made, Jupiter appeared. Concern begged Jupiter to bestow spirit upon that which she had formed. This wish Jupiter happily granted her. However, when Concern wished to give her name to that which she had made, Jupiter protested and demanded that his name be used. While Concern and Jupiter were disputing over the name, Earth arose and demanded that her name be used as it was she who had offered a piece of her body. The disputing parties sought out Saturn as judge, and he submitted the following decision: "You, Jupiter, as you have given the spirit, shall take the spirit at death. You, Earth, as you have given the body, you shall then again receive the body. However, Concern, since she has first formed this creature, may possess it as long as it lives. And as there is a dispute concerning the name, so let it be called "homo" as it has been made out of earth (humus).

The fable clearly expresses the point that human beings have their source in concern, and concern will permeate their being as long as they live. Humanity's being-in-the-world has the indelible stamp of concern. Also, the fable is explicit in showing that it is Saturn (time) who submits the final decision relative to the nature of humankind, making it clear that temporality provides the ontological ground and inner meaning of this creature that has been formed by concern.

Features of Dasein

The peculiar task of Heidegger's phenomenological ontology is that of a delineation of the constitutive features of *Dasein*, who has been defined as Concern. The three foundational features of *Dasein*, all of which have attached to them a temporal significance, are factuality, existentiality, and fallenness.

The factuality of *Dasein* characterizes humanity's naked "thereness"—humanity's abandonment or "thrownness." As human beings disclose themselves in the various concerns of their being-in-the-world, they find that they have been thrown into a world without consultation and abandoned to the chance factors that have already constituted them. They discover themselves as already brought into being, a fact among facts, part of a going concern, involved in situations that they have not created and in which they must remain as long as they are. In Heidegger's analysis of factuality, people can anticipate the significance of temporality as the final ontological meaning of concern. Factuality expresses primarily the directionality of pastness. *Dasein* reveals himself as *already* being-in-the-world. *Dasein* is already begun and has a past through which he has been defined and shaped. His factuality is his destiny.

The second constitutive structure of *Dasein* is existentiality. This structure points to humanity's disclosure of itself as a project and a possibility. Humanity is that which it has been but also that which it can become. People find themselves thrown into the world but also experience freedom and responsibility to transform the world and redefine themselves in their concerns with it. This involves an apprehension of human being in terms of possibilities. *Dasein* as possibility is projected into the future. Thus, existentiality is temporally rooted in futurity as factuality is rooted in the past. In a sense, existentiality and factuality are polar elements of human being. By virtue of their factuality, human beings are always already thrown into a situation; by virtue of their existentiality, they exist as possibility and understand themselves as moving into a future.

The third structural element in the ontological constitution of *Dasein* is fallenness. Fallenness points to the universal tendency of the human being to lose himself or herself in his or her present preoccupations and concerns, alienating himself from his unique and personal future possibilities. Fallen man exists as mere presence, retreating from his genuine self, which always involves his past and his future. He thus becomes a reduced self. The fallenness of human being receives its most trenchant expression in the movements of gossip, curiosity, and ambiguity. Gossip is an unauthentic modification of speech that simply repeats the accepted, everyday, conventional, and shallow interpretations of the public. No decisive content is communicated, because gossip is concerned only with a reiteration of the clichés that reflect the present and restricted world horizons of the anonymous one. Curiosity, which is always allied with gossip, indicates the insatiable human desire to explore everything in the present environment simply for the sake of discovering novelty—not for the purpose of authentic understanding but simply to engage in pursuits that will provide momentary distraction. Ambiguity is the lack of comprehension and singleness of purpose that results when the self has forfeited its unique possibilities in its preoccupation with the present. Thus, factuality, existentiality, and fallenness constitute the three basic ontological structures of human being. These structures are correspondingly rooted in the three modes of temporality—past, future, and present. Factuality qualifies *Dasein* as already-in-the-world, having arrived from a past; existentiality qualifies him as purposive or as existing in-advance-of-himself; and fallenness qualifies him as present with the world in everyday concerns.

Anxiety

A phenomenological description that seeks to penetrate to the immediate experience of being-in-the-world will need to give disciplined attention to the phenomenon of anxiety. Anxiety is described by Heidegger as a ground-determinant of the human situation. Anxiety is the basic mood that discloses the threatening character of the world by confronting the human beings with their irremovable finitude. Anxiety, first of all, should not be confused with fear. Fear has a definite object that can be specified within the region of either the environmental world or the communal world. A utensil, an object, or a person constitutes the source of fear. However, the source of anxiety remains indeterminate. That which threatens cannot be localized or specified. It remains indefinable. The source of anxiety is nothingness. Through anxiety people encounter the nothingness that is constitutive of their finitude. Anxiety, properly understood, is an intentional disclosure. It is an instance of pretheoretical intentionality, pointing to and revealing a most vital aspect of one's being-in-the-world. The theoretical intentionality of pure thought can never disclose nothingness, because thought is always directed to an object, but nothingness can never be objectivized or conceptualized. It can be experienced only on a pretheoretical and preobjective level. The interior of human being remains opaque to purely theoretical analysis. It can be penetrated only through preobjective elucidation and description.

This accounts for Heidegger's emphasis on the phenomenological importance of humanity's "preconceptual understanding of Being." The nothingness, preobjectively disclosed through anxiety, brings *Dasein* face to face with his radical finitude. The accentuation of the principle of finitude is a theme that runs throughout the whole of Heidegger's philosophy. His *Daseinsanalytik* is in its central intention a philosophy of human finitude. In this disclosure of nothingness and finitude anxiety also reveals the contingency of human existence and the threat of meaninglessness. Anxiety breaks down the superficial, surface realities that conceal humanity's true predicament and reveals the world as something strange and uncanny. The trusted world of everyday and mediocre concerns collapses. What was previously a refuge of security and contentment now becomes strange and puzzling. The world has nothing more to offer. Its former significance is reduced to insignificance. All protections and supports vanish. Nothing remains.

Death

As anxiety discloses humanity's finitude, so also it discloses its indelible transitoriness—its "being-unto-death." The death that is examined in Heidegger's phenomenological analysis is not the death of the "death-bed" (that is, death understood as the biological termination of empirical reality). Such a view of death is an objectivized view that can be understood only by the

one observing, never by the one who has to die. The being-unto-death of which Heidegger speaks is an experience of death that interpenetrates one's subjectivity. It is a death that one understands and appropriates in one's existential concerns. It is a mode of existence that *Dasein* takes over as soon as he is.

Death is a phenomenon that embraces the whole of life and entails a responsibility for life. In anticipating his final and irrevocable limit of being-in-the-world, *Dasein* appraises himself in the light of the finite possibilities that precede his end, shoulders his responsibility for these possibilities, and authentically chooses himself as a whole. As had already been taught by Søren Kierkegaard, death makes a difference for life. The anticipation of death infuses every choice with existential urgency. Our possibilities are limited by our final end—which is always imminent. As soon as a person is born, he or she is old enough to die. Thus, that person must seek to take over death by affirming himself or herself with the whole of his or her being in every decisive moment. For the most part, however, human beings engage in a retreat or flight from their having to die, losing themselves in an unauthentic being-unto-death, whereby death is objectivized and externalized as an on-hand factuality which befalls people in general but no one in particular. This is the death of the anonymous one. An authentic being-unto-death, on the other hand, is an awareness of death as a unique possibility which I, and I alone, will have to face. Numerous responsibilities are transferable and can be carried out by proxy. However, no such transferability is possible for the task of dying. There is no dying by proxy. Every *Dasein* must die his own death.

Conscience and Guilt

Conscience and guilt play a dominant role in Heidegger's *Daseinsanalytik*. Conscience is defined as the "call of concern" which summons us to an awareness of our existential guilt. The human being as such is guilty. Guilt is an inevitable and irreducible determinant of human being. The guilt that is under discussion in *Being and Time* is quite clearly not a moral quality that a person may or may not possess. It is a determinant of one's finite existence as such.

The concept of guilt in Heidegger's analysis is a transmoral concept. The moral view of guilt is rooted in an ontology of on-handness, wherein guilt is externalized and defined as a "thing" or an on-hand reality. The common expression of such an unauthentic, external view of guilt is the court-scene representation in which a person is pronounced guilty by an external judge. The transmoral concept of guilt understands guilt as a structural implication of finitude and nothingness. *Dasein* as a field of concern is basically a structure of finite possibilities, which he is free to actualize in his concrete choices. These possibilities are primarily rooted in the future; however, the past also holds possibilities that can be repeated. Thus, in his temporal existence *Dasein* is ever projected into one or another of his possibilities, choosing one and excluding another. Choice involves an inevitable sacrifice or exclusion of possibilities. In every choice, *Dasein* is "cutting off" possible alternatives that might have been but are not. These nonchosen possibilities remain structurally a part of *Dasein*'s being and constitute one expression of the nothingness of his existence:

> The nothingness which we have in mind belongs to *Dasein*'s being-free for his existential possibilities. This freedom *is* only in the choice of one, which means not-having-chosen and not-being-able-to-choose the other.

Conscience calls me to my possibilities, but I must always sacrifice some of these possibilities in choosing others. In actualizing one, I am not actualizing another, thereby becoming guilty. Every action implies guilt, but it is impossible to exist without acting. Thus, guilt is an irremovable quality of human being.

Resolution and Time

One would not be too far amiss in saying that the crowning phenomenological concept in Heidegger's *Daseinsanalytik* is resolution. Anxiety has disclosed nothingness and finitude and has revealed a world without supports. The existential reality of death has made human beings aware of their ephemeral or transitory being. Conscience has summoned *Dasein* to an acknowledgment of his inevitable guilt. However, people must drive beyond these discontinuities of existence and af-

firm their being. They do this through resolution. Resolution thus becomes a *sine qua non* for authentic existence.

This resolution is given its final meaning in Heidegger's seminal interpretation of the character of human time. Heidegger's analysis of time is in a real sense the focal point of the whole discussion in *Being and Time*. Central to Heidegger's analysis is his distinction between the quantitative, objective, and scientifically measured clock time and the qualitative, subjective time of human concern. Quantitative time is understood as an endless, passing, irreversible succession of discrete, objectivized nows. Nows are conceptualized as on-hand entities, thus betraying the restriction of this view of time to the region of on-handness. In "clock time" present moments are viewed as discrete entities. Some moments have gone by and we call them the past. They are no longer real. Some moments are yet to come and we call them the future. They are not yet real. Only the present is real. Qualitative or existential time, as contrasted with clock time, understands time as an ecstatic unity. The past, future, and present are inseparable phases of the care-structure of human existence:

> Temporality temporalizes itself fully in each ecstasy, i.e., in the ecstatic unity of the complete temporalizing of temporality there is grounded the wholeness of the structural complex of existentiality, factuality, and fallenness, which comprises the unity of the care-structure.

In existential time, the past is *still* real and the future is *already* real. Whereas quantitative time gives priority to the present, existential time gives priority to the future. Humanity's concerns are primarily oriented to the future. However, the past retains its significance in an existential view of time. The past is never existentially finished. It holds possibilities that can be repeated. Thus, we find Heidegger insisting on the importance of the notion of repetition—a notion that was introduced into modern philosophy by Kierkegaard.

Existential time provides the ontological horizon for humanity's self-understanding of its historicity. *Dasein* exists historically, which means that he is always arriving from a past, moving into a future, and deciding in the present what he is to become. The authentic self faces the future in resolution. Human beings achieve integrity when they apprehend themselves in their temporal and historical movements, acknowledge their past and future possibilities, appraise themselves in the light of their final possibility (death), and choose in the moment with the *whole* of their being. Such a self is unified or authentic. Authenticity and inauthenticity thus receive their final clarification in Heidegger's discussion of time and history. The inauthentic self of the anonymous one is a reduced self—a self that has lost itself by virtue of its fall into the mode of on-handness and its consequent sacrifice to the present. The anonymous one exists in a depersonalized and objectivized mode, in which he has dispersed himself in present concerns to the neglect of both future and past. The time that becomes normative for the anonymous one is the quantitative time of the clock and the calendar. However, this time applies only to the mode of on-handness.

The final meaning of inauthenticity is thus found in the tendency of human beings to reduce themselves and other selves to on-hand reality—to a thing or an object—that has no temporal significance beyond its simple presence as a discrete now. The authentic time of human existence is a unique, qualitative time in which past and future are always copresent. *Dasein* exists authentically when he acknowledges the unique qualitative time of his personal being and seeks to unify the three ecstasies that are structurally a part of his being as long as he is. These ecstasies are unified in resolute choice. The resolute *Dasein* thus achieves or wins his authenticity when he takes over his unique past, anticipates his unique future, and chooses in such a manner that his past and future are integrated. The past is held in memory, the future is courageously faced, and the moment is creatively affirmed as the "opportune time" for decisive action.

Calvin O. Schrag

Additional Reading

Beistegui, Miguel de. *Heidegger and the Political*. New York: Routledge, 1998. A comprehensive look at Heidegger's political and social views.

Biemel, Walter. *Martin Heidegger: An Illustrated Study*. Translated by J. L. Mehta. New York: Harcourt Brace Jovanovich, 1976. Biemel, a student under Heidegger, elucidates Heidegger's concern for Being and truth in an accessible analysis of seven works, including *Being and Time*. Dozens of black-and-white photographs of Heidegger and his contemporaries, a five-page chronology, and a twenty-page bibliography (including English translations and important secondary works) contribute to this introduction to Heidegger's thought.

Dallmayr, Fred. *The Other Heidegger*. Ithaca, N.Y.: Cornell University Press, 1993. While arguing against the idea that Heidegger's political involvement with National Socialism can be separated from his philosophical writings, Dallmayr makes an insightful and accessible case in a series of essays composing this book for why Heidegger's involvement does not imply that his philosophy should be rejected. There is, Dallymayr claims, an "other Heidegger" whose work can be read in a political but nonfascist light.

Dastur, Françoise. *Heidegger and the Question of Time*. Translated by François Raffoul and David Pettigrew. Atlantic Highlands, N.J.: Humanities Press, 1998. Referencing more than twenty works by Heidegger, this book is a clear and insightful introduction to Heidegger's question of time and being. It is for the expert in Heidegger as well as the novice.

Guignon, Charles, ed. *The Cambridge Companion to Heidegger*. London: Cambridge University Press, 1993. A collection of thirteen essays by highly respected scholars, published for the first time, on a variety of aspects of Heidegger's philosophy, including the influence of his thinking on psychotherapy, ecology, and theology. A valuable part of this collection is its bibliography, which contains a list of the publication schedule for the more than one hundred volumes of Heidegger's collected works in German, along with a list of secondary sources in English for students and others interested in the writings of the thinker whom the American philosopher Richard Rorty, one of the contributors to this book, called one of the three most important philosophers of the twentieth century.

Poggeler, Otto. *Martin Heidegger's Path of Thinking*. Translated by Daniel Magurshak and Sigmund Barber. Atlantic Highlands, N.J.: Humanities Press, 1987. Originally published in German in 1963, Poggeler's work is the most renowned critical study of the development of Heidegger's early metaphysical work into his later, nonmetaphysical thinking. For this translation of the text of the second German edition, Poggeler wrote a helpful preface and afterword.

Rée, Jonathan. *Heidegger*. New York: Routledge, 1999. An excellent biographical introduction to the thoughts of the philosopher, clearly presented and requiring no special background. Bibliography.

Steiner, George. *Martin Heidegger*. New York: Viking Press, 1978. Intended for the general reader, Steiner's short work, published soon after Heidegger's death, intertwines a short biography of the philosopher and an exposition of *Being and Time*, with a nod toward Heidegger's later works. Clarifies the central themes of Heidegger's philosophy. A brief chronology of Heidegger's life, a short bibliography of English titles, and an extensive index supplement a helpful text.

Wolin, Richard. *The Politics of Being: The Political Thought of Martin Heidegger*. New York: Columbia University Press, 1990. Motivated by the increased recognition in the 1980's of Heidegger's involvement with Nazism, Wolin seeks here to unearth political themes in Heidegger's philosophy from *Being and Time* through his later critiques of technology and humanism. From this perspective, he argues that Heidegger's involvement with National Socialism was not a "momentary lapse" of thinking but reflective of an endemic blindness to the concrete specifics of modern social life.

Zimmerman, Michael E. *Heidegger's Confrontation with Modernity: Technology, Politics, Art*. Bloomington: Indiana University Press, 1990. A critical, in-depth account of Heidegger's views on the nature of modern technology, from the perspective of the political context within which these views were formed. Zimmerman's readable style makes this book an excellent source for the general reader interested in this aspect of Heidegger's complicated work.

Dan Barnett, updated by Diane P. Michelfelder

Heraclitus of Ephesus

Heraclitus formulated one of the earliest and most comprehensive theories of the nature of the world, the cosmos, and the soul. His theory that the soul pervades all parts of the universe and its inhabitants stood in contrast to the ideas of his more mechanistic contemporaries.

Principal philosophical work: *Peri physeos,* c. 500 B.C.E. (partial translation, *The Fragments of the Work of Heraclitus of Ephesus on Nature,* 1889; also as *The Cosmic Fragments,* 1954)

Born: c. 540 B.C.E.; Ephesus, Greece
Died: c. 480 B.C.E.; place unknown

Early Life

According to the third century biographer Diogenes Laërtius (whose biographies provide some of the only information about the Greek philosophers), Heraclitus was born in the city of Ephesus to an important family that had an ancient and respected reputation. Through his family, he inherited public office, but he resigned in favor of his brother. When his friend Hermodorus was expelled from Ephesus, Heraclitus protested publicly and subsequently withdrew from public life. Heraclitus was a man of great personal integrity whose main purpose in life was to find the truth and proclaim it for the benefit of humankind, irrespective of the consequences. He attacked the sacred festival of the Bacchanalia, condemned the worship of images of the gods, and spoke unkind words about Pythagoras, Xenophanes, Hecataeus, and Hesiod. His arrogance was legendary. Heraclitus insisted that he was the sole bearer of the truth. He thought that common people were too weak of wit to understand the truth, claiming that his work was meant for the few who were intelligent.

To complicate the difficulty presented by this posture, his writings (those that survived) present special problems. Aristotle and Theophrastus observed that his statements were sometimes ambiguous, incomplete, and contradictory. It is no wonder that his contemporaries named him the Riddler, the Obscure One, and the Dark One.

Heraclitus was well aware of their criticism, but he was dedicated to his own high purposes.

Life's Work

The major work of Heraclitus that has come down to us, of which only fragments remain, was titled *Peri physeos.* He dedicated the work to Artemis and left a scroll of it in her temple, an act that was not unusual in that culture. Heraclitus would not qualify as a scientist; his talent was more that of the mystic. He had the ability to see further into the nature of things than others did. He was the first to unify the natural and the spiritual worlds, while others saw only the discrete components of nature. Anaximander and Heraclitus were both impressed with the ceaseless change of the temporal world and formulated theories about the primal matter of the universe. Anaximander's primal matter was colorless and tasteless, and otherwise had no characteristics. For Heraclitus, however, that which underlay the world of form and matter was not substance but process.

Heraclitus saw the world as a place where change, at every level and every phase of existence, was the most important phenomenon. The basic element of change, and at the heart of the process, was fire. The processes governing the world involved the four elements: fire, water, air, and earth. According to Heraclitus, fire was the element from which the others devolved, and it was always in motion. It was fire in the form of body heat that kept animal forms in motion; it was also able to transform and consume the other

Heraclitus of Ephesus. *(Library of Congress)*

basic elements. In essence, air was hot and wet, water was cold and wet, earth was cold and dry, and fire was hot and dry. Under certain circumstances, each of the four elements could be transformed into another (enough water could quench fire; a hot enough fire could reduce earth to ash, or water to steam). All the possible transformations were happening at any given time somewhere in the universe, such as in the cooking of a meal, the thawing of the winter ice, the volcanism of Mount Etna—and even in phenomena known to Heraclitus, such as the atmospheric disturbances of the sunspot cycle or the explosion of a supernova.

Heraclitus described two fundamental directions of this change. In the downward path, some of the fire thickens and becomes the ocean, while part of the ocean dies and becomes land. On the upward path, moist exhalations from the ocean and the land rise and become clouds; they then ignite (perhaps in the form of lightning) and re-

turn to fire (presumably the fiery ether, which was thought to dwell in the heights of the sky). If the fiery clouds from which the lightning comes are extinguished, however, then there is a whirlwind (a waterspout, perhaps), and once again the fire returns to the sea and the cycle is complete. All this transformation was not, however, simply random motion. There was a cosmic master plan, the Logos. Nothing in the English language translates Logos perfectly. As it stands in the beginning of the Gospel of John, it is usually translated as the Word, which is clearly inadequate in context and requires a definition. In Heraclitus's time, Logos could mean reputation or high worth. This meaning devolved from another definition of Logos: narrative or story.

The flexibility of the word has been a source of considerable debate. The three most important meanings of the word are (1) general rule or general principle, (2) the carrying out of a general principle, and (3) that which belongs distinctly to the realm of humanness, the faculty of reasoning. First and foremost, the Logos is the universal law, or plan, or process, that animates the whole cosmos. The Logos is the cosmos; it inhabits the cosmos. It is also what makes the difference between the sleeping human and the awakened human. It is, in humans, the wisdom to perceive that the Logos (on the highest level of abstraction) is immanent in the cosmos, that it is the universe's governing principle. That is the fountainhead of true knowledge in Heraclitus's system. All humans have the Logos in common. What they specifically have in common is the realization or perception that they are a part of the whole, which is the Logos. Without that realization they are fundamentally asleep. Within the slumbering human, the Logos lies dormant. Even if humans are technically awake, however, they can still be subject to error if they follow their own private "truth," that is, their own inclinations, and prefer their subjectivity more than they value the Logos. The self-dependence that one would call individuality could then be considered a violation of the Logos.

Though the physical senses are not attuned to the perception of the Logos, they are important in the process that leads to wisdom. For example, the ability to see is a prerequisite that may eventually lead to the perception that there is a plan to the universe. The senses are the mediators between that which is human and that which is cosmic. They are the windows that, during waking hours, connect the human with the portion of the Logos that can be perceived. During sleeping hours those channels are closed and the direct participation in the cosmos ceases. Respiration then becomes a channel by which the direct access can be maintained; the act of breathing maintains minimal contact. The Logos can be considered the soul of the universe. Each awakened human has a portion of higher enlightenment: the soul. Logos, Soul, and Cosmic Fire are eventually different aspects of the same abstraction—the everlasting truth that directs the universe and its conscious constituents. According to Heraclitus, the enlightened soul is hot and dry, like fire, which is why it tends upward, in the direction of the fiery ether. Soul and ether are the same material.

Soul is linked to Logos, but its roots are in the human body that it inhabits. Soul is possibly the healing principle in the body: Heraclitus likened the soul to a spider that, when its web is torn, goes to the site of the injury. Soul is born from moisture and dies when it absorbs too much water. Drunkenness was to Heraclitus a truly bad habit: A moist soul had diminished faculties as its body was also diminished, in that its intellect was stunted and its physical strength lessened.

Though the body was subject to decomposition, some souls seem to have been exempted from physical death (becoming water). Certain situations, among them dying in battle, tune the soul to such a heightened state (with the soul unusually motivated and not weakened by illness and old age) that it merges directly with the world fire. After death, there seems to be no survival of personal identity, though it is likely that the soul-stuff is merged with the Logos and that the Logos is the source of souls that exist in the physical world. Evidently, soul material follows a cycling process of its own. Heraclitus saw that the world was a unity of many parts, but the unity was not immediately manifest. The oneness of the world was the result of an infinite multiplicity. Heraclitus thought that the key to understanding this multiplicity was to look upon the world in terms of the abstract concept of harmony.

Pythagoras had previously used musical harmony in explaining the attunement and orderliness that he saw in the universe. Heraclitus, however, used the concept of harmony in a different way. He believed that harmony existed only where and when there was opposition. A single note struck on a lyre has no harmony of itself. Any two notes struck together, however, form a tension or a contrast between the two sounds, creating a continuum of possible notes between the two notes that have been struck. In terms of a continuum of hot and cold temperatures, not only do the extremes exist, but so also does the continuum exist, bounded by the extremes. At every point between the extremes of hot and cold, there is an identifiable point that has a specific temperature that is a function of both extremes.

Similarly, every virtue has a corresponding vice. Neither extreme on this scale is especially significant in human behavior: Few people, if any, represent extremes of either virtue or vice; most live in the continuum between. Ethical considerations motivate good individuals to tend toward the good in a choice between good and evil, and the measure of one's soul is where one stands on the continuum defined by good and evil. Heraclitus's most controversial statement on the subject was that the opposites that define the continuum are identical. Hate and love, therefore, would have to be one and the same. The absence of either defining term destroys the continuum, and without the continuum the two extremes cannot relate to each other. They define a world in which the people are passionate haters and ardent lovers, with no real people in between. The harmony that Heraclitus discerned was dependent on the tension between two opposites. The cosmos was, for him, a carefully and beautifully balanced entity, poised between a great multiplicity of contrasting interests, engaged in continual strife. The sum total of all these contrasting interests, however, was the harmony that no one saw except the truly enlightened souls. Only the Logos, which was One, and which created and tuned the harmony, was exempt from the balancing of opposites.

Perhaps the best known of Heraclitus's observations is that everything in the universe is constantly moving and changing. He considered all matter to be in a state of constant transformation from one form to a different form and, at the same time, from one set of physical qualities to another. Not only did he believe that the Logos bestowed life on all its parts, but he also believed that the forms of matter were intrinsically alive and that the flux was a function of the life within the matter. All life was caught up in the constant change: Everything was involved in processes of decomposition and in the reconstitution of new forms from the products of decay.

As the Greeks viewed the world, they saw only the portions of the movement that were available within the limits of their senses. Though they were not aware of the whole spectrum of movement, they were intelligent enough to extrapolate from what they could perceive. A continuous stream of water wearing away a stone was to them a good reminder of the fact that many processes of change were not perceptible in their time scale.

Heraclitus summed it up poetically in his famous analogy: "You cannot step twice into the same river, for fresh waters are flowing on." From one second to the next, the flux of things changes the world; though the river is the same river, the flux of things has moved its waters downstream, and new water from upstream has replaced the old. According to Diogenes Laërtius and others, "The cosmos is born out of fire and again resolved into fire in alternate periods for ever." One line of interpretation is that the world is periodically destroyed by a universal conflagration. More plausible, however, is the assumption that this is a restatement of Heraclitus's doctrine that fire is the one primal element from which all others derive and into which all elements are eventually transmuted by the workings of the eternal flux. In support of this argument is a phrase from the remaining fragments of Heraclitus's work: "From all things one, and from one all things." In Heraclitus's cosmology, however, there was the concept of a Great Year that occurred every 10,800 years, at which time the sun, moon, and other heavenly bodies returned to a hypothetical starting place. These bodies, though they were not exempt from the principle of constant flux, were permanent in their forms and in their heavenly paths. Beyond the measured paths of their orbits was the fiery ether of the unmoving Logos.

Influence

Heraclitus was quite unlike his contemporaries, both in terms of his personality and in the nature and scope of his thoughts. Whereas the works of his contemporaries were more in the line of primitive scientific inquiry, the endeavors of Heraclitus were more closely akin to poesy and perhaps prophecy. His aim was not to discover the material world but to seek out the governing principles within and behind the physical forms. In this respect, he was the most mystical of the Greeks.

Though the body of Heraclitus's work is faulted by time, by problems of interpretation, and by obscurity of the text (some of which was solely Heraclitus's fault), it is clear that he believed he had provided a definitive view of the processes that govern the cosmos and the workings of the human soul. His ideas were novel and daring in their time. At the center of his cosmos is the concept of constant change, which masks the concept of unity: All things are in balance, yet all things are in motion and transition, with fire playing the central role, and the Logos disposing and directing the parts. The Logos also governs human actions, reaching into the deeper parts of the personality, with the Oversoul touching the soul material within, fire outside calling to the fire within to awake, to look, to learn, to become, and to unite.

Richard Badessa

Heraclitus: Fragments

Type of philosophy: Metaphysics
First transcribed: Peri physeos, c. 500 B.C.E. (partial translation, *The Fragments of the Work of Heraclitus of Ephesus on Nature,* 1889)
Principal ideas advanced:
◇ There is a Logos, a rationale, by which all things are one.
◇ Opposites are the same (in several respects).
◇ Although opposites are unified by their interdependence, they exist in a state of constant strife.

◊ Everything is fire in that everything is involved in an eternal process of change and exchange.

◊ Failure to understand the rationale is the root of all evil.

Ancient tradition has termed Heraclitus "obscure," although many of the passages in his fragmentary *Peri physeos* (on nature), which consists of fewer than 150 sentences, are very clear in their intent and content—for instance, the denunciation of his fellow citizens:

The Ephesians ought to hang themselves, every one who is of age, and leave the city to the boys. They who threw out Hermodorus, the worthiest man of them, saying: "Let no one of us be the worthiest, but if there is one, let him go somewhere else, among others."

or his compliments to his eminent predecessor:

Learning many things does not teach one to have intelligence; else it would have taught Hesiod and Pythagoras, also Xenophanes and Hecataeus.

or his estimate of pious individuals:

They "purify" themselves by staining themselves with different blood, as if one who stepped into mud should wash it off with mud. However, one would be thought mad, if any man should see him behaving this way. And they pray to these idols, just as if one were to have a conversation with a house—knowing naught of the nature of gods and heroes.

or such remarks about human imbecility as "Dogs bark at every one they do not know" and "Donkeys would choose garbage rather than gold." Besides Hermodorus, only Bias of Priene escaped Heraclitus's contempt, and that was because Bias had said, "Most men are bad."

Logos

Heraclitus despised other men because he had made a discovery that he thought so obvious and important that failure to appreciate it was inexcusable. This was the discovery of what he called the Logos, a word that cannot be translated satisfactorily; it means not only "word" but almost anything else connected with words or what words stand for: account, discourse, argument, fame, reason, formula, pattern, rationale. One common rendering is "rationale."

Heraclitus's book began thus:

Of this Rationale [Logos], which is eternal, men turn out to be ignorant, both before they hear it and when they hear it for the first time. For although all things occur in accordance with the Rationale, they are like novices when they are tested by such words and works as I work out, distinguishing each thing according to its nature and explaining what it is. However, such things as they do when they are awake escape other men, just as they forget about what they do when asleep.

To judge from the wildly divergent interpretations of Heraclitus's teaching that have been offered since his time, people are as ignorant of Logos now as when they heard it for the first time.

"Listening not to me but to the Rationale, it is wise to agree that all things are one." This is the succinct account of the content of the Logos, which *is* the unity of all things. What Heraclitus meant is best explained by considering first the view he rejects. Most people suppose that the world is full of a number of things, each on its own, comprising a miscellaneous aggregation. The "learning many things" practiced by people such as Pythagoras and Hesiod consists of classifying the ingredients of the aggregate in accordance with a "table of opposites" and of explaining how these opposites came into being. Understanding is analysis.

This approach is utterly mistaken, Heraclitus protests. Opposites are not capable of existing: "They do not understand how what differs agrees with itself; back turning connection, as in bow and lyre." About a sixth of the extant fragments deal with opposites. They show four senses in which opposites are "the same," as Heraclitus puts it, with characteristic paradox. First, even common sense ascribes unity to what when "analyzed" proves to be full of so-called opposites:

Over those who step into the same rivers, different and again different waters flow.

The way of letters [as in a line of writing] is straight and crooked. It is one and the same.

Beginning and end are common on the circumference of a circle.

Second are polar opposites:

They would not know the name of Justice if these things [injustices] did not exist.

Sickness makes health pleasant and good; hunger, satiety; weariness, rest.

Third, there is the special kind of polar opposition that consists of the regular succession of one thing by its opposite, so that if the one perished, so would the other:

The teacher of most men is Hesiod. They understand that he knew many things—he who did not recognize day and night; for they are one.

The cold things get hot, hot gets cold, wet gets dry, parched gets damp.

Fourth, many oppositions are "subjective," dependent on the point of view or nature or interests of the observer, not on essential natures:

Swine rejoice in filth.

Sea is the cleanest and the dirtiest water: for fish it is drinkable and salubrious, but for men it is undrinkable and poisonous.

Doctors who cut and burn complain that they get no adequate pay for doing these things.

The way up and down is one and the same. [That is, the same road is "the road up" to valley dwellers and "the road down" to hill dwellers.]

Heraclitus summarizes:

Things taken together are wholes and not wholes; being brought together is being parted; concord is dissonance; and out of all things, one; and out of one, all things.

Insistence on the unity (interdependence) of opposites should not be mistaken for a denial of the existence of opposition. On the contrary, the business of opposites is to oppose, and the strife of opposites is the basic fact of existence. "It is nec-

essary to know that war is common, and justice is strife, and all things happen in accordance with strife." "War is father of all, king of all, and he shows some to be gods and some to be men; he makes some slaves and some free." "Homer deserved to be thrown out from amongst the contestants and beaten; and Archilochus likewise," their offense having been pacifism; but to pray for the cessation of warfare amounts to desiring the end of the world. Process, not substance, was Heraclitus's fundamental ontological category.

However, if the world does not consist of unrelated things, neither is it a chaos of haphazard events. What happens does so according to "measures"; the pattern of the measures is the Logos, or Justice. "The sun will not overstep measures; if he did, Furies, guardians of Justice, would find him out." "This cosmos, the same for all, no one of gods nor of men has made, but it always was and is and will be everliving fire, being kindled in measures and being extinguished in measures." "Wisdom is one thing: to know the Rationale of how all things are steered through all."

The World as Process

Philosophical speculation (as distinguished from mythology) about the nature of things had existed for hardly a century when Heraclitus wrote. His predecessors had taken it for granted (perhaps by inheritance from creation myths) that the world was made of one basic stuff, which had existed in an undifferentiated condition "in the beginning." They conceived their problems to be two: to identify this basic stuff (Thales, water; Anaximander, "the Boundless"; Anaximenes, mist; Pythagoras, number/atoms) and to describe the process of differentiation that had produced the world as we know it.

Heraclitus set himself in opposition to this tradition. The world, as a measured process, is eternal, in all its complexity. To be sure, it is "ever-living fire," but "fire" is chosen as symbolic of process, not as a "basic stuff" put forward as an alternative to water or mist or what-not. "All things are exchange for fire, and fire for all things, just as merchandise is exchange for gold and gold for merchandise" has often been cited against the present interpretation, but all the statement means is that the so-called elements merge into one another in the world process, that nothing is absolutely and eternally distinct from anything else. An obscure fragment purports to describe the exchanging: "Fire's turnings: first sea; of sea one half is earth, the other half is lightning-flash. Sea is poured out, and it is measured in the same proportion as that which it had before the earth arose."

Religion and Immortality

Though Heraclitus was scornful of popular belief, he thought, like Xenophanes, that religion should be reformed, not rejected utterly. His religious position is perhaps not too misleadingly described as pantheistic:

> God: day-night, winter-summer, war-peace, satiety-hunger. He changes in the same way as when there is a mixing [of oil] with spices, it is called after the fragrance of each.

According to this fragment, God is the organized totality of things, the unity of all apparent opposites. God, as one might expect, takes the objective view:

> To God all things are fair and good and just, but men suppose some things to be just and some unjust.

That Heraclitus thought his conception of God to be a purification of the popular notion is suggested by this fragment:

> That which alone is wise is one. It is unwilling and willing to be called by the name of Zeus.

Heraclitus taught immortality, but only in the (somewhat attenuated) sense that the soul, like everything else in the world process, is not a stuff but a process that undergoes successive phases. "There await men, when they die, such things as they do not hope for nor expect." "Immortals-mortals, mortals-immortals, living one another's death, dying one another's life." "Death to souls is to become water, to water death is to become earth, but from earth water comes into existence, and soul from water." Although "For souls it is delight to get wet," still "When a man is drunk, he is led by an immature boy, stumbling, not heeding where he steps; his soul is wet." Hence, "A dry soul is wisest and best."

Law and Evil

On the basis of this fragment Heraclitus has some claim to consideration as the founder of the philosophical theory of natural law:

> Those who speak with intelligence must take their strength from what is common to all, as a city from law, and much more strongly. For all human laws are nourished by the one divine. It has as much power as it wishes and it suffices for all and it prevails.

The one divine law is, of course, the Logos, which Heraclitus conceives not only as the formula of what *is* but also as the criterion of what ought to be: "The people should fight for the law just as for the city wall." His political views were decidedly undemocratic. Besides the denunciation of Hermodorus's banishers, three other fragments may be cited in this connection: "One man to me is ten thousand, if he is best"; "Also it is law to be persuaded by the counsel of one"; and "Every beast is driven to the pasture with a blow."

Like Socrates, Heraclitus in effect equated moral turpitude with lack of (intellectual) understanding. Failure to apprehend the Logos, that which is "common," is the root of all evil. "Thus one ought to follow what is common. However, although the Rationale is common, the many live as if they possessed private understanding." Heraclitus frequently compares "the many" to sleepers, since "For men awake there is one common cosmos, but men asleep turn away, each one, into a private world." "It is not right to act and talk like men asleep." Unfortunately it is not clear from the extant fragments just what alteration of behavior would ensue if one decided to "follow the common"—other than that one would not get drunk, nor throw out Hermodorus.

Heraclitus the Individual

"A man's character is [determines] his destiny," Heraclitus said, and the remark applies especially to himself. Though there is no reliable biographical information about him, Heraclitus's severe, haughty, enigmatic, yet pithy and curiously attractive style reveals him as a person. No one in Greek history before Socrates is so sharply delineated as an individual. It was Heraclitus's style that ensured the preservation of much of his book (which must have been a short one) through copious quotations by later writers. It was his style that led inevitably to distortions and misinterpretations of his teaching.

The two statements still most commonly attached to the name of Heraclitus are "Everything flows" and "You cannot step into the same river twice." Because of these, Heraclitus is summarized in the histories of philosophy as having taught a doctrine of perpetual change, and he is set off against the Greek philosopher Parmenides, who said that there is no such thing as change. However, many scholars doubt that either of these sentences is a genuine Heraclitean fragment; both are believed to be Platonic paraphrases that are, to say the least, misleading. Though Heraclitus, as a process philosopher, was committed to the view that reality is activity, the universality of change was not central in his thought by any means; what he stressed was rather the *ordered and eternal pattern* that intelligence (as contrasted with "learning of many things") could discern in the flux of existence—the flux itself being so obvious as not to deserve comment. As for rivers, it will be recalled that what Heraclitus actually said was that one *could* step into the same river as often as one pleased—but that when one did, "different and again different waters" would flow over one's feet, the point being to illustrate the relation of transitory particulars to a fixed pattern.

In later antiquity the Stoics found in Heraclitus's pantheism and natural law doctrine much that was congenial to their own philosophy. In consequence they looked upon him (rather sentimentally) as their progenitor. In the course of accommodating his doctrines to theirs, he was made out to have taught that fire is the basic stuff of the universe and that the world process moves in cycles, each of which is terminated by a general conflagration.

The actual teachings of Heraclitus (as distinguished from ex post facto quoting of his apothegms to decorate opinions independently arrived at) had little influence on the course of Greek philosophy. Unlike his Milesian and Pythagorean quasi contemporaries, Heraclitus made no contribution to the development of natural science. Perhaps he should be counted the founder of philosophical ethics for having related a moral code to a *Weltanschauung*, but the evidence bearing on this matter is slight, and it does not appear that he worked out this connection in any detailed way. Although his insistence on the Logos as the proper object of understanding is important, credit for it must be shared with the Milesians and Pythagoreans, his sneers at their superficiality notwithstanding.

However, as a stylist, phrase maker, and critic, Heraclitus is unique. This is not said by way of patronizing him. Heraclitus compared himself to the "Sibyl with raving mouth uttering things mirthless and unadorned and unperfumed." She "reaches over a thousand years with her voice." Heraclitus has surpassed her by many years.

Wallace I. Matson

Additional Reading

Burnet, John. *Early Greek Philosophy*. 1892. 4th ed. Reprint. London: A&C Black, 1975. Chapter 3 is devoted to Heraclitus and is probably the best of the nineteenth century English works that discuss Heraclitus. It has considerable insight and is readable without being dated.

Cohen, S. Mark, Patricia Curd, and C. D. C. Reeve, eds. *Readings in Ancient Greek Philosophy: From Thales to Aristotle*. Indianapolis: Hackett, 1995. Good introduction to Greek philosophers and their writings. Heraclitus's fragments are presented in straightforward English without commentary.

Dilcher, Roman. *Studies in Heraclitus*. New York: Olms, 1995. Intensive examination of Heraclitus. The first chapters examine the existing fragments as they relate to the conditions of human existence. The later chapters attempt to give coherence to his philosophy and resolve obscure or puzzling statements. Ends with a broad perspective of his work.

Kirk, G. S. *Heraclitus, the Cosmic Fragments*. 1954. Reprint. Cambridge, England: Cambridge University Press, 1962. A deep and thorough analysis of some of the Heraclitian fragments, this volume focuses on the "cosmic" fragments—those that are relevant to the world as a whole, the Logos, the doctrine of opposites, and the action of fire.

Kirk, G. S., and J. E. Raven. *The Presocratic Philosophers: A Critical History with a Selection of Texts*. 1957. 2d ed. Cambridge, England: Cambridge University Press, 1995. One of the chapters provides a very good analysis of Heraclitus. The book itself is one of the very best on Greek thought and the individual Greek philosophers.

Mourelatos, Alexander. *The Pre-Socratics: A Collection of Critical Essays.* 1974. Rev. ed. Princeton, N.J.: Princeton University Press, 1993. A collection of critical essays covering the major contemporaries of Heraclitus. Included in the book are four fine essays on Heraclitus.

Robinson, T. M. *Heraclitus: Fragments: A Text and Translation with a Commentary.* 1987. Reprint. Toronto: University of Toronto Press, 1991. Good first approach to Heraclitus. The introductory section examines his life and offers an overview of his work and contemporary testimony. Heraclitus's fragments are presented with side-by-side Greek text and English translation followed by concise commentary. Study concludes with a summary of his philosophical thinking, short paragraphs on Heraclitus's peers, and a detailed bibliography.

Schur, David. *The Way of Oblivion: Heraclitus and Kafka.* Cambridge, Mass.: Harvard University Press, 1998. Schur examines Heraclitus's and Kafka's work and finds similarities between the two.

Sweet, Dennis. *Heraclitus: Translation and Analysis.* Lanham, Md.: University Press of America, 1995. Opens with a brief look at Heraclitus's life. The rest examines the fragments, detailing Greek text and English translation plus commentary on facing pages. The study concludes with an analysis of Heraclitus's main themes that permeate the fragments.

Wheelwright, Philip. *Heraclitus.* 1959. Reprint. Princeton, N.J.: Princeton University Press, 1981. An excellent and well-written volume, the text reads very well because footnotes and matter not relevant to main points are relegated to the end of the book. Includes a very good bibliography.

Wilcox, Joel. *The Origins of Epistemology in Early Greek Thought: A Study of Psyche and Logos in Heraclitus.* Lewiston, N.Y.: E. Mellen Press, 1994. A critical evaluation of Heraclitus and his thought.

Richard Badessa, updated by Terry Theodore

Abraham Joshua Heschel

Heschel, a Jewish philosopher and theologian, was a leader in the Civil Rights and anti-Vietnam War movements of the 1960's and a driving force in improving relations between Christians and Jews.

Principal philosophical works: *Die Prophetie*, 1937; *The Earth Is the Lord's: The Inner Life of the Jew in East Europe*, 1950; *The Sabbath: Its Meaning for Modern Man*, 1951; *Man Is Not Alone: A Philosophy of Religion*, 1951; *Man's Quest for God: Studies in Prayer and Symbolism*, 1954; *God in Search of Man: A Philosophy of Judaism*, 1955; *The Prophets*, 1962; *Who Is Man?*, 1965; *The Insecurity of Freedom*, 1966; *Between God and Man: An Interpretation of Judaism*, 1975.

Born: January 11, 1907; Warsaw, Poland, Russian Empire (now Poland)
Died: December 23, 1972; New York, New York

Early Life

Abraham Joshua Heschel was the youngest of five children of Moshe Mordechai Heschel and Reizel (née Perlow) Heschel. His mother and father were descended from Hasidic rabbis or rebbes, nobles in the Jewish world. Heschel grew up among people whose life was devoted to the observance and study of Judaism. He was considered a prodigy in the sacred Hebrew texts, including the "Hebrew Bible" (the term Heschel preferred to "Old Testament") and the Talmud (Jewish civil and religious law). He spoke and was literate in Yiddish, Hebrew, German, and later English. As a teenager, he published his first articles on Talmudic literature. Heschel earned his reputation as a scholar and gifted writer with the publication of *Maimonides: A Biography* (1935), an interpretation of the life of the great twelfth century rabbi, physician, and philosopher.

In 1937, Martin Buber, the distinguished philosopher and educator, chose Heschel as his successor at the center for Jewish education and learning in Berlin. Heschel led educational activities connected with the German Jewish cultural renaissance that flourished during the early part of the Nazi regime. In 1938, Heschel and the other Polish Jews living in Germany were arrested and deported to Poland. He taught for eight months in Warsaw at the Institute for Jewish Studies. Heschel's mother and three of his sisters died in the Holocaust. Heschel himself narrowly avoided death three times. With the exception of Zalman Shazar, the writer who later became president of Israel, few of Heschel's childhood friends survived the Holocaust. Heschel believed the only enduring answer to the Holocaust is Jewish spiritual vitality. The Holocaust magnified his passion for social justice and his reverence for God. He was horrified by the threat of the destruction of the Jewish people and their traditions during the Holocaust. He felt it was his duty to Jews and non-Jews to preserve and revitalize the Jewish tradition. He saw his role as saving the Jewish soul from oblivion. In 1938, he helped establish the Institute for Jewish Learning in London.

Life's Work

In 1940, Heschel became an associate professor of philosophy and rabbinical studies at the Hebrew Union College in Cincinnati, Ohio. In 1945, he became a professor of Jewish ethics and mysticism at the Jewish Theological Seminary of America in New York, the center of the Conservative movement in the United States. He published a number of works, including *The Earth Is the Lord's*, *Man Is Not Alone*, *The Sabbath*, *Man's Quest for God*, *God in Search of Man*, and *The Prophets*.

In the early 1960's, Heschel became involved in issues of human suffering. He first gained national attention in 1960 when he addressed the first White House Conference on Youth. A year later, he played an active role at the White House Conference on the Aged. He became a friend and colleague of civil rights leader Martin Luther King, Jr., in 1963. In 1965, Heschel joined civil rights leaders such as King, Ralph Abernathy, Ralph Bunche, and Andrew Young in a protest march in Selma, Alabama. Heschel said he was praying with his feet when he was protesting against discrimination. Shortly after the Selma march, Heschel cofounded Clergy and Laymen Concerned About Vietnam, which became one of the strongest organizations opposed to the Vietnam War. He also enlisted the prominent Catholic priest Daniel Berrigan in the fight against continued U.S. involvement in the war in Vietnam.

In his 1951 review of *Man Is Not Alone*, Protestant theologian Reinhold Niebuhr predicted that Heschel would become a commanding and authoritative voice in the religious life of not only Jews but also everyone in the United States. In the mid-1960's, Heschel was involved with Vatican II, a council called by the pope to develop reforms in the Roman Catholic Church. In his discussions with Pope Paul VI and other Catholic leaders, Heschel advocated that the Church strengthen its relations with the Jews and members of other non-Catholic religions. Heschel initiated a movement to raise worldwide consciousness about the suppression of religious freedom among Jews in the Soviet Union. It was after reading Heschel's books that Elie Wiesel, a writer who won the 1986 Nobel Peace Prize, said he felt compelled to visit the Soviet Union and write *The Jews of Silence* (1966).

Heschel, unlike many other modern Jewish theologians, emphasized the limitations of reason in grasping humankind's dependence on the humanity and ultimate reality of God. Through his often lyrical and poetical style, he attempted to evoke an intense intimacy with the divine. He conveyed his ideas not through abstract philosophical and theological concepts but through evocative imagery. He aimed to help people recover an all-involving awareness of awe, radical amazement, and ultimately faith in the living God. His goal was to transform people's very consciousness so that they live, think, and pray in ways compatible with God's concern. He described his approach as an attempt to rediscover those questions for which religion provides answers.

Heschel's life and work are a synthesis of the traditional piety and learning of Eastern European Jewry and the philosophy and knowledge of Western civilization. He sought through his studies of the ancient and medieval sources of Judaism to offer an authentic and modern theology to the Jews of his generation. He wanted to help them with the problems and perplexities

Abraham Joshua Heschel. *(Library of Congress)*

they faced daily. He rejected the idea that any rational method or philosophical system could ever adequately prove God's existence and reality. Heschel believed that by penetrating pious people's minds, he might be able to help them appreciate and then accept the reality of God. Most of all, he believed that philosophers, theologians, religious leaders, and everyday people must be personally involved in solving moral, political, and social problems such as racial discrimination. Heschel said the standard of Jewish theology is the degree to which it affects the life of the Jew, his thoughts, and his deeds. He believed in the dignity of every person. In a June 16, 1963, letter to President John F. Kennedy, he said religious leaders had lost the right to worship God because they had failed to fight educational and housing discrimination against African Americans. Heschel believed his task was to restore the world to the kingship of God. He believed he was speaking and writing about God in God's presence.

Heschel's daughter, Susannah, a noted Jewish scholar in her own right, said the words that best describe her father's life and work are moral grandeur and spiritual audacity. He wrote and acted with the passion of a holy man, a man of faith, and the joy of being a Jew. His Jewishness infused everything he did. For Heschel, a life lived in response to the ineffable wonder of God was the only authentic human life. He believed that reality is infinitely more rich and complex than words can disclose. His teachings centered on how people can discover and embrace God's presence. He sought to show each person how to find a path to God. He wanted to demonstrate how God relates to people. He argued that religion is a leap of action and deeds rather than a leap of faith or thought. Heschel wrote about human qualities that people can cultivate in response to the world around them. His task was to show people how to perceive God's presence.

Heschel's work is a synthesis of the whole Jewish religious tradition from the Hebrew Bible, the Talmud and its compilation of Jewish civil and religious law, ancient and medieval philosophy, the mysticism of the Kabbalah, and Hasidism. Heschel's teachings may be described as mystical and prophetic. For Heschel, the Hebrew Bible was holiness in words; it is not humanity's book about humankind, but rather God's book

about humankind. Humankind, he said, should aspire to an immediate union with God. Ultimate reality is found in that union. For Heschel, the energy of Judaism derives from a person's encounter with the mystery of existence, with God, and with the meaning beyond mystery. His ultimate goal was to transform humanity's very consciousness so that people live, think, and pray in ways that are compatible with God. Humanity is precious to God, so it is humanity's responsibility to rise to God's standards. Heschel affirmed the absolute dignity of every human being. He defined religion as an answer to people's ultimate questions about their relationship with God.

To Heschel, the Hebrew Bible is the record of humanity's encounter with God and God's involvement in human life. Each individual must hear the voice of the prophets in the Bible in the context of that person's own life situation. Living is what people do with God's time and with God's world. Human beings must be inspired to understand the message. The central pillar of Heschel's theology was his belief that God needs humanity for the attainment of his ends in the world. Religion is a way by which humanity identifies itself with these ends and serves them. This mutual relation imposes a responsibility on both God and humanity. Ultimately, religion is not based on humanity's awareness of God, but on God's interest in humanity. Human beings, he said, stand for the great mystery of being God's partner. God, Heschel said, is deeply affected by human deeds. He suffers and rejoices as history unfolds. God is affected by what people do. People who commit evil acts put God in exile, unable to bring about redemption. Faith requires a leap of action, accepting the responsibility for creating a just society, for bringing an end to war and to evil, and for making possible our redemption and the end of God's captivity.

Influence

In deed and word, Heschel strove to recapture the religious dimension of life, which centers on the relationship between God and humanity. He had the power to speak to souls in search of God and exhibited an unshakable confidence in God's love for humankind. He was keenly aware that reality is infinitely richer and more complex than any words or abstract concepts can disclose.

Heschel interpreted Jewish tradition through such works as *Man Is Not Alone* and lived it through his religious and social activism. He was the first Jewish scholar appointed to the Union Theological Seminary in New York. After Heschel's death, the Catholic periodical *America* took the unprecedented step of devoting its entire March 10, 1973, issue to his memory. He was successful in preventing the inclusion of any reference to the conversion of Jews to Catholicism in any of the documents issued by the Vatican II council. The council's pronouncement on the Jews was the first Church statement devoid of any expression of hope for the conversion of Jews. Heschel holds the honor of being the first non-Christian writer ever referred to by a pope. Heschel's legacy played an important role in the formation of the Jewish Renewal movement. He was above all a great teacher and charismatic activist. Heschel taught people how to think and live religiously. He taught people how to confront the confusing complexities and difficulties of life—celebration, death, evil, joy, and suffering. Heschel was, as the theologian Reinhold Niebuhr predicted in 1951, a commanding and authoritative voice in Jewish and religious life in the United States.

Fred Buchstein

Man Is Not Alone

A Philosophy of Religion

Type of philosophy: Jewish philosophy, metaphysics, philosophy of religion
First published: 1951
Principal ideas advanced:

◇ Philosophers can neither prove nor disprove the existence of God.
◇ Faith is a spontaneous feeling for God's presence.
◇ Evaluating faith in terms of reason is like trying to understand love and beauty as algebraic equations.
◇ Only people who are willing to stake their whole lives on the truth of the invisible reality that is God will have faith in him.

◇ God is a partner in humanity's struggle against evil and for justice, peace, holiness, and doing the work of God's creation.
◇ Judaism teaches that humanity is in need of God because God is in need of humanity.
◇ Jewish existence is living a life shared with God and compatible with the presence of God.
◇ The Hebrew Bible is the story of God's quest for righteous people.

Man Is Not Alone is a masterly analysis of faith and the search for authentic religious expression. Abraham Joshua Heschel was most concerned with the *act* of believing, not the *contents* of believing, as were many philosophers and theologians. What makes Heschel distinctive among Jewish thinkers is his belief that God needs people as partners in the work of creation.

Heschel's perspective is that of an interpreter of the Hebrew Bible (Old Testament) and Judaic tradition. He deeply and personally felt the horrors, pain, and sorrow of the Holocaust, which he viewed as a threat to the future of Jews and the traditions of Judaism. He struggled to kindle his contemporaries' faith in God and to preserve the Jewish perspective. Heschel believed that God needs humanity to do the work of his creation, so he devoted his life to reawakening people's faith in God and alerting them to their need to do God's work as his partner. Humanity is endowed with the ability to fulfill what God demands. Sin, in Heschel's view, is the failure to fulfill one's obligations to God. He ignites people's sense of the ineffable, their amazement, and their wonder that the world and they themselves even exist. He urges people to live a pious life.

Man Is Not Alone is a systematic exposition of Jewish ethics, faith, mysticism, and prayer. Heschel said God requires people to act justly, love mercy, walk humbly with him, and revere the Sabbath. Ultimately, religion is not based on people's awareness of God, but on God's need of human beings as partners. This means no one is ever truly alone, as God is everywhere.

The Ineffable
The book focuses on the problem of God and problem of living from a Jewish perspective. It opens with an exploration of the ineffable—Heschel's word for the reality that lies beyond people's abil-

ity to articulate it. People encounter the ineffable; people do not create it. The ineffable is conceivable despite its being inexpressible or even unknowable. It is a universal perception. The concept of the ineffable accounts for the diversity of humanity's attempts to describe reality in words. When people sense the ineffable, they are immediately as certain of the value of the world as they are that it exists. People are compelled to pay attention to that which lies beyond their grasp.

Heschel wrote that human beings must stand in radical amazement that they exist at all. Sadly, Heschel said, too many people have lost their will to wonder. A life without wonder is not worth living. After Heschel resurrects people's sense of the ineffable, he urges them to revel in the awe and wonder that the world and they themselves exist. He then leads readers to the awareness that people are objects of God's concern. Further, he says, people are obliged to be partners with God in doing his work. Religion begins with people's sensing the ineffable, with an awareness of a reality beyond their logical concepts. People must open themselves to encounters with God. People first must possess an intuition of a divine presence and then acknowledge his essence.

Acknowledging God

Heschel differs from the speculative philosophers and theologians who proceed from an idea of God's essence to a belief in his existence. He proceeds from an intuition of God's presence to his essence. The root of religion is the question of what people do with their awe and wonder. People can either accept the presence and reality of God or accept the absurdity of denying it. For Heschel, the issue is not whether God exists, but whether people acknowledge there is a God. God exists and people must be faithful, intelligent, and intuitive enough to affirm that reality. Belief is born when mind and soul agree. God is not an abstract concept derived from philosophical investigations. Rather, people know God exists because of immediate and self-evident insight.

God sues for people's devotion as soon as they long to know him. Faith is people's aspiration to maintain their responsiveness to the living God. Humanity must first sense the ineffable, then react to God's expectations. Heschel shows people

how to respond to their obligations to God and their fellow human beings. He says God is neither an explanation of the world's enigmas and horrors nor a guarantee of salvation. The only thing people know about God is his name, which is ineffable. Neither an image nor a definition of God exists. Although people cannot express what they know about God, God expresses his will to them. People know through God himself that he is not beyond good and evil. For Heschel, the notion that God is a perfect being is just pure insolence. Neither biblical nor rabbinical literature attributes perfection to God. For Heschel, the ultimate principle of religion and ethics is that people feel obliged to do good because it is good. Wickedness is a disease, and evil is identical with death. Evil alienates people from other human beings and from God.

Religion begins where experience ends. It is at that point that people acquire the perception of being perceived. The essential content of Heschel's prophetic revelation is that people comprehend only what God asks of people. According to Heschel, the Hebrew Bible is the record of God's vision of humanity. The Hebrew Bible is the story of God's quest for the righteous person, not a history of the Jewish people. It reveals what God asks of humanity. It shows people how to commune with God's will. God is not the object of discovery but the subject of revelation. The Hebrew Bible shows that people know nothing about the attributes of God. All people can ascribe to God is his existence. Asking why people believe is like asking why people perceive. People trust in God because he is the living God. People arrive in the dimension of the holy when they grow beyond their self-interest, when they are concerned about the interest and welfare of others. God exhibits pure concern for his creatures. From the Hebrew Bible, people learn only about God's acts done for the sake of humanity—acts of creation, acts of redemption, and acts of revelation. We also learn that people should be faithful to the concerns of God. The only attribute the Hebrew Bible ascribes to God is that he is the Merciful One.

Faith in Action

According to Heschel, people forced God into exile or hiding through their acts of evil and horror. Humankind forsook its covenant with God. Humanity can rely on God only if God can rely on humanity. Having faith in God means justifying God's faith in humanity. Faith is a communion between God and humanity. Heschel says people must live their lives as if the fate of all time depends on a single moment and a single act. Whatever people do to other people, they do to God. People must strive to become what they are able to become. The true meaning of existence is found in fulfilling other people's needs. Living the religious life means serving God's ends, which he needs people's help to achieve. Humanity is thus indispensable to God. Humanity is not an innocent and passive bystander in the universe. Whatever one does to another person, one does to God. Ignoring God means defying him.

To Heschel, all religion begins with a sense that something is asked of people. That something is an ultimate commitment to God. The Judaism of the Hebrew Bible and rabbinical tradition defines religion as people's awareness that God is interested in them. Judaism teaches people never to be pleased with what they are. Happiness for Jews is having the vision of a goal that is yet to be reached. A life lived with God is the central idea of Judaism. The core of the Jewish religion is the quest for right living, right here, right now. Judaism is a theology of the common deed.

According to Heschel, piety is putting faith into action. The pious life is compatible with God's presence and will. Pious people are at peace with this life because of their attitude of reverence. When calamities occur, pious people do not grumble or lapse into despair. They do not do so because they regard nature and their own thoughts, life, and destiny as the property of God. Pious people recognize that all life and all their possessions are gifts of God. Every person—regardless of gender, mind, possessions, and race—is made in the image of God. Pious people believe they are obligated to give back to God what they have received from him by serving God. They have pledged their allegiance and faith to God. Piety is a life spent in pursuit of God's will. Pious people believe it is their destiny to contribute. They place their entire life at the disposal of God. Humanity is independent and free only before God. People know that it is their destiny to aid and to serve God's will. Their reward is in the here and now, not the hereafter.

The Return of Wonder

The publication of *Man Is Not Alone* in 1951 was widely hailed as a significant event. The prominent Protestant theologian Reinhold Niebuhr, for example, said the book revealed how to accept the ineffable reality of God. In hindsight, he was correct in predicting that Heschel would become a commanding and authoritative figure in the life of Jews and non-Jews in the United States and elsewhere in the world. Other contemporary reviewers suggested the book represented a breakthrough in the prevalent poverty of religious thought and expression. Theologians and philosophers had forgotten the living God and were single-mindedly focused on proving the existence of an abstract God. They had lost their sense of the ineffable and radical amazement at the very existence of a living God. In his book, Heschel wrote that God is not an object of cognition, and reason cannot furnish people with the clue to the ultimate reality of God. People possess an intuition of God's presence and voice. God is waiting and looking for humanity and reveals himself in people's everyday deeds.

Heschel's reputation as one of the leading Jewish thinkers has grown with time. For many Jews and non-Jews alike, he restored the place of awe, radical amazement, and wonder in their lives and religion. Heschel helped many people recognize the power of prayer to shift the center of living from self-consciousness and self-importance to surrender to God's voice and will. He resurrected the living God, the God who cares passionately about the quality of human life. He sought to turn people's focus to God and to encourage them pray to him.

Fred Buchstein

Additional Reading

Friedman, Maurice. *Abraham Joshua Heschel and Elie Wiesel: You Are My Witnesses*. New York: Farrar, Straus, Giroux, 1987. This book features an assessment of Abraham Joshua Heschel's life and work by a noted expert on Martin Buber and other Jewish thinkers. Friedman also includes a revealing account of his personal relationship with Heschel.

Granfield, Patrick. *Theologians at Work*. New York: Macmillan, 1967. The author, a theologian, interviewed Heschel on a variety of topics, such as cooperation between Christians and Jews, evil, and God. The interviews show Heschel's commonsense approach to theology and his opinion of the Jewish thinker Martin Buber.

Heschel, Susannah, ed. *Moral Grandeur and Spiritual Audacity: Essays by Abraham Joshua Heschel*. New York: Farrar, Straus, Giroux, 1996. Heschel's daughter, a noted Jewish scholar, has written a compelling and revealing short biography of her father as an introduction to the book. She includes stories on Heschel's relationship with Martin Luther King, Jr., and Pope Paul VI. She says the title of the book is the best description of her father's work and legacy.

Kaplan, Edward K., and Samuel H. Dresner. *Abraham Joshua Heschel: Prophetic Witness*. New Haven, Conn.: Yale University Press, 1998. This book, the first of two planned volumes, is a comprehensive biography of Heschel. The volume traces Heschel's life in Europe and ends with his immigration to the United States in 1940. It is based on interviews with Heschel's friends and family, archival documents, and previously unknown writings by Heschel. The authors portray Heschel's charisma and shortcomings. It is an important work on an important Jewish thinker.

Kasimow, Harold, and Byron L. Sherwin, eds. *No Religion Is an Island: Abraham Joshua Heschel and Interreligious Dialogue*. Maryknoll, N.Y.: Orbis Books, 1991. This collection includes remembrances of Heschel written by his daughter Susannah Heschel and others who knew him as a friend and teacher. The second part of the book contains an assessment of Heschel's message from a variety of viewpoints, including those of Protestants, Catholics, Muslims, and Hindus.

Merkle, John C. *Abraham Joshua Heschel: Exploring His Life and Thought*. New York: Macmillan, 1985. The author, a theologian, collected a variety of essays that remember Heschel the man and assess Heschel the biblical theologian, philosopher, poet, and social critic.

_____. *The Genesis of Faith: The Depth Theology of Abraham Joshua Heschel*. New York: Macmillan, 1985. This work is a thorough and valuable exploration and assessment of Heschel's doctrines.

Moore, Donald J. *The Human and the Holy: The Spirituality of Abraham Joshua Heschel*. New York: Fordham University Press, 1989. The author, a theologian, examines Heschel from a Christian perspective and assesses Heschel's spiritual legacy. This account is an affectionate one of Heschel as a person, a thinker, and a contributor to stronger bonds between Christians and Jews. It also shed lights on Heschel's prominent role in the Vatican II council.

Fred Buchstein

Hildegard von Bingen

The first major German mystic, Hildegard, in her prolific writings and extensive preaching, exerted a widespread influence on religious and political figures in twelfth century Europe.

Principal philosophical works: *Scivias*, 1141-1151 (English translation, 1986); *Liber vitae meritorum*, 1158-1163 (*The Book of the Rewards of Life*, 1994); *Liber divinorum operum*, 1163-1173 (also known as *De Operatione Dei*; *Book of Divine Works with Letters and Songs*, 1987); *The Letters of Hildegard of Bingen*, 1994-1998 (2 volumes); *Secrets of God: Writings of Hildegard of Bingen*, 1996.

Born: 1098; Bermersheim near Alzey, Rheinhessen (now in Germany)
Died: September 17, 1179; Rupertsberg near Bingen (now in Germany)

Early Life

Born in 1098 in Bermersheim near Alzey, Rheinhessen (in modern Germany), Hildegard von Bingen was the tenth and last child of Hildebert von Bermersheim, a knight in the service of Meginhard, Count of Spanheim, and his wife, Mechtild. At her birth, her parents consecrated Hildegard to God as a tithe. As early as the age of three, Hildegard had her first vision of a dazzling white light, which she was later to call the *umbra viventis lucis* (shadow of the living Light), which appeared to her as reflected in a *fons vitae* (shining pool). Other visions followed, along with accurate premonitions of the future. When she was eight years old, her parents entrusted her to the care of the learned Jutta of Spanheim, a holy anchoress attached to the Benedictine Abbey of Mount Saint Disibode.

Hildegard's visions continued during her adolescence, but embarrassed when she began to realize that she was alone in seeing them, she began to keep them to herself, confiding only in Jutta. In spite of ill health, Hildegard began her studies under Jutta, learning to read and sing Latin. Her further education was entrusted to the monk Volmar of Saint Disibode, who, over time, became her lifelong friend, confidant, and secretary. At age fourteen, she took vows and received the veil from Bishop Otto von Bamberg, the hermitage of Jutta having by this time attracted enough followers to become a community under the Rule of Saint Benedict.

The next two decades were formative years for Hildegard: She acquired an extensive knowledge of the Scriptures, the church fathers and later church writers, the monastic liturgy, science, medicine, and philosophy. From her later writings, it is possible to trace specific writers she studied during this period: Saint Augustine, Boethius, Saint Isidore of Seville, Bernard Silvestris, Aristotle, Galen, Messahalah, Constantine the African, Hugh of Saint Victor, and Alberic the Younger. Meanwhile, she continued to experience the charisma of her mystical visions. When Jutta died in 1136, Hildegard, at thirty-eight, was unanimously elected abbess by the nuns of her community.

Life's Work

The turning point in Hildegard's life came in 1141, when she received a commandment from God: "Write what you see and hear! Tell people how to enter the kingdom of salvation!" She initially went through a period of self-doubt: How could she, *ego paupercula feminea forma* (a poor little figure of a woman), be chosen as a mouthpiece for God?—and was concerned as to whether others would give credence to her visions. She finally confided fully in her confessor, the monk Godfrey, who referred the matter to his abbot, Kuno. Kuno ordered Hildegard to write down some of her visions, which he then submitted to the Archbishop of Mainz. The archbishop

Self-portrait by Hildegard von Bingen from a facsimile of the lost *Codex Rupertsberg. (Erich Lessing/Art Resource)*

an extensive correspondence of more than one hundred letters to popes, emperors, kings, archbishops, abbots, and abbesses; she also began to journey throughout Germany and France preaching against the abuses and corruption of the Church. As her visions led her to an active role in church and social reform, she came to accept her link with the tradition of the female prophets (Deborah, Olda, Hannah, Elizabeth).

In 1147, when Pope Eugenius III held a synod in Trier, he appointed a commission to examine Hildegard's writing. Bernard of Clairvaux, with whom Hildegard had corresponded, spoke affirmatively of her. Subsequently, in a letter to Hildegard, the pope approved her visions as authentic manifestations of the Holy Spirit and, warning her against pride, gave her apostolic license to continue writing and publishing. Hildegard, in return, wrote the pope a long letter urging him to work for reform in the Church and the monasteries. The woman who initially had felt timid serving as a mouthpiece for the Word of God was beginning to speak with the uncompromising sense of justice that was to characterize her prophetic and apostolic mission for the rest of her life.

With the pope's endorsement of her visions, Hildegard's renown and the number of postulants at her convent grew, and she determined to separate from the monastery of Saint Disibode and to found a new community at Rupertsberg, near Bingen, a site that had been revealed to her in a vision. Despite the objections of the monks of Saint Disibode and their abbot, Kuno, who would lose prestige and revenue with her departure, Hildegard used family connections with the Archbishop of Mainz to secure the property and personally oversaw the construction of a convent large enough to house fifty nuns. In 1150, she moved to Rupertsberg with eighteen other nuns. As abbess, Hildegard managed to obtain exclusive rights to the Rupertsberg property from Abbot Kuno in 1155, and several years later it was arranged that she would respond directly to the Archbishop of Mainz as her superior rather than to the abbot of Saint Disibode.

determined that Hildegard's visions were indeed divinely inspired, and Hildegard ultimately came to accept a view of herself as a woman chosen to fulfill God's work.

A ten-year collaboration between Hildegard and her secretary Volmar began, as she dictated to him her principal work, *Scivias,* an abbreviation for *Scito vias Domini,* or "know the ways of the Lord," consisting of twenty-six visions dealing with the relationships and interdependence between the triune God and humans through the Creation, Redemption, and Church. The visions also contained apocalyptic prophecies and warnings, which would motivate Hildegard to begin

Under Hildegard's leadership, the new community flourished, as did her own work and creative production. In 1151, she completed *Scivias*, concluding the work with a liturgical drama set to music. *Ordo virtutum* (1151) is the earliest known morality play and a dramatic work of considerable originality and merit. Between 1151 and 1158, seventy-seven individual hymns and canticles that she had written for her nuns were collected in a lyrical cycle entitled *Symphonia harmonia caelestium revelationum* (the harmonious symphony of heavenly revelations), which, according to Peter Dronke, contains "some of the most unusual, subtle, and exciting poetry of the twelfth century." Her music, ranging in mood from tranquil lyricism to declamatory intensity, includes some of the finest songs written in the Middle Ages.

Hildegard, who in addition to her responsibilities as abbess served in the convent infirmary, commenced work on two books on natural history and medicine. Characterized by careful scientific observation, Hildegard's medical and scientific studies contain the prototypes of some modern methods of diagnosis and anticipate certain later discoveries such as circulation of the blood and psychosomatic illness. She also wrote a commentary on the Gospels, an explication of the Rule of Saint Benedict and one of the Athanasian Creed, and the lives of Saint Rupert and Saint Disibode.

It was primarily for her mystical trilogy that Hildegard was known in her day: *Scivias*, a treatise on ethics titled *The Book of the Rewards of Life*, and *Book of Divine Works*, a vast cosmology and theodicy. It is these works, together with her letters, that primarily account for the late twentieth century renaissance in Hildegard scholarship. The illuminated manuscript of *Scivias* that was prepared at her scriptorium in 1165 is of interest not only to modern theologians and art historians but also to the layperson desiring access to her prolific and sometimes abstruse work.

Known by her twelfth century contemporaries as the *prophetissa* Teutonica, the Sibyl of the Rhine, Hildegard continued, into her seventies and eighties, to travel widely in Germany and France, providing spiritual direction and preaching. Pilgrims flocked to her convent; her advice was sought by popes and archbishops, emperors and kings, religious and laypersons of all classes. Her influence in twelfth century Europe was considerable. Through the years, she corresponded with four popes—Eugene III, Anastasius IV, Adrian IV, and Alexander III—and with two German emperors, Conrad III and his son and successor Frederick I Barbarossa, whom she rebuked for supporting an antipope. She also sent letters to Henry II of England and his queen Eleanor, the divorced wife of Louis VII. She corresponded with Bernard of Clairvaux and preached his crusade in her travels. She corresponded continuously with the Archbishop of Mainz and with bishops and clergy throughout Germany, the Low Countries, and central Europe. Moreover, she maintained a personal correspondence with twenty-five abbesses of various convents. Constant and uncompromising themes in her letters were condemnation of the abuses and corruption within both church and secular government and the need for social justice, compassion, and wisdom.

The year before her death, when she was in her eighties, Hildegard faced a difficult ethical trial. Her community was placed under interdict for having buried in the convent cemetery a revolutionary youth who had been excommunicated. Hildegard refused to have the body exhumed and removed as ordered; instead, she blessed the grave with her abbatial staff and removed all traces of it. In her view, although the young man had been excommunicated, because he had been absolved and reconciled with the Church before dying, he merited a sacred burial. The interdict forbade the community to hear Mass, receive the Eucharist, or sing the Divine Office. As painful as the interdict was to Hildegard, her sense of justice and her fidelity to her "living Light," no matter what the cost to her, led her to withstand the pressure to give in; she would not let the letter of the law stand before the spirit of the law. Hildegard wrote numerous letters of protest to the appropriate authorities, until finally her argument prevailed and the interdict was removed. Six months later, in 1179, she died.

Influence

The first major German mystic, Hildegard has never been formally canonized (three proceedings were initiated in the thirteenth and fourteenth centuries, but none was ever completed), yet she is included in the martyrologies and in the Acta Sanctorum under the title "saint," and in 1979, Pope John Paul II, on the eight hundredth anniversary of Hildegard's death, referred to her as "an outstanding saint." Through her preaching, writings, and correspondence, she actively influenced the decisions and policies of religious and political leaders of her day. The founder of the Rhineland mystic movement, she influenced later medieval mystics, including Mechtild of Magdeburg and Meister Eckhart. Further, the themes of ecology, social responsibility, the cocreativity of human beings, feminine aspects of the divine, and the interconnectivity of the cosmos in her visionary writings have been noted by Creation-centered theologians in the twentieth century.

Although philosophically Hildegard accepted the Catholic medieval view of woman's subordination to man, based on the doctrine of the Fall, her visions encouraged her to become highly independent in her thinking, actions, and creations. She made significant contributions in her medical writings. Her poetry, music, and liturgical drama *Ordo virtutum* are original in form and ideas. Her visionary works, while they also provide a compendium of contemporary thought, are a unique phenomenon in twelfth century letters, as are the manuscript illuminations that accompany them. Considering the originality of her visionary cosmology, it is not surprising that Hildegard has been compared to both Dante Alighieri and William Blake.

Jean T. Strandness

Secrets of God

Writings of Hildegard of Bingen

Type of philosophy: Ethics, metaphysics, philosophical theology
First published: 1996
Principal ideas advanced:

⋄ God, or ultimate reality, is love and mutual interconnectedness; human beings, created in God's image, find their true identity in inter-connectedness (*veriditas*) with God, one another, and all of creation.

⋄ It is through embodying such mutual interconnectedness in one's historical place and time that the individual grows and reaches fulfillment; at the same time, human society is bettered as individuals work toward the establishment of just government.

⋄ *Veriditas*, or interconnectedness, means greenness and symbolizes the life that develops and flows when God's Trinitarian love is placed at the center of reality and of one's consciousness.

⋄ Jesus Christ's desire to become incarnate in this world was the epitome of God's desire to be united with humanity through an outpouring of love; Mary, the mother of Christ, was the human embodiment and model of *veriditas*, for she became the womb through which God became present in human form.

⋄ *Ariditas*, or dryness or aridity, a lack of fruitfulness, can be brought about by "Godforgetfulness," a centering of human consciousness in material things rather than in the spiritual reality of God's love.

⋄ Aridity causes people to be unable to live within the tensions of polar opposites—the feminine and the masculine, good and evil—and unable to discern the good or evil consequences of each choice before it is made.

⋄ *Rationalitas*, or understanding or reason, is not mere intellectual clarification but comes about through love and interconnectedness with God and with reality as it was meant to be; it derives from mutual interrelatedness with others and with the elements of the cosmos, a kind of connected knowing.

Secrets of God: Writings of Hildegard of Bingen is a representative selection of all the works written by Hildegard of Bingen. It includes not only extensive excerpts from her philosophical works but also portions of her writings in biography, physics, and medicine. To reflect Hildegard's artistic accomplishments, the collection contains samples of her liturgical poetry and four of her mandala-like illustrations.

Hildegard wrote during the twelfth century at a time when the Church, while externally engaged in crusades against "infidels," was badly in need of internal reform. It was a time of transition and turbulence when nation-states were forming, commerce was expanding, European cities were flourishing, and a new era of learning was beginning to challenge the influence of monastic culture. As a Benedictine nun, Hildegard herself was steeped in monastic culture, and its influence can be seen throughout her writing. Saint Benedict's Rule of Life called for reading and reflecting on Scripture and listening and seeing all things with an open heart so that one could find God's voice wherever it manifested itself. It was a life of constant discernment and conscious awareness. Hildegard received her prophetic call in 1141 and continued writing until she finished her last visionary work in 1174.

Scivias

Secrets of God first presents excerpts from Hildegard's initial work, popularly known as *Scivias* (1141-1151; English translation, 1986), an abbreviation for the full Latin title *Scito vias Domini*, or "know the ways of the Lord." The work is divided into three separate books, containing six, seven, and thirteen visions respectively. *Scivias* initiates a structure for the communication of visions. She first describes the vision she has received and then transmits the explanation of the vision that she heard as a voice from heaven. The explanation is usually an allegorical interpretation of the vision, contains points on doctrine or morality that are backed up by Scripture, and ends with an admonition that remains constant throughout each book. Given Hildegard's theological grounding in the Trinity, it is not surprising that the three books of *Scivias* focus on three doctrinal areas: Creation, the work of the Father; Redemption, the work of the Son; and Sanctification, the work of the Holy Spirit.

The prologue to *Scivias*, included in *Secrets of God*, presents the intense vision in which God commanded her to share what she saw and heard. The excerpts from the first book of *Scivias* reveal Hildegard's belief that while human beings live in a fallen world because of the sin of Adam and Eve, that was never God's intention. People, along with all the other elements of creation, are longing for the same rebirth that God desires. The second book of *Scivias* reveals Hildegard's belief that the Incarnation of the Son and his act of Redemption are the primal points of Christian doctrine and the embodiment of God's loving and continued presence in the world. Although Hildegard dwells on all the sacraments of the Catholic Church, only two, baptism and matrimony, appear in *Secrets of God*; however, these selections are sufficient to make clear Hildegard's emphasis on the sacraments as a means of greater interconnectedness between people. The third book of *Scivias* contains visions that describe an allegorical building, the "edifice of salvation," which God upholds and in which virtues dwell. Through the building imagery, Hildegard gives an account of God's salvific work through history. Through the personification of various virtues, Hildegard discusses her conception of the moral life. The vision dealing with the virtue of discretion, a virtue key in Hildegard's philosophy, serves to illustrate Hildegard's moral concerns. Another vision included is that of the last judgment when history ends in a triumph of virtue and renewed creation.

The Rewards of Life and Divine Works

Hildegard's *The Book of the Rewards of Life* consists of six visions, all of which are variations on an immense figure of a man. Superimposed on the image of the world, he stretches from what Hildegard calls "the heaven" to "the abyss." From this vantage point, the man observes the interaction between the powers of light and the powers of darkness. In all, thirty-five vices and their oppositional virtues are presented. Collectively, the work demonstrates the opposing forces that shape human ethical behavior. It also demonstrates Hildegard's keen insight into human behavior, probing into people's deepest desires and defenses. *Secrets of God* conveys the almost apocalyptic initiating vision and gives a sense of Hildegard's ethical terrain, emphasizing especially humanity's need to become aware of deeply ingrained and socially set patterns of thinking, feeling, and interaction that defend a comfortable but sterile way of life.

Hildegard began *Book of Divine Works with Letters and Songs* in 1163 and completed it in 1173. Consisting of three books, it is considered Hildegard's most mature work on cosmology, salvation history, and eschatology, or things dealing with the end of the world. It emphasizes humanity's favored place in creation and argues that humanity, creation, and God are intimately interrelated. *Secrets of God* conveys Hildegard's holistic vision. It begins with her vision of *rationalitas*, a fiery human figure who is the Word who brought forth and sustains all life. As the visions continue, he is revealed as Love, the matrix or womb of all life.

Natural History and Medicine

Between 1151 and 1158, Hildegard composed *Physica* (*Natural History*; also known as *The Book of Simple Medicine*) and *Causae et Curae* (*Causes and Cures*; also known as *The Book of Compound Medicine*). Unlike the previous books, these are not structured in a visionary form although a mystical introduction may have existed at one time. *Physica* has nine parts, each of which is devoted to a category of creatures. *Causae et Curae* begins with an account of cosmology and the place of human beings within creation. It also contains a treatise on humoral medicine that shows Hildegard's departure from some traditionally held beliefs. It also offers a description of more than two hundred diseases, giving remedies for many of them. Finally it offers some astrological predictions based on the phases of the moon at the time of conception. *Secrets of God* gives a representative sampling of the various divisions of these books.

Songs and Biographies

Hildegard was a musician as well as a philosopher, theologian, herbalist, and abbess of a large and thriving convent. More than seventy of her various liturgical songs, probably composed for use in her convent, were collected into *Symphonia armonie celestium revelationum* (*Symphony of the Harmony of Celestial Revelations*, 1988). To complete its survey of Hildegard's writings, *Secrets of God* features two of her biographies, those of Saint Rupert and Saint Disibodi, and some specimens of her vast correspondence.

Hildegard's Legacy

The variety of people from all walks of life who corresponded with Hildegard during her lifetime attests the impact she had on her contemporaries. However, her work lay virtually forgotten for more than eight hundred years after her death. In the late twentieth century, Hildegard's own order of nuns, the Benedictines, eagerly researched, translated, and published Hildegard's works, making her works available to the German-speaking world. They attracted both scholars and people seeking spiritual guidance. In 1979, on the eight hundredth anniversary of Hildegard's death, the bishops of Germany petitioned Rome to have her declared a Doctor of the Church. Her influence has been rapidly spreading to other countries, especially to the United States. *Secrets of God* attempts to open the broad range of Hildegard's works to an increasing number of readers who are interested in all aspects of Hildegard's thinking. Feminist scholars are interested in the feminist aspects of God revealed in Hildegard's visions and perceptions of the divine. Practitioners of homeopathic medicine are intrigued by her natural remedies. Other scholars are at work to make her medieval mind-set and the anagogical structure of her work accessible to the modern consciousness.

Christine R. Catron

Additional Reading

Craine, Renate. *Hildegard: Prophet of the Cosmic Christ*. Spiritual Legacy series. New York: Crossroad, 1997. This volume covers the life and works of Hildegard of Bingen, a phenomenal woman born hundreds of years before her time. A visionary, mystic, author, artist, musician and composer, holistic healer, theologian, and Benedictine abbess, Hildegard did not accept her gift until the age of forty-two but still left behind a vast legacy that is discussed in this revealing biography.

Dronke, Peter. *Women Writers of the Middle Ages*. Cambridge, England: Cambridge University Press, 1984. A substantial study of the nature of Hildegard's visionary experiences and their influence on the development of her cosmological thought. Focuses on Hildegard's autobiographical writings, her letters, and her medical treatises, including excerpts from selected text and letters in the Latin original and in translation.

Newman, Barbara. *Sister Wisdom: St. Hildegard's Theology of the Feminine*. Berkeley: University of California Press, 1987. A comprehensive scholarly study that examines Hildegard's contributions within the context of twelfth century thought and also as part of the sapiential tradition.

_____, ed. *Voice of the Living Light: Hildegard of Bingen and Her World*. Berkeley: University of California Press, 1998. Compiled in conjunction with the nine hundredth birth anniversary of Hildegard of Bingen, the nine essays in this book offer an intriguing look at the life and work of this remarkable woman. She was the first woman given permission by the pope to write theological books, and she also preached openly to both the clergy and the common people.

Pernoud, Regine. *Hildegard of Bingen: Inspired Conscience of the Twelfth Century*. Translated by Paul Duggan. New York: Marlowe, 1998. In addition to discussing the writings and visions of this influential twelfth century abbess, Pernoud provides information about Hildegard's life. He offers insight into the turbulent political times she lived in and the effect she had on princes, the populace, and popes, through her correspondence.

Jean T. Strandness, updated by Lisa A. Wroble

Hippocrates

Hippocrates is credited with separating the practice of medicine from magic and superstition, inaugurating the modern practice of scientific observation, and setting the guidelines for high standards of ethical medical practice.

Principal philosophical works: *Corpus Hippocraticum*, fifth to third centuries B.C.E. (*The Genuine Works of Hippocrates*, 1849, 2 volumes; also known as *Hippocrates*, 1923-1995, 8 volumes, and *The Medical Works of Hippocrates*, 1950).

Born: c. 460 B.C.E.; Island of Cos, Greece
Died: c. 370 B.C.E.; Larissa, Thessaly

Early Life

Hippocrates was born on the island of Cos and lived from about the end of the fifth century through the first half of the fourth century B.C.E., according to two references to him in the dialogues of the Greek philosopher Plato. Though little else can be thoroughly documented, many legends, possibly true in parts, have been offered by commentators regarding Hippocrates' early life. According to tradition, Hippocrates was one of several sons of Praxithea and Heracleides. He probably had the education suitable to an individual of his background, which would include nine years of physical education, reading, writing, spelling, music, singing, and poetry. After another two years at a gymnasium, where he would have had intensive training in athletics, it is conjectured that Hippocrates studied medicine under his father, a member of the priest-physician group known as Asclepiads. This training was a form of apprenticeship in a medical guild.

In addition to his training, which consisted of following a physician and observing his treatment of patients, Hippocrates is believed to have traveled to the nearby islands of the Aegean Sea, to the Greek mainland, and possibly to Egypt and Libya, to study the local medical traditions. He is thought to have met the philosopher Democritus and the rhetorician Gorgias.

His sons Thessalus and Draco carried on the family tradition of medical practice. As testimony to his fame, legend also has it that King Perdiccas of Macedonia asked Hippocrates and another physician, Euryphon, to examine him and that Hippocrates helped him to recover from his illness.

Hippocrates was equally renowned as a teacher, giving rise to the image of the "Tree of Hippocrates" beneath which students sat and listened to him. Plato, a younger contemporary, referred to Hippocrates the Asclepiad as a model teacher of medicine. Some historical accounts suggest that Hippocrates habitually covered his head with a felt cap, though the reason for this habit is only a matter of speculation. This description did, however, help twentieth century archaeologists identify a likeness of him.

Life's Work

That Hippocrates was a well-known Greek physician who lived in the period of golden achievements in Greek history is undisputed. The rest of his achievements remain a matter of scholarly debate, centered on the problem of *Corpus Hippocraticum*, a substantial body of writings whose authorship seems to be spread out over different historical periods.

The medical views expressed in this collection are usually referred to as the ideas of Hippocratic medicine, acknowledging the inability to confirm which of the writings can be attributed to Hippocrates himself. Of the approximately sixty unsigned treatises that constitute the collection, only two are definitively known to have been written by Hippocrates' son-in-law, Polybus, because another famous ancient writer, Aristotle, quoted from them.

The normal historical tendency has been to attribute those that are written with authority and good sense and that seem to be of the approximately right time period to Hippocrates and the rest to other authors. The debate over the authorship of the *Corpus Hippocraticum* itself has produced an enormous body of scholarship; one tentative point of agreement is that the earliest essays are from the fifth century B.C.E. and the latest about two centuries later. To cloud the matter even further, the Hippocratic writings themselves are inconsistent, suggesting that the collection incorporates the thinking of different schools of medical practice.

The collection is historically important precisely because it had more than one purpose: to establish medicine as a practice distinct from philosophy and religion and, in furtherance of this goal, to collect information about this separate discipline in writing for the future edification of patients and physicians. Part of this effort involved debate with other schools of thought, such as the Cnidian school.

The centers of medical teaching were often in the temples of healing known as Asclepieions. The two most famous ones of the time were on Cos and Cnidus, between which there was a traditional rivalry and a fundamental difference in approach to medical practice. The Cnidus practitioners, under the guidance of the chief physician, Euryphon, seemed to have been much concerned about the classification of diseases and continued the tradition of deductive knowledge of disease derived from the practice of ancient Greece, Babylonia, and Egypt. Hippocrates was of the Coan school, which worked more inductively, concentrating on observation and treatment of the entire patient and taking into account the mental as well as the physical state.

The first important contribution of the Hippocratic writers—to separate medicine from the shackles of religion, superstition, and philosophy—is apparent in the first text of the collection, *Peri archaiēs iētrikēs* (*Ancient Medicine*, 1849), which is a reminder that medicine had previously been very much a matter for philosophical speculation. This essay estab-

lishes medicine as a branch of knowledge with its own rational methods and describes a practice that calls for skill, craft, art, and observation of patients.

Hippocratic medicine recognized disease as a natural process and suggested that most acute diseases are self-limited. The symptoms of fever, malaise, and other apparent sicknesses were not considered to be mysterious spiritual symptoms but merely the body's way of fighting off the poison of infection. Epilepsy, for example, much feared as a mysterious, sacred affliction, is discussed as a medical problem. The focus of Hippocratic medicine was on regulation of diet, meaning not merely nutrition but exercise as well. The adjustment of diet to the physical state of the patient was thus viewed as the original function of medicine, and the importance of the

Hippocrates of Cos. (*Library of Congress*)

kind of food and its preparation to treat sickness was recognized early.

The Hippocratic writers mention other ideas equally surprising in their modern relevance and influence, such as the notion that great changes, whether in temperature, periods of life, or diet, are most likely to lead to illness. Thus the collection of four books entitled *Peri diaitēs* (*Regimen*, 1931) starts with the argument that health is affected by the totality of diet and exercise; the age, strength, and constitution of the individual; the seasonal changes; variations in wind and weather; and the location in which the patient lives. The Hippocratic idea that a local condition must be treated in conjunction with the general condition, the whole constitution (*physis*) and the complex relations to the environment, is also remarkably similar to the modern notion of holistic healing.

Though many of the other practices and theories have been discarded medically, some were influential for so long that they have been incorporated into the history of Western culture. For example, among the most influential theories set forth in the Hippocratic collection is the idea that the human body is composed of four fluid substances: blood, phlegm, yellow bile, and black bile. Perfect health results from the balance of these fluids in the body. Concomitantly, an excess or deficiency or imperfect mixture results in pain, sickness, and disease. The influence of this theory is apparent in many classics of Western literature, such as the plays of William Shakespeare and Ben Jonson.

Hippocratic medicine was also conservative, seeking primarily to help the sick when it would be beneficial. Medicine was defined by three purposes: It should relieve suffering, reduce the severity of the illness, and finally, abstain from treating that which was beyond the practice of medicine. The physician's job was to help the natural recovery process with diet and regimen, to be administered only after careful observation of the individual symptoms and the patient's constitution. The remedies recommended were mild and adapted to the various stages of the disease; drugs were relatively rare. Most important, sudden and violent measures to interrupt the natural course of the disease were forbidden. The Coan school believed in prognosis, in pre-

dicting, from the experience of long and careful observation, the course of the disease and furthermore in telling the patients and their friends, so that they could be mentally prepared for what might follow, even if it were death. This dictum prevented the physician from prescribing ineffective or expensive treatments simply to remain busy; it is thought that the Hippocratic physician would not even undertake the treatment of a hopeless case, though he probably did his best to make the patient as comfortable as possible.

The most important view in the Hippocratic collection—the most important because it is still unchanged over the course of two thousand years—is the clearly expressed concept of the medical profession as it is summed up in the Hippocratic oath. The doctor is defined as a good man, skilled at healing. Perhaps for this definition alone, the man who is thought to have written or inspired the Hippocratic writings has been called the father of medicine, a title that suggests the ideal of the philosopher-physician—similar to the ideal of the philosopher-king—a person with moral character as well as practical skills.

Influence

Leaving aside the question of authorship of the Hippocratic writings, it is clear why the figure of Hippocrates, for whom the collection is named, is so revered: The keen observations of human behavior and health recorded in these pieces remain fruitful reading.

The Hippocratic writings include a book of more than four hundred aphorisms, pithy observations that have been absorbed, though sometimes in a much altered form, into the English language, influencing those outside the medical field. The most famous of these, popularly remembered as "Life is short, Art long," is a distillation of the following:

> Life is short, whereas the demands of the (medical) profession are unending, the crisis is urgent, experiment dangerous, and decision difficult. However, the physician must not only do what is necessary, he must also get the patient, the attendants, and the external factors to work together to the same end.

Others are commonsense pronouncements: "Restricted or strict diets are dangerous; extremes must be avoided"; "People who are excessively overweight (by nature) are far more apt to die suddenly than those of average weight"; "Inebriation removes hunger (for solid foods)."

If much of the rest of the body of medical knowledge represented by Hippocrates has long since been surpassed, its spirit has not. Hippocrates and his colleagues changed the attitude toward disease, freeing medicine from magic and superstition and insisting on the importance of observation over philosophical speculation. The Hippocratic writings established medicine as a separate discipline with a scientific basis, setting down in writing the medical knowledge of the time regarding surgery, prognosis, therapeutics, principles of medical ethics, and relations between physicians and patient, thus laying the foundations and formulating the ideals of modern medicine.

Shakuntala Jayaswal

Hippocrates: Works

Type of philosophy: Ethics, metaphysics
First transcribed: Corpus Hippocraticum, fifth to third centuries B.C.E. (*The Genuine Works of Hippocrates,* 1849, 2 volumes; also known as *Hippocrates,* 1923-1995, 8 volumes, and *The Medical Works of Hippocrates,* 1950)
Principal ideas advanced:
◇ Diseases are due to natural causes, as opposed to divine or magical causes.
◇ What medical science can and cannot do to heal patients is determined.
◇ Medical ethics is promulgated in the Hippocratic oath.
◇ Medicine is a profession; physicians are healers who have been trained and who follow a certain code of behavior.
◇ Proper treatment of illness requires the proper equipment and thorough observation of the patient.
◇ Case studies and procedures of diagnosis and prognosis provide an empirical study of symptoms.
◇ The environment affects an individual's health.

Before the fourth and fifth centuries B.C.E., there was no written record of medical practices in the Western world. Medicine was largely the job of healers who used herbal remedies; women who had knowledge of the healing powers of certain plants were often consigned to caring for the sick. In ancient Greece, however, healing became a profession, and the mostly male, literate doctors recorded their experiences with patients and their theories of how diseases spread in numerous essays, some of which were quite polemic as the writers defended their common mode of practice against possible detractors. About seventy of these essays (only sixty still exist), all anonymous, were collected and are known as the writings of Hippocrates, a physician who practiced during the time of Plato.

The writings in the Hippocratic collection were revolutionary because they usually attributed disease to natural causes and not, as was commonly held to be true, to the influence of demons or evil forces. When the cause of a disease could not be determined or when traditional remedies were not effective, early peoples turned to religious healing. This consisted of amulets and talismans to ward off the evil, prayer, and ceremonial requests to the gods. Healing also relied on incantations and the playing of music for the sick. Another method of treatment was dream healing, in which the cure was revealed to the patient in a dream or the patient was miraculously healed by a god while dreaming. In Greek culture, however, the power of divine forces was trivialized by many philosophers and physicians. This was even reflected in Greek mythology, in which the god of medicine Asclepius was granted the power to heal the sick, yet he did so not by supernatural means but by incantations, drugs, bandages, and surgery.

The *Corpus Hippocraticum* contains about sixty essays, including the Hippocratic oath and a collection of aphorisms. Greek language experts are certain that the essays were written from the fifth to third century B.C.E. and hence cannot have a single author. Beginning in the second century, scholars have tried to determine which of the essays were written by Hippocrates, but these efforts have not provided a definite answer. Fewer than a dozen essays are usually claimed to be the product of Hippocrates. The essays can be categorized according to topic: the nature of and the means of curing the human body, the characteristics of a good doctor and an ethical medical practice, case histories and treatments of illness, prognostics, and environmental factors of health.

The Art of Medicine and Ethics

Some of the Hippocratic writings consist of essays that attempt to establish a theory of medicine as it pertains to the practice of healing, the composition of the human body, and the causes of disease. *Peri archaiēs iētrikēs* (*Ancient Medicine*, 1849) explains the origin of medicine as a means to cure the sick. It discusses diet, body fluids, and the effects of applying heat and cold to the patient. *Peri technēs* (*The Art of Medicine*, 1923) is less concerned with practice and cynically notes the patient's desire for the relief of distressing symptoms rather than true health and the patient's tendency to ignore the doctor's orders. It also points out the limitations of medicine, which cannot treat all known disorders and therefore must treat only curable ones. *Peri diaitēs* (*Regimen*, 1931) delves into the nature of the human body, pointing out sexual differences, reproduction, embryology, and the four humors: blood, phlegm, yellow bile, and black bile. Other essays of this type discuss the nature of the universe, the soul, and the composition of living things.

The most famous Hippocratic work, *Orkos* (*The Oath*, 1849), deals with ethics. The first part of the oath highlights the important, almost sacred, nature of medical training, the value of the medical teacher, and the need to teach the art to those bound by the oath. The second part states that a physician under the oath should not hurt, deliberately kill, seduce, or reveal any confidential matter concerning a patient. Other essays dedicated to ethics are concerned with the characteristics of a good doctor. The brief article *Nomos* (*The Law*, 1849) discusses the difficulty of maintaining the reputation of the medical profession if a practicing physician does not have knowledge, schooling, and experience of the sacred, noble science of medicine. *Peri iētrou* (*The Physician*, 1923) asks that a doctor be clean, dignified, just, thoughtful, and caring. *Peri euschēmosynēs* (*Decorum*, 1923) says that a physician must dress simply, be patient, be self-controlled, be able to express himself or herself, accept the limi-

tations of healing, and be able to get along with diverse types of people. The last two articles also discuss the proper equipment needed for a doctor's office and a clinic and how to outfit a portable bag to be taken on house calls. *Parangeliai* (*Precepts*, 1923) discusses fees, quacks, professional consultation with other physicians, and the need for a doctor to be charitable, honest, open to helpful knowledge, and kind and reassuring to patients.

An Observation-Based Medicine

Case histories appear in *Epidemiōn* (*The History of Epidemics*, 1780). The author typically gives the name of the patient if known, along with the sex and age. The condition of the patient during the first visit is recorded, followed by a description of symptoms as well as the day they each first occurred. The case history ends with either the death or the recovery of the patient. If the patient recovers, the cause of the relief is then explained, usually by a release of body fluids. *Peri diaitēs oxeōn* (*Regimen in Acute Diseases*, 1849) provides the ancient physician with advice concerning diet, exercise, bloodletting, purgation, and bathing for the seriously ill patient. *Peri nousōn* (*Diseases*, 1988), *Peri pathōn* (*Affections*, 1988), and *Peri tōn entos pathōn* (*Internal Affections*, 1988) continue to offer advice for medical disorders such as lung inflammation, ulcers of the head, water on the brain, fever, colic, nasal polyps, dysentery, diarrhea, arthritis, tumors, hepatitis, and jaundice. Notably, many times the symptoms of the disease are described, but no steps for treatment are given. Other articles discuss treatment of wounds to the head, broken bones, dislocated joints, ulcers, fistulae, hemorrhoids, and epilepsy. The last is noteworthy to modern scholars because it denies any divine nature to the disease and provides a careful description of a disorder that is not as physically observable as, for instance, a wound.

Prognostikōn (*Prognosis*, 1597) advises the physician to observe the patient as much as possible. This includes learning the medical history of the patient and the circumstances surrounding the onset of the disease or injury and determining symptoms and other necessary information the patient does not tell the doctor out of inability to speak, willfulness, or forgetfulness. The article then lists explanations of various symptoms.

Aphorismoi (*The Whole Aphorismes of Great Hippocrates*, 1610; commonly known as *Aphorisms*), a list of more than four hundred pithy statements of medical observations and treatment divided into seven sections, was the first essay of Hippocratic writings to appear in English. These aphorisms continue the advice of the *Prognosis* and provide observations about human health in general. For example, one aphorism warns that overweight people are more likely to die suddenly than people of normal weight. Some aphorisms are trivial or have since proven to be untrue, including the beliefs that sneezing cures hiccups and that women cannot be ambidextrous. Many of the aphorisms concern the characteristic health problems of each stage of life, from childhood to old age, and they include observations about the effects of weather and environment on illness.

Peri aerōn hydatōn topōn (*Airs, Waters, Places*, 1597) continues these observations about external forces, which scholars find significant because they show that ancient physicians were able to understand that environmental elements caused illnesses, a fairly sophisticated observation. They were not able, however, to determine the exact causes of disease this way, as they lacked knowledge of viruses and microorganisms. *Airs, Waters, Places* hence appears to modern readers to be highly speculative, erroneous, and even racist compared to the more empirical articles dedicated to the precise observation of symptoms. The first part of the article describes the effect of the wind and the location of dwellings on health. A city facing east, for example, provides the best situation for good health. A subsequent section explains the best places to procure drinking water, pinpointing which water is cleanest, such as rain water, and which water is to be avoided, such as water from melted snow. Times of the year, such as the equinox or the rising of Sirius, determine how severe certain illnesses will be if they occur at these times. The rest of the article discusses the personality and physical characteristics of the known races of the world, based on the climate in which they are located.

Impact on Medical Ethics

Hippocratic writings founded Western medicine. Since the time of Hippocrates, advances in medicine have depended on clinical observation,

treatment of specific illnesses, and prescribed regimen. The name of Hippocrates and any writings associated with him quickly became sacrosanct. In the years 200 B.C.E. to 100 C.E., the works were acknowledged as fine examples of empirical medical practice, and Diocles, a significant Greek physician, collected the works to assist him in his practice.

The Roman physician Galen based his theory of medicine on Hippocrates, and Galen's works remained influential for centuries afterward. He criticized those physicians who lost sight of Hippocratic methods of medicine; in particular, he complains of his contemporaries Asclepiades and Erasistratus for not observing the true effects of disease and for rejecting the theory of humors as espoused in Hippocratic writings.

During the medieval period in Europe, Greek medical manuscripts were preserved. A few of the Hippocratic works remained as medical textbooks until the nineteenth century. The theory of humors remained in the popular culture until the seventeenth century, as personalities were classified as one of four types. Sanguine, phlegmatic, choleric, or melancholic people existed according to which of the four humors, blood, phlegm, choler (yellow bile), or melancholy (black bile), dominated their bodies.

The seventeenth century was also the period of the Enlightenment. Hippocratic medicine had been revived in the sixteenth century by Paracelsus, who disparaged the theory that sickness was caused by sin, who invented chemical drugs to cure illnesses, and who discovered causes and effective treatments of physical disorders.

During the seventeenth century, advances were made as vivisection was once more allowed and thinkers such as Francis Bacon advocated a Hippocratic approach to medical science. Following such discoveries as William Harvey's explanation of the circulation of the blood and his inconclusive study of reproduction, both based on experimental investigation, medical researchers reverted to seeking out magical or simplified methods of curing illnesses, such as a "magic touch" to cure scrofula, as advocated by English physician Richard Wiseman. This approach was roundly criticized by Thomas Sydenham, "the English Hippocrates," who supported a return to the clinical observation of Hippocrates.

Since the Enlightenment, medical science has advanced so rapidly that ancient medicine has become more the province of history and philosophy than of practicing physicians. Hippocrates, however, remains a familiar name because of the continuing existence of the Hippocratic oath, which modern physicians acknowledge as a useful ethical guide to the practice of medicine.

Rose Secrest

Additional Reading

Amundsen, Darrel. *Medicine, Society, and Faith in the Ancient and Medieval Worlds*. Baltimore, Md.: The Johns Hopkins University Press, 1996. A scholarly yet accessible history of ethical issues in medicine in the ancient and medieval worlds, including the ethics of the Hippocratic oath. Comprehensive footnotes and index.

Coulter, Harris L. *Divided Legacy: A History of the Schism in Medical Thought*. Vol. 1 in *The Patterns Emerge: Hippocrates to Paracelsus*. Washington, D.C.: Wehawken, 1975. The subtitle of the first volume refers to two patterns of thought, rational and empirical, dominating medical history. The author places Hippocrates in the empirical tradition. Provides an extensive bibliography and index. Lists quotations from original writings.

Edelstein, Ludwig. *The Hippocratic Oath: Text, Translation, and Interpretation*. Baltimore, Md.: The Johns Hopkins University Press, 1943. This monograph argues that the Hippocratic oath represented the opinion of a small segment of Greek medical society, was based on Pythagorean principles, and served as a voluntary oath of conscience between teacher and student.

Heidel, William Arthur. *Hippocratic Medicine: Its Spirit and Method*. New York: Columbia University Press, 1941. Heidel discusses the close connections among science, philosophy, history, and medicine in the period of Hippocratic medicine. Provides notes and sources.

Journal of the History of Medicine and Allied Sciences 51, no. 4 (October, 1996). This issue is dedicated to the Hippocratic oath and its influences. It opens with a new translation of the oath, with a commentary by Heinrich von Staden, and continues with a history of the oath's influence during the Middle Ages (by Carlos Galvão-Sobrinho), the Renaissance (by Thomas Rütten), and modern times (by Dale Smith). Each article is extensively footnoted, and the citations provide a comprehensive overview of recent scholarship on the Hippocratic oath and its influence on later ages.

Levine, Edwin Burton. *Hippocrates*. New York: Twayne, 1971. Levine introduces the problems of scholarship in identifying authorship of the Hippocratic writings. The discussion focuses on ideas presented in various selected essays. Includes notes, an index, and an extensive annotated bibliography.

Moon, Robert Oswald. *Hippocrates and His Successors in Relation to the Philosophy of Their Time*. 1923. Reprint. London: Longmans, Green, 1979. A series of lectures delivered by a physician to physicians, this work briefly categorizes the philosophies underlying the practice of ancient medicine before and after Hippocrates. Index.

Phillips, E. D. *Greek Medicine*. London: Thames and Hudson, 1973. Phillips traces practical and theoretical achievements of Greek medicine up to Galen. Includes selected references to the Hippocratic collection, an appendix on the cult of Asclepius, illustrations, an extensive bibliography, and indexes.

Tempkin, Owsei. *Hippocrates in a World of Pagans and Christians*. Baltimore, Md.: The Johns Hopkins University Press, 1991. Authoritative scholarly analysis of the construction of Hippocrates' biography in the Greco-Roman world and of the transformation that occurred to Hippocratic ideas and ideals as the Greco-Roman world converted from pagan to Christian. Provides notes, sources, extensive bibliography, and index.

Shakuntala Jayaswal, updated by Robert Baker

Thomas Hobbes

A pioneer of modern political principles, Hobbes wrote the English language's first great work of political philosophy.

Principal philosophical works: *De Cive*, 1642, rev. ed. 1647 (*Philosophical Rudiments Concerning Government and Society*, 1651); *Human Nature*, 1650; *De Corpore Politico*, 1650; *Leviathan*, 1651; *The Questions Concerning Liberty, Necessity, and Chance*, 1656; *Behemoth: The History of the Causes of the Civil Wars of England*, 1679.

Born: April 5, 1588; Westport, Wiltshire, England
Died: December 4, 1679; Hardwick Hall, Derbyshire, England

Early Life

There is a self-generated folklore regarding Thomas Hobbes's birth and the relation of that birth to his political ideas. According to Hobbes's autobiography, his mother was much alarmed by the approaching Spanish Armada, an alarm that led to his premature birth on April 5, 1588. Thus, Hobbes claimed to have been born with an especially keen aversion to violence; he and fear were born twins, according to Hobbes. If his mother's timidity explains his reverence for peace, however, what explains the ardor and stubbornness with which Hobbes later developed and presented his political theory? The personality of Hobbes's father may present the answer. A "choleric man," Hobbes's father was a vicar who abandoned his family after taking part in a brawl in the doorway of his church.

Along with an older brother and sister, Thomas was reared in the household of an uncle, Francis Hobbes. At the age of four, Thomas was sent to school at the Westport church, where he proved to be an able student. Subsequently, his education was put into the hands of Robert Latimer, a classicist with an extraordinary knack for teaching. Latimer took special pains to develop Hobbes's natural abilities. In 1603, Hobbes set off for Magdalen Hall, Oxford. He was put off by Oxford's archaic curriculum. As a result, he did not always attend lectures, choosing instead to haunt bookshops in search of materials that would better stimulate and satisfy his curiosity.

After receiving his bachelor's degree in 1608, Hobbes took a position as tutor in the household of William Cavendish, who later became the second earl of Devonshire. This arrangement was an extraordinarily happy one and an important one for Hobbes's further intellectual development: The Devonshire house was far more stimulating an environment than Oxford, and Hobbes thrived there, deepening his study of various subjects within the liberal arts. In 1610, Hobbes accompanied his pupil on a tour of Europe. There Hobbes studied French and Italian. Back in England, Hobbes continued his explorations of the life of the mind, making the acquaintance of Francis Bacon in the early 1620's. A significant figure in the history of science, Bacon championed the inductive method. Hobbes's irreverence for Scholasticism was probably reinforced by Bacon's.

In 1629, Hobbes completed an English translation of Thucydides's account of the Peloponnesian War. Some Hobbes scholars have concluded that this work was selected because of the suspicion it casts on democracy. Although there is little evidence to support that supposition, the translation does point out that Hobbes was primarily a classicist at this point in his life. His intellectual focus, however, was about to undergo the first of two important changes.

Also in 1629 (having left the Cavendish household upon the second earl's death in 1628), Hobbes again traveled to Europe, this time as a companion to the son of Sir Gervase Clifton. It

Thomas Hobbes. *(Library of Congress)*

Life's Work

The political strife in England led Hobbes to proceed with what was to be the third part of an all-embracing work of natural philosophy and ethics. *The Elements of Law, Natural and Politic* was circulated in manuscript form by Hobbes in 1640 (and published in 1650 in two parts, *Human Nature* and *De Corpore Politico*). Written in Latin, the work begins with a theory of "man," moving on to a discussion of the "citizen." Given the unruliness of human nature, Hobbes concluded, men could live together in peace only if they submitted to an absolute sovereign. In the context of the time, this seems to make Hobbes a clear monarchist, but Hobbes based his defense of absolutism not on divine right but rather on expediency and consent. Expediency causes men to enter into a contract with the sovereign in which they exchange most of their natural freedom for the security of stable (that is to say, *absolute*) government. Thus Hobbes is a "social contract" theorist.

This stance did not please the Royalists any more than it did Parliamentarians. The latter rejected Hobbes because his theory supported absolute monarchy. The former understood all too well the dangerous implications of social contract theory, for consent, unlike divine right, can be withdrawn. Thus, when the Civil War began to gain full steam in 1640, Hobbes quickly exiled himself to the safety of Paris, "the first of all that fled," as he himself put it. In Paris, Hobbes took up the relatively safe project of writing "objections" to the work of René Descartes, but his political pen had been far from quieted. In 1642, Hobbes published *De Cive*, in which he argued that, rightly understood, a Christian state and a Christian church were united under the leadership of the sovereign. Hobbes was faced with a world in which religious radicalism had become a source of acute political strife. To Hobbes, the stewardship of religion by the secular ruler was a safeguard against religious fanaticism, holy wars, and even intolerance. In 1647, an expanded version of *De Cive* was published, and in 1650 the manuscript

was on this trip, according to John Aubrey's *Lives of Eminent Men* (1813; also known as *Brief Lives*, 1898), that Hobbes fell "in love with geometry." This love of geometry not only altered the course of Hobbes's intellectual efforts but also was to have a substantial effect on the form in which he later chose to express his political ideas. In 1630, Hobbes was called back into the service of Devonshire, this time as tutor to the third earl. In 1633, Hobbes again was able to visit Europe, where he renewed his interest in geometry and science and where he reportedly met briefly with Italian mathematician and physicist Galileo.

In 1637, Hobbes returned to an England that was on the eve of a bitter and bloody civil war, its government and guiding political beliefs about to undergo more than a half-century of ferment. This historical context again shifted the focus of Hobbes's work, combining with his background and personality to make him both a notorious and a respected political theorist.

of *The Elements of Law, Natural and Politic* was published in two parts, *Human Nature* and *De Corpore Politico* (of the body politic).

In 1651, Hobbes published the centerpiece of his political philosophy, *Leviathan*. Wonderfully written in the brash, colorful English of the day, *Leviathan* is remarkably consistent with Hobbes's earlier political treatises. Like them, it seeks to establish his political theory on a scientific basis, proceeding from point to point nearly in the manner of a geometric proof. Nor had Hobbes's substantive position changed. He still argued that absolute rule was needed in order to ensure civil peace but that the sovereign's power was based on consent. Where Leviathan broke new ground was in its unforgettably graphic portrayal of the "state of nature" (that is, the situation that precedes and leads to the social contract) and the addition of two lengthy sections in which Hobbes complements his secular arguments with an examination of the political principles suggested by Scripture and by true Christianity.

Life in the state of nature, according to Hobbes, is "solitary, poore, nasty, brutish, and short." Everywhere there is the fear of violent death. Indeed, the state of nature is actually a state of war, with each person the potential enemy of every other. There is equality in the state of nature, but it is an equality based on mortality, since even the strongest can be overcome by force or guile. There is also an abundance of liberty, since people have a right to anything they can take and hold. With this natural liberty, however, comes acute insecurity: One's possessions (and indeed one's very life) are constantly in jeopardy. Given these conditions, human societies are not likely to prosper or grow comfortable enough to develop and enjoy the arts, letters, and other advantages afforded by civilization.

It is this bleak picture that justifies the need for voluntary submission to an absolute sovereign. People's fear of violent death propels them toward a state of peace. Natural laws, based in reason, show how peace can be achieved—that is, by entering into a contractual relationship with an absolute sovereign. The establishment of such a common power alone can ensure civil peace. In Hobbes's view, stability could be achieved only where sovereignty was undivided and absolute. Otherwise civil authority would come undone,

and the brutishness of the state of nature would reassert itself.

To this justification of absolute rule, rooted in human psychology and rational argument, Hobbes added two lengthy sections based on Scripture. In "Of a Christian Commonwealth," he argues that a theologically pure city of God is not possible in this life and that a truly Christian commonwealth is that which effectively preserves peace. In "The Kingdom of Darkness," Hobbes cites scriptural evidence to refute the arguments of those who would in fact subordinate civil peace to theological purity, using the metaphor of darkness to suggest both the absence of truth and the presence of Satan. Thus, Hobbes argued for a secular state with a minimalist public religion aimed at ensuring popular allegiance to the sovereign, who in turn ensures civil peace. What people wished to believe privately was of no interest to Hobbes or the state. This position challenged both Papists and Presbyterians, who argued that ecclesiastical authority ought to be supreme. As was suggested above, religion, to Hobbes, was too much a source of social conflict and schism to be elevated to a station of sovereignty. Though religion is interestingly absent from Hobbes's portrayal of the state of nature, it certainly did play a prominent role in the English Civil War. Such divisiveness, Hobbes believed, must be minimized by keeping public religion under the control of civil authority.

Hobbes closed *Leviathan* with a section titled "Review and Conclusions," in which he handled the tricky question of where one's allegiance belongs, should a sovereign be successfully overthrown or conquered. For Hobbes, obligation ended when the sovereign could no longer honor his side of the contract. At this point, a new contract comes into force with the newly established sovereign. Some observers have accused Hobbes of taking this position because of the imminent victory of Oliver Cromwell over the Royalists. Indeed, Hobbes did return to England shortly after Cromwell came to power, despite the fact that he had maintained close contact with Charles II while both were in France. Nevertheless, Hobbes's position regarding conquest is consistent with the rest of his political theory. The establishment and maintenance of stable political authority constitute the first priority for Hobbes. Forming a resistance movement to prolong conflict instead of allowing for the emergence of a new order clearly contravenes the goal of civil peace.

In any case, Hobbes's return to England was harmonious, and harmony remained after the restoration of the English monarchy under Charles II in 1660. To be sure, Hobbes had his enemies; he was accused of being an atheist, and "Hobbism" became a term of abuse, denoting the worst kind of freethinking and godlessness. Nevertheless, Charles II extended to Hobbes the protection of the Crown and the security of a very decent pension. For his part, Hobbes avoided writing openly on politically sensitive topics, though he continued to answer personal charges and wrote extensively on mathematics and philosophy. Not surprisingly, Hobbes came back to political themes on occasion, most conspicuously in a dialogue titled *Behemoth: The History of the Causes of the Civil Wars of England* (composed around 1668 but not published until 1679), but he allowed this and other political works to be suppressed in order to avoid a new round of accusations. Instead, notorious at home and a celebrity abroad, Hobbes kept what was for him a low profile, constantly writing, engaging in lively discourse over the philosophical issues of the day, and, late in his life, returning to the classics to produce translations of Homer's *Iliad* and the *Odyssey* (both c. 800 B.C.E.). Hobbes died at Hardwick Hall in Derbyshire on December 4, 1679.

Influence

Hobbes failed to establish an authoritative methodology for political discourse, and his defense of absolutism was soon neutralized by various constitutional theorists, including John Locke in his *Two Treatises of Government* (1690), and by the course of English history. Yet Hobbes's legacy is substantial, in terms of both his general approach to political theory and his conclusions about human nature and political institutions.

Many college courses in modern political philosophy begin with Hobbes. What does it mean to say that Hobbes was a "modern"? A number of things: For one, it recognizes the secular nature of Hobbes's methodology. Hobbes based his olitical theory on observation and reason rather than revelation or metaphysics. As such, he can be seen as a founding father of modern politi-

cal inquiry and social science in general.

Also distinctly modern is Hobbes's emphasis on individualism and self-interest (or egoism). For Hobbes, a convincing political prescription must recognize the essential selfishness of human nature and also be consistent with the dictates of rational self-interest. In fact, for Hobbes self-interest is utilized as an ordering principle. This formula for human harmony serves as the basis for contemporary free market economics and liberal democracy (or, as it is called by some, interest-group liberalism).

Hobbes can also be linked to the development of utilitarianism and legal positivism, solidifying his status as a source of modern thought. All this, however, refers primarily to Hobbes's approach to questions of human conduct rather than to his conclusions. Have his answers become completely obsolete?

There is no doubt that absolutism has gone out of vogue. Indeed, the concept of absolutism has been relegated to the junk heap of history, with authoritarianism, totalitarianism, corporatism, and other designations (some more or less scientific, others clearly ideological) being put forward. Hobbes's absolutism was both conceptually and practically tame compared to modern-day dictatorships. Hobbes was speaking of a form of government with natural limitations. His sovereign, bereft of contemporary propaganda devices and free of modern political religion, lacked both the power and the incentive to exercise totalitarian control. Alas, the natural limits on power assumed by Hobbes are no longer operative, if they ever were.

Nevertheless, there is a profound validity to Hobbes's political theory. There are, first, some political situations that resemble the Hobbesian state of nature sufficiently to recommend Hobbes's conclusions. True, in these instances, there is usually the confusion of faction and fanaticism, elements not present in Hobbes's conception of the state of nature, but these complexities do not contravene the clear need for a well-established common power to maintain peace and order as a prerequisite for further political progress. As Hobbes pointed out, a minimum of civil order is a prerequisite for liberty that is truly secure.

There is also something universal about Hobbes's realism. Indeed, there is even a discernible

Hobbesian element in U.S. politics—reflected, for example, in the 1787-1788 series of papers known as *The Federalist*. In number 51 James Madison wrote that government is "the greatest of all reflections of human nature," since "if men were angels, no government would be necessary." Like many other American statesmen, Madison feared tyranny and sought an effective form of limited government as a safeguard, but, like Hobbes, Madison also feared anarchy and lawlessness. Without effective government, the vicious side of human nature would create a situation in which neither property nor individuals were secure. Thus, while he did not demonstrate the need for absolute government, Hobbes did provide a powerful argument for the necessity of stable government, given the dark side of human nature.

Ira Smolensky

Leviathan

Type of philosophy: Ethics, political philosophy
First published: 1651
Principal ideas advanced:

◇ A human being is a group of material particles in motion.

◇ The state—the great Leviathan—is an artificial man in which sovereignty is the soul, officers the joints, rewards and punishments the nerves, wealth its strength, safety its business, counselors its memory, equity and law its reason and will, peace its health, sedition its sickness, and civil war its death.

◇ Reasoning is the manipulation of names; truth is the correct ordering of names.

◇ Desire is motion toward an object, and aversion is motion away; the good and bad are understood by reference to desire and aversion.

◇ In a state of nature, there is a war of every man against every man; to secure peace, men make contracts establishing a sovereign power who is not subject to civil law since by his will he creates law.

◇ Of the three forms of sovereignty—monarchy, aristocracy, and democracy—monarchy is the most effective in securing peace.

Leviathan is primarily a treatise on the philosophy of politics. It also contains important discussions—some brief, some extended—on metaphysics, epistemology, psychology, language, ethics, and religion. In this work, Thomas Hobbes develops his views from a metaphysics of materialism and a mechanical analogy in which everything is a particle or set of particles moving in accordance with laws. Though he was at one time secretary to English philosopher and essayist Francis Bacon, his inspiration came from Galileo, the Italian mathematician and physicist. Hobbes was unusual in being an early empiricist who recognized the importance of mathematics.

In *Leviathan*, the realism of Florentine man of affairs and political writer Niccolò Machiavelli, the emphasis on sovereignty of French legalist and politician Jean Bodin, and the attempt of Dutch jurist Hugo Grotius to modernize the conception of natural law by relating it to mathematics and the new science are combined and developed with great originality, clarity, and flair for pungent statement to constitute one of the masterpieces of political philosophy.

Natural Philosophy and Civil Philosophy

Hobbes divides all knowledge into two classes, Natural Philosophy and Civil Philosophy. The former is the basis for the latter and consists in turn of two parts, First Philosophy, comprising laws of particles in general such as inertia, causation, and identity, and Physics, which deals with the qualities of particles. These particles, singly or in combination, may be permanent or transient, celestial or terrestrial, with or without sense, with or without speech. A person is a group of particles that is permanent, terrestrial, sensible, and loquacious. Physics contains not only optics and music, which are the sciences of vision and hearing in general, but also ethics, which is the science of the passions of people, poetry, rhetoric, logic, and equity. The four last are respectively the study of people's use of speech in elevated expression, in persuading, in reasoning, and in contracting. Civil Philosophy deals with the rights and duties of the sovereign or of subjects.

The Mechanical Model

Hobbes makes extensive use of the mechanical model in constructing his system. Life is motion;

therefore, machines have artificial life. The heart is a spring, the nerves are strings, and the joints are wheels giving motion to the whole body. The commonwealth is an artificial man in which sovereignty is the soul, officers are the joints, rewards and punishments are the nerves, wealth is its strength, and safety is its business; counselors are its memory, equity and law are reason and will, peace is its health, sedition is its sickness, and civil war is its death. The covenants by which it comes into being are the counterpart of the fiat of creation.

It is apparent that the model is highly oversimplified. That simplicity is, nevertheless, the basis for much of the force the model carries. Hobbes does not hesitate to ignore the model if ill suited to his purpose, as it is in many cases where he has to deal with the details of psychology, religion, and social and political relations.

Human Faculties

The simplest motion in human bodies is sensation, caused by the impact of some particle upon a sense organ. When sensations are slowed by the interference of others, they become imagination or memory. Imagination in sleep is dreaming. Imagination raised by words is understanding and is common to man and beast.

Ideas ("phantasms" for Hobbes) proceed in accordance with laws of association or of self-interest, as in calculating the means to a desired end. Anything we imagine or think is finite. Any apparent conception of something infinite is only an awareness of an inability to imagine a bound. The name of God, for example, is used that we may honor him, not that we may conceive of him.

Hobbes considered speech the noblest of all inventions. It distinguishes human beings from beasts. It consists in the motion of names and their connections. It is a necessary condition of society, contract, commonwealth, and peace. It is essential to acquiring art, to counseling and instructing, and to expressing purpose. It is correspondingly abused in ambiguity, metaphor, and deception.

When a person manipulates names in accordance with the laws of truth, definition, and thought, he or she is reasoning. Truth is the correct ordering of names—for example, connecting by affirmation two names that signify the same thing.

Error in general statements is self-contradiction. Definition is stating what names signify. Inconsistent names, such as "incorporeal substance," signify nothing and are mere sounds. The laws of thought are the laws of mathematics, exemplified best in geometry, generalized to apply to all names. Reasoning is carried on properly when we begin with definition and move from one consequence to the next. Reasoning is therefore a kind of calculating with names. According to Hobbes, everything named is particular but a general name can be imposed on a number of things that are similar. He anticipated fundamental distinctions of Scottish philosopher and skeptic David Hume and later empiricists in maintaining that conclusions reached by reasoning are always conditional.

Hobbes extended the mechanical model in his discussion of the passions by holding that endeavor begins in the motions of imagination. Desire, which is the same as love, is motion toward an object which is therefore called "good." Aversion, which is the same as hate, is motion away from an object which is therefore called "bad." Other passions are definable in terms of these two. Fear is aversion with the belief that the object will hurt; courage is aversion with the hope of avoiding hurt. Anger is sudden courage. Religion, a particularly important passion, is publicly allowed fear of invisible powers. When the fear is not publicly allowed, it is superstition. The whole sum of desires and aversions and their modifications carried on until the thing in question is either done or considered impossible is deliberation. In deliberation, the last appetite or aversion immediately preceding action is will. In searching for truth the last opinion is judgment.

Since desires are endless, happiness is not a static condition but a process of satisfying desires. All motivation is egoistic. Humanity's basic desire is for power, which, like all other desires, ends only in death.

Religion

Hobbes completes the foundations for the development of his political theory with an analysis of religion. It is invented by human beings because of their belief in spirits, their ignorance of causes, and their devotion to what they fear. This explains why the first legislators among the Gentiles always claimed that their precepts came from God or some other spirit, and how priests have been able to use religion for selfish purposes. Religion dissolves when its founders or leaders are thought to lack wisdom, sincerity, or love.

Natural Law

Hobbes develops his political theory proper in terms of the time-honored concepts of equality, the state of nature, natural law, natural rights, contract, sovereignty, and justice. In his hands, however, they receive treatment that is very different from that of his predecessors, the Greeks, Saint Thomas Aquinas, Jean Bodin, and Hugo Grotius, as well as from that of his successors, English philosopher John Locke and his followers in the liberal tradition. Machiavelli's views on egoism and the need for absolute power in the sovereign anticipated Hobbes but were not developed in detail as a general political philosophy.

In their natural state, according to Hobbes, men are approximately equal in strength, mental capacity, and experience, and everyone has an equal right to everything. If they were without government, the conflict arising from their desires, their distrust, and their ambition would lead to a state of war of every man against every man. In such a state there would be no property, no justice or injustice, and life would be "solitary, poor, nasty, brutish and short." Fortunately, both passion (in the form of fear of death, desire for a long and reasonably pleasant life, and hope of achieving it) and reason (in the form of knowledge of the articles of peace in the form of the laws of nature) combine to provide a basis for the establishment of civil society and escape from universal strife.

The first law of nature is to seek the peace and follow it. The second, a necessary means to the first, is

> that a man be willing, when others are so too, as farre-forth as for Peace and defence of himself he shall think it necessary, to lay down this [natural] right to all things; and be contented with so much liberty against other men as he would allow other men against himselfe.

This is to be done by making contracts with others. A necessary condition for the operation of the second law of nature is that men perform their contracts, which is the third law of nature. For contracts to be valid, it is necessary, in turn, that a sovereign power be established who will make it more painful to commit injustice, which is the breaking of a contract, than to live justly, which is the keeping of contracts. Contracts without the sword, Hobbes reminds us, are only words that guarantee no security. The first three laws of nature, then, combined with the nature of man as a complex set of particles moving in accordance with various sets of laws—not only strictly mechanical laws but also what might be called egoistic and hedonistic laws—are the source of society, sovereignty, and justice.

Additional laws of nature, subordinate to the first three, or special cases, though not specified as such by Hobbes, require the practice of fidelity, gratitude, courtesy, forbearance, fairness, justice, equity, the recognition of natural equality, and the avoidance of contumely, pride, and arrogance. The whole doctrine of natural law, called by Hobbes a "deduction," can be summarized in the general law: Do not do unto another what you would not want him to do to you. Hobbes considers these laws of nature "eternal and immutable," because breaking them can never preserve the peace. The science of laws is true moral philosophy. He concludes this discussion of natural law with a remark whose significance has usually been ignored but must be appreciated if parts 3 and 4 of *Leviathan* are to be understood. These "laws," so far, are not properly named; they are only theorems, binding to be sure, *in foro interno* (that is, to a desire they should be effective) but not *in foro externo* (that is, to putting them into practice). If, however, it can be shown that they are delivered in the word of God, who by right commands in all things, then they are properly called laws and are in fact binding.

The Leviathan and the Sovereign

In working out the details of the second and third laws of nature, Hobbes maintains that to achieve peace, contentment, and security it is necessary that men agree with one another to confer their power upon a man or group of men of whose acts each man, even a member of a dissenting minority, will regard himself the original author:

This is the Generation of that great LEVIA-THAN or rather (to speak more reverently) of that *Mortal God*, to which we owe under the *Immortal God* our peace and Defence.

One may consequently define a commonwealth as

One Person, of whose Acts a great multitude, by mutuall Covenants one with another, have made themselves every one the Author, to the end he may use the strength and means of them all, as he shall think expedient, for their Peace and Common Defence.

This person is sovereign. All others are subjects.

The covenant generating the sovereign is not between the sovereign and the subjects but only among subjects that they will obey whatever ruling power the majority may establish. The covenant may be explicit (actually written) or it may be implicit (for example, in force by virtue of a conquering force remaining in the conquered country). The covenant is an agreement to refrain from interfering with the sovereign's exercise of his right to everything. The concept of consent is not present, at least not in the sense it carried later with Locke. Making the covenant is the one political act of subjects. Their proper role is to obey as long as the sovereign is able to protect them, unless he should order them to kill, wound, or maim themselves or to answer questions about a crime they may have committed. Even these are not restrictions of the sovereignty of the ruler, but only liberties that subjects retain under the laws of nature. Politically and legally, in Hobbes's system, there is and can be no legal limitation on sovereignty. There is no right of rebellion, for example, since the sovereign is not bound by any contract, not having made one. Subjects have only the legal rights granted them by the sovereign. The sovereign is the only legislator; he is not subject to civil law and his will—not long usage—gives authority to law.

More specifically, the sovereign must have the power to censor all expression of opinion, to allocate private property, to determine what is good or evil and what is lawful or unlawful, to judge all cases, to make war or peace, to choose the officers of the commonwealth, to administer rewards and punishments, to decide all moral or religious questions, and to prescribe how God is to be worshiped.

There are, says Hobbes, only three forms that sovereignty may take: monarchy, aristocracy, and democracy. Other apparent forms merely reflect attitudes. For example, if someone dislikes monarchy, then he calls it tyranny. Although his arguments would support any absolutism, Hobbes shows a strong preference for monarchy in claiming that it is the best means of effecting peace. The interests of the monarch and his subjects are the same. What is good for the monarch is good for the people. He is rich, glorious, or secure if they are, and not if they are not. He will have fewer favorites than an assembly. He can receive better advice in private than any assembly. There will be no argument and disagreement in making decisions, and they will stand more firm. Divisive factionalism and the consequent danger of civil war will not arise. Hobbes admits that monarchy has some problems about succession but says they can be met by following the will of the sovereign, custom, or lineage.

Hobbes maintains that a commonwealth established by acquisition in acts of force or violence differs from one established by institution, peaceably and with something approaching explicit covenant, only in having its sovereignty based upon fear of the sovereign rather than upon mutual fear of the subjects.

No matter how established or what its form, however, there are certain causes of dissolution that Hobbes warns must be avoided: insufficient power in the sovereign to maintain peace, permitting subjects to judge what is good or evil, considering violation of individual conscience a sin, considering supernatural inspiration superior to reason, considering the sovereign subject to civil law, permitting subjects absolute property rights, dividing sovereign power, regarding tyrannicide as lawful, permitting the reading of democratic books, and believing there are two kingdoms, spiritual and civil.

The Christian Commonwealth

The all-important task of showing that there are not two different kingdoms and at the same time showing that the theorems of the first two parts of *Leviathan* are in fact laws, and as such binding obligations, are Hobbes's main points in discussing the nature of a Christian commonwealth. The essential mark of a Christian is obedience to God's law. God's authority as lawgiver derives from his power. His laws, which are the natural laws, are promulgated by natural reason, revelation, and prophecy. In the first two parts of *Leviathan*, knowledge of natural laws and their implications have been found out by reason. Laws are, therefore, only conditional theorems. To be shown to be unconditional laws, they must be shown to be the will of God. In fact, Hobbes argues—using extensive quotation and acute, though one-sided, analysis of terms in Scripture and in common speech—all theorems of reasoning about the conduct of human beings seeking happiness in peace are to be found in Scripture. Hobbes concludes that there is no difference between natural law known by reason and revealed or prophetic law. What is law, therefore, depends upon what is Scripture.

Scripture, Hobbes argues—again with extensive quotation, analysis, and interpretation—is what is accepted as Scripture in a commonwealth and is nothing apart from its interpretation. If it is interpreted by conscience, we have competition and a return to the state of nature with its war made fiercer by religious conviction and self-righteousness. All the same arguments for commonwealth apply in particular, therefore, more strongly to the generation of a Christian commonwealth. This is a civil society of Christian subjects under a Christian sovereign. There is no question of opposition between church and state because there is no distinction between them. There are not two laws, ecclesiastical and civil—only civil. There is no universal church, since there is no power on earth to which all commonwealths are subject. Consequently, obedience to civil law is necessary for a person's admission into heaven. Even if a sovereign is not Christian, it is still an obligation and law for a Christian to obey him, since those who do not obey break the laws of God.

When these truths are obfuscated by misinterpretation of Scripture, demonology, or vain philosophy, then, says Hobbes, a kingdom of darkness arises. He applies, in some detail, the test of asking, "Who benefits?" to a number of doctrines in each category and concludes that the Presbyterian and Roman clergy, particularly the popes, are the authors of this darkness, for they gain temporal power from its existence. Hobbes adds that the errors from which the darkness arises are to be avoided, in general, by a careful reading of *Leviathan*. Some of the darkness arising from vain philosophy, for example, can be remedied by more careful attention to Hobbes's doctrines of language. These will show that the function of the copula can be replaced by the juxtaposition and ordering of words, thus removing the darkness that arises from the reification of *esse* in its counterparts *entity* and *essence*. These words, says Hobbes, are not names of anything, only signs by which we make known what we consider to be consequences of a name. Infinitives and participles similarly are not names of anything. When people understand these and other facts about language, they can no longer be deluded by mistaken interpretations of Scripture, demonology, or vain philosophy. In this instance they will no longer be deluded by the doctrine of separated essence and consequently will not be frightened into disobeying their sovereign.

Assessment and Influence

There are flaws in Hobbes's philosophy. He is often crude in his vigor, achieving a logical solution of a problem by omitting recalcitrant details. His errors, however, are usually due to oversimplification, not to being muddleheaded, superstitious, or unclear. No matter how wrong, he is never unintelligible. Moreover, he could not in his own day, and cannot now, be ignored. The partisans of England's civil war, the Puritans and Cavaliers, could both condemn him, but both Cromwell and Charles II could draw on his doctrines. U.S. president Abraham Lincoln appealed to Hobbes's doctrines of covenant and unity of the sovereign power to justify the use of force in dealing with secession.

Hobbes's philosophy, in its outline, development, method, and logic, very strongly affected later developments of political and ethical thought. It is doubtful that anyone has stated so strongly the case for political authority or more strongly supported the thesis that unity, not consent, is the basis of government, and conformity to the sovereign will is its strength. His influence is clearly apparent in the doctrines of sovereignty and civil law formulated by John Austin, an English writer on jurisprudence. His methods of argument about the nature of law prepared the way for Jeremy Bentham, English ethical and social philosopher, and the movement for scientific legislation based on pleasure, pain, and self-interest. In moral philosophy it is not too much to say that the subsequent history of ethics would not have been the same without Hobbes. Reactions by British moralist and quasi rationalist Richard Cumberland and the Cambridge Platonists, on one hand, and by English essayist Lord Shaftesbury and British moralist and empiricist Francis Hutcheson, on the other, developed into the eighteenth century opposition between reason and sentiment that is reflected in many of the problems that occupy moral philosophers today.

Bernard Peach

Additional Reading

Dietz, Mary G., ed. *Thomas Hobbes and Political Theory*. Lawrence: University Press of Kansas, 1990. A series of significant essays covering contemporary thinking on Hobbes, issued from the Benjamin Evans Lippincott symposium "The Political Philosophy of Thomas Hobbes, 1599-1988," held at the University of Minnesota in 1988.

Johnston, David. *The Rhetoric of Leviathan: Thomas Hobbes and the Politics of Cultural Transformation*. Princeton, N.J.: Princeton University Press, 1986. An important postmodern reading of *Leviathan*.

Mace, George. *Locke, Hobbes and the Federalist Papers: An Essay on the Genesis of the American Political Heritage*. Carbondale: Southern Illinois University Press, 1979. A controversial work in that Mace argues that *The Federalist* reflects a more Hobbesian than Lockean view, and also that Hobbes was, indeed, the greater thinker of the two. Places both Locke and Hobbes in the context of the founding of the United States.

Macpherson, C. B. *The Political Theory of Possessive Individualism: Hobbes to Locke*. New York: Oxford University Press, 1962. Macpherson argues that both Hobbes and Locke reflected the possessive individualist premises of emerging capitalist society, mistaking these premises for eternal principles of human nature. The book, therefore, constitutes a critique of Hobbes's "realism" about human nature.

Martinich, A. P. *A Hobbes Dictionary*. Oxford, England: Blackwell, 1995. One in a series of invaluable Blackwell Philosophic Dictionaries.

Rogers, Graham Alan John, ed. *Perspectives on Thomas Hobbes*. Oxford, England: Clarendon Press, 1988. A collection of essays published in association with the important fourth centenary Hobbes conference organized by the British Society for the History of Philosophy.

Sorrell, Tom. *The Cambridge Companion to Hobbes*. Cambridge, England: Cambridge University Press, 1996. An essential reference book by a leading British Hobbes scholar.

_____. *Hobbes*. London: Routledge, Kegan, Paul, 1986. A useful introduction to the thought of Hobbes.

Wolin, Sheldon. *The Politics of Vision: Continuity and Innovation in Western Political Thought*. Boston: Little, Brown, 1960. A popular and stylish textbook on the history of political philosophy with a lengthy chapter on Hobbes. He is seen as a prophet of modern society, in which impersonal rules and competition between interests have come to replace notions of a close-knit political community.

Ira Smolensky, updated by David Barratt

Paulin J. Hountondji

Through a critique of "ethnophilosophy" and an endorsement of a critical, "scientific" understanding of philosophy, Hountondji compelled a reassessment of traditional African philosophy and an examination of the relationship among philosophy, science, and development.

Principal philosophical works: *Libertés: Contribution à la révolution Dahoméenne*, 1973; *Sur la philosophie africaine: Critique de l'ethnophilosophie*, 1977 (*African Philosophy: Myth and Reality*, 1983); *Recherche théorique africaine et contrat de solidarité*, 1978.

Born: 1942; Abidjan, Ivory Coast, French West Africa

Early Life

French West Africa, during Paulin J. Hountondji's youth, was still under colonial rule by Europeans. The Ivory Coast, Dahomey (now Benin), and other nation-states such as Senegal and Guinea were territories of France, moving toward independence. French influence, linguistic and cultural as well as political, remained strong: Talented African students were caught between empire and independence. Hountondji graduated from secondary school in 1960, the year Dahomey gained its independence, and following a long tradition, he continued his education in France.

In Paris during the 1960's, Hountondji absorbed the Marxist combination of revolutionary socialist politics and "scientific" philosophy. He graduated from the prestigious École Normale Supérieure in 1966 with a degree in philosophy and did doctoral work under the guidance of the Marxist philosopher Louis Althusser. His doctoral thesis, on the phenomenology of Edmund Husserl, was completed in 1970. Both Husserl and Althusser understood philosophy as a science. For Husserl, the role of philosophy was to give a precise and systematic description of immediately given phenomena, thus avoiding speculation and ensuring certainty. For Althusser, philosophy was the critical identification of the object of each specific science and the under-

standing of the conditions, especially socioeconomic, under which the science produces its distinctive object. These perspectives are not identical, but both emphasize that philosophy is the method of critically understanding the creation of knowledge.

Life's Work

Hountondji began his academic career in France, teaching at the University of Besançon from 1967 to 1970. His fundamental concern, however, was not merely to teach philosophy or even to practice neo-Marxist critical theory but rather to introduce to Africa an understanding of philosophy appropriate to problems of development. Accordingly, Hountondji quickly returned to the continent of his birth, holding university positions first in Zaire and from 1974 at the National University of Benin in Cotonou.

While in Zaire, at the National University at Lumumbashi, Hountondji began his work as an "activist philosopher." In 1972, he founded *Cahiers Philosophiques Africains* (African philosophy journal), and in 1973, he became the executive general secretary of the Inter-African Council for Philosophy. His purpose in these endeavors was twofold: first, to provide continent-wide communication among philosophers and thus aid the professionalization of the discipline in Africa; and second, to advance his own understanding of philosophy as critical and scientific. He had already begun to articulate that understanding in a series of lectures and articles that, after being revised and supplemented, formed the basis of *African Philosophy: Myth and Reality*.

During this period, Hountondji became involved in the politics and administration of Benin. Benin (then Dahomey) had become independent in 1960; however, its political situation was completely unsettled during the 1960's and early 1970's. Brief periods of highly factionated civilian rule were punctuated by a series of military coups. Finally, in October, 1972, Major (later General) Mathieu Kerekou seized power.

Kerekou's Beninois revolution transformed political and economic life. Over the next several years, Dahomey became Benin, recalling the power of a precolonial empire. Much of the economy was placed under state control, and existing political parties were replaced by Kerekou's Parti de la Revolution Populaire du Benin. Marxism-Leninism was proclaimed as the official state ideology. Hountondji's exact role in the revolution is impossible to determine, but some facts are known. In 1973, he published a book on the revolution, and in 1974, he became a professor at the National University. His philosophical leanings were clearly Marxist, and some of Hountondji's educational suggestions, as described in *African Philosophy*, were implemented in Benin. It should be noted that Hountondji's writings emphasize the need for political freedom if philosophy and science are to flourish and that Benin's revolution, while ultimately unsuccessful in establishing socialism, was relatively nonrepressive.

By the mid-1970's, the first phase of Hountondji's philosophical thinking was complete. The publication of *African Philosophy* established his position as the leading critic of "ethnophilosophy." As an Althusser-educated Marxist, Hountondji had learned to read any philosophic statement as an emanation of its socioeconomic situation. He therefore placed ethnophilosophies—that is, representations of "traditional African philosophy"—in the context of African development or, more precisely, African nondevelopment. To Hountondji, ethnophilosophy legitimized and even celebrated an Africa that was precolonial, colonial, or some combination of the two and that was far inferior, in technological terms, to European and other Western nations.

To end that inferiority, a revolution was needed—a philosophical, not political, revolution. The pivot of that revolution, for Hountondji, was understanding that only critical philosophy is able to distinguish genuine from spurious science. Because genuine, or natural, science is empirical, methodical, and experimental, only science "liberated" from tradition and prejudice by critical philosophy could lead to development. Therefore, the conditions for development were the critique of ethnophilosophy by critical philosophy; the consequent replacement of mythical, magical, metaphysical ethnophilosophy by critical philosophy; and the endorsement by critical philosophy of empirical natural science and Marxist political economy. Hountondji believed the political revolution would quicken the process of replacing the traditional and developing the modern.

For Hountondji, ethnophilosophy was the rival of critical philosophy. He considered it a weak, inferior pretender to the status of "philosophy" although it existed on the same logical level as genuine philosophy. It was therefore necessary and appropriate to attack ethnophilosophy in order to start the argument about "African philosophy" and to drive ethnophilosophy from the intellectual field. Ethnophilosophy was, in good Marxist fashion, to be relegated to the junkheap of history. In the future, broadly speaking, science—not myth—would form African minds.

It is not surprising, then, that Hountondji's attention was drawn increasingly to the question of science. During the 1980's, he published a series of articles inquiring into the status of science in Africa. A substantial portion of his argument is continuous with that of *African Philosophy*: African science remains underdeveloped and dependent in relation to that of Europe and North America. Further, this lack of development is the analog and perhaps even an aspect of African economic underdevelopment.

On the other hand, Hountondji was having important second thoughts about ethnophilosophy and about what "science" is. (Alternatively, it may be argued, he was engaging in dialectical analysis.) He made two very important intellectual moves during this period. First, his basic countercategory to critical philosophy became "ethnoscience" rather than ethnophilosophy. Second, ethnophilosophy, in effect, descended a logical level; that is, ethnophilosophy became one of the ethnosciences, together with ethnobotany, ethnolinguistics, and so on.

The cumulative effect of these two moves was close to a conceptual revolution in Hountondji's thought. Ethnophilosophy as an ethnoscience is no longer in direct competition with "true," critical philosophy. Additionally, ethnoscience now assumes the same status as "genuine" Western science in relation to philosophy. This formal equality is not necessarily substantive equality: In any given area and for any given purpose, Western science may (or may not) be more valid and useful than ethnoscience. However, in Hountondji's estimation, the ethnosciences of precolonial Africa have provided valid knowledge and have proven themselves useful. They also represent a possible counterforce to African dependence on Western science. In this revised view, the task of philosophy remains formally the same: to evaluate the status of any given body of knowledge as science. Now, however, critical philosophy regards the ethnosciences much more dispassionately; that is, it no longer automatically dismisses them but instead inquires systematically into their validity and utility.

It is obvious, then, that Hountondji's later understanding of the term "science" had broadened considerably. This change had not occurred in a political vacuum, in Africa generally or in Benin specifically. During the 1960's and early 1970's, the newly independent African nations were viewed as "developing countries." Development was expected to be fairly rapid, to be along Western economic and technological lines, and to result in "modern societies." However, these anticipated changes have not occurred in any uniform fashion, leading to critical reconsideration of the concepts of "development" and "science."

Hountondji's movement away from Marxist orthodoxy is connected with the decline and demise of Kerekou's regime in Benin. That regime succeeded in providing much-needed political stability, surviving until 1990, but it failed to provide either social harmony or economic development. Increasing dissatisfaction and unrest were catalyzed by the worldwide liberalization movement of the late 1980's. In Benin, a National Conference, held in February, 1990, declared itself sovereign. The People's Republic of Benin ceased to exist, and a new, republican constitution was overwhelmingly approved in December, 1990.

The new regime included Hountondji. He became minister of national education in the transitional government of 1990 and continued in that post in the provisional government of 1991. With the new constitution fully, if not always firmly, in place, Hountondji became minister of culture and communications in 1992. He remained in the government until 1994, when he returned full-time to his university position. While in office, Hountondji helped put in place policies long espoused in his writings, including raising educational standards and teaching the various sciences in a variety of native languages. The latter policy, however, was opposed by parents who believed that their children were comparatively advantaged by instruction in French and was changed. Hountondji's writing includes a qualified acceptance of this "liberal democratic" repudiation of one aspect of ethnoscience.

Influence

In the early 1970's, Hountondji was a young philosopher with a clear mission—or so it seemed. He wanted to be a driving force in making Africans philosophically mature, that is, capable of understanding the world in terms of scientific and dialectical materialism. The critique of ethnophilosophy was, in its larger dimensions, a critique of all African traditionalism and thus of "underdevelopment" in all its aspects. The critique was timely. Many educated Africans wanted development to occur as quickly as possible. Hountondji's critical philosophy offered a means of sweeping away presumably outdated assumptions and institutions. Critical philosophy was contemporary and thus, for Africa, the wave of the future.

However, critical philosophy was in a paradoxical position. On one hand, its very essence is standing apart from everything subject to its critical scrutiny (which, as Hountondji insists, requires a political regime supportive of free inquiry). However, on the other hand, critical philosophy attacked ethnophilosophical traditionalism and, at least implicitly, promised development. It thus opened itself to evaluation by political and economic standards. Simply put, if modernizing Marxist regimes failed politically or economically, critical philosophy would probably be judged to have failed along with them.

This paradox or contradiction is evident throughout Hountondji's career and reveals itself in critical responses to his work. Hountondji moved between academic and administrative positions, in effect attempting a conjunction as old as classical Greek political philosophy, the uniting of philosophy and political power. Greek philosopher Socrates believed this union to be highly improbable; however, in any case, it is certain that political office mitigates the pure Socratic critical posture that Hountondji values. Additionally, critics have seen in the failure of Marxist regimes such as Benin's reasons both to reject critical philosophy and to associate its practitioners with an elitism ignorant of or opposed to the situation of the "African masses."

These problems and criticism should be given due weight, but Hountondji's considerable achievements remain. He set out to initiate a discussion of the nature of African philosophy and succeeded brilliantly. In critical philosophy, he provided a model of intellectual activity attuned to practical development. In his political and administrative work, he helped put this model to a practical test in an African society. Having discovered through experience some of the weaknesses of this critical scientific model, Hountondji reformulated his early rejection of ethnophilosophy into a position quite respectful of African ethnosciences. Throughout his career, he was the engaged philosopher willing to question his own strongly held critical positions in the light not merely of historical reality but also of the opinions of other thoughtful human beings.

John F. Wilson

African Philosophy

Myth and Reality

Type of philosophy: African philosophy, ethics, social philosophy

First published: Sur la philosophie africaine: Critique de l'ethnophilosophie, 1977 (English translation, 1983)

Principal ideas advanced:

◇ Hitherto, what has passed for African philosophy has been a form of pseudophilosophy called "ethnophilosophy."

◇ Ethnophilosophy is a combination of myth, tradition, and ethnography that falsely implies that Africans possess a single philosophical outlook.

◇ The source of ethnophilosophy is traditional oral discourse, which emphasizes memory and renders impossible the development of a critical perspective

◇ Ethnophilosophy is, implicitly, a neocolonial project that purports to understand Africans in spiritual terms and thus impedes practical, material development.

◇ In order to develop intellectually and practically, Africans require critical philosophy, the first task of which is to thoroughly critique ethnophilosophy.

◇ The further task of critical philosophy is to aid scientific development by distinguishing true, practically useful knowledge from that which is spurious.

◇ The political condition for the development of critical philosophy in Africa is the creation of regimes that allow complete freedom of inquiry and discussion.

In the seventy-five years before World War II, Africa was colonized, in large part by European missionaries. These Catholic and Protestant Christians penetrated deeply into Africa geographically, psychologically, and not least, philosophically. Therefore, when "African philosophy" was noted or recorded, the work was done mostly by religious men, either European missionaries such as Placide Tempels or their African pupil-successors such as Alexis Kagame and John S. Mbiti. Of course, these men emphasized the religious dimensions of African life and philosophy, and perhaps because they were adherents to a single religion, they also portrayed the unity of that religious-philosophic outlook across sub-Saharan Africa. However, from the perspective of those trained in a rigorous, secular philosophical tradition, African philosophy was little more than neocolonial ideology. Colonizers or their Christianized students were placed in the privileged position of representing African intellectual reality. They represented that reality as largely unrelated to economic and political (material) conditions. Paulin J. Hountondji, an African educated in French neo-Marxism, sought to redress this imbalance with a vigorous attack on "ethnophilosophy" in his critical work *African Philosophy*.

African Philosophy is divided into two parts, "Arguments" and "Analyses." Evidently, this was an editorial decision intended to balance the book in number of chapters (four in each part) and in pages per part. However, both chapter 8, "True and False Pluralism," and a fifteen-page "Postscript" are much more arguments than analyses of individual African philosophers. Thus roughly three-fourths of the work is Hountondji's attack on ethnophilosophy and his defense of critical philosophy. With the exception of the "Postscript," all the material had been published in some form before being revised and collected as *African Philosophy*.

Philosophy Defined

Despite being a collection of articles, the work possesses remarkable unity. Its unity is due to the simple fact that, in essence, it is an argument about one word, "philosophy." Hountondji, Marxist though he may be, is completely the modern French philosopher, that is, the Cartesian, in departing from a single "clear and distinct" idea. This idea is that, in "science," words have a precise, unequivocal meaning. Above all, philosophy, as word, as discipline, and as practice, has a precise meaning, because philosophy is the fully conscious, intentional, critical examination of all discourses that claim to be knowledge. Because critical examination presupposes the most careful study, it follows that any discourse being critically examined must first be stabilized in writing.

All sciences, then, but especially philosophy, must be textual. This textualization—that is, the representation in writing of traditional African philosophy—is precisely what the ethnophilosophers accomplished. Tempels's *Bantu Philosophy* (1959) might be considered the first text in this philosophical subdiscipline. Hountondji rejects this idea on several grounds. First, African philosophy must be authored from inside, by Africans, but Tempels is a European, doing "European science." Alexis Kagame's *La Philosophie bantu-rwandaise de l'être* (1955; the Bantu-Rwandese philosophy of being), authored by a Rwandan, is more legitimately African philosophy—because it is African. However, strictly speaking, in two senses, it is not philosophy. At most, such a reconstruction is a presentation of traditional wisdom, not of critical analysis. Additionally, these ethnophilosophical representations presuppose an "unconscious" unanimity among all Africans on the nature of things. The ethnophilosophers hold that there is one and only one traditional African philosophy.

Ethnophilosophy and Philosophy

Hountondji's position is that the African philosophy of the ethnophilosophers is a myth and that the ethnophilosophers are the mythmakers. Their myth is not about indigenous African gods and goddesses or spirits and heroes, who have a kind of reality for many traditional, noncritical Africans. Instead, the myth of the ethnophilosophers is Africa. Africa is presented exotically to Europeans and other Westerners as a simple, soulful place whose inhabitants, equally simple, are nearly devoid of economic and political concerns. The myth of Africa and Africans is, in essence, neocolonial ideology. It serves, Hountondji believes, two oddly related purposes. First, it elevates Europe over Africa intellectually and technologically and thus implicitly justifies European dominance. Second, African soulfulness restores spiritual health to materialistic Europeans, even as they continue to control Africa in the name of civilization and development. In sum, ethnophilosophy is the very "finest" sort of ideology: It makes the conqueror feel both morally justified and spiritually redeemed by the conquest.

Ethnophilosophy, then, is both bad philosophy and, if politically influential, bad ideology. Nevertheless, from Hountondji's perspective, it serves two necessary purposes. First, insofar as ethnophilosophy is authored by Africans, it marks the beginning of a textual tradition of African philosophy. Again, it is important to be "clear and distinct" on this point: Any given expression of ethnophilosophy is the view of some philosopher, not of Africans in general. Second, ethnophilosophical texts give the critical philosopher something with which to work. They are thus indispensable to the initiation of philosophy as a historical process.

Ethnophilosophy is a very halting first step. It is not true scientific discourse, nor is it even a systematic compilation of what has traditionally passed for "science" in Africa. (Hountondji does not use the term "ethnoscience" in *African Philosophy*.) Nevertheless, ethnophilosophy is the beginning of that profound transformation from oral cultures to literate civilizations in Africa. In a word, it straddles the border between myth and science.

With writing, science becomes possible. It is no longer necessary to devote the bulk of a society's intellectual energy merely to remembering. For Hountondji, every oral culture is dominated by the fear of forgetting: This obsession renders such a society not merely traditional but dogmatic. However, once writing takes hold, the mind is able to "look down" on what it thinks it knows. It can regard its knowledge critically, as something both secured in writing and open to inspection. At this point, true philosophy begins to exist. Philosophy is, in a sense, the highest form of science, because it scrutinizes every established body of knowledge. However, philosophy is not wisdom. Neither is it merely science. Instead, philosophy is a process that restlessly and endlessly examines and criticizes any organized discipline that claims to be knowledge.

This understanding of genuine philosophy presents the sharpest contrast with ethnophilosophy. Assuming the existence of a single, coherent statement of African philosophy that truly represented the worldview of all Africans, this would be doctrine, not philosophy. In Hountondji's opinion, what has made Europe powerful and progressive and Africa subordinate and static is that, for Europeans, philosophy is a history. Moreover, it is a history that includes science and politics. Philosophy rests on the various sciences, but it does not take them for granted. Instead, it subjects all limited or dogmatic formulations to searching criticism, in the process establishing a continuing, progressive history. For this process to proceed, political freedom, especially freedom of criticism, is necessary. No religious, scientific, or political dogma can be permitted to silence critical philosophy.

Politics and Philosophy

It is within this framework that Hountondji explains both the "Analyses" included in *African Philosophy* and the relationship between philosophy and politics. An article on the work of Anton-Wilhelm Amo, an eighteenth century African-German philosopher, and two pieces on the writings of Kwame Nkrumah, the twentieth century Ghanaian philosopher and political leader, are intended to begin the process of creating a history of African philosophy. Not surprisingly, Hountondji's reading of Amo and Nkrumah is especially alert for signs of ethnophilosophy; he finds none in the former but regrettable elements of it in the latter. The implicit message seems to be that Africans do philosophy best when they are philosophers first and Africans a distant second.

The critical reading of Nkrumah is in keeping with Hountondji's position on the relation between philosophy and politics. He draws a fine but very significant distinction between "political theory" and a "theory of politics." It is not completely clear whether political theory (or philosophy) is the combination of politics and philosophy or the subordination of philosophy to political purposes. What is clear is that political theory entails a loss of autonomy for both philosophy and politics. Each is "infected" with things extraneous to it—politics with irrelevant (and, for Hountondji, unreal) metaphysical issues, philosophy with the ideological baggage of politics. "Political philosophy," then, is all but indistinguishable from ethnophilosophy.

A theory of politics, on the other hand, is a legitimate and worthwhile philosophical contribution. Here again is the clarity and distinctness of Hountondji's most fundamental thesis: Philosophy is philosophy only when it functions critically. In this instance, philosophy should ruthlessly, and fearlessly, expose all the tricks of the political trade. It should especially discern and discuss the ways in which politics uses ideology to mystify and mislead. In this philosophical critique of politics, the contrast with science is always implicit and often explicit. Science deals with what is real, the material world and its processes; politics, like ethnophilosophy, dwells mostly in the realm of the imaginary.

Success and Criticism

African Philosophy fulfilled Hountondji's intention: It revolutionized the subdiscipline. It was recognized immediately as a major statement, and its author became the leader of the "antiethnophilosophers." In a positive vein, a new school in African philosophy emerged, that of "professional" or "rationalist" philosophers. Hountondji became one of the most prominent African philosophers. Influence was accompanied by honors. *African Philosophy* shared the Melville Herskovits Award of the African Studies Association in 1984.

African Philosophy also succeeded in a deeper sense. One of Hountondji's theses in the book is that African philosophy is in fact pluralistic, but that this pluralism is concealed by the ethnophilosophical pretense of unanimity. Hountondji's clarity on both "real" philosophy and "reality" forced every self-respecting African philosopher to take a position in relation to critical philosophy. Of course, the positions articulated varied widely—which is, no doubt, what Hountondji anticipated. Pluralism became a reality in African philosophy. Soon additional schools that went beyond ethnophilosophy and critical philosophy came into existence.

Because Hountondji took aim so very clearly at ethnophilosophy, not surprisingly, Hountondji's views were targeted by others. A fair amount of the criticism was, if not strictly personal, directed largely at Hountondji's sociological situation. Critics said Hountondji was a European-educated intellectual who had been thoroughly assimilated to non-African ways. As a result, his views are Eurocentric, elitist, and out of touch with the reality of ordinary African lives. Moreover, the sort of top-down, authoritarian Marxist development that Hountondji advocates goes against the communal African grain and has proved to be unsuccessful. Naturally, this sort of criticism refuses to tackle Hountondji using his own terms—terms that sharply separate philosophy and politics. On the contrary, it assumes that he is doing primarily political philosophy and that the criterion of evaluation in this field is practical success or failure.

This criticism returns the discussion to the essential question raised by *African Philosophy:* Is a nonideological, nonpolitical understanding and practice of philosophy possible? Or, as Hountondji himself is inclined to acknowledge, does every philosophical stance carry with it political implications? Assuming the latter to be true, the question may be rephrased as follows: Should the philosopher, as a matter of moral principle, conduct each inquiry and analysis in a manner as self-consciously open and dispassionate as possible? Hountondji's response in *African Philosophy*—a response that links science and philosophy, if not necessarily modernity—is in the affirmative.

John F. Wilson

Additional Reading

Althusser, Louis, and Étienne Balibar. *Reading Capital.* Translated by Ben Brewster. London: Verso, 1979. First published in French in 1968. Althusser wrote parts 1 and 2. A difficult, densely argued work but indispensable for understanding Althusser's shaping of Hountondji's notion of "science." Chapter 7, "The Object of Political Economy," is a brief, reasonably accessible summary statement.

Appiah, Kwame Anthony. *In My Father's House: Africa in the Philosophy of Culture.* New York: Oxford University Press, 1992. A subtle, interesting work by a leading Anglo-African professional philosopher, writing here in a mode quite sympathetic to ethnophilosophy. Hountondji is interpreted conventionally, with no attention to his later writing. Winner of the Herskovits Award for 1993.

Apter, Andrew. "*Que Faire?* Reconsidering Inventions of Africa." *Critical Inquiry* 19 (Autumn, 1992): 87-104. Developed from a 1989 African Studies Association roundtable in which Hountondji took part. Apter attempts to bridge the gap between ethnophilosophy and critical philosophy by arguing that traditional Yoruba cosmological rituals were implicitly critical of power holders.

Bell, Richard H. "Narrative in African Philosophy." *Philosophy* 64 (July, 1989): 363-379. An argument that the understanding of African philosophy should include narrative palaver as well as texts, and a partial endorsement of Hountondji's work as belonging to the dialectical rather than universalistic branch of critical philosophy.

Chachage, C. S. L. "Discourse on Development Among African Philosophers." In *African Perspectives on Development*, edited by Ulf Himmelstrand et al. London: James Currey, 1994. A brief, very useful discussion of five phases in the development of African philosophy. Hountondji's work is placed in the fourth phase, which is then treated critically by the fifth.

Floistad, Guttorm, ed. *African Philosophy*. Vol. 5 in *Contemporary Philosophy: A New Survey*. Dordrecht, Netherlands: Martinus Nijhoff, 1987. A collection of papers reflecting Hountondji's distinctions, categories, and criticism.

Imbo, Samuel Oluoch. *An Introduction to African Philosophy*. Totowa, N.J.: Rowman & Littlefield, 1998. An excellent introduction to African philosophy. Hountondiji's universalism is positioned against Leopold Senghor's Negritude.

Mudimbe, V. Y. *The Invention of Africa*. Bloomington: Indiana University Press, 1988. Usefully places Hountondji in a sociological context but repeats the standard "antiethnophilosophy" interpretation without noting Hountondji's insight into Africa as invented. Contains an extensive bibliography. Shared the Herskovits Award for 1989.

Senghor, Leopold Sedar. *On African Socialism*. Translated by Mercer Cook. New York: Frederick A. Praeger, 1964. A clear, thoughtful statement of African political philosophy by Senegal's poet-statesman. Sharply criticized by Hountondji for its "soft, humanistic, communal socialism" in contrast to the "scientific" Marxist variety.

Serequeberhan, Tsenay, ed. *African Philosophy: The Essential Readings*. New York: Paragon House, 1991. May be usefully compared with the Floistad volume because it reflects a later, more critical orientation toward Hountondji's work.

_____. *The Hermeneutics of African Philosophy*. New York: Routledge, 1994. A work in the dominant, postcritical mode of African philosophy in the 1990's. Hountondji's work is read as Eurocentric and neocolonialist, out of touch with both African Marxism and the sentiments of the "indigenous masses."

Tempels, Placide. *Bantu Philosophy*. Translated by Margaret Read. Paris: Presence Africaine, 1959. First published in French in 1945. For Hountondji, the prime example of "ethnophilosophy." It was to redirect the path of African philosophy that Hountondji subjected Tempels's work to scathing criticism.

John F. Wilson

Huineng

Although Huineng was the sixth patriarch of Chinese Chan (Zen) Buddhism, most Buddhist practitioners and scholars believe that the true tradition of Chinese Chan began with him. His brand of Buddhism was the first to display distinctly Chinese characteristics.

Principal philosophical works: *Liuzu tan jing*, c. 677 (*Sutra Spoken by the Sixth Patriarch*, 1930; better known as *The Platform Sutra of the Sixth Patriarch*, 1967)

Born: 638; Southwest Guangdong, China
Died: 713; Guangdong, China

Early Life

Few details of Huineng's early life are known. The traditional account of Huineng's life, which follows, appears in *The Platform Sutra of the Sixth Patriarch*. His father, Luxing Tao, a native of the northern Chinese city of Fan Yang, was a government official. For unknown reasons, Huineng's father was stripped of his position and banished to the southern Chinese city of Ling Nan, in the Xin Zhou district. At that time, northern China was the seat of culture, and those who lived in the south were considered barbarians.

Not long after his banishment, Luxing Tao, now a commoner rather than a respected official, died, leaving his wife and child destitute. Because his family was poor, Huineng was uneducated and lacked the means to make a good living. He became a woodcutter, scratching out a meager living and doing his best to support his mother.

Life's Work

One day, while he was delivering a load of firewood, Huineng overheard a man reciting the Diamond Sutra, a Buddhist text that holds an important place in the Chan (Zen) tradition. When he heard the instruction, "You should activate the mind without dwelling on anything," he experienced a degree of enlightenment. When Huineng asked about the text, the man said that he had learned it from Hongran, the fifth Chan patriarch.

Shortly thereafter, by good fortune, Huineng met a man who gave him enough money to support his mother and urged him to visit Hongran. After he had arranged for his mother to be cared for, Huineng traveled to Dong Chan monastery to meet the fifth patriarch. When Huineng met Hongran, the patriarch asked him where he was from and what he wanted. Huineng said that he was from the south and that he wanted to become a Buddha. Hongran responded, "Southerners have no Buddha-nature. How can you attain Buddhahood?" Huineng answered, "As far as people are concerned, there are North and South, but how could that apply to the Buddha-nature?" Huineng's question demonstrated to Hongran that his visitor had an unusual grasp of Chan, and Hongran told Huineng to remain at the monastery as a layperson, pounding rice in the mill and cutting firewood. Huineng did so, working at the monastery but not meditating with the monks.

After eight months had passed, Hongran decided that it was time to choose his successor. He told the monks that he wanted each of them to compose a verse that expressed their understanding of the Buddhist teachings. He intended to give the robe and bowl of the Chan patriarchs to the monk who wrote the best verse. The monks did not do what they were asked, however, since they believed that Shenxiu, who was foremost among them, would win the contest easily.

Shenxiu wrote a verse but was too anxious to give it to Hongran in person, so he wrote it on a wall. It read:

The body is the tree of enlightenment.
The mind is like a clear mirror on a stand.
Diligently wipe it off again and again,
Don't let it gather dust.

Hongran praised the poem and required the monks to memorize it. When Huineng heard one of the monks reciting the verse, he found it wanting, and that night he took a boy who could write to the wall on which Shenxiu's poem had been written. Huineng recited his own verse and had the boy write it next to Shenxiu's:

Enlightenment basically has no tree,
And the clear mirror has no stand;
Originally there is not a single thing;
Where can dust gather?

The monks did not know who had written the new verse, but they all praised its author, saying that he must be a living Buddha. When Hongran read the verse, he knew that it had been written by Huineng. Fearing that the monks would be angry that a mere layperson had bested them in understanding, Hongran said that the verse was the work of one who had no true understanding.

The monks forgot about the verse and went about their business, but that night Hongran paid a secret visit to Huineng. Hongran asked, "Is the rice whitened yet?" Huineng said, "It's whitened but has not had a sifting yet." Hongran struck the mortar three times, whereupon Huineng sifted some rice three times. The words and actions of both men had a hidden meaning. Because the Chinese character that means "sifting" has the same pronunciation as the character that means "teacher," Huineng was indicating that he was ready for complete enlightenment but needed the aid of a teacher. When Hongran struck the mortar three times, he was instructing Huineng to meet him in his room at the third watch that night. At the third watch that night, Huineng entered Hongran's room.

Hongran expounded the Diamond Sutra to Huineng, who experienced complete enlightenment. In that way, the fifth patriarch transmitted the teaching, and with it the robe and bowl of the patriarchs, to Huineng, who had become the sixth patriarch. Hongran went on to say that the robe had become the cause of dissension and that Huineng should not transmit it to anyone. He advised Huineng to leave the monastery at once and go into hiding.

Huineng did as he was told, but the monks soon realized that Hongran had chosen his successor, and they guessed, because of a comment that Hongran made, that he had chosen Huineng. Huiming, a bad-tempered monk who had been a general before he entered the monastery, took several hundred people and went after Huineng, intending to take the robe and bowl from him. Huiming overtook Huineng and was about to attack him when Huineng put the bowl and the robe on a rock, saying, "This robe symbolizes faith—why fight over it?" Huiming tried to pick up the robe and the bowl but was unable to budge them. Huiming was terrified and said, "I have come for the teaching, not for a robe." He asked Huineng to expound the true essence of Buddhism, and the patriarch said, "Since you came for the Dharma, you should stop all entanglements and not give rise to a single thought; then I will explain it for you." Huiming remained still for a very long time, preparing his mind. Then Huineng said, "Don't think of good, don't think of evil: At this very moment, what is your original face?" When he heard those words, Huiming experienced great enlightenment. After he had asked for further instruction, he left Huineng in peace.

Following his master's instructions, Huineng went into hiding in the forest, avoiding further pursuers. After spending ten to fifteen years in hiding, where he lived with a group of hunters (whose profession was thoroughly un-Buddhist), Huineng reemerged. He traveled to a monastery where the teacher Yin Zong was expounding the Nirvana Sutra. While he was there, Huineng overheard an argument between two monks who were watching a flag that was blowing in the wind. The first monk said that the flag was moving, and the second said that the wind was moving. Huineng said to the monks, "Neither the flag nor the wind is moving. It is your minds that are moving." The monks were impressed, and Huineng was asked to give a talk on the meaning of the sutras. It was obvious to all that Huineng was a man of remarkable understanding, and Yin Zong asked him if he was the sixth patriarch. When Huineng admitted that he was, Yin Zong asked Huineng to accept him as a disciple. Only then was Huineng, who had never studied or practiced in any formal manner, ordained as a monk.

After that, Huineng taught openly. He and his followers founded what has become known as the Southern School of Chan. In the meantime, Shenxiu had begun teaching, in spite of the fact that he had not received the transmission from Hongran, and he was regarded by many Chan Buddhists as the sixth patriarch. Shenxiu did, however, admit that Huineng's understanding was superior to his own. Shenxiu enjoyed the support of the government, and the school that he founded came to be known as the Northern School of Chan. Ultimately, however, the Southern School became recognized as authentic, whereas the Northern School died out.

Influence

It is significant that Huineng experienced complete enlightenment and became the sixth patriarch without becoming a monk or engaging in formal meditation practice. He emphasized the fact that the purpose of meditation was to enable the practitioner to directly perceive the truth—that is, to experience enlightenment. In his view, enlightenment and meditation were the same thing. Formal meditation without enlightenment was not true meditation. He also viewed the study and recitation of Buddhist texts, unless they were combined with the cultivation of enlightenment, as a waste of time.

Huineng's views were controversial in his day, although they are now viewed as correct by most Buddhist scholars and practitioners. In the Indian Buddhist tradition, formal study was generally considered to be extremely important, and that tradition lived on in the Northern School of Chan. Shenxiu had been a highly regarded Confucian scholar before he converted to Buddhism, and there was a strong intellectual component in his version of Chan. He and his followers could

not accept Huineng's radical approach, which was strongly influenced by the native Chinese religion of Daoism. It is the influence of Daoism on Buddhism that gave Chan Buddhism after Huineng its distinctly Chinese character. Buddhist scholar D. T. Suzuki wrote that the fact that Huineng's Chan survived and Shenxiu's Chan died out indicates that Huineng's approach was in accord with the Chinese way of thinking and Shenxiu's was not.

After Huineng's death, his followers went out of their way to emphasize his lack of education, and it is worth noting that they may have been overzealous in doing so. It is clear from accounts of Huineng's teaching that he had a thorough grasp of the history of Buddhism and was familiar with the sutras. He was certainly not ignorant of the Indian tradition, and he did not reject study and practice outright; he simply held that study and practice without enlightenment led nowhere.

Another important element of Huineng's Chan was his insistence that enlightenment, when it came, came instantly. Shenxiu and his Northern School held that enlightenment came gradually, step by step. Huineng believed that enlightenment, which entailed direct perception of the truth, came or did not come. How could direct perception come in installments? It simply was or was not there. For this reason, Huineng's Southern School is sometimes called the Sudden School, while Shenxiu's Northern School is sometimes called the Gradual School.

After Huineng began to teach openly, his followers began to record his teachings, and after his death the results of their work were collected in a volume that also included an autobiography of the sixth patriarch. Many versions of the work exist, and it goes by many titles, including *The Platform Sutra of the Sixth Patriarch*. The work is often referred to as the Platform Sutra or Altar Sutra. The fact that it is called a sutra is significant because the word is most often reserved for the teachings of Shakyamuni, the historical Buddha and founder of Buddhism. Huineng's work is the only one by a Chinese author to be called a sutra, which indicates the respect that it is accorded by Buddhists. The work is still widely used by Zen practitioners.

Shawn Woodyard

The Platform Sutra of the Sixth Patriarch

Type of philosophy: Buddhism, Chinese philosophy, ethics, metaphysics
First transcribed: Liuzu tan jing, c. 677 (*Sutra Spoken by the Sixth Patriarch,* 1930; better known as *The Platform Sutra of the Sixth Patriarch,* 1967)
Principal ideas advanced:

◇ Perfect, Buddha wisdom is in everyone.

◇ Insight into one's original, pure nature is possible only by putting that nature into practice.

◇ To attain insight into one's Buddha-nature, one's mind must be free from attachments and error.

◇ The practice of direct mind leads to sudden enlightenment.

◇ Through no-thought (not being distracted by thought while thinking), one's original nature, the true reality, is thought.

◇ The original wisdom and such meditation are one.

The Platform Sutra of the Sixth Patriarch is generally regarded as the basic classic of Chan (Zen) Buddhism. The work is reputed to be a record of the teachings of the great Chan master Huineng, as expressed in his remarks delivered in the Dafan Temple in Shaozhou in or about the year 677, and as recorded by his disciple Fahai. The most authentic version of the work is regarded by such scholars as Wing-tsit Chan and Philip B. Yampolsky, who translated the work in 1967, to be the *Dunhuang* manuscript, found in a cave in Dunhuang, northwest China, in 1900.

A Legendary Rise

Huineng was born in 638 in southwest Guangdong, but few details of his life are known. The prevailing legends, embellished by commentators over the years, tend to agree on the following biographical items: Huineng was born in 638 into a humble family, the Lu family, and was a firewood peddler. In his early twenties, he was inspired by a reading of the Diamond Sutra, and he traveled to the north to visit the fifth patriarch, who was an exponent of the sutra.

Legend has it that Huineng was appointed sixth patriarch after having served a stint under the fifth patriarch as a pounder of rice and having subsequently impressed the patriarch with a poem requested of all his disciples by the fifth patriarch. Whether or not the story is true, it appears clear that Huineng did "receive the robe" as sixth patriarch in 661, just a few months after arriving in Huangmei to visit the fifth patriarch.

In 676, after several years of preaching in south China, Huineng moved to Guangzhou. He had become a Buddhist priest at the age of thirty-nine. The following year (so the story goes), he was invited to lecture in the Dafan Temple in Shaozhou. There his remarks were recorded by his disciple Fahai, and the resultant work is, or at least provided the foundation for, *The Platform Sutra of the Sixth Patriarch.*

Huineng is honored as the Chan master who initiated the Southern School of Chan Buddhism in opposition to the Northern School led by Shenxiu, another student of the fifth patriarch. The Northern School maintained that enlightenment would come gradually as a result of practicing formalized procedures of meditation; the Southern School argued that meditation must be free, a matter of allowing the pure Buddha-nature to reveal itself, and that enlightenment would be sudden. According to Chan, although this difference of opinion about the speed of enlightenment was present as a matter of emphasis, the two schools differed more fundamentally in their concepts of mind, the Northern School maintaining that the mind or Buddha-nature, common to all persons, cannot be differentiated and that its activities are functions of the true reality, while the Southern School argued that the pure mind can function only in quietude or "calmness," and only after having freed itself from the false or erroneous mind with its attachments to individual thoughts. In any case, according to Chan, the Southern School became the most influential force in the development of Zen Buddhism in China from the ninth century.

As translated by Wing-tsit Chan, the heading of *The Platform Sutra of the Sixth Patriarch* is as follows:

The Platform Scripture Preached by the sixth patriarch, Hui-neng, in the Ta-fan Temple in Shao-chou, the Very Best Perfection of Great Wisdom Scripture on the Sudden Enlightenment Doctrine of the Southern School of Zen, one book, including the Giving of the Discipline that Frees One from the Attachment to Differentiated Characters for the Propagation of the Law. Gathered and recorded by disciple Fa-hai.

As translated by Yampolsky, the heading is:

Southern School Sudden Doctrine, Supreme Mahāyāna Great Perfection of Wisdom: The Platform Sutra preached by the sixth patriarch Hui-neng at the Ta-fan Temple in Shaochou, one roll, recorded by the spreader of the Dharma, the disciple Fa-hai, who at the same time received the Precepts of Formlessness.

Meditation and Wisdom
The Platform Sutra of the Sixth Patriarch recounts that Huineng lectured to more than ten thousand monks, nuns, and followers, all gathered in the lecture hall of the Dafan Temple. His topic was the *dharma* (law) of the perfection of wisdom (of the original, pure wisdom of the Buddha-nature). Huineng begins with an autobiographical account. The material is interesting, but it has little philosophical or religious import. In section 12, Huineng declares that he was determined or predestined to preach to the officials and disciples gathered there in the temple, and he maintains that the teaching is not original with him but has been handed down by the Sage Kings. Sections 13 through 19 contain the fundamental teachings of Huineng. In 13, Huineng declares that calm meditation and wisdom are a unity, that such meditation is the substance of wisdom, and that wisdom is the function of meditation.

The Buddhist doctrine, here implicit, is that everyone shares the Buddha-nature (wisdom) and that if one can turn one's mind inward and not be distracted, one can receive enlightenment. Wisdom and meditation are one in that meditation (of the kind advocated by Huineng) is regarded as the function or practice of the original nature. Hence, Huineng declares that meditation exists in wisdom, and wisdom is within meditation. Neither gives rise to the other, he insists. If the mind and words are both good and the internal and external are one, then wisdom and meditation are one.

The Importance of Practicing
Huineng next stresses the critical importance of practicing—actively attaining—a straightforward or direct mind. A straightforward mind requires having no attachments and attending to no differentiating characters, thereby realizing that all is one; there is a unity of nature in everything. To achieve such realization in the practice of the straightforward mind is *samadhi* of oneness, a state of calmness in which one knows all *dharmas* to be the same. However, the calm realization of oneness is not, as some people think, a matter of simply sitting without moving and not allowing erroneous thoughts to rise in the mind. To act in this way is to make oneself insentient, and that is not in accordance with the Way, the *dao*, which can work freely only if the mind is free from things. If one attempts, as some people do, to view the mind and keep it inactive, they become radically disturbed and never achieve enlightenment.

Huineng indirectly criticizes the Northern School in his description of the meditation method that, in effect, renders people insensible and inactive; and he continues his criticism in section 16 when he states that the deluded teachers recommend a gradual course to enlightenment, while the enlightened teachers practice the method of sudden enlightenment. In this passage, Huineng clearly states that to know one's own mind or to know one's original nature is the same thing, and if people differ in coming to enlightenment it is because some people are stupid and deluded while others know the method of enlightenment.

Huineng then remarks that everyone has regarded "no-thought" as his main doctrine. His remark ties in with what he had just been saying about meditation method, for the doctrine to which he alludes is the meditation method he endorsed, a method that came to be identified with the Southern School. Put informally, the statement of method would be put injunctively, "Practice no-thought," and sense would be made of the injunction by presuming the point to be that the mind will be open to its nature, will be able to "think" (intuit) the pure nature common to all within oneself, only if it is not distracted by thoughts *about* things, including the thought about achieving enlightenment by not thinking about anything else. The truth is, one cannot achieve awareness even of the Buddha-nature by thinking *about* it.

No-Thought
Huineng speaks of no-thought as the main doctrine (of meditation), of "non-form as the substance" and of "non-abiding as the basis" (to follow Yampolsky's translation). He then adds that "Non-form is to be separated from form even when associated with form. No-thought is not to think even when involved in thought. Non-abiding is the original nature of man." Presumably, as the next passage (of section 17) implicitly indicates, the original Buddha-nature is absolute, in no way dependent on, related to, or attached to any particular being or characteristic of being; hence, "non-abiding" (nonattachment) is the original nature of humanity. When involved in the thought consisting of the awareness of original nature (or while succeeding in the practice of freeing the mind), one is not thinking this or that. In that sense, the thinking of the original nature is no-thought. As scholar Chan translates, "If one single instant of thought is attached to anything, then every thought will be attached. This is bondage. But if in regard to *dharmas* no thought is attached to anything, that is freedom."

To be separated from forms is not to attend to the characters of things; it then happens, so Huineng preaches, that the substance of one's nature is pure. One must not be affected by external objects and one must not turn one's thought to them. However, one must, of course, *think*—that is, one must think the pure nature of true reality. No-thought is thought free from the error of attending to external things and characters and from all attachment. If one's pure nature is allowed to function, as it will if there is no-thought, then true reality becomes the substance of thought.

Sitting in Meditation
Huineng speaks of "sitting in meditation" (in section 18). He contends that this teaching does not call for looking at the mind or at the purity of one's nature. The objects of such viewing are illusions, and to suppose that one is looking at objects or that there are such objects to look at is to be deluded. However, if delusions are avoided,

then the original nature is revealed in its purity. Purity has no form, Huineng argues, and hence one cannot grasp the form of purity and then pass judgment on others. Deluded people are quick to find fault with others because they (the deluded) presume themselves to know the form of purity. By criticizing others, such persons violate the *dao*, the true Way.

Sitting in meditation, then, is not a matter of looking for forms or characters; sitting in meditation is, rather, to be free and not to allow thoughts to be activated. Hence (Huineng concludes in section 19), true meditation is the achievement of internal calmness and purity. To "see" the original nature and in purity and freedom to *be* the original nature—to meditate and to be wise—are one and the same. Meditation is the practice of original wisdom; wisdom is the internal subject of meditation.

The remaining sections of *The Platform Sutra of the Sixth Patriarch* are concerned with provoking ritualistic attention to the central features of Mahayana Buddhism or are taken up with miscellaneous material, most of it probably added by later writers.

Whether or not the ideas represented in *The Platform Sutra of the Sixth Patriarch* were actually enunciated by Huineng and recorded by Fahai, they represent the central doctrines of Chan Buddhism of the Southern School and are of philosophical and historical interest whatever their origin. In many ways, *The Platform Sutra of the Sixth Patriarch* can be seen as an argument for intuition as the way of enlightenment, in opposition to those who argue for the way of intellect and its distinctive mode, analysis.

Ian P. McGreal

Additional Reading
Blyth, R. H. "The Platform Sutra." In *Zen and Zen Classics: Volume 1*. Tokyo: Hokuseido Press, 1960. Blyth, an early student and translator of Japanese Buddhist and literary texts, has some interesting things to say about Huineng and his followers. Blyth's comments should, however, be read with care. He was extremely opinionated, and sometimes he draws the wrong conclusions. He is incorrect, for example, when he disagrees with Huineng and states, "If the body is different, the [Buddha-]

nature is different. If the Buddha-nature is the same, the body is the same."

Dumoulin, Heinrich. "The High Period of Chinese Zen." In *A History of Zen Buddhism*. Boston: Beacon Press, 1969. This chapter contains a brief section on Huineng and contains discussions of the sixth patriarch's significance in the history of Zen.

Keizan. "Huineng." Translated by Thomas Cleary. In *The Transmission of Light: Zen in the Art of Enlightenment by Zen Master Keizan*. San Francisco: North Point Press, 1990. Cleary has done an excellent job of translating Keizan's *Denkōroku*, which is one of the most important works in the Japanese Zen tradition. Keizan's work tells the enlightenment stories of fifty-three Buddhist patriarchs but it is intended as an instructional work for Zen practitioners. The chapter on Huineng is brief but extremely powerful.

Nan Huai-Chin. "The Sixth Patriarch of Zen." In *The Story of Chinese Zen*. Boston: Charles E. Tuttle, 1995. Many Buddhist scholars and translators have no true understanding of their subject, and much of their work is misleading or simply wrong. Nan Huai-Chin, however, is a contemporary Zen master, and his work is accurate and reliable. This chapter on Huineng corrects various errors that other scholars have made regarding the sixth patriarch. Highly recommended.

Suzuki, D. T. "From Zen to the Gandavyūha." In *Essays in Zen Buddhism: Third Series*. London: Luzac, 1934. This chapter includes discussions of Huineng's contributions to Zen Buddhism. Suzuki contends that true Zen began with Huineng. His discussions of the differences between the thought of Bodhidharma, the first Chan patriarch, and that of Huineng are particularly interesting.

_____. *The Zen Doctrine of No-Mind: The Significance of the Sûtra of Hui-neng*. Edited by Christmas Humphreys. York Beach, Maine: Samuel Weiser, 1993. Devoted to the teaching of Huineng, this book includes the technique and purpose of Zen training.

Shawn Woodyard

David Hume

Hume's philosophical writings undermined earlier reliance on reason as a guide for action and made major advances in the theory of perception and ethics.

Principal philosophical works: *A Treatise of Human Nature: Being an Attempt to Introduce the Experimental Method of Reasoning into Moral Subjects*, 1739-1740; *Essays, Moral and Political*, 1741-1742 (enlarged as *Essays, Moral, Political, and Literary*, 1758); *Three Essays, Moral and Political*, 1748; *Philosophical Essays Concerning Human Understanding*, 1748 (best known as *An Enquiry Concerning Human Understanding*, 1758); *An Enquiry Concerning the Principles of Morals*, 1751; *Political Discourses*, 1752; *The History of England*, 1754-1762 (6 volumes); *Four Dissertations*, 1757; *A Concise and Genuine Account of the Dispute Between Mr. Hume and Mr. Rousseau*, 1766; *The Life of David Hume, Esq., Written by Himself*, 1777; *Dialogues Concerning Natural Religion*, 1779.

Born: May 7, 1711; Edinburgh, Scotland
Died: August 25, 1776; Edinburgh, Scotland

Early Life

David Hume was born into a middle-class family, but his father died when he was quite young, leaving him, as the second son, with a patrimony of fifty pounds per year and a precarious living. He went to Edinburgh University with his older brother at the age of twelve, and after three years of study he left without taking a degree, as was the custom at the time. Hume spent the next three years reading the Greek and Roman classics rather than the legal tomes he was supposed to master for a career in the law. Hume's reading of the classics inclined him to a career in letters (philosophy, history, criticism), and he set about reading at various libraries to prepare himself for the essays in philosophy and morals he planned to write. By 1729, he had already set out the plan for his first work, but such intensive study had an effect on his health, so he began to exercise and transformed, in his own words, "a tall, lean and rawbon'd" young man into the "most sturdy, robust, healthful-like Fellow you have seen."

Hume had some difficulties in his first job as a clerk in Bristol. The work was not congenial, and he was named in a paternity suit as well. He therefore went to France in 1734, where his fifty pounds would enable him to live more comfort-ably and where he could read and study more widely. He spent a year at Reims and two years at Anjou, where he took advantage of the Jesuit library where René Descartes had studied. After three years of studying and writing, Hume had almost completed his first major work, *A Treatise of Human Nature*, and he returned to England in expectation of "literary fame."

Life's Work

Hume's *A Treatise of Human Nature* saw publication in 1739 but was, for the most part, ignored by the public; Hume said it "fell dead-born from the Press." There is still some debate among scholars about Hume's intentions in the treatise. The most common view until the mid-twentieth century was that Hume was attempting to undermine or subvert the philosophies of John Locke and George Berkeley. Later scholarship, however, suggested that Hume was attempting to apply the Newtonian model developed in natural philosophy (now known as physics) to moral philosophy. The most important aspect of Hume's program was an assault on the primacy of reason in human affairs. As Hume said in his famous dictum, "Reason is and ought to be the slave of the passions, and can never pretend to any other office than to serve and obey them." What Hume attempted to do was banish that inaccurate reliance on reason and all formulations of "ought" in moral issues by showing how people really lived and acted; Hume's philosophy is based on common sense and not on deductive premises. Hume's solution is to propose that "custom" and the "passions," not reason, lead people to act.

Other aspects of *A Treatise of Human Nature* that deserve mention are Hume's attempt to construct a theory of perception based on sense impressions rather than innate ideas. For Hume, ideas are "derived from simple impressions." Nevertheless, while Hume believed in the existence of the objects of perception, he realized that he could not prove that they existed. The scholar Nicholas Capaldi defended Hume's theory of perception, but he acknowledged problems and inconsistencies in it. More important for later philosophy is Hume's theory of causation, which attempts to destroy the Aristotelian theory of "essences" (what makes an object what it is when it is interacting with something else) and replace it with a Newtonian concept that defines an object by the qualities it appears to possess.

After the failure of *A Treatise of Human Nature*, Hume wrote political essays that were more successful and more lucrative, but he still needed a permanent position. He was encouraged to apply for the vacant professorship of ethics at Edinburgh University. Hume was obviously highly qualified but was rejected by the "zealots" for his supposed atheism. Hume defended his position in a pamphlet and accepted a position as tutor to the mad Marquess of Annandale. During these years he rewrote *A Treatise of Human Nature* to clarify certain positions and to tone down others that had offended some readers. The result of these revisions was published as *An Enquiry Concerning Human Understanding*.

An Enquiry Concerning Human Understanding clarifies some sections of *A Treatise of Human Nature*, adding two chapters as well. However, the chapters that were added, "Of Miracles" and "Of Particular Providence and of a Future State," led to controversy. Hume tests all reports of miracles by the rules of evidence and logic and finds them so deficient that he finds a person's belief in miracles to be nothing less than miraculous. Hume is not as direct in his rejection of the arguments for God's providence; he simply sets it aside, saying, "No new fact can ever be inferred by the religious hypothesis." There is no evidence that Hume ever denied the existence of God, but he opposed basing religion on such dubious grounds.

David Hume. *(Library of Congress)*

Hume extended his commonsense approach to morality with the publication of *An Enquiry Concerning the Principles of Morals* in 1751. In his search for a viable source for morality, Hume changed the concept of "sympathy" in *A Treatise of Human Nature* to one of "benevolence," a common idea in the eighteenth century. He makes this change clear in *An Enquiry Concerning the Principles of Morals*:

> Everything which contributes to the happiness of society, recommends itself directly to our approbation and good will. Here is a principle which accounts, in great part for the origin of morality: And what need we seek for abstruse and remote systems, when there occurs one so obvious and natural.

Hume also contrasts the principle of "benevolence" to that of "self-love," and he asserts, "I hate or despise him, who has no regard to any thing beyond his own gratifications and enjoyments."

During this period, Hume supported himself by taking a position first as judge advocate and later as aide-de-camp to General James St. Clair. The general's projected military expedition to Canada never became operational, but Hume did later take part in a military embassy with St. Clair to Vienna and Turin. Hume's *An Enquiry Concerning the Principles of Morals* was not immediately successful, so on his return to Scotland, he began to write *Dialogues Concerning Natural Religion* (which was not published until three years after his death, in 1779) and *The History of England*. *The History of England* was published in six volumes from 1754 to 1762, and they did provide Hume with the literary fame for which he longed. Hume's *The History of England*, ironically, was far better known and respected in the eighteenth century than were his enduring philosophical works, which were ignored or denounced for atheism.

Dialogues Concerning Natural Religion is in the form of a Socratic dialogue with four speakers: Pamphillus (the narrator), Cleanthes (a deist), Demea (an orthodox believer), and Philo (a skeptic). The subject of the dialogue is the "science of natural religion," which is based on scientific evidence and reasoning rather than revealed or institutional religion. Cleanthes advances the argument from design as proof of God's existence and nature. This argument is rejected by both the ortho-dox Demea and the skeptical Philo. At the end of the dialogue, Pamphillus acts as a sort of referee and states: "I cannot but think that *Philo's* principles are more probable than *Demea's*, but those of *Cleanthes* approach still nearer to the truth." This sudden shift at the end has puzzled many commentators, and as a result some have said that Philo speaks for Hume and others that Cleanthes does. Richard H. Popkin supports his view that Cleanthes speaks for Hume by comparing those views to Hume's other writings. If Cleanthes does speak for Hume, then the widespread notion that Hume rejected religion altogether is inaccurate, although he did oppose institutional religion throughout his life.

From 1763 until 1767, Hume served as private secretary to the Earl of Hertford, who was appointed British ambassador to France. In France, Hume received the fame and even adulation he never found in England. The French recognized Hume as an important philosopher, and he had a receptive audience in the *philosophes* of Paris. He also had perhaps his closest relationship with a woman while in Paris. His friendship with the Comtesse de Boufflers soon became a more intimate relationship; they maintained a correspondence for many years, but marriage was impossible.

Hume returned to Scotland in 1767 and began revision of the *Dialogues Concerning Natural Religion*. For once, he had no financial worries; his writing and appointments gave him an income of one thousand pounds per year. He became ill in 1775 and died on August 25, 1776, in a tranquil mood despite the impertinent questions about his beliefs posed by Scottish author James Boswell and others.

Influence

Hume was a man of the eighteenth century, the period of the Enlightenment, or the Age of Reason. It is often forgotten, however, that a major part of Hume's work was intended to show the limits of reason. He extolled common sense and distrusted any theory that was not soundly based on human experience. He never lapsed, however, into empiricism but instead retained a skeptical mind about the certainty of the objects of our perceptions. Many critics have complained that Hume's philosophy is merely negative and skeptical, but Hume specifically rejected the extreme form of skepticism called Pyrrhonism, and many of his deconstructions prepared the way for other philosophers. For example, Immanuel Kant made his debt to Hume quite clear: "I honestly confess that my recollection of David Hume's teaching was the very thing which many years ago first interrupted my dogmatic slumber." Hume also had a direct influence on such nineteenth century utilitarians as Jeremy Bentham and John Stuart Mill. Mill's essay *On Liberty* (1859) is clearly indebted to Hume.

There are lapses and inconsistencies in Hume's philosophy, and his psychological solutions to philosophical problems are of little value today. Nevertheless, Hume's achievement remains significant. He may not have solved the problem of the existence of the objects of perception, but he showed that Berkeley's idealism and Locke's empiricism were inadequate. In addition, Hume's rejection of metaphysics became a favorite theme for the twentieth century poststructuralists. Hume scholar John Passmore sums up Hume's achievement: "He [Hume] is pre-eminently a breaker of new ground: a philosopher who opens up new lines of thought, who suggests to us an endless variety of philosophical explorations."

James Sullivan

A Treatise of Human Nature

Being an Attempt to Introduce the Experimental Method of Reasoning into Moral Subjects

Type of philosophy: Epistemology
First published: 1739-1740
Principal ideas advanced:

◇ All human knowledge comes from impressions and ideas; the impressions are more forceful and lively than the ideas.

◇ By the use of memory and imagination, people preserve and arrange their ideas.

◇ People have no abstract, general ideas but only ideas of particular things that can be considered collectively by the use of general terms.

◇ Certainty comes from the intuitive recognition of the similarity or differences in ideas, or from

the demonstrative process of connecting a series of intuitions—as in arithmetic and algebra.

◇ People's knowledge of causal relationships is simply the habit of expecting events of one kind to follow events of another kind with which they have been observed to be conjoined; there are no necessary relationships between events.

◇ People have good reason to be skeptical about all conclusions reached by the use of reason or on the basis of sense experience.

David Hume's *A Treatise of Human Nature* is his earliest philosophical work and the one that contains the most complete exposition of his views. Apparently it was planned when he was in his early twenties, when he claimed to have discovered a "new scene of thought." The work was composed during a sojourn in France from 1734 to 1737 and was revised shortly thereafter in an unsuccessful attempt to gain the approbation of Bishop Joseph Butler. The first book of *A Treatise of Human Nature* was published in 1739, and the other two the next year. Hume had hoped that his views would attract a great deal of attention; instead, the work "fell dead-born from the Press." His novel theories did not attract attention until after he had published a more popular version in *Philosophical Essays Concerning Human Understanding* (1748; best known as *An Enquiry Concerning Human Understanding*, 1758). *A Treatise of Human Nature* was subjected to a full-scale attack by Thomas Reid in 1764. By this time, Hume was so successful as an author, especially on the basis of his essays and *The History of England* (1754-1762), that he refused to defend his first book and called it a juvenile work. Over the years, it has become increasingly important as the fullest and deepest statement of Hume's philosophical views; book 1 of *A Treatise of Human Nature* has come to be regarded as one of the finest achievements of English philosophy.

Science Applied to Moral Subjects

On the title page of book 1, Hume announces that *A Treatise of Human Nature* is "an attempt to introduce the experimental Method of Reasoning into Moral Subjects." In the preface, he explains that he intends to develop a "science of man" by applying Sir Isaac Newton's experimental method to human mental behavior. Following in the footsteps of various English and Scottish moral philosophers, and of the French skeptic Pierre Bayle, he hoped to discover the limits of human knowledge in such areas as mathematics, physics, and the social sciences (the moral subjects). By scrupulously observing human life, Hume thought he could discover certain general laws about human thinking and behavior. He admitted at the outset that it was probably not possible to uncover "the ultimate qualities of human nature," but he thought it should be possible to learn something about the origin and nature of what we think we know.

All of our information, Hume writes, is composed of impressions and ideas. The only difference between these is that the former strike us more forcefully and with greater vivacity than do the latter. Ideas and impressions can be simple or complex, the simple ones being those that cannot be divided into parts or aspects, while the complex ones are composed of simple ones. There is a great deal of resemblance between the impressions and the ideas. The simple ideas, in fact, exactly resemble simple impressions in all respects except with regard to their force and vivacity. Further, in terms of their appearance in the mind, the simple impressions always precede the simple ideas (except for one unusual case that Hume brings up). The complex ideas are composed of simple parts that are exactly like the simple ingredients of impressions that we have already experienced, though the complex idea itself may not actually be a copy of any complex impression. These discoveries about impressions and ideas indicate, Hume says, that all of our ideas are derived from experience (the world of impressions) and that we have no innate ideas in our minds—that is, ideas that are not based on what we perceive.

The Basis of Knowledge
In the first part of *A Treatise of Human Nature*, Hume proceeds to explore the bases of our knowledge. We possess two faculties, memory and imagination, for dealing with the ideas that we receive. The memory preserves the ideas in the exact order in which they entered the mind. The imagination, on the other hand, is free to arrange the ideas in any manner that is desired.

However, contrary to what might be expected, our imaginations do not function at random. Instead, we imagine ideas in ordered sequences, so that whenever a particular idea comes to mind, related ideas automatically follow it, according to certain principles of the association of ideas that Hume calls "a kind of ATTRACTION, which in the mental world will be found to have as extraordinary effects as in the natural." Ideas tend naturally to be associated when they are similar or when they are contiguous in time or space or when they stand in the relation of cause and effect. The importance of association is brought out when Hume comes to discuss causality in part 3.

Before applying these "discoveries" about the way we think, Hume takes up a few other questions. He argues first for a point the philosopher George Berkeley had previously made, that we possess no abstract general ideas but only ideas of particular things. General terms, such as "man" or "triangle," designate the collections of similar particular ideas that we have acquired from experience.

A Theory of Mathematics
Hume then tries to explain mathematics as being about particular experiences. He knew relatively little about mathematics and based many of his views on comments in philospher Pierre Bayle's *The Historical and Critical Dictionary* (1695-1697). Hume's empirical mathematical theory has generally been regarded as, perhaps, the weakest part of his book, though he was always proud of having shown that mathematics is "big with absurdity and contradiction." Hume conceived of arithmetic as being a demonstrable science dealing with relations of quantity, whereas geometry was thought of as an empirical science dealing with observable points. Because of the limitation of our ability to see and count the points, the theorems in geometry are always to some degree uncertain.

Sources of Knowledge
The most famous part of *A Treatise of Human Nature* is the third part of book 1, which treats "Of Knowledge and Probability." Genuine knowledge is gained by an intuitive inspection of two or more ideas to see if they stand in a particular relationship to each other. We can be completely

certain by intuition that two ideas do or do not resemble each other, or that they differ from each other, or that one has more or less of a given quality than another—for instance, that one is darker than another. Such knowledge is certain in that it depends solely on what one "sees" when two or more ideas are brought together by the imagination, but it gives us relatively little information. By connecting a series of intuitions, we gain the sort of demonstrative knowledge that occurs in arithmetic and algebra. Intuition and demonstration are the sole sources of complete certainty and knowledge.

Causality

Our information about the causal relation of ideas does not arise from an intuitive examination of our ideas, and almost all of our information about what is happening beyond our immediate experience is based upon causal reasoning. How do we decide which ideas are causally related? When we examine two ideas, or two impressions that we think are so related, we find that we do not perceive any necessary or causal connection between them. We perceive only that the ideas are contiguous and successive. We do not, however, perceive that they are necessarily connected in any way, although we do feel that there must be more to the sequence than merely one idea following after another. We believe that one of the ideas must make the other occur. However, Hume asks, what evidence do we have for such a belief, and where do we acquire the belief? If we admit that we do not perceive any necessary connection between events, then Hume suggests that we ought to ask ourselves why we believe that every event must have a cause and why we believe that particular causes necessarily must have certain effects.

When the first problem is examined, we discover something that is surprising. Even though we all believe that every event must have a cause, this proposition is not intuitively obvious, nor can it be demonstrated. When we conceive of events, we neither see them as caused nor necessarily think of them in terms of their causes. Because of the freedom of our imagination, each event can be thought of separately and independently. If events can be thought of as uncaused, it is also possible that they occur uncaused. If that

is a genuine possibility, then there can be no valid demonstration proving the impossibility of uncaused events. The demonstrations that had been offered by previous philosophers, Hume believed, are all unsatisfactory. They beg the question in that they assume what they are attempting to prove: namely, that every event has a cause. Apparently the causal principle, which is neither self-evident nor demonstrable, is so basic that we all accept it for reasons that seem to be unknown.

Causes and Effects

To explore the matter further, Hume turns to the other problem: What is the basis for our belief that particular causes have particular effects, and how do we infer one from the other? The actual constituents of our causal reasoning, he asserts, are a present impression of sense or memory, an imagined idea of a related event, and an unknown connection between them. When we hear a certain sound, we think of somebody ringing the doorbell. Why and how do we infer from the impression to its supposed cause? Many other ideas might have come to mind. When we hear the sound, we do not, at the same time, experience its cause, yet we implicitly believe that said cause must also be occurring to produce the perceived effect. This reasoning process is not a logical one, Hume maintains, since there is no *reason* for us to think of one idea rather than another when a particular experience takes place.

If reason cannot be what makes us connect events causally, perhaps experience is responsible. We find that when a sequence of events is constantly repeated in our experience, and when the events are conjoined, we tend to associate ideas about them in our minds. Then, when we experience just one of the events, we also think of the other. One of them we call the cause and the other, the effect. What is there in the fact that certain events have been constantly conjoined in the past that leads us to think of them as causally related? Hume points out that if the process involved were a rational one, we would have to presuppose that the principle of the uniformity of nature was true. This principle asserts that "instances, of which we have had no experience, must resemble those, of which we have had experience, and that the course of nature continues always uniformly the same."

The Limits of Experience

Hume next questions whether we possess any evidence that this principle is true, or that it has to be true. Since we can readily imagine that the world might change in many respects in the future, it is not possible to demonstrate that nature must be uniform. Our experience up to the present moment does not constitute evidence as to what the future course of nature will be, or must be. Just because the sun has risen every day up to now does not prove that it has to rise tomorrow. We can judge the future only if we know that nature is uniform. However, our information up to this point is only that, so far, nature has always been uniform. Experience can provide us with no clue about what has to be the case in the future. Hence, we can neither demonstrate nor prove from experience that the all-important principle of the uniformity of nature is true, even though much of our reasoning about the world depends upon it.

The acceptance of this principle, Hume contends, is a fundamental characteristic of human nature. We have a habit or custom that operates upon us for unknown and unknowable reasons. After we have experienced the same sequence of conjoined events several times, then, when we perceive one of the conjuncts, habit or custom leads us to think of the other, and to think of it in a lively and forceful way. Although we are able to think of any idea we wish, we are led psychologically to think only of a particular conjoined idea and to conceive of it with some of the force and vivacity of its conjoined impression. Such force and vivacity constitute our belief in the actual occurrence of the conjoined item. In terms of this explanation, the principle of the uniformity of nature is more a principle about how we think and feel than it is one about the order of events in the world.

Causation Rooted in Imagination

Hume uses his discovery of the psychological origins of our belief in the uniformity of nature to explain the basis for our conviction that there is a necessary connection between events. The necessary connection is never perceived, no matter how often the same sequence is observed. However, after a constant conjunction of events has been perceived many times, we then feel that one of the conjuncts causes or produces the other. It is not any discoverable fact about the events that makes us believe this, but rather our psychological attitude toward the events. We possess a fundamental propensity or determination of the mind to think of a conjoined idea after experiencing the conjunct or thinking of it, once we have perceived the constant conjunction of the two in our experience. This determination, which is a strong feeling, is the necessary connection that we think exists between events. Although it is felt in us, we have a tendency to conceive of it as existing in the events themselves. This idea is actually a feature of the way we think about events, rather than a feature of them. Thus, the term "cause" can be defined as "An object precedent and contiguous to another, and so united with it in the imagination, that the idea of the one determines the mind to form the idea of the other, and the impression of the one to form a more lively idea of the other."

Knowledge vs. Belief

In Hume's explanation of causality, he joins Nicolas de Malebranche's contention that there is no necessary connection between events with his own psychological account of how we react to the uniformities in experience. Because of our habits, we expect the future to resemble the past, and we feel that when we observe certain events, their constant conjuncts must also be taking place, even if we cannot observe them. We have no actual knowledge of what is taking place, but only beliefs. Because we can never be completely sure that our beliefs correspond to the actual state of affairs, our causal information is always, at best, only probable.

Hume sees the task of the sciences as that of carefully establishing bases for "reasonable belief" by collecting data about the constant conjunctions that occur in human experience and organizing these data in terms of scientific laws. These laws provide a form of rational expectation in that they allow us to predict the future course of events on the basis of detailed information about what has happened up to now. The scientist, like anyone else, expects, through personal habits and propensities, that the future will resemble the past. Science, for Hume, is not the search for the "real" cause of events but for the best available probable predictions about the course of nature, founded on correlations of constant conjunctions of events and the psychological habits of human beings.

Hume's Skepticism

After presenting his explanation of the source of our information, the nature of our beliefs about the world, and the character of scientific "knowledge," Hume turns in part 4 of *A Treatise of Human Nature* to the full statement of his skeptical views. He first presents a series of reasons to show why we should be doubtful of the conclusions that we come to because of our reasoning and those that we come to because of our sense experience and our attitudes toward it. Then Hume contends that though there are basic difficulties with regard to both our reason and our senses, we still have to believe many things because of our psychological structure. Unfortunately, what we believe is often either indefensible or contradictory.

The argument offered to engender a "scepticism with regard to reason" purports to show that even the most certain conclusions of reasoning are actually only probable and that their degree of probability diminishes the more that we examine them. Because we all make mistakes, every time we reason there is a possibility that we may err. When we check our reasoning, it is still possible that we have erred in our checking, that we will err in checking our checking, and so on. Each judgment that we make about the merits of our reasoning is merely probable, and the combined probability, Hume says, will get smaller and smaller the more we judge our judgments of our judgments of our judgments. Hence, if this checking process were conducted indefinitely, we should begin to lose confidence even in our most certain reasonings in arithmetic or algebra.

With regard to our sense information, Hume insists that we are naturally convinced that the objects we observe exist continuously and independently of us. However, as soon as we begin to examine this belief we find that it is completely unjustified and that it conflicts with what we know about our impressions. Neither sense information nor valid reasoning can supply any basis for concluding that there are independent and continuous objects. If our imaginations, through some propensities, supply us with this belief, it is still "contrary to the plainest experience." All that we ever perceive are impressions which, as far as we can tell, are definitely dependent on us. An alteration in our sense organs, or in the state of our health, changes what we perceive. In view of this, we should not think that our perceptions are things that exist independently from us, continuing to exist even when not perceived. However, Hume observes, no amount of argument on this subject makes us give up our natural belief in the existence of the external world.

The discussions of the bases for skepticism indicate that for Hume even complete skepticism is impossible because of the force of natural belief. "Nature, by an absolute and uncontrollable necessity has determined us to judge as well as to breathe and feel." Nature forces us to accept certain views, in spite of the evidence for or against them. Philosophy, Hume said elsewhere, would make us into complete skeptics, were not nature so strong. Philosophy would make us completely skeptical about the status of the objects that we perceive with our senses, but nature prevents us from taking the philosophical arguments seriously.

In his discussion of our knowledge of ourselves, Hume brings out a similar point. We all believe that we possess a personal identity that continues throughout our lives. However, when we try to discover the entity we call "ourselves," we discover that all that we are acquainted with is the succession of impressions and ideas. By certain psychological habits and propensities, we have created a fiction that makes us believe that we are also aware of an identical self that perseveres through all our various experiences.

Hence, there is a type of complete skepticism that results from a careful and profound study of human nature. In theory, we realize that there is inadequate evidence to support the bulk of what we believe about the world. Our reasoning and our senses are too unreliable to support these beliefs, which are due to our psychological character and not to any legitimate conclusions of rational processes. Some of these natural beliefs conflict with one another. Hume contends that the factors that make us connect events causally in our experience should make us disbelieve in the continuous and independent existence of sense objects. The more we examine human nature, the more we should realize how dubious and unreliable human opinions are. In the conclusion to book 1 of *A Treatise of Human Nature*, Hume points out that his skepticism even undermines his faith in his psychological findings.

The Limits of Skepticism

However, nature prevents us from carrying out this skeptical attitude to its final destructive conclusion. Regardless of the difficulties, in practice we find that we have to believe all sorts of things, even incompatible things. When we go out in the world, the skeptical doubts lose their force; we are overwhelmed by our natural feelings and beliefs, and we act and live in the same way anyone else does. Hume's final advice is that one should be skeptical when one has to be, and be a natural believer when one must, while realizing that neither of these attitudes has any final justification. In periods when doubts are not being taken seriously, one can go on to examine other aspects of the human world, as Hume does in books 2 and 3 of *A Treatise of Human Nature*, and search for laws about human passions. (One of his findings in this regard is that reason is, and ought only to be, the slave of the passions.)

A Treatise of Human Nature has been a rich source of many contemporary views. The more empirical side of it has greatly influenced the logical positivists and the language analysts. Some of the psychological analysis of human belief and behavior has influenced the pragmatists and instrumentalists. The extreme skepticism and irrationalism have had some impact on neo-orthodox theologians. It is for these reasons that *A Treatise of Human Nature* is regarded by many as one of the best philosophical works in the English language.

Richard H. Popkin

An Enquiry Concerning the Principles of Morals

Type of philosophy: Ethics
First published: 1751

Principal ideas advanced:

◇ The purpose of ethical inquiry is to discover those universal principles on which moral praise and blame are based.

◇ Benevolence is approved partly because of human sympathy and partly because of its social utility, but justice is approved for its utility alone.

◇ Utility accounts for the worth of such virtues as humanity, friendship, integrity, and veracity—and it is by its utility that government is justified.

◇ Theories that attempt to explain all human conduct as springing from self-love are mistaken.

◇ Whatever is worthwhile is so by virtue of its utility or its agreeableness.

◇ Moral judgment is essentially a matter of sentiment, not reason.

David Hume's *An Enquiry Concerning the Principles of Morals* is a philosophical classic that grows older without aging and that remains lively with a wisdom that speaks to the present. It is not the most profound of Hume's works or the most original, being to some extent a revision of book 3 of Hume's masterpiece, *A Treatise of Human Nature* (1739-1740). However, its author considered it the best of his works, and many critics have agreed with that judgment.

Dealing decisively with major ethical issues, the work presents in clear, carefully organized form an analysis of morals. It continues the attack begun by philosopher Joseph Butler against the self-love theory (psychological egoism) of Thomas Hobbes and, in so doing, achieves a measure of objectivism frequently either overlooked or denied by Hume's critics. On the other hand, after preliminary recognition of the significant but auxiliary role of reason in moral judgments, Hume sides with the eighteenth century school of sentiment against the ethical rationalists, on grounds shared today by those who regard ethical judgments as emotive utterances. However, while Hume is frequently cited as a predecessor of the latter philosophers, he avoids the utter relativism and moral nihilism frequently, but erroneously for the most part, attributed to them. Hence, although it would be worthwhile to read *An Enquiry Concerning the Principles of Morals* for its historical importance alone, it also has a unique relevance to some fundamental problems of ethical philosophy, particularly to those concerning the nature of moral judgment.

Although *An Enquiry Concerning the Principles of Morals* can be clearly understood without previous reading of Hume's other works, it is an application to ethics of the theory of knowledge and methodology presented in *A Treatise of Human Nature* and *Philosophical Essays Conerning Human Understanding* (1748; best known as *An Enquiry Concerning Human Understanding*, 1758), and its interest is enhanced by familiarity with those books. Like them, *An Enquiry Concerning the Principles of Morals* contains a measure of skepticism that, while fundamental, has been greatly exaggerated and widely misunderstood. Indeed, one of the chief merits of Hume's philosophy lies in the "mitigated" skepticism that recognizes the limits of human reason without succumbing to what he calls Pyrrhonism, or excessive skepticism, which in practice would make belief and action impossible. However, those who accuse Hume of the latter skepticism must ignore one of his chief aims: to apply the Newtonian method of "philosophizing" to a study of human nature.

The Origins of Morals

The object of the study is to trace the derivation of morals back to their ultimate source. Hume's proposed method was to analyze the virtues and vices of human beings in order "to reach the foundation of ethics, and find those universal principles, from which all censure or approbation is ultimately derived." Because this was a factual matter, it could be investigated successfully only by the experimental method, which had proved itself so well in "natural philosophy," or physical science.

This "scientific" approach will appeal to many modern readers, but herein lies an ambiguity that, in spite of the clarity of Hume's style, has misled some critics. One must realize that Hume was at this point writing of ethics as a descriptive study *about* morals—about acts, characters, and moral judgments. In this sense, ethics is a behavioral science and its statements are either true or false. That may suggest what today would be called an objectivist position, but Hume was not describing the way in which moral attitudes are affected;

moral judgments, strictly speaking, are matters of sentiment, although before they can properly occur reason must furnish all the available relevant information. To avoid misinterpretation, it is hardly possible to overemphasize this distinction between inductive conclusions *about* moral acts and judgments, on one hand, and moral approvals and disapprovals themselves, on the other.

Social Virtues: Benevolence and Justice

Hume's analysis begins with an examination of the social virtues, benevolence and justice, since their explanation will have relevance to other virtues as well. Such benevolent sentiments and characters as are described by words such as "sociable" or "good-natured" are approved universally. However, it is not the mere fact of approval but the principle underlying it that is the object of investigation. We approve benevolence in part because of the psychological principle of what Hume calls *sympathy*, an involuntary tendency in an observer to experience the same emotions he or she observes in a fellow human being, but the more immediate reason for such approval is that we perceive the utility (usefulness, conduciveness to happiness) of this virtue. When we praise a benevolent person, Hume says, we always make reference to the happiness and satisfaction that person affords to society. Because benevolence is regarded as one of the highest virtues, in turn it reflects the fundamental importance of utility. Even in our nonmoral judgment of value, usefulness is a paramount consideration.

In cases of uncertainty about moral questions, Hume adds, there is no more certain way of deciding them than by discovering whether the acts or attitudes involved are really conducive to the interests of society. Hume describes several reversals in the estimation of practices, such as generosity to beggars, when it was seen that their tendencies were harmful rather than helpful, as had been supposed at first.

Whereas benevolence is approved partly but not exclusively for its beneficial consequences, justice has merit for no other reason. (One must realize that Hume conceives justice as concerning only property relations, thus omitting "fair play" and equality, ordinarily considered essential to the concept; actually he accounts for impartiality by his account of truly moral judgment, as is shown below.) To prove this apparently controversial claim, Hume cites a number of cases in which the connection of justice and utility is demonstrated by their joint occurrence or nonoccurrence, increase or diminution. Too many and too lengthy to admit adequate recapitulation here, Hume's arguments may be suggested briefly by a few illustrations: In situations of superfluity or of dearth of material goods, the observation of property distinctions becomes useless and is suspended; a virtuous person captured by outlaws flouting justice would be under no restraint from justice if the opportunity to seize and use their weapons arose, since regard for ownership would be harmful; societies suspend international justice in times of war because of its obvious disadvantages.

Examination of particular laws confirms this explanation of justice; they have no other end than the good of humankind, to which even the theorists of natural law are forced to appeal ultimately. Particular laws would in many cases be utterly arbitrary and even ridiculous, were it not that the general interest is better served by having specified rules rather than chaos. In individual cases the fulfillment of justice may even be detrimental, as when an evil person legally inherits a fortune and abuses it, but consistent observance of the law is ultimately more useful than is deviation.

Were individuals completely self-sufficient, again justice would not arise, but actually people mate and then rear children; subsistence of the family requires observance within it of certain rules. When families unite into small societies and societies engage in commerce, the domain of utilitarian rules of property enlarges accordingly. Thus the evolution of social groups shows a direct proportion between utility and the merit of justice.

In finding the essence of justice and its moral obligation in utility alone, thus making it of derivative rather than intrinsic value, is Hume degrading this virtue? Not so, he insists:

For what stronger foundation can be desired or conceived for any duty, than to observe, the human society, or even human nature, could not subsist without the establishment of it; and will still arrive at greater degrees of

happiness and perfection, the more inviolable the regard is, which is paid to that duty?

Utility as the Basis for Society

At the end of his section on justice he repeats his conclusion that utility accounts for much of the merit of such virtues as humanity, friendship, and public spirit, and for all that of justice, fidelity, integrity, veracity, and some others. A principle so widely operative in these cases can reasonably be expected to exert comparable force in similar instances, according to the Newtonian method of philosophizing. Hume then finds utility to be the basic justification for political society or government, and he notes that "the public conveniency, which regulates morals, is inviolably established in the nature of man, and of the world, in which he lives."

However, is utility itself a fundamental principle? We may still ask *why* utility is approved, to what end it leads. The alternatives are two: It serves either the general interest or private interests and welfare. Hume recognizes the plausibility of the self-love or self-interest theory, holding that all approvals are ultimately grounded in the needs and passions of the self, but he claims to prove decisively the impossibility of thus accounting for moral judgments.

The skeptical view that moral distinctions are inculcated through indoctrination by politicians in order to make people docile is very superficial, Hume says. While moral sentiments may be partially controlled by education, unless they were rooted in human nature the terminology of ethics would awaken no response.

However, granted this response, must it still be traced to self-interest, perhaps an enlightened self-interest that perceives a necessary connection between society's welfare and one's own? Hume thinks not. We often praise acts of virtue in situations distant in time and space, when there is no possibility of benefit to ourselves. We approve some virtues in our enemies, such as courage, even though we know that they may work to our harm. When acts praised conduce to both general and private welfare, our approbation is increased, but we still distinguish the feelings appropriate to each. Now if the first two considerations are rejected by arguing that we approve what is not really to our own interest by imagining our personal benefit had we been in the situation judged, Hume replies that it is absurd that a real sentiment could originate from an interest known to be imaginary and sometimes even opposed to our practical interest.

Even the lower animals appear to have affection for both other animals and us; surely this is not artifice, but rather disinterested benevolence. Why then deny this virtue to humankind? Sexual love produces generous feelings beyond the merely appetitive, and common instances of utterly unselfish benevolence occur in parent-child relationships. It is impossible, Hume holds, to deny the authenticity of such affections as gratitude or desire for friends' good fortune when separation prevents personal participation.

However, if the evidence is so clear, why have self-love theorists been so persistent? Hume blames a love of theoretical simplicity. The self-love theory, as Butler forcibly argues, mistakenly attempts to reduce all motivation to this one principle and so is psychologically false. Human beings have physical appetites, each having its own object; that of hunger is food, that of thirst is drink. Gratification of these needs yields pleasure, which may then become the object of a secondary, interested desire: self-love. Unless the primary appetites had occurred, there could have been no pleasures or happiness to constitute the object of self-love. However, the disinterested primary passions also include benevolence or desire for others' good, satisfaction of which then similarly yields pleasure to the self. Hence self-love actually presupposes specific and independent needs and affections, which complexity is again shown by occasional indulgence of some particular passion, such as the passion for revenge, even to the detriment of self-interest.

Because self-love cannot account for our moral approval of utility, then the appeal of the latter must be direct. In any theoretical explanation, some point must be taken as ultimate, else an infinite regression occurs; hence we need not ask why we experience benevolence—it is enough that we do. Actually, however, Hume further explains it by reference to sympathy, the almost inevitable emotional reaction to the feelings of others. Yet Hume is careful not to claim that "fellow-feeling" is necessarily predominant over self-love; both sentiments vary in degree. However, in normal

people there is a close correlation between strong concern for one's fellows and sensitivity to moral distinctions. Benevolence may not be strong enough to motivate some people to *act* for the good of another, but even they will feel approval of such acts and prefer them to the injurious.

Universality in Moral Judgments

Having not only admitted interpersonal differences in sympathy but acknowledging also intrapersonal variations of feelings for others, how can Hume account for any uniformity and objectivity in our moral judgments? Here he offers one of his most significant contributions to ethics. Even while our sentiments vary, we may judge merit with practical universality, analogously to judgmental correction of variations in sensory perception. Though we do not all, or always, perceive the same physical object as having the same color, shape, or size, as when we approach an object from a distance, we do not attribute the variations to the object; instead we imagine it to have certain stable, standard qualities. Such adjustment or correction is indispensable to mutual understanding and conversation among people.

Likewise, human interests and feelings vary. Thus, moral discourse would be impossible unless people took a general rather than a private point of view:

> The intercourse of sentiments . . . in society and conversation, makes us form some general unalterable standard, by which we may approve or disapprove of characters and manners.

Although our emotions will not conform entirely to such a standard, they are regulated sufficiently for all practical purposes, and hence ethical language becomes meaningful:

> General language . . . being formed for general use, must be moulded on some more general views, and must affix the epithets of praise or blame, in conformity to sentiments, which arise from the general interests of the community.

In order for this standard to be effective, there must of course be a sentiment or emotion to implement it, and here again Hume produces a telling argument against the self-interest theory. Self-love is inadequate to the prerequisites of the concept of morals, not from lack of force but because it is inappropriate. Such a concept as this implies (1) that there be in existence a universal sentiment producing common agreement in approving or disapproving a given object, and (2) that this sentiment comprehend as its objects actions or persons in all times and places. None but the sentiment of humanity will meet these criteria. Hume's account of a "general unalterable standard" based principally on social utility and hence on benevolence is strongly objectivistic and balances subjectivistic strains in his ethics; it also provides the impartiality apparently neglected by his definition of justice.

Other Virtues

Having thus accounted for our approval of qualities conducive to the good of others, Hume continues his analysis of virtues and finds three other classifications. "Qualities useful to ourselves" ("ourselves" here meaning persons exhibiting the qualities) may be approved also for general utility, but primarily for benefit to the agent; examples are discretion, frugality, and temperance. Now a second major division and two other categories of virtues are added: the "agreeable" (pleasant or enjoyable) to their possessors or to others. "Qualities immediately agreeable to ourselves," approved primarily for the satisfying feelings aroused, are such as greatness of mind and noble pride, though some, like courage and benevolence, may also be generally useful. Good manners, mutual deference, modesty, wit, and even cleanliness illustrate "qualities immediately agreeable to others."

Only when the analysis is almost completed does Hume offer the first formal definition of "virtue" as a "quality of the mind agreeable to or approved by every one who considers or contemplates it." A second definition, better summarizing the work's results, is that "Personal Merit consists altogether in the possession of mental qualities, *useful* or *agreeable* to the *person himself* or to others." A definition of value in general follows: "Whatever is valuable in any kind, so naturally classes itself under the division of *useful* or *agreeable*, the *utile* or the *dulce*. . . ."

Readers familiar with the history of ethics will thus see hedonistic and utilitarian themes which received subsequent expression in Jeremy Bentham and John Stuart Mill. The only goal of Virtue, Hume says, is cheerfulness and happiness; the only demand she makes of us are those of careful calculation of the best means to these ends and constancy in preferring the greater to the lesser happiness. Such an obligation is *interested*, but the pleasures it seeks, such as peace of mind or awareness of integrity, do not conflict with the social good, and their supreme worth is almost self-evident.

Reason vs. Sentiment

Having discovered what he calls the true origin of morals through the experimental method, Hume is now ready to return to the issue of Reason versus Sentiment that he mentions at the beginning of *An Enquiry Concerning the Principles of Morals* but defers for settlement until the end. Throughout the book, statements occur that indicate his final position, but unfortunately there are also a number that appear to make moral judgment a matter of reason. This ambiguity is dispelled by Hume's final treatment showing that moral judgment proper is noncognitive and affective in nature. It is true that reason is indispensable to approval or disapproval, for it must provide the facts that pertain to their objects. Very detailed and precise reasoning is frequently required to determine what actually is useful in a given case; nothing other than reason can perform this function. In view of the importance of the question, of whether moral judgment is rational or sentimental (affective), to both the eighteenth century and ours, Hume's full recognition of the auxiliary role of reason must be kept in mind. However, he cannot agree with those rationalists who hold that moral judgments can be made with the same mental faculties, methods, and precision as can judgments of truth and falsity, and who frequently make comparisons between our knowledge of moral "truths" and those of mathematics and geometry.

Besides the evidence of the origin of moral sentiment from benevolence, there are perhaps even more cogent arguments based on comparison of the two types of judgment. The judgments of reason provide information, but not motivation, whereas blame or approbation is "a tendency, however faint, to the objects of the one, and a proportionable aversion to those of the other." That is, moral "judgment" is essentially affective and conative, while rational judgments are neither. Although reason can discover utility, unless utility's *end* appealed to some sentiment the knowledge would be utterly ineffective.

Rational knowledge is either factual or relational (logical or mathematical) in nature; its conclusions are either inductive or deductive. However, the sentiment of blame or approbation is neither such a conclusion nor an observation of fact; one can examine at length all the facts of a criminal event, but one will never find the vice itself, the viciousness, as another objective fact in addition to those of time, place, and action. Neither is the vice constituted by some kind of relation such as that of contrariety, for example, between a good deed and an ungrateful response, since an evil deed rewarded with good will would involve contrariety but the response then would be virtuous. The "crime" is rather constituted such by the sentiment of blame in the spectator's mind.

In the process of rational inference, we take certain known facts or relations and from these deduce or infer a conclusion not previously known; but in moral decisions, says Hume,

> After every circumstance, every relation is known, the understanding has no further room to operate, nor any object on which it could employ itself. The approbation or blame which then ensues, cannot be the work of the judgment, but of the heart; and is not a speculative proposition or affirmation, but an active feeling or sentiment.

This is one of the clearest and most definitive statements of Hume's position on moral judgment.

Finally, reason could never account for ultimate ends, as can be shown very shortly by asking a series of questions about the justification of an act. For example, if one says he exercises for his health and is asked why he desires health, he may cite as successive reasons its necessity to his work, the necessity of work to securing money, and the use of money as a means to pleasure. However, it would be absurd to ask *why* one wished pleasure or the avoidance of pain. Similarly we have seen that virtue appeals to sentiments that neither have nor require any further explanation. Whereas the function of reason is to discover its objects, that of moral (and aesthetic) sentiment (or taste) is to confer value.

Hence, in a radical sense, moral distinctions are subjective, but the subject from which they derive is the whole human race, and individual subjectivity is corrected by the general unalterable standard. *An Enquiry Concerning the Principles of Morals* thus affords both a naturalistic, empirical description of the origin of moral values and a persuasive account of an ethical norm by which consistent judgments may be made, without appealing to a doubtful metaphysics. It is in this eminently sane recognition of the functions and limits of both reason and emotion that modern readers can learn much from David Hume.

Marvin Easterling

Dialogues Concerning Natural Religion

Type of philosophy: Metaphysics, philosophy of religion
First published: 1779
Principal ideas advanced:

◇ The argument from design is an argument that attempts to prove God's existence on the basis of signs of adaptability in nature, but it is an unsatisfactory argument because, although plausible, it does not demonstrate with logical certainty the truth of the claim that the universe was designed.

◇ Furthermore, if we try to deduce the nature of God from the characteristics of nature regarded as God's handiwork, God must be finite, imperfect, incompetent, and dependent.

◇ It is possible that order in nature is the result of a natural generative process.

◇ A priori arguments designed to prove God's existence are inconclusive and establish only that something, not necessarily God, may have been a first cause.

◇ Although the cause of order in the universe probably bears some resemblance to human intelligence, nothing can be concluded concerning the moral character of such a cause.

David Hume's *Dialogues Concerning Natural Religion* is one of the most famous works criticizing some of the arguments offered by philosophers and theologians to establish the existence and nature of God. Hume, who was known as the Great Infidel in his own time, began writing the work around 1751. He showed the manuscript to several of his friends, who dissuaded him from publishing it because of its irreligious content. Over the years, he revised the manuscript many times and just before his death in 1776 made his final revisions. He was very much concerned to make sure that the work would be published shortly after his death. In his will, he first asked his friend the economist Adam Smith to arrange for the publication of the manuscript. When Smith refused, Hume next tried to get his publisher to do so, and when he also refused, Hume altered his will, instructing his nephew to take charge of the matter if the publisher had not done so within two years of his death. Finally, in 1779, the work appeared, gaining both immediate success and notoriety. It has remained one of the classic texts in discussions about the nature of the evidence presented to prove the existence of God and the character of his attributes.

Dialogues Concerning Natural Religion is patterned after Roman philosopher Cicero's work on the same subject, *De natura deorum* (44 B.C.E.; *On the Nature of the Gods*, 1683), in which a Stoic, an Epicurean, and a Skeptic discuss the arguments about the nature and existence of the gods. Both Cicero and Hume found that the dialogue form enabled them to discuss these "dangerous" subjects without having to commit themselves personally to any particular view. They could allow their characters to attack various accepted arguments and positions, without themselves having to endorse or reject any specific religious view.

The Case for a Deity

Hume begins *Dialogues Concerning Natural Religion* with a letter from Pamphillus, a young man who was a spectator at the discussion, to his friend Hermippus. Pamphillus explains that the dialogue form is most suitable for discussing theology, because the subject, on one hand, deals with a doctrine, the being of God, that is so obvious that it hardly admits of any dispute, while on the other hand, it leads to philosophical ques-

tions that are extremely obscure and uncertain regarding the nature, attributes, and decrees and plans of God. The dialogue form, presumably, can both inculcate the "obvious" truth and explore the difficulties.

After having Philo and Cleanthes debate the merits of skepticism in part 1, Hume presents Philo and the orthodox Demea as agreeing that human reason is inadequate to comprehend divine truths. They concur in the view that there is no doubt concerning the existence of a deity but that our natural and rational information is insufficient to justify any beliefs concerning the nature of the deity. Philo sums up the case by asserting that our ideas are all based on experience and that we have no experience at all of divine attributes and operations. Thus, the nature of the Supreme Being is incomprehensible and mysterious.

The Argument from Design

Cleanthes immediately objects and states the theory that Hume analyzes in great detail throughout *Dialogues Concerning Natural Religion*. The information and evidence that we have about the natural world, Cleanthes insists, enable us to infer both the existence and nature of a deity. He then presents what is called "the argument from design," an argument that had been current in both ancient and modern theological discussions but that had become extremely popular in the form in which it was stated by the physicist Sir Isaac Newton. Look at the world, Cleanthes declares, and you will see that it is nothing but one vast machine, subdivided into smaller machines. All the parts are adjusted to one another, so that the whole vast complex functions harmoniously. The adaptation of means to ends through all of nature exactly resembles the adaptation that results from human design and intelligence. Because natural objects and human artifacts resemble one another, we infer by analogy that the causes of them must also resemble one another. Hence the author of nature must be similar to the mind of man, though he must have greater faculties because his production is greater.

Philo proceeds to criticize the argument from design by pointing out first that the analogy is not a good one. The universe is unlike a human-made object, such as a machine or a house. Also, we discover causes only from our experience: for example, from seeing houses being built or machines being constructed. We have never seen a universe being produced, so we cannot judge if it is made analogously to human productions. We have perceived many causal processes other than human design, processes such as growth and attraction. For all that we can tell from our experience, any of these may be the cause of the natural world.

Cleanthes insists, in part 3, that the similarity of the works of nature to the works of human art is self-evident and undeniable. When we examine various aspects of nature in terms of the latest scientific information, the most obvious conclusion at which we arrive is that these aspects must be the result of design. By citing several examples, Cleanthes tries to show the immense plausibility of the argument from design. (In other works, Hume always stressed the fact that a reasonable person could not help being impressed by the order and design in nature and could not avoid coming to the conclusion that there must be some sort of intelligent orderer or designer of nature. However, Hume also insisted, as he did repeatedly in *Dialogues Concerning Natural Religion*, that no matter how convincing the argument may be, it is not logical and can be challenged in many ways.)

To counterattack, Hume has Demea point out another failing of the argument from design. If we gained knowledge about God by analogy with the human mind, then we would have to conclude that the divine mind is as confused, as changeable, as subject to influence by the passions, as is that of the human being. Such a picture of God is incompatible with that presented by traditional religions and by the famous theologians. In fact, as Philo and Demea point out in parts 4 and 5, if the argument from design is accepted, then strange theology will ensue. Because the human mind is finite, by analogy so is God's mind. If God's mind is finite, God can err and be imperfect. If we have to judge God's attributes from the effects of which we are aware, what can we actually ascertain about God's nature? We cannot determine, from looking at the world, whether it represents a good achievement, as we have no standards of universe-construction by which we can judge. We cannot tell if the world that we perceive was made by one God or by many deities. If one takes the analogy involved in the argument from design seriously, all sorts of irrelevant conclusions are possible and any conclusion about the type of designer or designers is pure guesswork:

> This world, for aught he [man] knows, is very faulty and imperfect, compared to a superior standard; and was only the first rude essay of some infant Deity, who afterwards abandoned it, ashamed of his lame performance; it is the work only of some dependent, inferior Deity; and is the object of derision to his superiors: it is the production of old age and dotage in some superannuated deity; and ever since his death, has run on at adventures, from the first impulse and active force, which it received from him. . . ."

These and all sorts of other hypotheses are all possible explanations, by means of the argument from design, of the order in the universe.

Other Theories: Growth and Chance
Philo, in parts 6-8, maintains that other explanations can be offered to account for the order in the world besides the explanation of a designer, and that these alternatives can be shown to be at least as probable. Two theories are considered, one that order results from a generative or growth process and the other that order is simply the chance result of the way material particles come together. Over and over again, we see order develop in nature as the result of biological growth. Seeds grow into organized plants. We do not see any outside designer introduce the order. Hence, if we judge solely by our experiences, one genuine possibility is that order is an unconscious result of the process of generation. The world, for all that we can tell, generates its own order simply by developing. Since every day we see reason and order arise from growth development, as it does in children maturing, and never see organization proceeding from reason, it is a probable as well as a possible hypothesis to suppose that the order in the world comes from some inner biological process in the world, rather than from some designing cause outside it.

Even the hypothesis of the ancient Greek philosopher Epicurus, that the order in the world is the result of "the fortuitous concourse of atoms" and that there is no external or internal designing or organizing force, suffices to account for the world as we know it. From our experience, it is just as probable that matter is the cause of its own motions as that mind or growth is. Also, nothing that we perceive proves that the present order of things did not simply come about by chance. Philo concludes the discussion on this point by asserting that an empirical theology, based solely on information gained from experience, would be inadequate to justify acceptance of any particular hypothesis about the source or cause of order in the world, or any particular religious system about the nature of the force or forces that govern the universe.

A Priori Arguments

Demea, the orthodox believer, who has agreed with Philo's attack up to this point, now contends, in part 9, that there are rational a priori arguments, not based on any empirical information whatsoever, that show that there must be a divine being. Demea states the classical theological argument that there must be a first cause, or God, that accounts for the sequence of causes occurring in the world. Hume has Cleanthes challenge this argument by introducing some of the skeptical contentions about causality and the inconclusiveness of a priori arguments that Hume had presented in his *A Treatise of Human Nature* (1739-1740) and his *Philosophical Essays Concerning Human Understanding* (1748; best known as *An Enquiry Concerning Human Understanding*, 1758). Further, Hume points out that even if the a priori were legitimate, and even if it actually proved that there must be a first cause, or a necessarily existent being, it still would not show that this being had to be God. Perhaps the material world is itself the first cause, the cause of itself.

The Nature of Deity

With this criticism, Hume concludes his considerations of arguments purporting to establish the existence of God and turns to what can be known about God's nature or attributes. At the beginning of part 10, Philo and Demea rhapsodize about the misery and weakness of human beings, which Demea presents as the reason that they must seek God's protection. Philo uses the same informa-

tion about the human plight to indicate that we cannot infer moral qualities of a deity from what is going on in the human world. If we knew what the deity is like, we might be able to explain, in terms of God's perfect plan, why the evils of this world occur and why there is so much human misery. However, since we do not know God's nature, we are not able to infer that he is perfect, wise, and good, from our limited knowledge of the dismal and painful existence of human beings.

Demea offers a religious explanation of the evils: namely, that our present existence is just a moment in the course of our existence. The present evil events will be recompensed and rectified in another realm, in an afterlife. However, Cleanthes insists, if human beings are to judge of divine matters from their experience, they have no information to support this religious supposition. The only way in which they can accept a belief in a benevolent deity is to deny Philo and Demea's thesis that human life is absolutely miserable. To this, Philo replies that the occurrence of any evil, any misery, any pain, no matter how small a part of human life it might be, raises difficulties in ascertaining if God has the moral attributes accepted by traditional religions. If God possesses infinite power, wisdom, and goodness, how does anything unpleasant happen?

Cleanthes argues, in part 11, that if one goes back to his analogy between the human and the deity, an explanation can be offered. If the author of nature is only finitely perfect, then imperfections in the universe can be accounted for as attributable to God's limitations. Philo, in turn, argues that present experience provides no basis whatsoever for any inference about the moral attributes of the deity, and that the more we recognize human weaknesses, the less we are capable of asserting in support of the religious hypothesis that the world is governed by a good and benevolent deity. If we knew that a good and wise God existed, then we might be able to account for the evils in this world by the theories of either Demea or Cleanthes. However, if we have to build up our knowledge and our hypotheses from what we experience, then we will have to admit that there are four possibilities concerning the first causes of the universe: that they are completely good, that they are completely bad, that they are both good and bad, and that they are neither good nor bad. The good and the evil events in human experience make it difficult to conclude from our experience alone that one of the first two possibilities is the case.

As Philo explores the four possibilities and seems to be leaning toward the last, Demea realizes with dismay that he and Philo are not really in accord. Demea stresses the incomprehensible nature of God, the weakness of human intellectual capacities, and the misery of human life as the basis for accepting orthodox theology. Philo employs the same points to lead to an agnostic conclusion, that we cannot know, because of our nature and God's, what God is actually like, and whether there is any explanation or justification for the character of the experienced world. Demea apparently accepted revealed information as the basis for answering the questions that human beings, by their own faculties, could not, while Philo turned only to human experience for the answers and found that no definite ones could be given. As soon as Demea sees how wide the gap is between them, he leaves the discussion, and Philo and Cleanthes are left on the scene to evaluate the fruits of their arguments.

Skeptics and Dogmatists

In the last part, 12, Philo offers what has been taken as a summary of Hume's own views about religion. Everywhere in nature there is evidence of design. As our scientific information increases, we become more, rather than less, impressed by the order that exists in the universe. The basic difficulty is that of determining the cause or source of the design. The difference between the atheist and the theist, and between the skeptic and the dogmatist, on this matter is really only a verbal one. The theist admits that the designer, if intelligent, is very different from a human being. The atheist admits that the original principle of order in the world bears some remote analogy to human intelligence, though the degree of resemblance is indeterminable. Even a skeptic like Philo has to concede that we are compelled by nature to believe many things that we cannot prove, and one of them is that there is in the universe order which seems to require an intelligent orderer. The dogmatist has to admit that there are insoluble difficulties in establishing any truths in this area

as well as in any other. The skeptic keeps pointing out the difficulties, while the dogmatist keeps stressing what has to be believed.

When these arguments are taken into account, Philo points out, we are still in no position to assess the moral character of the designer. The evidence from the observable world is that works of nature have a greater resemblance to our artifacts than to our benevolent or good acts. Hence, we have more basis for maintaining that the natural attributes of the deity are like our own than for maintaining that his moral attributes are like human virtues. As a result, Philo advocates an amoral, philosophical, and rational religion. In 1776 Hume added a final summation:

> The whole of natural theology . . . resolves itself into one simple, though somewhat ambiguous, at least undefined, proposition, *that the cause or causes of order in the universe probably bear some remote analogy to human intelligence.*

Nothing more can be said, especially concerning the moral character of the cause or causes.

The dialogue concludes with two perplexing remarks. Philo announces as his parting observation that "[t]o be a philosophical sceptic is, in a man of letters, the first and most essential step toward being a sound, believing Christian." This contention, which was made by all the Christian skeptics from Michel de Montaigne to Pierre Bayle and Bishop Pierre-Daniel Huet, may have been a sincere conviction on their part. In Hume's case, there is no evidence that his skepticism led him to Christianity but rather that it led him away from it.

At the very end, Hume has Pamphillus, the spectator, evaluate the entire discussion by saying that "*Philo's* principles are more probable than *Demea's*; but those of *Cleanthes* approach still nearer to the truth." Critics have variously interpreted this ending, pointing out that Pamphillus and Hume may not agree and that this conclusion may have been intended to quiet possible critics. Others have held that Hume himself may have felt, in spite of his devastating criticisms of Cleanthes's position, that it contained more truth than Philo's almost complete skepticism.

Dialogues Concerning Natural Religion has been a central work in discussions about religious knowledge ever since its publication. It is generally recognized as presenting the most severe criticisms of the argument from design, in showing its limitations as an analogy and as a basis for reaching any fruitful conclusions about the nature of the designer of the world. Because in the work Hume discusses only the natural evidence for religion, some later theologians, especially Søren Kierkegaard, have insisted that Hume's arguments only make more clear the need for faith and revelation as the sole basis of religious knowledge.

Richard H. Popkin

Additional Reading

Ayer, A. J. *Hume.* New York: Hill & Wang, 1980. This brief introduction to Hume's life is both well written and useful. The chapter on aims and methods is especially good.

Chappell, V. C., ed. *Hume: A Collection of Critical Essays.* Garden City, N.Y.: Doubleday, 1966. This collection of twenty-one essays by such acknowledged authorities as Ernest Mossner and Anthony Flew is valuable to students of Hume.

Hanson, Delbert J. *Fideism and Hume's Philosophy: Knowledge, Religion, and Metaphysics.* New York: Peter Lang, 1993. Fideism holds that belief in some religious theory must be sustained by faith alone. Michel de Montaigne and Blaise Pascal were Fideists. Hanson takes issue with the concept that Hume was a skeptic and attempts, in this book, to support that argument.

Hausman, David B., and Alan Hausman. *Descartes's Legacy.* Toronto: University of Toronto Press, 1997. This book is about the thought of René Descartes, George Berkeley, and Hume. Two chapters concentrate on Hume. The entire study is written from the point of view of Descartes's philosophy; Berkeley and Hume are contrasted with Descartes.

Herdt, Jennifer A. *Religion and Faction in Hume's Moral Philosophy.* Cambridge, England: Cambridge University Press, 1997. Herdt takes a new look at Hume's writings about religion and suggests a new interpretation.

Jenkins, John J. *Understanding Hume.* Edinburgh, Scotland: Edinburgh University Press, 1992. Offers a short biography, then spends the bulk of the book discussing Hume's philosophy, primarily by explicating Hume's *A Treatise of Human Nature.*

Norton, David Fate, ed. *The Cambridge Companion to Hume.* Cambridge, England: Cambridge University Press, 1993. Two biographical sketches follow eleven essays by scholars discussing the philosophy of Hume.

Passmore, John. *Hume's Intentions.* 3d ed. London: Duckworth, 1980. A valuable discussion of what Hume said and intended. Passmore corrects earlier imprecise and biased views of Hume.

Penelhum, Terence. *David Hume: An Introduction to His Philosophical System.* West Lafayette, Ind.: Purdue University Press, 1992. A short biography of Hume, a discussion of his philosophical system, and a number of annotated excerpts from his writing.

Pompa, Leon. *Human Nature and Historical Knowledge: Hume, Hegel, and Vico.* Cambridge, England: Cambridge University Press, 1990. The beginning of the book is devoted to a discussion of Hume's theory of history and his thoughts about the past.

Popkin, Richard H. *Introduction to Hume's "Dialogues Concerning Natural Religion."* Indianapolis, Ind.: Hackett, 1980. Excellent introduction to a fine edition of one of Hume's most interesting works.

Price, John Vladimir. *David Hume.* New York: Twayne, 1968. As the author says, "This book is a general introduction to . . . Hume . . . designed primarily for the reader who knows little about Hume."

_____. *The Ironic Hume.* Austin: University of Texas Press, 1965. Price investigates an aspect of Hume's practice that is ignored by others. He also suggests some important changes in interpretation that result from Hume's use of irony.

Quinton, Anthony. *Hume.* New York: Routledge, 1999. An excellent biographical introduction to the thoughts of the philosopher, clearly presented and requiring no special background. Bibliography.

Wilson, Fred. *Hume's Defence of Causal Inference.* Toronto: University of Toronto Press, 1997. A lengthy attempt to justify Hume's arguments and rules about causal inference. For the specialist.

James Sullivan, updated by Dwight Jensen

Edmund Husserl

Husserl is known as the founder of phenomenology, regarded by many as one of the most significant movements of the twentieth century.

Principal philosophical works: *Philosophie der Arithmetik, Logische und psychologische Untersuchungen,* 1891; *Logische Untersuchungen,* 1900-1901 (*Logical Investigations,* 1970, 2 volumes); *Ideen zu einer reinen Phänomenologie und phänomenologischen Philosophie,* 1913, rev. ed. 1976 (*Ideas: General Introduction to Pure Phenomenology,* volume 1, 1982; volume 2, 1989; volume 3, 1990); *Vorlesungen zur Phänomenologie des inneren Zeitbewußtseins,* 1928 (*On the Phenomenology of the Consciousness of Internal Time, 1893-1917,* 1991); *Formale und transzendentale Logik,* 1929 (*Formal and Transcendental Logic,* 1969); *Méditations cartesiennes: Introduction à la phénomenologies, par Edmond Husserl,* 1931 (also published as *Cartesianische Meditationen und Pariser Vortrage,* 1950; *Cartesian Meditations: An Introduction to Phenomenology,* 1960); *Erfahrung und Urteil: Untersuchungen zur Genealogie der Logik,* 1939 (*Experience and Judgment: Investigations in a Genealogy of Logic,* 1973); *Die Krisis europäischen Wissenschaften und die transzendentale Phänomenologie: Ein Einleitung in die phänomenologische Philosophie,* 1954 (*The Crisis of European Sciences and Transcendental Phenomenology: An Introduction to Phenomenological Philosophy,* 1970).

Born: April 8, 1859; Prossnitz, Moravia, Austrian Empire (now Prost)

Died: April 27, 1938; Freiburg im Breisgau, Germany

Early Life

Edmund Husserl was born on April 8, 1859, in Prossnitz, Moravia (then part of Austria), to a German-speaking Jewish family. (The Jewish connection would later become a liability, even though Husserl had become an Evangelical Lutheran in 1886. Throughout his life, he remained deeply moral and religious but not within the framework of a particular sect.) He passed the *Gymnasium* examinations in 1876 and studied in Leipzig, Berlin, and Vienna, concentrating on mathematics and science as well as philosophy. He gained his Ph.D. in 1882 from Vienna with a thesis in mathematics. After several years of study with the Catholic philosopher Franz Brentano, he moved to Halle, where in 1887 he qualified himself as a privatdocent (unpaid lecturer) and where he remained until 1901. The years at Halle were years of doubt and difficulty, but gradually, through his struggles with the prob-

lems of mathematics and logic, he developed his own distinctive system of ideas. It was during this period that he married Malvine Steinschneider, his ever-loyal wife; they had three children, one of whom was killed at the Battle of Verdun.

Life's Work

In 1900-1901, Husserl published his first important work, *Logical Investigations.* In 1901, he was invited to the University of Göttingen as an *ausserordentlicher Professor.* Husserl's position in the university was not an entirely happy one; his colleagues in the other faculties did not appreciate his work. He owed his promotion to the rank of *ordentlicher Professor* to the intervention of the Prussian minister of education. By this time, however, the new discipline of phenomenology was proving appealing not only to German students but also to foreigners, and Husserl is said to have had as many as twelve nationalities in his seminar at once.

In defining the term "phenomenology," it must be remembered that Husserl's thought was still evolving at the time of his death; he left

Edmund Husserl. *(Library of Congress)*

but can also be considered a method, perhaps simply one among many, suitable for the solution of some philosophical problems but not of others. Phenomenology begins with the analysis of consciousness or experience—they come to the same thing in the end, for consciousness is always intentional, pointing to something outside the ego. While this analysis is going on, the philosopher "brackets" all irrelevant considerations, such as the operations of empirical science and the conjectures of metaphysics about the reality of the material world. These latter are not pronounced meaningless as by the positivists; they are bracketed, or put aside for the moment, perhaps to be used on another occasion or by another thinker, but not to be allowed to confuse the present investigation.

Husserl eloquently describes the "stream of consciousness" (or experience) in which from time to time the ego singles out some "thing" (which is most easily conceived as an object but could be a memory or a mood) for special attention, viewing it from various aspects, so that eventually some "essence" emerges that is not identical with any specific perception. Note, however, that phenomenology does not deal with a shadow or symbol or illusion of some Kantian *Ding-an-sich* (thing-in-itself) that is supposed to be the ultimate reality; experience is real enough in itself, and the thing-in-itself has been bracketed. Although the stream of experience must include feelings and emotions as they enter into experience, and although the things of experience are given intuitively, this world is also the world of logic and mathematics. In the end, Husserl acknowledges that the only absolute reality is the pure ego and its life; all the external world, including other egos, is "contingent" and might turn out not to exist after all. In practice, however, Husserl treats the world and other egos as confirmed by experience.

In 1916, Husserl was called to an *ordentlicher* professorship at Freiburg. In spite of the grief and disillusionment caused by the war, he was now at the peak of his authority and prestige. Even in the aftermath of World War I, he had invitations to lecture abroad, first in London and later in Amsterdam and Paris. His philosophy, however,

behind an enormous amount of manuscript that has gradually been edited and published. His ideas are difficult and sometimes invite confusion with trains of thought that they superficially resemble or that they are connected with historically, such as existentialism. His battle cry "to the things themselves" is deceptive, since it suggests materialism, which he was trying to refute; his "bracketing" might be wrongly taken to suggest the rejection of the things bracketed. Finally Husserl was an inspiring but not an authoritarian teacher; therefore, although he had numerous disciples, they do not necessarily reproduce his thought.

Phenomenology can be considered a philosophy, some would say the only true philosophy, was changing. Even before the war, some of his disciples feared that he was becoming "transcendental" in his attempts to found a universal philosophical science on a foundation of phenomenology. He was becoming moralistic, hoping that phenomenology would establish the ethical autonomy of humanity. After his retirement in 1928, he would face further disappointments.

When Husserl retired in 1928, his position went to Martin Heidegger, whom he regarded as his chief disciple and logical successor. However, the works that Heidegger was publishing at the time seemed to point in an entirely new direction; Heidegger would eventually be hailed as an existentialist. Husserl was deeply hurt, but worse was to come. Nazi leader Adolf Hitler came to power in 1933, and for a time, at least, Heidegger supported him. Husserl was excluded from the university and silenced in Germany; many of his associates believed it necessary to distance themselves from him and his ideas. Others remained loyal, however, and as late as 1935 Husserl was still able to lecture in public and did so with great force and eloquence in Vienna and Prague, which had not yet fallen to Hitler. In 1937, Husserl's health began to fail, and he died on April 27, 1938.

Influence

Husserl's ultimate position in the history of philosophy is uncertain. His editors complain of the "partisan reception" of his posthumous material and the "uneven character of its discussion." The phenomenon of phenomenology is believed to be important, but the nature of the importance is hard to define.

A scholar of Husserl's eminence is expected to end his career in a flurry of banquets and celebrations, but Husserl's end better fits his character. His years of unrewarded toil as an unpaid teacher, his puritanical devotion to his work, and the uncompromising standards of clarity and logic by which he judged his own work find a fitting culmination in the defiant lectures that he delivered in the shadow of Hitler and a second world war. If he could not establish ethical autonomy for humanity, he could at least establish it for himself.

John C. Sherwood

Ideas

General Introduction to Pure Phenomenology

Type of philosophy: Epistemology, phenomenology
First published: Ideen zu einer reinen Phänomenologie und phänomenologischen Philosophie, 1913, rev. ed. 1976 (English translation, volume 1, 1982; volume 2, 1989; volume 3, 1990)
Principal ideas advanced:
◊ Natural sciences are, by nature, dogmatic; the phenomenologist must undertake a critical study of the conditions under which knowledge is possible.
◊ To distinguish within experience that which *experiences* from that which *is experienced*, one must suspend natural beliefs; this suspension of belief is made possible by a method of bracketing by which one talks not about trees and the self as items external to experience but of the "trees" and the "perceptions" of experience.
◊ *Noema*, that which is perceived, is dependent upon *noesis*, the perceiving; but *noema* has the kind of being peculiar to essences.
◊ The absolute forms of essences, which owe their actuality in consciousness to acts of perceiving, are *Eideia*, eternal possibilities of quality, related to other *Eideia* by external relations.

The term "phenomenology," as it is used by Edmund Husserl and his disciples, designates first of all a principle of philosophical and scientific method. The usual method of natural science proceeds from a body of accepted truth and seeks to extend its conquest of the unknown by putting questions to nature and compelling it to answer. The phenomenological method adopts a softer approach. Setting aside all presuppositions and suppressing hypotheses, it seeks to devise techniques of observation, description, and classification that will permit it to disclose structures and connections in nature that do not yield to experimental techniques. It has been widely fruitful in psychology and the social sciences, as well as in epistemology and value theory.

Husserl, in his *Logische Untersuchungen* (1900-1901; *Logical Investigations*, 1970, 2 volumes), did much to advance general phenomenological studies. However, he had in view a specifically philosophical application of the technique that many of his associates did not completely grasp or failed to share. *Ideas* was written with a view to clearing up the distinction between phenomenological psychology, which he regarded as a legitimate but secondary science, and phenomenological philosophy, which, he was prepared to maintain, is the foundation of all science. When a sociologist or psychologist conducts a phenomenological investigation, he or she puts aside all the usual theories and assumptions that have governed research in that field, but he or she cannot shed all presuppositions (such as, for example, the belief in the existence of the external world, the constancy of nature). As Greek philosopher Plato saw, every science must proceed upon some assumptions—except philosophy. To fulfill its promise, the phenomenological approach must bring one at last to an absolutely presuppositionless science. Pure phenomenology, or phenomenological philosophy, is, in Husserl's opinion, precisely that. It has long been the aspiration of philosophers to make their science an absolute one, one that rids itself of all presuppositions and stands with open countenance before pure Being. Husserl stands in this tradition.

Phenomenology is not to be confused with "phenomenalism," a name sometimes given to extreme forms of empiricism, such as that of philosopher Ernst Mach, which maintains that nothing is real except sense-data. In fact, this is one of the misconceptions that phenomenology is designed to overcome. If the empiricists are right, the unity and order which one is accustomed to find in the world are not given in experience but put there by the activity of the mind. Genetic psychology, which seeks to explain the origin of various mental habits and responses, would therefore hold the key to understanding one's whole view of the world. A good example is philosopher John Stuart Mill, who in his *A System of Logic* (1843) undertook to explain the force of syllogistic reasoning in terms of associationist psychology. Other positivists and pragmatists have attempted to create a psychological theory of knowledge and of valuation. Husserl argued, however, that the empiricists were wrong, that they did not come to their conviction about the absence of order and intelligibility in the pure data of expe-

rience by examining what is given there, but had it as an Idol of the Theater (to use philosopher Francis Bacon's term). It follows that they have misconceived the task of psychology in supposing that it can discover in the mind laws that give rise to the meaning of the world and that it is incumbent upon one to set about developing new accounts of logic, knowledge theory, aesthetics, and ethics that stand on their own evidence. In place of *psychologism* (a misconceived psychology or science of the soul), what is needed, if justice is to be done to experience, is *phenomenology* (a science of phenomena, or appearances).

Husserl takes his place, then, in the forefront of those twentieth century philosophers who have sought to reaffirm the autonomy of various philosophical disciplines against psychology. He was equally concerned to turn back the tide of the popular-scientific view of the world that he called naturalism. The particular sciences, by nature, are dogmatic. That is to say, they proceed without examining the conditions under which knowledge is possible. This is not to be held against them. However, when anyone attempts to build a natural philosophy on the findings of the sciences, this uncritical procedure opens the way to skepticism because the categories in terms of which one grasps natural events are unsuited to take account of conscious events, including the pursuit of scientific truth. It seems innocent enough to explain consciousness in terms of natural causes until one recollects that matter and the laws that govern its behavior are themselves part of experience. This, according to Husserl, is the point at which philosophers must step in. Their primary task, in fact, will be to distinguish within experience the part that experiences from the part that is experienced.

Suspending Belief

There are many overtones of the French philosopher René Descartes in Husserl's writings. Descartes, in order to escape from the ambiguities and uncertainties of ordinary, natural experience, developed a method of doubting. By bringing under question the whole phenomenal world, he laid bare a world of logical forms that he could not doubt. Husserl adopts a similar method. He talks of "suspending" natural beliefs, including the fundamental conviction of every healthy mind that there is a world "out there," that there are other selves, and so on. People are asked to "alter" this natural standpoint, to "disconnect" their beliefs about causation and motion, to "put them out of action." This is, of course, only a methodological procedure, in order to help people overcome their animal bias and make it possible for them to take a coolly intellectual view of things. Greek philosophy used the term *epochē* to indicate the suspense of judgment. Husserl presses this term into his service.

To make his meaning clear, Husserl uses the example of looking with pleasure into a garden where an apple tree is blossoming. From the natural standpoint, the tree is something that has transcendent reality in space and time, and the joy of perceiving it has reality in the psyche of a human being. However, Descartes reminds one that perceptions are sometimes hallucinations. One passes, therefore, from the natural to the phenomenological standpoint, bracketing the claims of both the knower and the known to natural being. This leaves one with "a nexus of exotic experiences of perception and pleasure valuation." One can now speak of the content and structure of the situation without any reference to external existence. Nothing is really taken away from the experience; it is all there in a new manner. One can now speak of "tree," "plant," "material thing," "blossoming," "white," "sweet," and so forth and be sure that one is talking about only things that belong to the essence of our experience. Similarly, at the opposite pole, one can distinguish "perceiving," "attending," "enjoying," and other ego acts. These each have their special characters and repay analysis.

Acts and Objects

Husserl was at one time a student of philosopher Franz Brentano, who had said that what distinguishes mental acts from nonmental acts is that the former invariably refer to something other than themselves. Drawing from the Scholastics, he said that these acts are "intentional." Husserl makes constant use of this discovery. To designate the ego acts, which are not limited to cognition but also include various attitudes such as doubting and supposing as well as volitions and feelings, he uses the Greek word *noesis* (literally, a perceiving). To designate the corresponding objects, for instance, "tree," "fruitful," and "charming," he uses the corresponding word *noema* (literally, that which is perceived).

An important part of the analysis of consciousness consists in tracing the relation between these. In each case, the *noesis* is real and fundamental, but *noema* is dependent and, strictly speaking, unreal. In the example, "the perceiving of the tree" is actual and constitutive of "the tree perceived." However, conversely, though it does not have reality, *noema* has being, which is lacking to *noesis*: That is, *noesis* is composed entirely of essences, which are eternally what they are and stand in necessary or a priori relations with each other. The same thing is true of volition and other modes. "The valuing of the tree" is a *noesis*. It has the same reality as "the perceiving of the tree." Correspondingly, "the value of the tree" is a *noema*. It does not have reality, but it has the same kind of essential being as the structure and properties that make up the object of cognition. The value characters likewise take their place in an a priori system together with other values.

As long as one's interest is directed primarily toward the life of the mind, one will be chiefly interested in exploring the various *noeses*. Husserl's delineation of these is subtle and perceptive and goes a long way toward persuading the reader of the necessity of this descriptive groundwork, although, as is sometimes true of the drawings of a microscopist, one may have difficulty in recognizing in it the familiar features of the mind. His account of "meaning," for example, should be studied by those who are interested in semantics, and his analysis of "sentiment" and "volition" provides an instructive approach to the question of the relation between emotions and values. One thing is common to all *noeses*, according to Husserl: All are at bottom *thetic*, or postulational. Husserl speaks of them as *doxa* (Plato's word for "opinion"). This does not imply that some *noeses* are not characterized by "certainty," just as others are characterized by a "sense of likelihood" or "doubt." However, in any case, this certainty is what is commonly called a "moral certainty." The conviction is a mode of the "perceiving" rather than a function of anything lying in the "perceived."

However, in the present work, Husserl does not consider mental acts per se. He studies them because they provide the key to the various grades and types of objects that make up the *noemata*. Corresponding to "perception," there is the realm of "colors," "shapes," and "sizes"; and corresponding to "perceptual enjoyment," there are "dainty" pink and "gloriously" scented. These qualities owe their actuality in consciousness to the *noeses*, but they are part of an order of being that is absolute and independent. Husserl calls all such absolute forms or essences *Eideia*, to avoid the ambiguities of such words as ideas and essences. They are eternal possibilities, each perfectly definite and distinct from every other but also linked with every other in a system of eternal relations. Thus, "pink," "white," and "green" are species under the genus "color"; and "color" itself stands in a hierarchy of perceptual "qualities." A similar hierarchical structure embraces the *noema* of value.

Universal Relations

Husserl, who began his philosophical studies as a logician, was preeminently interested in the grammar of meaning. He claims that, on a very abstract level, all *noema* exemplify universal relations that can be formulated in a *Mathesis Universalis* such as Gottfried Wilhelm Leibniz conceived. However, the theorizing logician does not do justice to the wealth of formal relations that lie before the phenomenologist:

> Its field is the analysis of the a priori shown forth in *immediate* intuition, the fixing of immediately transparent essence and essential connexions and their descriptive cognition in the systematic union of all strata in pure transcendental consciousness.

It begins by distinguishing various regional ontologies, of which the "formal region" exploited by the logician is only one. "Material regions" are numerous.

The region of the physical thing will serve as an example. The question presents itself as follows: How are we to describe systematically the *noeses* and *noemata* that belong to the unity of the intuitionally presenting thing-consciousness? Leaving aside the noetic factor, the problem is to analyze the essential connections by which "appearances" present themselves as "one and the same thing." The analysis discloses that a mere *res extensa* is conceivable apart from the idea of a *res materialis* and a *res temporalis*. However, as a matter of fact, a thing as presented to people involves all three of these. Hence, there are strata and formations constituting the thing. Each of these unities must be analyzed in turn. The problem of "presentation in space" must here be faced. Although, according to Husserl, its meaning has never yet been completely grasped, it now appears in clear light—namely, by "the phenomenological analysis of the *essential* nature of all the noematic (and noetic) phenomena, wherein space exhibits itself intuitionally and as the unity of appearances."

In the present volume, as is proper in an introduction, Husserl is able only to indicate the direction that the investigation must take. One must look to his other works and those of his disciples to see the analyses carried out in detail. Although Husserl worked chiefly in the field of epistemology, his disciples carried the method into axiology and philosophical anthropology (Max Scheler), aesthetics (Theodor Lipps), sociology (Karl Mannheim), comparative religion (Rudolph Otto), and ethics (Nicolai Hartmann), not to mention the "existentialism" of Martin Heidegger and Jean-Paul Sartre. For the ordinary reader, these developments are probably more interesting and fruitful than is pure phenomenology.

Husserl's significance as a philosopher is that, like philosophers René Descartes and Immanuel Kant, he appeared at a time when the foundations of science were themselves threatened, and irrationalism, skepticism, and nihilism threatened the very nerve of Western civilization. He sought to revive knowledge, to make possible once again a rational view of the world and of the human enterprise. He was conscious of being the continuer of a long tradition and, with some reluctance, admitted to falling under the classification of idealist. He most resembles Kant, and his work can be summed up as the search for the transcendental conditions that make "meaning" (scientific, ethical, aesthetic, religious) possible.

Jean Faurot

Additional Reading

Dreyfus, Hubert L., ed. *Husserl and Cognitive Science*. Cambridge, Mass.: MIT Press, 1982. An attempt to build bridges between Edmund

Husserl and current developments in analytic philosophy, philosophy of language, and cognitive psychology. The text focuses on Husserl's notion of intentionality as the key to such dialogue.

Farber, Marvin. *The Foundation of Phenomenology: Edmund Husserl and the Quest for a Rigorous Science of Philosophy*. 3d ed. Albany: State University of New York Press, 1968. A still unrivaled comprehensive and clear explanation of Husserl's life work.

Hopkins, Burt C., ed. *Husserl in Contemporary Context: Prospects and Projects for Phenomenology*. Boston: Kluwer, 1997. Examination of Husserl's thought and its contribution to phenomenology.

Kockelmans, Joseph. *Edmund Husserl's Phenomenology*. West Lafayette, Ind.: Purdue University Press, 1994. Kockelmans provides an overview of the principal themes of Husserl's thought that is both faithful and clear. He focuses especially on Husserl's own summary of phenomenology in his article for the *Encyclopedia Britannica*.

Landgrebe, Ludwig. *The Phenomenology of Edmund Husserl*. Ithaca, N.Y.: Cornell University Press, 1981. As one of Husserl's closest co-workers, Landgrebe understood that Husserl's phenomenology was a process of continually inquiring into its own foundations, radicalizing itself by this process of a never-ending return to its origins. In this text, Landgrebe continues that Husserlian dialogue, taking several of Husserl's basic themes and continuing that work of reflection.

Mensch, James R. *After Modernity: Husserlian Reflections on a Philosophical Tradition*. Albany: State University of New York Press, 1996. A lucid examination of Husserl's thoughts.

Mohanty, J. *Edmund Husserl's Theory of Meaning*. The Hague: Nijhoff, 1964. This remains the clearest summary of Husserl's ideas about meaning from his *Logical Investigations*. Mohanty looks at Husserl's thought in the light of

subsequent developments while being very faithful in his presentation of Husserl's own ideas.

Natanson, Maurice. *Edmund Husserl: Philosopher of Infinite Tasks*. Evanston, Ill.: Northwestern University Press, 1973. A very lucid introduction to Husserl's thought, examining it fully in the light of his later developments of the concepts of the life-world and transcendental subjectivity. Striking illustrations make difficult points remarkably clear.

Ricœur, Paul. *Husserl: An Analysis of His Phenomenology*. Evanston, Ill.: Northwestern University Press, 1967. Ricœur presents a perceptive yet critical view of Husserl's thought, especially by examining the texts *Ideas* and *Cartesian Meditations*. Ricœur's commentary, while very fair, also anticipates his own development of a more existential and hermeneutical phenomenology.

Sallis, John, ed. *Husserl and Contemporary Thought*. Atlantic Highlands, N.J.: Humanities Press, 1983. Sallis assembled a most cogent group of essays. Prominent Husserl scholars examine Husserl's work in the light of recent philosophical argumentation.

Sokolowski, Robert. *Husserlian Meditations*. Evanston, Ill.: Northwestern University Press, 1974. This exposition and commentary on Husserl's thought is wide-ranging, systematic, and remarkably clear. It focuses particularly on meaning and truth, or "how words present things."

Steinbock, Anthony. *Home and Beyond: Generative Phenomenology After Husserl*. Evanston, Ill.: Northwestern University Press, 1995. Steinbock demonstrates the value of Husserl's thought by applying Husserlian phenomenology in an original study of the social world and the concrete matters of life and how to live it. In doing so, he aptly refutes critiques of Husserl's thought as too formalistic or abstract.

John C. Sherwood,
updated by Christopher M. Aanstoos

I Ching

Derived from ancient divination traditions, the *I Ching* or *Yi Jing* (eighth to third century B.C.E.; English translation, 1876; also known as *Book of Changes*, 1986) identifies recurring situations arising from the dynamic interaction of *yin* (darkness) and *yang* (light); considered the fountainhead of traditional Chinese philosophy, the work began to exert a substantial influence on Western thought in the twentieth century, particularly with respect to philosophy of mind.

Authorship and Context

The *I Ching* holds the preeminent position in Chinese literature, with only the *Dao De Jing* (late third century B.C.E.; *The Speculations on Metaphysics, Polity, and Morality, of "the Old Philosopher, Lau-Tsze,"* 1868; better known as *Dao De Jing*) as a serious rival in terms of influence. Tradition accords it the highest position of the Five Confucian Classics—*I Ching*, *Shu Jing* (classic of history), *Shi Jing* (classic of poetry), *Chun Qiu* (spring and autumn annals), and *Li Ji* (*Book of Rites*, 1885)—not only for its antiquity but also for its breadth of wisdom, according to legends derived from semidivine sages. In *Lunyu* (late sixth or early fifth century B.C.E.; *Analects*, 1861), Confucius sets the book above all others and states that, at age seventy, he would need fifty more years to begin to penetrate its wisdom. The work was considered so essential to Chinese tradition that the first Qin emperor spared it from the general burning of the books in 213 B.C.E. During the Han Dynasty (207 B.C.E.-220 C.E.) that followed, the work was singled out as an ur-text comprehending the whole of Confucianism and was even cited, erroneously, as a source for the other classics.

Yet despite millennia of scrutiny by literary scholars, the book itself remains very much a mystery and, like its own mantic utterances, seems to defy straightforward critical investigation. The "original" date and authorship of the text are impossible to establish because it has grown by the steady accretion of exegesis into a complex, multilayered work. Though ultimately derived from the divination practice for which it is still used, the *I Ching*—referred to by diviners simply as "the Oracle"—has come to encompass a whole cosmology based upon natural transformation. In the West, this oracular aura still clings to the work. The Jesuit scholars who introduced the *I Ching* to Europe had not only their orthodoxy but also their sanity questioned for their trouble. Minds no less than Gottfried Wilhelm Leibniz, who tried to explicate the work in terms of binary mathematics, have been baffled in the attempt to open it to a Western audience. Only in the twentieth century, with the attention of thinkers such as Carl Gustav Jung, has the philosophic depth of the work generally come to be appreciated in the West.

The traditional source of the *I Ching* is not, in the strict sense, literary, but rather takes the form of eight trigrams, lineal forms comprising combinations of broken and unbroken lines. These trigrams each have symbolic names and natural associations, as shown in the table, "The Eight Trigrams of the *I Ching*."

Tradition attributes these symbols to Fu Xi (third millennium B.C.E.), the legendary first emperor credited with the introduction of agriculture, herding, fishing, and writing. Legend asserts that the sage ruler discovered the trigrams on the back of a turtle as it rose from the waters of the Yellow River; from these patterns he intuited the law of change evident in the course of the seasons and the movement of the heavens. Most likely the product of ancient divination lore, the eight primary trigrams illustrate the essential situations within the natural cyclic process of growth and decay.

Over time, this simple system was considered insufficient to represent the complexity of change, and the eight original trigrams were doubled and permutated into the sixty-four hexagrams that remain the foundation of the *I Ching*. While this amplification may have taken place as early as the fabled Xia Dynasty (c. 2200-1766 B.C.E.), a few tantalizing references to lost works that include hexagrams date from the Shang Dynasty (1384-1122 B.C.E.). The first written version of what forms the kernel of the *I Ching* is usually attributed to King Wen (also known as Wenwang, flourished twelfth century B.C.E.), a historical figure whose son founded the Zhou Dynasty (1122-221 B.C.E.). According to tradition, King Wen, a model governor of a small province, was unjustly jailed by the Shang emperor (who forced Wen to eat his son's flesh in order to show his loyalty). Wen avoided execution by performing hexagram divination for the imperial court and, during his confinement, purportedly rearranged sixty-four hexagrams into their present order and for each one wrote a brief commentary. These *Tuan* texts—often referred to as "judgments" or "decisions"—form the basis of the *I Ching*.

King Wen's son Wuwang eventually overthrew the Shang emperor, thereby establishing the Zhou Dynasty. Upon Wuwang's death, his brother Zhougong, known as the duke of Zhou, acted as regent until Wuwang's heir attained his majority. A model of the cultivated Chinese gentleman, the duke of Zhou continued his father's studies into the *I Ching* and is traditionally recog-

nized as the author of the *Yao* texts, commentaries corresponding to each line of the hexagrams. Whether either King Wen or the duke of Zhou was actually the author of the text attributed to him remains open to critical debate. Some linguists suggest that the *Tuan* and *Yao* texts are so deeply embedded in oral traditions of Shang divination practice that they must predate the culturally less sophisticated Zhou. However, others note the lack of oceanic and coastal imagery in the texts as evidence that they originated among the landlocked Zhou. Moreover, while the texts may represent a compilation of ancient oral divination traditions, the consistency of vocabulary and symbols suggest either a single editor or, more likely, a group of court scribes working under imperial auspices. The Zhou Dynasty left a definitive enough impression upon the text that in this form it is still commonly referred to as *Zhou Yi*; it would take almost a millennium before a subsequent incarnation of the text would become established in the Confucian canon and acquire its present name. The influence of the Zhou Dynasty also seems responsible for the ethical nature of the *Tuan* and *Yao* texts, which are more in character with the staid, moralistic Zhou than the relatively decadent Shang, whose leaders, in addition to divination, practiced human sacrifice and mass burials. The texts also seem to reflect the profound changes in the social system introduced by the Zhou rulers, who replaced the divine monarchy of the Shang with a feudal arrangement based on subjugation of everyone—

The Eight Trigrams of the *I Ching*

Qian (The Creative) Heaven	*Zhen* (The Arousing) Thunder	*Kan* (The Abysmal) Water	*Gen* (Keeping Still) Mountain
Kun (The Receptive) Earth	*Li* (The Clinging) Sun	*Sun* (The Gentle) Wind	*Dui* (The Joyous) Lake

Confucius, depicted playing the lute under a plum tree in this twelfth century drawing, is believed to have written the Great Commentary on the *I Ching*. *(Library of Congress)*

have achieved canonical status. There are actually only seven distinct commentaries, though the first three have two sections (making a total of ten). The seven commentaries of the Ten Wings are the *Xiang Zhuan* (commentary on the images, or lineal forms of the hexagrams), *Tuan Zhuan* (commentary on the judgments), *Wen Yan* (commentary on the words of the text), *Za Gua* (miscellaneous notes on the hexagrams), *Xu Gua* (commentary on the sequence of the hexagrams), *Shuo Gua* (discussion of the trigrams), and *Xi Ci Zhuan* (literally, the commentary on the appended judgments, but more commonly referred to as the *Great Commentary*). All of these works seem to be of a much later date than the *Zhou Yi*, and most appear to have a congregate nature as anonymous hands added layer upon layer of close reading of the primary texts.

Of these appended commentaries, the *Great Commentary* not only has been the most influential but also most directly bears the stamp of Confucius. Although Confucius may have authored the document, it seems more likely that a record of his statements on the text—much like those recorded in *Analects*—was used by disciples such as Zi Xia to give the document its present form. At once a justification and explication of the *I Ching*, the commentary interprets the work's cosmological symbolism in terms of an ethical humanism that, no doubt, would have been quite foreign to the Shang diviners who perfected the hexagram system. It assembles and analyzes a sequence of particular hexagrams—with titles such as Conduct, Duration, Increase, Decrease, Oppression, and Gentleness—as guideposts for the individual's self-development. The commentary is particularly Confucian in its nostalgic emphasis on the Zhou ideal of the "superior person" (*junzi*), who is virtuous, modest, reflective and, above all, submissive to the natural and social orders. The *Great Commentary* is quick to interpret the *Tuan* and *Yao* texts in terms of the decay of the contemporary social order—a preoccupation that directs

including the emperor—to the Mandate of Heaven. Lastly, the *Zhou Yi* betrays the patriarchal bias of the Zhou Dynasty: It reverses the Shang order of the first two hexagrams, giving primary place to the creative (associated with Heaven and father) rather than the receptive (associated with Earth and mother).

Next to King Wen, the name of Confucius is most often associated with the composition of the *I Ching*. Tradition ascribes to him the authorship of the Ten Wings, or appended commentaries on the *Zhou Yi* text. These sections are considered ancillary to the primary text but nevertheless some scholars to place its composition well after the death of Confucius in the tumultuous Warring States period (475-221 B.C.E.). In accordance with its Confucian origin, it seems to favor the *yang* lines of the hexagrams (representing light, masculinity, hierarchy, and rationalism) at the expense of the *yin* (representing darkness, femininity, organic unity, and intuition). Perhaps the best example of such hyperrationalism is its insistence that the shape of certain hexagrams served as archetypal images for technological innovations such as fishing nets (hexagram 30, the Clinging) and the plow (hexagram 42, Increase).

Because the *I Ching* escaped the burning of the books in 213 B.C.E., it became a central focus of the reemergent philosophic traditions during the Han Dynasty. Although the Confucian tradition remained the dominant approach, other traditions such as the Misfortune School linked the sequence of the hexagrams to a Daoist system of divination. Perhaps the most sustained philosophical inquiry to arise from the *I Ching* has concerned teleological speculation regarding the origin of *yin* and *yang*. During the Han Dynasty, Yang Xiong developed a system in the *Tai Xuan Jing* (before 18 C.E.; *The Classic of the Great Dark*, 1983), which posited the concept of *xuan*, or dark energy, as a transcendental state prior to the dissociation of *yin* and *yang*. Though better known for his commentary on the *Dao De Jing*, third century scholar Wang Bi also wrote an influential commentary of the *I Ching* that brought the subtlety of Daoist metaphysics to the text, invoking supreme nonbeing as the ultimate source of *yin* and *yang*. The neo-Confucians reclaimed the text during the Song Dynasty (960-1279 C.E.), reestablishing the Ten Wings as the canonical commentary and even banning heterodox interpretations such as those of Yang Xiong and Wang Bi. In place of *xuan* and supreme nonbeing, Zhou Dunyi (1017-1073 C.E.) offered the monadic concept of *tai ji* (the great absolute) as the ground of *yin* and *yang*. However, Zhu Xi (1130-1200 C.E.) located their source in the dyadic relationship of *li* (principle) and *qi* (energy).

Western scholars have compared the relation of *li* and *qi* to the Aristotelian distinction between form and matter. However, they have noted that the teleological system of the *I Ching* differs substantially from that common to classical Western philosophy in that *li* presupposes a view of nature as a constantly evolving organic whole rather than an essentially closed system based upon a priori or transcendental forms. Indeed, some contemporary scholars consider *I Ching*'s philosophical foundation in the idea of change as inherently antithetical to Western thought—at least that prior to the modern existentialist movement, which denied the priority of "being" to "becoming." Like much of the Daoist thought that it both encompasses and transcends, the *I Ching* anticipates the philosophies of Western thinkers such as Pierre Teilhard de Chardin and Alfred North Whitehead, both of whom view ultimate reality as an organic and ever-changing unity better understood as a process rather than a fixed being or substance.

Perhaps the work's most immediate contribution to Western thought concerns the philosophy of mind. As a direct result of his research into the text, Carl Gustav Jung coined his term "synchronicity" to justify the reality of seemingly irrational mental phenomena such as déjà vu or luck. In contrast to the Cartesian model of direct linear causation (in which event *A* causes event *B*, which in turn causes event *C*), Jung borrowed the *I Ching*'s model of change, which presupposes that all events are unique, independent occurrences that do not "cause" other events so much as correspond to or "resonate" within them (because all events share the internal dynamism of *yin* and *yang* forces).

Luke A. Powers

Overview

Type of philosophy: Chinese philosophy, ethics, metaphysics

First transcribed: I Ching (Yi Jing), eighth to third century B.C.E. (English translation, 1876; also known as *Book of Changes*, 1986)

Principal ideas advanced:

◇ The great absolute (the *tai ji*) generated the two primal forces, the *yin* (the passive, female, dark aspect) and the *yang* (the active, male, light aspect).

Three Hexagrams of the *I Ching*

Qian

_____
_____
_____
_____
_____
_____

Kun

____ ____
____ ____
____ ____
____ ____
____ ____
____ ____

Zhun

_____
____ ____
____ ____
____ ____
_____
_____

◇ The two primary forces generated the four images; the four images generated the eight trigrams.

◇ The eight trigrams combine to form sixty-four hexagrams, images composed of six lines, each representing a fundamental creative form of the universe.

◇ All possible situations and changes are shown by the hexagrams.

◇ The superior person consults the *I Ching* to be in accord with the eternal *dao* (the Way).

The *I Ching* is one of the three so-called "mystical scriptures," the other two being the *Dao De Jing* (late third century B.C.E.; *The Speculations on Metaphysics, Polity, and Morality, of "the Old Philosopher, Lau-Tsze,"* 1868; better known as *Dao De Jing*) and the *Zhuangzi* (c. 300 B.C.E., *The Divine Classic of Nan-hua,* 1881; also known as *The Complete Works of Chuang Tzu,* 1968; commonly known as *Zhuangzi,* 1991). Initially a book of divination, the *I Ching* grew over the centuries with the addition of commentaries and came to be venerated not only as a profound image of the forces of the universe but also as a source of wisdom.

The book is the work of many authors, and there is no consensus concerning their identity. Chinese scholar Wing-tsit Chan notes that tradition ascribes the eight trigrams (of which the sixty-four hexagrams are composed) to the legendary emperor Fu Xi (third millennium B.C.E.), the sixty-four hexagrams to King Wen (also known as Wenwang, flourished twelfth century B.C.E.), the two texts to him or the duke of Zhou (died 1094 B.C.E.), and the Ten Wings (appendixes or commentaries) to Confucius; but Chan points out that most modern scholars reject these claims and that one must simply conclude that the work is the "product of many hands over a long period of time."

Six Trigrams of the *I Ching*

Zhen   _____ _____   The Arousing, Thunder
        __ __
        _____

Kan   _____ _____   The Abysmal, Water
        _____
        _____ _____

Gen   _____   Keeping Still, Mountain
        __ __
        __ __

Sun   _____   The Gentle, Wind
        _____
        _____ _____

Li   _____ _____   The Clinging, Sun
        _____ _____
        _____

Dui   _____ _____   The Joyous, Lake
        _____
        _____

The first two hexagrams of the *I Ching*, as shown in the table, "Three Hexagrams of the *I Ching*," are particularly important and have received special attention from the commentators. The first is *qian*, the creative, heaven, and the second is *kun*, the receptive, earth. The trigram composed of three *yang* lines is itself called *qian*. The hexagram *qian* is, then, a pair of *qian* trigrams. The *qian* trigram is an image of the creative power of the universe. A *yang* line is an active, strong, male symbol; three such lines, composing the *qian* trigram, make up the image of creativity and heaven; the image is of power and, as applied to the family, of the father. The *qian* trigram is one of the fundamental eight symbols on which the entire imagery of the *I Ching* is built. A pair of *qian* trigrams, forming the *qian* hexagram, is the first symbol, the symbol of the universe itself, its power and its creative force, its pervasive activity as the origin of ceaseless movement and change.

The second hexagram is *kun*. *Kun* as a hexagram is composed of two *kun* trigrams; only *yin* lines appear. *Kun* is accordingly the image of the passive, the receptive, the female, the mother, earth.

The remaining six basic trigrams, *zhen*, *kan*, *gen*, *sun*, *li*, and *dui*, are shown in the table "Six Trigrams of the *I Ching*." The hexagrams of the *I Ching* are formed from the basic trigrams. The *first* trigram is the *bottom* one; the *first* line of the hexagram is the *bottom* line. The third hexagram, *zhun*, can be described as *zhen kan* (*zhen* below, *kan* above).

According to Chinese scholar Fung Yu-lan, the lines of the hexagrams were suggested by tortoise shell cracks, to which diviners attended in an earlier period. Over the centuries the significance of the hexagrams was developed, and the present-day version of the work contains the original text (that Confucius reputedly knew) with the appendices and commentaries.

The Sixty-Four Hexagrams

The main text of the *I Ching* consists of the sixty-four hexagrams, each followed by an explanation, or "judgment," of the hexagram considered as a whole, then by propositions or judgments on the six lines considered separately. For example, the judgment for *qian* (the creative) is "Supreme blessing; an augury of advantage."

The judgment, or "oracle," for each of the six lines of the hexagram *qian*, beginning at the bottom, follows: (1) "A dragon lies hid: there should be no expenditure"; (2) "Discloses a dragon in the field: advantageous to have audience of the great man"; (3) "A knight goes vigorously throughout the day (but) at night is more or less cautious: danger, (but) not of misfortune"; (4) "Something leaping up in an abyss: no misfortune"; (5) "A dragon flying in the heavens: advantageous to have audience of the great man"; (6) "An overbearing dragon, there is cause for censure (? repentance)."

The Ten Wings

According to tradition, the *guaci* or "judgment" for each hexagram—an explanation of the six-line image considered as a whole—was written by King Wen; the comments (*Yao* text) on the individual lines of each hexagram were written by the Duke of Zhou. However, the part of the book that accounts primarily for its eminence as a work of philosophical literature is the set of commentaries entitled the Ten Wings. Although there are seven commentaries, they are known as the Ten Wings because three of them have two parts, each related to the two parts of the basic text, part 1 covering the first thirty hexagrams, part 2 covering the remaining thirty-four.

The *Tuan Zhuan* (commentary on the judgments), contains the first two wings. The *Xiang Zhuan* (commentary on the images, or the abstract meanings involved) contains wings three and four. Wings five and six are the two parts of the *Xi Ci Zhuan* (the *Great Commentary*, a commentary on the appended judgments). The *Great Commentary* concentrates on the basic ideas of the trigrams (on the trigrams as basic "ideas" or "forms"). The *Wen Yan* (commentary on the words of the text) is a discussion of the first two hexagrams. The eighth Wing is the *Shuo Gua*, which comments on the symbolic import of the trigrams. A commentary on the order of the hexagrams, the *Xu Gua*, is the ninth Wing, and the tenth Wing, the *Za Gua*, adds various random comments on the hexagrams.

Yin and Yang

Insofar as it is possible to abstract a metaphysical thesis from the *I Ching*, it is that the universe owes its origin and its order to the *dao*, the fundamental primal way of being. In the beginning there was the great absolute (the "great ultimate" or "great primal beginning"), the *tai ji*. According to the *Great Commentary*, the great absolute gave rise to two primal creative forms, the *yang* (the positive power, active, male, light) and the *yin* (the negative, or receptive, passive, female, dark). These contrary but complementary features are manifest in Heaven (*yang*) and Earth (*yin*); Heaven is the creative, while Earth is the receptive. All movement and rest are subject to the universal laws of change, laws that are determined by the relationships of higher to lower, inferior to superior in aspects of the universe. Consequently, everything is ordered within a unified cosmos. The *yang* is creative, strong, firm; hence, it is the principle, power, or image of movement; the yielding *yin* is the dark (as opposed to the light) principle, the principle of rest.

In the hexagrams, the solid and broken lines (the *yang* and the *yin* lines) are so related to one another (imaging relationships in the universe) as to represent either a state of equilibrium or a condition of movement and displacement. Hence, according to the *Great Commentary*, the eight trigrams succeed one another and make intuitively perceptible both the form and cause of change.

Change in the universe may be recognized as a process of manifestation, the continual concrete manifestation of the abstract aspects and relationships mirrored by the hexagrams. To understand the aspects and relationships, the principles of change, the laws of the universe, is to understand all possibilities and actualities, to know in any given situation (as shown by the appropriate hexagram) how to act—whether to move or to be at rest—and accordingly how to fit in with the *dao* of things.

The hexagrams themselves would not provide a basis for moral judgment had not the sages recognized their revelatory power and fixed it for ordinary comprehension through the appended judgments. As the *Great Commentary* points out, as images of movement in accordance with the laws that reflect the interaction and interpenetration of the complementary basic aspects of the universe, the hexagrams show how good fortune and misfortune come about: Given the aspects affecting one another in any particular situation,

it becomes apparent, so it is argued, that certain lines of action will be fortunate, others unfortunate. One must recognize the occasion of positive change—when a yielding line is converted to a firm one—and of retrogressive change—when the opposite occurs. The "superior person"(*junzi*) attains tranquillity by acting in an appropriate way as determined by his or her understanding of the lines in their relationships and of the judgments appended to them.

The *Da Zhuan* comments on the effects of the *I Ching* on those who learn from it: "The Master said: Is not the Book of Changes supreme? By means of it the holy sages exalted their natures and extended their field of action. Wisdom exalts. The mores make humble. The exalted imitate heaven. The humble follow the example of the earth." The task for anyone who would acquire wisdom and act rightly is to relate "heaven," the creative power of the ideal, to "earth," the field of human action. Hence, the *Da Zhuan* continues, "Heaven and earth determine the scene, and the changes take effect within it. The perfected nature of man, sustaining itself and enduring, is the gateway of *dao* and of justice."

Ethics

The *I Ching* also has an ethical dimension. It states that the primary law of conduct is that of relating oneself to the *dao* of the universe by grasping the character of situations (shown by the hexagrams) and merging into the systematic changes (made evident through the lines and commentary on the lines).

The virtues are manifestations of the creative aspects of the universe, whether the creative takes the form of action or of patient and persevering reception. To be superior, one is told, one must make oneself strong, persevere in one's efforts whatever the initial difficulties, learn from the teachers, be prepared for the right moment but be willing to rest until that moment comes, be reflective, gain the strength that comes from cooperative effort, use the "taming power" of friendly persuasion when in a weak position, participate in heaven's influential effects, hold to principles when the morally inferior are in control, obey the will of heaven, and be modest, enthusiastic, tolerant, protective, fair, temperate, and firm.

The virtue appropriate to a situation depends on how the forces making for change are distributed in that situation. One is wise to attend to the sages, whose comments on the diagrams penetrate their significance and relevance and enable anyone who would be superior as a person to make some progress in attaining a state of harmony with the *dao*, the way of the universe. The names of the hexagrams suggest the virtues promulgated by the *I Ching*, the first two being fundamental (the following list is, of course, partial): The Creative, the Receptive, Union, Peace, Fellowship, Modesty, Enthusiasm, Contemplation, Grace, Innocence, Resoluteness, Pushing Upward, the Gentle, the Joyous, Inner Truth.

Part 1 of the *I Ching* is at once an account of beginnings, fundamental change, laws of change, the essential and influential forms, and the virtues applicable to all persons. Part 2 concentrates on social relationships and begins with situations relating to courtship and marriage; the virtues are not the "inner" virtues of self-development but virtues relating to others and to one's commerce with them.

The *I Ching* is not the curious amalgamation of cryptic remarks that many Westerners suppose it to be. Despite its long history of generation, it is a coherent and philosophically significant work. It is philosophy in the grand and traditional sense: a description of the universe relevant to spirit, an image intended to be both revelatory and inspiring.

Ian P. McGreal, updated by John K. Roth

Additional Reading

Lee, Jung Young. *Embracing Change: Postmodern Interpretations of the "I Ching" from a Christian Perspective*. Cranbury, N.J.: Associated University Presses, 1994. Though some of the connections of *I Ching* wisdom to Christian traditions seem a stretch, this work provides a thought-provoking introduction to the Chinese "sacred" text in terms accessible to a Western audience.

Needham, Joseph, and Wang Ling. *Science and Civilization in China*. 5 vols. Cambridge, England: Cambridge University Press, 1956. This seminal work places the *I Ching* within the framework of Chinese intellectual history. The authors argue that the work and divination practice in general impeded the development of scientific thought in China.

Shaughnessy, Edward. *Before Confucius: Studies in the Creation of the Chinese Classics*. Albany: State University of New York Press, 1997. A collection of critical essays, several of which focus on the historical sources for images in the *Zhou Yi*, a forerunner of the *I Ching*.

Shchutskii, Julian K. *Researches on the "I Ching."* Translated by William McDonald, Tsuyoshi Hasegawa, and Hellmut Wilhelm. Princeton, N.J.: Princeton University Press, 1979. Originally published in 1935 in the Soviet Union, this dissertation provides a good critical history of *I Ching* studies up to that time both in China and the West.

Watson, William. *Early Civilization in China*. London: Thames and Hudson, 1966. This work separates fact from legend in its discussion of sage emperors such as Fu Xi; it also includes historical information on the archaic divination practices from which the *I Ching* developed.

Whincup, Greg. *Rediscovering the "I Ching."* Garden City, N.Y.: Doubleday, 1986. The author seeks to isolate the older elements of the text to reveal an *I Ching* devoted more to practical divination than abstract speculation.

Wilhelm, Hellmut. *Change: Eight Lectures on the "I Ching."* Translated by Cary F. Baynes. Princeton, N.J.: Princeton University Press, 1960. An excellent short introduction to the hexagram system and its philosophical underpinnings, written by the son of famed *I Ching* translator Richard Wilhelm.

Wilhelm, Hellmut, and Richard Wilhelm. *Understanding the I Ching: The Wilhelm Lectures on the Book of Changes*. Princeton, N.J.: Princeton University Press, 1995. A series of eight lectures on the *I Ching* that endeavor to explain the philosophy.

Luke A. Powers

Luce Irigaray

By reexamining many of the major texts of Western philosophy, Irigaray has attempted to articulate the ways in which language, particularly the language of psychoanalysis, limits women.

Principal philosophical works: *Le Langage des déments*, 1973; *Speculum de l'autre femme*, 1974 (*Speculum of the Other Woman*, 1985); *Ce sexe qui n'en est pas un*, 1977 (*This Sex Which Is Not One*, 1985); *Et l'une ne bouge pas sans l'autre*, 1979; *Amante marine: De Friedrich Nietzsche*, 1980 (*Marine Lover of Friedrich Nietzsche*, 1991); *Le Corps-à-corps avec la mère*, 1981; *Passions élémentaires*, 1982 (*Elemental Passions*, 1992); *La Croyance même*, 1983; *L'Oubli de l'air: Chez Martin Heidegger*, 1983; *Ethique de la différence sexuelle*, 1984 (*An Ethics of Sexual Difference*, 1993); *Parler n'est jamais neutre*, 1985; *Sexes et parentés*, 1987 (*Sexes and Geneaologies*, 1993); *Le Temps de la différence*, 1989 (*Thinking the Difference: For a Peaceful Revolution*, 1994); *Je, tu, nous*, 1990 (*Je, Tu, Nous: Toward a Culture of Difference*, 1993); *The Irigaray Reader*, 1991; *J'aime à toi: Esquisse d'une félicité dans l'histoire*, 1992 (*I Love to You: Sketch for a Felicity Within History*, 1996).

Born: 1930; Belgium

Early Life

Little is known of Luce Irigaray's early life. She was born in Belgium and spent her childhood there. In 1955, she received a master's degree in philosophy and literature from the University of Lovain, completing a thesis on the writer Paul Velery. In 1956, she became a secondary schoolteacher in Brussels, Belgium, a post she retained until 1959.

Life's Work

In 1959, Irigaray moved to Paris and began studying for what was to be the first of many advanced degrees she was to receive in France. In 1961, she received a master's degree in psychology from the University of Paris, and in 1962, she was awarded a diploma in psychopathology from the Institut de Psychologie de Paris. Also in 1962, she accepted a position at the Fondation Nationale de Recherche Scientifique in Belgium, where she remained until 1964, when she returned to Paris as an assistant researcher at the Centre National de Recherche Scientifique. She remained attached to this organization and was named its director of research in 1986. Upon her

return to Paris, she began work on more advanced degrees. In 1968, she completed a doctoral degree in linguistics at the University of Paris X at Nanterre.

In 1974, she was awarded another doctorate, this time in philosophy, from the University of Paris VIII. She also obtained psychoanalytic training at the Freudian School, where she studied with Jacques Lacan, many of whose texts she was later to examine and reinterpret in her own writing. During her time as a student, she was also an instructor at the University of Paris VIII at Vincennes. Her first dissertation, which dealt with the language patterns of mentally disturbed individuals—specifically, victims of senility—was later published, and she refers to the information she gleaned in this study in other works.

Her second dissertation, however, was the cause of great controversy. The work, *Speculum of the Other Woman*, reexamined the basic tenets of Freudian theory, criticizing the extremely patriarchal system Sigmund Freud had created and Lacan was in many senses continuing. Irigaray went on to obtain her doctorate with highest distinction, but she was an outcast in the Freudian School after the publication of *Speculum of the Other Woman*. She also found considerable difficulty in finding teaching positions in the Paris universities because her views were seen as far too radical.

However, Irigaray continued to produce an astonishing corpus of work, all the while working as a private psychoanalyst and continuing her work with the Centre National de Recherche Scientifique. During the 1970's, when the women's movement was growing rapidly in France, she participated in demonstrations and rallies designed to help legalize contraceptives and provide women open access to medical abortion. Although she never joined any particular group, she continued to use her position as a respected feminist critic to advance the causes of women socially.

As Irigaray's work began to be translated into English and other languages in the 1980's, her fame as a philosopher, psychoanalyst, and linguist grew. She spoke at numerous scholarly conferences and was named the Jan Tinbergen Chair of Philosophy at Erasmus University in Rotterdam in 1982. During her tenure at Erasmus, she produced a series of lectures that was later published as *An Ethics of Sexual Difference*. The University of Bologna invited her to give a seminar in 1985, and in that year, she also returned to teach in Paris at the École des Hautes Études en Sciences Sociales. In June, 1987, she presented a monthlong seminar at the International Summer Institute of Semiotic and Structuralist Studies in Toronto, Canada. In 1988, she began a two-year teaching assignment at the College International de Philosophie in Paris, and in 1989 and 1990, she also taught at the Centre Americain d'Études Critiques. She continued to publish in book form and in scholarly journals, and her impact grew steadily as more of her works were translated.

Influence

Irigaray's work in the area of language and its relation to women's oppression in the West has been her most important contribution for feminist philosophers, but her work is also deemed crucial by literary theorists, students of gender theory, sociologists, and linguists. Her texts are extremely difficult to read because she assumes that her readers are familiar with her earlier works as well as the major philosophical texts of the Western canon. She also engages in a great deal of word play whereby she bends grammar, creates new words, uses hyphens and italics to highlight familiar words, and uses sentence fragments and other unorthodox constructions to make her points. Because one of her enduring points is that language is inadequate to express certain truths, especially female truths, her use of language is part of her message as much as the contents of her essays. Nevertheless, the unusual way in which she expresses her powerful ideas has no doubt estranged some of her potential readers, just as it has endeared her to many others. As her work continues to receive attention throughout the world, Irigaray will no doubt cement her position as one of the most important voices of the modern age.

Vicki A. Sanders

An Ethics of Sexual Difference

Type of philosophy: Ethics, feminist philosophy
First published: Ethique de la différence sexuelle, 1984 (English translation, 1993)
Principal ideas advanced:

◊ Sexual difference is one of the most pressing philosophical issues of the modern age.

◊ The transition to a new age of interaction requires that people rethink their traditional conceptions of space, time, and the inhabiting of place, but this is difficult because language determines how people perceive these concepts.

◊ The traditional use of language, which sees woman as something less than complete, has privileged men and required women to give up their individuality in order to serve as the "place" where men find something of themselves.

◊ Woman might regain her subjectivity in reality and in language in different ways, including the rediscovery of wonder and expanding the meaning of the caress, thus returning the primacy of touch over language.

This collection of essays originated as a series of lectures delivered by Luce Irigaray at Erasmus

University in Rotterdam during the second semester of 1982, when she was serving as the Jan Tinbergen Chair of Philosophy. By this time, Irigaray's controversial writing on the subjects of language, psychoanalysis, and gender were already well known, and the lectures contained in this book expand on her previously published ideas regarding the connection between language, culture, and women's place or lack of place in society. Her style of writing is highly unusual, combining elements of traditional literary theory and analysis with extremely unusual methods of composition. Irigaray uses strange punctuation, a multitude of hyphenated and created words, sentence fragments, and other grammatical techniques in an attempt to use what she regards as a flawed instrument, language, to contain her sometimes radical ideas.

Women and Sexual Differences

Irigaray begins her first essay, "Sexual Difference," by describing why the work of understanding sexual difference is so important to the modern world. She describes the role of God in most patriarchal societies as the creator of all space, in which time operates, which means that God is time itself, operating within the space created. Therefore, God is the only creature conceived of as beyond time, and God is always male in patriarchal societies. This is not helpful to the woman who seeks to find her identity, so something new must be found. Irigaray states that the constitution of a sexual ethics would require a return to what French philosopher René Descartes called the first passion, wonder. The rediscovery of wonder between man and woman—being able to look at the other sex as though one does not already know all about them—would be an important first step in the new sexual ethics Irigaray wishes to create.

In the second essay, "Sorcerer Love," Irigaray provides a reading of Plato's *Symposion* (c. 388-368 B.C.E.; *Symposium*, 1701), particularly "Diotoma's Speech," to show how women are denied the use of language. Diotoma does not speak but is spoken for, yet she manages to introduce a new ethic that stands in opposition to the traditional dialectical model. Diotoma rejects all certainty, including the certainty of language itself. Diotoma also realizes that love's real importance lies

in its role as a mediator between pairs of opposites.

The third essay, "Place, Interval," is a reading of book 4 of Aristotle's *Physica* (Second Athenian Period, 335-323 B.C.E.; *Physics*, 1812), in which he wrestles with the concept of place and how place can be required for a thing to exist but is not the thing itself. Irigaray sees this argument as particularly significant because woman in the traditional Western conception has been assigned the role of place for man but not for herself. Woman is something that allows man to exist but cannot exist herself within this scheme.

Essay 4, "Love of Self," raises the question of self-love with relation to men and women and how this love differs. Irigaray concludes that love of self is more complicated for women than it is for men because the woman must attempt to love herself while serving as the principal mirror through which the man sees and loves himself. Men are also disadvantaged because women cannot truly love anyone else (including men) if they cannot love themselves. The ways in which women and men relate to language mirror the ways in which they relate to each other and to the world. The necessary conditions for women to love themselves include removing the hierarchy of the mother's and father's functions in relation to children, reassociating love and eroticism, allowing women to form meaningful social groups, and reestablishing the existence of a female divine.

Self-Love and Relationships

Essay 5, "Wonder," is Irigaray's reading of René Descartes's *Les Passions de l'âme* (1649; *The Passions of the Soul*, 1950), in which she returns to the idea of wonder as the essential element lacking in people's modern understanding of the passions. If man and woman were again able to inspire surprise and wonder so that people felt as if they were seeing something eternally new, sexual ethics would be favorably altered. Wonder provides the appetite to appreciate the other without preconceived knowledge, and wonder inspires a sort of reverence. Wonder could provide the essential third element now lacking between men and women in all their relations with each other.

Essay 6, "The Envelope," is Irigaray's reading of Baruch Spinoza's *Ethica* (1677; *Ethics*, 1870) in which she examines the concept of God. In her view (and her choice of pronouns), God exists on its own with no outside agency predicating it. Man also has a creator/created relationship with woman because woman as mother is the container from which man arises and woman as lover is the location of the man's image of himself. Therefore, woman's effort is exhausted in providing identity for man, first as his mother and then as his lover. By reconsidering the roles of both, Irigaray suggests that men and women could be given wider scope.

Essay 7, "Love of Same, Love of Other," states that love of self among women, particularly in the feminine, is nearly impossible, except in the childish relationship of daughter and mother. However, psychoanalyst Sigmund Freud states that this early attachment must be destroyed by girls in order for them to become attached to men and become objects to attract male attention. This paralyzes the self-love of women as well as love between women, who compete with each other for men. In order to love each other or love the feminine in themselves, women must begin to love their own bodies and love the bodies of others. Women must become both mothers and daughters to each other; they must love with a maternal and a filial love.

Women need a language of their own, outside the supposedly neutral but actually deeply sexed language currently in use. Women must think about this sexism within language and attempt to circumvent it. Irigaray likens this to thinking about the mucous membranes of the body, which connect the body most immediately to the outside world (as language does), but which most people take entirely for granted unless they become irritated. Language has traditionally served men, and Irigaray urges the reader to think about its activities and especially its limits.

Language and Women
Essay 8, "An Ethics of Sexual Difference," examines the myth of Antigone. Like Antigone, woman has traditionally been walled up in a small space and deprived of a voice to speak because she upsets the male balance of the world, represented by Creon. Irigaray is convinced this is the present-day status of woman because the so-called universal is really the male element, and

women have been completely removed. There is not even a neuter space, only the male and the not-male that woman represents. This is also true in science, though science purports to be objective and neutral. Science does not speak to women, Irigaray asserts, because the language of scientific discourse does not allow it to; that language is and always has been male. This language is like air, which is the most essential element of all life but which is constantly completely ignored by most living beings. She indicates that people must again begin to think about air—and about all the unquestioned and unnoticed assumptions of language—more directly in order to arrive at a new sexual ethics that is workable.

Essay 9, "Love of the Other," attempts to pin down even more directly the hidden effects of sexism in language. Irigaray suggests that people think they control language, but in fact, it controls them by limiting how and what they are able to think, to talk, or to write about. Making reference to her own study of the utterances of mentally disturbed men and women and linguistic studies of students, Irigaray points out that men tend to make remarks that are self-referential, whereas women tend to make remarks entirely referential to the outside world. These two examples show the differences in how men and women view themselves in society. Irigaray assumes that women are trying to gain access to discourse—by use of the women's movement and other methods—but the dichotomy between thought and the feminine remains constant in Western culture. Removing this distinction would benefit both women and men immensely by opening up alternate realities to them, across which real communication would be possible for the first time.

Touching and Looking
Essay 10, "The Invisible of the Flesh," is a reading of Maurice Merleau-Ponty's *Le Visible et l'invisible* (1964; *The Visible and the Invisible*, 1968). Irigaray states her agreement with Merleau-Ponty that, in order to come to some meaningful understanding of the world, people must return to a moment of experience that predates language. By doing so, people can get a new understanding of all things because language is the primary

method by which people think and understand or believe that they understand. However, language is circular in that it always returns to itself as an ultimate reference. Therefore, some other path to knowledge must be found. According to both Merleau-Ponty and Irigaray, this prediscursive moment would be achieved through touch and also the look, which is a variant of touch. She equates this knowledge acquired by touching with Original Sin because Adam and Eve were warned not only not to eat of the forbidden fruit but also not to touch it as well. She suggests that perhaps the male interpretation of God, which has so often equated touch with evil carnality, is at fault in our lack of attention to this knowing that is acquired by touch. Man has traditionally claimed the privilege of the look in Western culture, but Irigaray suggests that this is illusory and that women have special access to the knowledge of touch by virtue of their status as mothers and lovers.

The eleventh and final essay, "The Fecundity of the Caress," is a reading of Emmanuel Lévinas's *Totalité et infini: Essai sur l'extériorité* (1961; *Totality and Infinity: An Essay on Exteriority*, 1969) and a final attempt to discuss ways in which the language of touch might give people access to knowledge that is forbidden in the strictures of language. Irigaray suggests that sensual pleasure can give people passage to parts of the world that are closed off by the confines of a sexed language system. Through a series of almost ecstatic short utterances, Irigaray describes a sensual moment in which men and women might bridge the gap that separates them and gain an understanding of each other and the world that has never before been available. Because women have usually been relegated to the status of mother, infant, or animal, their intimate knowledge of the body and of touch—as opposed to the knowledge that is described in sexed male language—has been ignored and ridiculed. If women were allowed to escape their traditional configurations and became once again figures that inspire wonder and astonishment, a new ethic might be achievable. This new ethic would call for a return to the flesh, a way of ordering the world that predates language and exists in the more nebulous world of the touch, the body's knowing without speech.

Irigaray's writing is extremely dense and diffi-

cult to follow because she assumes the reader has a wealth of prior knowledge to draw on and is well read in the major philosophical texts of the Western world. Additionally, she attempts to use language in unusual ways, to better make her points about the effects of language on our thought and especially the limits of words in truly expressing certain concepts, particularly feminine ones. However, even though her books are not readily accessible to the novice, her examinations of the interactions between language and culture, and particularly language and psychoanalysis, have been very influential. Feminist critics have been especially interested in her insights on traditional philosophical texts and her examinations of how language deals with the differences between men and women.

Vicki A. Sanders

Additional Reading

Chanter, Tina. *Ethics of Eros: Irigaray's Rewriting of the Philosophers*. New York: Routledge, 1995. Chanter provides an informative overview of Irigaray's use of traditional Western philosophical texts and how these texts serve as a basis for her language analysis while she provides new insight to these well-known works.

Mortley, Raoul. *French Philosophers in Conversation: Levinas, Schneider, Serres, Irigaray, LeDoeuff, Derrida*. New York: Routledge, 1991. In chapter 4 of this text, Irigaray provides her answer to the author's two questions about the importance of sexual difference in language. Her answers help illuminate many of the chief ideas found in *An Ethics of Sexual Difference* and give a brief overview of her ideas on language and sexuality in general.

Nordquist, Joan. *French Feminist Theory (III): Luce Irigaray and Helen Cixous*. Social Theory: A Bibliographic Series 44. Santa Cruz, Calif.: Reference and Research Services, 1996. This publication provides an exhaustive list of all material relating to Irigaray available in English as of the date of its publication, including books, essays, interviews, dissertations and theses, articles, and keyword-in-title indices.

Ross, Stephen David. *Plenishment in the Earth: An Ethic of Inclusion*. Albany: State University of New York Press, 1995. This text examines several of Irigaray's texts in detail and is interesting because it provides a male response to many of her theories, which is relatively unusual because most of the theorists and critics who study her are women. The book also attempts to place her in the context of several other important women philosophers of the twentieth century, as well as more traditional male thinkers.

Whitford, Margaret. Introduction to *The Irigaray Reader*, by Luce Irigaray. Oxford: Basil Blackwell, 1991. Whitford's introduction gives those unfamiliar with Irigaray's works an excellent starting point for these difficult texts, portions of which are provided in English.

Vicki A. Sanders

Alison M. Jaggar

One of the founders of feminist philosophy, Jaggar is noted for bringing rigorous analysis to bear on the claims of various theories about women's subordination.

Principal philosophical works: *Feminist Politics and Human Nature*, 1983; *Living with Contradictions: Controversies in Feminist Social Ethics*, 1994; *Morality and Social Justice: Point Counterpoint*, 1995 (with James P. Sterba, Milton Fisk, William A. Galston, Carol C. Gould, Tibor Machan, and Robert Solomon).

Born: September 23, 1942; Sheffield, England

Early Life

Alison Mary Jaggar was born Alison Mary Hayes in Sheffield, England. Her early academic work was in British institutions; she received a B.A. from Bedford College of the University of London in 1964 and an M.Litt. from the University of Edinburgh in 1967. In 1970, she earned a Ph.D. from the State University of New York at Buffalo.

The title of her dissertation was "On Communication in Philosophy: A Study of the Problems Involved in the Re-Expression of Theoretical Philosophical Statements." Her initial question when embarking on the project was whether different "schools" or traditions could be compared and evaluated against each other. However, the project's eventual focus became the possibility of translation between different philosophical traditions and especially translation into "ordinary language." She concluded that "ordinary language" may carry implicit beliefs about the world that contradict the claims of some philosophical theories, and hence an accurate translation or paraphrase may be impossible. However, Jaggar also determined that because of its flexibility, ordinary language can be the best medium for explaining theories outside their original terms of discourse and suggested some methods that could be used to make these concepts clearer.

This dissertation contains many themes that surface in Jaggar's later work, including an interest in links between different philosophic theories. The feminist writers whose work she later analyzed and evaluated offer many examples of the overlap (and occasionally the lack of connection) between philosophic and ordinary terms.

Life's Work

Although she pursued a nontraditional specialty, Jaggar followed a conventional academic career path. Upon receiving her doctorate, she served as an assistant professor of philosophy at Miami University from 1970 through 1972 and as associate professor at the University of Cincinnati from 1972 through the rest of the decade. In 1975, she also taught at the University of Illinois, Chicago Circle, as a visiting professor. During this period, Jaggar published several articles. The first, in 1973, was a continuation of her dissertation topic. Others, on ethics and on sexual equality, followed. These were forays into questions that would become central in her work.

In the 1970's, equal opportunity for women in employment became national policy backed by law in the United States. Before these changes, many inequitable practices were commonplace. For example, in many workplaces, a woman employee was routinely asked to resign when her pregnancy became obvious, regardless of her ability to perform her job. The passage of equal employment measures and the implementation of affirmative action ended many accepted business practices. In the mid-1970's, Jaggar, bringing her philosophical background and beliefs to a real-life situation, dealt with some of the dilemmas in "Affirmative Action with Respect to Women in Academia: The Law and Its Implementation" and "Relaxing the Limits on Preferential Treatment." These were articles directed at an audience outside, as well as within, the field of philosophy.

In 1977, she designed and taught the first course to be offered at any academic institute in the United States in feminist philosophy. During the late 1970's and the early 1980's, academics were beginning to regard the feminist critique of society less as radical "street" rhetoric and more as a subject for academic scholarship. Feminism gained recognition both as a new approach within existing disciplines and in new curricula known as women's studies. Jaggar's work, in the classroom and in her writing, gave impetus to this trend. It was also a happy concurrence of a scholar's interests and a movement on the verge of gaining academic respectability as a subject.

In 1978, Jaggar and Paula Rothenberg coedited *Feminist Frameworks: Alternative Theoretical Accounts of the Relations Between Women and Men*, a collection of documents from varied perspectives, including those on the antifeminist side of the debate. Jaggar's 1983 book, *Feminist Politics and Human Nature*, set basic parameters for the field of feminist philosophy. It describes and analyzes four "schools" of feminist thought according to their theory, political strategies, and ideals of the good society. Its categories are still used as a starting point for most new work in the field, although as Jaggar herself predicted, time has created some shifts and reevaluations among the categories.

In 1982, Jaggar was promoted to a full professorship at the University of Cincinnati and, in 1984, was named Obed J. Wilson Professor of Ethics. During the 1980's, Jaggar published about a dozen articles in addition to her trailblazing book and received several fellowships and research grants. She also taught as a visiting professor at the University of California, Los Angeles, and at Rutgers University. In 1989, she coedited *Gender/Body/Knowledge: Feminist Reconstructions of Being and Knowing*, a collection on feminist epistemology, with Susan R. Bordo.

In 1991, she was appointed professor of philosophy and women's studies at the University of Colorado at Boulder. During the 1990's, she continued to publish a variety of works, including many articles on feminist ethics. In *Living with Contradictions: Controversies in Feminist Social Ethics*, she brings together examples of practical rather than theoretical dilemmas as described by those people (not always women) experiencing them. *A Companion to Feminist Philosophy* (1998), a massive survey volume Jaggar coedited with Iris M. Young, contains articles defining the topic from regional and historical perspectives as well as those taking topical approaches.

Another arena in which Jaggar has been a pathfinder is that of making "womanspace" within the

Alison M. Jaggar. *(Courtesy of Alison Jaggar)*

profession of philosophy itself. She was a founding member of the Society for Women in Philosophy and has been chair of the American Philosophical Association's Committee on the Status of Women. She often states that she considers feminist scholarship to be inseparable from feminist activism.

Over the course of her career, Jaggar maintained her vision and goal of attaining a more equitable society. In her major work, *Feminist Politics and Human Nature*, she claims that socialist feminism is the best approach for achieving this goal. Although her basic position remains the same, she altered and expanded on her views on a number of aspects discussed in this 1983 book. For instance, whereas previously she tended to dismiss liberal feminists' emphasis on individual rights, she came to consider such rights as necessary in any foreseeable society, stating that black and non-Western women might bring different perspectives and needs to the debate and that socialist feminism would need to expand to include them. In her 1990's work on social ethics, she suggests that other arenas, such as militarism and the environment, may also fall within the scope of feminist concern.

Jaggar's interest in ethics has emphasized the crucial insights a feminist perspective can bring to the field. Both the perennial questions of ethics and the new dilemmas raised by bioengineering and other technology may look somewhat different from the "woman's standpoint" (a term adapted by feminist philosophy).

Influence

As a founder of feminist philosophy as an academic field, Jaggar played a major role in shaping its parameters and terms of discourse. Other feminist philosophers have used the categories she established, refining them, adding to them, and arguing with them, but in each case building upon the links and distinctions Jaggar set forth. Equally important, perhaps, has been Jaggar's legitimization of the radical writings from the early women's liberation movement. By treating these statements as valid examples of feminist positions, she brought them into an arena where opposition had to be based on reasoned argument (or at least its semblance) rather than emotional reactions.

Her *Living with Contradictions* has been successful in bringing ethical dilemmas "down to earth" from the rarefied heights of ethical theory. Few other such texts exist, except in the specialized field of bioethics, and this work's influence on the teaching of ethics may be substantial.

Jaggar has been less successful in her effort to have feminist theory recognized as a part of political philosophy. Whether from "jurisdictional" barriers or for other reasons, mainstream political philosophy has continued to focus on the public realm. Partly because of Jaggar's work, however, the feminist approach is now an accepted part of social theory, ethics, and epistemology as well as a part of the fields of feminist philosophy and women's studies.

Emily Alward

Feminist Politics and Human Nature

Type of philosophy: Ethics, feminist philosophy, political philosophy
First published: 1983
Principal ideas advanced:

◇ Writings of the women's movement fall into one of four philosophical traditions: liberal, Marxist, radical, and socialist feminism; although much feminist work does not exactly fit these categories, these divisions provide useful parameters for thinking about feminist issues.

◇ Both liberal and Marxist feminism base their concerns and strategies on a preexisting philosophical system and view of human nature: Liberalism views humans as autonomous individuals acting rationally to attain their own interests, and Marxism views humanity as evolving from the interaction of material conditions and conscious human efforts to use and control resources in society.

◇ Radical feminism, in contrast, does not draw on a coherent theory of human nature but is building one that emphasizes humans embodied as either men or women and that regards sex as the fundamental class division in human society.

◇ Socialist feminism, a still-developing category, combines the Marxist concept of human nature as historically determined with the radical insistence that sex is as fundamental a division as is economic class; therefore, it aims at creating a future in which both categories of this "class" (men and women) will be irrelevant to peoples' life prospects.

Written about twenty years after the birth of the women's movement in the 1960's, *Feminist Politics and Human Nature* analyzes that movement's writings and goals as political theory. Alison M. Jaggar attempts to sort the varied and often contradictory statements of the feminist movement into coherent systems of thought. In doing so, she traces the assumptions about human nature that underlay each system and its implied or explicit "solutions" to women's inequality.

To many, the feminism of the 1960's and 1970's was an entirely new way of looking at the world. Early advocates for the women's movement looked back to the suffragists of the nineteenth century and traced the emergence of feminist consciousness to societal sexism that persisted even during the 1960's antiwar and Civil Rights movements. In addition, during the 1960's, feminist writers were discovering the hidden history of women, showing how people's assumptions about things as diverse as pronoun usage, witchcraft trials, and the scientific method were all filtered through a cultural mindset that defined men as the norm.

Categories of Feminist Thought

Jaggar's book can be read, in part, as a response to the dizzying variety of protests, insights, and proposals for change produced during the formative years of the women's movement. It sorts and categorizes that movement's important writings by philosophical "schools," provides a framework that later theorists can refine or argue against, and evaluates these categories not only for intellectual adequacy but also in an attempt to show the best guides to future strategy and action.

In her two opening chapters, Jaggar argues for the acceptance of feminist thought as political philosophy. Feminist discourse is concerned with questions of freedom, justice, and equality, concepts debated by political philosophers for centuries. Feminists of the latter part of the twentieth century have merely broadened the debate, she says, by insisting that such questions also be asked in arenas outside the traditional "public square"—questions about the ways family life is organized, for example, and even about the dynamics of intimate relations.

Jaggar points out that the feminist use of the terms "oppression," "domination," and "liberation" implies an ongoing struggle. Most politics deals with conflicts between different classes or groups of people with different, sometimes incompatible, interests. Feminism also deals with the division of society into classes, not necessarily according to wealth and similar markers. It also proclaims the need for change and the belief that human actions can alter conditions formerly regarded as "givens" of natural law or human society. Jaggar cautions, however, that the idea of what it means to be "liberated" will change as the ongoing struggle progresses. As more events and patterns are revealed to be susceptible to human control, the definition of freedom will expand.

Jaggar ends the opening chapters by explaining the book's purpose: to sort the many feminist analyses and statements of women's situation into a few fundamental theories or paradigms. Jaggar identifies four basic feminist paradigms: liberal feminism, Marxist feminism, radical feminism, and socialist feminism. Because she views the politics of each paradigm as flowing from its theory of human nature, she examines both in detail.

Liberal Feminism

Liberal feminism grows out of Western liberal philosophy, whose origins Jaggar traces to the triumph of capitalism over feudalism. In this tradition, the most defining and important mark of being human is rationality. The capacity for reason is shared by almost all humans, but it is a trait held by individuals, not groups. Individuals act rationally to attain their own desires and interests; governments exist to promote as much opportunity as possible for them to do so, while keeping one individual's "pursuit of happiness" from violating that of others.

Early feminists argued that the principles of liberalism apply equally to women and men. In the women's movement of the 1960's and 1970's, liberal feminists put forth the idea that individuals can attain the freedom that lets them develop their own potential only if opportunities and societal expectations are not dictated by sex. This led to a sequence of strategies. Reasoned argument was followed by action to overturn sex-based inequalities under law. For matters not settled effectively by legal changes, liberal feminists developed projects to "level the playing field," including child-care facilities, battered women's shelters, and job training programs for women. In addition, much liberal feminist effort has been aimed at abolishing sex-specific expectations in the workplace, child rearing, and schooling.

Jaggar admits that liberal feminism has been successful in improving women's legal status in all Western countries. However, she finds many problems with both the theory and practice of liberal feminism. Its theory of human nature, emphasizing autonomous and self-centered individuals, discounts the experience of most women's lives. Its elevation of reason maintains the mind-body split that has devalued both women and the material world in which all humans reside.

As for the politics of liberal feminism, Jaggar suggests that equality of opportunity may not be an appropriate, or even achievable, goal. Feminists might do better to ask whether their goal is to become "imitation men" in a system similar to the present one or to leave open the possibility of other modes of democracy and social good. Liberal feminism, Jaggar concludes, aims at reforming an existing social and political system rather than replacing it with a new one more in the interests of women.

Marxist Feminism

Marxist political philosophy sets forth *praxis* as the defining feature of human nature. Praxis is the conscious use and alteration of the material world to provide for human needs. Praxis is viewed as operating in human evolution by a dialectical process (contemporary non-Marxists might say "feedback") involving the human body, mind, and society. Marxism attributes most social ills to the division of society into classes, which it traces to the appearance of private property when agriculture was invented.

Writing in the mid-nineteenth century, however, Karl Marx focused upon the class division wrought by the Industrial Revolution, that between owners of the means of production (capitalists) and workers.

Traditional Marxist feminists reflect this analysis. Their political program held that other inequities would be solved, or at least mitigated, once the capitalist system is abolished and society reorganized upon Marxist principles of equality, nonalienated work, and common ownership of the means of production. In the meantime, working-class women are assumed to share the class interests of their mates. Housewives can best deal with their situation by joining the wage economy, which gives them independent economic power vis-à-vis their husbands and enables them to join the struggle for a new system.

Marx's collaborator Friedrich Engels constructed a theory about the evolution of the family based on men's property interests replacing a very early matrilineal stage, but it was not carried over into the Marxist political program. Both Marx and Engels regarded the existing division of labor within the family as natural and not accessible to political analysis (or change.)

Jaggar finds the Marxist view of human nature more satisfactory than the liberal view. It allows for historical and cultural forces and for shared interests that go beyond the individual. It avoids the dichotomy between mind and body created by the liberal emphasis on reason. She especially likes the Marxist idea that human social arrangements can affect human nature, which means that both are under conscious human control. She also finds its concepts of "class" and of "alienation" fruitful for feminist analysis.

Marxist feminism falls short on theory, she says, because although it notes a sexual division of labor in both the family and the workplace, it fails to explain it. In practice, she finds, most Marxist structures have turned out to be sexist. They are led by men, depict male industrial workers and male intellectuals as heroic figures, and tend to be highly centralized. Jaggar believes women in existing Marxist states are somewhat better off than before, but that major inequalities persist. Marxist feminism fails because its central concept of class is seen only in "economistic" terms.

Radical Feminism

Radical feminism, unlike the liberal and Marxist varieties, appears to be a totally new school of thought, originating in the 1960's women's movement. Its writings have seldom been called philosophy. The term encompasses a wide variety of claims, theories, and insights. Although those based on women's own experiences predominate, radical feminism has also drawn from many other sources in the twentieth century milieu, especially those of alternative culture. In her book, Jaggar says that radical feminism lacks a central theory of human nature or of women's oppression. However, she discerns several recurring themes in its writings and practices.

One is that the most significant division in society is by gender, a sex-based class structure. This structure is held to exist at so deep a level that its effect on other differences and problems is often invisible. A related belief is that the line traditionally drawn between the public and private spheres is meaningless. Domination in one sphere supports that in the other, so that the personal is truly political.

Radical feminists may define female biology as the problem or the solution, or they may identify the purported existence of two sexes as the problem. (Andrea Dworkin's and Monique Wittig's works assert that human biology itself is a social construct.) Most radical feminists agree, though, that recognitions drawn from women's bodily experience are important sources of knowledge. At the same time, they hold a strong belief that women's subordination is innately connected with the spheres of sexuality and procreation. Hence, radical feminists commonly believe that true liberation requires a transformation in such practices. The specifics of what practices need to be radically changed and how forms the content of much radical feminist debate.

Jaggar praises radical feminism for its creative energy, its celebration of women, and its inclusion of human reproductive biology within the sphere of political discourse. However, she believes it does not yet deal well with the problems of human sexual differences that it brings to the fore. It rightly points out their centrality in human social arrangements but tends to wrongly infer that women's biology *causes* their oppression. Jaggar also objects to the concept of patriarchy as a system of universal male dominance, believing it inaccurate.

The politics of radical feminism have featured a drive for the formation of a separate female culture. This culture would cultivate values opposite those prevailing in the male culture, values such as sensitivity to others, closeness to nature, and emotional openness. Although Jaggar seems sympathetic to such efforts, she believes that radical feminism does not have a program whose scope matches its transformative vision. Withdrawing from the dominant culture is not an option for most women, who are bound by ties of affection or common interest to men. Even the most dedicated lesbian separatist has to live in a world where men wield power over her life. Jaggar observes that the most successful achievements of women's culture have been the ones that Marxists term "superstructural forms": art, music, fiction, and spirituality.

Socialist Feminism

Socialist feminism is a "younger sister" of these other philosophies. In her book, Jaggar describes it as a paradigm still in the formative stages. It draws elements from both Marxist and radical feminism, yet has the potential to go beyond. It could, she believes, reconcile many "either-or" conflicts and point the way to more adequate theory and more effective means of transforming society. Jaggar makes it clear that this is her preferred mode of feminist thinking, while adding that it also has some conceptual and practical problems.

It is fair, if oversimplistic, to say this paradigm aims to reconcile the two theories regarding the main source of society's conflict, which Marxism sees as class and radical feminism as sex. This will involve, at minimum, accounting for women's subordination in both the marketplace and in the procreative and maintenance work of family life. Marxism's historical approach complements the passionate value reversals of radical feminism. For example, it shows that traits now used to devalue women would have no meaning in other settings: "Emotionality" was a virtue during the Renaissance, and being "dependent" merely means being a part of society in feudal cultures. Social feminism is starting to go beyond these insights drawn from Western history and to look at the patterns of women's subordination in other cultures, which may be quite different. Jaggar concludes that socialist feminism is very far from having a coherent theory, but it is well on its way. She also expects it to incorporate parts of the radical feminism movement in future.

Socialist feminism's ultimate aim is to abolish both class and gender distinctions. To do so requires changes in many social systems: the attainment of real reproductive freedom (the details of which change with changing technology), the equal involvement of men in family life, the degendering of wage levels, and the continuance of some separate women's organizations as interim, experimental institutions. Jaggar expects this agenda will be accompanied by dramatic, even wrenching, social turmoil, but considers it achievable as well as desirable.

Call for Feminist Epistemology

Feminist Politics and Human Nature ends with Jaggar emphasizing the need to develop a feminist epistemology, a way of describing reality that reflects the experience of all women. The book has been very influential in women's studies and feminist philosophy. It played a major role in establishing the latter as a field of study, and it remains a central text for those doing academic work in either field. As Jaggar herself has commented, even those scholars who disagree with her have defined their positions in reference to this book and theory.

The impact of Jaggar's book in the ordinary world is less apparent. As a call-to-arms, it lacks the outrageousness and color of many primary women's movement writings. Although it is more accessible than much contemporary philosophy, its theoretical approach has probably limited its audience to the semiconverted, at least.

Some of the book's minor points have been overtaken by events. Very few Marxist societies now exist to provide models for Marxist feminism, and highly paid professions such as law and medicine have become less exclusively male. Nonetheless, *Feminist Politics and Human Nature* remains a basic source for analysis and further development of feminist thought.

Emily Alward

Additional Reading

Bryson, Valerie. *Feminist Political Theory: An Introduction*. London: Macmillan Press, 1992. An alternate overview of feminist political thought, Bryson's book pays much attention to the historical background of modern feminism. She discusses Jaggar chiefly in terms of the latter's attempt to connect Marxist theory and reproductive labor.

Kensinger, Loretta. "(In) Quest of Liberal Feminism." *Hypatia* 12, no. 4 (Fall, 1997): 178-197. This article questions Jaggar's accepted divisions and other theorists' categories of feminist thought. For example, Kensinger examines Jaggar's description of liberal feminism, calling its boundaries unclear if not invisible, and concludes that "telling any story of feminism obscures its motion." She notes that Jaggar had partially anticipated this problem in her remark that theory changes constantly to reflect changing social realities.

Maynard, Mary. "The Reshaping of Sociology? Trends in the Study of Gender." *Sociology* 24, no. 2 (May, 1990): 269-290. In this overview article, Maynard questions the sorting of feminists into various schools of thought. She speculates that categories such as Jaggar's reflect the factionalized nature of the women's movement during the late 1970's and the early 1980's.

Emily Alward

William James

Seeking to reconcile a deep commitment to scientific thought with the emotional nature of human beings and longing for some kind of religious faith, James helped create and popularize the modern science of psychology and the uniquely American approach to philosophy called pragmatism.

Principal philosophical works: *The Principles of Psychology*, 1890; *The Will to Believe and Other Essays in Popular Philosophy*, 1897; *Human Immortality*, 1898; *Talks to Teachers on Psychology*, 1899; *The Varieties of Religious Experience*, 1902; *Pragmatism: A New Name for Some Old Ways of Thinking*, 1907; *A Pluralistic Universe*, 1909; *The Meaning of Truth: A Sequel to "Pragmatism,"* 1909; *Some Problems of Philosophy*, 1911; *Memories and Studies*, 1911; *Essays in Radical Empiricism*, 1912; *Collected Essays and Reviews*, 1920.

Born: January 11, 1842; New York, New York
Died: August 26, 1910; Chocorua, New Hampshire

Early Life

William James was born on January 11, 1842, the eldest son of Henry and Mary (Walsh) James. His parents, who were of Scottish and Scotch-Irish ancestry, had four other children and provided one of the most remarkable home environments on record. There is little doubt that his childhood as part of this unusual family was instrumental in creating William James, the psychologist and philosopher, just as it helped mold his brother Henry, the equally famous American novelist.

Henry James, Sr., was a restless, perhaps even tortured, intellectual with a religious bent, able to pursue his own private quest for truth because of a small inheritance. His family naturally became part of his search, and conversation around the Jameses' dining table was more like a philosophical seminar than typical family chatter. The children were encouraged to think and to question and even to defend their ideas under the watchful eyes of their parents. Education was considered too important to be left to chance. Henry, Sr., moved his family from the United States to Europe and back again several times, enrolling his children in numerous schools in an attempt to find the perfect atmosphere for learning. This varied and unsettled experience gave both William and his brother Henry an excellent command of languages and the basics of a liberal education without providing in-depth knowledge in any particular area. The gypsylike introduction to the academic world and family debates did provide, however, a healthy respect for diversity and a tolerance for other opinions, including sometimes very strange ones, that marked William James throughout his life.

As a youth, James was of slight to medium build with blue eyes and a less-than-robust constitution. Gradually, the determination to overcome his tendency toward physical and emotional illness became an important undercurrent in his celebrated attitude toward life. If by the force of will a sickly, neurotic youth could transform himself into a dynamic professor who seemed to his students perpetually engaged in productive thought, then others were also free to make such transformations. His mature outlook was open and optimistic, and his personality, dominated by humor and tolerance, made him almost impossible to dislike. His students nearly worshiped him, and his many friends and acquaintances in the intellectual community of the world, even when they disagreed violently with his ideas, loved the man himself.

Yet the surface of this congenial thinker hid a storm raging beneath.

William James. *(Library of Congress)*

to long for the certainty it provided. He later paid homage to his father's ideas when he published some of the elder James's letters in *The Literary Remains of Henry James* (1885).

The inability to please his father even haunted James's choice of vocation. When William was eighteen, the family had moved to Newport, Rhode Island, where he could study art with William M. Hunt. His father was not happy with this choice, but he was even less happy when his eldest son abandoned art a year later and entered the Lawrence Scientific School at Harvard University. This decision proved to be a significant turning point. Not only did it begin a lifelong connection between William James and Harvard but it also began the gradual development of his personality beyond the influence of his family. The process would be difficult and never complete, but it was well on its way when the young man gravitated almost naturally toward medical school at Harvard. His studies were interrupted for a year so he could accompany the famous anthropologist Louis Agassiz on an expedition to the Amazon, but James still received his M.D. in June, 1869.

Too unstable emotionally to begin a medical practice, he remained in a state of semi-invalidism until he was appointed instructor in physiology at Harvard in 1872. Characteristically, James believed that the conquest of his emotional problem was made possible by a philosophical conversion. While in Europe during a phase of his medical education, he had been introduced to the ideas of the French philosopher Charles-Bernard Renouvier, whose stress on free will helped James reject the paralyzing fear of determinism. James's struggle for personal independence would reach a climax of sorts with his marriage to Alice H. Gibbens of Cambridge, Massachusetts. By all accounts, the union was a happy one and eventually produced five children. More important, however, the establishment of his own family at the advanced age of thirty-six coincided with the beginning of his productive career.

Life as part of the James family had been challenging, but it had not produced happiness. As a young man, William continually struggled with bouts of emotional illness that at times necessitated an almost total retreat from the active world. At the center of the problem was the inability to reconcile his growing commitment to the rationalistic, scientific outlook of his age with the deep religious faith of his father. The elder James, who had rejected established religion as a young man, had been introduced to the ideas of Emanuel Swedenborg when William was two years old. Though Henry, Sr., was never able to become a strict follower of the Swedish theologian, he constructed his own system of belief that became a necessary spiritual consolation. His son could never accept his father's simplistic faith, yet he always respected it and sometimes seemed

Life's Work

In the same year as his marriage, James agreed to a contract with Henry Holt and Company for the publication of a textbook on psychology. The agreement was, in part, recognition of his growing influence in an area of study that was undergoing transformation from a kind of mental philosophy into a laboratory science. During his European travels, James had been influenced by the experimental approach to psychology current in Germany, and he taught his first course in psychology in 1875. His approach was revolutionary. Rather than the vague, often theological, speculation that characterized psychology in American universities, James started with physiological psychology, stressing the relationship between body and mind, and insisted on a thoroughly empirical approach. He soon established one of the first laboratories dedicated to psychological research in the United States.

His proposed textbook on psychology took almost as long to mature as James himself had. Scheduled for publication in 1880, the book did not appear until 1890, as *The Principles of Psychology*. It was hardly a textbook; instead, James had produced a monumental study covering the entire field as it stood in 1890 and proposing numerous theories that would influence psychology for years to come. Yet the work was not the empirical tour de force that one might expect. In spite of his dedication to science, James never liked laboratory research, and his own contribution was more impressionistic and philosophical than scientific. Moreover, the enthusiastic reception of his work owed as much to literary eloquence as it did to sound research.

In fact, James had already tired of experimental psychology before *The Principles of Psychology* was ever published. Though he would continue to be influential in the field and engage in numerous scholarly debates, his primary interest had turned to philosophy. It was not as much a change of direction as it was a change of emphasis. Since youth, he had been interested in philosophical speculation, and he taught his first course in philosophy in 1879. Much of his psychological work had philosophical overtones, and he was appointed professor of philosophy at Harvard in 1885. He had also exhibited an unusual interest in psychic phenomena, infuriating many of his fellow psychologists with his tolerant attitude toward the claims of spiritualists, mediums, and such dubious ideas as telepathy. This tendency was not an indication that James actually accepted parapsychology without qualification. Instead, it was a continuation of his quest for a reconciliation between the human need for spiritual meaning and the human commitment to rational inquiry. This problem became the core of James's philosophical questioning for the last decade of the nineteenth century.

James had been thinking about the problem for most of his life and had published essays on the subject while writing *The Principles of Psychology*. He began to draw these ideas together with the publication in 1897 of his collection of essays *The Will to Believe and Other Essays in Popular Philosophy*. He carried his ideas further when invited to give the Gifford lectures on natural religion at the University of Edinburgh. Ill health prevented him from appearing until 1901-1902. These lectures, published under the title *The Varieties of Religious Experience*, are his most definitive attempt at reconciling his empirical scientific approach with religion and the spiritual world. Although his conclusions would hardly please the most orthodox, they stand as a ringing defense of the "right" to believe beyond physical evidence and an important recognition of the limitations of science, which James believed had erected a new orthodoxy as limiting as the old.

The remainder of James's life would be dedicated to defining and explaining his approach to philosophy, which he generally called pragmatism. The term was borrowed from his friend and fellow student Charles S. Peirce. Though Peirce clearly meant something different from James by the term, it was James who popularized it and made it part of American philosophical tradition. Unfortunately or perhaps fortunately, depending on one's perspective, most of James's writing was directed toward a popular rather than a philosophical audience. As a result, many of the principles of pragmatism actually depend upon which pragmatist is responsible for the explanation. This vagueness, however, is probably inherent in the doctrine and is, at least partially, responsible for its widespread acceptance.

James's final philosophical position had been evolving throughout his life and rested on a concept of the human mind that he had explained in his famous *The Principles of Psychology*. In this sense, James always remained a psychologist, but he carried his psychological perspective into the world of metaphysics. Very early in his intellectual development, James had committed himself to what he called "radical empiricism," which was firmly in the tradition of philosophers David Hume and John Stuart Mill and against the dominant rationalism implicit in the most influential philosophical school of his era, German idealism. Idealism, James believed, led to a concept of the "absolute" that resulted in a deterministic universe, something he could not accept. Yet materialism, the chief opponent of idealism, also leads to a deterministic universe. James sought the middle ground, which, above all, would be useful to humankind.

Usefulness is perhaps the key to understanding James's version of pragmatism. The meaning of an idea can be judged only by the particular consequences that result from it. If an idea has no real consequences, then it is meaningless. When placed in the context of James's radical empiricism, which accepts reality as that which is experienced, this doctrine means that human motives play a key role in human beliefs. Such an approach would have its most radical impact on the philosophical conception of truth. To James, this hallowed term should not apply to some mysterious ontological reality. Instead, it should refer only to one's beliefs about the world. To be true, an idea must refer to some particular thing and have "cash value," that is, satisfy the human purpose for which it was intended. It is important to remember that for James and for most pragmatists, this does not mean simply practicality or what might be called pure subjectivism. Rather, truth should be tied to rigid empirical criteria and motivations designed to maximize human values.

James spent the balance of his life defending his ideas in numerous essays and lectures, most of which have been published in various collections. In his last years, he became the best-known philosopher in the English-speaking world, and his ideas were seen as America's answer to the sterile speculations of continental rationalism. To answer those who criticized his tendency toward popularization, James hoped to bring his theories together in a complete metaphysical argument.

Unfortunately, the project was never completed. His less-than-robust health failed him, and he died at his country home in New Hampshire on August 26, 1910.

Influence
Never the ivory-tower intellectual, James always tried to live his own philosophy. For him, philosophy could never be separated from the real needs of human beings, and the answers he sought, even in the rarefied atmosphere of metaphysics, must have use beyond the lecture halls of universities. This explains his own tendency to simplify his ideas, which, while leading to philosophical sloppiness, made them available to people without the training or the inclination for abstract thinking. It also explains his commitment to contemporary causes, such as his opposition to imperialism during the presidency of William McKinley, his general opposition to war, and his defense of unpopular ideas such as faith healing. James was always concerned first and foremost with the real fate of human beings.

His philosophy would become one of the most important intellectual influences in American life, particularly in the twentieth century. Like his famous personality, which made him so popular with friends and students, his ideas were essentially optimistic and positive. To him, the universe was pluralistic and capable of being understood. Humankind was not a passive victim of the cosmos but an active agent, whose role was essentially creative. Although people might not be able to change the dictates of nature, they could change the conditions of their own environment.

David Warren Bowen

The Principles of Psychology

Type of philosophy: Epistemology, philosophical psychology
First published: 1890
Principal ideas advanced:
◇ Psychology is the study of phenomena such as consciousness, self, habits, and the conditions of these phenomena's development and change.

◇ Consciousness is a stream of inner thoughts that are ever-changing, continuous, personal, and selective.

◇ The part of consciousness with which we are most intensely involved is called the self. The self consists of those values and interests with which we are most identified, our social roles and commitments, and cherished possessions and relationships.

◇ Habits are automatic reactions to situations acquired by frequent association with these situations. Habits keep society predictable and save consciousness for challenging new situations.

◇ We actively interpret perceived objects and events in line with our expectations and orient them in space and time.

◇ Some ideas are based upon associations between objects or events that occur close together frequently. Conceptual associations are formed by comparing the memory images of objects to detect essential similarities.

◇ Instinctive tendencies are built into human beings, but their exact expression is greatly modified by experience.

This textbook marked an important transition from mental philosophy to scientific psychology and from a narrow focus on the structure of consciousness to the psychological study of the purpose and processes of human functioning. At the time of its publication in 1890, the idea from associationistic philosophy that complex thought results from the mechanical compounding of correlated sensations was still the prevailing assumption of experimental psychologists. These psychologists used their own introspections to attempt the dissection of conscious experience into its elements.

William James was influenced by strands of thought outside this tradition. Influencing James's psychological viewpoint were naturalist Charles Darwin and his ideas about adaptive evolutionary change, philosophical pragmatism with its notion that all theories should be judged by their practical usefulness, and a scattering of German psychologists, called "act psychologists," who viewed psychology as the study of psychological processes. James therefore posited a more practical, more dynamic view of a human being pulsating with change, actively selecting the relevant from the world of experience, and combining this experience in adaptive ways. These themes were soon to become the dominant approach in early twentieth century American psychology, which was called "functional." Themes from James continue to reverberate throughout psychological thinking into the twenty-first century.

Antecedents of Mental Life

James defines psychology as the science of mental life, both its phenomena and its conditions. By phenomena, James means such human characteristics as consciousness, the self, desires, habits, emotions, thoughts, and perceptions. By conditions, James refers to all the antecedents of this mental life. Such antecedents include innate predispositions, the brain, and associations formed from experience.

The antecedent innate predispositions James called instincts. James cited some forty such built-in tendencies to direct activity to certain classes of goals. His list of instincts included the entire gamut of human motives, from fear, pugnacity, and acquisitiveness to sympathy, sociability, and curiosity. The actual expression of each of these directional tendencies becomes greatly modified by experience. One can learn indirect methods of expressing each tendency, or even learn to inhibit the tendency completely in most situations. Since such instincts as curiosity and fear inevitably conflict with each other, inhibition is inevitable. Through associative learning, instincts become linked to specific objects as well. We learn to crave specific foods and to love specific people.

Experience also plays an antecedent role in forming mental associations between ideas that frequently occur together—"horse and carriage," for example. Associations are also formed based upon the logical similarities between ideas. The association between an apple and a banana, both classifiable as fruit, is such a logical relationship. Each of these types of similarities is reflected in corresponding links in underlying brain processes. The brain, James speculates, involves several levels of linkage, with simple associations, such as reflexes and habits, linked at lower levels of the brain. The more abstract, logical associations are reflected in "diffuse excitement" in the higher brain centers of the cerebrum. James is most specific about underlying physiological processes in his discussion of emotion. He is emphatic that the underlying physiological reaction comes before the emotional feeling that interprets this process. In the words of James, "We do not shudder because we are afraid; we are afraid because we shudder."

Consciousness

Phenomena, as studied by psychologists, include consciousness, the self, and habits. Consciousness consists of dynamic and ever-changing mental activity. A moment in this ever-changing stream of consciousness never returns again in exactly the same fashion. Consciousness is continuous. The consciousness of any given moment is linked with relevant memories from the past and intentions for the future. Consciousness is personal. The conscious memories of each of us are endowed with a warmth and intimacy that eludes a simple acquaintance with objective events. It is my consciousness. My thoughts are owned by me. Consciousness is selective. The consciousness of each of us selects from the confused world of events and memories the information most relevant to our concerns and interests. Although much of our conscious experience can be put into words, parts of this experience are too complex or too unique to label. Like every aspect of organisms, consciousness has adaptive significance. It permits a flexible response to new challenges and problems.

The Self

Part of our conscious experience reflects our strongest personal involvements and is endowed with special meaning and value. This part James calls the self. The self includes all that a person can call "my." It includes one's family, friends, cherished possessions, the "material self." It includes one's significant interactions with others and the roles played in such interactions, the "social self." It includes one's central and most valued characteristics, sensibilities, and values, the "spiritual self." It includes the feeling of identity that gives unity to our experience, the "pure ego." Aside from our actual self, each of us carries around a picture of ourselves as we would like to be, the "ideal self." How close each person is to his or her ideal self influences self-esteem—

or, in the famous equation of James, esteem reflects one's success divided by one's pretensions. James notes that competition between the various social selves may force us to pick and choose. Each person's self is unique. This uniqueness has sometimes been given transcendent importance by the older religious term, the "soul."

Other aspects of human functioning may lie outside conscious awareness. For example, habits are automatic, learned reactions made to frequently recurring situations. Habits are established by the refinement of sensory-motor arcs in the nervous system and become more precise and refined with practice. Habits become more firmly established with age. They serve as a powerful conservative force that keeps society operating in its accustomed way, the "great fly wheel of society." They allow a quick, adaptive response to recurring situations, making it possible for us to save conscious thought for new situations and special challenges.

Consciousness operates upon the environment by the processes of selective attention, perception, concept formation, and reasoning. In each of these operations, the individual is viewed as actively responding to the environment rather than passively receiving messages from it. By attention is meant the selective focusing of consciousness to become alerted to only part of thousands of bombarding stimuli. Intense, exciting, and vivid stimuli are likely to be noticed. Stimulus objects in line with the individual's expectations and interests are also more likely to compel attention. James uses the term "will" to suggest the sustaining of attention on a single idea, one reflecting the self perhaps, suppressing conflicting instinctual pressures in order to complete a sequence of activity.

Perception

The sensory information once awarded attention must then be perceived. Although every experience is essentially new, we deal with each new experience by identifying it with memory images of similar objects and events in the past. Objects seen only partially or dimly, once identified, are endowed with solidity and wholeness. The object must also be placed into a context of space and time. We automatically see objects at a distance from us, assigning them places in space. Spatial concepts are developed in each of us by first localizing sensations felt by the body, learning something about the "real" sizes of objects, and thereafter seeing such familiar objects at given distances and directions from us. Events must also be placed in time or else each episode would become like "the light of the glow worm and quickly fade away." Our orientation to periods of time such as months and years is dependent upon our placing in symbolic memory a sequence of key episodes as markers. Into this sequence we place individual events.

A final perceptual task is separating the real from illusion and fantasy. James suggests that we accept as real all that is not contradicted by an overwhelming preponderance of information. We accept as real the physical reality of our senses, certain shared abstract truths, the beliefs of our culture, beliefs about the supernatural world, and certain convictions that relate to one's particular self.

Perceived images then enter the stream of consciousness. Many of the loose associations of reverie are based upon simple contiguity and repetition. An ordered conceptual system results from comparing objects and combining them within systems of useful similarities. Domesticated animals that bark we may denote as dogs. The essence of the similar property can be understood only by differentiating the concept from similar objects that are just enough different no longer to be included. That animal makes doglike sounds but is not domesticated; it is a jackal.

Reasoning

Reasoning involves the further requirement that we come up with precisely the association that solves a particular problem. Of all the associations we can dredge up, we must locate the one that fits. Abstract thinking involves the use of labels that fit a large number of individual objects that are particularly useful in reasoning because they make available to the reasoner more possible solutions. James notes how often the more creative levels of reasoning seem to involve an intuitive process.

Memory

Memory is also dependent upon these associative links. We remember material best when many such links have been formed, when our interest in the material is high, and when we can direct our attention in a systematic search for associations. Strong links are sometimes formed with the conditions under which the material was originally stored. Material learned under hypnosis, for example, can sometimes be retrieved only when the subject is in a hypnotized state.

Legacy for Contemporary Psychology

James's assumptions about the broad nature of psychological science, more than those expressed in any other work of the time, fit contemporary views. James assumed that developmental processes involve an interaction of nature and nurture. Almost all contemporary developmental psychologists hold this view, with little support for the alternative empirical view that the environment molds all. James maintained that brain processes reflect psychological experience at many levels, with abstract thought reflecting diffuse excitement of the higher brain centers. This view has been supported by a century of research. Little support for the alternative view of specific thoughts localized in specific brain areas remains. A decade before Sigmund Freud, James hypothesized that important behavioral tendencies and certain states of consciousness lie outside self-awareness. Few contemporary psychologists question the validity of an unconscious so broadly construed. James's emphasis upon the selective nature of attention and the importance of personal factors in perception were given a new importance in the psychology of the late twentieth century when the "cognitive revolution" once again made the study of such mental processes scientifically respectable. James never saw a computer, but much of what he said about conceptualization and reasoning is quite compatible with modern computer models of these processes.

The Principles of Psychology anticipates the framework of assumptions underlying scientific psychology. It also contains the germ of many ideas that were later to become implemented in specific traditions of practice and research. James's characterization of the self has been particularly influential. The importance of self-validation and the treatment of wounded self-esteem became the central objectives of the humanistic psychotherapy of Carl Rogers. The proposition that "a man has as many social selves as there are individuals who recognize him" has become the very cornerstone of contemporary social psychology. Research on possible selves, on self-attribution, on strategies of self-enhancement proceeds apace. Like James's description of habit and of consciousness, James's characterization of the self is still quoted word for word in contemporary psychology texts. To this day, no one has said it better.

Thomas E. DeWolfe

The Will to Believe and Other Essays in Popular Philosophy

Type of philosophy: Ethics, philosophy of religion, pragmatism
First published: 1897
Principal ideas advanced:

◊ Decisions between hypotheses proposed to our belief are genuine options when they are living (of vital concern to us), forced (no third alternative is possible), and momentous (presenting a unique opportunity of considerable importance).

◊ Whenever a genuine option cannot be settled on intellectual grounds, it is right and necessary to settle it according to our passional inclinations.

◊ The religious option concerning the belief in God is a genuine option that promises most to the person who has the passional need to take the world religiously.

◊ We possess free wills that are not determined; determinism, the theory that decisions are causally determined, fails to account for the sense of human freedom.

Now a classic, this work takes its title from one of ten separate essays written at different times. Originally presented as lectures to academic clubs, these writings express "a tolerably definite philosophic attitude" that William James named "radical empiricism," an ordinary person's empiricism, which takes experience as it comes, "seeing" even matters of fact as subject to possible future reinterpretation and rejecting dogmatic monism in the face of the obvious plurality of the things

making up the universe. James also wanted to make a case for our right to believe some moral and religious views for whose certainty the evidence can never fully be on hand. Sympathetic to a wide range of philosophical viewpoints, James sought to give intellectual significance to the role of the emotions in specified contexts. He also criticized the prevailing academic opinion that only scientific methods can produce an adequate understanding of the human condition.

The first four essays—"The Will to Believe," "Is Life Worth Living?," "The Sentiment of Rationality," and "Reflex Action and Theism"—are concerned directly with religious problems. Two others, "The Dilemma of Determinism" and "The Moral Philosopher and the Moral Life," also give some attention to religious aspects of ethical problems. A final essay, "What Psychical Research Has Accomplished," defends scholars who inquire into the possibility that mental life may involve phenomena that escape our ordinary scientific criteria. The remaining essays—"Great Men and Their Environment," "The Importance of Individuals," and "On Some Hegelisms"—show James's concern to find commonsense facts philosophically interesting, to criticize some unexamined assumptions of rationalism, and to resist the spread of absolutist and totalist theories that swallow up the individual in an "environment," overlook human differences by stressing only similarities, and ignore diversity in emphasizing unity.

Three broad types of subject matter receive treatment in James's book: the nature and motives of philosophizing, the justification of religious and moral beliefs, and the nature of the moral enterprise. A common theme also runs through what would otherwise be a collection of unrelated essays: the problem of the relation of evidence to specific human beliefs. If the book has a positive thesis, it is that people may rightfully hold certain religious, moral, and metaphysical beliefs even when conclusive evidence for their adequacy is absent. James resists the positivistic tendency of his age to assume that scientific methods will prove able to decide all important questions about existence. Similarly, he expresses criticism of any extreme rationalistic reliance on logic as the sole criterion of philosophical adequacy. There are some beliefs that are truths in the making. "And often enough our faith beforehand in an uncertified result *is the only thing that makes the result come true*," he writes. One comes to understand that James is moved to philosophical activity by a desire to justify the rightness of certain beliefs—that God exists, that people possess free will, that moral effort represents a genuinely objective worthiness, that pain and evil cannot justify suicide, and that practical as well as theoretical needs ought to influence one's philosophical outlook.

The book's historical influence partly stems from the nature of the problems addressed by the author. Most of these problems are close to ordinary human experience. James also reassures those thinkers who, unconvinced that a completed metaphysical system is really possible, want to resist making a forced choice between philosophical certainty and philosophical skepticism. Philosophical argument can take place fruitfully somewhere on this side of certainty, according to James. Yet such argument need not lapse into arbitrariness. Logic is a subservient instrument. It is subject to the felt needs of religious, moral, and practical demands. James argues that a qualified moral idealism need not lead to sentimentalism in escaping the twin threats of pessimism and nihilism. Some philosophical viewpoints are relatively more adequate than others, even though no one viewpoint can hope to exhaust the whole domain of reality. Such a generous spirit animates James's essays that even critics who are unpersuaded by some of the arguments nevertheless recognize in them the evidences of a rare and gifted philosophical mind.

The Nature and Motives of Philosophizing

The book's opening essay is crucial for the broad way it sketches the nature, purposes, and possibilities of philosophizing. Written in 1879, "The Sentiment of Rationality" states convictions that are presupposed in James's more restricted discussions of topics in religious and moral philosophy. A number of basic questions caused James to write this essay. What is the philosophic quest really about? What are the conditions that any philosophy must meet if it is to be accepted? How can one know that the philosophic demand for a peculiar kind of rationality has been satisfactorily met?

Philosophic pursuit of a rational conception of existence marked by universality and extensiveness succeeds whenever a feeling of intellectual "ease, peace, rest" is the result. Any adequate philosophy must satisfy two kinds of human distress. One is theoretical: the intellectual concern to form a general conception of the universe. The other is practical: the moral and religious desire to include our passional natures in any philosophical consideration of how we are to act and what we should believe.

Two cravings gnaw at the philosopher. Intellectual simplification is always one philosophic need. Simplification requires reduction of the world's numerous details to fewer significant abstractions that stress similarities. Theoretical life would be an impossibility without such abstractions. The other need is the clear demand for recognition of the perceived differences among things. Philosophic rationality results only when each of these competing impulses receives serious consideration. James insists that philosophizing involves a continuous, yet never fully successful, synthesizing of these two cravings—a mark of whose successful handling is the feeling that some original puzzlement no longer proves irritating to the mind. As an activity, philosophizing must involve the whole person. Philosophizing must therefore often give way to hosts of other intellectual quests since its own unique function is to discover a general picture of "the hang of things."

An important conviction operates at this point in James's development. It is that any metaphysical conception must remain open to future possible theoretical anxiety. Our need of a philosophic view of the nature of things results only in partial and temporary satisfaction. Any instance of the feeling of rationality can itself founder on the shoals of the question about its justifiability. Even if the world *is* a certain way, it *might* yet be otherwise. Thus the worry about "nonentity" arises, named by James "the parent of the philosophic craving in its subtilist and profoundest sense." Through awareness of a possible other state of affairs, people can lose the feeling of rationality once gained. No single logically consistent system can still people's theoretical demands when they are faced by the query: Why just this sort of world and no other? "Every generation will produce its Job, its Hamlet, its Faust, or its Sartor Resartus." Mystical ecstasy can realize the psychological equivalent of the feeling of rationality when logic proves inadequate. Yet "empiricism will be the ultimate philosophy," for even the mysteriousness of existence depends on an irreducible fact about a universe that is dissatisfying to our theoretical demands.

Exclusive concern with the theoretical impulse leads people to skepticism or to a sense of wonder about the universe. One or the other arises when a completed metaphysical system begins to wane. Does the matter end here? Denying that it does, James argues that now the practical life acquires a heightened rational significance. Practical demands play a role in one's choice of a philosophy when systems exist whose logical methods are equally sound. People's belief that their wills can influence the future must receive justification in any important philosophical system. People can adopt that philosophy which most fully satisfies certain moral and aesthetic requirements of human nature.

The better philosophy is always relevant to people's expectations about the future. Yet there is no one, final, "better" philosophy. For example, a philosophy that retains the notion of substance will remain a perennial contender for human acceptance. Similarly, idealism will remain a challenging possibility for thinkers requiring an identification of the universe with our personal selves, materialism for thinkers wanting an escape from self. James concludes that temperamental differences are important in the quest after the sentiment of rationality. To be humanly acceptable, a philosophy must limit moral skepticism and satisfy people's belief that they "count" in the creation of a future world. According to James, no philosophy can succeed that ignores the practical craving for a world that is partly responsive to people's future expectations, their human faiths, and their commonsense conviction that moral striving genuinely counts for something.

Moral and Religious Beliefs
Take the question "Does God exist?" James rejects the agnostic argument that one ought never to hold beliefs for which conclusive evidence is lacking. Reasonable persons seek both to avoid

error and to attain the maximum amount of truth. Yet there may be questions such that neither "yes" nor "no" replies are justified by existing evidence but to which people may rightfully give an affirmative belief-response. James insists that the matter of God's existence is such a question, as are questions about the importance of the individual, the value of life versus suicide, and the possible existence of human free will. *How* people treat such questions is important. James argues that people may believe certain statements for reasons of the heart when conclusive evidence is lacking, and the beliefs help to initiate future discoveries of a practical kind. This thesis forces James to consider the problem of the relation of evidence to belief.

Belief involves a willingness to act on some hypothesis. James insists that any proposition may serve as a hypothesis—though he is not always clear about the form of such a hypothesis. Ordinarily, a proposition such as "This litmus paper is blue" is not considered a hypothesis because it lacks a proper hypothetical form. A proposition of the form "If this litmus paper is put into a given solution, it will turn red" is a hypothesis capable of some testing, provided that the proper details are supplied. However, James had in mind statements of moral and religious belief whose adoption by people might result in bringing about a desired truth. One may help to make another person's attitude friendly toward oneself by adopting a believing attitude toward the statement "X is friendly toward me." Belief in some propositions is a requirement for their future possible verification. According to James, religious beliefs may often be of this kind. Religious beliefs involve one in assenting to statements for which conclusive evidence is absent. James wants to defend the right to hold such beliefs if they meet specified conditions. A person has an option to believe certain hypotheses in religion and morals if the hypotheses are living rather than dead, forced rather than avoidable, and momentous rather than trivial.

What makes a hypothesis "living," "forced," and "momentous" is its relation to a thinker's interests. The test here seems to be predominantly psychological and cultural, for an individual's interests are what they are, however caused. James admits that not everyone will find the same hypothesis living, forced, and momentous, giving the example of a Christian confronted with the command, "Be a Theosophist or be a Mohammedan." Yet James insists that the God-hypothesis confronts people with a genuine "option," meaning that such an option is living, momentous, and forced. He argues that the agnostic who neither affirms nor denies God's existence has already decided against such an existence. The agnostic decides to give up all hope of winning a possible truth in order to avoid a possible error in a situation for which evidence must in principle be inconclusive. The agnostic's right to disbelieve in this case is no greater than the religious person's right to believe.

A critic may say at this point that James's way of arguing may encourage people to choose their beliefs by an individualistic criterion of psychological comfort—something on the order of the command: "Believe what you need to believe." James warns his readers that he is countering academicians' disregard of the passional aspects in human decision making and that the right to believe occurs only in a matter that "cannot by its nature be decided on intellectual grounds." James apparently thinks the genuine religious option concerns the *thatness* of God's existence rather than the choice of an existing institutional means for expressing one's decision to believe in God's existence. Yet he does seem to argue, on the other hand, that those who are agnostics choose to treat the God-hypothesis as a dead one. Moral and religious options are such that, if the believer takes an affirmative stance regarding a belief, they promise that the better aspects will win out in the universe and a person will be better off for believing. One might put even the God-hypothesis in a psychological form: "If you believe that God exists, even now you will be benefited." Yet it is not clear that James would wish to regard the force of the central religious hypothesis as purely psychological.

The Moral Life

In discussing features of the moral landscape, James once again shows his distrust of intellectual abstractions and generalizations. He is convinced that philosophers can never produce an airtight, finished moral system. Nor can moral philosophers dogmatically solve all issues in ad-

vance of actual situations. Yet James openly defends two general moral notions. One is that human demands and obligations are coextensive. The second is that people have a right to believe they are free. Any genuinely moral philosophers place their own cherished ideals and norms in the scales of rational judgment even as they realize that no one standard measure is attainable that will apply to all occasions. The moral philosopher holds no privileged status for deciding concrete instances of conflict in human demands. James insists that the moral philosopher "only knows that if he makes a bad mistake the cries of the wounded will soon inform him of the fact."

James advances the thesis about coextensiveness of demands and obligations in the essay "The Moral Philosopher and the Moral Life." There are no intrinsically "bad" demands, since demands are simply what they are. Without them, there could be no basis of moral life. James seeks to give due recognition to biological and psychological facts. He wants an "ethical republic." Terms such as "good" and "bad"—whose meanings constitute the metaphysical function of moral philosophizing—refer to objects of feeling and desire. Only "a mind which feels them" can realize moral relations and moral law. James insists that the moral philosopher must "vote for the richer universe"—that which can accommodate the widest possible range of human wants. Yet James fails to make clear how the philosopher may determine what should pass as the richer universe if all demands have equal status in principle. On this issue James seems to appeal to intuition, for he argues that "the nobler thing *tastes* better"—indicating that he recognized that some demands are more appealing than others.

Determinism

The most suggestive essay concerned with a moral issue is "The Dilemma of Determinism," in which James argues that, though no proof is possible, the human being does possess free will. This is a unique defense of indeterminism, which presupposes a metaphysical position: namely, that the universe is in reality a pluriverse containing objective possibilities of novelty. The problem that concerns him is that of the relation of freedom to chance rather than of freedom to cause. "Chance" is a relative word that tells one nothing about that on which it is predicated. "Its origin is in a certain fashion negative: it escapes, and says, Hands off! coming, when it comes, as a free gift, or not at all." James disliked the contemporary distinction between "hard" and "soft" forms of determinism. The "soft" form of determinism argues that causality is quite compatible with responsible action and ethical judicability. What James wanted to discover is the metaphysical view necessary to determinism. He concluded it is a view that takes possibilities never actualized as mere illusions. James insists that determinism is unable to give adequate account of human feelings about possibility—the feeling that the universe contains genuine choices or alternatives, objectively real risks. Indeterminism insists that future volitions can be ambiguous, and "indeterminate future volitions *do* mean chance."

According to James, determinism results in an unavoidable dilemma. It must lead either to pessimism or to subjectivism. People share a universe that daily calls for judgments of regret about some things happening in it. However, if events are strictly necessitated, they can never be otherwise than what they are. In this case, human regrets suggest that, though some feature of the universe could not have been different, yet it would have been better if it were different. Such reasoning leads to pessimism. James argues that people can give up pessimism only if they jettison their judgments of regret. People can perhaps regard regrettable incidents—including the most atrocious murders—as teleological links in a chain leading to some higher good. Murder and treachery then cease to be evils. However, a definite price must be paid for such a teleological optimism, because the original judgments of regret were themselves necessitated on the determinist's position. Some other judgments should have existed in their place. "But as they are necessitated, nothing else *can* be in their place." It seems then that, whether people are pessimists or optimists, their judgments are necessitated.

Subjectivism and Indeterminism

One escape from this pessimism-optimism impasse is to adopt subjectivism. The practical impulse to realize some objective moral good can be subordinated to a theoretical development of an understanding of what is involved in goodness and evil. The facts of the universe can be valued only insofar as they produce consciousness in people. Subjectivism emphasizes the knowledge of good and evil in order to underscore the nature of human involvement. Experience rather than the objective goodness or badness of experience becomes the crucial factor for any moral subjectivism. However, the indeterminist must reject subjectivism because it fails to do justice to people's empirical notions of the genuinely *moral* significance of human experiences. In addition, subjectivism leads to mere sentimentality and romanticism.

James concludes that common sense informs people that objective right and wrong involve real limits. Practical reason insists that "conduct, and not sensibility, is the ultimate fact for our recognition." Only indeterminism can make sense out of this practical insistence on objective right and wrong. Yet indeterminism does not argue that Providence is necessarily incompatible with free will. In an example involving chess, James shows how Providence can be like a master chess player who, though knowing the ultimate outcome of the game, must face unpredictable moves by an amateur player. On the other hand, James concludes that indeterminism gives people a special view: "It gives us a pluralistic, restless universe, in which no single point of view can ever take in the whole scene." James concludes that people have a right to be indeterminists and to believe in free will even in the absence of a persuasively final proof.

Whitaker T. Deininger, updated by John K. Roth

Pragmatism

A New Name for Some Old Ways of Thinking

Type of philosophy: Epistemology, pragmatism
First published: 1907
Principal ideas advanced:
◇ Pragmatism is both a philosophical method and a theory of truth.
◇ As a method, it resolves metaphysical disputes by asking for the practical consequences of alternative resolutions.

◇ Once a distinction of practice is made, theoretical difficulties are likely to disappear.

◇ As a theory of truth, pragmatism claims that ideas are true insofar as they are satisfactory; to be satisfactory, ideas must be consistent with other ideas, conformable to facts, and subject to the practical tests of experience.

Occasionally a book succeeds in giving influential expression to an attitude and a set of principles that eventually make up a historically important philosophical movement. This is the case with William James's *Pragmatism*. Borrowing the term from his philosophical contemporary Charles S. Peirce, James attempted in a series of published lectures to popularize and defend "a number of tendencies that hitherto have lacked a collective name." Pragmatism came to dominate the American intellectual scene as well as to gain recognition as a uniquely American philosophical position. James's book still serves as a sympathetic if sometimes polemical introduction to the pragmatic movement. Its eight related essays discuss the origin and meaning of pragmatism as well as suggest how the pragmatic method can be applied to troublingly perennial problems in metaphysics and religion. The contents give evidence of James's belief that philosophizing, as a technical concern, must always involve consequences for the life of common sense and ordinary people.

The Need for Pragmatism

Given the question "Can a philosopher settle all philosophical disputes disinterestedly?," James replies in the negative. The point is not that philosophers ought to ignore claims of logic and evidence. Rather, the point is that philosophical "clashes" involve more than logic and evidence. James insists that no philosopher can wholly "sink the fact of his temperament," however responsibly one seeks to give "impersonal reasons only for [one's] conclusions." A philosophical attitude necessarily becomes colored by a person's temperament. In "The Dilemma in Philosophy," which opens *Pragmatism*, James argues that a fundamental opposition in temperament has marked the history of thought: that between rationalism and empiricism. The rationalist values "abstract and eternal principles"; the empiricist,

"facts in all their crude variety." Aware that so hard and fast a distinction can serve only a rough-and-ready use, James suggests that clusters of traits tend to distinguish the rationalist from the empiricist. Rationalists are tender-minded, intellectualistic, idealistic, optimistic, religious, free-willist, monistic, dogmatical. Empiricists are tough-minded, sensationalistic, materialistic, pessimistic, irreligious, fatalistic, pluralistic, skeptical.

This rule-of-thumb distinction between two attitudes James applies to his view of the existing philosophical situation. This situation is one in which even children "are almost born scientific." Positivism and scientific materialism tend to dominate the scene, favoring the empirically minded outlook. Yet people also seek to preserve an element of religiousness. James insists that a philosophical dilemma arises that is unacceptable to his contemporaries: to adopt a positivistic respect for empirical facts that ignores religion, or to keep a religiousness that is insufficiently empirical. James will settle for neither alternative. He asserts that the common person as philosopher demands facts, science, and religion. Ordinary people cannot find what they need in the philosophical country store. Materialists explain phenomena by a "nothing but" account of higher forms in terms of lower, while religious thinkers provide a choice between an empty transcendentalist idealism (whose Absolute has no necessary relation to any concretely existing thing) and traditional theism (whose compromising nature lacks prestige and vital fighting powers). Rationalist elements in idealism and theism emphasize refinement and escape from the concrete realities of ordinary, everyday life. The result is that for the common person's plight, "Empiricist writers give him a materialism, rationalists give him something religious, but to that religion 'actual things are blank.'"

For this dramatically staged intellectual predicament, James has a philosophical hero ready in the wings. It is "the oddly-named thing pragmatism." Pragmatism is offered as a philosophy that can salvage the religious values of rationalism without perverting people's many-sided awareness of facts. It can also take account of the way temperamental demands inevitably affect foundations of philosophical systems. What

James promises for his generation is a kind of philosophical synthesis that locates personal ways of seeing things squarely in the heart of philosophical subject matter. What that involves he describes in two essays: "What Pragmatism Means" and "Pragmatism's Conception of Truth."

Pragmatism as Method

Pragmatism is both a method and a theory of truth. The method can be used by widely different philosophical persuasions. Its function is chiefly that of settling metaphysical disputes. Metaphysical arguments involve "notions" about which one can always ask whether the notions lead to any practical consequences. Such notions must be shown to make a difference in human conduct if they are to prove meaningful. Two Jamesian examples can illustrate what is meant here. One example concerns an argument about whether, if a person circles a tree around whose trunk a squirrel is also moving, one can say the person "goes round" the squirrel. James shows how the answer depends on what is meant by "round." If one means by "going round" that the person is in successive places to north, east, south, and west of the squirrel, then he does go round the animal. If one means, on the other hand, that the person is behind, then to the right of, then in front of, and then to the left of the squirrel, then the person may not actually go round the squirrel, since the animal may move simultaneously with the person's movements. James concludes that an argument of this kind, if analyzed, turns out to be a verbal one.

Another example illustrates how the pragmatic method is compatible with many possible results. James asks his readers to view the method as being like a corridor in a hotel, whose doors open into many rooms that contain thinkers involved in a variety of intellectual pursuits. These pursuits may be metaphysical, religious, or scientific. Metaphysically, one room may harbor a person working out an idealistic system, while another may shelter a thinker attempting to show that metaphysics is an impossibility. James insists that the pragmatic method is neutral regarding the kinds of thought going on in the rooms. Nevertheless, he insists that as a theory of truth, pragmatism favors the nominalist's preference for

particulars, the utilitarian's stress on what is useful, and the positivist's dislike of metaphysical speculations and merely verbal solutions of problems. James believes that when people employ words such as "God," "Matter," "the Absolute," "Reason," and "Energy," they should use the pragmatic method in seeking to show how such notions can have practical effects.

Pragmatism as Theory

As an instrumentalist theory of truth, pragmatism views sharp distinctions between logic and psychology with great suspicion. Ideas are instruments that help to dispel doubt when inherited bodies of opinion no longer produce intellectual ease. Belief means the cessation of doubting. However, what makes a belief true? James asserts that an idea is true if it permits the believer to attain "satisfactory relations with other parts of our experience." This genetic conception of truth—influenced by Darwinian biology—sees ideas as true for specified situations, always in principle subject to change and reevaluation. Some critics interpret James's emphasis on the contextual truth of an idea as meaning people may believe whatever happens to make them comfortable. James rejects any wish-fulfilling conception of pragmatic truth. He states conditions that any idea must satisfy to qualify as workable. These conditions are quite conservative: Ideas must prove consistent with other ideas (including old ones) conformable to existing facts, and subject to experiential corroboration and validation.

James is mostly critical of rationalistic metaphysical ideas leading to no observable differences in domains of human conduct. He rejects claims about *the* Truth. Nevertheless, he will consider even theological ideas as possibly true as long as their proponents can show them to affect some actual person's behavior. "Truth lives, in fact, for the most part on a credit system." Truth concerns matters of fact, abstract things and their relations, and the relations of an idea to the entire body of one's other beliefs. Ideas unable to conform to men's factual knowledge simply cannot have what James calls "cash-value."

James's relevant essays about truth sometimes raise questions that they do not satisfactorily answer. Some critics accuse him of advocating a subjectivist theory of truth. Elsewhere, James defends his views by suggesting two kinds of criteria for testing the meaning of any proposition. First, a proposition has meaning if it leads to observable consequences in experience. Second, a proposition is meaningful if someone's belief in it leads to behavioral consequences. James seems to employ the first view when he writes about scientific and factual knowledge. He uses the second view when discussing certain moral and religious beliefs. It is the second view that worries some critics, who think that, if taken literally, it can justify as true any psychologically helpful belief.

Applications of Pragmatism

Most of the remaining essays in *Pragmatism* seek to illustrate how the pragmatic method and theory of truth may be applied to specific problems. These are predominantly philosophical rather than scientific problems. In "Some Metaphysical Problems" and "The One and the Many," James applies his generous theory of meaning to such problems as the meaning of substance, the relative values of materialism and spiritualism, the problem of evil, the debate about freedom of the will, and the merits of monism and pluralism as cosmological notions. "Pragmatism and Common Sense" discusses three kinds of knowledge whose truth-claims are perennial. "Pragmatism and Humanism" and "Pragmatism and Religion" indicate how pragmatism can mediate in disputes among hard-headed empiricists and abstract rationalists.

Taking the traditional puzzles about substance, design in nature, and free will, James argues that such metaphysical issues often lead to no genuine consequences for action if treated in solely intellectual terms. "In every *genuine* metaphysical dispute some practical issue, however conjectural and remote, is involved." Metaphysical arguments thus concern something other than what seems the case. Influenced by the thing-attribute aspect of grammar, people worry about substance because they suppose a *something* must support the external and psychological objects of our perceivable world beyond what these objects are experienced *as*. James asks us to imagine that a material or spiritual substance undergoes change without altering our perceptions of its supposed

attributes. In such a case, our perception of the properties would be the same as before. It follows that the notion of substance as standing for something beyond perceived qualities of objects can add nothing to our actual knowledge of the things in the world. Only in the Catholic claims about the Eucharist can the notion of substance have any practical use—a religious one. Similarly, arguments whether God or matter best explains the origin and development of the universe are unimportant so far as the observable facts go. Only one's expectations about the future can make the theist-materialist issue important. The pragmatic method leads to a slight "edge" for theism, according to James, since the belief in God "guarantees an ideal order that shall be permanently preserved." *What* the world is like, even if God created it, remains a matter for patient scientific labors to discover. The theistic conception of the world's origin permits people a kind of enjoyment that materialism excludes. Morally, theism is preferable since it refuses to take human disasters as the absolutely final word, while materialism denies the eternity of the moral order.

The Design Question

The question of whether there is design in the world is also pointless if raised with scientific intent. The design issue is really a religious one. It is not open to purely rational solution. The significant aspects of the issue concern *what* that design may be, as well as the nature of any possible designer. James applies a similar treatment to the determinism-versus-free-will controversy. To decide in favor of free will means to accept a faith that the universe can be improved through human effort. James calls this faith in improvability "meliorism." In turn, such a belief requires rejection of any absolute monistic conception of the cosmos. It requires belief in the notion that reality is a multiverse. The universe is neither simply one nor an absolute randomness. It is a pluriverse that contains specific kinds of unity as well as directly experienced "gaps." It is not *now* an absolute unity in light of our experience, but we may hope for such a completed unity as a possible future cosmic event.

James insists on the misleading nature of traditional metaphysical disputes. Metaphysical arguments seem to concern problems that human intellect can solve if only that intellect "gets them right." Yet, they are really practical problems. They are significant only when found to express hidden religious and moral issues. The pragmatist favors a decision for free will, belief in God's existence, faith in an increasing unity in a pluralistic universe, and hope that elements of design exist as grounds for one's belief in meliorism. Faith may rightfully decide when human reason proves insufficient. The reason is that such faith expresses confidence in the promise of the future and results in beneficial consequences for our present living.

James rejects metaphysical monism for moral and religious reasons. Monism implies a certain completedness about the universe even now. This completedness requires the denial of free will and, if God exists, of a worthwhile God. Nevertheless, James's pluralism includes the view that many kinds of unity compose the universe. Intellect aims neither at variety nor unity, but at totality. The world contains important unities but is not a total unity. Some parts of the world are continuous with others, as in spacetime; practical continuities appear (as in the notion of physical gravity); and there are systems of influence and noninfluence which indicate existence of causal unities. Furthermore, there are generic unities (kinds), unities of social purpose, and aesthetic unities. These are experienced. Yet, James says, we never experience "a universe pure and simple." Pragmatism therefore insists on a world as containing just as many continuities *and* disjunctions as experience shows to exist.

The only ultimate unity may be an absolute knower of the system. Even the system may not always be considered to be a necessary unity, since the world may exist as eternally incomplete—actually subject to addition and loss. Our knowledge of such a world grows slowly, through scientific criticism, common sense, and philosophic criticism. No one can demonstrate conclusively which, if any, of these ways of knowing is the truest. Common sense builds up customary ways of organizing the materials of experience. It uses such concepts as thing, same or different, kinds, minds, bodies, one time, one space, subjects and attributes, causal influences, the fancied, the real. Scientific criticism adds

more sophisticated notions—such as "atoms" and "ether"—casting some doubt on the adequacy of commonsense concepts. The philosophical stage gives no knowledge quite comparable to the other two. Philosophical criticism does not make possible description of details of nature. Our decisions about which philosophical views to adopt must turn on practical rather than theoretical criteria. On the other hand, choice between common sense and scientific notions will rest on existence of kinds of corroboration which, in principle, will always be lacking in the cases of competing philosophical claims.

The essays in *Pragmatism* express a loosely stated yet consistent philosophical viewpoint. Through them runs the excitement of discovery that, if only the pragmatic method be adopted, many old and perplexing issues can be translated into practical ones. James seems eager to help people discover the metaphysical views that will conform to their experienced needs. On the other hand, he wants to insist on binding tests when the pragmatist handles common sense and science. He is less insistent on such tests in religious and moral domains. His major thesis is that "all true processes must lead to the fact of directly verifying sensible experience *somewhere*, which somebody's ideas have copied." His generosity remains attractive even to some critics who reject his philosophical conclusions.

Whitaker T. Deininger, updated by John K. Roth

Additional Reading

Allen, Gay Wilson. *William James*. New York: Viking Press, 1967. This reliable and readable biography situates James in his social and historical context.

Bauerlein, Mark. *The Pragmatic Mind: Explorations in the Psychology of Belief*. Durham, N.C.: Duke University Press, 1997. A helpful treatment of James's views about the relationships among belief, consciousness, the human will, and knowledge, and claims about truth.

Cotkin, George. *William James, Public Philosopher*. Baltimore: The Johns Hopkins University Press, 1990. Cotkin explores the social and political context in which James worked and draws out James's contributions to the important debates of his day as well as the lasting implications of his work.

Croce, Paul Jerome. *Science and Religion in the Era of William James*. Chapel Hill: University of North Carolina Press, 1995. Assess how debates about science and religion informed James's philosophy.

Myers, Gerald E. *William James: His Life and Thought*. New Haven, Conn.: Yale University Press, 1986. A well-written, carefully researched, comprehensive study of James's life and thought.

Perry, Ralph Barton. *The Thought and Character of William James*. Nashville, Tenn.: Vanderbilt University Press, 1996. A reprint of a classic by a well-respected philosopher, this book contains valuable information about James's life and work.

Putnam, Ruth Anna, ed. *The Cambridge Companion to William James*. Cambridge, England: Cambridge University Press, 1997. Significant essays by well-qualified James scholars interpret and assess a wide range of topics and problems in his philosophy and psychology.

Roth, John K. *Freedom and the Moral Life: The Ethics of William James*. Philadelphia, Pa.: Westminster Press, 1969. Focuses on key themes in James's moral philosophy and evaluates the significance of James's ethics.

Seigfried, Charlene Haddock. *Pragmatism and Feminism: Reweaving the Social Fabric*. Chicago: University of Chicago Press, 1996. An important interpreter of James's philosophy appraises continuities and discontinuities between American pragmatism and feminist theory.

Simon, Linda. *Genuine Reality: A Life of William James*. New York: Harcourt, Brace, 1998. A worthwhile account of James's life and his pioneering work in psychology and philosophy.

Suckiel, Ellen Kappy. *Heaven's Champion: William James's Philosophy of Religion*. Notre Dame, Ind.: University of Notre Dame Press, 1996. A study of the themes and lasting significance of James's philosophy and its emphasis on religion.

Taylor, Eugene. *William James on Consciousness Beyond the Margin*. Princeton, N.J.: Princeton University Press, 1996. Explores James's interests in and theories about human consciousness, psychology, religious experience, and other forms of experience.

Wild, John. *The Radical Empiricism of William James*. Garden City, N.Y.: Doubleday, 1969. Shows how James's psychology and pragmatism relate to European phenomenology and existentialism.

David Warren Bowen, updated by John K. Roth

Karl Jaspers

In his early career, Jaspers played an important role in establishing the foundations of clinical psychiatry, and in his mature years, he was one of the major philosophers to lay the groundwork for the existential movement. After World War II, he attempted to develop a world philosophy that would promote human unity based on freedom and tolerance.

Principal philosophical works: *Allgemeine Psychopathologie*, 1913 (*General Psychopathology*, 1962); *Psychologie der Weltanshauungen*, 1919; *Philosophie*, 1932 (2 volumes; *Philosophy*, 1969-1971, 3 volumes); *Vernunft und Existenz*, 1935 (*Reason and Existenz*, 1955); *Existenzphilosophie*, 1938 (*Philosophy of Existence*, 1971); *Die Shuldfrage*, 1946 (*The Question of German Guilt*, 1947); *Von der Wahrheit*, 1947 (*Truth and Symbol*, 1959); *Der philsophische Glaube*, 1948 (*The Perennial Scope of Philosophy*, 1949); *Vom Ursprung und Ziel der Geschichte*, 1949 (*The Origin and Goal of History*, 1953); *Die Frage der Entymythologisierung*, 1954 (with R. Bultmann; *Myth and Christianity*, 1958); *Die großen Philosophen*, 1957-1981 (3 volumes; *The Great Philosophers*, 1962-1993, 3 volumes); *Die Atombombe und die Zukunft des Menschen*, 1958 (*The Future of Mankind*, 1961; also known as *The Atom Bomb and the Future of Man*); *Der philosophische Glaube angesichts der Offenbarung*, 1962 (*Philosophical Faith and Revelation*, 1967); *Karl Jaspers: Basic Philosophical Writings, Selections*, 1986.

Born: February 23, 1883; Oldenburg, Germany
Died: February 26, 1969; Basel, Switzerland

Early Life

Born and reared near the North Sea in Oldenburg, Germany, Karl Theodor Jaspers was the eldest of three children in an upper-middle-class family whose ancestors had lived in northern Germany for generations. His father was a successful lawyer who served as president of the city council as well as a bank director. Never in good health, during childhood Jaspers suffered from serious diseases that developed into a chronic dilation of the bronchial tubes, which led to cardiac decompensation (the heart's inability to maintain normal circulation). These severe health problems meant that Jaspers had limited energy for physical activity, leading him to think seriously about the significance of human existence.

In his early years of school, Jaspers was not an especially outstanding student, but he did gain a reputation for a spirit of independence. Having a strong dislike for discipline and regimentation, during his high school years he was in constant conflict with the school authorities. In 1901 and 1902, he studied law at the Universities of Heidelberg and Munich, but, not finding this field compatible with his interests, he decided to study natural science to learn as much as possible about the universe. Between 1902 and 1908, he studied medicine at the Universities of Berlin, Göttingen, and Heidelberg. After passing the state examination to practice medicine, he wrote his dissertation, *Heimweh und Verbrechen* (1909; nostalgia and crime). In 1909, he took a job as a volunteer research assistant at the psychiatric clinic of the University of Heidelberg, a position that he held for six years; in 1910, he married Gertrud Mayer, a German Jew who was the sister of his closest friend.

Life's Work

At the Heidelberg clinic, Jaspers chose to work in his own way, at his own pace, and with his own choice of patients. He was allowed this independence because he agreed to work without a salary. Jaspers was very dissatisfied with the conditions of clinical psychiatry, especially the emphasis on organic medicine, the limited attempts at therapy, and the failure to consider individual differences. In his clinical work, Jaspers was influenced by philosopher Edmund Husserl's method of phenomenology—the direct observation and description of phenomena combined with an attempt not to depend on causal theories. His early work *General Psychopathology* was one of the first serious attempts to present a critical and systematic synthesis of the modern methods available in psychiatry, making Jaspers one of the best-known German psychiatrists.

In spite of this success, Jaspers's interests were moving in the direction of general philosophy; the same year that he published his book, he was able to enter the philosophical faculty as the specialist in empirical psychology at Heidelberg. Although his work was not appreciated by Heinrich Rickert and other philosophers at the university, his academic advance was rapid. By 1921, he was a full professor of philosophy, and in 1922, he occupied the second chair of that field.

Jaspers's intellectual development was reflected in his published lectures *Psychologie der Weltanschauungen* (psychology of worldviews). In this work, Jaspers investigated the limits of the philosophical knowledge of humankind, and he anticipated all the major themes of his later works. Emphasizing the differences between philosophy and science, he argued that the latter was based on empirical data, providing objective facts that are apodictically certain. In contrast, Jaspers considered philosophy to be directed at subjective insight into the nature of being, using intuitive methods that resembled Eastern mysticism. His system, while founded on belief, recognized the validity of modern science, searching for a philosophy that would transcend scientific knowledge while remaining free of dogmatism. Jaspers believed that human existence was the center of all reality, and he argued that in contrast to inanimate objects, human existence included the freedom for self-determination.

Jaspers developed these germinal ideas during the 1920's and early 1930's, and during these years, he worked in association with Ernst Mayer and Martin Heidegger. In 1932, he published his three-volume work *Philosophy*, which was his most systematic account of the so-called existential philosophy. Jaspers argued that philosophy was primarily an activity in which people gain illumination into the nature of their existence and that content and doctrines are relatively unimportant—not to be considered as objectively true or false. Influenced by Søren Kierkegaard, he used the term "existence" to refer to a sentient subject (or soul) possessing self-awareness and freedom. Although he rejected theism and divine revelation, Jaspers sought for a vague form of transcendence that was not knowable by empirical data, with the individual find-

Karl Jaspers. *(Archive Photos)*

ing hints of this reality through symbolic "ciphers" as found in myths or religious teachings. In the realm of ethics, Jaspers focused on the goal of "authentic existence," which primarily meant to seek truth and to stand by one's convictions.

Jaspers seriously underestimated the appeal of National Socialism (Nazism), and he was taken by surprise when Adolf Hitler assumed power in 1933. Unlike many academicians, he made no concessions to the Nazi government, and unwilling to forsake his Jewish wife, he became an enemy of state. Until 1937, he was allowed to teach and publish, and his book *Reason and Existenz* developed the key concept of "the encompassing," which referred to the spiritual and material reality that surrounds human existence. When removed from his professorship at Heidelberg, he was allowed to present a final group of lectures, published in the short book *Philosophy of Existence*. While emphasizing metaphysics, these lectures did imply an anti-Nazi stance in their defense of individualism, their advocacy of seeking truth, and their focus on spirituality.

In 1942, Jaspers received permission to emigrate to Switzerland, but his wife would have been required to remain behind. He refused to leave without her, and she was soon forced to hide in the home of friends. If arrested, both of them had decided, they would commit suicide. In 1945, he learned that his deportation was scheduled for the middle of April, but fortunately U.S. troops occupied Heidelberg two weeks before the appointed date. Although disillusioned by the Nazi period, Jaspers used this time to write a revision of *General Psychopathology* and to complete his large book on logic, *Truth and Symbol*.

After the German surrender, Jaspers spent most of his energy trying to provide a theoretical basis for the rebuilding of the universities and helping promote the moral and political rebirth of the nation. In the book *Die Idee der Universität* (1946; *The Idea of the University*, 1959), he called for the complete de-Nazification of the teaching staff and for the return of the autonomous university of the years before 1933. Believing that an acknowledgment of national guilt was necessary for a moral rebirth, Jaspers argued in *The Question of German Guilt* that those who actively participated in crimes against humanity (such as the

Holocaust) were morally guilty, while those Germans who passively tolerated Nazi crimes were only politically responsible. He hoped that the German people would accept this sense of collective guilt and responsibility, allowing for a higher level of democracy and moral sensitivity. Jaspers was disappointed when his writings did not appear to have any impact on the emerging society, and in 1948, he accepted a professorship in philosophy in Basel, Switzerland. Many Germans bitterly resented his emigration.

Jaspers was convinced that the modern developments in science and nuclear weapons meant that nationalism had become a dangerous anachronism and that it was necessary for humankind to strive for a new unity based on a world confederation, a project that was elaborated in *The Future of Mankind*. This utopian dream would be accomplished gradually through democratic means, and in the short term, Jaspers supported the United Nations and decolonization. Radical change would require a new mode of thinking, to which Jaspers referred as "world philosophy," with the fundamental ideas developed in *Philosophical Faith and Revelation*. Because all thinking ultimately relies on faith, Jaspers looked to humanity's commitment to a common transcendence approached through the ciphers of various cultures, resulting in a new attitude of tolerance.

In formulating his world philosophy, Jaspers took a renewed interest in the history of philosophical thinking, writing the erudite book *The Great Philosophers*. In *The Origin and Goal of History*, one of the philosopher's most important contributions was the concept of the axial period (from 800 to 200 B.C.E.), during which time the religious and philosophical foundations of the existing civilizations came into being.

With his ambitious aspirations for humanity, Jaspers was disappointed with developments of the postwar world, especially with the conservative climate in Germany. He wrote a bitter critique of German democracy in *Wohin treibt die Bundersrepublik?* (1966; *The Future of Germany*, 1967), a book that was widely criticized in West Germany. In response, Jaspers returned his German passport and applied for Swiss citizenship. In 1968, his physical condition deteriorated rapidly, and he died early in 1969, three days after his eighty-sixth birthday.

Influence

Although Jaspers rejected the label of "existentialist," he was one of the philosophers who had a great influence on this diverse movement in the postwar period. As a popular teacher for a long time and as author of thirty books, Jaspers inspired large numbers of students to think about the meaning of human existence and to engage in the act of philosophizing. Never attempting to establish a school of thought or to argue the truth of particular doctrines, Jaspers is not remembered for particular ideas as much as for a general style and mood in metaphysical speculation.

Authorities agree that much of Jaspers's thought was rather vague and ambiguous—at times contradictory. Because he emphasized the subjectivity of the individual thinker, not making a clear distinction between truth and knowledge about the truth, his philosophy can be classified as a form of idealism, and he was a strong critic of materialism, positivism, and scientism. Although not committed to any particular religion, he expressed a mystical temperament, appearing to be overwhelmed by a generalized spirituality that he considered to be the ground of being. He tended to use common words, such as "existence," in a specialized sense, and some of his favorite words (for example, "the Encompassing") are open to multiple connotations and interpretations. When Sebastian Samay once asked Jaspers what he thought about some of his commentators, Jaspers replied: "Their work is excellent, but you know, they are much too clear. They have tried to do away with many of my ambiguities." In the years after World War II, however, Jaspers's works in philosophy and government became more widely read and cogently argued, reflecting his growing concern for the social values of reason, justice, and democracy.

Although Jaspers always insisted that he was not a hero during the Nazi era, he clearly demonstrated much moral courage in standing by his wife and refusing to renounce his convictions. In like manner, he demonstrated considerable strength of character in doing productive work in spite of a weak physical condition. As much as for his philosophical and psychological writings, Jaspers deserves to be remembered for these personal characteristics.

Thomas T. Lewis

Reason and Existenz

Type of philosophy: Existentialism, metaphysics
First published: Vernunft und Existenz, 1935 (*Reason and Existenz*, 1955)
Principal ideas advanced:

◇ No description of Existenz is possible; Existenz can be clarified only by reference to concrete situations.

◇ Existenz is the freedom of an individual, the possibility of decision; because one exists in this special sense, one is that which one can become in one's freedom.

◇ The Encompassing is that which one encounters; considered as Being-in-itself, the Encompassing appears only in and through the Being-which-we-are—one knows what confronts one only in terms of what one is because of it.

◇ Reason and Existenz develop mutually and are interdependent.

◇ In existential communication, the self first comes to full consciousness of itself as a being qualified by historicity (determination in time), uniqueness, freedom, and communality.

The five lectures that constitute *Reason and Existenz* were delivered at the University of Groningen, Holland, in the spring of 1935. In these lectures, the author knits together the various themes that are elaborated in his many philosophical writings. *Reason and Existenz* is thus both a helpful summary of and an excellent introduction to the author's philosophy.

Ezistenz and Philosophy

Jaspers defines philosophy as the elucidation of Existenz (*Existenzerhellung*). (The term "Existenz" is retained because the English "existence" is not its equivalent.) This elucidation of Existenz needs to be sharply contrasted with any attempt at a *conceptualization* of Existenz through objectively valid and logically compelling categories. Jaspers denies that a unifying perspective of the content of existential reality is possible. Nevertheless, a clarification of or elucidation of Existenz as it expresses itself in concrete situations can be productively undertaken. According to Jaspers, the philosopher is the one who strives for such clarification.

Jaspers finds in the concrete philosophizing of Søren Kierkegaard and Friedrich Nietzsche a profound exemplification of the philosophical attitude. Both, in their interest to understand existential reality from within, had serious reservations about any program that intended to bring thought into a single and complete system, derived from self-evident principles. Any claim for a completed existential system affords nothing more than an instance of philosophical pretension. Existenz has no final content; it is always "on the way," subject to the contingencies of a constant becoming. Kierkegaard and Nietzsche, in grasping this fundamental insight, uncovered the existential irrelevancy of Georg Wilhelm Friedrich Hegel's system of logic. It was particularly Kierkegaard, in his attack on speculative thought, who brought to light the comic neglect of Existenz in the essentialism and rationalism of Hegel. Kierkegaard and Nietzsche further laid the foundations for a redefinition of philosophy as an elucidation of Existenz through their emphasis on the attitudinal, as contrasted with the doctrinal, character of philosophy. They set forth a new intellectual attitude toward life's problems. They developed no fixed doctrines that can be abstracted from their thinking as independent and permanent formulations. They were both suspicious of scientists who sought to reduce all knowledge to simple and quantifiable data. They were passionately interested in the achievements of self-knowledge. Both taught that self-reflection is the way to truth. Reality is disclosed through a penetration to the depths of the self. Both realized the need for indirect communication and saw clearly the resultant falsifications in objectivized modes of discourse. Both were exceptions—in no sense models for followers. They defy classification under any particular type and shatter all efforts at imitation. What they did was possible only once. Thus the problem for us is to philosophize without being exceptions, but with our eyes on the exception.

Encompassing and Being

At the center of Jaspers's philosophizing is the notion of the *Umgreifende*. Some have translated this basic notion as the "Comprehensive"; others have found the English term, the "Encompassing," to be a more accurate rendition of the origi-

nal German. The Encompassing lies beyond all horizons of determinate being, and thus never makes its appearance as a determinable object of knowledge. Like philosopher Immanuel Kant's noumenal realm, it remains hidden behind the phenomena. Jaspers readily agrees with Kant that the Encompassing as a designation for ultimate reality is objectively unknowable. It escapes every determinate objectivity, emerging neither as a particular object nor as the totality of objects. As such, it sets the limits to the horizon of humanity's conceptual categories. In thought, there always arises that which passes beyond thought itself. Humanity encounters the Encompassing not within a conceptual scheme but in existential decision and philosophical faith. This Encompassing appears and disappears only in its modal differentiations. The two fundamental modes of the Encompassing are the "Encompassing as being-in-itself" and the "Encompassing as being-which-we-are." Both of these modes have their ground and animation in Existenz.

Jaspers's concern for a clarification of the meaning and forms of being assuredly links him with the great metaphysicians of the Western tradition, and he is ready to acknowledge his debt to Plato, Aristotle, Baruch Spinoza, Hegel, and Friedrich Wilhelm Joseph Schelling. However, he differs from the classical metaphysicians in his relocation of the starting point for philosophical inquiry. Classical metaphysics has taken as its point of departure being-in-itself, conceived either as Nature, the World, or God. Jaspers approaches his program of clarification from being-which-we-are. This approach was already opened up by the critical philosophy of Kant, which remains for Jaspers the valid starting point for philosophical elucidation.

The Encompassing as being-which-we-are passes into further internally articulated structural modes. Here empirical existence (*Dasein*), consciousness as such (*Bewusstsein überhaupt*), and spirit (*Geist*) make their appearance. Empirical existence indicates oneself as object, by virtue of which one becomes a datum for examination by the various scientific disciplines such as biology, psychology, anthropology, and sociology. In this mode of being, one apprehends oneself simply as an object among other objects, subject to various conditioning factors. One is not yet properly known as human. One's distinctive existential freedom has not yet been disclosed. One is simply an item particularized by the biological and social sciences for empirical investigation.

The second structural mode of the being-which-we-are is consciousness as such. Consciousness has two meanings. In one of its meanings, it is still bound to empirical reality. It is a simple principle of empirical life that indicates the particularized living consciousness in its temporal process. However, we are not only particularized consciousnesses that are isolated from one another; we are in some sense similar to one another, by dint of which we are disclosed as consciousness as such. Through this movement of consciousness as such, one is able to understand oneself in terms of ideas and concepts that have universal validity. *Dasein,* or empirical existence, expresses a relationship of humanity to the empirical world. Consciousness as such expresses a relationship of humanity to the world of ideas. Ideas are permanent and timeless. Therefore, one can apprehend oneself in one's timeless permanence.

The influence of the Greek philosopher Plato upon the thought of Jaspers becomes clearly evident at this point. People participate in the Encompassing through the possibility of universally valid knowledge in which there is a union with timeless essences. As simple empirical consciousness, people are split into a multiplicity of particular realities; as consciousness as such, people are liberated from their confinement in a single consciousness and participate in the universal and timeless essence of humanity.

Spirit constitutes the third modal expression of the Encompassing which-we-are. Spirit signifies the appetency toward totality, completeness, and wholeness. As such, it is oriented toward the truth of consciousness. It is attracted by the timeless and universal ideas that bring everything into clarity and connection. It seeks a unification of particular existence in such a way that every particular would be a member of a totality.

There is indeed a sense in which spirit expresses the synthesis of empirical existence and consciousness as such. However, this synthesis is never completed. It is always on the way, an incessant striving that is never finished. It is at this point that Jaspers's understanding of spirit differs from that of Hegel. For Hegel, spirit drives beyond itself to its own completion, but not so for Jaspers. On one hand, spirit is oriented to the realm of ideas in which consciousness as such participates and is differentiated from simple empirical existence; on the other hand, spirit is contrasted with the abstraction of a timeless consciousness as such and expresses kinship with empirical existence. This kinship with empirical existence is its ineradicable temporality. It is a process of constant striving and ceaseless activity, struggling with itself, reaching ever beyond that which it is and has. Yet it differs from empirical existence in that empirical existence is unconsciously bound to its particularization in matter and life, by virtue of which it can become an object in a determinable horizon. As empirical existence, people are split off from each other and become objects of scientific investigation. Spirit overflows every objectivization and remains empirically unknowable. It is not capable of being investigated as a natural object. Although it always points to its basis in empirical existence, it also points to a power or dynamism that provides the impetus for its struggle toward meaning and totality.

It is through the Encompassing being-which-we-are that one has an approach to the Encompassing as being-in-itself. Being-in-itself never emerges independently as a substantive and knowable entity. It appears only in and through the being-which-we-are. In this appearance, it is disclosed as a limit expressing a twofold modification: the world and transcendence. The being-which-we-are has one of its limits in the experience of the world. The world in Jaspers's philosophy signifies neither the totality of natural objects nor a spatiotemporal continuum in which these objects come to be. It signifies instead the horizon of inexhaustible appearances that present themselves to inquiry. This horizon is always receding, and it manifests itself only indirectly in the appearances of particular and empirical existence. It is never fully disclosed in any one of its perspectives and remains indeterminate for all empirical investigation. The Encompassing being-which-we-are has its other limit in transcendence. Transcendence is that mode of being-in-itself that remains hidden from all phenomenal experience. It does not even manifest itself indirectly. It extends beyond the horizons of world orientation as such. It remains the completely unknowable and indefinable, existentially posited through a philosophical faith.

Existenz and Reason

All the modes of the Encompassing have their original source in Existenz. Existenz is not itself a mode, but it carries the meaning of every mode. It is the animation and the ground of all modes of the Encompassing. Thus, only in turning one's attention to Existenz can one reach the pivotal point in Jaspers's philosophizing. In Existenz, one reaches the abyss or the dark ground of self-hood. Existenz contains within itself an element of the irrational and thus never becomes fully transparent to consciousness as such. Consciousness is always structurally related to the universal ideas, but Existenz can never be grasped through an idea. It never becomes fully intelligible because it is the object of no science. Existenz can only be approached through concrete elucidations—hence, Jaspers's program of *Existenzerhellung*. Existenz is the possibility of decision, which has its origin in time and apprehends itself only within its temporality. It escapes from every idea of consciousness as well as from the attempt of spirit to render it into an expression of a totality or a part of a whole. Existenz is the individual as historicity. It determines the individual in one's unique past and unique future. Always moving into a future, the individual, as Existenz, is burdened with the responsibilities of decisions. This fact constitutes one's historicity. Existenz is irreplaceable. The concrete movements within one's historicity, which always call one to decision, disclose one in one's unique individuality and personal idiosyncrasy. One is never a simple individual empirical existent that can be reduced to a specimen or an instance of a class; one is unique and irreplaceable. Finally, Existenz, as it knows itself before transcendence, reveals itself as freedom. Existenz is possibility, which means freedom. Humanity is that which one can become in one's freedom.

As the modes of the Encompassing have their roots in Existenz, so they have their bond in Reason. Reason is the bond that internally unites the modes and keeps them from falling into an unrelated plurality. Thus Reason and Existenz are the great poles of being, permeating all the modes but not coming to rest in any one of them. Jaspers cautions the reader against a possible falsification of the meaning of Reason as it is used in his elucidation of Existenz. Reason is not to be construed as simple, clear, objective thinking (*Verstand*). Understood in this sense, Reason would be indistinguishable from consciousness as such. Reason, as the term is used by Jaspers, is closer to the Kantian meaning of *Vernunft*. It is the preeminence of thought that includes more than mere thinking. It not only includes a grasp of what is universally valid (*ens rationis*) but also touches upon and reveals the nonrational, bringing to light its existential significance. It always pushes toward unity, the universal, law, and order but at the same time remains within the possibility of Existenz. Reason and Existenz are thus inseparable. Each disappears when the other disappears. Reason without Existenz is hollow and culminates in an empty intellectualism. Existenz without Reason is blind, incessant impulse and irrational striving. Reason and Existenz are friends rather than enemies. Each is determined through the other. They mutually develop each other and through this development find both clarity and reality. In this interdependence of Reason and Existenz is an expression of the polar union of the Apollonian and the Dionysian. The Apollonian, or the structural principle, dissolves into a simple intellectual movement of consciousness, a dialectical movement of spirit, when it loses the Dionysian or dynamic principle. Conversely, the Dionysian passes over into irrational passion that burns to its own destruction when it loses its bond with the Apollonian.

Communication

The reality of communication provides another dominant thesis in the philosophy of Jaspers. Philosophical truth, which discloses Existenz as the ground of the modes and Reason as their bond, can be grasped only in historical communication. The possibility of communication follows from the ineradicable communality of humanity. No one achieves humanity in isolation. People exist only in and through others and come to an apprehension of the truth of their Existenz through interdependent and mutual communal understanding. Truth cannot be separated from communicability. However, the truth that is expressed in communication is not simple; there are as many senses of truth as there are modes of the Encompassing being-which-we-are. In the community of one's empirical existence, it is the pragmatic conception of truth that is valid. Empirical reality knows no absolutes that have a timeless validity. Truth in this mode is relative and changing, because empirical existence itself is in a constant process of change. That which is empirically true today may be empirically wrong tomorrow because of a new situation into which one will have passed. All empirical truth is dependent upon the context of the situation and one's own standpoint within the situation.

As the situation perpetually changes, so does truth. At every moment, the truth of one's standpoint is in danger of being refuted by the very fact of process. The truth in the communication of consciousness as such is logical consistency and cogent evidence. By means of logical categories, one affirms and denies that which is valid for everyone. Whereas in empirical reality, truth is relative and changing because of the multiple fractures of particulars with one another in their time-bound existence, in consciousness as such there is a self-identical consciousness that provides the condition for universally valid truths. The communication of spirit demands participation in a communal substance. Spirit has meaning only in relation to the whole of which it is a part. Communication is thus the communication of a member with its organism. Although each spirit differs from every other spirit, there is a common agreement as concerns the order that comprehends them. Communication occurs only through the acknowledgment of their common commitment to this order. Truth in the community of spirit is thus total commitment or full conviction. Pragmatic meaning, logical intelligibility, and full conviction are the three senses of truth expressed in the Encompassing being-which-we-are.

However, there is also the will to communicate Reason and Existenz. The communication of Existenz never proceeds independently of the communication in the three modes of the Encompassing being-which-we-are. Existenz retains its membership in the mode of empirical existence, consciousness as such, and spirit; but it passes beyond them in a "loving struggle" (*liebender Kampf*) to communicate the innermost meaning of its being. The communication of Existenz is not that of relative and changing particulars, nor is it that of an identical and replaceable consciousness. Existential communication is communication between irreplaceable persons. The community of Existenz is also contrasted with the spiritual community. Spirit seeks security in a comprehensive group substance. Existenz recognizes the irremovable fracture in being, accepts the inevitability of struggle, and strives to open itself for transcendence. Only through these movements does Existenz apprehend its irreplaceable and essentially unrepeatable selfhood and bind itself to the historical community of selves who share the same irreplaceable determinants. It is in existential communication that the self first comes to a full consciousness of itself as a being qualified by historicity, uniqueness, freedom, and communality.

Reason plays a most important role in existential communication. Reason as the bond of the various modes of the Encompassing strives for a unity in communication. However, its function is primarily negative. It discloses the limits of communication in each of the modes and checks the absolutization of any particular mode as the full expression of Being. When empirical existence is absolutized, the essence of humanity is lost; one is reduced to an instance of matter and biological life, and one's essence becomes identified with knowable regularities. One is comprehended not in one's humanity, but in one's simple animality. The absolutization of consciousness as such results in an empty intellectualism. One's empirical reality is dissolved into timeless truths, and the life of the spirit remains unacknowledged. When spirit becomes a self-sufficient mode, the result is a wooden culture in which all intellection and creativity are sacrificed to a communal substance. None of the modes is sufficient by itself. Each demands the other. Reason provides the internal bond through which their mutual dependence can be harmoniously maintained.

Philosophical Logic and Faith

For Jaspers, the truth of Reason is philosophical logic; the truth of Existenz is philosophical faith. Philosophical logic and philosophical interpenetrate, as do Reason and Existenz themselves. Logic takes its impulse from Existenz, which it seeks to clarify. Philosophical logic is limited neither to traditional formal logic nor to mere methodology; it prevents any reduction of humanity to mere empirical existence or to a universal consciousness. Philosophical logic is negative in that it provides no new contents, but it is positive in establishing the conditions for every possible content. Philosophical faith, the truth of Existenz, confronts humanity with transcendence and discloses one's freedom. Philosophical faith is contrasted with religious faith in that it acknowledges no absolute or final revelation in time. Transcendence discloses a constant openness in which humanity apprehends itself as an "inner act," more precisely, an act of freedom. Faith is an acknowledgment of transcendence as the source of humanity's freedom. The highest freedom that humanity can experience is the freedom that has its condition in a source outside itself.

Calvin O. Schrag

Additional Reading

Ehrlich, Leonard. *Karl Jaspers: Philosophy as Faith.* Amherst: University of Massachusetts Press, 1975. An analysis of Karl Jaspers's understanding of philosophical thought as the expression of faith, in the underlying unity of the subjective and the objective, examining such key themes as the role of freedom and transcendence.

Kaufmann, Walter. *From Shakespeare to Existentialism.* Garden City, N.Y.: Anchor, 1960. This fine review of existentialism includes a chapter focused on Jaspers. Kaufmann's penetrating scholarship dispels some misunderstandings of Jaspers and places him in the context of the existential movement with respect to Friedrich Nietzsche in particular, while sharply criticizing Jaspers's own understanding of Nietzsche and Sigmund Freud.

Olson, Alan M., ed. *Heidegger & Jaspers.* Philadelphia: Temple University Press, 1994. The work of Heidegger and Jaspers is presented and studied.

Samay, Sebastian. *Reason Revisited: The Philosophy of Karl Jaspers.* Notre Dame, Ind.: University of Notre Dame Press, 1971. An examination of Jaspers's philosophy, particularly with respect to the relations of subject and object, being and reason, and transcendence. Very detailed, but somewhat dated in his conclusions about the influence of Jaspers's thought.

Schilpp, Paul, ed. *The Philosophy of Karl Jaspers.* Rev. ed. Chicago: Open Court Publishing, 1981. In addition to an autobiographical summary, this book offers commentaries by twenty-four prominent scholars who critically examine many diverse aspects of Jaspers's work, such as death, guilt, suffering, communication, history, citizenship, religion, art, and psychopathology. They address their remarks directly to Jaspers, who replies. Bibliography.

Wallraff, Charles F. *Karl Jaspers: An Introduction to his Philosophy.* Princeton, N.J.: Princeton University Press, 1970. A fine introductory study of Jaspers's life and thought, including a critical analysis of his terminology and a useful bibliography.

Thomas T. Lewis,
updated by Christopher M. Aanstoos

Saint John of the Cross

Saint John of the Cross contributed to the renewal of monastic life and to the development of mystical theology during the golden age of the Catholic Reformation. His most lasting contribution has been to Western mysticism.

Principal philosophical works: *La subida del Monte Carmelo*, 1578-1579 (*The Ascent of Mount Carmel*, 1864, 1922); *Cántico espiritual*, 1577-1586 (*A Spiritual Canticle of the Soul*, 1864, 1909); *Llama de amor viva*, 1582 (*Living Flame of Love*, 1864, 1912); *The Complete Works of St. John of the Cross*, 1864, 1934, 1953 (includes *Noche escura del alma*, c. 1585; *Dark Night of the Soul*, 1864); *Poems*, 1951.

Born: June 24, 1542; Fontiveros, Spain
Died: December 14, 1591; Úbeda, Spain

Early Life

Juan de Yepes y Álvarez (Saint John of the Cross) was born on June 24, 1542, in Fontiveros, Spain, a town of five thousand inhabitants situated on the Castilian tableland. His father, Gonzalo de Yepes, was the son of a prosperous local silk merchant. Gonzalo was disinherited for marrying Catalina Álvarez, an impoverished and orphaned Toledan, apprenticed to a weaver in Fontiveros. John was the third son born to this union. The death of his father following a prolonged illness when John was only two left John, his mother, and his siblings in dire poverty.

Seeking help, Catalina left Fontiveros, going initially to the province of Toledo but later settling in Medina del Campo, a city of thirty thousand. In Medina, there was a doctrine, or catechism, school. As much an orphanage as an educational institution for the poor, this school received John as a student. Children were fed, clothed, catechized, and given a rudimentary education. Apprenticeship in various trades was also part of the program of the doctrine school. Little is known of the four trades that John tried, except that his efforts were unsuccessful. Because in later life John was fond of painting and carving, his failure, perhaps, was one of premature exposure rather than of aptitude. John was next at-

tached to the Hospital de la Concepción, where he worked as a male nurse, begged alms for the poor, and continued his studies. Academic success caused him to be enrolled at the Jesuit Col-

Saint John of the Cross. (*Library of Congress*)

lege, situated barely two hundred yards from the hospital. Founded in 1551, this school enrolled forty students at the time John was in attendance, probably from 1559 to 1563. John's teachers recalled his passionate enthusiasm for books. With a good education in the humanities, John in 1563 found his life's vocation, taking the dark brown habit and white cloak of the Carmelites.

Life's Work

At the age of twenty-one, John entered the small community of the Carmelite brothers in Medina, then a fellowship of perhaps six members. The order of Our Lady of Mount Carmel had been founded four centuries earlier, in 1156, in Palestine by Saint Berthold as one of extreme asceticism and of great devotion to Mary. By the sixteenth century, it admitted female as well as male members. The so-called Original or Primitive Rule of 1209 had been relaxed, the order following a Mitigated Observance. Why John selected this order is not known. Perhaps it was his love of contemplation, his devotion to the Virgin, or his practice of extreme asceticism that attracted him to the Carmelites. John of Yepes now took the name Fray Juan de Santo Matia (Brother John of Saint Mathias), though five years later, when, on November 28, 1568, he professed the Carmelite Primitive Rule, he would change his name to Fray Juan de la Cruz (Brother John of the Cross). As a monastic reformer, John was to make a lasting contribution to Christianity.

Following his profession as a Carmelite, John continued his education at the College of San Andres, a school for sixteen years attached to the famed University of Salamanca. A good Latinist and an excellent grammarian, John took classes in the college of arts at Salamanca from 1564 to 1567. Perhaps seven thousand students were matriculated at the University of Salamanca at that time. Taught by a faculty known throughout Spain and the Habsburg lands, the young monk next turned his attention to theology, attending lectures in divinity in 1567-1568. At Salamanca, John was taught a clear-cut Thomism and was deeply immersed in the philosophy of Aristotle and the theology of Saint Thomas Aquinas. Concurrently, John was a master of students at San Andres.

Following his ordination as a priest in 1567, John met Saint Teresa de Jesús of Ávila. Daughter of a noble Spanish family, Teresa had entered the Carmelite Convent of the Incarnation (Mitigated Observance) at Ávila in 1535. Teresa had become persuaded that discipline was too relaxed and that there ought to be a return to the Primitive Rule of the Carmelites. Her followers were called Discalced Carmelites, in opposition to the Calced Carmelites, who continued to follow the Mitigated rather than the Primitive Rule. Within a year of his meeting with the remarkable Mother Teresa, John was committed to the so-called Teresian Reforms of the Carmelite order. For that reason, in November, 1568, John was made professor of the Primitive Rule of the Carmelites at Duruelo. Resolving "to separate himself from the world and hide himself in God," John sought a strictly contemplative life. That wish was never granted, for John was often sought as a counselor and confessor (for the laity and the religious) and as a popular and persuasive preacher.

Soon John became subprior, then novice master, and finally rector of a new house of studies founded at Alcalá. This was a creative time for John, who was able to integrate the intellectual and the spiritual life and who could combine contemplation with active service, including becoming Teresa's confessor after 1571. John found "the delights which God lets souls taste in contemplation," but he was advised by Teresa that "a great storm of trials" was on the horizon.

Disputes between the Carmelites who followed the Primitive Rule and those who held to the Mitigated Observance caused John to become a focus of attention. Following an initial imprisonment in 1576, John was seized on December 2, 1577, by some of the Calced Carmelites and taken to Toledo, where he was commanded by superiors to repent of his reforms. This was yet another step in the antireformist policies that had prevailed in the Carmelite order since a general chapter meeting in 1575. Because John refused to renounce the reforms, he was imprisoned for some nine months in a small cell. There was only one small opening for light and air. John's jailers were motivated by "vindictiveness . . . mingled with religious zeal," for they believed that his reforms of the order were a very great crime and revealed a stubborn pride and insubordination. John accepted his imprisonment, with its insults, slanders, calumnies, physical sufferings, and agonies of soul, as a further labor by God to purify and refine his faith.

In August, 1578, John escaped from his captors and fled to southern Spain. The separation of the two branches of the Carmelite order, the Calced and the Discalced, occurred in 1579-1580. John became the rector of a Discalced Carmelite college in Baeza in Andalusia, serving also as an administrator in the Reformed Carmelite order and becoming prior of Granada in 1582 and of Segovia in 1588. John, vicar provincial of his order's southern region, was a member of the governing body of the society by 1588.

John's contemporary, Eliseo de los Martires, described him as "a man in body of medium size" and one of "grave and venerable countenance." His complexion was "wheaty," or "somewhat swarthy," and his face was filled with "good features." Normally John wore a mustache and was often fully bearded. Dressed in "an old, narrow, short, rough habit," one so rough it was said that "the cloak seemed to be made of goat-hair," John reminded many of a latter-day John the Baptist. John impressed those he met with his purity of character, his intensity of spirit, his austerity of life, his profound humility, his fondness for simplicity, and his honesty and directness in speech. Contemporary biographers also recalled his sense of humor, noting that he delighted in making his friars laugh, often sprinkling his spiritual conversation with amusing stories.

Perhaps John's greatest legacy to the world community is his writing about the interior life. During his trials, tribulations, and travels, John wrote of his encounters with God. These extensive treatises on the mystical life are a unique combination of his poems and his commentaries on those poems. *A Spiritual Canticle of the Soul*, part of which was said to have been composed while John was on his knees in prayer, is such a synthesis of poetry and commentary. That poetry is both didactic and symbolic, practical and devotional. The ancient threefold route of the soul to God is described in *A Spiritual Canticle of the Soul*. One moves from purgation (or confession of sin, the emptying of the self) to illumination (or instruction, revelation of God, filling with the divine) and then to union or perfection (going beyond a sense of separation to one of complete integration with God). This ongoing colloquy of

Christ and the soul draws on the rich imagery of courtship and love, starting with the soul's search for the Beloved, continuing to an initial meeting, then describing the perfect union, and concluding with a discussion of the poignant desire for an everlasting intimacy with the Eternal, a longing that can only be fulfilled in eternity. *The Ascent of Mount Carmel* is also a discussion of how the soul can attain mystical union with God. The journey to God contains a "dark night" because the spirit must quite literally mortify, or put to death, sensory experience and sensible knowledge and then maintain itself by pure faith. Following such purgations, as well as those that come from the faith experience itself, the soul enters into a transforming union with God. This is truly a passion, for it combines both intense suffering and ecstatic pleasure, the two components of overwhelming love. In *Living Flame of Love*, the spiritual marriage, or divine union, is further described.

Though he longed only for contemplation, John once more was caught up in controversy. In 1591, he found himself banished to Andalusia. After some time in solitary life, John became extremely ill, going to Úbeda for medical attention. Following extreme pain, John died at Úbeda on December 14, 1591. In his dying moments, John requested the reading of the Canticle of Canticles, the moving love poem of the Old Testament. Interpreting it as an allegory of the soul's romance of God, John commented, "What precious pearls."

Influence

Although controversial during his lifetime, John was commended by the Catholic Church, following his death, as both a saint and teacher. Beatified by Pope Clement X in 1675, John was canonized in 1726 by Benedict XIII. In 1926, Pius XI declared him a doctor of the Church, one of perhaps thirty Catholics deemed a theologian of outstanding intellectual merit and personal sanctity, to be received universally with appreciation.

John surely was a mighty doctor of the Church, embodying the profound spirituality of the Catholic Reformation in Spain, drawing on the same religious energies that inspired Teresa, Ignatius of Loyola, the founder of the Society of Jesus, and Francis Xavier, a missionary evangelist of Asia. He will forever be one of the treasures of the Roman Catholic tradition.

As reformer, master, saint, doctor, poet, and seer, John transcended the limits of one country or creed. His significance goes beyond his accomplishment in enriching the piety of Roman Catholicism and enhancing the literature of his native Spain. John's profound mysticism causes him to be ranked alongside the great religious seekers of all human history—with the saints of Hinduism, the sages of Buddhism, the Sufis of Islam, the seekers of Daoism, the teachers of Confucianism, the visionaries of Protestantism, and the holy men and women of Orthodoxy and Asian Christianity. As such, John of the Cross is one of the major figures of world religion, combining intellectual rigor with a vigorous work ethic, wrapping both in a profound and appealing spirituality.

C. George Fry

Dark Night of the Soul

Type of philosophy: Ethics, philosophical theology
First transcribed: Noche escura del alma, c. 1585 (English translation, 1864, in *The Complete Works of St. John of the Cross*)
Principal ideas advanced:

◇ For spiritual illumination to take place, the senses must undergo a "cleansing" darkness.

◇ This purgation cannot occur by the efforts of the will, only by passive acceptance of the "dark night."

◇ Three signs of the "dark night" are "aridity" of prayer and life, inability to restore former satisfaction, and inability to meditate.

◇ Meditation after this "purgation" can be devoid of mental images.

◇ Confrontation with one's own spiritual imperfections during this "dark night" leads to anguish and suffering, though knowledge of God's mercy keeps it from becoming despair.

Juan de Ypes y Álvarez, who took as his reformed religious name Juan de la Cruz, or John of the Cross, wrote his *Dark Night of the Soul* near the end of his life as a fourth part of a previous book,

La subida del Monte Carmelo (1578-1579; *The Ascent of Mount Carmel*, 1864, 1922). Much of what is obscure in *Dark Night of the Soul* is clarified by reading *The Ascent of Mount Carmel*, though the metaphysical nature of the subject matter makes understanding inevitably difficult. Nevertheless, *Dark Night of the Soul* is a systematic description of John's actual experience, not a theoretical work.

The general religious-historical context for all of John's work is Saint Teresa of Avila's reform of the Carmelite order. John's participation in Saint Teresa's reform contributed to his spiritual and theological development, though it led to political dangers within the Carmelite order. By representing a higher ideal, a stricter observance of the rule of the Carmelite order established three hundred years earlier, John and others like him posed a threat to the rest of the order, who seemed lax by comparison. Even within the reform movement (known as the Discalced, or "without shoes," a reference to the ideal of poverty), disagreements arose. The Discalced reformers called for a more active missionary role in the community for Carmelite priests, and John defended the exclusively contemplative life.

These disagreements were not just academic: They led to John's brief imprisonment in 1576 and again for some nine months in 1577. It was in this period of crisis that John wrote some of his most powerful poetry, especially "The Spiritual Canticle." One key to understanding the thought of John is that all of his theological works began as poetry, and only later, at the request of nuns and priests attempting to understand the thought and experience behind them, did he work out a systematic theology as prose commentaries to these poems.

The Poem and Commentaries

It was in this manner that John wrote *Dark Night of the Soul*. In 1578, a year after his imprisonment, John was named superior of the monastery of El Calvario in Andalusia. There he wrote the poem beginning "En una noche oscura," or "On a dark night"—the kernel of *Dark Night of the Soul*. In his talks with the nuns of El Calvario, John began to see the value of writing down his commentaries on his poems. If Christian theology originates in commentaries on Scripture, which in many cases is poetry, then commentaries on Christian poetry might be almost as valuable.

John's commentaries on the *Dark Night of the Soul* poem, however, did not begin until 1585. At that time he was prior of the Discalced monastery of Los Martires in Grenada, which benefitted from the generosity of a wealthy lady, Señora Ana de Peñelosa. It was Ana who asked John to write his commentaries on his poems, for her edification. Among them was *Dark Night of the Soul*, completed by 1585.

The Passive Night

The structure of thought in *Dark Night of the Soul* is an extension of that of the previous work, *The Ascent of Mount Carmel*, basically a fourfold pattern representing the progress of the soul in contemplative prayer. Because John's contemplative prayer progresses by two modalities, active/passive and spiritual/sensual, four combinations are possible. The four different types of "night" in his spiritual experience are, in sequence, the active night of sense (described in the first book of *The Ascent of Mount Carmel*), the active night of spirit (*The Ascent of Mount Carmel*, books 2 and 3), the passive night of sense (*Dark Night of the Soul*, book 1), and passive night of spirit (*Dark Night of the Soul*, book 2).

Dark Night of the Soul, then, deals exclusively with the passive form of the spiritual darkness John called "night." The passivity is considered a progression from the active nights discussed in *The Ascent of Mount Carmel*, because in the passive nights described in *Dark Night of the Soul*, the soul has learned to submit to God's will, realizing that further illumination is up to God and is not subject to any action on the part of the individual. This passivity must be understood in that context, however, for it does not imply inactivity. In fact, the image that John uses is a concentration of the mental faculties into the "single act" of union with God.

Before discussing the passive night of sense, which is the subject of book 1, John describes the soul of the individual contemplative just before entering that night. The contemplative at this point John calls a "beginner," and he describes the purgation of many imperfections in the beginner (chapter 1). The next six chapters each deal with one of the seven capital sins purged by

this dark night: pride, avarice, luxury, wrath, gluttony, envy, and sloth. Chapter 8 begins the explication of the poem by expounding the first line. Chapter 9 describes the signs by which the soul knows it is making progress in the "dark night," and chapter 10 offers advice on enduring the deprivations of that night. The remaining four chapters explicate the rest of the first stanza of the poem, and list the spiritual benefits of the passive night of sense.

By "passive night of sense," John refers to a withdrawing of sensual images in prayer that would have, before this night, appeared as consolation to the contemplative. The presence of images in prayer is associated with the spirituality of Saint Ignatius of Loyola, a contemporary with whom John corresponded. It is also a staple of the Roman Catholic practice of praying the rosary: Each decade of beads represents a specific event in the lives of Mary and Jesus, on which the individual contemplates while reciting the prayers. The sensory images that appear in this type of contemplation are seen by the individual receiving them as gifts from God. When these gifts are withdrawn in the passive night of sense, the individual feels abandoned by God. Moreover, because of a heightened discrimation, the individual is aware of spiritual imperfections previously hidden from view, and so feels that such apparent abandonment is justified. Thus, spiritual progress paradoxically leads to feelings of isolation and spiritual "dryness."

In book 2, before going on to the second stanza of the poem, John revisits the first stanza from the point of view of the last stage of contemplation, the passive night of the soul. He follows the same pattern he employed in the first book, beginning by analyzing the imperfections of the soul about to enter this final night. Because the soul has already passed through the purgation of the passive night of sense, it no longer suffers the imperfections mentioned in book 1. It does, however, experience other imperfections (chapter 2) and other pains and griefs (chapters 5-8). John assures the reader, however, that the pains of this dark night are merely purgative, preparing the way for the divine illumination to follow (chapter 9). In chapter 15, John begins explicating the second stanza of the poem, which expresses much more of the illumination following the passive night of spirit. The fundamental image in this section is that of a ladder by which the soul climbs to God (chapter 18). The image is not original with John, as he acknowledges with references to Saints Bernard and Thomas Aquinas (chapter 19). The rest of the book is an exposition of the remainder of the poem.

An Approach to Prayer

Although John implies a progression through the four steps mentioned (and the *Dark Night of the Soul* concentrates on only two of them), they are not as clearly distinguished in John's writings as they are in this outline. Although book 1 of *Dark Night of the Soul* studies the passive night of sense, for example, we find descriptions of the same phenomenon in books 3 and 4 of *The Ascent of Mount Carmel* under the rubric "active night of spirit." This is only apparently a contradiction: It is the passivity of the senses that allows for the enlightenment of the spirit, so that passive night of sense and active night of spirit are rather two ways of speaking about the same contemplative experience. John's interest is in describing as accurately as he can what he experienced in prayer, not in developing a system. In fact, an attempt to systematize too much what happens in prayer works against the ethos of grace that John stressed throughout his writings: The dark nights, whether active or passive, sensual or spiritual, come at God's will, not the contemplative's. This insistence on an important doctrinal issue of the day, the role of individual efforts in salvation, reflects the influence of the Council of Trent, which defined the doctrine of Justification for Catholics in 1547.

The approach to contemplative prayer espoused by John is part of a tradition of Western spirituality known as the *via negativa*, or negative way to union with God. It is "negative" not in an evaluative sense but in a logical one: The "positive" way of contemplation involves images associated with God. However, because God is greater than any image, which involves the limitations of human senses, some thinkers advocate approaching God by means of eliminating all images, which can become a barrier to full contact with God. Twentieth century commentators on John have observed the affinity of his "negative way" with forms of contemplation in eastern re-

ligion, such as the Zen *koan*, or the use of a mantra or chant to disengage the mind from discursive thought. There is, however, a long tradition of the *via negativa* in Western thought going back to Plotinus.

The influence of the mystical theology of John is still felt not only in the Roman Catholic Church but also in intellectual circles outside of that faith, particularly in the field of the psychology of consciousness. In the last two decades of the twentieth century, several fruitful scholarly studies comparing John's spirituality with Jungian psychology have enriched the understanding of the Spanish mystic among modern readers. Among Catholic thinkers, John's preeminence among the Church's teachers has been assured not only by his beatification in 1675 (a preliminary declaration of a holy person's worthiness of veneration, often a prelude to canonization) and his canonization in 1726 but also by his being declared in 1926 a doctor of the Church. That declaration makes John one of only three dozen spiritual writers in the two-thousand-year history of the Church whose teachings have been designated especially worthy of note, and of particular authority to the faithful.

John's influence on Western culture, particularly in Spain, also includes his poetic influence. By adapting the *lira* form of his predecessor Garcilaso de Vega to the Hebrew poetry of the Song of Songs, John explored the relationship of erotic imagery to the union of the soul with God. The relationship of the contemplative to God is essentially that of a passionate love. Although it transcends the merely sensual (hence the dark night of sense precedes the dark night of spirit), it is no less intense a passion than that of the worldly lover for the beloved: In fact, it is more intense, for God's love for people is infinite, in a way that no human lover's can be. This notion is played out in the works of many Christian poets after John.

John R. Holmes

Additional Reading

Crisógano de Jesús Sacramentado, Father. *The Life of Saint John of the Cross.* Translated by Kathleen Pond. New York: Harper & Brothers, 1958. A thoroughly documented and detailed biography of Saint John of the Cross as a person and as a Carmelite friar. Illustrations, charts, notes, and references make this a necessary resource for the serious scholar.

Cugno, Alain. *Saint John of the Cross: Reflections on Mystical Experience*. Translated by Barbara Wall. New York: Seabury Press, 1979. This concise study attempts to understand John from a philosophical rather than a theological or mystical viewpoint. It explores such major themes in the philosophy of religion as the absence of God, the meaning of mysticism, the role of desire in religion, and the doctrine of the Kingdom of God.

Duohan, Leonard. *The Contemporary Challenge of John of the Cross: An Introduction to His Life and Teaching*. Washington, D.C.: ICS Publications, 1995. This biographical work looks at the life of Saint John of the Cross and what it means to modern people. Includes bibliographical references.

Frost, Bede. *Saint John of the Cross, 1542-1591, Doctor of Divine Love: An Introduction to His Philosophy, Theology, and Spirituality*. London: Hodder and Stoughton, 1937. This classic study of John's thought attempts to do justice to the complexity and variety of his writings. The author admits the difficulty inherent in any attempt to understand John's thinking about mystical experience, given that language proves inadequate to describe it.

Gaylord, Mary Malcolm, and Francisco Marquez Villanueva, eds. *San Juan de la Cruz and Fray Luis de Leon: A Commemorative International Symposium*. Newark, Del.: Juan de la Cuesta, 1996. This collection of works from a symposium examines mysticism in literature, focusing on John of the Cross and Luis de Leon. Includes index.

Gicovate, Bernard. *San Juan de la Cruz*. New York: Twayne, 1971. The author provides a compre-hensive general introduction to John's life, poetry, and prose texts. Written with the student of literature in mind, this book explores John's literary technique as well as his religious philosophy. Includes bibliography.

Hardy, Richard P. *Search for Nothing: The Life of John of the Cross*. New York, Crossroad, 1982. Hardy wrote this biography to explore John's humanity and make his personality accessible to the modern reader. Hardy provides a necessary corrective to more traditional accounts of John's life.

Payne, Steven, ed. *John of the Cross: Conferences and Essays by Members of the Institute of Carmelite Studies and Others*. Washington, D.C.: ICS Publications, 1992. This collection of essays deals with John's thinking on a variety of theological topics, useful to the scholar as well as the general reader. Each essay includes bibliographical notes.

Perrin, David Brian. *For Love of the World: The Old and New Self of John of the Cross*. San Francisco: Catholic Scholars Press, 1997. This work examines the beliefs of John of the Cross and places him within the history of the Catholic church. Includes index.

Ruiz, Federico, et al. *God Speaks in the Night: The Life, Times, and Teaching of John of the Cross*. Translated by Kieran Kavanaugh. Washington, D.C.: ICS Publications, 1991. This book commemorates the fourth centenary of John's death with almost one hundred short essays authored by Spanish Carmelite scholars and is lavishly illustrated with beautiful color photographs and illustrations. Organized around the central events of John's life, this volume provides a wealth of information of use to the scholar as well as the general reader. Includes an index of names and places.

C. George Fry, updated by Evelyn Toft

Hans Jonas

Jonas's philosophical works treat, principally, Gnosticism, existentialism, ethics, and metaphysics. The philosophical edifice that Jonas constructs is broadly based on metaphysics and the premise that there is a logical bridge between "being" and moral obligation; between "what is" and "what ought to be."

Principal philosophical works: *Augustin und das paulinische Freiheitsproblem: Eine philosophische Studie zum pelagianischen Streit*, 1930; *Gnosis und spätantiker Geist*, volume 1, *Die Mythologische Gnosis*, 1934; *Gnosis und spätantiker Geist*, volume 2, *Von der Mythologie zur mystischen Philosophie*, 1954; *The Gnostic Religion: The Message of the Alien God and the Beginnings of Christianity*, 1958; *The Phenomenon of Life: Toward Philosophical Biology*, 1966; *Philosophical Essays: From Ancient Creed to Technological Man*, 1974; *The Imperative of Responsibility: In Search of an Ethics for the Technological Age*, 1984; *Mortality and Morality: A Search for the Good After Auschwitz*, 1996.

Born: May 10, 1903; Mönchengladbach, Germany
Died: February 5, 1993; New Rochelle, New York

Early Life

Hans Jonas began studying philosophy at Freiburg in 1921 and completed his doctorate on Gnosticism in 1928 under the supervision of Martin Heidegger and Rudolf Bultmann at the University of Marburg. Heidegger was the most renowned philosopher of his day, and Bultmann was, perhaps, the most influential New Testament scholar of the first half of the twentieth century. In 1924, Jonas had come with Heidegger from Freiburg to Marburg, and it was there that he met Bultmann and established what would be a lifelong friendship. Upon Bultmann's death in 1976, Marburg University conducted a memorial at which Jonas delivered an academic lecture. In this lecture, Jonas recounted that it was in a New Testament seminar taken under Bultmann that the intellectual environment of primitive Christianity was first opened up to him. It was in this seminar that Jonas learned of Gnostic Christianity, and it was Bultmann who encouraged him to pursue the investigation of this topic for his dissertation, published in 1930. Jonas's study of Gnosticism went on for many years, and in 1958,

having narrowed the scope of his two previous volumes on Gnosticism published in Germany in 1934 and 1954, he finalized his research and published it in English under the title *The Gnostic Religion: The Message of the Alien God and the Beginnings of Christianity*.

Life's Work

The two disciplines of philosophy and theology were formative with respect to the life work of Jonas. Jonas had studied at the University for the Science of Judaism in Berlin between 1921 and 1924, and Jewish theology would have an enduring importance for him. In 1933, having completed his doctoral work, Jonas fled Germany to London as a result of Hitler's Law for the Reconstitution of the German Civil Service, which prohibited Jews from placement in universities. He vowed that he would not return to Germany except as a soldier in a conquering army.

In 1935, Jonas emigrated to Jerusalem and, at the onset of World War II, enlisted in the British Army. He volunteered for combat duty and served for five years in Italy and Germany. It was not until the war's end that Jonas discovered that his mother had been executed at the concentration camp in Auschwitz. Jonas later wrote an essay on the problem of evil in connection with the Holocaust, "The Concept of God after Auschwitz" (1968). It was during World War II that Jonas entered what he would later call the "second stage of his theoretical life." In part, the transition resulted from his separation from his books and the tools of research while in combat; partly it was a consequence of being confronted by "the apocalyptic state of things" and "the proximity of death." He could not do formal research, but he was not prevented, as he put it, from "thinking." He thought about "the very foundations of our being" and "the principles by which we guide our thinking on them." While in Jerusalem before the war, he had spent his days absorbed with the second volume of his classic work on Gnosticism. The war, and a change in Jonas's intellectual priorities postponed publication of the second volume until 1954. Jonas married Elinore Weiner in 1943 and again enlisted in the military in 1948, this time on the side of the Israelis in their effort to gain independence.

By his own account, the years spent in war had a profound effect on his philosophical-theological outlook. Through the atrocities of war, he came to be more conscious of human mortality and the fundamental similarities that human beings have with other organisms: biological life, death, hunger, and pain, and, most important, purposiveness. The existential characteristics of a human being must be seen to include these value-laden, "somatic" elements. This rethinking of philosophy established his philosophical agenda for the next two decades. On the whole, his task during this period could be characterized as a revival of both nature philosophy, an ancient but abandoned Western tradition, and ethical objectivism.

In 1949, Jonas and his family left Israel under the firm conviction that peace would be long in coming between Arabs and Jews and his philosophical studies and academic goals would be hampered as a result. They arrived in Montreal, Canada, where he was the recipient of a fellowship. In 1951, he secured a position as an assistant professor of philosophy at Carleton University, Ottawa. Jonas went to the United States in 1955 and obtained a position as professor of philosophy at the New School for Social Research in New York.

Jonas gained recognition in the United States in 1964 when he was asked to give the inaugural lecture at an international gathering of scholars honoring Heidegger at Drew University. The theme of the gathering was the relevance of Heidegger's philosophy for contemporary Protestant theology. Heidegger was scheduled to give the opening lecture but withdrew because of his health. In his place, Jonas took the podium and used the opportunity to confront Heidegger's Nazi affiliations and ideology. On this occasion, Jonas criticized Heidegger's notion that "fate" plays an integral part in Christian faith. Jonas proclaimed that such a doctrine militates against the responsibility to choose and offers no hope for a norm that would inform the ethical dilemma posed by the "call of German destiny" under the führer, Adolf Hitler. When Jonas had completed his lecture, he was received with a standing ovation by the very people who had come to honor Heidegger. Jonas was convinced that from the time of Socrates, philosophy had been shown to be unique among the branches of learning. It alone shaped the conduct as well as the thinking of its disciples with respect to the pursuit of the good. Many years later, Jonas wrote:

Therefore, when the most profound thinker of my time fell into step with the thundering march of Hitler's brown battalions, it was not merely a bitter personal disappointment for me but in my eyes a debacle for philosophy.

Jonas wrote three important treatises that map his intellectual pilgrimage. Jonas's classic work on Gnosticism and primitive Christianity, *The Gnostic Religion*, examines the basis of metaphysical dualism. Gnosticism, which thrived during the first three centuries of the Christian era, was a philosophical-religious movement that embraced a dualism according to which matter was evil and God was utterly transcendent. The human task was to gain "gnosis," or "knowledge," so that after death the soul would be reunited with God and freed from material, bodily existence.

Jonas's later works aim at countering the ethical nihilism mandated by both Heidegger's existentialism and Gnosticism. Jonas considered existentialism and Gnosticism to be flawed in the same way; both affirmed a dualism between authentic human existence and nature, or the material world. They shared the common tenet that there are no moral laws in the cosmos or in nature to which human beings are responsible. For Gnosticism, it is because the world is positively evil; for existentialism, it is because human beings create values and therefore are not themselves subject to any moral law. According to Heidegger, only human beings have purposes and therefore "exist." Nature, which includes nonhuman living organisms, takes on meaning only within this world of humanity. Jonas believed that since the time of French philosopher René Descartes, philosophy had embraced one side of a dualism, the side of mind, or consciousness. The metaphysical dualism of Gnosticism and Christianity lives on in the thought of Descartes, phenomenology, and existentialism.

Jonas relies on some of Heidegger's own tenets to remap the "existential" so as to include all organisms. In *The Phenomenon of Life: Toward a Philosophical Biology*, Jonas contends that purposive existence is not unique to human beings; it is evident in all living things. All living nature is purposive, free, and therefore value-laden. In a paper first presented to the Royal Palace Foundation in Amsterdam on March 19, 1991, and published in *Mortality and Morality: The Search for the Good After Auschwitz* under the title "The Burden and Blessing of Mortality," Jonas declares, "Life says 'yes' to itself. By clinging to itself it declares that it values itself." All living organisms, according to Jonas, exhibit concern for their own existence as evidenced by the evolution of the survival techniques that they employ. This value that is to be associated with life is derived from the possibility of death, and this only in organic beings.

The challenge posed by Gnosticism and Heidegger's existentialism apparently could be countered only by an extensive investigation into the domain of metaphysics, and it is in this conceptual region that Jonas distinguishes himself. At a conference in Bonn, "Industrial Society and an Ethics for the Future," in October, 1985, Jonas delivered a lecture that was later revised and published under the title "Toward an Ontological Grounding of an Ethics for the Future" (1996). The lecture and the article summarize the important themes of his earlier, major monograph, *The Imperative of Responsibility: In Search of an Ethics*

for the Technological Age. His concern is to preempt the nihilist retort that there is nothing in the notion that nature makes value decisions or that nature has intrinsic value that makes human beings bound by duty to such value. Jonas maintains that "purpose as such" is that in nature that is "good in itself," and as the essence of life, it presents to the human will a summons to ethical responsibility for the preservation of life in its highest evolutionary form, human life. The argument in this work also supports an ethical obligation to all "being," including nonhuman living nature. Although Jonas considers theology to be of great value, he denies that the existence of a creator God is necessary as a foundation for ethics. The imperative of responsibility is grounded in nature itself. Jonas asserts, however, that faith is not necessarily contrary to reason, and faith in the God of Judaism is compatible with Jonas's own ethical and metaphysical views.

Jonas's 1996 publication *Mortality and Morality* brings together the full range of his philosophical and theological pursuits in the form of a compilation of his most important essays, five of which were translated into English for the first time.

An important element of Jonas's general ontology that unifies the external and internal worlds—those of matter and subjective purpose—into a "psychophysical totality of reality" is the disruptive place that the emergence of human thought has in the evolution of ecological systems. The relatively late arrival of humankind in the evolutionary continuum has resulted in an impairment of the equilibrium of nature. Jonas notes that philosophy has traditionally fixated on human actions in social contexts but has not given adequate attention to the human being as an acting and, potentially, disruptive element in nature. The writings of Jonas go some distance in providing a philosophy of nature that sets forth principles for environmental ethics.

Influence

Jonas attempts to explicate a conceptual connection between metaphysics and ethics; a connection and purpose that has, in modern philosophy, been largely disavowed. The work of Jonas regarding method represents a return to speculative philosophy, which aims toward a sort of comprehensive explanation of the cosmos and the place of humanity in it. At the same time, he integrates scientific principles and disciplines such as evolution and biology into his analysis, resulting in a contemporary and informed philosophy of nature. His early and late works reveal a place in his thinking for God, as understood from a vantage point of liberal Judaism, but he does not believe that the notion of a creator God is fundamentally necessary to the grounding of ethics. Jonas contends that the practice of philosophy should make its practitioners moral, as it did with Socrates. Jonas's life and his work are a tribute to that ancient notion.

Darryl L. Henry

Mortality and Morality

A Search for the Good After Auschwitz

Type of philosophy: Ethics, metaphysics
First published: 1996
Principal ideas advanced:

◇ Organic life is distinguished from inanimate nature by the activity of metabolism.

◇ Metabolism involves the organism's capacity and freedom to use inanimate matter for its own survival purposes.

◇ Value enters the universe as a result of the possibility of mortality and the importance that the organism places on its own survival.

◇ The perception, on the part of human beings, that the continuance of their own metabolic existence is valuable is, at the same time, a perception of obligation to promote that value by preserving life.

◇ There is a logical bridge between what *is*, understood as a metabolic struggle to preserve life, and what *ought to be*, understood as a duty to preserve life.

◇ Human beings are biological organisms with the unique capacity to form representative ideas including the idea of the good that makes possible the extension of moral obligation beyond that of mere preservation of life, to the preservation of a quality of life.

◇ The God of Judaism exists, but belief in God is not necessary for a grounding of ethics.

Hans Jonas tackles one of the most troublesome problems in all of philosophy: establishing an objective ground for ethics. He contends that ethics is based on value that is contained in nature itself. Jonas draws on a sparse number of what he believes to be fertile truths, which serve as the seed and ground of most, if not all, of what he writes in the essays collected in *Mortality and Morality*. These truths are that philosophy has lapsed into a study of one part of reality, the study of mind, at the expense of the other part, the philosophy of nature. German idealism in the forms of neo-Kantianism, phenomenology, and existentialism neglects the organic basis of mind and therefore distorts what it means to be a human being. This idealism descends from French philosopher René Descartes's metaphysical dualism, which took the form of a bifurcation of the mental and the material. According to Jonas, the living organism with its indissoluble inwardness and outwardness is the undeniable evidence against dualism, and it serves as the starting point for the development of a uniform theory of being.

Evolution and Freedom

In the first essay of *Mortality and Morality*, "Evolution and Freedom: On the Continuity Among Life-Forms," Jonas asserts that the Western philosophical tradition has made the fundamental mistake of ascribing certain features exclusively to humanity, although, according to Jonas, these features are also characteristic of nonhuman organisms. Organic life is a continuum that includes humanity and is identified by key capabilities and functions including metabolism, motility, appetite, feeling, perception, imagination, art, and thinking. There is, however, an ascending order to organic existence according to the knowledge and power of an organism or its perception and action. Jonas maintains that not all organisms in this ascending order have "mind" or "will," but all organisms do possess "freedom" and that this is the property that distinguishes organic life as such.

"Freedom," in Jonas's vernacular, has an unusual meaning. It is to be contrasted with lifeless matter and is to be associated with metabolism, the fundamental characteristic of all living organisms. Jonas asserts that things that have metabolic processes display freedom. The freedom of the most primitive organisms is the freedom to transcend matter and to use it. In its most developed form, in humans, freedom is the freedom to form ideas and to choose ways of life. This, he admits, runs counter to the usual understanding of freedom as something unique to the mind and will of human beings. Jonas, however, is concerned with giving an account of humanity that, according to principles of evolutionary biology, positions humans in nature and as a part of nature. One barrier to an understanding of Jonas's philosophy can perhaps be overcome if one keeps in mind that human beings can be differentiated from other life-forms on the basis of functions and capabilities, but human beings are not in "metaphysical isolation" from other life-forms. Jonas contends that it is the nature of living organisms, humans in particular, to have an interest in preserving their own existence and that this interest is evidenced in the striving to sustain metabolism.

Jonas makes a demarcation between the purely physical universe and organic life: The former functions according to immutable law; the latter in accordance with freedom. Sometime during the evolutionary process, organic life separated from mere matter. Matter, of course, is indispensable for organic life, but through metabolism—the exchange of matter with the environment—the material parts of the organism are only temporary contents. There is, in other words, no persisting material substratum in any living organism. This suggests the organism's transcendence of material existence in the direction of freedom. Metabolism is the basis for all sophisticated capabilities and functions that are characteristic of *animal* life, including feeling, perception, and motility, but even in the most primitive organisms, metabolism represents a departure from material necessity. Jonas suggests that what is unique to living things is their ability to alter their own matter for the purpose of their own preservation. This is the theoretical payout of the philosophically indigent notion of metabolism, and it seems to be at the heart of Jonas's notion of freedom and responsibility. From these humble beginnings, Jonas erects a philosophical edifice that builds a bridge from the meaning of life to the duty to preserve it, but as a preliminary

to this all-important task, he must first show the basis for a distinction between the "subject" that carries the responsibility and the "object" to which it is responsible.

Jonas contends that another way of looking at freedom is in terms of "selfhood." He observes that the altering of matter by an organism puts matter at the disposal of an organism and that the continued striving of the organism in its self-preservation can be described as "self-concern." Jonas is sensitive to the charge of anthropomorphizing, but he has stipulated exactly what is meant by self-concern; it involves the acquisition and use of matter for the continued existence of the organism. This self-concern carries with it the notion of selfhood and subjectivity.

Humans, Other Animals, and Mortality

In "Tool, Image, and Grave: On What Is Beyond the Animal in Man," Jonas compares and contrasts humans and other animals. The distinguishing feature of humans is the ability to form representative ideas, which Jonas views as a mark of greater freedom and responsibility. He notes that humans have a surplus of capacities and capabilities that have nothing to do with biology and survival. Humans have, for example, self-generated purposes that afford luxuries, not merely necessities. Jonas evaluates the significance of human artifacts that, he thinks, point decisively to particular and unique human qualities. A tool is produced as a result of an *idea* in the human imagination that as an expression of freedom is imposed on matter. This idea, or form, in the imagination is not the result of any biological function of the organism as is the case with a spider and its web, for example. Image making, such as that which produced early rock drawings, is biologically useless. The interest that humans have in such a nonpractical exercise is associated with the freely created *idea* from which the image is derived. The image is a representation of a general sort, and it is understood by its creator to be such. Jonas contends that other animals do not have the aptitude to differentiate, in this way, between perceptions and representations. Lastly, on the subject of the "grave," he notes that commemoration of the dead through burial is associated with beliefs pertaining to things invisible and immaterial. The grave signifies the unique human capacity to reflect on one's own origin and destiny and to have a concept of self. The human endowment of being able to form ideas that are representations and not mere perceptions is the source of the human ability to be concerned with what *ought to be*, not merely with what *is*.

In "The Burden and Blessing of Mortality," Jonas observes that all life is mortal. The real threat of annihilation, or death, is with every organism from the beginning. The organism, however, clings to life by performing its metabolic processes, and, in so doing, attributes value to itself. In fact, it is only because of the possibility of life's cessation that there can be this "clinging" and this "value." Life, then, is the source of all value.

Preserving Human Life

In "Toward an Ontological Grounding of an Ethics for the Future," Jonas attempts to show that the very nature of humanity entails a responsibility to preserve humanity. He tries to do what, throughout much of the history of philosophy, has been considered improper: to show that facts about reality imply ethical duties. Jonas made the case in "Tool, Image, and Grave" that the eidetic aptitude in human beings is a distinguishing mark. This aptitude, the capacity to represent things by general ideas, makes possible the idea of self and what a human "self" *ought* to be.

The key philosophical move made by Jonas, in grounding ethics in nature, is the affirmation that the value every organism places on its own existence—as evidenced by a clinging, against all obstacles, to metabolic life—is the source of all value in the universe. The very perception, or apprehension, of value is the perception of something that should be. This involves a perception of a responsibility to preserve value and, most important, human life, because it is this value that humans perceive firsthand in their own struggle to survive. By means of the ability to form representative ideas, humans form notions of what humanity should be and, from this, a sense of moral obligation. In the remainder of the essay, Jonas examines the threat that modern technology poses to life. Jonas sets a course in the direction of establishing a theory of environmental ethics.

Religion

The remaining essays in *Mortality and Morality* are devoted to theological topics. As indicated by the title of part 2, "A Luxury of Reason: Theological Speculations After Auschwitz," Jonas views theology as a "luxury" of reason rather than as a necessity. As was demonstrated in part 1, ethics is grounded in nature, not in the existence of God. Jonas, however, is interested in theology and has much to say on the subject. For example, Jonas asserts that immortality is not an object of knowledge and therefore cannot be proven or disproven. Jonas examines various views of the afterlife and speculates that what are immortal are human deeds, not human souls. Human deeds live on in the mind of God and form God's developing image. Throughout part 2, Jonas attempts to articulate biblical concepts in terms that are compatible with modern thought. His presupposition is that faith must be compatible with reason.

Jonas does not subscribe to many of the orthodox teachings of Judaism, and he attempts to demythologize the unnatural and irrational elements in the religious tradition. For example, he denies that God is all-powerful and cites the Holocaust as proof of it. Either God is not complete in love or God is not complete in power, and it is preferable to believe the latter. In addition, he denies divine interventions in nature. Miracles did not and do not happen, but this does not impinge on faith; although, in the case of Christianity and the resurrection and ascension of Christ, the denial of miracles is far more problematic than in Judaism.

It remains to be seen how the thought of Jonas will influence ethical theory and metaphysics. His treatment of God, ethics, and metaphysics reveals a bold attempt to circumscribe the entire universe. This classical, speculative approach to philosophy is reminiscent of the Greek philosophers Plato and Aristotle. It is not, however, an approach that has been highly regarded among philosophers in the twentieth century. What distinguishes Jonas, however, is the assimilation of certain accepted principles of modern thought into his ethical theory, especially those coming out of the biological sciences. The intriguing and innovative rendering of the otherwise plain notion of metabolism, for example, together with the philosophical freight that Jonas makes it carry, is reason enough to think that his writings could catch the attention of a wide audience. In the latter part of the twentieth century, his writings inspired a number of European environmentalists, who found in his works a rigorous, philosophical justification for their causes.

Darryl L. Henry

Additional Reading

Lubarsky, Sandra B., and David Ray Griffin, eds. *Jewish Theology and Process Thought*. Albany: State University of New York Press, 1996. A compilation of essays in honor of Hans Jonas, including one essay by Jonas. An essay by John B. Cobb notes the parallels between Jonas's doctrine of God and process theology, particularly with respect to God's manner of relation to the world.

Spicker, Stuart F., ed. *Organism, Medicine, and Metaphysics: Essays in Honor of Hans Jonas on His Seventy-fifth Birthday, May 10, 1978*. Boston: D. Reidel, 1978. Includes essays by Charles Hartshorne and Strachan Donnelley that contrast Jonas's view of organisms with that of Alfred North Whitehead.

Wellmer, Albrecht. *Endgames: The Irreconcilable Nature of Modernity*. Translated by David Midgley. Cambridge, Mass.: MIT Press, 1998. A look at some of Jonas's fundamental ideas in the context of German social thought.

Darryl L. Henry

Carl Jung

Jung, the founder of analytic psychology, is probably best known for his descriptions of the orientations of the personality, "extroversion" and "introversion." His theories of universal symbolic representations have had a far-reaching impact on such diverse disciplines as art, literature, filmmaking, religion, anthropology, and history.

Principal philosophical works: *Zur Psychologie und Pathologie sogenannter occulter Phänomene*, 1902; *Über die Psychologie der Dementia praecox: Ein Versuch*, 1907 (*The Psychology of Dementia Praecox*, 1909); *Wandlungen und Symbole der Libido*, 1912, rev. ed. *Symbole der Wandlung*, 1952 (*The Psychology of the Unconscious*, 1915; rev. ed. *Symbols of Transformation*, 1967); *Die Psychologie der unbewussten Prozesse*, 1917 (*The Psychology of the Unconscious Processes*, 1917); *Psychologische Typen*, 1921 (*Psychological Types*, 1923); *Modern Man in Search of a Soul*, 1933; *Analytical Psychology: Its Theory and Practice*, 1935; *Psychology and Religion*, 1938; *Psychologie und Alchemie*, 1944 (*Psychology and Alchemy*, 1953); *Aion: Untersuchungen zur Symbolgeschichte*, 1951; *Synchronizität als ein Prinzip akausaler Zusammenhange*, 1952 (*Synchronicity: An Acausal Connecting Principle*, 1955); *Antwort auf Hiob*, 1952 (*Answer to Job*, 1954); *Mysterium Coniunctionis*, 1955; *Erinnerungen, Träume, Gedanken*, 1962 (with Aniela Jaffé; *Memories, Dreams, Reflections*, 1963); *Man and His Symbols*, 1964; *Briefe*, 1972-1973 (*Letters*, 1973); *The Freud/Jung Letters*, 1974.

Born: July 26, 1875; Kesswil, Switzerland
Died: June 6, 1961; Küsnacht, Switzerland

Early Life

Carl Gustav Jung was descended from a long line of physicians and theologians. His father, Johann Paul Achilles Jung, was a pastor of the Swiss Reformed Church, as were eight of his uncles. His mother, Emilie Preiswerk, suffered from a nervous disorder that often made her remote and uncommunicative; his father was reportedly irritable and argumentative. Because his parents were of little comfort or support to him as a child, and because his sister, Johanna Gertrud, was born nine years after he was, Jung spent much of his childhood alone. Jung's adolescence was a time of confusion and probing, especially about religious matters. His religious conflicts, however, were eventually supplanted by other intellectual interests. Before concentrating on the study of medicine at the University of Basel in 1895, he explored biology, archaeology, philosophy, mythology, and mysticism, subjects that laid the foundation for the wide-ranging inquiries he undertook throughout his life.

After receiving his degree in medicine, Jung decided to specialize in psychiatry. Consequently, in 1900 he went to the Burghölzli, the mental hospital and university psychiatry clinic in Zurich, where he studied under the famous psychiatrist Eugen Bleuler. While working at the Burghölzli, Jung published his first papers on clinical topics, as well as several papers on his first experimental project: the use of word-association tests (free association). This project later gained for him worldwide recognition. Jung concluded that the word-association process could uncover groups of emotionally charged ideas that often generated morbid symptoms. The test evaluated the patient's delay time between introduction of the stimulus and the response, the appropriateness of the response word, and the patient's behavior. A significant deviation from normal denoted the presence of unconscious affect-laden (emotion-laden) ideas. Jung coined the term "complex" to describe this combination of the idea with the strong emotion it aroused.

In 1906, Jung published a study on dementia praecox that was to influence Bleuler when the latter designated the term "schizophrenia" for

Carl Jung. *(Library of Congress)*

the illness five years later. In this work, Jung hypothesized that a complex produced a toxin that impaired mental functioning and caused the contents of the complex to be released into consciousness. Thus, the delusional ideas, hallucinatory experiences, and affective changes associated with the psychosis were to be viewed as more or less distorted manifestations of the originally repressed complex. Jung, in essence, was venturing the first psychosomatic theory of schizophrenia; although he subsequently abandoned the toxin hypothesis in favor of disturbed neurochemical processes, he never relinquished his belief in the primacy of psychogenic factors in the origin of schizophrenia.

Life's Work

By the time that Jung first met Sigmund Freud in Vienna (1907), he was well acquainted with

Freud's writings. As a result of their meeting, the two men formed a close association which lasted until 1912. In the early years of their collaboration, Jung defended Freudian theories and Freud responded to this support with enthusiasm and encouragement.

In 1910, Jung left his position at the Burghölzli to focus on his growing private practice. It was during this time that he began his investigations into myths, legends, and fairy tales. His first writings on this subject, published in 1911, manifested both an area of interest that was to be sustained for the rest of his life and a declaration of independence from Freud in their criticism of the latter's classification of instincts as either self-preservative or sexual. Although Jung's objections to conceiving the libido in primarily sexual terms were already apparent at this early stage, the significance of these objections became clear only much later, in his studies of the individuation process.

It was not only intellectual disagreements, however, that led to the rupture between Freud and Jung. Jung objected to Freud's dogmatic attitude toward psychoanalysis—his treating its tenets as articles of faith, immune from attack. This attitude diminished Jung's respect for Freud (although Jung's writings reveal that he, too, was prone to dogmatic assertions). Thus, while Freud worked to establish causal links extending back to childhood and, in so doing, posited a mechanistic account of human behavior, Jung attempted to place human beings in a historical context that gave their lives meaning and dignity, which ultimately implied a place in a purposeful universe. In their later writings, both men became increasingly concerned with social questions and expressed their ideas in more metaphysical terms. Hence Freud weighed the life instinct against the death wish, and Jung discussed the split in the individual between the ego and the shadow (the latter being the animal side of the psyche).

After breaking with Freud, Jung underwent a prolonged period of inner turmoil and uncertainty about his theories. Like Freud, he used self-analysis (dream interpretations, specifically) to resolve his emotional crisis. Yet this was also a time of creativity and growth, leading to Jung's unique approach to personality theory. Both a milestone in Jung's career and the signal of his break with Freudian psychology, *The Psychology of the Unconscious* was the book in which his own point of view began to take definite shape. In this work, Jung interprets the thought processes of the schizophrenic in terms of mythological and religious symbolism.

The theme that unifies most of Jung's subsequent writings is individuation, a process that he viewed as taking place in certain gifted individuals in mid-life. While he believed that Freud and Alfred Adler had many valuable insights into the problems encountered during the maturation process, he considered their investigations limited. Jung's particular concern was with those people who had achieved separation from their parents, an adult sexual identity, and independence through work, but who nevertheless underwent a crisis in mid-life.

Jung viewed individuation as a process directed toward the achievement of psychic wholeness or integration. In characterizing this developmental journey, he used illustrations from alchemy, mythology, literature, and Western and Eastern religions, as well as from his own clinical investigations. Particular signposts on the journey are provided by the archetypal (universal) images and symbols that are experienced, often with great emotion, in dreams and "visions," and that, in addition to connecting the individual with the rest of humankind, signify his or her unique destiny. In his writings on the "collective unconscious" and the archetypal images that are its manifestation, Jung maintained that cultural differences cannot wholly account for the distribution of mythological themes in dreams and visions. He writes of many patients who, while completely unsophisticated in such matters, describe dreams that exhibit striking parallels with myths from many different cultures.

It has been pointed out, however, that there appears to be a basic ambiguity in Jung's various descriptions of the collective unconscious. At times, he seems to regard the predisposition to experience certain images as comprehensible in terms of some genetic model. At other times, he

emphasizes the numinous quality of these experiences, maintaining that archetypes demonstrate communion with some divine or world consciousness.

The latter part of Jung's life was relatively uneventful. He lived in Zurich, where he pursued private practice, studied, and wrote. Unfortunately, he left no detailed accounts of his clinical activities, although throughout his works there are scattered anecdotes from his professional experience as a psychotherapist. His great interest in religious questions is often treated as an embarrassment by practicing psychotherapists, and the problems with which he struggled are viewed as esoteric. Nevertheless, his popularity as a thinker derives from precisely this subject matter and from his belief that life is a meaningful journey. He studied Eastern religions and philosophy but saw himself as inescapably belonging to the Judeo-Christian tradition, although he was in no sense an orthodox believer. In a late work, *Answer to Job*, he pictures Job appealing to God against God and concludes that any split in the moral nature of humanity must be referred back to a split in the Godhead. The book is often obscure, but Jung asserts that in contemplating the future, he became more inclined to view the division in humankind as an expression of divine conflict.

In his memoirs, written shortly before his death, Jung appears more detached and agnostic and denies having any definite convictions. He concludes the book with a statement about his own feelings of uncertainty, maintaining that the more uncertain he felt about himself the more he felt a kinship with all things. It seemed to him as though the alienation that separated him from the world was transferred to his own inner world and revealed an "unexpected unfamiliarity" with himself.

Influence

Jung's effect on therapeutic practice has been relatively minimal. He has been ardently attacked on a number of grounds, especially by Freudian analysts. They claim that archetypes are metaphysical constructs whose existence cannot be proved, and that the idea of the collective unconscious violates accepted principles of psychology and evolution. He is also criticized for his failure to offer any coherent model of personality development and for resurrecting an outdated concept of the unconscious. Others simply dismiss him as a mystic or ignore his work because he does not offer experimental evidence for his observations.

Whatever the opinion about his theories, however, Jung's impact on the field of modern psychology has been extensive; his theories widened the scope of thinking about the human mind. For example, the word-association test has become a standard instrument of clinical psychology; a number of rating scales have been devised for testing the introversion-extroversion dimension of personality; his concept of individuation has been incorporated into some of the most renowned theories of personality development; and finally, the comparative studies of mythology, religion, and the occult that he undertook in his search for archetypes have shed new light on the universal aspects and dynamics of human experience and have influenced psychological thinking about humans as symbol-using beings.

Genevieve Slomski

Memories, Dreams, Reflections

Type of philosophy: Epistemology, philosophical psychology
First published: Erinnerungen, Träume, Gedanken, 1962 (English translation, 1963)
Principal ideas advanced:
◇ Human psychic life is made up of conscious and unconscious elements. In order to be whole, people must become more aware of the language of the unconscious and the forms in which it expresses itself.
◇ Dreams and visions are messengers of the unconscious; properly interpreted, they can lead to conscious understanding of the wholeness of psychic life.
◇ Western people have much to learn about the psyche from non-European and "primitive" mythologies and cultures.
◇ If it is to adapt to the needs of modern life, Christianity must develop its doctrine to accommodate the idea of the coexistence of opposites within God.

For many years, Carl Jung resisted the idea of writing an autobiography. However, in 1957, when he was eighty-two years old, he agreed to furnish material for such a work to his assistant, Aniela Jaffé. Jung soon became involved in the task himself, and most of the material in the book comes directly from his own hand. It is not an autobiography in the usual sense, because it does not present a chronological account of the outer events of his life. Biographical details emerge only peripherally and are secondary to Jung's main purpose, which is to set forth insights into his inner mental processes and intellectual development. What results is a series of snapshots that shed light on how Jungian psychology, one of the most important achievements of the twentieth century, came into being.

Memories of Early Years
After a prologue in which Jung explains that the only significant events in his life were those in which the unconscious elements within him, the eternal dimension of human life, erupted into the transitory world of the conscious personality, Jung devotes his first three chapters to memories of his childhood, his schooldays, and his years at the university.

Jung's visionary capacity was apparent even when he was a young child. He recounts the earliest dream he could remember, which occurred when he was between three and four years old. In the dream, he saw a hole in the ground and then descended a stone stairway, passed through a doorway, and came to a golden throne. Standing on the throne was what he first thought was a huge tree trunk. Then he realized that it resembled human flesh. He was terrified, and when he heard the voice of his mother saying that the thing was the "man-eater," he became even more alarmed.

This dream haunted Jung for years; only decades later did he realize that what he had seen was a ritual phallus. He interpreted this as a vision of a subterranean god who was a counterpart of the Jesus that his parents so often mentioned. As a child, he had therefore been initiated into the realm of darkness, the underground world that was mysteriously linked with the world above. His intellectual development had begun.

Another milestone came when Jung was nine. For reasons unknown to him at the time, he carved a two-inch mannequin, complete with top hat and boots, out of a school ruler. He placed the mannequin in his pencil case along with a smooth oblong stone, which he painted to look as though it was divided into an upper and lower half. He hid the pencil case where no one could find it. As a result of these and other ritual actions he performed in connection with his secret possession, he felt safe. Whenever a difficult situation arose he would think of the contents of the case and be calmed. The mannequin episode lasted for about a year. Jung then forgot about it until the age of thirty-five, when he came across in his studies images of "soul-stones" in mythology, representing the life-force, and depictions of the small gods of the ancient world, such as the one that stands on the monuments of Asklepios. He then realized the connection between his childhood mannequin and stone and these archaic mythological representations, and he concluded that archaic elements must enter the individual psyche without any direct transmission. (His father's library contained none of the mythological information.) This realization became the basis of Jung's theory of the archetypes of the collective unconscious.

As a child and youth, the idea of God interested Jung, but he felt ambivalent about the figure of Jesus. His curiosity could find no satisfaction in the dry Christianity of his father, a parson. In their occasional awkward discussions about the matter, his father would insist that Jung must simply believe; the young Jung would reply that he wished to experience and to know directly, not merely accept a dogma. When he began exploring his father's library, he grew frustrated because he could find no theological works that explained the dark aspects of God.

It was at about this time that Jung began to sense two dimensions of his own existence: the individual self, limited to his own ego, with its hopes, fears, and desires, and a more cosmic, timeless "true" self that he could discover in solitude and that brought him peace. He called these "number one" and "number two" personalities, and later he realized that every human being possesses this double existence, although relatively few are conscious of it. In Jung's own life, it was the call of the "number two" personality that was to prove dominant.

Spiritualism and Psychiatry

Studying medicine at the University of Basel, Switzerland, Jung became interested in psychic or spiritualistic phenomena—events for which there appeared to be no rational explanation. When he expanded his studies to psychiatry, he knew that he had found his vocation: a discipline in which his interest in objective and subjective nature might be combined. In 1900, Jung accepted a position in a mental health clinic in Zurich. Five years later, he became lecturer in psychiatry at the University of Zurich and senior physician at the psychiatry clinic.

Jung's reflections on his thirteen years in Zurich form the substance of chapter 4. His main interest lay not in making diagnoses and compiling lists of symptoms but in the psychology of his patients, what actually was taking place in their minds. He came to understand that each patient was an individual with a unique story that could, if understood by the therapist, be used as an aid in healing. It was his interest in this area that drew Jung to the work of Sigmund Freud, and his relations with Freud form the subject of chapter 5. Although Jung found that Freud's techniques of dream analysis and interpretation were useful, he disagreed with Freud on one vital issue: Jung did not regard all neuroses as caused by sexual repression or sexual trauma. Eventually this led to his break with Freud. He believed Freud was obsessed with the sexual theory and had elevated it to the status of a dogma. In addition, Freud did not accept the reality of the psychic phenomena that had long interested Jung, nor did he accept the notion of an impersonal substratum of the psyche that Jung, stimulated by a series of powerful dreams, was beginning to formulate.

Break with Freud

In chapter 6, "Confrontation with the Unconscious," Jung describes a period of great turbulence that followed his break with Freud. During this time he was driven to experiment with the images that welled up in his mind from the unconscious, in dream and vision. As the incessant stream of images came to him over a period of years, he felt extreme tension, as if he were contemplating an alien, incomprehensible world. Inner and outer worlds seemed irreconcilable to him, and he encountered for the first time the voice he gradually recognized as belonging to his anima, the feminine element within his psyche. He abandoned his academic career and gave himself over wholly to what he called the service of the psyche, because he felt that it was of vital importance not merely to him personally but to humanity as a whole.

Mandalas

In 1918, Jung entered a more peaceful phase of his psychic studies, when he discovered the form of the mandala, drew many mandalas himself, and interpreted them as an expression of the self, of the psyche's thrust toward wholeness. In reflection, he states that those six intense years, from 1912 to 1918, were the most important of his creative life; all his later work flowed out from the material he accumulated during that period.

In the following chapter, Jung presents a brief summary of the genesis of many of his works and explains why he was drawn to the study of gnosticism and alchemy. He regarded the latter, with its strange symbolism, as a historical counterpart of his own development of the psychology of the unconscious.

Lessons from World Cultures

After a chapter in which Jung describes how he built his own house in Bollingen, near Zurich, to correspond to the archetypal principles that operated in his own psyche, he goes on to discuss his travels in non-European cultures: in North Africa; among the Pueblo Indians in New Mexico; in Kenya, Uganda, and India; and trips to Ravenna and Rome. What emerges from these accounts is Jung's awareness of what European people have lost and what they have inflicted, or are poised to inflict, on non-European cultures. The Europeans think that they have overcome or left behind the emotional, instinctive life that they observe in the Arab or the African, but they have paid a high price for doing so. Europeans have will and rationality, but they no longer possess the intense vitality of life that is a characteristic of nonwhite cultures. Jung found that he identified with these foreign cultures more than he had anticipated, largely because they expressed elements of life that had been blocked from European consciousness.

In late chapters, Jung discusses the intense visions that accompanied his recuperation from a heart attack in 1944 and his reflections on the possibility of life after death. On the latter issue, he offers no definitive view but suggests that, as long as we confine ourselves to the rational intellect, we will remain ignorant of how far life might extend. He points out that the unconscious, through dreams, can send hints of things that otherwise we would not know and that the psyche is not bound by space and time. On the evidence of his own dreams, he suggests the probability that something of the psyche continues after physical death, but whether it is conscious of itself remains an unanswered question.

The Importance of Myth

In the final chapter, Jung offers his views about the world situation. He was writing at the height of the Cold War, in which the world was divided into two power blocs, one materialistic and atheistic, the other professing a religion, Christianity, that no longer had any vitality. Jung urges that the Christian myth be allowed to continue to grow and adapt to changes in consciousness if it is once more to become a living faith. In particular, Christianity must go beyond the dualism that has always lain just beneath its monotheistic façade and find a way to represent God as a synthesis of opposite forces. Because this is the way the human psyche is structured, it must also be reflected in the macrocosmic myth by which humanity lives. Then the doctrine of the Incarnation could be understood as the human confrontation with the opposites, and the synthesis of them in the wholeness of the self could be understood as the personality experienced in its full depth and range, conscious and unconscious. Such a development in Christianity would once more fit humankind into the universe and restore to life the meaning it has lost.

Assessment and Impact

Jung himself was ambivalent about *Memories, Dreams, Reflections*. He requested that it not be included in his collected works because he did not regard it as a scientific work, finding it impossible to consider his own life as a scientific problem; he could only tell a story that reflected his own truth. Jung was also apprehensive regarding the reception of his memoir because he had been shaken by the harsh criticism to which another of his late works, *Antwortauf Hiob* (1952; *Answer to Job*, 1954), had been subjected. He therefore asked that the book not be published in his lifetime, a condition he believed would also give him the detachment and calm he needed to reflect on his life.

Despite Jung's misgivings, *Memories, Dreams, Reflections* has proved lastingly popular. From the outset, reviewers were generous in their praise. "To be able to share Jungian emotions is surely an almost necessary capacity of the free mind," wrote Philip Toynbee in *The Observer*, a sentiment echoed by many. Subsequently, along with *Man and His Symbols* (1964), another work intended for the general reader that was supervised by Jung and published posthumously, *Memories* has become the means by which many readers encounter Jung's thought for the first time. It endures as a compelling record of the inner life of one of the most profound minds of the twentieth century.

Bryan Aubrey

Additional Reading

Hall, Calvin S., and Vernon J. Nordby. *A Primer of Jungian Psychology*. New York: New American Library, 1973. A standard (and thorough) introduction to the basic Jungian concepts of the structure, dynamics, and development of the normal personality.

Jacobi, Jolande. *The Psychology of C. G. Jung*. 8th ed. Translated by Ralph Manheim. New Haven, Conn.: Yale University Press, 1973. In this introductory work, consisting of a profile of Jung's major theories, Jacobi broadens the scope of her *Der Weg zur Individuation* (1965; *The Way of Individuation*, 1967) to give an overview of Jung's contributions to the field of analytic psychology.

McLynn, Frank. *Carl Gustav Jung*. New York: St. Martin's Press, 1997. This evenhanded, unbiased biography chronicles Jung's life from birth to death. McLynn not only explains Jung's theories and documents his contributions to psychotherapy but also provides insights into the controversies of Jung's life, from his time as a protégé of Sigmund Freud and the quarrel that left them bitter enemies to his alleged anti-Semitism and womanizing.

Mattoon, Mary Ann. *Jungian Psychology in Perspective*. New York: Free Press, 1981. This book not only offers an insightful overview and brief discussion of the major concepts of Jung's psychology but also attempts to evaluate those concepts. It gathers, for the first time, the results of empirical studies in which Jungian hypotheses have been tested. It also includes a comprehensive bibliography of works on Jungian psychology.

Progoff, Ira. *Jung's Psychology and Its Social Meaning*. New York: Dialogue House Press, 1981. Progoff's study is a comprehensive statement of Jung's psychological theories and an interpretation of their significance for the social sciences. It sets the specialized concepts of Jung's psychology specifically into the context of his whole system of thought and, more generally, considers Jung's work in its historical context.

Singer, June. *Boundaries of the Soul: The Practice of Jung's Psychology*. New York: Anchor, 1994. Recognized as the classic introduction to Jungian psychology, this book explains key elements of Jung's thought. It provides examples of the applications of Jungian psychology both clinically and in the business world (such as the concept of personality types, masculine/feminine relationships) and also incorporates case histories into the understanding of psychotherapy and the inner workings of the human mind.

Genevieve Slomski, updated by Lisa A. Wroble

Immanuel Kant

Kant vindicated the authority of science while preserving the autonomy of morals by means of a new system of thought called critical or transcendental philosophy.

Principal philosophical works: *Der einzig mögliche Beweisgrund zu einer Demonstration des Daseyns Gottes,* 1763 (*The Only Possible Ground for Demonstration of the Existence of God,* 1798); *Träume eines Geistersehers erläutert durch Träume der Metaphysik,* 1766 (*Dreams of a Spirit-Seer, Illustrated by Dreams of Metaphysics,* 1900); *Allgemeine Naturgeschichte und Theorie des Himmels,* 1775 (*The Universal Natural History and Theory of the Heavens,* 1900); *Kritik der reinen Vernunft,* 1781 (*The Critique of Pure Reason,* 1838); *Grundlegung zur Metaphysik der Sitten,* 1785 (*Fundamental Principles of the Metaphysics of Ethics,* 1895; better known as *Foundations of the Metaphysics of Morals,* 1950); *Kritik der praktischen Vernunft,* 1788 (*The Critique of Practical Reason,* 1873); *Kritik der Urteilskraft,* 1790 (*The Critique of Judgment,* 1892); *Die Religion innerhalb der Grenzen der blossen Vernunft,* 1793 (*Religion Within the Boundaries of Pure Reason,* 1838).

Born: April 22, 1724; Königsberg, Prussia (now Kaliningrad, Russia)
Died: February 12, 1804; Königsberg, Prussia

Early Life

Immanuel Kant was the son of a harness maker and the grandson of a Scottish emigrant. As a child, Kant was especially close to his mother, a serene woman who possessed an incisive curiosity about the natural world and a great native intelligence. As one of nine children in a devout Lutheran Pietist family, Kant was reared to respect inner tranquillity, industry, truthfulness, godliness, and order as the highest goods in human life. Kant's mother died when he was thirteen, but he remembered her throughout his life with deep devotion; he told his friends that she had planted and nurtured the first seed of good in him and that her teachings had both opened his mind and provided a healing influence on his life.

Perhaps the most remarkable feature of Kant's life, especially in the light of his profound and pervasive influence on the history of Western thought, is his provinciality. Kant never left the environs of the town of Königsberg in which he was born. He was educated in the local high school, the Collegium Freidericianum, and later at the University of Königsberg. After completing his baccalaureate studies in 1746, he worked as a tutor for a number of local families. He was able to maintain his studies while working as a tutor and so was able to take his master's degree at Königsberg in 1755. That same year, he was appointed to the post of *privatdocent* (private lecturer) in the university. He gave regular courses of lectures, which continued through his 1770 appointment to the professorship of logic and metaphysics. Kant's early lectures and writings covered diverse topics, including physical geography, anthropology, mathematics, and theoretical physics, as well as logic, metaphysics, and moral philosophy.

Life's Work

Kant did his most original and important work quite late in his life. His project of critical philosophy began with *The Critique of Pure Reason,* on which he worked between 1775 and 1781. This work aimed to resolve the disputes of all contemporary and traditional metaphysics by reinterpreting the conditions for human knowledge. Kant viewed the whole history of metaphysical inquiry as a series of failures to establish conclusive truths of first principles concerning God, human freedom, and immortality. In particular, he observed that rational cosmology (that is, metaphysical speculation concerning the nature of the world and its origin) was prone to generate conflicting demonstrations that appeared to be equally valid. Kant named these conflicting arguments "antinomies," and he found them to be in a sense inherent in reason itself. In Kant's view, the preponderance of antinomies in the history of thought cast doubt on the whole enterprise of metaphysics.

Juxtaposed to his preoccupation with the self-contradictory nature and uncertainty of metaphysics were Kant's deep convictions about the value and trustworthiness of Isaac Newton's mathematical science. Mathematics and natural science yielded genuine knowledge. Kant took this as a clue to the sort of reformation that was called for in metaphysics. By inquiring into what made mathematical science possible, Kant hoped to uncover the conditions under which true metaphysical knowledge is possible.

Here is Kant's seminal discovery: What makes knowledge possible in mathematics or physics is humanity's possession of necessarily true propositions that are universally recognized as correct without any reference to experience. An example of such a proposition in mathematics is "The sum of the angles in a triangle is equal to two right angles." The possession of such truths proves that people's cognition of the world is not necessarily a product of experience or the functioning of their senses. From one's senses one obtains raw intuitions, but these intuitions do not constitute authentic cognitions. Raw intuitions become substantive cognitions only when they are processed actively by the mind. The mind organizes and synthesizes the raw intuitions according to innate rules. Without the raw intuitions given by the senses, a person could not be aware of any object, but without the active participation of the mind, that person could form no conception of any object.

Kant reasoned that the certainty of science rested on the purity of its truths—that is, their independence of sensation. Nothing that was given to sense experience from the outside could

be guaranteed even by science, for an additional observation might reveal an alternate sequence that would prove the scientist's first conclusion to be neither always nor inevitably true—neither universal nor necessary. If observational science was to be certain, it must proceed from propositions that were pure of sensation, that were a priori, or "present from the very first."

From this discovery, Kant devolved a new, chastened metaphysics, free of the liabilities of all previous metaphysical inquiry. He had determined that the mind actively supplied certain concepts to intuition or sensation before that raw material was perceived and subsequently cognized, before its being registered as experience at all. Accordingly, it was also clear that humans are not immediately in touch with things as they are in themselves. It is as if one views the world through a particular set of rose-colored glasses,

Immanuel Kant. *(Library of Congress)*

glasses that one can never remove. Thus, according to Kant, previous metaphysicians had been misguided in their aspirations to know about the ultimate nature of things. What one can know, or make certain claims about, is one's experience of things (the appearances of things), not things-in-themselves. Kant said that one must take for granted that "things-in-themselves" are real per se, but that they are not directly known to one. Rather, one knows the appearances of these things, as mediated through one's mind's perceptual and cognitive apparatus. What one has no experience of, including the nature and existence of God and the fate of the soul, one can access only by faith, not speculative knowledge. Thus, the new Kantian metaphysics confined itself to determining the necessary features of all objects of possible experience and to determining the structures of the mind that themselves impart to all objects of possible experience the features that they of necessity have.

This strict limitation on objects of knowledge, this restriction on the valid application of pure human reason, did not end in pure skepticism for Kant. He claimed that he found it necessary to deny knowledge in order to make room for faith. With the elimination of dogmatic metaphysics, he had silenced those who made knowledge claims or arguments on either side of speculative metaphysical issues. It was of no use, for example, to argue for or against God's existence, or to try to prove that people have or do not have free will. Such issues were beyond the ken of human understanding. Objections to morality and religion therefore carried no weight, since they mistook what was beyond the limits of human experience to be legitimate objects of human understanding. This engendered the other substantial phase of the Kantian philosophy, the writings on ethics and religion.

Although Kant set limits on speculative reason, he granted a practical employment of reason that articulated postulates, articles of faith, in matters where discursive knowledge was impossible. Kant saw that humans as a matter of fact made moral commitments and acted as if they had free will. This did not involve an illegitimate metaphysical knowledge claim but rather a postulate born of practical necessity. Kant's *Foundations of the Metaphysics of Morals*

and his *The Critique of Practical Reason* were devoted to working out such rational principles of morality.

Kant's analysis of morality revealed that an agent's goodness was neither some quality of his behavior nor a quality of his desire to cause some particular state of affairs. Goodness involved doing one's duty solely for the sake of so doing. Duty was what conformed with the moral law that Kant called the "categorical imperative," which stipulated that an action was moral if and only if one could will that it should become a universal law. The categorical imperative thus enunciated a purely formal, logical criterion for morality whose hallmark was a demand for complete impartiality.

The next ten years of Kant's life were spent in vigorous productivity. Among the twenty or so books and treatises composed during this time were enormously influential works on aesthetics, *The Critique of Judgment*; on rational theology and ethics, *Religion Within the Boundaries of Pure Reason*; and the famous essay on political theory, *Perpetual Peace*, in which Kant proposed the creation of a federation or league of nations as an antidote to international conflict resolution. Kant's powers began to fail in his last years. He gave up lecturing in 1799, and as he lost his eyesight and intellectual clarity, he slowly faded away. Almost all of Königsberg and many persons from all over Germany attended his funeral.

Influence

Kant said that his project could be codified in the following three questions: What can I know? What ought I to do? For what may I hope?

These questions have occupied every philosopher in the history of Western thought, but Kant's answers to them dramatically altered how they were approached by all of his successors. No one before Kant had regarded human minds as actively operative organisms that drew their material from the senses while shaping this material autonomously, according to their own laws. His discovery that the mind forms its cognitions itself supplanted all previous epistemological theories and quickly became a philosophical commonplace. Since Kant, no one has been able to neglect the transforming and intrusive influence of the observer's cognizing process upon the object of observation. This insight spawned the whole twentieth century analytic movement in philosophy, which emphasizes logic and theory of knowledge and rejects metaphysics. It also gave rise to anti-Kantian theories of human experience offered by Georg Wilhelm Friedrich Hegel, Edmund Husserl, John Dewey, and Alfred North Whitehead.

The influence of Kant's deontological, anti-naturalistic moral views was very strong, especially among later ethical intuitionists. Yet it is a mistake to separate Kant's ethical thought from his overall system. The richest meaning of the moral doctrines emerges when the doctrines are seen as the central focus of his overall systematic approach to philosophy. The whole system yields a doctrine of wisdom concerning the human condition: What humans can know is extremely limited, but this fact need not be regarded as regrettable or disappointing, for it testifies to the wise adaptation of our cognitive faculties as human beings to our practical vocations. If we had a clearer vision of the true natures of things, we would always do what we ought, but then we would not be acting out of a pure motive to do our duty. We would be acting, rather, out of fear or hope of reward. Thus we would lose the opportunity to manifest goodwill, which Kant called the only thing in the world (or even out of this world) which can be taken as good without qualification.

Patricia Cook

The Critique of Pure Reason

Type of philosophy: Epistemology, metaphysics
First published: Kritik der reinen Vernunft, 1781 (English translation, 1838)
Principal ideas advanced:

◊ To establish the possibility of metaphysics as a science, it must be shown that synthetic a priori truths are possible.

◊ Synthetic a priori truths are universally and necessarily true (hence, a priori), but their necessity cannot be derived by analysis of the meanings of such truths (hence, they are synthetic).

◊ The two sources of knowledge are sensibility and understanding.

◊ Space and time are the a priori forms of sensibility (intuition); we are so constituted that we cannot perceive anything at all except by casting it into the forms of space and time.

◊ The a priori conditions of our understanding are called the categories of our understanding. The categories of quantity are unity, plurality, and totality; the categories of quality are reality, negation, and limitation; the categories of relation are substance and accident, cause and effect, and reciprocity between agent and patient; the categories of modality are possibility-impossibility, existence-nonexistence, and necessity-contingency.

◊ The principles of science that serve as presuppositions are synthetic a priori; the possibility of such principles is based upon the use of a priori forms of intuition together with the categories of the understanding.

Immanuel Kant's *The Critique of Pure Reason* is an established classic in the history of epistemology. First published in 1781 and then revised in 1787, it is the fruit of Kant's later years and, as such, clearly reflects the insight and wisdom of a mature mind. It is a work in which the author attempted to conciliate two conflicting theories of knowledge current at his time: British empiricism as represented by John Locke, George Berkeley, and David Hume, and continental rationalism as represented by René Descartes, Gottfried Wilhelm Leibniz, and Christian von Wolff. The latter theory maintained that important truths about the natural and the supernatural worlds are knowable by pure reason alone, independently of perceptual experience, whereas the former held that perceptual experience is the source of all our legitimate concepts and truths of the world. Kant believed that both these doctrines were wrong, and he tried in *The Critique of Pure Reason* to correct the pretensions of each while saving what was sound in each.

Metaphysics as Science
Kant began his inquiry by asking why metaphysics had not kept pace with mathematics and natural science in the discovery of facts about our world. Celestial mechanics had been developed

by German astronomer Johannes Kepler at the beginning of the seventeenth century and terrestrial mechanics by Italian mathematician and physicist Galileo later in the same century, and the two theories were soon united into one by English physicist and mathematician Sir Isaac Newton. These developments represented astonishing progress in natural science, but Kant could detect no parallel progress in metaphysics. Indeed, in metaphysics he saw only interminable squabbling with no apparent method for settling differences. He therefore asked whether it is at all possible for metaphysics to be a science.

Metaphysics can be a science, Kant reasoned, only if there exists a class of truths different in kind either from the straightforward synthetic truths of nature discoverable through sense experience or from the straightforward analytic truths that owe their validity to the fact that the predicate term is contained in the subject term of such judgments—in other words, to the fact that they are true by virtue of the meanings of their terms, true by definition. This distinction is illustrated by the statements "Peaceful resistance is effective" (synthetic) and "Peaceful resisters shun violence" (analytic). This distinction had been recognized by Hume, who regarded it as exhausting the kinds of statements that can be true or false. However, Kant believed that there are statements neither empirical nor analytic in character—synthetic a priori statements. These are statements that are true neither by definition nor because of facts discoverable through sense experience. Rather, they can be seen to be true independently of sense experience; in this sense, they are a priori and necessarily true, because no sense experience can possibly confute them. Kant believed that all mathematical statements are of this sort: for example, "Seven plus five equals twelve." He also believed that synthetic a priori truths constitute the framework of Newtonian science. However, if such truths exist, Kant next asked himself, how are they possible?

A Priori Bases for Human Knowledge

They are possible, he said, if it can be shown that human knowledge is dependent upon certain concepts which are not empirical in origin but have their origin in human understanding. However, even before he revealed the existence of such concepts, Kant attempted to show in the first major division of *The Critique of Pure Reason*, entitled the "Transcendental Esthetic," that a priori considerations form the basis even of human perception or sensibility. This view was important to Kant, for in his proposed Copernican revolution in epistemology, the two sources of knowledge are sensibility and understanding working in inseparable harness together. He had already written in the introduction to *The Critique of Pure Reason* that all knowledge begins with experience, but it does not necessarily arise out of experience.

What are these a priori foundations of sensibility? According to Kant, they are space and time. He reasoned that all objects of perception are necessarily located in space and time. Such objects may vary over a period of time in color, shape, size, and so on and still be perceptible objects, but they cannot be deprived of space and time and still remain perceptible. Even to establish ourselves as perceivers, and objects in our environment as objects of perception, requires the use of spatial and temporal terms—hence, the concepts of space and time. As percipients, we regard perceived objects as separate from or distant from us, and we realize that our perceptions themselves, whether of external objects or of our own thoughts and feelings, succeed one another in time. We cannot represent them otherwise and still sensibly preserve the meaning of the terms "perceiver" and "object of perception." In this sense, space and time deserve recognition as presuppositions of sense experience. All our empirical, descriptive characterizations of perceptible objects take for granted their fundamental nature as objects in space and time. That is why Kant calls space and time "forms of intuition," in order to distinguish them from the "contents" of sense experience. To be sure, portions of space and moments of time can be perceived, but such parts must always be understood as forming parts of an underlying continuum of space and time. (British phenomenalists such as Berkeley and Hume were not in agreement with this interpretation of space and time.)

Categories of Human Understanding

Believing that he had already exhibited the dependency of human knowledge upon conditions prior to immediate sense experience, Kant next proceeded to a consideration of the a priori conditions of human understanding. In Kant's view, all knowledge is the product of human understanding applied to sense experience. Does the understanding organize the contents of sense experience according to its own rules—rules that must originate elsewhere than in sense experience if their function is to categorize it? Such rules exist indeed, declared Kant, and he called them the "categories of the understanding." He argued that there are twelve such categories and that they can be discovered and classified by careful scrutiny of the logical forms of the judgments we characteristically make about the world. For example, if we look at our categorical judgments, we see that they contain a referring expression that we call the grammatical *subject* and a characterizing expression that we call the *predicate*. In "Beethoven was a great composer," the referring or subject term is "Beethoven," and our characterizing or predicate term is "great composer." Now a tremendous number of the factual claims we normally make are of this same basic form—*substance* and predicated *property*—and for Kant, therefore, the concept of substance deserves the status of a category of knowledge. Under it are subsumed all the substance-words in our conceptual scheme of things—"table," "tree," "moon," "nail," and so on—which denote material objects in our environment. It is thus a familylike concept denoting all those objects that have *substantiality* in common, something that none of the individual terms in this category does.

Much the same point can be made about the concept of *causality*, to take another of Kant's categories, which he derived from the form of hypothetical or conditional judgments—our "if . . . then" judgments. "If water is heated under normal atmospheric conditions to 212 degrees Fahrenheit, it will boil" and "If one suppresses his guilt-feelings, one will become neurotic" are examples of hypothetical judgments that assert a causal connection between the states of affairs mentioned by the antecedents and consequents of such judgments. Such judgments also appear frequently in our factual reports on the world and suggest that the concept of causality is an important and fundamental concept in our way of recording experience. It is a concept embracing numerous words in our language, such as "create," "produce," "bring about," and "make," all of which are causal terms. By virtue of designing such a large family of terms, the concept of causality must be regarded as one of the relatively few root concepts or categories at the basis of our conceptual scheme that give this scheme its flavor by influencing it throughout. The importance of causality is something that Kant clearly saw, even though it had been missed by the British phenomenalists.

Many philosophers have disagreed with Kant over his number and selection of categories, as well as his method of arriving at them, but they have not taken issue with him as to the existence of categories in our conceptual framework and their importance in any account of human knowledge. However, many others have rejected Kant's major contention that human knowledge is dependent upon such categories as substance and causality and so have sided with Hume, who, not finding anything answering to such categories in immediate sense experience, proceeded to dismiss them as fictitious. Kant, of course, agreed with Hume that substance and causality are not to be found *in* sense experience, but he insisted nevertheless that they are necessary ingredients in a world about which we can hope to have knowledge. The Kantian point is sometimes made by saying that unless one assumes that the general features referred by one's judgments persist in time and are public entities independent of any particular percipient, there can be no confirmation judgments and consequently no knowledge at all. Kant saw this simple but essential point when he stated that the categories are necessary conditions for our having any knowledge whatsoever.

He also saw that categories such as substance and causality are by no means arbitrary impositions upon sense experience, as is sometimes implied by Hume and his followers, but are useful concepts, since sense experience testifies to a great amount of orderliness in the world rather than to a befuddling chaos. It is the presence of order observable by all that vindicates the use of such ordering principles as substance and causality—they would have no utility whatever in a chaotic world.

Principles of Newtonian Science

It is chiefly as ordering principles that Kant viewed the categories. What they order or synthesize in his partly phenomenalistic theory of knowledge are the items of experience: colors, shapes, sizes, sounds, tactile impressions, odors, and so on. However, Kant believed that there is a problem in showing how such a priori principles can be applied to empirical data, and he thought that the answer to this problem is to be found in the mediatory power of time, which, as seen above, is an a priori ordering form which is a necessary condition of sense experience. Kant proceeded to relate the categories to the concept of time, and it was this merger of the concepts of substance, causality, and time that paved the way to his discussion of the presuppositions of Newtonian science. Kant believed that there are three such presuppositions: namely, the principles of the conservation of matter, of universal causality, and of the universal interrelation of all things making up the natural world. (In the Newtonian view of the universe, all objects were considered to be made up of material particles governed in their behavior by the universal laws of motion and attraction.)

Such principles are not analytic truths, according to Kant, because their denials are not self-contradictory, nor are they empirical generalizations, because we know them to be necessarily true, and no empirical generalization is ever necessarily true. They must therefore be genuine synthetic a priori truths, and their possibility arises from the fact that they utilize a priori concepts whose use is indispensable to human knowledge and yet whose only sanctioned cognitive use is in relation to the objects of sense experience in the manner dictated by the principles in question themselves.

Kant's argument in this respect is somewhat circular, though it has been defended as illuminating by thinkers who believe that any examination of basic principles must inevitably be circular in that they must be elucidated in terms of one another. However, his argument has not been convincing to many others who, although granting that Kant isolated the main presuppositions of the scientific thinking of his day, do not concede that the presuppositions are synthetic a priori. Such critics argue that it is one thing to show

that certain concepts are not empirical in origin and another to show that the judgments in which they figure are a priori. Concepts such as substance and causality may indeed underlie our factual discourse about the world and so be necessary and ineradicable concepts to intelligible and informative discourse, but it is not at all evident that the principles in which they occur—such as that the quantity of substance remains invariant throughout all physical transformations—are necessarily true. Such principles may be fruitful guideposts in scientific inquiry, yet not be true or false judgments at all, merely heuristic rules in the way that Kant himself was to regard certain metaphysical concepts, as we shall see shortly.

The Transcendental Dialectic

Up to this point Kant's concern was to explore the foundations of scientific knowledge and to disclose the dependency of such knowledge upon a handful of forms, concepts, and principles. In this exploration, he clashed sometimes head-on, sometimes obliquely, as we have seen, with accounts of human knowledge provided by British empiricists. However, his conclusions thus far were also brewing trouble and embarrassment for continental rationalism as well—for what follows from showing that concepts such as causality and substance are presuppositions of empirical knowledge? It follows, Kant said, that their use independent of sense experience is illegitimate and can result only in conceptual difficulties and empty noise. Kant's initial concern was to determine whether people can fruitfully engage in metaphysical speculation. In his time, such speculation chiefly revolved around such matters as the immortality of the soul, the origin and extent of the universe, and the existence and nature of God. Was a science of such matters really possible? In the third and concluding portion of his inquiry, called "Transcendental Dialectic" (that dealing with the categories and principles he had termed the "Transcendental Analytic"), Kant's answer to this burning question was an unequivocal no.

Kant identified the main concepts of the aforementioned metaphysical issues as the psychological idea (or soul), the cosmological (or world), and the theological idea (or God), and he considered the author of such ideas to be human reason rather than human understanding or sensibility. However, why is human reason unable to develop these ideas cogently and scientifically? Kant's chief explanation for this debility was that nothing in sense experience corresponds to the ideas of pure reason, and thus there can be no control over their speculative use.

Cartesians and Leibnizians, for example, argued that the soul was an immaterial, simple, and therefore indestructible substance. However, where is the empirical support for such claims? It does not exist, said Kant, and furthermore the reasoning leading up to such conclusions is wholly fallacious. These Cartesians and Leibnizians have treated the "I think," or *cogito*, that is presupposed by all acts of knowing as the logical subject of our judgments, analogous to the way in which "Beethoven" is the subject of the judgment "Beethoven became deaf in his later years." Furthermore, Cartesians and Leibnizians have argued that just as "Beethoven" designates a real person, so does the knowing subject of the *cogito*. Kant's rebuttal to this argument consisted of saying that it is an analytic truth that acts of knowing presuppose a knower, but the existence of the knower is an empirical question that cannot be inferred from an analytic truth whose validity is founded upon the meaning of terms. The existence of the soul as well as its properties must remain an empirical question, and the concept of substance is properly applied only to the self that is the object of empirical psychology.

The Limits of Reason

Kant next turned to metaphysical speculation about the universe at large. People have always asked themselves with respect to the universe whether it had a beginning in time or has always existed, whether it is finitely or infinitely extended in space, and whether it was created. Kant showed that no definitive answers to such questions are possible. Indeed, he argued that reasoning can establish with equal cogency alternative answers to such questions. His explanation for such a disconcerting and paradoxical state of affairs in metaphysics was that one cannot regard the universe as a substance or given entity in the way a desk, for example, can be so regarded. It is of course meaningful to ask when

a certain desk was made, how it was made, and what its spatial boundaries are. Such questions can be settled empirically, for we can trace the history of the desk and have it before us to measure. However, this investigation of the properties of the desk and the countless ones like it which we undertake in our daily lives occur within the framework of the universe, so that the questions that can significantly be raised about things within the universe cannot significantly or profitably be asked of the universe itself. If the categories of substance and causality have as their proper epistemic function the characterization of given and possible objects of perception, it is an improper use of such categories to apply them to what is neither a given nor even a possible object of perception such as the universe. Because it is not such an object, the universe cannot serve as a check or control upon our speculations about it, and it is this basic consideration again which explains reason's incompetence in this area.

Can human reason do any better, then, in the area of theological speculation? Can it, in the absence of empirical evidence, produce convincing arguments for God's existence, his benevolence, omniscience, and so forth? Kant surveyed the standard arguments or alleged proofs for the existence of God and concluded that none of them has any real force. He found that arguments that use the facts of existence, design, and causality in nature to support claims on behalf of divine existence not only make an unwarranted leap from the known to the unknown but also fall back on the ontological argument for the existence of God as propounded successively by Saint Anselm, Descartes, and Leibniz. This famous and captivating argument begins with the premise that God is the being greater than which nothing is conceivable, and—with the help of a subordinate premise to the effect that existence in the real world is better than existence merely in idea—proceeds to the conclusion that God must exist, for if God did not exist, God would not then be the greatest conceivable entity.

Kant's rebuttal of the ontological argument consists of saying that all existential statements of the form "X exists" are synthetic a posteriori and must be established on empirical grounds. If the major premise of the ontological argument is analytic, then existence is included in the definition of "God" and one has, in effect, defined God into existence. However, Kant asked, can we by definition define anything into existence, or must we not look beyond our concept of something in order to determine whether it genuinely exists? Kant added that it is in any case a mistake to view existence as a predicate like any other, because in all statements in which referring expressions such as "God" occur as subject terms, the existence of the denoted object(s) is not asserted by such statements but rather taken for granted in order to see what is attributed truly or falsely to the denoted object(s). However, if existence is taken for granted in this way, then as far as the ontological argument is concerned, one has assumed the very point in question and the argument is question-begging.

The results of Kant's inquiry into classical metaphysics prompted him to reject the view that the leading concepts of such speculation have any constitutive place in human knowledge at all. Such concepts do not enter into the weblike structure of our knowledge of the world, as do the categories in his view. However, Kant did not progress further to the Humian conclusion that metaphysical works containing these concepts should therefore be consigned to the flames. On the contrary, he argued that although such concepts do not have a constitutive role in human knowledge, they nevertheless have a vital regulative function in the scientific quest, for they posit a systematic unity to the world and so stimulate scientists to look for connections in nature, even between such diverse elements, say, as falling apples and orbiting planets. It is pure reason, with its concept of an ordering, purposeful, and wholly rational God, for example, which proposes for investigation the idea that the world created by God must be rationally constructed throughout and so reward experimental inquiry by people similarly endowed with reason. No other faculty of the mind was for Kant capable of such a stirring vision.

In this remarkable conclusion to his inquiry into the contributing factors of human knowledge, Kant plainly conceded enormous importance to pure reason, although not that exactly which rationalists defended. He therefore appeased the rationalists no more than he did the British empiricists.

Implications for Later Philosophy

Many philosophers since Kant have appreciated his middle road between rationalism and empiricism, even if they have not been able to accept the details of this reasoning, and they have credited Kant with the rare ability to raise problems worthy of philosophical investigation.

Other philosophers have not been impressed by Kant's strictures against rationalism and empiricism, and they have borrowed from his meticulous genius (happily wedded to broad vision) what suits their purposes while ignoring what does not. Thus German philosopher Georg Wilhelm Friedrich Hegel, for example, was stimulated by Kant to seize upon pure reason's dialectical tendencies—so futile in Kant's view—and erect upon such tendencies a complete picture of history and the world—quite often at the expense of empirical facts. Latter-day phenomenalists such as John Stuart Mill and Bertrand Russell persisted in the search for the foundations of human knowledge among sense data (more lately in conjunction with formal logic), which in all their fleeting transiency are so much unlike Kant's enduring and causally ordered substances.

However, most philosophical critics assent to the rich stimulation of Kant's ever-surprising fertile mind and rank him among the great philosophers of all time.

Erling Skorpen

Foundations of the Metaphysics of Morals

Type of philosophy: Ethics, metaphysics

First published: Grundlegung zur Metaphysik der Sitten, 1785 (Fundamental Principles of the Metaphysics of Ethics, 1895; better known as Foundations of the Metaphysics of Morals, 1950)

Principal ideas advanced:

◇ Nothing is unconditionally good except the good will.

◇ The good will, which is the rational will, acts not merely in accordance with duty but from duty.

◇ The good will is obedient to the moral law.

◇ Duty consists in observing the categorical imperative: Act only according to that maxim by which you can at the same time will that it should become a universal law.

◇ A second form of the categorical imperative is: Act so that you treat humanity, whether in your own person or in that of another, always as an end and never as a means only.

◇ A third form of the categorical imperative is: Act always as if you were legislating for a universal realm of ends.

Immanuel Kant holds in *Foundations of the Metaphysics of Morals* that ethics, like physics, is partly empirical and partly a priori. This work deals only with the a priori part in that it is based entirely on the use of reason without recourse to experience. Everyone must recognize, Kant writes, that since moral laws imply absolute necessity, they cannot be merely empirical. For example, "Thou shalt not lie" applies not merely to all human beings but to all rational beings. Its ground, therefore, must be found in pure reason. Moreover, what is done morally must be not only in accordance with law but also for the sake of law; if this were not its motivation, different circumstances of the agent would call forth different responses.

This book, issued as a preliminary to an intended metaphysic of morals, *Kritik der praktischen Vernunft* (1788; *The Critique of Practical Reason*, 1873), comprises a critical examination of purely practical reason and establishes the supreme principle of morality. The order of inquiry is from common moral knowledge to the supreme principle (analysis), then back to application in practice (synthesis).

Good Will

Kant begins by claiming, "Nothing in the world—indeed nothing even beyond the world—can possibly be conceived which could be called good without qualification except a *good will*"—not intelligence, wit, judgment, courage, or the gifts of fortune. Possession of these is a positive evil if not combined with good will, which indeed is the indispensable condition even of worthiness to be happy. Although moderation, self-control, and calm deliberation are all conducive to good will, they can also characterize the cool villain and

make that evil person even more abominable. The goodness of the good will does not depend on its accomplishments; it "would sparkle like a jewel in its own right, as something that had its full worth in itself," even if external circumstances entirely frustrated its actions.

The good will is the rational will. Why has nature appointed reason to rule the will? Not for the sake of adaptation, which would be more efficiently accomplished by instinct. Moreover, when a cultivated reason makes enjoyment its end, true contentment rarely ensues. Reason, then, is intended for something more worthy than production of happiness. Being a practical faculty, yet not suitable for producing a will that is good merely as a means (instinct would do better), reason must be given us to produce a will good in itself. Everyone knows, at least implicitly, according to Kant, the concept of a will good in itself. We need only bring to light that to which we give first place in our moral estimate of action.

Duty

Kant considers the concept of duty, distinguishing between what is done *in accordance with* duty (but motivated perhaps by a natural inclination or a selfish purpose) and what is done *from* duty. Moral import is clearly seen only in those cases in which, on account of absence of inclination, duty is exhibited as the motive. It is our duty to be kind, and amiable people are naturally inclined to kindness. However, do they act from duty or from inclination? Ordinarily we cannot be sure which; however, suppose that someone in such deep sorrow as to be insensible to the feelings of others yet tears himself out of this condition to perform a kind action. We see, then, that that person's action has genuine moral worth. Conversely, we know a person who by nature is unsympathetic yet behaves beneficently; that person must be acting from duty, not from inclination.

Moral worth attaches to action from duty even with respect to the pursuit of happiness, according to Kant. Everyone has an inclination to be happy, and particular inclinations toward what are regarded as the particular constituents of happiness. Still, all these subtracted, the duty to pursue one's happiness would remain, and only the dutiful pursuit would have true moral worth. (Pursuit of happiness is a duty because unhappiness could tempt one to the neglect of other duties.) The commandments to love our neighbors and our enemies should be read as requiring us to exercise beneficence from duty; love cannot be commanded.

A central idea in Kant's work is that the moral worth of action performed from duty lies not in its purpose but in the maxim (rule, or principle) by which it is determined. Otherwise, moral worth would depend on inclinations and incentives, which, as we have seen, cannot be the case. "Duty is the necessity of an action executed from respect for law," writes Kant. One cannot have respect for a mere consequence or inclination, but only for what can overpower all inclination; this can be no other than law itself. To be an object of respect is the same as to be valid as a source of command. The law determines the will objectively; subjectively one is determined by respect for the law; this subjective element is the maxim of one's action, that one ought to follow the law whatever one's inclination. Respect, the conception of a worth that overrides self-love, can be present only in a rational being.

The only kind of law the conception of which is capable of determining the will without reference to consequences must be the notion of conformity to law as such. That is to say: Never act in such a way that you could not also will that your maxim should be a universal law requiring everybody in these circumstances to do this action. This is what the common reason of humankind has constantly in view in moral matters, Kant claims.

For example, might one extricate oneself from a difficulty by making a false promise? A prudential calculation of consequences might or might not recommend this course. However, to determine whether it is consistent with duty, one need only ask whether one could wish that everyone in difficulty might extricate himself or herself similarly. One sees that the maxim would destroy itself, for if it were a universal law, no one could derive any help from lying, since no promise made in a difficult situation would be believed. Hence there is no difficulty in deciding whether a proposed course of action would be morally good; one need only ask oneself whether one's

maxim could become a universal law. If not, it must be rejected and the action forgone. Reason compels respect for universal legislation. Every other motive must defer to duty.

Common reason habitually employs this test: "What if everybody did that?" It is the advantage of practical over theoretical reason to be everybody's possession. Ordinary people are as likely to hit the mark as philosophers—indeed, more so, being less liable to be led astray by subtle fallacies. Nevertheless, philosophy is called upon to buttress reason against the assaults of inclination and against specious arguments on their behalf. That is why a metaphysic of morals is required.

Although only what is done from duty has moral worth, it is not possible to be certain in even one instance that an action was in fact done from duty. Some philosophers have indeed attributed all motivation to self-interest. They may be right as a matter of psychology, for how can we be sure that what we most sincerely and carefully conclude to be action from duty was not in reality prompted by some hidden impulse of inclination?

Duty, therefore, is not an empirical concept, according to Kant. Moreover, its universality and necessity also show its nonempirical nature. Nor could it be derived from examples, how would we know in the first place that the cases were fit to serve as examples if we did not presuppose knowledge of the concept? Even if we consider the actions of God, we must antecedently possess the concept of duty in order to judge them as moral. Duty, therefore, is a concept a priori. While this fact is obvious, it nevertheless needs to be explicitly argued for, on account of the popularity of empirical rules recommended as bases of morality. It is a mistake to try to popularize morality by holding out the inducement of happiness. On the contrary, the picture of disinterested duty has the strongest appeal—even to children—because here reason recognizes that it can be practical.

Imperatives

Kant argues that if reason, which tells us what principles of action are objectively required, infallibly determined the will, we would always choose the good. However, in fact, the will is affected also by subjective incentives that clash with the dictates of reason. Thus the will, when not completely good (as it never is in human beings), experiences the pull of reason as constraint. This command of reason, the objective principle constraining the will, is also called an imperative. A perfectly good or *holy* will, being always determined to action only by objective laws, would not experience constraint.

According to Kant, imperatives are either *hypothetical*, commanding something to be done in order to achieve a desired end (If you want *X*, do *A*), or *categorical*, commanding an action as objectively necessary (Do *A*, and never mind what you desire). Hypothetical imperatives are further subdivided into rules of skill, which tell what to do in order to achieve some end that one may or may not wish to achieve (heal a person, or poison him) and counsels of prudence, telling what to do to achieve happiness, the one end that all rational beings in fact do have. However, the counsels of prudence are still hypothetical, depending on what the agent counts as part of his happiness. Only the categorical imperative is the imperative of morality.

How are imperatives possible—how can reason constrain the will? There is no problem with respect to rules of skill, since it is an analytic proposition that whoever wills the end wills the indispensable means. Because the notion of happiness is indefinite and infallible, means for attaining it cannot be prescribed; counsels of prudence do not strictly command, but only advise. Still, there is no difficulty here as to how reason can influence the will. The puzzle arises only with respect to the categorical imperative.

The Categorical Imperative

We cannot show by any example that a categorical imperative does influence the will. When someone in trouble tells the truth, it is always possible that not the categorical "Thou shalt not make a false promise" influenced his will but the hypothetical "If thou dost not want to risk ruining thy credit, make no false promise." Hence, the question of the possibility of the categorical imperative must be investigated a priori. Moreover, the categorical imperative is synthetic a priori—a priori in that the action prescribed is necessary, synthetic in that the content of this action is not derived analytically from a presupposed volition.

The categorical imperative is simply the demand that the subjective principle of one's action, one's maxim, should conform to the objective law valid for all rational beings. Therefore, Kant contends, there is only one categorical imperative: "Act only according to that maxim by which you can at the same time will that it should become a universal law." Here are some of Kant's examples:

1. Suicide. Maxim: Out of self-love, I shorten my life. However, a system of nature in which this maxim was law would be contradictory: The feeling impelling to improvement of life would destroy life. Therefore, the maxim could not be a law of nature, and the action is contrary to duty.

2. False promises. A universal law of nature that people in trouble escape by making false promises is incoherent, as they would never be believed.

3. Is it alright to amuse oneself at the expense of failing to develop one's talents? While it could be a law of nature that all people do this, a rational being could not *will* it to be a law of nature, for rationality entails willing that faculties be developed.

4. Should we help other people, or is "Every man for himself" morally permissible? A world could exist without altruism; but again, a rational person could not will it, for that person's will would conflict with itself. There must often be occasions when a person needs the love and sympathy of others, from which he would be cutting himself off.

Examples 1 and 2, in which the idea of the maxim as law of nature is self-contradictory, show strict duties. Examples 3 and 4, in which the maxim could be law of nature but not willed to be, illustrate meritorious duties. If we were perfectly rational, then every time we thought of transgressing duty, we would notice a contradiction in our will. However, in fact, we experience no such contradiction but only antagonism between inclination and what reason prescribes. This does show us, however, that we acknowledge the validity of the categorical imperative.

Kant contends that the form of the categorical imperative can also be deduced from the consideration that "rational nature exists as an end in itself." Rational beings (persons) do not exist as mere means to some other end but as themselves bearers of absolute worth. Every person thinks of his or her own existence in this way, and the rational ground for so doing is the same for all others. It is therefore not a merely subjective principle of action, but objective. The categorical imperative can thus be phrased as follows: "Act so that you treat humanity, whether in your own person or in that of another, always as an end and never as a means only." This principle also condemns suicide (which is using oneself merely as a means to maintaining a tolerable life up to its conclusion) and false promising, and it shows the merit of self-development and altruism.

The notion of rational beings as ends leads, in Kant's ethics, to another formulation of the categorical imperative. We can form the conception of a universal realm of ends, an ideal society of completely rational beings. Such beings would act toward each other not from interest but from pure practical reason; that is, they would always do their duty. This action would be in conformity to the laws of reason, which they had imposed upon themselves. Therefore, "Act always as if you were legislating for a universal realm of ends."

The categorical imperative, in all its forms, is the principle whereby a rational being gives a law to himself or herself. It is thus the principle of autonomy (self-legislation). All other principles, based on interest, are heteronomous (other-legislation), the "other" being the object determining the will: riches, say, or happiness, or any external object of interest. All heteronomous principles are spurious. The worst is that based on happiness, which is neither empirically nor conceptually connected with morality and virtue. It undermines morality by making the difference between virtue and vice to be a mere matter of calculation instead of a difference in kind. The appeal to a moral sense can furnish neither an objective standard of good and bad nor a basis for valid judgment; nevertheless, it does have the merit of ascribing intrinsic worth and dignity to virtue. Morality based on an ideal of perfection is empty and involves circular reasoning, as it does not explain our moral ideals but presupposes them. Theological morality, based on the notion of the divine will, either presupposes an independent standard or tries to base morality on the notions of glory, dominion, might, and vengeance—a system directly opposed to morality. All these heteronomous moralities look not to the action itself but to the result of the action as incentive: "I ought to do something because I will something else" is a hypothetical imperative, and hence not a moral imperative.

Free Will

Kant attempts to show not that the autonomous will is actual but that it is possible. To show even this much is difficult, Kant admits, inasmuch as if nature is a system of effects following by natural laws from their causes, and if human beings are part of nature, it seems that every human action is necessitated by natural causes, and thus could not be otherwise than it is. The will could not then be autonomous, "a law to itself," unless it is free.

Kant's strategy in establishing the possibility of freedom depends on the distinctions, elaborated in *Kritik der reinen Vernunft* (1781; *The Critique of Pure Reason*, 1838), between things as they are in themselves and things as they appear to us. With regard to conceptions that come to us without our choice, such as those of the senses, we can know only how they appear, not how they are in themselves. This applies even to one's self-concept: One knows oneself only as one appears to oneself and is ignorant of the reality underlying the appearance. However, a person finds in himself or herself the faculty of reason, which transcends the conceptions given through the senses. A person must therefore conclude that his or her ego, as it is in itself, belongs to the intelligible world (world of things-in-themselves). The upshot is that an individual has a dual citizenship. In the world of the senses, one's actions are explainable in terms of natural causation, thus heteronomously. As a denizen of the intelligible world, however, the causality of one's will is and must be thought of under the idea of freedom, as autonomous.

If we belonged only to the intelligible world, all our actions would conform to the law of freedom and would be moral. If we belonged only to the sensible world (as nonrational animals do), all our actions would be effects of natural causation—that is, determined by incentives. Belonging as we do to both worlds, we experience the dictates of practical reason as *ought*; even in following material incentives, we are conscious of what reason requires. We must assume, although we cannot prove, that there is no ultimate contradiction between natural necessity and freedom in human action. The assumption is justified, for there is no contradiction in a thing-in-itself's being independent of laws to which the thing-as-appearance must conform. In this way we can "comprehend the incomprehensibility" of the unconditional necessity of the moral imperative.

Whitaker T. Deininger

The Critique of Practical Reason

Type of philosophy: Ethics
First published: Kritik der praktischen Vernunft, 1788
(English translation, 1873)
Principal ideas advanced:

◇ Morality can claim objectivity and universality only by being founded on pure reason itself.

◇ Moral laws are universal and categorical because of their form, not their empirical content.

◇ The fundamental law of the pure practical reason is so to act that the maxim of the will could always function as a principle establishing universal law.

◇ Were it not for the moral law, people could never know themselves to be free; for humanity, "thou ought" implies "thou canst."

◇ The rational postulates of the practical reason are that people are free, that the soul is immortal, and that God exists.

None of Immanuel Kant's writings can be understood without a clear recognition of the "Copernican revolution" in philosophy effected by his first critique, *Kritik der reinen Vernunft* (1781; *The Critique of Pure Reason*, 1838). Previously, the predominant rational tradition in Western philosophy was founded on the assumption of reason's capacity for discovering the forms or essential structures characterizing all things. Whether the form of "treeness" was an innate aspect of every existent tree (as Greek philosopher Aristotle believed) or a transcendent form in which each existent tree participated (as Greek philosopher Plato held), the capacity of reason for perceiving such forms was not doubted. The medieval controversy over "universals" centered not in reason's ability for such perception but in the nature of this rational activity.

From the first questioning of the nominalists, however, through the break between self and "exterior world" in the philosophy of René Descartes, doubt as to the precise authority of rational apprehension increased. Human error and empirical deception began to be seen as intervening between perceiver and perceived, thus raising powerfully the question of the criteria for truth. The Aristotelians, especially from the time of Saint Thomas Aquinas on, affirmed that knowledge begins with sense perception; however, because of reason's capacity for extracting forms, human knowledge not only possessed the qualities of necessity and universality but also made possible an inductive knowledge of transempirical realities.

It was the empiricists, especially David Hume, who provided the most serious challenge to this rationalist claim. Centering his attack on the problem of universal causality (cause and effect as universally operative), Hume raised the question of necessity. On what grounds, he asked, can one insist that, *of necessity*, all "effects" have causes and, similarly, that such causes *necessarily* produce identical effects? Hume's conclusion was that the category of causality, like all human ideas, is derived from sense impressions, having the status simply of a habitual assumption and expectation; human ideas are forever bereft of necessity.

Answering the Empiricists
It was Kant who saw the seriousness of this empiricist challenge. Reason was bankrupt as an agent of knowledge if it could no longer claim necessity, and thus universality, for its findings. Humanity and the world had been severed, and skepticism seemed the inevitable result.

The answer provided by Kant's first critique was a revolution, a complete reversal of the previous conception of the knowing process. If human knowledge cannot claim a necessity that is resident within the empirical world itself, it is possible, nevertheless, to claim universality for it if the locus of necessity is within the universal operations of human reason. With this new conception of rational necessity and universality, Kant proceeded to exhibit what he conceived to be the necessary operations of rational apprehension, the manner in which the understanding, by its very structure, has perceived and organized, and of necessity will always perceive and organize, whatever realities encounter it.

As Kant interpreted it, Hume's error was in seeing subjective necessity as grounded only in habit instead of being a result of the a priori structure of reason. If the latter is the case, rational necessity and universality are guaranteed, although on a far different basis from before. For Kant, the forms perceived through sense experience are the product of the categories of the human mind, but now the externality so encountered is never known as it is in itself (as _noumenon_), but only in its relation to humanity (as _phenomenon_).

Although reason attempts to complete this knowledge by bringing it into a comprehensive unity, it is barred from success in this speculative operation by certain antinomies, both sides of which are in harmony with a person's phenomenal knowledge. In the area of speculative psychology, these antinomies make it impossible to affirm a soul existing apart from the physical. In the area of speculative cosmology, the consequence of the antinomies centers in the impossibility of establishing human beings as free of the determined processes of cause and effect. In the area of speculative theology, the antinomies negate the possibility of proving the existence of God. In all cases, the antinomies defy resolution of these questions _either_ positively or negatively.

As a result, reason, in its theoretical function, is barred from any cognitive penetration into the noumenal. This does not mean that the noumenal realm is necessarily unlike a person's phenomenal knowledge of it and that human categories do not apply there; rather, the problem is that pure reason can provide no guarantee of any correspondence.

What is most significant about the first critique is that, while Kant revives the old Platonic distinction between noumenon and phenomenon, as he explored reason along the narrowly Aristotelian lines of his day (as a strictly cognitive activity), the Platonic distinction became a severe human limitation. Plato had stressed the noetic aspects of reason, which was deeply imbued with an intuitive or mystical quality. However, in the preface to the second edition of the first critique, Kant gave indication that he was moving toward a broader, or more Platonic, conception of reason: "I have found it necessary to deny _knowledge_ [of supersensible reality] in order to make room for _faith_." Although faith, for Kant, was to be understood largely in moral terms (stemming from his pietistic background), we have here a beginning indication of his recognition of modes of human apprehension far broader than simply discursive or cognitive reason. Much of the impetus for exploring this possibility came from Kant's tremendous interest in ethics, made urgent by the seemingly undermining affect of his first critique upon this realm. His understanding of the experience of the form of duty, like Plato's experience of the form of the good, has about it a near mystical quality.

Pure vs. Practical Reason

The Critique of Practical Reason is of major importance not only as the attempt to create a purely rational ethic but also as a defense of a nondiscursive mode of apprehension, as an insistence that the "rational" is not restricted in meaning to the "cognitive." It is this point that Kant develops further in the third critique, _Kritik der Urteilskraft_ (1790; _The Critique of Judgment_, 1892), in terms of beauty and the purposiveness of nature. In order to understand these points, one must beware the misleading title of the second critique. In distinguishing between _pure_ reason and _practical_ reason, Kant is not speaking of two human agents or loci of activity; in both critiques he is speaking of pure reason as such, but in the first he is concerned with its theoretical or speculative function, in the second with its practical or ethical function. For Kant, this second function is the activity known as will. It is his purpose to show that will is not divorced from reason, controlled internally by drives or impulses, or externally by pleasure stimuli. In its fulfilled operation, it is a purely rational enterprise; it is pure reason in its practical operation which must *control* drives and *determine* external ends.

Likewise, in this realm it was Hume who haunted Kant, for Hume understood reason as being the pawn of passions, and morality as being rooted in subjective feeling. Just as Kant's answer in the cognitive realm depended on exhibiting the a priori or categorical laws of human cognitive activity, so his answer in the second critique depended on discovering the a priori or categorical laws of the rational will. Morality could claim objectivity and universality only by being founded not on experience but on pure reason itself. The task of the second critique, then, is to discover the a priori or necessary principles of the practical reason.

The Problem of Freedom

At the heart of the problem of ethics is the problem of freedom; without freedom, morality is an impossibility. However, according to the first critique, since all things are seen, of necessity, under the category of causality, all things are seen as determined. Yet, Kant insists, the same noumenon-phenomenon distinction applying to the object of such knowledge applies to the subject as well. It is humanity as phenomenon who is seen under the category of necessity, but the nature of the noumenal person remains unknown. Although the speculative function of reason strives for an understanding of the human "soul," the antinomies, as we have seen, left the matter of freedom for the noumenal self as "problematic but not impossible." If Kant can exhibit the will as free, he believes, he can also show the capacity of pure reason to determine the will's total activity.

If there is to be an objective ethic, an ethic based on freedom, the only possibility for it can be reason presupposing nothing else but itself, for a rule can be objective and universal only if it is not subject to any contingent, subjective conditions. Thus, moral *laws* cannot be based on the pleasure principle, for the objects of pleasure and pain can be identified only empirically, thus having no objective necessity. Further, hedonism can make no legitimate distinction between higher and lower pleasures; only if reason is able to de-

termine the will can there be a higher faculty of desire than base feeling. Likewise, there is no objective, universal basis for an ethic of happiness, for happiness is simply the general name for satisfaction of desire.

Consequently, maxims (subjective, personal principles) of people's commonplace activity can claim the ethical status of law not according to their content, which is always empirically gained, but only according to their form. Every maxim can be tested for such universality of form by inquiring whether that maxim, if made a universal law, would negate itself. For example, all people seeking only their own happiness would soon render happiness impossible; thus, the goal of individual happiness is judged to be lacking the universality required of a moral law.

Now, since it is only the form of the maxim that makes objective claim upon the will, the will must be seen as independent of the natural law of cause and effect; that is, we have here a case in which the will operates in isolation from the phenomenal realm. The act is rooted totally in reason itself. This is the heart of Kant's ethic—"freedom and unconditional practical law imply each other." Since freedom cannot be known through the theoretical function of reason, its objective reality is discovered by experiencing the moral law as duty, as a rational necessity. This means that the pure practical laws are discovered in the same manner as the pure theoretical laws, by observing what reason directs in indifference to empirical conditions. Without the moral law, Kant insists, people would never know themselves to be free; "thou ought" implies "thou canst."

The Categorical Imperative

For Kant, the fundamental law of the pure practical reason is this: "So act that the maxim of your will could always hold at the same time as a principle establishing universal law." Such rational control of the will is objective, for the legislation is made in indifference to any contingencies. Yet a distinction must be drawn between a *pure* will and a *holy* will; although the moral law is a universal law for all beings with reason and will, because the free person has wants and sensuous motives, that person is capable of maxims that conflict with the moral law. Thus, this law comes to people as a "categorical imperative." It is categorical because it is unconditioned; it is an imperative because it is experienced as "duty," as an inner compulsion provided by reason. Holiness is above duty, but in this life it remains the ideal to be striven for, but never reached. Each maxim must strive for unending progress toward this ideal; it is such progress that deserves the name "virtue."

Kant's formulation of the moral law is, in effect, a philosophical statement of the Golden Rule. As Kant says, the moral law of universality alone, without the need of any external incentive, arises as duty "to extend the maxim of self-love also to the happiness of others." Put on a commonsense level, Kant's moral formula is rooted in the integrity required by reason. It is self-evident that reason, to be rational, must operate in complete self-consistency; since the rational is the universal, reason qua reason must consent to will only that which can consistently be willed universally.

For Kant, the demand of duty is unmistakable and can, without difficulty, be perceived by the simplest person. Where the difficulty arises is in following the imperative. Kant's estimate of humanity is such that he goes so far as to maintain that the good act is done only when duty and inclination are in conflict. What he really means here is that aversion is a sign that the individual has gone beyond self-interest to real duty. It is necessary to insist, Kant maintains, that satisfaction follows but does not precede awareness of the moral law; there is certainly a "moral feeling" that should be cultivated, but duty cannot be derived from it.

Six Ethical Systems

Kant's rejection of all ethical theory but his own formal principle provides a helpful summary of alternative ethical systems. Of the subjective type, there are two kinds: external and internal. In the former, philosophers such as Michel de Montaigne root ethics in education, while others, such as Bernard Mandeville, see its basis in a civil constitution. Of the internal variety, Epicurus sees physical feeling as central, while Francis Hutcheson grounds ethics in "moral feeling." There are likewise internal and external types within the objective ethical systems. The former is the ethic of perfection, held by Christian von

Wolff and the Stoics; the latter is the "will of God" ethic of theological morality. The subjective group Kant quickly discards as empirically based and thus, by definition, failing to meet the requirements of universal morality. Also, the objective types, though rational, depend on a content that, within the confines of Kant's first critique, can be gained by empirical means only; consequently, these too must be disqualified as neither universal nor necessary.

People's capacity for obeying the moral law in independence of empirical conditions establishes, for Kant, the objective fact of their free, supersensible (noumenal) nature. As Kant puts it, the necessity of the practical reason makes freedom a rational postulate. Freedom is not known, in the theoretical sense, but it must be subjectively affirmed as necessary. This does not mean that freedom is simply subjective, but that its objectiveness is perceived through reason's practical rather than theoretical operation. Moral need has the status of law, while the antinomies render the completions of speculative reason hypothetical or arbitrary. Thus, the former provides the certitude that the latter lacks, establishing the factuality of freedom as valid for both the practical and pure reason. Here we see the breadth of Kant's conception of reason: Such a moral postulate is both objective and rational, even though it is not cognitive.

Because it is Kant's concern to show that it is pure (speculative) reason itself that is practical, the postulates of reason in its practical function become objective for reason as such. In actuality, the practical function is prior and the speculative function must submit to it, for "every interest is ultimately practical, even that of speculative reason being only conditional and reaching perfection only in practical use." The result of this insight is that the agnosticism of the first critique is transcended by the second, for while still insisting upon his former severe limitations on speculative reason, Kant here provides an alternative mode for metaphysical affirmation. This is most apparent in the two additional moral postulates that Kant draws from the postulate regarding freedom. What is required by the moral law is complete "fitness of intentions," which would be holiness. However, since this is impossible for finite humanity, the practical reason requires that one affirm an "endless progress" in which such fitness can be completed. Because such progress requires the immortality of the soul, this affirmation becomes an objective postulate of the practical reason. Such a proposition is not demonstrable, but is "an inseparable corollary of an a priori unconditionally valid practical law." Thus the second antinomy of speculative reason is practically resolved.

Likewise, a third postulate is involved. The postulate of immortality can be made only on the supposition of a cause adequate to produce such an effect; thus, one must affirm as an objective postulate the existence of God, an affirmation sharing the same necessary status as the other two moral postulates. A further basis for this postulate rests in the fact that although finite existence supports no necessary connection between morality and proportionate happiness, such a connection is morally necessary.

Pure Rational Faith

The affirmation of such postulates Kant calls the activity of "pure rational faith," for although they are objective (necessary), freedom, the soul, and God are not known as they are in themselves. This, he affirms, is in truth the essence of "the Christian principle of morality." It is from morality that religion springs, for religion is nothing more than "the recognition of all duties as divine commands."

Because morality involves the moral law, with the form of an action, it follows that no "thing" is good or evil; such designations properly apply only to an acting will. Good and evil are defined only after and by means of the moral law; to reverse this procedure is to develop an empirical, subjective ethic. It is the practical judgment that determines the applicability of a universal maxim to a concrete act. To make an application such as this is very difficult, for it is here that the laws of freedom (the noumenal realm) are applied to the laws of nature (the phenomenal realm). Such a meeting is possible because the moral law is purely formal in relation to natural law. That is, it raises this question: If this proposed act should take place by a law of nature of which you were a part, would your will regard it as possible? The center of the moral act thus rests in one's intentions, not in consequences. If the

right act occurs but not for the sake of the moral law, it is not a moral act. The only incentive that is valid is the moral law itself.

For human beings as they are, their natural feelings of self-love are ever at war with the moral law. The very fact that morality resides in law reveals the severe "limitation" of humanity. The moral law is victorious only if all inclinations and feelings are set aside out of respect for the moral law, in and of itself. An act not performed out of such a sense of duty is inevitably tainted with the self-pride of believing goodness to be a spontaneous reflection of one's nature.

Problems of Application

Perhaps the major difficulty in Kant's ethic is the problem of application. There are few acts that a performer would not defend as universally valid if the hypothetical performer and situation were in every way identical with those of the actual performer. Every evil has been defended by the exigencies of person and circumstance. Kant's moral formula is designed to eliminate all such individualized decisions. Yet to the degree that the formula is interpreted, not in such a particularized fashion but in an absolutely universal sense, its inadequacy becomes evident. Total truth-telling, total promise-keeping, and the like, all have obvious moral exceptions. Likewise, how is one to resolve conflicts between these objective duties? Furthermore, law for its own sake tends to be elevated above the individual persons between whom moral relations arise.

Kant's moral position has stimulated generations of heated conflict. For certain theologians, Kant's ethic seems to be only an ethic of the Fall and not a redemptive ethic; for others, it is a classic Protestant ethic, judging human pretension and incapacity. For philosophers, the difficulty, as with Saint Anselm's ontological argument, rests in its deceptive simplicity (despite the difficulty of its expression). Such a position is uncomfortable in its rather wholesale rejection of consequences, moral incentives, absolute good, and the like. However, there is no denying Kant's realistic appraisal of human capacity, the absolute quality of moral activity and yet the relativity of concrete ethical situations. It may be that Kant's ethic is too simple, discards too much, and is too uncompromising, but consequent ethicists have found it impossible to bypass this second critique.

In regard to their larger ramifications, Kant's critiques have been a powerful damper on speculative metaphysics. Philosophically, they have stimulated an exploration of noncognitive modes of human apprehension; theologically, they have encouraged exploration of the moral dimensions of religion and of theological method.

W. Paul Jones

The Critique of Judgment

Type of philosophy: Aesthetics, ethics
First published: Kritik der Urteilskraft, 1790 (English translation, 1892)
Principal ideas advanced:

◇ Judgment in general is the faculty of thinking the particular as contained under the universal; if a judgment brings the particular under a given universal, it is determinant, and if it discovers a universal by which to judge a given particular, it is reflective.

◇ Taste is the faculty of judging an object by a satisfaction (or dissatisfaction) that is not dependent on any quality of the object itself. The satisfaction is a subjective response to the mere representation of the object; hence, it is disinterested.

◇ Even though beauty is subjective, it is universal; the beautiful is that which pleases universally because it satisfies the will as if it served a purpose.

◇ The sublime is found when a formless object is represented as boundless, even though its totality is present in thought.

Since its publication, *The Critique of Judgment* has been of highest importance to the philosophy of art and of religion. It met opposition as radically skeptical and destructive of theology; indeed, Immanuel Kant intended to set limits on religious thinking. It opened promising new pathways in aesthetics, still found highly worthy of exploration.

The work is based wholly on the psychology of faculties and the logic Kant adopted in *Kritik*

der reinen Vernunft (1781; *The Critique of Pure Reason*, 1838) and *Kritik der praktischen Vernunft* (1788; *The Critique of Practical Reason*, 1873). The former treats the faculty of *understanding*, which, presupposing natural law, brings people their knowledge of nature. The latter treats *reason* ("practical" reason, will, or desire), which presupposes freedom and legislates for people in accordance with moral law. While writing the first two critiques, Kant believed that the faculty of pleasure and pain could have no critique, being passive only. However, he came to regard this faculty to be the same as judgment, which subsumes representations under concepts, always accompanied by a feeling-response. He declared finally that judgment could have a *regulative* critique of its own, showing its functions and limitations, even though the faculty brings us no objective knowledge. Indeed, *The Critique of Judgment* would show the ground of union between understanding and reason, although their presuppositions had seemingly forced them irrevocably apart.

The desire or will, when realized, is actually a natural cause, specifically that cause which acts in accordance with concepts. Concepts are of two kinds, natural concepts and concepts of freedom. The understanding carries on a theoretical legislation through natural concepts resulting in knowledge; the practical reason carries on a moral legislation through precepts resulting in choices of actions. Understanding and reason legislate over the very same territory of experience, yet without conflicting. However, the practical reason presupposes a *supersensible substratum*, which cannot be experienced but which is necessary as a condition of freedom of choice. The understanding can give knowledge only through intuition, which can never reach the *thing-in-itself*; the concept of freedom, on the other hand, represents its object as a *thing-in-itself* but cannot give it intuition. The region of the thing-in-itself is supersensible, but while we cannot *know* it, we can *impute* reality to it. This must be a *practical* reality founded on our necessity of acting, not on any source of substantive knowledge concerning it. To postulate such a substratum enables us to transfer our thought between the realm of nature and the realm of freedom and think according to the principles of each in turn.

The Principle of Judgment

The deduction of the principle of judgment is crucial to the book. "Judgment in general," says Kant, "is the faculty of thinking the particular as contained under the universal." Either the universal or the particular might be given. If the universal is given, then the judgment that brings the particular under it is *determinant*; the judgment brings knowledge according to a priori law and with finality. However, if the particular is given, then the judgment must find for itself a law to judge by, in the absence of a concept. Hence it is *reflective*, and if the judgments delivered are to be regarded as laws, this must be on the assumption of some underlying unifying principle. The principle must be this: As universal laws of nature have their ground in our understanding (as shown in *The Critique of Judgment*), particular empirical laws must be considered in accordance with such a unity as they would have if an understanding had furnished them to our cognitive faculties, so as to make possible a system of experience according to particular laws of nature. The concept of an actual object contains its purpose; the principle of judgment that we take, then, on these suppositions, is *purposiveness* in nature. (For nature to realize a purpose would be to carry out a "particular law of nature.") *If* nature were guided by an understanding, then purposiveness would underlie its variety as the unifying factor. This concept of purposiveness is a priori—it provides a principle for reflecting upon nature without needing specific experience of nature. Yet we can never prove real purpose in nature; we only justify our way of thinking about it.

The faculty of judgment functions also as the faculty of pleasure and pain. When the understanding shows us an order of nature and the judgment apprehends it under the aspect of purposiveness, we feel pleasure because the attainment of any aim is bound up with the feeling of pleasure. Because the ground of this feeling is a principle a priori, the judgment is valid for every person. The *imagination* is the faculty of a priori intuitions; our pleasure arises when the judgment of purposiveness places the imagination in agreement with the understanding—shows a form such as an understanding would furnish.

The judgment of taste represents purposiveness without mediation of a concept. However, purposiveness may also be represented objectively as the harmony of the form of an object with the possibility of the thing itself, according to some prior concept that contains the basis of this form. A concept of an object may be realized in two ways: A person may make an object that fulfills his or her preconceived concept, or nature may present an object realizing a concept that we supply. Thus we can regard *natural beauty* as the presentation of the concept of subjective purposiveness, and *natural purposes* as the presentation of the concept of an objective purposiveness. Hence, *The Critique of Judgment* is divided into the "Critique of the Aesthetical Judgment" (considering the former), involving the feeling of pleasure, and the "Critique of the Teleological Judgment" (treating the latter), involving the understanding and reason, according to concepts. Although the aesthetical judgment is the special faculty of taste, the teleological judgment is not a special faculty but only the reflective judgment in general, judging of certain objects of nature according to reflective principles.

Aesthetic Judgment

True to his critical logic, Kant considers in turn the quality, quantity, relation, and modality of the judgment of taste, in a subdivision called the "Analytic of the Aesthetical Judgment." Then in its "Dialectic," he resolves an antinomy or contradiction that arises in aesthetics.

By the *aesthetical*, Kant means that element whose determining ground can be no other than subjective. Consequently, the aesthetic apprehension does not depend on existential relations of the judged object with other things (its usefulness, for example) but only on the relation of the *representation* of the object to the observing subject. In contrast, the pleasant and the good always involve a representation not only of the object but also of some connection of the judging subject with that object; hence, they bring an interested rather than a free satisfaction. Taste is the faculty of judging of an object, or of the method of representing one, by a satisfaction (or dissatisfaction) which as to quality is entirely disinterested. The object of such satisfaction is called beautiful.

Because the satisfaction does not depend on a particular relationship with a particular subject, it may be thought of as resting on something present in everyone and hence binding universally. Because this element inheres in the subject, not in the objects judged, the quantity is a "subjective universality." What we postulate is that all rational minds are constituted alike in the relation of their cognitive faculties. For a representation to be capable of becoming a cognition at all requires *imagination* for bringing together in ordered fashion the manifold of phenomena, and *understanding* for providing a concept under which the representations may be united. However, this requires as its condition a free play in the action of imagination and understanding. Aesthetic pleasure must be communicable among all minds so constituted. What the judgment of taste asserts as universally valid is not some attribute of the object (as in the claim that something is pleasant or good), but rather the claim of our presupposition of the communicability of aesthetic pleasure among subjects. As to quantity, then, the beautiful is that which pleases universally without requiring or providing a concept.

A purpose is a concept of an object insofar as the concept is regarded as the cause of the object. When we can think of an object only as though caused by a concept, *for us* that object has purposiveness, even though we cannot know whether it has purpose. That is, it has *purposiveness without purpose*. The mere form of purposiveness is given, and it is that in which we take pleasure. As to relation, beauty is the form of the *purposiveness* of an object, so far as this is perceived in it *without any representation of a purpose.*

The modality of the judgment of taste is necessity. It is, however, neither objective necessity nor practical necessity, like those respectively of understanding and reason, but *exemplary* necessity. It requires the assent of all "to a judgment which is regarded as the example of a universal rule that we cannot state." This assent may be expected only on the assumption introduced above, the communicability of our cognitions. Under this presupposition, an individual has a right to state his judgment of taste as a rule for everyone and thus assert of all subjects the particular judgment arising from his or her own experience. The

beautiful, then, is that which without any concept is cognized as the object of a *necessary* satisfaction.

Judgment of the Sublime

The judgment of the sublime has the same quality, quantity, relation, and modality as that of the beautiful, but there are important differences. The beautiful pleases through its form and its bounds, but the sublime is found when a formless object is represented as boundless, even though its totality is present in thought. Hence, while beauty is a satisfaction in quality, the sublime is a satisfaction in respect to quantity. Furthermore, in the sublime, the form may seem to violate purposiveness and be quite unsuited to our presentative faculty. It rather should be said that the object is fit for the presentation of a sublimity found in the mind, producing in us a feeling of purposiveness of our powers, independent of nature.

The sublime has two kinds: the mathematical and the dynamic. Whereas that of the beautiful is restful, the judgment of the sublime stirs a movement of the mind that is judged as subjectively purposive and is referred either to the cognition, generating (A) the mathematically sublime, or to the will, generating (B) the dynamically sublime.

With regard to (A), we can always think something still greater than whatever the senses give us. While we cannot have an intuition of the infinite, which is absolutely great, we can comprehend it logically. To do this without contradiction presupposes a supersensible faculty. Thus we refer to the ideas of reason (God, freedom, immortality). Comparing the objects of nature, however grand, with these ideas, we gain a feeling of respect for our own destination according to the law of reason.

With regard to (B), on observing in nature mighty objects from which we are in no danger, if we can think of a case in which we would fear them, we feel the emotion of the sublime. It calls up a comparison with our own power, which is small physically but which, in our *rational* faculty, has a superiority to nature even in its immensity, in the sublimity of the mind's destination.

The judgment of either kind of sublime is thus not so much upon the object but on our state of mind in the estimation of it. Like the judgment of the beautiful, the judgment of the sublime postulates a common faculty, in this case the feeling for the legislation of reason—that is, for what is moral.

Characteristics of Aesthetic Judgment

Kant considers it requisite to provide a *deduction*, or proof of its grounds, for any judgment claiming necessity. However, since the judgment of taste is neither cognitive nor practical, it can draw its necessity from no concepts. Rather, it has a twofold peculiarity: It claims the universality of a singular, not a universal, proposition, and it claims the necessary assent of everyone a priori, but cannot depend on a priori grounds of proof for doing so. Because of what they are, Kant asserts, the explanation of these peculiarities suffices as a deduction. As to the necessity, although the judgment of each individual improves with exercise, at each stage it claims the necessary assent of others. It claims autonomy. If it submitted to external principles, it would be something other than taste. As to quantity, since it judges without a concept, this must always be singular: "This tulip is beautiful," never "All tulips are beautiful," since the universal subject term of the latter is a concept and brings the understanding into the process. Obviously, then, no objective principle of taste is possible, and no rule can be given to art. Rather, the principle of taste is the subjective principle of judgment in general, operating on the condition solely of the faculty of judgment itself.

Unlike mere labor or science or commercial handicraft, beautiful art is free. Yet we must be conscious of it as art and not nature, to keep it within the framework that will allow it to please in the mere act of judging. Beautiful art is the work of genius, which is the "innate mental disposition (*ingenium*) through which nature gives the rule to art." Genius is an original productive talent, not a capacity for following rules. Its products serve as examples setting standards for others. Natural beauty is a beautiful thing, but artificial beauty is a beautiful representation of a thing. In some beauties, such as the latter, inevitably a concept enters, and enjoyment through reason as well as aesthetic judging enters with it. Taste, but not genius, is a requisite for judging works of beautiful art. Genius is a faculty of pre-

senting *aesthetical ideas*, representations of the imagination that occasion much thought where no single thought is adequate. This is a particular kind of the play that harmonizes the imagination and the understanding. It goes beyond the limits of experience to find presentations of such completeness that they have no example in nature, presentations that will communicate the aesthetic pleasure to others.

The chief aesthetic problem of Kant's times was how to controvert seriously matters of taste, as though taste had an objective standard, when we also assert that there is no disputing tastes. Kant cast the problem as an antinomy in the "Dialectic of the Aesthetical Judgment." The thesis is "The judgment of taste is not based upon concepts, for otherwise it would admit of controversy (would be determinable by proofs)." The antithesis is "The judgment of taste is based on concepts, for otherwise, despite its diversity, we could not quarrel about it (we could not claim for our judgment the necessary assent of others)." The apparent contradiction is resolved when we recognize that "concept" has a different reference in each proposition. A concept may be either determinable or not. The thesis refers to determinable concepts; the antithesis refers to the one indeterminable concept, the supersensible, on which the faculty of judgment rests. So understood, both are true, and the contradiction disappears.

The beautiful is the symbol of the morally good, in that it gives pleasure with a claim for the agreement of everyone else. It makes the mind feel an elevation of itself above mere pleasantness of sensation and enables it to estimate the worth of others in this regard also. For just as the reason does in respect to the practical, the judgment gives the law to itself with respect to objects of pure aesthetic satisfaction. The propaedeutic to the beautiful arts lies in humane studies, not in precepts, and it reaches art through the social spirit and the communication that is distinctive of humanity. Taste "is at bottom a faculty for judging of the sensible illustration of moral ideas."

Purpose

The sequel of the study of purposiveness in nature without purpose is the study of the basis of judging nature as having purpose—the "Critique of the Teleological Judgment." We have absolutely no grounds to ascribe purpose objectively to nature, but must regard purpose as a principle supplied by ourselves for bringing this phenomenon of nature under rules wherever the laws of mechanical causality do not suffice to do so.

A purpose is a concept that functions as a cause of that of which it is the concept. In order to see the possibility of a thing as a purpose, it is a requisite that its form is not possible according to natural laws and that the empirical knowledge of its cause and effect presupposes concepts of reason. The things regarded as natural purposes are organized, living beings. The understanding takes causes to be immediate preceding conditions (efficient causes) of their effects, but the reason can think a final cause. For a thing to be a natural purpose, its parts must be possible only through their reference to the whole, and they should so combine in the unity of the whole that they are reciprocally cause and effect of each other. Thus nothing is in vain in it. The being so constituted may be regarded as the product of both efficient causes and final causes, an organized and self-organizing being—in a word, a *natural purpose*. Organized beings give the basis for teleology, as they first afford objective reality to the concept of a natural purpose. From regarding them, we are carried further, reflectively to regard the mechanism of all of nature as subordinated according to principles of reason.

The reflective judgment must subsume presentations under a law not yet given; hence, it must serve as principle for itself. Therefore it needs maxims for its reflection, so as to attain to concepts and cognize nature even according to empirical laws. Among its maxims the following antinomy arises. Thesis: All production of material things and their forms must be judged possible according to merely mechanical laws. Antithesis: Some products of material nature cannot be judged to be possible according to merely mechanical laws. However, these are maxims, not substantive propositions. The concepts involved in maxims of the judgment (including "mechanical laws") are not accorded objective reality but are merely guides to reason. Now the thesis may be acceptable as a maxim of the determinant, and the antithesis of the reflective judgment. Hence, no contradiction in fact exists between them.

To unite the mechanism of nature and the principle of purposes, teleology places the supersensible tentatively at the basis of phenomenal nature, but of it we can have no theoretical knowledge whatever. We should explain everything in nature by mechanism as far as this is in our power. However, we should acknowledge that some things, which we cannot even state for investigation without a concept of a purpose of reason, must finally be accounted for by purposes.

For anything in nature, if we ask why it exists, the answer is either that it rose solely out of nature's mechanism without design, or else that it has somewhere a designed ground as a contingent being. If the latter, we can say either that its purpose lies in itself, a final purpose, or that the ground of its existence is external to it in another natural being. Apparently, humanity is the only reality we can regard as the ultimate purpose of creation here on earth, for humans are the only creatures "who can form a concept of [their] purposes and who can, by [their] reason, make out of an aggregate of purposively formed things a system of purposes." That within us that is to be furthered as a purpose must be either what nature could perhaps satisfy, our happiness, or else our aptitude and skill with which we can turn nature to all kinds of purposes, our culture. However, if we make happiness our whole purpose, a purpose dependent upon nature, this renders us incapable of positing our existence as a final purpose and of being in harmony with it. The culture of skill, and particularly of the will, of discipline, makes us receptive of higher purposes than nature itself can supply. Through culture of the beautiful arts and the sciences, we are prepared for a reign in which reason alone shall have authority.

The Moral Law

The moral law, as the rational condition of the use of our freedom, obliges us a priori (as shown in *The Critique of Practical Reason*) to strive for the highest good in the world possible through freedom. The highest physical good is happiness. However, reason supposes virtue to be the worthiness to be happy, and it is impossible to represent virtue and happiness as connected by natural causes or as harmonized in life. Thus, to represent to ourselves a final purpose consistent with the moral law, we must assume a moral world cause. While the final purpose cannot be regarded as having objective reality, it has subjective practical reality by being embodied in our actions toward the highest good. Through it we gain the possibility of thinking the world has a purposive order, although we gain no proof of the existence of its original Being. "For the existence of the original Being as a Godhead, or of the soul as an immortal spirit, absolutely no proof in a theoretical point of view is possible." Faith (as *habitus* or disposition, not act) is the moral attitude of reason toward belief in something unattainable by theoretical cognition. The mind assumes that, since it is so commanded, the duty to attain the highest good is possible to fulfill. It has grounds for such a faith in the faculty of the reason freely to legislate in accordance with the moral law. Only freedom, among the three pure rational ideas—God, freedom, and immortality—proves its objective reality by its effects in nature; thus it renders possible the reconciliation in thought and nature of God, immortality, and freedom.

John T. Goldthwait, updated by John K. Roth

Additional Reading

Allison, Henry E. *Idealism and Freedom: Essays on Kant's Theoretical and Practical Philosophy*. New York: Cambridge University Press, 1996. An important interpreter of Immanuel Kant explores relationships between Kant's theory of knowledge and his moral philosophy.

Bohman, James, and Matthias Lutz-Backmann, eds. *Perpetual Peace: Essays on Kant's Cosmopolitan Ideal*. Cambridge, Mass.: MIT Press, 1997. The contributors appraise Kant's theories about and hopes for a universal rationality that would encourage shared moral understanding and reduce political conflict.

Cassirer, Ernst. *Kant's Life and Thought*. Translated by James Hayden. New Haven, Conn.: Yale University Press, 1981. Written by an important twentieth century philosopher, this book offers a readable intellectual biography of Kant.

Caygill, Howard. *A Kant Dictionary*. Cambridge, Mass.: Blackwell, 1995. A reliable reference guide that helps to clarify key concepts and ideas in Kant's philosophy.

Copleston, Frederick. *A History of Philosophy: Modern Philosophy*. Garden City, N.Y.: Doubleday, 1964. Copleston devotes several lucid chapters to Kant and his significance in the history of philosophy.

Guyer, Paul. *Kant and the Claims of Taste*. New York: Cambridge University Press, 1979. A careful and detailed study focusing on Kant's understanding of beauty and goodness and how we make judgments about them.

_____, ed. *The Cambridge Companion to Kant*. Cambridge, England: Cambridge University Press, 1992. Helpful essays by contemporary Kant scholars shed important light on key aspects of Kant's theory of knowledge, metaphysics, ethics, and religious thought.

Hare, John E. *The Moral Gap: Kantian Ethics, Human Limits, and God's Assistance*. New York: Oxford University Press, 1996. A study of the strengths and weakness of Kant's influential moral philosophy.

Kemp, John. *The Philosophy of Kant*. New York: Oxford University Press, 1968. A brief, readable account of Kant's theory of knowledge, moral philosophy, and aesthetics.

Jones, W. T. *A History of Western Philosophy: Kant to Wittgenstein and Sartre*. New York: Harcourt, Brace, 1969. Provides a good starting point for readers who want a clear and basic introduction to Kant's philosophy.

Schott, Robin May, ed. *Feminist Interpretations of Immanuel Kant*. University Park: Pennsylvania State University Press, 1997. Essayists bring the perspectives of feminist scholarship to bear on Kant's method and thought.

Walker, Ralph. *Kant*. New York: Routledge, 1999. An excellent biographical introduction to the thoughts of the philosopher, clearly presented and requiring no special background. Bibliography.

Wolff, Robert Paul, ed. *Kant: A Collection of Critical Essays*. Garden City, N.Y.: Doubleday, 1967. Important scholars contribute essays on a wide range of themes and issues in Kant's philosophy.

Patricia Cook, updated by John K. Roth

Søren Kierkegaard

Kierkegaard's challenge to neat systems of philosophical thought, such as that propounded by Georg Wilhelm Friedrich Hegel, has highlighted his philosophical influence. His predominant assumption, that existence is too multiform to be systematized, is at the basis of existentialism and indeed much of Continental philosophy.

Principal philosophical works: *Enten-Eller*, 1843 (*Either/Or*, 1944); *Gjentagelsen*, 1843 (*Repetition*, 1993); *Frygt og Bæven*, 1843 (*Fear and Trembling*, 1939); *Philosophiske Smuler*, 1844 (*Philosophical Fragments*, 1936); *Begrebet Angest*, 1844 (*The Concept of Dread*, 1944); *Stadier paa Livets Vej*, 1845 (*Stages on Life's Way*, 1940); *Afsluttende uvidenskabelig Efterskrift*, 1846 (*Concluding Unscientific Postscript*, 1941); *Opbyggelige Taler I forskjellig Aand*, 1847; *Christelige Taler*, 1848 (*Christian Discourses*, 1939); *Synspunktet for min Forfatter-Virksomhed*, 1859 (wr. 1848-1849; *The Point of View for My Work as an Author*, 1939); *Sygdommen til Døden*, 1849 (*The Sickness unto Death*, 1941); *Indøvelse i Christendom*, 1850 (*Training in Christianity*, 1941); *Hvad Christus dømmer om officiel Christendom*, 1855 (*What Christ's Judgment Is About Official Christianity*, 1944); *Til Selvprøvelse*, 1857 (*For Self-Examination*, 1940).

Born: May 5, 1813; Copenhagen, Denmark
Died: November 11, 1855; Copenhagen, Denmark

Early Life

Søren Aabye Kierkegaard was the last of seven children born to Michael Pedersen Kierkegaard and his second wife, Ane Sørensdatter (Lund); she had been the maid of Michael's first wife, who died childless after two years of marriage. The elder Kierkegaard, an affluent businessperson, had been born in poverty and virtual servitude, rising by dint of hard work and good fortune to the comfortable status the family enjoyed at Søren's birth.

Despite such prosperity, the Kierkegaard household was haunted by early death. Two of Søren's siblings died before he was nine; his mother and three more siblings died in a span of less than three years before his twenty-first birthday. Michael was never able to overcome the belief that these deaths were punishment for the unpardonable sin he committed when, as a boy of eleven, tending sheep and bitter at his lot, he cursed God.

The influence of the somber elder Kierkegaard on his gifted son is certain, but the extent to which it permeated Kierkegaard's character and influenced his writings throughout his life is difficult to estimate. A key passage from Kierkegaard's journals suggests that his father's inadvertent revelation of some past misdeeds permanently altered their relationship:

> An affair between the father and son where the son finds everything out, and yet dare not admit it to himself. The father is a respectable man, God-fearing and strict; only once, when he is tipsy, he lets fall some words that arouse the most dreadful suspicions. Otherwise the son is never told of it and never dares to ask his father or anybody else.

Regarding this incident, Kierkegaard scholar Frederick Sontag says that it thrust Kierkegaard into a "period of dissipation and despair," causing him for a time to neglect completely his theological studies at the university.

In addition to his father's influence, Kierkegaard was indelibly marked by his engagement to Regina Olsen. He met her for the first time at a party, when she was fourteen. She was captivated by his intellectual sagacity; he later admitted that that had been his design. They both endured a difficult period of waiting until she was nearly eighteen before they became engaged. Yet, having endured such a lengthy period of waiting, within days after the engagement had been effected Kierkegaard was convinced that it was a mistake. Some years after he had broken the engagement, he wrote in his journal:

> I said to her that in every generation there were certain individuals who were destined to be sacrificed for the others. She hardly understood what I was talking about. . . . But just this spontaneous youthful happiness of hers, set alongside my terrible melancholy, and in such a relationship, must teach me to understand myself. For how melancholy I was I had never before surmised; I possessed no measure for conceiving how happy a human being can be.

In 1841, not long after breaking his engagement, Kierkegaard successfully defended his doctoral thesis and departed for Berlin, where he stayed for several months attending lectures. Within two years, he published his first books, the product of an intense period of creativity, and his career was fully launched.

Life's Work

Kierkegaard was a powerful and prolific writer. The bulk of his corpus was produced within a period of about seven years, spanning 1843-1850. Appreciative readers of Kierkegaard's writings can be thankful for the voluminous groundswell of production that came in his early thirties, for he died a young man of forty-two. During the course of his writing career, he pursued several recurring themes; it would be misleading, however, to treat his work as though he had systematically moved from one arena to another in a planned, orderly fashion.

Indeed, Kierkegaard's decided distrust of the systematizing of philosopher Georg Wilhelm Friedrich Hegel had pushed him in the direction of an existential methodology that would be expressive of his whole personality. Rather than creating a system for the whole of reality that was necessarily linked by chains of reasoning, Kierkegaard created in his writings psychological experiments centered on persons confronting life situations. By so doing, he avoided both the strict rationalism and the idealism so characteristic of analytic philosophers and pulled his readers into existential consideration of life's dilemmas.

Kierkegaard considered his life and his works as an effort to fulfill a divinely appointed task. This conviction had led to his breakup with Regina because of what he called his destiny "to be sacrificed for the others." It also led him to the realization that his vocation was to confront his contemporaries with the ideal Christian life. He saw that as his purpose in life and consequently

Søren Kierkegaard. *(Library of Congress)*

chose to lay aside every weight that would hinder him from "willing that one thing."

Denmark had appropriated Hegelianism as the proper mode of informed thinking. Indeed, the Danish had even allowed Christianity to be absorbed into the Hegelian system. Hence, the Christian ideal of individuals choosing Christ was lost: Every person in Denmark was nominally a Christian. When applied to the Church, the totalizing attempt prefigured in Hegel made everyone a Christian by birth. It was within this context, and for the purpose of confronting this attitude, that Kierkegaard arose to do battle in print. He described himself as a "midwife," helping to bring forth authentic individuals. His goal was nothing short of arousing his age from its complacence. Whereas Hegelianism might encourage rigors of thought, it made things easy through its promise of certainty. Kierkegaard, on the other hand, made things difficult by thrusting the individual into the fray, thereby teaching him what it truly means "to become a Christian."

An important aspect of many of Kierkegaard's works had to do with his method. For his philosophical works, he used a variety of often-flamboyant pseudonyms, such as Victor Eremita, Constantine Constantius, Virgilius Haufniensis, Johannes Climacus, and Anti-Climacus. At the same time, under his own name, he produced a number of devotional works and religious meditations. Kierkegaard's indirect communication has caused not a little bewilderment. He himself addressed what he referred to as his "polynymity" rather than "pseudonymity" in an appendix to *Concluding Unscientific Postscript*. Given his consistent and unwavering emphasis on "choice," it is reasonable to assume that Kierkegaard believed that this method of presentation enhanced his ability to confront the reader. As long as pseudonyms were used, his readers were not free to see what "Kierkegaard, the authority" had to say about the issues. Readers would thus be thrown back on themselves, having to choose an interpretive stance for themselves.

Because Kierkegaard was a difficult writer, ahead of his time, he received little income from his writings, depending largely on his substantial inheritance. Moreover, as a brilliant, acerbic, and uncompromising critic of his society, he was frequently embroiled in controversy; in his later years, he worked in great isolation. Near the end of his life, Kierkegaard wrote several books that dealt explicitly with Christianity. *For Self-Examination* challenged his readers to view themselves in the light of New Testament descriptions of Christianity rather than simplistically accepting the terms that the established church was propounding. His *What Christ's Judgment Is About Official Christianity* views the relationship between the state and Christianity. He shows that the official Christianity of which every Dane partook was far from New Testament Christianity.

On October 2, 1855, Kierkegaard collapsed while walking in the street. The nature of his final illness is not certain. He was hospitalized, accepting his fate with tranquillity. He died on November 11, 1855.

Influence

At the time of his death, and for a long period thereafter, Kierkegaard's works were little known outside Denmark. Both his striking originality and the fact that he wrote in Danish delayed recognition of his achievement. By the early twentieth century, however, a wide diversity of thinkers reflected his influence, which has continued to grow since that time; he is often hailed as "the father of existentialism."

Even Kierkegaard's most explicitly philosophical writings, it should be noted, bear an undeniable theological character. In *Philosophical Fragments*, he plumbs the epistemological depths of how a historical consciousness can confront an eternal consciousness and come away with what one might call "knowledge." In other words, to what degree can eternal truth be learned within the categories of time or space? In *Concluding Unscientific Postscript*, he confronts the objective problem of the truth of Christianity. The issue involved here is often referred to as "Lessing's ditch." Gotthold Ephraim Lessing believed that there exists an intellectually impossible leap from the contingent truths of history to the necessary truths of divine revelation. Kierkegaard looked at this problem and concluded that "a leap of faith" was required for the individual bound by finiteness and historical necessity to encounter eternal truth. This assertion has caused most to claim that Kierkegaard equated truth with subjectivity.

Stephen M. Ashby

Either/Or

Type of philosophy: Ethics, existentialism
First published: Enten-Eller, 1843 (English translation, 1944)
Principal ideas advanced:

◇ The aesthetical mode of existence is exemplified by both romantic hedonism and abstract intellectualism; both the sensualist and the intellectual fail to commit themselves decisively and thereby to achieve existence and selfhood.

◇ Only through choice is authentic selfhood attained; life is a matter of either/or.

◇ The aesthetical way leads to boredom, melancholy, and despair.

◇ In turning toward decision and commitment because of despair, the self passes from the aesthetical stage to the ethical.

◇ In the ethical stage, in virtue of having chosen itself, the self becomes centralized, unified, and authentic.

◇ The third stage of development is the religious, but no stage is sufficient by itself; the ethical stage transfigures the aesthetical, and the religious transfigures the ethical.

In *Either/Or*, Søren Kierkegaard seeks to elucidate the contrasts and interrelationships between what Kierkegaard called the aesthetical and the ethical modes of existence. Like most of Kierkegaard's writings, *Either/Or* was not published under his own name but under one of several pseudonyms. The heterogeneous literary style employs lyrical aphorisms, orations, psychological analyses, drama reviews, and philosophical formulations.

In the first part of the work, the aestheticist, who expresses his views through these various literary forms, is designated as *A*. In the second part, the ethical thinker, who bears the pseudonym of Judge William, is designated as *B*. In one of his later works, *Afsluttende uvidenskabelig Efterskrift* (1846; *Concluding Unscientific Postscript*, 1941), Kierkegaard explained the central theme of *Either/Or* by informing the reader that *A* is an existential possibility, superior in dialectics and highly gifted in the use of wit and poetic style, who nevertheless remains unable to commit himself in decisive action, and thus never exists at all in the true sense. *B*, on the other hand, represents the ethical person whose whole life is transformed into inwardness, passion, and commitment.

Judge William elucidates the content of the ethical in the form of a letter addressed to *A*. The communication of ethical truth demands a form or style that is commensurate with it. Ethical truth is existential and concrete, as contrasted with the theoretical and abstract, and consequently requires for its expression a form that has the personal quality of a dialogue or a letter. This constitutes the form of indirect communication. At the outset, Judge William reminds the aestheticist of the biblical story of the Prophet Nathan and David as a supreme example of this form of communication. King David listened attentively to the prophet's parable but remained in a state of theoretical detachment. He intellectualized the parable as an objective story that applied only to the mythical stranger. Not until the Prophet Nathan made the application explicit in his statement "Thou, O King, art the man" did David apprehend the existential relevance of the parable. The Prophet Nathan used the form of indirect communication. This is also the form used by Judge William.

The Aesthetical Way

The aesthetical mode of existence has two primary expressions—romantic hedonism and abstract intellectualism. Wolfgang Amadeus Mozart's *Don Giovanni* is depicted as the classical representative of the sensual or hedonistic view of life, and Johann Wolfgang von Goethe's *Faust: Eine Tragödie* (1808; *The Tragedy of Faust*, 1823) expresses the aesthetical personality of abstract intellectualism. Kierkegaard's archenemy, the Hegelian rationalist, also falls victim to the latter expression. For both the sensualist and the intellectualist, inward existence and commitment are accidental and remain a matter of indifference. Neither is able to shoulder responsibility and commit the self to action. They lack the ethical pathos that characterizes *B*.

The view of life that characterizes the hedonist is portrayed by the young lover in the "Diary of a Seducer," who carries through his seduction with a diabolical cunning. The young lover is a prototype of Mozart's Don Giovanni character: He experiments with numerous possibilities but never commits himself to the responsibility of actualizing any particular one in earnestness and seriousness. He experiments with the techniques of seduction but never commits himself in a promise. He experiments with love but never commits himself in marriage. In his aesthetical experimentation, the young lover retains the proper abstractness and indifference. Every woman is, for him, a *woman in general*. Insofar as the young lover has a guiding principle, it is the hedonistic principle that enjoyment or pleasure constitutes the only end of life. The necessary internal conditions for the attainment of this life of pleasure are physical beauty and health; the necessary external conditions are wealth, glory, and high status. However, these conditions provide no ethical pathos for a committed life, and it is precisely a committed life that the young lover seeks to avoid. He lives only in the moment, an erotic present in which the satisfaction of a desire is maximized. Then the moment passes, and a new desire asserts its claim to thrive. His whole life becomes a discontinuous succession of passing from one moment to the next. His personality thus lacks unity and continuity. He has dispersed or lost himself in the present to the neglect of his past and his future. He no longer retains his past in memory, and he retreats from the future that confronts him with the responsibility of decision.

The speculative intellectualist suffers the same loss of selfhood as the romantic hedonist. Whereas the hedonist loses himself in the immediacy of the erotic present, the speculative thinker loses himself in the immediacy of his thought. The speculative thinker seeks to comprehend the whole of reality through the categories of a universal logic. However, in such a system, the concretely existing subject really does not matter. Just as for the sensualist every woman is a woman in general, so for the intellectualist all reality is dissolved into general categories. Speculative thought sees only the general movement of history, explained through the mediation of logical categories, and forgets the individual who apprehends himself within his particular and concrete history. Thus, both the hedonist and the speculative thinker evade the responsibility of decision. Both flirt with the realm of possibility but neither makes the leap into existence. The

hedonist escapes from the future and responsibility for dispersing himself in momentary pleasures. The speculative thinker evades choice by playing the role of a detached observer who speculates about the general movements in world history, but who never participates in his own inner history with pathos and inwardness. Expressing the Socratic irony of which Kierkegaard was a master, his pseudonym is made to say:

> To the philosopher world history is concluded, and he mediates. Hence, in our age as the order of the day we have the disgusting sight of young men who are able to mediate Christianity and paganism, are able to play with the titanic forces of history, and are unable to tell a plain man what he has to do in life, and who do not know any better what they themselves have to do."

The speculative thinker reduces existence to thought, sacrifices involvement for detached observation, and substitutes a reflective deliberation on universal history for the responsibility of concrete, personal decision. The common denominator of both expressions of aesthetical existence is a retreat from the reality of choice. In both cases, the self has not yet found itself. Only through choice is authentic selfhood attained. This demands an awareness that life is a matter of either/or. However, the either/or is a matter of indifference for the hedonist and the intellectualist alike. The aestheticist moves in a realm in abstraction from inwardness and existence.

Boredom and Despair

The aesthetical mode or stage of existence leads to boredom and melancholy, and finally to despair. *Either/Or* and the writings of Kierkegaard as a whole contain graphic descriptions of the enveloping character of the moods of boredom, melancholy, and despair. Boredom is depicted as an aesthetical determinant that has plagued humankind from the very beginning.

> The gods were bored, and so they created man. Adam was bored because he was alone, and so Eve was created. Thus boredom entered the world, and increased in proportion to the increase of population. Adam was

bored alone; then Adam and Eve were bored together; then Adam and Eve and Cain and Abel were bored *en famille*; then the population of the world increased and the people were bored *en masse*.

The aesthetical life of pure pleasure, as well as that of pure thought, leads to an abyss of boredom and tedium. Now it is necessary to distinguish two forms of boredom. In one form, boredom is apprehended as an intentional mood that is directed toward a particular object, event, or person. One is bored with a book, a movie, or a boorish conversant. This form of boredom is merely a surface phenomenon that does not yet disclose humanity's true situation. In the second and more genuine form of boredom, one is bored not with an intentionally specified object or person—one is bored with oneself. Humanity is confronted with a nameless emptiness that threatens life itself with a loss of meaning. This form of boredom brings one to a more intensified awareness of one's predicament.

The enigmatic, nameless emptiness that characterizes genuine boredom is also an existential determinant of melancholy individuals. If melancholy individuals are asked what it is that weighs on them, they are prone to reply, "I know not, I cannot explain it." Melancholy is a "spiritual ailment" or a "hysteria of the spirit" that confronts people with the abyss of emptiness and meaninglessness and reveals the disquietude and discontinuity of their existence. However, for the most part, the individuals who are subject to the disquieting moods of boredom and melancholy refuse to accept the condition and seek to conceal it through various diverting activities.

Like the philosopher Blaise Pascal, Kierkegaard saw how people seek to escape from themselves through diversions that provide momentary distraction. The continuing search for diversion is the basis of the "rotation method" described in the first part of the work. People are bored with life in the country, so they move to the village; they become bored in the village, so they move to the city; they then become bored with their homeland and travel abroad; they become bored with life in a foreign land, and then entertain the possibility of an endless journeying to alleviate their boredom. Melancholy individuals also engage in a self-defeating and frustrating search for diversion.

It is in the Roman emperor Nero, says the author, that one finds the example *par excellence* of a melancholy nature that had given itself over to an endless search for diverting distractions. Nero sought to divert himself through an immersion in pleasure. He appointed "ministers of pleasure" who were entrusted with the task of finding novel ways to satisfy his desires. Only in the moment of pleasure could Nero find distraction from his melancholy. "Then he grasps after pleasure; all the world's cleverness must devise for him new pleasures, for only in the instant of pleasure does he find repose, and when that is past he gasps with faintness." When the instant of pleasure passes, Nero again plunges into melancholy. Hence a new desire must be created so that another momentary gratification may occur. However, there is no end to this sort of thing, and Nero finds himself sucked into an abyss of meaninglessness and emptiness. Finally in his need for pleasure-producing distraction, he orders the burning of Rome, but when the last embers die, he again gyrates into an appalling melancholy. This description of Nero's nature, we are reminded by the author, has not been undertaken as an occasion to thank God along with the Pharisee that we are different from Nero. Nero is "flesh of our flesh and bone of our bone," which is to say that in Nero, a universal determinant of human existence becomes transparent.

Despair is the most intensive expression of the threat of meaninglessness and emptiness; it constitutes the culmination of the aesthetical mode of existence. The aesthetical life proves itself to be despair. In despair, the self experiences a loss of hope because diversion no longer provides its momentary satisfaction. Aestheticists realize that they cannot find themselves outside of themselves—neither in their hedonistic and sensual pursuits nor in the abstractions of their speculative thought. To discover their genuine selfhood, they must turn inward. They must turn toward earnestness, passion, decision, commitment, and freedom. Only in this movement will they be able to collect themselves out of their dispersed and dissipated existence and become a unified and integrated self. Despair is thus an intensification of subjectivity that constitutes the gateway to authentic or genuine selfhood. In "choosing" despair, the self gives birth to itself and passes from the aesthetical stage of indecision to the ethical stage of decisive commitment.

The Ethical Way

The ethical stage is the stage of decision and resolute commitment. The act of choice is an intensification of the ethical. Even the richest personalities, writes the author, must be accounted as nothing before they have chosen themselves. On the other hand, the poorest personalities are everything for having chosen themselves. Choice liberates the self both from the immediacy of pleasure and from the immediacy of reflection or pure thought and makes possible the discovery of genuine selfhood. Through decision and commitment, the self becomes integrated and "centralized." Aestheticists are always "eccentric" in that they seek the center of themselves in the periphery of hedonist or intellectualistic concerns—that means that they have lost their selves. Ethical people, by virtue of having shouldered their responsibility in decision, have their center within themselves. Their lives are centralized and unified. The unity of the ethical self is not a unity that is anchored in some residual ego or abiding substratum. The self is not an object that can be abstractly defined as having a permanent nature or a substantial fixity. Unity is achieved, not given. The self achieves or attains its unity and integrity through choice.

Choice thus becomes the central category for the ethical thinker. This is the category that lies closest to the heart and thought of Judge William. Not being a logician, he has no lengthy and impressive list of abstract categories—he has only one concrete denomination: choice. Choice involves freedom, an either/or, and in this can be found the greatest treasure that humans can possess. Judge William explains to the reader the central intention of his ethical elucidations when he writes:

> For freedom, therefore, I am fighting. . . . I am fighting for the future, for either/or. That is the treasure I desire to bequeath to those whom I love in the world; yea, if my little son were at this instant of an age when he could thoroughly understand me, I would say to

him, "I leave to thee no fortune, no title and dignities, but I know where there lies buried a treasure which suffices to make thee richer than the whole world, and this treasure belongs to thee, and thou shalt not even express thanks to me for it lest thou take hurt to thine own soul by owing everything to another. This treasure is deposited in thine own inner self: there is an either/or which makes a man greater than the angels."

Judge William's central intention of calling the aestheticist to an awareness of freedom and the importance of choosing is understood as an expression of the Socratic task of attaining self-knowledge. "Know thyself" and "Choose thyself" are conjunctive rather than disjunctive tasks. The knowledge that was the concern of Socrates was an ethical knowledge, and ethical knowledge can be achieved only through choosing. The self becomes transparent to itself only in decisive action.

Romantic and Conjugal Love

In the person of Judge William is the concrete exemplification of the ethical mode of existence. He is a married man who has committed himself in conjugal love. As such, he is contrasted with the young lover of the "Diary of a Seducer," who dissipates himself in his various experiments with romantic love. Romantic and conjugal love are thus understood as existential qualities that differentiate the aesthetical and the ethical. Romantic love is experimental and nonhistorical, lacking continuity. Conjugal love expresses an inner history that gives it constancy and stability.

The romantic hedonist lives in the present, which he experiences in abstraction from existence. The present becomes an instantaneous now, defined as the occasion for enjoyment. The past loses its existential significance, and the future is never really faced. The young lover seduces a girl, and after the moment of seduction passes, all is over. The moment then becomes part of an abstracted past that has significance only as an object for melancholy recollection. Romantic love knows no repetition. The romantic hedonist lives his life as though it were a discrete succession of instantaneous nows, each coming to be and passing away into a past that is bereft of existential importance. Everything is concentrated in the present, which is apprehended as embodying full reality. Conjugal love, on the other hand, strives for repetition. The ideal husband is one who is able to repeat his love every day. The married man thus carries within himself the memory of his past, anticipates his future, and undertakes his daily tasks and decisions in the context of his integrated wholeness. His past, future, and present are unified. It is thus that time and history become of paramount importance for conjugal love. The constancy and continuity of conjugal love are made possible through a unification of the self in its inner history.

In distinguishing between romantic and conjugal love, Judge William does not intend an absolute disjunction. He speaks of marriage as the true transfiguration of romantic love. Marriage is its friend, not its enemy. Romantic love is not left behind in the transition to the ethical sphere. It becomes transfigured through the constancy of conjugal love. In the ethical stage, romantic love is historicized and apprehended in terms of its temporal significance. The aesthetical always remains in the ethical, but it remains as a *relative* and *dependent* mode of existence. "By the absolute choice the ethical is always posited, but from this it does not follow by any means that the aesthetical is excluded. In the ethical the personality is concentrated in itself, so the aesthetical is absolutely excluded or is excluded as the absolute, but relatively it is still left." The romantic hedonist absolutizes the aesthetical as the final and self-sufficient dimension of existence. The ethical person appropriates the aesthetical in its relativity and transforms it by the existential determinants of choice and commitment. At one point in his letter, Judge William speaks of the three stages (aesthetical, ethical, and religious) as "three great allies." The spheres or stages of existence are not temporally successive levels of development, excluding each other in a hierarchical ascent. They are modes of existence, always in some sense present, penetrating the personality in its process of becoming. They constitute the existential cross section of the self and coexist interdependently throughout its history. No sphere is sufficient by itself. The absolutization of one of the three spheres brings about a suffocation of the self.

Choice

The phenomenon of time, which plays such an important role in ethical existence, is the focus of a profound analysis of German philosopher Georg Wilhelm Friedrich Hegel's teaching on the alienated or unhappy consciousness. Hegel had already taught that the alienated consciousness is the self that is never present to itself, being absent from itself either in the past or in the future. The author agrees that Hegel was right in thus defining the realm of the unhappy consciousness but argues that he was wrong in understanding it abstractly rather than existentially. Hegel "beheld the kingdom from afar off." The author understands himself to be a native inhabitant of the realm. Consciousness is alienated from itself when it is severed either from its past or from its future. The alienated consciousness has lost the memory of its life and has nothing for which to hope. Thus, it culminates in despair. The unified consciousness has within it both pastness and futurity. Memory and hope are unified in the center of personality. The ethical person attains this unified consciousness in the moment of decisive action. In the act of choice, the past is taken up, the future is acknowledged and faced, and the self is centralized.

The touchstone of the decision through which the self achieves its unity and integrity is inwardness. An authentic choice is a choice made inwardly in passion and earnestness. The accent falls on the *way of choosing* rather than on *what is chosen*. In the ethical sphere, people are educated in *how* to choose. Their first concern is not with the choice of the "right" but with the earnestness and inwardness that determines the movement of choice. This does not mean that the ethical thinker has no interest in the moral content of choice. It does mean, however, that the moral content cannot be abstracted as a *what*—as an objectively determined and legislated moral standard. An action made solely because of external standards is bereft of moral content. Only that action that proceeds from the depths of inwardness qualifies the self as ethical. Judge William has little interest in a table of virtues that delineates abstract moral requirements. Ethical action is not a matter of following virtues. It is a matter of self-knowledge and self-commitment. Like German philosopher Friedrich Nietzsche's strong person, Kierkegaard's ethical person exists "beyond good and evil."

Either/Or concludes with a prayer and a sermon. This is a reminder to the reader that the ethical stage is not the final dimension of existence but is itself transfigured by a religious state. As the ethical stage transfigures the aesthetical, so the religious transfigures the ethical by introducing the existential determinants of suffering, guilt, sin, and faith. However, _Either/Or_ does not carry the existential elucidation beyond the ethical. One of the reasons Kierkegaard wrote _Stadier paa Livets Vej_ (1845; _Stages on Life's Way_, 1940) was to give proper due to the religious stage.

Calvin O. Schrag

Philosophical Fragments

Type of philosophy: Existentialism, metaphysics, philosophy of religion
First published: Philosophiske Smuler, 1844 (English translation, 1936)
Principal ideas advanced:
◇ People can be separated into three groups, depending on the values they hold: The aesthetes want entertainment, pleasure, and freedom from boredom; ethical people live for the sake of duty, taking on obligations in order to be bound to discharge them; and religious people live in order to obey God.
◇ The Socratic idea of religious truth is that truth in religious matters is not unique, that one learns religious truths by recollection of what one has learned in the realm of Ideas.
◇ The alternative position (the Christian view) is that God in time (Jesus Christ) is the teacher of people, that faith is an organ of knowing, that knowledge comes through the consciousness of sin, and that in a moment of decision a person's life can be changed.

Søren Kierkegaard's _Philosophical Fragments_ is the central work in a series of books marked by a consistent theme, a most unusual manner of presentation, pervasive irony, and a single-minded effort to present Christianity in a fashion

that requires the reader to reach some sort of decision about it. The irony of Kierkegaard is evident even in the title of the book: _Philosophical Fragments_. Very few philosophers would entitle their main work a "fragment" or try to present the core of their position in fewer than one hundred pages.

The Three Stages

To read Kierkegaard with some degree of understanding, it is necessary to have some knowledge of the general plan of his literary work. One of the essential features of his philosophical position is the doctrine of the "stages." Kierkegaard believed that people can be separated into three groups, depending on the values they hold as fundamental. He calls these three groups "aesthetes," "ethicists," and "religionists."

Aesthetes are people who live for the interesting; they want entertainment and variety in their lives and seek to avoid boredom, which they regard as the worst evil that can overtake them. They live to find immediate satisfaction and avoid making any long-term commitments. All people have the aesthetic as the basic material of their lives; many remain in the aesthetic stage throughout life. However, some people move into another sphere, the ethical.

Ethicists live for the sake of doing their duty; they replace struggles over the interesting versus the boring with those involving the good versus the bad. The kind of person German philosopher Immanuel Kant had in mind when he urged people to do their duty rather than follow their inclinations is the kind of person Kierkegaard called the ethical person. Ethicists' lives are successful if they take on as many obligations to other people as possible and do their best to discharge these obligations.

Kierkegaard contrasted the ethical person with the aesthete in his first book, _Enten-Eller_ (1843; _Either/Or_, 1944), by posing the question of love and marriage. Aesthetes fall in love, live for a multitude of engagements (but no marriages), and want romance in the Hollywood sense. Ethicists do not fall in love but rather choose to love, want a short engagement so that they may enter the state of being married (and thereby become duty-bound to another person for the remainder of their days), and find their romance in daily routine rather than in secret, passionate moments.

A great many people with this kind of ethical concern base the ethical rules that govern their lives in God's will. For such persons, there is no difference between being ethical and being religious. However, Kierkegaard felt that the Christian religion demanded a different orientation from that which characterizes the ethical person. Kierkegaard did not believe that the Christian concept of sin could be explained by saying that to sin is to break an ethical rule. Sin is not violation of rule but violation of the person of God. Kierkegaard contrasted the ethical person's orientation with the religionist's orientation in *Frygt og Bœven* (1843; *Fear and Trembling*, 1939), in which he considered the problems arising out of biblical figure Abraham's intended sacrifice of his son, Isaac. As Kierkegaard saw it, Abraham had to choose between the ethical demand to avoid murder and the religious command from God that he sacrifice his son. Kierkegaard raised the question whether it might not be the case that religious commitment sometimes requires a person to suspend his ethical concern. The religious person may at times face the temptation to be good rather than holy.

Indirect Communication

Another feature of Kierkegaard's writing is the technique Kierkegaard called "indirect communication." This technique implied that the doctrine of the stages should not be stated directly. The representatives of the various stages should not be described from the point of view of an external observer but presented "from within," so to speak. To this end, Kierkegaard often adopted pseudonyms in his books. He felt he could best present the aesthetic stage by imagining an aesthete, then writing out what such a person would say. *Either/Or*, for example, is an extended correspondence between "a young man" and his older friend, Judge William. Kierkegaard does not directly enter the picture, and he offers no judgment between the two views of life presented by the young man and the judge; the reader is left to decide. Kierkegaard was quite successful in this matter, even presenting the imaginary characters with different writing styles. The young man writes beautifully, is poetic, sensitive, and lyrical; the judge writes in a pedestrian style, lecturing as he goes, paying little attention to literary graces.

The pseudonymous author of *Philosophical Fragments* is Johannes Climacus—one who is writing about something that is at the climax of the total problem that concerned Kierkegaard throughout his literary and philosophical career. Climacus is detached, ironic, and supposedly noncommitted on the immediate problem he is considering—namely, the possibility of giving a different view of religious truth from that presented by Socrates. Socrates is used in the book as a foil, as a man holding a position against which an alternative view can be seen more sharply. Christianity, as Kierkegaard understood it, is the alternative, of course, but although the reader understands this quite early in the book, the position is not called Christianity until the last paragraph.

Religious Truth

The "Socratic" position that Climacus assumes in the book is a rather common interpretation of the Socrates of Plato's dialogues. It may be stated briefly as follows: Truth in religious matters does not differ from other kinds of truth. The point of religion is to hold true beliefs about God and to act in accordance with them. Coming to hold true beliefs, in religion as in other areas of human concern, is essentially a matter of recollection, of remembering what a person knew in the realm of the Ideas before birth but forgot when the soul was imprisoned in the body. The teacher, in this case, does not introduce anything new to the learner but merely serves as midwife, helping the learner to recall what he or she once knew. After the recollection occurs, the learner adjusts to the true propositions, and the teacher drops out of the knowing relation. The teacher is an occasion, but not a condition, for knowing.

The essential elements in the (Christian) alternative position regarding religious truth are set forth quite openly by Kierkegaard's pseudonym in the "Moral" that he appends to *Philosophical Fragments*. The Christian "hypothesis" (as Climacus calls it) differs from the Socratic position, as sketched above, in assuming *faith* as an organ of knowing, in presupposing that there can be a *consciousness of sin* in people, in supposing that there can be a *moment of decision* that changes the course of a person's life, and in assuming a different kind of *teacher* from Socrates—namely, God in time (that is, Jesus Christ). The detachment of Climacus can be seen in the fact that he states these new assumptions so clearly in this "Moral," thus enabling the reader to reject Christianity simply and yet with understanding, if he so desires. Furthermore, Climacus merely states that the hypothesis he has been elaborating differs from Socrates' position in these respects. The question of which hypothesis is true is an entirely different question, he says, and he makes no effort to settle this latter question.

Now if Socrates is right, Climacus argues, the truth is within a person. The teacher merely helps pupils realize what they had known all along. In such a case, a person is in the truth rather than in error. In addition, the teacher is not important, because the teacher neither removes the learner from error nor introduces the individual to new truth. Further, the time at which a learner recalls the truth is not important. All in all, the situation is similar to what happened with most, if not all, people when they learned the basic elements of arithmetic: They can no longer remember from whom they learned them or when. The important thing is that two and two make four, and they always have and always will.

The alternative to this view obviously involves assuming that one is not naturally in the truth but is naturally in error. If this is the case, then the teacher must first give the learner the condition for leaving error and apprehending truth. Then the teacher must provide the truth for the learner to apprehend. The moment at which the learner leaves error and apprehends truth is now quite important and decisive for the learner. In addition, the teacher must be more than an ordinary person, because the teacher is essential to the learner's apprehension of the truth. Indeed, the teacher is so crucial that he or she is even necessary in order that the learner may recognize that he is in error. Such a teacher, Climacus says, one could appropriately call "Savior."

These elements in Climacus's alternative hypothesis are obviously elements in the traditional Christian account. The fact that one is naturally in error rather than in the truth and also that one does not even recognize such a condition clearly refer to the Christian doctrine of sin, and Climacus does call being in error "sin." The truth that one gains from the teacher is just as obviously the faith that Christians possess. The very unusual teacher who is essential to coming into the truth is, as Climacus calls him, "God in time"; that is, Jesus of Nazareth. The crucial moment in which a person leaves error for truth is the conversion experience that is the object of so much preaching in Christian churches. Climacus leaves no doubt that these identifications are appropriate because he often speaks to the reader about what he has written, citing the original sources of the "hypothesis" he is developing.

In outline, then, the account in *Philosophical Fragments* is a very familiar one, differing from the usual Christian account only in the words used to express it and in the reference to the Socratic alternative. There are, however, some implications of Climacus's simple account that are deserving of further treatment. Two matters should be looked into further here: Climacus's account of "the Absolute Paradox," and the question of the "disciple at second hand."

Absolute Paradox

The Absolute Paradox is a discussion of the philosophical significance of the Christian claim that God was incarnate in Jesus of Nazareth. The Socratic view that the truth is somehow within humanity and needs only to be drawn out by a skillful teacher such as Socrates implies that the human mind is adequate for knowing the truth, even religious truth. If, on the contrary, people do not have the truth within themselves in some sense, then what a person ought to know or needs to know is beyond the self—it is the unknown. Or, as Climacus calls it, it is "the other," the absolutely other. However, if it is the absolutely other than humanity, then a person's reason is not competent to know it. Yet people, if they are to achieve the truth, must come to know this absolutely other. To this end, so Christians hold, God—the absolutely other—became incarnate in humanity; that is to say, the absolutely other became not absolutely other. This requires us to say, then, that the Unknown (God) is both absolutely other and not absolutely other than humanity. This statement, clearly, is a self-contradiction.

One of the senses of the word "paradox" is such that a paradox is an apparent contradiction that is seen, on examination, not to be a contradiction. Thus, it is paradoxical to say of a certain member of a group, who is very talkative, that he says less than anyone else in the group. Here, at first glance, it looks as if we are saying that the person both talks a great deal and does not talk a great deal. However, the puzzle is resolved quickly when attention is called to the way the words "talk" and "say" are used; namely, although he *talks* a great deal, he *says* very little. Most of his talk is insignificant; it is idle chatter. Such a paradox, then, can be resolved by making some kind of distinction between the apparently incompatible predicates.

In saying that his paradox is "Absolute," however, Climacus seems to be saying that it cannot be resolved. The reason the paradox cannot be resolved lies in the uniqueness of the particular paradox in question. It is essential to Climacus's paradox that the word "absolutely" be included. God both is and is not *absolutely* other than humanity. If one said of Jones that he is other and not other than Smith, one could go on to specify the similarities and differences between the two people: Both are philosophers, but one is interested only in logic, while the other is interested only in ethics. They are alike, yet they differ. However, if Jones were said to be *absolutely* other than Smith, then no comparisons could be made at all. When using the expression "totally different" in ordinary speech, one usually intends to emphasize a difference that is really only partial. One means that two things differ fundamentally in *some* (but not all) respects. However, Climacus is using "absolutely other" in a rather strict way, and this means that even to express the total difference is to go beyond the strict limits of language and understanding. Strictly speaking, one cannot even mention a total difference between two things. The very mention of them indicates at least one respect in which they are not totally different; namely, they are alike in that they can be talked about.

If this is the case, however—that God or the Unknown is both totally like and totally unlike humanity and that one should not even be able to state this—then the paradox Climacus is expressing cannot be resolved. It cannot be resolved be-cause the very language of this paradox, in one sense at least, does not have meaning. The paradox is absolute. Yet one must express oneself—or at least Christian people feel that they must express themselves. There is an urge in people, Climacus feels, which drives them to try to express the inexpressible. (Reason, Climacus says, seeks its own downfall.) To come at this point in a somewhat different way, most people can remember trying to express the uniqueness of their beloved in a language that has its power in virtue of expressing the common features, the repeatable elements, the universally instanced qualities of experience. People try to express the unique in terms of the common, and the result is often the paradoxical or the trite.

If Christianity is true, then its central claim—that God was incarnate in Jesus of Nazareth—leads to a paradox, a paradox that cannot be resolved as paradoxes usually are. However, there is also another sense of the word "paradox" that is involved in the discussion in *Philosophical Fragments*. Another meaning of the word (its etymological meaning) is "contrary to the received opinion." The Absolute Paradox is paradoxical also in this sense, and this leads to another point Climacus makes in connection with the paradox.

Climacus's discussion of the Absolute Paradox is followed by a section in which he claims that humanity's response to the paradox is to be offended. The religious person, having passed through the "moment" and having changed from being in error to being in the truth (to having faith), upsets ordinary value commitments. Some of Jesus' remarks, at least as they are reported in the Christian Scriptures, surely run counter to the prevailing values of everyday life. Common sense surely does not suggest that one turns the other cheek when a person strikes one, nor does it agree that the meek shall inherit the earth. What people usually adopt as a pattern for life is in conflict with the pattern set forth in the Christian Gospels. People usually want "success" rather than "peace" (in the Christian sense). Therefore, the Christian recommendation, based on its being a revelation from a transcendent God, offends people. Why should one love one's neighbor rather than sell to him or her at a profit? Because God says so. However, this recommendation is unreasonable. True enough, but who is to say that God is reasonable? Did not God reveal himself in a most unexpected way? Namely, as the apparently illegitimate son of a poor Nazarene woman, born outside wedlock and in the ancient equivalent of a garage? The Christian account is so contrary to the received opinion of what is of real value that it offends the hearer. Such is Climacus's observation.

Another consequence of the Christian account is that if God revealed himself in Jesus of Nazareth, then it seems he gave special advantages to those who were contemporary with Jesus and knew Jesus personally, advantages that are denied to those who are not contemporaries of Jesus. Climacus argues that the immediate followers of Jesus, the "contemporary disciples," enjoyed no advantage over the noncontemporary, the "disciples at second hand." The paradox is the key to Climacus's position here. What the contemporary *saw* was not God but the man Jesus. It was not apparent or obvious to a normal observer that Jesus was more than simply a good man. The divinity that Christians attribute to Jesus was not evident to the senses but represented an additional characteristic about Jesus that people recognized only in the light of what traditionally has been called the gift of grace from God. People did not naturally look at Jesus and see his divinity; they beheld only his manhood. Only if God granted grace to the observer, did the observer "see" the divinity of Jesus. Again using the traditional Christian terminology, even the Apostles could not recognize the divinity of Jesus without having been enlightened by the Holy Spirit. Thus, the contemporary disciple enjoyed no advantage over the disciple at second hand insofar as Jesus' divinity is concerned. The only advantage the contemporary enjoyed concerns Jesus' manhood, his historical existence. Indeed, if there is any advantage, it is the advantage that the disciple at second hand enjoys in having the testimony of several generations that the man Jesus is also God. The reiteration of this claim brings it home as a possibility in a way that the contemporary disciple did not experience.

Such, then, is the position set forth by Kierkegaard, through the pseudonym "Johannes Climacus" in the *Philosophical Fragments*. It is what is at the heart of the (religious) "existentialist" position to which Kierkegaard gave the name. The

position is elaborated, by the same pseudonym, in a much longer and more involved book, *Afsluttende uvidenskabelig Efterskrift* (1846; *Concluding Unscientific Postscript*, 1941)—that runs to more than five hundred pages as compared with the ninety-three pages of *Philosophical Fragments*— but it is the same position nevertheless. It is stated clearly and succinctly in the *Philosophical Fragments* as a hypothesis; in the *Concluding Unscientific Postscript*, an attempt is made to discuss what would happen if a sophisticated person were to attempt to put into operation in his or her own life what is discussed merely as a possibility in the *Philosophical Fragments*. In Kierkegaard's later work, Climacus concerns himself with the personal question: How do I become a Christian? However, the later work depends on *Philosophical Fragments*, and *Philosophical Fragments* is really the central statement of Kierkegaard's position. Rarely does one find such an important question as the philosophical account of Christianity stated with the precision, clarity, and wit that Kierkegaard exhibits in the *Philosophical Fragments*. Kierkegaard was possessed of a keen intellect, a logical passion, and an ability to give expression to one of the most significant alternatives in Western civilization in a manner that retains the kernel of Christianity, yet makes possible its discussion in the modern milieu. To have done this is a philosophical and literary achievement of the first order.

Robert E. Larsen

Concluding Unscientific Postscript

Type of philosophy: Existentialism, metaphysics, philosophy of religion

First published: Afsluttende uvidenskabelig Efferskrift, 1846 (English translation, 1941)

Principal ideas advanced:

◊ Subjective thinkers are engaged thinkers who by activity commit themselves to an understanding of the truth, which, by the manner of their existence, they are; they seek to comprehend themselves not as abstractions but as ethically engaged, existing subjects.

◊ Only individuals matter; existence is individual in character.

◇ Existent individuals are people in the process of becoming; they move into an uncertain future.

◇ Because death is imminent, every choice has infinite worth and every moment is a unique occasion for decisive action; each individual achieves being through decision.

◇ In their development, thinkers may pass through the aesthetical stage (in which they experiment but do not commit themselves), the ethical stage (in which they act decisively and commit themselves), to the religious stage (in which their sin is acknowledged and they commit themselves to God).

Søren Kierkegaard has been called the Danish Socrates, and *Concluding Unscientific Postscript* demonstrates his claim to that title. In this work, Socrates is acknowledged as the illustrious Greek who never lost sight of the fact that a thinker remains an existing individual. The Socratic maieutic method, with its use of ignorance, irony, and dialectics, pervades the work.

The Socratic method is used by Johannes Climacus (Kierkegaard's pseudonym) to elicit from the reader an awareness that truth is subjectivity. The doctrine of "the subjective thinker" stands at the center of this classic, and it provides the pivot point around which all the themes revolve. Subjective thinkers are *engaged* or *involved* thinkers, whose thought, directed toward a penetration of their inner consciousness, moves in passion and earnestness. They find in the theoretical detachment of objective reflection a comic neglect of the existing individuals who do the reflecting. Objective reflection tends to make subjects accidental and transforms their existence into something indifferent and abstract. The accent for subjective thinkers falls on the *how*; the accent for objective reflection falls on the *what*. Objective truth designates a "what" or an objective content that can be observed in theoretical detachment. Subjective truth is a "how" that must be inwardly appropriated. Truth as subjectivity thus becomes inward appropriation. Truth, subjectively appropriated, is a truth that is *true for me*. It is a truth which I *live*, not merely observe. It is a truth which I *am*, not merely possess. Truth is a mode of action or a manner of existence. Subjective thinkers live the truth; they *exist it*.

Hegel and Descartes

One need not proceed far into the pages of *Concluding Unscientific Postscript* to become aware that Kierkegaard's archenemy, against whom his Socratic, ironical barbs are directed, is German philosopher Georg Wilhelm Friedrich Hegel. Johannes Climacus finds in the systematized, objective, and theoretical reflection of Hegel's philosophy a fantastic distortion of truth and an ingenious system of irrelevancy. Climacus never tires of lampooning the system. Hegelians, in neglecting the crucial distinction between thought and reality, erect a system of thought that comically excludes their own existence. They seek to comprehend themselves as expressions of abstract, universal, and timeless categories; thus they lose themselves as concrete, particular, and temporal existents.

> One must therefore be very careful in dealing with a philosopher of the Hegelian school, and, above all, to make certain of the identity of the being with whom one has the honor to discourse. Is he a human being, an existing human being? Is he himself *sub specie aeterni*, even when he sleeps, eats, blows his nose, or whatever else a human being does? Is he himself the pure 'I am I?' . . . Does he in fact exist?

Hegelians afford an instance of philosophical comedy in which there is thought without a thinker. They erect a marvelous intellectual palace in which they themselves do not live. The subject, in Hegel's objective reflection, becomes accidental, and truth as subjectivity is lost.

French philosopher René Descartes shares Hegel's fate of falling under the Kierkegaardian irony and devastating intellectual lampooning. It was Descartes who provided modern philosophy with *Cogito, ergo sum* ("I think, therefore, I am") for its foundation. Now either the "I" that is the subject of the *cogito* refers to a particular existing human being, in which case nothing is proved (If I *am* thinking, what wonder that I *am*!), or else the "I" refers to a universal pure ego. However, such an entity has only a conceptual existence, and the *ergo* loses its meaning, the proposition being reduced to a tautology. The attempt by Descartes to prove his existence by the fact that he thinks leads to no real conclusion, for insofar as he thinks, he has already abstracted from his own existence. Descartes had already prepared the stage for the later Hegel's identification of abstract thought and reality. Contra Descartes, Climacus is ready to defend the claim that the real subject is not the cognitive subject, but rather the ethically engaged, existing subject. In both Descartes and Hegel, he finds that cognition and reason have been viciously abstracted from the concrete particularity of existence.

Existence and Individuals

Subjective thinkers emphatically reject the rationalists' reification of reason, but they in no way deny the validity of thought so long as it is existentially rooted. Subjective thinkers are indeed thinkers who make use of thought in seeking to penetrate the structures of their subjectivity and so to understand themselves in their existence. The nobility of Greek thinkers (particularly Socrates) is that they were able to do this. They existed in advance of speculation and the system. Subjective thinkers are both thinkers and existing human beings. This is a truth, says Climacus, a statement that, deserving emphasis, cannot too often be repeated, and the neglect of which has brought about much confusion. Kierkegaard was by no means an opponent of thought. He insisted only that thought be placed back into existence, following its vicious abstraction by Hegel. "If thought speaks deprecatingly of the imagination, imagination in its turn speaks deprecatingly of thought; and likewise with feeling. The task is not to exalt the one at the expense of the other, but to give them an equal status, to unify them in simultaneity; the medium in which they are unified is *existence*."

When subjective thinkers thus make the movement of understanding themselves in their existence, they discover that in the order of reality (as distinct from the order of abstract thought), individuals—and individuals alone—exist. Existence is indelibly individual in character. Kierkegaard's philosophy is a crusade for the reality of the concrete individual. "The individual" (*Enkelte*) was Kierkegaard's central category. It is in this category that he saw bound up any importance that he as a subjective thinker might have. This category was so decisive for his whole literary effort that he asked that it be inscribed on his tombstone (and it was). The human self is not humanity in general. Humanity does not exist; only individual human beings exist. Existential reality resides not in the genus or in the species but in the concrete individual. Universals, like crowds, are abstractions that have neither hands nor feet.

Becoming

To exist means to be an individual, but to exist also means to be in the process of becoming. "An existing individual is constantly in process of becoming; the actual existing subjective thinker constantly reproduces this existential situation in his thoughts, and translates all his thinking into terms of process." Although Hegel in *Wissenschaft der Logik* (1812-1816; *Science of Logic*, 1929), had much to say about processes in which opposites are combined into higher unities, his doctrine of becoming is ultimately illusory because it does not understand process from the point of view of concrete existence. Logic and pure thought can never capture the existential reality of becoming, for logical entities are *states of being* that are timeless and fixed. In the moment that Hegel wrote *Science of Logic* with the intention of encompassing the whole of reality, he forfeited the concrete becoming in which subjective thinkers find themselves disclosed. In *Concluding Unscientific Postscript*, Climacus satirizes the Hegelian system:

I shall be as willing as the next man to fall down in worship before the System, if only I can manage to set eyes on it. Hitherto I have had no success; and though I have young legs, I am almost weary from running back and forth between Herod and Pilate. Once or twice I have been on the verge of bending the knee. However, at the last moment, when I already had my handkerchief spread on the ground, to avoid soiling my trousers, and I made a trusting appeal to one of the initiated who stood by: "Tell me now sincerely, is it entirely finished; for if so I will kneel down before it, even at the risk of ruining a pair of trousers (for on account of the heavy traffic to and fro, the road has become quite muddy),"—I always received the same answer: "No, it is not yet quite finished." And so there was another postponement—of the System, and of my homage.

System and finality are correlative concepts. However, existence, which is constantly in the process of becoming, is never finished. Thus, an existential system is impossible. Reality itself is a system, but a system only for God. There can be no system for an existing individual who always stands in the throes of becoming.

As existence involves individuality and becoming, so assuredly does it involve the future. One exists in a process of becoming by facing a future. Subjective thinkers are passionately and earnestly interested in the time of immediate experience as it qualifies their existence. Time for existing subjects is not a time in general—an abstract, cosmic time that is spatialized through objectivizing categories. Their interest has to do with the time of their inner experience—time as it is concretely lived rather than abstractly known. In subjective thinkers' immediate experience of time, the future has priority. Their lives are lived primarily out of the future, for in their subjectivity they understand themselves as moving into a future. This future generates uncertainty and anxiety. Tomorrow may rob one of all one's earthly goods and leave one desolate. Subjective thinkers, when they penetrate to the core of their subjectivity, thus find the uncertainty of life itself. Wherever there is subjectivity, there is uncertainty.

Death is one of the most ethically significant uncertainties of life. Subjective thought discloses death as an imminent possibility. However, for the most part, people devise means of concealing this imminent possibility. They approach the fact of death through the eyes of objective reflection and thus conveniently transform it into something in general. Viewed *objectively*, death is a general and universal occurrence that befalls all forms of life. Viewed subjectively, death is an imminent uncertainty that pertains to one's particular existence and that makes a difference for one's individual decisions. Death is thus apprehended not as a generalized empirical factuality but as a task or a deed. "If the task of life is to become subjective, then the thought of death is not, for the individual subject, something in general, but is verily a deed." Death, subjectively understood, becomes a task in that it is defined in terms of its ethical expression. It is experienced and appropriated in an anticipatory conception

in such a way that it transforms the whole of a person's life. When death is existentially appropriated, then every decision receives a singular importance. If death is imminent, every choice has infinite worth, and every moment is a unique occasion for decisive action. Death makes a difference for life.

Choices and Action

In the subjective movements of their engaged existence, subjective thinkers disclose their existence as qualified by individuality, becoming, time, and death. Already in these movements, the pathway is opened for decisive action. The category of decision becomes a centralizing concept for subjective thinkers. In facing a future, existing subjects are called to decision. Thus subjective thinkers are at the same time ethical thinkers. They understand their personal existence as a task and a responsibility. They must choose in order to attain their authentic selfhood. Their essential humanity is not given but is achieved through decision. The greatness of humankind lies in possession of an *either/or*. This either/or becomes a matter of indifference for the Hegelian. In Hegel's timeless categories, there is no place for decisive action or ethical commitment.

> Ethics has been crowded out of the System, and as a substitute for it there has been included a something that confuses the historical with the individual, the bewildering and noisy demands of the age with the eternal demand that conscience makes on the individual. Ethics concentrates on the individual, and ethically it is the task of every individual to become an entire man; just as it is the ethical presupposition that every man is born in such a condition that he can become one.

The objective reflection that is so peculiar to the system transforms everyone into an observer. However, existing individuals are actors as well as observers. They make choices that affect the whole of their lives. They are engaged in action that is decisive for themselves as well as for others. The ethically existing subject is thus of utmost importance; but for Hegelians, who are concerned with the general developments of world history and the meditation of opposites in this world history, the ethical subject remains unacknowledged.

Kierkegaard regarded the existentially decisive act for the ethically engaged subject as not an external action but rather as an internal decision. It is inward passion rather than external consequences that constitutes the criterion of ethical action. The person who does not own a penny can be as charitable as the person who gives away a kingdom. Suppose, says Climacus, that the Levite, who found the man that had fallen among thieves between Jericho and Jerusalem, was inwardly concerned to help sufferers in distress. Let us suppose further that when he met the victim he was frightened at the possibility of robbers nearby and hastened on, lest he also become a victim. He failed to act, giving no help to the sufferer. However, after having left the victim, he was overcome by remorse and hurried back to the scene but arrived too late. The Samaritan had already helped the victim in his distress. If this were the sequence of events, would one not have to say that the Levite acted? Indeed he acted, says Climacus, and in an inwardly decisive sense, even though his action had no external expression.

The Three Stages of Existence

Much time is devoted in *Concluding Unscientific Postscript* to a delineation of the "stages" or "existence spheres"—a delineation that Kierkegaard had already undertaken in two of his earlier works, *Enten-Eller* (1843; *Either/Or*, 1944) and *Stadier paa Livets Vej* (1845; *Stages on Life's Way*, 1940). However, for the first time, his writings contain an analysis and description of irony and humor as transitional stages between the aesthetical and the ethical, and the ethical and the religious, respectively.

The *aesthetical stage* is the stage of experimentation. Aestheticists are those who experiment with various possibilities but never commit themselves in passionate choice. They experiment with love but never commit themselves in marriage. They experiment with thought but never commit themselves in action. A constant flight from the responsibility of decision characterizes aestheticists. Thus they lack the decisive content of subjectivity—inwardness, earnestness, and passion. It is only in the ethical

stage that these decisive determinants appear.

The transition to the *ethical stage* is by way of irony. Climacus speaks of irony as the "boundary zone" between the aesthetical and the ethical. The purpose of irony is to rouse one from one's unauthentic aesthetical floundering to an ethical consciousness. Irony elicits the discrepancy between the inward and outward, as this discrepancy is expressed in life. Irony makes one aware of the discrepancy between one's inward lack of wisdom and one's outward claim of its possession. It makes one aware that one's outward profession of virtue betrays an inward lack of it. Irony constitutes the first awareness of the ethical, seeks to bring these suppressed discrepancies to light, and thus drives beyond itself to the next stage.

The ethical stage is the sphere of decisive action and self-commitment. The ethical person has resolutely chosen the self and exists in passion and in inwardness. The personality of the aestheticist is dispersed because of floundering in possibilities. The personality of the ethical person is unified or centralized because the individual has been able to commit the self to definite modes of action. However, the ground of this unification and the ultimate source of this commitment is not disclosed until the self apprehends itself in the movements of the religious sphere. Although in tension, the ethical and the religious are so close, says Climacus, that they are in constant communication with one another. It is for this reason that the two stages are often hyphenated and designated as the ethico-religious sphere. The "boundary zone" between the ethical and the religious is humor. The ethical thinker drives beyond the ethical to the religious through the expression of humor, in which there is a protest against the externalization of ethical norms and standards. The humorist is aware of this externalization, which tends to become identified with the religious, contests it as the proper measure, but still is unable to establish a God relationship in terms of religious passion. Kierkegaard's *Frygt og Bœven* (1843; *Fear and Trembling*, 1939) incomparably expresses this suspension of an externalized ethics through the movement of faith, exemplified by biblical figure Abraham in the intended sacrifice of his son Isaac. Only when existing subjects have apprehended their relationship to God as a relationship qualified by inwardness and passion do they proceed to the religious stage.

The new determinant that is introduced in the *religious stage* is the determinant of suffering. Suffering is the highest intensification of subjectivity. In it lies the fullest expression of inwardness. The suffering that is acknowledged in this stage, however, must not be confused with the poetic representations of suffering peculiar to the aesthetical stage, nor with the reflection *about* suffering that is always qualitatively different from the fact of suffering, nor with suffering as a simple outward ethical manifestation. Religious suffering is an expression of an inward God relationship, like that of biblical figure Job, which remains opaque to the aesthetical and ethical consciousness.

The religious stage is internally differentiated by two levels of existence—religiousness *A* and religiousness *B*. Religiousness *A* is the religion of immanence. Religiousness *B* is the "paradoxical religiousness," that in which the qualitative distinction between God and humanity is disclosed and God's presence in time is revealed in the paradox of Christ. The distinction between *A* and *B* also expresses the corresponding distinction between guilt-consciousness and sin-consciousness. Guilt, properly understood, is a determinant of religiousness *A*; sin is a determinant of religiousness *B*. Guilt is a disrelationship of the subject with the self. It points to an internal fissure within consciousness that results because of an alienation from the individual's absolute *telos*. It is still a movement within immanence. In religiousness *B*, guilt becomes sin. The disrelationship of the subject with the self is now apprehended as a disrelationship with God. The existing subject can acquire a guilt-consciousness through the purely human movement of dialectics in which he or she understands the self as alienated from the self in the process of becoming. However, sin-consciousness requires a disclosure by God so as to reveal to humanity that guilt is at one and the same time an implication of sin. The pagan can have no consciousness of sin. Sin-consciousness emerges only in the subject's awareness of the self as existing in a disrelationship with God. This God is a God who has entered time and history.

It is thus that religiousness *B* finds its supreme expression in Christianity, with its teachings of the "Absolute Paradox" or "Deity in time." As the "paradoxical religiousness," religiousness *B* affirms a qualitative distinction between God and humanity. God is wholly and utterly transcendent to the temporal order. Thus, religiousness *B* breaks with religiousness *A*. There is no natural kinship between the eternal and the temporal. Thus, the advent of eternity in time is disclosed as a paradox. Christ is the Absolute Paradox who reveals God in time, makes one aware of one's sin, and calls a person to faith and decisive commitment through which sin is overcome.

In his analysis and description of the religious stage as the crown and culmination of the three stages (which must be understood not in terms of temporal sequences of successive development, but rather in terms of copresent qualifications of subjectivity), Kierkegaard makes his central intention quite apparent. The leading question that concerns Climacus is already put to the reader in the introduction: "The subjective problem concerns the relationship of the individual to Christianity. To put it quite simply: How may I, Johannes Climacus, participate in the happiness promised by Christianity?" It is significant that in the appendix, "For an understanding with the reader," the question is reiterated: "Now I ask how I am to become a Christian." This is indeed Kierkegaard's central question, posed not only in *Concluding Unscientific Postscript* but in all of his other writings as well. Explaining his own perspective as an author, Kierkegaard informs his readers in his book *Synspunktet for min Forfatter-Virksomhed* (1859; wr. 1848-1849, *The Point of View for My Work as an Author*, 1939) that underlying the whole of his literary work is the central concern of how to become a Christian—a task that is extremely difficult in Christendom.

Calvin O. Schrag

Additional Reading

Allen, Diogenes. *Three Outsiders: Pascal, Kierkegaard, Simone Weil.* Cambridge, Mass.: Cowley Publications, 1983. The chapter on Kierkegaard examines his time period and its influence on his ideas. The author discusses how Georg Wilhelm Friedrich Hegel influenced Søren Kierkegaard by breaking the hold of the eighteenth century Enlightenment on European philosophy. Also includes the influence of Socrates on Kierkegaard.

Bloom, Harold, ed. *Soren Kierkegaard*. Modern Critical Views series. New York: Chelsea House, 1989. A collection of essays discussing the importance of Kierkegaard and his philosophy. The editor's introduction places Kierkegaard in historical context, relating him to Georg Wilhelm Friedrich Hegel and others.

Evans, C. Stephen. *Kierkegaard's "Fragments" and "Postscript": The Religious Philosophy of Johannes Climacus*. Atlantic City, N.J.: Humanities Press, 1983. An analysis of the two books that Kierkegaard wrote under a pseudonym in which he reveals much of his religious philosophy. Evans's book is basically a commentary on the two books by Kierkegaard.

Hannary, Alastair, and Gordon D. Marino. *The Cambridge Companion to Kierkegaard*. Cambridge, England: Cambridge University Press, 1998. The sixteen essays in this volume look at Kierkegaard's contribution to philosophical, theological, and spiritual issues. Contains bibliography and index.

Lowrie, Walter. *Kierkegaard*. 2 vols. Gloucester, Mass.: Peter Smith, 1970. This is the definitive biography of Kierkegaard, written by one of the most prominent translators of his writings. Traces Kierkegaard's life chronologically, providing a list of dates for major events and publications. Also includes a helpful fifteen-page synopsis of Kierkegaard's works.

Pattison, George and Steve Shakespeare. *Kierkegaard: The Self in Society*. New York: Macmillan, 1998. This volume presents twelve essays from the 1995 meeting of the Kierkegaard Society of the United Kingdom. These essays challenge the notion of Kierkegaard as an extreme individualist.

Rae, Murray. *Kierkegaard's Vision of the Incarnation: By Faith Transformed*. Oxford: Clarendon Press, 1997. Rae, chaplain at the University of Auckland, examines Kierkegaard's view of the Incarnation. His sympathetic interpretation contrasts with that of many other commentators. Contains an extensive bibliography.

Ree, Jonathan, and Jane Chamberlain, eds. *Kierkegaard: A Critical Reader*. Oxford, England: Blackwell, 1998. The nine essays in this work attempt to determine the role of Kierkegaard's work in philosophy and religion in modern society. Includes index.

Sontag, Frederick. *A Kierkegaard Handbook*. Atlanta, Ga.: John Knox Press, 1979. A systematic approach to Kierkegaard's philosophy, which Kierkegaard himself avoided. A study of major concepts that provides a companion reader to the student of Kierkegaard.

Stack, George J. *Kierkegaard's Existential Ethics*. Tuscaloosa: University of Alabama Press, 1977. An explanation of the ethical concepts in Kierkegaard's existentialism. This volume examines the philosopher's connection to the developing philosophy of nihilism and helps readers understand how his personal struggles affected his philosophy.

Walker, Jeremy. *Kierkegaard: Descent into God*. Montreal: McGill-Queens University Press, 1985. Walker examines Kierkegaard's remarks on the importance of Socrates, discusses his ethical positions, and attempts to reveal the effect of personal sorrows on his philosophy. The title refers to the philosopher's difficulty in explaining exactly how a person becomes a believer in God.

Westphal, Merold. *Kierkegaard's Critique of Reason and Society*. Macon, Ga.: Mercer University Press, 1987. A discussion of different aspects of Kierkegaard's philosophy. Chapter 6, "Kierkegaard and the Logic of Insanity," is a lecture-essay that discusses the difficulty in understanding many of Kierkegaard's concepts.

Stephen M. Ashby, updated by Glenn L. Swygart

Martin Luther King, Jr.

As founding president of the Southern Christian Leadership Conference, King espoused non-violent resistance, spearheading the movement that led to the 1964 Civil Rights Act and the 1965 Voting Rights Act.

Principal philosophical works: *Stride Toward Freedom: The Montgomery Story*, 1958; *The Measure of a Man*, 1959; *Strength to Love*, 1963; *Why We Can't Wait*, 1964; *A Martin Luther King Treasury*, 1964; *The Trumpet of Conscience*, 1967; *Where Do We Go from Here?*, 1967; *The Words of Martin Luther King, Jr.*, 1983, 1987; *A Testament of Hope: The Essential Writings and Speeches of Martin Luther King, Jr.*, 1986, 1991; *The Papers of Martin Luther King, Jr.: Called to Serve*, 1992; *The Papers of Martin Luther King, Jr.: Rediscovering Precious Values*, 1994.

Born: January 15, 1929; Atlanta, Georgia
Died: April 4, 1968; Memphis, Tennessee

Early Life

Martin Luther King, Jr., was born in Atlanta, Georgia, on January 15, 1929, the second child of the Reverend Michael Luther and Alberta Williams King. He was originally named Michael Luther King, Jr., but after the death of his paternal grandfather in 1933, King's father changed both his and his son's first names to Martin to honor the grandfather's insistence that he had originally given that name to his son in the days when birth certificates were rare for African Americans. Nevertheless, King was known as M. L. or Mike throughout his childhood. In 1931, King's father became pastor of the Ebenezer Baptist Church on Auburn Avenue, only a block away from the house where King was born.

King's father was both a minister and a bold advocate of racial equality. His mother was the daughter of the Reverend Adam Daniel Williams, who had preceded King's father as pastor of Ebenezer and had established it as one of Atlanta's most influential black churches. Both of King's parents believed in nonviolent resistance to racial discrimination. He grew up under the strong

Martin Luther King, Jr. *(Library of Congress)*

influence of the church and this family tradition of independence.

King was a small boy, but vigorously athletic and intellectually curious. He enjoyed competitive games as well as words and ideas. Intrigued by the influence of his father and other ministers over their congregations, young King dreamed of being a great speaker. African American historian Lerone Bennett, noted:

> To form words into sentences, to fling them out on the waves of air in a crescendo of sound, to watch people weep, shout, *respond*: this fascinated young Martin. . . . The idea of using words as weapons of defense and offense was thus early implanted and seems to have grown in King as naturally as a flower.

King excelled as a student and was able to skip two grades at Booker T. Washington High School and to enter Morehouse College in 1944 at age fifteen. At first he intended to study medicine, but religion and philosophy increasingly appealed to him as the influence of Morehouse president Dr. Benjamin E. Mays and Dr. George D. Kelsey of the religion department grew. Mays, a strong advocate of Christian nonviolence, sensed in King a profound talent in this area. In 1947, King was ordained a Baptist minister, and after graduation the following year, he entered theological studies at Crozer Theological Seminary in Pennsylvania.

During his studies at Crozer and later in a doctoral program at Boston University (1951-1954), King deepened his knowledge of the great ideas of the past. Especially influential upon his formative mind were the Social Gospel concept of Walter Rauschenbusch, the realist theology of Reinhold Niebuhr, and, above all, the nonviolent reformism of Mohandas K. Gandhi. In Gandhi, King found the key to synthesizing his Christian faith, his passion for helping oppressed people, and his sense of realism sharpened by Niebuhrian theology. Later King wrote:

> Gandhi was probably the first person in history to lift the love ethic of Jesus above mere interaction between individuals to a powerful and effective social force on a large scale. . . . It was in this Gandhian emphasis on love and nonviolence that I discovered the method for social reform.

King realized that nonviolence could not be applied in the United States exactly the way Gandhi had used it in India, but throughout his career King was devoted to the nonviolent method. In his mind, Gandhi's concept of *satyagraha* (Truthforce) and *ahimsa* (nonviolence) were similar to the Christian idea of *agape*, or unselfish love.

In Boston, King experienced love of another kind. In 1952, he met Coretta Scott, an attractive student at the New England Conservatory of Music. They were married the following year at her home in Marion, Alabama, by King's father. Neither wanted to return to the segregated South, but in 1954, while King was finishing his doctoral dissertation on the concepts of God in the thinking of Paul Tillich and Henry Nelson Wieman, he received a call to pastor the Dexter Avenue Baptist Church in Montgomery, Alabama. Their acceptance marked a major turning point in their own lives, as well as in American history.

By then King was twenty-five years old and still rather small at five feet, seven inches. With brown skin, a strong build, large pensive eyes, and a slow, articulate speaking style, he was an unusually well-educated young minister anxious to begin his first pastorate. As the Kings moved to the city that had once been the capital of the Confederacy, they believed that God was leading them into an important future.

Life's Work

King quickly established himself as a hardworking pastor who guided his middle-class congregation into public service. He encouraged his parishioners to help the needy and to be active in organizations such as the National Association for the Advancement of Colored People (NAACP). Montgomery was a rigidly segregated city with thousands of African Americans living on mere subsistence wages and barred from mainstream social life. The U.S. Supreme Court decision of 1954, requiring integration of public schools, had hardly touched the city, and most blacks apparently had little hope that their lives would ever improve.

An unexpected event in late 1955, however, drew King into his first significant civil rights activism. On December 1, Rosa Parks, a local black seamstress, was ordered by a bus driver to yield her seat to a white man. She refused, and her arrest triggered a 381-day bus boycott that led to a U.S. Supreme Court decision declaring the segregated transit system unconstitutional. King became the principal leader of the Montgomery Improvement Association, which administered the boycott, as thousands of local blacks cooperated in an effective nonviolent response to legally sanctioned segregation.

Quickly, the "Montgomery way" became a model for other southern cities: Tallahassee, Mobile, Nashville, Birmingham, and others. In January, 1957, King, his close friend Ralph David Abernathy, and about two dozen other black ministers and laypersons met at the Ebenezer Baptist Church to form a South-wide movement. Subsequent meetings in New Orleans and Montgomery led to the formal creation of the Southern Christian Leadership Conference (SCLC), which King used as the organizational arm of his movement.

From this point onward, King's life was bound with the southern nonviolent resistance movement. Its driving force was the heightened confidence of thousands of blacks and their white supporters, but King was its symbol and spokesperson. He suffered greatly in the process. In 1958, while promoting his first book, *Stride Toward Freedom*, an account of the Montgomery bus boycott, he was stabbed by a black woman. He was frequently arrested and berated by detractors as an "outside agitator" as he led various campaigns across the South. By early 1960, he had left his pastorate in Montgomery to become copastor (with his father) of the Ebenezer Baptist Church and to give his time more fully to SCLC.

Not all of King's efforts were successful. A campaign in Albany, Georgia, in 1961 and 1962 failed to desegregate that city. At times, there were overt tensions between King's SCLC and the more militant young people of the Student Nonviolent Coordinating Committee (SNCC), which was created in the wake of the first significant sit-in, in Greensboro, North Carolina, in February, 1960. King supported the sit-in and the Freedom Ride movements of the early 1960's, and he was the overarching hero and spiritual mentor of the young activists, but his style was more patient and gradualist than theirs was.

King's greatest successes occurred between 1963 and 1965. To offset the image of failure in Albany, the SCLC carefully planned a nonviolent confrontation in Birmingham, Alabama, in the spring of 1963. As the industrial hub of the South, Birmingham was viewed as the key to desegregating the entire region. The campaign there was launched during the Easter shopping season to maximize its economic effects. As the "battle of Birmingham" unfolded, King was arrested and wrote his famous "Letter from Birmingham City Jail," in which he articulated the principles of nonviolent resistance and countered the argument that he was an "outside agitator" with the affirmation that all people are bound "in an inextricable network of mutuality" and that "injustice anywhere is a threat to justice everywhere."

The Birmingham campaign was an important victory. Nationally televised scenes of police chief Eugene "Bull" Connor's forces using fire hoses and trained dogs to attack nonviolent demonstrators stirred the public conscience. The administration of John F. Kennedy was moved to take an overt stand on behalf of civil rights. President Kennedy strongly urged the Congress to pass his comprehensive civil rights bill. That bill was still pending in August, 1963, when King and many others led a march by more than two hundred thousand people to Washington, D.C., later dubbed the March on Washington. At the Lincoln Memorial on August 28, King delivered his most important speech, "I Have a Dream," calling upon the nation to "rise up and live out the true meaning of its creed, that all men are created equal."

After the March on Washington, King reached the height of his influence. Violence returned to Birmingham in September when four black girls were killed at the Sixteenth Street Baptist Church. In November, President Kennedy was assassinated. Yet in July, 1964, President Lyndon B. Johnson signed into law the Civil Rights Act, which ended most legally sanctioned segregation in the United States. Later in 1964, King was awarded the Nobel Peace Prize. Increasingly, he turned his attention to world peace and economic advancement.

In 1965, King led a major campaign in Selma, Alabama, to underscore the need for stronger voting rights than those provided in the 1964 Civil Rights Act. The result was the 1965 Voting Rights Act, which gave the federal government more power to enforce African Americans' right to vote. Ironically, as these important laws went into effect, the ghettos of northern and western cities were erupting in violent riots. At the same time, the United States was becoming more deeply involved in the Vietnam War, and King was distressed by both of these trends. Beginning in 1966, he attempted nonviolent campaigns in Chicago and other northern cities, but with less dramatic successes than those of Birmingham and Selma.

King's opposition to the Vietnam War alienated him from some of his black associates and many white supporters. Furthermore, it damaged his relationship with the Federal Bureau of Investigation (FBI) and the Johnson administration. Many observers have seen his last two years as a period of waning influence. Yet King continued to believe in nonviolent reform. In 1968, he was planning another march on Washington, this time to accentuate the plight of the poor of all races. In April, he traveled to Memphis, Tennessee, to support a local sanitation workers' strike. On the balcony of the Lorraine Motel on April 4, he was shot to death by James Earl Ray. King's successor, Ralph David Abernathy, carried through with the Poor People's March on Washington in June.

King was survived by Coretta and their four children: Yolanda Denise (Yoki), Martin Luther III (Marty), Dexter, and Bernice Albertine (Bunny). Soon after King's death, Coretta established the Martin Luther King, Jr., Center for Nonviolent Social Change. This organization, along with the SCLC, would continue King's work.

Influence

King embodied a number of historical trends to which he added his own unique contributions. He was the author of five major books and hundreds of articles and speeches. His principal accomplishment was to raise the hopes of black Americans and to bind them in effective direct-action campaigns. Although he was the major spokesperson of the black Civil Rights movement, he was modest about his contributions. Just before his death, he declared in a sermon that he wanted to be remembered as a "drum major for justice." The campaigns he led paved the way for legal changes that ended more than a century of racial segregation.

Above all, King espoused nonviolence as a means of social change. That theme runs through his career and historical legacy. In the tradition of the great Mohandas K. Gandhi, he left a decisive mark on U.S. and world history, and his dream of a peaceful world inspired many individuals and subsequent movements. In 1983, the U.S. Congress passed a law designating the third Monday in January a national holiday in his honor.

Thomas R. Peake

Why We Can't Wait

Type of philosophy: Ethics, social philosophy
First published: 1964
Principal ideas advanced:

◇ Nonviolent protest is an effective and moral response to violence. It brings benefits to the individual, the community, the nation, and the world as a whole.

◇ Peace is not found in the absence of conflict but in the functioning of a just society committed to equality.

◇ In the face of evil, moderation or gradualism is unacceptable, because it allows for the continuation of immoral and undesirable actions.

◇ The laws of humankind must conform to a higher ideal of justice, one that emanates from God but that can be understood through the concepts of equality, human improvement, and democratic participation.

◇ The historical legacy of unjust treatment requires compensation in the form of social programs designed to foster equality and opportunity.

Martin Luther King, Jr.'s *Why We Can't Wait* was written in 1963 and published in early 1964. The Civil Rights movement in the United States had achieved several notable successes in the previous months, including President John F. Kennedy's support for a civil rights bill and the March on Washington, during which King delivered his famous "I Have a Dream" speech. However, King and his supporters had received criticism for their efforts, with some observers charging that they expected too much, while more militant activists declared that they asked for too little. Moreover, the civil rights legislation was stalled in Congress. *Why We Can't Wait*, then, was a book of its time, in which King presents historical examples and ethical arguments to explain the Civil Rights movement and to exhort supporters to continue in their efforts at a crucial juncture in U.S. history. It has also stood the test of time as the articulation of the concept of nonviolent resistance and its necessity in combatting social injustice.

Racial Discrimination

King opens the book with a brief introduction that compares the lives of two black children, a boy living in Harlem, New York, and a girl living in Birmingham, Alabama. Both children endure poverty and a world of limited opportunity. By drawing this comparison, King asserts that racial discrimination and its damaging affect on African Americans is a national problem, not one confined to the South. Although discrimination is not as overt in the North, King notes, it is nonetheless as crippling and unjust as the segregation practiced in the South. Later in the work, King asserts that racial discrimination is also damaging to whites. Using Birmingham as an example, King illustrates the ways in which segregation has diminished the quality of life for the white community. Refusing to abide by a court order to integrate parks, for example, the city instead closed them; the baseball team disbanded rather than accept black players; and at least one touring symphony orchestra refused to visit Birmingham because it would not perform before segregated audiences. Although black Americans bore the most onerous burdens of racism, King makes it clear that all Americans suffer when injustice is allowed to prevail.

Despite the opening image of despair, the introduction ends on a positive note, with the boy and girl preparing to take the first steps necessary to improve their lives. King then explores the motivations behind their resolve. In examining the causes of what, in the language of his day, he refers to as the "Negro Revolution," King explains the frustration that African Americans shared regarding the slow pace of change in the United States. The 1954 Supreme Court decision

in *Brown v. Board of Education*, which prohibited racial segregation in public schools, had offered hope to African Americans. However, in subsequent decisions, the Court had weakened the impact of the *Brown* decision. In the 1960 presidential election, Democratic candidate John F. Kennedy had promised support for civil rights, but once in office he appeared satisfied with limited gains. King notes that at the same time the federal government backed away from its commitment to civil rights, it positioned itself as a defender of liberty and democracy abroad.

Frustration stemmed from other sources besides the failures of the government officials. During the early 1960's, the United States experienced an economic boom, from which, for the most part, African Americans received little benefit. Discrimination prevented them from realizing any real gains or new opportunities. Meanwhile, Africans and Asians were achieving newfound political power, ending generations of white colonialism. Finally, King points to the powerful symbolism of the hundredth anniversary of the Emancipation Proclamation as another source of discontent and a spur to action for civil rights activists. Government inaction and continued poverty in an era of plenty, the pride in the achievements of other oppressed peoples abroad, and the unpleasant truth that the promise of freedom inherent in the Emancipation Proclamation had not fully come to pass—all prompted African Americans to take a revolutionary stance in their struggle to end racial discrimination.

Nonviolence as Revolution

Having identified and justified the causes of dissatisfaction, King proceeds to detail the means for carrying out this revolution. Although he praises the strategy of pursuing legal victories that the National Association for the Advancement of Colored People (NAACP) had conducted for decades, he argues that this strategy is slow and often results in only token victories. On the other hand, he condemns those who call for violent revolution, claiming that bloodshed will result only in "racial suicide" as whites retaliate with greater violence. King advocates nonviolence as the only alternative to these positions. He marshals several arguments in support of nonviolence as an effective means of achieving a civil rights revolution.

King points to the economic boycotts during the American Revolution and to Mohandas K. Gandhi's leadership against British colonial rule in India as examples of nonviolence that have proven effective in the past. However, historical evidence does not explain the reasons for the success of nonviolent protest. Nonviolence works because it possesses a moral authority that sheer physical strength and brutality lack. King believes that although Americans retain a frontier mentality that demands response and retribution, they will recognize the superiority of the moral position that those who practice nonviolence hold.

King maintains that nonviolence will be especially effective in securing civil rights for African Americans because it will bring to light the unjust and brutal behaviors practiced by the whites opposed to integration. For centuries, blacks have lived in fear of violence perpetrated at night or in some isolated jail cell. By bringing the beatings into the streets before news cameras and newspaper reporters, nonviolent protesters will gain the support of Americans throughout the nation who are horrified by the atrocities they witness on their televisions.

Nonviolence also brings various benefits to the community and the individual. King claims that a nonviolent "army" is an egalitarian force. Each member of this army, regardless of wealth or social status, faces the same consequences, the same risk of a beating or imprisonment. Thus, nonviolence strengthens bonds within the community. In addition, nonviolence requires a level of courage and self-discipline that contributes to an individual's self-esteem. Far from being an act of cowardice, as some critics implied, nonviolence demands a brave heart. It serves as a constructive channel for feelings of anger and frustration.

Letter from Birmingham City Jail

The heart of *Why We Can't Wait* is the chapter entitled "Letter from Birmingham City Jail," which King wrote while incarcerated for violating a court injunction against protesting. Addressing his letter to eight clergymen who had counseled moderation during the crisis in Bir-

mingham, King defends his actions and explains why nonviolent direct action is appropriate. Moderation, King informs his critics, is satisfied with a negative peace. However, the absence of conflict does not signify the presence of justice. King seeks a positive peace, one in which all people receive the respect due them as human beings. The nonviolent protests raise tensions in the community until a sense of crisis prevails, creating situations that at first glance seem distant from peace. Far from being an unfortunate side effect of the protests, crisis is necessary because it creates the need for a solution. Negotiations will ensue, and individuals will seek justice in their society. Thus, rather than replacing the process of legal battles that the NAACP had called for, nonviolent direct action creates the circumstances that allow for that strategy to take place.

In their criticism of King, the eight clergymen had pointed out that King broke the law when he led protesters through the streets of Birmingham. How can he speak of justice, how can he look to the courts and the government for assistance, when he is willing to ignore the law to achieve his goals? King maintains the existence of a moral authority higher than the law of the land; the law of the land can be ignored or even used as a tool by the segregationists opposed to civil rights. While he does explicitly refer to the law of God and cites theologians including Saint Augustine, Saint Thomas Aquinas, and Paul Tillich in his argument, King offers a definition of justice that is also available to nonbelievers. A just law is one that improves the human personality and seeks equality. It is created by all the people. The segregation laws are therefore unjust. They distort and degrade both African Americans and whites. They codify and punish differences, placing one group in society above another. Finally, laws promoting racial discrimination do not express the will of the people, because African Americans have been denied their right to vote. According to King's concept of justice, the Birmingham law against protesting was intended to thwart justice, not protect it, and therefore must be broken.

However, violating unjust laws must be a public act, and those who engage in civil disobedience must accept the consequences, including imprisonment. By accepting the punishment, the nonviolent protester shows respect for the concept of the law while illustrating the destructiveness of the unjust law. This perspective allows King to regard breaking unjust laws as a moral act. He argues that social injustice demands a response because it endangers justice throughout the entire society. Because King defines "time" as neutral, allowing it to pass without action is inexcusable. To counsel patience, to urge blacks to wait, is to agree to the existence of an intolerable evil, the denial of justice to an oppressed minority. Thus, the title of the work refers not only to the impatience that African Americans feel toward the slow pace of change; it is also the recognition of a moral imperative, the necessity of attacking injustice.

Healing Through Redress

King concludes his work with thoughts regarding the completion of the task at hand. When will the job be finished? Revising the laws in accord with the higher standards of justice that King has outlined is only the first step toward equality. Merely repealing the segregation acts is not enough, because the historical legacy of racism and discrimination will remain as a burden to African Americans. The passage of time has allowed evil to do its work; society must now offer remedies for the damage that has been done. King rejects compensation as atonement; rather, he views it as a corrective that will allow African Americans to assume their rightful place as equals in society, possessing the same opportunities as their fellow citizens. King again offers historical evidence to support his argument, using the GI Bill of Rights and the Marshall Plan as domestic and international examples of the United States' willingness to assist the disadvantaged. In keeping with his contention that racism has also injured whites, he advocates economic assistance to whites who suffered as racist policies depressed the southern economy.

In closing, King claims that the Civil Rights movement will bring a healing to the United States. King speaks of a sense of unity and brotherhood that will pervade the nation. Perhaps more important in his estimation is the change that nonviolence will bring to people across the globe. The successful use of nonviolence in the United States will prompt others to employ it as a strategy for ending discrimination and abuse. King hopes that a new adherence to the doctrine of nonviolence will bring an end to all violence and lead to an era of peace.

King published six books and several articles during his lifetime. However, his impact on American life stemmed largely from his prominence as a public figure and his powerful oratory. He is remembered more for his speeches—especially the "I Have a Dream" speech that he delivered in August, 1963—than for his writings. The only exception is the "Letter from Birmingham City Jail." Largely ignored when it was first written, the letter was reprinted in several national magazines after the Birmingham campaign received national attention. Nonetheless, *Why We Can't Wait* serves as a useful introduction to King's thought.

Thomas Clarkin

Additional Reading

Ansbro, John J. *Martin Luther King, Jr.: The Making of a Mind*. Maryknoll, N.Y.: Orbis Books, 1982. This study of King's intellectual and spiritual development is based on extensive primary material from King's student days as well as his later writings. Ansbro focuses on the pivotal role of nonviolence based on *agape* in King's social theology. The work's thematic organization is complex.

Branch, Taylor. *Parting the Waters: America in the King Years, 1954-1963*. New York: Simon & Schuster, 1988. This Pulitzer Prize-winning work offers the most comprehensive account of King's early career.

_____. *Pillar of Fire: America in the King Years, 1963-65*. New York: Simon & Schuster, 1998. The second volume in Branch's history of King and the civil rights era, this work contains a wealth of detail that is at times overwhelming.

Fairclough, Adam. *Martin Luther King, Jr*. Athens: University of Georgia Press, 1995. This slim volume serves as a superb introduction to students interested in King's life and impact.

Friedly, Michael, and David Gallen. *Martin Luther King, Jr. The FBI File*. New York: Carroll & Graf, 1993. The extended introductory essay is followed by material from King's FBI file, and includes excerpts from tapes that the FBI secretly made of King's private conservations.

Garrow, David J. *Bearing the Cross: Martin Luther King, Jr., and the Southern Christian Leadership Conference, a Personal Portrait*. New York: William Morrow, 1986. Garrow carefully documents King's personal life and the origins and progress of the Civil Rights movement. He pays particular attention to internal struggles, including King's sexual temptations and his agonizing awareness that his life was at risk.

_____. *The FBI and Martin Luther King, Jr.: From "Solo" to Memphis*. New York: W. W. Norton, 1981. This work examines the roots and nature of the FBI's opposition to King and demonstrates that serious efforts were made to discredit King as a national leader.

King, Coretta Scott. *My Life with Martin Luther King, Jr*. Rev. ed. New York: Henry Holt, 1993. This book is a valuable personal account of the King family, but it must be balanced by schol-arly accounts. The revised edition does not differ significantly from the original edition, which was published shortly after King's death.

Lewis, David Levering. *King: A Critical Biography*. 2d ed. Urbana: University of Illinois Press, 1978. A reprint with some modifications of the 1970 edition, this account is a critical biography rather than a eulogy of King.

Washington, James, ed. *A Testament of Hope: The Essential Writings and Speeches of Martin Luther King, Jr*. San Francisco: Harper San Francisco, 1991. This collection includes material that King wrote or said from throughout his career. However, the brief introductory essay does not provide an analytical framework from which to study the excerpts.

Thomas R. Peake, updated by Thomas Clarkin

Saul Kripke

Kripke provided technical and conceptual advances in modal logic but is more widely known for his work in the philosophy of language, in particular for initiating the causal theory of reference.

Principal philosophical works: "A Completeness Theorem in Modal Logic," 1959; "Semantical Considerations on Modal Logic," 1963; "Identity and Necessity," 1971; "Naming and Necessity," 1972; "Outline of a Theory of Truth," 1975; "Is There a Problem About Substitutional Quantification?," 1976; "Speaker's Reference and Semantic Reference," 1977; "A Puzzle About Belief," 1979; *Naming and Necessity*, 1972 (article), 1980 (book); *Wittgenstein on Rules and Private Language: An Elementary Exposition*, 1982; "A Problem in the Theory of Reference: The Linguistic Division of Labor and the Social Character of Naming," 1986.

Born: November 13, 1940; Bay Shore, New York

Early Life

Saul Aaron Kripke, son of Myer Samuel and Dorothy Evelyn (Karp) Kripke, attended Harvard University, where he received a B.A. degree in 1962. In 1959, as a student, he distinguished himself by publishing an influential paper in the prestigious *Journal of Symbolic Logic*. Upon graduation, he received a Fulbright scholarship. A member of the Society of Fellows at Harvard in philosophy and mathematical logic, he served his alma mater as a lecturer from 1963 to 1966, when he left to take an appointment at Rockefeller University, where he stayed for ten years. In 1976, he became the McCosh Professor of Philosophy at Princeton University.

Life's Work

Kripke's earliest writings and influence were in the field of modal logic. Where "standard" formal logic deals with the syntax and semantics of inference, modal logic extends these to characterize and systematize inferences involving the modalities of possibility and necessity. For example, "standard" logic does not allow the inference "If it is necessary that p, then p" or "If p, then it is possible that p." Various systems of modal logic have been constructed to handle such inferences.

One way of talking about such systems is to speak of "possible world semantics." Although the world is the actual world, with a particular structure and history, things could have been different; facts could have been contrary to what they are. An intuitive way to speak of this is to talk of possible worlds, that is, worlds like the real world, but different in some respect or other.

To say that a proposition is possibly true simply means that, although it is false in the real world, it is true in some possible world. To say that a proposition is necessarily true simply means that it is true in all possible worlds (including the real world). Kripke's first paper, "A Completeness Theorem in Modal Logic," established that a formal modal system is complete: This means that any proposition p, either it or its negation, could be proven in that system (in other words, all valid inferences are shown to be valid in that system). This paper was followed by several others in the 1960's, most notably "Semantical Considerations in Modal Logic," in which Kripke elaborated on both technical aspects of modal logic and their wider implications and applications, including in the fields of ontology and philosophy of language.

It was these implications and applications of results in modal logic that brought Kripke his greatest renown. In 1972, he published *Naming*

Saul Kripke. *(Princeton University, Office of Communications)*

contingent properties associated with those names. For example, the name "Saul Kripke" attaches to a particular object not because of any contingent property that might be true of that particular object (for example, that he is the McCosh Professor of Philosophy). This is because there are possible worlds in which Saul Kripke is not the McCosh professor, but there are no possible worlds in which Saul Kripke is not Saul Kripke. Publication of *Naming and Necessity*, including its proposal of a new theory of reference and names, made Kripke a well-known figure not only in the community of logicians but also in the philosophical community at large.

His groundbreaking work in semantics continued throughout the 1970's, highlighted by two more influential writings: one on truth, "Outline of a Theory of Truth," and one on belief, "A Puzzle About Belief." The former presented his attempt to provide a theory that both resolved paradoxes involving truth and captured basic intuitions about natural languages. Truth paradoxes have been long-standing in philosophy, the most famous being the liar paradox. This paradox is illustrated by the following sentence: "Everything I say is a lie." If that sentence is true, then I am lying when I say that everything I say is a lie, which means that I am not lying. Another way to characterize this paradox is "This sentence is false." If the sentence is false, then it must be true. A standard response to this paradox has been to speak of different levels of language, such that the content of that sentence is on one level, but when speaking about that sentence (for example, by calling it true or false), people are at a different level. The first level is often said to be the object language and the second level is said to be the metalanguage. Kripke, however, argued that with natural languages, people do not conceive of themselves as using different levels and do not speak of "truth-level-one," "truth-level-two," "truth-level-three," and so on. A second concern for him was that, again with natural languages, people want to speak of

and Necessity, widely regarded as his most influential work and immediately considered a landmark in the philosophy of language. As the title indicates, he drew a connection between the modal element of necessity and the semantic issue of naming. The natural point of contact between these two, for Kripke, was the Leibnizian principle of the indiscernibility of identicals; that is, if two objects are identical, then they are indiscernible (or have all properties in common). If two objects really are identical, that is, if "$a = b$" is true, then, said Kripke, that identity would hold across all possible worlds (so that "$a = b$" would be necessarily true). From this starting point, Kripke questioned and ultimately rejected the view that names attach to objects in virtue of truth-value gaps, times when we do not want to (or cannot) say that a given sentence is true or false. He addressed these problems using tools of mathematical logic to characterize what he calls a "fixed point" language. Critics of his outline claimed that certain truth paradoxes remain unexplained; however, supporters claimed that his approach, though incomplete, is more promising than other approaches.

The second influential paper (on belief) returned to issues of reference, truth, and what speakers have in mind. A legitimate intuition about the truth of sentences is that coreferential terms can be substituted in them without changing the truth value of those sentences. For example, if "Cicero was lazy" is true, then, if Cicero equals Tully, "Tully was lazy" also would be true. This sort of substitutivity, however, breaks down in belief contexts. That is, while it might be true that I believe Cicero was lazy, not knowing that Cicero equals Tully, I might not believe that Tully was lazy. Relating back to Kripke's view that names are rigid designators and so should be interchangeable without affecting the truth value of the sentences in which they occur, belief contexts are problematic. The problem is not epistemological (I just don't know that Cicero equals Tully), but semantic (the truth values of the sentences are different).

Kripke extends this problem beyond that of substitutivity of coreferential terms in belief contexts to simple, ordinary contexts of disquotation and translation. (The principle of disquotation is as follows: If a normal English speaker, on reflection, sincerely assents to *p*, then he believes that *p*. The principle of translation is that if a sentence of one language expresses a truth in that language, then any translation of it into any other language also expresses a truth in that other language.) Kripke's puzzle is exemplified by the following case: Pierre, a normal French speaker who hears about the wonders of London, comes to believe "Londres est jolie" (London is pretty). However, if Pierre later learns English and visits London but sees only the seamy side of the city without realizing that this is the city he used to know as 'Londres,' Pierre comes to believe "London is not pretty." Does Pierre, or does he not, believe that London is pretty? Remembering that the issue is semantic, not epistemological, Kripke

insisted that "As any theory of truth must deal with the liar paradox, so any theory of belief and names must deal with this puzzle."

Kripke's work on these semantic problems and issues led to his second book, *Wittgenstein on Rules and Private Language*, which, like his earlier writings, generated enthusiasm and controversy. He suggested that the philosopher Ludwig Wittgenstein's rejection of private languages revealed a much deeper concern with the very possibility of rule following in language, which, in turn, revealed concern about matters of meaning, truth, and knowledge.

In *Philosophical Investigations* (1956; bilingual English and German edition), Wittgenstein claimed that language was rule-governed and required publicity; there could be no private language. Obeying the rules of language entailed publicity. The very meaning of words requires rule-governedness, as does people's ability to use and understand the meanings of words. Kripke asserted that Wittgenstein was actually addressing a "skeptical paradox," namely, there was no way to properly account for what it is to follow a linguistic rule. If this is so, it strikes at the very core of meaning and language itself. How can one know if one is following a rule? It cannot just be based on the fact that one has followed, or believed that one has followed, a rule in the past, because past cases might not completely reveal the nature of the rule or correctly extrapolate that rule to new cases. (This is Scottish philosopher David Hume's old problem of induction applied to linguistic rules.) If there is no way to account for rule following and if the meanings of words are dependent upon this, the very notion of meaning is in jeopardy.

Wittgenstein resolved his own paradox, said Kripke, by dropping the assumption that meaning is based on truth conditions and by adopting the view that meaning instead is based on assertability or justification conditions. Wittgenstein's notions of language games and meaning as use, which require a sociality to both language and meaning, were part of this adopted view. As Kripke put it, "The solution turns on the idea that each person who claims to be following a rule can be checked by others." This requirement of publicity was part and parcel of Kripke's writings on semantics all along. Yet the apparent endorsement of Wittgenstein's handling of this paradox, with its commitment to extrasemantic factors to account for meaning, suggests some movement on Kripke's part away from his earlier separation of the semantics and pragmatics of language.

Influence

It is safe to say that in the second half of the twentieth century, Kripke was as influential in the fields of logic, ontology, and philosophy of language as any other philosopher. In particular, his nascent causal theory of reference became the dominant theory. Concepts that he introduced, such as rigid designators, became standard terminology. His early work in quantified modal logic was truly groundbreaking. His writings, often very technical but always clear and succinct, displayed the seriousness and rigor of twentieth century analytic philosophy. At a time when analytic philosophy as a whole came under criticism as being removed from the concerns of everyday people and even of other academic disciplines, Kripke maintained a seriousness of purpose and focus of thought to wrestle with perennial philosophical issues such as truth and meaning while demanding clarity of explanation. To understand contemporary philosophy of language, one must understand the work of Kripke.

David Boersema

Naming and Necessity

Type of philosophy: Epistemology, philosophy of language
First published: 1972 (article); 1980 (book)
Principal ideas advanced:

◇ The descriptivist theory of naming and reference should be rejected; the proper view of reference is the causal theory of reference.

◇ Proper names are rigid designators, that is, they designate the same object in all possible worlds in which the object exists.

◇ Because names are rigid designators, if identity statements, such as "Mark Twain is Samuel Clemens," are true, they are necessarily true.

◇ Like proper names, natural kind terms, such as "water," "gold," and "tiger," function as rigid designators, and therefore, if identity statements involving them, such as "Water is H_2O," are true, they are necessarily true.

A long-standing concern for philosophers has been the issue of meaning, not just the meaning of things such as the meaning of life or the meaning of freedom but also the meaning of words and sentences. What words and sentences mean, how they "have meaning," and how speakers can use them to mean things have been debated as far back as Plato's *Cratylos* (c. 388-368 B.C.E.; *Cratylus*, 1804). Many twentieth century philosophers addressed the issue of reference, how words refer to objects.

The Descriptivist Theory

Saul Kripke's *Naming and Necessity* consists of revised transcriptions of three lectures given at Princeton University in 1970. The first lecture provides a brief historical survey of the descriptivist theory, particularly the version associated with philosophers Gottlob Frege, Bertrand Russell, John Searle, and several others. This theory asserts that a speaker succeeds in referring to an object by having some descriptions in mind that the speaker associates with that object. For example, one is able to refer to Aristotle (the object) by having some descriptions in mind that one associates with that object (such as "the most famous student of Plato" or "the teacher of Alexander the Great"). The typical types of linguistic units that are used to refer to objects are names, pronouns, and definite descriptions (such as "the largest cat in the city").

Throughout much of the twentieth century, the discussion about reference centered on whether the descriptions associated with reference had to be true of the object being referred to, whether a single description was sufficient for reference to succeed, and the intention of a speaker (for example, could someone refer to Aristotle without intending to, especially if reference required having descriptions *in mind*). This discussion was often framed in terms of whether or not names had meanings. Frege claimed that names have both a reference and a sense. For example, the name "Venus" refers to a particular object, but the name "Venus" means (or has the sense) "the second planet from the sun." The major critic of the view that names had meanings was John Stuart Mill, who claimed that they served only a referential role. By the 1960's, Searle had identified some difficulties facing the view of names held by Frege and Russell; he insisted that no single description could capture how names function. Rather, speakers have a cluster of descriptions that are associated with referring to an object. It is the descriptivist theory in general and this cluster theory in particular that Kripke rejects in *Naming and Necessity*.

Before proceeding to a discussion of Searle's cluster version, Kripke draws several conceptual distinctions, distinctions that he views the descriptivist theorists as overlooking or failing to appreciate. One distinction is that between speaker reference and semantic reference, or what a speaker refers to when using a name and that to which the name itself refers. Although one might be referring to (or trying to refer to) one person by using a particular name, the name itself might very well refer to, or pick out, someone else. For example, if one says, "I really detest Plato's *Ethica Nicomachea*," one might be referring to Aristotle, the actual author, but the name "Plato" does not refer to Aristotle. By insisting on speakers having descriptions in mind for reference to succeed, descriptivists confuse this distinction, says Kripke.

A second distinction, related to the first, that Kripke draws is identity versus identification. The identity of an object (and of the semantic reference of a name) is a metaphysical issue. How people come to identify that object, its identification, is an epistemological issue. It might well be the case that one identifies Aristotle as the most famous student of Plato or the teacher of Alexander the Great, but those means of identification do not constitute the identity of Aristotle (or the semantic reference of the name "Aristotle"). According to Kripke, descriptions that one has in mind might *fix* the reference of a name in some contexts, but they certainly do not *determine* the reference of the name nor the identity of the object named (and they definitely do not, he says, give the meaning of a name, since names do not have meanings).

In Kripke's view, names are rigid designators.

To understand the importance of this claim, one must understand the notion of possible worlds. The world has a particular structure and history. However, things could have been or could be different. Although in fact (in this world), Richard Nixon won the 1968 U.S. presidential election, he might not have. Indeed, it is possible that Nixon might never have entered politics at all. Each of these possible but not actual situations (often called "counterfactual situations") can be spoken of as a "possible world." Although in the real world, Nixon won the 1968 election, in a possible world, he did not. In *Naming and Necessity*, Kripke says rigid designators is a term that designates the same object in all possible worlds. Therefore, although the definite description "the winner of the 1968 U.S. presidential election" designates Nixon in this world, in one possible world, it designates Hubert Humphrey (in a world in which Humphrey beat Nixon), and in another possible world, it designates Barry Goldwater. Therefore, the description "the winner of the 1968 U.S. presidential election" is not a rigid designator because it designates different objects in different possible worlds. Names, however, says Kripke, are rigid designators; they designate the same object across different possible worlds. In other words, the name "Nixon" (or "Richard Milhouse Nixon") always refers to the same person. How else could people make sense of counterfactual claims about him? The reference stays put, so to speak, while the descriptions change.

The Cluster Theory and the Causal Theory

The second lecture constituting *Naming and Necessity* involves a thorough analysis and critique of Searle's cluster version of the descriptivist theory. Kripke identifies six theses of this theory: First, to every name or designating expression X, there corresponds a cluster of properties, C. Second, one of those properties (or some conjointly) are believed by the speaker to uniquely pick out some individual object. Third, if most (or a weighted most) of the cluster of properties C are satisfied by one unique object Y, then Y is the referent of the name X. Fourth, if no unique object is picked out (satisfies the cluster of properties C), then X does not refer. Fifth, the statement "If X exists, then X has most of the cluster of properties C" is known a priori by the speaker.

Sixth, the statement "If X exists, then X has most of the cluster of properties C" expresses a necessary truth (for the speaker).

Kripke offers a number of specific examples to show that each of these theses is wrong. He does this by showing that having descriptions in mind is neither necessary nor sufficient for reference. There are plenty of cases, he says, in which one refers to someone even though one has no, or no true, descriptions that uniquely pick out a particular object. For example, it might well be that I have no descriptions associated with the name "Feynman" that will pick out a unique object. Perhaps my only description in mind is "some physicist or something." Nevertheless, the name "Feynman" refers to Richard P. Feynman, not to someone else. Therefore, having certain descriptions in mind is not necessary for successful reference. In addition, they are not sufficient, as Kripke's Gödel example illustrates. Suppose that all the descriptions (or cluster properties C) are satisfied by a unique object, but the unique object is not the person to whom the speaker is trying to refer. Suppose that the descriptions (the cluster properties C) are, unbeknownst to the speaker, satisfied by Schmidt, not Gödel. Does the name "Gödel" now refer to Schmidt? Kripke answers in the negative. The speaker's beliefs about Gödel and about Schmidt might have been false, but "Gödel" refers to Gödel and not to Schmidt.

Having shown the descriptivist theory to be "wrong from the fundamentals," Kripke outlines a different view of reference. This view, known primarily as the causal theory of reference, focuses on three factors: first, the initial baptism of an object (where there is a causal connection to an object such that the name is associated with that object); second, the historical passing on of that name, such that later uses of the name are historically linked to the initial association of name and object; third, the intention to have speaker reference correspond to semantic reference (the speaker having the intention to refer to the same object as did the person from whom the speaker acquired the name). The first factor emphasizes the causal component of objects; the second factor emphasizes the public nature of language, including reference; and the third factor emphasizes the use that speakers make of names in the act of referring.

Names and Identity

Having rejected the descriptivist theory and reiterated that names are rigid designators, Kripke proceeds to claim that identity statements involving names are in fact necessary, not contingent. Names refer semantically and are not dependent on descriptions that speakers have in mind (the referent of a name is independent of epistemological factors). Therefore, although one might come to discover truths about someone, including truths about identity (which means one does not know those truths a priori), those identity truths are necessary. For example, if it is true that Cicero is Tully or Gaurisanker is Everest, then even though a speaker might not have known it, the identity holds, and because names designate the same object in all possible worlds, then the identity statement will be true in all possible worlds (that is, it will be necessarily true). Just as identity, which is metaphysical, is not the same as identification, which is epistemological, so necessity is not the same as a prioricity.

In the third lecture, Kripke extends this understanding of names and necessary identity statements to natural kind terms, that is, names of kinds of objects rather than names of individual objects. Just as one might have certain descriptions associated with a name that is used to refer to a particular individual (for example, one uses "the most famous student of Plato" to talk about Aristotle), but those descriptions do not constitute the semantic reference of the name, one might also have properties associated with a natural kind term that nonetheless do not uniquely pick out that kind. For example, the phenomenal properties of being yellow, malleable, and shiny might be the properties used to talk about gold, but they are not definitive of gold. They might be helpful in terms of identification, but they do not secure identity. Instead, there exist certain essential properties that are necessarily true of the kind (for gold, these properties are its atomic number; for tigers, their genetic structure).

The impact of Kripke's critique of the descriptivist theory of reference has been, for most philosophers, to demolish it. Although various responses and criticisms have been leveled against Kripke's claims, for the most part, the causal theory has become the widely accepted view of reference. Philosophers in other areas, such as philosophy of biology and philosophy of law, appeal to the causal theory in making claims outside concerns about language. Some professional philosophers have raised concern over the question of whether and to what extent his views, especially regarding possible world semantics, were independent of the work of Ruth Barcan Marcus.

David Boersema

Additional Reading

Davies, Martin. *Meaning, Quantification, Necessity: Themes in Philosophical Logic*. London: Routledge & Kegan Paul, 1981. Davies discusses Saul Kripke's work in the context of modal logic and its connections with meaning, truth, and reference. Fairly technical.

Devitt, Michael. *Designation*. New York: Columbia University Press, 1981. Devitt extends Kripke's views on reference by trying to flesh out his causal theory of reference.

Dummett, Michael. *Truth and Other Enigmas*. Cambridge, Mass.: Harvard University Press, 1978. Collection of essays on logic and language, including an influential critique of Kripke's view of reference.

Forbes, Graeme. *The Metaphysics of Modality*. Oxford: Clarendon Press, 1985. A clear introduction to modal logic that includes explanations of Kripke's contributions.

French, Peter A., Theodore E. Uehling, Jr., and Howard K. Wettstein, eds. *Studies in the Philosophy of Language*. Vol. 2 in *Midwest Studies in Philosophy*. Morris: University of Minnesota Press, 1977. Excellent anthology of papers on various issues related to meaning, reference, and names. Kripke's "Speaker's Reference and Semantic Reference" is included.

Humphreys, Paul, and James H. Fetzer, eds. *The New Theory of Reference: Kripke, Marcus, and Its Origins*. Dordrecht: Kluwer, 1998. This is a collection of papers that focuses on the controversy of whether, and to what extent, Kripke's view of reference, especially its connections to quantified modal logic, was anticipated by the work of Ruth Barcan Marcus.

Katz, Jerold J. *The Metaphysics of Meaning*. Cambridge, Mass.: MIT Press, 1990. An introduc-tory but sophisticated treatment of several philosophers on the nature of meaning, including Ludwig Wittgenstein, W. V. O. Quine, and Kripke.

Linsky, Leonard. *Names and Descriptions*. Chicago: University of Chicago Press, 1977. A clear, sophisticated introduction to issues of reference, existence, and modality, including a thorough discussion of Kripke's notion of rigid designators and necessity of identity.

_____. *Referring*. London: Routledge & Kegan Paul, 1967. Very clear survey of theories and concerns regarding reference before the publication of Kripke's work.

McGinn, Colin. *Wittgenstein on Meaning: An Interpretation and Evaluation*. Oxford: Basil Blackwell, 1984. Clear and thorough introduction to Wittgenstein on meaning, including a critique of aspects of Kripke's interpretation of Wittgenstein, particularly the role of community.

Salmon, Nathan U. *Reference and Essence*. Princeton, N.J.: Princeton University Press, 1981. Technical treatment of the theory of direct reference (causal theory) and its relation to essences.

Searle, John. *Expression and Meaning: Studies in the Theory of Speech Acts*. Cambridge, England: Cambridge University Press, 1979. This book responds to Kripke's criticisms of Searle's views on reference and proper names.

_____. *Intentionality: An Essay in the Philosophy of Mind*. Cambridge, England: Cambridge University Press, 1983. This book includes Searle's response to criticism by Kripke.

_____. *Speech Acts: An Essay in the Philosophy of Language*. Cambridge, England: Cambridge University Press, 1969. This book contains several essays in which Searle elaborates on the theory of reference and proper names that Kripke rejects.

Teorema 17, no. 1 (Winter, 1998). This special issue commemorates the twenty-fifth anniversary of the publication of Kripke's *Naming and Necessity*. Eight papers discuss and respond to various aspects of Kripke's book.

David Boersema

Jiddu Krishnamurti

Krishnamurti maintained that only individual transformation of the human mind can bring peace and harmony to the world, and that every individual transformation contributes to the world revolution necessary to escape decades of global wars and environmental degradation.

Principal philosophical works: *At the Feet of the Master*, 1910; *Education as Service*, 1912; *Towards Discipleship*, 1926; *By What Authority? Ommen Camp Fire Talks, 1927*, 1927; *Come Away*, 1927; *The Path*, 1927; *The Search*, 1927; *Who Brings the Truth?*, 1927; *The Song of Life*, 1931; *Authentic Report of Twelve Talks Given by Krishnamurti at Ojai Camp, 1934*, 1934; *Education and the Significance of Life*, 1953; *The First and Last Freedom*, 1954; *Commentaries on Living, from the Notebooks of J. Krishnamurti*, 1956; *Commentaries on Living, from the Notebooks of J. Krishnamurti, Second Series*, 1958; *Commentaries on Living, from the Notebooks of J. Krishnamurti, Third Series*, 1960; *This Matter of Culture*, 1964; *Think on These Things*, 1964; *Freedom from the Known*, 1969; *Talks with American Students, 1968*, 1970; *The Only Revolution*, 1970; *The Urgency of Change*, 1970; *The Impossible Question*, 1972; *Tradition and the Revolution*, 1970; *The Awakening of Intelligence*, 1973; *Beyond Violence*, 1973; *Krishnamurti on Education*, 1974; *Beginnings of Learning*, 1975; *Krishnamurti's Notebook*, 1976; *J. Krishnamurti Talking with Student and Staff at Brockwood Park School on Inward Flowering*, 1977; *Truth and Actuality*, 1977; *The Wholeness of Life*, 1978; *Early Writings*, 1978?; *Exploration into Insight*, 1979; *From Darkness to Light: Poems and Parables*, 1980; *The Network of Thought*, 1982; *Krishnamurti's Journal*, 1982; *Krishnamurti at Los Alamos, 1984*, 1984; *The World of Peace*, 1985; *The Ending of Time*, 1985; *Krishnamurti to Himself: His Last Journal*, 1987; *The Future Is Now: Last Talks in India*, 1988; *Meeting Life: Writings and Talks on Finding Your Path Without Retreating from Society*, 1991; *Freedom, Love, and Action*, 1994.

Born: May 22, 1895; Madanapalle, Andhra Pradesh, India
Died: February 17, 1986; Ojai, California

Early Life

Jiddu Krishnamurti was born in Madanapalle, a small town in South India near Madras, where he lived with his family until they moved to Madras, after the death of his mother and when he was a young teenager. His name is from Sri Krishna, a Hindu god and an eighth child, like Jiddu. He was frequently beaten in school because he did not learn his lessons. Then he was discovered by C. W. Leadbeater of the Theosophical Society, a group led by noted English writer Annie Besant. In 1911, she arranged for Krishnamurti and his brother Nitya, who died of tuberculosis in 1925, to go to England for training to become the reembodiment of the Buddhist spiritual teacher Lord Maitreya, as head of a new religious organization, the Order of the Star in the East. For years, Krishnamurti served as a vehicle for the society's teachings, traveling to many cities in India, the Netherlands, France, and the United States.

Life's Work

Krishnamurti made his permanent home in California's Ojai Valley, where he spoke and taught for the duration of his long life. His method was to talk informally to the hundreds, and then thousands, who came to visit and hear what he had to say. However, he began to doubt that he was all that the society had made him believe. In 1929, after a vision, he disbanded the Order of the Star in the East (claiming some sixty thousand members) and pronounced that no truth could be found by any formal organization or philosophy. In the same year, he started a school near his birthplace, in Rishi Valley, India, for an education without pressure of tradition. In later years, he established five more schools in India: in Rajghat (on property purchased by Besant), Uttar Kashi in the Himalayas, Bangalore, Chennai, and Mumbai. He repudiated all religions and political groups, all ideals and ideologies, all cultures and nationalities, and, most dramatically, his own spiritual authority. He began a rigorous and arduous career of constant world travel, lecturing to all who would listen.

Krishnamurti attacked the root problem of conformity through pressures of education in his 1953 work *Education and the Significance of Life*. In the first and second series of his *Commentaries on Living*, he discussed specific problems caused by the obstacles of hopes, fears, illusions, beliefs, and prejudices.

In the 1960's, Krishnamurti engaged in extensive dialogues with David Bohm, a theoretical physicist who taught at the University of London.

They discussed the nature of time, consciousness, the brain, and, above all, the transformation of humankind and the future of humanity. These experiences are background to the third series of *Commentaries on Living*, in which Krishnamurti returns to the varied fears and ideas that interfere with free consciousness. However, most important was *Krishnamurti's Notebook*, based on seven months in 1961 and 1962 when Krishnamurti kept a daily record of his perceptions and states of consciousness of the Otherness whose immensity and benediction filled the spaces of his life.

In 1964, *Think on These Things* was published to become one of Krishnamurti's most popular works. It is made up of discussions he had with students, teachers, and parents in the schools in India. Although this work does not systematically develop any particular theme, the recurring motif of the work is a concern for right education to cleanse world consciousness. In 1968, a time of

Jiddu Krishnamurti brings his message to a group at the Logan estate near Bristol, Pennsylvania, in 1932. *(Library of Congress)*

great unrest on college campuses in the United States, Krishnamurti conducted similar discussions with students. In these discussions, published in 1970 as *Talks with American Students, 1968*, Krishnamurti shows students a way to explore the true meaning of freedom and rebellion.

In 1968, Krishnamurti was videotaped for the first of many times. In the same year, he joined others in establishing the Brockwood Park School in England, and seven years later he founded the Oak Grove School in the United States. The paradox and irony of his message are captured in the title of *Freedom from the Known*, in which true education is shown to begin with asking basic questions to which individuals must find individual answers. The irony is that the student must unlearn before learning these truths, and the paradox is that knowledge must be emptied from the mind in order for true education to occur. This and previous concerns were brought together in a collection called *Freedom, Love, and Action*, drawn from meetings with students throughout the 1960's.

In 1971, Krishnamurti gave a talk in New York City, in which he focused on the fundamental significance of relationships. Without overcoming social and psychological divisions, there can be no revolution of consciousness. Whatever corruption there may be in the world, it comes from individual division of consciousness, and unless this division is healed, there can be no significant social relationships. The key to healing lies in attention to loneliness, the plight of so many in the world but especially in the United States. Love is the way out, but love must pass by the dangers of lust into passion, where sorrow lies. Beneath sorrow is death, which also must be confronted as part of living.

This message is published in *The Impossible Question*, which takes the questioner toward the encounter with death. Asking about impossibilities will force the mind to explore origins buried beneath ideas which are culture's possibilities. Probing questions lead into a process which Krishnamurti called meditative, although he often attacked traditional forms of meditation as practiced in his home country. The point of these lessons is captured in *The Awakening of Intelligence*, which includes conversations with Jacob Needleman, Alan Naude, Swami Venkatesananda,

and Bohm on teaching, traditional beliefs, fragmented consciousness, and psychological revolution without violence. This last theme is repeated and expanded in *Beyond Violence*, where it is given greater urgency by recognition that high technology has intensified our awareness of mass violence.

Krishnamurti focused on the problems of education. Out of his many dialogues with students and teachers, he came to realize that all problems can be reduced—in origin, formulation, and resolution—to the problem of education. In a series of talks from 1974 to 1976, he articulated his thoughts on this subject, and he published them in *Krishnamurti on Education* and *J. Krishnamurti Talking with Student and Staff at Brockwood Park School on Inward Flowering*. The first book covers talks with teachers in India, the second with teachers in England in September, 1976, and with students in England in October, 1976.

In *Truth and Actuality* and *The Wholeness of Life*, Krishnamurti returns to the underlying challenge of all education: confronting truth in the problems of everyday living. Individual misery is a symptom of cultural chaos and history. The mind must be saved from this chaos and freed to find its original energies, long dissipated by layers of culture and tradition. This can happen only when the individual has the courage to abandon all securities, from religious beliefs to family values. A free mind, which is the only healthy mind, must accept danger as its proper medium.

The many dialogues and discussions with Bohm led to several areas of agreement and understanding, although there were strains as each believed the other was being manipulated by others to serve selfish purposes. Nevertheless, they represented a serious effort to unite science and imagination in a single, integrated model. The scientist had been persecuted by American politicians attacking communism, and the philosopher was criticized for leading people away from traditional values of nationalism. What brought them together in a positive way was Bohm's theory of implicate order, in which matter and consciousness are one.

An important publication that gave further expression to insights polished by talks with Bohm and others was *The Network of Thought*, in which Krishnamurti compares bad education with computer programming, in which minds are turned into biological and emotional machines to fit into preconceived patterns, or mental networks, for controlling social and political behavior. Self-observation without thought is the paradoxical way to break out of these networks.

The idea that bad education has disturbed harmony throughout the world is the message behind *The World of Peace*, which was published with parallel texts in both English and German, from talks at Brockwood Park in England in 1983. In this work, Krishnamurti invites his audience to be free from the blind illusions of the self as the only basis for world peace.

The appeal of his insights to scientists took Krishnamurti in March, 1984, to the National Laboratory Research Center at Los Alamos, New Mexico, where he participated in a seminar on the subject of creativity in science. The resulting publication was *Krishnamurti at Los Alamos, 1984*. Later, his discussions of this and other matters with Bohm were published as *The Ending of Time*, in which Krishnamurti emphasized that the setting of goals interferes with genuine creativity for scientists and, indeed, for every person. Self-centered thinking confuses and destroys clear perception of reality. Only love and compassion can move one toward the reality that lies beyond thought and time.

Krishnamurti's final talks in India in 1985 were published in 1988 as *The Future Is Now*, a call to each person to accept responsibility for the pain and chaos of the world. The posthumously published *Meeting Life* gently suggests that revolution can occur in quiet ways, when problems are observed by minds free of ideas and ideals, the clutter of tradition and history. The paradox, he repeats, is that all of being is fulfilled when people let go of everything, as in death, the subject of his final utterances, published as *Krishnamurti to Himself*.

Krishnamurti died at ninety years of age on February 17, 1986, at his home in Ojai, California. His body was cremated and his ashes scattered to discourage followers from localizing his memory as an object of worship.

Influence

Krishnamurti's life and thought have established themselves in many ways. In books, films, work-shops, schools, and the Krishnamurti Foundation, his talks have been widely disseminated in nearly fifty languages during his life and since his death. The profound impact of his influence was felt by such thinkers as David Bohm, George Bernard Shaw, Bertrand Russell, Aldous Huxley, Joseph Campbell, Albert Einstein, Jackson Pollock, and even Charlie Chaplin. All testify to the enduring influence of his ideas on individual consciousness and the need for spiritual revolution to eliminate chaos in the world. As a result of this influence, an increasing number of schools and educational institutions have been encouraged to teach that people are whole human beings and not merely tools of nations or religions or ideologies. Science has been influenced to attend to interrelationships of observer with observed. Lacking system, Krishnamurti's teachings have lacked the sanctions usually accorded to Western products of the Greek philosophical tradition, but in his lack of system lies Krishnamurti's greatest appeal to minds left unsatisfied by analytical reason alone. For that reason, his philosophy embodies features of universality that transcend the limitations of East and West, science and religion, individuals and societies.

Richard D. McGhee

Think on These Things

Type of philosophy: Ethics, Indian philosophy, metaphysics
First published: 1964
Principal ideas advanced:
⬦ Education is preparation to understand life as a whole.
⬦ Discontent becomes creative when one is discontented with everything.
⬦ Clear attention requires removal of prejudices of all kinds.
⬦ The search for truth is the search for God.

Jiddu Krishnamurti's philosophy cannot be separated from religious intuition. Like Theosophy, it emphasizes intuition and revelation and derives from the Hinduism of India, in which the human and the divine are realized as one through reincarnation, transmigration, and karma: Each person struggles to achieve wisdom and self-liberation in Nirvana. Krishnamurti retains the substance of both Theosophy and Hinduism, but he rejects the forms and names, even as he rejects any organized religion or body of beliefs.

The book is a collection of Krishnamurti's discussions with students, teachers, and parents in India. There are twenty-seven chapters, each of which opens with Krishnamurti's exposition of a main theme, followed by his answers to questions posed by his listeners.

Education

The first is a discussion of education as preparation to understand life as a whole experience. Even ambition can interfere with freedom, because it limits energies and interferes with unbiased attention to reality. People so inhibited must revolt against everything, including society, religion, and tradition. Chapter 2 examines the problem of freedom as caused by wishing to become something. It can be solved only when education begins at childhood to cultivate the self free of goals set by others. Freedom is restricted by all institutions, including education, because it is limited by claims of absolute belief and needs to pursue knowledge.

Love

Next, freedom requires love. There can be no dependence of any kind, including dependence on family or nation. Love can itself be misleading and a dependence, so long as it causes a wish for something in return. Listening carefully is the theme of the fourth session. If happiness is to be possible, a person must learn to listen well. The mind is like a river. One must watch it flow past in its restlessness. It is important to distinguish the discontent of this restlessness from the discontent of struggles to succeed at becoming something in the world. Discontent can be creative or destructive. The creative kind emanates from the mind which observes itself as it is, rather than observing the world as a goal for measuring success.

Beyond Ego

It is extraordinarily difficult to grasp the whole of life, which is the subject of the sixth discourse.

The mind has to get outside the limits placed on its energies by a selfish society and history. Individuals prepared by education as a training for a job will never conceive the wholeness of their lives; a single spoke in a wheel cannot conceive of the rim and the hub that lie beyond it. The person who wants to revolutionize the world must first get rid of the wish to revolutionize, because that is to set a goal and is a symptom of ego. Failure to do so leads to opposition and destructive competition. Conflict always issues from such desires and pursuits. Competition breeds chaos and violence. To prevent that from occurring, ambition must be dissolved by love. The eighth chapter examines orderly thinking, which seems necessary for learning. However, the very effort to be orderly is pernicious and undermines genuine learning, because it eliminates so much of reality, setting limits on the mind. When loving minds are open to all experience, the world is created anew as a whole, self-affirming process.

Mind and Revolution

The crucial importance of an open mind is the subject of the next talk. Most people consider thinking to be a matter of calling upon memory, but that is wrong. Real thinking is a matter of current attention to what actually exists. Memory is a weight that interferes with real thinking. Clear attention requires removal of prejudices of all kinds, since they screen and filter experience in such a way as to reduce reality. The truly open mind will be simple and austere in its repose. Simplicity is an attribute of inward beauty because it indicates the abandonment of acquisitiveness and selfishness. It comes to the mind through love for all things of the world.

Tradition presses for conformity; truth cries out for revolt. In the eleventh chapter, revolution is emphasized as most fit for a free and open mind. Not only must the mind revolt against the patterns within society, but it must also revolt against all of society itself. The mind is like a prisoner who can revolt to demand improved conditions within the prison and still be a prisoner, or revolt to escape from the prison itself. It is only outside the walls of society's prison that genuine freedom can be found. This freedom comes to innocence. Thus, the next section probes the actual achievements promoted by Krishnamurti. The innocence here is a quality of openness and tolerance, rather than a matter of obedience to morals or laws.

Equality

Free of the walls and open to God as Truth, the mind affirms equality. This occurs because no one is superior to any other when everyone drops ambition for success. Schools ought to create an atmosphere in which this happens, where each person feels confident in his or her own innocence of purpose. The thirteenth chapter indicates the paradoxical truth that equality is possible only when all are free, and freedom exists only when all are equal. Individuals enjoy freedom and equality when they break free of traditions imposed on them by conventional education. The fourteenth chapter examines a matter often associated with successful learning: self-discipline. This subjection to rigor of thought is rejected as a dulling process in which the sharp mind is ground down to accept conformity. If integration occurs, no discipline is needed, because integration is the totality of being in all its dimensions.

Any form of inducement discourages freedom and equality. Even the inducement to reward will be detrimental. The fifteenth talk explores the nature of cooperation and sharing as products of freedom and equality. An agreement on a common goal is an inducement, and so it also subverts genuine freedom. If the goal or the plan is more important than the process of cooperation, there is no freedom; when the goal dissolves or the idea evaporates, so will the freedom and the cooperation. The joy of doing something together is the only reliable measure, and it can occur only when there is no hope of reward or fear of punishment for failure. The next discussion turns around the idea of renewal. It begins with a question about the signs of deterioration in all things of the world, including the body but also the mind; minds deteriorate because they have been made heavy and dull by the weight of history and tradition.

The River: Metaphor for Life

Chapter 17 employs a favorite image to make its point: Life in its flow and process is like the movement of a river, wide and deep. To this may be compared a pool that is stagnant and heavy with scum. This contrast is used to compare the lives of individuals, most of whom stagnate in their pools of habit and decay. To escape, they must break through barricades and free their life force to flow into and with the great river. The barricades are such things as family, ambition, gods, and fear of death. The next discussion describes a free mind as an attentive one. The practice of attention is not easy, because it requires notice of the gaps in, as well as the facts of, existence. One must observe absence as well as presence, nothing as well as something. Distinction is required between an act of attention that narrows and one that widens the mind.

Learning, Religion, and Mental Freedom

Barricades to mental freedom examined in chapter 19 are knowledge and tradition. There is a kind of knowledge that is more hindering than helpful to understanding: the knowledge taught as beliefs and ideals that divide rather than unite people. Such knowledge is destructive because it prevents the discovery of truth and God, who is all of being and reality. To overcome this kind of knowledge requires an attention that is sensitive to everything, including even unconscious processes of the mind itself. Drawing on previous discussions of inward beauty, the next chapter examines what it means to be religious. Krishnamurti's answer is that a religious person is one who is sensitive to reality. This reality, in all its details, is a totality that includes forms of ugliness as well as beauty. The mind that loves is the mind sensitive to all reality.

Because opening the mind is learning, there is a question about the purpose of this learning. The simple answer is that understanding truth and God is the purpose of learning. Concentration without tension and attention without elimination are attributes of the learning that is open to the truth of what is, rather than what might be or should be. Chapter 21 compares love, like life, to the flow of a river, and so again the point is made that a free mind is a loving mind and a flowing process. Love unites the perceiver with the perceived, the thinker with the thought, and in that unity is creative stillness.

The discussion in chapter 23 deals with a particularly difficult notion: that people need to be alone even though they are constantly seeking diversions that take them away from themselves. Because people are empty and dull, they cannot endure being alone with themselves. They need to fill this emptiness of boredom. The attentive mind, loving as it does, will not be aware of boredom because it is that to which it attends: It is the same as the object of its observation. The subject is the object, and so there can be no feeling of loneliness or boredom. A discussion of the energy of life follows. In this, Krishnamurti cautions against using discipline to learn, because it can destroy the energy required for genuine learning. Teachers and education can destroy learning when they compel the young to curtail their energies in efforts of memory and habits of belief handed down by tradition and history. When love is missing from learning, lost in gadgets and deadened by memory, that learning languishes and dies.

The mind energized by love to identify with the object of its learning is one capable of living effortlessly. Krishnamurti describes a scene in which a boat glides along a river with the work done by the wind. This is a picture of the kind of mind that can be attained and that can revolutionize reality. It must come as a consequence of simple attention to the mind itself. When that happens, the mind ceases to struggle, and, without surprise, the subject of the mind is lost in the object of the mind. With all his talk of mind, Krishnamurti stresses, ironically, in chapter 26, that the mind is not everything. The discussion turns around the problems that technology poses for genuine learning, because technology is a production of abstract reasoning, or mind as separate from heart. Krishnamurti says that this is a matter of filling the heart with things of the mind, and it must be reversed for world revolution to occur.

Learning as God-Seeking

The final chapter is a conclusive discussion that learning is seeking God because God is truth. Education should prepare students for this learning, not dissipate their energies and distract them with pressures to conform to political and religious ideals, to train for jobs, and to bend to the dehumanizing and divisive pressures of societies and nations. The revolution for which Krishna-

murti calls is like the ever-widening circle of energy caused by a pebble thrown in the lake of life.

Think on These Things is a collection of discussions that Krishnamurti repeated many times in many places to many different audiences. It looks back on decades of his thinking and anticipates still more years of similar thoughts. It nevertheless had a unique impact on people living in the time of its original publication in 1964, the height of the Cold War and fear of nuclear holocaust. The yearning of people for peace and quiet was nourished by Krishnamurti's wisdom, and the perplexity of new discoveries in quantum physics was relieved by reflective observations that the behavior of atomic particles could be reconciled with the behavior of human observers.

Richard D. McGhee

Additional Reading

Blau, Evelyne. *Krishnamurti: 100 Years*. New York: Stewart, Tabori, and Chang, 1995. A stirring assortment of recollections, writings, and photos published as a tribute to denote the centennial of Krishnamurti's birth.

Chandmal, Asit. *One Thousand Suns: Krishnamurti at Eighty-five and the Last Walk*. New York: Aperture, 1995. A becoming tribute to Krishnamurti's life and work.

Huxley, Aldous. Foreword to *The First and Last Freedom*. New York: Harper, 1954. The main theme of Jiddu Krishnamurti is that hope lives in individuals, not in societies. Huxley met and often spoke with Krishnamurti, near whom he lived in California. Both men were critical of organized religion, national politics, and technology for suppressing and discouraging free thought and full human development.

Jayakar, Pupul. *Krishnamurti: A Biography*. New York: Harper & Row, 1986. An appreciation of the man and his ideas, this biography lacks a larger vision of the evolving context for Krishnamurti's development in a rapidly changing world. The significance of Krishnamurti to Indian and Eastern cultures, however, is evident.

Krishnamurti, J. *Limits of Thought: Discussions Between J. Krishnamurti and David Bohm*. New York: Routledge, 1998. In this book Bohm and Krishnamurti survey human nature and an individual's relationship to society, yielding insights on cosmic order, death, and human thought.

Lutyens, Mary. *Krishnamurti: The Years of Fulfillment*. London: Farrar, Straus & Giroux, 1983. The second volume in Lutyens's biography, this provides a detailed account of Krishna-murti's activities during the period of his greatest influence. Although there are other volumes, this one is the most focused on the years Krishnamurti's basic ideas and teachings were formulated.

Richard D. McGhee

Julia Kristeva

Kristeva linked semiotics and literary criticism by treating literature as a psychological, historical, and political phenomenon. Her analyses employ concepts from both psychology and political philosophy.

Principal philosophical works: *Séméiotiké: Recherches pour une sémanalyse*, 1969 ("The System and the Speaking Subject," 1973); *Le Texte du roman*, 1970; *La Révolution du langage poétique*, 1974 (*Revolution in Poetic Language*, 1984); *Des Chinoises*, 1974 (*About Chinese Women*, 1977); *Polylogue*, 1977 (partial translation, *Desire in Language: A Semiotic Approach to Literature and Art*, 1980); *Pouvoirs de l'horreur: Essai sur l'abjection*, 1980 (*Powers of Horror: An Essay on Abjection*, 1982); *Histoires d'amour*, 1983 (*Tales of Love*, 1987); *Au commencement était l'amour: Psychanalyse et foi*, 1985 (*In the Beginning Was Love: Psychoanalysis and Faith*, 1988); *The Kristeva Reader*, 1986; *Soleil noir: Dépression et mélancolie*, 1987 (*Black Sun: Depression and Melancholia*, 1989); *Étrangers à nous-mêmes*, 1988 (*Strangers to Ourselves*, 1991); *Les Nouvelles Maladies de l'âme*, 1993 (*New Maladies of the Soul*, 1995).

Born: June 24, 1941; Silven, Bulgaria

Early Life

Born in Bulgaria in 1941, Julia Kristeva received her early education from a French religious order and her college training at the University of Sofia. She arrived in Paris in 1966 to begin studies toward a doctoral degree; this step turned into a permanent emigration for her, and her professional life in effect began in Paris. In 1967, her articles began to appear in the leading intellectual journals, *Critique*, *Langages*, and *Tel Quel*. Owing to her close association with the latter, Kristeva tended to be grouped with the poststructuralist school of thought about language and culture. She had, however, a distinctive voice from the very first. Having been introduced to Western literature through the innovative Russian critic Mikhail Bakhtin, she arrived prepared to make a unique contribution at the moment when Paris was most receptive to nontraditional, non-Western approaches to Western culture.

After defending her doctoral dissertation, *Revolution in Poetic Language*, Kristeva was appointed to a chair in linguistics at the University of Paris VII. She served on the editorial board of *Tel Quel* from 1970 to 1983. With a group from *Tel Quel*, she made a three-week visit to China in 1974; from this experience came her perceptive study *About Chinese Women*. Kristeva married the French novelist and theorist Philippe Sollers in 1970 and had a son in 1976. She completed professional training in psychoanalysis, opening her own practice in 1979.

Life's Work

Kristeva's work linked literary theory and semiotics. She treats literature as a psychological, historical, and political phenomenon. Although her range of erudition is multicultural, her focus is most often on French literature, with Russian a significant secondary source. James Joyce heads the wide-ranging list of literary sources outside the Russian and French.

The first stage of Kristeva's critical writings, roughly from the years 1967 through 1974, includes "The System and the Speaking Subject," *Le Texte du roman* (works of fiction), and *Revolution in Poetic Language*. In this stage, Kristeva was concerned with elaborating the tools of criticism. She validated Bakhtin's concept of literary polyphony as an important stage in the novel and his understanding of "poetic language" as a concept much broader than poetry. She validated French avant-garde critic Roland Barthes's insights into the existential "negativity" of language and the preeminence of history and politics over literature. She expanded the inventory of critical terminology with numerous new terms, such as "intertextuality," "paragram," "genotext," and "phenotext." Of these, "intertextuality" has gained the widest acceptance; it refers to the transposition of one system of signs into another, refreshing the connotations of both. She affirms the application, begun by colleagues such as Barthes and Jacques Derrida, of semiotics to literature; in so doing, she emphasizes that the semiotic approach is a post-Symbolist approach and carefully distinguishes between the traditional symbols and the innovative concept of "signs" in literature. In this first stage, Kristeva's approach was at its most severely technical or structuralist. For example, she applied calculus in her definition of an omniscient narrator opening a story with a description of a hero in the third person:

> The subject of utterance (S_d) coincides with the zero degree of the subject of enunciation (S_t), which can be designated either by the "he/she" nonperson pronoun or by a proper name. This is the simplest technique found at the inception of the narrative.

In an anthology of her early writings, taken from many sources and available only in English as *Desire in Language*, Kristeva puts her approach into focus: "One of the problems for semiotics is to replace the formal, rhetorical division of genres with a typology of texts." For her, the most important genre in need of semiotic redefinition is the novel, particularly in its subversive role, from François Rabelais to Louis-Ferdinand Céline, as the carrier of what Bakhtin called the "carnivalesque" (joyous, sensual, mocking) impulse in Western culture. She views the novel dynamically, as a process or operation. The importance of the differing stylistic and psychological threads weaving through the novel is emphasized as the real key to the distinctness of the genre. She sounds a distinct extraliterary note in a chapter entitled "The Ethics of Linguistics": Both linguis-

tic and literary analysis deserve a larger role in the interpretation of history and culture than has previously been seen. In semiotic fashion, a parallel is assumed among all manifestations of culture, with literary and language codes participating in the same processes as, for example, ethical and legal codes. In the late nineteenth century, "something quite new [entered] . . . Western society and discourse . . . subsumed in the names of [Karl] Marx, [Friedrich] Nietzsche, and [Sigmund] Freud." She finds a parallel between these thinkers' shattering of various codes and the code shattering of such twentieth-century writers as the Russian Futurists and Céline. In Kristeva's words, "a code . . . must be shattered in every revolutionary beginning."

Kristeva's increased emphasis on Freudian (and Lacanian) psychology is apparent in *Powers*

Julia Kristeva. *(Gamma Liaison)*

of Horror. Here, Freudian analysis is the predominant tool used in a bold survey of most of the range of human discourse, culminating in a nearly definitive study of Céline. The work is rewarding for its flashes of genuine eloquence about a kaleidoscope of writers, illuminated and connected in new ways. For example, on Marcel Proust: "the delightful interlacing of Proustian sentences, which unfold my memory and that of my language's signs down to the silent, glowing recesses of an odyssey of desire"; and the Marquis de Sade: "the Sadean narrative machine unveils, beneath the power of terror, the playful reckoning of sexual drive coiled up in death." There is also a convincing interpretation of the New Testament as having innovated an inextricable link between sin and beauty and a less easily defensible reinterpretation of the Old Testament along Freudian-Lacanian lines. A genuinely witty insight into Céline's *pointillisme* (his addiction to using three dots in lieu of any other form of punctuation) is the suggestion that it represents his obsession with the three points of the Oedipal triangle. Kristeva's chiefly psychologically oriented stage as a critic continued with *Tales of Love.* At the same time, her openly political orientation matured into a broader human view in which politics is less important.

Kristeva is complex and difficult, seeking to express the heretofore inexpressible in her work. She relies to a considerable extent upon paradox to express insights that appear to be beyond logic, for example: "Torn between being the guardian of the law and the instance which disavows the law, hasn't philosophy turned away from thought?" In her second, most politicized phase, Kristeva threw a gauntlet to her orthodox counterparts, challenging them to find their way through her multidimensional thinking (about the self, the other, and the Lacanian nonsubject nonobjects of an alienated consciousness): "No scholar, no orthodox theoretician can find his way through any of my essays, unless he has personally experienced this four-sided duel."

Although Kristeva's fundamental theories have evolved and matured, their provenance is not completely forgotten. Though identified with the leftist intellectual movement of France and agreeing with many of its ideals, Kristeva occupies a unique position as a radical anti-Marxist.

In her own words: "I am an exile from socialism and Marxist rationality." Yet far from seeing the latter as outmoded and moribund, she viewed it as an opponent to be fought with the sharpest weapons: "We must attack the very premises of this rationality . . . and dismantle them patiently and meticulously, starting with language and working right up to culture and institutions." Because one cannot use language and logic to dismantle language and logic, Kristeva has, perhaps in spite of herself, contributed to the achievement of new levels of theoretical meticulousness.

D. Gosselin Nakeeb

Strangers to Ourselves

Type of philosophy: Ethics, social philosophy
First published: Étrangers à nous-mêmes, 1988 (English translation, 1991)
Principal ideas advanced:

◊ The foreigner is a wanderer with no sense of belonging.

◊ From very early times, foreigners have been viewed with suspicion.

◊ Foreigners trouble native people because they threaten the established tradition.

◊ Throughout history there have been cosmopolitans, who wished to feel at home in any country.

◊ Christianity succeeded as a religion partly because it appealed to foreigners.

◊ The Renaissance was a time of New World discoveries and explorations, a time in which cosmopolitanism was prevalent.

◊ Human rights are distinct from civil rights. However, if one is not a citizen, often human as well as civil rights are denied.

◊ Psychoanalyst Sigmund Freud's study of the unconscious revealed the stranger within each person; the "strangeness" or foreignness within each person is projected onto others; thus, one is a stranger to oneself and to others.

Strangers to Ourselves is a reflection on foreignness and foreigners. It sympathizes with the problems and thoughts of the foreigner as well as those of people who live with foreigners and even with the troublesome discovery of finding the foreigner in oneself. Because Julia Kristeva was born in Bulgaria and settled in France, she herself in some ways reflects the foreigner, and she sympathizes with this point of view. She expresses concern that France is becoming a kaleidoscope of nationalities in which immigrants do not give up their particularities and in which a new homogeneity is not likely or desirable. This book received the Henri Hertz Prize, awarded by the Chancellerie des Universités de Paris for the best book by a faculty member.

The title of the first chapter, "Toccata and Fugue for the Foreigner," refers to the idea that a foreigner is never completely at home in a new country even when he or she has been there for a number of years. A musical form, the toccata rushes from here to there, briefly touching on each note. The foreigner is a wanderer who never feels a sense of belonging. Possessed with a driving ambition, the person will take any and all jobs and try to be the best at whatever that may be. The foreigner lives with a sense that those at home have been abandoned, and although one's mother tongue has been forgotten, there is an awkwardness in speaking the new language. Worst of all, the foreigner feels that no one is listening and no one deeply understands. Kristeva uses an example from Vladimir Nabokov's novel *The Real Life of Sebastian Knight* (1941). Knight wanders; he cannot find a home, a partner, or a language. Even his memories are constantly changing.

Ancient Views of Foreigners

In the remaining chapters of the book, Kristeva traces attitudes toward the foreigner throughout history. The Greek author Aeschylus tells of the Danaides, women of Egypt who fled their native land, became foreigners in Greece, and married Greek men. Thus, Greece is in part built on exogamous relationships. The foreigner in Greece, however, was not a citizen but a suppliant, under the protection of the law.

In Homeric times, the ancient world closed in on itself, and foreigners were greeted with suspicion and hostility. Classical times gave birth to the word "barbarian," which is believed to have originated with people who were inarticulate in the Greek language and whose efforts to speak

sounded like "bla-bla" or "bara-bara" to the Greeks. In the writings of Euripides, the barbarian is already portrayed as an enemy of democracy.

The Stoics had a sense of the cosmopolitan. The king Menander said, "I am a man, and nothing human is foreign to me." The Stoics believed that all humankind is bound in concentric spheres that include the entire universe, from citizens to the stars. Distinctions faded between Greeks and barbarians, between free persons and slaves, and even between men and women. However, this idea remained a utopian one. Zeno of Citium, the founder of Stoicism, wrote a cynical piece in which he imagined a world with no distinct states. There were no marriages, schools, courts, money, or temples, and cannibalism, incest, and prostitution reigned. The Greeks remained a closed society. Even in Alexandria, Greeks married among themselves.

Jews and Christians

In her next example of attitudes toward foreigners, Kristeva notes that even though the Jewish people think of themselves as chosen by God, chosenness does not mean exclusivity. She cites the example of Ruth, an ancestor of David, who was a Moabite, but who was dedicated to the fulfillment of a divine global design.

Christianity was founded on the principle of hospitality. In accordance with the cosmopolitanism of late Hellenism, Saint Paul preached that Jesus came as a stranger, and the church was to include all people. No distinctions were made between Greek and Jew, slaves and free people, and men and women. Saint Augustine spoke of two cities: Babylon, representing selfishness, and Jerusalem, representing community. The people of God were to be united not by erasing differences but by forgiving them. A whole industry sprang up around the welcoming of foreigners, which gradually turned into hospitality for Christians only. In the late Roman Empire, Rome became concerned with protecting itself from outsiders. Pagans were mistrusted, and heretics became foreigners, even in their own country.

In her fifth chapter, Kristeva pauses in her historical survey to suggest that a foreigner can be defined only in negative terms. A foreigner is one who does not have the same nationality, one who is outside of a social group. She questions whether one is fully human if one is not a citizen. In many countries, the foreigner is excluded from public service, has no right to own property, and is more easily subject to arrest. When one is denied the right to vote, one is reduced to being a passive object, having no control.

Changing Attitudes

Kristeva next looks at the Renaissance, the era of explorers and discoveries in the New World. She examines Italian writer Dante Alighieri's *La divina commedia* (c. 1320; *The Divine Comedy*, 1802), which he wrote while in exile. Deprived of a homeland, Dante imagined a Christian universalism. He envisioned a political monarchy in which small communities would be harmonized within a spiritual design. Italian philosopher Niccolò Machiavelli envisioned a balance between the individual and the state, but he advocated that the state use terror and strength to occupy conquered nations. He had no concern for international justice. French writer François Rabelais wrote of an expedition to China in which water was a symbol for the course of psychic investigation into myth, dream, ideal, wealth, and happiness. English statesman Thomas More's *De Optimo Reipublicae Statu, deque nova Insula Utopia* (1516; *Utopia*, 1551) illustrated a place in which people abhor tyranny, share wealth, abolish private property, and respect culture and religion. French essayist Michel Eyquem de Montaigne advocated that people respect the strangeness in others because they sometimes find strangeness in themselves. He condemned the forced conversion of the Jews to Christianity and defended other religions and races. In the Renaissance, Kristeva says, a natural human universality was taking shape. Geographical publications increased, atheistic principles were discovered, and the goodness of the "savage" was idealized. Supranational bodies were beginning to be conceived.

During the Enlightenment, attitudes toward the foreigner took a different direction. French political philospher Montesquieu believed that humans would join together naturally, but that government policies should guarantee this. He held a kind of borderless philosophy in which human rights superseded citizen's rights and higher political systems overshadowed the na-

tion. All people had rights whether or not they were citizens. The freedom of the individual was more important than the unity of society. During the Enlightenment, the "savage" or stranger became the alter ego of the philosopher, the figure onto which one projected one's inner self.

Kristeva then gives three examples from the Enlightenment. First, in French philosopher Denis Diderot's *Le Neveu de Rameau* (1821, 1891; *Rameau's Nephew*, 1897), the nephew is the stranger who wants to challenge, invert, shock, and contradict. He is, however, expelled from the gathering because of his outrageousness. The second example is from the writings of Fougeret de Monbron. A cosmopolitan, he said, has no fixed abode, and is nowhere a foreigner. He said that "the universe is a kind of book, of which one has read only the first page when one has seen only one's country." His tone, however, is negative and hateful. He can only appreciate his own country because he has seen the incivilities of others. The third example concerns the German philosopher, Georg Wilhelm Friedrich Hegel. According to Hegel, because culture is foreign to the natural human body, it forces everyone to take into account what is strange and other. All three of these views take a somewhat ambivalent tone toward the strange, the other. The foreigner is fascinating, but somewhat dangerous and threatening.

The Revolution and Nationalism

In the last section of chapter 7, Kristeva gives three examples of French attitudes toward foreigners during the French Revolution. In 1790, the National Assembly declared that all foreigners who had lived in France for five years could be naturalized. It also proclaimed that it would never declare war against any people. During the Revolution, however, "foreign agents" were held responsible for losses. In 1793, all foreigners were asked to leave France, and foreign generals were asked to leave the army. Nationalism became paramount. In 1794, a new law forbade any former nobility and foreigners to stay in Paris. The possessions of the English and the Spanish were impounded, and all were excluded from public service.

In contrast, Anacharsis Clootz, who took his name to show his rejection of Christianity and joined the Revolution in 1790, wanted to do away with the idea of "foreign" and ceaselessly proclaimed his cosmopolitan ideas. However, he failed to object when steps were taken against foreigners and when the political winds shifted against cosmopolitanism. He was guillotined in 1793.

Political philosopher Thomas Paine, the son of an English Quaker, violently attacked the aristocracy and monarchy of England. In his *Rights of Man* (part 1, 1791; part 2, 1792), he spoke of his confidence in humanity and his optimism regarding the French Revolution. While an honorary French citizen living in France, Paine stated that Louis XVI should be imprisoned but not guillotined. Because of his Quaker faith, he opposed the death penalty, and this belief led to his imprisonment when the National Convention of France voted for the death penalty. Paine was saved by U. S. President James Monroe, who declared him a U.S. citizen.

German philosopher Immanuel Kant realized the importance of nations remaining distinct but at the same time working in collaboration, of promoting cosmopolitanism, and of respecting differences. He said that nature separates peoples by language and religion, and therefore only separation and union will guarantee universal peace. French philosopher Jean-Jacques Rousseau expressed the idea that a national community can be tolerable only if it is subservient to the happiness of its members. In the 1800's, however, nationalism became a political concept, where the supreme good was not the individual but the nation as a whole. German philosopher Johann Gottfried von Herder said that although all people are brothers and sisters in their origins, they become differentiated on the basis of language and civilization. Therefore, Germany could claim superiority over other nations.

The Stranger Within

After psychoanalyst Sigmund Freud's contributions to philsophical thought, the "strange" lost its pathological aspect. Freud perceived the foreigner as being within each person. One projects onto others what one experiences as dangerous or unpleasant. This results in a loss of boundaries between the self and the other. People all become foreigners to themselves and to each other.

Kristeva's work, including *Strangers to Ourselves*, made considerable impact on various areas of study: linguistics, psychoanalysis, political science, philosophy, and art and literary criticism. For Kristeva, in the field of art, human expression of any kind is an attempt to return to the maternal body. Art shows how bodily impulses long for expression and allows people to revisit the realm of the maternal. Feminist authors are particularly interested in this aspect of her philosophy. Although some of Kristeva's writings concern women, she remains critical of the women's movement, which she says is negative and reactive and does not take into consideration the complexity of masculine-feminine interactions.

Winifred Whelan

Additional Reading

Fletcher, John, and Andrew Benjamin, eds. *Abjection, Melancholia and Love: The Work of Julia Kristeva*. London: Routledge, 1990. Stemming from a 1987 conference at the University of Warwick on the work of Julia Kristeva (which she also attended), this collection of ten explanatory and critical essays deals with a number of her seminal ideas such as the "abject," the "semiotic chora," " primary narcissism," and adolescence and perversion. The book includes Kristeva's own article, "The Adolescent Novel."

Grosz, Elizabeth. *Sexual Subversion: Three French Feminists*. Sydney: Allen & Unwin, 1989. This text contains an excellent introductory glossary with some basic terms of postmodern thought, as well as a lucid explanation of several components of Kristeva's work including the semiotic and the subject. It provides a basic explanation of French feminism as well as additional writings on the work of Luce Irigaray and Michèle Le Doeuff.

Guberman, Ross Mitchell, ed. *Julia Kristeva Interviews*. New York: Columbia University Press, 1996. This diverse collection of twenty-three interviews given by Kristeva covers her intellectual influences, views on socialism and feminism, concepts of avant-garde practice and psychoanalysis, and other issues.

Kim, C. W. Maggie, Susan M. St.Ville, and Susan M. Simonaitis, eds. *Transfigurations: Theology and the French Feminists*. Minneapolis, Minn.:

Fortress Press, 1993. Using North American feminism as a foil, this volume of essays introduces characteristic components of leading French feminists, including Kristeva, and the relationship of their thought to the larger context of feminist theology.

Lechte, John. *Julia Kristeva*. London: Routledge, 1990. Part of a series of books on twentieth century thinkers edited by British scholar Christopher Norris, this text offers a careful reading of Kristeva's work within the realm of semiotics.

Moi, Toril, ed. *The Kristeva Reader*. New York: Columbia University Press, 1986. This book contains an excellent selection of Kristeva's work from the late 1970's to the early 1980's. The articles are accompanied by brief and insightful explanations that contextualize Kristeva's work within the larger French intellectual environment.

Oliver, Kelly. *Ethics, Politics, and Difference in Julia Kristeva's Writing*. New York: Routledge, 1993. A series of critical essays that generally focus on Kristeva's works concerning identity within the symbolic and the "ethico-political" subject.

_____, ed. *The Portable Kristeva*. New York: Columbia University Press, 1997. A collection of Kristeva's writings strongly representative of her work during the 1980's and 1990's, this book is organized topically and offers a solid introduction to some of Kristeva's seminal ideas.

_____, ed. *Reading Kristeva: Unraveling the Double-Bind*. Bloomington: Indiana University Press, 1993. A volume that offers myriad ways of interpreting Kristeva's complex ideas. It provides a succinct summary of many of her notions within the context of those both critical and supportive of her ideas.

Smith, Anna. *Julia Kristeva: Readings of Exile and Estrangement*. New York: St. Martin's Press, 1996. An in-depth and accessible reading of Kristeva, this text discusses the concepts of exile and estrangement in relationship to the female intellectual and metaphors of habitation.

D. Gosselin Nakeeb, updated by Linda R. James

Thomas S. Kuhn

Departing from traditional philosophy of science, Kuhn argued that science does not evolve only by the steady accumulation of knowledge but also by periodic conceptual revolutions. He emphasized that in its pursuit of knowledge, science is a social process.

Principal philosophical works: *The Copernican Revolution: Planetary Astronomy in the Development of Western Thought*, 1957; *The Structure of Scientific Revolutions*, 1962; *The Essential Tension: Selected Studies in Scientific Tradition and Change*, 1977; *Black-Body Theory and the Quantum Discontinuity, 1894-1912*, 1978; *The Trouble with the Historical Philosophy of Science*, 1992.

Born: July 18, 1922; Cincinnati, Ohio
Died: June 17, 1996; Cambridge, Massachusetts

Early Life

Thomas Samuel Kuhn was born on July 18, 1922, in Cincinnati, Ohio. He attended Harvard College, where he earned a bachelor of science degree in physics in 1943. For the next two years, he worked for the Radio Research Laboratory in Cambridge, helping develop military technology for the United States Office of Scientific Research and Development. He continued his studies in physics, completing his master's degree in 1946 and his doctorate in 1949. His dissertation, "The Cohesive Energy of Monovalent Metals as a Function of Their Atomic Quantum Defects," prepared him as a specialist in solid-state physics, and he published three professional papers on physical and mathematical subjects. In 1948, he married Kathryn Louise Muhs. They had two daughters and a son.

While working on his dissertation in 1947, Kuhn began to study the history and philosophy of science. James Conant, then the president of Harvard, introduced Kuhn to the subjects, asking him to teach an experimental course for undergraduate nonscience majors on the history of science. As part of his preparation, Kuhn read the Greek philosopher Aristotle's *Physica* (c. 330 B.C.E.; *Physics*, 1812). It puzzled him how the ancient philosopher could have so misunderstood the na-

ture of motion and why generations of thinkers had taken his ideas so seriously. Suddenly, according to Kuhn, he experienced a "eureka" moment. To Aristotle, he realized, motion was only a special case of general changes of quality: The fall of a stone from gravity, like fog rolling in or a child's growth, was not a state but a *change of state*. Aristotle's views suddenly made sense. Kuhn further realized that theories become outmoded when scientists undergo a basic cognitive shift in how they view natural phenomena, as they did after the seventeenth century when, following Sir Isaac Newton's first law of motion, they began regarding motion as a state in itself. This startling perception, Kuhn later said, made his jaw drop. It also seeded his career in philosophy.

Life's Work

From 1948 to 1951, Kuhn was a junior fellow in the elite Society of Fellows of Harvard University. The fellowship allowed him to read further in science history, concentrating on physics. In 1951, he joined the Harvard faculty as an assistant professor of general education and the history of science. The same year, he delivered a series of lectures at the Lowell Institute in Boston. In his courses and lectures, he developed the idea that the history of science was not a steady, orderly accumulation of knowledge, as philosophers of science had long argued. Instead, Kuhn found

Thomas S. Kuhn. *(Princeton University Library)*

bium coelestium (1543; *On the Revolutions of the Celestial Spheres*, 1939) was the product not only of mathematics, Kuhn showed, but also of new analyses of motion, explorations of the Atlantic Ocean, and the Renaissance's increasing emphasis upon human experience as a guide to knowledge. More important, Kuhn argued that for Copernicus's theory to succeed, despite its greater simplicity than Ptolemy's model, scientists had to undergo a fundamental realignment in their thinking. For example, they could no longer view Earth as central to the universe and therefore unique. Such entrenched assumptions underlaid Ptolemy's theory as well as other Renaissance astronomical theories competing with Copernicus's for acceptance. The realignment brought by the Copernican revolution had profound repercussions for theology and society and, therefore, was social as well as scientific, Kuhn held.

periods of disorder, confusion, and rivalry in every branch of science. Science evolves discontinuously, he concluded.

More than a decade passed before Kuhn fully articulated his philosophical explanation for these discontinuities. First, he studied a specific discontinuity in depth: the Sun-centered model of the heavens proposed by Nicolaus Copernicus and its acceptance. Influenced by Conant and philosopher Stanley Cavell, Kuhn wrote his historical analysis while on sabbatical, with the help of a Guggenheim Foundation grant. *The Copernican Revolution* anatomizes the history of an idea in the tradition of Arthur O. Lovejoy's *The Great Chain of Being* (1936), which Kuhn admired. He chose Copernicus's work, he wrote, because it allowed him to trace how concepts in different realms of thought could merge to produce a new outlook on nature. Copernicus's cosmological model began as a mathematical revision of Ptolemy's Earth-centered model of the universe, published in the *Mathēmatikē syntaxis* (c. 150 C.E.; *Almagest*, 1948) and dominant in Western astronomy afterward. Copernicus's *De revolutionibus or-*

In the fall of 1956, Kuhn left Harvard to become a full professor at the University of California, Berkeley. He concentrated on a philosophical analysis of his historical studies and completed a manuscript while on a fellowship at Stanford University's Center for Advanced Study in Behavioral Sciences during 1958 and 1959. After thorough revisions, it appeared as *The Structure of Scientific Revolutions* in 1962, part of a series of philosophical monographs for the International Encyclopedia of the Unified Sciences.

The Structure of Scientific Revolutions lays out a schematic theory for the evolution of science in general and scientific specialties. It draws upon several famous historical examples, mostly from physics and astronomy, but more to illustrate Kuhn's system than to substantiate it. The weight of his argument is abstract, logical, and epistemological rather than historical. Three key features of the argument attracted particular attention. First is the idea that science relies on paradigms, a term that Kuhn borrowed from linguistics. Grammatical patterns, called paradigms, guide speakers in using the correct forms of words for specific contexts. Examples of paradigms include the use of "are" following "they" or the addition of an *s* to indicate plurality in a noun. Similarly, Kuhn contended that paradigms of received ideas guide scientists' interpretation of data acquired by observing natural phenomena. These paradigms underpin Kuhn's emphasis upon theoretical structures in *The Structure of Scientific Revolutions*. Second was Kuhn's distinction between normal science and scientific revolutions. Normal science consists of researchers solving problems by applying the prevailing scientific paradigm, a mixture of theory and assumption that scientists share in their profession. History shows, however, that scientists frequently encountered data that the prevailing paradigm could not satisfactorily explain. To Kuhn, such anomalies lead to a period of crisis in a scientific discipline as some scientists persist in applying the established paradigm while other, usually younger, colleagues test novel theories. The crisis ends when a new theory that accounts for the anomalies wins general acceptance. The process of change entails a shift from one paradigm to another, and such fundamental change is a revolution. Third, Kuhn's system presents a scientific revolution as a phenomenon among a community of workers; therefore, it is social.

In 1964, Kuhn moved to Princeton University, becoming M. Taylor Pine Professor of the History of Science in 1968. The next year, he issued a second edition of *The Structure of Scientific Revolutions* with a long afterword in which he tried to clarify some of the vagueness that other philosophers found in his theory. In 1972, Kuhn also joined the Princeton-based Institute for Advanced Studies, the United States' premier think tank. The growing fame from *The Structure of Scientific Revolutions* brought further challenges to his ideas and daunting intellectual opponents. Among them were Sir Karl Popper and Paul Feyerabend, two other major figures in the philosophy of science. Most battles were collegial. Popper, a generation older than Kuhn, made suggestions that broadened his philosophical knowledge, and Feyerabend, a contemporary, became a friend. Some philosophers, however, resented Kuhn because, trained as a physicist, he was an outsider.

A collection of essays and lectures, *The Essential Tension: Selected Studies in Scientific Tradition*

and Change, came out in 1977. The selections defend, refine, and extend the basic arguments in *The Structure of Scientific Revolutions* from historical and philosophical viewpoints. The book shows that Kuhn was not only quick to recognize defects in his philosophy, intellectually wide-ranging, and generous in his acknowledgment of others' ideas but also relentlessly persevering.

In 1978, Kuhn published *Black-Body Theory and the Quantum Discontinuity, 1894-1912*, the last major work to appear during his lifetime. It is a mathematically sophisticated historical study of contributions to quantum theory by Max Planck, Albert Einstein, Paul Ehrenfest, and others. As much as any episode in science, the development of quantum theory qualifies as a revolution, and many writers have called it one, but not Kuhn. He refers to Planck's work as a "turning point" and says that quantum properties required a "fundamental reconstruction" of established theory. Terms such as "revolution" and "paradigm shift" do not appear. Although it avoids the terminology of *The Structure of Scientific Revolutions*, the study nevertheless applies Kuhn's philosophical system. At times it appears as if Kuhn were avoiding his earlier terminology, which had been corrupted in popular usage, to show that his ideas still accurately describe science history.

Kuhn and his wife were divorced in 1978. He later married Jehane Barton. In 1979, he left Princeton for the Massachusetts Institute of Technology and in 1982 was appointed to the Laurance S. Rockefeller Professorship in Philosophy, teaching in both the linguistics and philosophy departments. He retired in 1991. During his teaching career, he impressed colleagues and students with his fierce commitment to his work.

He could be irascible with people who willfully misinterpreted his work, and he argued for his ideas passionately. That commitment earned him many honors and awards. His election as president of the Philosophy of Science Association in 1988 reflected his increasing acceptance by other philosophers, and he held memberships in the National Academy of Science, History of Science Society, Leopoldina Academy, British Academy, and American Academy of Arts and Sciences. He received the Howard T. Behrman Award for achievements in humanities at Princeton in 1977, the History of Science Society's

George Sarton Medal in 1982, and the John Desmond Bernal Award from the Society for Social Studies of Science in 1983. Two foreign and three American universities awarded him honorary degrees.

After retiring, he continued to refine his philosophy of science, studying especially how the mind works and the influence of language on the development of sciences. He was completing a manuscript that thoroughly explicates the ideas first presented in *The Structure of Scientific Revolutions* when he died of throat cancer in 1996 following a two-year illness.

Influence

The Structure of Scientific Revolutions is Kuhn's most influential book. It went through three editions, sold a total of more than a million copies, and was translated into twenty-five languages. The book transformed Kuhn from a respected science historian to an intellectual celebrity not only in academic circles but also with the general public as other thinkers, often to Kuhn's dismay, freely interpreted and reapplied his concepts. "Paradigm" entered the vocabulary of popular culture, used loosely for almost any type of intellectual edifice, such as aesthetic theory, art criticism, political trends, or strategy in sports; "paradigm shift" also was applied in nonscience contexts, frequently by social scientists.

Although Kuhn insisted he was "pro-science" and that the goal of science was increasingly accurate understandings of nature, many of his readers took him to mean that science was merely a sequence of social arrangements, the arbitrary replacement of one paradigm with another by majority rule and no different from any political or societal process. They interpreted Kuhn as denying any strict rationality in science. Accordingly, opponents charged Kuhn with being a relativist and an antirealist. Some admirers, by the same token, applauded him because they thought he proved that science had no more claim on truth than any other human thought system—religion, astrology, or philosophy, for example. Kuhn vigorously denied he was a relativist, but writers who were hostile to science continued to cite him in support of their own contentions. He once remarked in exasperation that he preferred his critics to his followers.

The controversies over his ideas and the wide currency of his terminology testify to his pervasive effect on intellectual discourse. In fact, Kuhn has been called the most influential historian and philosopher of science in the second half of the twentieth century. During a Massachusetts Institute of Technology commencement address in 1996, Vice President Al Gore echoed that judgment, praising Kuhn for clarifying the relation between science and society and thereby helping each person cope with the world's increasingly rich technological culture.

Roger Smith

The Structure of Scientific Revolutions

Type of philosophy: Epistemology, philosophy of science
First published: 1962
Principal ideas advanced:

◇ Science evolves not continuously but in periods of normal research punctuated by crises in theory that produce a revolution, which in turn resolves into another period of normal research.

◇ Scientists within a discipline form a community whose education has united them in relying on a certain paradigm—a collection of theories, facts, and methods—that guides them in discovering and solving problems.

◇ A revolution entails a paradigm shift, which involves a change in the meaning of basic concepts and terminology.

◇ Rival scientific schools within a discipline cannot effectively communicate with each other because the assumptions and theories of each are incommensurable, or untranslatable.

Knowledge of nature's workings and the ability to put that knowledge to practical use depends upon the doctrine of empiricism, the development of ideas on the basis of experimentation and observation. This doctrine itself evolved from the declining reliance during the Renaissance upon Christian doctrine and the Bible to explain new phenomena and increasing emphasis upon human experience as a source of knowledge. During the early twentieth century, a group of logical positivists, including England's Bertrand Russell and Austria's Ludwig Wittgenstein, rejected all metaphysical doctrines and held that true knowledge comes from human experience alone, particularly via its most rigorously controlled form, the scientific method: the accumulation of data under controlled conditions, construction of theories on the basis of the data, and verification of theories by experimentation and observation in accordance with objective standards of logic. Although subsequent adherents to this school often called themselves logical empiricists and insisted that theories cannot really be verified, only falsified, the underlying assumption is that the history of science has been the unbroken accumulation of knowledge in an orderly, unified sequence.

In *The Structure of Scientific Revolutions*, Thomas S. Kuhn disagrees with the logical positivists almost completely. Although he also believed that scientists aim for an increasingly accurate understanding of nature, he found that a community of scientists, such as physicists or biologists, often goes through periods of divisive disagreement over theory and the nature of data. The final triumph of one faction of a scientific field over another involves the interactions of people. Science is a social process as well as a knowledge-gathering enterprise.

Kuhn concentrates on the structure of scientific development in order to offer a schematic explanation applicable not only to individual disciplines and subdisciplines but also to science as a whole. Kuhn concerns himself with only the pure sciences and not the social sciences or applied sciences, and he specifically addresses the cognitive (or epistemic) function of science. He does not explore science's ultimate value or truth or its place in human culture.

A Challenge to the History of Science

The introduction challenges the view of the history of science that predominated before publication of *The Structure of Scientific Revolutions* in 1962. That view held science to be a sequence of datable discoveries, inventions, and theories. It served a small but attitude-building function in science education because it formed part of the received knowledge in textbooks. Textbooks covered contemporary knowledge but not its development, seldom explaining scientific history in depth. Historians such as Alexander Koyré, Kuhn points out, were unable to support the development-by-accumulation view of science textbooks because it was sometimes impossible to determine precisely who made a discovery or when. If such questions as who or when were not always relevant, then a continuous, orderly development is at best a conveniently fictional image of science. Kuhn promises that his book will offer a new image drawn from a close examination of history.

In the first chapter, Kuhn argues that the methods of science alone cannot guarantee a unique answer to a question about nature. A researcher who is versed in the standards of evidence and logic in science but who is not trained in a particular discipline such as chemistry might devise any number of mutually incompatible answers to a problem in chemistry by applying standard scientific techniques. It is prior experience in a discipline, gained from scientists' education and their professional careers, that guides a researcher to an answer that is useful to the discipline and compatible with it. Therefore, specialized training helps determine the types of questions that scientists will ask about the aspect of nature they study and the sorts of answers that they are likely to produce.

The Cycle of Science

Science, however, does not automatically settle into a routine of scientific training followed by application of textbook-conveyed knowledge, especially when the discipline is new, Kuhn explains in the second chapter. History reveals many instances in which a discipline consisted of several schools of thought at odds with each other about basic conceptions. During the late Renaissance, for example, some astronomers held, following Ptolemy, that Earth was the center of the universe and everything revolved around it; followers of Tycho Brahe thought Earth was the center and the Sun revolved around it, but that everything else revolved around the Sun; and Copernicans placed the Sun at the center, around which Earth and the other planets revolved. All three schools derived their distinct cosmologies in ways generally compatible with the same mathematics and methods of observation. What distinguishes such rival schools, Kuhn proposed, is not that one is more or less scientific than another but that each has a view incommensurable with the others. Incommensurability, or untranslatability, is a key term in Kuhn's philosophy: The basic conceptions of one scientific school do not correspond to those of another. When proponents of one school argue with those of another, the two sides are apt to talk past each other rather than communicate meaningfully.

Eventually, one theory prevails. Elaborated on and passed on by professional education, it provides succeeding generations of researchers with a shared set of assumptions, theory, facts, and methods with which to analyze new problems and phenomena. Kuhn termed this shared professional knowledge a "paradigm." In the third through fifth chapters, he discusses the paradigm-guided pursuit of scientific knowledge. It inaugurates the mature phase of a science, during which normal, or routine, science reigns. Specialists agree on what constitutes an acceptable problem, how to go about investigating it, and how to fit data to established theory in solving it. Most scientists spend their entire careers posing and solving problems in accordance with an established paradigm, assuming that they have a fundamental grasp of how nature behaves.

In chapters 6 through 8, a key section of *The Structure of Scientific Revolutions*, Kuhn considers what happens when a paradigm fails to support a scientist's assumption. First, evidence of a fundamental novelty accumulates from experiments, or equipment behaves in an unexpected way that the scientific establishment cannot explain. Newtonian mechanics, for example, could not explain experimenters' failure to detect a theoretical all-pervading ether, and classical physicists were perplexed by the seemingly paradoxical behavior of light as both a particle and a wave. The impulse of most scientists is to suppress such anomalies, Kuhn says, in order to defend the assumption in their paradigm that the anomalies appear to contradict. However, when normal science repeatedly fails to satisfy professional expectations, anomalies cannot be suppressed for long. A young scientist, or one new to a disci-

pline, inevitably reexamines the evidence from a fresh, nontraditional viewpoint. In his special theory of relativity, Albert Einstein demonstrated that no ether need exist in order to explain the dynamics of light; ether thereby vanished as a scientific problem. Quantum mechanics grew out of the puzzle over light's dual nature and accepted that light can behave like a particle or a wave, depending upon how it is observed. New theoretical concepts, such as Einstein's positing light as a constant and the uncertainty principle of quantum mechanics, are difficult for many scientists to accept.

A period of crisis follows for the discipline. Scientists divide into schools, and controversy over basic assumptions prevails. One faction gradually dominates and establishes a new set of commitments for the profession that serves as the basis for practicing the science. That is, a new paradigm takes over. However, the new paradigm does not just supply a new theory. It forces the reevaluation of the prior paradigm and the knowledge it had produced because it is fundamentally incompatible with the new viewpoint. The new paradigm transforms the imagination of scientists. This process of transformation is a scientific revolution.

The cycle of normal science, crisis, and paradigm shift is not incremental, as previous philosophy of science assumed, and because its course is not predictable, it is not strictly logical. Kuhn admits that there is some arbitrariness involved in starting a revolution and in the shape the new paradigm will take because that depends upon unexpected, accidental discoveries and the unorthodox methods of innovators. Nevertheless, the innovations cannot be entirely arbitrary. They must be more fruitful in problem solving than the previous paradigm. Accordingly, succeeding paradigms are better and better approximations of truths about nature.

In the ninth and tenth chapters of *The Structure of Scientific Revolutions*, Kuhn illustrates his structural scheme for scientific revolutions with four signal episodes in the history of science: the cosmological model of Nicolaus Copernicus in the Renaissance, the mechanics of Sir Isaac Newton and the new chemistry of Anton Lavoisier during the Enlightenment, and the relativistic dynamics of Einstein early in the twentieth century. Each, he contends, not only changed science fundamentally but also eventually changed the worldview of Western culture.

Textbooks and the Goal of Science

In chapter 12, Kuhn returns to the influence of science textbooks, which more than any other single influence imbue scientists with the traditional paradigm of their profession. Textbooks before *The Structure of Scientific Revolutions* implied that a paradigm was the logical outcome of the discoveries and hypotheses that led to it by ignoring those discoveries and ideas that did not contribute to it. Thereby, textbooks gave the appearance of continuity, which Kuhn calls "unhistoric stereotypes," and obscured the revolutionary ferment that led to a paradigm.

In the final chapter, Kuhn takes up a related, troubling question: How can the development of science through revolutions, in which some degree of arbitrariness exists, be reconciled with the progress of science in uncovering useful truths about nature? Kuhn offers only the outline of an answer, admitting that much more study of scientific communities is required to settle the question. His discussion draws upon an analogy with Darwinian evolution. Just as there is no ultimate goal of biological evolution, according to Charles Darwin, so Kuhn suggests there is no goal for science. Instead, the equivalent of natural selection takes place from competition among rival schools of thought, a process that produces the fittest way to conduct science until something new in the environment of scientific evidence challenges it. Science grows increasingly articulated and specialized (the equivalent of speciation) as it evolves.

No single modern book about the philosophy and history of science so deeply stirred up controversy and inspired further analysis as *The Structure of Scientific Revolutions*. The challenge to long-standing assumptions about science history prompted such heated discussions among philosophers of science and scientists themselves that science history is said to have pre-Kuhnian and post-Kuhnian periods. Regularly, books and articles appeared and conferences were held about the book, and Kuhn forcefully defended and elaborated his ideas until his death in 1996. One colleague predicted that Kuhn's book would be one of the few philosophical monographs of the twentieth century to be remembered in centuries to come.

The Structure of Scientific Revolutions also had a deep effect on popular culture. By the late 1960's, when the book became commonly assigned reading in philosophy courses, antiestablishment fervor among college students and intellectuals was strong. Because Kuhn recognized that some arbitrariness affects science, readers searching for reasons to reject authority misread Kuhn to mean that all human systems are arbitrary—that everything is relative—and so no unassailable truths create authority. Despite Kuhn's objections, antiscience intellectuals continued to cite *The Structure of Scientific Revolutions*. At the same time, terms such as "paradigm" and "scientific revolution" entered the general intellectual idiom.

Roger Smith

Additional Reading

Giere, Ronald N. *Explaining Science: A Cognitive Approach*. Chicago: University of Chicago Press, 1988. This book surveys the philosophical theories of science and includes an extensive review of Kuhn's philosophy. Many of the discussions are largely developed from Kuhn's concept of revolutions in science.

Horgan, John. "Reluctant Revolutionary." *Scientific American* 264, no. 5 (May, 1991): 40-9. In an interview, Kuhn reveals his frustration with those who misused or misinterpreted his ideas about scientific revolutions. He discusses modifications he made to his theory, particularly in the definitions of "paradigm" and "incommensurability." Horgan depicts both Kuhn's personality and ideas with clarity.

Horwich, Paul, ed. *World Changes: Thomas Kuhn and the Nature of Science*. Cambridge, Mass.: MIT Press, 1993. An introduction by the editor and essays by nine scholars discuss how Kuhn's ideas differ from those of previous philosophers. The essays take historical or philosophical approaches in their arguments. In "Afterwords," Kuhn comments on the essays, refining his views about incommensurability and defending himself against charges of relativism and antirealism.

Hoyningen-Huene, Paul. *Reconstructing Scientific Revolutions: Thomas S. Kuhn's Philosophy of Sci-*

ence. Chicago: University of Chicago Press, 1993. The author "reconstructs" Kuhn's theory of scientific development as articulated in *The Structure of Scientific Revolutions*. His purpose is to clarify the fundamentals of the theory and end the confusion produced by the diverse interpretations of Kuhn's vaguely defined terms. This volume is most helpful for readers familiar with the controversies produced by Kuhn's book.

Margolis, Howard. *Paradigms and Barriers: How Habits of Mind Govern Scientific Beliefs*. Chicago: University of Chicago Press, 1993. Margolis applies his own analysis of cognition to Kuhn's concept of the paradigm shift. Specifically, Margolis finds that habits of mind, pervasive and normally beneficial, sometime pose barriers in the face of novel phenomena or theories. A paradigm shift occurs when the barrier is overcome and new habits of mind replace old. His argument, he insists, reveals that relativism has a limited role in the methods of science.

O'Hear, Anthony. *Introduction to the Philosophy of Science*. Oxford, England: Clarendon Press, 1989. O'Hear discusses Kuhn's paradigm-centered theory at length and somewhat unsympathetically. He specifically compares Kuhn's ideas with those of Karl Popper and examines the historical evidence upon which Kuhn relied. The book, which summarizes the philosophy of science as a whole, is readable and well-suited to readers new to the subject in general and Kuhn in particular.

Thagard, Paul. *Conceptual Revolutions*. Princeton, N.J.: Princeton University Press, 1992. Thagard bases his own theory of scientific revolutions on Kuhn's ideas. He seeks to add a psychological and computational approach for analyzing conceptual transformations, hierarchies, combinations, structures, sources, and explanatory coherence. In so doing, he summarizes Kuhn's work and shows its wide influence.

Roger Smith

Jacques Lacan

Lacan was the single most important figure in the development of psychoanalysis in twentieth century France. His powerful rereading of Freud's work and rethinking of Freud's fundamental concepts made him a key figure in French intellectual life from the 1950's until his death.

Principal philosophical works: *De la psychose paranoïaque dans ses rapports avec la personnalité*, 1932; "Le Problème du style et la conception psychiatrique des formes paranoïaques de l'expérience," 1933; "Fonction et champ de la parole et du langage en psychanalyse, 1956 (*The Language of the Self: The Function of Language in Psychoanalysis*, 1968); "Le Séminaire sur 'La Lettre volée,'" 1956 ("Seminar on 'The Purloined Letter,'" 1973); "L'Instance de la lettre dans l'inconscient: Ou, La Raison depuis Freud," 1957 ("The Insistence of the Letter in the Unconscious," 1966); "Le Désir et son interprétation," 1959-1960 ("Desire and the Interpretation of Desire in *Hamlet*," 1977); "Hommage fait à Marguerite Duras du *Ravissement de Lol V. Stein*," 1965; *Écrits*, 1966 (*Écrits: A Selection*, 1977); "Of Structure as an Inmixing of an Otherness Prerequisite to Any Subject Whatever," 1970; *Le Séminaire: Livre XI, Les Quatre Concepts fondamentaux de la psychanalyse*, 1973 (*The Four Concepts of Psychoanalysis*, 1977); *Télévision*, 1974 (*Television*, 1987); *Le Séminaire: Livre XX, Encore*, 1975 (partial translation, *Feminine Sexuality*, 1982); *Le Séminaire: Livre I, Les Écrits techniques de Freud*, 1975 (*Freud's Writing on Technique*, 1987); *Écrits inspirés*, 1975; *Proposition du 9 octobre 1967*, 1978; *Le Séminaire: Livre II, Le Moi dans la théorie de Freud et dans la technique de la psychanalytique*, 1978 (*The Theory of the Ego in Psychoanalytic Theory and Practice*, 1987); *Le Séminaire: Livre III, Les Psychoses*, 1981; *Annuaire et textes statutaires*, 1982; "Joyce le symptôme," 1982; *Les Complexes familiaux*, 1984 (*The Family Complexes*, 1988); *Le Séminaire: Livre VII, L'Éthique de la psychanalyse*, 1986; *The Works of Jacques Lacan*, 1986; *Joyce avec Lacan*, 1987.

Born: April 13, 1901; Paris, France
Died: September 9, 1981; Paris, France

Early Life

Jacques Marie Émile Lacan was born on April 13, 1901, into an upper-middle-class Parisian family. His academic training focused first on medicine, then on psychiatry. He studied with the distinguished French psychiatrist Louis-Nicholas Clérambault, receiving his doctorate in 1932 with a thesis on the relationship of paranoia to personality structure. While still working as a psychiatrist, Lacan began studying psychoanalysis with the distinguished Freudian analyst Rudolf Loewenstein and in 1934 became a member of the Paris Psychoanalytic Society.

During the 1930's, a complex set of influences helped form the mind of the young Lacan, laying the foundation for the mature work that would make him a luminary in the febrile Parisian atmosphere of the decades following World War II. In addition to his growing absorption in the thought and teaching of Sigmund Freud, Lacan associated closely with the Surrealist circle of artists and writers and contributed essays and poems to Surrealist publications. This Surrealist connection attests his lifelong fascination with language and its power to shape human life.

Lacan was also strongly influenced, as were many others of his generation, by the teaching of the Russian émigré thinker Alexandre Kojève. It was primarily through Kojève's lectures between 1933 and 1939, at the École Normale Supérieure, on Georg Wilhelm Friedrich Hegel—with particular emphasis on the *Phänomenologie des Geistes* (1807; *The Phenomenology of Spirit*, 1872; also known as *The Phenomenology of Mind*, 1910)—that the work of the great German philosopher had a major impact on French thought. Thus, at the same time that Lacan was immersing himself in Freud's theories, he was attending Kojève's lectures emphasizing the Hegelian account of the problems for the development of human self-consciousness. This complex of Lacan's interests in the 1930's—psychiatry, Freud, Surrealism, Hegel—typifies what would always mark his work: a breathtaking catholicity of scope buttressed by remarkable erudition, reminiscent of Freud himself.

Lacan's position as an important thinker within Freudian psychoanalysis was first established for an international audience in 1936, when he spoke at the Fourteenth Congress of the International Psychoanalytic Association. In this address, Lacan presented his theory of the mirror stage. He argued that the earliest development of the human ego (somewhere between six and eighteen months) occurred on the basis of the infant's imagined relationship with its own body as first perceived in a mirror and with that of the significant others—typically the mother—in its life. Lacan's conclusion was that the human ego is never a coherent entity, even from its very inception. This moment, 1936, at which Lacan chose to present his developing theory is significant, for it was at this time that Freud's daughter Anna and others following her lead were beginning to argue for the coherence of the ego and to elaborate its varied mechanisms of defense and adaptation. Thus Lacan's first step onto the international psychoanalytical stage veered toward a possible schism from the keepers of Freudian orthodoxy, thereby prefiguring the series of rifts and splits within the psychoanalytic movement that Lacan would repeatedly provoke later in his career.

Life's Work

Lacan was a dominant intellectual presence in French cultural life for three decades, and his influence radiated far outward from its psychoanalytic base into disciplines such as philosophy, literary criticism, and linguistics and into broader, interdisciplinary fields such as feminism and some variants of Marxism. The extent of Lacan's impact both within and beyond psychoanalysis highlights what he himself considered to be his primary purpose as analyst and writer: to

revivify psychoanalysis by a radical return to Freud's work and to do so by putting Freud's thought in touch with the latest developments in contemporary thought. For Lacan, these two intentions were inextricable, and together they define the originality of his contribution to twentieth century thought and the breadth of his influence.

Lacan's published work consisted primarily of essays, the most important of which were collected and published as *Écrits: A Selection*. Yet his most immediate impact on the French intellectual public came not from his writings but rather through the biweekly seminars (actually public lectures) that he conducted for more than three decades, very few of which appeared in print during his lifetime. Lacan's verbal brilliance, personal flamboyance, and intellectual charisma fused in lectures that became veritable performances attended by important thinkers from many fields in French culture.

The impact Lacan had on French psychoanalysis was pervasive as well as divisive. No one escaped his influence, but that influence provoked repeated divisions and splits. In 1953, Lacan and several colleagues broke with the Paris Psychoanalytic Society, the official French branch of the International Psychoanalytic Association, and formed a new Société Française de Psychanalyse. Then in 1964, Lacan reformed his analytic society, calling it L'École Freudienne de Paris, only to dissolve it in 1980 to create a new organization he called La Cause Freudienne. These schismatic moves bear witness to Lacan's growing worry that his teachings were becoming too institutionalized and thereby rigid and narrow, a fear similar to Freud's earlier concern that the professionalization of psychoanalysis as a branch of medicine would unduly constrict its applicability in the broad arenas such as education, where Freud hoped his science's impact would be most profound. Lacan's ambitions for his own rethinking of Freud's work were equally far-reaching.

Lacan's protean thought defies summary, but certain emphases within it can be isolated as indicative of major currents within his work. He always stressed that the core of Freud's vision lay in *Die Traumdeutung* (1900; *The Interpretation of Dreams*, 1913) and the works that immediately followed it. There the core concepts of psycho-analysis—the unconscious and sexuality—were first developed and elaborated. Lacan argued that Freud perceived that the unconscious could be understood as having a structure. In his own reworking of Freud, this was one of the places where Lacan turned to contemporary thinkers to elaborate upon a core Freudian insight, typified by his most frequently quoted phrase: "The unconscious is structured like a language." Twentieth century linguists such as Ferdinand de Saussure and Roman Jakobson had argued that when human beings acquire the use of speech, they are subsumed into a symbolic order that preexisted them as individuals and that could be shown to have a systematic structure. Because the unconscious makes itself visible and audible primarily through speech (as well as symptoms, dreams, and involuntary acts of omission and commission), Lacan emphasized that the unconscious has a structure like that of language and hence can be systematically examined.

In a related vein, and with important cues taken from the work of the anthropologist Claude Lévi-Strauss on kinship structures and totemic relationships, Lacan theorized that the human subject is situated within different orders, or planes of existence, which he called the Imaginary, the Symbolic, and the Real. The Imaginary evolves out of the mirror stage but extends into adult life; it is the realm of all false or fantasized identifications that a human subject makes with an Other. The Symbolic is the realm of social and cultural symbolism and of language. Entrance of the child into the domain of the Symbolic with the acquisition of language means that the laws of language and society come to dwell within the youngster, thus laying the foundation for social, mediated relationships with others that are different from the self-centered but alienating relationships of the Imaginary. This constituted Lacan's reworking of Freud's fundamental concept of the Oedipus complex. Finally, the Real for Lacan was everything that was neither within the Imaginary nor the Symbolic; hence, in a typical Lacanian paradox, the Real was what could not be known directly about a human subject.

Lacan's unorthodox approach to psychoanalytic training was as provocative and disturbing as his revisions of Freudian theory on the basis of

linguistic concepts or his attempts to reevaluate the status of psychoanalytic knowledge in the light of the new directions emerging from other disciplines. The classic psychoanalytic session lasts fifty minutes, but Lacan introduced shorter sessions of varying length, some lasting only a few minutes. This tampering with a cornerstone of psychoanalytic practice was a key factor in helping to precipitate Lacan's break with the Paris Psychoanalytic Society in 1953. From Lacan's point of view, sessions of variable length better preserve the overall movement of a patient's discourse during the course of an analysis, while adherence to the standard length session is constraining and rigid for both patient and analyst.

Over and over again, both in his theoretical work and in his practice as a psychoanalyst, Lacan sought to challenge the limits to psychoanalysis, limits he thought had been created by Freud's disciples. He sought to recapture the radical core of Freud's vision in his own work and to transmit it to his audiences with the aid of what he took to be the best tools available in the intellectual milieus with which he was familiar. His achievement was similar but far more extensive than that of his early mentor Kojève. Just as the Russian philosopher was almost singlehandedly responsible for the widespread impact of Hegel's thought on French intellectual life after the 1930's, so Lacan was the single most important figure in the rather belated reception of Freud in twentieth century French cultural life.

Influence

With the publication of *Écrits* in 1966, Lacan became not only a thinker known in French intellectual circles but also an intellectual presence of major importance in Western culture. Practitioners of a variety of the intellectual disciplines that the French call the human sciences found inspiration in Lacan's work, and his influence spread beyond Western Europe to various parts of the world. There was widespread interest in Lacanian ideas in South American psychoanalytic circles. His work proved to be a fertile source for new approaches in cinema criticism and literary studies in England and the United States as well as on the European continent. Especially after his 1972-1973 seminar (published in 1975 and partially translated as *Feminine Sexuality*), in which he turned his attention to the place of love and sexuality in psychoanalysis with particular attention to female sexuality, his thought became a focus of much critical attention by European and American feminist theorists. As scholar Malcolm Bowie has noted, part of the reason for Lacan's profound impact on European thinking after World War II was that "his writing proposes itself consciously as a critique of all discourses and all ideologies." For Lacan, as for Freud before him, psychoanalysis was to be the basis for a self-critique of Western culture itself, not merely of individuals within it, although, like his great predecessor, Lacan never abandoned the idea that the fundamental basis of Freud's science was the spoken dialogue between analyst and analysand.

The implications of Lacan's work were always disturbing. His thought can be seen as part of a broader twentieth century critique of the notion of a unified human subject, thus placing his work alongside that of his Parisian contemporaries. Where Lacan's peculiar originality lay was in his understanding of the radicality of Freud's discoveries and in his desire to push the consequences of those discoveries to their logical limits. In doing so, he may indeed have become, as the philosopher Ellie Ragland-Sullivan writes, "the most important thinker in France since René Descartes and the most innovative and far-ranging thinker in Europe since Friedrich Nietzsche and Sigmund Freud."

Michael W. Messmer

The Language of the Self

The Function of Language in Psychoanalysis

Type of philosophy: Epistemology, philosophical psychology, philosophy of language

First published: "Fonction et champ de la parole et du langage en psychanalyse," 1956 (English translation, 1968)

Principal ideas advanced:

◇ Language is the principal tool to be used by psychoanalysts and, in fact, is the only tool that provides real access to the unconscious.

◇ Language is a system that uses words, but it has a greater existence than a mere collection of words.

◇ Language is the tool by which people form and understand social relations, and it is associated with the rule of the father and with the rule of law.

◇ Language always assumes a hearer and anticipates a response, and this reciprocity is the principal method by which both individuals and society order themselves.

This work was first presented by Jacques Lacan at a conference of psychoanalysts and addresses the particular problems psychoanalysts face in dealing with patients. The context of this work led Lacan to begin it by sharply rebuking other practitioners whom he sees as using faulty techniques for dealing with analysis. Although he is dealing primarily with the function of language in the psychoanalytic process, his ideas about the differences between words and language and about the ways in which people use language to define themselves and order their world have much broader implications.

The Importance of Speech

In the introduction, "The Function of Language in Psychoanalysis," Lacan asserts his firm belief that language—particularly speech—is the only sound tool for analysts to use with their patients. He reminds his colleagues that the analysts' speech or lack of speech and their capacity to listen are factors in the process of analysis as much as the patient's talking. He states his goal of convincing his listeners that linguistic research should be primary in their training because language is the only path to the inner truth of their patients.

In the first section, "The Empty Word and the Full Word," Lacan states that the word is the only thing that really passes between patient and doctor in the analytic process and that the speaking of the words is itself a crucial step. Often the analyst says nothing while the patient talks and talks, but this very silence allows the process of language to work itself out in the patient; patients discover themselves by talking, with no response except the act of listening on the part of the analyst. Words, Lacan points out, are used to create imaginary identities but are also used to destroy them. The second party in the process—the listener—provides the speaker with a framework on which to hang thought, and this allows the speaker to return finally to some reality. Even when a subject is lying or deliberately not telling the truth, the discourse, or act of sharing language between the two, is serving some function.

As an example, Lacan cites psychoanalyst Sigmund Freud's study of his patient Anna O. and the discovery that describing a traumatic event from the past that produced physical or mental symptoms could alleviate the symptoms immediately. The "naming" of the trauma through language allowed the subject to be free of its effects. By this example, Lacan attempts to show that language has powers quite apart from its ability to communicate information between people.

In this section, Lacan also describes the various ways in which language can be used to communicate. For example, he states that the unconscious part of a subject's mind is revealed in those parts of language that are not under his or her direct control, such as physical aspects (including pronunciation), vocabulary, use of metaphor and simile, and omissions. Often, subjects give information by what they refuse to say or are unable to say. It is the task of the analyst to discover the truth found in these empty spaces.

Language, according to Lacan, is a process of speaking whereby one's history is made real. Therefore, even before children are able to speak, they are unconsciously organizing their experiences according to the verbal model; in other words, they are writing their histories. The task of the analyst is to help people restate these histories in a pattern that is meaningful and helpful to them. Lacan concludes this section with a statement on the omnipresence of discourse in the human experience. If discourse—speaking, hearing, and replying—is the unifying factor of human existence, language has a primary importance in all human relations, not just psychoanalysis.

Symbols, Words, and Language

In the second section, "Symbol and Language," Lacan interprets Freud's work on symbols and signs and how they interact or fail to interact with language. Lacan returns to Freud's texts to remind the reader that dreams, considered the ultimate pure expression of the human unconscious, take the form of stories or narratives; they are based on language models. Dreams, therefore, can be seen as languages trying to express themselves, and the same can be said of psychological or physical symptoms—they are a language trying to make itself understood.

At this point, Lacan begins to draw distinctions between the word and language. The word is part of language, but the word cannot exhaust the meaning of language without using language as a tool. The law of the land, for example, is written in words, but to understand it, one must do more than simply understand the meaning of each individual word used to compose a law. One must understand the sense of the words together, the meaning of the whole, to have a real grasp of what the law is saying. Language, therefore, includes words, but is more than the sum of its parts. Words are symbols in the use of language, but language is more complex and implies understanding not only the various meanings of individual words but also the ways in which they relate to each other and to objects, people, or events in real life.

In addition, words are not the whole of language, Lacan states, because even though animals can be made to recognize the sound of certain words and to respond in a desired way, words are not merely a collection of sounds. Words have meaning in language because they relate to concepts as well as concrete objects, and this can be understood only by humans, the users of language. Language always refers back to itself and assumes a large body of knowledge on the part of the participant. To use language, one must do more than merely speak the sounds of words. One must understand an enormous and complicated system of references and signals and be able to use them in different contexts and to constantly modify them as the process of using language unfolds over time. Language completely envelopes people's lives, and it is by and through language that people understand themselves and the world that surrounds them.

Lacan provides an extremely telling example of a man who is working in production and sees himself as a member of the proletariat. Because he identifies himself as such, he participates in a strike that shuts down production at a plant. In this case, even though the word "proletariat" defines a concept, rather than a concrete object, its meaning is real for the man who names himself as part of this group. His use of this name to refer to himself and his condition causes him to act in a way that affects the world of concrete objects and potentially alters history.

The Analyst's Task

In the final section, "Interpretation and Temporality," Lacan reasserts his belief that unless psychoanalysis returns to the primacy of the word, it will become increasingly meaningless. The task of the analyst is to understand the myriad ways in which language operates in and around people and to apply this knowledge to the way an individual uses language. In analysis, he says, symbols are always markers of something the subject is repressing; however, the symbols themselves are not aware of their function as screens for this repressed material. Therefore, the task of the analyst must be to understand the symbolic in language and tease out the meaning through the process of discourse.

Lacan cites the example of Austrian zoologist Karl von Frisch and his work with bee communication to show how "bee dancing" is different from human language. The dancing of bees and language use among humans are similar in that both are intended to convey information. The bee wants to show its fellows where nectar is located and uses an elaborate system of body movements to indicate direction, distance, and other pertinent factors. However, even though this dancing conveys very specific and detailed content, Lacan asserts that it is not the same as language. The primary difference is that with bees, the signs are always fixed in a definite relationship that does not change. The bees always perform the same movements to show "ten feet to the left," whereas language is infinitely adaptable and is able to change to fit the needs of individual speakers at any given moment. For example, using language, a person might say "ten feet to the left," "over by the violets," or "next to the fence but a few feet up from the apple tree," and so on, with nearly infinite permutations. Further, the "fence" in question might be picket, chicken wire, hurricane fencing, or a thousand other variations—language develops in use to meet the needs of its users.

In summation, Lacan contends that language is always a subjective exercise, because a speaker always assumes a hearer and anticipates a response. The speaker—whether the subject of psychoanalysis or an everyday individual—shapes speech to conform to various sets of norms (social, cultural, economic, relational) and always assumes a certain listener who is also shaping a response to what is said and heard. Even when talking to the self, one assumes that another part of one's personality or mind will hear and shape a reply. Language always seeks the response from the other, whether the other is really another individual or merely one's own unconscious. Language therefore identifies people to themselves as well as to others.

The impact of Lacan's language analysis on modern thought would be hard to overstate. His elucidations of Freud's major texts and theories provided a wealth of information for not only psychoanalysts but also sociologists, linguists, literary theorists, and feminists. His insights into the functions of language and his clear examinations of how language orders the individual's view of the self and affects the relations people form with each other in society are extremely important to all modern critical thought. Though Lacan was at times the focus of resentment and could be very petty in his disdain for those who did not agree with his methods (as the introduction to this work shows), he became increasingly significant in the latter part of the twentieth century, especially in the 1970's and 1980's.

Vicki A. Sanders

Additional Reading

Benvenuto, Bice, and Roger Kennedy. *The Works of Jacques Lacan: An Introduction*. New York: St. Martin's Press, 1986. A straightforward, chronologically oriented discussion of Jacques Lacan's key writings from his early years until his death.

Bowie, Malcolm. "Jacques Lacan." In *Structuralism and Since: From Lévi-Strauss to Derrida*, edited by John Sturrock. Oxford: Oxford University Press, 1979. This essays provides a brief introduction to Lacan's thought and is a good place to begin reading about him.

Clement, Catherine. *The Lives and Legends of Jacques Lacan*. Translated by Arthur Goldhammer. New York: Columbia University Press, 1983. Originally published in France in 1981, this book by a former disciple of Lacan is a provocative meditation on the meaning and significance of his life and work in and for contemporary culture.

Evans, Dylan. *An Introductory Dictionary of Lacanian Psychoanalysis*. London: Routledge, 1996. A lucid explanation of many of Lacan's technical terms, how he came to change them during his career, and some of his influences.

Feldstein, Richard, Bruce Fink, and Maire Jaanus, eds. *Reading Seminars I and II: Lacan's Return to Freud*. New York: State University of New York Press, 1996. This book offers a series of in-depth essays that discuss theoretical foundations and clinical applications of Lacan's work. Authors include Jacques-Alain Miller, Colette Soler, and Slavoj Žižek.

Felman, Shoshana. *Jacques Lacan and the Adventure of Insight: Psychoanalysis in Contemporary Culture*. Cambridge, Mass.: Harvard University Press, 1987. A complex work that explores the implications of Lacan's work for the practice of reading and interpretation in contemporary culture.

Gallop, Jane. *Reading Lacan*. Ithaca, N.Y.: Cornell University Press, 1985. A series of powerful psychoanalytic readings of Lacan's work by a literary critic. This book both demonstrates the importance of Lacan's thought for work in the humanities in general and is a representative instance of the impact Lacan's thought has had on feminist theory.

Grosz, Elizabeth. *Jacques Lacan: A Feminist Introduction*. London: Routledge, 1995. A lucid overview of Lacan's work from a feminist perspective, providing an introduction to many of his seminal ideas as well as both objections and support from feminist thinkers.

Leader, Darian, and Judy Groves. *Introducing Lacan*. 1996. Reprint. New York: Totem Books, 1998. The comic book presentation of Lacan, which provides an amusingly illustrated and basic outline of many of the philosopher's ideas, is an excellent resource for a beginner.

Marini, Marcelle. *Jacques Lacan: The French Context*. Translated by Anne Tomiche. New Brunswick, N.J.: Rutgers University Press, 1992. A succinct overview of Lacan's work in general and the cultural context of his professional life.

Roudinesco, Elisabeth. *Jacques Lacan: Outline of a Life, History of a System of Thought*. Translated by Barbara Bray. New York: Colombia University Press, 1997. An extensive and carefully researched account of Lacan's life by a French scholar and historian of psychoanalysis in France.

Turkel, Sherry. *Psychoanalytic Politics: Freud's French Revolution*. 2d ed. New York: Guilford Press, 1992. Lacan is the central figure in this account of the reception of Freud and psychoanalysis in French culture in the decades after 1945.

Žižek, Slavoj. *Looking Awry: An Introduction to Jacques Lacan through Popular Culture*. Cambridge, Mass.: MIT Press, 1997. An accessible and eloquent account that elucidates key Lacanian notions through an application to certain components of film and fiction in popular culture.

Michael W. Messmer, updated by Linda R. James

Julien Offroy de La Mettrie

La Mettrie carried the Cartesian mechanism to its logical endpoint by positing, on the basis of his medical understanding, that a human being is a mechanism and that happiness arises from the effects of sense stimuli on this mechanism.

Principal philosophical works: *Histoire naturelle de l'âme*, 1745 (*Treatise on the Soul*, 1996); *L'Homme-machine*, 1747 (*Man a Machine*, 1750; also known as *L'Homme Machine: A Study in the Origins of an Idea*, 1960); *Discours sur le bonheur: Ou, L'Anti-Sénèque*, 1747 (*Anti-Seneca: Or, The Sovereign Good*, 1996); *L'Homme plant*, 1748 (*Man a Plant*, 1994); *Les Animaux plus que machines*, 1750; *Le Petite Homme à longue queue*, 1751; *Œuvres philosophiques*, 1757 (3 volumes).

Born: December 25, 1709; Saint-Malo, Brittany, France
Died: November 11, 1751; Berlin, Germany

Early Life

Julien Offroy de La Mettrie came from a comfortable background in Saint-Malo, a busy port town in northwestern France. His father was a merchant in the textile trade and a part of the bourgeoisie that made up the city's informal governing class. There was enough money to educate the young La Mettrie very well. His early studies in the humanities were carried out in the *collèges* (private secondary schools) of Coutances and Caen; from there he went on to the Collège du Plessis in Paris. For a time he felt a religious calling and became interested in the Jansenist movement; little evidence of this phase remains, unless it be a later acceptance of a mechanistic causality of human thought and behavior reminiscent of the Jansenist conviction of predestination. In 1725, at the age of sixteen, he entered the Collège d'Harcourt, where Cartesianism was newly introduced, to study natural philosophy. He received his bachelor's degree two years later. Thereafter he appears to have found his calling, and he entered the medical school at the University of Paris, shifting later to Reims, where he received his bachelor's and doctorate in medicine in 1733.

La Mettrie went into medical practice in Reims and was never totally divorced from practice for the remainder of his short life. It must be emphasized that his knowledge of anatomy and medicine, gained at a time when both were advancing rapidly, underlay his philosophical views about the mechanism that is the human animal. New skills in dissection, and new medicines from the iatrochemists, became available month by month during this time, and it was easy to reach the exciting conclusion that the human animal-machine would be explicable within the lifetimes of scientists and physicians of the eighteenth century.

After qualification as a physician, La Mettrie moved to Leyden to further his studies with the Dutch chemist-physician Hermann Boerhaave. During his time there, he translated a number of Boerhaave's texts on diseases, medicine and pharmaceuticals, and chemistry, and composed works of his own on treatment of vertigo and of venereal diseases, as well as reminiscences of his medical practice. La Mettrie married in 1739. He and his wife, the widow Marie-Louise Droneau, produced two children: a daughter in 1741, as well as a son in 1745 who did not survive childhood. The marriage also did not survive, and in 1742, La Mettrie removed to Paris, where he became personal physician to the duc de Grammont, and shortly thereafter the medical officer to the duc's regiment in the Gardes Françaises. He took part in a number of engagements in the War of the Austrian Succession, which added to his medical skills and observations but left him permanently opposed to human bloodshed.

Life's Work

During the eight years that remained to him, La Mettrie poured out a remarkable series of writings, most of which succeeded in getting him in trouble with some individual or group. In 1745, he published *La Volupté* (sensual delight), dedicated to the Marquise du Chatelet for her "personal contribution" to the subject matter of the book. In the same year, he produced his first major philosophical writing, *Treatise on the Soul*. This work was composed as the result of a serious illness and fever that overcame him during the last of the battles in which he was involved, the Siege of Freiburg. Observing the confusion of thought brought about by his physical state, he concluded that "thought is only the result of the organization of the machine [which is the human mind], and . . . the disruption of its authority greatly influences that part of ourselves that the metaphysicians call the soul." From this observation it is a short step to the conclusion that human thought and behavior are produced by purely mechanical causes and that the soul, if it exists at all, very likely is as well. Of course, La Mettrie is not speaking from intellectual speculation but from medical experience. He had observed and performed dissections of the brain and nervous system and was familiar with the postmortem evidence that such-and-such a brain lesion was responsible for a particular delusion or disability in the patient before death. He could quite possibly have extended these observations in battlefield medicine, noting how head injuries affected the senses and physical abilities of the wounded. When he spoke of mechanical causes, he spoke with authority.

This did not sweeten the answers of his critics, however. They railed against the "pernicious statements spread through his book on the materialism and mortality of the soul, on the eternity of the world, and on Atheism." La Mettrie was forced to give up his position with the Gardes Françaises, and his book was ordered burned by the public hangman in Paris. His medical competence was great enough that he moved on to a position as military hospital inspector for Lille, Ghent, Brussels, Antwerp, and Worms. However, he was not to be satisfied with one battle when he could produce two with a little extra effort. Disgusted by the self-serving incompetence of the medical establishment, particularly in France, in 1746 he produced *Politique du médicine* (the politics of medicine). The negative response was predictable, and with both clerics and physicians now opposed to him, La Mettrie found it wise to flee to Holland in the fall of 1746, not because any formal legal process faced him but because he feared the deviousness and caprice of the French judicial system.

Julien Offroy de La Mettrie. *(Liaison Agency Network)*

He took up residence in Leyden, with its memories of student days and the time of apprenticeship to Boerhaave, but this calming effect did not last. Within a year, he produced an ironic comedy, *La Faculté vengée* (1747; the medical establishment revenged), continuing his attack on the physicians whom he regarded as charlatans. By the end of 1747, he published the work for which he is best remembered, *Man a Machine* (literally, "man, a mechanical device").

In *Man a Machine*, he takes the last steps in the long trek from French philosopher René Descartes's assertion, more than a century before, that animals are machines, and humans are machines also but possess souls that can relate them to God. La Mettrie draws on his extensive medical knowledge of the anatomy and physiology discovered in that intervening century: that muscular tissue is itself motile, for example, under electrical or other stimulus, thereby eliminating Cartesian mind-body duality with mind as sole causal agent; that disease of the body can cause disease of the mind, or soul; that extreme fatigue, hunger, or the effect of drugs can alter consciousness and even rational thought; that animals can be trained to do many of the things humans can do; that animals appear to possess emotions analogous to those of humans; and so on. His conclusion is that both animals and humans are mechanisms that think and feel and that no outside cause is necessary to account for this condition, nor is there any necessity to postulate a soul or an afterlife.

The ethics that follows from this formulation is that of natural law, a variation on the Golden Rule of not doing that which we would not want done to us. This is shared by animals, at least in the limited cases cited by La Mettrie. It further follows that because humans have only their sensations, perceptions, and mechanical causes to take into account, the object of people's existence must be the happiness that proceeds from these sources. Such happiness, because it proceeds from mechanical or physiological causes only, may even take the form of actions that are considered monstrous by society at large. Individuals who find happiness in this way must be punished by society, but from a medical standpoint they should be treated with compassion. The theology of *Man a Machine* is dismissive. A supreme being might very probably exist, but this is a possibility of little everyday consequence. Such a being would not necessarily be worshiped, nor would it conduce to morality, any more than its absence would lead to immorality. It was clear that atheism—nonbelief—was the preferred belief.

This time the reaction to La Mettrie's views was immediate and vicious. Thousands of pages of refutation and vilification appeared from Catholics and Protestants alike, even in normally liberal and tolerant Holland. The book had been published anonymously, so that the publisher Luzac was the only person who could be called to account. Called he was, before the Consistory of the Walloon Church of Leyden, and required to produce all copies of the book for destruction, to disclose the name of the author, and to apologize and promise never to make such an error of faith again. He conformed with the first and last of these demands but later produced and marketed a number of copies of *Man a Machine* to satisfy his own conviction that ideas must have free access. La Mettrie in the meantime had been identified as the author and found it necessary to flee Holland with his publisher's help. He accepted an offer from Frederick II of Prussia to become "physician extraordinary" and *lecteur* to the king, as well as a member of the Royal Academy of Sciences of Prussia.

At Potsdam, he continued both his philosophical and his antimedical establishment writings, the latter in *L'Ouvrage de Pénélope* (1748; Penelope's work), which enlarged on the earlier *Politique du médicine* with devastating satire on medical practice and particular physicians. In 1748, he also published *Anti-Seneca: Or, The Sovereign Good*, in which he enlarged on his views of happiness as a kind of health—that is, as the pleasurable well-being of the man-machine, available to all regardless of moral, social, or intellectual considerations. This earned for him an undeserved reputation as a voluptuary which—given his fondness for the table and for the ladies, as well as his fondness for scandalizing the disapproving—led to a distaste that spread far beyond the court at Potsdam. Other publications of his last years are *Man a Plant*, an extended analogy between the human or animal life and that of plants; *Les Animaux plus que machines* (1750; animals are more than machines), an attack by irony on animistic biology, with its postulated animal soul; *Le Système d'Epicure* (1750; *The System of Epicurus*, 1996), a confused examination of the origin of species; and two medical treatises of 1750, *Traité sur la dyssenterie* (treatise on dysentery) and *Traité de l'asthme* (treatise on asthma).

La Mettrie clearly enjoyed his life in court and his relation to the highly cultivated Frederick II (he of the flute concerti and the graceful prose style, who had nonetheless carved his empire out of former Habsburg territory), and his position in the Royal Academy of Sciences, presided over by Pierre-Louis Moreau de Maupertuis, who also hailed from Saint-Malo. Despite these personal pleasures, he longed to return to France and tried to enlist the aid of Voltaire, who was part of Frederick's court for a time, to get influential friends to intercede for him.

Whether La Mettrie would have succeeded became moot when he died in the fall of 1751, a month short of his forty-second birthday. The circumstances of his death provided a field day for his detractors: At a dinner given by Lord Tyrconnel, France's ambassador to Prussia, he consumed a large quantity of a pheasant-and-truffle pâté. It is conjectured that the pâté was spoiled or bacterially contaminated, for he fell ill and no treatment could prevent his death a few days later. Conventional critics saw in this a divine punishment for gluttony and a refutation of materialism, and a story even circulated that La Mettrie had repented and come back to the church on his deathbed. Frederick II, after ascertaining the facts, wrote a laudatory *Éloge de La Mettrie* (elegy for La Mettrie), which was read before the Royal Academy of Sciences and laid to rest this and other scurrilous allegations. La Mettrie's body was buried in the French Catholic Church at Friedrichstadt.

Influence

La Mettrie's thoroughgoing mechanism had some influence on his contemporaries, mainly a kind of cover that allowed them to develop their own anticlerical, sometimes atheistic views surreptitiously while someone else acted as the lightning rod. Among these were the encyclopedist Denis Diderot and his colleague Paul-Henri-Dietrich d'Holbach, as well as the later "Ideologue" and materialist Pierre-Jean-Georges

Cabanis, who was born after La Mettrie's untimely death. Materialism remained a thread of thought, or the foundation for thought, throughout the centuries following the eighteenth, but La Mettrie's specific contributions fell from attention rather quickly. Whether this was because they were so explicitly based on scientific observations that were superseded in the great upsurge of medical and biological discovery of the nineteenth century, or simply because La Mettrie had gone as far as it was reasonably possible to go with mechanism as a philosophy, is impossible to say. He has since been recognized as a forerunner of current mechanism, particularly in the science of behaviorism, but without detailed connection of his ideas with those of today.

Robert M. Hawthorne, Jr.

Man a Machine

Type of philosophy: Metaphysics
First published: *L'Homme-machine*, 1747 (English translation, 1750; also known as *L'Homme Machine: A Study in the Origins of an Idea*, 1960)
Principal ideas advanced:

◇ Both animals and people are machines that feel.

◇ The soul is a material part of the brain, as is shown by the fact that when the body is diseased, so is the soul.

◇ Humans are distinguished from other animals by their larger brains and by their ability to use language.

◇ Although it is highly probable that a supreme being exists, this information has little practical value.

The French philosopher René Descartes declared that all animals except humans are "machines," very complicated automata, responding to external stimuli in a mechanical way. Humans alone, because they possess immaterial souls, are conscious and endowed with free will and therefore capable of being virtuous or sinful. However, Julien Offroy de La Mettrie denied the existence of any sharp distinction between humans and other animals. In his *Histoire naturelle de l'âme*

(1745; *Treatise on the Soul*, 1996), he raised a strong objection to Descartes's calling brutes "machines," thereby denying that they think and feel. However, three years later, he changed his terminology (not his doctrine) and argued that animals are machines that feel, and so are humans. "The human body is a machine which winds its own springs; . . . the soul is but a principle of motion or a material and sensible part of the brain." *Man a Machine*, the better-known translation of *L'Homme-machine*, is somewhat of a misnomer. Although in English it seems strange to call a man or a dog a *machine*, it makes sense to speak of them as *mechanisms*, which is what La Mettrie meant. Hence his philosophy is often referred to as mechanism.

Body and Soul

Man a Machine is for the most part a treatise on physiological psychology, containing also certain ethical and antitheological reflections. It is in the form of an oration, without subdivisions. La Mettrie begins with a defense of experience and observation as foundations of knowledge even about the soul, as against the claims put forward for revelation as a source superior to reason. "If there is a God, He is the Author of nature as well as of revelation; . . . if there is a revelation, it can not contradict nature." Although nature certainly stands in need of interpretation, so does the Bible. Concerning the soul, the requisite "experience and observation . . . are to be found throughout the records of the physicians who were philosophers, and not in the works of the philosophers who were not physicians. . . . Only the physicians have a right to speak on this subject." According to La Mettrie, theologians have the *least* right.

What experience and observation show the philosopher-physician about the soul is that its character is patently dependent on bodily conditions. When the body is diseased, so is the soul. A genius may be reduced to idiocy by a fever; it sometimes happens, conversely, that "the convalescence of an idiot produces a wise man." Extreme bodily fatigue produces a sleep amounting to the temporary extinction of the soul. The effects of opium, wine, and coffee are cited. In addition, diet influences character. The English are savage because they eat their meat red and

bloody. In La Mettrie's opinion, the English diet accounts for their vices of "pride, hatred, scorn of other nations, indocility and other sentiments which degrade the character"—but education can counteract this. Extreme hunger and prolonged sexual abstinence can produce raving maniacs. When the body degenerates in old age, so does the soul. Female delicacy and male vigor correspond to the different bodily constitutions of the sexes. When one looks through a gallery of portraits, one "can always distinguish the man of talent from the man of genius, and often even an honest man from a scoundrel." Differences in national character correspond to differences in climate. In sum, "the diverse states of the soul are always correlative with those of the body."

Comparative mammalian anatomy, especially brain anatomy, bears out and explains this conclusion. Humans are the most intelligent of animals because they have the largest and most convoluted brains. The descending order of intelligence—monkey, beaver, elephant, dog, fox, cat—is also the descending order of brain size and complexity. La Mettrie makes three generalizations about animals: "1st, that the fiercer animals are, the less brain they have; 2nd, that this organ seems to increase in size in proportion to the gentleness of the animal; 3rd, that . . . the more one gains in intelligence the more one loses in instinct." However, among humans, brain defects are not *always* gross: "A mere nothing, a tiny fibre, something that could never be found by the most delicate anatomy, would have made of Erasmus and Fontenelle two idiots."

The higher animals can do surprising things when properly trained. It would be interesting to attempt to teach an ape to speak by application of the methods used so brilliantly with deaf-mutes. If one chose a fairly young ape, "one with the most intelligent face, and the one which, in a thousand little ways, best lived up to its look of intelligence," the experiment might well succeed. Then the ape "would no longer be a wild man, nor a defective man, but he would be a perfect man, a little gentleman, with as much matter or muscle as we have, for thinking and profiting by his education." For humans are not distinguished qualitatively from the other animals except in possessing language. Language itself is not an inherent possession of the human species as such, but must have been invented by certain geniuses who taught it to the others.

Knowledge consists of the comparison of the sensory ideas (images) produced in the brain, and this comparison can hardly proceed without language, a system of symbols for classifying. This comparison La Mettrie calls "imagination," and he asserts: "All the faculties of the soul can be reduced to pure imagination. . . . Thus, judgment, reason, and memory are not absolute parts of the soul, but merely modifications of [the] medullary screen upon which images of the objects painted in the eye are projected as by a magic lantern." Hence, all talent and genius is fundamentally the same thing: lively imagination. "Man's preeminent advantage is his organism. . . . An exaggerated modesty (a rare fault, to be sure) is a kind of ingratitude towards nature." There is nothing wrong with taking pride not only in skill, learning, and virtue, but even in mind, beauty, wealth, nobility; these, "although the children of chance, all have their own value."

Nature and Natural Law

It is wrong to try to distinguish humans from other animals by the former's alleged exclusive acquaintance with natural (moral) law. Natural law is "a feeling that teaches us what we should not do, because we would not wish it to be done to us." It manifests itself to *me* when, for example, I feel remorse after bad conduct; my belief that *you* have a similar experience can only be based on my inferences from your behavior. However, we see the same signs in animals, such as the "crouching and downcast air" of a dog that has offended its master. La Mettrie cites the story of Androcles and the lion to prove that animals feel gratitude. If, however, it is maintained that despite appearances, animals do not really have any awareness of natural law, then it follows that people do not either, for "man is not moulded from a costlier clay; nature has used but one dough, and has merely varied the leaven." However, in fact, remorse and gratitude are universal, even among the most hardened criminals. These persons commit their atrocities from morbid impulses, and they are punished adequately by their consciences. It would be better to hand them over to doctors than to burn them or bury them alive, as is the custom.

It is clear that for these reasons, virtue is its own reward, and that "Nature has created us all solely to be happy—yes, all of us from the crawling worm to the eagle lost in the clouds." La Mettrie developed the ethical implications of this doctrine in his *Discours sur le bonheur: Ou, L'Anti-Sénèque* (1747; *Anti-Seneca: Or, The Sovereign Good,* 1996).

La Mettrie next turns his attention to religion. It is highly probable, he says, that a supreme being exists; but this is "a theoretic truth with very little practical value." It does not follow that a highest being ought to be worshiped just because it exists; nor does religion (as everyone knows) ensure morality, any more than atheism excludes it.

The "zealous writers" who pile up evidences of design in nature to prove the existence of an intelligent Creator are misguided. "Either the mere structure of a finger, of an ear, of an eye, a single observation of Malpighi proves all, . . . or all the other evidences prove nothing." For even if it is admitted that these facts rule out the possibility of a merely "chance" universe, the existence of a supreme being is not thereby proved, "since there may be some other thing which is neither chance nor God—I mean, nature." All people know is that there is an infinite variety of ingenious mechanisms in nature; people know nothing of their ultimate causes; in this situation, recourse to God is a mere disguise of ignorance. "The weight of the universe therefore far from crushing a real atheist does not even shake him."

At this point, La Mettrie writes (more astonishingly than convincingly): "Such is the *pro* and the *contra,* and the summary of those fine arguments that will eternally divide the philosophers. I do not take either side." A friend of his, however, "an abominable man," maintained to him that "the universe will never be happy, unless it is atheistic." The extirpation of religion would put an end to religious wars. "Nature, infected with a sacred poison, would regain its rights and its purity. Deaf to all other voices, tranquil mortals would follow only the spontaneous dictates of their own being, the only commands which can never be despised with impunity and which alone can lead us to happiness through the pleasant paths of virtue."

The Mechanical Nature of the Body

Returning to the subject of the soul, La Mettrie next shows that it is not necessary to postulate the soul as a principle or cause of motion of the body because muscular fiber is inherently motile. He offers ten observations and experiments in proof. One is that portions dissected from polyps regenerate into whole polyps; the other nine are concerned either with spontaneous motions of parts of organisms severed from bodies or with the motion of parts of the body after death. "The soul is therefore but an empty word, of which no one has any idea, and which an enlightened man should use only to signify the part in us that thinks."

La Mettrie describes at considerable length the physiology of reflex and involuntary movements to illustrate the mechanical nature of the body. He cites, among other things, the phenomenon of erection. The bodily effects of emotional states show, moreover, that there is no sharp division between what is under control of the will and what is not. Though La Mettrie does not deny (or even discuss) the "freedom of the will," he remarks that the will "cannot act save by permission of the bodily conditions." However, having shown (to his satisfaction) that the body is self-moved and that consciousness is a property of its organized matter, not an independent substance, La Mettrie confesses that he can go no further in explanation. "The nature (origin) of motion is as unknown to us as that of matter."

La Mettrie praises Descartes for having proved that animals are machines. His insistence on the distinctness of mental from material substance was, according to La Mettrie, a ruse to throw the theologians off the scent; for the analogy of humans with animals is so striking that it could only be overlooked by "animals and machines which, though upright, go on all fours." There is no contradiction in the notion of a thinking, feeling, moral animal-machine. "Thought is so little incompatible with organized matter, that it seems to be one of its properties on a par with electricity, the faculty of motion, impenetrability, extension, etc." Only pride and prejudice lead people to resist these conclusions. However, "matter contains nothing base, except to the vulgar eyes which do not recognize her in most splendid works." La Mettrie again states that im-

mortality is not impossible. To suppose it out of the question would be to reason like caterpillars who can have no conception of their coming metamorphosis. People should admit that they are invincibly ignorant in this domain and will remain so.

Materialists

La Mettrie concludes by picturing the wisdom, justice, tranquillity, reverence (for nature), gratitude, affection, tenderness, kindliness, pity, and forgiveness—in a word, the happiness—of the materialist.

> Convinced, in spite of the protests of his vanity, that he is but a machine or an animal, the materialist will not maltreat his kind, for he will know too well the nature of those actions, whose humanity is always in proportion to the degree of the analogy proved between human beings and animals; and following the natural law given to all animals, he will not wish to do to others what he would not wish them to do to him. Let us then conclude boldly that man is a machine, and that in the whole universe there is but a single substance differently modified. . . . Such is my system, or rather the truth, unless I am much deceived. It is short and simple. Dispute it now who will.

More than two centuries after La Mettrie, one is likely to smile wryly at the pretty picture of grateful lions regulating their conduct by the Golden Rule, and at the conviction that once religion is gone, all will be well—as if religion were something imposed on people from outside, contrary to "the spontaneous dictates of their own being." However, these amiable eighteenth century ideas should not deceive anyone into supposing that La Mettrie was a naïve thinker. He deserves the credit (or blame) for many insights usually attributed to such philosophers as Jean-Jacques Rousseau, Étienne Bonnot de Condillac, Claude-Adrien Helvétius, and Paul-Henri-Dietrich d'Holbach. His brief remarks on the relation of evidence to conclusion in the design argument for the existence of God penetrate to the essential logical point in a manner not inferior to the more celebrated critiques of David Hume and Immanuel Kant.

Materialists, at least since Lucretius, argued that no chasm separates humans from the rest of nature and that the soul must be material, or a property of matter, because mental states obviously vary with the condition of the body. La Mettrie did not have a new argument; he only added to the old one such evidence as was available to him from recent investigations of brain anatomy. However, just as La Mettrie questioned the relevance of piling up evidence for design in nature for the purpose of proving a Great Designer, so here also one can ask whether more and more detail about the *dependence* of soul on body strengthens the conclusion that soul *is* body. Except for theological considerations (which La Mettrie justifiably ignored), philosophers who were well aware of all the facts concerning the effects of bodily constitution on the soul still upheld the separateness of body and soul for three reasons: First, one's thoughts and feelings, of which one is directly aware, are obviously neither bodies nor properties of bodies; it makes no sense to raise questions about them as to where they are or how big they are. Second, one knows that the self has an identity that no material thing, or property, could have, for anything that occupies space can be divided, whereas one has no notion of what it would be like to split oneself into two selves. Third, matter is essentially inert; if it moves, there must be a cause of its motion; and one's experience reveals that volition, which is mental, is capable of moving the body.

La Mettrie paid attention to the third objection; he gave good reasons for denying the inertness of matter, especially organic matter. An answer to the second is implicit in his writing: The unity of the self is only a unity of functions, and when the organism is malformed (as in congenital idiocy or deafness), the corresponding functions ("faculties") are absent.

There is discernible in La Mettrie the bare beginning of a materialist reply to the first objection. He says that "judgment, reason, and memory are not absolute parts of the soul, but merely modifications of [the] medullary screen upon which images of the objects painted in the eye are projected as by a magic lantern." That is, when an image is formed on the retina, it is transmitted by the optic nerve to the visual cortex, and the

visual sensation is the resulting "modification" or "brain-event." This doctrine requires considerable argumentation and explication before it becomes plausible, and La Mettrie provides none. However, he has at any rate progressed beyond the view of Descartes, according to whom the immaterial soul somehow "inspects" (directly, infallibly, and unintelligibly) the "medullary screen." In any case, it would be unreasonable to complain of La Mettrie that he did not, once and for all, explain how one is to conceive the identity of thought and brain process—that is, solve the mind-body problem, still one of the most vexing questions on the philosophical agenda.

La Mettrie was the first, the most consistent, and the most extreme of the eighteenth century French materialists. He was a thinker of great originality who insisted on expressing his thoughts in print, well knowing that to do so would expose him to the rage of fanatical obscurantists. In fact, he was forced to flee from France to Holland, thence to Prussia, where Frederick II granted him asylum. In Potsdam, he resumed the practice of medicine. He enjoyed but two years of security and prosperity; he died at the age of forty-one. (The pious claimed that epicurean gluttony was the cause of death.) Frederick himself composed his eulogy, saying of him:

> La Mettrie was born with a fund of natural and inexhaustible gaiety; he had a quick mind, and such a fertile imagination that it made flowers grow in the field of medicine. Nature had made him an orator and a philosopher; but a yet more precious gift which he received from her was a pure soul and an obliging heart. All those who are not imposed upon by the pious insults of the theologians mourn in La Mettrie a good man and a wise physician.

Wallace I. Matson, updated by John K. Roth

Additional Reading

Brehier, Emile. *The History of Philosophy*. Vol. 5 in *The Eighteenth Century*. Translated by Wade Baskin. Chicago: University of Chicago Press, 1967. Contains a short but sound discussion of the development of materialism in the middle of the eighteenth century.

Rosenfield, Leonora Cohen. *From Beast-Machine to Man-Machine: Animal Soul in French Letters from Descartes to La Mettrie*. 1940. Rev. ed. New York: Octagon Books, 1968. This older volume is indispensable for the understanding of the progression of mechanism.

Wellman, Kathleen Anne. *La Mettrie: Medicine, Philosophy, and Enlightenment*. Durham, N.C.: Duke University Press, 1992. Gives medical background of Julien Offroy de La Mettrie's philosophical views.

Robert M. Hawthorne, Jr.

Susanne K. Langer

Langer's philosophy brought attention to the importance of symbol making in human mental activity. Her best-known work, *Philosophy in a New Key*, sold more than 500,000 copies during Langer's lifetime.

Principal philosophical works: *The Practice of Philosophy*, 1930; *An Introduction to Symbolic Logic*, 1937; *Philosophy in a New Key: A Study in the Symbolism of Reason, Rite, and Art*, 1942; *Feeling and Form: A Theory of Art*, 1953; *Problems of Art: Ten Philosophical Lectures*, 1957; *Reflections on Art: A Source Book of Writings by Artists, Critics, and Philosophers*, 1958; *Philosophical Sketches*, 1962; *Mind: An Essay on Human Feeling*, 1967, 1972, 1982 (3 volumes).

Born: December 20, 1895; New York, New York
Died: July 17, 1985; Old Lyme, Connecticut

Early Life

Susanne Katherina Knauth was the second of three daughters born to a well-to-do family of German immigrants living in Manhattan. Her father was a corporate lawyer who also owned a substantial portion of the German American bank of Knauth, Nachod, and Kühne. Her mother's family owned a textile plant in Germany. This background meant that Knauth enjoyed a great many material and cultural advantages during her childhood.

Music and art were central to the life of this wealthy, cultivated family. However, Knauth's father opposed higher education for women, and he discouraged his daughters from entering college. This attitude made life difficult for Knauth, who had developed an interest in intellectual questions. After her father's death, her mother helped her gain admission to Radcliffe College, a prestigious women's college and the sister school to the then all-male Harvard. She was therefore already twenty years old when she began her advanced education. In 1920, she earned her B.A. degree from Radcliffe.

During her senior year at Radcliffe, she became acquainted with William Leonard Langer, a Harvard graduate student who later became a prominent historian. Years afterward, in his autobiography, Langer confessed that his future wife seemed more interested in logic and music than in romance, and he expressed the view that Knauth's mother and sisters had talked her into agreeing to marry him. The wedding was held in early September of 1921, and Susanne Knauth acquired the surname that would appear on all of her philosophical writings. The couple then left immediately for ten months in Europe, where William Langer was to do research for his doctorate in history, funded by a fellowship and a generous monetary wedding gift from Susanne's mother.

After their return to the United States, Susanne enrolled as a graduate student in philosophy. Once a week, she would usually take the train from Worcester, Massachusetts, where her husband had taken a teaching position at Clark University, to Cambridge, Massachussets, to attend the Harvard lectures on logic by Henry Sheffer or to take part in a seminar run by the famous philosopher Alfred North Whitehead. Whitehead's use of the idea of symbolic modes of thought in science influenced Langer greatly, and her philosophy is sometimes seen as an effort to extend Whitehead's symbolic approach to artistic expression.

She gave birth to two sons: Leonard, in 1922, and Bertrand, in 1925. Despite the increasing responsibilities of family life, she earned a master's

Susanne K. Langer. *(National Archives)*

intellectual and logical character of symbols, paying little attention to the symbolization of feeling, the hallmark of her later writings. She presented logical symbols as a response to the inadequacy of natural language for conveying precise ideas in scientific fashion.

After the publication of *An Introduction to Symbolic Logic*, Langer became dissatisfied with the reduction of human experience to logic and began to believe that feeling could also be interpreted in terms of symbols. The year 1942 saw two critical events in Langer's life: She was divorced from her husband, and she published *Philosophy in a New Key*. The basic theme of her most popular book was the distinction between discursive and nondiscursive symbols. Discursive symbols, found in scientific and natural language, are those that give form to the logical concepts of discourse. Nondiscursive symbols, found in art, give form to feeling. Langer maintained that attention to symbolic activity as a basic function of the human mind was the "new key" struck by modern philosophy.

Although *Philosophy in a New Key* met with wide acceptance among educated readers in general, it received relatively little attention from professional philosophers. Many academic reviewers dismissed her book as a popularization of the literature on signs and symbols. Some saw her thinking as derived from the writings of the German philosopher Ernst Cassirer, whose work Langer appreciated. Langer acknowledged Cassirer's influence and translated his book *Sprache und Mythos* (1925; *Language and Myth*, 1946). Her skillful writing did indeed present philosophy in a manner that general readers could understand and enjoy, and she did succeed in introducing many nonspecialists to concepts of symbolic forms. Her originality may have been underestimated, though, because few philosophers of symbolism have given as much careful and systematic attention as Langer did to the role of symbolism in the nonrational mental life of humans. Further, other philosophers who worked on signs and symbols frequently overlooked

degree in philosophy from Harvard in 1924 and a doctorate in 1926. Her first book, *The Cruise of the Little Dipper, and Other Fairy Tales*, a study of myth and fantasy, was published in 1924.

Life's Work

After finishing her doctoral degree, Langer worked as a tutor at Harvard and taught at Radcliffe, Wellesley, and Smith Colleges. Her first strictly philosophical work, published in 1930, was *The Practice of Philosophy*. Seven years later, she completed a textbook, *An Introduction to Symbolic Logic*. This book showed the interest in symbols that was to characterize her thinking throughout her life, but in it she emphasized the symbolization in art, and none of them, including Cassirer, produced a comprehensive theory of art.

Philosophy in a New Key went through three editions, with the second appearing in 1951 and the third appearing in 1957. By the time of the second edition, Langer was already seeing this book as a preface for an extended philosophy of art. While at Columbia University, where she taught from 1945 to 1950, she received a Rockefeller Foundation grant to write *Feeling and Form: A Theory of Art*. In this book, she developed a theory of art as consisting of symbolic forms that express feelings. She clarified her distinction between the discursive and expressive functions of communication through symbols. Language is discursive; it conveys ideas and deals with facts. Art, on the other hand, is expressive. It presents the subjective parts of experience and inner perceptions by making these audible or visible. This makes feeling, the nondiscursive area of human life, available to contemplation and understanding by externalizing it in a visible or audible form. Langer describes language as an indirect and representational symbol system, in which abstract logical and factual relationships are expressed by words that represent those relationships. She describes art as a symbol system that presents the structures and relationships of concrete feelings directly.

Langer's publications did not give her immediate success in an academic career. She worked at a string of temporary teaching positions, often holding several part-time jobs simultaneously after her divorce. She served as an untenured lecturer during her years at Columbia University. Her professional difficulties were probably due in large part to a bias against women in universities. In 1954, she obtained her first tenured position, at Connecticut College, which was at that time a women's college.

In Connecticut, she refined the theory of art offered in *Feeling and Form*. In *Problems of Art*, she moved away from using the term "symbolic forms" to describe artistic products. She felt uncomfortable with this term because she feared that it implied that works of art could be taken as representing some inner state, as having a meaning. She began using instead the term "expressive forms," which better communicated her view that artworks embody their

sense or "import" rather than refer to it.

Langer remained an active member of the faculty at Connecticut College until 1962, when she became an emeritus professor, a status for distinguished faculty members who are retired from regular university activities but remain associated with a university. She assembled a variety of approaches to thinking about art in *Reflections on Art*. In 1960, in recognition of her achievements, Langer was elected to the American Academy of Arts and Sciences. In the year of her retirement from active teaching, she published a collection of short pieces on philosophy called *Philosophical Sketches*.

During the last two decades of her life, Langer worked in her colonial home in Old Lyme, Massachussetts, on a massive work of philosophical investigation, *Mind: An Essay on Human Feeling*, which appeared in three volumes. In this final work, Langer sought to offer a detailed argument that aesthetics and human consciousness are intricately intertwined and interdependent. Moreover, she maintained that both consciousness and aesthetics can be explained by an investigation of the evolution of the human mind.

Much of Langer's work had been dedicated to the argument that art consists of images that present the forms of feeling. Through art, human beings present or make conscious all aspects of the human mind and the human personality. In the three volumes of *Mind*, she sought to show how her view of the nature of mental activities could be based in evolutionary biology.

Feelings evolved in organisms, she argued, as adaptive responses to their environments. Feelings of tiredness or hunger, for example, tell organisms when to sleep or eat. For many animals, other animals became part of their environment. Adapting to other animals, especially to those of the same species among social animals, led to the development of the exchange of signs of feeling so that animals could respond to one another.

In one organism, the human, the evolutionary elaboration of a part of the nervous system, the neocortex, led to the development of subjective feelings, of feelings cut off from the world outside. These were not just ideas but also emotions and sensations. In order to maintain contact among the subjective worlds of individual humans, human organisms evolved symbolic thinking to represent concepts and present feelings in ways that could be part of a shared reality. Symbolic thinking constituted consciousness because those who represent concepts and present feelings to a shared reality also engage in representation and presentation to themselves.

Influence

Langer won a wide readership outside the university setting. *Philosophy in a New Key* remained in print more than half a century after it first appeared, and it is one of the best-selling books in the history of Harvard University Press. It has long been required reading in university courses in a variety of fields, including anthropology, art history, literature, and religion, in addition to philosophy.

Langer is most familiar to those interested in the philosophy of art and aesthetics, but others concerned with symbol-making activities have also found her ideas useful. The anthropologist Clifford Geertz, for example, made extensive use of Langer's work in his book *The Interpretation of Cultures* (1973), one of the key theoretical texts of modern anthropology.

Although Langer was not a feminist, some feminist scholars have developed an interest in her work. These scholars have maintained that Langer's emphasis on feeling and her linking of the activities of thinking and feeling were feminist approaches that challenged traditional, primarily discursive, male-dominated philosophy.

Although appreciation of Langer's work has grown among academic philosophers, especially among those who work in aesthetics, some still regard her writings as essentially popular compilations of the works of other philosophers who have worked on symbolism, such as Charles S. Peirce, Alfred North Whitehead, and Ernst Cassirer. However, in the first chapter of *Philosophy in a New Key*, Langer maintains that philosophical thinking becomes widely relevant, and therefore popular, when it raises a new set of questions that alter widely held perspectives on human life. Langer's ability to arouse interest in questions of symbolism within a broad readership, as well as her provocative theories of artistic expression, made her one of the most influential philosophers of the twentieth century.

Carl L. Bankston III

Philosophy in a New Key

A Study in the Symbolism of Reason, Rite, and Art

Type of philosophy: Aesthetics, epistemology
First published: 1942
Principal ideas advanced:

◇ Symbolism is a new and increasingly important issue in philosophy.

◇ Human beings understand their world through symbols.

◇ Symbols are related to human experience through denotation and connotation.

◇ Denotation is the relationship between a symbol and the object to which it refers; connotation is the relationship between a symbol and the conception of the object.

◇ Through denotation and connotation, symbols present pictures of the human experience.

◇ Human experience consists both of reason and of feeling; therefore, there are at least two kinds of symbols.

◇ Discursive or logical symbols, such as words or mathematical symbols, are primarily denotational and represent objects and the relationship between objects.

◇ Presentational symbols, which are primarily connotative, present concepts of prerational feeling and describe the forms of relationships among feelings.

Early twentieth century philosophy saw a turn away from attempts to define an objective reality that exists apart from human participants and toward attempts to define what humans can say about the world. With the work of eighteenth century philosopher Immanuel Kant, it became accepted that humans know phenomena, or ideas of things, and not things-in-themselves. Therefore, clarifying ideas and the ways that ideas are expressed eventually came to be seen as one of the chief jobs of philosophy, if not the sole job of philosophy.

Because of the interest in clarifying the expression of ideas, a concern with meaning, in language and in mathematics, dominated the work of many of the most influential philosophers of the first half of the twentieth century. This concern led a number of philosophers to focus on symbols, meaningful sounds or objects that express thought and make communication possible. One of those philosophers was English philosopher Alfred North Whitehead, who worked on symbolic modes of thought in science. Susanne Langer studied with Whitehead while he was teaching at Harvard University. She was also heavily influenced by the early work in logic of the Austrian Ludwig Wittgenstein and by the thinking of the German Kantian philosopher Ernst Cassirer on symbolic forms.

In addition to her academic training in philosophy, Langer studied music throughout her life. Thus, while Whitehead and Wittgenstein had concentrated on attempting to describe how human reason is expressed through symbols, Langer extended the study of symbolism to prerational, or nondiscursive, areas of life. She discussed how religious rites and artworks, as well as reason, may be seen as symbolic expressions.

Symbolism as the "New Key"

Langer introduces her work by suggesting that the answers that philosophers give are often less significant than the questions that they pose. The questions asked at different points in time indicate varying concerns and imply varying frameworks of thought. The most ancient Greek philosophers, such as Thales and Anaximenes, turned their attention to the question of the ultimate composition of the universe. Socrates, however, showed a new concern when he asked, "What is truth?" He was no longer interested chiefly in which answer about the universe was true, but in what truth itself may be and in what the value of truth may be. Much later, at the beginning of the modern era, the division of the world into inner experience and outer world generated questions about what humans can know about the world around them. Many of these questions, however, came to be seen as irrelevant and uninteresting as modern science stimulated a growing concern with testable facts. The facts of science, though, are not objects but concepts, representations of the world. Mathematics, the chief tool of most scientists, does not consist of things but of symbols that describe the relationships among things. Langer maintains that the "new key" in philosophy, the new philosophical framework, is symbolism.

Signs and Symbols

Langer distinguishes symbols from signs. Signs indicate things. To a trained dog, the spoken word "dinner" can indicate that a meal is about to be served. Symbols, however, represent things as well as indicate them. The word "dinner" may indicate to a human that food will arrive, but it can also stand for the idea of dinner and relate this idea to other ideas. People spend much of their lives engaging in symbolization, in relating ideas to other ideas. However, a large part of human expression has seemed perplexing and impractical to philosophers, since many modes of expression, including ritual and art, do not convey logical meaning. Langer suggests that these modes of expression are symbolic transformations of experiences that cannot be conveyed by means of language alone.

The meaning of signs and symbols has both a logical and a psychological aspect. Logically, anything that has meaning must be capable of conveying the meaning. Psychologically, anything that has meaning must have meaning for someone, for a subject. The logical relationship between a sign and its object is a one-to-one correlation. One part of the pair, the object, is more interesting to the subject, the person involved, and the other part, the sign, is more readily available. Symbols follow a more complex logic. In addition to the object, the symbol, and the subject, there is a conception. In other words, the symbol refers not just to the concrete object but also to the abstract idea of the object. The word does not simply indicate the dinner about to arrive; it also refers to the idea of dinner in discussions, for example, of cooking. The denotation of a symbol is its relationship with the object. The connotation of a symbol is its relationship with the conception of the object. The three most common meanings of the word "meaning," then, are signification, denotation, and connotation.

Langer based her view of the nature of symbols on the "picture theory" of language proposed by Wittgenstein in his early work. Wittgenstein proposed that propositions or statements present pictures of some part of reality. In this view, both things and relations among things are projected into language. Some of those influenced by the early Wittgenstein argued that because language is a picture of some state of things, in order to be meaningful statements either must be true by definition or must be provable as true or false. Statements that cannot be logically worked out in the manner of equations or at least proven in theory do not provide a picture of any state of affairs outside language. Therefore, mystical, metaphysical, and poetic statements are simply confused thinking or expressions of emotion that are mistaken for meaningful propositions.

Language as Symbol

Philosophy in a New Key accepts the argument that only statements with a clear, provable relationship to arrangements of objects are meaningful in language. However, it rejects the assumptions that language is the only means of expressing thought and that everything that cannot be expressed through thought is merely formless emotion. Instead, Langer maintains that language is one form of symbolism, discursive symbolism, in which objects and relationships among objects are represented. There is also, however, a nondiscursive symbolism made up of presentational forms. Feelings have definite forms that can be presented to thought through arrangements of shapes or sounds.

In her discussion of language, Langer suggests that even this primary form of discursive symbolism may have its roots in connotation, in the emotional significance that concepts hold for human beings. She points out that the speech of small children seems to arise from playing with sounds and with ideas attached to sounds and objects, rather than from practical desires to communicate needs. Expression through language enables people to bring objects, events, and actions into their minds, to hold onto things by means of their symbols.

Ritual and Myth as Symbol

Sacramental rituals and myth are two areas of human symbol making, areas that have often been ignored or misunderstood by philosophers who approach the mind only in terms of reason. Sacred objects are symbols that express powerful psychological reactions to fundamental experiences such as life and death. These psychological reactions often result in physical movements, such as raising one's hands or dropping to one's knees. When these movements become repeated gestures before the sacred objects or group, the gestures are formalized as rituals.

While ritual, according to Langer, originates from significant movements, myth originates from fantasy. The most subjective and private form of fantasy, in her view, is the dream. Folktales are somewhat less private, because they are shared and traditional stories, but they still express individual fears and desires. Myth expresses general ideas, conceptions of the state of humanity and the universe, in the form of fantasy. Langer sees mythological thinking, as an expression of general ideas, as a necessary forerunner of metaphysics. In turn, metaphysics, consisting of abstract statements about the ultimate nature of things, is the forerunner of the abstractions of science.

Music as Symbol

In the eighth chapter of *Philosophy in a New Key*, entitled "On Significance in Music," Langer presents her theory of music. She rejects the two most common theories of expression in music, the self-expression theory and the semantic theory. The first holds that music is the pouring out of the emotions of the composer or performer. If this were the case, according to Langer, it would be difficult to explain the difference between a musical composition and a sigh or a scream. The semantic theory, the theory that music is a language that conveys messages, also seems inadequate to her. If music is a language, what is the meaning of each of its notes and what information does it communicate? Her own theory adopts parts of each of these others. Music does express feelings but not as an outpouring of emotion. It also has symbolic significance but not discursive significance. Instead, it is the logical expression of feelings. It formulates the inner life of human beings and presents this inner life to conscious awareness.

A Fabric of Meaning

Langer summarizes her general view by arguing that people live in a fabric of meaning. Even facts are not realities that are automatically given but are instead intellectually formulated events. To formulate events intellectually is to conceive of them as symbols. Philosophy should therefore concern itself with symbols in order to clarify meanings. A philosophy that knows only inductive or deductive logic will overlook a vast array of symbols and find itself unable to explain much of human life.

Critical Responses

One of the best-selling books published by Harvard University Press, *Philosophy in a New Key* communicated philosophical thinking about signs and symbols to a wide readership and made work in this area available to nonspecialists. Going through several editions, the book remained in print more than half a century after it first appeared, regularly appearing on required or recommended reading lists for college courses in such diverse disciplines as general philosophy, linguistics, English, anthropology, and art.

Professional philosophers have sometimes regarded *Philosophy in a New Key* as a popularization of the ideas of Whitehead, Cassirer, and Wittgenstein. It has been criticized for its reliance on the early Wittgenstein's "picture theory" of language, a theory Wittgenstein himself apparently rejected in his later work. Some critics have also objected to Langer's portrayal of human history as a march of progress, from the folktales and emotional reactions of "primitive savages" to the sophisticated abstractions of "civilized people."

Langer herself presented her book as an introduction to the "new key" of philosophers of symbolism. Nevertheless, it was an effective synthesis of many different thinkers. Moreover, Langer herself struck a new key in the attention she gave to nondiscursive, nonrational forms of thought. She was also an early exponent of the idea that shared symbols create human communities and that what people can know depends on what symbols are available to them. This view of the symbolic nature of community has become a common one among social scientists, and the prominent anthropologist Clifford Geertz acknowledged Langer's influence.

Among philosophers of art and music, Langer's ideas are widely known but not widely accepted. However, respect for her theory of music has been growing among philosophers of music. In his book *The Corded Shell* (1980), the influential theorist Peter Kivy acknowledged similarities between Langer's ideas and his own ideas on expressiveness in music. Others, such as philosopher of music Lars-Olof Åhlberg, have recognized Langer's contribution to the philosophy of music.

Carl L. Bankston III

Additional Reading

Langer, William L. *In and Out of the Ivory Tower: The Autobiography of William L. Langer.* New York: Neale Watson Academic Publications, 1977. In this autobiography, Susanne K. Langer's husband from 1921 to 1942 discusses their courtship and marriage but devotes little attention to his former wife's work as a philosopher.

Lyon, Arabella. "Susanne K. Langer: Mother and Midwife at the Rebirth of Rhetoric." In *Reclaiming Rhetorica: Women in the Rhetorical Tradition*, edited by Andrea A. Lunsford. Pittsburgh: University of Pittsburgh Press, 1995. In a feminist view of Langer's work, Lyon discusses the philosopher's life and writings and maintains that it is scandalous that historians of ideas have paid so little attention to this widely read thinker. She defends Langer's originality and creativity and points out how Langer's ideas differed from those of philosophers such as Ernst Cassirer, who are sometimes thought to be the sources of Langer's work.

Percy, Walker. *The Message in the Bottle: How Queer Man Is, How Queer Language Is, and What One Has to Do with the Other.* New York: Farrar, Straus & Giroux, 1980. The novelist Walker Percy makes use of Langer's work in this book of essays on language and meaning. Chapter 14, "Symbol as Need," presents a discussion of Langer's view of symbolization as a basic human need.

Carl L. Bankston III

Gottfried Wilhelm Leibniz

Though never formally an academic philosopher, Leibniz was one of the greatest intellectuals of his day: a metaphysician, theologian, philologist, historian, genealogist, poet, inventor, scientist, mathematician, logician, lawyer, and diplomat. He contributed to the development of rationalist philosophy and corresponded with or personally knew virtually every major European thinker in every field of inquiry.

Principal philosophical works: *Dissertatio de arte combinatoria*, 1666; *Discours de métaphysique*, wr. 1686, pb. 1846 (*Discourse on Metaphysics*, 1902); *Nouveaux essais sur l'entendement humain*, wr. 1704, pb. 1765 (*New Essays Concerning Human Understanding*, 1896); *Essais de Théodicée sur la bonté de Dieu, la liberté de l'homme et l'origine du mal*, 1710 (*Theodicy: Essays on the Goodness of God, the Freedom of Man, and the Origin of Evil*, 1951); *La Mondologie*, wr. 1714, pb. 1840 (also published as *Lehrsütze über die Monadologie*, 1720; *Monadology*, 1867); *Principes de la nature et la grâce fondés en raison*, wr. 1714, pb. 1768? (*The Principles of Nature and of Grace*, 1890); *The Philosophical Works of Leibnitz*, 1890; *Philosophical Papers and Letters*, 1956 (2 volumes); *Philosophical Essays*, 1989.

Born: July 1, 1646; Leipzig, Saxony (now in Germany)

Died: November 14, 1716; Hanover (now in Germany)

Early Life

Gottfried Wilhelm Leibniz was born into an academic family; his mother's father was a professor, as was his own father (who died when Leibniz was six). Leibniz was intellectually gifted; he taught himself Latin and read profusely in the classics at an early age. When he was an adolescent, Leibniz began to entertain the notion of constructing an alphabet of human thought from which he could generate a universal, logically precise language. He regarded this language as consisting of primitive simple words expressing primitive simple concepts that are then combined into larger language complexes expressing complex thoughts. His obsession with this project played an important role throughout his life.

Leibniz was formally educated at the University of Leipzig, where he received his bachelor's and master's degrees for theses on jurisprudence, and at the University of Altdorf, where he received the doctorate in law in 1666. He declined a professorship at Altdorf and entered employment as secretary of the Rosicrucian Society. Eventually he was employed as a legal counsel by Johann Philipp von Schönborn, a governing official of Mainz.

Life's Work

Leibniz's philosophy was rationalist. Rationalists believe that the origins of our knowledge lie in the fundamental laws of human thought (reason) instead of in human experience of the world; empiricists, by contrast, believe that knowledge derives from our experience of the external world via the senses. In fact, Leibniz argued that the laws of science could be *deduced* from fundamental metaphysical principles and that observation and empirical work were not necessary to arrive at knowledge of the world. What was needed instead was a proper method of calculating or demonstrating everything contained in certain fundamental tenets. For example, he believed that he could deduce the fundamental laws of motion from more basic metaphysical principles. In this general conception, he followed in the intellectual footsteps of French philosopher René Descartes. The great problem with interpreting

Leibniz's contribution to this tradition of thought is that he published only one major book during his lifetime, and it does not contain a systematic account of his full philosophy. Therefore, it is necessary to reconstruct his system from the short articles and the more than fifteen thousand letters he wrote.

Leibniz's youthful dreams of constructing a perfect language quickly evolved into a theory of necessary and contingent propositions. He claimed that in every true affirmation the predicate is contained in the subject. This idea evolved from his conception of a perfect language that (in all of its true, complex statements) would perfectly reflect the universe. The true propositions of this language are necessarily true, and all necessary propositions are, according to Leibniz, ultimately reducible to identity statements. Such a conception was more plausible in the case of purely mathematical statements because, for example, "4 = 2 + 2" can be equated with "4 = 4." Yet this conception seemed impossible in the case of contingent statements, for example, in "the house is blue." Leibniz avoided this problem by arguing that the necessity in what appears as contingent truths can be revealed (or resolved) only through an infinite analysis and therefore can be carried out in full only by God. It follows that, for humans, all contingent truths are only more or less probably true. Such truths are guaranteed by the *principle of sufficient reason*, which states that there must be some reason for whatever is the case. Necessary truths, or truths of reason, on the other hand, are guaranteed by the *principle of contradiction*, which states that the denial of such a truth is a contradiction (though this can be known only by God). A logical principle closely related to the principle of sufficient reason is the notion of the identity of indiscernibles, now known as Leibniz's law. This principle states that it is impossible for two things to differ only numerically, that is, to be distinct yet have no properties that differ; if two things are distinct, there must be some reason for their distinctness.

Leibniz had elaborated the rudiments of his metaphysical system while at Mainz, but it was during his sojourn in Paris that his philosophy matured. In 1672, he was sent to Paris on a diplomatic mission for the German princes to persuade Louis XIV to cease military activities in Europe and send forces to the Middle East. Leibniz remained in Paris for four years, and though he failed to gain an audience with the monarch, he met frequently with the greatest minds of the day, including Christiaan Huygens, Nicolas de Malebranche, Antoine Arnauld, and Simon Foucher. He also carried out studies of the mathematics of Blaise Pascal and René Descartes and actually built one of the first computers—a calculating machine able to multiply very large numbers. While residing in Paris, he also made a brief trip to England, where he met with chemist and

Gottfried Wilhelm Leibniz. *(Library of Congress)*

physicist Robert Boyle and visited the Royal Society, to which he was elected.

When he returned to Hanover, he accepted a post as director of the library to John Frederick, the duke of Brunswick, where he remained for the next ten years. It was only after working with Huygens in Paris on the nature of motion that Leibniz finally came to grips with the problem of the continuum. On his return trip from Paris, during which he visited Baruch Spinoza in Holland, he composed "Pacidius Philalethi" (1676), an extended analysis of this subject. This issue is traced back to the ancient Greeks and concerns the problem of resolving the motion of an object into its motions over discrete parts of space. If the body must pass through each successive parcel of space between two points, then it can never get from one point to another because there is an infinity of such discrete parcels between any two points. It was in the context of this problem of motion and the continuum that Leibniz developed, in 1676, the differential calculus, publishing his results in 1684. Sir Isaac Newton had already discovered the calculus but did not publish his results until 1693, several years after Leibniz published his discoveries. Priority of discovery is accorded to Newton, although the consensus is that they arrived at the calculus independently.

Leibniz argued that Cartesian physics renders motion ultimately inexplicable on the basis of fundamental concepts because it is grounded in the notion of matter as extension and does not accommodate dynamic properties. For Leibniz, the fundamental tenet is that activity is essential to substance. Substantial being is what is simple—what can be conceived by itself and what causes itself. The term "monad" was adopted by Leibniz to refer to this fundamental unit of existence. Monads are metaphysical entities that are not extended and are not of a material nature but are units of psychic activity. All entities are monadic, from God, the supreme monad who has created all the other grades of monads, to the lowest grade of being. The universe of monads is divided into two realms on the scale of perfection, that of nature and that of grace. Because monadic substances are psychic rather than material, Leibniz's philosophy has been labeled "panpsychistic idealism." On the level of phenomena, Leibniz retained a mechanical model:

Matter in the phenomenal realm is "secondary matter," composed of monadic substances and having mass. Yet, according to Leibniz, substances and monads do not interact with each other. The universe consists of an infinity of such monadic substances, individuated by the principle of indiscernibility and each of which undergoes changes. This change in the monad occurs entirely because of its own nature, according to a logically necessary law and not because of effects coming to it from outside. All of these changes in the monads have been harmonized by God into what appears as a causal order. Leibniz referred to this as the "way of preestablished harmony" and likened it to the synchronized sounding of two clocks. Because each monad/substance is completely independent of all the others, Leibniz said (in his later writings) that they are "windowless"; that is, they do not look out on the world. Though this conception may appear to be rather unusual, it does account for the plurality of existents in the universe, because the substances are infinite and independent of one another.

The changes of a monad are changes in the degree to which it expresses the universe. This expression or "perception" occurs on all levels of being; all individuals express the rest of the universe through the changes that occur in them. Because each individual represents all individuals, metaphysical accommodation is made of the unity of the universe in the diversity of an infinity of monads. An exhaustive specification of the nature of one substance/monad would give an exhaustive specification of the natures of all other substances/monads (from a particular point of view). Because such a specification would be logically necessary (in any true assertion the predicate is contained in the subject), the complete description of the universe is a tautology, though this could be fully known only by God.

The characteristics of the monad, activity and perception, are analogous to the features of the mental lives of human beings. In connection with the notion of perception, Leibniz later introduced the notion of "apperception." In *The Principles of Nature and of Grace*, he distinguished between perceiving the outer world and apperceiving the inner state of the monad (which is self-consciousness in a human being). In fact, differences between monads relate to their degree of clarity of perception and the presence of perception or apperception. At the bottom of the hierarchy of being are monads with confused perception and unselfconscious appetition. Leibniz's theory of human understanding is developed in his *New Essays Concerning Human Understanding*, written in response to John Locke but not published in Leibniz's lifetime. The perceptions of the human soul are expressions of the perceptions occurring in the body and are confused and unclear. Because all changes occur according to internal principles, all the ideas of the human mind are innate.

Leibniz was the first thinker to employ explicitly the notion of the unconscious, which he did in connection with the distinction between apperception and perception—not all perceptions are apperceived. These perceptions he refers to as "petites perceptions," and he gives as his favored example the sound of a wave crashing on the beach: The sound is composed of tiny perceptions of droplets hitting the beach, of which one is unaware though one is perceiving them.

During his years in Hanover, Leibniz grew very close to Sophia, the wife of his patron Ernest Augustus, First Elector of Hanover, and to Sophia's daughter Sophia Charlotte, who became the first queen of Prussia. Leibniz discussed many philosophical ideas with them, and from these conversations arose his only major work published during his lifetime, *Theodicy*. In this text, Leibniz argued along Augustinian lines that evil exists in the world because the world could not be as good as it actually is without the evil that it contains. In fact, out of all the possible universes, Leibniz believed, this universe contains the greatest amount of good. This conception earned for Leibniz's theories the appellation "philosophy of optimism."

Toward the end of his life, Leibniz became embroiled in an intellectual dispute with Samuel Clarke, a disciple of Newton. Leibniz claimed that Newtonian physics had contributed to a general decline of religion in England. Clarke defended Newtonian physics against this charge, while Leibniz attacked Newton's conceptions on philosophical grounds in a series of letters. Leibniz asserted that the notions of absolute space and absolute time violated the principle of sufficient reason and that the concept of gravity introduced the incomprehensible notion of action at a distance. Leibniz had earlier argued that space and time have no substantive existence and are only the ordered relations between coexistent entities and the ordering of successively existent entities, respectively. The death of Leibniz ended the debate with Clarke, who immediately published the correspondence. In spite of his extensive contacts with savants throughout Europe, Leibniz's death on November 14, 1716, was relatively unnoticed.

Influence

Leibniz had remained in the humble employ of royal patrons his whole life, though at one point he was offered the position of head librarian at the Vatican, which he declined to accept. In 1700, the Berlin Society of Sciences was founded, and Leibniz was elected president for life. Throughout his life, Leibniz speculated about grandiose social-intellectual projects. He advocated the Christian conquest of the pagan lands, the compilation of a universal encyclopedia of human knowledge, the reuniting of the Protestant and Catholic churches, and the restoration of peace in Europe under the Holy Roman Empire. In a true Enlightenment spirit, Leibniz also advocated the establishment of scientific academies throughout the world and actually corresponded with Peter the Great concerning such an academy for Russia. In spite of such visionary plans, Leibniz was very conservative politically; he did not criticize existing institutions and was opposed to innovation in moral and religious matters. Yet he was friendly to all, avid of learning of the world from everyone he encountered.

Leibniz had a tremendous influence on his contemporaries. Virtually all philosophers in Germany were Leibnizian during the years after his death. One early Leibnizian who proved to be equally influential in Germany was Christian von Wolff. Wolff had corresponded with Leibniz from 1704 to 1716 on mathematical and philosophical topics. Wolff taught the Leibnizian system to Martin Knutzen, who in turn taught it to Immanuel Kant, who long remained a Leibnizian. One of Kant's early essays in metaphysics was on the principle of sufficient reason and its relation to the logical principles of identity and contradiction. Writing in the light of the Lisbon earthquake of 1756, Voltaire bitterly satirized the philosophical optimism of Leibniz (along with Alexander Pope) in his work *Candide: Ou, L'Optimisme* (1759; *Candide: Or, All for the Best*, 1759). Leibniz's philosophical influence is still evident to this day. His law concerning the identity of indiscernibles is the starting point of much of the work done in the twentieth century on semantics, and his notions of necessity and possibility are the ancestors of work by contemporary modal logicians on the nature of necessity.

Mark Pestana

Theodicy

Essays on the Goodness of God, the Freedom of Man, and the Origin of Evil

Type of philosophy: Metaphysics, philosophical theology
First published: Essais de Théodicée sur la bonté de Dieu, la liberté de l'homme et l'origine du mal, 1710 (English translation, 1951)
Principal ideas advanced:
◇ The truths of philosophy and theology cannot contradict each other.
◇ If God is all-good, all-wise, and all-powerful, how did evil come into the world?
◇ The answer is that some error is unavoidable in any creature less perfect than its creator; furthermore, all possible worlds contain some evil, and evil improves the good by contrast.
◇ Because humans have free will, they are responsible for their acts; God's foreknowledge of the course of human inclinations did not involve predestination.
◇ The soul is coordinated with the body by a preestablished harmony.

For all of the continental rationalists, including René Descartes, Baruch Spinoza, and Gottfried Wilhelm Leibniz, God occupied a large and a systematic place. Much could be made of all that these thinkers owe to medieval theology, but the point is that they were centrally interested in the nature of God and God's relationship to the natural world. The way in which this problem is worked out by Leibniz has much to do with his

solution to other problems. Moreover, there is evidence that Leibniz looked upon himself (to a considerable extent) as a theologian and was most proud of his contributions there. He wished to bring peace between Catholics and Protestants, and his writing had some effect along this line. Particularly, Leibniz wanted to provide rational solutions for traditional theological issues, and he made it his major goal to provide a reconciliation between traditional religious views and philosophical thought through demonstrating their essential harmony.

The *Theodicy* has a unique place among the classical writing in philosophical theology, for it is one of the first attempts to "justify the ways of God to man" in straightforward and philosophical terms. Previous theological views had dealt with the issue of God's choice and creation of this particular natural order, but many had bracketed this topic as being beyond rational scrutiny, and few had set out to answer it directly and in detail. Theodicy, the discussion of God's orderings insofar as they concern human purposes, became a major part of philosophical theology after Leibniz's treatise.

Leibniz was among those who considered Christianity's merit to be its rational and enlightened nature, as contrasted with at least some other religions. Along with rationalism went a tendency to minimize the differences in nature between God and humanity. Leibniz shared in this tendency, stating that the perfections of God are those of the human soul, even though God possesses them in boundless measure. Leibniz was also an optimist about the essential goodness of humans and the possibility of their perfection, and it is probably this view of the nature of humanity that more than any other single factor led Leibniz into his "best of all possible worlds" doctrine.

The Nature of God
Human freedom and the justice of God form the object of this treatise, and Leibniz's aim was to support both while minimizing neither. To do this would justify God's ways to humanity; people would be more content to receive what God has ordained once the logic and harmony of God's plan were grasped. God does whatever is best but does not act from absolute necessity. Na-

ture's laws allow a mean between absolute necessity and arbitrary decrees. In this way, both God's and human actions were to be explained and reconciled.

God (for Leibniz) is deeply involved in the affairs of humanity, continually creating them, and yet God is not the author of sin. Evil has a source somewhere other than in the will of God; God permits moral evil but does not will it. Leibniz hoped that this view would offend neither reason nor faith. Consciously, Leibniz set out to modify the strictness of the necessity he found in the works of Thomas Hobbes, Spinoza, and Descartes. These philosophers had not been interested in a Christian doctrine of evil, for such a doctrine requires that humanity be given greater freedom in order to remove evil from God's immediate responsibility.

Reason Supports Faith

In *Theodicy*, Leibniz assumes that the truths of philosophy and theology cannot contradict each other. God acts in creation according to general rules of good and of order. Mysteries may be explained sufficiently to justify belief in them, but one cannot comprehend them. In explaining this, Leibniz distinguishes between logical or metaphysical necessity (whose opposite implies contradiction) and physical necessity. Even miracles must conform to the former, although they may violate the latter. Reason is the ultimate norm: No article of faith must imply contradiction or contravene proofs as exact as mathematics.

The Problem of Evil

When one considers evil, one asks what reasons, stronger than those that appear contrary to them, may have compelled God to permit evil. God is subject to the multitude of reasons and is even "compelled" by them. Leibniz infers that God must have had innumerable considerations in mind, in the light of which he deemed it inadvisable to prevent certain evils, for nothing comes from God that is not consistent with goodness, justice, and holiness. God must have been able to permit sin without detriment to his perfections; the weight of the reasons argues for it. Humans are essentially in the same circumstance in which God was in finding it necessary to permit certain evils.

Because reason is a gift of God even as faith is, Leibniz argues, contention between them would cause God to contend against God. Therefore, if any reasoned objections against any article of faith cannot be dissolved, then the alleged article must be considered as false and as not revealed. Reason and faith can be reconciled. Yet reason is still faced with its central problem: How could a single First Principle, all-good, all-wise, and all-powerful, have been able to allow evil and to permit the wicked to be happy and the good unhappy? Since Leibniz's time, philosophical inquiry into theological problems has often begun with this question.

Leibniz did not attempt to make the connection between God and moral evil an indirect one, which has been the traditional method. An evil will, he says, cannot exist without cooperation. An action, he asserts, is not, for being evil, the less dependent on God. Thus, Leibniz makes the solution to the problem of evil directly a matter of accounting for God's action, because nothing can come to pass without his permission. God is the first reason of things.

The cause of this world, Leibniz writes, must be intelligent, for the First Cause has to consider all possible worlds and then fix upon one to create. Such an intelligence would have to be infinite, and united to a goodness no less infinite, it cannot have chosen other than the best of all possible worlds.

It may be, for instance, that all evils are almost as nothingness in comparison with the good things that are in the universe. Whence did evil come then? We must consider that there is some original imperfection, due to the creature's limited nature, in the creature before sin. Leibniz adopts this view of "original sin," that some error is unavoidable in principle in a creature that must be less perfect than the being who creates it.

Other reasons for evil may be given: There is evil in all of the possible worlds, and so no choice could avoid it entirely. Evil often makes us savor good the more because of it—evil in that sense is necessary to any good. Human will is responsible for its own actions; but this explanation simply leads Leibniz into a consideration of God's foreknowledge and the question of divine predestination. Leibniz indulges in hairsplitting, distinguishing between what is certain and what is necessary. The will is inclined toward the course it adopts, and in that sense its action is and always has been "certain" in God's knowledge. However, the action of humanity's will is not necessary, although this means merely that its opposite does not involve a logical contradiction. Such "contingency" Leibniz allows to remain.

Free Will vs. Predestination

God always chooses the best but is not constrained to do so. This is the extent of his freedom. Another natural sequence of things is equally possible, in the logical sense, although God's will is determined in the choice it makes by the preponderating goodness of the natural order he chooses—that is to say, the natural order that actually exists. Everything is certain and determined beforehand in humanity's action, although this is not the absolute necessity that would find any alternative logically contradictory. The necessity comes from the goodness of the object chosen.

The prevailing inclination always triumphs. In that sense, Leibniz cannot conceive of either God or humans acting irrationally, and hence the actions of both God and humanity are necessary. The whole future is determined. However, because people know neither what the future is nor what it is that God foresees or has resolved, people must still do their duty, according to the reason God has given them and the rules he has prescribed. In the midst of an expansive metaphysical doctrine of possible worlds and the infinity of possible choices open to God, Leibniz adopted a conservative theological view of predestination. A radical in metaphysics, he was almost a reactionary in his view of the fixed relation of God to the world.

Like many conservatives, Leibniz tried—and believed that he had succeeded—to reconcile absolute foreknowledge on God's part with human freedom. His answer is as old as Augustine's. People are free in that their actions flow from their own will, but the action of the will in turn is dependent on its causes, which ultimately run back to God. Notwithstanding this dependence of voluntary actions on other causes, Leibniz still believed that the existence within people of a "wonderful spontaneity" is not precluded. This makes the soul independent of the physical influ-

ence of all other creatures, although Leibniz was careful not to say that it is also independent of God.

Preestablished Harmony

The doctrine of preestablished harmony is introduced to reconcile the difficulty. It was predestined from the beginning that God's design and humanity's volition should coincide: to Leibniz this seems to be a satisfactory solution. It is the typical solution of the rationalist. A reason has been given, and the whole scheme is seen to fit into a logical framework in which there is no contradiction or ultimate disharmony. Whereas one might begin with the premise that human freedom must at all cost be allowed for, Leibniz begins with the idea that all factors should be accounted for by a rational framework.

Preestablished harmony again accounts for the coordination of the soul and body. Like Spinoza's "parallel attributes," God ordained at the time of creation a logical ordering in which the soul's actions coincide with the body's movements. Like Descartes and Spinoza, Leibniz was thoroughly convinced that there is no interaction but there is a rationally determined plan of agreement. God has arranged beforehand for the body to execute the soul's orders. God has accommodated the soul to the body. Actually, the design of the world is simply an extension of God's perfection. Just as the rationalists of this era saw God and the human soul as being very close by nature, so also they viewed the natural order as an extension of the divine nature through creation. Although it is less than God, the created order essentially exhibits the same qualities as does divinity itself.

God is inclined toward every possible good, in proportion to the excellence of that good. God, before decreeing anything, considered among all the possible sequences of things that one which God afterward approved. God grants his sanction to this sequence (the present natural order) only after having entered into all its detail. From such a description of God's rational selective activity comes the doctrine of the best of all possible worlds.

In most traditional accounts of ultimate origin, the First Cause moves because it is good and outgoing, not grudging. However, in all classical and in most medieval schemes such a god has no real choices to make. Leibniz presents a modern metaphysical framework in that he stresses the infinitely wide range of alternatives open to God. The philosophical solution, however, is traditional. God selects according to fixed norms. It makes sense to say that classical thinkers also considered this world to be the best possible, but they believed that God had no alternatives. Leibniz simply set classical theory into a wider context of possibilities but continued to agree to God's fixed goodness and to his necessary selection and creation.

Christ and Salvation

In *Theodicy*, Leibniz takes up traditional and primarily theological questions concerning Christ and salvation. His answers here are not startlingly novel, except that Leibniz transferred miracles, belief in the nature of Christ, and a Christian doctrine of salvation into a thoroughly rational framework. Leibniz wanted the doctrines of traditional Christianity to be amenable to his philosophical scheme of metaphysics. In the process of demonstrating this mutual harmony, like all philosophical theologians, he was pushed into giving some rather far-fetched accounts of some difficult religious notions—for example, the assertion of the existence of all human souls in seed in their progenitors since the very beginning of things. Obviously such an idea would be helpful in establishing a religious notion of original sin in Adam; but it is hardly likely to be confirmable by the microscopic observations Leibniz's rationalism suggests.

Both Leibniz's questions and his answers are repetitious. *Theodicy* sets out to refute certain doctrines that Leibniz opposed (particularly those of Pierre Bayle). Leibniz did this partly by reference to and elaboration of certain of his famous theories (preestablished harmony, the essential goodness of God's choice), but primarily his weapon was the repetition of his own position. As a rationalist, Leibniz evinced the traditional irritation at finding that someone else did not find his reasoning as persuasive as he himself did and that his opponent continued to hold different theories. Despite this defect, *Theodicy* illustrates how important works do not always have the technical rigor and logical tightness that one might suppose. Leibniz repeats his maxims and principles;

he does little to explore them in detail. Yet Leibniz is dealing with questions of great moment and common interest, and his proposed solutions are interesting and suggestive. More precise and cogent pieces of philosophical analysis have proved to be less interesting over the years, but Leibniz's sometimes tedious and often loose reflections on the crucial issues of theology are still very much alive.

Frederick Sontag, updated by John K. Roth

Monadology

Type of philosophy: Metaphysics
First published: La Mondologie, wr. 1714, pb. 1840 (also published as *Lehrsätze über die Monadologie,* 1720; English translation, 1867)
Principal ideas advanced:

◇ Monads are the elements of all things; they are simple substances, created all at once out of nothing; they can neither be altered in quality nor changed internally by any other created thing.

◇ No two monads are perfectly alike; for every individual monad there is some internal difference that accounts for its particular nature.

◇ Perception and apperception are the two chief types of activities by which monads exhibit their natures.

◇ Humans are distinguished from animals by their knowledge of necessary and eternal truths; humans reason according to the principles of contradiction and sufficient reason.

◇ Only through God's mediation is interaction or knowledge of any sort possible; although the monads are isolated, they function and perceive according to God's preestablished harmony.

◇ This is the best of all possible worlds, for God's goodness made him choose it from the infinite number of possible universes.

Monadology is undoubtedly Gottfried Wilhelm Leibniz's best-known work. Because it is a condensed statement of his main philosophical principles, written late in life, there is good reason for this popularity. On the other hand, its popularity is somewhat strange, because Leibniz himself gave no title to the manuscript and it was not published during his lifetime. Written in French in 1714, it was first published in German in 1720. Not until 1840 did the original French version appear, and the title *La Monadologie*, given to the work at that time, has remained. Although *Essais de Théodicée sur la bonté de Dieu, la liberté de l'homme et l'origine du mal* (1710; *Theodicy: Essays on the Goodness of God, the Freedom of Man, and the Origin of Evil*, 1951) represents Leibniz's philosophical and theological interests more directly, and his *Nouveaux essais sur l'entendement humain* (wr. 1704, pb. 1765; *New Essays Concerning Human Understanding*, 1896) undoubtedly provoked more immediate interest, *Monadology* remains important as a brief metaphysical sketch.

Monadology has been called an "encyclopaedia of Leibniz's philosophy," and one of its drawbacks is that in a strict sense, the reader needs to know Leibniz's other writings in order to understand its contents properly. Support can be found for considering *Theodicy* to be a more central work from the fact that Leibniz himself added references in the margin of his manuscript (later named *Monadology*) referring particularly to passages in *Theodicy* where the views were more fully expressed. Yet *Monadology* can be, and usually has been, read alone. As such, it stands in a tradition of brief yet comprehensive metaphysical expositions that have an influence out of proportion to their length.

Monads

Particularly in view of the fact that Leibniz did not himself title *Monadology*, the work could just as easily be called "on substance" or "on the modes of being." In subject matter, *Monadology* follows the great tradition of metaphysics in trying to define what the ultimate substance of the world is and in trying to arrange a hierarchy to account for all the possible modes of existence. *Monadology* is divided into ninety brief paragraphs, each summarizing some fundamental point. The first paragraph opens with a description of a monad, thus introducing Leibniz's most famous doctrine and the single principle in terms of which his entire metaphysics is developed.

Like Baruch Spinoza, whom he knew and admired, Leibniz was impressed with mathematical

rigor, and he reflects this love of simplicity and brevity in his philosophical writing. *Monadology* is not an intricately structured work like Spinoza's *Ethica* (1677; *Ethics*, 1870), but the same love of clarity and of a single First Principle is clearly evident in both. Leibniz, who was equally famous as a mathematician, is read by mathematically and logically inclined philosophers as well as by speculative metaphysicians and theologians.

A monad, Leibniz tells us, is a simple (indivisible) substance that enters into compounds, and a compound is an aggregation of simple things. Monads are the elements of all things, the atoms of all nature; they are indestructible because no such simple substance can be destroyed by natural means. Nor can they come into existence artificially within natural limits because they could not, by their very nature, be formed from anything else. Spinoza's "substance" was so large that it became absolutely infinite and included both God and the world as ordinarily conceived. Leibniz's substances, on the other hand, are the smallest and simplest conceivable entities.

Creation and annihilation are the means of entrance and exit for monads, and here Leibniz's theological dimension is most evident. They are, Leibniz says, created "all at once," which is a condensed reference to the traditional doctrine of creation *ex nihilo*, just as "annihilation" has similarities to traditional eschatological views. Because monads are conceived as having such extra-mundane means of entrance and exit, it is not really surprising that Leibniz asserts that the monads cannot be altered in quality or changed internally by any other created thing. This has overtones of traditional doctrines of predestination, but Leibniz puts it in his dramatic and famous phrase that the monads "have no windows" through which anything could come in or go out. Each is a self-contained, self-developing entity. The means of their coordination will be explained later.

However, if monads cannot be altered from without, they would all be identical and indistinguishable were it not for internal differences in quality. The monads derive the qualities they have from internal differences. This is another way of saying that Leibniz denies that there is any general or external principle of individuation. Leibniz then reverses the emphasis from trying to account for a principle of individuation and difference among monads to asserting, in a more radical note, that every monad is absolutely different from every other. No two are perfectly alike; in even the most similar some internal difference of intrinsic quality can be found.

Perception and Apperception

Having covered the basic questions concerning monads as such in eight brief paragraphs, Leibniz then sets forth more general metaphysical principles, built upon the doctrine of the monads as the ultimate simple components of all things. Every created being (and the monad itself is a created thing) is subject to change. All natural changes of the monad come from an internal principle, and the pattern of change that a group of monads characteristically exhibits is its nature. The nature of a thing is its pattern of activity. Perception and apperception (or consciousness) are the two chief types of activity of a monad or of a group of monads, and all activity may be categorized under these two headings. The activity that produces change from one perception to another is what Leibniz calls "appetition," and nothing but perceptions and their changes can be found in a simple substance like a monad.

Monads have a kind of self-sufficiency, an internalized and purposeful plan of activity, which is what makes them their own source of their internal activities. Because they have this self-directive action as well as perceptions and desires, they may be called souls, although this title is to be reserved only for those whose perception is distinct and is accompanied by memory.

One perception comes only from another perception, as a motion comes only from another motion. Therefore, every present state of a monad is a consequence of its preceding state. So understood, any present moment has within it much more of the future than either the past or the present. Leibniz's theory of monads, although in a sense deterministic, is a view that is directed primarily toward the future. Certainly all activity and perception have this orientation. However, humans are unique and are to be distinguished from animals, despite the basic similarity between our component parts and theirs. Such a distinction of humans from animals must

be based on a distinction of degree; humans have knowledge of necessary and eternal truths, but animals do not.

Reason and Fact

Leibniz began in his theory of monads with a description of a common nature that all things share. Beginning with this separation of humans from animals in virtue of humanity's knowledge of eternal truths, Leibniz concentrates primarily on humanity and God, and for this reason the common, shared substance receives less emphasis. For humans, knowledge of necessary and eternal truths raises them to a knowledge of themselves and of God. Reflective self-consciousness has been introduced. People have a knowledge of necessary truths, and they may think about God's nature—all of which requires a unique type of reasoning.

People's reasoning is founded on two great principles: the principle of contradiction, which separates the true from the false, and the principle of sufficient reason. The latter tells us that for every fact there is a reason sufficient to account for the fact regardless of whether the reason can be known. Truths in turn are to be divided into two kinds: those of reasoning and those of fact. Truths of reasoning are necessary, and their opposite is impossible; truths of fact are contingent, and their opposite is possible.

The Nature of God

Leibniz then offers his arguments for God's existence. The sufficient or final reason for things must be outside the sequence or series of particular contingent things, however infinite the series may be. Thus, the final reason for all things must be a necessary substance, and this substance is called God. There needs to be only one God because this God is sufficient to account for the variety of particulars.

Such a God is absolutely perfect because perfection as Leibniz defines it is nothing but the presence of positive reality, and God, as an unlimited sequence of possible beings, must contain as much reality as possible. To separate humanity from God, Leibniz asserts that created beings derive their perfections from God but their imperfections from themselves because God is infinite but humanity must be limited. God's infinity seems to be the chief source of his perfection and is the quality that separates him most radically from humanity because both are composed of basically similar monads.

Leibniz modifies Saint Anselm's ontological argument for God's existence. Instead of using Anselm's phrase, "necessary existence," Leibniz writes, "He must necessarily exist, if He is possible." This changes Anselm's point and shifts the question of God's existence to one of demonstrating the possibility of a God. Nothing can interfere with the possibility of an infinite God's existence (this part of the reasoning is traditional), but the possibility of a God must first be established (this is new).

One of Leibniz's most famous, and disputed, doctrines is that of the creation of monads. He has asserted that none can be brought into being or destroyed by natural causes, but this leaves open the question of a divine origin. God, it turns out, is the only uncreated monad; all the rest are created or derivative. This process Leibniz calls "fulguration," and it seems to be not a single act but an activity of God continued from moment to moment. Because no further explanation of this important doctrine of the origin of monads is given nor any further definition of the key term "fulguration" (except a reference to *Theodicy*), this theory of Leibniz has been the source of much discussion.

The Best of All Possible Worlds
Only through the mediation of God can one monad affect another; and one affects another only in the sense that, in predestinating things from the beginning, God may have considered one monad in determining the activity of another in relation to it. God is said to have a "will" that regulates things according to a principle of the best, but this does not allow him any alternatives in design. This is Leibniz's most famous doctrine, that God has in fact created the best world which it was possible for him to devise.

God does have an infinite number of possible universes to choose from, it is true, but only one of them could become actual through his creative activity. Fitness, or degree of activity in perfection, determines him, so that in that sense his activity in creation is not really free. When all that must be considered and balanced is in-

cluded, there are no alternatives to the world he did create. His goodness makes him choose it, and his power makes him produce it.

People are not at all cut off in this world. Each living thing is a perpetually living mirror of the universe. It sometimes seems as if people live in many different worlds, but these are in truth nothing but aspects of a single universe, viewed from the special point of view of each monad. Being joined in this way, people are not really independent. Everybody feels the effect of all that takes place in the universe. Each created monad thus represents the whole universe within itself. All nature shares in this interconnectedness, down to matter itself. There is nothing fallow, nothing sterile, nothing dead in the universe, no chaos, no confusion save in appearance.

Preestablished Harmony
God alone is completely without body, although this means merely to be a monad of a special type. The births and deaths of natural bodies are not abrupt transitions (no transition for Leibniz is abrupt). Birth and death are gradual changes. Body and soul both follow their own laws (no soul is without body except God). The body and soul of any entity agree, despite their variant laws, through the "preestablished harmony" of all substances that God has arranged. This is a modern metaphysical version of the traditional theological doctrine of foreordination. Souls act according to the laws of final causes through appetitions, ends, and means. Bodies act according to the laws of efficient causes or motions. Through God's original design, the two realms are in harmony with each other.

Minds are able to enter into a kind of fellowship with God. The totality of all such spirits composes the City of God, and this is the moral world within the natural world. This moral world and natural world are, like body and soul, in perfect harmony. God as architect satisfies in all respects God as lawgiver. The world exceeds all the desires of the wisest people, and it is impossible to make it better than it is. On this high note of optimism, *Monadology* ends.

Monadology in Context
One thing that should be noted is that the famous doctrine of the monads occupied only the first

part of the unnamed treatise, and in the later sections the traditional theological problems are taken up with less and less mention made of the theory of the monads. *Monadology* is not the tightly knit and interlocking statement of doctrine it is often thought to be. Within this brief treatise many important theories are merely mentioned; few are argued at all. More independence probably exists between the various theories here than is often recognized, and certainly other of Leibniz's writings need to be studied (primarily *Theodicy*) before any appraisal at all can be made. What is to be found within the ninety brief paragraphs of the treatise is, without question, a reflection of Leibniz's attempt to meet and to deal with every major philosophical and theological problem.

Frederick Sontag

Additional Reading

Adams, Robert Merrihew. *Leibniz: Determinist, Theist, Idealist*. New York: Oxford University Press, 1994. An important philosopher of religion explores Gottfried Wilhelm Leibniz's philosophical theology and its views regarding evil, goodness, and the nature of God.

Aiton, E. J. *Leibniz: A Biography*. Boston: A. Hilger, 1985. A worthwhile account of Leibniz's life, including his place in the scientific, philosophical, and religious worlds of his time.

Copleston, Frederick. *A History of Philosophy: Modern Philosophy*. Garden City, N.Y.: Doubleday, 1964. Copleston situates Leibniz in the history of Western philosophy and provides a helpful introduction to Leibniz's major views.

Deleuze, Gilles. *The Fold: Leibniz and the Baroque*. Minneapolis: University of Minnesota Press, 1993. A significant French philosopher takes stock of the contributions and implications of, as well as problems in, Leibniz's thought.

Hostler, John. *Leibniz's Moral Philosophy*. New York: Barnes & Noble Books, 1975. This study of the ethical dimensions of Leibniz's metaphysics argues that the metaphysics is worked out in the framework of his systematic moral ideas.

Jolley, Nicholas, ed. *The Cambridge Companion to Leibniz*. New York: Cambridge University Press, 1995. Important scholars contribute significant essays on wide-ranging aspects of Leibniz's philosophy.

MacDonald, Ross G. *Leibniz*. New York: Oxford University Press, 1984. This introduction to Leibniz's thought contends that he hoped to create a synthesis of all knowledge traditions.

Mates, Benson. *The Philosophy of Leibniz: Metaphysical Underpinnings*. London: Oxford University Press, 1986. A reliable introductory study that covers all aspects of Leibniz's metaphysics.

Rescher, Nicholas. *Leibniz: An Introduction to His Philosophy*. Totowa, N.J.: Rowman & Littlefield, 1979. Argues that Leibniz's unorthodox metaphysical system ultimately aims at providing a formation for traditional views in ethics and religion.

Riley, Patrick. *Leibniz' Universal Jurisprudence: Justice as the Charity of the Wise*. Cambridge, Mass.: Harvard University Press, 1996. An exploration of Leibniz's ethics and political theories and of his interest in international relations.

Rutherford, Donald. *Leibniz and the Rational Order of Nature*. New York: Cambridge University Press, 1995. Concentrates on the rationalism of Leibniz's thought, including the idea that ours is the best of all possible worlds.

Wilson, Catherine. *Leibniz's Metaphysics: A Historical and Comparative Study*. Princeton, N. J.: Princeton University Press, 1989. Wilson shows how Leibniz developed his distinctive metaphysical system, taking into account his historical context and his place within the philosophical debates of his day.

Woolhouse, R. S., ed. *Gottfried Wilhelm Leibniz: Critical Assessments*. New York: Routledge, 1994. In this collection, Leibniz scholars take stock of his theories, their implications, and their lasting value.

Mark Pestana, updated by John K. Roth

Emmanuel Lévinas

With the claim that ethics, rather than ontology, is "first philosophy," Lévinas launched a major critique of the Western philosophical tradition, suggesting that philosophy is finally the wisdom of love in the service of love.

Principal philosophical works: *La Théorie de l'intuition dans la phénoménologie de Husserl*, 1930 (*The Theory of Intuition in Husserl's Phenomenology*, 1973); *De l'évasion*, 1935 (article), 1982 (book); *De l'existence l'existant*, 1947 (*Existence and Existents*, 1978); "Le Temps et l'autre," 1947 (*Time and the Other*, 1987); *En découvrant l'existence avec Husserl et Heidegger*, 1949; *Totalité et infini: Essai sur l'extériorité*, 1961 (*Totality and Infinity: An Essay on Exteriority*, 1969); *Autrement qu'être: Ou, Au-delà de l'essence*, 1974 (*Otherwise than Being: Or, Beyond Essence*, 1981); *De Dieu qui vient à l'idéeI*, 1982; *Éthique et infini*, 1982 (*Ethics and Infinity*, 1985); *À l'heure des nations*, 1988 (*In the Time of the Nations*, 1994); *Nine Talmudic Writings*, 1990; *Levinas: Basic Philosophical Writings*, 1996.

Born: January 12, 1906; Kaunas, Lithuania
Died: December 25, 1995; Paris, France

Early Life

Through his early education, Emmanuel Lévinas was thoroughly steeped in Russian culture and Jewish orthodoxy. He read, in Russian, the great novelists Aleksandr Pushkin, Nikolai Gogol, Fyodor Dostoevski, and Leo Tolstoy, and the Bible in Hebrew. In 1923, Lévinas left Lithuania (a few intermittent years, including the revolutions of 1917, had been spent with his family in the Ukraine) for Strasbourg, where he began his general university education in psychology, sociology, Latin, and philosophy. Among the important philosophical influences at this time were the canon of philosophers Plato, Aristotle, René Descartes, and Immanuel Kant. Especially important, however, for Lévinas was the work of philosopher Henri Bergson, in particular his work on time as duration and as a release from static "scientific time."

While in Strasbourg, and through a colleague's chance invitation to read Edmund Husserl's *Logische Untersuchungen* (1900-1901; *Logical Investigations*, 1970), Lévinas discovered the thought of this philosopher and the emerging philosophical discipline called phenomenology. This discovery prompted Lévinas to travel to Freiburg (Breisgau) to study with the master during the academic year 1928-1929. In phenomenology, Lévinas found a discipline that allowed the philosopher to think non-naïvely about the constitution of reality via an analysis of the intentional stance of consciousness. By intentionality, Husserl meant the mental context in which things appear as the things that they are. The mind moves out toward reality, intends it, and in so doing, places it within a meaningful context or horizon.

While in Freiburg, Lévinas came upon Husserl's successor, Martin Heidegger, and his text *Sein und Zeit* (1927; *Being and Time*, 1962). Heidegger was very important in Lévinas's interpretation of phenomenology because he proposed an existential phenomenology, that is, a phenomenology firmly rooted in human existence as it occurs day to day. As Lévinas put it, in Heidegger's work, one learned to hear the "verbality" of the phrase "to be." Lévinas wrote a dissertation, *The Theory of Intuition in Husserl's Phenomenology*, which philosopher Jean-Paul Sartre credited as introducing phenomenology to the French-speaking world and which also began a long conversation, appreciative but also critical, with the phenomenological tradition. Lévinas's subsequent philosophical work would frequently take as its point of departure the axioms of either Husserl or Heidegger.

Lévinas's experiences during World War II shaped his later work; the philosopher described his writings as being dominated by "the presentiment and the memory of the Nazi horror." The "Nazi horror" took many forms, including Heidegger's involvement with National Socialism and the murder of many of Lévinas's family members. Lévinas was saved from the extermination camps (though not the work camps) because of his French uniform. After the war, he continued his work in phenomenology through a variety of increasingly critical studies of Heideggerian ontology. In several essays, he struggled to develop his own voice, a voice that would find international acclaim in his state doctoral thesis *Totality and Infinity*.

In addition to his philosophical training, Lévinas continued his studies in Hebrew and Talmudic exegesis. These works were of a more confessional nature, and beginning in 1957, Lévinas lectured annually on Talmudic passages. He published several books on the exegesis of the Talmud and the interpretation of modern Judaism.

Life's Work
In his earlier career, Lévinas had remained on the margins of French philosophical life, in part because of his involvement with, and eventual directorship of, the École Normale Israélite Orientale. The mission of this school was to promote the emancipation of Jews living in the Mediterranean regions by training qualified teachers. Because the school was in Paris, Lévinas took advantage of lectures being offered at the Sorbonne by Léon Brunschvicg and Alexandre Kojève. He also met several philosophers who later rose to prominence: Jean-Paul Sartre, Jean Hyppolite, Gabriel Marcel, and Jean Wahl.

During the 1930's, Lévinas worked primarily as an interpreter of the phenomenology of Husserl and Heidegger. He wrote several expository essays, some of which would later be gathered together and published as *En découvrant l'existence avec Husserl et Heidegger* (1949; Husserl and Heidegger's discovery of existence). During this period, he also cotranslated Husserl's *Cartesianische Meditationen* (1931; *Cartesian Meditations*, 1960) into French. Lévinas had planned to write a book on Heidegger but never did, partly because he was disappointed by Heidegger's in-

volvement with the Nazis and partly because he was drafted by the French army in 1939. He served as an interpreter of Russian and German until his capture by the Germans.

After the war, Lévinas published a short book *Existence and Existents*, which showed a more critical position with respect to Heideggerian phenomenology. Rather than arguing from beings to Being, as Heidegger had, Lévinas proposed that one must move from essence or being, which he termed the anonymity of the "there is," to particular existing beings if one was to get at the true sense of things. Before what Heidegger called the generosity of Being, there is a chaotic indeterminacy to being that precedes all giving or creativity. Lévinas's short book did not receive a great deal of attention. It was written in a rather difficult style and dealt with themes in phenomenology that were only beginning to be understood. However, at the invitation of Wahl, Lévinas gave a series of lectures dealing with time at the Sorbonne in 1946-1947, and their publication was more widely received.

At the age of fifty-five, Lévinas received his state doctorate, which brought international renown and a full-time academic post at the University of Poitiers. This position would be followed by an appointment at the University of Paris-Nanterre in 1967 and the Sorbonne (Paris IV) in 1973, where he became honorary professor in 1976. The publication of his doctoral work, *Totality and Infinity*, immediately established Lévinas as a highly original thinker.

The main contours of Lévinas's work were developed in a few essays written in the 1950's, but the revolutionary character of his thought was not revealed until after the publication of *Totality and Infinity*. Lévinas claims that Western philosophy, because of its commitment to Greek ontology, is characterized by a totalitarian impulse that does violence to the integrity and transcendence of otherness. He insists that the human and the divine other cannot be made to fit within a monism of being, even though this has been the consistent goal of a great many philosophers. Though Lévinas does incorporate Hebrew experience in his description of the human/human and human/ divine encounter, it would be a mistake to think that he is simply substituting a biblical for a philosophical account. Lévinas argues for his philosophical positions in ways that do not require a belief in the scriptural traditions. In fact, in texts of Plato and Descartes, he finds moments that indicate precisely the sort of transcendence that he envisions. In the *Politeia* (c. 388-366 B.C.E.; *Republic*, 1701) Plato spoke of the Good that is "beyond being," and in the *Meditationes de Prima Philosophiae* (1641; *Meditations on First Philosophy*, 1911), Descartes spoke of the idea of the infinite that exceeds thought and overwhelms it, leading the mind not to comprehension but to worship.

Lévinas's point is that these sorts of texts reveal an honesty that acknowledges the integrity of the other but at the same time senses that the activity of reason must correspond to the matter with which it deals. Critical knowing, rather than being the dogmatic exercise that pronounces meaning upon the world, comes about as learners are attentive to the other and allow themselves to be taught by others. Given that the other is the teacher, the self and the other form an asymmetrical relationship, one in which the self as learner is beholden to what the other presents. The other person is not the self's alter ego but is transcendent with respect to the self. This is the beginning of an account that stresses the ethical nature of the knowing situation. As soon as the self encounters another, a claim has been put upon the self to respect and be responsible for one's own alterity or otherness. Ethics is "first philosophy" because every pursuit of wisdom, if it is attentive to the integrity, even sanctity, of the other arises out of a moral claim placed upon the knower.

In the 1960's, Lévinas had to respond to the questions of many sympathetic and critical readers. Is it even possible to think beyond being if being is the very orbit within which all thought must move? Lévinas recognized that though his work was primarily inspired by the phenomenological method, what he was finally pointing to was something transphenomenological. The difficulty involved in Lévinas's work was elaborated in his second major text *Otherwise than Being: Or, Beyond Essence*. In this work, Lévinas concentrated on the modalities that govern and orient a subject that is attentive and responsive to otherness. He produced a careful description of proximity, vulnerability, inspiration, and responsibility. Lévinas's radical claim is that a subject who has undergone a heteronomous conversion (who has relinquished the drive for comprehension and control) will be so responsible for the other as to be substituted for the other, even to the point of death. As knowers, people are witnesses to otherness and are called to give an account of the other's integrity, an account that finally must move beyond abstract speech to the "ethical language" that gives to the other with open hands.

In his later years, following retirement from his academic post, Lévinas continued to lecture widely on themes enunciated in his major works. Before his death, he was working on a theme that interested him in the earliest stages of his career, namely, a conception of time as diachronous rather than synchronous. He also continued work on problems in religion and the nature of death. Throughout this period, his work on Talmudic texts as well as issues associated with Judaism and modern culture carried on at a steady pace.

Influence

Lévinas's work is perhaps the most significant attempt to move beyond the phenomenology of Husserl and Heidegger. He influenced many friends and students, including philosophers Paul Ricœur, Jacques Derrida, Adriaan Peperzak, and Jean-Luc Marion. In good phenomenological style, Lévinas's work prompts his readers to return to beginnings. What is the original situation out of which human action and thought emerge? What does it mean to be responsible knowers? How do we construct a just and peaceable world? What is the meaning of death? These are perennial questions that cannot be avoided. Lévinas guides his readers in thinking about and developing answers to these questions.

Norman Wirzba

Totality and Infinity

An Essay on Exteriority

Type of philosophy: Ethics, metaphysics
First published: Totalité et infini: Essai sur l'extériorité, 1961 (English translation, 1969)

Principal ideas advanced:

◇ Western philosophical method is totalitarian in nature; it consistently denies and dissimulates the otherness of reality, reducing it to sameness in thought.

◇ The drive to sameness is grounded in the concrete life of an autonomous thinking being, a being that, in striving to maintain itself, finds the world around it as the arena for work and enjoyment.

◇ Further examination of concrete life reveals that the other, primarily the face of another human being, breaks through the enjoyment of ego-centered existence and shows it to be unjust and irresponsible; totality is beset by infinity, or put another way, immanence is circumscribed by transcendence.

◇ A phenomenological description of the "ethical relation," or what Lévinas also calls the "face-to-face" relation, leads to a reconsideration of the nature of thought as desire, of experience as responsibility, and language as discourse.

Emmanuel Lévinas's *Totality and Infinity* can be understood as a response to two large crises, one cultural and one philosophical. When the book was written, Europe had recently come through two bloody wars, World Wars I and II, which demonstrated on a scale never before seen the barbarity of humanity against humanity. The depth of this crisis was seen in the genocidal programs carried out by nations that were supposed to represent the best of the Western tradition. In response to this crisis, Lévinas asks if there is not an eschatological hope available to people, a hope sustained and nourished by the life of one's responsibility to another, that will redirect the pessimism and despair that the witness of history ought to teach people.

On the philosophical level, phenomenology, as it was defined by Edmund Husserl and Martin Heidegger, promised to put philosophy on a new and rigorous path. Husserl envisioned phenomenological philosophy as the science that would lead people past the relativism and naturalism that ruled the day; however, Heidegger believed that phenomenology evoked the sense of long-forgotten Being and by doing so would lead humanity into authentic existence. Neither of these attempts, in Lévinas's view, addressed the crucial philosophical problem of how to address and overcome the violent tendencies latent within Western philosophical practice. Because Lévinas believed that philosophical reflection is inherently totalitarian in nature, he attempted to work out a modality of thinking that welcomes and is responsible to the infinite. This form of thinking uses a description of the ethical situation, what Lévinas calls the "face-to-face" encounter, and hopefully leads to peace rather than war.

The preface of *Totality and Infinity* states that war, as it appears in history and in thought, is the context for the work as whole. Lévinas claims that war is inextricably tied with the totalitarian and violent nature of thought and that people have known this at least since the time of the Greek philosopher Heraclitus, who pronounced that "war is the king of all" and that "all things come to be according to strife and opposition." Although the exercise of thought might be given over to the discovery of a unity or harmony among all things, what is in fact discovered is reason's complicity in the skill of winning wars between nations, communities, and people. To understand the nature of this violence, one must see beyond the surface to the injury that might be done against another, to the refusal on the part of the one who violates to acknowledge the otherness or integrity of the one violated. Violence is not simply an action, but a mode of seeing and holding the world. In short, the violent act finds its root in the blindness or dissimulation of exteriority. Lévinas calls this a totalitarian vision because totalities are all-encompassing. They do not allow the reality of anything "outside" or "beyond" the totality that might challenge it or put it into question. However, if there is no exteriority, no otherness or infinity, then rational thought is condemned to the maintenance of war, and moral reflection is shown to be a mockery. Lévinas argues that the possibility for peace depends on a prior possibility that the exercise of reason can become truly attentive to the integrity and transcendence of the other and in so doing can become a genuinely critical reason.

Otherness, Sameness, and Ethics

The first section begins with an analysis of the appearance of otherness within thought. Can the other appear "as other," or must otherness always be a feature of the thinker's frame of reference and thus not genuinely other but more of the same? Although the history of philosophy has tended to be governed by sameness, as when the aim of a thought is always directed by the a priori conditions that make each thought possible or when reason is grounded in a thinking being who sets the terms for rationality, Lévinas nonetheless claims that it is possible to find moments within the tradition where the ubiquity of sameness is called into question. One of these would be the persistence of metaphysical desire. By this desire, Lévinas means the tendency to seek out that which is absolutely other, that which is not of this world. To be sure, metaphysicians have often claimed to grab hold of the metaphysical world they seek, but in this grasp, they forget the desire that propelled them forward in the first place. Desire is not to be confused with need. A need can be met and filled, but it is the essence of desire to desire beyond that which could possibly complete it. Metaphysical desire thus prepares a rupture within the totality of thought and, in so doing, clears a space for genuine otherness to make itself felt.

Lévinas is also aware that metaphysics has often taken the form of an ontology, a science that pertains to the being of things. Being becomes the theoretical category in terms of which all things are understood. However, this metaphysical desire, because it is allied with the drive for comprehension, denies metaphysical desire and the otherness of what is known; Lévinas developed this theme at much greater length in *Autrement qu'être: Ou, Au-delà de l'essence* (1974; *Otherwise than Being: Or, Beyond Essence*, 1981). It is Lévinas's view that theoretical ontology, when left to its own terms, finally leads to frustration because of the sense that the freedom that invests the categories of understanding is arbitrary, perhaps even dogmatic or naïve. What is lacking is the possibility of critique. Any critique of the categories has to come from beyond the autarchic theoretical practice that legitimates knowing. In short, it has to come from the other, specifically another person, who comes to one from beyond thought and calls one's thinking into question. Lévinas terms this calling into question of sameness by otherness "ethics." Ethics, as Lévinas

uses the term, does not deal so much with a moral theory as it does with the intersubjective encounter between self and other that accomplishes the critical essence of knowledge.

In the second section of *Totality and Infinity*, Lévinas analyzes the basic egoism of life. He maintains that human life, before it is a theoretical or practical life, is driven by enjoyment and happiness. As he puts it, "life is love of life." The drive to life is worked out in terms of the people nourishing themselves on and living from the world they encounter. Lévinas calls this drive egoistic because throughout the course of a person's life, the goal of enjoyment remains sovereign. In other words, the subject of existence is autonomous, a law unto itself, dictating the terms in which the world is met, engaged, and consumed. The life of enjoyment is thus the essence of what Lévinas has called the "drive to sameness."

The other is reduced to sameness through labor. A sense of a person as a task or project to be completed has always existed, gaining prominence after the dawn of modern science and technology. As free individuals, people decide their fates and determine their own courses of action. To safeguard and promote the liberty of individuals to maximize their enjoyment of the world, political and economic structures such as liberal democracy and free-market capitalism are inevitably devised. However, the enjoyment that "lives from" the world must eventually acknowledge its dependence on others and thus call into question the sovereign movement of an autonomous person. Lévinas argues that in the very play of enjoyment and happiness, human freedom is shown to be arbitrary and unjust. As he puts it, only the freedom that can be ashamed of itself founds truth.

The Face of the Other

Section three carries out a phenomenological analysis of the "face of the other" as the occasion for redirecting one's freedom to responsibility and eventually continuing on into justice and peace. The face presents the exteriority that calls into question the machinations of thought and thus makes thought's totality and sameness tremble. Lévinas turns to the face of another person because it, better than anything else, refuses to be contained by the theoretical gesture that threatens to comprehend it. It is not the bare physicality of the face that interests Lévinas but its "ethical resistance," or its capacity to say no to all the meaning bestowals people would otherwise confer upon it. The face is thus the mark of the integrity, even sanctity or holiness, of the other person.

The face manifests itself primarily as speech. The face "speaks," not only in terms of the phonetic words it may utter but also in the very expression of bearing witness to itself. This expression, which has little to do with the communication of the other person's interior states, founds language and communication because it evokes from one, if one is attentive, a response. Language is not enacted in a sovereign consciousness but comes to be in the ethical relation that acknowledges and welcomes the other person. Language is created in the community freely established across the distance between beings. The essence of language is discourse, the relation with the other. The first and primary rationality would thus live in discourse. In this analysis of discourse as the basis for language, Lévinas finds the occasion for the redefinition of reason as the welcoming of the face of the other.

In the fourth and final section, Lévinas gives several short and somewhat enigmatic analyses of love and eros, fecundity, filiality, and fraternity, all with the aim of addressing how the ethical relation of the self-other is to be worked out in a history governed by violence. In certain respects, he is invoking an eschatological time in which the particularity of the self-other relationship is expanded into a universal program of justice and peace.

Lévinas's Impact

Totality and Infinity was the work that first brought Lévinas international acclaim. Because of its difficulty and originality, however, it was easily misunderstood. In the years following its publication, Lévinas wrote several essays, as well as the equally important *Otherwise than Being*, that refined and developed its themes. His work was appropriated by Jacques Derrida, for instance, because it manifests the supreme attention to and welcoming of otherness that Derrida thinks is vital to the work of deconstruction. His

work has also been influential within the fields of psychoanalysis, literary theory, feminism, and political theory, primarily because of Lévinas's profound analysis of the face of the other and its dissimulation in the history of thought. More recently, his work has been of great interest to theologians interested in how speech and thought about God as the "supremely other" is to be possible. There is little doubt that Lévinas's work, beginning with *Totality and Infinity*, will continue to exert its influence, for in it we find one of the most serious, and certainly one of the most profound, reflections on the violent character of human thought and history.

Norman Wirzba

Additional Reading

Bernasconi, Robert, and Simon Critchley, eds. *Rereading Levinas*. Bloomington: Indiana University Press, 1991. This collection of essays by several of Emmanuel Lévinas's major interpreters covers a wide range of themes, including the philosopher in relation to deconstruction, his later works, Lévinas and the feminine, and his thought in relation to the philosopher Maurice Blanchot, psychoanalysis, and the care of animals. It includes a lengthy essay by Jacques Derrida on Lévinas's later work.

Cohen, Richard A., ed. *Face to Face with Levinas*. Albany: State University of New York Press, 1986. This early collection of essays on Lévinas is valuable for its contextualization of Lévinas's thought. It includes an important and accessible interview conducted by Richard Kearney that covers a wide range of philosophical issues. Several other essays deal with Lévinas's method and his relation to the history of philosophy.

Davis, Colin. *Levinas: An Introduction*. Notre Dame, Ind.: University of Notre Dame Press, 1996. Davis, who is not a philosopher, introduces the broad themes of Lévinas's work in a style accessible to those who are not conversant with European philosophy.

Derrida, Jacques. *Adieu à Emmanuel Lévinas*. Paris: Galilée, 1997. Provides expert criticism and interpretation of Lévinas's work.

Gibbs, Robert. *Correlations in Rosenzweig and Levinas*. Princeton, N.J.: Princeton University Press, 1992. This volume focuses primarily on

Lévinas's relation to and development of Jewish thought. It highlights in fresh and interesting ways, via discussions on language, reason, and social theory, what a Jewish critique of Greek philosophical practice might resemble.

Llewelyn, John. *Emmanuel Levinas: The Genealogy of Ethics*. London: Routledge, 1995. This text provides a more advanced interpretation of Lévinas's overall work. Llewelyn traces the chronological and logical development of Lévinas's ideas, arguing that his many texts form a systematic whole. Included in this volume are chapters on Lévinas's early work on death and time, the significance of the face, the nature of responsibility and language, and the question of God.

Peperzak, Adriaan. *Beyond: The Philosophy of Emmanuel Levinas*. Evanston, Ill.: Northwestern University Press, 1997. An important collection of essays, some expository, some critical, written for the more advanced reader.

_____, ed. *Ethics as First Philosophy: The Significance of Emmanuel Lévinas for Philosophy, Literature and Religion*. London: Routledge, 1995. This wide-ranging collection of papers was first presented at an international conference on the impact, potential or realized, of Lévinas's thought on other disciplines such as theology, psychoanalysis, and literary theory. Most of Lévinas's major interpreters are represented.

_____. *To the Other: An Introduction to the Philosophy of Emmanuel Levinas*. West Lafayette, Ind.: Purdue University Press, 1993. Peperzak's text is an excellent introduction to the range of Lévinas's work. It provides a broad outline of Lévinas's overall work and then sharpens various themes with a close reading of and commentary on the essay "Philosophy and the Idea of the Infinite" (which appears in the volume). Peperzak concludes with interpretive essays on Lévinas's two major philosophical works *Totality and Infinity* and *Otherwise than Being*. A useful bibliographical essay is included.

Norman Wirzba

C. I. Lewis

One of the leading American philosophers of his generation, Lewis responded to developments in logic and science by combining philosophical analysis with pragmatism. He also drew renewed attention to Kantian ethics.

Principal philosophical works: *A Survey of Symbolic Logic*, 1918; *Mind and the World-Order: Outline of a Theory of Knowledge*, 1929; *Symbolic Logic*, 1932 (with Cooper Harold Langford); *An Analysis of Knowledge and Valuation*, 1946; *The Ground and Nature of the Right*, 1955; *Our Social Inheritance*, 1957; *Values and Imperatives*, 1969; *Collected Papers*, 1970.

Born: April 12, 1883; Stoneham, Massachusetts
Died: February 3, 1964; Menlo Park, California

Early Life

Clarence Irving Lewis grew up in small Massachusetts towns and in the White Mountains of New Hampshire. Later he commented that mountains and deep woods had always had special meaning for him. His parents were orthodoxly religious. His father, who worked in a shoe factory, was quiet and thoughtful and had strong convictions concerning social betterment. He belonged to the Temperance movement, admired Fabian socialism, and joined the Knights of Labor. After involvement in a strike, he was blacklisted by the employers, losing both his job and his home. The family was condemned to years of meager existence.

To help his family, C. I. Lewis early began to undertake part-time and summer farm and factory work. When he was thirteen, he started to think speculatively about the cosmos, questioning the biblical account of it. He later described this as the period of the most intense and furious thinking he ever experienced, his native skepticism clashing explosively with his orthodox upbringing. When he was fifteen and doing summer farm work in the White Mountains, his employer, an elderly woman, encouraged him by revealing that she too had heretical thoughts and by listening at length to his. A year or two later, he began to read about the history of Greek philosophy and found that many of his speculations had been anticipated by the pre-Socratics.

Lewis received a solid education at the public high school of Haverhill and determined to go on to college. He entered Harvard in 1902. Tuition at that time was $150 per year; he had accumulated enough savings from his earlier work so that he was able to enter, and by continuing to do part-time work as a waiter and tutor, he was able to pay his way. He hastened to take his bachelor's degree in three years, however, to minimize expense.

At Harvard, President Charles W. Eliot's system of free electives was in place, and Lewis chose to study mainly philosophy. This was the golden age of Harvard philosophy, and his professors included philosophers and psychologists such as Josiah Royce, William James, Hugo Münsterburg, and later George Santayana and Ralph Barton Perry. It was Royce whom Lewis described as his own paradigm of a philosopher; Lewis admired what he called Royce's ponderous cogency and respected Royce's absolute idealism, though he did not accept it.

After completing his undergraduate program, Lewis found work as a teacher of English for three years. During this period he married his high-school sweetheart, and soon their first child was born. In 1908, Lewis returned to Harvard for graduate work in philosophy, again studying speedily in order to save money. He earned his doctoral degree in 1910, and in 1911 he secured a

C. I. Lewis. *(AP/Wide World Photos)*

teaching position in philosophy at the University of California, Berkeley.

Life's Work

At Harvard, Royce had encouraged Lewis to study new developments in symbolic and mathematical logic, and at Berkeley, Lewis began teaching in this area. Feeling the need for a better textbook, he set out to write *A Survey of Symbolic Logic*. This was a useful contribution at the time but in 1932 was superseded by *Symbolic Logic*, which Lewis wrote in collaboration with C. H. Langford. Both books devoted most of their space to presenting in accessible form results originated by others.

There is, however, one new contribution to logic that Lewis introduced in these books: the theory of what he called "strict implication." This was in opposition to philosopher Bertrand Russell, who had studied the truth-functional conditional, which he had called "material implication." A truth-functional conditional with false antecedent is true regardless of whether its consequent is true; Russell had confusingly expressed this point by saying that a false proposition implies any proposition. Lewis was incensed at this, because in the usual language of logic, to say that one proposition implies another is to say that the latter can validly be inferred from the former; however, it is not true in general that from a false proposition one may validly infer every proposition.

Lewis's response was to introduce the notion of strict implication and to construct a formal system for it. Strict implication is the relation that holds between one proposition and another when, if the former is true, the latter must with logical necessity also be true. Lewis drew up sets of axioms for the theory of strict implication, employing also the correlative notion of possibility: a proposition being understood to be possible in this sense when and only when its negation is not logically impossible. In Lewis's system, an impossible proposition does strictly imply any proposition, but no proposition strictly implies others merely because of its falsity. Lewis had begun the branch of logic that has come to be called "modal logic."

In 1920, Lewis was called back to Harvard to join its philosophy faculty. He remained until his retirement in 1953. Lewis became an admired teacher at Harvard, noted for his eloquence in courses on the theory of knowledge and on Immanuel Kant's philosophy. Tall and dignified, usually in a tweed suit, he had a mustache and often wore a pince-nez.

Lewis's position as a significant American philosopher rests primarily on two large works, *Mind and the World-Order* and *An Analysis of*

Knowledge and Valuation. Both books deal mainly with epistemological issues.

The earlier book is the more successful of the two because of its livelier style and its greater timeliness. The philosophical issue most prominent in this book is the nature of a priori knowledge, which had become a source of controversy in the 1920's. Lewis was confident that there is an important distinction to be drawn between propositions such as those of logic and mathematics, which are knowable a priori without need of sensory evidence, and empirical propositions knowable only on the basis of sensory observation.

Rationalists had held that the human faculty of reason sees intellectually into the essential nature of reality, providing us with substantive information a priori; Kant had held that our faculty of sensibility provides us with pure intuitions that inform us a priori about the structure of space and time. Lewis rejected these views, holding that the mind cannot acquire information in such ways. Lewis's view of a priori knowledge was that it is wholly analytic; it does not convey any substantive information but has to do only with the conceptual structures we create. We choose what concepts to employ in classifying the patterns of our experience. The set of concepts we choose to use changes and evolves over time. Whatever concepts we employ at a given time, there will be necessary truths about the relationships of their meanings, truths that we can know a priori merely by reflection on what we mean by our words or symbols.

Lewis went on to add that, in his view, a priori knowledge is made by mind and is capable of being altered. He called his view "conceptualistic pragmatism," thereby suggesting linkage with the pragmatic philosophies of Charles S. Peirce, William James, and John Dewey. Lewis recognized that they did not share any clear common doctrine, but still, for Lewis, pragmatism stood for the idea that human activity can create truth. He thus seemed committed to the exciting but disturbing idea that any a priori truth can be altered by us if we choose to do so.

Much that Lewis had to say about a priori knowledge is impressive and plausible. There is an unresolved tension, though, between his insistence, on one hand, that a priori truths are neces-

sarily true, and his insistence, on the other hand, that they are under our control. If it is a necessary truth that five plus seven equals twelve, then this sum cannot be otherwise, and if it cannot be otherwise, we cannot make it be otherwise.

Here it may be that Lewis was not distinguishing sufficiently between the truth that five plus seven equals twelve and the symbolism we use to convey this truth: $5 + 7 = 12$. We could, of course, change our symbolic conventions, letting the numeral 5 stand for six and the numeral 7 stand for eight, in which case the expression "$5 + 7 = 12$" could convey something false rather than something true. Yet this would not mean that we had made five and seven no longer equal to twelve; it would mean only that we had altered our way of expressing this necessary, unalterable truth.

In *An Analysis of Knowledge and Valuation,* Lewis gives more emphasis to elaborating his theory of empirical knowledge. He introduces several distinctive notions of his own. He speaks of what he calls expressive statements, which he thinks of as worded in a private language one can use to formulate for oneself the indubitable content of one's immediate sense experience. What he calls "terminating judgments" are predictions involving expressive statements. A terminating judgment says that if some specified sense experiences occur, and if one consciously acts in a certain way, then in all probability other specified sense experiences will occur. Such terminating judgments often can be decisively verified or falsified. Nonterminating judgments are complex logical combinations of innumerable terminating judgments; they can never be finally verified or falsified. Lewis's view is that ordinary judgments about physical objects are nonterminating judgments.

This position looks rather like phenomenalism, that is, the reduction of talk about the external world to talk about immediate experience. Lewis does not want to dissolve the physical world into sense experience, however. For him, it is only what he calls the "intensional meaning" of ordinary judgments about physical objects that can be translated into complexes of expressive statements. Their denotational meaning he holds to be independent of the intensional meaning. Here Lewis seems committed to something like Kant's distinction between phenomena and things-in-themselves. The view is puzzling, because we might have expected that the intensional meaning of a judgment would determine its denotation; it is not easy to see how denotation is to be understood if it is independent of intension.

The final section of *An Analysis of Knowledge and Valuation* deals with value judgments. Rejecting all noncognitivist theories, Lewis defends a form of naturalism, arguing that value judgments are a type of empirical judgment. There are immediate experiences of satisfaction of which we can be aware, and ordinary value judgments are empirical predictions that such experiences will arise in connection with specified objects.

In his last decade, Lewis devoted himself mainly to writing about ethics. His *The Ground and Nature of the Right*, *Our Social Inheritance*, and the posthumous *Values and Imperatives* belong to this period. He saw moral obligation as necessarily linked with value: One's moral obligation is to do what will promote value. This view is akin to utilitarianism, but, contrary to the utilitarians, Lewis held that there are incommensurable kinds of good experiences, so we cannot establish what our moral obligations are merely by adding up the quantities of potential good that alternative actions would probably achieve. Lewis did not discuss the objection that utilitarianism is incompatible with justice, an objection that some later philosophers have emphasized.

Lewis advocated something like a Kantian categorical imperative: his principle that like cases should be judged the same way, or that one ought always to abide by universal rules applicable to everyone. He calls this a "rational principle" and presumably would have classified it as an analytic truth, although, as he states it, it seems rather substantive.

Influence

Lewis made an original contribution to logic by inventing modal logic. His work in epistemology helped spread in the United States a major new view of a priori knowledge as wholly analytic. His work on empirical knowledge and on value theory has been less widely influential, but his view of ethics contributed to a renewal of interest in Kantian ethical principles.

Stephen F. Barker

Mind and the World-Order

Type of philosophy: Epistemology, pragmatism
First published: 1929
Principal ideas advanced:

◊ A priori truths are definitive in nature; they specify the real because of antecedently determined criteria of what is to be called "real."

◊ Empirical truth is never more than probable, because descriptions of matters of fact are hypothetical propositions, pragmatic in character.

◊ Knowledge is the result of interpreting the sensuously given by means of a priori concepts; thus, there is no contradiction between the relativity of knowledge (to the concepts) and the independence of the object (understood in terms of the given).

◊ To know is to have reason to expect that, were we to act in certain ways, our experience would present the character we expect.

◊ The a priori has its origin in mind, but its applicability is a function of the world order; a world which would not, relative to some interpretative act of mind, exhibit order is practically inconceivable.

Pragmatism, sometimes called the characteristically American philosophy, is usually considered to have been best exemplified in the writings of William James, Charles S. Peirce, and John Dewey. The position is sometimes called "humanism" (for example, the point of view developed by the English philosopher F. C. S. Schiller) and sometimes called "instrumentalism." Although there were many variations in the specific philosophies of these individuals, they shared a belief in the relativity of truth to the concrete verification processes and to the practical role that humanity plays in the world. In general they also were in agreement in being more or less hostile toward metaphysics, at least of an absolutistic sort, and feeling that a view of the universe that "made no difference" to the common person, either in the sense that it could not be confirmed or disproved by observable phenomena or in the sense that it did not help one to live a better life, was really meaningless, and that indulgence in speculation of this kind was a waste of time.

C. I. Lewis had many of the same interests that

Peirce did, and like Peirce he made important contributions to the fields of the philosophy of science and symbolic logic. Lewis's *A Survey of Symbolic Logic* (1918) is one of the standard works in this area. In *Mind and the World-Order*, this broad knowledge of the nature of deductive systems and of the difference between a priori and a posteriori cognition is used to develop a position that Lewis called "conceptualistic pragmatism." It has much in common with the views of the earlier pragmatists, and Lewis frankly acknowledges his indebtedness to these philosophers, but it also has certain distinctive aspects. For this reason it deserves careful consideration as an important philosophical position. Lewis modified pragmatism to make it more compatible with the methodologies of the mathematical and natural sciences.

Three Principles

Lewis attempts to reduce his point of view to three principles: First, a priori truths are not forms of intuition or categories that determine the content of experience; they are, rather, definitive in nature and limit reality only in the sense that whatever is called "real" is selected from experience by means of criteria that are antecedently determined. Second, the application of any a priori concepts to a particular experience is hypothetical because it is instrumental or pragmatic; consequently, empirical truth is never more than probable. Third, no belief in the conformity of experience to the mind or its categories is required, for a complete nonconformity of these two aspects of knowledge is inconceivable.

Definition of Philosophy

To explain these principles Lewis begins with an analysis of philosophical method. Philosophy is not "another science," nor is it a substitute for science. It is the critical and reflective application of the mind to experience. It deals with what is already familiar to us, but it analyzes this familiarity into the clear ideas that constitute it. Philosophy begins with the experiences of reality, goodness, and validity, which we all have, and attempts to clarify these notions by critical consideration of what is implicitly in them and therefore does not transcend experience. (A person with no sense of reality will not acquire one by

the study of metaphysics.)

More specifically, this analysis of experience involves the discovery of *categories*—the formulation of the criteria of reality. Experience does not determine its own categories; *mind* provides these criteria and they are imposed upon the given by our active attitude. Philosophy is not empirical if this claim means that it takes what is merely given to the mind as the totality of experience; nor is it analytic in the sense that it accepts a ready-made experience. Philosophy is not rationalistic if this claim means that it forces reality into a procrustean bed, but it is rationalistic in the sense that it is particularly concerned with that aspect of experience that the mind contributes by its interpretive act.

Knowledge

Analysis of knowledge reveals two elements: the concept and the sensuously given. The former is the product of thought; the latter is merely presented and involves no such activity. The conceptual element is a priori, and philosophy can be defined as the study of the a priori in the sense that it undertakes to define, or explicate, such concepts as the *good*, the *right*, the *valid*, and the *real*. The pure concept and the sensuously given do not limit each other; they are mutually independent. Knowledge is the result of interpreting the given by means of concepts. Consequently, there is no knowledge in the mere awareness of the given. Furthermore, all empirical knowledge is only probable because it is based on the application of a temporally extended pattern of actual and possible experiences to something that is immediately given, and this pattern may have to be revised in view of what future experiences disclose. However, the independence of the conceptual and the given in no way prevents us from having valid knowledge. Nor does it in any way restrict the possibility of finding concepts under which any conceivable experience can be subsumed.

Experience: Given and Conceptual

There are two theories of experience, Lewis argues, which do not accept the partition of experience into the given and the conceptual. One of these eliminates the conceptual entirely and reduces experience to the given. This theory is exemplified by Henri Bergson and the mystics. Its inadequacy can be clearly seen in its inability to handle the fact of error. If mind is pure receptivity, that with which it coincides in knowledge must always have the same objectivity, and we can never make mistakes. The other theory eliminates the given and reduces knowledge to the conceptual. This is the position of the idealists. Its inadequacy lies in its failure to recognize in knowledge an element that we do not create by thinking, one that we cannot, in general, displace or alter. This element is always ineffable, for if it is describable, concepts must have been brought in. It is an abstraction, for it never exists in isolation in any experience or state of consciousness. It is given *in*, not *before*, experience. It is made up of "qualia," which are repeatable and recognizable but have no names. They are fundamentally different from the universals of logic. They may be characterized by such terms as "the given," "the data of sense," "the sensuous," and "the given in its feeling character," provided one does not in the use of this terminology give the qualia merely a psychological status.

The conceptual element of experience, on the other hand, is quite different from the given. It is the construction, or interpretation, which is put upon the given. It is not to be understood in terms of any imagery or any psychological state of an individual mind. On the contrary, it is defined as "that meaning which must be common to two minds when they understand each other by the use of a substantive or its equivalent." Verifying the commonness of meaning in the case of any concept takes one of two routes: exhibiting the denotation by a behavioral act, or employing a definition. The former is unsatisfactory because it does not enable us to determine *uniquely* the meaning of the concept. The latter specifies the meaning directly in terms of a pattern of other concepts: A is defined in terms of B and C, and these are defined by other concepts. This is obviously a process that is never completed, but it does enable us to ascertain a genuine identity of meaning in two minds. It should not be interpreted as an analysis of meaning in the sense of a repeated dissection of a meaning into other meanings until one is reached which is no longer relational; *every* concept is a pattern of other concepts. To argue this definition of concepts on the grounds (a) that when we use a concept we "seldom have in mind" such a pattern of concepts, and (b) that we may have a meaning which we cannot state in terms of such a pattern without further thought, is to overlook the fact that concepts play a role in knowledge which is primarily practical; meanings may be exhibited implicitly in the consistency of behavior, as well as explicitly in the statement of definitions.

Perceptual Knowledge

Having indicated that experience consists of two elements, the given and the conceptual, Lewis proceeds to ask what is involved in our perceptual knowledge of objects. His first task is to show that there is no knowledge by mere acquaintance; that is, knowledge *always* transcends the immediately given. This view requires him to distinguish, on the one hand, between qualia and our immediate awareness of them, and, on the other, between objects and our knowledge of them.

Qualia are subjective and have no names in normal language; they can be indicated by such phrases as "looks like" or "appears to be." Because they are immediately given, they have no need of verification and we cannot possibly be mistaken about them. However, if we take the simplest concepts, for example, "blue" or "round," we can see that what they embrace are not qualia but patterns of relations. This is shown by the steps that we would take in order to confirm our judgment that a given penny, say, is round: We might walk around it or view it from a different angle, we might pick it up and turn it in our fingers, we might move toward it or away from it. In each case, we are attempting to confirm certain predictions that are involved in the supposition that it really *is* round. If these do not turn out as anticipated, we withdraw our judgment.

The objective reality of the property consists in what would verify it and in what would disprove it. Thus, the existence of an objective property is not constituted by the presentation of a given quale but by the presentation of a given quale *plus* the concept of an ordered relation of different qualia tied up with certain conditions of behavior. The concept *means* this pattern of qualia. It therefore extends temporally beyond the given quale, permitting the pattern to be confirmed or disproved as an interpretation of the given, and it always prescribes possible ways of acting toward the presented object. *Without* such a pattern we could never identify an object.

However—unfortunately, perhaps—even with such a pattern, we cannot surely identify an object, because the pattern always contains unrealized future experiences and because a certain pattern may serve to identify different qualia. Also, different patterns may be applicable to the same quale. Our perceptual knowledge of an object is consequently more than mere acquaintance with a quale; when we ascribe objectivity to a presentation, the "acquaintance with" changes into "knowledge about" and we have a conceptual interpretation of what is presented. Knowledge consists of that part of the flux of experience that we ascribe to ourselves and that we change by our activities, and of that part that is objective and that we cannot predicate of ourselves. The world is bigger than the content of our direct experience only because we are active beings, only because we can say to what is revealed in our experience, "If we should do this, then we should experience that," and we find that the carrying out of these actions often reveals new truths about the world.

No Knowledge Without Interpretation

In further elaboration of this theory of knowledge, Lewis shows that the examination of the problem of how we know has been guided since René Descartes by an erroneous belief in the incompatibility of three alternatives: knowledge is not relative to the mind; the content of knowledge is not the real; and the real is dependent on mind. He proceeds, first, to show that there is no contradiction between the relativity of knowledge and the independence of the object. Indeed, relativity *requires* an independent character in what is thus relative. The fact, for example, that the weight of an object can be determined only relatively to a standard, such as a pound or a gram, does not imply that weight "in itself" has no meaning and that the object is therefore outside the category of weight. The concept of weight is an interpretation that *transcends* this relativity because it is a relational pattern exhibited by the independently real object. Furthermore, one should not, on the grounds that mind

cannot be known, argue from the dependence of knowledge on mind to the conclusion that such knowledge cannot be of the real.

For I do know my mind, Lewis argues, though I learn it only in its commerce with real objects. In other words, I can learn the relation between mind and object by varying the object and noting the variation in its appearances and subjective manifestations, and by varying the mind and noting the resulting variations in the object. Finally, the fact that mind may have unrecognized limitations in its capacity to know the real does not imply either that knowledge is deceitful or that we must forever remain ignorant of the real.

Having shown that there is no knowledge without interpretation, Lewis examines the consequences of this fact. One of these is that there must be at least *some* knowledge that is a priori. The reasons for this are easy to see. Interpretation represents an activity of the mind and is always subject to test by future experience. The mere fact that interpretation reflects the character of past experience is not sufficient; there must be an assumed orderliness in experience that will entitle us to *expect* a certain kind of future on the basis of what the past has disclosed. This knowledge that nature is orderly must be *necessarily* true and independent of the particular character of experience. Knowledge of this kind is a priori.

Explaining A Priori Knowledge

After proving that certain historical conceptions of the a priori, which identify it with that which is psychologically undeniable, that which is self-evident, or that whose denial implies its affirmation, are erroneous, Lewis turns to an explanation of the a priori. The a priori has nothing to do with anything that is inescapable; it always permits of alternatives. It has its origin in an act of mind, thus exhibiting mind's creativity and not its dependence on anything inside or outside itself. Mind is, of course, limited in the sense that our perceptual organs are restricted to a certain range of stimuli; dogs can smell things that we cannot smell, and eagles can see things that we cannot see. However, these things are not beyond the range of our *conception*, though they are beyond the range of our *perception*. Could there be anything, then, which *is* beyond the range of our conception? Obviously not, for in saying that an object is conceivable, we are really saying something whose opposite makes no sense; the alternative to what can be experienced could not even be phrased. However, although the range of the *conceivable* cannot be determined by any act of mind, the range of the *real* might be so determined. Science, in fact, does precisely this. It prescribes the character that reality must possess. Consequently, when we say that we experience dream objects, or fairies, or mermaids, science tells us that these kinds of "objects" cannot possibly be real.

A priori principles are required to limit reality; they are not required to limit experience. An interpretation is a priori only in the sense that it prescribes for a particular case and is thus not subject to recall even if the particular should fail to conform to the prescription. On the other hand, an interpretation is a posteriori if it is abandoned when the case does not fit. Let us suppose, for example, that we set up the categorial interpretation of scientific reality as "the realm in which every event has a cause." Now let us further assume that we come upon what is presumably a genuine miracle. We have two alternatives: we can say that the miracle did not really happen, or we can say that real events can happen without any natural causes. If real events must always have natural causes, then the miracle could not have been real; but if real events generally have causes (but might not), then the particular case could constitute an exception to the generalization. In the former case our interpretation is a priori; it can be maintained in the face of all experience, *no matter what*. In the latter case our interpretation is empirical and subject to disconfirmation in terms of experience. Lewis illustrates his point by the story of the man who boastfully made out a list of the names of all the men whom he could whip. When one burly man, whose name appeared on the list, approached him belligerently and insisted that he could not be whipped, the maker of the list said, "All right; then I'll just rub your name off." His original boast had no a priori character.

The apparent problem, of course, is how to get the empirical and the a priori together. However, the real problem, according to Lewis, is not to "get them together" but to discover their copresence in all cases of knowledge. The analysis of knowledge reveals the following five phases: (1) the immediate awareness of the given, exemplified by "This looks round"; (2) judgments about presented objects, exemplified in "This object *is* round"; (3) the a priori development of abstract conceptual schemes, exemplified in such mathematical judgments as "In a Euclidean triangle, the sum of the angles equals 180 degrees"; (4) the categorical knowledge implied in our interpretation of reality, exemplified in the judgment, "If this is a round object, then if I change my position in a certain way, it will appear elliptical"; and (5) empirical generalizations, such as "All swans are white."

Misunderstanding is sure to arise if we fail to distinguish phase 1 from phase 2. Merely to be aware of an appearance (a quale) is, as we have seen, not knowledge. However, to judge that an object *is* round, rather than *appears* round, is knowledge. What makes it knowledge is the fact that it rests for its corroboration on a judgment of the kind indicated in phase 4: "If this object is round, then I can expect certain other appearances to reveal themselves." In fact, when I say that it is round, I assert implicitly *everything the failure of which would falsify the statement*. This is a priori and regulative in character, for it commits me to saying, "If I find that the presented object does *not* confirm my predictions of its other appearances, I shall deny that it is round."

An a priori proposition always has this characteristic. For example, the statement "All swans are birds" is a priori because if any creature originally designated as a swan were discovered not to be a bird, the designation "swan" would be withdrawn. On the other hand, an empirical generalization, such as "All swans are white," might be contradicted if we found a black swan. Thus, an a priori proposition does not assert any limitation of experience; it asserts merely that we are tentatively trying out a certain categorical system that is so compactly organized that if one of its concepts does not fit reality, its other concepts will also not fit, and we should therefore abandon it and try another. Only if we have such a rigid scheme can we have knowledge of reality at all, for if an object is to be identifiable in terms of a certain concept, we must be provided with a criterion by means of which we can decide whether the object exemplifies the concept. If we were to change our criterion whenever an object failed to exemplify it, we could never have any criteria and we could never have knowledge. It *does* follow, of course, that our knowledge of objects can be probable only, never certain, for no matter how many predictions concerning the expected appearances of the object have been confirmed, there is always the possibility that the next one will not be; all verification is partial and a matter of degree. If we demand, therefore, something more than this, and require that in order to save us from skepticism empirical knowledge must be *certain*, we are doomed to disappointment.

The Question of Order

Lewis concludes with a chapter entitled "Experience and Order." If all knowledge is in terms of concepts and concepts are of the mind, the application of concepts to experience demands a certain orderliness in the world. The givenness of certain qualia must be a clue to certain expected sequences, and the occurrence of these sequences in the past must be a valid ground for our belief in their occurrence in the future. This is commonly called the "assumption of the uniformity of nature."

Lewis tries to show just what is involved in this necessary "uniformity." It can be expressed in three principles. Principle A says that "it must be false that every identifiable entity in experience is equally associated with every other." This assumes merely that there are *some* recurrent sequences in nature; that is, there are things of such nature that concepts can be applied to them. Principle B states that whenever we have cases in which Principle A does not apply (namely, in which the sequences seem to be "random"), we can extend these situations through certain identifiable entities in such a way as to make them satisfy Principle A. For example, if we can find no order among events, we can pass to simpler elements by deeper analysis, or to a larger whole containing the original constituents, or to a higher level of abstraction by disregarding irrelevant aspects. In each case, we will find order where there had previously appeared to be none. Principle C affirms that "the statistical prediction of the future from the past cannot be generally invalid, because whatever is future to any given

past, is in turn past for some future." This states simply that the person who uses as a basis for prediction a statistical generalization that is continually revised in terms of actual observations cannot fail to make more successful predictions than one who does not.

A world that exhibits these principles is certainly not an inconceivable one. Indeed, since all we want to assure ourselves of is the *probability* of our apprehensions and our generalizations, not their *certainty*, we can hardly imagine a world that would *not* provide a basis for such knowledge. For certain modes of cognition and irreducible variety in the world would be completely irrelevant. Moreover, our demand for uniqueness in the individual thing seems to require a world of unlimited variety. However, in most modes of understanding the uniformity is not *discovered* in the world but *imposed on the world* by our own categorical procedure. What we are really saying, therefore, when we assert that the world is orderly is merely that there must be apprehensible things and objective facts—and to this conclusion there seems to be no conceivable alternative except the nonexistence of everything.

A. Cornelius Benjamin, updated by John K. Roth

Additional Reading

Colella, E. Paul. *C. I. Lewis and the Society Theory of Conceptualistic Pragmatism: The Individual and the Good Social Order.* San Francisco: Mellen Research University Press, 1992. Examines the individual and the social order in Lewis's version of pragmatism.

Gowans, Christopher W. "Two Concepts of the Given in C. I. Lewis: Realism and Foundationalism." *Journal of the History of Philosophy* 27, no. 4 (October, 1989): 573-591. This essay examines realism and foundationalism in Lewis's beliefs.

Luizzi, Vincet. *A Naturalistic Theory of Justice: Critical Commentary on, and Selected Readings from, C. I. Lewis' Ethics.* Washington, D.C.: University Press of America, 1981. This volume looks at ethics and justice from Lewis's point of view.

Quine, Willard V. "Truth by Convention." Reprinted in *Readings in Philosophical Analysis*, edited by Herbert Feigl and Wilfred Sellars. New York: Appleton-Century-Crofts, 1949. Lewis's younger colleague Quine examines the view that a priori statements are based on conventions of language.

_____. "Two Dogmas of Empiricism." In *From a Logical Point of View*. Cambridge, Mass.: Harvard University Press, 1953. This famous article attacks the view, held by Lewis and many others, that there is a legitimate philosophical distinction between a priori and empirical statements.

Rosenthal, Sandra B. *The Pragmatic a Priori: A Study in the Epistemology of C. I. Lewis*. St. Louis: W. H. Green, 1976. This volume looks primarily at the epistemology of Lewis while emphasizing the pragmatic dimension.

Saydah, J. Roger. *The Ethical Theory of Clarence Irving Lewis*. Athens: Ohio University Press, 1969. This volume presents a detailed study of the ethical position held by Lewis.

Schilpp, Paul Arthur, ed. *The Philosophy of C. I. Lewis*. La Salle, Ill.: Open Court, 1968. Contains an autobiographical statement by Lewis, more than a dozen essays on his philosophy by others, his own fairly brief replies to those comments, and a bibliography of his writings.

West, Cornel. *The American Evasion of Philosophy: A Genealogy of Pragmatism*. Madison: University of Wisconsin Press, 1989. This readable survey of American pragmatism contains only a few references to Lewis because it emphasizes the social dimension. It is nevertheless helpful for placing Lewis in relation to other pragmatists.

Stephen F. Barker

Lin Yutang

Lin's descriptions of Chinese philosophy and character in his nonfiction and novels were major sources through which Western readers learned to appreciate Chinese life and thought.

Principal philosophical works: *My Country and My People*, 1935; *The Importance of Living*, 1937; *The Vigil of a Nation*, 1944; *From Pagan to Christian*, 1959.

Born: October 10, 1895; Changchow, Fukien Province, China
Died: March 26, 1976; Hong Kong

Early Life

Lin Yutang, the son of a Chinese Presbyterian minister, was educated in missionary schools that taught him Calvinist theology and forbade him to study Chinese philosophy or participate in Chinese folk traditions. From 1911 to 1916, he went to St. John's College in Shanghai, a college supported by American Episcopalians, where all major courses were taught in English. His father, who had reluctantly sold the family home to put an older son through college, was forced to borrow money to finance Lin's education but refused to help Lin's brilliant older sister continue her schooling. When she died of bubonic plague shortly after her marriage, Lin felt pangs of guilt; he was thereafter sympathetic to Chinese feminists. While at St. John's, Lin began to doubt Christian doctrine and abandoned his intent to train for the ministry.

From 1916 to 1919, he taught English at Tsinghua College in Beijing and immersed himself in Chinese literature and folklore. In 1919, he agreed to an arranged marriage with a neighbor's daughter. Although his wife remained a pious Christian while Lin drifted further and further away from his original faith, the marriage lasted. In 1919, Lin took advantage of a meager scholarship to go to the United States with his wife for a year of graduate study in comparative literature at Harvard; then he and his wife moved to Ger-many, where the hyperinflation of the German mark greatly improved the standard of living their few dollars had previously allowed. After attending classes at Jena University, Lin earned a Ph.D. in linguistics from Leipzig University in 1923, submitting a thesis on archaic Chinese phonetics.

From 1923 to 1926, Lin was a professor of English at Beijing University, where he supported student protests against the weakness of the Chinese government in resisting foreign aggression and became involved in street fights alongside his students. When he learned that he was on a list of fifty radical professors who were to be arrested and killed, he fled south and taught at Amoy University (now Xiamen University) and in Hankou in 1926 and 1927. For six months in 1927, Lin served as assistant to the minister of foreign affairs in the Nationalist government before abandoning active politics, moving to Shanghai in 1928, and devoting himself to writing.

In 1932, he founded a humor magazine, *Lunyu banyuegan* (analects fortnightly), which became one of the most popular magazines in China, especially among college students. In 1934 and 1935, Lin started two other magazines in which he encouraged individualistic expression through brief informal essays. The irony and sarcasm with which Lin commented on life and politics in China won him the title Master of Humor and also provided a technique for social criticism that kept him out of jail as he tested the Nationalist government's tight censorship controls. Lin satirized the Nationalist government, its Communist critics, and traditionalists longing to retreat into the imperial past. As a result, he was attacked from all angles of the political spectrum. He received death threats from people he offended and was criticized as trivial and self-indulgent by Communists for not following their ideological directives.

American novelist and China expert Pearl Buck admired Lin's work. She urged him to write an English-language description of Chinese culture and life that would help Americans understand and sympathize with China, and she arranged a contract with her publisher. The success of the book changed the course of Lin's life.

Life's Work

Lin set out to demonstrate in *My Country and My People* that China was still a vibrant and creative

Lin Yutang. *(Library of Congress)*

society despite its thousands of years of existence and could therefore survive its current weaknesses and problems. He admired classical Chinese philosophy for generating a practical, commonsense attitude toward life, but he did not view the traditional emphasis on family as wholly admirable. Lin praised the Chinese concept of extended family as a major cultural force making for social stability. However, he noted that too often the elevation of family ties over national interests led to nepotism and corruption. This was especially true because of the chaotic state of Chinese politics in the 1930's when independent warlords and Communist armies challenged the Nationalist government for control at the same time that the Japanese threatened the country.

In the second part of the book, Lin discussed the circumscribed life of women, even after the liberating effects of the revolution of 1911. He described the literary revolution that occurred when the influence of Western literature encouraged using colloquial language to replace the formal language of the classics and praised the rich legacy of fine arts that China still enjoyed. The last chapter, "The Art of Living," celebrated the humanistic attitudes toward life encouraged by the inherited Chinese philosophical traditions. An epilogue expressed Lin's hope that the residual strengths of China would overcome the current collapse of order and that an effective leader would emerge from the chaos to prepare the way for a government of law and justice.

My Country and My People became an immediate best-seller and was widely translated in Europe and South America. Reviewers were uniformly complimentary. Lin's publisher arranged a significant advance for his next book and in May, 1936, Lin and his family sailed for New York, where Lin intended to spend a year writing a volume expanding on the philosophical themes he had sketched in his concluding chapter. The outbreak of open warfare between China and Japan in July, 1937, changed his plans; except for brief visits to China in the 1940's, Lin spent most of the next thirty years in the United States, where he published more than thirty novels, translations, and nonfiction works in English.

The Importance of Living was even more successful than Lin's first book; it went through forty printings in the United States and was translated into fifteen languages. Reviews were preponderantly positive. It was Lin's most important and influential book, and it made him the foremost interpreter of the customs, aspirations, fears, and thoughts of the Chinese people to the Western world.

Chinese reviewers' reactions to Lin's books were not always as favorable as those of English-language reviewers; Lin did not support any of the major political or literary factions in China, and he was condemned from all sides. Many Chinese in the United States disliked his frank descriptions of Chinese problems and feared that talk of warlords, bandits, nepotism, and corruption would lower American opinions of China. Proponents of the Nationalist government objected to his revelation of government authoritarianism; they found particularly objectionable his *A History of the Press and Public Opinion in China* (1936) because of its description of government propaganda and censorship activities. Chinese Communists were infuriated by Lin's disdainful rejection of Marxism and denounced him as superficial and irresponsible. Some sober-minded Americans, impressed by reports of the horrors of the Sino-Japanese War, found the subtle humor of his prose irritating; he seemed clever and witty at the wrong moment in history.

Moment in Peking: A Novel of Contemporary Chinese Life (1939) continued Lin's effort to increase American understanding of China, this time through an epic 815-page novel that chronicled the life of three middle-class Chinese families from 1900 to 1938. Beginning with the flight of these families from Beijing when the Boxer rebels captured the city, the narrative followed the lives of three generations as they struggled to survive the various disasters and chaos that marked twentieth century Chinese history, ending with the massive upheaval caused by the Japanese assaults on Shanghai and Beijing in 1937. Hailed as

a masterful narrative by reviewers, especially effective in its presentation of the life of women during these years, it became another best-seller. He attempted to continue his presentation of wartime China in *A Leaf in the Storm: A Novel of War-Swept China* (1941) but was less successful. Lin's only novel dealing with Chinese life in the United States, *Chinatown Family* (1948), describing the difficult rise to affluence of the children of a Chinese laundry worker as they assimilated American culture and values, received a mixed reaction from reviewers.

Lin had been skeptical of the willingness or ability of the Chinese Nationalist government under Chiang Kai-shek to counter Japanese aggression, but once actual warfare broke out and Chiang's armies began to fight, Lin joined in calls for all factions in China and the United States to rally behind the Nationalists. He helped raise money for the relief effort, lectured on the Chinese war effort, and in 1943 flew into China to observe the war firsthand. *The Vigil of a Nation*, in which he recounted his trip, became one of his most controversial books. Lin described the war already in progress between the Nationalists and the Communists, calling Chiang's regime authoritarian and repressive but finding it decidedly preferable to the totalitarian rigor of the Communists. Lin's call for all-out U.S. support of the Nationalists upset and offended many American liberals who still hoped that the two sides could be reconciled.

The triumph of the Chinese Communists saddened Lin, who grew more and more conservative. In *From Pagan to Christian*, after describing his childhood education as a Presbyterian and his gradual disillusionment with Christian theology, Lin devoted three lengthy chapters to exploring the religious aspects of Confucianism, Daoism, and Buddhism. Although he believed each had much wisdom to offer, he found none fully satisfying. Lin asserted that at no time did his belief in reason lead him to stop believing in God, but he could not find any satisfactory form of worship. His discovery of a Presbyterian church in New York that stressed the teachings of Jesus rather than theological dogma permitted him to return to the church of his childhood.

In 1966, Lin left the United States for Taiwan. At that time the only major Chinese writer to settle on the island, he was hailed by the government, which built a home for him and after his death preserved it as the Dr. Lin Yutang Memorial Library. On the island and after moving to Hong Kong in the early 1970's, he concentrated on his lifelong ambition to produce a Chinese-English dictionary of modern usage, which was finally published in 1972.

Influence

Lin was at the peak of his influence during the 1930's and 1940's. Most American critics and writers turned to his books for information on China. He became the best-known Chinese cultural envoy to the United States and the favorable image of China held by many Americans was largely shaped by his works. Although he continued to publish new volumes almost yearly in the 1950's and 1960's and some received respectful reviews, none sold in the numbers to which he had become accustomed. Modern Library editions of his anthologies were major sources of information on Chinese thought, but intellectuals began to treat him as a not very profound popularizer. The noted critic Edmund Wilson set the theme when he dismissed Lin's work as that of "a Chinese for Women's Club discussions, for Book-of-the-Month Club choices, for big publishers' advertisements."

In the 1980's, however, Lin's reputation began to recover. When the Chinese Communist regime relaxed its ideological rigor after the death of Mao Zedong, Lin received recognition as a major Chinese author. Lin translated only one of his English-language works into Chinese, but translations of many of his works became available in China. A ten-volume collection of his novels was published, a lengthy television series based on *Moment in Peking* became a success when shown on the national network, and his essays praising democratic procedures proved popular with college students. Chinese in Taiwan, pleased by Lin's support of the Nationalist government, had always recognized his work; a history of modern Chinese literature published in Taiwan in 1971 devoted three chapters to him in its discussion of the 1930's.

Lin's reputation in the United States was slower to rebound. The 1997-1998 issue of *Books in Print* listed only five works by the author. Both

The Importance of Living and *The Importance of Understanding* (1960)—an anthology that Lin translated to serve as a companion to *The Importance of Living*—have been reprinted and are available to those interested in learning about Chinese thought. *My Country and My People*, no longer in print, is now a historical document, providing glimpses of life in pre-Communist China. Critical reexaminations of Lin's work have been few and rather limited. There are, however, signs of change. Two doctoral dissertations devoted to Lin at prestigious universities, Columbia in 1991 and the University of California, Berkeley, in 1996, indicate that his reputation and the value of his work are receiving serious reconsideration.

Milton Berman

The Importance of Living

Type of philosophy: Chinese philosophy, ethics, philosophy of religion
First published: 1937
Principal ideas advanced:

◇ The highest personal ideal of classical Chinese culture is to develop a spirit of detachment that provided a sense of freedom and encouraged an intense joy of living.
◇ The Daoist tradition teaches how to attain an attitude of detachment that permits one to appreciate life's comedies even while one is experiencing life's tragedies.
◇ The Confucian tradition teaches how to attain what Lin calls the Spirit of Reasonableness, which produces a sense of tolerance and sympathy for all.
◇ The best philosophy of living combines aspects of Daoism and Confucianism.
◇ Religion should stress moral values, not doctrine.
◇ Chinese literature and philosophy do not propose either dogmas or extreme theories, but stress common sense and reasonableness.

Writing at a time when China appeared weak and divided against itself, Lin Yutang, unable to resist adequately the brutally aggressive activity of the Japanese military, set out through his work to increase American understanding and support for China. Because China was considered the underdog in the struggle with Japan, many Americans were sympathetic to the Chinese, but few knew much about China. In his first major work, *My Country and My People* (1935), Lin described sources of strength in the life of the Chinese people that he believed would help the nation survive its problems. In *The Importance of Living*, he examined the ideas that permitted the Chinese people to maintain a sense of human dignity in the face of cynicism and totalitarian threats. Using his mastery of English prose style, Lin attempted to popularize the "wisdom of the Orient" and make it accessible to the general reader through the use of irony and gentle humor.

In his preface, Lin informed the reader that the book was a personal testimony based on his own experience of thought and life. He warned against judging any philosopher or poet solely on the basis of how he was presented in this work, since each individual would inevitably be incompletely revealed within it. Using gentle irony, Lin apologized for the fact that he was not a trained philosopher. He refused to claim any originality because the ideas he covered had been discussed by many before him.

The opening chapter asserted that the highest ideal of Chinese culture was a person with a sense of detachment, "which enables one to go through life with tolerant irony and escape the temptations of fame and wealth and achievement." The sense of detachment provided a feeling of freedom that permitted a keen and intense joy of living. To illustrate this phenomenon, the book explained the philosophies and art of living that the Chinese had developed over the centuries.

Living a Full and Happy Life

Unlike the traditional Christian theological approach stressing the doctrine of Original Sin, the Chinese view of life stressed the importance of living in harmony with nature. Recognizing that humans live on earth and not in heaven, Chinese poets and philosophers did not need to reject the human body. They could accommodate the recognition of personal mortality and the realization of life's impermanence. The Daoist philosopher

and poet Zhuangzi expressed this sense of evanescence poetically when he described awakening from a dream in which he was a butterfly and wondering whether he was truly Zhuangzi dreaming he was a butterfly or a butterfly dreaming he was Zhuangzi. Confucius prosaically reduced the basic desires of human beings to two fundamental aspects: alimentation and reproduction, or more simply, food and drink and family. Lin argued that only the achievement of true harmony with nature could improve human beings, and therefore the education of one's senses and emotions was even more important than the education of one's mind.

Although there was much disagreement between Chinese philosophers on many points, they did concur that people must be both wise and unafraid to live a full and happy life. The positive Confucian approach and the quiet Daoist view could be combined into a philosophy that Lin considered to be that of the average Chinese. The apparent conflict between calls for action and inaction could be resolved; when they were merged together they became complementary and made for contentment with life on earth. Mixing these two outlooks created a harmonious personality, which was the acknowledged aim of all culture and education; this harmonious personality would experience a joyous love of life.

As an adherent of materialism, Lin rejected the distinction between material and spiritual happiness and refused to distinguish between the joys of the mind and joys of the flesh. In a chapter entitled "The Importance of Loafing," Lin urged the necessity of leisure to permit the achievement of a life of inner calm that led to an intense enjoyment of the life of nature. Awareness of mortality made the Chinese scholar's enjoyment of life all the more intense. For Lin, "Chinese philosophy may be briefly defined as a preoccupation with the knowledge of life rather than the knowledge of truth." The basic question it asks is "How are we to live?"

Lin examined Chinese answers to this question in a series of chapters that are essentially collections of familiar essays. Chapter 8, "The Enjoyment of the Home," is mostly about family. Lin argues that ancestor worship is misunderstood if it seen as a religion. Rather, it promotes a valuable sense of family consciousness and family honor, although it can also lead to abuses such as those pointed out in *My Country and My People*. The chapter ends with a section titled "On Growing Old"; Lin praises the Chinese reverence for age and expresses his shock when encountering the American denial of becoming elderly. Chapter 9, "The Enjoyment of Living," contains ten short essays devoted to such topics as "On Sitting in Chairs," "On Tea and Friendship," and "Some Curious Western Customs" regarding the rules of when to take off one's hat and how to shake hands.

Chapters entitled "The Enjoyment of Nature" and the "Enjoyment of Travel" use quotations from Chinese poetry and prose to illustrate what Lin considers proper approaches to these pleasures. In "The Enjoyment of Culture" Lin argues that "the aim of education or culture is merely the development of good taste in knowledge and good form in conduct." He especially praises the joys of reading. In an example that reflects centuries of Chinese experience with censorship, he quotes a Chinese scholar who thought that the experience of reading a banned book behind closed doors on a snowy night was one of life's greatest delights.

A Pagan and a Christian

In the next-to-last chapter, Lin describes his religious views. Belief in the importance of humankind is the essence of the humanism he espouses, but he is also concerned about the meaning and destiny of the world around him. Lin argues that religion should not attempt to dictate to science but should confine itself to the realm of moral conscience; failure to do so lies at the root of his dislike of existing churches. Lin rejects belief in personal immortality and considers the Christian preoccupation with it as pathological. He explains at length why he considers himself a pagan.

Born the son of a Christian pastor and educated in missionary schools that cut him off from classical and popular Chinese culture, Lin intended to become a Christian minister. However, he gradually lost his faith and began to reject Christian doctrines. In his theology class, Lin discovered that some theologians question the doctrine of virgin birth, and he was enraged that

Chinese believers had to assent categorically to this doctrine before being baptized, even though theologians of the same faith regarded it as an open question. Lin concluded that theologians are the greatest enemies of Christian religion. He could not continue to believe in the doctrines of Original Sin or Redemption. Although the Christian believer lived in a world governed and watched over by a God who played a personal role, that of a kindly father, in the believer's life, the pagan lived in the world as an orphan and must, therefore, take care of himself. It was this fear of living without the support of a loving God that caused Lin to hesitate before he finally proclaimed himself a pagan. As a pagan, Lin found life and belief much simpler. He still believed in God but hesitated to say so for fear of being misunderstood. In *From Pagan to Christian* (1959), Lin described his return to the religion of his childhood.

Common Sense and Reasonableness

The final chapter, the "Art of Thinking," examines the nature of humanized thinking that Lin believed to be central to Chinese literature and philosophy. Common sense and the spirit of reasonableness crushed all theories and dogmas:

> China, therefore, becomes a land where no one is trying very hard to think and everyone is trying very hard to live. It becomes a land where philosophy itself is a pretty simple and common sense affair that can be as conveniently put into two lines of verse as in a heavy volume. It becomes a land where there is no system of philosophy, broadly speaking, no logic, no metaphysics, no academic jargon; where there is much less academic dogmatism, less intellectual or practical fanaticism, and fewer abstract terms and long words.

Chinese philosophy is, consequently, accessible to the average literate person. In contrast, the trend toward specialization and cutting up of knowledge in Western scholarship has made philosophy a subject that even educated people believe they can do without. Lin finds this "a strange anomaly of modern culture, for philosophy, which should lie closest to men's bosom and business, has become most remote from life."

Rather than stressing logic, Chinese philosophy stresses common sense and the spirit of reasonableness. Reasonable thinking is humanized thinking, and the reasonable person is the highest type of cultivated human being. Where the logical person is too often self-righteous and therefore inhuman as well as wrong, the reasonable person suspects he or she could be mistaken and is therefore likely to be right. Lin rejects the theories of fascism and communism, but he is even more terrified by the fanatical methods that their logical theories inspire. He reassures his readers that the human mind is capable of better things and concludes with hope "that eventually we shall be able to live peaceably because we have learned to think reasonably."

Appreciation of Lin

Reviewers in the United States and Europe hailed *The Importance of Living* as the most useful and impressive revelation of Chinese thought available to the average reader. This volume and the anthologies of Chinese literature and philosophy that Lin compiled—*The Wisdom of China and India* (1942), *The Wisdom of Confucius* (1943), *The Wisdom of Laotse* (1948), and *The Importance of Understanding* (1960), a translation of selected prose and poetry that served as a companion volume to *The Importance of Living*—were the major sources of knowledge of Chinese thought for several generations of Americans.

Although both *The Importance of Living* and *The Importance of Understanding* were kept in print, Lin's reputation faded considerably during the 1960's and 1970's. His books began to seem dated, and few teachers cited his work as the first place to send an inquiring student. When interest in Lin resurfaced in mainland China in the 1980's, his English-language novels were translated and presented as a series on national television, and his early essays attracted Chinese students. The work remains a charming, if highly personal, exposition of the ideas of classical Chinese writers, written in an easily accessible prose style.

Milton Berman

Additional Reading

Chan, Wing-Tsit. "Lin Yutang, Critic and Interpreter." *College English* 8 (January, 1947): 163-169. This article sketches Lin's life, including praise as well as negative reactions to his books on China, and criticizes him for overemphasizing the role of Daoism in Chinese thought.

Cheng Lok Chua. "Golden Mountain: Chinese Versions of the American Dream in Lin Yutang, Louis Chu, and Maxine Hong Kingston." *Ethnic Groups* 4 (May, 1982): 33-59. This essay examines Lin's novel, *Chinatown Family*, which describes the difficulties Chinese immigrants faced in reconciling their dreams of material wealth with the Confucian ideal of the family.

Davidson, Robert F. *Philosophies Men Live By*. New York: Holt, Rinehart and Winston, 1962. Davidson analyzes *The Importance of Living* as a work of twentieth century hedonism carrying on the tradition of the Cyrenaics and Epicureans.

Fairbank, John K., and Albert Feuerwerker, eds. *Republican China 1912-1949, Part 2*. Vol. 13 in *The Cambridge History of China*. Cambridge, England: Cambridge University Press, 1986. This volume is invaluable for understanding what Lin experienced during his years in China. The few references to him are in the chapter describing literary trends from 1927 to 1949.

Kim, Elaine H. *Asian American Literature: An Introduction to the Writings and Their Social Context*. Philadelphia: Temple University Press, 1982. Kim scorns Lin's writings as superficial; she considers him a Chinese aristocrat who had little understanding of the reality of Asian American life that he attempted to describe in *Chinatown Family*.

Lai Ming. *A History of Chinese Literature*. New York: John Day, 1964. Although there are few direct references to Lin, the book contains a useful description of the tradition in which he wrote and his position in the Chinese literary debates during the 1920's and 1930's.

Recken, Stephen L. "Fitting-In: The Redefinition of Success in the 1930's." *Journal of Popular Culture* 27 (Winter, 1993): 205-222. This article portrays *The Importance of Living* as one of many books and articles that urged Americans to reduce their material expectations during the Great Depression.

Scott, A. C. *Literature and the Arts in Twentieth*

Century China. Gloucester, Mass.: Peter Smith, 1968. Scott dismisses Lin as a lightweight Chinese journalist who succeeded in the United States because of his mastery of English prose style.

Wilson, Edmund. "The Americanization of Lin Yutang." *The New Yorker* 20 (February 3, 1945): 78-81. Well-known critic Wilson finds little of value in Lin's works.

Milton Berman

John Locke

Locke combined the rational, deductive theory of René Descartes and the inductive, scientific experimentalism of Francis Bacon and the Royal Society. He gave the Western world the first modern theory of human nature and a new synthesis of the individualistic concept of liberty and the theory of government that was emerging out of the debates over natural law.

Principal philosophical works: *Epistola de Tolerantia*, 1689 (*A Letter Concerning Toleration*, 1689); *A Second Letter Concerning Toleration*, 1690; *Two Treatises of Government*, 1690; *An Essay Concerning Human Understanding*, 1690; *A Third Letter for Toleration*, 1692; *Some Thoughts Concerning Education*, 1693; *The Reasonableness of Christianity as Delivered in the Scriptures*, 1695; *Some Thoughts on the Conduct of the Understanding in the Search of Truth*, 1706.

Born: August 29, 1632; Wrington, Somerset, England

Died: October 28, 1704; Oates, Essex, England

Early Life

John Locke was born in the small English village of Wrington, in Somerset, on August 29, 1632. His father, John Locke, was a local attorney of modest means. His mother, née Agnes Kneene, was the daughter of a local tanner. Both parents were educated Puritans, and while the home atmosphere was austere, it was also intellectual. Locke's father was a stern and taciturn man who seemed little interested in his son during his youth but grew friendlier as Locke became an adult. Agnes Locke was ten years older than her husband and thirty-five when John, her first son, was born. She was a pious and affectionate mother. Locke had only one brother, Thomas, born August 9, 1637. Shortly after John Locke's birth, the family moved to Belluton and a larger and more comfortable farmhouse.

Locke's early education was at home. By 1647, at the age of fifteen, his father had arranged for him an appointment to Westminster School, located next to Westminster Abbey in London. Headmaster Richard Busby was a remarkable teacher with definite conservative sympathies toward the Royalists and the Church of England. Even though Parliament had gained the upper hand in the Civil War with the king, Busby kept his post. Although he was not able to influence Locke toward either political or religious orthodoxy, Busby apparently cooled his pupil's zeal for the Puritan faith. In 1650, Locke was elected a King's Scholar. This meant that he boarded in the school instead of private quarters outside and, more important, would be eligible for a scholarship to Oxford or Cambridge when he was graduated. Locke studied Latin, Greek, Hebrew, and Arabic in order to read the great books written in those languages. In 1651, Locke's brother, Thomas, also came to Westminster. In later years, Locke criticized boarding schools severely for the cruelty and violence they encouraged, indicating that those were not happy years for him. Only four of his schoolmates remained his friends in later life.

Locke grew to be tall and slender, a handsome man with a long, sensitive, and patrician face, a high forehead, large, dark, expressive eyes, a full mouth, and a dimpled chin. In later years, he often wore a wig in the style of his times, but he never lost his own hair. Locke did not change much as he grew older, except that his hair turned white and his face grew thinner.

In May of 1652, when he was twenty, Locke was last on a list of six Westminster students elected for scholarships to Christ Church, Oxford, where he enrolled the next November. Al-

John Locke. *(Library of Congress)*

though Oxford had suffered greatly during the English Civil War, it had become a more settled place by the time Locke arrived. The curriculum was still medieval, and three and a half years' study in logic, metaphysics, and classical languages were required for the bachelor's degree. Latin was the spoken language, and all students attended religious services twice daily. While at Oxford, Locke acquired the lifelong idiosyncrasy of using ciphers, invisible ink, code names, and other devices to keep secrets. He seems to have cultivated an aura of romantic mystery for himself, an unexpected trait for someone renowned as the founder of the Age of Reason.

When Locke earned his B.A. in 1656, he decided to begin the three years of study required for the master of arts degree. What attracted him was not the regular curriculum with its methodology of disputation (he saw little chance of finding truth in that way) but rather the new learning, just making its appearance in the sciences, with its empirical methodology. He attended meetings to discuss the discoveries of Andreas Vesalius, William Harvey, William Gilbert, and Paracelsus, among others, whose work was based on observation. This was the beginning of a lifelong study of science, medicine, and experimental philosophy. Locke concluded that unquestioning adherence to tradition and trusting emotional convictions were the two principal causes of human error; Royalists and Puritans, respectively, were his prime examples. Locke practiced medicine throughout his adult life and seems to have had something of a gift for it, but he was never much of a scientist. As a philosopher of the empirical and rational method of the scientific search for knowledge, however, he had few peers.

For Oxford, these were hard years as the political fortunes of the Royalist and Parliamentarian factions shifted back and forth and were reflected in changes at the university. Since religion was still a matter of state at this time, each political shift brought a different religious focus. Out of these struggles grew an interest in toleration among the students and scholars at Oxford. Within the context of this debate, Locke concluded that toleration was a nice idea but impractical. He thought religious zealots, such as most Puritans, had proved dangerous to society's peace and security, while Catholics were always suspect because their allegiance to the pope could too easily make them traitors. Later in his life, Locke would take a more liberal stand, but the change grew out of experience, not principle. Interestingly, some of his arguments against toleration were cribbed from Thomas Hobbes's great work *Leviathan* (1651), although Locke never acknowledged his debt to Hobbes (not unusual in Locke's time).

Locke was also beginning to think seriously about the concept of natural law, especially the idea that it incorporated a moral code that was knowable to rational beings and compelling once known. His ideas on the subject were as yet poorly formed. The theory was not new; it dated back to the Greek Stoics and had been adopted by medieval Christianity as the law of God. The idea of natural law was then reclaimed in the Renaissance by secular interests as the basis for a new theory of government and was a popular issue for scholarly debate in Locke's time. It was the Greek and Renaissance forms that interested Locke. He rejected the medieval theory that humankind innately knew the law of nature as it applied to human conduct. He was already moving toward a theory that explained all knowledge as the result of experience.

Life's Work

Locke's father died on February 13, 1661, and his one brother, Thomas, died in late 1663. That left him alone in the world, for his mother had died in 1654. Locke's father had left him some land and a few cottages, which provided him a small but adequate income the rest of his life. Locke had numerous female friends throughout his life and seems to have been close to marriage at least twice. For reasons on which he chose not to comment, however, he remained a bachelor.

Christ Church elected him lecturer in Greek the same year that his father died, and in 1663 he was appointed lecturer in rhetoric. During these early years as a teacher, Locke periodically considered becoming a clergyman to advance his career. Permanent faculty members customarily took holy orders. His dislike of theology and his interest in science, however, seem to have been the deciding factors, and he never did so. His great friend and scientific mentor, and the leading scientist of the day at Oxford, was Robert Boyle. Boyle advised Locke to concentrate on scientific research and leave theology to those who loved disputation.

In 1665, while the Great Plague was ravaging London, King Charles II and his court came to Christ Church for an extended stay. Locke may have met the king at that time, because Locke was offered the post of secretary to the diplomatic mission in Brandenburg, Germany. What interested Locke most while on this assignment was how easily Brandenburgers accepted religious differences. A change in his thoughts on

toleration dates from this experience. Locke was offered several other posts with diplomatic missions but declined, preferring to stay at Oxford.

In the summer of 1666, Locke met Anthony Ashley Cooper, then Baron Ashley and later the third earl of Shaftesbury. There immediately developed between them a deep respect and admiration which evolved into a collaboration. Cooper invited Locke to Exeter House, his London home, first as a houseguest and then as his personal physician. Locke accepted because he liked Cooper and the city and because many of his friends lived in London. Cooper knew most of the prominent intellectuals of his day and introduced Locke to them. In this environment, Locke, heretofore a minor Oxford scholar, amateur scientist, and unqualified medical practitioner, discovered his talent as a philosopher. While Locke did occasionally perform medical services for Cooper and his family, and in at least one instance may have saved Cooper's life, Locke was chiefly a friend, confidant, and adviser to Cooper in his many political activities, especially during his tenure as one of the king's leading ministers in 1672 and again in 1678.

Religion was a critical concern of English politics during the reign of Charles II. Although the king was personally willing to allow all Englishmen to worship as they pleased, Parliament was adamantly opposed to all but the Church of England. Complicating matters, Charles II's heir was his brother James, duke of York, who had publicly announced his conversion to Catholicism. Prompted by Cooper, who advocated toleration, Locke almost finished *A Letter Concerning Toleration* by 1667, although it was not published until 1689. In fact, most of his important works were not published until late in his life.

Locke was an overly cautious man in an unsettled political atmosphere. In *A Letter Concerning Toleration*, Locke distinguished between those actions and opinions that concerned politics and society and those that did not. He argued that toleration of the latter was necessary. Locke concluded that all Christian religions except Catholicism must be tolerated. Catholic allegiance to the papacy and the threat to social peace posed by all non-Christians disqualified both groups from toleration. For his day, that was a liberal position and, as a result of Locke's later fame, influential in the evolution of full toleration in England. Locke's personal religious convictions were few. He rejected nearly all dogma except a belief in God, and he argued for a rational interpretation of Christianity in all other matters.

Also as a result of Cooper's interest, Locke had become concerned about economics and matters of trade. Through Cooper's influence, Locke received appointments to public offices related to trade and commerce and invested in various commercial enterprises. Locke was meticulously careful with money and was very knowledgeable about finance; he always made a profit from his investments. He wrote several essays to protest government policies that he thought unwise or unfair.

In 1671, as a result of ill health, Locke went to France for an extended visit. While in France, he met Samuel von Pufendorf, Gottfried Wilhelm Leibniz, and a number of others connected to the French Royal Society. Locke traveled extensively in France and later in England because of his continuing respiratory problems, which were aggravated by the London smog. While traveling, he maintained an extensive correspondence with his friends.

By 1681, Cooper was out of government and involved in a plot to overthrow Charles II in order to put the king's bastard son, the duke of Monmouth, on the throne. The purpose was to prevent the king's legitimate heir, his brother James, from succeeding him and giving England a Catholic monarch. After the plot was discovered in 1682, it became dangerous for anyone to be associated with Cooper. This included Locke, who slipped out of England secretly and by February of 1683 was in Rotterdam. He lived in various cities in the Netherlands, part of the time in hiding to avoid extradition, and did not return to England until half a decade later. However, the period was a productive one for Locke. He spent the winter of 1684-1685 in Utrecht beginning work on *An Essay Concerning Human Understanding*, finishing it by late 1686. Before publishing it, he released several short, descriptive summaries to promote sales of the essay. The essay itself was not printed until 1690.

In *An Essay Concerning Human Understanding*, Locke was addressing three questions: How do we gain knowledge? How trustworthy is that knowledge? and What is the scope or extent of what can be known? Although Locke claimed to be approaching these questions empirically, an empiricist would not attempt to answer the third question, or even perhaps the second, before all knowledge was known. Locke was more indebted to the rationalism of René Descartes than he admitted. Empiricism, however, was the method he tried to use to demonstrate his conclusions, and, in the process, he presented a radically new view and definition of human nature. Locke was certain that people were born with minds empty of any knowledge and that the mind's only links with the external world were through the senses. The mind had the capability of forming abstract ideas after reflecting on sensory perceptions it received and of constructing from those ideas even more complex abstractions. Locke made a clear distinction between knowledge by reason, which can be empirically demonstrated, and faith or opinion, which he thought was ungrounded fantasy.

An Essay Concerning Human Understanding also contains an extensive discussion of language and the use of words. A major achievement of the essay was in separating faith from reason in types of philosophical inquiry and in demonstrating which would lead to trustworthy knowledge. Locke's was a view of human nature radically different from what Christian theologians had proposed. There was no place in Locke's scheme for Original Sin or predestination to evil; human behavior came from thought, which was learned and subject to the influence of reason and observation.

While in the Netherlands, Locke was involved in some other minor writing projects and in editing his *A Letter Concerning Toleration*. He also spent time visiting friends, including Antoni van Leeuwenhoek, the inventor of the microscope, and Prince William of Orange and his wife, Mary, who would become the next monarchs of England. Charles II had died in 1685 and was succeeded by James II, but by 1688, the English were so offended by their new king that they invited William and Mary to intervene and take the throne. Locke was delighted by their acceptance and the flight of James II. He made ready to return home immediately, having been offered space aboard Princess Mary's ship, and arrived in England on February 20, 1689.

King William offered Locke several diplomatic posts, but Locke refused to leave England and accepted only a part-time position as commissioner of appeals. Locke's Oxford position had been lost while he was in the Netherlands. He asked to have it restored but withdrew the request upon learning that someone else would be dispossessed. Locke was soon involved in finishing his great work of political philosophy, *Two Treatises of Government*, publishing it anonymously in 1690.

Locke had written the first drafts of the *Two Treatises of Government* back in 1681, when Cooper was planning to overthrow Charles II. Although Cooper's activities may have been part of Locke's inspiration, the issues raised were ones that had been under discussion among Europe's intellectuals for some time, and Locke was already familiar with them. The Glorious Revolution of 1688 made the *Two Treatises of Government* apposite again. There is no evidence to support Locke's statement that there were originally three treatises and that the longer middle one had been lost; scholars are at a loss to explain Locke's claim. The first treatise was written as a detailed refutation of Sir Robert Filmer's *Patriarcha* (1680), an undistinguished work in defense of autocracy that had become popular in Royalist circles. Although Locke cited Hobbes as his antagonist, Hobbes was unpopular and Locke's arguments were more clearly in opposition to Filmer's than to Hobbes's. The reason for the subterfuge is unknown.

The second treatise, *Of Civil Government*, proposed an alternative theory for the origins and purpose of government based on natural law. Locke maintained that because God had given each person a life, it was part of God's natural law that the individual was the only rightful owner of that life, that each had this right equally, and that the right was therefore inalienable. Besides life, there were the other primary rights of liberty and property, which were necessary to preserve life and without which an inalienable right to life could have little value. From these three, all other rights were derived. Locke argued that before government existed (which he called a state of nature), each person had sole responsibility for the defense of his or her own rights. For convenience and the better protection of their rights, especially property, people established societies with governments by consenting to a social contract. For Locke, it followed that the only legitimate reason a government had for existing was to preserve and protect rights. If the government then violated individual rights, it destroyed the social contract. This violation released the individual from any obligation and justified rebellion in order to establish a new social contract.

Between 1688 and 1690, the three most important of Locke's works were published. In the years following 1690, he published a number of lesser items, including a special edition of *Aesop's Fables* in 1691, printed in English and Latin to help children learn Latin; his first economics essay, written in 1672, *Some Considerations of the Consequences of Lowering of Interest, and Raising the Value of Money* (1692); *A Third Letter for Toleration*, in answer to a critic; *The General History of Air* (1692), edited for his old friend Boyle, who had died and left the manuscript in rough form; *Some Thoughts Concerning Education*; second, third, and fourth editions of *An Essay Concerning Human Understanding*, in which he expanded his arguments; *The Reasonableness of Christianity as Delivered in the Scriptures*; and vindications of several works that had been attacked by other writers.

Locke was also interested in current affairs. He was the dominant commissioner on the Board of Trade from 1695 to 1700 and undertook several projects to influence his friends in Parliament on economic issues. Specifically, he wanted Parliament to allow the censorship law to lapse in 1695 and to issue new coins with milled edges to prevent clipping. They did both.

Locke kept up the habit, formed during the years he was a member of Cooper's household, of creating discussion clubs. These usually met weekly in a tavern and discussed science, politics, philosophy, or all three. Members of the clubs had included Cooper, John Somers, Lord Pembroke, and other important members of the educated elite. He also found time to visit his many friends, including Sir Isaac Newton and Christopher Wren. By 1695, his asthma was so bad during the London winters that he moved permanently to the home of Lady Masham, his closest female friend, where he lived out the remainder of his life. He had become a famous man of letters in England and throughout Europe. A steady stream of friends, disciples, and dignitaries came to visit and pay their respects. Because of failing health, he refused, in 1697, the personal request of King William III to take the post of embassy secretary in Paris at a critical time in the negotiation of the Partition Treaties with King Louis XIV. He chose his young cousin, Peter King, as his heir and gave him help and advice to further his career as a lawyer and statesman. King became Lord High Chancellor of England for a time after Locke's death.

In 1700, Locke began having trouble with swelling in his legs, which kept him in bed for extended periods. Locke continually prepared himself for death, which, periodically, he thought was imminent. Nothing, however, ever interfered with his mental powers. Locke kept up a voluminous correspondence and read the latest important books and papers. His physical condition grew steadily weaker throughout 1703 and 1704, and on Saturday, October 28, 1704, he was unable to rise without help and died peacefully sitting in a chair shortly after 3:00 P.M. with Lady Masham by his side. Locke was buried quickly and privately in the nearby village churchyard of High Lever, as he had requested. He was seventy-two years old.

Influence

Locke left an extraordinary intellectual legacy. His essays on toleration were a major contribution on the subject and deserve some of the credit for the development of a more liberal government policy toward religious beliefs. *An Essay Concerning Human Understanding* created a new image of human nature substantiated by empirical observation. Locke objected to medieval rationalism because the premises of any disputation were determined by theology. Earlier philosophers had attempted to separate theology from rationalism but failed to provide an alternative means of substantiating their conclusions, resulting in some bizarre concepts in philosophy. Locke's insistence on empirical evidence gave the study of human nature a scientific basis, doing for the social sciences what Newton did for the natural sciences.

Locke's *Two Treatises of Government* constituted a synthesis of a long-standing debate among Europe's intellectuals. In his work, the combination of natural law theory and the concept of vested rights was clearly stated for the first time, transforming the latter into the principle of inalienable rights. These rights became a matter of universal principle and a specific manifestation of a new individualistic definition of liberty that would later make itself felt in such events as the American Revolution. Later, Enlightenment philosophies expanded Locke's ideas to create new visions of how a society should be structured and the ways in which progress could be achieved.

Richard L. Hillard

Of Civil Government

The Second Treatise

Type of philosophy: Ethics, political philosophy
First published: 1690, in *Two Treatises of Government*
Principal ideas advanced:

◇ In the state of nature, all people are free and equal; no person is by nature sovereign over other people.

◇ The law of nature governs the state of nature; reason reveals the law of nature, which is derived from God.

◇ In a state of nature, no one ought to harm another's life, health, liberty, or possessions; if anyone does harm another, the one harmed has the right to punish the other person.

◇ By one's labor, one acquires as one's property the products of one's labor.

◇ In order to remedy the inconveniences resulting from a state of nature in which everyone is judge of one's own acts, people enter into a contract, thereby creating a civil society empowered to judge people and to defend the natural rights of people.

◇ If a government violates the social contract by endangering the security and rights of the citizens, it rebels against the people, and the people have the right to dissolve the government.

The Glorious Revolution of 1688 saw the expulsion of James II from the throne of England and the triumph of Whig principles of government. James had been accused of abandoning the throne and thus violating the original contract between himself and his people. Two years later, John Locke's *Of Civil Government: The Second Treatise* appeared in *Two Treatises of Government* and was looked upon by many as a tract that justified in philosophical terms those historical events. The first treatise had been an argument against the view that kings derive their right to rule from divine command, a view held by England's royal family the Stuarts, especially James I, and defended with no little skill by Sir Robert Filmer in his *Patriarcha* (1680).

After rejecting Filmer's thesis, Locke looked for a new basis of government and a new source of political power. He recognized that the state must have the power to regulate and preserve property, and that to do so it must also have the right to punish, to use the death penalty and all lesser ones. In order to carry out the laws passed, the force of the community must be available to the government, and it must also be ready to serve in the community's defense from foreign injury. Political power by which the government performs these functions ought to be used only for the public good and not for private gain or advantage. Locke then set out to establish a basis for this power, a basis that he considered moral and just.

Natural Law as the Basis of Government

He turned to a concept used by political theorists since the time of the Stoics in ancient Greece: natural law with its concomitants, the state of nature and the state of war. Many philosophers have objected to the state of nature as a concept because history does not indicate that such a state existed. In *Of Civil Government* Locke tries to answer this objection by pointing to "primitive" societies known in his day, the nations of Indians living in the New World. However, that was not a strong argument and was not really needed by Locke. The concept of the state of nature can be used as a device to set off and point up the difference between a civil state in which laws are enacted by the government and a contrasting state in which either these laws are absent in principle or another set of laws prevails. In this way, the basis of civil enactments and the position of the individual within society may be better understood.

This applies also to the other concepts mentioned, the state of war and natural law. At any rate, Locke holds that in the state of nature one may order one's own life as one sees fit, free from any restrictions that other people might impose; in this sense, each individual and all others are equal. They are equal in a more profound sense from which, as it were, their right to act as independent agents comes; that is, as children of God. By use of reason, people can discover God's commands by which they should order their lives in the state of nature. These commands are called the "laws of nature." Thus, although one is free to act as one pleases in the state of nature, one is still obligated to act according to God's commands. This ensures that one's actions, although free, will not be licentious. The basic restriction that God's laws place on an individual is that one treat others as one would like to be treated. Because people are equal and independent, they should not harm one another regarding their "life, health, liberty, or possessions."

Free Will

Humanity's glory as well as its downfall has been free will, whereby one may choose to do or not to do what one ought to do. To preserve oneself from those who choose to inflict harm, one has the right to punish transgressors of the law. Reparation and restraint are the two reasons that justify punishment when one by one's acts has shown that one has agreed to live by a law other than that which common reason and equity dictate; that is, one has chosen to violate God's orders. The right to punish is thus a natural right by which people in the state of nature may preserve themselves and humankind from the transgressions of the lawless. This right is the basis for the right of governments to punish lawbreakers within the state; thus, Locke provides a ground for one aspect of political power that he had noted earlier.

The State of War

When an individual indicates through a series of acts that are apparently premeditated that he or she has designs on another's life or property, then that person enters into a state of war, a state of enmity and destruction, toward the intended victim. In the state of nature, people ought to live according to reason and, hence, according to God's commands. Each individual must be the judge of his or her own actions, for on earth there is no common superior with authority to judge between that person and another when a question of aggression arises and when relief is sought. One's conscience must be one's guide as to whether one is in a state of war with another person.

In the Declaration of Independence, the American colonists proclaimed that people had natural rights granted to them by their Creator and that governments were instituted by people with their consent to protect these rights. Locke, as pointed out, held these rights to be life, liberty, and property, whereas the Declaration proclaims them to be life, liberty, and the pursuit of happiness. It is interesting that Thomas Jefferson, the author of the Declaration of Independence, pondered whether to use "property" or "pursuit of happiness" and in an early draft actually had written the former. Much of Locke's discussion in *On Civil Government* influenced the statesmen and leaders of the colonies during the period of the American Revolution.

Property

Locke seems to use various senses of "property" in his discussions. Speaking quite generally, one might say that whatever was properly one's own—whatever God had endowed an individual with or whatever the legislature of the commonwealth had declared as legal possession—no one else had a claim to. In spelling out this idea, Locke starts first with one's own body, which is God-given and which no one has a claim upon; an individual has a right to be secure in his or her person. Included in this idea is the fact that life itself is a gift to which no one else has a claim, as well as the freedom to move about without restriction.

There is next the more common use of "property," which is often rendered "estate" and which refers to the proper possessions that one gains in working the earth that God has given people to use for the advantage of their lives and their convenience. Because working for one's own advantage and convenience involves the pursuit of happiness, it can be seen in what way the terms "property" and "pursuit of happiness" are inter-

changeable. This more common use of "property" is, nonetheless, related to the first use in Locke's theory. What is properly a person's own may be extended when, with regard to the common property that God has blessed people with for their use, a person mixes labor with it and makes it his or her own. Divine command prescribes, however, that one take no more than one needs, for to take more than one's share may lead to the waste of God's gift and result in want for others. Locke believed that there was more than enough land in the world but that it should be used judiciously; he does complicate matters, however, by stating that disproportionate and unequal possessions may be acquired within a government through the consent of the governed.

Locke's embryonic economic theory may be looked upon as an early statement of the classical or labor theory of value. This is especially so if we remember that aside from the "natural" or God-given articles of value that people have, they create objects of value by means of their own labor; more succinctly, labor creates value. This view was held by such influential thinkers in economic history as Adam Smith, David Ricardo, and Karl Marx. Locke had again provided a ground for the use of political power to regulate, preserve, and protect property in all its aspects by establishing its place in the state of nature prior to the institution of the commonwealth.

The Case for Government

Locke has shown that although people ought to live according to divine commands, some do not and thus turn the state of nature into one of war. Because there is no common superior on earth to whom one can turn for restitution, people are often left helpless. It is obvious that not every injury imagined is a wrong, that two individuals in conscience may disagree, and that those instances of obvious wrongs are not always rectifiable when people have only their own judgments and strength to depend upon. A disinterested judge, supported by more power than a single person has alone, may provide people with a remedy for the insecurity that exists in the state of nature. In the most general sense of "property," a commonwealth may provide the solution to its preservation and security by making public the laws by which people ought to live, by establishing a government by which differences may be settled through the office of known and impartial judges who are authorized to do so, and by instituting a police force to execute the law, a protection absent in the state of nature. People give up their rights to judge for themselves and to execute the laws of nature to the commonwealth, which in turn is obligated to use the power that it has gained for the ends that led to the transference of these rights. In giving up their rights, people consent to form a body politic under one government and, in so doing, obligate themselves to every member of that society to submit to the determinations of the majority. Note that everyone who enters into the society from the state of nature must consent to do so; hence, consent is unanimous and anyone who does not consent is not a member of the body politic. On the other hand, once the body politic is formed, its members are thenceforth subject to the vote of the majority.

In discussing consent and the general question "Who has consented and what are its significant signs?" Locke uses the traditional distinction between tacit and express consent. Although he is somewhat ambiguous at times, his position is apparently as follows. There are two great classes or categories of individuals within society, those who are members and those who are residents but not members. (A convenient and similar distinction would be those who are citizens and those who are alien residents.) Both these two groups receive benefits from the government and hence are obligated to obey it. By their presence, they enjoy the peace and security that goes with a government of law and order, and it is morally and politically justifiable that that government expect of them that they obey its laws. Those who are merely residents may quit the body politic when they please; their tacit consent lasts only as long as their presence in the state. Members, however, by their express consent create and perpetuate the society. They are not free to be or not be members at their whim; otherwise, the body politic would be no different from the state of nature or war from which its members emerged, and anarchy would prevail. Citizens usually have the protection of their government at home and abroad, and often, at least in the government Locke preferred, a voice in the affairs of their nation. Locke points out, however, that the people who form the commonwealth by their unanimous consent may also delegate their power to a few or to one (oligarchy or monarchy); but in any case it is their government.

Obligations of Government

There are certain aspects of government that Locke believed must be maintained to ensure that it functions for the public good:

(1) The legislative, which is the supreme governmental power, must not use its power arbitrarily over the lives and fortunes of the people. The law of nature still prevails in the governments of humankind.

(2) Nor should power be exercised without deliberation. Extempore acts would place the people in as great jeopardy as they were in the state of nature.

(3) The supreme power cannot take property from a person without that individual's consent. This principle applies also to taxation.

(4) The legislative power cannot be transferred to anyone else, but must remain in the hands of that group to which it was delegated by the people. In so acting, the legislature ensures that political power will be used for the public good.

Separation of Powers

Locke believed that the interests of the people would be protected more fully in a government in which the three basic powers—legislative, executive, and federative—were separate and distinct in their functions. The legislature need meet only periodically, but the executive should be in session continually, whereas the management of the security of the commonwealth from foreign injury would reside in the body politic as a whole. Strictly speaking, the federative power—treaty making and so forth—need not be distinguished from the legislative. It is interesting that the three branches of government in the United States include the judiciary rather than the federative, which is shared by both the executive and legislative branches of government. This structure reflects the influence of Montesquieu as well as Locke at the Philadelphia convention.

Government, which is made up of these three basic powers, of which the legislative is supreme, must not usurp the end for which it was established. The community, even after it has delegated its power, does not give up its right of self-preservation, and in this sense it retains forever the ultimate power of sovereignty. This power cannot be used by the community that is under obligation to obey the acts of the government unless that government is dissolved. It must be pointed out that the community is for Locke an important political concept. The exercise of its power after the dissolution of government is as a public body and does not involve a general return to the state of nature or war by its members. However, in what way is a government dissolved?

Violation of the Social Contract

When a government exercises power beyond right, when public power is used for private gain, then tyranny prevails. Such acts set the stage for the dissolution of government. It should be pointed out that in forming a community and in delegating power to a government, the people, especially in the latter case, enter into an agreement or, analogously, into a social contract with their government to provide them with security, preservation, and those conveniences that they desire, in exchange for the transference of their rights and the honor, respect, and obligation that they render to the government. The violation of their part of the contract leads the government to declare them (as individuals) outlaws, to use its police force to subdue them and its courts to set punishment for them.

In discussing dissolution in general, Locke points out that it can apply to societies and communities as well as to governments. It is seldom that a community is dissolved. If it does happen, it is usually the result of a foreign invasion that is followed by the utter destruction of the society. Governments, on the other hand, are dissolved from within. Either the executive abandons his or her office (as was done by James II) and the laws cannot be carried out, or the legislative power is affected in various ways that indicate a violation of trust. If, for example, the property of the subjects is invaded, or if power is used arbitrarily, then government is dissolved.

Obviously, it falls upon the community to judge when this power is being abused. Generally, Locke holds, the people are slow to act; it takes not merely one or two but a long series of abuses to lead them to revolution. In fact, he points out that the term "rebellion" indicates a return to a state of war and a denial of the principles of civil society. However, when this happens in the dissolution of government, it is the government that has rebelled and not the community; it is the community that stands for law and order and puts down the rebellion. Thus, Locke rather cleverly concludes his treatise not with a justification of the right of rebellion but, rather, with the right of the people to put down unlawful government, unlawful in that it violates the trust and the law of nature, leading to tyranny, rebellion, and dissolution.

Theodore Waldman

An Essay Concerning Human Understanding

Type of philosophy: Epistemology
First published: 1690
Principal ideas advanced:

◇ At birth the mind is a *tabula rasa*, or blank tablet; no one is born with innate ideas.

◇ All of our ideas come from experience, either from sensation or by reflection.

◇ All simple, uncompounded ideas come from experience, and the mind, by combining simple ideas, forms new complex ideas.

◇ The qualities of objects are either primary or secondary: primary qualities—solidity, extension, figure, mobility, and number—are inseparable from objects, but secondary qualities—such as colors and odors—are in the observer.

◇ The substance of objects is a something—we know not what—that we have to assume as the support of an object's qualities.

John Locke's *An Essay Concerning Human Understanding* is the first major presentation of the empirical theory of knowledge that was to play such an important role in British philosophy. The author had studied at Oxford, and later he became a medical doctor. Although he did not practice much, he was greatly interested in the developments current in medical and physical science, and there is some evidence that he first began to formulate his theory of knowledge in terms of considerations arising from medical researches of the day. Locke was a member of the Royal Society of England, where he came into contact with many of the important experimental scientists, such as Robert Boyle and Sir Isaac Newton. A discussion with some of his friends seems to have been the immediate occasion of the writing of *An Essay Concerning Human Understanding*, in which Locke attempted to work out a theory of knowledge in keeping with the developing scientific findings and outlook.

The completed version of the work dates from the period when Locke, along with his patron, the Anthony Ashley Cooper, the third earl of Shaftesbury, was a political refugee in Holland. After the Glorious Revolution of 1688, Locke returned to England and was quickly recognized as the leading spokesperson for the democratic system of government that was emerging in his homeland. The essay, first published in the same year as Locke's famous work in political philosophy, *Two Treatises of Government*, quickly established the author as the foremost spokesperson for the new empirical philosophical point of view that was to dominate English philosophy from then on.

Seeking the Origins of Human Knowledge

The question to which Locke addressed himself in his essay is that of "the origin[s], certainty, and extent of human knowledge, together with the grounds and degrees of belief, opinion, and assent." By using what he called "this historical, plain method," Locke hoped to discover where our ideas and our knowledge come from, what we are capable of knowing about, how certain our knowledge actually is, and when we may be justified in holding opinions based on our ideas. The value of such an undertaking, Locke asserted, is that one would thus know the powers and the limits of human understanding, so that "the busy mind of man" would then restrict itself to considering only those questions with which it was actually capable of dealing and would "sit

down in a quiet ignorance of those things" beyond the reach of its capacities.

Before commencing his investigations, Locke pointed out that human beings do, in fact, have adequate knowledge to enable them to function in the condition in which they find themselves. Therefore, even if the result of seeking the origin, nature, and extent of our knowledge leads us to the conclusion that we are unable to obtain complete certitude on various matters, this should not be grounds for despair, for skepticism, or for intellectual idleness. People have wasted too much time, Locke insisted, in bemoaning their intellectual situation or in disputing in areas in which satisfactory conclusions are impossible. Instead, he said, we should find out our abilities and our limitations, and then operate within them.

The Question of Innate Knowledge

The first book of *An Essay Concerning Human Understanding* deals with one theory about the origin of our ideas, the thesis that our knowledge is based upon certain innate principles that are supposed to be "stamped upon the mind of man." Locke severely criticized this theory, especially in the form in which it had been presented by thinkers such as Herbert of Cherbury. Adherents of this theory of innate ideas had maintained that the universal agreement of humankind regarding certain principles showed that these must be innate. Locke argued in opposition that the fact of universal agreement would be insufficient evidence as to the source of the principles in question. He also argued that, in fact, there actually are no principles that are universally agreed to, since children and idiots do not seem to know or believe the principles that are usually cited as examples of innate ideas. The way in which children acquire knowledge about the principles in question, through the learning process, further indicates that they are not born with innate ideas.

After having criticized the innate idea theory, Locke turned next to the positive side of his investigation. We do have ideas (an idea being defined as whatever is the object of the understanding when a person thinks); this is beyond any possible doubt. Then, if the ideas are not innate, where do they come from?

Empirical Origins of Knowledge

The second book of *An Essay Concerning Human Understanding* begins the development of a hypothesis about the origins of human knowledge, namely, the empirical theory. Let us suppose, Locke said, that the mind initially is just a blank tablet (a *tabula rasa*). Where, then, does it obtain its ideas? From experience, Locke proclaimed. Experience comprises two sources of ideas, sensation and reflection. We receive many, if not most, of our ideas when our sense organs are affected by external objects. We receive other ideas by reflection when we perceive the operations of our minds on the ideas that we have already received. Sensation provides us with ideas of qualities, such as the ideas of yellow or of heat. Reflection provides us with ideas such as those of thinking, willing, and doubting. These two sources, Locke insisted, give us all the ideas that we possess. If anyone has any doubts about this, let that person simply inspect his or her own ideas and see if there are any that have not come to him or her either by sensation or reflection. The development of children also provides a further confirmation of this empirical theory of the origin of human knowledge. As the child receives more ideas from sensation, and reflects on them, that child's knowledge gradually increases.

Ideas: Simple and Complex

Having thus answered the question concerning the origin of our ideas, Locke proceeded to investigate the nature of the ideas that we possess. All of our ideas are either simple or complex. A simple idea is one that is uncompounded, that contains nothing but one uniform appearance, and that cannot be distinguished into different ideas. An example of a simple idea would be the smell of a rose. A complex idea, in contrast, is one that is composed of two or more simples, such as a yellow and fragrant idea. The simples, Locke insisted, can neither be created nor be destroyed by the mind. The mind has the power to repeat, compare, and unite the simples, thereby creating new complex ideas. However, the mind cannot invent simple ideas that it has not experienced. The simples, in the Lockean theory of knowledge, are the building blocks from which all of our complex and compounded ideas can be constructed and accounted for.

Many of the simple ideas are conveyed by one sense, such as the ideas of colors, sounds, tastes, smells, and touches. One crucial case for which Locke argued is the idea of solidity, which he claimed we receive by touch. This idea is that of a basic quality of bodies. It is not the same as the space that bodies occupy, nor is it the same as the subjective experience of hardness that we receive when we feel objects. Instead, for Locke, solidity is akin to the fundamental physical notion of "mass" in Newtonian physics. It is that which makes up bodies. To those who doubted that they were actually acquainted with such an idea, Locke suggested that they place a physical object, such as a ball, between their hands and then try to join them. Such an experience, presumably, would provide a complete and adequate knowledge of solidity—or at least as complete and adequate an idea as we are capable of obtaining of any simple idea. The importance of this idea in Locke's theory will be seen shortly with regard to his theory of primary and secondary qualities.

Some of our ideas are conveyed by two or more senses. Locke included in this group the ideas of space or extension, figure, rest, and motion, which, he said, we receive by means of both sight and touch. Other ideas come from reflection. Still others are the result of both reflection and sensation. Included in this latter group are the ideas of pleasure and pain and the idea of power (which we gain from reflecting on our experience of our own ability to move parts of ourselves at will).

Qualities of Objects

If these are the types of ideas that we possess, classified according to their sources, can we distinguish those ideas that resemble actual features, or qualities of objects, and those that do not? The qualities of objects are divided by Locke into two categories, the primary and the secondary ones. The primary ones are those that are inseparable from bodies no matter what state the object may be in. This group includes solidity, extension, figure, mobility, and number. In contrast, the secondary qualities "are nothing in the objects themselves, but the powers to produce various sensations in us by their primary qualities," such as the power of an object, through the motion of its solid, extended parts, to produce sounds, tastes, and odors in us when we are affected by it.

Thus, in Locke's theory, objects possess primary qualities, the basic ingredients of Newtonian physics, and they possess secondary ones, which are actually the powers of the primary qualities to cause us to perceive features, such as colors, odors, and so on, which are not "in" the objects themselves. In terms of this distinction, we can say that our ideas of primary qualities resemble the characteristics of existing objects outside us, whereas our ideas of secondary qualities do not. The primary qualities of things are really in them, whereas the secondary qualities, as perceived sensations, are only in the observer. If there were no observers, only the primary qualities and their powers would exist. Hence, the rich, colorful, tasteful, noisy, odorous world of our experience is only the way *we* are affected by objects, not the way objects actually are. This distinction between our ideas of primary and secondary qualities led Locke to argue that some of our ideas give us genuine information about reality, while others do not.

The Idea of Substance

In the remainder of the second book of *An Essay Concerning Human Understanding*, Locke surveyed the various other kinds of ideas that we possess, those gained by reflection, those that are complexes, and so on. The most important, in terms of his theory and in terms of later philosophy, is the complex idea of substance. The idea of substance originates from the fact that in our experience a great many simple ideas constantly occur together. We then presume them to belong to one thing because we cannot imagine how these simple ideas can subsist by themselves. Therefore, we accustom ourselves to suppose that there must be some *substratum* in which the ideas subsist, and we call this substratum a substance. When we ask ourselves what idea we actually have of a substance, we find that our idea is only that of a *something* to which the constantly conjoined ideas belong. When we try to find out what this something is, we discover that we do not know, except that we suppose it must be a something that can support or contain the qualities that could produce the collection of simple

ideas in us. If we attempt to find out something more definite about the nature of substance, we discover that we cannot. What do color and weight belong to? If we answer, to the extended solid parts, then to what do these belong? It is, Locke suggested, similar to the case of the Indian philosopher who said that the world is supported by a great elephant. When asked what supported the elephant, he replied that it rested on a great tortoise. When asked what the tortoise rested on, he conceded and said, "I know not what." This, Locke asserted, is all that can finally be said of the nature of substance. It is something—we know not what—which we suppose is the support of the qualities that we perceive or that affect us.

Each constantly conjoined group of qualities we assume belongs to some particular substance, which we name "horse," "gold," "man," and so on. We possess no clear idea of substance, either in the case of physical things or in the case of spiritual things. However, we find that we cannot believe that either the physical qualities or the mental ones that we always experience together can exist without belonging to something. Therefore, although we have no definite ideas, we assume that there must be both bodies and spirits underlying and supporting the qualities that give rise to our ideas. Our inability to obtain clear ideas of substances, however, forever prevents us from gaining genuine knowledge about the real nature of things.

Ideas and Reality

At the end of the second book of *An Essay Concerning Human Understanding*, Locke evaluated what he had discovered about the nature of our ideas. This evaluation commences the examination of the problem of the extent and certitude of our knowledge, which is developed at length in the fourth book. Our ideas are real, Locke contended, when they have a foundation in nature and when they conform with the real character of things. In this sense, all simple ideas are real because they must be the result of genuine events and things (since the mind cannot create them but receives them from experience). However, not all real ideas are necessarily adequate representations of what does in fact exist. Ideas of primary qualities are both real and adequate.

Ideas of secondary qualities are real but only partially represent what is outside us. They represent powers that exist but not features corresponding to the ones that we perceive. The ideas of substances that we have are very inadequate, because we are never sure that we are aware of all the qualities that are joined together in one substance, nor are we sure of why they are so joined. Hence, some of our ideas tell us what is really outside us, whereas other ideas, caused by what is outside us or by our reflection on our ideas, do not adequately represent "real" objects.

Later philosophers, such as George Berkeley and David Hume, were to argue that once Locke had admitted that some of our ideas were neither representative of reality nor adequate to portray reality, he could not then be certain that *any* of our ideas actually correspond to real features of the world. Hence, they contended that Locke, in trying to build from an empirical theory of knowledge to genuine knowledge of reality, had actually laid the groundwork for a skeptical denial of the contention that people can know anything beyond the ideas in their own minds. Locke's theory rested on maintaining that our ideas of primary qualities resemble genuine characteristics of reality. However, the opponents argued, primary qualities are really no different from secondary qualities, as we know them, and hence we have no assurance from the ideas themselves that some are real and adequate and others are not.

Words and Language

The third book of *An Essay Concerning Human Understanding* appears to deal with some unrelated topics, those concerning the nature of words and language. This book, which evoked the interest of those concerned with linguistic philosophy, covers problems normally dealt with in anthropology, psychology, linguistics, and philosophy.

Two points that are raised are of central importance to Locke's main theme of the nature and extent of our knowledge and played a role in the later history of empirical philosophy. One of these is Locke's theory concerning the meaning and referent of general terms, such as "man" and "triangle." All things that exist, Locke asserted, are particular, but by abstracting from our ideas of things, by separating from them particular details or features, we finally form a general idea. In this way, we arrive at the general abstract ideas about which we reason. Berkeley and Hume both challenged Locke on this point and insisted that we do not, in fact, possess any abstract general ideas. Hence, they insisted that an empirical account of our ideas of so-called general terms must be developed from the particular ideas that we have.

One of the general terms that Locke claimed gained some meaning from the abstracting process is "substance." However, when he analyzed what we might mean by the term, Locke distinguished between what he called "the nominal essence" and "the real essence" of a substance. The nominal essence is that abstract general idea of a substance formed by abstracting the basic group of features that constantly occur together. The real essence, in contrast, is the nature of the object that accounts for its having the properties that it does. The nominal essence describes what properties a substance has, whereas the real essence explains why it has these properties. Unfortunately, Locke pointed out, we can never know the real essence of anything, since our information, which we abstract from, deals only with the qualities that we experience and never with the ultimate causes that account for the occurrence of these properties. Thus, our knowledge of things is sure to be sharply curtailed because of the fact that we will never discover the reasons why things have the characteristics that they have.

Knowledge as Comparison of Ideas

The fourth and last book of *An Essay Concerning Human Understanding* deals with knowledge in general, with the scope of knowledge, and with the question of how certain we can be of such knowledge. Our knowledge deals only with ideas, since these are the only items with which the mind is directly acquainted. What constitutes knowledge, according to Locke, is the perception of the agreement or disagreement of two ideas. Ideas may agree or disagree in four ways. They may possibly be identical or diverse. They may be related in some respect. They may agree in coexisting in the same subject or substance. They may agree or disagree in having a real existence outside the mind. All of our knowledge, Locke insisted, falls under these headings. We know either that some ideas are the same or different, or that they are related, or that they always coexist, or that they really exist independently of our minds.

If these are the kinds of items that we can know about, how can we gain such knowledge? One source of our knowledge is intuition, the direct and immediate perception of the agreement or disagreement of any two ideas. The mind "sees" that black is not white and that a circle is not a triangle. Also, "this kind of knowledge is the clearest and most certain that human frailty is capable of." Anyone who demands more certainty than that gained by intuition "demands he knows not what, and shows only that he has a mind to be a sceptic, without being able to be so." All certain knowledge depends upon intuition as its source and guarantee.

The Problem of Certitude
We acquire knowledge not only by directly inspecting ideas but also through demonstrations. According to Locke, when we know by demonstration, we do not see *immediately* that two ideas agree or disagree, but we see *immediately* by means of connecting two ideas with others until we are able to connect them with each other. This process is actually a series of intuitions, and each step in a demonstration is therefore certain. However, because the steps occur successively in the mind, error is possible if we forget the previous steps or if we assume that one has occurred if it actually has not. Intuition and demonstration are the only two sources of certain knowledge.

However, there is another source of knowledge that has a degree of certitude assuring us of truths about particular experiences. This kind of knowledge goes beyond bare probability but does not reach genuine certainty. It is called "sensitive knowledge," which is the assurance that we have on the occurrence of specific experiences, that certain external objects actually exist that cause or produce these experiences. We cannot reasonably believe, Locke insisted, that all of our experiences are imaginary or are just part of a dream. Hence, we have sensitive knowledge, a degree of assurance that something real is going on outside us.

The Extent of Human Knowledge
In terms of these kinds of knowledge, types of sources, and degrees of certainty, it is now possible to outline the extent of human knowledge and to evaluate what we can actually know about the real world. We can gain knowledge only to the extent that we can discover agreements or disagreements among our ideas. Because we can neither intuit nor demonstrate all the relations that ideas can have with one another, our knowledge is not even as extensive as our ideas. In almost all cases, we can determine with certainty whether our ideas are identical or different from one another. We can tell if our ideas are related to others only when we can discover sufficient intermediary ideas. In fields such as mathematics, we keep expanding our knowledge as more connections between ideas are intuited or demonstrated. The areas in which we seem to be most limited in gaining knowledge are those dealing with the coexistence and real existence of ideas. Because we can never know the real essence of any substance, we can never know why any two ideas must necessarily coexist. We never discover why particular secondary qualities occur when a specific arrangement of primary qualities exists. We are aware of the fact that certain ideas occur over and over again in combination, but we do not know why they do this. With regard to real existence, we are, Locke maintained, intuitively certain of our own existence and demonstratively certain that God exists. We are only sensitively certain that anything else exists, which means that we have serious assurance that objects other than ourselves and God exist only when we have experiences that we feel must be caused by something outside us. Our assurance in these cases is limited to the actual moment when we are having these experiences. Once an experience is over, we have no certitude at all that the object that caused the experience still continues to exist. All that we can know about an object when we know that it exists is that at such times it actually possesses the primary qualities that we perceive, together with the power to produce the other effects that we experience.

This assessment of the extent of our knowledge indicates, according to Locke, that we can never know enough to develop a genuine, certain science of bodies or of spirits, because our information about their existence and their natures is so extremely limited. However, we can obtain sufficient knowledge and probable information to satisfy our needs in this world, so we should not despair or become skeptical just because investigation has revealed how limited our knowledge actually is and how uncertain it is in many areas.

Foundations of Empiricism

Locke's *An Essay Concerning Human Understanding* represents the first major modern presentation of the empirical theory of knowledge. In developing an account of human knowledge in terms of how it is derived from experience, what its nature is, and how limited it is, Locke provided the basic pattern of future empirical philosophy. In attempting to justify some basis for maintaining that we can have some knowledge of some aspects of reality, Locke raised many of the problems that have remained current in philosophical discussions up to the present time. Empiricists after Locke, such as Berkeley and Hume, showed that if one consistently followed out the thesis that all of our knowledge comes from experience, one could not be certain that substances exist or that anything exists beyond the ideas directly perceived. Locke's *Essay* is the source of many of the methods, ideas, and problems that have prevailed in philosophy, especially in British and American epistemology, ever since its first publication.

Richard H. Popkin

Additional Reading

Ayers, Michael. *Locke*. New York: Routledge, 1999. An excellent biographical introduction to the thoughts of the philosopher, clearly presented and requiring no special background. Bibliography.

Brantley, Richard E. *Locke, Wesley, and the Method of English Romanticism*. Gainesville: University of Florida Press, 1984. Brantley alleges that John Locke influenced John Wesley, the founder of the Methodist Church, and that Wesley's work influenced the eighteenth century Romantic poets.

Chappell, Vere, ed. *John Locke: Theory of Knowledge*. New York: Garland, 1992. Thirty critical essays about the philosopher and his ideas concerning knowledge, reprinted from their original locations. This book is volume 8 in a series; Locke's philosophy of politics is contained in volume 9.

Kramer, Matthew H. *John Locke and the Origins of Private Property*. Cambridge, England: Cambridge University Press, 1997. A detailed analysis of Locke's theories about the rewards of labor and the relationships between labor and ownership.

Lennon, Thomas M. *The Battle of the Gods and Giants*. Princeton, N.J.: Princeton University Press, 1993. This book is about René Descartes and Pierre Gassendi, but a forty-page chapter and a few pages at the end of the book are devoted to Locke's inheritance from both philosophers.

Schouls, Peter A. *Reasoned Freedom: John Locke and the Enlightenment*. Ithaca, N.Y.: Cornell University Press, 1992. Compares Locke to Descartes, then invites comparison to other philosophers, such as Michael Oakeshott, by presenting Locke's defense of reason and his explications of freedom, self-determination, and education.

Seliger, M. *The Liberal Politics of John Locke*. London: George Allen & Unwin, 1968. Seliger attempts to explain the ambiguities and contradictions of Locke and thereby explain his system. He has more argument with opinions about Locke than he has with Locke.

Tully, James. *A Discourse on Property: John Locke and His Adversaries*. Cambridge, England.: Cambridge University Press, 1980. Locke's theories of property have long caused argument among political thinkers. This book is Tully's attempt to reconsider what Locke said.

Zuckert, Michael P. *Natural Rights and the New Republicanism*. Princeton, N.J.: Princeton University Press, 1994. Locke (and many others) wrote about "natural rights." This book about the thought of a number of philosophers features text about Locke and his influence on the Americans, on questions about natural law, on government, and on property.

Richard L. Hillard, updated by Dwight Jensen

Lucretius

Lucretius synthesized primary tenets of Greek Epicureanism and atomism and offered a rational, nontheological explanation for the constituents of the universe; he did this in Latin hexameter verse and developed a philosophical vocabulary for the task.

Principal philosophical work: *De rerum natura*, c. 60 B.C.E. (*On the Nature of Things*, 1862).

Born: c. 98 B.C.E.; probably Rome
Died: October 15, 55 B.C.E.; Rome

Early Life

It is much easier to show why most of what has been written about the life of Titus Lucretius Carus is incorrect, doubtful, or malicious than it is to arrive at a reliable account. Relatively little can be deduced from his poem, and there are no substantive contemporary references to him. Consequently, too much credence has been given to the jumbled biographical note written by Saint Jerome, which itself was derived from an unreliable account by the Roman historian Gaius Suetonius Tranquillus. Saint Jerome miscalculates Lucretius's dates of birth and death; also, it is unlikely that Lucretius was driven insane by a love potion and wrote *On the Nature of Things* during periods of lucidity. The latter story seems to have arisen from Lucretius's treatment of love in section 4 of the poem.

Several details of Lucretius's early life can, however, be inferred with relative certainty. His name is a strange combination that implies both servile (Carus) and noble origins (from the kinship grouping *Gens Lucretia*), but he was likely closer to the middle class of his contemporary Cicero. Though Cicero himself did not emend Lucretius's poetry, as Saint Jerome reports, it is likely that his brother Quintus Cicero oversaw its publication. Like Cicero, Lucretius appears to have evinced an early interest in philosophy, influenced by the Alexandrian movement, though his own poetry has an old Roman spirit reflecting his readings of Quintus Ennius. Cicero thought that Lucretius had the "genius" of Ennius and the "art" of the Alexandrians.

Lucretius lived through the turmoil caused by the civil war between aristocrat Lucius Cornelius Sulla and populist Gaius Marius as well as the conspiracy of Lucius Sergius Catilina. He also witnessed the consequent decline of Roman republican government. Perhaps this political uncertainty directed him to the comfortable philosophy of Epicurus, which held that the goal of human existence should be a life of calm pleasure tempered by morality and culture. The atomism of Democritus and Leucippus, which held that the material universe could be understood as random combinations of minute particles (*atomoi*), provided a rational and scientific means of explaining the cosmos and avoiding what Lucretius came to see as the sterile superstitions of religion.

In all, the impressions one has of Lucretius at this early stage in his life are of a young man of good background and a good education who is eager not for the political arena or personal advancement but to explain the world in a reasonable way to Romans with similar education who would read his verse. In addition, he aimed to make living in that rationally explained world as pleasant an experience as possible.

Life's Work

One can only guess how Lucretius lived during the years he was writing *On the Nature of Things* from its dedication to Gaius Memmius. Memmius held the office of praetor in 58 B.C.E. and fancied himself a poet, primarily of erotic verse

Lucretius. *(Corbis/Bettmann)*

The times in which Lucretius lived cried out for reasonableness. Educated Romans saw the obvious conflict between their elaborate mythology and their religion, which glorified deities who did everything from seducing women to causing mildew. Even so, Rome continued to fill the various priestly colleges, to take auspices as a means of determining favorable outcomes, and to celebrate public games in honor of these very deities. A century later, Rome would deify its emperors, partly to shift its religious observances to personalities who were incontestably real and partly to curb the spread of imported cults such as Mithraism and what came to be known as Christianity.

Lucretius had solved this problem, for himself at least, and outlined his position on religion in *On the Nature of Things*. The creative force of nature is real; it is personified in the goddess Venus. The deities are simply personifications of various aspects of nature, and human beings can free themselves of superstition by seeing the world as constantly recombining *atomoi*. Death itself is nothing more than atomic dissolution, a preparation for new arrangements of atoms and new creation. If human beings can accept death in these terms, they can cast aside the fear that binds them to religious superstition. This acceptance will prepare them to see that life's purpose is to maximize pleasure and minimize pain.

Neither of these theories is new; they are derived from the atomism of Democritus and Leucippus and the teachings of Epicurus. What is new is Lucretius's synthesis and his offering it as rational scientism to educated Roman readers. One reason almost nothing is known about Lucretius's personal life is undoubtedly his determination to practice these ideas. Removing himself from the fray to seek philosophical calm would necessarily have resulted in a lack of contemporary biographical references, but it is precisely on this score that Lucretian Epicureanism is most misunderstood. It is just the opposite of egocentric gratification, because Lucretius couples it with the mechanics of atomism. Seen in this way, the individual is merely a part in the world ma-

in the style of Catullus. Memmius's shady political dealings eventually caught up with him, and he was driven into exile; nevertheless, it is reasonable to assume that Lucretius received some financial support from him. Memmius figures less importantly in the body of the poem, however, and his name is used in places only for metrical convenience.

Details of the poem show the kind of atmosphere Lucretius wished to escape, essentially that of his own city in the final years of the republic. The world is filled with gloom, war, and decay. The poet wishes to stand on a hill, far removed from wickedness and ambition, and watch the waste and destruction. Passages such as these reveal a man who yearned for tranquil anonymity. Other writers, such as Cicero, would find themselves propelled into a political maelstrom that would ultimately destroy them; Lucretius was determined to avoid this fate.

chine; immortality exists, but only in the myriad indestructible *atomoi* that constitute each part.

One can only guess how Lucretius first encountered Epicureanism. There were Greek professors in Rome during the first century B.C.E. who taught the theories of Epicurus. Cicero mentions non-Greek Epicureans who wrote treatises Lucretius might easily have read. The ease with which Lucretius deals with the technical vocabulary of atomism suggests that he was accomplished in Greek. (This would be expected of any educated Roman.) He no doubt read Epicurus, Democritus, and Leucippus in the original language.

Reading Greek gave Lucretius access to other sources, such as Empedocles, the philosopher-poet who wrote *Peri physeos* (fifth century B.C.E.; *On Nature*, 1908). What the modern world calls "natural selection" comes to Lucretius through Empedocles, as does the principle of attraction and repulsion, which Lucretius sees as "love" and "hate." Lucretius's hexameter meter is used by Empedocles but also by Homer. Indeed, Lucretius borrows from Homer, Euripides, Thucydides, Hippocrates, and various early Roman poets.

Though his philosophy is Greek, Lucretius maintains a very Roman insistence on the primacy of law. In *On the Nature of Things*, for example, he notes that human beings moved from primitive status to society only after they had agreed on a social contract. Language improved on gesture, and social order prevailed. It is worth noting that similar ideas later appear in the creation account of Ovid in *Metamorphoses* (c. 8 C.E.; English translation, 1567). Though Lucretius failed to convert the Roman masses, he obviously made inroads among his successors in poetry. Vergil read him, too, and while Vergil's work is more elegant, there can be little doubt that he was impressed by Lucretius's descriptions of nature; one can easily see their influence in Vergil's pastoral poems.

The random nature of the *clinamen* ("swerve") that atoms make when they recombine must have troubled Lucretius, since he is generally insistent on the orderly cycle of nature. This bothered others, too, but it is the only way to explain natural differences atomically. The *membranae* ("films"), which are thrown from objects and thereby produce visual impressions, are another artificial means of describing a natural phenomenon, but *On the Nature of Things* is, on the whole, free of such difficulties.

The poem's six books show evidence of unfinished composition, but one cannot deduce Lucretius's premature death from this fact. The Victorian poet Alfred, Lord Tennyson perpetuated Suetonius's marvelous fiction of Lucretius's insanity and death by a love potion, but the author of *On the Nature of Things* was a very sane man whose entire reason for living was to bring rationality to an irrational world.

Influence

Lucretius privileged the creative force of nature, but he in no sense resembled the English Romantic poets in their wonderment at its powers. He was the rare combination of natural scientist, philosopher, and poet, and he strove for clarity and reasonableness in what he wrote. He clearly was not the gaunt, love-crazed, mad genius of Suetonius and Saint Jerome, but an evangelizer who appealed to an educated audience, much like modern-day writers of popular science.

Lucretius thus became a symbol that served the purposes of those who wrote about him. Because the facts of his life remained a mystery, even to the generation that immediately followed his own, he could be portrayed by Suetonius as foreshadowing the Roman Empire's vice, by Saint Jerome as representing pagan degeneracy, and ultimately by Tennyson as typifying egocentric gratification. Even so, as is true of many great lives, work overshadows personality, and this is clearly what Lucretius intended, for *On the Nature of Things* opened a world of what would otherwise have remained esoteric Greek philosophy to a popular audience. What is more important, Lucretius presented these ideas as a means of dealing with his own troubled world.

Were one to cancel out Lucretius's masterly synthesis of Epicureanism and atomism, his contribution to both Roman poetry and the Latin language would remain. Nearly one hundred technical words adapted from the Greek appear within six books of hexameter verse, the epic meter of Homer and of Lucretius's fellow Roman Ennius. That Lucretius's work inspired the succeeding generation of Roman poets, which included both Vergil and Ovid, attests its immediate influence. The modern reader, armed with contemporary science and psychology, can object only to the mechanics of the natural phenomena Lucretius discusses; his plea to cast aside superstition and fear strikes a welcome note.

Robert J. Forman

On the Nature of Things

Type of philosophy: Metaphysics
First transcribed: De rerum natura, c. 60 B.C.E. (English translation, 1862)
Principal ideas advanced:

◇ Nothing is ever generated from nothing; nature consists of atoms moving in void.

◇ Atoms naturally move downward, but when some swerve from their course, collisions occur; free will in human beings is a similar phenomenon.

◇ Everything in nature is different from every other thing; the number of atoms of each shape is infinite, although the shapes of atoms are not infinite in number.

◇ Sensed qualities are produced by combinations of atoms of various shapes, sizes, and weights.

◇ The soul is composed of atoms; hence, at death the soul dies with the body.

Lucretius's *On the Nature of Things*, which many consider to be the greatest didactic poem in any language, is an exposition of the philosophy of Epicurus. No divergence of doctrine, however minute, is to be found between Lucretius and his master.

After an invocation to Venus, symbolic of the loveliness, fruitfulness, and peace of nature, Lucretius eulogizes Epicurus as the deliverer of humankind from the superstitious terrors of religion:

When human life lay foul before the eyes, crushed on the earth beneath heavy religion, who showed her face from the regions of heaven, glowering over mortals with horrible visage, first a Greek man dared to lift mortal eyes against her and to stand up to her; nei-

ther stories of gods nor thunderbolts nor heaven with menacing growl checked him, but all the more they goaded the spirited manliness of his mind, so that he longed to be first to break through the tight locks of nature's portals. Thus the lively force of his mind prevailed, and he journeyed far beyond the flaming walls of the world and traversed the whole immensity with mind and soul, whence victorious he reports to us what limit there is to the power of each thing, and by what law each has its boundary-stone set deep. And so religion in turn is cast down under foot and trampled; the victory exalts us to heaven.

People make themselves miserable through fear of divine caprice in this life and of hellfire after it. Lucretius argued that the first fear comes from ignorance of the workings of nature and the latter from the false belief in an immortal soul. The cure for both is an understanding of materialist philosophy. "Thus of necessity this terror of the mind, these darknesses, not the rays of the sun nor the bright arrows of daylight will disperse, but nature's aspect and her law."

You may think, says Lucretius to Memmius (the Roman official to whom the poem is dedicated), that the materialist philosophy is unholy. Not so: "On the contrary, that very religion has very often given birth to criminal and impious deeds." For instance, the sacrifice of Iphigenia by her father. "*Tantum religio potuit suadere malorum!*—so much of evil has religion been able to put over!"

Nature and Atoms
The first law of nature is "Nothing is ever generated from nothing, by any divine force." This Lucretius takes to be amply proved by experience. If something could come from nothing, then anything could beget anything, or things would pop up out of season, or adult humans and trees would appear all at once. The observed regularity of birth and growth implies fixed seeds of all things or, in other words, sufficient causes of all that happens. Nor can anything disappear into nothing; if it could, then already in the infinity of time nothing would be left. "By no means then do any of the things that are seen

perish utterly; since Nature refashions one thing out of another, nor permits anything to be born unless aided by the death of something else."

Nature consists of atoms ("seeds," "beginnings"—Lucretius does not use the Greek word) too small to be seen, but nevertheless real. The winds, odors, heat, and cold show that real things can be invisible, and the drying of wet clothes and the gradual wearing away of rings and stones proves that the things we can see are made of tiny particles. Because things move, there must be void space for them to move in. Visible objects contain much void, as is proved by differences in density and by the free passage of heat and sound through apparently solid objects, of water through rocks, and of food through the tissues of the body. Besides atoms and void, no third kind of thing exists; everything else that has a name is either an essential or accidental property of these two.

Atoms are absolutely solid, containing no void within them, and therefore are internally changeless. If they were not, there would be no large-scale objects left, for all would have been pulverized in infinite time. Moreover, if things were infinitely divisible, then the sum of things and the least thing would be equal, both containing an equal, infinite, number of parts—an absurd situation, according to Lucretius.

After refuting (what he takes to be) the rival theories of Heraclitus, Empedocles, and Anaxagoras, Lucretius proceeds to prove that the universe is infinite in space. If it were not, what would happen if you went to the edge of it and shot an arrow? Either the arrow would stop, because there was something beyond to stop it, or it would not, and again there would be space beyond the presumed boundary. The number of atoms in infinite space is also infinite, for because their general tendency is to fly apart, a finite number in infinite space would have to so spread out that the average density would be near zero, which is against observation. There is no center to the world and no antipodes. (All the ancient atomists continued to hold that the earth was a flat disc, even though schools such as the Pythagoreans and Aristotelians, less scientific in their general principles, had long known better.)

Book 1 concludes with a well-known passage, more applicable to the progressive nature of science than to the fossilized dogmas of Epicureanism:

> These things you will learn thus, led on with little trouble; for one thing will grow clear from another, nor will blind night snatch away the road and not let you perceive Nature's ultimates. Thus things will kindle lights for things.

The proem to book 2 is the longest ethical passage in the poem, depicting the peaceful serenity of the Epicurean's life, contrasted with the troubled existence of the unenlightened, who in getting and spending lay waste their powers.

The Qualities of Atoms

Atoms move either by their own weight or by blows from other atoms. Left to themselves, atoms move "downward" (Lucretius fails to define what down means in an infinite, centerless universe), all at the same speed, faster than light, because the void offers no resistance. No atom, then, would ever have hit another if it were not for the fact that "at quite an uncertain time and at uncertain places they push out a little from their course." Thus one hits another, the second a third, and so on. Lucretius also employs this "swerve," which is supposed to occur not just "in the beginning" but in the present, to account for free will in human beings.

Everything in nature is different from every other thing: Each lamb knows its own mother, one blade of wheat is not exactly like the next. The atoms also differ in their shapes. Lightning, though it is fire, "consists of more subtle and smaller figures." Honey is sweet because, being made of smooth and round bodies, it caresses the tongue and palate, while the hooked atoms of wormwood tear them. (According to atomism, all the senses are varieties of touch.) The *shapes* of atoms are not infinite in number. If they were, Lucretius infers, there would have to be some that were of enormous size. However, the number of atoms of each shape is infinite. Not every kind of particle can link with every other—that would produce monstrosities.

All combustibles contain particles capable of tossing fire abroad. Anything (such as a fruit) that has color, taste, and smell must contain at least three kinds of constituent atoms. However, no atom *by itself* has color, savor, or odor; the properties of atoms are simply solidity, size, shape, and weight. Colors and the other sensed qualities are products of atomic *arrangements*. If colors were embedded in the ultimate constituents of matter, we should be unable to account for their rapid changes without violating the principle nothing-from-nothing. Lucretius has another argument: Because color is not essentially bound up with the shape of a thing, if atoms were themselves colored, we should expect all visible things to exist in all possible colors.

Nor are individual atoms endowed with consciousness. For sense depends on vital motions, and hence depends on birth. Heavy blows can produce unconsciousness, which ought not to happen if consciousness were independent of atomic arrangements. Pain is the result of a disturbance, but an atom cannot be (internally) disturbed. In addition, consciousness of each atom would lead to all sorts of absurdities, such as that not only a man but also his semen would be conscious.

Lucretius makes brilliant use of the atomistic principle that just as an indefinitely large number of meanings can be conveyed by rearranging the letters of the alphabet, "so also in things themselves, when motion, order, position, and figure are changed, the things also are bound to be changed."

There are other worlds, like this one, in the infinite universe. Indeed, the vastness and complexity of the universe is itself proof that the whole is not governed by gods: it would be too much for them. Or, if you assume intellects adequate for the task, it then becomes inexplicable why there is evil and confusion in the world.

Growth and decay pertain to worlds as much as to individuals. The vital powers of this earth are wearing out. "Indeed, already the broken and effete earth has difficulty in creating little animals, though it once created all the kinds at once, and gave birth to the huge bodies of wild beasts."

The Mind and the Soul

Lucretius distinguishes between the mind (*animus, mens*), which is what thinks in us, and the soul (*anima*), which is the vivifying principle: "seeds of wind and hot vapor, which take care that life shall stay in the limbs." Both, of course,

are made of atoms, "extremely subtle and minute." They form a unity: "Mind and soul are joined to each other and form one nature, but the chief, so to speak, that which rules the whole body, is the Reason. . . . It is situated in the middle region of the chest." Besides atoms of wind, air, and hot vapor, the mind also contains a fourth, unnamed kind of atom, "than which nothing finer or more mobile exists." This "very soul of the whole soul" has to be postulated to account for consciousness, which *is* the motion of this superfine substance. Lucretius is a consistent materialist; consciousness is not for him an unexplained product of atomic motions, distinct from them but, like color, an "accident" of atoms of a certain kind in a certain arrangement. In other words, consciousness is an atomic process.

Souls differ in their compositions: Lions have more heat, deer more wind, oxen more air. People also differ from one another; their temperaments depend on the makeup of their souls. However, Lucretius is quick to add: "So tiny are the traces of the natures, which Reason could not dispel from us, that nothing prevents us living a life worthy of the gods."

The soul particles are few in number compared to those of the flesh, as we know from our inability to sense very slight stimuli. It follows from the atomic nature of the soul that it is dispersed at death; hence consciousness ceases. Lucretius deems this point so important that he reinforces it with a multitude of observations. Lucretius points out that understanding grows with the body and decays with it; that the soul is affected by bodily diseases besides having some of its own; that mental ills can be cured by material medications; that "dying by pieces" in paralysis and the twitches of recently severed limbs show that the soul is divisible and therefore destructible; and that there must be *some* soul-fragments left in the body after death to account for the generation of worms in the corpse. He also points out that if the soul is immortal, we should remember our past existences (to the ancients, the immortality of the soul implied preexistence as much as life *post mortem*). To reply that the soul loses its memory at the shock of birth "is not, I think, to stray very far from death."

Animals have souls appropriate to their bodily constitutions. Thus, the transmigration hypothesis—that souls should queue up to get into a body—is not only incomprehensible but ridiculous. In general, each thing has its appointed place: that of the soul is the body. If the soul were immortal, there would be a tremendous grotesqueness in its being so intimately linked with a mortal thing (as Lucretius contends elsewhere, there could never have been any centaurs, because the disparity in growth rates between the limbs of equine and human beings render them incompatible). Immortal things are so because they cannot be assaulted (atoms), because they offer no resistance to blows (void), or because there is no room for them to scatter. None of these applies to the soul. Therefore, fears of hell are foolish.

> Death, therefore, is nothing to us, nor does it concern us in the least, inasmuch as the nature of the mind is held to be mortal. And just as we felt no ill in time gone by when the Carthaginians came from all quarters to the attack, when all things under the high shore of heaven shook and trembled in horror at the fearful tumult of war, and it was in doubt to which of them would fall the rule of all things human by land and sea—so, when we shall not exist, when there shall have been a parting of body and soul by whose union we are made one, you may know that by no means can anything happen to us, who will then not be, nor move our feeling; not if earth is confounded with sea and sea with sky.

Perception

The theory of vision in atomism is that objects constantly throw off "idols" or "semblances," very thin films, of which the snake's discarded skin furnishes an example. Such "idols" enter the eye and jostle the atoms of the mind, resulting in vision. The less said about this doctrine—which, as ancient critics pointed out, cannot even explain why people cannot see in the dark, or how people can get the "idol" of an elephant into our eye—the better. Although the Epicurean theory is patently false and ridiculous, its ancient rivals are unintelligible.

All perceptions are true, according to the Epicureans, even those in imagination and dreams—which are perceptions of finer idols that enter the body otherwise than through the eyes. It is in inferences from perception that errors arise. Epicurus held that the gods really do exist because they are perceived in dreams. They live in the peaceful spaces between the worlds, in "quiet mansions that winds do not shake, neither do clouds drench them with rainstorms nor the white fall of snow disturb them, hardened with bitter frost; ever a cloudless sky covers them, and smiles with light widely diffused." The gods are, in short, ideal Epicureans. The mistake of people is in their false inferences that these beings trouble themselves with *humans* or even know of their existence. *True* (Epicurean) religion consists in taking these blessed beings as models and making one's own life, as far as possible, like theirs.

In his discourse on perception and imagination, Lucretius takes the opportunity to state another important principle of materialist philosophy, the denial of purposive causation. One must not suppose that our organs were created *in order to* perform their appropriate functions: This is "back-to-front perverse reasoning, for nothing at all was born in the body so that we might be able to use it, but what is once born creates its own use."

This book concludes with a discussion of sex, genetics, and embryology, containing the philosopher's denunciation of the passion of love as "madness." It is best, Lucretius says, not to fall in love at all; but if you do, you can still be saved if only you will open your eyes to "all the blemishes of mind and body of her whom you desire."

The Origin of the World

The world was not created by the gods. If they set out to create a world, where could they get the plan for it other than through observation of nature? Lucretius explains the origin of the world this way:

> So many beginnings of things, of many kinds, already from infinite time driven on by blows and by their own weights, have kept on being carried along and hitting together, all trying to unite in all ways, creating whatever conglomerations were possible among them, so that it is no wonder that they have fallen into those dispositions also and come through

those passages by which the present sum of things is carried on by renewal.

However, even if we knew nothing of this concourse of atoms, we ought still to reject the hypothesis of divine creation, on account of the many evils in the world. Most of the earth is uninhabitable sea, mountain, and desert; what can be lived in requires laborious clearing and cultivation, the fruits whereof are uncertain. Why are there wild beasts, diseases, untimely deaths, the helplessness of human infancy?

The world is young, for discoveries—such is the Epicurean philosophy—are still being made. The heavy earth-seeds came together and squeezed out the smoother and rounder, which went to make sea, stars, sun, and moon. Lucretius gives five alternative explanations of the revolutions of the heavens; one is free to take one's choice as long as gods are not introduced.

First bushes appeared on the earth's surface, then trees, then, by spontaneous generation, birds and beasts. "Wherever there was an opportune spot, wombs grew, grasping the earth with their roots." Many monsters (though no centaurs) came out of them; in the end, all perished except those few that were capable of feeding and protecting themselves and begetting offspring. Although this account contains the notion of survival of the fittest, it is hardly an improvement over the fantasies of Empedocles and distinctly inferior to the evolutionary speculations of Anaximander, who in the sixth century B.C.E. had already freed himself from the prejudice of fixity of species.

Civilization

Lucretius next proceeds to a reconstruction of the history of civilization. This passage, which has nothing to do with atomist principles, is a marvel of shrewd deduction, confirmed in almost all its details by modern anthropology and archaeology. His principle of reasoning is that certain discoveries could not have been made unless others had preceded them; for example, woven textiles must have come after iron, which is necessary for making various parts of the loom. (Although he was mistaken, the method is promising.)

Fire came first and made possible stable family relationships and the development of human sympathy. "Then too neighbors began to join in friendship, anxious neither to harm nor be harmed among themselves." Language arose in these primitive societies, first as mere animal cries, but developing by the assignment of conventional names. Then came kings and cities and property and gold. Then revolts broke out against absolute rulers, leading to the rule of law. Religion, unfortunately, also arose. Metallurgy was discovered accidentally: first that of copper, silver, and gold, later bronze and iron.

Though this account, quite unlike most ancient philosophies, shows a knowledge of technology and of the idea of progressive development, Lucretius did not consider material progress an unalloyed blessing. Life was on balance no more secure in his day than in times of savagery; then one might be eaten by a wild beast, but one did not have to contend with looting armies. Then one might have poisoned oneself through ignorance; however, for Lucretius the danger was that someone else might poison you very skillfully. Lucretius the materialist wrote:

> Thus the race of men labors always in vain, and uses up its time of life in idle cares, truly because it has not learned what the limit of getting is, nor at all how far true pleasure can increase. And this, little by little, has raised life up to the height and stirred up from below the great tides of war.

Book 6 consists of miscellaneous Epicurean "explanations" of phenomena such as thunder, lightning, and earthquakes, the natural causes of which need to be understood lest they provide material for religion to use to frighten people. The poem ends abruptly after a translation of Thucydides's description of the plague at Athens in the second year of the Peloponnesian War.

Wallace I. Matson, updated by John K. Roth

Additional Reading

Bréhier, Émile. *The Hellenistic and Roman Age.* Translated by Wade Baskin. Chicago: University of Chicago Press, 1965. Deals with Epicurus, Lucretius, and atomistic metaphysics in the broad context of ancient Greek and Roman philosophy.

Clay, Diskin. *Lucretius and Epicurus.* Ithaca, N.Y.:

Cornell University Press, 1983. A helpful comparative study of the metaphysical and ethical philosophies of two important thinkers from the ancient world.

Copleston, Frederick. *A History of Philosophy: Greece and Rome*. Garden City, N.Y.: Doubleday, 1962. Copleston provides a brief but clear discussion of Lucretius in his chapter on "Epicureanism."

Dalzell, Alexander. *The Criticism of Didactic Poetry: Essays on Lucretius, Virgil, and Ovid*. Toronto: University of Toronto Press, 1997. Explores how Lucretius used poetic forms to express his philosophical views.

Gale, Monika. *Myth and Poetry in Lucretius*. Cambridge, England: Cambridge University Press, 1994. Lucretius's distinctive use of poetic imagery is analyzed in a study that sheds light on his methods and metaphysics.

Jones, W. T. *A History of Western Philosophy: The Classical Mind*. New York: Harcourt Brace, 1969. In a chapter on ancient atomism and materialism, Jones discusses Lucretius in a clear and accessible way.

Pelikan, Jaroslav. *What Has Athens to Do with Jerusalem? Timaeus and Genesis in Counterpoint*. Ann Arbor: University of Michigan Press, 1997. Reflects on the similarities and differences between biblical views and other important philosophical outlooks from the ancient world, including the Epicurean outlook amplified by Lucretius.

Sedley, D. N. *Lucretius and the Transformation of Greek Wisdom*. Cambridge, England: Cambridge University Press, 1998. Shows how Lucretius built on and departed from Greek traditions that informed the context in which he worked.

Segal, Charles. *Lucretius on Death and Anxiety: Poetry and Philosophy in "De Rerum Natura."* Princeton, N.J.: Princeton University Press, 1990. Shows how Lucretius developed his understanding that death is not to be feared.

Robert J. Forman, updated by John K. Roth

Jean-François Lyotard

Writing on philosophy, politics, and aesthetics, Lyotard made the link between postmodernism and poststructuralism, engaged the problems of psychoanalysis, Marxism, and deconstruction, and examined the way society legitimizes knowledge and discourse.

Principal philosophical works: *Le Phénoménologie*, 1954 (*Phenomenology*, 1991); *Discours, figure*, 1971; *Dérive à partir de Marx et Freud*, 1973 (partial translation, *Driftworks*, 1984); *Économie libidinale*, 1974 (*Libidinal Economy*, 1993); *La Condition postmoderne: Rapport sur le savoir*, 1979 (*The Postmodern Condition: A Report on Knowledge*, 1984); *Le Différend*, 1983 (*The Differend: Phrases in Dispute*, 1988); *Le Postmoderne expliqué aux enfants: Correspondance, 1982-1985*, 1986 (*The Postmodern Explained to Children: Correspondence, 1982-1985*, 1992); *Heidegger et "les juifs,"* 1988 (*Heidegger and "the Jews,"* 1990); *L'Inhumain: Causeries sur le temps*, 1988 (*The Inhuman: Reflections on Time*, 1991); *Peregrinations: Law, Form, Event*, 1988; *The Lyotard Reader*, 1989; *Leçons sur l'Analytique du sublime: Kant, "Critique de la faculté de juger,"* 1991 (*Lessons on the Analytic of the Sublime: Kant's "Critique of Judgment,"* 1994); *Toward the Postmodern*, 1993.

Born: August 10, 1924; Versailles, France
Died: April 21, 1998; Paris, France

Early Life

Jean-François Lyotard was an intellectual committed to political action whose life's work in philosophy emerged slowly. He was a secondary school teacher in French Algeria from 1950 to 1952 before the start of the Algerian war for national liberation, a cause he actively and publicly supported. In 1954, he published his first book, *Phenomenology*, a work heavily influenced by the philosopher Martin Heidegger. In this book, Lyotard defined the intellectual's role as that of understanding history in terms made available through phenomenology. Subsequently, his politics became increasingly radical, and he adopted an anti-Soviet form of Marxism. From 1954 to 1964, he was a member of the editorial board of *Socialisme ou Barbarisme*, a Marxist periodical that was critical of the totalitarianism of the Soviet Union. During this time, he also contributed articles to the periodical *Pouvoir ouvrier* (worker power). His antagonism to authoritarianism led him to join an intellectual movement that in May, 1968, expressed its sympathies with the student

and worker riots that shook French life; many of the student organizers of these riots were students of Lyotard, who was working as a lecturer at Nanterre University at that point.

Life's Work

Lyotard began the work for which he is best known with the publication of his doctoral dissertation, *Discours, figure* (conscious and unconscious communication). In the dissertation, Lyotard rejects the structuralism that had dominated French thought in the 1960's and relies on Sigmund Freud's distinction between the conscious and the unconscious to distinguish between the conscious element of communication (discourse) and the unconscious (figure), the latter of which he, following Freud, associates with desire and libido. In contrast to the structuralism of the day, which focused on the form of a work of art, Lyotard argued that on the figural level, art communicates the disruptive force of desires. The work of Paul Cézanne, for instance, overturns the power of representation in favor of unleashing figures associated with feelings and desire. Thus, in an argument that Lyotard would continue in his far more difficult and less well received 1974 work, *Libidinal Economy*, art is valued for its ability to release desire. This later book puts this aesthetic notion to work in the realm of politics, where Lyotard finds the disruptive traces of libidinal drives, whose power to disrupt any dogma show the limits of Marxist, or any, totalizing theory.

A theoretical problem that inevitably occurs in the absence of a totalizing theory is the problem of judgment. Without a single, clear frame of reference, how can art or actions that proceed from different assumptions be judged good or bad? Although *Discours, figure* and *Libidinal Economy* are both more interested in unleashing the energy of the libido and of art than they are in making precise judgments, it is exactly this question of judgment to which Lyotard would turn his attention in his later work and which would make for his most lasting contribution to philosophy.

The Postmodern Condition: A Report on Knowledge defines the postmodern as a state marked by an unwillingness to accept any grand narratives. The overarching narratives that have been used to justify science and the arts—for instance, the belief that technology will lead to a better life for all, or that the history of civilization is the history of the march toward enlightenment—are met with incredulity instead of firm belief. Thus, Lyotard believed those in the generation following World War II were living through an age of a legitimation crisis—one in which there was no single narrative, no mutually understood common goal, by which society could justify its actions.

It is society's lack of a standard for satisfying the fundamental disputes that Lyotard faces in the work that may be his most important contribution to philosophy, *The Differend: Phrases in Dispute*. The term *différend* is used by Lyotard to mean disputes that defy litigation within any set of rules because they are disputes that arise from the irreconcilable difference between sets of rules. For an example of what Lyotard means, contrast an American Indian claim to land based on centuries of tribal care of that land and of its use as a burial ground with a mining interest's claim to that land based on deeds and federal laws. Because different forms of legitimation are involved in each claim, there cannot be one "court" equally suited to evaluating each claim

(indeed, the notion of a court already entails certain presuppositions about how such a dispute is to be handled).

Lyotard's catch-all term for thought, speech, artistic and political events is "phrases," a word he uses to emphasize the primacy of the individual event over any given context. For instance, the phrase "I can come over to your house later" can be given any number of meanings (or "linkages" in Lyotard's terminology), but fundamentally it exists to be interpreted. Thus, the *différend* is, in the words of his book's subtitle, a "phrase in dispute," but one in which the conflict is not resolvable by deference to any higher-order organizing principle. Among his examples of how such disputes arise, Lyotard imagines a laborer trying to claim to an arbitrator that his hours of work are not a commodity that he owns but hours of his life. It would not be received as a relevant argument; labor-capital relations are premised on the assumption that the laborer sells work *as* a commodity, and disputes are arbitrated on the same assumption. Thus, the laborer who voices such a dispute is silenced by the arbitration process that cannot "hear" him.

Similarly, and more powerfully, Lyotard writes at length about remembering the Holocaust. Survivors of the Nazi Germany death camps are faced with the burden of knowing that the horror of Auschwitz and similar camps exceeds the power of words or language to convey it. Thus, to speak about it is to give a false impression—the impression that it can be understood by those who have not lived through it, that it is imaginable. However, not to speak about it allows the experience to be forgotten or distorted. This produces a conflict: No system of interpretation exists that can accurately understand the testimony (or silence) of Holocaust survivors, but Holocaust survivors must nonetheless speak and therefore further the misinterpretation of the Holocaust while trying to further the interpretation of it.

Lyotard's response to this dilemma is to advocate a return to reading not as a process of extracting correct interpretations out of texts but as a process of sensitively reexamining that which we think we know. Just as an avant-garde artist such as novelist James Joyce or composer Arnold Schoenberg creates a sublime work of art that defies any contemporary standards of beauty, so a reader (as an interpreter of culture) can recognize the outbursts of pleasure or displeasure that indicate that our frame of interpretation is inadequate to understanding the "phrases" at hand. Lyotard's challenge, then, is to achieve an aesthetics and a political ethics based on rumination, not with the goal of achieving a perfect frame of reference but as an obligation to what has been forgotten or ignored or overlooked.

Among Lyotard's most interesting attempts to develop his concept of the *différend* was his book *Heidegger and "the Jews,"* written as his contribution to the question of how European thinkers who are indebted to Heidegger should address his infamous association with the Nazi Party and his refusal to completely condemn this association. Although Lyotard's evaluation of Heidegger seems to be somewhat harsher than that of some of his contemporaries, including Jacques Derrida, he is less interested in defending or attacking Heidegger than in analyzing the dispute as irresolvable by any single court of opinion; that is, he sees it as a *différend*. This approach opened him to charges of intellectual obscurantism because he was analyzing a politically provocative issue in terms unfathomable to any but his closest readers.

Influence

Among the French philosophers of postmodernism and poststructuralism who became prominent following the 1968 student uprisings—Jacques Derrida, Michel Foucault, Julia Kristeva, and Luce Irigaray, among others—Lyotard can fairly be said to be the one most concerned with justice. In relating poststructuralism to postmodernism (which had developed as theoretical and artistic movements, respectively, with little relation to one another), he called attention to the political importance of each. After Lyotard, it became clear that postmodernism's tendency to shake off the grand narratives of the past was a historically conditioned example of the free play of language exposed by Derrida. Lyotard, however, went a little further, demanding a politics based on the inclusion of the free play that always escapes the totalizing politics of rabid Marxism or dogmatic capitalism.

Thomas Cassidy

The Postmodern Condition

A Report on Knowledge

Type of philosophy: Aesthetics, epistemology, social philosophy
First published: La Condition postmoderne: Rapport sur le savoir, 1979 (English translation, 1984)
Principal ideas advanced:

◊ The postmodern period is defined as a period of incredulity toward legitimating metanarratives, or grand narratives.

◊ Social law and order, which once took their authority from legitimizing narratives, now take their authority from science; science, however, in turn, takes its authority from narratives that promise science will lead to freedom and power.

◊ Science is moving toward a postmodern scientific sensibility, one that can accept indeterminacy and avoid grand narratives.

◊ We are entering into an age of little narratives instead of grand narratives.

Shortly after the publication of *Économie libidinale* (1974; *Libidinal Economy*, 1993), Jean-François Lyotard began work on what would become *Le Différend* (1983; *The Differend: Phrases in Dispute*, 1988). The earlier work maintained that any totalizing system was necessarily based on repression of the libido; the latter would reaffirm this earlier position but also begin to posit a way back, one that allowed for careful, nonsystematic reading that would be sensitive to what its tools of interpretation could not understand. In the process of writing this work, he was asked by the Conseil des Universités of Quebec to produce of report on the state of knowledge in the Western world. The result was *The Postmodern Condition: A Report on Knowledge*.

Postmodernism

Lyotard's use of the word "postmodern" was somewhat capricious. The term was already much in use to denote a trend in art, literature, and architecture marked in part by a glib use of irony, a free and sometimes jarring use of allusions to and quotations of earlier forms, and a repudiation of the forms and aims of modernism, especially its high aestheticism. By using the word "postmodern" in his report, Lyotard was asserting a connection between this state of affairs that he was examining and that implied by the poststructuralist writing of Jacques Derrida and Michel Foucault, which is that the narratives used to support Western culture and science are no longer credible.

Additionally, his laudatory use of the term "postmodern" was a rebuke to the work of Jürgen Habermas, a German philosopher and sociologist who had identified what he called "communicative action"—reasoned, unselfish discourse—as the key to completing what he considered to be the incomplete project of modernity, namely, the establishment of equitable social institutions along rational guidelines. The simple use of the term "postmodern" implied that pursuing the goals of modernity was perhaps an antiquated enterprise; an overreliance on rationality, in Lyotard's thinking, always leads to a suppression of intuition and desire, the font of creativity. Habermas recognized the rebuff and responded in print, and indeed, the rest of Lyotard's life was punctuated by intellectual sparring between the two philosophers.

However important the debate between Lyotard and Habermas was in shaping *The Postmodern Condition*, it had little to do with the work's enthusiastic reception. Rather, because of its relative clarity and brevity and because it offered an intellectually rigorous attempt to explain what was meant by the term "postmodern," which had been in vogue for some time, when the book was translated into English, it was widely received as a statement asserting the poststructuralist concepts behind postmodern artistic practices.

Legitimation

Lyotard begins *The Postmodern Condition* by pointing out how the field of knowledge has changed in the years since World War II. No field has grown faster than computer science and its corollary fields. Indeed, whole new sciences have been created that are devoted to the speedy transmission of knowledge. Therefore, Lyotard maintains, knowledge has come to be valued less for its own inherent worth than for its utility. Knowledge has an exchange value; it is worth something. In the words of Marxist analysis, one

might say it has been commodified. The measure of knowledge is no longer "Is it true?" but instead "What is its value?" Thus, knowledge is treated as a form of wealth, something of monetary value, an association that is very widely understood because knowledge is indeed key to building wealth in the corporate world. Further, the success of such scientifically created knowledge appears to legitimize the forms of society that created it. Without such legitimation, a legislator has no authority to pass laws that will be accepted as the norm. Technological prowess serves as a concrete example of social prowess and allows the legislator to demonstrate in concrete terms that the contemporary, scientifically advanced society is working well.

However, scientific advances are not the only ways that societies assure themselves of their own legitimacy. Science, Lyotard claims, has always existed side by side with narrative legitimation; societies have also always authorized themselves through narrative, a form of legitimation next to which science has always rested somewhat uneasily. As an anthropological example of legitimation through narrative, he refers to the storytellers of the Cashinua Indians of South America, who begin their stories with their group's name, thereby affirming their right to speak as Cashinuas. The rhythmic form of the narrative, consisting of "interminable monotonous chants," reduces the listener's awareness of ordinary time and brings the listener into fuller and unwary participation in the narrative. The listener is initiated (and reinitiated) into the tribe through narrative. The goal of the narrative is to bring the listener into harmony with the values and aims of the tribe.

Though this example may seem very specialized to the Cashinua, what Lyotard wishes the reader to see is that this is the way that mythology and mythological epics—such as Homer's *Iliad* (c. 800 B.C.E.; English translation, 1616)—have been used by Western society. These also are unifying narratives. However, since the beginning of the modern period, starting in the late seventeenth century, we have been living in a society legitimated by metanarratives that tell us that society is moving toward greater emancipation and rationality, and scientific progress is the hallmark of both. We are assured that scientific advances will increasingly liberate us from degrading labor to free ever more of our time and, further, that the light of rationality will dispel the darkness of myth under which our ancestors labored. In the metanarrative of the Enlightenment, knowledge emerges as the hero who will usher in a new golden age of humanity.

When it comes to explaining exactly what caused this narrative to lose credibility, Lyotard is vague. He talks about late nineteenth century nihilism but offers as his most compelling argument the proposition that scientific knowledge, to legitimize itself, must do so scientifically. To legitimize itself in terms of a nonscientific narrative of the life of the human spirit necessarily delegitimizes it by embracing a nonscientific hypothesis; to eschew that path is to renounce the Enlightenment's universalizing metanarrative of the progress of humanity through scientific knowledge. This is an interesting philosophic argument, one that Lyotard attributes to the late nineteenth century German philosopher Friedrich Nietzsche, but why this argument should have waited a century to have made its importance felt is a question Lyotard avoids in this work, although some of his later writings argue that the ovens of the Holocaust made the presentation of technology as the servant of human liberation an untenable narrative.

Postmodern Society

This leads us to the postmodern period, a period marked by what Lyotard calls "incredulity" toward metanarratives. Narratives that claim to announce the truth for all people for all time have no credibility. If science has no standing as a good in itself, if it is not the tool for the liberation of all people, then the only credible goal for research shifts from finding what is true to finding what is useful—what knowledge will help the financial backers of research accumulate power and wealth? This further leads to the state into which he indicates that Western universities have fallen, in which the goal of the university shifts from an inquiry into values to the dissemination of predetermined skills that are useful to industry. Industrial society needs many computer scientists, teachers, and doctors; it does not need an untethered search for truth.

Thus painted, the picture of postmodern society (a picture that is deeply indebted to the writings of Theodor Adorno and Max Horkeimer on the developments of capitalism in industrialized society) seems remarkably dreary. However, for Lyotard, all is not gloom. He sees positive developments in what he calls postmodern science: fractal geometry, Heisenberg's uncertainty principle of quantum mechanics, and other fields of science that challenge a totalizing worldview. Drawing on the theories of Paul K. Feyerabend and Thomas Kuhn, he argues that in fact postmodern science develops not along a consistent set of mutually agreed on principles but along separate and constantly shifting principles. Science no longer tells a unified story; molecular chemists, astrophysicists, and subatomic theorists see different "truths" that are fundamentally incommensurable with one another. The postmodern scientist is the author not of the grand narrative, but of the little narrative, a project Lyotard implies will be the cultural work of the postmodern condition.

Some Criticisms

Commentators have found many flaws with this argument, starting from Lyotard's stretching of the word "narrative" into shapes that are unrecognizable (a flaw he himself freely admitted, though he continued to stand by its usefulness for his purpose). More important, though, his critics have noted that the descriptions of science provided by Kuhn and Feyerabend are not descriptions of "postmodern" science but of science in general. Furthermore, the science Lyotard seems to champion is not so cheerfully postmodern as he would have it; it has not entirely abandoned "grand narratives" but merely set them aside, while the work for such things as a unified field theory (which would explain the unity of the four basic forces of nature) goes on.

Finally, many commentators have had trouble avoiding the self-evident contradiction in Lyotard's account. *The Postmodern Condition* tells a metanarrative about the demise of the metanarrative. Thus, Lyotard is caught in exactly the trap in which he claims science is caught when it seeks to legitimate itself through narrative or avoid legitimating itself all together. If his narrative is credible, it proves him wrong because it itself is a metanarrative. If, on the other hand, metanarratives really had lost all credibility, Lyotard would have no credulous way of saying it. In sum, for his narrative to speak with authority, it has to speak with no authority, an ironic contradiction that does not entirely discount his work but does imply that the straightforward narrative form he used for *The Postmodern Condition* is not finally able to contain what he wants it to contain, therefore making the far more obscure, playful, and aphoristic style of *The Differend* almost a necessity.

Some Answers

Appended to the English-language edition of *The Postmodern Condition* was a short essay, "What Is Postmodernism?," which dealt with the issue of postmodernism more directly as it related to aesthetic (as opposed to scientific) culture, the realm in which the term "postmodern" had achieved its greatest prominence. This essay is important in that it asserts a direct connection between modernism and postmodernism and because it can provide some insight into the paradox Lyotard creates for himself in *The Postmodern Condition*. The postmodern, he asserts, "is undoubtedly a part of the modern," not at its end "but in its nascent state."

Using examples from art, he points out that among the great modernist painters, Paul Cézanne attacked the Impressionists, Pablo Picasso challenged Cézanne, and Marcel Duchamp challenged the very notion of art. Modernism he understands as the art that tries to make visible something that is unpresentable. Artists such as James Joyce and Marcel Proust will each find different ways to attempt to make visible that in life that cannot be made visible. The implicit project of bringing to visibility something that is not visible implies a deep metanarrative of progress. However, the incredulity toward any preexisting metanarrative also marks these modernists as postmodern. However unhelpful this blurring of distinct terms might be to those attempting a taxonomy of artistic movements, it is helpful in positing a connection between modernism and postmodernism that is alive and ongoing.

This essay also comments on the main text. The stance Lyotard is taking in *The Postmodern Condition* is that he is trying to make something visible that he believes to be invisible; even if it cannot be made visible, his attempts to do so show him to be a conscientious modernist, a stance he shifts in his decidedly more postmodern *The Differend*. Because of its lively tone and free use of cultural references, this essay, like this book itself, has been widely quoted and cited, but one cannot say that it has been widely understood.

Thomas Cassidy

Additional Reading

Bennington, Geoffrey. *Lyotard: Writing the Event*. Manchester, England: Manchester University Press, 1988. The first influential book-length study of Jean-François Lyotard's work. It is a necessary commentary for those interested in studying Lyotard in depth.

Connor, Steven. *Postmodernist Culture: An Introduction to Theories of the Present*. Cambridge, Mass: Blackwell, 1989. Though not an intensive analysis of Lyotard, this introduction to postmodernism does have an excellent discussion of *The Postmodern Condition* and might be a better starting point than any of the books focused on Lyotard.

Rachjman, John. "Presence of Mind." *Artforum* 37, no. 1 (September, 1998): 27-41. A personal reminiscence published shortly after Lyotard's death that does an excellent job of summarizing some of the philosopher's more important beliefs, especially as relating to art and to technology.

Readings, Bill. *Introducing Lyotard*. New York: Routledge, 1991. Though too difficult to serve as an introduction to the philosopher, this volume is a worthwhile and serious study of Lyotard's work.

Rojek, Chris, and Bryan S. Turner, eds. *The Politics of Jean-François Lyotard*. New York: Routledge, 1998. Leading authorities in cultural and philosophical studies attempt to answer the numerous questions still being asked about Lyotard.

Sim, Stuart. *Jean-François Lyotard*. New York: Prentice Hall, 1996. A worthwhile introduction to Lyotard. Includes a bibliography and index.

Williams, James. *Lyotard: Towards a Postmodern Philosophy*. Malden, Mass.: Polity, 1998. A succinct, keen, and well-researched introduction to Lyotard.

Thomas Cassidy

Niccolò Machiavelli

Machiavelli initiated a pragmatic mode of political discourse that is entirely independent of ethical considerations derived from classical philosophy and Christian theology.

Principal philosophical works: *Dell' arte della guerra*, 1521 (*The Art of War*, 1560); *Discorsi sopra la prima deca di Tito Livio*, 1531 (*Discourses on the First Ten Books of Titus Livius*, 1636); *Istorie fiorentine*, 1525 (*The Florentine History*, 1595); *Il principe*, 1532 (*The Prince*, 1640).

Born: May 3, 1469; Florence (now in Italy)
Died: June 21, 1527; Florence (now in Italy)

Early Life

The year 1469 has a dual significance in the historical annals of Florence, since it marks both the date of Lorenzo de' Medici's ascension to power and that of Niccolò Machiavelli's birth. The boy was reared in a household consisting of his parents, Bernardo and Bartolomea, along with two older sisters and a younger brother. Bernardo, a tax lawyer and petty landowner of modest means, was a man of pronounced scholarly proclivities with a genuine passion for Roman literature. Machiavelli's own schooling in the principles of Latin grammar and rhetoric began at the age of seven. The study of arithmetic, however, was deferred until several years later. Although the family was too poor to own many books, it did possess a copy of the first three decades of Livy's survey of ancient Roman history. This work must have been a favorite of both father and son, because it was eventually sent to the bindery when Niccolò was seventeen years of age. Little is known for certain about the next decade in Machiavelli's life. There is some evidence that indicates that he may have spent most of the years between 1487 and 1495 in Rome working for a prominent Florence banker.

The political climate in Florence had altered drastically in the years immediately preceding Machiavelli's return from Rome. Lorenzo de' Medici had died in 1492, succeeded by his eldest son, Piero, an inept youth barely twenty years of age. Piero was soon confronted with a major crisis when King Charles VIII of France invaded Italy in 1494 to lay claim to Naples, and Piero's feckless conduct vis-à-vis the French monarch met with such revulsion on the part of his fellow citizens that they resolved to banish the entire Medici clan from the city forever. Soon thereafter, control of the Florentine republic fell into the hands of an austere Dominican friar from Ferrara, Girolamo Savonarola.

Although Savonarola made considerable headway in mitigating the dissolute moral conditions that pervaded Florence, he had considerably less success with his self-imposed mission to restore Christian virtue to the Roman Catholic Church. His adversary in this struggle was the Spaniard Rodrigo Borgia, whose reign as Alexander VI is generally conceded to represent the moral nadir in the history of the papacy during the Renaissance. Savonarola's persistent challenges to papal authority led to his being formally excommunicated by the Roman pontiff; this event emboldened the friar's political adversaries into taking direct action to destroy him. The climax of this struggle occurred on May 23, 1498, when Savonarola and his two closest confederates in the Dominican Order were escorted to the main square in Florence and hanged atop a pile of brush and logs that was thereupon set ablaze by the hangman. Several hours later, the charred remains of the three men were tossed into the Arno River. Machiavelli witnessed Savonarola's rise and fall at first hand and viewed the episode as an object lesson on the dangers of being "an unarmed prophet."

Life's Work

Savonarola's demise turned out to be highly beneficial with respect to Machiavelli's own personal fortune, for a few months thereafter he was called upon to serve in the newly reconstituted municipal government in several important posts. Its chief executive, Piero Soderini, appointed him both head of the Second Chancery and secretary to the Council of Ten for War. It remains unclear why an inexperienced young man of twenty-nine from an impoverished family should have been elevated to these key offices. Most likely, it was his keen intelligence that recommended him to Soderini, for each of the artists for whom Machiavelli chose to pose has fully captured this character trait. In addition to showing the bemused cynicism of his facial expression, artists depicted Machiavelli as a slender man with thin lips and penetrating eyes. He was, in short, a man whose crafty countenance must have caused others to be on their guard while conducting official business with him.

Despite his initial lack of diplomatic experience, Machiavelli was routinely commissioned to undertake sensitive missions to other Italian states as well as to the courts of Louis XII in France and Maximilian I in Germany. Diplomatic activities such as these played a vital role in Machiavelli's development as an uncompromising exponent of political pragmatism. Most instructive of all in this context were his extensive contacts with Cesare Borgia in Romagna during 1502-1503. It was this illegitimate son of Pope Alexander VI who best exemplified the quality of manliness, or *virtù*, that Machiavelli most admired in a political and military leader. Borgia's meteoric career was, however, terminated abruptly as a result of the death of his father in 1503. The new pope, Julius II, was an inveterate enemy of the entire Borgia clan and soon sent Borgia into exile, where he later died.

Julius was also responsible for terminating Machiavelli's career as a civil servant. When Louis XII of France invaded Italy and succeeded in establishing control over the Duchy of Milan, Julius proceeded to form a political coalition known as the Holy League, whose aim was to drive the invader from Italian soil. Soderini, despite Machiavelli's advice, refused to permit Florence to join the coalition and insisted on its maintaining strict neutrality throughout the entire conflict. After the expulsion of the French, Julius decided to punish the Florentine republic and compelled its citizenry to accept the return of the Medicis. Both Soderini and Machiavelli were immediately dismissed from office. On February 23, 1513, moreover, Machiavelli was falsely accused of being part of a conspiracy to reestablish the republic and was put to torture on the

Niccolò Machiavelli. *(Library of Congress)*

1147

rack. Though lack of evidence compelled the authorities to release him, he feared rearrest and decided to retire to his ancestral villa at Sant' Andrea, near Florence, together with his wife, Marietta Corsini, and their six children.

His retirement from public life at age forty-three enabled Machiavelli to study Roman literature and to compose many original works. His major political treatises are *The Prince* and *Discourses on the First Ten Books of Titus Livius*. Because Machiavelli focuses on issues pertaining to the governance of principalities in *The Prince* and of republics in *Discourses on the First Ten Books of Titus Livius*, these works constitute, in effect, a unified exposition of the author's political theories and should therefore be studied in conjunction with each other. The title of the latter work is, however, misleading to the extent that this work is not really a commentary on Livy's history of ancient Rome. Machiavelli subscribed to a cyclical view of history based on the theories propounded by the Greek historian Polybius, and he used *Discourses on the First Ten Books of Titus Livius* to draw parallels between the events depicted by Livy and the political situation of his own time. He next tried his hand at writing comedies for a brief period. The most celebrated of his works in this genre is *La Mandragola* (pr. c. 1519; *The Mandrake*, 1911), the other two being adaptations of plays by Terence. Foremost among the other books that Machiavelli wrote at Sant' Andrea are *The Art of War* and *The Florentine History*. In *The Art of War*, Machiavelli argues strongly in favor of the greater efficacy of native militias as opposed to mercenary armies, and in *The Florentine History*, he chronicles the city's fortune from the fall of the Roman Empire to the death of Lorenzo the Magnificent.

Even though Machiavelli had been an ardent supporter of the republic headed by Soderini, he considered himself to be a professional civil servant above all else and burned with a desire to be of service to his native city. Machiavelli, in fact, wrote *The Prince* for the express purpose of getting the Medici family to recognize his political sagacity and offer him employment in the new regime. Within a few years, the responsibility of governing Florence passed into the hands of Lorenzo de' Medici, to whom Machiavelli decided to dedicate *The Prince*. Lorenzo,

however, showed no interest in the treatise. Lorenzo died prematurely in 1519 at the age of twenty-seven and was succeeded by Cardinal Giulio de' Medici, under whose administration of the city's affairs Machiavelli's personal fortunes improved somewhat. He was entrusted with a few minor diplomatic missions on behalf of the Medicis. More important, it was Giulio who commissioned Machiavelli to write *The Florentine History*.

Giulio de' Medici became Pope Clement VII in 1521 when the immediate successor to Pope Leo died after a brief reign of twenty months. A series of diplomatic missteps on the part of Clement led to the horrendous sack of Rome in 1527 by mercenaries in the service of the German emperor Charles V. The citizens of Florence took advantage of the occasion and expelled the Medicis from their own city for the sake of reestablishing the republic. Machiavelli expected to be reinstated in the posts that he had held under Soderini. The Florentines, however, took a dim view of Machiavelli's previous association with the Medicis and declined to entrust him with any posts in the new regime. Bitterly disappointed, Machiavelli died in Florence a scant few months after the city had regained its liberty. The eclipse of the Medicis turned out to be a short one because Pope Clement and Emperor Charles were quick to reconcile their differences. The Medicis returned to Florence in 1530, but this time they did so as a hereditary nobility. The city's days as an independent republic were thus ended forever.

Influence

Machiavelli's political writings have elicited an unusual number of disparate reactions over the course of time. The negative viewpoint was initiated by the Roman Catholic Church when it decided to ban open dissemination of Machiavelli's works by placing his complete works on its Index of Prohibited Books in 1559. Oddly enough, even though an English translation of *The Prince* did not appear until 1640, it was the frequent allusions to Machiavelli that occur in plays by Elizabethan dramatists such as Christopher Marlowe and William Shakespeare that did most to popularize his image as an evil counselor. It is generally assumed that the Elizabethan public had already derived a measure of familiarity with the contents of *The Prince* from earlier French translations of the work. Philosopher Sir Francis Bacon, on the other hand, took a more favorable view of Machiavelli and hailed him as a fellow empiricist who described "what men do, and not what they ought to do." French philosopher Jean-Jacques Rousseau went even further in vindicating Machiavelli by contending that the real purpose of *The Prince* was to expose the modus operandi of tyrants and thereby to advance the cause of democracy. In modern times, however, *The Prince* has frequently been called "a handbook for dictators."

Whatever may be said for and against Machiavelli's political doctrines, it is necessary to recognize that he himself was deeply committed to a republican form of government. Even after one concedes Machiavelli's genuine patriotism and his deeply held commitment to republican virtues, there are a number of disquieting elements in his political philosophy that cannot easily be dismissed. There is, for example, his excessive taste for violent and cruel solutions to political problems, as reflected in his unabashed admiration for the bloody deeds of Cesare Borgia. Similarly, he held the view that morally reprehensible actions in terms of Christian standards are fully justifiable if perpetrated for what have come to be known as "reasons of state." For these and other reasons, Machiavelli continues to be a disturbing figure in the cultural pantheon of Western culture.

Victor Anthony Rudowski

The Prince

Type of philosophy: Ethics, political philosophy
First published: Il principe, 1532 (English translation, 1640)
Principal ideas advanced:
◇ In order to win and retain power, one is fortunate if one is born to power, for the individual who rises to power by conquest or treachery makes enemies who must be eliminated.
◇ If a prince must be cruel—and sometimes he must to retain power—he should be cruel

quickly, and he should cause great injuries, for small injuries do not keep a person from revenge.
◇ A prince should be concerned for the people he governs only to the extent that such concern strengthens his hold on the state.
◇ Although a prince can sometimes afford to be virtuous, flattery, deceit, and even murder are often necessary if the prince is to maintain himself in power.

Great political thinkers often write about specific historical situations and yet succeed in making recommendations that apply to times other than their own. Niccolò Machiavelli must be numbered among such thinkers. An Italian patriot deeply involved in the diverse political maneuvers of sixteenth century Italy, he addresses advice to Lorenzo de' Medici which, first written in 1513 and later published as *The Prince* five years after his death, marks him as one of the most controversial, enduring, and realistic political theorists of the modern world.

In this short book, Machiavelli undertakes to treat politics scientifically, judging people by an estimate of how in fact they do behave as political animals rather than by ideal standards concerned with how they ought to act. The hard-headedly consistent refusal of the author to submit political behavior to moral tests has earned the named "Machiavellian" for amoral instances of power relations among nation-states and other organized groups. The power divisions of Machiavelli's Italy are now seen to have been prophetic of the massive national rivalries that followed in the Western world. The problems encountered by Renaissance princes endured long after the princes themselves fell before more powerful enemies. Machiavelli understood how success is always a minimal condition of political greatness. In *The Prince*, he presents a manual of advice on the winning and retention of power in a world containing extensive political factionalism and lust for dominion.

Historical Context
Critics who are clearly aware of the amoral aspects of Machiavelli's political recommendations sometimes attempt to gain him a sympathetic hearing in unfriendly quarters. They do so by

placing *The Prince* in its limited historical setting and relating its contents to certain biographical facts about the author. They tell how Machiavelli longed for one ultimate goal: the eventual political unification of Italy as an independent state under one secular ruler, strong enough to rebuff the growing might of powerful neighbors like Spain and France. The armies and policies of these neighboring countries had already seriously influenced internal affairs even in Machiavelli's beloved Florence. Critics often suggest that Machiavelli's subordination of religion to the temporal aims of princes followed from his hatred of the political machinations of the Roman Catholic Church, which, by maintaining a series of temporal states, helped to keep Italy divided. The state of affairs created by the Church also invited foreign intrigues and corrupted the spiritual life of the Italians. In this context, another peculiarity of *The Prince* deserves mention: its total unconcern for forms of government other than monarchical ones. This unconcern might suggest that Machiavelli favored the monarchical form over the republican form. However, such a view would be false. In *Discorsi sopra la prima deca di Tito Livio* (1531; *Discourses on the First Ten Books of Titus Livius*, 1636), Machiavelli openly expressed preference for republics whenever the special conditions for their existence could be obtained. He tells his readers in *The Prince* that he has discussed republics elsewhere.

Such historical insights help to gain for *The Prince* a more understanding reading by those who reject its sharp separation of politics from morals. Yet the fact is clear that, whatever its author's motives, *The Prince* does ignore all moral ends of organized life and instead emphasizes the need to maintain sovereignty at all costs. Coldly, calculatingly, Machiavelli tries to show princes the means they must use in seeking power as an end in itself. He does not discuss moral rules. Discouraging to unsympathetic critics is the extent to which actual political life often seems to fit Machiavelli's somewhat cynical model.

The Monarch's Rise to Power

Machiavelli classifies possible governments as either republics or monarchies. In *The Prince*, he confines his analytic attention to the latter. Any monarch with a legitimate inheritance of power and traditions is most favored. The reason is that, unlike newly risen rulers, he need offend the people less. Established rulers reap the benefits from forgotten past abuses that led to the established system. People who rise to power by virtue of conquest or favorable circumstances must confront incipient rebellions. They must also make more promises than the established ruler, thus falling under various obligations. Machiavelli believed newly created rulers must perform their cruelties quickly and ruthlessly. They must never extend cruelties over a long period of time.

Machiavelli insists that if a prince must cause injuries, he should cause great injuries, for small injuries do not keep a person from revenge. In any case, what the prince does must fit the circumstances and the nature of his particular dominion. Not all princes should attempt to use the same methods. All princes must act, however. For example, they should never postpone war simply to avoid it. In political conflicts, time is neutral regarding the participants; it produces "indifferently either good or evil."

Newly created monarchs often find themselves involved with members of a mixed state. Extreme difficulties confront a ruler in such situations. Mixed monarchies often require rule over possessions whose citizens do not share the monarch's language. A common language and nationality help make ruling easier for the monarch, especially if his subjects' experience of freedom has been a limited one. There are two general ways in which to treat subjects who lack the monarch's nationality and language. One is that the monarch can take residence among the subjects. To do so permits a ready response to contingent problems and allows the subjects to identify themselves with the person of the ruler. The other is for the ruler to establish select colonies at key positions in the subjects' territory. Such colonies cost little. Their injured parties are also often scattered, thus proving easier to handle. If he maintains such colonies, the monarch should use diplomatic maneuvers aimed at weakening the stronger neighbors and protecting the less powerful ones. Machiavelli uses historical examples here, as he does elsewhere in *The Prince*. For example, he admires the manner in which the Romans anticipated contingencies in governing their colonies and acted promptly, if sometimes brutally, to meet them. On the other hand, Machiavelli asserts that Louis XII of France made basic blunders in a similar situation.

Ruling Foreign Subjects

There will be times when the ruler must govern subjects accustomed to living under laws of their own. Machiavelli coldly suggests three methods of ruling these. First, the ruler can totally despoil them, as the Romans did to certain rebellious cities. Second, he can make his residence among the subjects, hoping to keep down future rebellions. If he chooses neither of these alternatives, the ruler must permit the subjects to live under laws of their own. In this event, he must exact tribute from them. If possible, he should also put control of the laws in the hands of a few citizens upon whose loyalty he can count. It is dangerous to ignore the activities of people accustomed to living in freedom if they are part of one's sovereign state. The reason is that "in republics there is greater life, greater hatred, and more desire for revenge; they do not and cannot cast aside the memory of their ancient liberty, so that the surest way is either to lay them waste or reside in them."

Acquiring Power

Machiavelli shows great interest in how people acquire their rule over possessions. Methods of ruling must be made adaptable to differences in manner of acquisition. For example, rulers may obtain their power as a result of someone else's abilities, or they may win power by their own abilities. Machiavelli judges the do-it-yourself method as the surest; there is no substitute for princely merit. Also, the prince should command his own military forces without depending too heavily on aid from allied troops. The wise prince will imitate great personal models, because life is primarily a matter of imitative behavior. The prudential prince must show careful regard to the right circumstances for seizing power. Once in power, he can use force if he possesses soldiers loyal to himself. Machiavelli warns princes to beware the flattery of their subjects. They should especially show suspicion of the flattery of their ministers, who are supposed to advise them. Machiavelli's model of the state seems to be the Renaissance city-state: small in population and territorial extent. As an example of a ruler who arises by virtue of talent, he mentions Francesco Sforza of Milan. Cesare Borgia is used to illustrate the nature of successful ruling by a prince whose power initially results from conditions created by others.

In all, there are four ways in which a prince can attain political power: by his own abilities, by the use of fortunate circumstances (wealth or political inheritance), by wicked conduct and outright crime, and by the choice of his fellow citizens. Machiavelli does not condemn the ruler who succeeds by using criminal techniques. Thus, Agathocles, the ancient Sicilian, used such methods in rising from a military rank to kill off the rich men and senators of Syracuse. Yet Agathocles used such excessive cruelty that Machiavelli warns scholars not to include him "among men of real excellence." Instances of power criminally seized and successfully held lead Machiavelli to suggest that cruelty is intrinsically neither good nor bad. Cruelty must be said to have been used well "when all cruel deeds are committed at once in order to make sure of the state and thereafter discontinued to make way for the consideration of the welfare of the subjects."

Nonetheless, Machiavelli never asserts that cruelty is the best means of attaining power. His judgment here as elsewhere is a hypothetical one: If the situation requires cruelty for the realization of power, then the prince must do what is necessary. Thus, although Machiavelli prefers methods that do not involve cruelty, he refuses to condemn the prince who uses cruelty.

The conditional nature of Machiavelli's recommendations about seizing power becomes evident when he discusses the case of the prince who rises by the consent of his fellow citizens. This situation is the most promising for a prince. However, it rarely happens. Thus, this case cannot serve as a universal model. Chosen in such a manner, a prince need not fear that people will dare to oppose or to disobey him: "The worst a prince can fear from the people is that they will desert him." On the other hand, if his power stems from the nobility, the prince must fear both their possible desertion and their possible rebellion. In order to prepare for a rebellion, the people obviously require trained leaders. Thus, a prudent ruler supported by the people must attempt to retain their favor. A prince initially supported by the nobles can win over the people by making himself their protector. If he succeeds, he may end up stronger than the prince originally chosen by the people, for the people will appreciate the benefactor who guards them against internal oppression.

Maintaining Power

Machiavelli is never so cynical as to argue that a wise prince can endlessly ignore the needs of his own people, yet he justifies a concern for the people solely in terms of its value toward guaranteeing a continuing rule. Realistically, Machiavelli insists that the prince must lead an army. This is true even of churchmen who manage ecclesiastical states. Force or the threat of force serves as the basis of the state. Times of peace should never be permitted to divert the ruler's mind "from the study of warfare." In peaceful times, the prudent ruler estimates future events. By thought and preparation, he gets ready to meet such events.

A morbid sense of the contingency of human events runs through the book. Any ruler must show concern for changes of fortune and circumstance. The prince should show caution in delegating any of his own powers. Machiavelli hardly ever discusses economic or ideological problems. Normally, the prince of whom he writes is a single man bent on political self-preservation and the quest for methods by which to coerce his enemies into submission or inaction. The picture is one of a ruler feverishly studying the histories and actions of great people to be ready for the possible day when relatively stable conditions may alter for the worse. The reader concludes that, in Machiavelli's view, stability in politics is extremely rare. Yet Machiavelli understands that no prince can stand completely alone. Some powers must be delegated. Some people must be favored over others. How the prince treats his friends and subjects will always influence future political events. The prince should work to create a character able to make sudden adjustments in terms of his own self-interest. The most successful ruler must "be prudent enough to escape the infamy of such views as would result in the loss of his state." He must never

cultivate those private virtues which, in a public man, can prove politically suicidal. He should develop vices if these will help to perpetuate his rule.

Generosity is a value in a prince only if it produces some benefit and no harm. A wise ruler will tax his subjects without becoming miserly. Yet he should prefer the name "miser" to a reputation for generosity that may prevent him from raising monies needed to maintain security. Generosity can more easily lead to the subjects' hatred and contempt than can miserliness. The prince can even show mercy if it is not interpreted as mere permissiveness. The cursedly cruel Borgia proved more merciful than the Florentine rulers who lost the city to foreigners. As long as he keeps his subjects loyal and united, the ruler may sometimes act strenuously against them. Especially is this necessary in newly created monarchies. Machiavelli advises the prince to be both loved and feared but choose being feared over being loved. The subjects obey a prince who can punish them.

In maintaining order, the prince has some rules of thumb to follow. He should keep his word unless deceit is specifically called for. He should use admired private virtues if they do not interfere with the play of political power. A conception of human nature operates here. Machiavelli thinks the plain man is capable of some loyalty to a ruler. However, such a man is easily led. "Men are so simple," Machiavelli writes, "and so ready to follow the needs of the moment that the deceiver will always find someone to deceive." A prince must know how and when to mingle the fox's cunning (the ability to avoid traps) with the lion's strength (capacity to fight the wolves). He should often conceal his real motives. Internally, he must avoid conspiracies. Externally, he should keep enemies fearful of attacking. Against conspirators, the prince always has an advantage. Conspirators cannot work in isolation; thus they fear the existing laws and the threat of detection. Only when the population shows some open hostility need the prince genuinely fear conspirators.

Machiavelli realizes that people seldom get to choose the circumstances most favorable to their political hopes. They must settle for what is possible rather than for the ideal. Princes must avoid the lures of utopian political constructions, "for how we live is so different from how we ought to live that he who studies what ought to be done rather than what is done will learn the way to his downfall rather than to his preservation." Machiavelli regards people as weak, fickle, and subject to changing loyalties. These psychological traits are the bedrock on which a wise prince must build his policies.

Nonetheless, the author of *The Prince* understands that success in politics, however rationally pursued, is beyond the complete control of any person. The Renaissance worry about Chance and Fortune (qualities so important as to be personified in the imagination as well as the literature of the time) haunts the final pages of Machiavelli's book. Large-order events in the world often seem to drive people onward, much like "the fury of the flood." Yet not all events happen fortuitously. People are half free to shape their political lives within the broader forces of the universe. That prince rules best, therefore, whose character and conduct "fit the times." It will be better for the ruler to be bold rather than cautious. Fortune is like a woman, "well disposed to young men, for they are less circumspect and more violent and more bold to command her." Thus Machiavelli argues for a partial freedom of will and action within a world largely made up of determined forces.

Modern Import

The Prince stands as a classic example of realistic advice to rulers seeking unity and preservation of states. Its picture of human nature is somewhat cynical, viewing humanity as vacillating and in need of strong political direction. Yet the work is not modern in one sense; namely, it fails to discuss ideological aspects of large-scale political organization. Machiavelli's prince is one who must learn from experience. His conclusion is that ruling is more like an art than like a science. What is somewhat modern is the realistic emphasis on tailoring political advice to the realization of national ends whose moral value is not judged. *The Prince* is therefore a fascinating if sometimes shocking justification of the view that moral rules are not binding in the activities of political rulers.

Whitaker T. Deininger

Additional Reading

Bondanella, Peter E. *Machiavelli and the Art of Renaissance History*. Detroit: Wayne State University Press, 1973. This astute study constitutes a chronological survey of Machiavelli's development as a literary stylist. Focuses on the compositional techniques that he employed in depicting the character and conduct of heroic personages. Lacks a formal bibliography, but there are copious endnotes for each chapter.

Grant, Ruth Weissbourd. *Hypocrisy and Integrity: Machiavelli, Rousseau, and the Ethics of Politics*. Chicago: University of Chicago Press, 1997. This work challenges the usual standards for political ethics and sheds light on Machiavelli's argument for the necessity of hypocrisy. Grant interprets the writings of Machiavelli as pro-hypocrite and the writings of Rousseau as anti-hypocrite and balances them in a conceptual framework encompassing the moral limits of compromise, and integrity in political behavior.

Machiavelli, Niccolò. *Machiavelli and His Friends: Their Personal Correspondence*. Translated by James B. Atkinson, edited by David Sices. De Kalb: Northern Illinois University Press, 1996. Arranged chronologically and with an introduction and historical annotations by the translator, these 257 letters written to Machiavelli, and 84 written by him, offer a broad view of the life, people, places, and crucial events of Renaissance Italy. Covering thirty years in Machiavelli's adult life (from 1497 to his death in 1527), this annotated personal correspondence provides insight into the man considered to be the first modern political theorist and his associates, some the most influential thinkers of Italian Renaissance.

Pitkin, Hanna Fenichel. *Fortune Is a Woman: Gender and Politics in the Thought of Niccolò Machiavelli*. Berkeley: University of California Press, 1984. This pioneering study of gender as a factor in political theory depicts Machiavelli as a misogynistic authoritarian. It is particularly useful in clarifying the manner in which Machiavelli employs the concepts of *fortuna* and *virtù*. The text is extensively annotated and supplemented by a highly detailed index and a useful bibliography of works cited.

Sullivan, Vickie B. *Machiavelli's Three Romes: Religion, Human Liberty, and Politics Reformed*. De Kalb: Northern Illinois University Press, 1996. Drawing on Machiavelli's writings from *The Florentine History*, *The Prince*, and *Discourses on the First Ten Books of Titus Livius*, the author provides a unique and important study of Machiavelli's political thought. She offers a new understanding of Machiavelli's religious views, maintaining that he uses both pagan and Christian elements in his political philosophy.

Victor Anthony Rudowski,
updated by Lisa A. Wroble

Alasdair MacIntyre

MacIntyre makes a radical critique of much modern philosophy from a historicist and Aristotelian position, engaging a wide range of other academic disciplines.

Principal philosophical works: *Marxism: An Interpretation*, 1953 (republished in 1968 as *Marxism and Christianity*); *The Unconscious: A Conceptual Analysis*, 1958; *Difficulties in Christian Belief*, 1959; *A Short History of Ethics*, 1966, 2d ed. 1998; *Secularization and Moral Change*, 1967; *Herbert Marcuse: An Exposition and a Polemic*, 1970; *Against the Self-Image of the Age: Essays in Ideology and Philosophy*, 1971; "Epistemological Crises, Dramatic Narrative, and the Philosophy of Science," 1977; *After Virtue: A Study in Moral Theory*, 1981, 2d ed. 1985; "The Relationship of Philosophy to Its Past," 1984; "Relativism, Power, and Philosophy," 1985; "Whose Justice? Which Rationality?," 1988; "Reply to Dahl, Baier, and Schneewind," 1988; *Three Rival Versions of Moral Enquiry: Encylopaedia, Genealogy, and Tradition*, 1990; *First Principles, Final Ends, and Contemporary Philosophical Issues*, 1990; "Précis of 'Whose Justice? Which Rationality?,'" 1991.

Born: January 12, 1929; Glasgow, Scotland

Early Life
Alasdair Chalmers MacIntyre was born the only son of two Scottish doctors, both graduates of Glasgow University. He was educated privately and at Epsom College, an English public school south of London. His interests began to focus on the classics (Latin and Greek), and in 1947, he enrolled at Queen Mary College, London University, as a classics major.

After graduating in 1950, he pursued graduate study in philosophy at Manchester University. His classical studies gave him a sound grounding in Greek philosophy because he could study the works of Plato and Aristotle in the original language, and his later writing on Roman jurisprudence and the early church theologians was made surer by his access to the original Latin of those texts.

Life's Work
After receiving his M.A. at Manchester, MacIntyre was appointed lecturer in the philosophy of religion there in 1951. Two years later, he published his first book, *Marxism: An Interpretation*, republished in 1968 as *Marxism and Christianity*, a title that better expresses its subject matter. At the time, MacIntyre saw himself as both a Christian and a Marxist, and the book is an expression of this combined stance. However, the tensions between the two were already apparent, and between the two editions, he dropped his allegiance first to Marxism and then to Christianity.

However, on republishing the book, he refused to revise it, noting that "one cannot entirely discard either [Marxism or Christianity] without discarding truths not otherwise available." He notes a number of similarities between the two. They are both constantly being refuted and yet survive. Both wish to exempt themselves from historical relativities, which means neither finds it easy to distinguish foundational truths from temporal responses to particular social situations. Attempts to demythologize either Marxism or Christianity leave only platitudes, and any radical criticism of the secular present is lost. MacIntyre saw demythologizing as a basically liberal enterprise, seeking to mask the illiberal realities of the established order. It is significant that his later work attempted to preserve this radical and ideological critique of the present, while presenting a sophisticated acceptance of historical relativism to ground his work concretely.

Later in life, he reclaimed his earlier allegiance to Christianity, especially to the Reformed tradition of his Scottish Presbyterian parents, although he also called himself an "Augustinian Christian," going back to older roots. However, he never renewed his allegiance to Marxism, though he continued to view it with respect as one of the few coherent systems the modern age produced. Its failures, he later came to see, were in practice. The Communist Party as institution, just as the Catholic Church as institution, became problematic. As Marxism assumed power, it changed into something else, such as utilitarianism or Weberian economics.

More central to his teaching at this time was his *Difficulties in Christian Belief*, actually published after he left Manchester in 1957 to take up a post as lecturer in philosophy at Leeds University in the north of England. The book was one of a series published by the Student Christian Movement, a theologically liberal publishing house. The view taken in this work was that philosophy can help the religious believer engage in meaningful thinking about difficulties presented by Christianity (and often by other belief systems) without attempting to solve them all or abandoning discussion of them. He covers the usual list of difficulties—evil, miracles, proof, morality, immortality—but stresses that difficulties are not doubts. His conclusion is still to trust—people do not enter God's kingdom by argument but by trust.

MacIntyre's other interests in this early period were Freudianism and the process of analytic psychology, as reflected in the 1958 publication of *The Unconscious: A Conceptual Analysis*. At this stage, MacIntyre mostly concerned himself with the relationship of philosophy with other academic disciplines or discourses and the search for how philosophy could open up such areas fruitfully.

His commitment to pursuing ethics as a career within academic philosophy was helped by two periods of research, the first at Nuffield College, Oxford, where he was a research fellow 1961-1962, and the second at Princeton University, as senior fellow with the Council of Humanities in 1962-1963. These two stints were followed by his appointment as fellow and preceptor in philosophy at University College, Oxford. His three-year tenure at this post was marked by the publication of *A Short History of Ethics* in 1966. It soon became a standard textbook in undergraduate philosophy classes throughout the English-speaking world. It was written in the concise but narratively clear style that was to become a hallmark of his writing.

In his next book, *Secularization and Moral Change*, MacIntyre wrote, "We have to learn from history and anthropology of the variety of moral practices, beliefs, and conceptual schemes." This and his earlier 1966 text demonstrate his belief in the importance of knowing the historical context before being able to understand the strengths and weaknesses of any philosophical position. *A Short History of Ethics* claims morality emerges out of human history; moral decisions are not some sort of individualistic function of the self, detached from cultural context.

MacIntyre had clearly established himself as an Aristotelian, modified by the medieval theology of Saint Thomas Aquinas. However, he was willing to consider the thought of those outside the traditional philosophical boundaries; for example, in *A Short History of Ethics*, he discussed German religious reformer Martin Luther and political philosopher Niccolò Machiavelli, and elsewhere, the novelists Laurence Sterne and Jane Austen. These writers are all relevant to historicist philosophical enquiry and demonstrate the breadth of his interests.

On the strength of his growing academic reputation, he gained his first professorial appointment, as professor of sociology at the University of Essex, a post he held from 1966 to 1970. The school was a new university and, at that time, was one of the centers of radical student politics in Britain. Sociology students were particularly involved. Interestingly, MacIntyre was willing to take a sociology post at a demanding time for academics rather than stay in a safe philosophy haven in Oxford.

His own stance is reflected in two books published during this time: *Herbert Marcuse: An Exposition and a Polemic* and *Against the Self-Image of the Age: Essays in Ideology and Philosophy*, a collection of his articles and papers. His own engagement with sociology is reflected in *Sociological Theory and Philosophical Analysis: A Collection* (1970), which he coedited with Dorothy Emmett.

Although his rejection of Christianity and Marxism was maintained in these books, he remained committed to ideology as such, which, he argued, was needed more than ever to fill "the cultural desert created by the liberal intelligentsia."

MacIntyre later said of this period that he was preoccupied with the basis for the moral rejection of Stalinism. He realized he could not return to the liberalism against which Marxism emerged because he still accepted the Marxist criticism of liberalism. In fact, he saw that Marxism was weakened by taking on board some of the liberal agenda, as it was doing during this period. He was also convinced of the importance of philosopher Georg Wilhelm Friedrich Hegel, the departure point for much Marxist thinking and for much else. He edited *Hegel: A Collection of Critical Essays*, published in 1972.

In 1970, MacIntyre left England to continue his career in the United States. His first professorial post in the United States was at Brandeis, as professor of the history of ideas, a post he held for two years. This was followed by a lengthier stay (1972-1980) at Boston University, where he was university professor in philosophy and political science. During this period, he wrote *After Virtue: A Study in Moral Theory*, by far his most groundbreaking piece of philosophy and the fullest statement yet of his historicist virtue ethicism.

MacIntyre, who had one son and three daughters by previous marriages, wed Lynn Sumida Joy in 1977. In 1979, he won a National Endowment for the Humanities award, as he did again in 1987 and 1988; in 1984, he was awarded a Guggenheim Fellowship. These awards enabled him to do further research, for instance into David Hume, the Scottish Enlightenment philosopher, about whom he wrote extensively in "Whose Justice? Which Rationality?" The grant from the National Endowment for the Humanities enabled him to spend a year at the Hastings Center, New York, at the Hastings Institute of Society, Ethics and the Life Sciences, founded in 1969 to focus on applied ethics. He was particularly concerned with developing ethical concepts for science and medicine. A similar concern for education was evidenced by *Education and Values* (1987), being the 1985 Richard Peters lectures given to the Institute of Education of London University, which MacIntyre shared with Anthony Quinn and Bernard Williams.

During the 1980's, his reputation led to his gaining several prestigious posts, first at Wellesley College, where from 1980 to 1982 he was Luce Professor. He subsequently became the W. Allen Jones Distinguished Professor of Philosophy at Vanderbilt University and, in 1988, the McMahon/Hank Professor of Philosophy at Notre Dame University. He received honorary doctorates at Swarthmore (1983), Queen's University (1988), and Williams College (1993). Other honors included the presidency of the eastern division of the American Philosophical Society for 1984 and being named Fellow of the American Academy in 1985.

In the seven years after *After Virtue*, he published only one other book, *Revisions: Changing Perspectives in Moral Philosophy*, which he coedited with Stanley Haverwas. Then in 1988, he published the promised sequel to *After Virtue*, "Whose Justice? Which Rationality?" This article originated as part of the 1982 Carlyle Lectures at Oxford University, on "Some Transformations of Justice." Its structure is again historicist, beginning with classical notions of justice and practical reasoning but spending longer on Thomas Aquinas and his integration of Aristotelian and Christian (Augustinian) schemata. The longest sections actually deal with post-Reformation Scottish philosophy, which MacIntyre sees as having stayed true to Aristotelianism until its "betrayal" by Hume. In some ways MacIntyre was trying to get back to his Scottish roots and disavow his anglicization.

Two major works followed in quick succession: *Three Rival Versions of Moral Enquiry: Encyclopaedia, Genealogy, and Tradition* and *First Principles, Final Ends, and Contemporary Philosophical Issues*, both published in 1990. In 1995, he was appointed arts and science professor at Duke University, North Carolina.

Influence

MacIntyre's impact was twofold. First, he made philosophical thinking available to nonphilosophers by bringing philosophy in to serve other disciplines and areas of concern, including religious faith, sociology, medicine, psychology, and politics, and by writing in a way accessible to nonexperts, as in *A Short History*.

Second, he created a foundation whereby he can critique contemporary thought from a traditional viewpoint, while maintaining the reality of modern pluralism and avoiding a reactionary conservatism. This knife-edge endeavor is accomplished by reinterpreting the Thomist enterprise of finding an absolute concept of truth and yet holding the necessity of a historicist approach. People have to philosophize from within time. What students need to be taught is not to dialogue but to engage in conflict.

Critics have questioned his portrayal of disarray in modern philosophy and his particular historical readings. Certainly the historicist approach does seem like reinventing the map for each separate excursion. On the other hand, MacIntyre does rescue readers from temporal provincialism, a problem of modernism.

David Barratt

After Virtue

A Study in Moral Theory

Type of philosophy: Ethics
First published: 1981
Principal ideas advanced:

◇ The project of post-Enlightenment ethics has failed and was bound to fail because it had detached itself from any sort of tradition or context.

◇ The sign of this failure is the interminability of its disagreements and its fragmentedness.

◇ All philosophical enterprises need to be historically grounded and their claims understood in terms of an ongoing, modifiable tradition.

◇ The source of the post-Enlightenment failure was its radical rejection of the Aristotelian tradition that had been widely accepted in classical, Christian, Jewish, and Islamic cultures.

◇ Aristotelian ethics, reinterpreted historically, is still a far more coherent community-based moral system than any of the post-Enlightenment systems, which have largely been reduced to individualistic emotivism.

◇ The main features of this type of ethics are the following of certain practices directed toward certain ends, needing virtues to produce both internal and external goods.

◇ Such virtue-led ethics stand in contrast to rules-led systems; these ethics are applicable, and should be applied, to a wide range of cultural activities.

After Virtue: A Study in Moral Theory represents perhaps the widest-ranging and most far-reaching example of Alasdair MacIntyre's historicist and Aristotelian thinking. MacIntyre developed the work as a conscious response to the failure of modern philosophy in general, and contemporary moral philosophy in particular, to find any means to resolve its disputes. The work was also a reaction to what MacIntyre calls "armchair" philosophy and to the fragmentation of academic disciplines. As such, it became a determined effort to link philosophy with other forms of knowledge, particularly history and sociology. A working knowledge of theology and literature is also noticeable as cultural evidence of moral thinking and valuing.

In this, MacIntyre is typical of "virtue" ethicists. Where he differs from certain proponents of virtue ethics is his adherence to and restatement of Aristotle's teleology. He is skeptical of all attempts to separate ethics from ends, though these are not to be described in any utilitarian sense. He acknowledges that different lists of virtues have been produced by different cultures but sees this as a historical inevitability rather than as a weakness. The real concern is to be able to discern virtues as productive of inner goods, not as simulations aimed only at externals and reducible to utilitarian ends or rule-based systems.

After Virtue consists of eighteen chapters with a preface; an additional chapter was added to the 1985 second edition as an answer to some of MacIntyre's critics. The book can be divided into two halves: Chapters 1 through 9 form a historical examination of post-Enlightenment moral philosophy and its failure, and chapters 10 through 18 restate the Aristotelian alternative. The second part can be further subdivided: Chapters 10 through 13 trace the development of classical moral philosophy, particularly virtue ethics, from heroic societies through the Middle Ages, and chapters 14 through 18 look at the fortunes of virtue ethics in same period, seeking to redefine virtue ethics in a continuing Aristotelian format.

A Critique of Modernism

MacIntyre's critique of post-Enlightenment moral philosophy points to a much wider radical critique of modernism as a whole. This critique, in the first part of *After Virtue*, has three elements: the features of modernism, the philosophers of modernism, and the failures of modernism.

The main features of modernism can be categorized under its philosophy, its characters, and its fictions. Its philosophy MacIntyre sees as emotivism, wherein all moral truth statements are reducible to personal expressions of approval or disapproval and can therefore have no universal import. Under emotivism, "All X is good" comes to mean "I like X" or "I approve of X." MacIntyre traces emotivism back to philosopher G. E. Moore, who wrote at the turn of the nineteenth and twentieth centuries. The "characters" of modernism, that is, the types that most exemplify its values, MacIntyre sees as the bureaucratic manager, the therapist, and the rich aesthete (as exemplified in the novels of Henry James). All are manipulators, the essence of modernist individuality being to manipulate or be manipulated. To be manipulated is to lose one's own liberty.

MacIntyre also delineates the fictions of modernism, much as Charles Dickens did in his novel *Hard Times* (1854) with its "fictions of Coketown." Two of MacIntyre's fictions are, in fact, the same: the fiction of utilitarianism (there are all sorts of happinesses and miseries, not just one reductivized one) and the fiction that "facts" are morally neutral, unattached to any value system. Other fictions are those of "rights," "universalism" (that is, philosophic "universals" detached from any social context), and "managerial efficiency." The first two fictions stem from the overarching fictiveness of the eighteenth century Enlightenment, which MacIntyre clearly sees as a philosophic disaster area. "Managerial efficiency" is a fiction because just as value-free facts do not exist, value-free efficient management is an impossibility. The more impersonal and amoral management is, the less creative and motivated those who are being managed will be, and therefore, the less efficient.

According to MacIntyre, the key figures in this failed Enlightenment enterprise were Scottish philosopher David Hume, German philosopher Immanuel Kant, and Danish writer Søren Kierkegaard. All rejected Aristotelianism, especially its communal and teleological dimensions; all therefore had to search for new grounds on which to base the choice for moral action. Hume excluded reason as a possible basis and claimed that therefore it must be the passions. Kant, on the other hand, rejected the passions, grounding his ethics in practical reason. Kierkegaard rejected both grounds, claiming the basis of ethics was a criterionless choice. MacIntyre cites Kierkegaard's *Enten-Eller* (1843; *Either/Or*, 1944), with its choice of the aesthetic self versus the moral self, as representative of the writer's views on this subject.

The Failures of Moral Philosophy

MacIntyre traces the continuing search for new groundings for a moral self through the nineteenth century from John Stuart Mill and other utilitarians to G. E. Moore and into the twentieth century with French philosopher Jean-Paul Sartre. It is in the German philosopher Friedrich Nietzsche, however, that MacIntyre sees the logical outcome of post-Enlightenment ethics. Nietzsche is the seer of modernity; Nietzsche's disgust with all rational attempts to ground morality exemplifies it. His substitution of will for reason has made him appealing to certain postmodern thinkers. MacIntyre argues that although Nietzsche thought he had ended *all* rational moral philosophy, in fact, he had merely killed off the post-Enlightenment enterprise.

The failures of modern moral philosophy are manifold. The main areas of failure for MacIntyre are its rejection of a sense of tradition and of a sense of community, which leads, ultimately, to the disappearance of the self; the separation of "is" and "ought" (the naturalistic fallacy is fallacious); and its claims that the social sciences are scientific and, therefore, their truths are not moral claims. In fact, for the social sciences, one must allow for unpredictability (political philosopher Niccolò Machiavelli's notion of *fortuna* is cited); effective organizations actually allow for a high degree of it. The eighteenth century prophecy of scientifically managed social control has not been fulfilled, only the imitation of it.

Virtue

The fallacy of the is/ought distinction stems from the rejection of Aristotelianism, where goodness is a *virtue*, a quality of being, not a set of rules. Nietzsche's criticism of moral philosophy for not answering the question "What sort of person ought I to become?" is partially a result of the rejection of Aristotelian notions of ends (*teloi*) and virtues. MacIntyre returns the reader to what has wrongfully been rejected.

However, one of MacIntyre's problems with Aristotle is that although he is a historicist, Aristotle is not. In fact, Aristotle believed he had dealt with most previous philosophical problems, and the past could therefore be discarded. MacIntyre reinterprets Aristotle within his cultural context. In this sense, he is not a classical Aristotelian.

MacIntyre begins his account within heroic societies, especially Homeric Greece. For him, the main feature of heroic ethics is its narrative structure. He develops this concept of narrativity throughout the second part of *After Virtue*. The epic generates epic virtues, which do not distinguish action from being, the physical from the moral. In Greek, "virtue" originally meant excellence of any kind. It was also communal, and MacIntyre rejects Nietzsche's account of the heroic virtues as a fiction of nineteenth century individualism. As heroic community moved into the Greek city-state, virtues became linked to politics: The good man was the good citizen. The typical narrative structures now became fourfold: tragedy, comedy, philosophic discourse, and the legal system. All contained elements of conflict between the older epic narrative and the newer political ones. Aristotle saw such conflict as bad; MacIntyre was more relaxed about it.

Aristotle divided the virtues into those of the intellect and those of character. Education and exercise were the means to develop them. The virtues became a person's character, moving the individual toward *telos*, which Aristotle defined as *eudaimonia* ("blessedness, happiness, prosperity") and were not an external means but integral to life. The key text cited is the *Ethica Nicomachea* (Second Athenian Period, 335-323 B.C.E.; *Nicomachean Ethics*, 1797).

MacIntyre then fast-forwards his account to the Middle Ages, to see how Aristotelian ethics were developed in a fragmented society becoming Christianized. He examines the fusions of Christianity and Aristotelianism in the twelfth century, particularly in the work of philosopher Peter Abelard (he is surprisingly brief on Saint Thomas Aquinas). The four cardinal Greek virtues of justice, prudence, temperance, and courage were joined to the three Christian virtues of faith, hope, and charity (love). However, Abelard emphasized the rival Greek philosophy of Stoicism, seeing the real moral battleground to be the will rather than the reason. Stoicism also denies *telos*: One wills to do what is right because it is right.

MacIntyre suggests that Stoicism becomes influential where the law displaces the virtues, as in fragmented societies. However, as medieval society unified, Aristotelian concepts predominated, the virtues became communal and also reconciliatory, as love demands forgiveness. Importantly, the Christian narrative became the quest: The virtues thus became those qualities that enable men to survive evils on their historical life journey.

The Practice of Virtue

In chapters 14 and 15, MacIntyre reformulates a definition of the virtues that will withstand Nietzschean pessimism. The notion of a "practice" is the ground for his definition. Just as the professions recognize good practice, so should human life. Virtues can then be defined as those qualities necessary to achieve the goods *internal* to those practices. The gaining of *external* goods can only lead to simulation—Jane Austen is a writer whose work exemplifies the discerning of such falsity.

However, virtues must contribute to the good of the whole life. MacIntyre stresses the unity of the narrative quest for each human life. Only such a narrative quest makes intelligible particular actions and settings. Its *account* establishes individual entity as subject (of that narrative) by making the subject *accountable*. Integrity (to which he links constancy) is therefore, for him, the prime virtue.

Lastly, virtues are related to the pursuit of a good for all human beings, but this can be established only in a community and within an ongoing social tradition. As with the poet T. S. Eliot, such tradition is constantly being modified and can be kept alive only by the exercise of the virtues. Every practice has its own history and its own community.

Having defined a practice of virtue, MacIntyre concludes his historical account, seeing in the perhaps unlikely combination of the Jacobins, Jane Austen, and William Cobbett the last true representatives of the classical tradition of the virtues. MacIntyre says that in the final quarter of the twentieth century, people are in a new dark age: They await a new Saint Benedict to lead them to a new virtuous community.

Moral Philosophy and Modern Times

Upon its publication, MacIntyre's *After Virtue* struck chords in at least three areas. First, its historicism accords with developments in literary, historical, and philosophic theory that stand out against historical postmodernist theory. Second, its holistic approach to human life and academic institutions is part of a groundswell of modern culture that is protesting against the increasing fragmentation, privatization, and bureaucratization of modern institutions and life. Third, its plea for a return to traditional values and its emphasis on the virtue of a sense of tradition appealed to the radical right, especially in the United States, where MacIntyre's impact has been most keenly felt.

However, perhaps his biggest impact is in his attempt to make moral philosophy accessible to the educated layperson and the virtuous citizen. His style and approach, although logically rigorous, nevertheless are amenable to readers from various disciplines and concerns who wish to see a renewal in public life. Although he takes philosophy out of its armchair, MacIntyre also seeks to take it out of the postgraduate classroom and return it to the marketplace. The impact of *After Virtue* lies therefore in the opening up of traditional ways of thinking morally, not only to make a radical critique of modernism (including Marxism) but also as a strengthening and encouraging of an alternative, albeit minority, community, engaged in a traditional quest for a virtuous life.

David Barratt

Additional Reading

Casey, John. *Pagan Virtue: An Essay in Ethics*. Oxford: Clarendon Press, 1990. A very useful general discussion on virtue ethics from a distinguished moral philosopher.

Engelhardt, H. Tristram, Jr., and Daniel Callahan, eds. *Knowledge, Value, and Belief*. Hastings, N.Y.: Hastings Center, 1977. This contains a chapter on MacIntyre's earlier work, put within the context of the Hastings Center Institute of Society, Ethics, and Life Sciences, with its focus on applied ethics, and where MacIntyre worked for a year.

Fuller, M. B. *Making Sense of MacIntyre*. Brookfield, Vt.: Ashgate, 1998. This book attempts to understand and pinpoint some of MacIntyre's philosophical positions.

Gunnemann, Jon P. "Habermas and MacIntyre on Moral Learning." In *The Annual of the Society of Christian Ethics*. Boston: Society of Christian Ethics, 1994. Gunnemann notes that MacIntyre dismisses Jürgen Habermas's Kantianism in *Three Rival Versions*, and that Habermas also dismisses MacIntyre. He looks at differences and areas of moral convergence, suggesting that Habermas does better in accounting for moral constructions and understanding other traditions, but MacIntyre does better on questions of moral identity.

Gutting, Gary. *Pragmatic Liberalism and the Critique of Modernity*. New York: Cambridge University Press, 1999. A critical analysis of the work of Alasdair MacIntyre, Richard Rorty, and Charles Taylor.

Horton, John, and Susan Mendus, eds. *After MacIntyre*. Notre Dame, Ind.: University of Notre Dame Press, 1994. Horton and Mendus bring together a collection of critical essays on MacIntyre, exploring especially his criticisms of the Enlightenment. The opening essay elucidates succinctly MacIntyre's development since *After Virtue*. The collection as a whole balances elucidation and critique. There are sixteen essays, including one by MacIntyre.

McCann, Dennis P., and M. L. Brownsberger. "Management as a Social Practice: Rethinking Business Ethics After MacIntyre." In *The Annual of the Society of Christian Ethics*. Knoxville, Tenn.: Society of Christian Ethics, 1990. The authors see MacIntyre as having uncritically assimilated Aristotle's prejudice against commerce. They take one of MacIntyre's "social characters," the business manager, and challenge his concept of him, and thus his critique of modern liberal societies. The article does this, however, within the context of MacIntyre's theory of social practices, which they wish to retain.

McMylor, Peter. *Alasdair MacIntyre: Critic of Modernity*. London: Routledge, 1994. The fullest account so far of MacIntyre's thinking, especially his radical critique of contemporary philoso-phy and culture. McMylor acknowledges both the strengths and weaknesses of such a critique.

Von Dohlen, Richard F. *Culture War and Ethical Theory*. Lanham, Md.: University Press of America, 1997. This book contains a chapter on MacIntyre's philosophical theories.

David Barratt

Moses Maimonides

Through his classification of Jewish law, life, and observance, as defined in the Torah, Mishnah, and Talmud, and his further interpretation of the philosophical bases of Judaism in the light of Aristotelian thought, Maimonides influenced Jewish and Christian scholarship and trends, an influence that continues to the present.

Principal philosophical works: *Iggereth Hashemad*, c. 1162; *Kitab al-Sirāj*, 1168 (partial translation, *The Eight Chapters of Maimonides on Ethics*, 1912); *Mishneh Torah*, 1185 (books 1-2, *The Book of Knowledge and the Book of Adoration*, 1974; books 3-14, *The Code of Maimonides*, 1949-1979); *Dalālat al-Hā'irīn*, 1190 (*The Guide of the Perplexed*, 1881-1885); *Millot ha-Higgayon*, before 1204 (*Maimondes' Treatise on Logic*, 1938); *Kitab al-Fara'id*, before 1204; *Iggerot ha-Rambam*, before 1204 (*Epistles of Maimonides: Crisis and Leadership*, 1985).

Born: March 30, 1135; Córdoba (now in Spain)
Died: December 13, 1204; Cairo, Egypt

Early Life

Moses Maimonides (born Moses ben Maimon, whose Arabic name was Abū 'Imrān Mūsā ibn Mayumūn ibn 'Ubayd Allāh) was a child of destiny, recognized as such by the family and society into which he was born. His birth as son of the renowned Maimon ben Joseph was regarded as so important that the day, hour, and minute were recorded, as well as the fact that it occurred on the eye of Passover, which fell on the Sabbath. The young Maimonides (sometimes referred to as the Second Moses) was extraordinarily sensitive to his religious and intellectual heritage and to an awareness of his destiny, to be a leader of his people. As a result of this precocity, the child spent no time playing or attending to his physical health, lest such activities interfere with his life's mission.

Although Maimonides' boyhood and physical characteristics are not recorded, biographical accounts place much emphasis upon his intellectual development. His major teacher was his father, who was a Talmudic scholar, a member of the Rabbinical Council, *dayan* (judge) of Córdoba (a position held for generations in the family), and an acknowledged scholar and writer in the areas of Bible exposition, Talmudic commentary, astronomy, and mathematics. The young boy's knowledge expanded from other sources as well: Jewish scholars, his relatively untroubled interactions with the life and scholars of the Spanish and Arab communities of Córdoba, and countless hours reading the manuscripts in his father's library. In turn, Maimonides, entrusted with the education of his younger brother, David, began to develop his classification skills as he transmitted his own knowledge to the younger boy.

When Maimonides was thirteen, the religiously fanatical Almohad faction captured Córdoba. Jews and Christians were initially forced to choose between apostasy and death but later were allowed the third option of emigration. Historical sources are unclear as to how long Maimonides' family remained in Córdoba, in what other cities they lived, or whether they formally converted or professed belief in the other monotheistic religion while continuing to practice Judaism. In their writings, both Maimonides and his father addressed the difficulties of living as a Jew and the minimum expectations afforded the still-practicing Jew in a hostile environment. Clearly, between 1148 and 1160, when the family settled in Fez in Morocco, Maimonides, in addition to his other activities, was collecting data for the three great works of his career.

Moses Maimonides. *(Library of Congress)*

During the family's stay in Alexandria, Maimonides' father died, and his brother David drowned. David's death was particularly grievous, as Maimonides wrote: "For a full year I lay on my couch, stricken with fever and despair." At age thirty, Maimonides began to support himself and David's wife and children financially by putting to use the medical career for which he had prepared during his years in Fez. Embarking upon his dual career of Jewish scholarship and medicine, Maimonides made notable contributions that remain relevant and significant to the present day. His personal life remains obscure, but his letters indicate that his first wife died young. He remarried in 1184 and fathered a girl and a boy, Abraham, who later followed in his father's path of scholarship and leadership. In fact, ten generations of the Maimonides family followed as leaders of the Cairo community.

Life's Work

Maimonides' twofold scholarly approach throughout his life was to examine existent knowledge in a field through classification followed by integration. In clear and succinct form, he would then publish the results, which had a major impact as each succeeding generation continued to find new, contemporaneous, and ever-relevant meanings in his writings.

The achievements of Maimonides, one of history's "men for all seasons," are broad and deep. He has been equally influential in four areas: religion, philosophy, psychology, and medicine. In the fields of religion and religious thought, Maimonides made his significant impact primarily through two major works: *Kitab al-Sirāj* and *Mishneh Torah*. The first was written in Arabic, the second in Hebrew. *Kitab al-Sirāj* is a commentary on the Mishnah, the early compilation of Jewish law. Maimonides' intent in this work was to clarify for Jews the complex discussion of law of which the Mishnah is composed and to provide

In Fez, Maimonides studied medicine, read extensively, and wrote while his father and brother established a thriving jewelry business. Although ostensibly involved with the Arabic community, the family remained faithfully Jewish. This period of accommodation with Muslim leaders and thought was broken by the prominence given to Maimonides' *Iggereth Hashemad* (letter concerning apostasy), which reassured the many Jews who were similarly accommodating to their environment. Because this leadership position thrust upon Maimonides threatened the family's security, they immigrated to Palestine in 1165. After remaining five months in Acre, the family settled in Egypt, living first in Alexandria and then in Cairo.

an understandable framework of guidelines for living a life satisfactory to God. Probably the most important section of the *Kitab al-Sirāj* is the statement of Maimonides' articles of faith, the basic principles of Judaism, which include the existence of a Creator, the unity of Deity, the incorporeality of God, the external nature of God, the worship and adoration of God alone, the existence of prophecy, the greatness of Moses as a prophet, the gift of the law to Moses by God on Sinai, the immutability of the law, the knowledge by God of the acts of humanity, reward for the righteous and punishment for the wicked, the coming of the Messiah, and the resurrection of the dead.

The *Mishneh Torah* continues the explanation of Jewish law with a codification by subject of the content of the massive Talmud in fourteen books, each representing one area of Jewish law. The work begins with a statement of purpose, followed by book 1 on God and humanity. It ends with a poetic longing for the Messianic age, when "the earth will be filled with the knowledge of God as the waters cover the sea."

Maimonides' contributions to religion and religious thought overlap his contributions in philosophy. His major philosophical contribution, however, is *The Guide of the Perplexed*, in which he addresses and reconciles the rationalist Aristotelian philosophy with Jewish beliefs and faith. His treatments of philosophical constructs include discussions of God, Creation, prophecy, the nature of evil, Divine Providence, and the nature of humanity and moral virtue.

More than his other writings, *The Guide of the Perplexed* has become part of mainstream philosophy rather than remaining unique to Judaism. One reason for its generalized significance may be that it represents the beginnings of psychotherapy. In the section on the nature of humanity and moral virtue, Maimonides defines a life satisfactory to God as one that approaches happiness through development of intellect and control of appetites by morality, referring especially to control of the sexual drive. This work also represents a bridge between Maimonides' contribution in the second area, philosophy, and his major contributions to both the third and fourth areas: psychology and medicine.

In the study of medicine, Maimonides' significant contribution was in his clear, textbook descriptions of major areas of the discipline that he describes metaphorically as one of the "strange women [in addition to his betrothed, the Torah] whom I first took into my house as her handmaids [and who have] become rivals and absorb a portion of my time." Maimonides' medical writings date between 1180 and 1200 and include most notably *A Physician's Prayer*, his "aphorisms" (*The Medical Aphorisms of Moses Maimonides*, 1970, 1972), an encyclopedia, a glossary of drug names, a work on married life, and treatises on asthma and poisons and their cures.

Influence

Maimonides' contributions span and integrate history. His contributions begin with his scholarship in religion and religious thought that explores concepts and events from Creation to the giving of the Torah, to the canonization of prophetic thought in the Mishnah and the Talmud. His scholarship then moves to philosophical contributions that integrate the Jewish world of antiquity with the Greek world of Aristotle and with the Arabic worlds of Spain and Egypt of the twelfth century. In his contributions to psychology and medicine, Maimonides foreshadows today's practices in healing and Freudian thought.

History shaped Maimonides' insights as he codified and synthesized Jewish literature. In turn, Maimonides guided the insights of his contemporaries and those of succeeding generations as he responded to the realities of medieval Spain and the traditions of Aristotle, developing a new blend of faith and rationalistic thought. He influenced the thought of succeeding scholars by providing new religious, philosophical, psychological, and medical foundations on which to build the concept of a good life.

June H. Schlessinger and Bernard Schlessinger

The Guide of the Perplexed

Type of philosophy: Jewish philosophy, metaphysics, philosophical theology
First transcribed: Dalālat al-Hā'irīn, 1190 (English translation, 1881-1885)

Principal ideas advanced:
◇ Those who have become perplexed about religious matters as a result of studying philosophy can be helped by realizing that scriptural writings may often be understood in a figurative sense.
◇ It is precisely because of the difficulty of understanding the divine that metaphor becomes useful in religious utterances.
◇ Once the necessity for an indirect approach to religious matters is admitted, faith becomes a way of relating oneself to a Being whose mystery is understood metaphorically.

"From Moses to Moses there was none like Moses" is a famous phrase that indicates something of Maimonides' place of importance in Jewish thought. The First Moses represents the origin of the great Jewish religious tradition and the Jewish Law. The Second Moses stands for an attempt to reconcile this inherited tradition with the growing Arabian and Western philosophy and culture that were being absorbed in the eleventh century.

Intellectuals of his age were perplexed by the disparity between the Law, which meant so much to them, and the philosophical sophistication they could not resist acquiring. For them, Maimonides provided *The Guide of the Perplexed*, as well as a new summary of the Law, both of which were so successful that they have become classics in the religious tradition as well as in secular philosophy.

The Perplexed

Maimonides addressed *The Guide of the Perplexed* to those who had studied philosophy and had acquired knowledge and who "while firm in religious matters are perplexed and bewildered on account of the ambiguous and figurative expressions employed in holy writings." Moses' audience was from the beginning firmly committed to its religious tradition; but now that philosophy had penetrated religion, the question was never one as to whether religion should be maintained but only how it was to handle its philosophical content. Maimonides wrote for those whose religious roots were deep and who had held to religious practice:

The object of this treatise is to enlighten a religious man who has been trained to believe in the truth of our holy Law, who conscientiously fulfills his moral and religious duties, and at the same time has been successful in his philosophical studies.

It is not difficult to see why such people were "lost in perplexity and anxiety," caught in tensions they could not easily resolve. Their religious training was too deeply ingrained even to consider surrendering it, and yet the new sophistication made philosophy naturally attractive. It is not that such people had for the first time become intellectuals—because as Jews, they had inherited a long and subtle intellectual tradition—but that formerly reason had worked only within the Law, and afterward, philosophy took this same reason outside the Law and offered it new and alien foundations. This was the general cause for concern, but *The Guide for the Perplexed* focuses on the particular problem of trying to explain certain words in Scripture central to the religious tradition whose common interpretation sets them at odds with philosophical refinements. Reason never ceased to accept the Law, but it found it difficult to accept any teaching based on a literal interpretation of the Law.

Furthermore, the perplexity had to be met by finding a way to live with it, because to surrender either the Law or the newly found philosophy was unacceptable. Maimonides' attempt is never to try to remove the source of the anxiety, as might seem natural, but to try to find a way in which to adapt to it. To surrender religion would mean to break down the context that gave meaning and continuity to Jewish life, but to surrender philosophy would be no service to religion either because it would leave religion still disturbed by the unanswered philosophical questions. To reject philosophy would not remove the objections with which philosophy perplexes religion. Because there could be no escape from perplexity, it had to be met and accepted as the starting point.

Metaphor as an Answer

Maimonides' first step toward meeting this perplexity is the ancient one of suggesting that the offending words in Scripture may also be understood in a figurative sense. Although this is the general line of Maimonides' reply, he was quick to see that it would provide only temporary relief from perplexity unless backed up by an explanation as to why it was necessary to use figurative language in the first place. This he began to do by explaining that even in natural science, some topics are not fully explained, that most difficult problems cannot be thoroughly understood by any one of us, and that, because people differ in degree of intelligence, truth is withheld from most ordinary people, and, therefore, their objections can be ignored. The necessity for metaphor, it seems, cannot be explained until people are convinced that reason allows only a few to reach great heights, and that even here they must all accept final limitations.

If such is the case, we are forced back to metaphor as the most adequate means available for expressing what we do know. If all obscurity could be removed from the subject, then literal terms could be used without reservation. Because literal description is completely successful only where all tinges of mystery can be removed, the acceptance of metaphorical expression depends upon the existence of some sense of mystery where God is concerned. The purely philosophical mind might have difficulty accepting mystery, even in the case of God, but Maimonides wrote for an overtly religious person, for whom the sense of mystery in the divine nature did not seem at all abnormal.

Maimonides was not fooled into thinking that an allegorical interpretation of religious literature is a full explanation to a philosophical mind. Instead, the intent of this method was to show the philosophical-religious mind that to ask for a complete exposition in these matters is an exorbitant demand. The difficulty of understanding a literal impossibility arises only for the intelligent because the ill-informed do not recognize an impossibility when it appears. Yet intelligent observers who can admit the plausibility of a secret meaning need not reject the difficult religious doctrine at once, because they can treat it allegorically, as well as literally, to see if it may be accepted in this second mode. For Maimonides, the literal meaning was never to be rejected but was always to be retained along with the more subtle metaphorical treatment.

All of this can serve to relieve philosophical perplexity, but, interestingly enough, it can do so only for one made sensitive to the limitations of human reason through a religious tradition. Without the religious sensitivity, no solution can be found. The religiously untrained person simply cannot see the need for metaphorical expression. It takes some acquaintance with God, which only a religious discipline is likely to provide, to convince one of how difficult a matter it is to deal with the divine.

When the mind comprehends one thing, it tends to think that it can comprehend everything, but it is just this view of knowledge that must be guarded against if the metaphorical method is to be successful in dealing with human perplexity. If there are no limitations set for the mind, everything would theoretically be open to literal interpretation. Metaphor can become meaningful when the mind finds that it cannot go everywhere directly. Metaphor is the shortest distance between two points only when the direct path is not open to the human mind.

Mystery and Literalness

Here is the paradox: The religious spirit, which feeds on the sense of the final mystery within the divine nature, leads to perplexity when brought into contact with philosophical optimism and its literal, one-level mode of statement. Yet the only hope for the reconciliation without surrender is that a sense of divine mystery might force one to see that a frontal attack is not possible in the case of God. Thus, allegorical interpretation provides a genuine basis of latitude that alone is generous enough to retain both the religious sense of a divine mystery never fully disclosed, together with a philosophical directness whenever possible.

Such an interpretation of mystery and literalness together, which requires metaphorical expression, opens the way for a genuine meaning for faith. "By 'faith' we do not understand merely that which is uttered with the lips, but also that which is apprehended by the soul, the conviction that the object of belief is exactly as it is apprehended." If God is not directly approachable by literal means, faith always concerns something seen only incompletely through the figure of a symbol. Such belief cannot be compelled; however, if the necessity for indirect approach is admitted in the case of objects exceeding the limits of direct grasp, metaphor becomes meaningful and faith an appropriate and possible way of relating oneself to such a Being. If all things were open to direct knowledge, a relation of faith could only seem unnecessary and inappropriate.

Metaphor and Negative Theology

Metaphor is not a completely successful or controllable means of communication. People can employ only inadequate language where God is concerned, and metaphor is the best method at their disposal, because it allows the mind to get around barriers by subtle and indirect means. "We therefore make the subject clearer, and show to the understanding the way of truth by saying He is one but does not possess the attribute of unity." This seems to contradict ordinary expression, but by negating part of the phrase in the figurative statement, the sensitive mind passes on to a grasp of God's nature, which could not be given by direct statement. What we learn from this example is that "we cannot describe the Creator by any means except by negative attributes." Metaphor and negative theology, then, are natural companions.

Positive assertions about God allow the imagination to mislead one, whereas proof by negation leads one gradually to more perfect knowledge of God. The mystery involved in the divine nature turns the ordinary situation around, so that one can be convinced that certain qualities must be negated, whereas one cannot be as sure of positive attributes as one might be in an ordinary instance. The method of negative attributes is necessary "to direct the mind to the truth that we must believe concerning God," but it could be adopted only by one who felt the presence of mystery in the divine nature and realized the inappropriateness of frontal attack.

One's only complete knowledge concerning God, it turns out, "consists in knowing that we are unable truly to comprehend Him." God alone comprehends himself, and one not made aware of these matters too quickly jumps to the conclusion that people can know nothing about God at all. The truth lies somewhere in between, and it requires the energy of religious interest to keep from slipping into either extreme. God may be approached, but only by indirection. The negative method provides the mind with positive apprehensions of the divine nature but not such

that all mystery is removed because God remains never fully comprehended by any being other than himself.

Maimonides' Guide

Thus, Maimonides has provided a context in which perplexity may be stabilized, but it is not a simple solution. He speaks to people whose sense of religious tradition is basic to them, and thus he is able to call on their religious discipline to hold a flexible position that does not go all the way in either direction. The use of metaphor allows the literal meaning of the ordinary religious language to remain, while making room for the more subtle and refined meaning of terms in philosophical usage. A willingness to grant metaphor as legitimate and applicable depends upon an agreement that knowledge reaches its limits at least in the case of God, and it is almost inconceivable that one should allow this limit to be placed on knowledge philosophically unless one had experienced some feeling of the mystery present at the center of the divine nature. Recognizing the difficulty, people employ the negative method to protect them while they look directly into the light, and the knowledge they achieve will not seem contradictory as long as it is regarded as at least partly metaphor and symbol. If people's religious sense is strong enough to feel this, they can accept metaphor and control the anxiety that philosophical sophistication has brought to them. This is the guide for the perplexed, but only for one whose perplexity stems from a strong religious tradition and its accompanying sense of the mystery encountered whenever the mind is turned toward God.

Turning to Maimonides' doctrine of nonliteral or metaphorical interpretation, we have to ask what it is that allows such duality of meaning without simple equivocation of terms. Maimonides' answer is that this is possible only when people deal with a kind of existence not capable of reduction to a single level, and they are not likely to grant this if they have lost all sense of mystery in the divine nature. Philosophy can be counted on to take the mystery out of the natural order, as well it should; but it cannot be asked to provide feeling for the irreducible mystery in the divine nature. The cultivation of the religious life provides the datum on which philosophy applies itself to develop theology—that is, the rational statement of the divine insofar as this is possible. However, if theology is not to become pure philosophy, the devotional life must have provided it with some sensitivity regarding the difficulty of handling God on one's own terms.

In spite of this rather clear framework and simple objective, the casual modern reader is likely to be struck by the elaborate scholarly nature of much of *The Guide of the Perplexed*. The opening pages are entirely given over to an exegesis or analysis of the use of certain Hebrew terms, all of which are central to Jewish religious thought. Interspersed is a discussion of the limits of human intellect as well as an appraisal of the value of studying metaphysics. Such a diversity gives a correct picture of the blend of religious thought, scholarly study of concepts, and traditional philosophy that makes up *The Guide of the Perplexed*. Then follows a consideration of the nature of God and of God's attributes.

Major Theological Issues

The scope of *The Guide of the Perplexed* is as wide as all traditional theology and religious thought. It is by no means simply a piece of philosophical apologetic, as might be thought from its title. Maimonides correctly sees that the only adequate way to provide a guide out of any perplexity is to discuss all the major theological issues. To do so successfully is to provide the best, most substantial guide that can be produced. After considering the traditional attributes of God (such as unity and incorporeality), the second Moses begins part 2 with a discussion of twenty-six propositions employed by philosophers to prove God's existence.

Next comes the question of creation versus the eternality of the universe, and Maimonides sets forth as best he can the way in which a doctrine of creation *ex nihilo* can be justified philosophically. Prophecy and the prophets then occupy him, as one might almost guess, for the Jewish tradition demands that prophecy be made acceptable. Visions are discussed, but evil and divine providence are the two central problems in this section. A religious belief in God runs into its greatest philosophical difficulty in trying to reconcile its conception of divinity with the evils and difficulties of the world.

What Maimonides has provided is a comprehensive summa of religious belief and philosophical tradition. Out of this meeting, a theology is born, although its material setting within the literature of Judaism makes it appear less abstract than most modern questions. *The Guide of the Perplexed* is a vast compendium of philosophical and religious material, which is then given shape through Maimonides' attempt to draw answers out of this combination. The towering position of influence that he occupies within the Jewish tradition gives some measure of his success.

Philosophy and religion in certain areas treat the same questions, but they do so in different ways and in different settings. When they are kept apart, as they can be in some ages, no conflict arises. Whenever an age becomes generally sophisticated philosophically, perplexity is bound to come. To those who can drop neither perspective, some reconciliation of the two bodies of material must be made. Out of the attempt to reconcile philosophy and religion, each age arrives at a new theological perspective, which has implications for both technical philosophy and the religious life.

Frederick Sontag, updated by John K. Roth

Additional Reading

Benor, Ehud. *Worship of the Heart: A Study of Maimonides' Philosophy of Religion.* Albany: State University of New York Press, 1995. Benor explains and evaluates the key points in Moses Maimonides' philosophical understanding of religion and Judaism in particular.

Botwinick, Aryeh. *Skepticism, Belief, and the Modern: Maimonides to Nietzsche.* Ithaca, N.Y.: Cornell University Press, 1997. Appraises the contributions and implications of Maimonides' philosophy for later developments in philosophical criticism and religious belief.

Buijs, Joseph A., ed. *Maimonides: A Collection of Critical Essays.* Notre Dame, Ind.: University of Notre Dame Press, 1988. Well-qualified Maimonides scholars offer helpful interpretations and criticisms of Maimonides' philosophy.

Dodds-Weinstein, Idit. *Maimonides and Saint Thomas on the Limits of Reason.* Albany: State University of New York Press, 1995. Compares and contrasts two great medieval thinkers on issues concerning reason, revelation, and religion.

Faur, Josâe. *"Homo Mysticus: A Guide to Maimonides's Guide for the Perplexed*. Syracuse, N.Y.: Syracuse University Press, 1999. A helpful aid in understanding Maimonides' contribution to mysticism.

Fox, Marvin. *Interpreting Maimonides: Studies in Methodology, Metaphysics, and Moral Philosophy*. Chicago: University of Chicago Press, 1990. A scholarly study of Maimonides' approaches to and views about the nature of reality and ethics.

Hartman, David. *Maimonides: Torah and Philosophic Quest*. Philadelphia: Jewish Publication Society of America, 1976. Attempts to reconcile Maimonides' hidden theories with those he openly expounded and integrates Maimonides' religious views with his philosophical doctrines.

Heschel, Abraham Joshua. *Prophetic Inspiration After the Prophets: Maimonides and Other Medieval Authorities*. Edited by Morris M. Faierstein. Hoboken, N.J.: Ktav, 1996. A leading Jewish theologian and philosopher evaluates Maimonides' contributions to religious tradition and to understandings of revelation in particular.

Kellner, Menachem Marc. *Maimonides on Judaism and the Jewish People*. Albany: State University of New York Press, 1991. Kellner clarifies Maimonides' influential interpretation of Jewish tradition and the significance of Jewish life.

Strauss, Lev. *Philosophy of Law: Contributions to the Understanding of Maimonides and His Predecessors*. Albany: State University of New York Press, 1995. A helpful interpretation of Maimonides' views on law, ethics, and religious tradition.

Weiss, Raymond L. *Maimonides' Ethics: The Encounter of Philosophic and Religious Morality*. Chicago: University of Illinois Press, 1991. An illuminating study that show how Maimonides understood the similarities and differences between the ethical outlooks of philosophy, religion, and Judaism in particular.

June H. Schlessinger and Bernard Schlessinger, updated by John K. Roth

Nicolas Malebranche

Malebranche sought to reconcile René Descartes's mechanistic philosophy with the God-filled universe of Saint Augustine and the Neoplatonists, and he preserved the centrality of God's action in his doctrine of occasionalism.

Principal philosophical works: *De la recherche de la vérité*, 1674-1675, 6th ed. 1712 (*Treatise Concerning the Search After Truth*, 1694, best known as *The Search After Truth*); *Conversations chrétiennes*, 1676; *Traité de la nature et de la grace*, 1680 (*Treatise of Nature and Grace*, 1694); *Méditations chrétiennes et métaphysiques*, 1683; *Traité de morale*, 1683 (*A Treatise of Morality*, 1699); *Recueil de toutes les réponses à M. Arnauld*, 1684-1694; *Entretiens sur la métaphysique et sur la religion*, 1688 (*Dialogues on Metaphysics and on Religion*, 1923); *Traité des lois de la communication du mouvement*, 1692; *Entretiens sur la mort*, 1696; *Entretien d'un philosophe chrétien et d'un philosophe chinois*, 1708; *Réflexions sur la prémotion physique*, 1715; *Œuvres complètes de Malebranche*, 1958-1967.

Born: August 6, 1638; Paris, France
Died: October 13, 1715; Paris, France

Early Life

Nicolas Malebranche's father, also named Nicolas, was a secretary to King Louis XIII. He and his wife, Catherine de Lauzon, had a number of children, of whom Nicolas was the youngest. A malformation of the spine led to Malebranche's education at home until age sixteen, when he entered the Collège de la Marche, from which he graduated in 1656 as Maitre ès Arts. He spent the next three years at the Sorbonne; in 1660, he joined the Congregation of the Oratory and was ordained in 1664. He would spend the rest of his life in the Oratory of the Rue St.-Honoré, but these first four years permanently shaped his thought and philosophy. The order took its theological tone from its founder, Cardinal Bérulle, who was both a devoted follower of Saint Augustine, with his doctrine of God's grace, and a personal friend of philosopher René Descartes. Malebranche's discovery of Descartes's *Traité de l'homme* (1662; in Latin as *De Homine*, 1664; *Treatise of Man*, 1972) launched him on a study of the mathematics and physics that underlay Cartesian thought. By 1674-1675, his first major work, *The Search After Truth*, had appeared. It contained the essence of Malebranche's thinking; the works that followed amplified its conclusions, tightened its presentation, and responded to critics.

Life's Work

The Search After Truth contains many of the essential correspondences and differences between Descartes's and Malebranche's thinking, and it provides comparisons between them. Both men concluded that the universe is composed of three elements: mind, body, and God. Both agreed that body is defined entirely by extension—that is, by its pure physical existence, in much the same way that matter is defined in present-day textbooks as that which possesses mass and occupies space (mass frequently was left out of consideration before English physicist Isaac Newton demonstrated the effects of its magnitude in the seventeenth century). Body could have no inherent motion but must be set into motion by an external cause; it cannot be a causal agent.

Mind is a separate substance from body. Both thinkers conclude that the known world is a world of ideas held in the mind; the body, being separate, can give no information about that world. For Descartes, both animals and humans are mechanical devices composed of body animated by mind. The distinction between them is that humans possess a soul that, according to a chain of careful Cartesian reasoning, connects humanity to God. People's certainty about the world in which they live and move, then, is guaranteed by God. Their certainty about what they know, however, is a mathematician's certainty: What people perceive clearly and distinctly is what they know in that mind that exists separately from the body. The clarity and distinction is almost Euclidean: People can know the existence of a triangle, or the relation of its sides and angles to those of another triangle, without appealing to God for specific certification of this knowledge. By extension, people can know that mind causes body to move and accomplish the actions of everyday life.

For Malebranche, the relation between God, mind, and body is much more subtle. To begin with, neither body nor mind is a causal agent. The sole cause in the universe is God. What a

person perceives as cause and effect—for example, the motion imparted to a body on collision—is in fact the result of God's intervention, in accordance with rules he has himself laid down. This doctrine is called occasionalism—that is, each apparent cause-effect occurrence is actually an *occasion* of God's intervention. The part mind plays in this is that mind is the essential element that makes a human being. Malebranche sets aside completely the notion of a body-mechanism actuated by mind, in favor of his occasionalist causality. People are thinking beings only, their existence contained solely in their perception of ideas that form an *intelligible extension* (in contrast to the physical extension that is the only attribute of body). This intelligible extension of ideas lies in God—indeed, Malebranche affirms, along with Saint Paul, that people see all things in (or through) God—though intelligible extension is not identical with God. The ideas he speaks of are archetypes or Platonic ideals, eternal and infinite; people understand them incompletely, and only as God illuminates them.

What Malebranche is doing in this God-centered development of Cartesian thought is expressing a thoroughly Augustinian admixture of theology and metaphysics—that is, of the unseen world of God and of the origin and being of the seen world about people. He is in no way confused in treating these things together. Where Descartes had said that he preferred to concentrate on metaphysics and leave theology to theologians, Malebranche saw no reason to separate the two. Both are legitimate parts of a universe that has its being in God. This fits with, or even proceeds from, his theodicy, or explanation of how God's wisdom and power can be reconciled with imperfection and evil in the world. God acts in the simplest ways possible, and according to intentions that have the character of physical laws, as manifested in the causality of occasionalism. If these actions (drought, say, or famine) appear imperfect to humanity, this is because people have not recognized that the

Nicolas Malebranche. *(Library of Congress)*

sum of the actions makes for the best world possible.

Malebranche's two major contributions to Cartesian philosophy—occasionalism and his doctrine of seeing all things in God—are thus presented in his first work, along with his theodicy. *The Search After Truth* went through six editions during Malebranche's lifetime, and Malebranche added an *Éclaircissements* (Elucidations) in the course of them. Subsequent writings amplified and clarified his views, as well as presenting more specific defenses of Roman Catholic theology. These include *Conversations chrétiennes*, a justification of Catholicism; *Treatise of Nature and Grace*; *Méditations chrétiennes et métaphysiques*), an explanation of Malebranche's system of philosophy and a defense against his critics; *A Treatise of Morality*, a demonstration of Christian ethics; *Dialogues on Metaphysics and on Religion*, Malebranche's second major presentation of his philosophy, presented not as a treatise but as a three-person dialogue in the style of Plato; *Entretiens sur la mort*, a supplement to the *Dialogues on Metaphysics and on Religion*; and a number of lesser works in philosophy, physics, and mathematics.

Influence

Malebranche's ideas attracted adverse criticism almost from their first publication. The most acute and unsparing critic was Antoine Arnauld, author of the major Jansenist treatise *De la fréquente communion* (1643; on frequent communion) and coauthor with Pierre Nicole of the Jansenists' *La Logique: Ou, L'Art de penser contenant, outre les regles communes, plusieurs observations nouelles propres à former le jugement* (1662; *Logic: Or, The Art of Thinking*, 1685, known as the Port-Royal logic). Jansenism was a movement within the Roman Catholic Church that attracted many French clergy; its principal theological convictions were a rigorous predestination, an insistence that the soul could be converted to God only within the Church and by God's freely given grace, and the view that frequent communion was unnecessary for the converted. Arnauld's *Des vrayes et des fausses idées: Contre ce qu'enseigne Iaideur de La recherche de la vérité* (1683; *On True and False Ideas*, 1990) objected to Malebranche's ideas about grace but chose to attack them through the more vulnerable ideas about vision

in God. Arnauld considered false the view that ideas exist separately from perceptions, and only in the mind of God, as representative entities or archetypes. He felt that this view arose because of a confusion about what constitutes the presence of an idea in the mind, leading to the false notion that an object can be perceived only if a representative entity in the mind of God acts as a surrogate for it.

Throughout *Des vrayes et des fausses idées*, Arnauld distances himself from his opponent by referring to him as "the Author of the 'Search After Truth,'" or even just "this Author." In later publications, he focuses on his real concern, Malebranche's overreliance on reason and his consequent softness on grace as the only means of salvation. A long polemic exchange occurred, and Arnauld even managed to have *Treatise of Nature and Grace* placed on the Church's Index of Prohibited Books; later *The Search After Truth* was added. The battle between Arnauld and Malebranche ended only with the death of the former in 1694; some of his objections were published posthumously, but Malebranche did not hesitate to have the last word after that. The result of this activity, and of lively exchanges with other critics that sharpened his thinking and the published expressions of his views, was that Malebranche became a leading philosophical figure in the latter part of the seventeenth century. To be a *malebranchiste* was to concur in the ideas of a recognized and respectable school of metaphysical thought.

If Malebranche was a major influence during his lifetime, his ideas persisted in the eighteenth century, if only by way of reaction to them. Philosopher John Locke, Malebranche's contemporary, reacted to Malebranche's doctrine of vision in God, in a published essay, and agreed that people's knowledge and existence lie only in their ideas, although he did not take Malebranche's extreme view that this knowledge is a reflection of the representative entities in the mind of God. Irish philosopher Bishop George Berkeley argued that ideas and their qualities arise in the mind through people's perceptions, although their continued existence is guaranteed by God. Scottish philosopher David Hume took the last step in this skeptical direction and explained humans' being as nothing but perceptions, and their notions of causality as nothing but the familiarity of repeated sequences of events. This brought Cartesian metaphysics to a standstill that had to wait to be resolved by philosopher Immanuel Kant at the end of the eighteenth century.

Malebranche's original contributions to Cartesian philosophy, as expressed in *The Search After Truth* and the *Treatise of Nature and Grace*, were the doctrines of occasionalism and of the vision of all things in God. He published the last edition of *The Search After Truth* in 1712. In the summer of 1715, he fell ill while visiting a friend in Villeneuve St. Georges, outside Paris. He returned to the Oratory a few days later but apparently did not recover fully. He died in October of that year.

Robert M. Hawthorne, Jr.

Dialogues on Metaphysics and on Religion

Type of philosophy: Metaphysics, philosophy of religion
First published: Entretiens sur la métaphysique et sur la religion, 1688 (English translation, 1923)
Principal ideas advanced:

◊ Human beings exist as thinking beings; they are not material bodies.

◊ The only world we know is an intelligible world, the world of our ideas, but because the ideas have an eternal, infinite, necessary character that is independent of people's conception, they must be features of an intelligible extension.

◊ Intelligible extension has its locus in God, but it should not be identified with God.

◊ People understand certain truths only because God illuminates the ideas.

◊ When an event involving the body occurs, an event involving the soul occurs as a result of God's action; in this manner, human beings have feelings—this is the theory of occasionalism.

◊ The universe contains three types of beings: God, mind, and body; of the three, God alone is an active agent in the universe.

Nicolas Malebranche was the chief Cartesian philosopher of the late seventeenth century. He was a member of the Augustinian religious order of the Oratory in Paris, where he originally devoted himself to the studies of ecclesiastical history, biblical criticism, and Hebrew. At the age of twenty-six, he came across a work by René Descartes and was so impressed by its method and the theory it contained that he devoted the next several years to studying Cartesian philosophy and mathematics. The first fruits of these studies appeared in 1674-1675 in his famous work *De la recherche de la vérité* (1674-1675, 6th ed. 1712; *Treatise Concerning the Search After Truth*, 1694, best known as *The Search After Truth*), in which he developed his modified version of Cartesian philosophy. The work was immediately successful and was translated into several languages, including English. It was studied and discussed by major thinkers everywhere and soon led to a series of polemical controversies between Malebranche and his opponents. His *Dialogues on Metaphysics and on Religion* presents a more literary and definitive version of his theory, as well as answers to many of his critics. It has remained the most popular expression of Malebranche's theory of knowledge and his metaphysics.

Malebranche's views were tremendously influential in their own day. For a period, he was the most important metaphysician in Europe, providing the theory that was debated everywhere. Among the thinkers who were greatly influenced by Malebranche's views were Irish philosopher George Berkeley and Scottish skeptic David Hume. Although his works were severely criticized by the Jesuits, and some of his writings were placed on the Roman Catholic Church's Index of Prohibited Books, Malebranche had, and continues to have, an enormous influence among French philosophers.

The First Dialogue

Dialogues on Metaphysics and on Religion is written more in the style of Saint Augustine than in that of Plato. It presents a statement of Malebranche's theories rather than a discussion of philosophical issues. In it, two spokespersons for Malebranche expound his views to a student, Aristes, and correct the latter's misunderstandings.

The first dialogue begins with Theodore instructing Aristes in the method of finding philosophical truth. Understanding should be gained through reason; hence, for the time being, faith is not taken as a source of knowledge. The sensuous or material world should be ignored, so that the senses and the imagination will not interfere with the pursuit of rational knowledge. With this much in mind, the analysis of what rational truths people can possess is begun.

The analysis proceeds as follows. Because nothing, or nonbeing, can have no qualities, I, who think, must exist. (I have at least the quality of thinking; hence, I cannot be nothing, or nonexistent.) What, however, am I? I am not a body, because a body is only a piece of extension. When I examine my idea of a body, the only properties that I find belonging to it are extensional ones, relations of distance. Thought is not a property or type of extension, because thoughts cannot be defined in terms of distances, and because they can be conceived without reference to any properties of extension. Hence, people's conception of themselves is totally different from their conception of bodies. (Malebranche offers these considerations as evidence that people are not material bodies.)

When people examine their ideas, they find that what they are directly acquainted with is an intelligible world, and not a material one. People know ideas, and not physical things. Even if all material objects disappeared, people's ideas might remain the same. Because everything that a person can know is an idea, it is only the intelligible world that directly concerns people. When people inspect this intelligible world of ideas, they find that it has an eternal, immutable, and necessary structure that is not in any way dependent on their thinking about it. Truths, such as 3 x 3 = 9, are always true and they must be true. One does not decide or will that they be true; instead, one is forced to recognize and accept their truth. Furthermore, the truths of the intelligible world are infinite, in that they apply to an infinite number of objects; hence, these necessary and unchangeable truths must apply not only to the limited, finite number of things in a person's mind but also to what Malebranche calls "intelligible extension"—the entire rational world of concepts.

All of this is intended to show that the world of intelligible extension, the realm of true ideas, cannot be a feature of a person's mind. Intelligible extension has a structure unlike that of oneself, in that it is eternal, infinite, immutable, and necessary. Hence, although a person is aware of certain aspects of intelligible extension, it must be located elsewhere, in something that possesses the actual characteristics of the intelligible world—namely, God.

The Second Dialogue

The second dialogue deals with the nature and existence of God. Malebranche emphatically denies that intelligible extension is God. Such a view would be similar to that held by Baruch Spinoza. Instead, Malebranche contends that the recognition of intelligible extension makes people realize *that* God is, because he alone can be the locus of intelligible extension. This does not state, however, *what* God is. In fact, people know of God only in relation to what he makes people know, or by what he illuminates. Anytime that a person has any knowledge, that person knows that God exists, but one can never know his nature.

To clarify this point, Malebranche argues that God is unlimited Perfection or Being or Infinite Reality. No human idea can represent such a Being, because all human ideas are determinate. In this lifetime, a person cannot attain a clear idea of what God is; people only can see that he is, and how he is related to everything that people know. People realize that the proposition "There is a God" is obviously true, and that God's essence includes his existence, but they cannot understand what his nature really is.

According to Malebranche, "We see all things in God," but we do not actually see him. The ideas we have that constitute knowledge do not properly belong to our own minds, but rather to intelligible extension. Because of the characteristics of intelligible extension, it must be located in God; hence, whenever we know something, we are seeing a truth in God, and seeing it because he illuminates it for us. In this respect, Malebranche's theory of knowledge differs sharply from that of Descartes. According to the latter, people establish truths about reality from the clear and distinct ideas in their own minds.

Descartes contended that because God gave people these ideas, and because he is no deceiver, whatever is clear and distinct about human ideas must be true of the real universe as well. Critics have noted that Descartes never succeeded in building a bridge from his ideas of reality. Malebranche removes the need for such a bridge building by insisting that the ideas are not located in people's minds, but are instead in God's Mind. A truth is a direct observation of intelligible extension in God, and people see what is God's Mind because he illuminates the ideas and enables people to see them. Thus, Malebranche's theory is a type of direct Platonic realism. The only truths are truths about the world of ideas, and these are known not by inference from the contents of human minds but by direct vision of the Divine Mind.

Ideas and the Senses

In the third, fourth, and fifth dialogues, Malebranche discusses the relationship of ideas to sense information. Ideas are intelligible. This means that they can be defined, so that people can understand why they have the characteristics they do. In terms of this conception of "ideas," the only ideas people have are divine ones. People do not have an idea of themselves because they do not know their own natures completely, and people cannot make themselves know themselves. People do not have ideas of their sense experiences, which Malebranche calls "feelings," because they cannot give clear definitions of them.

In a famous passage, Aristes and Theodore appropriately illustrate this point by discussing music. When one tries to make intelligible the real reason why people hear the sounds they do, the explanation is in terms of the mathematical relationships of vibrating strings, and not in terms of experienced qualities. The mathematical relationships can be defined in terms of the ideas involved in intelligible extension; however, the sounds cannot be defined, only "felt." In addition, no intelligible connection can be discovered between the vibrations and the felt sounds. (Does a certain sound experience *have* to be the result of vibrations of a certain frequency?)

What people can understand relates only to the realm of ideas, the realm of intelligible exten-

sion. Sense qualities are not features of mathematical ideas, for, as far as is known, they are only feelings in people. There is nothing in the mathematical relationships that people can understand about moving bodies that explains the occurrence of these feelings. The ideas that people have of bodies allow understanding of them in terms of the principles of mathematical physics without reference to feelings.

Then, what accounts for having feelings and experiencing them in some orderly relation to physical events? In giving his answer, Malebranche presents his theory of *occasionalism*. Bodies cannot cause feelings, because bodies are only extended objects moving. People cannot be the cause of their feelings, because they have no control of them. God, then, must be the cause, giving people a certain set of feelings whenever certain physical events occur. There must be laws of the conjunction of the soul and the body by which God operates on both substances, so that when an event happens to one, a corresponding event happens to the other. Each of these events is the "occasion" but not the cause of the other's occurrence. There is no necessary connection between a physical event and a mental event. God, acting according to general laws he has laid down, causes two independent sets of events, the physical ones and the feelings and ideas. The mind and the body have no contact with each other; however, God wills incessantly and produces a sequence of physical events that are correlated with a conjoined series of mental events. By means of the system God employs, people ascertain, through discovering the general laws God provides, what is necessary for self-preservation. Feelings alert people to bodily needs, so that they seek food when they have the feeling of hunger, and so on.

The sense "feelings" that God provides serve not only as warning signs for the care and maintenance of people's bodies (which they otherwise would know nothing about, because their knowledge is only about ideas) but also as the occasions for becoming aware of truths about ideas. The diagrams employed in mathematics, which are only sensations, cannot teach since they do not contain the pure ideas; however, they can function as cues, attracting attention to the truths people can learn from reason. Learning actually consists of a person being made aware of some fact about the intelligible world, and of being made aware of this fact by God, who alone has the power to make a person think and know.

Metaphysical Theory

The sixth and seventh dialogues bring out the crucial characteristics of Malebranche's metaphysical theory, showing why God is the sole causal agent in the universe. The universe contains three types of beings: God, whose existence can be demonstrated from his definition; mind, which can be directly apprehended through its mental processes, though it cannot be clearly known; and bodies, whose existence is known only by Revelation. The last point startles Aristes, so Theodore examines the evidence available for the existence of bodies.

People do not know bodies by ideas, because their ideas are of intelligible extension, and not of physical extension. They do not feel bodies, because their feelings are only modifications of their own souls, caused by God in consequence of his general laws. In terms of what people know and feel, it is quite possible that bodies do not exist at all. Human knowledge and experience could be exactly the same, because God directly causes all, whether bodies exist or do not exist. In fact, Malebranche goes on to argue, it cannot be shown that bodies must exist, but it can be shown that God need not create bodies. If God is infinitely perfect, there is no reason why he has to create anything. It is compatible with God's nature either that he has created a physical world or that he has not. If it could be shown that he had to create a physical world, then God would not be perfect (and, as Malebranche interprets this term, self-sufficient). He would require something other than himself; namely, what he had to create. Because, by definition, God is dependent on nothing, if he created a physical world, he did it arbitrarily and not necessarily. What Malebranche, in effect, claims is that no necessary conclusion about the nature of created things follows from the concept of an all-perfect, omnipotent deity.

If all of this is accepted, then is there any reason to believe that bodies do, in fact, exist? First, some proofs are convincing but not conclusive. The constancy of human experience, along with

people's natural inclination to attribute experiences to bodies, persuades them that there are bodies. This persuasion, however, could be erroneous, because people know that they could have the experiences they do, together with an inclination to believe certain things about these experiences, without there being any bodies—God could produce all such effects in them. The decisive evidence, according to Malebranche, is given by faith, in the statements that appear in the beginning of the book of Genesis, which states that God created heaven and earth. (Bishop Berkeley later disputed whether the text in question says anything about whether God created a physical world, or whether it refers only to a world of ideas.)

In the seventh dialogue, the climax of this metaphysical view is reached. A third character, Theotimus, is introduced, who is a spokesperson for Malebranche's theological views. Theodore and Theotimus together defend the theory that God alone is an efficacious agent in the universe. It already had been shown that unaided minds have no power, but receive only those ideas and feelings that God wills to give them. Now it is argued that bodies are also powerless, because their sole defining properties are extensional, that is, relations of distance. Bodies exist only because of God's will, and their particular location at any moment must also be the result of God's will. If all this is the case, then obviously bodies cannot be the cause of their own motions, or of the motions of each other—only God can be. The same point can be brought out from God's side. If he is omnipotent, then nothing besides God can have any power to act. If it did, then there would be something God could not do, namely, control the actions of a particular object. God's omnipotence implies, according to Malebranche, that God is the only possible active agent in the entire universe. This point is made in the striking assertion that not all the angels and demons acting together can move a bit of straw unless God so wills.

Then what makes the world operate? In general, it is God's will. In particular, the world proceeds according to general laws that God provides. Malebranche insists that God wills according to the principle of economy that the smallest set of fixed laws should be employed.

God can change everything at any moment, because he is the only active agent; however, because he wills in keeping with his principle of economy, effects continue to occur in lawful sequences, which people can learn through the study of nature. The world as people know it, because it is the effect of God's will, can only be described, never explained. People never know any reason *why* events happen, beyond the general formula that God so wills them. There is no necessary connection between events; hence, the created world must be known descriptively, not logically.

The remainder of *Dialogues on Metaphysics and on Religion* deals with Malebranche's theology. The author tries to show that his version of Cartesian philosophy is in accord with Christian doctrine and attempts to answer some of the theological objections that had been raised.

To an extent, Malebranche's theory represented the culmination of the grand tradition of seventeenth century metaphysical inquiry. Starting with Descartes, the "new philosophers" had tried to explain why the world discovered by modern science must have the characteristics it does. Malebranche, by consistently following out some of the main themes of Descartes, reduced the hope of reaching a rational explanation of the world to nothing, leaving only theology, instead of philosophy, as the source of knowledge about the world. Berkeley and Hume then followed some of Malebranche's insights, and Hume reduced the theological vision of Malebranche to a complete skepticism.

Richard H. Popkin

Additional Reading

Arnauld, Antoine. *On True and False Ideas*. Translated by Stephen Gaukroger. Manchester, England: Manchester University Press, 1990. Arnauld's penetrating criticism in a modern edition, but with Old French spelling.

Black, Andrew S. "Malebranche's Theodicy." *Journal of the History of Philosophy* 35, no. 1 (January, 1997): 27-44. Defense against objections by Antoine Arnauld.

Brehier, Emile. *The Seventeenth Century*. Vol. 4 in *The History of Philosophy*. Translated by Wade Baskin. Chicago: University of Chicago Press, 1966. Places Malebranche's thought in the context of Cartesianism and its followers and developers. Many references in this and Vol. 5, *The Eighteenth Century*, to Malebranche's influence on subsequent thinkers. Sound bibliography of primary and secondary sources.

Nadler, Steven M. *Malebranche and Ideas*. New York: Oxford University Press, 1992. A book-length version of an introduction written for a collection of Malebranche translations, with full scholarly apparatus.

Radner, Daisie. *Malebranche*. Assen, Netherlands: Van Gorcum, 1978. Shows Malebranche's relation to Descartes's philosophy in complete detail as regards his theories of physical reality.

Schmaltz, Ted. *Malebranche's Theory of the Soul: A Cartesian Interpretation*. New York: Oxford University Press, 1996. Schmaltz presents and defends many of Malebranche's arguments and shows how they are relevant to prevailing themes in the philosophy.

Watson, Richard A., and Marjorie Grene. *Malebranche's First and Last Critics: Simon Foucher and Dortous de Mairan*. Published for the *Journal of the History of Philosophy*. Carbondale: Southern Illinois University Press, 1995. Translations, with excellent introductions, of two volumes of criticism of *The Search After Truth*.

Robert M. Hawthorne, Jr.

Thomas Robert Malthus

The original professor of political economy, Malthus will be forever linked to discussions of the population problem. Terms such as "Malthusian economics" and "neo-Malthusianism" have achieved a permanent place in the English language and suggest the high level of controversy that his work engendered.

Principal philosophical works: *An Essay on the Principle of Population, As It Affects the Future Improvement of Society*, 1798; *Principles of Political Economy Considered with a View to Their Practical Application*, 1820; *Definitions in Political Economy*, 1827.

Born: February 13, 1766; the Rookery, near Dorking, Surrey, England

Died: December 23, 1834; Claverton, Bath, England

Early Life

Thomas Robert Malthus was born on February 13, 1766, at his father's estate, the Rookery, near Dorking, England. Some biographies incorrectly list February 14, the day of his baptism, as his birth date. His father, Daniel Malthus, was an Oxford-educated lawyer and a gentleman of some means, as well as an intellectual of the Enlightenment and a devotee of the French thinker Jean-Jacques Rousseau.

Malthus grew up in a genteel, intellectually invigorating environment provided by his father, who was caught up in the exciting ideas of the Age of Reason and the French Revolution. Indeed, Malthus's great work was initially a reaction to many of those ideas, especially the notion that through the use of reason, humankind could achieve perfection. Privately educated under a series of tutors, Malthus entered Jesus College of Cambridge in 1784 when he was eighteen. There he won prizes in Latin and English grammar, but his chief study was, as his father had suggested, mathematics. In that area, he was graduated as Ninth Wrangler (high honors) and was awarded a fellowship.

Upon graduation, Malthus took religious orders in 1788 and became a pastor in the Church of England, taking charge of the rectory in the village of Surrey in 1793. In 1804, he gave up his fellowship and married Harriet Eckersall, his cousin and eleven years his junior. A devoted family man, his home life appears to have been quite stable, and his wife was reputed to have been a charming hostess. He had three children, two sons and a daughter who died when she was seventeen, the one note of tragedy in his personal life.

Malthus was a handsome man, with an aristocratic nose, sharp eyes, and a high forehead. He dressed as a gentleman of the day and wore his curly hair short with sideburns. Contemporary sources generally indicate that his personality, despite the heated controversy that ensnared him, was genuinely amiable and pleasant. Even his worst enemies frequently noted his sincerity and fairness. He was, by all reports, a gentle man.

Life's Work

In 1805, Malthus received an appointment as professor of history and political economy at the newly founded East India College, the purpose of which was to train civil servants for work in India. This was the first such professorship established, and Malthus retained it until his death. He was a dedicated teacher, called "Pop" by his students.

By the time he left religious work for education, Malthus had already written the book that resulted in his historical significance: *An Essay on*

Thomas Robert Malthus. *(Library of Congress)*

the Principle of Population, As It Affects the Future Improvement of Society. Despite his other contributions, it was this work that marked him as a man of controversy. The original work was fairly short and was published anonymously, but it became widely read, quickly sold out, and generated considerable discussion, not all of it positive. From 1799 to 1802, Malthus traveled widely throughout Europe, collecting additional data on his theory that the growth of population would normally press uncomfortably against the supply of food. The 1803 edition was greatly expanded, and while critics still quote from the first edition, it is the 1803 version that represents the fuller accounting of Malthusian principles. During his lifetime, *An Essay on the Principle of Population* went through six editions, and both abridged and complete editions remain in print.

Malthus was both attacked and admired in his day. In 1819, he was elected a fellow of the Royal Society, and in 1821 he became a charter member of the Political Economy Club, along with David Ricardo, his close friend, and James Stuart Mill. In 1824, he received admission as a royal associate into the Royal Academy of Literature. Also a member of the French Institute and the Royal Academy in Berlin, in 1834, he became a charter fellow of the Statistical Society. During the Christmas vacation of 1834, he and his family visited his father-in-law at Claverton, Bath. There, on December 23, Malthus died of a heart attack. He is buried in Bath Abbey. His wife survived him by thirty years.

Students of Malthus and Malthusian economics can easily become confused by the controversy surrounding Malthus and particularly by arguments advanced in his name that actually bear no relation to the man or his ideas. It is best to begin by asking how Malthus came to write *An Essay on the Principle of Population* and what he said in the work. Malthus wrote his work in response to certain ideas put forth by the reforming Englishman William Godwin and the equally perfectionistic Frenchman, the Marquis de Condorcet. Simply stated, Godwin and Condorcet believed that with the use of reason and education, human progress could not end. They both foresaw continued physical, intellectual, and moral advancement until a perfect society resulted. In discussing these ideas with his father, Malthus entered certain objections to such a happy view, and his father suggested that he put them in writing, which Malthus did.

Like so many of his contemporaries, Malthus admired science and mathematics, and he believed in a natural law that would inevitably prevent human perfection. The secret lay in the mathematical relationships that he understood to govern the growth of population and the production of food. Population, he said, increased geometrically, while food or agriculture could be increased only arithmetically. Thus, the human population would increase by the following progression: 1, 2, 4, 8, 16, 32, 64, 128, and so forth. Food, however, would increase arithmetically: 1, 2, 3, 4, 5, 6, 7, 8. To many in this early age of science, and an age so eager to discover natural laws, the simple proof that Malthus offered seemed inescapable: Population growth was always threatening to outrun the capacity to increase food production.

Regarding what could be done about this situation, Malthus had little in the way of encouraging answers. In his day, there were no dependable methods of birth control (which was at any rate regarded as immoral), and abortion was illegal. The only natural limits to population growth appeared to lie in war, disease, and poverty. This depressing situation gave rise to attacks on Malthus and to his being called the Dismal Parson and to political economy becoming known as the Dismal Science. There were simply no checks on population that Malthus could find that did not come under the heading of either vice or misery. In the 1803 edition, Malthus introduced the notion that a possible curb on population growth might rest in what he called "moral restraint," by which he meant the social responsibility to bear no more children than parents could properly maintain. Although the addition of moral restraint is the greatest change that Malthus made in his theory, the inherent weakness of this restriction, since it depends on individual control, was obvious.

Influence

Viciously attacked during his lifetime, Malthus and his ideas became even less popular in the second half of the nineteenth century. Marxists were particularly bitter in finding that Malthusian economics was merely a tool of the capitalist society to keep the poor oppressed. Humanitarians found the theory hard-hearted and mean-spirited and rejected it vigorously. More important, the mathematical analysis employed by Malthus simply did not withstand rigorous scrutiny. Food, critics observed, was organic, and thus it also increased geometrically. Additionally, technological advances made in agriculture seemed almost to eliminate hunger. By 1900, Malthus was generally dismissed as a pseudo-scientist who had leaped to a gross generalization. The only school of thought that continued to embrace Malthus was that of some social Darwinists (Charles Darwin himself had been influenced by Malthus) who found the population theory acceptable in the light of their emphasis on the struggle for survival.

In the twentieth century, however, Malthus emerged as an important symbol in a concept known as neo-Malthusianism. Ironically, this movement advocated birth control, which Malthus opposed as immoral. Nevertheless, after World War II it became apparent that in many areas of the world, particularly in underdeveloped countries, population was growing at an alarming rate. As the prospect, and often the reality, of famine loomed in Africa and Asia, calls for government-sponsored birth control programs mounted. Some attempts to institute programs were made in India and China. The problem, however, continues, as does the image of Malthus in this important issue.

Whatever the flaws of his analysis, Malthus must be regarded as the father of demographic studies. In addition, he was an important and influential figure in the development of early nineteenth century economic thought. His influence on Darwin was of enormous importance, as was his work on the diminishing returns of agricultural production. The Malthusian legacy is most evident in the continued use and misuse of his name, which has become synonymous with population studies and the population problem.

Roy Talbert, Jr.

An Essay on the Principle of Population

As It Affects the Future Improvement of Society

Type of philosophy: Ethics, social philosophy
First published: 1798, rev. eds. 1803, 1806, 1807, 1817, 1826
Principal ideas advanced:
◇ Population increases geometrically; food increases arithmetically.
◇ Food is an essential of human life; "passion between the sexes" is a fundamental human quality and likely to remain so.

◇ The experience of the United States shows that, when not subject to the limitations of the supply of farmland, population will double in twenty-five years.

◇ Population and food tend to be in an uneasy balance, at the subsistence level.

◇ There are two kinds of checks on population growth: the preventive, in which the age of marriage is deferred until the breadwinner is able to support a family, and the positive, in which children die young for lack of adequate sustenance.

Thomas Robert Malthus lived through the last third of the Enlightenment and witnessed the stirring events of the French Revolution and the subsequent convulsions of the Napoleonic era. The progression of the French Revolution from modest, Enlightenment-based liberalism through radicalism to a violent reaction against the early liberalism no doubt affected Malthus, who came from a liberal family. The global conflicts of the Napoleonic era also led to the centralization of power in national governments, which meant that statistical information was collected on a much wider scale than before. The national censuses instituted in 1790 in the United States and in 1801 in Britain provided the numerical data on which mathematical models of society could be based. Malthus also benefited from the contemporary developments in mathematics, which in turn drew on new understanding in the field of astronomy, leading to the creation of mathematical models of the universe. Malthus was one of the first of a long line of thinkers of the nineteenth century to attempt to apply mathematical models to society.

The origin of *An Essay on the Principle of Population* is said to have been an argument Malthus had with his father over the view advanced by reforming Englishman William Godwin and the Marquis de Condorcet, among others, on the perfectibility of humankind. Malthus argued that the pressure of population on the means of subsistence ensures that the bulk of the population will live at a low level. If by chance the lot of an ordinary worker improved, he would immediately rush into marriage and bring into being numerous children whom he would be unable to support. He would then sink back into a marginal existence.

Malthus, reflecting his status as a clergyman, laid stress on the obligation that God imposed on every man to support his children. He further accepted the biblical urging to every person to multiply and be fruitful. Combining these two mandates of God meant that the prudent man would postpone marriage until he could clearly see how he could support his children. However, the poor had no sense of prudence; they married early and had abundant children, whom they were then unable to support, forcing them to rely on society through the "poor laws," the welfare system of the England of that time. The recent sharp increase in the "poor rates," the taxes levied on property owners specifically for the support of the poor, was, to Malthus, a clear demonstration of the operation of the principle of population.

Population and the Food Supply

In the first edition of *An Essay on the Principle of Population*, Malthus devotes many pages to refuting the ideas of Godwin and other Enlightenment thinkers on the perfectibility of humankind. In later editions, however, he eliminated these sections and replaced them with an exhaustive survey of the world's population, region by region, based on population data such as that collected in the 1801 and subsequent censuses in Britain. He also drew on information he had collected on two trips to Europe, in 1799 and 1802. He frequently drew comparisons with China, which he felt clearly exemplified the operation of the principle of population. However, a major benchmark was the data on population in the United States, enumerated in the 1790 and subsequent censuses. The average growth of the population of the United States indicated that, where no shortage of farmland existed, the population would double in twenty-five years; indeed, in some frontier communities, as quickly as every fifteen years. The first census in Britain, in 1801, caused him to revise some of the figures quoted in the first edition of *An Essay on the Principle of Population*, in which he had estimated the population of Great Britain as seven million. The census of 1801 revealed that, on the contrary, the British already numbered eleven million.

Using some of the new statistical data, Malthus demonstrates how the mathematical model underlying the principle of population would operate. In the first twenty-five years, the population and the food supply could very well increase at the same rate, from one to two; but in the second twenty-five years, the population would increase from two to four, whereas it was inherently unlikely that the food supply would increase by more than the amount it had increased in the preceding twenty-five years, that is, from two to three. In the third quarter-century, the discrepancy would be marked, as the population would now be eight times its size at the outset, and the food supply would be only four times as large. Thus, in as little as seventy-five years, half the population would be without food.

There has been substantial debate among economists as to whether Malthus had a concept of diminishing returns. He certainly did not use this concept to characterize his assertion that the food supply could not be increased at the same rate as population, in part because he understood the variable productivity of land. He accepted, as did his contemporary and ideological opponent, David Ricardo, that increasing agricultural output meant bringing into production marginal lands, that the best and most productive land would be the first that would be cultivated. He argued, based on his own observations of rural England, that doubling the agricultural labor force would not double the agricultural output because the additional labor would be put to work on "marginal" land. The more marginal the land, the less output could be expected from it, even if the labor input was equivalent to that on the best land.

Malthus grappled with, but never fully integrated into his thinking, the effect of emigration on the population. He acknowledged that the ability particularly of Englishmen to emigrate to the New World, where the supply of farmland was plentiful, had helped to postpone the inherent conflict between population and food supply within England, but he maintained that emigration did not fundamentally alter the operation of his principle. Also, the growth of industrial jobs did not undo the principle, for the fundamental constraint was the food supply.

Malthus maintained that a nation's ability to feed its own population was a necessary part of the sovereignty of any nation. Any country that became permanently dependent on foreign food supplies would lose its ability to act independently. In this observation, Malthus was reflecting the condition of England in his own times. An exporter of grain in the eighteenth century, except for a couple of years affected by adverse weather conditions, England was becoming an importer of grain. Malthus felt this conversion contained alarming prospects for England's future ability to conduct an independent foreign policy.

Implications for Policy

In attempting to make policy recommendations on the basis of his principle, Malthus first recommended abolishing the existing poor laws, under which indigent persons could receive financial support from public funds. At a certain date in the future, such support should end, and the indigent be told to look for help from private charities. Malthus's ideas played an important part in the intensive debate then occurring in England as to the appropriate welfare policy for the nation. His ideas clearly contributed to the attitudes of the politicians who reformed England's welfare system in the "New" Poor Law of 1834.

Malthus strongly favored a system of state-supported public education (which did not then exist), holding that educated men, especially if taught about the principle of population, would be more likely to postpone marriage until they could support their children. These ideas are reflected in many late twentieth century views on population that stress the education of women as central to solving population pressures in developing countries.

Malthus had a profound impact on social and political theorizing. His ideas have been used to support restrictions on immigration and to support birth control, although Malthus himself opposed artificial means of limiting births. Some of the startling improvements in agricultural output in the late twentieth century have been hailed as invalidating Malthus's principle of population, as has the striking slowdown in population growth in industrialized economies. On the other hand, the rapid population growth in underdeveloped countries has been seen as an affirmation of the principle of population, especially as indigenous food supplies prove increasingly inadequate. The jury is still out on the principle of population.

Malthus's use of mathematical models influenced nearly all twentieth century social theorizing. The collection of statistics, such as the censuses that Malthus quoted and manipulated in the second and subsequent editions of *An Essay on the Principle of Population*, has been expanded and refined enormously since Malthus's time. Statistics detailing the demographics of modern society have been collected in huge computer databases to make it easier to analyze the data and create predictive mathematical models. Nearly all contemporary social analyses use statistical material in support of their theses.

Economists debate whether Malthus used inductive or deductive reasoning. His assertion of the principle of population and his subsequent accounts of the conditions in various countries in the light of it suggest deductive reasoning; but his method of arriving at the principle, on the basis of observations of the world around him, especially rural England, is a classic case of inductive reasoning.

Nancy M. Gordon

Additional Reading

Appleman, Philip, ed. *Thomas Robert Malthus: An Essay on the Principle of Population, Text Sources, and Background Criticism*. New York: W. W. Norton, 1976. Contains selections from the writings of the Marquis de Condorcet and William Godwin and the first and second editions of *An Essay on the Principle of Population*, as well as responses, positive and negative, from critics of the nineteenth and twentieth centuries.

Dupaquier, Jacques, et al., eds. *Malthus, Past and Present*. New York: Academic Press, 1983. A selection of papers presented in 1980 at the International Conference on Historical Demography. Contains useful information on the influences on Malthus, the conditions of his time, and the neo-Malthusian movement.

Hollander, Samuel. *The Economics of Thomas Robert Malthus*. Toronto: University of Toronto Press, 1997. This lengthy study is the definitive view of Malthus's economic analysis.

James, Patricia. *Population Malthus: His Life and Times*. London: Routledge & Kegan Paul, 1979. An excellent biography.

Peterson, William. *Malthus*. Cambridge, Mass.: Harvard University Press, 1979. An intellectual biography that sets the work of Malthus in the context of early nineteenth century thought.

Turner, Michael, ed. *Malthus and His Time*. London: Macmillan, 1986. Further selections, somewhat more technical, from the 1980 international conference on historical demography.

Winch, Donald. *Malthus*. New York: Oxford University Press, 1987. Succinctly reviews Malthus's economic ideas in just more than one hundred pages.

Wood, John Cunningham, ed. *Thomas Robert Malthus: Critical Assessments*. 4 vols. London: Croom Helm, 1986. The one hundred reprinted articles and excerpts give a sweeping overview of reactions to Malthus's work.

Roy Talbert, Jr., updated by Paul B. Trescott

Mao Zedong

In 1949, Communist Party chairman Mao led the People's Liberation Army to victory over the Nationalist Party forces in China and established the People's Republic of China. He adapted Marxist-Leninist theory and practice to Chinese conditions and created a new doctrine that he later viewed as valid on a world scale.

Principal philosophical works: *Shi jia lun*, 1927 (speech; *Concerning Practice*, 1951); *Mao dun lun*, 1937 (speech), 1952 (book; *On Contradiction*, 1952); *Xin min zhu zhu yi lun*, 1940 (serial), 1952 (book; *China's New Democracy*, 1945); *Selected Works*, 1954-1962 (5 volumes); *Guan you zheng que qu li ren min nei bu mao dun di wen ti*, wr. 1957, pb. 1957 (*On the Correct Handling of Contradictions Among the People*, 1957); *Zai Zhongguo gong chan tang quan guo xuan quan gong zuo hui yi shang di jiang hua*, wr. 1957, pb. 1964 (*Speech at the Chinese Communist Party's National Conference on Propaganda Work, March 12, 1957*, 1966); *Ren di zheng que si xiang shi cong na li lai di*, 1964 (*Where Do Correct Ideas Come From?*, 1966); *The Writings of Mao Zedong, 1949-1976*, 1986-1992 (2 volumes); *Mao Zedong on Dialectical Materialism: Writings on Philosophy, 1937*, 1990.

Born: December 26, 1893; Shaoshan, Hunan Province, China

Died: September 9, 1976; Beijing, China

Early Life

Mao Zedong was born into a peasant family of some means. His father, seeing little value in education, forced him to leave school at age thirteen to work on the farm. Mao, however, had acquired a taste for reading, and novels about heroic bandits, peasant rebels, and notable rulers had fired his imagination. Continuing his reading, he came upon a book calling for the modernization of China and constitutional government. It motivated him to leave home and continue his studies. At age sixteen, he entered primary school, where he became acquainted with Western liberal thought. A book on heroes led him to admire nation-building military leaders and respect the martial virtues. A short stint in a revolutionary army led to his first encounter with the ideas of socialism.

In time, Mao settled on becoming a teacher and entered normal school in 1913, graduating in 1918. He acquired an effective writing style and ideas to write about. In short, he came to believe in the goodness of humanity, the malleability of human nature, the power of the human will, the potential inherent in the Chinese peasantry, and the need to adapt Western ways to Chinese culture. He was also involved in radical organizations and thus in laying a foundation for future political action.

In 1918, Mao was at the University of Peking, where he found enthusiasm for the Bolshevik Revolution and Marxism. Back in Hunan Province in 1919, he was a leader in the anti-Japanese, antigovernment May Fourth Movement. The following year, he became a primary school director and thereby attained status and influence. By 1920, he considered himself a Marxist, and in July, 1921, was present at the founding of the Chinese Communist Party.

Russian insistence on controlling the Chinese party split it into factions. Mao accepted Russian leadership and the official party position, including Communist membership in the Guomindang, or Nationalist Party, and support for a bourgeois nationalist revolution. In 1924, illness sent him back to Hunan, where a new peasant militancy convinced him that the poor peasantry was the true revolutionary class. After his failure to spark a revolt in 1927, Mao took his ragtag army to the Jingkang Mountains. He lost his major party positions, but he built his peasant army. Beginning in 1930, the Guomindang, now his enemy, began a series of attacks against Mao's new base area in Jiangxi, leading to the six-thousand-mile Long March that began in late 1934. By 1935, Mao was chairman of the party's politburo. A new phase had begun.

Life's Work
Mao had bested the Soviet-backed so-called Twenty-eight Bolsheviks, whom he had fought politically for control of the Communist Party. Of elite background, these members lacked an understanding of the masses. The relationship between the Chinese and Soviet parties would remain strained thereafter, especially since the Soviets backed the Guomindang, in their own strategic interests, and were willing to sacrifice the Chinese Communist Party accordingly. When Japan invaded China in 1937, the Soviets, concerned about their eastern territories, called for a Guomindang-Communist United Front, even though Mao's Yan'an base area was under Guomindang attack. Necessity, however, dictated such an alliance. The alliance was effected, both parties aware that it was but a temporary partnership.

During the Yan'an period, Mao developed what became Maoism. Contrary to Marxist-Leninist orthodoxy, he stressed the role of the peasantry over that of the proletariat. Similarly, his goal was to conquer the countryside through guerrilla warfare and encircle the cities, which would later be taken by conventional warfare. He also set forth the basis for his theory of "permanent revolution," holding that change is perpetual and conflict will continue even under communism. He also expounded his doctrine of the "mass line." In a protracted war, the zeal of the masses must be maintained by the party cadres. The masses being infallible, it was the task of the cadres to gather their scattered ideas, synthesize them, propagate them among the masses until they accept them as their own, and then test them through action.

Meanwhile, Mao won over the peasants through fair treatment. People of all classes were called to join the anti-Japanese war, with the national (middle and patriotic) and petty bourgeoisie, and even the landlords, assured of retaining their property, at least for the

Mao Zedong. *(Library of Congress)*

moment. A clash with the Guomindang in 1940-1941 ended the United Front. This necessitated the rectification campaign of 1942-1944, as Mao believed that the recruits needed disciplining through studying Marxism-Leninism. Also, as Mao's Sinification of Marxism was being ignored, he believed that it needed emphasizing. The tool was the so-called cult of Mao—Mao was supreme in matters of ideology and was proclaimed infallible. In 1945, "Mao Zedong Thought" was incorporated into the party constitution.

The final phase of the civil war began in late 1948. The Guomindang, led by Chiang Kai-shek, had lost both U.S. military aid and the confidence of the Chinese, and were weakened enough for the Communist People's Liberation Army to take the major cities. On October 1, 1949, the People's Republic of China was officially inaugurated. The revolution was not a socialist revolution but a "New Democratic Revolution." The government was a coalition of four elements defined as "the people": the proletariat, the peasants, and the national and petty bourgeoisie. The Communists, however, would exercise hegemony over these classes through force and exercise a dictatorship over elements designated as "reactionary." Thus landlords and corrupt merchants were subject to severe punishment, including death. Corrupt bureaucrats met the same fate. Lack of enthusiasm for Chinese involvement in the Korean War led to millions of executions.

Rapid economic development was Mao's immediate goal. In early 1952, he inaugurated the First Five-Year Plan, which was meant to be the first step on the road to socialism. In July, 1955, he began the rapid nationalization of remaining private enterprises and the collectivization of agriculture. The peasants lost their recently acquired lands and were merged into agricultural collectives.

Aware that enthusiasm for his policies was weak among intellectuals but convinced that they were true believers after years of thought reform, Mao sought to involve them with his "Let a Hundred Flowers Bloom" campaign. In 1956, intellectuals were encouraged to air their views. So vehement was the criticism of both the party and Mao that the campaign was ended in 1957, and the offenders were punished through hard and humiliating labor.

Convinced that being "red" was more productive than being "expert" and at odds with the Soviet Union over Nikita S. Khrushchev's de-Stalinization speech and Eastern European policies, Mao set out to prove that China could become a great power on its own and attain communism before the Soviet Union. Certain that the Chinese people could accomplish anything through sheer willpower, he launched his "Great Leap Forward" in 1958. Steel was produced in backyard furnaces, mines were worked as never before, and regimented agricultural communes were inaugurated. People and machines were pushed beyond endurance. Millions died, the soil was depleted, and the economy was wrecked for years to come.

Mao's prestige within the party was at its nadir. He blamed the local officials for the failures, but the party blamed him. He resigned his chairmanship of the republic, but he retained the party chairmanship and his public image was kept intact. He fended off a move to topple him by a party faction led by Defense Minister Peng Dehuai in 1959, but the intensity of the verbal attack returned him to the realm of mortality.

The years 1960 and 1961 saw Mao in seclusion as party leaders openly criticized him and reversed his economic policies. By 1963, with the aid of the army headed by Lin Biao, he was attempting to weaken the party bureaucracy and prepare for his restoration. He returned to seclusion from 1964 to mid-1966, supposedly dying but actually preparing for a spectacular return. It came with a swim in the Yangzi (Chang Jiang) River and a pronouncement of good health.

Mao, formerly a distant figure with a cultivated air of mystery, now appeared in public, as did his wife Jiang Qing, making her political debut. The cult of Mao was pushed to new heights. The army had been thoroughly indoctrinated, and the Red Guard, composed of Chinese youth directly under Mao, made its appearance. So, too, did their bible, the so-called little red book, which contained selections from Mao's writings. Formerly the Chinese were encouraged to study all of Mao's writings; now they had short excerpts from them. Their thinking had been done for them. All these events were linked to the Cultural Revolution. Anticipating another Great Leap Forward, Mao opted to eliminate his critics beforehand.

Moreover, Mao held that each generation must experience revolution at first hand. Accordingly, the Red Guard was turned loose on the bureaucracy. Educational institutions were devastated and a multitude of historical sites destroyed. Ultimately the army intervened to restore order.

By 1968, the party was being reconstructed and its primacy proclaimed. Lin Biao was designated as Mao's successor. Mao came to suspect Lin of plotting against him, however, and Lin died under mysterious circumstances in 1971. Mao remained largely in the background from 1972 to his death in 1976. Still, he led the criticism of elitist Confucianism, with which he linked Lin, and later of the bourgeois Right. The radical Left remained dominant because of Mao's presence. His death brought factional conflict into the open and left the future uncertain.

Influence

Piecing together the life and writings of Mao is akin to trying to solve a Chinese puzzle. While his life's story as told to Edgar Snow and related by him in *Red Star over China* (1937) is a vital source, scholars have found discrepancies that need explaining. Moreover, Mao's writings were repeatedly revised during his lifetime to support his claims to infallibility. Clearly, then, they were flawed, and his claims to be an original thinker of great import must be at least partially rejected. His theory and practice of guerrilla warfare, however, must be given due respect. His place in history as a military leader who withstood every conceivable adversity but survived to attain power is secure. Later military ventures against China's neighbors were a different story. The wars with India and Vietnam were less than successful, and successes in the Korean War less than what had been desired.

Mao's major claim to historical significance is his unification of China into a nation. From what amounted to a conglomeration of feudal principalities ruled by warlords, he fashioned a China that was more than a place on a map. Yet his brutality in forging and maintaining that unity, together with his megalomania and military aggressiveness, subjected him to substantial criticism. The China that he left was one devoid of much of its cultural heritage, destroyed in the name of progress. Mao's critics believe that

his immediate legacy to China was primarily oppression, repression, and suppression.

Robert W. Small

On Contradiction

Type of philosophy: Ethics, metaphysics, political philosophy
First published: Mao dun lun, 1937 (speech), 1952 (book; English translation, 1952)
Principal ideas advanced:

◇ Two basic outlooks on reality exist: the metaphysical and the materialist dialectical.
◇ Contradiction is central to the development of all things and ideas.
◇ The essence of each branch of thought is based on its inherent contradictions and their resolution.
◇ At any stage of development, one particular contradiction plays the leading role, and this item must be identified and dealt with in order to provide solutions.
◇ The central contradiction in the current struggle in China is that between the proletariat and the bourgeoisie.

In 1937, when *On Contradiction* was first delivered as a speech, the Chinese Communist Party, led by Mao Zedong, in response to an attack by Japan, had temporarily allied with the Guomindang, the revolutionary party led by Sun Yat-sen, which had overthrown the leaders of the Ching Dynasty in 1911. The speech was an attempt to explain both the current struggle and the upcoming development of the Communists in historical terms. Mao drew on the writings of Vladimir Ilich Lenin and Joseph Stalin, leaders of the Soviet Union, then the only nation in the world led by a Communist government. There are also considerable references to the works of Karl Marx and Friedrich Engels, nineteenth century German philosophers who initiated the ideas of communism, and through them, to the earlier works of German philosophers Immanuel Kant and Georg Wilhelm Friedrich Hegel.

Kant wrote of thesis, antithesis, and synthesis. Every philosophical situation can be seen as a conflict between two opposing points of view and the resolution between them, which leads to synthesis, a new system of thought. Marx used this system to discuss the proletariat, or working class, and the capitalist ruling class, and posited as their synthesis a new ruling class composed of the workers themselves. Mao draws on both these sources in two ways. The thesis-antithesis system is generalized as a series of societal contradictions and then particularized into the revolutionary struggle between communism and capitalism, in China and elsewhere.

Contradictions

Mao begins *On Contradiction* with a brief introduction summarizing two basic modes of thought. The metaphysical mode suggests that causes of events are external, including such factors as climate and geography. The method of dialectical materialism, to which the author subscribes, contends that basic causes are internal, central to the very nature of a situation or a physical entity. Dialectical materialism was founded by Hegel and was further codified and specifically related to class struggles by Marx.

At the basic level, all developments are determined by the contradictions inherent in a situation and the resolution of these contradictions. Mao states that such contradictions are universal and underlie all modes of thought. Thus, mathematics is based upon the contradiction between positive and negative quantities, electricity on positive and negative charges, and physics on action and reaction. Most pertinent to the present discussion, the struggle to achieve a communist state is based on the contradiction between labor, which produces goods and services, and the capitalist class, which owns and controls the means of production.

Change depends on particular contradictions. Every change in motion of matter is thus determined: Mechanical energy, heat, light, sound, and so on, determine the changes in the matter they affect. Essentially, this is a scientific statement, maintaining that changes in matter are determined by differences in various forms of energy.

In social development, the particular contradictions involve conflicts between groups of people. The contradiction between the rulers of a feudal society and the peasants who do the real work of that society leads to social conflict and democratic revolution. The later conflict between the capitalist rulers and the workers similarly leads to communist revolution.

It is essential at this stage to acknowledge that development of thought moves in two seemingly contradictory directions. Specific types of contradictions lead to general principles, and then, in turn, consideration of these principles allows the philosopher to make statements and predictions regarding future developments in other particular circumstances.

Changing Circumstances

Mao warned of the danger of accepting a general principle as universal and creating a stereotype that is used in an attempt to solve all problems. Particular problems may require different solutions. In China, he said, the situation had changed since the 1911 revolution that overcame the old feudal system. In 1911, the struggle was between the masses of Chinese people and the small ruling class, and the result was a democratic revolution. Afterward, the new rulers, led by Sun Yat-sen and the Guomindang, themselves became reactionary and, by the time Mao delivered his speech, needed to be opposed by the Communists. It is absolutely necessary to understand the opposing point of view, or a one-sided, stereotyped solution will lead to inevitable failure, Mao cautioned.

In 1937, Mao said, the most basic contradiction, or conflict, was with the imperialist designs of Japan. During this struggle, the Communists were allied with the Guomindang, but this alliance was to be recognized as temporary. Eventually, when the struggle with Japan was resolved, the Communist Party had to oppose the Guomindang itself and would ultimately triumph over that party. However, the most basic contradiction in society, Mao said, is the conflict between the social character of production and the private ownership of the means of production.

At any particular stage in development, there is a basic contradiction that underlies all others, and this basic contradiction changes over time. Thus, capitalists were originally an underclass opposed to the feudal rulers, and the bourgeoisie was a revolutionary class. As capitalism gained ascendancy and displaced the feudal aristocracy, the situation was drastically changed, and the capitalists in turn became the rulers. Eventually, the workers, in turn, must displace the capitalists and become the rulers themselves.

At every stage, it is necessary to determine the most basic contradiction involved, in order to provide resolution of that contradiction. If only superficial contradictions are recognized, the problems will not be resolved in any permanent way, and the ultimate result will be more contradictions and more conflicts. Only when the central problem is identified can it be truly resolved.

Every aspect of a current reality contains the seeds of its contradiction. Death cannot exist without life, nor above without below, fortune without misfortune. War contains the seeds of peace, and peace leads inevitably to war. It is interesting in this connection that Mao was certain that the condition of relative world peace that existed in 1937 was likely to lead to a second world war, which indeed came to pass shortly thereafter.

There is, therefore, a basic unity of contradictions, and any aspect of a situation may change into its opposite. The ruled become the rulers, the oppressed become the oppressors. The Guomindang, originally a positive force for democracy, became a reactionary ruling class. According to Mao, the Communist revolution, if it were to succeed over the long term, would have to contain the seeds of its own disintegration. The rule of the Communist Party would itself lead to the destruction of *all* political parties, and true rule by the people in general.

The Seeds of Contradiction

There are many forms of contradiction, some of which are far from obvious. It is only when contradiction becomes antagonism that true changes occur. Mao uses an example from physics here. Before a bomb explodes, it appears to be a single entity. It is only upon detonation that the conflicting substances within the bomb reveal their contradiction, and the conflict is resolved.

Similarly, societal conflicts may remain in apparent stasis for long periods of time, and only when contradiction becomes antagonism can these conflicts be resolved. For this reason, violent revolution is necessary for long-term social

changes to occur. In the Soviet Union, the October Revolution of 1917 was necessary to effect the destruction of the czarist regime. Afterward, philosophical conflicts between those led by Lenin and Stalin and those led by Leon Trotsky and Nikolay Ivanovich Bukharin had to reach ignition point before the struggle could become clear and the contradictions resolved.

It is only when capitalism leads to imperialism that ignition is reached and true socialist revolution can occur, a fact that Mao noted as most germane to China's conflict with Japan and with capitalist society in general. The war against Japan, while temporarily resulting in peace among Chinese political factions, would inevitably make class conflicts obvious. Then and only then would the Communist revolution succeed, Mao said.

The Japanese imperialist invasion was, indeed, a major step toward the outbreak of World War II. In ways that Mao did not predict directly, unusual alliances were formed during that war, including an alliance between the capitalist societies of Western Europe and the United States and the Communist government of the Soviet Union. On the other hand, very much as Mao foresaw, the defeat of the imperialist powers of fascism did lead almost instantly to a resurgence in the conflicts between capitalism and communism as well as to the Cold War that immediately followed World War II.

In China, the Communists were triumphant, and the People's Republic of China, with Mao as its leader, was proclaimed in 1949. Again, predictably, this new regime was opposed by the capitalist powers, especially the United States, which for decades supported the regime of Chiang Kai-shek, an anti-Communist, and refused to acknowledge the rulership of Mao's Communist Party. Predictably, once the Communists gained control of the Chinese government, there were many internal conflicts within the party, and Mao's own point of view was eventually discarded.

The Path of Communism

Half a century after Mao wrote *On Contradiction*, communism, which had become the political philosophy of the ruling class in two of the most populated nations in the world and in many smaller countries, came under attack. In the Soviet Union and Eastern Europe, it eventually collapsed altogether. In China, the years preceding the end of the twentieth century saw considerable social revolt.

Ultimately, Mao's analysis of social change was vindicated. Central to the ideas in *On Contradiction* and other essays of the period is the concept that all social conditions contain the seeds of their own contradictions, conflicts, and ultimate destruction by new events and conditions. Ironically, the success of communism created its own problems and its own underclasses. Communism did not, as Mao suggested, lead to the dissolution of political parties. Instead, the Communist regimes became the ruling classes, as had the feudal and capitalist classes before them, and the struggles continued. With all his criticism of dogmatists, Mao apparently did not foresee that the Communists, once they achieved real power, would become as dogmatic and intolerant as their predecessors. Finally, as Mao might have foreseen if he had carried his arguments a few steps further, communism became one more step in social development, leading to some as yet unforeseen successor system.

Since Mao's time, the struggle between capitalism and communism has seen many changes, as well as several alliances between the two conflicting systems of thought, including the alliance against the fascists and, as the twentieth century ended, a temporary alliance between the United States and the Soviet Union against imperialist Middle Eastern powers. This conflict, when it is resolved, will lead to another series of contradictions. In the final analysis, communism is clearly no more permanent a political situation than the older forms of government it displaced.

Marc Goldstein

Additional Reading

Becker, Jasper. *Hungry Ghosts: Mao's Secret Famine*. New York: Free Press, 1996. This study examines the famine that lasted from 1958 to 1962 and claimed an estimated thirty million lives. Becker concludes that Mao Zedong's flawed policies were to blame.

Chai, Winberg, ed. *Essential Works of Chinese Communism*. Rev. ed. New York: Bantam Books, 1972. A history of Chinese communism told largely through key documents and writings, including the most important of Mao's writings. The book is arranged in seven chronological chapters with a commentary on each. Includes an introduction.

Ch'en, Jerome, ed. *Mao*. Englewood Cliffs, N.J.: Prentice-Hall, 1969. This book contains a series of excerpts from the writings of Mao, his contemporaries, and historians. It also includes a lengthy introduction that can stand by itself as a short biography.

Karnow, Stanley. *Mao and China: A Legacy of Turmoil*. New York: Penguin Books, 1990. A revised edition of Karnow's 1972 *Mao and China from Revolution to Revolution*, this work examines Mao's entire life but focuses on the Cultural Revolution and its aftermath, including a discussion of the events in Tiananmen Square. A large book that is invaluable for the reader who wants detail.

Leys, Simon. *Chinese Shadows*. New York: Viking Press, 1977. Leys, a China specialist, shares observations made during travels through China in 1972 and 1976. He presents an account of the destruction of Chinese cultural heritage and of the oppression that he witnessed in China.

North, Robert C. *Chinese Communism*. New York: McGraw-Hill, 1966. This study places Mao's early years in the context of the development of the Communist Party. The last chapter includes material on the Sino-Soviet dispute. A chronology, maps, and numerous illustrations are included.

Rule, Paul. *Mao Zedong*. Leaders of Asia series. Queensland, Australia: University of Queensland Press, 1984. This very brief work offers a broad overview of Mao's life and career and could serve as an excellent introduction for high school students.

Schram, Stuart. *Mao Tse-tung*. Baltimore, Md.: Penguin, 1966. This biography concludes with beginning of the Cultural Revolution. Schram's examination of the formative influences that helped shaped the future Mao is particularly well done.

Snow, Edgar. *Red Star over China*. Rev. ed. New York: Grove Press, 1968. Snow was the first Westerner to observe the Chinese Communists and to interview Mao. A good starting point for the study of Mao. Snow's work includes interviews with Mao, a chronology, and ninety-three short biographies, including one of Mao.

Starr, John Bryan. *Continuing Revolution: The Political Thought of Mao*. Princeton, N.J.: Princeton University Press, 1979. A thematically organized study of Mao's political thought that discusses issues including class conflict and political organization.

Suyin, Han. *The Morning Deluge: Mao Tsetung and the Chinese Revolution*. Boston: Little, Brown, 1972. Suyin portrays Mao in a heroic light. The book ends rather abruptly, failing to offer a conclusion regarding Mao's importance.

Robert W. Small, updated by Thomas Clarkin

Gabriel Marcel

Marcel was a major figure in the mid-twentieth century development of French philosophy, as well as a significant dramatist. He was the first French thinker to explore phenomenological and existential themes in depth and became a key influence on the post-World War II French intellectual scene.

Principal philosophical works: "Existence et objectivité," 1925 ("Existence and Objectivity," 1952); *Journal métaphysique*, 1927 (*Metaphysical Journal*, 1952); *Position et approches concrètes du mystère ontologique*, 1933 ("On the Ontological Mystery," 1948); *Être et avoir: Philosophie de l'esprit*, 1935 (*Being and Having: An Existentialist Diary*, 1949); *Du Refus à l'invocation*, 1940 (*Creative Fidelity*, 1964); *Homo Viator: Prolégomènes à une métaphysique de l'espérance*, 1945 (*Homo Viator: Introduction to a Metaphysic of Hope*, 1951); *Le Mystère de l'être*, 1951 (volume 1, *Réflexion et mystère*; volume 2, *Foi et réalité*; *The Mystery of Being*, volume 1, *Reflection and Mystery*, 1950; volume 2, *Faith and Reality*, 1951); *Les Hommes contre l'humain*, 1951 (*Men Against Humanity*, 1952; also known as *Man Against Mass Society*, 1952); *The Existential Background of Human Dignity*, 1963.

Born: December 7, 1889; Paris, France
Died: October 8, 1973; Paris, France

Early Life

Gabriel Marcel was born on December 7, 1889, into a Parisian bourgeois family. His father had a distinguished career as a government official, diplomat, and curator, holding the rank of councillor of state and eventually holding posts in the Bibliothèque National and the Musées Nationaux. Marcel's mother died when he was four, an event that had a powerful formative influence on him in registering both the irrevocability of death and the mystery of abiding presence. His upbringing took place in an atmosphere essentially devoid of religious experience, his father being a cultured agnostic and his stepmother (his mother's sister) a nonreligious Jew who converted to a liberal humanist Protestantism. Young Marcel was thus reared in an environment where the basic values reflected those of the French Third Republic: reason, science, and ethical conscience.

Marcel was an early and brilliant academic achiever, passing his *agrégation* in philosophy at the very early age of twenty in 1910. This qualified him to teach at the *lycée* level in the French educational system (the secondary level), which

he later did sporadically. He never earned a doctorate, however, or became a university professor. During World War I, he worked for the French Red Cross, locating missing soldiers and communicating information concerning them to their relatives. Marcel's war experiences were a great shock, disturbing the securities of the rational bourgeois universe of his early years and starkly bringing home to him the tragic character of human existence. After this, his prewar philosophical training, highly abstract in character, came to seem arid and mechanical, and he sought a more concrete mode of philosophy, better able to do justice to the intimacies of human experience not touched by abstract forms of thought.

If World War I was the occasion for a philosophical conversion for Marcel, the decade of intense intellectual searching that ensued after the war's end culminated in the decisive event in his spiritual life—his conversion to Roman Catholicism on March 23, 1929. Marcel had for years been concerned with philosophical investigation of the character of personal existence and the experience of faith, so his conversion was a culmination of, rather than a turn from, the spiritual quest occasioned by his philosophical conversion. It also placed him in the company of a

Gabriel Marcel. *(Archive Photos/Agence France)*

number of other distinguished French intellectuals who converted to Catholicism in the years of the Third Republic, among them Paul Claudel, Charles Péguy, and Jacques Maritain.

Marcel's struggle against the systematic spirit that had characterized much of French philosophical inquiry after philosopher René Descartes built on the anti-Cartesian turn in French thought associated with the work of philosopher Henri Bergson. Three of Marcel's writings of the period 1925 to 1933 signaled his emergence as a major new intellectual voice in French philosophy: "Existence and Objectivity," *Metaphysical Journal*, and "On the Ontological Mystery." All the major themes of his mature work are evident in these texts. Variations on the themes that Marcel had begun to articulate within the framework of his emerging philosophical viewpoint received

exposition in a series of nine plays that he wrote in the years between 1914 and 1933. He later insisted on the intimacy of his philosophical and dramatic works, which were the theatrical embodiment in dramatic characters of the concrete examples on which much of his philosophical reflection rested.

Life's Work

Marcel called one of his books *Homo Viator: Introduction to a Metaphysic of Hope*, a title that captures several enduring themes of his mature work. *Homo Viator* means "man en route," or "man the journeyer." The phrase reveals Marcel's belief both that the task of the philosopher is always an exploratory one, a searching along the paths of human experience for those key themes that one must patiently explore, and that the philosopher's task itself mirrors the life situation of every human individual. Hope was one of those crucial experiences—faith, exile, fidelity, trust, witness, and despair were others—that Marcel conceived it to be the purpose of the philosopher to interrogate because they had been dismissed by the dominant schools of modern philosophy as inaccessible to or unworthy of philosophical scrutiny.

Marcel's method in approaching philosophical questions was always open, probing, and intuitive, what he called "concrete." Rather than publish systematic treatises, he published his philosophical workbooks, his daily journals of philosophical investigations, and his philosophical diaries—thinking in process. Later these "drillings" into the depth of human experience could be worked up into philosophical essays and given extended development, perhaps finally to receive fully organized treatment, as in his Gifford Lectures in 1949-1950, which were published in two volumes as *The Mystery of Being*, or his William James Lectures at Harvard in 1961-1962, which were published as *The Existential Background of Human Dignity*. Yet always Marcel's concern was to deny that the detached, disembodied *Cogito* ("I think") of Descartes could be the appropriate beginning for philosophy as he conceived it. For him, philosophy began more in wonder and astonishment than in curiosity and doubt, and the exploratory texts that constitute the bulk of his philosophical works were better vehicles than systematic treatises for capturing these foundational philosophical experiences.

A distinction crucial to Marcel's philosophical stance is the one that he made between primary and secondary reflection. Primary reflection is the realm of abstraction, objectivity, and universality; this is the world of the analytically verifiable, best exemplified in modern scientific and technological thought. The great threat from primary reflection for Marcel was that the spirit of abstraction was too likely to become imperialistic, tyrannizing over all domains of human experience. Hence, he opposed primary reflection to secondary reflection, the latter being the realm in which emphasis falls on the intuitive, on participation, and on dialogue. Herein Marcel emphasized over and over the possibility of human beings' penetrating the mystery of existence through confrontation with "presence" and "mystery" rather than with the "object" of primary reflection. He rejected any relationship of the philosopher to reality that could be described as that "of an onlooker to a picture." Rather, Marcel developed a "concrete philosophy" in which secondary reflection, approaching the world, the self, and other human beings through love, fidelity, hope, or another "concrete approach," could yield a knowledge that would illuminate human life as it is lived, although a kind of knowledge not verifiable by the techniques of primary reflection.

It is appropriate to characterize Marcel's sense of the necessity for a full, open relationship between beings, or between a person and what he or she confronts—a mystery or a presence—as dialogical. It is a relationship well characterized in the terms "I" and "thou," made popular through the work of the Jewish philosopher Martin Buber. To establish such a dialogical relationship with others and with the world demands a *disponibilité*, an availability or readiness of the self toward others and the world, as well as an involvement or engagement with the world. The origin of such a relationship lies in the experience of the body, of human incarnation. The self projects into the world its sense of bodily presence as it becomes aware of its own body, and this bodily

experience becomes the prototype for the way the world exists for the self. Just as the self cannot be separated from the body, so too it is inseparable from its situation in the world. It is impossible to abstract completely from those concrete situations that are constitutent of the human self, although one of the great temptations of primary reflection is to accomplish just such a complete separation of self from situation. Thus, a self that is open to the world, that can establish dialogical relations with it and with other people, can develop a participant knowledge of great ontological depth, something denied to the self that treats others as objects to be manipulated.

Marcel's sensitive probing of existential experiences revealed to him a deep-seated "exigence," or impulse, at the base of all human life, which he described as an impulse to transcendence. He was convinced that this "ontological exigence" in human beings testified to the existence of an inexhaustible presence that he called "being." His analyses of human experiences convinced him of the presence of this inexhaustible being, although it could be approached only obliquely through phenomenological description. Thus Marcel's mature philosophy came to rest on the assurance that through openness to such crucial human experiences as love, fidelity, and hope, it was possible to approach God in a fashion identical with the approach of his concrete philosophy to other persons. Through concrete human experience, being itself could be approached and the human "ontological exigence" proven to be more than what the French existentialist thinker Jean-Paul Sartre had called it: a "useless passion."

In one sense, Marcel's thinking was a call to restore simple human values—faith, trust, comradeship, love—in a world threatened increasingly by technological abstractions and political alienation. In *Men Against Humanity*, he brought his philosophical views to bear on an analysis of the social and political world of immediate postwar Europe. He worried that the dominance of technology was leading to a world ruled by despair, without hope; he blamed the increasing violence of the contemporary world on that spirit of abstraction against which he had conducted a long philosophical struggle. Although he never developed anything like a fully articulated social philosophy, his essays on social and political themes exhibit a marked congruence with his more speculative work. In both there are the consistent effort to give meaning and depth to central human experiences, the deep sadness at the varieties of human grief, and the desire to bring together the metaphysical certainty of the convinced Christian with the concrete awareness of real human relationships of the phenomenologist, which characterized Marcel's life work from beginning to end.

Influence

Marcel is often characterized as an existentialist, although he himself rejected that term. Such a characterization usually sees him as a theistic existentialist as opposed to the atheistic existentialism of Jean-Paul Sartre or Martin Heidegger. Although the differences between and among the various existentialist philosophers were many, and Marcel was certainly right to reject any term that served to conflate his views and those of people such as Sartre, whom he vehemently opposed, there is, nevertheless, a grain of truth in applying the label "existentialist" to him. He shared with other existentialist thinkers a passion to engage philosophically with the world of lived human experience, a profound distrust of the abstractions of scientific and technological thought, and a sensitivity to literature and art as perhaps more powerful tools than philosophy for the analysis of human existence. In his essay "Existence and Objectivity" and in his *Metaphysical Journal*, Marcel was deeply involved with many of the ideas that later became central to existentialism, and these texts were published before Karl Jaspers, Heidegger, and Sartre had published any of their major works. Thus, Marcel is rightly characterized as the first French existentialist.

Marcel's thought also demonstrates affinities with other important twentieth century European thinkers. His philosophical method, based on the intuitive approach of his concrete philosophy, in many respects parallels the work of the German phenomenologist Edmund Husserl, although Marcel worked independently of him. Similarly, Marcel's dialogical approach to existential concerns is reminiscent of the work of Buber, although his work began and was pursued independently of influence from Buber.

Marcel's concern with the philosophical description of bodily experience anticipates as well some of the major emphases in the work of the French thinker Maurice Merleau-Ponty. Marcel is also appropriately characterized as the first French phenomenologist.

Marcel belongs to that distinguished group of twentieth century French thinkers whom the historian H. Stuart Hughes called "philosophers who were Catholics." Like Péguy and Maritain, Marcel was a convert to Catholicism; like them, he lived in and wrote out of an ambiguous situation in which the society around him opposed the spiritual values to which he was committed. Writing against the grain of his world, Marcel developed a highly personalized, even idiosyncratic, philosophical stance, one he communicated best through essays, diaries, and other fragmentary forms. He himself provided the best descriptive term for his work when he called it neo-Socratic, for, like his chosen Greek forebear, Marcel as a thinker was concerned to show how important it is to pose problems correctly before even attempting their solution. In invoking the person of Socrates, Marcel associated his work with the constant questioning, risk taking, and ongoing dialogical approach of an earlier *homo viator* like himself.

Michael W. Messmer

The Mystery of Being

Reflection and Mystery *and* Faith and Reality

Type of philosophy: Ethics, existentialism, metaphysics

First published: Le Mystère de l'être, 1951 (volume 1, *Réflexion et mystère*; volume 2, *Foi et réalité*; English translation, volume 1, *Reflection and Mystery*, 1950; volume 2, *Faith and Reality*, 1951)

Principal ideas advanced:

◇ The peculiar task of philosophy is to describe what it means to be in a particular concrete situation.

◇ Existential thinking, the thinking of an involved self, is threatened by the interest in abstractions and by bureaucratic societies that reduce individuals to averages.

◇ Primary reflection is analytical; secondary reflection is recuperative, allowing the self to discover its being in action.

◇ The immediate encounter with the mystery of being is in terms of a lived participation; being is an internal relation; the self, or the body, is not an object of knowledge, but the subject who knows the self as he or she acts.

◇ To know others existentially is to encounter them not as things, but in acknowledgment of them as persons.

◇ Freedom is found when the self turns inward and becomes aware of its capability for commitment and treason.

Gabriel Marcel is one of the main figures associated with existential thought in France. His two-volume work *The Mystery of Being* is the final product of a series of Gifford Lectures that were given in 1949 and 1950 at the University of Aberdeen. Characteristic of *The Mystery of Being*, and one might say of Marcel's writings in general, is a philosophical approach that is oriented toward concrete descriptions and elucidations instead of systematic delineations. In this respect, the existentialism of Marcel has greater affinities to the thought of Søren Kierkegaard and Karl Jaspers than to that of Martin Heidegger and Jean-Paul Sartre. Marcel will have nothing to do with the system builders. A philosophical system, even though it may have an existentialist cast, as in Heidegger and Sartre, entails for the Marcel a falsification of lived experience as it is immediately apprehended.

The Concrete

On every page of Marcel's writings, the reader is forced to acknowledge the author's concentrated efforts to remain with the concrete. Existential thinking is the thinking of the "involved self." This involved self is contrasted by the author with the "abstracted self." The abstracted self, in its movement of detachment, escapes to a privileged and intellectually rarefied sanctuary—an "Olympus of the Spirit"—from which it seeks to formulate a global and inclusive perspective of the whole of reality. Marcel's concrete philosophical elucidations express a continuing pro-

test against any such Olympian view. "There is not, and there cannot be, any global abstraction, any final terrace to which we can climb by means of abstract thought, there to rest for ever; our condition in this world does remain, in the last analysis, that of a wanderer, an itinerant being, who cannot come to absolute rest except by a fiction, a fiction which it is the duty of philosophic reflection to oppose with all its strength." A person as an "itinerant being"—or as a wayfarer, as the author has expressed it in the title of another of his works, *Homo Viator: Prolégomènes à une métaphyqiue de l'espérance*, 1945 (*Homo Viator: Introduction to a Metaphysic of Hope*, 1951)—is always on the way, passing from one concrete situation to another. At no time can he shed his situationality and view himself and the rest of the world as completed. There is no thought or abstraction that can tear itself loose from the concrete situation of the involved self and lay a claim for universal validity. This, for Marcel, as already for Kierkegaard, is the grievous fault in all varieties of idealism.

Idealism fails to recognize the situational character of all human thinking. The philosophical reflection that the author prescribes is a reflection that retains its existential bond with the concrete situation. The peculiar task of philosophy is that of describing what it means to be in a situation. This task is a phenomenological one—phenomenological in the sense that it takes its point of departure from everyday, lived experience and seeks to follow through the implications that can be drawn from it.

Concrete existence is lost in the abstract movements of a detached reflection, but it is also threatened by the pervasive bureaucratization of modern life. In the chapter entitled "A Broken World," Marcel develops a penetrating analysis of the dissolution of personality in the face of increased social regimentation. Humans stand in danger of losing their humanity. The modern bureaucratized world tends to identify individuals with the state's official record of their activities. Personality is reduced to an identity card. In such a situation, people are defined in terms of replaceable functions rather than acknowledged as unique and irreplaceable selves. Creative activities are standardized and consequently depersonalized. Everything, including humans themselves, is reduced to a stultifying law of averages. In one passage, the author speaks of an equality that is obtained by a process of "leveling *down*" to a point where all creativity vanishes. The language and theme are reminiscent of Kierkegaard's critique of society in which he indicted the public for having effected a leveling process that virtually made the category of the individual extinct. This theme of depersonalization also links Marcel with two German existentialists, Jaspers and Heidegger. Jaspers described how the masses have become the masters of the people and reduced everything to an appalling mediocrity. Heidegger, in his notion of *das Man*, expressed basically the same theme. In a later work, *Les Hommes contre l'humain* (1951; *Men Against Humanity*, 1952; also known as *Man Against Mass Society*, 1952), Marcel pays special attention to this phenomenon, elucidating it in a descriptive analysis that is rich and penetrating.

Reflection

The leading question in Marcel's philosophy of the concrete is the question, "Who am I?" Only through a pursuit of this question can humans be liberated from the objectivizing tendencies in modern thought, and return to the immediacy of their lived experience. Reflection will illuminate this lived experience only as long as it remains a part of life. The author defines two levels of reflection—primary and secondary. Primary reflection is *analytical* and tends to dissolve the unity of experience as it is existentially disclosed to the involved self. Secondary reflection is *recuperative* and seeks to reconquer the unity that is lost through primary reflection. It is only with the aid of secondary reflection that humans can penetrate to the depths of the self. The Cartesian *Cogito* ("I think") is derived by primary reflection, and therefore it is viewed as a mental object somehow united with the fact of existence. However, this abstract reflection is already at a second remove from the reality of pure immediacy. If the "I exist" is to provide the Archimedean point, then it will need to be retrieved in its indissoluble unity as an immediate datum of secondary reflection. Existence, as Immanuel Kant had already shown in his *Kritik der reinen Vernunf* (1781; *The Critique of Pure Reason*, 1838), is not a property or a predicate that can be attached to a mental ob-

ject. Existence indicates an irreducible status in a given sensory context. Secondary reflection uncovers my existence as it is sensibly experienced *in act*. This apprehension of my existence *in act* is what Marcel calls the "existential indubitable." In asking about myself, I am disclosed as the questioner in the very act of posing the question. It is here that we find ourselves up against existence in its naked "thereness."

The living body is for the author a central phenomenon in secondary or recuperative reflection. Secondary reflection discloses my existence as an *incarnated* existence—an existence that is tied to a body that I experience as peculiarly and uniquely my own. The "existential indubitable" is manifested in the experience of my body as it actually lives. Primary reflection tends to dissolve the link between me and my body; it transforms the "me" into a universal consciousness and my body into an objectivized entity that is in fact only one body among many others. The original unity of the experience of myself as body is thus dissolved. Primary reflection takes up the attitude of an objectivizing detachment. The body becomes an anatomical or physiological object, generalized as a datum for scientific investigation.

It becomes evident that the Cartesian dualism of mind and body springs from primary rather than secondary reflection. The body in Descartes's philosophy is a substantive entity that has been objectivized and viciously abstracted from the concrete experience of the living body as intimately mine. Secondary reflection apprehends my body as an irreducible determinant in my immediate experience. On one hand, my body is disclosed as something that I *possess*, something that belongs to me. However, as I penetrate deeper, I find that the analogy of ownership does not succeed in fully expressing the incarnated quality of my existence. The analogy of ownership still tends to define the relation of myself to my body as an external one. It defines my body as a possession that is somehow accidental to my inner being. However, this is not so. My body is constitutive of my inner being. Properly speaking, it is not something that I have; it designates who I am:

My body is *my* body just in so far as I do *not* consider it in this detached fashion, do not put a gap between myself and it. To put this point in another way, my body is mine in so far as for me my body is not an object but, rather, I *am* my body.

It is at this point that the author's distinction between being and having becomes relevant. The phenomenon of being can never be reduced to the phenomenon of having. In *having*, the bond between the possessor and the possessed is an external relation; in the phenomenon of *being*, the bond is internal rather than external and is expressed by Marcel in the language of participation. Humans have or possess external objects and qualities, but they participate in being. The implications of this phenomenological distinction for the immediate awareness of the living body are evident. On one level of experience, my body is something that I have or possess. It is a material complex that is attached to myself, and defines me as a self with a body. However, on a deeper level of experience, I *am* my body, and I am my body in such a way that the simple materiality of my body as a possession is transcended. I *exist* as body, as an incarnated being for whom the experience of body and the experience of selfhood are inseparable phenomena. Speaking of my body is a way of speaking of myself. The body in such a view is existentialized. It is no longer an object possessed by a subject. It is apprehended as a determinant of subjectivity.

Participation

The immediate encounter with the mystery of being is thus in terms of a lived participation. The idea of participation, says the author, assumed importance for him even in the days of his earliest philosophical gropings. Although the language of participation would seem to betray a Platonic influence, the author makes it clear that the idea of participation includes more than an intellectual assent. Indeed, the foundational mode of participation is feeling, inextricably bound up with a bodily sense. The Platonic dualism of mind and body, with its perfervid intellectualism and depreciation of the senses, could not admit the existential quality of participation that Marcel seeks to establish. Marcel's favorite illustrations of feeling as a mode of participation are his illustrations of the link between the peasant

and the soil, and the sailor and the sea. Here, he says, one can grasp what participation means. The peasant's attachment to the soil and the sailor's attachment to the sea transcend all relationships of simple utility. The peasant does not "have" the soil as a simple possession. The soil becomes a part of his being. He becomes existentially identified with the soil. A separation of himself from the soil would entail a loss of identity and a kind of incurable internal bleeding. This bond through participation, expressed in the link between the peasant and the soil, points to the fundamental relation of humans to the mystery of being.

In Marcel's philosophy of participation, the notions of intersubjectivity, encounter, and community are decisive. In the second volume of *The Mystery of Being*, the author seeks to replace the Cartesian metaphysics of "I think" (*Cogito*) with a metaphysics of *intersubjectivity* that is formulated in terms of "we are." Philosophical reflection, he argues, must emancipate its inquiry from the solipsism of an isolated epistemological subject or a transcendental ego. My existence is disclosed only in the context of a "living communication" with other selves. "The more I free myself from the prison of ego-centricism," concludes the author, "the more do I exist." Embedded in all my existential reflections is a preliminary and precognitive awareness of a communal horizon of which I am inextricably a part. "I concern myself with being only in so far as I have a more or less distinct consciousness of the underlying unity which ties me to other beings of whose reality I already have a preliminary notion."

The basic phenomenon of communal intersubjectivity is further elucidated in the author's use of the notion of *encounter*. The intersubjectivity of human life becomes apparent only in the movements of personal encounter. Now the phenomenon of personal encounter expresses a relationship that is qualitatively different from that which obtains in a relationship between physical objects on the level of *thinghood*. Selfhood and thinghood constitute distinct modes of being, correspondingly requiring different modes of apprehension or knowledge. Another human self cannot be encountered as a thing. Every human self is a "thou" and must be encountered as a personal center of subjectivity. Only through encounter does one attain knowledge of another self. The French verb *reconnaître* is peculiarly suited to express the movement of encountering. The range of meaning in *reconnaître* is restricted if it is translated in its usual manner as "to recognize." The French usage denotes *acknowledgment* as well as *recognition*. In an encounter, another self is known when he or she is acknowledged as a person. Knowledge is acknowledgment.

Allied with notions of the encounter and *reconnaître* are the notions of *disponibilité* and *indisponibilité*, which are elucidated at some length in a previous work by Marcel, *Être et avoir: Philosophie de l'esprit* (1935; *Being and Having: An Existentialist Diary*, 1949). The two notions have been rendered into English respectively as *availability* and *unavailability*. Marcel suggests, however, that it would be more natural if one spoke of handiness and unhandiness. Self-centered people are unhandy. They do not make themselves and their resources available to other selves. They remain encumbered with themselves, insensitive to openness and transparence. They are incapable of sympathizing with other people, and they lack a requisite fellow feeling for understanding their situation. Handy and available selves are those who can transcend their private, individual lives and become open to a creative communion with other selves. They are ever ready to respond in love and sympathy. No longer enclosed upon themselves, they acknowledge the inner freedom or subjectivity of the other and thus reveal both themselves and the other as something other than object. It is Marcel's accentuation of the theme of creative intersubjectivity that most clearly contrasts his existential reflections with those of his fellow countryman Jean-Paul Sartre. In the existentialism of Sartre, the final movement culminates in a disharmonious and alienating egocentricism. In the existentialism of Marcel, the last measure and note is one of harmony—creative communality.

Mystery and Problem

The existential reflections in the author's two-volume work are geared to an elucidation of various facets of the presence of being. Being discloses itself as a mystery—hence, the appropriate title of his lectures, *The Mystery of Being*. In the concluding chapter of volume 1, the author erects a signpost for philosophical wayfarers to help them in their metaphysical journeyings. This signpost is the distinction between problem and mystery. A mystery is something in which I myself am involved. A problem is something from which I detach myself and I seek to solve. One is involved in mystery, but one solves problems. Mystery has to do with the experience of presence. Problem has to do with the realm of objects that can be grasped through the determination of an objectivizing reason. A problem is subject to an appropriate technique; it can be diagramed, quantified, and manipulated. A mystery by its very character transcends every determinable technique. Being is a mystery rather than a problem, and the moment that it is reduced to a problem its significance vanishes. By turning a mystery into a problem, one degrades it. When the mystery of the being of the self is subject to a problematic approach, which by definition objectivizes its content, then the personal and subjective quality of selfhood is dissolved. When the mystery of evil is translated into a problem of evil, as is the case in most theodicies, then the issue is so falsified as to render impossible any existentially relevant illumination.

In advancing his distinction between mystery and problem, however, Marcel is not delineating a distinction between the unknowable and the knowable. In fact, the unknowable belongs to the domain of the problematic. It points to the limiting horizon of that which can be conceived through objective techniques. The recognition of mystery involves a positive act or responsiveness on the part of self. It expresses a knowledge that is peculiar to its content—an immediate knowledge of participation as contrasted with an objectivizing knowledge of detachment. Knowledge is attainable both in the domain of mystery and in the domain of problem, but the knowledge in each case is irreducibly adapted to its intentional content.

In volume 2, the author concludes his philosophical reflections by showing that his philosophy of being is at the same time a philosophy of freedom. Although the notion of freedom is not given as much attention in the existentialism of Marcel as in that of Kierkegaard, Jaspers, and Sartre, it plays a significant role in his elucidations of concrete experience. Freedom is disclosed in the domain of mystery rather than in the domain of problem. Freedom can never be found in a series of external acts. Freedom is found only when the self turns inward and becomes aware of its capacity for commitment and treason. Freedom is disclosed in the subjective movements of promise and betrayal. I am free to bind myself in a promise, and then I am free to betray the one who has taken me into his trust. Freedom is thus disclosed in both its creative and destructive implications. Both fidelity and treason are expressions of a free act. This freedom, which is experienced only *in concreto*, moves within the mystery of humanity's inner subjectivity. As a problem, freedom can be nothing more than a series of objectively observable psychological states. As a mystery, freedom constitutes the inner core of the self.

There is an inner connection between faith and freedom, which is elaborated in volume 2. Faith is itself a movement of freedom in the establishment of bonds of commitment—both with other humans and with God. Faith is thus described as trust rather than as intellectual assent to propositional truth. Marcel distinguishes between *believing that* and *believing in*. Faith is not a matter of *believing that*. It is not oriented toward propositions that correspond to some objective reality. Faith is expressed through *believing in*. To believe in another person is to place confidence in him. In effect, this is to say to the other: "I am sure that you will not betray my hope, that you will respond to it, that you will fulfill it." Also, to have faith in God is to establish a relationship of trust in him. Humans are free to enter into a covenant with God, invoking a bond of trust and commitment, but they are also free to betray him and revoke the covenant.

Faith and freedom disclose the need for transcendence. Transcendence, for the author, is not simply a horizontal transcendence of going beyond in time—as it is for Heidegger and Sartre. Transcendence has a vertical dimension as well—a going beyond to the eternal. The experience of transcendence is fulfilled only through participation in the life of a transcendent being. Marcel's philosophy of being, unlike that of Heidegger and Sartre, is not simply a philosophy of human finitude. It seeks to establish a path that reaches beyond the finite and temporal to the transcendent and eternal.

Calvin O. Schrag

Additional Reading

Cain, Seymour. *Gabriel Marcel*. New York: Hilary House, 1963. This is a short introduction to the major themes of Marcel's thinking and proves a good starting point for further study.

_____. *Gabriel Marcel's Theory of Religious Experience*. New York: Peter Lang, 1995. An astute, interesting evaluation and interpretation of Marcel's thought on the religious meaning of human existence.

Gallagher, Kenneth T. *The Philosophy of Gabriel Marcel*. New York: Fordham University Press, 1962. Good overall study of Marcel's philosophical work, with an introduction by Marcel.

Hanley, Katherine Rose. *Dramatic Approaches to Creative Fidelity: A Study in the Theater and Philosophy of Gabriel Marcel (1889-1973)*. Lanham, Md.: University Press of America, 1987. This is the most extensive attempt in English to relate Marcel's philosophical and dramatic works.

Keen, Sam. *Gabriel Marcel*. London: Carey Kingsgate Press, 1966. This work is a good short survey of Marcel's philosophical work.

McCown, Joe. *Availability: Gabriel Marcel and the Phenomenology of Human Openness*. Missoula, Mont.: Scholars Press, 1978. Explores Marcel's focus on the concept of availability and its connections to phenomenology and theology.

Moran, Denis P. *Gabriel Marcel: Existentialist Philosopher, Dramatist, Educator*. Lanham, Md.: University Press of America, 1992. An overview of Marcel's biography and thought, with extended consideration of the relation of his work as a philosopher and dramatist to educational practice.

Schilpp, Paul Arthur, and Lewis Edwin Hahn, eds. *The Philosophy of Gabriel Marcel*. Library of Living Philosophers series. La Salle, Ill.: Open Court, 1984. Contains a number of essays on Marcel's work, as well as his own 1969 "Autobiographical Essay."

Michael W. Messmer, updated by William Nelles

Marcus Aurelius

Although renowned as the last of Rome's "good emperors," Marcus Aurelius is best remembered for his *Meditations*. These simply written private notes reflect the emperor's daily efforts to achieve the Platonic ideal of the philosopher-king and are the last great literary statement of Stoicism.

Principal philosophical work: *Tōn eis heauton*, c. 171-180 (*Meditations*, 1634)

Born: April 26, 121; Rome
Died: March 17, 180; Sirmium or Vindobona
  (modern Vienna)

Early Life

Marcus Aurelius Antoninus was born Marcus Annius Verus in Rome. His father was Annius Verus, a magistrate, and his mother was Domitia Calvilla, also known as Lucilla. The emperor Antoninus Pius was, by virtue of his marriage to Annia Galeria Faustina, the sister of Annius Verus, the boy's uncle. The emperor, who had himself been adopted and named successor by Hadrian, eventually adopted Marcus Annius Verus. The young man then took the name Marcus Aelius Aurelius Verus. The name Aelius came from Hadrian's family, and Aurelius was the name of Antoninus Pius. The young man took the title Caesar in 139 and, on becoming emperor, replaced his original name of Verus with Antoninus. Hence, he is known to history as Marcus Aurelius Antoninus.

Marcus Aurelius was well brought up and well educated. Later, he would write of what a virtuous man and prudent ruler his uncle and adoptive father had been. To the fine example set by the emperor was added the dedicated teaching of excellent masters. Letters exist that attest the boy's industry and the great expectations engendered by his performance as a student. He studied eloquence and rhetoric, and he tried his hand at poetry. He was also trained in the law as a preparation for high office. Above all, Marcus Aurelius's interest was in philosophy. When only eleven years of age, he adopted the plain, coarse dress of the philosophers and undertook a spartan regimen of hard study and self-denial. In fact, he drove himself so relentlessly that for a time his health was affected. He was influenced by Stoicism, a sect founded by the Greek philosopher Zeno of Citium in the fourth century B.C.E.

Life's Work

Antoninus Pius became emperor upon the death of Hadrian in July, 138. He adopted not only Marcus Aurelius but also Lucius Ceionius Commodus, who came to be called Lucius Aurelius Verus. The adoptive brothers could scarcely have been more different. Verus was destined to rule alongside Marcus Aurelius for a time despite his manifest unworthiness. He was an indolent, pleasure-loving man, whereas Marcus Aurelius was proving himself worthy of more and more responsibility. The year 146 was a highly significant one, for it was at about that time that Antoninus Pius began to share with Marcus Aurelius the government of the empire. Further, the emperor gave him Faustina, his daughter and the young man's cousin, in marriage. A daughter was born to Marcus Aurelius and Faustina in 147.

At the death of Antoninus Pius in March, 161, the senate asked Marcus Aurelius to assume sole governance of the empire. Yet he chose to rule jointly with Verus, the other adopted son. For the first time in its history, Rome had two emperors. Apparently, and fortunately for the empire, Verus was not blind to his inadequacies. He deferred to Marcus Aurelius, who was in turn tolerant of him. Marcus Aurelius cemented their relationship by giving his daughter Lucilla to Verus as wife. That their joint rule lasted for eight years was really a credit to them both.

The first major problem to be faced by the joint rulers was the war with Parthia. Verus was sent to command the Roman forces but proved ineffectual. Fortunately, his generals were able, thus achieving victories in Armenia and along the Tigris and Euphrates rivers. The war was concluded in 165, but as soon as Marcus Aurelius and Verus received their triumph—a huge public ceremony honoring the victors in war—Rome was struck by a virulent pestilence. As the plague spread throughout Italy and beyond, the loss of life was great.

At this time, barbarians from beyond the Alps were threatening to invade northern Italy. Although Marcus Aurelius was able to contain them, they would periodically renew their efforts. For the rest of the emperor's life, he would spend much of his time and effort in holding these warlike people at bay. Verus died suddenly in 169, and Marcus Aurelius became the sole emperor of Rome. His reign continued as it had begun, beset by difficulties on every hand. He was almost constantly in the field, campaigning against one enemy or another. He was on the Danube River for three years, prosecuting the German wars, and by 174, he had gained a series of impressive victories.

In 175, Avidius Cassius, who commanded the Roman legions in Asia, led a revolt against the emperor. Up to that time, Cassius had been a fine general, but when he declared himself Augustus, the emperor marched east to meet the threat. Before the emperor arrived, however, Cassius was assassinated by some of his officers. Marcus Aurelius's treatment of the family and followers of Cassius was magnanimous. His letter to the senate asking mercy for them has survived. During this time, Marcus Aurelius

suffered a severe personal tragedy. The empress, Faustina, who had accompanied her husband on the Asian march, abruptly died. Some historians have written that she was scandalously unfaithful and promiscuous, but their reports are contradicted by her husband's pronouncements. He was grief-stricken at her death, and his references to her are loving and laudatory.

It was during this decade of constant warfare, rebellion, and personal grief that Marcus Aure-

Marcus Aurelius *(Library of Congress)*

lius began to write the lofty, dignified contemplative notes that would come to be called *Meditations*. They were meant for no eyes but the emperor's, and their survival through the centuries is a mystery, although some scholars have no doubts as to their authenticity. They reflect Marcus Aurelius's sense of duty, his high-mindedness, and his apparent inner peace. Two themes dominate the *Meditations*: First, people, to the utmost of their ability to do so, should harmonize with nature; second, it is not the circumstances of one's life that produce happiness but one's perception of those circumstances. According to the emperor, happiness always comes from within, never from without. The *Meditations* are also marked by their author's common sense. He observes that when one is seduced by fame and flattered by others, one should remember their want of judgment on other occasions and remain humble. A great emperor might be expected to be self-assured, perhaps even self-centered and self-satisfied; Marcus Aurelius strikes the reader as more self-composed and self-contented.

Although the emperor's campaigns were generally successful (one victory, in which a fortuitous storm threw the enemy into a panic, was even viewed as a miracle), his reign was not unblemished. He was often forced to make concessions that allowed large numbers of barbarians to remain in Roman territory and that eventually resulted in a proliferation of barbarians within his own armies (some of his legions were already identifiably Christian in makeup). He also seems to have been blind to the vices of Commodus, his son and successor. It is the persecution of the Christians, however, which brings his record into question.

The constant state of war, aggravated by widespread pestilence, caused the populace to demand a scapegoat. The Christians were a natural target, since their repudiation of the ancient gods was thought to have brought divine retribution upon Rome. An ardent persecution was begun, especially in the provinces. At first, the persecutions seem to have progressed ad hoc. Eventually, however, a provincial governor appealed to the emperor for guidance. His directions were, by contemporary standards, severe. If the Christians would deny their faith, they would be released. Otherwise, they were to be punished. Those un-

repentant Christians who were Roman citizens were beheaded. The others were put to death in a variety of imaginative ways. Apologists for Marcus Aurelius have maintained that he had little to do with these persecutions, and they do seem out of character for the author of the *Meditations*. Still, in order to argue that Marcus Aurelius was in no way culpable, one must read history quite selectively.

In 180, the emperor was conducting yet another successful, though somewhat inconclusive, campaign, this time along the upper Danube. He fell ill with the plague or some other contagious malady and died on March 17 of that year.

Influence

The commemorative bust of Marcus Aurelius features a noble head, framed by curly hair and neat chin whiskers. The countenance is strong, honest, and handsome. Any idealization of the likeness is appropriate, for the emperor's demeanor as well as his words set one of the greatest examples in history. When his ashes were returned to Rome, he was honored with deification and, for long afterward, he was numbered by many Romans among their household gods. Commodus erected in his father's memory the Antonine column in Rome's Piazza Colonna. The emperor's statue was placed at the top of the column and remained there until Pope Sixtus V caused it to be replaced by a bronze statue of Saint Paul. The substitution is symbolic, as it was meant to be.

Throughout the Christian era, attempts have been made to associate the *Meditations* with Christian thought. Such efforts are understandable, for the emperor's self-admonitions to virtuous conduct for its own sake, steadfastness, magnanimity, and forbearance are congenial to the mind of the Christian apologist. The weight of evidence, however, indicates otherwise. Marcus Aurelius seems to have known little about the Christians, and what he knew, he did not like. Even granting that he was not deeply involved in their persecution, he clearly regarded them as fanatical troublemakers. He should be viewed, then, not as an incipient Christian but as the voice of paganism's last great moral pronouncements.

The emperor was an able but not a great military figure. He was an intelligent but not a brilliant thinker. As a writer, he was a competent but not a formidable stylist. In short, Marcus Aurelius was great because he brought a human quality to his leadership and made optimal use of his limited talents.

Patrick Adcock

Meditations

Type of philosophy: Ethics
First transcribed: Tōn eis heauton, c. 171-180 (English translation, 1634)
Principal ideas advanced:

◇ Nature is one, the divine substance, God or reason, so that virtue for humankind consists in being in harmony with the way of nature.

◇ Virtue is the highest good.

◇ The ideal Stoic wills to control the self in those respects in which control is possible—in desiring, believing, and responding.

◇ People's freedom, in a world in which all events are determined, is their power to assent or dissent to the course of events.

◇ Nothing that is according to nature can be evil; hence, death is not evil, nor are the ordinary misfortunes of life.

Marcus Aurelius Antoninus, at once emperor and philosopher, man of history and vulnerable man, created a personal record of his thoughts, the *Meditations*, that reveals much of the man and his world. He was a stoic (one who may suffer but who refuses to be moved by suffering) in that he survived the treacherous debaucheries of Lucius; Aurelius Verus, with whom he shared his empire, the rebellious uprisings of powerful tribes; famine and flood; the deaths of his children—except one, who became a tyrant—and the threat of Christianity. He may have tolerated faithlessness in his wife, but this lack of fidelity, on which he makes no comment, may have been nothing more than a rumor.

Stoicism and Nature

Marcus Aurelius, a stoic in his personal life, was also a Stoic, heir to the philosophic tradition initiated by Zeno of Citium and expanded and con-

tinued by Chrysippus of Soloi, Panaetius of Rhodes, Posidonius, Seneca the Younger, and Epictetus. What is central to Stoicism is not a stonelike stubbornness in a world of suffering but a strengthening faith in the way of nature. Nature is one, the substance of God. God is a divine fire that periodically consumes all things. However, although the divine conflagration turns all things and persons to fire—thus effectively uniting all in the purest form possible— things and persons will exist in the next cycle of existence; the cycles of existence and conflagration will succeed each other forever. Virtue for humankind is in willing to be in harmony with the way of nature. Pleasure and pain are irrelevant, if the only good is nature's way and obedience to that way. Thus, the stoical attitude is the consequence of a dedication to the Stoical ideal; it is not itself the essence of that ideal.

So conceived, Stoicism can be recognized as close in spirit to Daoism, the philosophy and religion of ancient China, in which obedience to the Dao, the "way" of the universe, is the highest virtue. Like Daoism, Stoicism involves the belief that nature, because it is the matter of God, works only toward the good—although the Chinese did not identify the cosmic power as fire or as God. Finally, to fix the idea of Stoicism, it is helpful to distinguish between Stoicism and Epicureanism. Although both the Stoics and the Epicureans fostered a life of moderation in which the passions would be controlled by will and reason, the Epicureans regarded pleasure as the highest good. Contrary to common belief, they did not endorse a program of wine, women, and song but rather a life of moderation in which the desire for peace and contemplation would take precedence over the desire for gratification of the senses. For the Stoics, virtue itself was the highest good, although it was generally believed that a modest kind of happiness would be the virtuous person's natural reward. Although there are other important differences, one can come to understand the essential distinction between Stoicism and Epicureanism by realizing that for the Stoics, virtue was the highest good, and for the Epicureans, happiness was the highest good and virtue only the means.

In Stoicism, particularly in the later philosophy as exemplified in the *Meditations*, the ethical elements received more emphasis than the metaphysical. The early philosophy was a pantheistic materialism—because it held that God is fire, and all nature is God—but later Stoics were not interested in developing these ideas, and insofar as fire was mentioned it was in a metaphorical, rather than a metaphysical, way.

Stoic Ethics

The Stoic ethics is not complicated; it is more an expression of dedication to nature's way and to the control of the self than it is a specific guide to the complexities of life. The wise person, the one who becomes the ideal Stoic, is one who wills to control the self in those respects in which control is possible: desiring, believing, and responding. The ideal Stoic also, like the Epicurean, refuses to be affected, in desires or attitudes, by matters beyond the individual's control or unworthy of concern.

Nevertheless, although the ethics of Stoicism is not complicated, problems develop in connection with the metaphysical ground of the ethics. If all nature tends toward the good, and if all events are causally determined—as the Stoics believed—how is it possible for people to err and how can they be held responsible for their actions? The Stoics were unanimous in giving assent to the claim that people are morally responsible and that their responsibility involves their freedom, and they were generally united in adhering to a strict determinism. The answer that won most favor among the Stoics and that seems to be influential in the thinking of Marcus Aurelius is that although, causally speaking, events could not be other than they are, in the act of assenting or dissenting, people play a critical role in the course of events; and it is in that moment of assent or dissent that people show their freedom and acquire their responsibility. At its most positivistic, this philosophy means that to attribute moral responsibility to people is simply to attribute to them the power, in the causal situation, of assenting or dissenting.

Although there are reflections of Stoical philosophy in the *Meditations*, the work itself is not a philosophic treatise. It is a record of the reflections of a philosophically tempered ruler, a person with moral sensitivity and intellectual awareness who never gave up the practice of examining his ideas, his motives, and his actions with the intention of refining himself. He is a generous and thoughtful man in his book, an honest man with a sense of his errors—but throughout the work, Marcus Aurelius seems to be sustained by a strengthening spirit, the fire, or *pneuma*, which is the cosmic principle of the universe. Whether or not the work was intended to be read by anyone other than the writer, the *Meditations* remains an intensely personal philosophic journal by one of the greatest of the Stoics.

The book begins with expressions of gratitude: to his grandfather Verus for having taught him to refrain from passion, to his father for having inspired in him manlike behavior, to his mother for teaching him to be religious and to "content myself with a spare diet," and to his great-grandfather for having encouraged him to acquire a good education. Other friends and teachers are remembered in charming fashion. Marcus Aurelius shows gratitude for having been taught to be humble as a prince while at the same time maintaining a sense of his responsibilities in public matters. He thanks the gods "That I was not long brought up by the concubine of my father; that I preserved the flower of my youth. That I took not upon me to be a man before my time, but rather put it off longer than I needed."

Understanding and Meditation

Within a few pages of the beginning of the *Meditations*, Marcus Aurelius writes that nothing is more important than understanding "the true nature of the world, whereof thou art a part," and he gives himself sober counsel:

> These things thou must always have in mind: What is the nature of the universe, and what is mine in particular: This unto that what relation it hath: what kind of part, of what kind of universe it is: And that there is nobody that can hinder thee, but that thou mayest always both do and speak those things which are agreeable to that nature, whereof thou are a part.

Again, in book 6, Marcus Aurelius writes:

> He that seeth the things that are now, hath seen all that either was ever, or ever shall be, for all things are of one kind; and all like one

unto another. Meditate often upon the connection of all things in the world; and upon the mutual relation that they have one unto another. For all things are after a sort folded and involved one within another, and by these means all agree well together.

To "meditate often"—this was both the duty and the practice of Marcus Aurelius. Even in the midst of war, while waiting for the next day's battle, he reflected on the "connection of all things" and attempted to understand the relation of himself, a part, to that nature of which he was a part.

He concerned himself with the problem of evil and considered whether death is evil. His conclusion was that because nature is the means by which people and God are united, whatever people find disagreeable is no true evil. He believed in both the justice and intelligence of the creative force in the universe and regarded it as inconceivable that nature would be so constituted as to allow both the good and the bad to happen to good and bad people "equally and promiscuously."

His advice to himself was to spend each moment as if it were the last moment of his life. If death comes, he argues, it brings people into the company of the gods—or it brings extinction—and in either case, a rational person should not be disturbed. In any event, what one loses at the moment of death is nothing more than the present moment—and it does not seem proper to complain about losing a moment of one's life. Thus he writes: "The time of a man's life is as a point; the substance of it ever flowing, the sense obscure; and the whole composition of the body tending to corruption." However, what of it? For one who by the use of philosophy allows the spirit to discipline the self, all things that happen are accepted contentedly, and one is assured by the conviction that "nothing that is according to nature can be evil."

The Stoic Ideal

It may sometimes seem that the ideal Marcus Aurelius constructed is beyond reach: In his regard for community, for other men, for the way of nature in all its manifestations, he constructed a moral pattern for himself (and, by implication, for others) that few people could hope to attain. He enjoins himself always to keep his thoughts on worthy matters, to think only of that which he would be happy to reveal were he asked to state his thoughts; he charges himself never to act against his will, or against community, or without examination of what he proposes to do; and he vows soberly to "let thy God that is in thee to rule over thee" so that his life might be so ordered that were he to die, he would be ready.

This Stoic ideal is so carefully considered and presented as the product of personal meditations that it carries with it no hint of moral pride or arrogance. Indeed, if Marcus Aurelius ever supposed he was successful in meeting the ideal, there is no sign of it in his book. The nobility of his character is revealed in the testimony from those who knew him—together with the spirit of the *Meditations*—a philosophic, universe-accepting, strenuous spirit forever exploring nature for intimations of divine intention.

Marcus Aurelius's determination "to stand in no need, either of other men's help or attendance, or of that rest and tranquillity, which thou must be beholding to others for" resembles American philosopher Ralph Waldo Emerson's call for self-reliance. Here again is no insensitive stubbornness but a sign of a faith in the way of nature.

Common Law

Marcus Aurelius argued that if reason is common to humankind, then reason's law is common law, and from common law can be derived the commonweal that makes the world a city and all people fellow citizens of it. He placed great faith in reason because he regarded it as an expression of the great ordering breath of God that pervades all nature. The concern for other human beings fills the *Meditations*, and the spirit is much like that of the Christianity that Marcus Aurelius never understood.

To live according to nature, to disdain rest and tranquillity, to be ready for death, to take misfortune as nothing evil, to be persistent in one's efforts to live like a human, to be happy as one who has faith in the purposes of God and nature, to live with the gods and to give allegiance to the god within, to honor reason and to use it as the divine in humanity whereby one both recognizes and participates in the community of all humanity, to regard happiness as the consequence of "good inclinations of the soul, good desires, good actions"—this is the genteel, impassioned Stoical philosophy that emerges from the pages of the *Meditations*. The common conception of Stoicism as a philosophy of endurance is destroyed in the face of the fact that Marcus Aurelius's Stoicism is well balanced, sympathetic, strenuous, idealistic, and demanding—a call to people to use their highest powers and to control their passions.

Much of the delight of the work comes not from its philosophy—although the Stoicism developed by Marcus Aurelius is in every respect admirable—but from the author's sprightly style, which while communicating the most serious of thoughts ever reminds us of the presence of the living thinker, a lover of humanity, action, and nature. Such an aphorism as "That which is not good for the beehive cannot be good for the bee" creates a pleasant image, expresses a sentiment, fixes an idea, and rounds out an argument. Again, reflecting on anger, he writes, "To them that are sick of the jaundice, honey seems bitter; and to them that are bitten by a mad dog, the water terrible; and to children, a little ball seems a fine thing. And why then should I be angry?"

One's heroes reveal much about a person. Marcus Aurelius writes: "Alexander, Caius, Pompeius; what are these to Diogenes, Heraclitus, and Socrates? These penetrated into the true nature of things; into all causes, and all subjects: and upon these did they exercise their power and authority. However, as for those, as the extent of their error was, so far did their slavery extend." With Marcus Aurelius, the philosopher takes precedence over the soldier and emperor.

Throughout all of his actions and reflections, Marcus Aurelius was sustained by an unconquerable faith. He wrote that neither time nor place can limit an individual's efforts to be a true person, and he regarded true personhood as made possible by reflection on God's ways as shown in the course of nature and by calm acceptance of all circumstances. Not to accept nature, for him, was not to accept law, and not to accept law was to be a fugitive from God. Yet to live in accordance with nature and to accept all things, to act as directed by reason, not passion—this was not a burdensome life, but a happy one: "How happy is man in this his power that hath been granted

unto him: that he needs not do anything but what God shall approve, and that he may embrace contentedly, whatsoever God doth send unto him?"

For the Stoic Marcus Aurelius, the answer was clear—and the assurance of his self-reliant faith is alive in his words: "Herein doth consist happiness of life, for a man to know thoroughly the true nature of everything; what is the matter, and what is the form of it: with all his heart and soul, ever to do that which is just, and to speak the truth."

Ian P. McGreal

Additional Reading

Arnold, E. Vernon. *Roman Stoicism*. Reprint. London: Routledge & Kegan Paul, 1958. A series of easy-to-follow lectures by a classical scholar. Four chapters discuss the thought of Marcus Aurelius Antoninus, which receives ample treatment.

Birley, Anthony. *Marcus Aurelius: A Biography*. London: Eyre & Spottiswoode, 1966. Rev. ed. London: Batsford, 1987. In this well-researched study, Birley aims to disinfect the image of Marcus Aurelius of numerous historical fictions. Includes an illuminating profile of the philosopher-ruler's early education as revealed through correspondence with his tutor Fronto.

Farquharson, Arthur Spenser Loat. *Marcus Aurelius: His Life and His World*. 2d ed. New York: William Salloch, 1951. A fine biography, especially with regard to Marcus Aurelius's birth, childhood, and education. Contains one of the few discussions of his home life. Situates the *Meditations* within Stoic philosophy and the literature of the age.

Guevara, Antonio de. *The Diall of Princes*. 1619. Translated by Thomas North. London: Alsop, 1619. Reprint. The Scholar's Library, No. 1. London: Philip Allan, 1919. A loosely organized historical romance by a sixteenth century Spanish courtier and bishop. Founded on the life and character of Marcus Aurelius, yet viewed from a Renaissance perspective, the book was written to put before the emperor Charles V the model of antiquity's wisest and most virtuous prince. Not essential reading, but interesting.

Hadot, Pierre. *The Inner Citadel: The Meditations of Marcus Aurelius*. Translated by Michael Chase. Cambridge, Mass.: Harvard University Press, 1998. This eminent scholar discerns the *Meditations* as spiritual exercises practiced in accordance with the Stoic method, particularly as espoused by Epictetus. Spirited and engaging, clear and accessible to the general reader, the book includes a fascinating concordance of the many quotations and literary allusions in the *Meditations*.

Marcus Aurelius Antoninus. "The *Meditations* of Marcus Aurelius." Translated and edited by George Long. In *Plato, Epictetus, Marcus Aurelius*, edited by Charles W. Eliot. 2d ed. New York: Collier & Son, 1937. Long's translation of Marcus Aurelius's work is accompanied by his brief and interesting life of the author. His companion essay, "The Philosophy of Anto-ninus," includes a useful explanation of Stoicism and traces its progress and decline in the Roman world.

Watson, Paul Barron. *Marcus Aurelius Antoninus*. 1884. Reprint. Freeport, N.Y.: Books for Libraries Press, 1971. A detailed and eloquent biography, suitable for the general reader. Though the book centers on his career as a ruler, the final chapter relates the events of his life to the philosophy embraced in the *Meditations*.

Wenley, R. M. *Stoicism and Its Influence*. Our Debt to Greece and Rome series. New York: Cooper Square, 1963. A rich exposition of Stoic doctrines and a defense of the importance of Stoicism against historians of philosophy who have tended to dismiss it. Discussions of Marcus Aurelius are sprinkled liberally throughout the text.

Patrick Adcock, updated by Grant A. Marler

Karl Marx

Marx's ideas concerning modes of economic distribution, social class, and the developmental patterns of history have profoundly influenced theories in philosophical and economic thought and have helped shape the political structure of the modern world.

Principal philosophical works: "Zur Kritik der hegelschen Rechtsphilosophie," 1844 (*Critique of Hegel's Philosophy of Right*, 1970); *Ökonomische und philosophische Manuskripte*, 1844 (*Economic and Philosophic Manuscripts of 1844*, 1947); *Die deutsche Ideologie*, 1845-1846 (*The German Ideology*, 1938); *Manifest der Kommunistischen Partei*, 1848 (with Friedrich Engels; *The Communist Manifesto*, 1850); *Grundrisse der Kritik der politischen Ökonomie*, 1857-1858 (*Foundations of the Critique of Political Economy*, 1973); *Zur Kritik der politischen Ökonomie*, 1859 (*A Contribution to a Critique of Political Economy*, 1904); *Das Kapital*, 1867, 1885, 1894 (*Capital: A Critique of Political Economy*, 1886, 1907, 1909; better known as *Das Kapital*).

Born: May 5, 1818; Trier, Prussia
Died: March 14, 1883; London, England

Early Life

Karl Marx was born into a Jewish family in the city of Trier in the southern Rhineland area. By the time the Rhineland was rejoined, after the Napoleonic Wars, to Protestant Prussia in 1814, his father, a public lawyer, had converted to Christianity. In 1830, the young Marx entered the Trier secondary school and pursued the traditional humanities curriculum. In the fall of 1835, he entered the University of Bonn as a law student, but he left the following year to enroll at the University of Berlin. His studies were concentrated on law, history, and the works of the then-leading philosophers Johann Gottlieb Fichte and Georg Wilhelm Friedrich Hegel.

Marx was graduated in 1841 after writing his doctoral dissertation, and he returned to Bonn, where he became involved with his friend Bruno Bauer in left-wing politics and in the study of the materialist philosophy of Ludwig Feuerbach. In April, 1842, he began writing radical articles for the *Rheinische Zeitung* (Rhenish gazette), and he assumed its editorship in Cologne that October. He married in June, 1843, and moved to Paris that October.

In August, 1844, Marx met Friedrich Engels in Paris, and the two began a productive collaboration. Marx's articles had angered the Prussian government, and in February, 1845, he moved to Brussels. In 1848, the year of revolutions in many European countries, Marx was ordered to leave Brussels; he returned to Paris and then to Cologne. He was again compelled to leave in 1849 and went to London, where he would remain for the rest of his life.

Life's Work

Marx's lifelong critique of capitalist economy began in part as an analysis of the then-dominant Hegelian system of philosophical idealism. Influenced to a degree by Feuerbach's materialism, Marx rejected Hegel's metaphysical vision of a *Weltgeist*, or Absolute Spirit. It was not metaphysical Spirit that governed history but rather material existence that determined consciousness. The ways in which an individual was compelled to seek physical necessities such as food, shelter, and clothing within a society profoundly influenced the manner in which a person viewed himself and others. As Hegel (and others) suggested, the course of history was indeed a dialectical process of conflict and resolution, but for Marx this development was determined to a great extent by economic realities. Whereas Hegel saw dialectical process (thesis/antithesis/synthesis)

as one of ideas, for Marx it was one of class struggle. Hence, Marx's position is called dialectical
materialism. He stood in staunch opposition to
the prior philosophical tradition of German idealism and thinkers such as Immanuel Kant,
Fichte, and Hegel. German philosophy, he believed, was mired in insubstantial theoretical
speculation when concrete and practical thought
about the relationship between reality—especially economic and political realities—and consciousness was needed. In general, Marx was a
synthetic thinker, and his views represent a mixture of German materialist philosophy such as
that of Feuerbach; the French social doctrines of
Charles Fourier, Comte de Saint-Simon, and
Pierre-Joseph Proudhon; and British theories of
political economy such as those of Adam Smith
and David Ricardo.

Marx's philosophical position of a dialectical
materialism suggests a comprehensive view of
social organization—which is, broadly
speaking, a dimension of human consciousness—in all its manifestations.
The determinant of all societal forms
is its economic base (*Basis*), that is, the
means of production and the distribution of its produced wealth. All aspects of human social interaction,
what Marx called the superstructure
(*Überbau*), are influenced and shaped
by the economic base and its consequent relationships of power among
social classes. The superstructure ultimately involves a society's educational, legal, artistic, political, philosophical, and scientific systems. The
nature of the economic base and above
all the power relationships of the
classes tend to be reproduced in an
overt or covert fashion in the various
dimensions of the societal superstructure. The pedagogical curriculum of
the school system, for example, might
reproduce or reinforce in some unconscious manner the inequality of the social classes on which the mode of production is based. Various aspects of
the artistic or cultural dimensions of a
society (a novel, for example) might
also incorporate in symbolic expres-

sion the nature of the economic base. Thus
Marx's economic theories provide an account for
a wide variety of phenomena.

In capitalist political economy, the individual
must sell his physical or intellectual labor—must
sell himself as a commodity—in order to survive.
Thus, Marx's early writings, such as *Economic and
Philosophic Manuscripts of 1844*, deal with the pivotal concept of alienation (*Entfremdung*) as a central aspect of the worker's experience in capitalism. Because the worker is reduced to an
exploited commodity or object, the worker experiences a condition of dehumanization (*Ent-
menschlichung*). The individual is alienated or divorced from his or her full potential as a human
being. Committed to long hours of labor in a
factory, the worker—man, woman, or child—has
no time to develop other facets of the personality.
In a capitalist society, individuals are estranged
not only from aspects of their own selves but also

Karl Marx. *(Library of Congress)*

from others in that the labor market is a competitive one and workers must outdo one another in order to survive. In its crudest form, capitalist economy, Marx would assert, is a kind of Darwinian "survival of the fittest," in which the weak (those who cannot work) must perish.

In *The German Ideology*, Marx discusses earlier forms of social organization, such as tribal or communal groups, in which the estrangement of the individual in industrialist society was not yet a crucial problem. His vision of an ideal socialist state would be one in which the individual might, for example, manufacture shoes in the morning, teach history in the afternoon, and play music in an orchestra in the evening. In other words, a person would be free to utilize or realize all dimensions of the self. This idealized notion of social organization in the writings of the young Marx indicates the utopian influence of Romantic thought upon his initial critique of capitalist society.

In 1848, after the Paris revolts of that same year, Marx and Engels published *The Communist Manifesto*, a booklet that has become the best-known and most influential statement of Marxist ideology. It presents a brief historical sketch of bourgeois society and suggests that capitalism will eventually collapse because of its inherent pattern of cyclical economic crises and because of the worsening situation of the worker class, or the proletariat, in all capitalist nations. The proletariat has become, they argue, more conscious of its situation, and a worker revolution is inevitable. The international communist party presents a revolutionary platform in which the workers are the ruling class in charge of all capital production. Marx and Engels call for a worker revolt to overthrow the "chains" that bind them.

In 1859, Marx published *A Contribution to a Critique of Political Economy*, which became a preliminary study for the first volume of his and Engels's planned multivolume analysis of capitalist political economy, *Das Kapital*. Marx actually completed only the first volume; the second and third were edited from his notes by Engels, who was helped on the third by Karl Kautsky. The former work is a technical economic analysis of the capitalist mode of production with the intention of revealing "the economic law of motion" that underlies modern (industrial) society.

In *Das Kapital*, Marx discusses economic issues such as the labor theory of value and commodities, surplus value, capital production and accumulation, and the social relations and class struggles involved in capital production. Capital accumulation, the central goal and justification of the system, is beset by certain internal contradictions, such as periodic episodes of moderate to extreme market inflation and depression and a tendency toward monopoly. These inherent conditions usually have their most deleterious effects upon the wage laborer. Such cycles will eventually lead to economic collapse or revolutionary overthrow by the proletariat. In general, Marx's analyses were flawed—especially the labor theory of value upon which much of this work is based—and could not account for adaptive changes in the capitalist system.

In December, 1881, Marx's wife, Jenny, died, and his daughter died the following year. Marx himself, after a life of overwork and neglect of his health, died in 1883.

Influence

Marx was a critical social and economic philosopher whose materialist analyses of bourgeois capitalist society initiated a revolution that has had profound effects on the development of human civilization. Despite some of the later ideological, and at times quasi-religious and fanatical, adaptations of his thought, the basic philosophical assumptions of Marx's approach remain humanistic and optimistic; they are based upon fundamental notions of the European Enlightenment—that is, that human reason can successfully alleviate the problems of life. Alienation is, for example, in Marx's view (as opposed to modern existential thought) a historical and societal phenomenon that can be overcome through a change in the social-economic order. Marxism has remained a vital intellectual position and therefore possesses much relevance to the modern world.

Subsequent developments of Marxist thought resulted in communist revolutions in a number of countries such as that led by the ideologue Vladimir Ilich Lenin within czarist Russia in 1917 and that of the popular leader Mao Zedong in the Republic of China in 1949. Unfortunately, these revolutions involved pogroms and mass executions of certain segments of the population, usually elements of the landed bourgeoisie. Such was the case under the rule of Joseph Stalin in Soviet Russia. These socialist governments became reified, for the most part, at the intermediate stage of a party dictatorship rather than the essentially free state of the people that Marx had envisioned.

Marx's philosophy has led to fruitful thought in areas other than social and economic thought. The notion that the power relationships of the economic base affect, in various ways, the manifestations of the societal superstructure has produced an analytical mode called ideological criticism, in which the hidden dimensions of class ideology are revealed in their social expressions. The concept has been especially productive in the fields of literature and the arts. Marxist analyses of literary texts have yielded new insights into the nature of literary production and its relationship to society at large. The Hungarian critic György Lukács, for example, wrote many excellent books and essays on the history of European literature, establishing a new model of Marxist interpretation and criticism.

Thomas F. Barry

Selected Works

Type of philosophy: Ethics, philosophy of history, social philosophy
First published: Various times
Principal ideas advanced:
◇ The postulation of transcendent divine beings is a function of humanity's incomplete and distorted self-identification.
◇ Incomplete human self-identification is a function of nonegalitarian and incompletely developed modes of production.
◇ The state is the ideologically legitimated power of ruling classes over laboring classes; its disappearance under genuine egalitarian and advanced productive and social conditions is thus necessary by definition.
◇ Socially mediated production on the basis of foresight and skill distinguishes human from animal production; blockages in the develop-

ment and expression of these basic capacities, reaching a peak in capitalism, are entitled "alienation."
◇ Human history can be represented and explained as a sequence of changes in the modes of production, upon which are raised corresponding sociopolitical structures and modes of thought.
◇ The capitalist mode of production and its corresponding social and ideological forms will predictably give way to a socialist order that expresses human capabilities and thus overcomes alienation.

The philosophical dimensions and interest of Karl Marx's work were largely underestimated for a variety of reasons. First, the general disrepute of "speculative" as opposed to "empirical" thought in the later nineteenth century led Friedrich Engels and his collaborators to stress the hardheaded empiricism, scientism, and even positivism of Marx's work when they undertook to turn it into the ideology of a mass movement during the 1880's. Marx himself was probably involved in this effort. In any case, its success was ensured by consolidation of power in Russia by a group of Marxists schooled exclusively in this view. Second, the manuscripts of Marx that could shed a different light on the origins and foundations of Marx's thinking were not widely available until the twentieth century. This fact is obviously not unconnected with the first. Here Marx's complicity derives from his habit of keeping his philosophical way of thinking out of view in the works he prepared or authorized for publication, largely in order to preclude any intimation of idealism, which he felt would undermine the urgency of his message to the working class.

However, four of Marx's works have thrown much light on his deeper philosophical roots, commitments, and habits. These works are Marx's "Zur Kritik der hegelschen Rechtsphilosophie" (1844; *Critique of Hegel's Philosophy of Right*, 1970); *Ökonomische und philosophische Manuskripte* (1844; *Economic and Philosophic Manuscripts of 1844*, 1947); *Die deutsche Ideologie* (1845-1846; *The German Ideology*, 1938); and *Grundrisse der Kritik der politischen Ökonomie* (1857-1858; *Foundations of the Critique of Political Economy*, 1973), a rich but unwieldy group of notebooks sometimes called the "rough draft of capital." It is on these works that the following sketch is based.

Precursors: Hegel and Feuerbach

Like his Young Hegelian companions, Marx as a graduate student began to suspect that Georg Wilhelm Friedrich Hegel's idealism leads to the unwarranted positing of transcendent entities—notably, Absolute Spirit. The point is not that Hegel takes this line; it is that he is unable, whatever his intentions, to escape it. By 1843, Marx had become especially intrigued by philosopher Ludwig Feuerbach's *causal* explanation of the positing of transcendent objects.

For Feuerbach, they are projections, roughly, of an "ideal self" displaced into another world because of factual restrictions placed on self-recognition and self-validation in this world. These restrictions come about generally from the domination of nature over humanity, but more particularly they arise whenever some people systematically dominate others. Given such an artificial division within the species "man" (as if differences between classes or races or other social groupings were like, or took the place of, differences between whole species), individual human beings are prevented from seeing in themselves what is characteristic of all people and seeing in all people what is characteristic of themselves. Full recognition and expression of one's "species being," then, is blocked. (An assumption of this argument is that rational persons basically experience themselves and other beings in terms of categories like natural kinds.) This blockage is expressed by the ascription of ideal human characteristics to divine beings.

For Feuerbach, the degree of progress in history, then, is marked by stages in which people take back into self-characterizations predicates that had been projected onto fantastic beings. This process culminates in the refusal to countenance, however bloodlessly and undescriptively, any divinity at all. In such ideal circumstances, there will be, by definition, no religion. Further, the only entities that will be ontologically certified are those that have their roots exclusively in sensory experience and that can be referred back to sensory particulars as their subjects. Hegel's philosophy, since it fails to pass this ontological test, is not nearly as far beyond religious thinking as its

author hopes. Meanwhile, however, Feuerbach's own theory remains deeply ambiguous about the relation it posits between empiricism and the demand that our experience is categorized in essentialistic terms such as "species being." The basic problem is that one may talk about kinds in ontological terms (roughly essentialism) without thoroughgoing empiricism, and vice versa. Feuerbach seems never to have faced this tension squarely, or even to have recognized it fully. The ambiguity is passed on to Marx. Feuerbach's theory does, however, propose a test for its own verification. It will be verified if there comes to exist a social reality that is jointly characterized by (a) a thoroughgoing empiricism, (b) the disappearance of religion, and (c) sufficiently democratic political institutions to express social equality.

What is crucial is that Marx deeply accepted this complex hypothesis. Some of his first works are an attempt to further Feuerbach's analysis by showing why merely formal democracy is not sufficient to bring about conditions (a) and (b). Marx became convinced, on the basis of contemporary sociological information, especially about America and France, that formal democracy not only can coexist with religion but also can bring about an intensification and interiorization of religious belief. These apparent countercases to Feuerbach's theory never led Marx to suspect the general thesis itself, but they did propel him to find some additional factor (d), which is alleged to be preventing the joint coexistence of (a), (b), and the "real or true democracy" needed for (c). Under the increasing influence of socialist literature, Marx came to find this additional factor in *pure private property*.

Thus, already in his crucial interpretation of Hegel's political philosophy, Marx shows that Hegel's countenancing of transcendent objects and his contempt for empiricism—indeed his whole "upside-down" ontology and epistemology, which makes particular space-time substances dependent on abstract universals rather than the opposite—is of a piece with his justification of antidemocratic politics and private property. The one supports the other. Within the political theory itself, moreover, where Hegel promises a solidarity between rulers and ruled, Marx finds marked "alienation" and "division." Deceptive idealist rhetoric to the contrary, there is no common mind in the state portrayed by Hegel, only the domination of some by others and naked self-interest by all. This estrangement at the political level, Marx concludes, is integrally connected to the justification of private property that Hegel built into his state-construct. It is at this point that Marx commits himself to the thesis that political community (in a Rousseauean sense) is possible if and only if private property is dismantled. Although he speaks of this as a *fulfillment* of democracy (as had the extreme left wing of the popular party during the great French Revolution), it is unclear whether Marx at this time was speaking of a fulfillment of a democratic *state* or had already come to believe what he later clearly proclaimed—that such a "democracy" requires the disappearance and delegitimation of the state itself. The state, in this latter view, comes *by definition* to refer to an institution functioning to restrict property to a particular class or set of classes. Its disappearance, therefore, in genuinely equal social conditions is analytically guaranteed.

Democracy and Property

However one analyzes Marx's views on "true democracy," it is certainly the case that by the time of his essay "On the Jewish Question" (which appeared in *Economic and Philosophic Manuscripts of 1844*), Marx held that formal democracy as a political institution exists merely to preserve bourgeois property rights. As these lead to human separation, competition, and the privatization of experience, they result in the religious-displacement illusions postulated by Feuerbach and in a political life which is something apart from, and dominating, the activities of the individual.

In other essays in the *Economic and Philosophic Manuscripts of 1844*, Marx deepened this analysis by showing *why* private property in its developed bourgeois form (where entitlement to property rests on no qualification beyond formal personhood) leads to this sociopolitical and religious alienation. He first situates this kind of private property in its larger context: that production and distribution system we call laissez-faire capitalism. He does this by way of an analysis of the writings of the political economists. He then more generally lays down what he thinks has since the beginning distinguished the human species from other animal species: a productive capability that is characterized by (1) the intervention of intelligence and foresight into the productive process and (2) a thoroughgoing social organization of production. (Marx couples these two characteristics in such a way that without the one, the other will not continually change and develop.)

These conjoint capacities express themselves in the creation of a "humanized nature" in which people *cooperate* to transform the found materials of their environment into objects that are media for self-expression and that thus permit mutual human recognition in a public sphere. In creativity conceived along artistic lines, then, Marx locates the *sine qua non* of the full mutual recognition that, in different ways, Hegel and Feuerbach were concerned to make possible. Marx's insistence on "social *praxis*" centers on this view of "transformative activity" as the locus of human expression, development, and recognition. This is humanity's "species being." Indeed, in a productive system that appears most distinctively human, self-expression and mutual recognition provide the motive for production, and the securing of more basic needs appears as a concomitant and by-product of the achievement of these recognition-needs. Conversely, where human production is centered on the preservation of "mere existence," human life appears less distinguishable from that of other species, and human production approximates the narrowness of animal production.

Capitalism vs. Socialism

Marx goes on to show that this latter pole is most closely approached in capitalism. Because of the complete dominance of pure private property under capitalism, workers are alienated (1) from the product of their work, since they do not own it, and it cannot therefore express them; (2) from the process of their work, since they sell their own labor capacity, which is their most basic human ("inalienable") attribute; and (3) from other people, since although capitalist production is de facto enormously cooperative and thus socialized, (1) and (2) prevent it from being experienced as the work of consciously cooperating human beings and as a product of their joint activity. Indeed, on the contrary, the economic system appears as something to which people subject themselves as to a fact of nature. It therefore becomes a fetish to them.

Socialism, Marx concludes, by removing private property, allows the basic defining dispositions of human beings to operate freely. This is a program whose time has come, because the skills, tools, and productive capacity of capitalism itself provide the necessary conditions for this fulfillment of human aspiration. Marx found such a call in contemporary communist propaganda literature, which, although frequently written by intellectuals, he took to be a genuine and spontaneous expression of the experience and intelligence of the working class itself. He was also delighted to find in this literature a concomitant rejection of religion and of formal democracy, and thus a confirmation not only of Feuerbach's thesis but also of his (Marx's) own interpretation of it. Marx's enormous and lasting confidence in the working class—which has presented great problems for Marxists—derives, one is tempted to conclude, from his astonishment that the working class had independently arrived at Feuerbach's and his own insights.

Productivity and History

Marx's strategy of situating types of property relations within larger and more comprehensive types of productive relations (first used in 1844), when combined with the judgment that humanity's productive activity is the most central aspect of human experience, suggests a larger project still: redoing Hegel's and Feuerbach's accounts of the historical development of humankind toward full self and mutual recognition on the basis of these presuppositions. Against Hegel, Marx stresses that successive types of consciousness do not unfold out of their own conceptual resources, but rather on the basis of changes in humanity's socially mediated interchange with the environment. Marx believed that Hegel had at one point grasped this in *Die Phänomenologie des Geistes* (1807; *The Phenomenology of Spirit*, 1868; also known as *The Phenomenology of Mind*, 1910), when he spoke of the slave's sense of self-identification as superior to the master's because the former's transformative interaction with nature gives a solidly achieved sense of self, while the latter is subject to the shifting tides of honor and opinion

in an elitist world cut off from its productive roots. However, these ideas were soon buried, and Hegel constructs his history as the history of consciousness moving on its own steam toward "theoretical" self-appropriation. Against Feuerbach, Marx stresses that the progressive taking back of alienated human properties from postulated divinities cannot be displayed as moving toward a passive, sensationalistic empiricism of the English sort, with its concomitant pleasure ethic, political indifference, and historical blindness. For Marx, people recognize their own essence (*Wesen*) in and by their productive activity, and therefore progressively in proportion as they make nature a home that expresses themselves ("humanized nature"). This Marx calls "active or practical materialism," as opposed to Feuerbach's "speculative" materialism.

The first attempt to carry out this historical project occurs in *The German Ideology*, on which Marx collaborated with Engels. What stands out in this account is a conscious attempt both to suppress the essentialistic language that had hitherto characterized Marx's thinking and to insist upon the empiricist credentials of the authors. What is to be traced is a *factual* history of the human race, in which changing forms of production determine corresponding sociopolitical patterns and legitimating ideologies. Essentialistic language would automatically imply, it is asserted, that the determination works the other way around, as in Hegel, and (it is now insisted) in the Young Hegelians as well. Nevertheless, looked at more closely, what we actually find here is a history with a high degree of quasi-logical and dialectical patterning, and a suspicion arises that the forecast of the coming socialist order with which the work culminates is derived as much from his dialectical machinery as from the empiricistic database on which we are merely *told* that it rests. It is plausible to think, then, that some essentialism, and indeed some Hegelian dialectic of consciousness, lurks inside these empiricist trappings. The resolution of this tension between contingent empirical fact and necessary quasi-logical unfolding in accounting for human history constitutes the most difficult and vital problem in the analysis of Marx's mature philosophical commitments. Two other problems are associated with it: (1) How is either empiricism or quasi logicism consistent with Marx's claim that human agents freely make their own history? and (2) How is Marx capable of exempting his own analyses from the sociopolitical and economic determinism on which, in his view, it would appear *all* intellectual products rest?

Two Marxes?

Orthodox Marxism had long committed itself and Marx to a rather deterministic theory of the kind worked out by Engels in *Herrn Eugen Dührings Umwälzung der Wissenschaft* (1878; *Anti-Dühring*, 1907) and *Dialektik der Natur* (1925; *Dialectics of Nature*, 1941) and had thus allowed Marx's insistence on free human activity to escape from view. The problem of self-referencing was also bypassed by simply asserting that Marxism is a "science" that grounds its judgments in the way that natural science does. The publication of the early manuscripts may well have scandalized proponents of these views, but it was always possible to take the tack of calling these manuscripts juvenilia. For several decades the central issue in Marx scholarship, then, centered on where precisely to draw the line between the young Marx and his mature scientific-deterministic successor, who presented in *Das Kapital* (1867, 1885, 1894; *Capital: A Critique of Political Economy*, 1886, 1907, 1909; better known as *Das Kapital*) the laws by which capitalism inevitably gives way to socialism.

The publication of *Foundations of the Critique of Political Economy*, however, demonstrated that the habits of mind frequently associated with the younger Marx were still operating in Marx's thinking while he was writing *Das Kapital*, if somewhat behind the scenes. Those who still wished to speak of two Marxes were then driven to think of them as two alternating sides of a single Marx that vied with each other until the end. More challenging approaches, however, have tried to demonstrate that the understanding of *Das Kapital* that the study of *Foundations of the Critique of Political Economy* makes possible shows a coherence of the later view with the earlier one at the expense of Marx's alleged scientism. The main point is to challenge the quasi-deterministic interpretation of *Das Kapital* itself. The correct disposition of these issues, however, is still far from accomplished.

David J. Depew, updated by John K. Roth

Additional Reading

Arnold, N. Scott. *Marx's Radical Critique of Capitalist Society: A Reconstruction and Critical Evaluation*. New York: Oxford University Press, 1990. Arnold provides a careful and detailed account of Marx's analysis of capitalism.

Avineri, Shlomo. *The Social and Political Thought of Karl Marx*. Cambridge, England: Cambridge University Press, 1969. Emphasizes the ways in which Marx's thought develops from his critique of Hegel.

Berlin, Isaiah. *Karl Marx: His Life and Environment*. 4th ed. New York: Oxford University Press, 1996. A prominent twentieth century interpreter offers a helpful study of Marx.

Bottomore, Tom, ed. *Interpretations of Marx*. New York: Blackwell, 1988. A worthwhile collection of essays by prominent scholars on various aspects of Marx's thought.

Carver, Terrell, ed. *The Cambridge Companion to Marx*. Cambridge, England: Cambridge University Press, 1991. Essays explain and criticize a wide variety of themes, problems, and methodological issues in Marx's philosophy.

Curtis, Michael, ed. *Marxism: The Inner Dialogues*. 2d ed. New Brunswick, N.J.: Transaction, 1997. Significant essays explore various interpretations of Marx's contributions to political, economic, and philosophical life.

Eagleton, Terry. *Marx*. New York: Routledge, 1999. An excellent biographical introduction to the thoughts of the philosopher, clearly presented and requiring no special background. Bibliography.

Fischer, Ernst. *How to Read Karl Marx*. New York: Monthly Review Press, 1996. Updates ways in which Marx may be interpreted and understood.

McLellan, David. *Karl Marx: His Life and Thought*. New York: Harper & Row, 1973. A reliable critical biography of Marx by a prominent scholar.

Rader, Melvin. *Marx's Interpretation of History*. New York: Oxford University Press, 1979. Evaluates the varied and at times competing interpretations of history that can be found in Marxist scholarship as well as in the philosophy of Marx itself.

Rosenthal, John. *The Myth of Dialectics: Reinterpreting the Marx-Hegel Relation*. New York: St. Martin's Press, 1998. An effort to reappraise the important relationship between Hegel and Marx.

Singer, Peter. *Marx*. New York: Oxford University Press, 1980. A brief but informative introduction to Marx's life and major ideas.

Smith, Cyril. *Marx at the Millennium*. Chicago: Pluto Press, 1996. Takes stock of the contribu-tions and implications of Marx's philosophy as the twentieth century draws to a close.

Suchting, W. A. *Marx: An Introduction*. New York: New York University Press, 1983. A good criti-cal biography of Marx presented chronologi-cally and by topic.

Thomas F. Barrry, updated by John K. Roth

Marcel Mauss

Combining strong philosophical training with sociological interests, Mauss was one of the key figures in twentieth century French sociology. Generally considered one of the pioneers of functionalist methodology, he made major contributions to sociological thought in the areas of the theory of religion, economic exchange, and primitive classification.

Principal philosophical works: "Esquisse d'une théorie générale de la magie," 1902-1903 (with H. Hubert; *A General Theory of Magic*, 1972); *De quelques formes primitives de classification*, 1903 (with Émile Durkheim; *Primitive Classification*, 1963); "Essai sur les variations saisonnières des sociétés Eskimo: Étude de morphologie sociale," 1904-1905 (with H. Beauchat; *Seasonal Variations of the Eskimo: A Study in Social Morphology*, 1979); "L'Art et le mythe d'après M. Wundt," 1909; "Essai sur le don: Forme et raison de l'échange dans les sociétés archaïques," 1923-1924 (*The Gift: Forms and Functions of Exchange in Archaic Societies*, 1954); "Rapports réels et pratiques de la psychologie et de la sociologie," 1924 ("Real and Practical Relations Between Psychology and Sociology," 1979); "Commentaires sur un texte de Posidonius: Le Suicide, contre-prestation suprême," 1925; "Effet physique chez l'individu de l'idée de mort suggérée par la collectivité (Australie, Nouvelle-Zélande)," 1926 ("The Physical Effect on the Individual of the Idea of Death Suggested by the Collectivity," 1979); "Wette, wedding," 1928; "Biens masculins et féminins en droit celtique," 1929; "Les Techniques du corps," 1936 ("Body Techniques," 1979); "Une Catégorie de l'esprit humain: La Notion de personne, cell de 'moi,'" 1938 ("A Category of the Human Mind: The Notion of Person, the Notion of 'Self,'" 1979); *Sociologie et anthropologie*, 1950 (*Sociology and Psychology*, 1979); *Œuvres*, 1969-1975.

Born: May 10, 1872; Épinal, France
Died: February 10, 1950; Paris, France

Early Life

Born and reared in a firmly orthodox Jewish family, Marcel Mauss was the nephew of Émile Durkheim, already at the time of Mauss's birth one of the leading figures in French sociology. Durkheim, who took pains to direct his nephew's education, both early and late, steered Mauss toward philosophical studies at Bordeaux, where he was thoroughly grounded in neo-Kantian thought. Later, at the École Practique des Hautes Études, Mauss turned to the history of religion, and in 1897-1898 he embarked upon a tour that included a period of study under British social theorist Edward Tylor, often considered the father of cultural anthropology. During his university years, Mauss also began an intensive study of languages, including Greek, Latin, Hebrew, and Sanskrit, that would serve him well throughout his career. By 1901, Mauss had assumed a teaching chair at the École Practique in the history of the religion and philosophy of "noncivilized" peoples, a position he held for the rest of his life.

Life's Work

Durkheim's intellectual influence on Mauss can hardly be overstated. The earliest fruit of their collaboration (which lasted until the elder man's death in 1917) was the study *Primitive Classification*. Its assemblage of factual materials reflects Mauss's more empirical bent, and the theoretical interpretation is largely Durkheim's. Considered a pioneering effort to uncover the origins of such classifications as space, time, number, and hierarchy in the social structure, *Primitive Classification* theorizes from data gathered from studies of Australian aborigines and the American Zuñi, as well as from traditional Chinese culture. The work's methodology, which seeks to establish formal correspondences between social and symbolic classifications, reflects Durkheim's lifelong insistence on the unity of all social phenomena—a conviction that Mauss shared. Although *Primitive Classification* has met with substantial criticism over the years, it remains an important and influential theoretical contribution.

Although *Primitive Classification* is the only major work formally coauthored by Durkheim and Mauss, it is important to note that all of Mauss's work was produced through intimate collaboration with the group of disciples and students that formed the Durkheim circle. As early as 1898, the Durkheim group founded *L'Année sociologique*, both the name of the journal in which most of their work first appeared and the moniker by which the circle itself was known. Aside from Mauss, the school of Durkheim included Henri Hubert and Paul Fauconnet. The emergence of such a school, whose thought and methodology were remarkably unified, was made possible first of all by the unsystematic nature of Durkheim's approach to sociology. Although the term *functionalism* has long been associated with the *Année sociologique*, the Durkheimian method was largely free of dogmatism. It amounted to a set of questions, problems, and suggestions applicable across a range of fields, including religion, law, morals, demography, and economics. Another reason for the emergence and cohesion of the school was Durkheim's conviction that sociology as a science must not be isolated from the process of political and social change. The Durkheim circle, and especially Mauss, were deeply committed democratic socialists and saw the ultimate purpose of their work as advancing social reform.

Most important, however, the Durkheimists were unified by their common commitment to an overriding methodological principle: The proper object of sociological study is the whole of society; no social fact should be studied in isolation from the total range of social phenomena. Mauss's own commitment to such a principle is evident in another early collaborative work, his *Essai sur la nature et la fonction du sacrifice* (1898; *Sacrifice: Its Nature and Function*, 1962), coauthored with Henri Hubert and first published in *L'Année sociologique*. In this study, Hubert and Mauss built

particularly upon the earlier work of Scottish Semitic scholar William Robertson Smith while rejecting his methodology. Sacrifice, according to Smith, should be understood in evolutionary or genetic terms. Thus, sacrifice as first practiced emerged out of primitive hunting and nomadic cultures and involved the immolation and consumption of totem animals in a communal meal. Later, according to this genealogy, the totemistic aspect of sacrifice disappears, while the communal aspect is refined, as in the religion of the Semites, whose sacrificial practices were the focus of Smith's theorizing. Against this genetic thesis, Hubert and Mauss argue for the methodological primacy of "typical facts." What is important, they claim, is not to establish a theory of sacrifice based upon a causal chain of historical descent, but to grasp what is most typical or representative of sacrifice across the total range of social praxis.

In attempting to bring this methodology to bear upon the reality of sacrifice and thus to formulate a general theory, Hubert and Mauss focus on two cultures whose sacrificial ethos was well documented: those of India (in the Vedas) and Israel. What is to be concluded from such a study, they argue, is that the most primordial component of sacrifice is the expulsion of a sacred spirit, whether pure or impure. Rites of expulsion, negotiating between the realms of the sacred and the profane, replace Smith's emphasis on communion as the fundamental element of sacrifice. In the quintessential sacrificial act, claim Hubert and Mauss, the separation between the divine and the human spheres is overcome. It is true that they recognize communion as one aspect of sacrifice, but they emphatically reject the notion that various kinds of sacrifices are the offspring of some earlier, simpler form. All the sacrifices of which people are aware, they argue, are already complex social forms. The apparently various sacrificial forms nevertheless possess a fundamental unity, which is in turn a question of process—a process that involves the establishment of a line of communication between the sacred and profane worlds by way of an intermediary, or sacrificial victim.

In the years before World War I, Mauss took a leading role in editing *L'Année sociologique*, and along with Hubert he directed its religious sociology section. In addition, he collaborated in the writing of several other sections and contributed a substantial number of reviews and notes. Under Mauss's direction, the journal became the principal means by which the discipline of sociology was established in France on a solidly professional basis. Its contributors were not only sociologists; they included members of a range of related fields in the social sciences, particularly those who shared the methodological aims of the journal.

World War I claimed the lives of a number of *L'Année sociologique*'s collaborators. The effects of the war, followed by the death of the journal's founder, Durkheim, threatened to bring a unique and profoundly influential project to a halt. In the years following his master's death, however, Mauss assumed the central role in the group and twice revived the journal after its collapse (once for several years in the 1920's, and again in the 1930's). Also during this period, while pursuing his own research, he devotedly edited posthumous works by Durkheim, Hubert, and others.

Although some historians have seen Mauss's contribution to sociology as merely a continuation of Durkheim's methods, others have detected a significant break. There can be no doubt that until the end of his career, Mauss carried on in the spirit of Durkheim and continued to adhere to the central vision of an integrated sociology, understood as the science of total social facts. On the other hand, with the publication of Mauss's single most important work, "Essai sur le don: Forme et raison de l'échange dans les sociétés archaïques" (1923-1924; *The Gift: Forms and Functions of Exchange in Archaic Societies*, 1954), a significant shift, amounting to a reform of Durkheimian method, is indicated. Whereas for Durkheim an integrated sociology was focused on the social *collective*, Mauss attempts in *The Gift* and in subsequent works to strike a balance between the collective and the individual. Collective ideas are no longer the primary locus of the cultural process; rather, a true understanding of people within the social milieu must also include the person in his or her individuality—an emphasis that opens the way for the integration of psychology into the sociological sphere in a far more significant fashion than Durkheim would have countenanced.

The Gift is among the earliest studies of gift exchange in primitive societies, and the first to inquire systematically into the norm of reciprocity that, according to Mauss, governs gift exchange. Relying, as was his custom, on the fieldwork of others, Mauss examines the rites of exchange in Melanesia, Polynesia, and the American Northwest, as well as in the premodern Germanic, Roman, and Brahmanic Indian cultures. Contrary to the prevailing view that primitive economies lacked markets, Mauss is able to show that economic life in the archaic world is part of a totality that includes religious, moral, legal, aesthetic, and mythological elements. In other words, each of these cultural elements is inextricably related to all the others, and no act of exchange can be interpreted narrowly as merely economic. In all the societies examined, Mauss finds clear evidence of what he terms obligatory, or reciprocal, gift exchange. Unlike the exchange of gifts in modern societies, primitive rites of exchange always involve the obligation to give gifts, to receive gifts, and to repay gifts given. Such obligations generally are accompanied by formal ritual and governed by a variety of sanctions. In most cases, exchange in the societies studied may be termed *total prestation*, a phrase that Mauss employs to suggest that within such cultures everything of real importance—birth, death, marriage, kinship, warfare, and so on—is intrinsically related to, or woven into the web of, gift giving. As for purely utilitarian forms of exchange, these either are nonexistent in archaic societies, or they exist only in a subsidiary fashion alongside the system of gift exchange. Finally, Mauss asserts that the object exchanged in primitive gift giving is itself in some sense a "person"; that is, a spirit (in Maori, the *hau*) inhabits the gift, which can never be alienated from the original giver. Thus, ownership in gift-giving societies is never absolute.

Underlying Mauss's study of prestation in primitive societies was a set of political commitments that were consistently held throughout his life. As early as 1904, he was taking part in a range of socialist activities, participating in support groups for striking workers, campaigning for democratic socialist candidates, and deeply involved in the cooperative movement. Both Durkheim and Mauss looked to the corporations of the high Middle Ages as exemplars of social and economic life, and they believed that the advent of capitalism had exacerbated social divisions to a pathological degree. Neither Mauss nor Durkheim, however, ever supported the communist alternative, fearing its totalitarian tendencies. Mauss's politics are strikingly in evidence in *The Gift*; in a final chapter, he upholds the reciprocal system of obligations as a model for the reform of modern economic life.

Although Mauss remained active as a teacher and a scholar throughout the 1920's and most of the 1930's, his career was effectively brought to an end by the German invasion of France and the subsequent disintegration of *L'Année sociologique*. A number of his scholarly projects remained unfinished at the end of his life, including works on the sociology of money and prayer, and the manuscripts are believed to have been destroyed during World War II.

Influence

Mauss's influence, both as a faithful disciple of Durkheimian functionalism and as an original theorist in his own right, has been extensive. As a central figure in *L'Année sociologique*, Mauss, especially after Durkheim's death, could be credited with maintaining the cohesion of the group and thus with advancing its influence as a sociological movement not only in France but to some degree in the Anglo-Saxon nations as well. Among French sociologists and ethnologists, such well-known figures as Georges Dumézil, Louis Dumont, and, most important, Claude Lévi-Strauss were directly inspired by Mauss—the latter having claimed for *The Gift* the status of a major turning point in the history of the social sciences. In the reciprocal pattern of exchanges that Mauss explored in *The Gift*, Lévi-Strauss found the essential formula for his own structuralist account of primitive mentality and social structure. Mauss's influence has also spread in more recent years into the broader areas of social theory and philosophy, as is evidenced by the profound impact *The Gift* has had and continues to have on the writings of Jean Baudrillard and, more recently, Jacques Derrida, the father of deconstructionist theory. For Baudrillard, especially, the patterns of symbolic exchange discussed in *The Gift* serve as a model whereby the simulacral

economies of postindustrial capitalism may be critiqued and supplanted.

Jack E. Trotter

The Gift

Forms and Functions of Exchange in Archaic Societies

Type of philosophy: Ethics, social philosophy
First published: "Essai sur le don: Forme et raison de l'échange dans les sociétés archaïques," in *L'Année sociologique*, 1923-1924 (English translation, 1954)
Principal ideas advanced:
◇ The exchange of gifts in primitive societies should not be studied in isolation from other aspects of archaic life such as the economic, juridical, moral, aesthetic, or religious.
◇ Gift exchange in primitive society, though appearing gratuitous, is in fact governed by a system of obligations.
◇ The system of obligatory gift exchange offers important lessons for the development of social solidarity in modern societies.

The Gift may best be understood within the context of Marcel Mauss's attempt to develop a sociological approach to economic phenomena. Contrary to the predominant understanding of economics, Mauss saw economic transactions not in isolation from other social phenomena, but as part of a social totality. This sociological approach to economic relations may be traced back as far as French mathematician and philosopher Auguste Comte's claims, in the 1800's, that economic theorists were mistaken in viewing the economy as an autonomous, fully rationalized entity.

A Theory of Gift Exchange

Mauss initiates his investigation into gift exchange in archaic societies by posing two questions: What is the principle by which a gift received must be repaid? and What force is there in the thing given that compels the recipient to make a return? Relying on the fieldwork of a number of anthropologists, Mauss focuses his inquiry primarily on the tribal customs of the peoples of Melanesia, Polynesia, and the American Pacific Northwest. Contrary to the standard view, according to which primitive societies lack economic markets in any but the most rudimentary sense, the evidence provided by a study of these cultures suggests strongly that such societies possess highly developed and symbolically elaborate markets for the exchange of economic goods.

Whereas the market in modern societies is understood to be a discrete sphere of fully rationalized activity, the primitive market is at once economic, moral, aesthetic, and religious. Market exchanges are not enacted, as in modern society, primarily between individuals but between groups, such as families, clans, and tribes. Also, although material objects of recognized value are often objects of primitive exchange, such exchange may additionally involve human beings (women and children), feasts, military aid, or highly symbolic "goods" such as entertainments. This system of exchange in the broadest sense of the term may be called *total prestation*.

Although archaic societies do engage in buying, selling, and barter, these transactions are subsidiary to and take place largely within the broader context of reciprocal exchange, or gift giving and receiving. Essential to an understanding of the system of reciprocal exchange is its *involuntary* nature. Primitive gift giving may appear to be gratuitous, but in fact it involves a delicate balance of expectations and obligations. It is not a discrete act but an elaborate continuation of social relations. Moreover, this obligatory system of gift exchange is hedged by powerful sanctions including, at the most extreme, acts of war.

Mauss distinguishes three types of obligation: the obligation to give gifts, the obligation to receive gifts, and the obligation to repay gifts received. Motivating the circularity of obligation is the belief, which Mauss illustrates with examples taken from Samoan culture, that gifts exchanged under obligation contain an intrinsically magical power, a *mana*. In Samoan culture this *mana*, or *hau*, which inhabits the gift is inextricably a part of its original owner and cannot, like a modern gift, be considered inert. Rather, the gift is a "person" in its own right and even when abandoned

by its owner can never truly be alienated from him or her. The *hau* that resides in the gift demands repatriation; the one who receives the gift must repay in turn through the giving of some equivalent gift.

Mauss summarizes the system of obligation in Samoa when he notes that in all instances of exchange, there are generally acknowledged rights and duties concerned with consuming and repaying existing alongside those concerned with giving and receiving. This pattern of reciprocity is highly symmetrical and is above all a pattern of spiritual bonds between things that are also persons. The system is also perpetual, an endless chain of giving and receiving, passing and repassing between individuals, families, clans, tribes, sexes, and generations, as well as between all of these and the gods.

Commonalities in Gift Exchange

Mauss declines to offer a general theory explaining how the system of gift exchange must have spread geographically; nevertheless, he finds common traits of the system not only in Polynesia, Melanesia, and the American Pacific Northwest but also among the pygmies of Africa and in Indo-European cultures. Among these common traits are the rules of generosity. To illustrate the rule-bound nature of obligatory generosity, Mauss examines the gift-giving rituals of the Andaman islanders in Southeast Asia. Here a friendly rivalry characterizes the exchange of presents, with highest distinction belonging to those who give the most valuable gifts. Although most of the needs of Andaman islanders are met through such obligatory exchanges, the primary purpose of exchange is not practical but moral. Exchange seeks above all to enhance amicable relations among those involved. So powerful is the bond created through the system of reciprocity that an identity of persons is thereby established. Parties to an exchange are placed under a perpetual obligation to exchange further gifts. Rites of reunion, weeping, and embracing may accompany such perpetual acts of giving and may be considered the symbolic equivalents of exchange.

Turning to the principles, motives, and intensity of gift exchange, Mauss finds the clearest examples in Melanesia, among the Trobriand islanders, whose system of prestation is called the *kula*, a form of exchange that must be further distinguished from the *gimwali*, a mere straightforward exchange of useful goods that functions in supplementary fashion within the total system, but which is regarded by the islanders as inferior to the more aristocratic *kula*. Whereas the *gimwali* is exemplified by aggressive bargaining, the *kula* is undertaken only by chiefs who, as representatives of their tribes or villages, exchange a variety of valuable goods in a highly ceremonial and apparently disinterested fashion. The term *kula* can be translated as "ring" and thus serves as a metaphor for the circularity of exchange, which among the Trobrianders involves maritime expeditions between islands on days specifically set aside for intertribal gift exchange and feasting. The circle of mutual obligation is dispersed over a vast territorial expanse, knitting together the various island tribes into a single cultural unit. Theoretically, the valuables of the *kula* never cease to circulate. The gift received is the property of the recipient, but this ownership is both possession and loan, a trust and a pledge of future giving.

Among the highly developed and wealthy tribes of the northwest coast of America, Mauss finds the most accentuated form of total prestation, the *potlatch*. During the summer months the northwest American tribes do their hunting and fishing, and in general accomplish most of the practical business of life. Radically distinct from this are the winter months, the period of the *potlatch*, which are feverish with the movement of tribes. This is the season of feasts, marriages, and visitations, and upon all such occasions the rituals of the *potlatch* are much in evidence. All the goods that have been hoarded during the summer months of industry are squandered without restraint in highly competitive rites of exchange and consumption. Central to the process of socialization mediated by the *potlatch* are the activities of various intertribal societies, such as the men's and women's societies of the Kwakiutl, which cut across tribal lines.

Two further traits associated with total prestation are especially evident among the northwest American tribes: credit and honor. According to modern economic theory, sale on credit is the product of a long evolutionary development and

was unknown among primitive tribes. The origins of credit, however, do not conform to the usual evolutionary model. Among the northwest American tribes, gift giving and receiving account for the whole of economic life. Within the context of such total prestation, the notion of credit is implicit. It is in the nature of the gift that it cannot be repaid at once; thus, the notion of time, so crucial to the idea of credit, is already well developed in the *potlatch* and similar systems. In paying a visit, contracting a marriage or alliance, making a treaty, or attending a feast, the idea of time—the deferral of counter-prestation according to a prescribed place and date—is ever assumed and woven into the fabric of the *potlatch*. Barter arises only later, by way of a simplification of the system of gift giving on borrowed time, or credit.

The role of honor is central to systems of gift exchange, particularly in the *potlatch*, to the degree that the prestige of an individual is tied closely to expenditure. In the *potlatch*, one not only returns gifts but returns them with interest. To do otherwise would compromise both individual and tribal honor. Among the northwestern American tribes, therefore, competitive gift giving is displayed in the most extreme forms and transcends the usual rituals of exchange. Some systems of *potlatch* require the expenditure of the whole of one's possessions, reserving nothing. Rivalry and antagonism, motivated by what may seem an exaggerated notion of honor, are basic elements of such systems. Political status, social rank, marriages, and alliances all are treated as a conflict of wealth. Accumulation of wealth occurs solely for the purposes of expenditure, or unadulterated destruction—for example, burning all one's possessions or casting them into the sea—to humiliate a rival.

Indo-European and European Cultures

Turning to an examination of gift exchange in Indo-European cultures, Mauss draws his examples from ancient Roman, Hindu, and Germanic custom. Here he wishes to establish that the distinction between "pure" gift giving and obligatory exchange is of relatively recent vintage even in such highly advanced civilizations. In ancient Rome, for example, where scholars generally assume a distinction between gift giving and obligatory exchange, the concept of the *nexum*, or legal bond, reveals a substratum of obligatory exchange. The oldest form of contract in Roman law, the *nexum*, reveals an affinity with the Melanesian *hau*, wherein the object exchanged is identified with the person who offers the object, thus establishing a personal bond and an obligatory element that the more familiar written contract of sale in modern exchange does not assume. In Brahmanic India, there is clear evidence of ritual of the *potlatch* type depicted in the *Vedas* and inscribed in the Brahmanic Code. Here again, the crucial similarity to the *potlatch* is the obligatory nature of gift exchange and the confusion of persons with objects given. Likewise, the obligatory nature of gift giving in premodern Germanic culture is evidenced by etymologies of the numerous cognates of the German term for gift giving (*geben*), as well as in elaborately documented studies of Germanic folklore. Moreover, the notion of the pledge, or *wadium*, in Germanic custom displays a clear affinity to the Roman *nexum*. In both cases, to give an object in exchange is also to give a part of oneself, a part that resides in the object and that may carry its own intrinsic sanctions in the form of magical spells.

Finally, Mauss offers a number of observations on the social and economic life of societies such as those of Europe. It is only in Western societies that people have been turned into purely economic animals. This has produced severe social consequences, most evidently in the rise of class warfare, which is itself but a symptom of widespread social disintegration. On the other hand, recent movements have led to a new awareness of the need for social solidarity and responsibility. The concept of social insurance, for example, undertaken by the state for the benefit of the old, the infirm, and the unemployed, is not so much a novel development as a return to the premodern system of total prestation. From this recognition, a further course of action should be deduced. It is crucial that in modern societies, the wealthy should come to understand themselves as the benefactors of the whole social body. Whether at the level of the state or on the part of individuals, a system of obligatory giving should become the binding force of society. Limits should be placed on those forms of economic activity undertaken for sheer profit alone, such as market speculation

and usury. Honor, disinterestedness, and corporate solidarity should become the watchwords of a revitalized civilization.

Historians of sociology generally agree that *The Gift* is Mauss's single most influential work. Certainly it was the first systematic attempt to elaborate the relationship between patterns of exchange and the social structure as a whole. The main line of influence of *The Gift* has been on French ethnology, particularly on the work of structural anthropologists such as Claude Lévi-Strauss, who regarded the work as a major turning point in the development of sociological method. In addition, *The Gift* has stimulated many further studies, including extensive fieldwork, on the problems of ceremonial exchange and kinship organization in primitive societies. Although specific aspects of Mauss's view of gift exchange have been challenged, his fundamental argument remains widely accepted.

Jack E. Trotter

Additional Reading

Durkheim, Émile, and Marcel Mauss. *Primitive Classification*. Edited and translated by Rodney Needham. Chicago: University of Chicago Press, 1963. Needham's introduction to this translation provides a reliable guide to the methodology employed by Durkheim and Mauss throughout their research and is particularly helpful in highlighting the significance of the principle of interpreting social "facts" only in relation to the totality of a social complex. *The Gift* is generally recognized as the outstanding example of this methodology.

Gane, Mike. *The Radical Sociology of Durkheim and Mauss*. London: Routledge, 1992. Although much of this volume by a well-known American sociologist deals with Durkheim and the philosophical school *L'Année sociologique*, chapter 6, titled "Institutional Socialism and the Sociological Critique of Communism," deals at length with the political involvements that informed and, to some degree, motivated the writing of *The Gift*. Gane depicts Mauss as a deeply committed democratic socialist opposed to the totalitarian extremes of communism, on one hand, and the alienating, socially irresponsible tendencies of capitalism on the other. Gane's reconstruction of Mauss's politics is particularly helpful in illuminating the final chapter of *The Gift*, which attempts to hold up the archaic economy of reciprocal exchange as a political model for modern times.

Godelier, Maurice. *The Enigma of the Gift*. Translated by Nora Scott. Chicago: University of Chicago Press, 1999. Provides an analyis of the work of Mauss.

James, Wendy, and N. J. Allen, eds. *Marcel Mauss: A Centenary Tribute*. New York: Berghahn Books, 1998. An homage to the work of Marcel Mauss that affirms the enduring significance of his ideas.

Lévi-Strauss, Claude. "French Sociology." In *Twentieth Century Sociology*, edited by Georges Gurvitch and Wilbert E. Moore. New York: Philosophical Library, 1945. Lévi-Strauss's introduction to French sociology is dedicated to Mauss and focuses largely on the contribution of Durkheim, Mauss, and *L'Année sociologique* to the development of modern sociology. Lévi-Strauss's work is particularly useful for an understanding of the close ties in the French tradition between sociological research and social criticism. Lévi-Strauss appraises the central importance of *The Gift* and reviews some early criticism of the work.

Raison, Timothy, ed. *The Founding Fathers of Sociology*. London: Scholar Press, 1979. This anthology is intended to introduce the student of sociology to the leading figures of the tradition, and it contains useful chapters on both Mauss and Durkheim. The chapter on Mauss, by Michael Wood, contains several insightful pages on *The Gift*, illuminating some of the central problems raised by the work. Wood's style is highly readable and should present no difficulties for the uninitiated.

Sahlins, Marshall. *Stone Age Economics*. Chicago: Aldine Atherton, 1972. This well-known text contains an outstanding chapter on *The Gift* ("The Spirit of the Gift") that examines Mauss's interpretation of the *hau* as the master concept of the work. Sahlins reviews the substantial criticism directed at this concept and contributes his own reinterpretation of the meaning of the *hau*. This chapter is outstanding for its explication of the tradition of political philosophy that lies behind *The Gift*, informing its fundamental assumptions.

Szacki, Jerzy. *History of Sociological Thought*. Westport, Conn.: Greenwood Press, 1979. No serious understanding of Mauss's work, including *The Gift*, is possible without some knowledge of his collaboration with the other members of the sociological circle that formed around Émile Durkheim, *L'Année sociologique*. Even *The Gift*, which bears only Mauss's name, was a collaborative work. Szacki is especially good at delineating the principles that bound the circle together and at demonstrating precisely where Mauss, Durkheim's most prominent student, parted company with the master.

Jack E. Trotter

John S. Mbiti

Collecting and synthesizing indigenous concepts of God, myths and stories, prayers, and proverbs into a religiously oriented "African worldview," Mbiti has explored the complex relationship between African and Christian ontology, theology, and ethics.

Principal philosophical works: *African Religions and Philosophy*, 1969, rev. ed. 1990; *Concepts of God in Africa*, 1970; *The Crisis of Mission in Africa*, 1971; *New Testament Eschatology in an African Background: A Study of the Encounter Between New Testament Theology and African Traditional Concepts*, 1971; *Love and Marriage in Africa*, 1973; *Introduction to African Religion*, 1975, rev. ed. 1991; *The Prayers of African Religion*, 1975; *Bible and Theology in African Christianity*, 1986.

Born: November 30, 1931; Mulango (Kitui), Kenya

Early Life

John Samuel Mbiti, one of six children born to Samuel Mutuvi Ngaangi and Valesi Mbandi Kiimba, was the first to survive; thus, John Samuel was surnamed "Mbiti" (literally "hyena," symbolically "a child vowed unto God"), the name being in effect a prayer in thanksgiving and for survival. His strongly Christian family saw to his religious Westernized academic education, through the African Inland Church; Alliance High School near Nairobi, Kenya; and University College of Makerere, Kampala, Uganda, an "external college" of the University of London. Influenced by a combination of his name, an early personal religious experience, and his undergraduate studies and teachers, Mbiti was moving toward the priesthood when he graduated from Makerere in 1953. He received another bachelor of arts degree and a bachelor of theology degree from Barrington College in Rhode Island in 1956 and 1957, lectured on religion in Kenya and in England in the late 1950's, and earned a Ph.D. in theology at Cambridge University in 1963. His doctoral dissertation, "Christian Eschatology in Relation to the Evangelisation of Tribal Africa," was of seminal importance for his subsequent theological and philosophical writing. His ordination in the Church of England followed his graduation from Cambridge.

Mbiti's development as a promising young Christian academic is, however, only half the story. He is a member of the Akamba people, who occupy Ukambani, an area in eastern and south-central Kenya. As a boy and a young man, Mbiti was systematically and deeply immersed in Christian life and doctrine. His education was Christian and Western; it was not traditional and African. There was, however, another, informal education for young Mbiti—Akamba stories and the art of storytelling. Evidently, Mbiti was fascinated by the entire process—the stories themselves, the dramatic and poetic narration, the moral and practical lessons they taught, and broadly, the entire vision of the Akamba world they presented. He wrote and published a novel, *Mutunga na Ngewa Yake* (1954), numerous poems and short stories, and an *English-Kamba Vocabulary* (1959). Beyond these, he sought out and recorded about fifteen hundred traditional stories, publishing a representative selection as *Akamba Stories* (1966).

By the age of about thirty, Mbiti was both a budding Christian theologian and a collector and student of materials illuminating portions of traditional African life. At the root of his activities was a profound sense of the needs of a changing Africa, especially its young people. Both Christianity (including Western technological civilization) and African traditionalism were necessary; neither alone was sufficient. Mbiti saw that a conjoining of these elements, a syncretism, must occur, and he would make a major contribution.

Life's Work

Mbiti's approach to the problem of syncretism has always been religious, but initially it was specifically theological. His 1963 Cambridge dissertation, published in 1971 as *New Testament Eschatology in an African Background*, inquires into the deepest psycho-spiritual grounds whereupon Africans and Christians might meet. These grounds are eschatological; that is, they draw on a concern, shared in traditional Akamba society and in Christianity, with the ultimate destiny of human beings. For each, as Mbiti reads the Akamba and the New Testament, this destiny is both otherworldly and corporate. After a relatively brief period of several generations as "living-dead," the Akamba lose individual personhood to a generalized spiritual status in the endlessly receding past, the Tene. Christians, too, understand their being spiritually, but not in the distant past—nor, Mbiti argues, in the future. Instead, they see their spirituality in the present/presence of Christ, whereby individuals become a "many-in-one."

New Testament Eschatology in an African Background is a learned, brilliant, spiritually infused work of comparative theology, much more than a work in "African religions." By 1964, Mbiti had been in the West for most of ten years, in a rarefied intellectual atmosphere. That year, he returned to Africa to teach in the Department of Religious Studies and Philosophy at Makerere University. As he studied, researched, and taught, he moved beyond Akamba to Africa, seeking to understand the worldview of sub-Saharan African peoples as a whole.

Mbiti's movement from theology to religion had parallels in his ecclesiastical and personal life. As a clergyman at Makerere, he had the duty of pastoral counseling, often on marriage problems. This counseling reflected and developed Mbiti's abiding concern with practical ethical issues. This concern, and its relation to broader philosophical questions, is manifest in his writings, especially *Love and Marriage in Africa* (1973).

He did not lack firsthand experience with married and family life. On May 15, 1965, Mbiti married Verena Siegenthaler, a teacher of languages and social worker. Verena and John had three daughters (Maria Mwende, Esther Mwende, and Anna Kavata) and a son (Kyeni Samuel). Mbiti became a devoted family man, drawing on this practical experience to help him formulate a well-developed philosophy of marriage incorporating traditional African, Christian, and modern liberal elements.

Throughout the 1960's and early 1970's, Mbiti engaged in extensive research into the beliefs and practices of literally hundreds of African peoples. Always a collector, he amassed roughly three hundred African concepts of God and more than three hundred African prayers, which he published as *Concepts of God in Africa* (1970) and *The Prayers of African Religion* (1975). He also collected roughly twelve thousand traditional African proverbs as a portion of the data for *African Religions and Philosophy* (1969) and *Introduction to African Religion* (1975).

As his research and writing proceeded, Mbiti became convinced of the truth of three fundamental propositions. First, there does exist a traditional African religion, generally held in common by most sub-Saharan peoples. One of the vital parts of this religion is the belief in a single supreme being. Second, African religion implies a philosophical worldview, an ontology, but this ontology is religious rather than more generally metaphysical. Third, African religion is both practical and pervasive throughout all areas of traditional African life, meaning that African religion and philosophy are inseparable from African practice.

None of these propositions implies that Africans are (necessarily) Christians, though Mbiti remained convinced that Christianity is the true religion, solving fundamental religious problems that elude traditional African religion. These religions are joined together, or syncretized, in this respect: Each involves a complete way of life, wherein ontology and spirituality are implicit in daily practice. They are thus set off against any modern Western ontological understanding, in which religion is merely one among a number of discrete areas of activity. Simply put, for the traditional African and the Christian, life is a religious whole, rather than a collection of unrelated or discordant parts.

As Mbiti studied traditional African peoples, he was aware that their ways of life were being changed rapidly by the process of modernization. In his understanding, these ways of life were not primarily secular and material: They were the expression of a people's deepest beliefs and their understanding of ultimate things. To change or lose African practices was tantamount to losing African religion.

While deeply sensitive to the magnitude of this loss, Mbiti remained aware of the power and appeal of the modern West. This helps to explain why, in 1974, he left Africa to join the Ecumenical Institute of the World Council of churches at Bossey (near Geneva), Switzerland, serving as director from 1976 until 1980. Traditional African religion is as vulnerable to change as traditional Africa, and both are subject to a modernization that has become worldwide. Ecumenism cannot simply or purely preserve the African religious worldview; however, it might enable Africa to make its contributions to a world religion that recognizes both the spiritual unity and diversity of human beings.

Naturally, Mbiti brought a heightened awareness of African religion to the Ecumenical Institute at Bossey. His first task was to keep the institute in existence; it faced major financial problems. He was able to do this, in the process demonstrating not merely his commitment but also his practical administrative and fund-raising skills. This accomplished, Mbiti turned his hand to making the institute more fully ecumenical. He promoted increased participation by Christian scholars and practitioners from Asia, Latin America, the Pacific Islands, and Africa. Titles of the institute's publications that he edited suggest the breadth of Mbiti's understanding of the Church: *African and Asian Contributions to Contemporary Theology* (1977), *Confessing Christ in Different Cultures* (1977), *Indigenous Theology and the Universal Church* (1979), and *Christian and Jewish Dialogue on Man* (1980).

Mbiti left the institute at Bossey in 1980. He became parish minister at the Reformed Church at Burgdorf, Switzerland, the next year. In 1983, he began concurrent service as a part-time professor at the University of Bern. He also served as a visiting professor at a number of European and American universities. His research and writing focused on the content of Christianity present in the daily lives of ordinary Africans, with special attention to oral theology, and he collected and studied sermons preached in marketplaces and extemporaneous occasional prayers. This is in keeping with both his very early interest in Akamba storytelling and his conviction that, for Africans, traditional and Christian religion are integral parts of everyday living.

Influence

Mbiti's work is that of a philosophical mediator. He engaged in the process of showing the connections between, and thus brought together, traditional African religions and Christianity, Africa and the West, religion and philosophy, and, most fundamentally, belief and practice. Although this project has much in it of political philosophy, its specifically spiritual dimension makes it practical theology.

The leading thesis of Mbiti's practical theology is this: What remains of traditional Africa provides the fullest possible view of human beings as *homo religiosus*. The tendency of Western critical philosophy has been to understand human beings politically, economically, scientifically, or historically. Each of these human types exists secularly—in the world and in time. Understood ontologically, human beings existing in time are subject to ultimate dissolution and destruction. Only if understood religiously and spiritually may human beings escape this temporal fate.

These ontological reflections explain Mbiti's preoccupation with time. His critics have charged that his linguistic analyses showing that Africans are oriented toward the past rather than the future are both overgeneralized and demeaning. These critics are eager to discover that some African peoples have a well-developed notion of the future. This critical activity, however, misses Mbiti's main point: African religion and philosophy are ontologically *superior* insofar as they avoid thinking in temporal terms. His chief ontological comparison has always been between African religions and Christianity, to the advantage of the latter because Christian spirituality does not fade into a dimly remembered past. Mbiti retained no doubt, however, that African ontology is more sound than any of the varieties of Western secularism.

Thus, with no particular effort except his own philosophical instincts, Mbiti has placed himself in a "postmodern" mode in two important respects. First, he has engaged in ethnic studies of indigenous peoples at the subnational level for nearly a half century. The foundation of these studies has been a respect for the philosophical awareness, religiously expressed, of these peoples. This approach has been labeled *ethnophilosophy*, to contrast it with the specialized and professionalized (and supposedly superior) variety. Mention of ethnophilosophy introduces the second postmodern aspect. If Mbiti is an ethnophilosopher, he is one whose religious ontology calls into question both the progressive, futuristic and the analyzing, differentiating tendencies of modern thinking. The view he urges people to take is of existence as a religious whole. This deep traditionalism is also a characteristic positive postmodern position.

Categorizing Mbiti as a postmodern, however, is as pointless as pinning the ethnophilosopher label on him. Mbiti does not reject modernity in favor of ethnic wisdom; both are part of contemporary Africa. If his work has emphasized the latter over the former, it is because he found it relatively neglected. Moreover, Africa is part of the world, and the world, for Mbiti, is part of a cosmic order in which the temporal is intelligible finally only in the light of the eschatological. In plainer terms, reflection on the human condition intimates a destiny beyond time and space, or beyond the natural to the supernatural. Mbiti has shown, in his life and through his writing, that African peoples share and practice this religious understanding.

John F. Wilson

African Religions and Philosophy

Type of philosophy: African philosophy, ethics, philosophy of religion
First published: 1969
Principal ideas advanced:

◇ African peoples have a philosophical and specifically ontological understanding of things, but that ontology is religious.

◇ The key to grasping this religious ontology is understanding the African notion of time, which is oriented to the past rather than the future.

◇ As Africans leave the present and move into the past, they increasingly assume the status of spirits.

◇ Traditional African religion is informal and practical, presented especially in proverbs and in stories about ancestors who have become spirits.

◇ The African system of ethics dictates a respect for age and authority, and it practically requires family life, because remembrance provides (limited) personal immortality.

◇ African religious philosophy provides collective cohesion but fails to resolve important theological problems and does not adequately prepare Africans for participation in the modern world.

Four fairly distinct philosophical and scholarly traditions form the background to John S. Mbiti's classic treatment of the African worldview. The first is the extensive anthropological literature on individual peoples, begun in the colonial period and continuing during African national independence following World War II. This work provided the data from which a more general "African" perspective might be developed. The second sort of research was specifically into religion, as missionaries and scholars became aware that Africans held well-developed religious views that were not merely "primitive" and "superstitious." A third and related scholarly strand was the growing interest in African philosophy, especially in the question of the ontology or "theory of being" implicit in African beliefs and practices. There was an increasing recognition of Africa's independence from Europe not only politically but philosophically: Africa was emerging as other than a dependent colonial stepchild. Fourth and finally, Mbiti as a Christian minister and an accomplished theologian was a representative of the long tradition of eschatological speculation into the ultimate destiny of human beings. Mbiti drew on all these traditions but was in the unique position of being a native African religious practitioner who combined all four, in his person and in *African Religions and Philosophy*.

A Theory of African Religious Life
The book is a comprehensive treatment of the African understanding of God and humanity. It is

comprehensive in the African, but not the Western, mode. It includes very little on politics and economics, and virtually nothing on history and science. Instead, it rests on the premise that to understand (traditional) African life is to accept this truth: Africans live in a religious universe and are participants in a religious drama. The book is intended to demonstrate this first principle, in order discussing time; God; other spiritual beings; human beings and their institutions, especially the family; death and the afterlife; spiritual power and spiritual "specialists"; ethics; and the developing historical situation in Africa. It is, in sum, African life as viewed from the "inside."

To hold that Africans are a religious people is to say that their understanding of being is spiritual. Mbiti distinguishes five ontological levels, in descending order: God; spirits, including both extra-human beings and deceased humans; living and nascent human beings; the remainder of biological life; and lifeless objects. There is also a sixth sort of being, a power or energy pervading all things. God controls this power, as do spirits to a lesser extent. This ontological hierarchy implies that material objects, with which the modern world is preoccupied, have relatively little reality.

This spiritual ontology illuminates and is illuminated by the African conception of time. That which is most real is spiritual, and that which is spiritual exists most fully in the past. Furthermore, the deeper in the past a (spiritual) being is, the more real it is. In general, each thing that is older is more real than each thing that is younger. Past beings are ontologically (and, Mbiti illustrates, ethically) superior to present beings; future beings barely exist, if they exist at all. Correspondingly, the past—in Swahili, the *Zamani*—has greater reality than the present, the *Sasa*, and it has far greater reality than the future. This ontology, coupled with Mbiti's analysis of East African verb tenses, is the basis of his extremely controversial contention that, traditionally, Africans have virtually no conception of future time.

Thus, movement from present toward past is movement toward being. Aging and then dying place each person on this path from the *Sasa* to the *Zamani*—toward one's ancestors, toward the spirits, and ultimately toward God. This would be very good religious news, except for two problems. The first is that African peoples believe that, deep in the *Zamani*, a close, happy relationship between humans and God was broken, either by accident or through human disobedience. Humans thus came to have a destiny in the *Zamani*, but not a union with God. The second problem is the nature of that ultimate destiny. The African belief is that personal identity is retained only as a "living-dead"; that is, in the first several generations following death when a person's family continues to remember that person. Once personal memory passes and the *Sasa* period is left completely, personality also passes. The person is lost in the collective immortality of undifferentiated spiritedness. The *Zamani* is thus a personal graveyard without the possibility of divine union.

These fundamental religious beliefs are thoroughly intertwined with African institutions and the African psyche. The orientation toward the past encourages a very deep traditionalism. That which is older is more real and more authoritative, and therefore should be revered, maintained, and continued. An endless cycle or pattern of repetition thus becomes the norm. This pattern is the human equivalent of the endless natural cycle. There is a future in the sense of things yet to be, but these things should be and probably will be as they have been previously. Observance of tradition helps to ensure this continuity and predictability.

The most important traditions are in a sense religious, but in the practical sense of being centered on marriage and family life. Traditional African life is family life in marriage, including the complex initiation rites that remove a person from childhood and ready him or her for marriage. Mbiti provides considerable, interesting detail on these rites, which powerfully impress on the individual the absolute necessity of procreation. One must marry and must have children, for religious reasons. Only children ensure the existence of future generations that will remember a person after his or her death, and thus provide the limited personal immortality possible on the *Sasa-Zamani* borderline.

African Forms of Worship
Mbiti argues forcefully that this homage to the departed should not be understood as ancestor worship. Africans worship God and other, lesser

deities. The line between religion and ethics nevertheless is indistinct. The ongoing relationship between the living and the departed might be termed the ethics of generation and generations. Implicit in generation is hierarchy. The debt that the living owe to parents, and parents before them, reaching back to God, is life. Givers of life, in its human and other forms, are superior to receivers; thus, there is no contradiction in worshiping a more remote God and a more proximate Earth Goddess, nor in holding that it is practically impossible for elders and betters to do wrong (because they have done such great good). African ethics is "corporate"—the individual is subordinate to the community—but not merely in the social or spatial sense. The community also, and even primarily, exists in time, reaching back in the deep *Zamani* to God. There thus exists an African spatial-temporal cosmos that is less material than ethical and spiritual.

The African reverence for and celebration of life might suggest a wholly positive attitude toward spirits. There is, however, a pronounced tension between spiritualism—or spiritism—and traditionalism. African peoples very much value continuity, predictability, and a routinized future. That which is out of the ordinary—the birth of twins is a common example—is unsettling and often considered evil. The African view of God is that He usually and perhaps always does good. Evil exists, however, and an effort is made to explain it. Evil does not exist by chance, nor as a result of the activity of the (usually) friendly and familiar living-dead. Instead, evil is caused by those depersonalized spirits which exist deep in the *Zamani*, remote from living people. The spirits have some relation to that power or force—the sixth ontological category mentioned earlier—which pervades the universe and operates across space and time.

Africans are very wary of this force, and they are both respectful and wary of those living persons who have unusual access to it. In this attitude toward spiritual power, Mbiti sees the paradoxical quality of intensely communal African life. Individuals are spiritually close but quite unsure how spiritual power will be used; to be spiritually open is to be spiritually vulnerable. On a practical level, spiritual specialists such as medicine men, mediums, and rainmakers func-

tion and are consulted. "Good magic" and/or protection against "evil magic" is sought. On the ontological and cosmological levels, however, the problem is difficult to address rationally, let alone resolve. If one believes the universe to be fundamentally spiritual, yet is unsure whether the spiritual power is good or evil, what attitude toward the universe does one adopt?

Limits of African Traditionalism

Mbiti sees, in this absence of a clear religious good news, the limitations of traditional African religious ontology. The lesser limitation is secular. The lack of a notion of a future that is dynamic, changing, and progressive ill prepares Africans for participation in the modern world. Mbiti, however, is far from convinced of the wisdom of many modern institutions, especially of formal intellectual education, which fails to prepare young people for practical family life.

It is not, then, the general African worldview that Mbiti finds inadequate: It is the specific understanding of a person's spiritual destiny and, by implication, the nature of the spiritual power itself. African corporate society, founded on traditionalism, does not sufficiently distinguish the individual from the group. This is mirrored on the ontological level by the loss of personhood to a generalized spiritual mass deep in the *Zamani*. Simply put, the person is spiritually lost. For Mbiti, Christianity rectifies this. It teaches that the spiritual power is unequivocally good: It is Christ's unconditional love for each human being. Acceptance of that love provides an ontological security and personal spiritual destiny not present in traditional African religions.

The Spread of Mbiti's Thought

Numbers alone never measure the impact of a book, especially one of philosophy, but they are a starting point. *African Religions and Philosophy*, in the original edition, was reprinted thirteen times and translated into Japanese, French, German, Korean, and Polish. The demand for a shorter, more simple version led Mbiti to publish *Introduction to African Religion* in 1975; it was reprinted nine times. In 1990, a revised and enlarged edition of *African Religions and Philosophy* was published, followed in 1991 by a revised edition of the *Introduction to African Religion*. It is safe to say that Mbiti has, together with Geoffrey Parrinder, taught traditional African religion to the world, and that, in emphasizing the cohesion of African religion, ontology, and ethics, he stands alone.

African theologians have rejoiced that one of their own has taken African religion seriously in a theological sense. As a work in religious ontology, *African Religions and Philosophy* contributes more than further information on African religions. It also goes beyond setting forth the philosophy behind African religious beliefs and practices, although Mbiti sometimes talks in these terms, and thus exposes the work to a purely philosophical critique centering on his notion of time. To do ontology is to consider premises about being, and it is Mbiti's thesis that African premises about being are religious. In other words, the African view is that being is divine, and that human "being" has in it an element or aspect of the divine.

This understanding places *African Religions and Philosophy* squarely in a tradition in which philosophy is not understood as critical, individualistic, and (therefore) modern. Mbiti is emphatic that "Africa" is unintelligible in these terms. It is far more intelligible in terms of all traditions of philosophical theology, including but certainly not limited to the Christian tradition. It is to be hoped, if not inevitably expected, that the lasting impact of Mbiti's work will be to help establish Africa's place in a renewed conversation about divine being.

John F. Wilson

Additional Reading

Evans-Pritchard, E. E. *Nuer Religion*. Oxford: Clarendon Press, 1956. The classic study of a particular African religion. The work is demanding, but at least the concluding "Reflections" should be read.

Gyekye, Kwame. *An Essay on African Philosophical Thought: The Akan Conceptual Scheme*. Cambridge, England: Cambridge University Press, 1986. Gyekye engages in a sustained critique of Mbiti's views, contrasting Akan (Ghana) notions of time with those of East Africans. Despite this, there is much agreement both on the value of studying indigenous philosophy and on its content.

Hountondji, Paulin J. *African Philosophy: Myth and Reality*. Translated by Henri Evans. Bloomington: Indiana University Press, 1983. Hountondji understands Mbiti as one of a number of "church ethnophilosophers" who, in emphasizing indigenous African spirituality, deflect attention from political and economic interests. An influential, controversial book.

King, Noel Q. *African Cosmos: An Introduction to Religion in Africa*. Belmont, Calif.: Wadsworth, 1986. A useful treatment by Mbiti's former colleague at Makerere University, with considerable attention to the religious rituals practiced by a number of African peoples. Contains some illustrations, a glossary of African religious terms, and an extensive annotated bibliography.

Munro, J. Forbes. *Colonial Rule and the Kamba*. Oxford: Clarendon Press, 1975. Discussing the period 1889-1939, Munro provides insight into the social circumstances in which Mbiti grew up. His exceptional educational achievements become especially evident.

Olupona, Jacob K., ed. *African Traditional Religions in Contemporary Society*. New York: Paragon House, 1991. A series of papers by African scholars intended to study African religion sympathetically, from the "inside." Mbiti's contribution, on women in African religion, attempts to counterbalance the disparaging patriarchal view.

Olupona, Jacob K., and Sulayman S. Nyang, eds. *Religious Plurality in Africa: Essays in Honour of John S. Mbiti*. Berlin: Mouton De Gruyten, 1993. A wide-ranging, occasionally uneven collection of essays in recognition of Mbiti as scholar and minister. Mercy A. Oduyoye's critique of his views on marriage is noteworthy, given Mbiti's recent defense of women. Contains biographical material and a complete Mbiti bibliography through 1987.

Oruka, H. Odera, ed. *Sage Philosophy: Indigenous Thinkers and Modern Debate on African Philosophy*. Leiden, The Netherlands: E. J. Brill, 1990. An interesting, engaging work in which Odera interviews a dozen "sages" and contrasts their indigenous but individual views with the holistic approach attributed to Mbiti. Critical essays by other African philosophers are included.

Parrinder, Geoffrey. *African Traditional Religion.* Reprint. Rev. ed. Westport, Conn.: Greenwood Press, 1970. A fine, widely available introduction to the subject. Parrinder communicates, briefly and clearly, his understanding (shared with Mbiti) that Africans traditionally live in a spiritual universe.

Serequeberhan, Tsenay, ed. *African Philosophy: The Essential Readings.* New York: Paragon House, 1991. Various viewpoints on the debate over the nature of African philosophy. Kwasi Wiredu's contribution, providing a critical but reasonably balanced assessment of Mbiti's work, is especially relevant.

Tempels, Placide. *Bantu Philosophy.* Translated by Margaret Read. Paris: Presence Africaine, 1959. Originally written in Dutch and first published in a French translation in 1945. In the book that triggered the debate on African philosophy, Tempels argues that, in Bantu ontology, force is being, and being force. It is paired with Mbiti's work as "ethnophilosophy."

John F. Wilson

George Herbert Mead

Trained in philosophy, Mead earned wide acclaim as a social scientist, playing a major role in establishing sociology and social psychology as disciplines. Drawing on pragmatism and behaviorism, he formulated social behaviorism, a pragmatic philosophy that offered a radical view of mind and self as developing out of society, via the acquisition and the use of language, rather than the other way around.

Principal philosophical works: *The Philosophy of the Present*, 1932; *Mind, Self, and Society*, 1934; *Movements of Thought in the Nineteenth Century*, 1936; *The Philosophy of the Act*, 1938.

Born: February 27, 1863; South Hadley, Massachusetts
Died: April 26, 1931; Chicago, Illinois

Early Life

George Herbert Mead grew up in Oberlin, Ohio, the son of Hiram Mead and Elizabeth Storrs Billings Mead, devout Congregationalists and prominent educators. His father was a professor (1869-1881) of sacred rhetoric and pastoral theology at the theological seminary at Oberlin College, the oldest coeducational liberal arts college in the nation. His mother served from 1870 to 1883 on the Women's Board of Managers and taught English at the college from 1881 to 1883. She distinguished herself as associate principal and as the innovative president (1890-1900) of Abbott Academy in Andover, Massachusetts; the school, later renamed Mount Holyoke College, is the oldest continuing women's liberals arts college in the United States.

George, a quiet, bookish boy, attended Oberlin College during the period 1879-1883, graduating with a bachelor's degree. The curriculum was limited in scope, comprising the classics, rhetoric, literature, and moral philosophy, together with mathematics and a smattering of the natural sciences—chemistry and botany. The classics program made a deep impression on him, and throughout his adult life he enjoyed reading classical texts in Greek and Latin.

Like many young scholars of his generation, Mead tried to teach school as a way of putting his degree to good use. He took a teaching position in Berlin Heights, Ohio, but was fired because he could not cope with the discipline problems he faced in the classroom. At loose ends, he spent the next three years in the Northwest, supporting himself alternately by tutoring and surveying, according to the weather. In the latter capacity, he worked for the Wisconsin Central Railroad, laying the first line from Minneapolis, Minnesota, to Moose Jaw, Saskatchewan, and from there to connect with the Canadian Pacific Railway (CPR).

Life's Work

Mead discovered what was to be his life's work at Harvard University, where during the year 1887-1888 he studied philosophy, graduating with a bachelor's degree. He studied with the leading lights, primarily idealist philosopher Josiah Royce and psychologist and pluralist philosopher William James. Mead lived with the James family and tutored the children as a means of earning some needed money. He found himself at the center of a number of intellectual crosscurrents, especially those that were transforming philosophy in terms of its connections with psychology and religion, and those creating the social sciences. An important academic debate at this time concerned the status of psychology, which had not yet emerged from its home in the philosophy department. Before the 1870's, psychology meant phrenology or Scottish mental philosophy; after the 1870's, it meant the study of mind or consciousness via introspection. Differ-

George Herbert Mead. *(Library of Congress)*

ent scholars defined mind or consciousness in different ways, variously employing biological, physiological, or behavioral concepts. Researchers soon realized that they needed laboratories if they were to test the theories that were being advanced.

Experimental psychology as it is now known began with Wilhelm Wundt, a physician and psychologist who taught at the University of Heidelberg. Wundt believed that before tackling metaphysical problems, psychology should try to understand the simplest experience via the methods of physiology. In 1867, he began teaching the first formal classes in psychology, which he called physiological psychology. In 1875, he established the first laboratory for experimental psychology at the University of Leipzig. This laboratory became the international center for training psychologists.

In the United States, the movement to establish the "new" experimental psychology as a discipline dates from the 1880's. Early in his career at Harvard, James in 1875 established a psychological laboratory so that he could give demonstrations in his classes, but he did little experimenting of his own. In founding his laboratory, he signaled that the new (experimental) psychology had come to the United States. At the time of Mead's studies with him, James was preparing his major work, *The Principles of Psychology* (1890). In it, James surveys contemporary psychological knowledge and shares his own discoveries and insights. As commentators point out, the concrete rendering of experience is a key element in the development of James's philosophy. He coined the term *stream of consciousness*, thereby contrasting his view with that of Wundt, who thought that consciousness consisted of discrete elements. His work advances the new psychology by presenting materials in philosophical form.

In Royce, Mead found a scholar who helped students from religious backgrounds, like Mead, see that the intellectual problems of the day could be explored through philosophy rather than theology. This versatile thinker published many papers and books in a variety of disciplines, always looking back to antecedents but also looking forward, with a philosophy that was profoundly religious yet scientifically logical.

In due course, Mead formulated his own research project, namely, to explain the origin of mind and self in terms of a basic (social) process, that of communication. Like Royce before him, Mead then went on an intellectual tour of the Continent, studying at the universities of Leipzig and Berlin. At Leipzig, he studied with Wundt, who helped him understand the functions of gestures; at Berlin, he studied with Wilhelm Dilthey, who helped him understand the social theory of the self.

In October, 1891, Mead and Helen Castle were quietly married. They would be intellectual companions for the next forty years. In 1892, their son, Henry, was born. About this time, philosopher, educator, and social critic John Dewey offered Mead a job teaching in the Department of Philosophy and Psychology at the University of Michigan at Ann Arbor. Mead accepted Dewey's offer, and the Meads returned to the United States. There, without a graduate degree, he taught a variety of philosophy courses, including experimental psychology, from 1891 to 1894.

As the new chairman of the philosophy department, Dewey had started assembling a group of thinkers who could reconstruct philosophy, making it applicable to the problems people face in everyday life. He had published several books on theoretical and applied psychology, including *Psychology* (1887) and *Applied Psychology* (1889). In this stimulating milieu, Mead began to assemble the elements of his social philosophy. He spent much time talking to Charles Horton Cooley, a colleague who studied how people interacted. Cooley believed that individuals and society make up two sides of the same coin: The self of the individual is a reflected appraisal of the reactions of others.

In 1894, Dewey moved to the University of Chicago to become chairman of the department of philosophy, psychology, and education, and by arrangement Mead moved with him. At the University of Chicago, over the course of nearly four decades, Mead taught a variety of courses, including advanced psychology, history of science, modern philosophy, advanced social psychology, and systematic pragmatism. He became associate professor in 1902 and full professor in 1907. Together with Dewey's other handpicked thinkers, Mead helped Dewey create the Chicago School of pragmatism, which was to dominate American philosophy during the first quarter of the twentieth century.

The move to a research-oriented university gave Dewey and Mead a great opportunity to develop their diverse interests. Increasingly, Dewey turned his attention to education. For example, in 1896 he established a laboratory school so that he could develop and test his psychological and pedagogic hypotheses. Along the way, he abandoned his Hegelian idealism and formulated his own version of pragmatism, which he called instrumentalism.

Guided by Mead's ideas, Dewey attempted to "humanize" the sciences. His instrumentalism explores the conditions under which reasoning occurs, together with the forms (or controlling operations) of thought that can be used to establish future consequences. In explaining human development in pragmatic terms, Dewey took his cue from Charles Darwin and conceptualized intelligence as an instrument people use when they face a conflict or challenge; he argues that ideas too are subject to the survival of the fittest. Accordingly, intelligence serves a practical, instrumental purpose: determining courses of action and anticipating consequences. Furthermore, whereas Hegel used the term *dialectic* to describe the way two opposite ideas clash to produce a third, entirely different idea, Dewey spoke of the dialectic of action as opposed to the dialectic of ideas. In this way, he avoided the dualism that had plagued philosophy. He argued that ideas are worthless unless they pass into action: Experience, not argument, proves who is right.

Mead's impact on Dewey can be detected in the latter's article "The Reflex Arc in Psychology" (1896), which served as the point of departure for later work in functional psychology and for Mead's social behaviorism. In this article, Dewey challenges the prevailing tendency to use the stimulus-response unit as the building block of psychological theory. The stimulus in a reflex is inseparable from the response, in that the response serves to modify the way the stimulus is perceived the next time. He argues that the reflex should be conceptualized as a circular arrangement, whereby the organism adapts to the environment, coordinating and integrating sensory and motor responses. This view anticipates Mead's conception of behavior as the constant adaptation to the environment.

As well as becoming involved in intellectual life at the University of Chicago, Mead immersed himself in the affairs of his community, especially in the fields of education (he was involved in Dewey's experimental school), municipal affairs (such as the Chicago stockyard project), and social welfare. As Dewey later explained, Mead saw no distinction in his pragmatic philosophy between thought and action.

Mead also made his mark as a superb lecturer who helped students to conceptualize sociology and social psychology. Conversation was his first medium of communication, writing a poor second. During the period 1894-1931, Mead published twenty articles in philosophy, six in psychology, and four in sociology, together with eighteen book reviews and four abstracts (mostly in psychology journals), along with thirty popular magazine and newspaper articles on social and educational issues. Several obituaries were addressed to small groups of professional readers. The only book he intended to write was *The Philosophy of the Present* (1932), based on the Carus lectures he delivered in 1930. This book, along with three books based on transcriptions of his lecture notes and papers, were published after his death.

One of these books, *Mind, Self, and Society*, edited by Charles W. Morris, shows that Mead modified pragmatism, as formulated by James and Dewey, and radical behaviorism, as formulated by John B. Watson, to great effect. Pragmatism, a uniquely American philosophy, is the product of cooperative deliberation and mutual influences. Charles Sanders Peirce, the founder of this school of thought, projected pragmatism as a method for explicating the meanings of philosophical and scientific concepts. He conveyed this idea by means of a memorable schema: The meaning of a proposition is its logical (or physical) consequences.

During the late 1890's, James revived and reformulated Peirce's pragmatism, projecting it as a metaphysics of truth and meaning. In a series of lectures, which he later published as *Pragmatism: A New Name for Some Old Ways of Thinking* (1907), he argued that, by means of the pragmatic method (or maxim), pragmatists try to interpret each notion by tracing its consequences; if no practical differences can be traced between two alternatives, they mean practically the same thing, and dispute is pointless. The point he makes is that ideas matter only if they make things happen. Dewey projected his version, instrumentalism, as a way of thinking experimentally, so as to organize, plan, or control future experience. He applied it to all areas of life, especially education.

James and Dewey tried to produce a philosophy that combined the interpretive, subjective study of human experience with the objective, scientific study of human conduct, one that conformed to the criteria borrowed from the natural

sciences. Mead called his approach social behaviorism to set it apart from psychological behaviorism. Psychologist John B. Watson pioneered the idea of psychological or radical behaviorism, explaining human behavior in terms of physiological responses to the environment. Watson, who had done graduate work at the University of Chicago, argued that to become scientific, psychology must abandon all nonobservable concepts. This meant studying observable, measurable behavior and its environmental causes and consequences, and ignoring consciousness altogether.

Like Watson, Mead recognized the importance of observable behavior, but unlike Watson he believed that covert aspects of behavior could be studied in terms of their behavioral context. He takes as his point of departure the social act, which comprises overt as well as covert aspects of human action. Studying the social act means understanding the behavior of the individual in terms of the behavior of the group of which the individual is a member. The social act, or symbol-mediated communication, requires the cooperation of at least two individuals. For Mead, communication was not a matter of communicating private meanings but of exchanging commonly understood signals and gestures, the very starting point of consciousness. He discovered the importance of gestures in naturalist Charles Darwin's book *The Expression of the Emotions in Man and Animals* (1872), which describes physical attitudes as well as physiological changes, such as blushing, as expressions of emotion. He also drew on Wundt in developing the idea of gestures as means for eliciting responses from other organisms—thus as parts of the social act. Thus, he argues that language derives from gestures, or the conversation of gestures. Mead wove these various ideas into his social behaviorism, the fundamental insight of which can be stated briefly: Mind and self emerge when gesture-mediated interaction becomes symbol-mediated interaction, when the participants in interaction transform themselves into social objects playing the communicative roles of speakers and hearers, thereby using language as a medium for reaching understanding, coordinating action, and socializing individuals via the mechanism of taking on the attitude of the other.

Influence

Mead played a vital role in the development of American pragmatism, and his philosophy of mind exerted a great influence on his colleagues, especially those in the nascent disciplines of psychology, sociology, and social psychology. Many thinkers regarded Mead's as a creative mind of the highest order. In a paper prepared for Mead's memorial service, Dewey observed that Mead's mind was the most original in philosophy in the America of the previous generation. He stated that one would have to go far to find a teacher of the time who started so many fruitful lines of thought and speculated on the loss to his own thought had he not had the benefit of Mead's seminal ideas.

Following the twists and the turns Mead took in formulating his theories can be difficult. In contrast to his colleagues, he published little, and he died before setting down his thoughts in book form. Dedicated students organized Mead's fugitive writings, together with their lecture notes, into an orderly medium so as to preserve his philosophical message.

Among philosophers, interest in Mead's work has remained lukewarm. Among social scientists, however, interest in his work grew through the twentieth century. Some sociologists speak of Mead as America's greatest sociological theorist. Dramaturgical theorists, ethnographers, phenomenologists, symbolic interactionists, and ethnomethodologists argue that his theories have yet to be exploited to their full potential.

Robert M. Seiler

Mind, Self, and Society

Type of philosophy: Metaphysics, philosophical psychology, social philosophy

First published: 1934

Principal ideas advanced:

◇ Mind and self can best be understood as having emerged from a more basic social process.

◇ There is no absolute separation between the social and the organic, and any pragmatic or behavioral account of human action that fails to recognize this fact is faulty.

◇ Novelty of response is possible for individual selves that, by the use of memory, can take advantage of past experience within society.

How George Herbert Mead's book came to be published tells something about the author's unusual stature as a professor. The book's contents primarily represent the careful editing of several sets of notes taken by appreciative students attending Mead's lectures on social psychology at the University of Chicago, especially those given in 1927 and 1930; other manuscript materials also appear in the book. For more than thirty years, Mead taught at the University of Chicago, exerting a powerful scholarly influence on students, colleagues, and professional acquaintances. His written contributions during his lifetime were confined to articles and reviews for learned journals. Nevertheless, as a result of the devotion of some of those he influenced, Mead has left to the learned world four published books, all of which appeared after his death. The other three books are *The Philosophy of the Present* (1932), *Movements of Thought in the Nineteenth Century* (1936), and *The Philosophy of the Act* (1938).

The Theory of Social Behaviorism

Mind, Self, and Society remains crucial for the manner in which its central concerns dominated all of Mead's philosophizing during the first three decades of the twentieth century. Mead thought that all aspects of human conduct, including those so often covered by terms such as *mind* and *self*, can best be understood as emergents from a more basic process. The four separate but related parts of the book present Mead's defense of a social behaviorism: "The Point of View of Social Behaviorism," "Mind," "The Self," and "Society."

Mead's attempt to state the nature of social behaviorism is related to the specific situation he found in the intellectual landscape. As a naturalist strongly influenced by the theory of biological evolution, Mead shows a typical suspicion of older dualistic accounts of the mind-body problem. He sets out to explain physical and mental events through one embracing theory. Thus, he rejects the view that a physico-psychological dualism exists that requires a theory to account for supposed differences between mental and nonmental forms of conduct or between human and nonhuman.

Mead's philosophical views are those of the pragmatists, for whom the function of intelligence is the control of actions rather than a supposedly disinterested description of metaphysical realities thought to be independent of experience. There is difficulty, however, for psychologists in avoiding a dualist theory if they retain in their vocabulary words such as "mind," "consciousness," "self-consciousness," and "self." This was Mead's initial problem. One answer of the day had come from John B. Watson, sometimes called the father of psychological behaviorism. Watson had argued that the scientific study of human conduct must confine itself strictly to those aspects of behavior that are externally observable. Accordingly, Watson insisted that psychologists give up using terms such as "mind" and "self," because what can be observed are brains and nervous systems in response to external stimuli.

Like Watson, Mead claims that any effort to understand human behavior by reliance on introspection of internal mental states produces a theoretical difficulty in that psychological explanations can never be subjected to experimental tests. Mead also insists that earlier philosophers made hasty and often illegitimate metaphysical capital out of the distinction between external and internal aspects of behavior. Thus, he shares Watson's general scientific aim: the statement of a thoroughly behavioral account of human action. Mead, however, criticizes Watson's physiological version of behaviorism as resting on too narrow a conception of what makes up an action. Words such as "mind" and "self" must be kept in the psychological vocabulary, but they should never be thought of as referring to entities or processes that stand outside the subject matter of behavioral analysis. Watson's views result from a heavy reliance on mechanical models as well as from too restricted a notion of the nature of reflex activity. By reducing experiences of a mental kind to explicitly physiological correlates, Watson produced a psychological behaviorism that Mead saw as leading inevitably to obvious absurdities.

Social Aspects of Action

Mead's claim is that psychologists need not "explain away" those features of conscious life that often prove embarrassing to strictly physiological analysts of conduct—minds and selves definitely exist. The narrow Watsonian model, however, fails to take their existence into account. The reason is that the model depicts conduct as created by an organism (containing a brain and a central nervous system) responding to numerous stimuli (response-provoking objects that are external to that organism). Here lies the source of Watson's incorrect view of what action involves, according to Mead. This view lacks an adequate awareness of the social aspect of action, especially human action. To produce an adequate behavioral theory of action, one needs a model demonstrating that the social aspects of human action belong partly to the organism itself rather than resulting from the relations between atomic organisms and external stimuli. What this means is that, in the case of human action, no absolute separation exists between the social and the organic.

The major problem for Mead is to explain how minds and selves appear in the social process. Minds and selves are exclusively features of human conduct. Mead admits that animals possess intelligence but denies that they have minds, even though animals also function in social contexts. The necessary conclusion is, then, that only social beings can be said to possess self-consciousness, and only human organisms are socially based emergents having this specific kind of mental life. Mead offers an explanation of this in terms of the emergence in the social process of what he calls _significant_ symbols. Such symbols are ultimately linguistic in form, but they evolve from the roles played in all organic conduct by gestures and responses to gestures. Certain gestures become significant symbols when they implicitly arouse in an individual making them the same responses that they explicitly arouse, or are supposed to arouse, in the individuals to whom they are addressed. Human organisms differ from other animal organisms in their ability to make use of significant symbols. For example, a dog that growls at another dog is making a gesture, but the dog cannot make use of a _significant_ gesture because it can never take the role of the "other" in a process of communication in the way that humans can and do. Communication involves this taking of the role of the other, self-consciously, in a social context. It is this ability possessed by human organisms that makes language and communication possible.

Mead does not argue that meaning exists only in linguistic form, but he does argue that language constitutes the most meaningful type of communication. For Mead, meaning is objectively *there* as a feature of social processes. He states that awareness of consciousness is not necessary for the presence of meaning in the process of social experience. Communication involves making available to others meanings that actually exist to be discovered and talked about. Significant symbols function to make the user of them aware of the responses they call out in those to whom they are directed. The significant symbol not only calls out in the user the awareness of others' responses to it; the symbol also functions to make those responses serve as stimuli to the user. This gives an anticipatory character to communication. The result is that users of such symbols can respond to them in novel ways, actually introducing changes into the social situation by such responses. In this view, ideas are anticipations of future expected actions made possible by the capacity to use significant symbols.

Emergence of the Self

This capacity of the human organism to use significant symbols is a precondition of the appearance of the self in the social process. The self is not like the body, which can never view itself as a whole. The self emerges from a process of social communication that enables viewing of oneself, as a whole, from the perspective of others. Mead treats this problem in terms of the phases of the self, the "me" and the "I." His effort is to understand this human capacity to adopt the attitudes of others toward oneself. Each response to a significant symbol presupposes that one can associate oneself with the set of attitudes making up the social group ("the generalized other") to which one belongs. In this manner, the "me" emerges as a phase of the self, for the "me" *is* that set of attitudes appropriated by the individual. The "I" as a phase of the self is that which makes possible the organism's response. The "I" can respond to the "me" in novel ways, meaning that, for Mead, social action is never simply imitative or literally repetitive.

Mead makes use of the notions of the game and play to illustrate his thesis. Games and play require participants to adopt the roles of the others involved. Just as in a game one can never get beyond the set of attitudes associated with the various roles of the different players, so in the case of the human mind and self there is no getting beyond the social process they presuppose. Without society involving a number of different roles, there would be nothing in terms of which a self could arise. Without the viewpoints of others that form the "me," there would exist nothing to which the "I" could respond.

Mead's treatment of the nature of the self permits him to take seriously features of "depth" psychology that Watsonian behaviorism overlooks. To understand a self means to understand something about the roles and attitudes of others as productive of that self. Here Mead finds a difference between the social lives of animals and men. Animal and human social communities involve organization, but in human social systems the organization reflects the self-conscious adoption of a number of roles, a thing impossible in animal communities. The strict organizational patterns found in bee and ant societies do not lead to significant communication or to the creation of a language. Although social life is necessary as a condition of the appearance of minds and selves, minds and selves do not always exist where there is social life. What emerges in the form of minds and selves from a social process is a genuine and irreducible reality.

Because the self exists only when an individual can know the attitudes of others in a community, it is normal for multiple selves to be present in each person. These attitudes form the possibility of a "me" that can become an object and response-provoking stimulus to an "I." The self can become an object to itself in a way in which a body cannot. The nature of the social community in which the self arises obviously influences the nature of that self. Mead states that normally, within the sort of community to which people belong, there is a unified self, but that it may be broken up. A person who is somewhat unstable nervously and in whom there is a line of cleavage may find certain activities impossible, and that set of activities may separate and evolve another self.

The pathological aspect of a multiple self concerns the possibility of "forgetting" forms of past experiences from which important elements of the self have emerged. In any existing social community, there must exist some fairly stable attitudes and roles if a self is to emerge at all, and it is the stable elements that permit language to possess a universal significance for communication. The symbols of a language permit a self to respond to the same meaning or object as would others in the group using that set of symbols. Linguistic confusions reflect social instability in that meanings are hardly fixed at all. Personality is unable to develop when rapidly altering social attitudes and roles fail to permit language to capture relatively stable meanings. The reason is that there can be no completely individual self. When a self does appear, Mead says, it always involves an experience of another, and there cannot be an experience of a self simply by itself.

In Mead's analysis of the self, the "me" reflects those features that make up the stable habit patterns of an individual's conduct. In a sense, the "me" is the individual's character insofar as it can issue forth in predictable forms of behavior. The "I" can arise as a phase of the self that permits some novelty of response because the "I" appears only in the memory of what the individual has done. Mead claims that individuals usually know what they have done and said only *after* they have acted and spoken. There is a retrospective stance to the self-awareness of the "I" that permits novel uses of this memory in new situations. Individuals are not compelled to respond in the same way they formerly did once there is a self; they can react in original ways to the attitudes of other members in the social community. In such reactions, the "I" always acts in terms of an appeal to a widened social community if it reacts against the existing practices of the group. Mead claims that the moral importance of the reactions of the "I," as a phase of the self, resides in the individual's sense of importance as a person not totally determined by the attitudes of the others. The "I" demands freedom from conventions and laws, and such demands, when they occur, imply that another community exists, if only potentially or ideally, in which a broader and more embracing self is possible of realization. The complete development of a self therefore requires both phases, the "I" and the "me"—established habits in a social situation that yet leave room for novel responses to new situations.

Each individual in a social community will have some element of a unique standpoint from which to react to the attitudes making up that community. The reason is that each individual can reflect on his or her own experiences within the social structure supporting his or her existence. Mead thinks that a rational social community will encourage development of self-responsible action rather than automatic responses by coercive external conditioning. Such a community will provide opportunity for the stereotyped kind of work that each person needs (if he or she is a healthy individual) plus opportunity for self-expression through unique responses to situations (so that the person does not feel "hedged in" and completely a conventionalized "me"). A rational community differs from a mob or a crowd, for in a rational community the individual can become a determinant of aspects of the environment. Great men such as Socrates, Jesus, and Buddha were able to influence the communities of their own day and age by their appeals to an enlarged potential community.

Contrasts with Earlier Theories

Mead's social behaviorism places him in opposition both to the individualistic and to the *partially* social explanations of mind. The individualistic theory argues that mind is a necessary logical and biological presupposition of any existing social process. Its adherents attempt to account for the social aspect of human existence in terms of contract theories of the origin of political and social life. The *partially* social theory admits that mind can express its potentialities only in a social setting but insists that mind is in some sense prior to that setting. Mead argues that his social behaviorism is in direct contrast to these competing theories in that mind presupposes, and is a product of, the social process. For Mead, the forms of social groupings tend toward either cooperative or aggressively competitive ones. Mead favors the former. He believes that the democratic ideal of full human participation in a variety of social situations (involving different roles) can best call out the wide range of human responses that mind makes possible. In a democratic society, the twin quests after universality of experience, economic and religious, can best be harmonized. Such a society also makes available a wider range of roles from which an individual can develop a self. It is clear that, for Mead, democracy involves a society that permits a rich variety of primary groups to exist.

Mead's attempt to state a consistent theory of social behaviorism may have failed. In fact, his position is a metaphysical rather than a scientific one; however, his views form a metaphysical defense of the democratic ideal in terms of the behavioral hopes of psychologists to bring human conduct under rational control. Mead is at least on the side of reason and rationality. He is stubborn in his refusal to give up terms such as *mind* and *consciousness*, and he is equally unwilling to discard the behaviorist model of the psychologists. He tries valiantly to widen the conception of the human act. The critical question remains, naturally, whether Mead or anyone can have the best of two possible worlds.

Whitaker T. Deininger

Additional Reading

Aboulafia, Mitchell, ed. *Philosophy, Social Theory, and the Thought of George Herbert Mead*. Albany: State University of New York Press, 1991. Brings together some of the finest critical studies of Mead, written by American and European thinkers working in diverse traditions.

Cook, Gary A. *George Herbert Mead: The Making of a Social Pragmatist*. Urbana: University of Illinois Press, 1993. Shows how Mead, from his youth until his last years, formulated his own unique solutions to the intellectual problems of his time, utilizing Mead's own published and unpublished writings.

Hamilton, Peter, ed. *George Herbert Mead: Critical Assessments*. London: Routledge, 1993. Brings together many papers arguing why Mead is important for symbolic interactionism, tracing his influence in social behaviorism and theories of the mind.

Joas, Hans. *G. H. Mead: A Contemporary Re-examination of His Thought*. Translated by Raymond Meyer. Cambridge, Mass.: MIT Press, 1997. Combines two approaches to great effect. The contextualist approach sketches his political and intellectual biography, showing how Mead, as he engaged the dominant theoretical and methodological issues of the day, developed his theories. The thematic approach, explicating Mead's later work in science, temporality, and sociality, offers an interpretation of the system of thought he was developing during the last decade of his life.

Miller, David L., ed. *The Individual and the Social Self: The Unpublished Work of George Herbert Mead*. Chicago: University of Chicago Press, 1982. Provides a superb edition of Mead's unpublished 1914 and 1927 class lecture notes in social psychology, together with a fine introduction, which presents Mead in terms of a revolt against Cartesian dualism and chronicles his rejection of John Locke, George Berkeley, and David Hume.

Mutaawe Kasozi, Ferdinand. *Self and Social Reality in a Philosophical Anthropology: Inquiring into George Herbert Mead's Socio-philosophical Anthropology*. New York: Peter Lang, 1998. An assessment of the role of philosophical anthropology in Mead's work.

Perinbanayagam, R. S. *Signifying Acts: Structure and Meaning in Everyday Life*. Carbondale: Southern Illinois University Press, 1985. Locates, for sociology and social psychology, the tradition that has come to be known as "symbolic interactionism," producing a full and faithful representation of the provenance, development, and contemporary cast of the tradition, based on the formulations of Charles Sanders Peirce, William James, John Dewey, and Mead.

Robert M. Seiler

Mencius

Through a lifetime of reflection, Mencius clarified and expanded the wisdom embodied in Confucius's *Lunyu* (late sixth or early fifth century B.C.E.; *Analects*, 1861), rendering Confucian ideas more accessible. His *Mengzi* eclipsed other interpretations of Confucius and gained acceptance as the orthodox version of Confucian thought.

Principal philosophical works: *Mengzi*, early third century B.C.E. (*The Works of Mencius*, 1861; commonly known as *Mengzi*)

Born: c. 372 B.C.E.; Zou, China
Died: c. 289 B.C.E.; China

Early Life

Mencius was born about 372 B.C.E. in the small principality of Zou in northeastern China, not far from the birthplace of Confucius, whose work Mencius spent his life interpreting. Knowledge of Mencius's early life is scarce. What evidence exists must be extracted from his own writing, most notably the *Mengzi*, although many biographical observations are found in the great historian Sima Qian's *Shi-ji* (first century B.C.E.; *Records of the Grand Historian of China*, 1960, rev. ed. 1993), a large work that has been translated in part many times and is best known by its original title.

Mencius was probably a member of the noble Meng family, whose home, like that of Confucius, was in the city-state of Lu, in what is now southwestern Shandong Province. Certainly Mencius's education was one that was common to the aristocracy, for he was thoroughly familiar with both the classical *Shi Jing* (c. 500 B.C.E.; *Book of Odes*, 1891) and the *Shu Jing* (c. 626 B.C.E.; *Book of Documents*, 1846), which together provided the fundamentals of his classical training. Moreover, he had a masterly grasp of Confucius's work and quoted it frequently, leading to the assumption that he studied in a Confucian school, purportedly under the tutelage of Confucius's grandson, who was himself a man of ministerial rank in the central state of Wei.

Known as Mengzi to his students, Mencius assumed the role of teacher early in life and never abandoned it. Rejecting material well-being and position as ends in themselves, he, like many Confucians, nevertheless aspired to hold office inside one of the courts of the Chinese states. He did indeed become a councillor and later the minister of state in Wei. In such positions, he tutored students, not all of them noble, in classical works: the dynastic hymns and ballads anthologized in the *Book of Odes* and state papers from archives that formed the *Book of Documents*. These were works from which, by the end of the second century B.C.E., Confucian precepts developed. During these early years of observation and teaching, Mencius gained disciples, furthered his interpretations of Confucius, and enjoyed considerable renown in many parts of China.

Life's Work

Mengzi was Mencius's principal work. It appeared late in his life. Had it incorporated less wisdom than his many years of diverse experiences and reflections allowed or a less lengthy refinement of Confucius's thoughts, it would not be likely to rank as one of the greatest philosophical and literary works of the ancient world.

Mencius garnered experience through his wanderings and temporary lodgments in various Chinese courts and kingdoms. He was fortunate to live in an age when, despite continuous political turmoil, dynastic rivalries, and incessant warfare, high levels of civility prevailed in aristocratic circles. Teacher-scholars, as a consequence, were readily hosted—that is, effectively subsidized—by princely families eager to advance their children's education and to instruct and invigorate themselves through conversation with learned men.

Some of Mencius's temporary affiliations can be dated. Between 323 and 319 B.C.E., Mencius was installed at the court of King Hui of Liang, in what is now China's Sichuan Province. He moved eastward about 318 to join the ruler of the state of Qi, King Xuan. Prior to his sojourn to Liang (although the dates are conjectural), Mencius visited and conversed with princes, rulers, ministers, and students in several states: Lu, Wei, Qi, and Song.

Mencius's journeyings were not feckless. They related directly to his philosophical and historical perceptions. Like Confucius, Mencius believed that he lived in a time of troubles in which—amid rival feudatories and warring states, divided and misruled—China was in decline. Also like Confucius, Mencius looked back fondly on what he thought had been the halcyon days of Chinese government and civilization under the mythical kings (2700-770 B.C.E.), when a unified China had been governed harmoniously.

Drawing on Chinese legends incorporated into literary sources familiar to him from the Xia (c. 2200-1766 B.C.E.), Shang (c. 1384-1122 B.C.E.), and Zhou (1122-221 B.C.E.) dynasties, Mencius concluded that the ideal governments of these earlier days had been the work of hero-kings—Yao, Shun, and Yu—whose successors had organized themselves into dynasties. These were the Sage Kings, who, like kings Wen and Wu of the Zhou family, had been responsible for China's former greatness. Their dissolute successors, however, such as the "bad" kings of the Xia and the Shang dynasties, were equally responsible for the subsequent debasement of the Sage Kings' remarkable achievements and erosion of their legacy.

For Mencius, a vital part of this legacy was the concept of the Mandate of Heaven. It was an idea that he ascribed to the early Zhou kings, who justified their authority by it. These kings asserted that they had received the mandate directly from the deity, who designated Zhou rulers as Sons of Heaven, viceroys of Heaven. Effectively, that charged them with the responsibilities of being the deity's fief holders. The Zhou kings, in turn, proceeded to impose lesser feudal obligations on their own fief holders and subjects. In Mencius's view, this arrangement was more than merely an arbitrary justification for Zhou authority; it was also a recognition of authority higher than that of humans. Because the Mandate of Heaven was not allocated in perpetuity, it was essentially a lease that was operative during good behavior. When rulers lost virtue and thereby violated the mandate, the punishment of Heaven descended upon them. Their subjects, their vassals, were constrained to replace them. It was on this basis, as Mencius knew, that the Zhou kings had successfully reigned for four centuries.

Equally important in this hierarchical scheme developed around the Zhou conception of the Mandate of Heaven, of Sage Kings functioning in response to it, were the roles of sage ministers. It was these ministers whom Mencius credited with the rise and harmonious rule of the Sage Kings. In times when the Mandate of Heaven had obviously been forgotten or ignored, Mencius wished not only that this ideal past would be restored but also that his presence at various courts would allow him to identify, assist, and guide potential Sage Kings, fulfilling the role of sage minister himself or through his disciples.

King Xuan of Qi was one of the rulers at whose court he served and for whom he envisioned greatness as the Ideal King. Xuan, however, appeared lacking in will. King Hui of Liang also showed some promise, but Mencius despaired of Hui when he revealed his desire to rule the world by force. Briefly, Mencius saw potential in the king of Teng, who ruled a small principality that, nevertheless, afforded a sufficient stage for a True King. That potential also went unrealized. To critics who charged that Mencius was simply unperceptive, his reply was that such rulers possessed ample ability but had not availed themselves of his services. After these encounters, despairing, he returned home to kindle his belief in the Ideal King in the hearts of his disciples.

The basis for Mencius's initial optimism lay in his interpretation of China's history, for it reassured him that great kings had appeared in cycles. About two hundred years lay between the reign of Tang, founder of the Shang Dynasty (c. 1384-1122 B.C.E.), and Wu, first ruler of the great Zhou Dynasty (1122-221 B.C.E.). Consequently Heaven's dispatch of another Sage King, according to Mencius, was overdue. In this interim and in expectation of the Sage King's appearance, people such as he, "Heavenly instruments," had divine commissions to maintain the ideal.

There is no evidence that Mencius, any more than Confucius, was successful in the realization of such dreams. Although Mencius served briefly as a councillor, and although his knowledge was profound as well as wide-ranging, he revealed more disdain for than interest in (or understanding of) practical politics in his own highly politicized environment. Furthermore, areas of intellection such as religion, ethics, and philosophy were densely packed with rivals. A number of these, such as Mozi the utilitarian or Yang Zhu the hedonist, enjoyed greater recognition and higher status than he did. Nor was Mencius ranked among the leading intellectuals or scholars of his day who were inducted into the membership of the famous Ji-Xia Academy.

Later generations would honor him, but in his own time, Mencius was a relatively obscure, evangelizing teacher whose views were merely tolerated, a pedagogue who never penetrated beyond the fringes of power, a man without a substantial following. These conditions help explain his occasional haughtiness, manipulative argumentation, and assertive promulgation of Confucianism. Nevertheless, not until two centuries after his death did Confucian principles gain significant influence.

Thus, Mencius's work can be examined for its intrinsic merit, outside the context of his own lifetime. He was, foremost, a devoted follower of Confucius. As such, he never wavered in the belief that it was not enough to be virtuous; people also had to model themselves after the Sage Kings. Antiquity represented the epitome of good conduct, good government, and general harmony. Consequently, the ways of old—or his interpretations of them—had to be accepted or rejected completely.

This position inevitably raised the issue of how the sages of yesteryear had become, both as people and as governors, such ideal models. Had

such gifts been divinely bestowed? Mencius believed that they were like all people. This response led him therefore into an elaboration of the central tenets of his philosophy, into an embellishment of Confucius, and ultimately into formulating his major contribution to thought.

Whereas Confucius left only one equivocal observation on human nature, Mencius—probably because the contention of his time demanded it—placed the essence of human nature at the center of his work. Discussions of humanity (*ren*) and of justice (*yi*) accordingly became his preoccupations, and, subsequently, because of Mencius, became the focus of Chinese philosophy.

In defining humanity, he declared unequivocally that all people were born sharing the same human nature and that human nature is good. Mencius sought to demonstrate this belief through his maxims and parables: All people were endowed with sympathy for those whose lives were at risk or who had suffered great misfortune; all people felt best when they were instinctively being their best. Thus, all people who cultivated *ren* were capable of indefinite perfectibility; they were capable of becoming sages. Furthermore, people would find *ren* irresistible, for it nullified the menaces of brute physical force (*ba*). Writing with fewer logical inhibitions than had been displayed by Confucius, Mencius asserted that all things were complete within every person: Everyone, in microcosm, embodied the essences of everything: the macrocosm.

Consequently, people who knew their own nature also knew Heaven. In asserting this, wittingly or not, Mencius again went beyond Confucius, for knowing oneself first in order to know everything suggested meditative introspection, whereas Confucius had disparaged meditation and insisted on the superiority of observation and the use of the critical faculty. Mencius stressed the real incentives for the cultivation of one's humanity. Those who did so enjoyed wisdom, honor, and felicity. When such people became kings, the state was harmoniously governed and prospered. In turn, such kings won over the allegiance of the world—which to Mencius, as to all Chinese, meant China. *Ren* therefore also afforded people prestige and moral authority that constituted power (*de*) far greater than any physical force.

Mencius was all too aware of the extent to which his everyday world indicated just the opposite, that is, the appalling conditions people had created for themselves. He was also aware of misapplications of force, either as a result of these problems or as a result of attempts to resolve them. Yet to Mencius, the failure to cultivate one's humanity lay at the root of these difficulties. He was not naïve about some of the causes of inhumanity. Poverty and the misery of people's environments, he conceded, often left little chance for cultivating one's humanity, but that lent urgency to the search for a Sage King who could mitigate or eradicate these conditions. He was also aware that people's appetites, as well as the conditions in which they lived, left little to differentiate them from other animals. Yet, the difference that did exist was a vital one: namely, their ability to think with their hearts.

Justice (*yi*) was a concomitant to Mencius's concept of humanity and was also central to his teaching. By justice, Mencius meant not only doing the right thing but also seeing that others received their rights. Clearly the "right things" consisted in part of rituals and formal codes of manners and of traditional civilities. They also embraced rights that were not necessarily embodied in law: the right of peasants to gather firewood in the forests, the right to subsistence in old age, and the right to expect civilities and to live according to traditional codes of behavior. If feeling distress for the suffering of others was, according to Mencius, the first sign of humanity, then feelings of shame and disgrace were the first signs of justice.

Mencius spent his lifetime forming his maxims and parables to illustrate what humanity and justice meant to him—or what he believed they should mean to all people. Appropriately for a teacher, he provoked more questions than he answered; he never arrived at his goal, nor did his disciples. He died about 289 B.C.E., probably near his place of birth on the Shandong Peninsula.

Influence

A devoted Confucian, Mencius expanded and clarified Confucius's *Analects* and the principles of his master as they were being taught and debated a century after Confucius's death. Mencius, however, went beyond Confucius by placing hu-

man nature and his belief in its essential goodness at the center of philosophical discussion. Officially ranked a sage, he stands among the world's most respected literary and philosophical geniuses.

Clifton K. Yearley and Kerrie L. MacPherson

Mengzi

Type of philosophy: Ethics, social philosophy
First transcribed: Mengzi, early third century B.C.E. (*The Works of Mencius*, 1861; commonly known as *Mengzi*)
Principal ideas advanced:

◇ Every human being is born good; hence, if one maintains one's original nature, one will remain good.
◇ In humanity's original nature, there is a sense of shame, a sense of courtesy, and a sense of right and wrong.
◇ If one relies only on one's sense perceptions without subjecting them to the control of the mind, one falls into evil ways and perverts one's original nature.
◇ If one allows the desire for personal gain to overcome one's righteousness and sense of social obligations, one also perverts one's nature.
◇ Ideal rulers are considerate of their subjects' interests and provide both moral leadership and adequate social welfare.
◇ Any person who practices the principles of humanity and righteousness with sincerity radiates the spiritual influence of the universe.

The exact date and authorship of this collection of philosophical dialogues and anecdotes have remained a subject of dispute for centuries, but there is no doubt about the existence of the man, Mencius (Mengzi), in the fourth to third centuries B.C.E. Mencius taught students, lectured to the rulers of his time, and expounded his political and moral philosophy in much the same way as most of the Confucians did.

When very young, Mencius lost his father, and his mother worked alone at a weaving loom to support her son. Mencius's childhood education is said to have been of the ideal kind, and his mother has been held in reverence by the Chinese as an ideal mother. It is said that she was so determined to cultivate her son's moral integrity at a very early age that she took extreme caution in her own speech and behavior in front of him. Once their landlord slaughtered a hog. When the young Mencius saw it, he asked his mother why. In jest his mother answered that the landlord was preparing a feast for him. Immediately afterward, she regretted her statement; in order to correct her untruthful statement, she sold her badly needed clothing to buy some meat with which she actually served him a good dinner. Another time, she was distressed by Mencius's fondness for play when she wanted him to concentrate on studies. After some ineffective admonition, she took out a knife and cut the warp on her loom. Because she could no longer weave, the family was without food. This drastic gesture impressed the young boy so much that he never again neglected his studies.

After studying with a disciple of Confucius's grandson, Mencius emerged in his adult life as a recognized standard-bearer of Confucianism. In his expositions on Confucius's teachings, however, Mencius ventured much further in metaphysical speculations than his master ever did. From Mencius, Confucianism gained a fully developed theory on human nature and a clear orientation toward idealism.

Innate Goodness

Mencius subscribed to the basic Confucian doctrine of *ren* (benevolence), but in elaborating on this doctrine he gave it a metaphysical basis. Confucius urged people to be humane toward others so that society might be harmonious and peaceful; Mencius urged people to be kind to others because, as he says, to be kind is humanity's natural propensity. People are born good, and evil ways are perversions. Every human being has innate goodness; hence, if one can maintain one's original nature, one will remain good. In Mencius's own language, this original good human nature is the "heart of the child," or the untainted heart. If unperverted, one's original childlike heart will lead one toward the good, just as "water naturally flows downward." If already perverted, one can attain salvation only by returning to one's original state of goodness.

How is this innate goodness of humanity observed? Mencius suggested looking at the sympathetic feeling that is a part of humanity's nature. He uses the following illustration: Anybody seeing a child about to fall into a well would immediately spring to the child's aid. One would do this without reflecting on the advantage and disadvantage of one's action; one would not think about what merit one would gain if one rescued the child, or what blame one would have to face if one refused to reach out a hand. One would leap to save the child because the peril of the child would spontaneously fill one with a sense of alarm. This example proves the existence of a sense of mercy in every person.

With similar illustrations, Mencius argued that he had proved the existence of a sense of shame, a sense of courtesy, and a sense of right and wrong in humanity's original nature. Together with the sense of mercy, these senses constitute the four good beginnings of humanity's development. According to Mencius, the sense of mercy is the beginning of *ren* (humanity); the sense of shame should lead people to righteousness; the sense of courtesy, if allowed to develop, will give people decorum; and the sense of right and wrong is the foundation for wisdom. As with a person's four limbs, these four senses are already inseparable parts of any person at birth. Also as with the four limbs, these four senses develop to their proper healthy proportions if people cultivate them; otherwise they wither away through misuse or desuetude.

Basing his argument on his observation of the uninstructed child, Mencius asserts in his work that humanity has intuitive ability and knowledge. He points out that every child "knows" how to love his or her parents, and as the child grows, he or she "knows" how to respect elder siblings. The former is true *ren* (humanity) and the latter is true *yi* (righteousness). Therefore, says Mencius, people are born with the innate knowledge to distinguish the right from the wrong and the innate ability to act according to the right.

The innate knowledge and ability of people, like their basic senses or feelings, are analogous to the seeds of a plant. To allow these seeds to germinate, Mencius brings forth another notion: the *cai* of humanity, or people's "natural powers." Thus if one exhausts one's natural powers, one will realize one's potential of being good, and one who does evil is failing to exercise one's natural powers. Although human nature is basically good, people can be led astray by their contact with the outside world. If people rely only on their sense perceptions (on seeing, hearing, taste, and so forth) without subjecting them to the control of their mind (heart), which is the office of thinking, then they fall into evil ways. Here Mencius's theory of the "mind" is something very comparable to "reason," but the mind of the Mencian doctrine is closely linked to his theory of a mystic *qi*. Mencius, in explaining his theory of innate knowledge, gives his view on the origin of evil, which is a subject not treated by Confucius himself.

Righteousness

Mencius never speaks of *ren* (humanity or benevolence) without mentioning *yi* (righteousness). He is not the first Confucian philosopher to use the term *yi*, but the emphasis certainly is his. Although "right," "fair," and "just" are all within the commonly accepted senses of the word *yi*, in Mencius's usage, this word most frequently stands for a concrete sense of justice and fairness. Mencius seems to stress the importance of fulfilling one's obligations toward other people. These obligations are social in nature. Thus, an unfilial son is not *yi* because he fails to repay his parents' kindness toward him, and a servant deserting his or her master is not *yi* because the individual fails to repay the master's favors. In this light, Mencius's *yi* does not suggest anything like the Western abstract concept of righteousness. However, there is at least one place where Mencius does seem to bring in an absolute righteousness. When he warns rulers not to abuse their subjects, Mencius states that rulers have an obligation to protect the interest of the people. Because rulers do not directly owe any favor to the people, Mencius in this case accepts an absolute standard of righteousness even though he fails to define it.

The social basis of the Mencian concept of righteousness creates perplexing problems when social obligations come into conflict with one another. A man is a righteous son to his father and a righteous minister to his king only as long as there is no conflict of interest between his father and his king, but this condition does not always

exist. There is an anecdote in this book that illustrates such difficulties. The story concerns a warrior in ancient China who encountered his own former teacher on the battlefield, on the opposite side of no-man's-land. Remembering his obligation toward his former teacher, the warrior should show his respect to his present enemy. However, as a loyal soldier to his lord, the warrior should shoot his former teacher to death. Caught in such a dilemma, the warrior won immortality and historical acclaim by a curious compromise. He broke off the points of four of his arrows and shot the arrows at his former teacher. Then he promptly withdrew with a clear conscience.

In contrast to the idea of righteousness, Mencius put *li*, or "profit" (not to be confused with *li*, or "rules of propriety"). He blamed humanity's departure from righteousness to seek personal gain for the disorder and unhappiness in society. Greed leads to strife as people, both in and outside the government, go after profit and fight for personal benefit. Only if everyone strives for that which is right and does what he or she ought to do, can the human community prosper in peace. This is what Mencius preached to the rulers and to his disciples alike. It should be noted, however, that Mencius did not dismiss the importance of material well-being, and the work is not always clear on how Mencius would draw the distinction between the desirable and the undesirable kind of profit.

Government and Rulers

That Mencius recognized the need for material well-being is evident in his political and economic ideas. His ideal government is one with both moral leadership and adequate social welfare. Like Confucius himself, Mencius advocated rule by moral excellence and humane feeling. Rulers must be considerate of their subjects' interests. If the ruler is benevolent, the state will prosper because people will not only flock toward it but also imitate its virtuous way of living. Because benevolent government could bring peace and prosperity to people without the need for any other action, Mencius's theory amounts to rule by moral magnetism.

Mencius was aware of the larger political and economic forces that were at work in society in addition to the moral forces in which he had great confidence. He realized that a state does not exist without people, so he advised the rulers that people must come first, the state second, and the king last. These are his often-quoted words: "People are the roots of the nation. If the roots are not firm, the nation collapses." Indeed the king must win the "hearts" of his subjects; otherwise, his administration will be doomed. Mencius urged the ruler to give to and to share with the people what they desire and not to do to them what they would not like. Because all human beings like the pleasures of life, the king must work to increase the pleasures of life and to share them with his people. Here Mencius clearly accepts public profit and material well-being for everybody as something good and moral that does not violate the principle of righteousness.

With these declarations, Mencius appears as a champion of the people against tyrannical governments. He is particularly remembered for his expressions in support of the people's right to revolt. There is enough in the sayings attributed to Confucius himself that implies this right to rebel. Confucius makes the observance of Heaven's will a necessary condition for the ruler to keep his throne, and he blames the king's loss of the Heavenly Mandate for the downfall of his dynasty. Mencius elaborates on this view and makes it explicit. He calls a person without *ren* (benevolence) a scoundrel, and a person without *yi* (righteousness) a scourge, both deserving defeat, even death, regardless of their social station.

Two Types of People

Much as Mencius championed the people's right to revolt against a tyrannical ruler, this Confucian sage did not believe in self-rule. In his work, Mencius upholds a natural division of labor in society on the basis of the different aptitudes of people. There are, he says, two types of people: those of brain and those of brawn. The former work with their minds and are destined to rule, while the latter work with their hands to feed the former and are to be ruled by the former. In this way, he affixes an unmistakable stamp of approval on the Confucian attitude that only the literati, who tend to monopolize education and literature, are fit to conduct the affairs of the government.

Mencius argued that between the two types of people exists a basic difference that helps to justify their separate destinies. Briefly, this difference lies in the spiritual fortitude of those with education. Mencius attributes a moral strength to the true scholar who, unlike the uneducated, is capable of maintaining a steadfast heart even when he or she is threatened with financial insecurity. For the ordinary person, an ensured material provision is necessary to keep him or her behaving properly. What the hungry stomachs of the common people would consume first, Mencius is saying here, are moral scruples. Consequently in the *Mengzi*, Mencius urges intelligent rulers to look after their people's livelihood first. He demands that rulers make certain that each farmer has around his house about an acre of land planted in mulberry trees, to enable anyone over fifty to be clothed in silk. Poultry and meat animals should be bred in season so that those over seventy will never lack a meat diet. In addition, Mencius would assign at least fifteen acres of land to any family of eight mouths in order to keep them all well fed. The establishment of schools to teach the people Confucian principles comes last because principles can take roots only in minds when stomachs are full.

Mencius's Mysticism

The difference between Mencius and Confucius comes into sharp relief when Mencius leaves the concrete and practical issues of the day to deal with the abstract. In the *Mengzi*, Mencius injects metaphysics into the Confucian system. He does so by going beyond Confucius in accepting Heaven at different times as a supreme being with a discerning moral will, as a fatalistic pattern, or as the authority that creates virtue and sets the standard of righteousness. Mencius starts with his theory of human nature and asserts that it is Heaven that gives people their innate knowledge contained in his mind (or heart—the Chinese word, *xin*, means both heart and mind). The mind, or innate knowledge, is what makes people great because by exercising their minds, people can come to "know" their original nature. Mencius's theory of untainted heart, however, is not the same as the mystic Daoist theory of untampered heart: The latter does not talk about humanity's mind and its importance.

The mysticism in the system of Mencius begins when he states that when people exercise their minds to the utmost, they will also come to "know" Heaven. The unerring and unwavering attitude to examine oneself in search of one's good nature is called, in Mencian terms, *cheng*, or sincerity. A person practicing the principles of humanity and altruism with "sincerity" can succeed in returning to his original nature, which is a part of Heaven. Consequently Mencius declares that "All beings are complete within man." The person who has attained this state is a perfect person, or a *junzi*. The *junzi* radiates a spiritual influence wherever he or she appears. Under the *junzi*'s influence, the ordinary people become good and the state becomes orderly. This spiritual influence, in most cases, is described by Mencius as *qi*, or the irresistible, all-pervading force.

The basic senses of the term, *qi*, include "air," "all gaseous matters," and "the air that surrounds a person." Mencius uses this term largely in the last sense. He assumes that a person with such an influential air around him or her must first possess that degree of spiritual perfection described above. In Mencius's ecstatic description of this all-pervading force, claiming that it flows "above and below together with Heaven and Earth," and that it "fills the entire universe between Heaven and Earth," the *qi* acquires puzzlingly mystic proportions.

However, this Mencian concept of *qi* need not be a puzzle if the basis of his theory is considered. According to him, people acquire this all-pervading force by practicing the principles of humanity and morality according to the dictates of Heaven, conceived as a supreme moral voice. The process of acquiring this force, then, is a constant doing of righteous deeds without stop or affectation. People can do so only when they use their minds to examine themselves and to rediscover the righteous senses (the four basic good senses already discussed) that come with their birth. In this analysis, the mystic *qi* of Mencius is no more than a moral force stated metaphorically.

Mencius's Legacy

These are the basic tenets of an idealistic philosopher who, next to the Song Dynasty (960-1279) philosopher Zhu Xi, perhaps did the most in establishing Confucianism as the controlling orthodoxy in Chinese thought for at least two millennia. Much, of course, has been read back into his book. Many apologists of Chinese tradition attempt to offer Mencius as the great champion of democracy in Eastern political thought. They cite Mencius's words on the importance of people but they overlook the Mencian pattern of social hierarchy. Almost every rebel in Chinese history quoted Mencius to support his revolt against the government. At the same time, every ruler found comfort in this work when he contemplated punitive campaigns to suppress rebellions. Above all, Mencius has been adopted by the Chinese state-socialists as their ancient spokesperson.

In the same manner, the mystic element in this work has been made use of by different schools of thought. The Daoists have always wanted to include Mencius in their ranks, and they are not entirely without justification. Certain basic elements of Daoist mysticism antedated, or at least coexisted with, Confucian thought. The theory of the all-pervading force of Mencius certainly has a familiar ring to the ears of a Daoist. These problems cannot be tackled before philological studies of the text can establish the indisputable authenticity of any statements attributed to Mencius in this book and can secure other corroborating evidence to make the full implications of these statements clear.

Kai-yu Hsu

Additional Reading

Creel, H.G. *Chinese Thought from Confucius to Mao Tse-tung*. Chicago: University of Chicago Press, 1953. A very clear text with a good chapter on Mencius. Includes a brief bibliography, selected readings, and a useful index.

Ivanhoe, Philip J. *Confucian Moral Self Cultivation*. New York: Peter Lang, 1993. This work provides a very good introduction to important Confucian philosophers such as Confucius, Mencius, and Xunzi.

_____. *Ethics in the Confucian Tradition: The Thought of Mencius and Wang Yang-ming*. Atlanta, Ga.: Scholars Press, 1990. Looks at neo-Confucian Wang Yang-ming's interpretation of Mencius. Includes chapters that contrast the two philosophers' approaches to the nature of morality, human nature, sagehood, the origin of evil, and self-cultivation. A good introduction to Mencius's thought.

Koller, John M., and Patricia Joyce Koller. *Asian Philosophies*. 3d ed. Upper Saddle River, N.J.: Prentice-Hall, 1998. A general introduction to Asian philosophy. Contains a brief section on the philosophy of Mencius within a chapter on the main concepts in Confucianism. A good introduction for beginners.

Mote, Frederick W. *Intellectual Foundations of China*. New York: Alfred A. Knopf, 1971. Contains intelligent scholarly essays, a select bibliography, and an index. The entries on Mencius are brief, but very good for placing him in context.

Nivison, David S. *The Ways of Confucianism: Investigations in Chinese Philosophy*. Edited by W. Van Norden. Chicago: Open Court, 1996. This work includes a substantial treatment of Mencius on issues such as weakness of will, virtue, motivation, and issues in translating Mencius. Includes an introduction by W. Van Norden

Richards, I. A. *Mencius on the Mind: Experiments in Multiple Definition*. London: Kegan Paul, Trench, Trubner, 1932. An enlightening work using linguistic methods developed in the West. Richards offers a critique of Mencius's method of argument. A very useful book in comparative philosophy.

Schwartz, Benjamin I. *The World of Thought in Ancient China*. Cambridge, Mass.: Harvard University Press, 1985. A scholarly study that compares the major issues in Chinese philosophy with Western philosophical concepts. Includes a very helpful chapter on Mencius. Provides a bibliography, notes, and an index.

Shun, Kwong-loi. *Mencius and Early Chinese Thought*. Stanford, Calif.: Stanford University Press, 1997. This work is the first of three proposed volumes on Confucian-Mencian ethics. This volume focuses on the texts of Mencius and their influence on early Confucian thinkers. It includes a thorough index, bibliography, and notes.

Verwilghen, Albert Felix. *Mencius: The Man and His Ideas*. New York: St. John's University Press, 1967. Provides an introduction to Mencius and his philosophy.

Waley, Arthur. *Three Ways of Thought in Ancient China*. Winchester, Mass.: Allen & Unwin, 1939. A standard among scholars. A very readable work with a helpful bibliography, glossary, and index. Includes good introductions and translations.

Clifton K. Yearley and Kerrie L. MacPherson,
updated by Tammy Nyden-Bullock

Maurice Merleau-Ponty

Merleau-Ponty, French philosopher and man of letters, was one of the most original and profound thinkers of the postwar French movement of existential phenomenology.

Principal philosophical works: *La Structure de comportement*, 1942 (*The Structure of Behavior*, 1963); *Phénoménologie de la perception*, 1945 (*The Phenomenology of Perception*, 1962); *Humanisme et terreur: Essai sur le problème communiste*, 1947 (*Humanism and Terror: An Essay on the Communist Problem*, 1969); *Sense et non-sense*, 1948 (*Sense and Non-Sense*, 1964); *Les Aventures de la dialectique*, 1955 (*Adventures of the Dialectic*, 1974); *Signes*, 1960 (*Signs*, 1964); *Le Visible et l'invisible*, 1964 (*The Visible and the Invisible*, 1968); *La Prose du monde*, 1969 (*The Prose of the World*, 1974).

Born: March 14, 1908; Rochefort, France
Died: May 4, 1961; Paris, France

Early Life

Maurice Merleau-Ponty's father died before his son was seven years old, and Maurice, his brother, and his sister were reared in Paris by their mother, a devout Catholic who gave her children a strongly religious upbringing. It was not until the 1930's that Merleau-Ponty eventually became discontented with the established Church and ceased to practice his faith. At one point in his life, he even admitted to being an atheist but then altered his position to one of agnosticism. His final position with regard to religion is not known; what is clear, however, is that some degree of reconciliation with the Church of his early years probably occurred before his sudden death in May of 1961, because a Catholic Mass was said at his funeral.

According to his own writings, Merleau-Ponty's childhood was happy, so happy that his adult years never quite provided him with the same sense of complete fulfillment. The death of his father while Merleau-Ponty was still very young is thought to have affected him immeasurably. He became extremely close to his mother and remained completely devoted to her until her death only a few years before his own.

Merleau-Ponty received his secondary education at the Lycée Louis-le-Grand and then studied at the École Normale Supérieure in Paris. Af-ter taking his *agrégation de philosophie* (a difficult postgraduate examination for teaching positions at *lycées* and universities in France) in 1931, he taught in a *lycée* at Beauvais for the next five years. He then held a research grant from the Caisse de la Recherche Scientifique for a year and subsequently took up teaching again, this time at the *lycée* in Chartres. In 1935, he returned to Paris as a junior member of the faculty at the school he had attended, the École Normale.

Life's Work

In the winter of 1939, after the Nazi invasion of Poland, Merleau-Ponty entered the army and served as a lieutenant in the infantry. While in the army, he wrote his first major work, *The Structure of Behavior*. Although the work was completed in 1938 when he was thirty years old, because of the war, the book was not published until 1942. Perhaps the most important thesis of this work is Merleau-Ponty's reinterpretation of the distinctions between the physical, the biological (or vital), and the mental dimensions of existence. These dimensions were treated by him as different levels of conceptualization at which human behavior could be studied, and they were distinguished by the degree to which the concepts used were useful and meaningful. Although Merleau-Ponty was very insistent upon the irreducibility of these distinctions, he also maintained that they were logically cumulative, such that biological concepts presuppose physical concepts and mental concepts presuppose both. Yet, at the same time that he defended this thesis of the logical interdependence of the physical and the mental, Merleau-Ponty rejected in principle all attempts to explain this relationship in causal terms. Merleau-Ponty's first work, then, was both a sustained and a powerful attack on behaviorism in psychology as well as a new philosophical interpretation of the experimental work of the Gestalt psychologists.

After the demobilization of France and during the German occupation, Merleau-Ponty again returned to teaching and writing. Continuing his critique of traditional psychology, in 1945, he published what was to become his masterwork: *The Phenomenology of Perception*. This second book examined what he viewed as traditional prejudices regarding perception in order to advance a "return" to things themselves. According to Merleau-Ponty, understanding the body itself involves a theory of perception. One is able to know oneself only through relationships with the world, and the world is not what one thinks it is but what one lives through. Drawing heavily

Maurice Merleau-Ponty. *(AP/Wide World Photos)*

upon, but also modifying, the phenomenological techniques of Edmund Husserl as well as the existential threads in the thought of Gabriel Marcel and Martin Heidegger, Merleau-Ponty, in this work, begins to construct a personal synthesis, an original philosophical interpretation of human experience. For this reason, he is considered to be one of the originators of contemporary existential philosophy and, in the opinion of one of his notable colleagues, Paul Ricœur, "was the greatest of the French phenomenologists."

After the occupation of France ended, Merleau-Ponty joined the faculty of the University of Lyon and at the same time (in 1945) became coeditor of the existentialist periodical *Les Temps modernes* with Jean-Paul Sartre, a former schoolmate and longtime friend. By 1950, Merleau-Ponty's reputation was established, and he took a position at the Sorbonne as professor of psychology and pedagogy. He was to remain in this post for only two years. Then, in 1952, he was appointed to a chair at the Collège de France. This was the chair that had been left vacant by the death of Louis Lavelle and that had previously been occupied by Henri Bergson and Édouard Le Roy. Merleau-Ponty, in fact, was the youngest philosopher ever to hold this position—one of the more prestigious in French academic life—and he retained it until his death in May, 1961. Merleau-Ponty was happily married to a woman prominent in her own right as a physician and psychiatrist in Paris, and they had one child, a daughter.

All Merleau-Ponty's work demonstrates a familiarity with both current scientific research and the history of philosophy, a combination that gives his work a more balanced character than that of the other existentialists. Another of his major concerns was with political and social philosophy as well as the problems of everyday politics. Consequently he wrote numerous newspaper articles on contemporary events and problems. His more sustained essays on Marxist theory and leftist politics, however, were gathered in two collections: *Humanism and Terror: An Essay on the Communist Problem* and *Adventures of the Dialectic*.

In the former work, Merleau-Ponty leaned so far in the direction of Marxist historicism as to argue that historical undertakings are to be judged retroactively by their success or failure and that to act "historically" is inevitably to submit oneself to this "objective" judgment of events, in which personal intentions, good or bad, are irrelevant. Simultaneously, however, he rejected the orthodox Marxist view that a scientific theory of the logic of historical development is accessible as a basis for such action. The latter work, exhibiting a new direction in the philosopher's social thought, contains a powerful critique of the French Communist Party, with which he had earlier sympathized. Marxism, in his opinion, was a timely device for thinking about human needs and contingencies in modern industrial society; however, he rejected its dogmatic rigidity, particularly its claims to predictive power and historical mission, and the nonliberating, totalitarian features that had become associated with it.

Well to the left of Sartre during the 1940's, Merleau-Ponty was close to the Communists from 1945 to 1950 and played a crucial role in linking existentialist and Marxist thought during that period. By 1955, however, he was no longer engaged in Marxist politics. In 1950 Sartre, on the other hand, began to move closer to Marxism. For some years after 1955, Sartre was occupied almost exclusively with the existentialism-Marxism debate, which since 1945 had continued to be an explosive issue in French intellectual and political life. The ideological split with Sartre led to an open break with him and to Merleau-Ponty's resignation from the editorship of *Les Temps modernes*. Nevertheless, Merleau-Ponty's political views remained decisive for Sartre, as the latter freely admitted in a memoir published after Merleau-Ponty's death.

Merleau-Ponty wrote essays and articles on language, literature, the aesthetics of film, and painting in the busy final decade of his life. In these essays, published as collections entitled *Sense and Non-Sense* and *Signs*, he sought to work out some of the implications of his thesis on the primacy of perception using Husserl as his fundamental reference point for epistemological grounding and dialogue. Merleau-Ponty had hoped to conclude his analysis of the prereflective life of consciousness with a survey of the major modes of reflective thought in which he would seek to determine their criteria for validity

and truth. At the time of his sudden death from a coronary thrombosis in 1961, he had written only incomplete fragments and sketches.

Influence

Merleau-Ponty's career included two principal aspects. He was, first, a professional philosopher and teacher of philosophy whose main body of work was done in the field of philosophical psychology and phenomenology. In addition, he was a man of letters who wrote extensively on political and aesthetic subjects and actively participated in the intellectual life of his time. Despite the fact that Merleau-Ponty is sometimes viewed as a kind of junior collaborator of Sartre, both his philosophical work and his more general writings reveal a mind and a mode of thought that developed in a fully independent manner and that are very different from Sartre's and, in terms of intellectual rigor and elegance, often demonstrably superior.

As in the case with other "existentialist" philosophers, Merleau-Ponty had no "disciples" in the strict sense of the word because his method was his life. To adopt his method then, would be to begin to experience the world in a new way, with a new philosophy, and not with a continuation of Merleau-Ponty's life and thought. Thus, it is not by virtue of his existentialism, Marxism, or phenomenology that he made his greatest contribution, but rather by virtue of the extent to which, through each of these, he was able to illuminate the human quality of existence. It is in and through his uniqueness that his impact will be felt most strongly.

Genevieve Slomski

The Phenomenology of Perception

Type of philosophy: Epistemology, existentialism, phenomenology
First published: Phénoménologie de la perception, 1945 (English translation, 1962)
Principal ideas advanced:
◇ The world is not (as realism contends) the cause of one's consciousness of it, but neither (as idealism contends) does one's conscious-

ness "constitute" the world by providing order and meaning to intrinsically meaningless "sensations."

◇ The human body is no mere "physical body" that can be understood in terms of purely causal relations between its parts and between itself and objects; as "lived" it is, rather, the bearer of one's most fundamental grasp of and orientation to the world, which provides the basis for one's more conscious, personal activities.

◇ The human mind is not sheer mind, possessing a pure rational comprehension of the world or of itself; human rationality is rooted in human perception, and self-knowledge is mediated through bodily expression and action in the world and through time.

◇ One is not determined by one's past, temperament, or situation, but neither is one radically free in relation to these motivations; one's freedom is found in accepting them and taking them up in free choices, in which one proffered motivation is refused only by accepting another, and which can only gradually modify the basic direction of personality.

The Phenomenology of Perception is Maurice Merleau-Ponty's second book, following *La Structure de comportement* (1942; *The Structure of Behavior*, 1963), a critique of psychological behaviorism. *The Phenomenology of Perception*, which incorporates some insights from the earlier work, defines the main lines of the philosophical position that Merleau-Ponty held for most of the rest of his life, with significant changes in the direction of his thinking clearly emerging only in the various fragments that were published posthumously as *Le Visible et l'invisible* (1964; *The Visible and the Invisible*, 1968).

The Phenomenology of Perception is in some respects less, but in many respects more, than its title suggests. It is not a systematic orderly analysis, along Husserlian lines, of perception regarded in isolation from other modes of human consciousness. Rather, it is a kind of ontology of human existence, in which perception is shown to play a most fundamental role. In the range of its topics—which include embodiment, sexuality, the relation between self and other, self-knowledge, temporality, and freedom—the work

is comparable to Jean-Paul Sartre's *L'Être et le néant* (1943; *Being and Nothingness*, 1956). Indeed, the influence of Sartre, who was Merleau-Ponty's friend and associate for many years, is often apparent, although Merleau-Ponty avoids the abstract oppositions and paradoxes of Sartre's thought and presents a subtler, more concrete conception of these matters.

In the working out of his position, Merleau-Ponty also comes to terms with such giants of modern philosophy as René Descartes, Immanuel Kant, and Georg Wilhelm Friedrich Hegel. His work also reflects his familiarity with twentieth century French thinkers such as Henri Bergson, Léon Brunschvicg, and Gabriel Marcel, and with psychological literature, particularly that of the Gestalt school. However, the most significant influence on his thinking is clearly phenomenology, as represented by Edmund Husserl, Martin Heidegger, and Max Scheler.

In the preface to his work, Merleau-Ponty says that phenomenology involves an attempt to recall the prescientific experience of the world on which scientific knowledge is based but which is often passed over by an attitude that (mistakenly) takes scientific knowledge to be absolute. He credits Husserl with developing the method by which the absolutist pretensions of science could be criticized but declines to follow Husserl in the idealistic direction that characterized much of his work. Phenomenological reflection does not lead, Merleau-Ponty says, to recognition of oneself as a "transcendental consciousness" somehow apart from the world but to the revelation of one's "being-in-the-world" ("being-in" to be understood as meaning not simple spatial location but "inhabiting" or "being involved in"). Moreover, reflection on "essences" does not disclose essences as a separate sphere of being but rather should serve as a means for clarifying concrete *existence*, one's living experience of the world and oneself.

Sensation and Consciousness

In the introduction, "Traditional Prejudices and the Return to Phenomena," Merleau-Ponty critically examines certain concepts and assumptions that have had the effect of obscuring, rather than illuminating, the true nature of our perceptual experience. Chief among such concepts is that of *sensation*. Sensations are usually conceived of as isolated, inner states that the perceiver undergoes as a result of external stimuli. The "constancy hypothesis" in psychology postulates that uniform stimuli produce uniform effects of this sort. However, this attempt to construct a causal account of perception is inadequate, Merleau-Ponty argues; nothing in one's actual experience corresponds to this concept of sensation. One's perceptual life is not composed of isolated states; in it, every element has some meaning in relation to the whole. Perceptual consciousness is not the sheer feeling of an inner state but is (in the phenomenological sense) intentional, is directed toward, is consciousness of something other than itself. The empiricists' conceptions of "association" and "projection of memories" or the rationalists' conception of (for example) "judgment" as processes that remedy the deficiencies of sensations reflect the inadequacy of the concept of sensation. Association and memory must somehow be suggested, "motivated" by present experience, which thus cannot be a blind sensation. Judgment is based on a perceptual field having some inherent structure, which it seeks to make explicit.

The fundamental error of both empiricist and rationalist accounts of consciousness, Merleau-Ponty argues, lies in what he calls the "prejudice in favour of the world." These accounts presuppose a conception of a fully determinate "objective" world and attempt to understand consciousness on this basis—either as a mere effect of this world or as objective knowledge of it—rather than beginning with an unprejudiced examination of that perceptual experience through which there comes to be a world for oneself. Such reflection will disclose perception as neither the passive undergoing of sensations nor the active, rational "constitution" of the "objective" world but as a living relation to an ambiguous, prescientific, perceptual world.

The Body

Having thus set the essential task of his work, Merleau-Ponty turns to the crucial topic of the body. His discussion—which occupies the first main division of *The Phenomenology of Perception*—proceeds largely through reflection on scientific findings about the body, findings that he contends have been seriously misinterpreted by scientists. He attempts to establish that the human body is not an object in the world (a mere "physical object") and that concept of the body is an abstraction from the concrete, "lived" body, which is one's point of view on, one's openness to, and the base of one's orientation toward the world. Because the theory of the body and the theory of perception are of necessity closely related, Merleau-Ponty's account of the body provides an avenue to disclosure of the concrete perceived world that underlies the "objective" world depicted by science.

Merleau-Ponty's reflections on the body are extraordinarily rich, and only some of their most basic themes can be indicated here. He points to a number of considerations that preclude the body's being adequately conceived of as an "object"—as something that is related to other "objects," or whose parts are related to one another, only externally and mechanically. The study of the nervous system has shown, he says, that no simple localization can be assigned to the ability to perceive a specific quality. Sensible qualities are not mere effects of stimuli but require that the body be somehow "attuned" for their perception, as the hand, in moving around an object, anticipates the stimuli that will reveal the object to it. Merleau-Ponty provides a particularly illuminating discussion of "phantom limb" experiences, in which people seem to feel (for example) pain in an amputated limb. He argues that this phenomenon can be explained neither in terms of mere physical factors (such as stimuli affecting the nerves that had been linked to the limb) nor purely psychological factors (such as memory of the lost limb or refusal to face its loss). Rather, a phantom limb is experienced when objects are implicitly taken to be manipulable, as they were before loss of the limb. It is a matter of one's projecting oneself into a practical environment, of one's embodied "being-in-the-world," of one's ambiguous concrete existence at a level before the abstract distinction of the "physical" and the "psychological." The body is no mere "thing"; it is a "body-subject," the seat of one's habits, of one's innate and acquired capacities and orientation toward the world. As such, it provides the general background from which one's most conscious, personal, and rational acts emerge.

Merleau-Ponty subsequently deals with the nature of bodily movement and its relation to perception. Consciousness does not move the body as one moves an "object" through space, he argues; rather, the body moves insofar as it "inhabits" space, insofar as it is oriented in relation to objects. One's perceptual powers are themselves intimately interrelated. The unity of the living body is the unity of a "style," comparable to the unity of a work of art; its powers work together in disclosure of the world.

Merleau-Ponty's account of the body concludes with discussions of sexuality and of "the body as expression and speech." His discussion of sexuality—which involves some very subtle reflections on Sigmund Freud—depicts it as a general atmosphere that suffuses life in such a way that it can neither serve as a total explanation of our existence nor be isolated from the other modes of our being-in-the-world. Neither a matter of mere "physiology" nor a matter of sheer consciousness, sexuality is a mode of one's being-in-the-world, a basic manner in which one embodied being can exist in relation to another.

In his discussion of speech, Merleau-Ponty criticizes empiricist psychologies that construe one's use of words as the mere result of physiological processes and rationalist conceptions that take words to be merely external accompaniments of thought, linked to it by mere association. Both of these views deprive the word itself of meaning. However, he argues, thought and speech—either external or internal—are essentially bound up with each other. Contrary to most of the philosophical tradition since Greek philosopher Plato, Merleau-Ponty denies that meaningful speech must be preceded or accompanied by a separate process of thinking. Rather, we think in speech; and although thinking sometimes seems to run "a step ahead" of speech, it nevertheless requires linguistic expression to establish itself. The phenomenon of speech must ultimately, he adds, be understood as similar to other modes of bodily "gesture"—their meaning is immanent in them. The whole expressive dimension of our embodied existence stands as one more proof that the rigid Cartesian dualism of thinking substance and extended substance is inadequate.

The Perceived World

In the second main division of *The Phenomenology of Perception*, Merleau-Ponty turns to an explication of the concrete structures of the perceived world. Again he attempts to delineate an alternative to both empiricism and rationalism. Both views, he argues, simply presuppose a fully determinate objective world. Empiricism locates the subject as a thing in that world, construes the relation of world to subject as causal, and constructs its account of experience on that basis. Rationalism takes the world to be for a knowing subject and analyzes experience accordingly. Neither takes its stand within that ambiguous living experience in which objects come to be. Accepting this task, Merleau-Ponty provides accounts of people's concrete experience of sensible qualities, spatial location, depth, movement, shape, size, the "natural thing" as a unity of sensible qualities, and finally of the world as that open unity that forms the ultimate horizon of all human experiences. Preeminent in all these experiences is the role of the body—its capacity to "merge into" a given perceptual situation (as when, without any thought, it manages to grasp the true colors of things despite abnormal lighting conditions that change the "objective" stimuli that are present), to respond to the solicitation of ambiguous data, to grasp through the unity of its perceptual powers the unity of qualities in a thing, and to be present through the perceptual field to a world that is ever incomplete.

People and the World

The last and perhaps most interesting chapter dealing with Merleau-Ponty's account of the perceived world examines "the other self and the human world" and draws on many of the basic insights developed in earlier sections. People not only are conscious of natural objects, he notes, but also perceive the artifacts and inhabitants of a cultural and social world—a human world. The first, the most basic "cultural object," he argues, must be the body of the other person; only on the foundation of one's perception of others is a cultural world made accessible. However, "objective thought" would make perception of the other impossible by construing all bodies as mere objects, and the subject as a pure "for itself," a sheer self-conscious, rational surveyor of the objective world. This would make it unintelligible that a body could ever be truly expressive of a subjectivity and that there could ever be another for-itself for one. However, as Merleau-Ponty has shown, one is not a sheer for-itself; one is, rather, an embodied, perceiving, behaving subject, and thus the other's body is not for one a thing, a mere in-itself. One's experience of embodied subjectivity allows one, before any sort of explicit analogy or judgment, to grasp another consciousness in its embodiment. The perceived world, as that unity that forever outruns one's determinate grasp of it, is also crucial here; as one's different perspectives "slip into" one another and are united in relation to the perceptible thing, so one's perspective and that of the other "slip into" one another and are united in the world, in which our communication is possible.

Language and the experience of dialogue play an important role. People's thoughts are woven together in living, reciprocal speech. However, Merleau-Ponty adds, the plurality of consciousnesses, their differences from one another, is an inescapable fact. For example, the anger or grief that I grasp in another's behavior does not have the same significance for both of us; he *lives* what I merely *perceive*. We have common projects, but each participates in it from his own perspective. Solitude and communication, Merleau-Ponty warns, must not be taken as exclusive alternatives; rather, they are two aspects of our ambiguous human condition. Thus I can recognize that the other is imperfectly known by me only if I do have experience of the other. Merleau-Ponty proceeds to criticize Sartre's claim that I must either make an object of the other or allow the other's "gaze" to make an object of me. Another person's gaze is felt as unbearable, Merleau-Ponty says, only if it replaces possible communication, and the latter retains its truth. He concludes by asserting that I am neither in society as one object among others, nor is society in me as an object of thought; rather, the social is a "dimension of existence" in which I live.

Self-Knowledge, Time, and Freedom

The final main division of *The Phenomenology of Perception* deals with "being-for-itself" and "being-in-the-world." Here Merleau-Ponty discusses self-knowledge (the *cogito*), temporality,

and freedom. Developing the position of Descartes, idealism has argued that objects must be for a subject which is for itself, which knows itself, which somehow contains within itself the key to every object that it could possibly encounter. However, the mind is not a sheer for-itself, Merleau-Ponty maintains; the *cogito* does not involve an absolute and total self-knowledge. Thus, he undertakes a critique of traditional doctrines of the *cogito*. He argues first that, contrary to Descartes, one can be no more certain that one sees than that the thing one sees exists. Nor does one possess absolute self-knowledge in respect to one's will or feeling; one can, for example, think that one is in love without truly being so. One does not know oneself so much in oneself, in some inner and immediate self-presence, as in action. It is by action and expression in the world and through the body that one achieves determinacy and clarity for oneself, so that the *cogito* is inherently conditioned by temporality. Thus, "I think" is dependent on "I am." Even in the sphere of so-called "pure thought"—geometrical thinking, for example—one's grasp of truth is dependent on one's bodily orientation to the world, through which one can fundamentally grasp what a "triangle" or a "direction" is. Moreover, thought is inherently dependent on speech, and the clarity achieved in a given thought is dependent on an always somewhat obscure context that has been formed by past acts of expression. The centrality of this phenomenon of "acquisition" in mental life points again to the inherent temporality of a person's grasp on truth.

These critical reflections on doctrines that would grant to the mind an absolute grasp of itself or of the world do not, however, lead Merleau-Ponty to reject the cogito altogether. There is, he says, a presence to self that precedes and conditions one's explicit grasp of oneself or of the world, a "tacit *cogito*" that precedes the "spoken *cogito*." However, this tacit *cogito* is inchoate and must be expressed in a verbal *cogito* in order to attain clarity. The ultimate subject, Merleau-Ponty concludes, is not a sheer self-present nonworldly ego that "constitutes" the world, but a being that belongs *to* the world.

The fundamental role of time in relation to all sorts of phenomena is indicated throughout *The Phenomenology of Perception*, but it becomes the explicit theme of Merleau-Ponty's reflections only in the penultimate chapter of the work. He begins by arguing that time is inseparable from subjectivity; without a subject, there is no present in the world, and without a present there can be no past or future. However, what is the fundamental relation of time and subjectivity? The subject cannot, he says, be simply located in the "now," and its consciousness of past and future explained in terms of physiological or psychological "traces" of the past. Such "traces," being purely present, could not ground one's opening onto past or future. However, neither could time be a constituted object for a nontemporal subject before whom past, present, and future were equally arrayed, for if they were all like present, there would be no time. Time, then, is inseparable from a subject, but this subject is itself inherently temporal, is situated in time, and grasps future and past on the horizon of a flowing present that accomplishes the transition between them. There is an essential interdependence between temporality and the "thrust" of concrete subjectivity toward a world and a future in which it can (in both senses of the term) "realize" itself.

The final chapter of *The Phenomenology of Perception* is a subtly reasoned and eloquently expressed reflection on human freedom. Initially, Merleau-Ponty notes, the only alternative to a causal and deterministic conception of the relation between the subject and the world (a conception that would, in effect, make a thing of consciousness) is a view of human consciousness as wholly free, independent of all motives, of nature, of one's past temperament and history. In this view—which is essentially that expressed by Sartre in *Being and Nothingness*—even obstacles to freedom are in reality deployed by it; it is the individual's choice to reach a certain destination that makes certain objects into obstacles.

However, Merleau-Ponty responds, this abstract conception of freedom would in effect rule it out completely. A wholly indeterminate freedom would lack even the possibility of committing itself, since the next instant would find it again indeterminate and uncommitted. Rather, he argues, a choice once made must provide some impetus to personality, must establish a direction that tends to conserve itself. Because one

is not a sheer self-conscious subject but an embodied being like other human beings, one's free choices take place against a background of possibilities that have a kind of preliminary significance. Thus mountains appear to be high whether or not one chooses to climb them. Because one is a temporal being, one's established character and habits, although they do not cause behavior, do incline one to certain choices.

Freedom is always, then, a taking up of some meaning or some motivation that is offered by one's situation in the world. One can reject one proffered meaning or motivation, Merleau-Ponty says, only by accepting another. Even if a person being tortured refuses to provide the information the torturers demand, this free action does not reflect a wholly solitary and unmotivated choice; it is supported by the person's awareness of unity with comrades, preparation for such an ordeal, or long-established belief in freedom.

Humanity is neither a mere thing nor a sheer consciousness. Human life involves a continual synthesis of the for-itself and the in-itself, a taking up and shaping of one's finite situation, a reciprocity of self and world. People are truly free not by denying their natural and social situation but by assuming it and living it. Thus philosophy recalls people to their concrete existence in the world, where, Merleau-Ponty suggests, their proper task is to commit their freedom to the realization of freedom for all.

John D. Glenn, Jr.

Additional Reading

Abram, David. *The Spell of the Sensuous*. New York: Pantheon Books, 1996. This book is not an analysis of Maurice Merleau-Ponty but a very vivid demonstration of his thinking, especially with regard to perception and language. Abram uses Merleau-Ponty's ideas with great power in developing his own original ecological philosophy.

Bannan, John. *The Philosophy of Merleau-Ponty*. New York: Harcourt, Brace & World, 1967. Bannan offers overviews of much of Merleau-Ponty's writings, especially with respect to consciousness's relations with the world and with others.

Barral, Mary. *The Body in Interpersonal Relations: Merleau-Ponty*. New York: University Press of

America, 1984. The author introduces Merleau-Ponty through an analysis of the importance he attaches to the body as the bearer of the dialectic of subjectivity and objectivity

Cataldi, Sue. *Emotion, Depth, and Flesh: A Study of Sensitive Space*. Albany: State University of New York Press, 1993. This book, a concrete application of Merleau-Ponty's philosophy of embodiment to a phenomenology of place, covers the experience of emotion and its relations to the body and space. Very readable, with intensely moving phenomenological descriptions of spaces as they are experienced.

Dillon, M. C. *Merleau-Ponty's Ontology*. Bloomington: Indiana University Press, 1988. Dillon presents Merleau-Ponty's effort to overcome a subject-object dualism through his original phenomenological ontology of the flesh as found in *The Phenomenology of Perception* and *The Visible and the Invisible*.

_____, ed. *Merleau-Ponty Vivant*. Albany: State University of New York Press, 1991. An excellent collection by premier Merleau-Ponty scholars engagingly taking up a number of the philosopher's significant themes. Their discussions help situate Merleau-Ponty in relation to late-twentieth century thought.

Langer, Monika. *Merleau-Ponty's Phenomenology of Perception*. Tallahassee: Florida State University Press, 1989. This text provides a very clear guide and commentary to Merleau-Ponty's most influential book, *The Phenomenology of Perception*. A chapter-by-chapter reading renders its insights with grace and fluidity.

Madison, Gary. *The Phenomenology of Merleau-Ponty*. Athens: Ohio University Press, 1981. Madison surveys Merleau-Ponty's major works very comprehensively but assesses the earlier works from the viewpoint of the later ones, looking particularly at Merleau-Ponty's ontological analysis of Being and existence.

Mallin, Samuel. *Merleau-Ponty's Philosophy*. New Haven, Conn.: Yale University Press, 1979. This book presents Merleau-Ponty's work as a unified and integrated whole. Mallin's method is to analyze extensively the concepts that are central and original to Merleau-Ponty.

Review of Existential Psychology and Psychiatry 18 (1982-1983). This special edition of a journal gathers a variety of provocative essays on Merleau-Ponty's work, relating it to psychoanalysis, phenomenological psychology, intersubjectivity, and sexuality. It also contains a new translation of a lecture course by Merleau-Ponty on the experience of others.

Surling, Laurie. *Phenomenology and the Social World: The Philosophy of Merleau-Ponty and Its Relation to the Social Sciences*. London: Routledge & Kegan Paul, 1977. Surling argues that Merleau-Ponty's philosophy can be understood as a dialectic between a discipline and a transcendental impulse and that it is this overall dialectical relationship that offers a coherent perspective on being in the world, especially on those areas of thought often considered to be the exclusive domain of the social sciences.

Genevieve Slomski,
updated by Christopher M. Aanstoos

Mary Midgley

Midgley combined critique and constructive commentary to bring philosophy to bear on contemporary issues. Her philosophy is marked by an emphasis on the importance of human nature and biology, the recognition and rejection of nonsense, and a resistance to smoothing out significant differences.

Principal philosophical works: *Beast and Man: The Roots of Human Nature*, 1978; *Heart and Mind: The Varieties of Moral Experience*, 1981; *Animals and Why They Matter*, 1983; *Women's Choices: Philosophical Problems Facing Feminism*, 1983 (with Judith Hughes); *Wickedness: A Philosophical Essay*, 1984; *Evolution as a Religion: Strange Hopes and Stranger Fears*, 1985; *Wisdom, Information, and Wonder: What Is Knowledge For?*, 1989; *Can't We Make Moral Judgements?*, 1991; *Science as Salvation: A Modern Myth and Its Meaning*, 1992; *The Ethical Primate: Humans, Freedom, and Morality*, 1994; *Utopias, Dolphins, and Computers: Problems in Philosophical Plumbing*, 1996.

Born: September 13, 1919; London, England

Early Life

Mary Midgley (née Scrutton), like German philosopher Immanuel Kant, flourished as a published philosopher in the later portion of her career. Born in London on September 13, 1919, she read "classical greats" at Somerville College. Leaving Oxford in 1942, she worked as a civil servant and a teacher of classics. She then became secretary to the distinguished classicist Gilbert Murray. After the war, she tutored students at Somerville College and began research on Plotinus, then took a position as lecturer at Reading University.

She married philosopher Geoffrey Midgley in 1950, when he was teaching at the University of Newcastle on Tyne. They had three sons, and while raising them, she worked in broadcasting, reviewed books (especially for the *New Statesman*), and conducted research on animal behavior, work that prepared her for her later flurry of writing. Her British Broadcasting Corporation appearances illustrate her deep commitment to bringing philosophy out of its isolation and reestablishing it as a significant contributor to culture and society. She began to teach again, part-time in 1965 and full-time in 1971. She retired in 1980 to devote herself to writing.

Life's Work

In 1978, Midgley published *Beast and Man: The Roots of Human Nature*, a book stimulated by her preparation for an adult education class she taught at her home university and for lectures at Cornell University, given at the invitation of the well-known philosopher Max Black. In this volume and in her *Animals and Why They Matter* in 1983, her concern is to assert the status of human beings as animals, members of the biological community, without reducing them to *mere* animals or diminishing their unique qualities. Her interest in science was again evident in her 1985 work, *Evolution as a Religion: Strange Hopes and Stranger Fears*, in which Midgley distinguished between evolutionary theory in biology and evolution as myth, and her 1992 publication, *Science as Salvation: A Modern Myth and Its Meaning*, a collection of essays based on her Gifford Lectures, which critiqued a variety of quasi-scientific proposals and prospects that optimistically offer different sorts of panaceas to problems of the human race.

In many of her other publications, Midgley examined issues of morality and knowledge. In her 1981 publication, *Heart and Mind: The Varieties of Moral Experience*, she argued that the supposedly sharp distinction between mind and heart, or thought and feeling, does not correspond to our actual mental states, which are typically affective and cognitive. Two years later, with Judith Hughes, she published *Women's Choices: Philosophical Problems Facing Feminism*, which focused on philosophy and feminism. Her 1984 publication, *Wickedness: A Philosophical Essay*, is concerned with evil in human affairs and the human heart. In 1989, she published *Wisdom, Information, and Wonder: What Is Knowledge For?*, in which she discussed the importance of understanding and the integration of theoretical and practical knowing. The mutual relevance of theory and practice, and of theoretical and practical reason, is one of her major themes. In *Can't We Make Moral Judgements?*, Midgley noted that those who answer the title question negatively make a considerable degree of moral commitment, and she argued that the reasons for answering the question negatively presuppose that the answer is in fact positive. While being sympathetic to and taking note of the reasons to be suspicious of moral judgment, she argued that accepting this position would leave us without sound basis for protesting both what those who embrace this suspicion deplore and what they ought to deplore.

Midgley's philosophical writings, considered as a whole, form an impressive, creative, and coherent body of work. Midgley, as part of her effort to bring philosophy back into public discourse, aimed her writing at the intelligent layperson at least as much as the professional philosopher or academic. Whether one agrees with her on specific points, her work can fairly be described as balanced, sensible, informed by relevant empirical data, and seasoned with a bit of iconoclasm toward views she regards as influential but simplistic. The result is accessible discussions of practical topics with recognition of the importance of theory to practice. Without writing down to her audience or avoiding relevant complexities, she wrote understandable prose on important topics.

Apparently as a matter of principle, though many of the topics on which she wrote are matters on which religious traditions have taken stances, she steadfastly avoided taking or opposing any religious standpoint. For example, in *Wickedness*, although she dealt with the problem of evil, she avoided a discussion of whether the existence of evil is evidence against the existence of God.

Can't We Make Moral Judgements? begins with a student's question that expresses a modern-day assumption: "But surely it's always wrong to make moral judgments?" The assumption behind the student's question is that no one is ever in a proper position to judge the conduct of another person. However, if one believes that judging others is wrong, one is making a moral judgment on everyone who does so. Even if no one ever knows the motives of another person—and motives are really not that inscrutable—it would not follow that torture or genocide could not be recognized as morally deplorable. In any case, the student was doing what he suggested was morally wrong by declaring something always forbidden. Similarly, the idea that morality is private expresses the notion that the things that morality deals with are not wrong and so may safely be allowed to go their own way, another (highly dubious) moral judgment.

It is widely accepted that needlessly harming others is wrong, and this view is doubly morally committed: It takes needlessly harming others to be morally impermissible and assumes some notion of what is harmful and therefore of what is the opposite of harmful, of what is helpful and healthy, of what is good. Midgley noted that those who are skeptical of our ability to judge the cultures of others tend to judge our past culture and accept criticisms of our culture when they are offered by those in other cultures who have been oppressed. It follows then, that in principle, one can make moral judgments regarding cultural practice. Midgley argued that the reasons typically offered for answering her title question negatively in fact justify an affirmative answer.

In *Animals and Why They Matter*, Midgley distinguished between two policies regarding animals, namely absolute dismissal (in which animals do not count at all) and relative dismissal (in which consideration of animals comes after all consideration of human concerns). Although she noted that human beings are also animals, for simplicity's sake, she contrasted animals and humans in this work. The distinction between absolute and relative dismissal is important, she argued, for two reasons. One is that the interests of animals and the interests of humans often do not compete, and when they do not, relative dismissal allows animal interests to be consulted, whereas absolute dismissal does not. The other reason is that one can build on relative dismissal to create what she regards as a better view, although absolute dismissal does not permit this. Her purpose, in effect, was to build on relative dismissal, arguing that the continuity between animal and human life—loneliness, play, ambition, fear, rivalry, and maternal affection—justifies a broad policy of avoiding cruelty to animals, showing compassion for them, and respecting them as sentient beings. All of this is done without denying that there are significant differences between human and nonhuman animals.

In *Beast and Man*, Midgley discusses the importance of human nature and biology, the recognition and rejection of nonsense, the habit of comparison, and the resistance to smoothing out significant differences, topics that are all characteristic of Midgley's thought and writing. The gist of the work is contained in the following:

> Man has his own nature, not that of any other species. He cannot, therefore, be degraded by comparison, if it is careful and honest, because it will bring out his peculiarities, it will show what is unique about him as well as what is not. Certainly he is *more* free than any other species. But that extra freedom flows from something natural to him—his special kind of intelligence and the character traits that go with it. It is not, and does not have to be unlimited. (In fact, unlimited freedom is an incoherent notion.) It is not added by his own will after birth, or by some external force called culture.

In *Utopias, Dolphins, and Computers: Problems in Philosophical Plumbing*, a collection of papers, Midgley compared philosophy to plumbing because philosophy deals with a complex structure that underlies culture, much as the pipes and valves of plumbing are the underpinnings of the water system; problems with either structure can have serious consequences. Both philosophy and plumbing serve vital needs, neither is typically open to an entirely new start, and both are hard to repair. Neither is optional, and both can be done either well or badly.

Midgley's stated concern in this book was representative of all her work: to bring philosophy to bear on various current issues, including the status of animals, the state of the environment, the position of women, and the plurality of interacting cultures. In the work, she combined critique with constructive commentary and made a serious effort to see the strengths of positions that were ultimately rejected. For example, social contract theory is the view that political authority derives only from the agreement of the people to be ruled by a sovereign whom each obeys for individual benefit. It was highly useful in the rejection of the divine right of kings and was based on a legitimate recognition of the value of the individual and the importance of autonomy. Nonetheless, the theory does not adequately cover the interests of those not capable of contracting, including children, the mentally disabled, or sentient nonhumans. Further, Midgley asserts, under the social contract theory, society is viewed as merely a logical construct of its members, each of whom is regarded as a sort of building block easily separable from others. However, people are related to family, friends, a spouse, and others in ways that make separation often costly and destructive.

Influence

Midgley, in some ways at least, is an Aristotelian, deeply interested in practical wisdom as well as theoretical understanding, convinced of the importance of biology, concerned to develop an accurate account of human nature, and inclined always to seek the mean between two extremes save in cases where this is plainly an error (between zero and infinity, there is no right number of murders to commit). She is also like Socrates, whom she much admired, in that she challenges theories that have gone well beyond their original scope and endeavor to explain everything. Her motivation in doing so is not merely her conviction that such theories, in their bloated versions, are false, but also her feeling that they are harmful. She deplores the isolation of philosophy from general culture and rejects the tendency of philosophers to write only for their peers, hence her devotion to writing nontechnical prose for wide audiences and the issue-oriented content of her books. She also employs nontechnical language because the topics she deals with are broad and she must bring to bear theories and data from various disciplines in order to relevantly discuss them.

Keith E. Yandell

Wickedness

A Philosophical Essay

Type of philosophy: Ethics
First published: 1984
Principal ideas advanced:

◇ Evil is something good gone bad; therefore, the world cannot be completely evil.

◇ Aggression is not always evil as a motive and in its aims, and various evils are not based on aggression.

◇ Human motives and concerns are naturally outer-directed in such a way as to favor goods for at least some others as well as for the self.

◇ An action can be both free and predictable; therefore, divine foreknowledge of free human action also seems quite possible.

The central theme of Mary Midgley's *Wickedness: A Philosophical Essay* is that the traditional analysis of evil as a privation is correct. Midgley adapts and adopts this analysis of evil as something good gone bad, as a parasite feeding on goodness. In this view, the notion of a completely evil world is logically inconsistent; evil cannot occur save as the perversion of something good. This view has Platonic and Augustinian sources. In *Wickedness*, the view that evil is to be seen as something good gone bad is developed and defended in connection with evolutionary theory and a rather Aristotelian view of human nature. The major opposing views are described and critiqued.

Dealing with Evil

One way of dealing with evil is to deny that it exists. This, Midgley notes, is often based on the view that to call anything evil is presumptuous and self-righteous; however, this entails assuming that being presumptuous and self-righteous is bad. Therefore, what begins as a denial of evil unintentionally ends up as an assertion to the contrary.

Another way of dealing with evil is to claim that its roots lie entirely in society and not in people, which suggests that evil can be eliminated if only one puts the proper social institutions in place. This view, Midgley clams, is typi-cally associated with the view that human beings start out not as creatures with a determinate nature, but as blank tablets or fully malleable clay. This, she suggests, is not what we find; it is incompatible with evolutionary theory and the discoveries of basic human biology. Furthermore, the attempt to find the roots of evil in society and not in people tends to focus on the question of whether aggression is innate, to which the required answer is negative. This assumes that a single motive is the source of all evil and is mistaken in two ways: (1) aggression is not always an evil motive and its aims (for example, defending the weak) are not always bad, and (2) there are various evils that are not based on aggression. Aggression, the tendency to attack, typically from anger, is found in many animals; in none is it simply the motive to destroy. It occurs in a context of motives and conditions that constrain its uses and effects. Like fear, whether it is good or bad depends on how it is used and what its effects are. Both fear and aggression, like pain, are typically responses to evils. Both fear and aggression are normal and frequently occur, within constraints, among individuals who continue in the same family or remain friends and in society, without necessarily being destructive of persons or personal relationships. Hence aggression is not always evil in itself or in its consequences. Further, there are obviously evils that are neither instances nor consequences of aggression.

The attempt to find the roots of evil not in people but in society, Midgley claims, is not sufficiently realistic; it does not take evil sufficiently seriously. Evil is no temporary problem solvable by social engineering; it arises from our natural motivations.

Freud and Motivation

In Midgley's discussion of views that oppose hers, psychoanalyst Sigmund Freud comes in for considerable discussion. Typically, Midgley argues, one explains any given human motive by reference to the good at which the motive aims. Indeed, she asserts, to explain a motive *is* to do this. However, obsessive self-destruction resists such explanation, and Freud offers an account of it that is incompatible with Midgley's perspective.

Earlier Freudian theory, she explains, follows philosopher Thomas Hobbes in regarding persons in a state of nature (outside society) as being in a permanent posture of war with one another, from which they escape by making a social contract based entirely on individual self-interest. Each person is viewed as essentially solitary rather than as inherently social, and the self's deepest wishes are thought of as always self-directed. The pleasure principle battles with the superego within each psyche. Society is viewed as alien to the self, not as the natural and positive result of people's interactive, cooperative endeavors. In this account, people live in societies only because they need protection. Later Freudian theory, faced with the horrors of World War I, offered an explanation of the varieties of destructive behavior, including self-destructive behavior. Freud views people as battling between one basic motive, Eros, and another, the death wish, which is viewed as having no good at which it aims. Such a motive is obviously contrary to Midgley's evil-as-the-perversion-of-good thesis and therefore invites her attention.

The doctrine that all motives aim at perceived self-interest is rejected even in Freud's earlier view, in which he saw sex as warring with self-preservation in each person. This, Midgley notes, implicitly recognizes an outer-directedness in human motives, a recognition that deserves further development. Human motives and concerns are naturally outer-directed in such a way as to favor good for at least some others as well as for oneself. Freud's later conception of a death wish as a basic human motive also rejects the doctrine that self-interest dominates human motives.

Midgley joins Freud in this rejection, adding that among human motives are some that target the best interests of others. Further, she argues that someone's having sheer destruction as an aim is a matter not of one's having a death wish as a fundamental motive but of various natural desires combining to produce aims that are not found among those targeted by those desires taken singly. She asserts that the combination of desires that aim at self-destruction becomes obsessive. Once obsessive, they are in effect detached from the rest of one's motives that would otherwise draw attention to themselves and counterbalance the desire to see harm done to another or oneself. An obsessional combination of desires exercises something like autonomy over the behavior of the person whose obsession they form. According to Midgley, there is no need for a death wish as a basic motive. There is instead a combination of motives that together, in obsessional isolation from the rest of one's system of motives, seek an end not among those sought by any of its constituent members. Motives for positive things combine to target a destruction none singly would seek, and when the combination of motives becomes obsessive, it breaks loose from the balancing influence of other motives that would otherwise and ordinarily limit the scope and depth of the destruction that is sought. Thus one can explain evil without subscribing to anything like a death wish. Further, there is no evolutionary necessity for a death wish; unlike child rearing, it is not something one needs to learn to do or can escape from.

The possibility of a negative connection between predictability and freedom is also discussed. Midgley argues that a free action may also be predictable, particularly if the action is one that the agent is known by the predictor to consciously have a good reason for performing. It seems correct that it is logically possible for an action to be predictable and free. Unless a prediction of an action is based on the predictor's knowledge that something will make it impossible for the person to act differently from the way predicted, a correct prediction of a freely performed action is possible. Therefore, divine foreknowledge of free human action also seems quite possible.

Possible Flaws

Along with its considerable strengths, there are also weaknesses in *Wickedness*. Some significant issues are not explored with convincing depth. There is, for example, a strong minority perspective among moral philosophers that favors moral relativism or otherwise rejects the view that moral propositions are true or false, that rests its case on the view that the world does not, or even cannot, contain the sorts of properties it must have if such propositions are to be either true or false. This view has been seriously presented in rigorous argument and deserves a careful discussion, which it does not receive in *Wickedness*.

In addition, some philosophical issues are simply not dealt with because, some critics suggest, they seem not to be topics one can even raise. Determinism is characterized as the belief that there is regularity in nature, a belief that makes engaging in science possible. Therefore, determinism will be true if people enjoy success in doing science. Determinism is thus described by Midgley as pragmatic and operational, not as a well-known metaphysical view that is concerned with a particular sort of relationship between earlier and later phenomena in which the occurrence of the earlier phenomena rules out any other later phenomena than those that actually occur. Determinism in this more robust sense is a concern to philosophers and nonphilosophers alike. Further, it is what most nonphilosophers and most philosophers mean by the word "determinism." It would be hard to find anyone who actually meant by "determinism" what Midgley means by the term. This is out of accord with her usual practice; she does not typically use familiar terms in peculiar senses.

Fatalism, determinism's main competitor in *Wickedness*, personalizes natural forces, treating them as things that control us. Construed as Midgley describes it, determinism is no enemy of freedom, whose opposite is sometimes slavery and sometimes lack of normal, rational control. It is fatalism, Midgley says, that opposes freedom. The resulting conceptual map has no obvious place for the classical dispute between (full-blown) determinists and libertarians.

Consider a fatalist view in which personalized natural forces result in a person's shouting curses. Replace it by a determinist view in which depersonalized physical forces result in a person's shouting curses. In the fatalist case, the personalized forces bring about something that they foresee and intend to occur. In the determinist case, the depersonalized causes bring about something that they do not foresee or intend; there is nothing such causes foresee or intend. However, in each case, the thing that brings something about is necessary and sufficient for what is brought about. Given this, and given that neither the forces nor the physical causes are under the shouter's control, can the person be free in his or her cursing? The question is perfectly

intelligible, as is the libertarian contention that the answer is negative. Yet on Midgleyian terms, the issues involved here cannot be so much as raised.

Consider also a version of fatalism that takes natural forces to be influences but not determining causes. In this view, there is room for libertarian freedom; one can personalize natural forces in such a manner that a fatalistic (full-blown deterministic) view results, and one can personalize natural forces in such a manner as not to produce such a view. If fatalism is the view that natural forces are somehow properly personalizable, fatalism can be metaphysically deterministic and it can be metaphysically nondeterministic. Midgley's map leaves out plainly possible alternatives, some at least of which are centrally relevant to the overall case she wishes to make.

Keith E. Yandell

Additional Reading

Griffiths, Sian, and Helena Kennedy, eds. *Beyond the Glass Ceiling: Forty Women Whose Ideas Shape the Modern World*. New York: Manchester University Press, 1996. This collection of essays, produced in association with the *Times* higher education supplement, portrays important and influential contemporary women. Includes a section on Midgley.

Irwin, T. *Plato's Moral Theory*. Oxford: Clarendon Press, 1977. This book discusses the ethics of Plato, the first great member of the evil-as-privation tradition to which Midgley's book belongs.

Maritain, Jacques. *Saint Thomas and Evil*. Milwaukee, Wis.: Marquette University Press, 1942. The book discusses Saint Thomas Aquinas's view of evil. Thomas, like Midgley, viewed evil as good gone bad.

Urmson, John. *Aristotle's Ethics*. Oxford: Blackwell, 1988. Excellent discussion of Aristotle's ethics, also relevant to Midgley's theory of evil.

Warnock, Mary, ed. *Women Philosophers*. London: Everyman, 1996. This collection of essays on women philosophers contains a section on Midgley.

Keith E. Yandell

John Stuart Mill

Desiring the greatest possible happiness for individual men and women and an England with the greatest possible justice and freedom, Mill questioned all assumptions about knowledge and truth and made what was observed the starting point of his discussions.

Principal philosophical works: *A System of Logic, Ratiocinative and Inductive: Being a Connected View of the Principles of Evidence, and Methods of Scientific Investigation*, 1843; *Essays on Some Unsettled Questions in Political Economy*, 1844; *Principles of Political Economy*, 1848; *Dissertations and Discourses*, 1859; *On Liberty*, 1859; *Considerations on Representative Government*, 1861; *Utilitarianism*, 1861 (serial), 1863 (book); *An Examination of Sir William Hamilton's Philosophy, and of the Principal Philosophical Questions Discussed in His Writings*, 1865; *Auguste Comte and Positivism*, 1865; *The Subjection of Women*, 1869; *Autobiography*, 1873; *Three Essays on Religion*, 1874.

Born: May 20, 1806; London, England
Died: May 7, 1873; Avignon, France

Early Life

John Stuart Mill was the eldest of nine children born to James Mill and Harriet Burrow. James Mill, the son of a shoemaker, with the help of his patron, Sir John Stuart, attended the University of Edinburgh, where he studied philosophy and divinity. He qualified for a license to be a preacher but soon lost his belief in God. In 1802, in the company of Sir John Stuart, who was then a member of Parliament, James Mill went to London to earn his living as a journalist.

Two years after the birth of John Stuart Mill, James Mill began his association with Jeremy Bentham, twenty-five years older and the founder of utilitarianism. James Mill became Bentham's disciple and the principal disseminator of utilitarianism. Along with free trade, representative government, and the greatest happiness of the greatest number, a major belief of utilitarianism is that education offers vast possibilities for improving humankind. The association between James Mill and Bentham, therefore, was to have a profound effect on the childhood, and indeed on the entire life, of John Stuart Mill, for he became the human guinea pig upon whom Bentham's ideas on education were enacted. Un-

der the direction of his father, John Stuart Mill was made into a Benthamite—in John's own words, "a mere reasoning machine."

James Mill began John's education at the age of three, with the study of Greek, and it was not long before the boy was reading Aesop's Fables. By the time he was eight and began the study of Latin, he had read a substantial body of Greek literature, including the works of the historian Herodotus and much of Plato. In the opening chapter of his *Autobiography* (begun in 1856 but published posthumously in 1873), Mill gives a detailed account of his prodigious feats of reading. Much of his studying was done at the same table at which his father did his writing. On the morning walks with his father, Mill recited the stories he had read the day before. In his *Autobiography*, he states: "Mine was not an education of cram. My father never permitted anything which I learnt to degenerate into a mere exercise of memory." The purpose of the education was to develop the greatest possible skills in reasoning and argumentation. Those skills then were to be used for the improvement of humanity.

In the year of John's birth, James Mill began to write a work that would be eleven years in the making, his *History of British India* (1818). In his *Autobiography*, John tells of his part in the making of that formidable work, reading the manuscript aloud while his father corrected the proof sheets. He goes on to say that the book had a great influence on his thinking. The publication of *History of British India* led directly to James Mill's appointment to an important position in the East India Company, through which he was able to have a considerable impact upon the behavior of the English in India.

The final episode in James Mill's education of his son was the work they did with David Ricardo's treatise *On the Principles of Political Economy and Taxation* (1817). On their daily walks, the father gave lectures to the son drawn from Ricardo's work. On the following day, the son produced a written account of the lecture, aimed at clarity, precision, and completeness. From these written accounts, James Mill then produced a popularized version of Ricardo, *Elements of Political Economy* (1821); this exercise in the thinking of Ricardo also formed the basis of one of John Stuart Mill's great works, the *Principles of Political Economy*. When he and his father finished with Ricardo, John was fourteen and was allowed to be graduated from James Mill's "academy."

John then spent a year living in France with Samuel Bentham, Jeremy's brother. When he returned to England, he began the study of law with John Austin, a lawyer who was a friend of his father and Bentham. During this period, Mill had one of the greatest intellectual experiences of his life, the reading of one of Bentham's great works, *Traité de législation civile et pénale* (1802), edited and translated into French by Bentham's Swiss disciple Étienne Dumont and later published in English as *Theory of Legislation* (1840). Mill was exhilarated by Bentham's exposure of various expressions, such as "law of nature" and "right reason," which, Bentham showed, conveyed no real meaning but served to disguise dogmatisms.

Mill also was greatly impressed by the scientific statement in this work of the principle of utility. Reading Bentham's statement of the principle "gave unity to my conceptions of things." Mill says in his *Autobiography* that at this time, all of his ideas came together: "I now had opinions; a creed, a doctrine, a philosophy." He had been transformed: "When I laid down the last volume of the *Traité,* I had become a different being."

In 1823, James Mill obtained for his son a position in the same department as the one in which he worked at the East India Company. For the next thirty-five years of his life, John Stuart Mill worked in the office of the Examiner of India Correspondence. This was for Mill his "professional occupation and status." He found the work wholly congenial and could think of no better way to earn a steady income and still be able to devote a part of every day to private intellectual pursuits.

Life's Work

It was in the *London and Westminster Review,* founded by Bentham, that Mill's first writings of

John Stuart Mill. *(Library of Congress)*

significance appeared in 1824 and 1825. Among others were essays on the mistaken notions of the conservative *Edinburgh Review* and on the necessity of absolute freedom of discussion. In 1826, however, at the age of twenty, Mill became seriously depressed and experienced what has come to be known as his "mental crisis," a period in his life discussed in detail in his *Autobiography*. Mill explains that at twenty, he suddenly found himself listless and despairing and that he no longer cared about the purpose for which he had been educated. He had to confess to himself that if all the changes in society and in people's attitudes for which he, his father, and Bentham were working were accomplished, he would feel no particular happiness. He had been taught that such accomplishments would bring him great happiness, but he realized that on a personal level he would not care. Thus, he says, "I seemed to have nothing to live for."

His *Autobiography* tells of his dramatic recovery. He read of a boy who, through the death of his father, suddenly had the responsibility for the well-being of his family thrust upon him. Feeling confident that he was capable of doing all that was expected of him, the boy inspired a similar confidence in those who were dependent on him. Mill claimed that this story moved him to tears: "From this moment my burden grew lighter. The oppression of the thought that all feeling was dead within me, was gone. I was no longer hopeless: I was not a stock or a stone." He says further that he learned two important things from his mental crisis. First, asking whether you are happy will cause you to be happy no longer. Second, stressing right thinking and good behavior is not enough; one must also feel the full range of emotions.

It is thought that the intensity of his relationship with his father was the main cause of Mill's crisis. He adored and worshiped James Mill and thus found it impossible to disagree with him. In recognizing the value of feeling, however, the son was rejecting his father's exclusion of feelings in determining what is desirable. As John came out of his depression, he let himself take an interest in poetry and art; William Wordsworth's poetry was a medicine to him, bringing him joy, much "sympathetic and imaginative pleasure." He was further helped in his emotional development

with the beginning, in 1830, of his platonic love affair with Harriet Taylor and, in 1836, by the death of his father.

In 1830, Mill began to commit to paper the ideas that were to go into his first major work, *A System of Logic*. Mill had come to believe that sound action had to be founded on sound theory, and sound theory was the result of sound logic. He was aware of too much argumentation that was not based on clear thinking; in particular, what were no more than habitual beliefs were frequently represented as truths. The subtitle of *A System of Logic* helps to explain Mill's intention: *Being a Connected View of the Principles of Evidence, and Methods of Scientific Investigation*.

Although Mill and the utilitarians regarded experience or observation as the exclusive determinant of truth, of considerable influence in both Great Britain and on the Continent were those who believed that truth could be known through intuition. Those who started with intuition, Mill believed, started with nothing more than prejudices, and these prejudices then provided justification for untrue doctrines and harmful institutions. In *A System of Logic*, Mill attempted to combat what he considered prejudices by establishing a general theory of proof. Insisting that "facts" were facts only if they could be verified by observation, Mill argued the necessity of ascertaining the origins of individual ideas and belief systems.

The publication of *A System of Logic* established Mill as the leader of his school of thought, now known as Philosophical Radicalism. *A System of Logic* became the most attacked book of its time, and Mill responded by revising to take account of the attacks. Over the remaining thirty years of his life, Mill took the book through eight editions. His response to the criticisms of *Principles of Political Economy* was similar; he saw that treatise through seven editions.

As *A System of Logic* was an attempt to overthrow the dominance of the intuitionists, *Principles of Political Economy* was an attempt to liberate economic thinking from his own utilitarian predecessors, especially his father and David Ricardo. In the preliminary remarks, Mill says:

It often happens that the universal belief of one age of mankind—a belief from which no one *was*, nor without an extraordinary effort of genius and courage, *could* at that time be free—becomes to a subsequent age so palpable an absurdity, that the only difficulty then is to imagine how such a thing can ever have appeared credible.

By 1848, the descriptions of economic activity by his predecessors had gained the status of natural law among the newly dominant middle class; to behave otherwise than to sell as dearly as possible and to buy as cheaply as possible, including human services, was to violate natural law. Mill thought it necessary to consider the effects of economic behavior on individuals and on society. He refused to accept the idea that there must be no interference with the playing out of economic forces.

Unlike his predecessors, Mill saw feasible alternatives to the system of laissez-faire and private property. He refused to accept the idea that there was nothing to be done about the suffering and injustices wrought by the system. He could not passively accept a system in which remuneration dwindles "as the work grows harder and more disagreeable, until the most fatiguing and exhausting bodily labour cannot count with certainty on being able to earn even the necessaries of life." He would consider communism as an alternative if there were no possibility of improving the system then at work. He insists, though, that a comparison with communism must be made "with the regime of individual property, not as it is, but as it might be made." Thus, Mill comes to advocate that the "Non-Interference Principle," sacred to his predecessors, must not be regarded as inviolable.

One of the markets in which interference by government is justified is education, which, as governed by the free market, was to Mill "never good except by some rare accident, and generally so bad as to be little more than nominal." Yet education is the key to elevating the quality of life. Well-educated persons would not only understand that true self-interest depends upon the advancement of the public interest but would also be thoroughly impressed with the importance of the population problem. Mill was a wholehearted Malthusian and believed that there could be no permanent improvement of society

unless population be under "the deliberate guidance of judicious foresight." Another of the many high points of *Principles of Political Economy* is the chapter on the stationary state, in which Mill rejects the desirability of indefinitely pursuing higher rates of economic development. Mill was "not charmed with the ideal of life held out by those who think that the normal state of human beings is that of struggling to get on, that the trampling, crushing, elbowing, and treading on each other's heels are the most desirable lot of human kind." The ideal economic state of society for Mill is that in which "no one is poor, no one desires to be richer, nor has any reason to fear being thrust back, by the efforts of others to push themselves forward."

On Liberty is one of the most influential works in all of Western literature. It is a justification of the value of individuality, to the individual and to the individual's society. Written during a period of rigid, although informal, social control, *On Liberty* is an encouragement for the individual to do and say whatever he or she wishes to do or say. The work consists of five chapters, the first of which is a history of the contention between liberty and authority. The objective of this introductory chapter is to show that whereas limiting political tyranny used to be a foremost goal, in his own time and country, it is the tyranny of public opinion that must be withstood and limited. The tyranny of the majority is an evil against which society must guard, for the tendency of the majority is to coerce others to conform to its notions of proper behavior and right thinking. Mill asserts that the "engines of moral repression" are growing and that a "strong barrier of moral conviction" must be raised against them.

In the chapter "Of the Liberty of Thought and Discussion," Mill argues the necessity of providing freedom for the expression of any and all opinions. Preventing an opinion from being expressed is an evil act against all humanity. Even if the opinion happens to be false, the truth could be strengthened by its collision with the false opinion. If, however, the silenced opinion happens to be true, an opportunity to move toward truth has been lost. Only when it is possible to hear one's own opinions contradicted and disproved can one feel confidence in their truth. Throughout history, the most eminent of persons have believed in the truth of what turned out to be foolish notions or have engaged in conduct that later appeared to have been irrational. Yet progress has been made; fewer people are prone to holding foolish opinions and behaving irrationally. That has happened because errors are correctable. People learn from experience, but they also learn from discussion, especially discussion on how experience is to be interpreted. "Wrong opinions and practices gradually yield to fact and argument: but fact and argument, to produce any effect on the mind, must be brought before it."

"Of Individuality, as One of the Elements of Well-Being" is perhaps *On Liberty*'s most potent chapter. In it, Mill argues that both the highest development of the individual and the good of society require that the individual be free to express his or her individuality. Mill regards individuality as a "necessary part and condition" of civilization, instruction, education, and culture. Different modes of living need to be visible in a society; where there is no individuality, there is no impetus for either other individuals or the society as a whole to improve. The visible individuality of some forces others to make choices, and it is only in making choices that various human faculties are developed—"perception, judgment, discriminative feeling, mental activity, and even moral preference." Where there are no opportunities to choose, the feelings and character are rendered "inert and torpid, instead of active and energetic." Human beings must be free to develop themselves in whatever directions they feel the impulse, and the stronger the impulses the better. Should eccentricity be the result, then it should be remembered that "the amount of eccentricity in a society has generally been proportional to the amount of genius, mental vigor, and moral courage which it contained." The chief danger of the time is that so few dare to be eccentric. "Every one lives as under the eye of a hostile and dreaded censorship." This suppression of individuality can make a society stagnant.

Soon after the appearance of *On Liberty*, Mill began work on *Utilitarianism*. About half the length of the former, it is, despite its title, a great humanistic work. Mill stretches Bentham's very limited concept of human motivation from the absolutely egotistic or selfish to include the altru-

istic. Bentham believed that experiences fell into one of two categories, pleasurable or painful, and that within each category there were quantifiable differences in such qualities as intensity and duration; Mill believed that in regard to pleasure there are two different kinds, higher and lower. The higher pleasures, which include knowledge, the experience of beautiful objects, and human companionship, Mill asserts, are more valuable than the lower, animal pleasures. Mill felt it necessary to make this distinction because whenever he came across the term "utilitarianism," the term seemed to sanction the lower pleasures and exclude the higher. Mill wished to rescue the term from the "utter degradation" into which it had fallen.

Rather than encouraging degradation, utilitarianism encourages the development of nobility. Truly noble persons always have the effect of making other people happy. Utilitarianism, therefore, could only attain its end—the greatest happiness of the greatest number—through the general cultivation of nobleness of character, not selfishness. Indeed, Mill insists, "In the golden rule of Jesus of Nazareth we read the complete spirit of the ethics of utility. To do as you would be done by, and to love your neighbor as yourself, constitute the ideal perfection of utilitarian morality."

Doing as one would be done to is at the heart of Mill's discussion of relations between the sexes in *The Subjection of Women*. Centuries-old customs and laws subordinated women to men, but the test of true virtue is the ability of a man and woman to live together as equals. One reason why they often do not is that the law favors men. That is seen particularly when the law returns women to the custody of the very husbands who have physically abused them. Another reason they do not usually live together as equals lies in what women are taught is proper behavior toward men. Women are taught to be submissive and to make themselves attractive, but men are not taught to behave similarly toward women. Such an imbalance in the way men and women relate to each other is doomed: "This relic of the past is discordant with the future and must necessarily disappear." Throughout his life, Mill sought equality and justice for women, not only because he believed strongly in the abstractions "equality" and "justice" but also because he believed that equality and justice in their relationships would improve and make happier both men and women. Mill's last years were devoted to public service.

A few months before his death, he was involved in beginning the Land Tenure Reform Association, for which he wrote in *The Examiner* and spoke publicly. Mill died at Avignon on May 7, 1873.

Influence

In the nineteenth century, Mill was England's most thoughtful and most wide-ranging writer on the subjects of how truth could be determined, what was good for the individual human being, and what was good for society as a whole. As a result of his consideration of these questions, he is known as a great champion of fundamental civil liberties and an opponent of all forms of oppression. He is one of the two great defenders in English, along with John Milton, of the necessity of the freedoms of thought, expression, and discussion.

For the most part, Mill's discussions in print are dispassionate and disinterested; he sincerely sought knowledge and truth, regardless of the sources from which ideas came. Without preconceptions of how it must have been, he sought to understand the past. Without contempt, he listened to and read his philosophical opponents in order to find and make use of whatever germs of truth there might be in their positions. He was always open to modifying and correcting what he had said previously. Aware of the brutality in humankind's past, he was never cynical about human nature or pessimistic about humanity's long-term future. He was optimistic about the desire and capacity of men and women to make themselves better persons, not all people certainly, but enough to have the net effect of improving society. He respected the complexity of human nature and human behavior. Never quick to rush to judgment, he saw that even an immoral action might have a sympathetic side or have qualities of beauty to it. Mill was a very wise man, the nineteenth century's Socrates, and generations of students have been nourished on his works.

Paul Marx

On Liberty

Type of philosophy: Ethics, political philosophy
First published: 1859
Principal ideas advanced:

◇ An individual's liberty can rightfully be constrained only in order to prevent one's doing harm to others.

◇ Certain areas of human freedom cannot rightfully be denied: the freedom to believe, the freedom of taste, and the freedom to unite (for any purpose not involving harm to others).

◇ Open expressions of opinions should not be repressed, for if the repressed opinion is true, one loses the opportunity of discovering the truth; and if the repressed opinion is false, discussion of its falsity strengthens the opposing truth and makes the grounds of truth evident; furthermore, the truth may be divided between the prevailing opinion and the repressed one, and by allowing expression of both, one makes recognition of the whole truth possible.

John Stuart Mill thought long and hard about the theoretical and practical problems connected with liberal democratic government. Actual service in the British Parliament brought him into intimate contact with applied politics. Beneath the surface of nineteenth century British political experience, Mill came upon the one problem he considered central to everyone's long-range interests. The clarity with which he stated this problem in *On Liberty* earned him a justified reputation as defender of the basic principles of liberalism. "The struggle between Liberty and Authority," he wrote, "is the most conspicuous feature in the portions of history with which we are earliest familiar, particularly in that of Greece, Rome, and England." The individual's relation to the organized power of state and popular culture requires that people draw the line between what in principle rightly belongs to each. The liberal task concerns how people are to meet the necessary demands of organized life without destroying the rights of the individual.

Mill mentions two ways in which people gradually subdued sovereign power after long and difficult struggles. First, select groups within a given political domain worked to compel the rulers to grant them special immunities. Second (and historically a later phenomenon), people managed to win constitutionally guaranteed rights through some political body which represented them. These historical tendencies limited the tyrannical aspects of sovereign power without raising questions about the inherited right of the sovereign to rule.

Guarding the Individual's Rights

A later European development involved the replacement of inherited rulers by people elected for periodic terms of governing. This was the aim of popular parties in modern European affairs, according to Mill. People who once wanted to limit governmental powers when such government rested on unrepresentative principles began to put less stress on the need of limitation once government received its justification by popular support—for example, through elections. "Their power was but the nation's own power, concentrated, and in a form convenient for exercise." However, Mill criticizes European liberalism for failing to understand that popularly supported governments may also introduce forms of tyranny. Mill's essay refers to this phenomenon as "the tyranny of the majority." Earlier thinkers asked who could protect people from the tyranny of an inherited rule, but modern Europeans asked who would protect people from the tyranny of custom. The individual citizen's independence is threatened in either instance. Individuals need protection from arbitrary rulers and also from "the tyranny of the prevailing opinion and feeling." Even a democratic society can coerce its dissenters to conform to ideals and rules of conduct in areas that should belong solely to the individual's decisions.

The chief concern of modern politics, then, is to protect the individual's rights from governmental and social coercion. Mill argues that the practical issue is even narrower—"where to place the limit," which liberal minds agree is needed. Mill understands that organized life would be impossible without some firm rules. People can never choose to live in a ruleless situation. "All that makes existence valuable to anyone, depends on the enforcement of restraints upon the actions of other people." However, the question

is which rules are to prevail. Satisfactory answers remain to be realized. Existing rules, which vary from one culture and historical epoch to another, tend to become coated in the clothing of apparent respect through force of custom; they come to seem self-evident to their communities. People forget that custom is the deposit of learned ways of acting. Few realize that existing rules require support by the giving of reasons, and that such reasons may be good or bad. Powerful interest groups tend to shape the prevailing morality in class terms. People also often act servilely toward the rules created by their masters.

Mill credits minority and religious groups, especially Protestant ones, with having altered customs by their once heretical resistance to custom. However, creative groups out of step with prevailing modes of action and thought often sought specific changes without challenging in principle the existing rules of conduct. Even heretics sometimes adopted a bigoted posture toward other theological beliefs. As a result, many religious minorities could simply plead for "permission to differ." Mill concludes that religious tolerance usually triumphed only where religious indifference also existed side by side with diversified bodies of religious opinion.

Authority and the Individual

A criterion by which rightful interference in an individual's personal life can be determined is offered by Mill. Individuals and social groups may so interfere only for reasons of their own self-protection. Society has a coercive right to prevent an individual from *harming* others, but it may not interfere simply for the individual's own physical or moral good. In this latter domain, one may attempt to convince but not to compel an individual to change his or her views or actions. Mill adds a further qualification, namely, that the individual must possess mature faculties. Children, insane persons, and members of backward societies are excluded from the use of the criterion. Moreover, the test whether interference is proper can never involve abstract right but only utility—"utility in the largest sense, grounded on the permanent interests of man as a progressive being." Failures to act, as well as overt acts causing harm to others, may be punished by society.

The question is then raised as to how one is to interpret the notion that unharmful acts belong solely to the agent. What are the rights belonging to a person that can never lead to harm to others? There are three broad types of such rights, according to Mill. The types are "the inward domain of consciousness," "liberty of tastes and pursuits," and "freedom to unite, for any purpose not involving harm to others." Mill insists that no society or government may rightfully deny these areas of fundamental human freedom. People must be permitted and even encouraged to seek their good "in their own way." This means that the repressive tendencies of institutions, including churches and sects, must continually be curbed. Mill points out how even Auguste Comte, the famous French sociologist, encouraged a form of despotism over individuals in society in the name of positivistic rationality. Mill insists that any successful resistance to the individual's coercion by opinion or legislation requires defense of the right to think and to express one's views in the public marketplace.

Mill's famous book addresses several aspects of the problem concerning the relation of authority to the individual: first, the nature of one's freedom of thought and public discussion of controversial ideas; second, the ways in which individuality is a necessary element in one's well-being; and third, the limits of society over the individual. A concluding chapter shows some practical applications of the liberal principles that Mill has defended.

Expression of Opinion

The first argument against repression of open expression of opinion is that the repressed opinion may be true. Those who silence opinion must act on the dogmatic assumption that their own viewpoint is infallible. However, if a given opinion happens to be true, people can never exchange error for its truth as long as discussion is curtailed. On the other hand, if the controversial opinion is false, by silencing discussion of it, people prevent more lively truths in existence from gaining by the healthy collision with error. No government or social group should be permitted to claim infallibility for the limited perspective that any given group must inevitably hold toward events. "The power itself is

illegitimate," Mill argues, insisting that "the best government has no more title to it than the worst."

Mill lists a number of possible objections to his first argument in defense of free discussion: One should not permit false doctrines to be proclaimed; people should never allow discussion to be pushed to an extreme; persecution of opinion is good in that truth will ultimately win out; and only bad individuals would seek to weaken existing beliefs that are useful. None of these objections proves persuasive to Mill. He answers by asserting: A difference exists between establishing a truth in the face of repeated challenges that fail to refute it and assuming a truth to prevent its possible refutation; open discussion holds significance only if it applies to extreme cases; many historical instances show that coercive error can interfere with the spread of true opinions; and, finally, the truth of an opinion is a necessary aspect of its utility. Mill reminds people how very learned persons joined with those who persecuted Socrates and Jesus for holding opinions that later won many adherents. Such persecution often involves the bigoted use of economic reprisals, about which Mill says: "Men might as well be imprisoned, as excluded from the means of earning their bread."

Mill's second argument for open discussion concerns the value it holds for keeping established truths and doctrines alive. Such discussion challenges people to know the reasons for their beliefs—a practice that forms the primary basis of genuine education. Without challenge, even accepted religious doctrines become lifeless, as do ethical codes. Discussion of false opinions forces those holding existing truths to know why they hold the opinions they do. Mill points out that even in the natural sciences, there are instances when alternative hypotheses are possible. Experience indicates that in religious and moral matters, one should expect a great range of viewpoints. Organized intolerance of opinions that conflict with the official views kills "the moral courage of the human mind." Mill agrees with the critics who assert that not all people can hope to understand the reasons for their received opinions, but he reminds the critics that their own point involves the assumption that someone is an authority regarding those reasons. Consolidation of opinion requires open discussion. Mill's judgment is that with no enemy at hand, "both teachers and learners go to sleep at their post."

The third argument for free discussion rests on the possibility that competing views may share the truth between them. Even heretical opinions may form a portion of the truth. To the objection that some opinions, such as those associated with Christian morality, are more than half-truths, Mill replies by stating that this morality never posed originally as a complete system. Christian morality constituted more a reaction against an existing pagan culture than a positive ethical doctrine. People's notions of obligation to the public stem from Greek and Roman influences rather than from the teachings of the New Testament, which stress obedience, passivity, innocence, and abstinence from evil. Mill's conclusion is that the clash of opinions, some of which turn out to be errors, proves helpful to the discovery of truth.

The question about how freely people may act is more difficult. Mill agrees with those who insist that actions can never be as free as opinions. Actions always involve consequences whose possible harm to others must receive serious consideration. People need long training in disciplined living to achieve the maturity required for a responsible exercise of their judgmental capacities. Yet individuality constitutes an inescapable element in the end of all human action, which is happiness. For this reason, people must not permit others to decide all issues for them. The reasons are that others' experience may prove too narrow or perhaps it may involve wrongful interpretations; alternatively, it may prove correct and yet unsuited to a given individual's temperament. It may also become so customary that people's passive acceptance of the experience retards their development of numerous unique human qualities. The person who always acquiesces in others' ways of doing things "has no need of any other faculty than the ape-like one of imitation."

Curbs on Individuality

What concerns Mill is that society shows a threatening tendency to curb individuality. The pressures of social opinion lead to a deficiency of individual impulses, a narrowing of the range of human preferences, and a decline in spontaneity. At this point, Mill, who usually speaks favorably

of Protestant resistance to earlier orthodox doctrines, singles out Calvinism for harsh criticism. Modern society evinces dangerous secular expressions of the earlier Calvinist insistence that people perform God's will. The emphasis was on strict obedience. So narrow a theory of human performance inevitably pinches human character. As an ethical teleologist and a utilitarian, Mill holds that the value of human action must be determined by its tendency to produce human self-realization. Obedience can never be an adequate end of human character.

Mill insists that democratic views tend to produce some conditions that encourage the loss of individuality. A tendency exists "to render mediocrity the ascendent power among mankind." Political democracy often results in mass thinking. To protect human individuality, people must show a great suspicion of averages, for the conditions of spiritual development vary from person to person. In fact, Mill argues that democracy needs an aristocracy of learned and dedicated people who can guide its development along progressive paths. What Mill calls "the progressive principle" is always antagonistic to the coercive stance of customary modes of thinking and acting. Such a principle operates only in contexts that permit diversity of human types and a variety of situations. Mill laments that the latter condition seemed on the wane in nineteenth century England. He suggests, also, that the slow disappearance of classes has a causal relation to the growing uniformity in English society. His general conclusion, expressed as a warning, is that the individual increasingly feels the compulsions of social rather than governmental coercion.

Societal Interventions

To what extent may society influence the individual? Mill asserts that society can restrain people from doing damage to others' interests as well as require people to share the burdens of common defense and of protection of their fellows' rights. Society may rightfully establish rules that create obligations for its members insofar as they form a community of interests. Education aims at developing self-regarding virtues in individuals. Individuals who are persistently rash, obstinate, immoderate in behavior, and filled with self-conceit may even be subject to society's disapprobation.

However, society must not punish a person by legal means if the individual acts in disapproved ways regarding what that person thinks to be in his or her own good. "It makes a vast difference both in our feelings and in our conduct toward him," Mill warns, "whether he displeases us in things in which we think we have a right to control him, or in things in which we know that we have not." Mill rejects the argument that no feature of a person's conduct may fall outside the area of society's jurisdiction. A person has the right to make personal mistakes. Finally, Mill argues that society will tend to interfere in a person's private actions in a wrong manner and for the wrong reasons. Religious, socialistic, and other forms of social censorship prove unable to develop adequate self-restraints. A full-blown social censorship leads, in time, to the very decline of a civilization.

Mill concludes his work by pointing out the circumstances under which a society can with justification interfere in areas of common concern. Trade involves social aspects and can be restrained when it is harmful. Crime must be prevented whenever possible. There are offenses against decency that should be curbed, and solicitation of others to do acts harmful to themselves bears watching. Mill writes: "Fornication, for example, must be tolerated, and so must gambling; but should a person be free to be a pimp, or to keep a gambling-house?" The state may establish restrictions of such activities, according to Mill. Finally, Mill argues that the state should accept the duty of requiring a sound education for each individual.

Whitaker T. Deininger, updated by John K. Roth

Utilitarianism

Type of philosophy: Ethics
First published: 1861 (serial), 1863 (book)
Principal ideas advanced:

◇ Those acts that produce the greatest happiness for the greatest number of persons are right and good.

◇ An act derives its moral worth not from its form but from its utility.

◇ Although it is the intrinsic worth of pleasure that gives value to acts conducive to pleasure, some pleasures are better than others in quality.

◇ The proof of the value of pleasure is that it is desired, and the proof of the claim that some pleasures are better than others is that experienced, rational people prefer some pleasures to others.

◇ Justice is the appropriate name for certain social utilities by which the general good is realized.

The central aim of John Stuart Mill's *Utilitarianism* is to defend the view that those acts that produce the greatest happiness of the greatest number of people are right and good. This ethical position did not originate with Mill. An influential predecessor, Jeremy Bentham, earlier championed pleasure and pain as the sole criteria for judging what is good and bad. The utility yardstick measures good by asking: Does an act increase pleasure, and does it decrease pain? Bentham's crude "Push-pin is as good as poetry" interpretation of the yardstick led to numerous criticisms. Therefore, Mill states the principle of utility in its most defensible form both to counter some specific criticisms of it and to make clear what the sanctions of the principle are. He also offers a proof of the principle. The work concludes with a discussion of the relation of utility to justice.

Foundations of Morals
Utilitarianism opens with the author's lament that little progress has occurred through centuries of ethical analysis. Ethical philosophers seeking to define the nature of "good" have left a number of incompatible views to their intellectual posterity. Mill admits that history of scientific thought also contains confusion about the first principles of the special sciences. Yet this is more to be expected in the sciences than in moral philosophy. Legislation and morals involve practical rather than theoretical arts. Because such arts always aim at ends of action rather than thought, they require agreement about a standard by which the worth of those ends can be evaluated. There is greater need of fixing the foundation of morals than of stating the theoretical principles underly-

ing bodies of scientific knowledge. The sciences result from accumulation of many particular truths, but in moral philosophy "A test of right and wrong must be the means, one would think, of ascertaining what is right or wrong, and not a consequence of having already ascertained it."

Ethical intuitionists insist that people possess a natural faculty that discerns moral principles. Against them, Mill argues that appeal to a "moral sense" cannot solve the problem of an ultimate ethical standard for judging acts. No intuitionist claim about knowledge of moral principles can provide a basis for decisions regarding cases. Intuitionist and inductive moral theorists usually disagree about the "evidence and source" grounding moral principles. Clearly, then, the main problem facing moral philosophers is that of justifying their judgments in the light of a defensible principle.

Mill asserts that even those philosophers who wish to reject the greatest-happiness principle must invoke it. For example, the German philosopher Immanuel Kant claimed that the basis of moral obligation involves a categorical imperative: "So act that the rule on which thou actest would admit of being adopted as a law of all rational beings." Mill insists that numerous, even contradictory, notions of duties can follow from this imperative. Kant's noble effort thus leads to decisions that can be shown to be immoral only because the consequences of some universally adopted acts would be unwanted by most people.

The fact that people tacitly employ the utility yardstick is not the same as a proof of its validity. Mill offers to present such a proof. He makes clear that no absolutely binding proof, "in the ordinary and popular meaning of the term," is possible. To give a philosophical proof means to advance reasons directed at one's rational capacities. Philosophical proofs are their own kinds of proofs. It is in this sense of proof that Mill promises to make good after he has first more fully characterized the utilitarian doctrine.

Pleasure and Utilitarianism

Mill must first perform an important polemical function in replying to critics who have problems with the utilitarian doctrine. The polemic is to serve the persuasive goal of winning over critics

to a proper understanding of utilitarianism, whose basic view of life is "that pleasure and freedom from pain are the only things desirable as ends." A corollary to this claim is that all things desirable are so either for the pleasure they can directly produce or for ways in which they serve as means to other pleasures or preventions of pain. Aware that some thinkers view his idea as a base moral conception, Mill states a number of outstanding objections to it. He argues that the objections represent either misunderstandings of the utilitarian doctrine or, if they contain some truth, views that are not incompatible with it.

Mill rejects the argument that utilitarianism chooses to picture human nature at the lowest animal level. Clearly, animals are incapable of experiencing many pleasures available and important to people. Every "Epicurean theory of life" also admits that intellectual pleasures are more valuable than those of simple sensation. "It is quite compatible with the principle of utility to recognize the fact that some kinds of pleasure are more desirable and more valuable than others." Pleasures must be judged in terms of quality as well as quantity. Mill suggests a way in which the value of two possible pleasures may be determined. Only that person who, out of wide experience, knows both pleasures can decide and can thus state a comparative judgment. Apparently Mill believed this test is adequate. He assumed that the experienced person actually knows the worth of competing pleasures in a manner that is not simply psychological but objective. Rational beings should choose pleasures of higher quality. Not all people are equally competent to render decisive judgments. In a striking sentence Mill writes: "It is better to be a human being dissatisfied than a pig satisfied."

Answers to Utilitarianism's Critics

In *Utilitarianism*, Mill replied to a number of other important criticisms of the utilitarian doctrine.

First, the utilitarian greatest-happiness principle is said to be too exalted in expecting human beings to adopt a disinterested moral posture. Mill's reply is that in serving the interests of one's fellow creatures, the motive may be either self-interest or duty. The resulting act rather than the motive must be judged, though the motive of duty can influence people to honor the character of the doer as well. People can promote the general interests of society without always fixing "their minds upon so wide a generality as the world, or society at large."

Second, to the charge that utilitarianism will make people cold and unsympathizing, Mill answers that people should show interest in things other than those concerned with standards of right and wrong. Yet it is necessary to emphasize the need of making judgments of right and wrong and to supply moral standards for human behavior.

Third, Mill calls simply false the view that utilitarianism is a godless doctrine. Religiously inclined people can use the utilitarian standard to determine what in detail the will of God means for human action.

Fourth, some critics complain that utilitarianism will end in expediency. Mill's rebuttal is that the utility principle does not justify acts that result only in the pleasure of the lone individual. The social standard must always operate.

Fifth, Mill argues that utilitarianism can account even for the actions of martyrs and heroes. Heroism and martyrdom involve individual sacrifices whose ultimate aim is an increase in the happiness of others or of society as a whole.

Other criticisms—that utilitarianism overlooks lack of time for people to decide the results of given actions and that utilitarians may use the doctrine to exempt themselves from moral rules—are shown to apply equally to other ethical doctrines.

Sanctions

Mill goes on to admit that other questions about a moral standard can be raised. For what reasons should any person adopt the standard? What motivates one to apply it? There are two possible kinds of sanctions for utilitarianism—external and internal sanctions. Desire of favor and fear of displeasure from one's fellows or from a sovereign God constitute the utilitarian principle's external sanctions. Given feelings of affection for other people or awe for a God, people may act also out of unselfish motives that can "attach themselves to the Utilitarian morality, as completely and powerfully as to any other."

Conscience makes up the internal sanction of the principle. Mill defines conscience as "a pain, more or less intense, attendant on violation of duty." This sanction is really a feeling in the mind such that any violation of it results in discomfort. Even those who think moral obligation has roots in a transcendental sphere act conscientiously only insofar as they harbor religious feelings about duty. There must be a subjective feeling of obligation. However, is this feeling of duty acquired or innate? If innate, the problem concerns the objects of the feeling. Intuitionists admit that principles rather than the details of morality get intuited. Mill argues that the utilitarian emphasis on regard for the pleasures and pains of others might well be an intuitively known principle. Some regard for interests of others is seen as obligatory even by intuitionists who insist on yet other obligatory principles. Mill thought that any sanction provided by a transcendental view of the origin of obligation is available to the utilitarian doctrine.

Nevertheless, Mill's view was that people's notions of obligation are actually acquired. Though not a part of human nature, the moral faculty is an outgrowth of it. This faculty can arise spontaneously in some circumstances as well as benefit from proper environmental cultivation. The social feelings of humankind provide a basis of natural sentiment that supports the utilitarian doctrine. "Society between equals can only exist on the understanding that the interests of all are to be regarded equally." Proper education and social arrangements can encourage the moral feelings toward virtuous activity. By education, people can learn to value objects disinterestedly which, in the beginning, they sought only for the sake of pleasure. Mill claims that virtue is one good of this kind.

Proof of the Utility Principle

In *Utilitarianism*, Mill raises a question as to whether the utility principle can be proved. It is difficult to understand what kind of question Mill thought he was asking. The setting for this question appears to involve something like the following: When someone asks if the principle has any sanctions, it is as if he were to ask, "Why should I seek the good even if the utility principle is sound?" However, when someone asks for a proof of the principle, it is as if he were to inquire, "How can I know *that* the utility principle is true?" Strangely, this question comes up only after Mill has already refuted a whole range of criticisms of the utilitarian doctrine as well as shown the sanctions that support it.

Mill argues that "the sole evidence it is possible to produce that anything is desirable, is that people do actually desire it." One difficulty with this assertion concerns the word "sole." Even if it is true that nothing can be desirable that is not desired by someone, would it follow necessarily that one's desire of an object is sufficient evidence of its desirability? If not, what besides desire would account for an object's desirability? Contextually, it would appear that Mill might have to agree that though everything desirable must be desired, not everything desired need be desirable. This would follow from his earlier claim that some pleasures are qualitatively better than others. A human being who desired to live like a pig would seek to evade realizing the highest kind of happiness available to him or her. To this argument, Mill might have wanted to reply that, in fact, no one really does want to live like a pig. Yet the most controversial aspect of Mill's proof occurs when he insists that "each man's happiness is a good to that person, and the general happiness, therefore, a good to the aggregate of all persons." Some philosophers call this statement an example of an elementary logical fallacy—attribution of a property applicable to the parts of a collection to the collection itself. The utilitarian stress on people's obligation to seek the happiness of the greatest number raises a question about the relation of individual pleasures to social ones. A person may desire to drive at high speeds as an individual, yet not have grounds for making desirable the changing of the speed rules. What Mill wants to emphasize is that in conflicts between social and individual interests, the individual interests must often give way.

Ultimately a conception of human nature must serve as justification for Mill's use of the utility principle. The proof runs to the effect that people are, after all, naturally like that. If they do not seek happiness directly, they seek other ends as a means to it. To a skeptic convinced that the principle cannot be proved by an appeal to human nature, Mill might have said: "Obviously, you misunderstand what you really desire." In this case, the utility principle is proved in that it conforms to what people are like. On this basis, however, it seems peculiar to want to argue that people *ought* to use the principle in making moral judgments. To say that people ought to act in a given way is to imply that they may not.

Justice and Utility

The concluding chapter of *Utilitarianism* discusses the relation of justice to utility. The idea of justice tends to impede the victory of the utilitarian doctrine, according to Mill. People's sentiment of justice seems to suggest existence of a natural, objective norm that is totally divorced from expediency and hedonistic consequences. Mill's task was to indicate how the utilitarian doctrine could accommodate this sentiment and nevertheless remain the sole acceptable standard for judging right and wrong.

One must examine objects in the concrete if one wants to discover whatever common features they may contain. This is true of the idea of justice. Several fundamental beliefs are associated in popular opinion with notions such as "just" and "unjust." Justice involves respect for the legal and moral rights of other people. It implies the wrongfulness of taking away another's moral rights by illegal or even legal means. There can be bad laws. The notion of desert is also important. This notion entails belief that wrongdoing deserves punishment and the doing of right deserves reciprocation in good acts. Justice cannot mean doing good in return for evil, according to Mill. Nevertheless, people may waive justice when they are wronged. Furthermore, people ought not to break promises that are willingly and knowingly made. This is so even in the case of implied promises. Justice precludes a breach of faith. Finally, justice implies impartiality and equality in the treatment of people and claims. This means that people ought to be "influenced by the considerations which it is supposed ought to influence the particular case in hand." Mill concludes that several general features rather than one are common to these opinions about justice. Turning to the etymology of the word, he asserts that the primitive meaning of justice is "conformity to law." The Greeks and

Romans, recognizing the possibility of bad laws, came to view injustice as the breaking of those laws that ought to be obeyed. The idea of justice in personal conduct also involves the belief that a person ought to be forced to do just acts.

To say that justice accepts the idea of the desirability of compelling people to do their duty tells people what justice is about. Yet it does not distinguish justice from other branches of morality. According to Mill, justice involves the notion of perfect obligation. Duties of perfect obligation imply the existence of a correlative right in a person or persons. "Justice implies something which it is not only right to do, and wrong not to do, but which some individual person can claim from me as his moral right." This view of justice admits a distinction between moral obligation and the domains of beneficence and generosity. In people, the sentiment of justice becomes "moralized," spread over a social group or community. Justice then involves the feeling that one ought to punish those who harm members of that community. People's need of security plays a role here as does the idea of right. Justice involves a belief that there are rights that morally society must defend. Thus justice is compatible with the utility principle, for "when moralized by the social feeling, it only acts in directions conformable to the general good."

The idea of justice requires belief in a rule of conduct applicable to all people, plus a sentiment that sanctions the rule. This sentiment, which insists that transgressors be punished, is compatible with the utility principle if the idea of justice is taken to refer to special classes of moral rules. These are the rules without which the realization of the general good would be impossible. An important example of such rules would be those forbidding one person to harm another. Such rules presuppose the utilitarian doctrine that one person's happiness must be considered as important as another's. Mill's conclusion is that "Justice remains the appropriate name for certain social utilities which are vastly more important, and therefore more absolute and imperative, than any others are as a class."

Utilitarianism is a book of significance for thinkers concerned about the problem of moral fairness in a social setting. Mill attempted to show that people's notions of obligation can be made compatible with the utility principle. What animates the work is Mill's clear conviction that even the more exalted moral claims of intuitionists and Kantian moralists make sense only if the utilitarian doctrine is the true one. Only with justice and binding rules of obligation can people achieve the greatest happiness of the greatest number.

Whitaker T. Deininger

Additional Reading

Berger, Fred R. *Happiness, Justice, and Freedom: The Moral and Political Philosophy of John Stuart Mill.* Berkeley: University of California Press, 1984. A thorough evaluation of the moral and political contributions and implications of John Stuart Mill's utilitarianism.

Berlin, Isaiah. *Four Essays on Liberty.* London: Oxford University Press, 1969. Essays on some of the issues raised by Mill in his *On Liberty.*

Carlisle, Janice. *John Stuart Mill and the Writing of Character.* Athens: University of Georgia Press, 1991. A study of Mill's life and thought in relation to ideas of virtue and character.

Copleston, Frederick. *A History of Philosophy: Modern Philosophy.* Garden City, N.Y.: Doubleday, 1967. Several chapters in this standard history of philosophy focus in lucid ways on utilitarianism and Mill's philosophy in particular.

Crisp, Roger, ed. *Routledge Philosophy Guidebook to Mill on Utilitarianism.* New York: Routledge, 1997. Helpful articles clarify Mill's understanding of utilitarian philosophy.

Donner, Wendy. *The Liberal Self: John Stuart Mill's Moral and Political Philosophy.* Ithaca, N.Y.: Cornell University Press, 1991. A carefully developed interpretation of the basic themes and arguments in Mill's political philosophy and ethics.

Dworkin, Gerald, ed. *Mill's "On Liberty": Critical Essays.* Lanham, Md.: Rowman & Littlefield, 1997. Noted Mill scholars address the perspectives, problems, and prospects contained in Mill's famous study of liberty.

Lyons, David. *Rights, Welfare, and Mill's Moral Theory.* New York: Oxford University Press, 1994. Interprets how Mill understood human rights and responsible public policy within the framework of his utilitarianism.

Mazlish, Bruce. *James and John Stuart Mill: Father and Son in the Nineteenth Century*. New York: Basic Books, 1975. A thorough discussion of the entangled personalities and ideas of the two Mills.

Riley, Jonathan. *Liberal Utilitarianism: Social Choice Theory and John Stuart Mill's Philosophy*. New York: Cambridge University Press, 1988. A thoughtful discussion of Mill's philosophy and its relationship to contemporary political and economic policy.

Robson, John. *The Improvement of Mankind*. Toronto: University of Toronto Press, 1968. A clearly written and helpful examination of Mill's social and political thought.

Ryan, Alan. *J. S. Mill*. London: Routledge & Kegan Paul, 1974. Focuses on Mill's major works and relates them to the issues of his time.

Schneewind, Jerome B., ed. *Mill: A Collection of Critical Essays*. Garden City, N.Y.: Doubleday Anchor Books, 1958. A good collection of articles by various authorities on many aspects of Mill's philosophy.

Skompski, John, ed. *The Cambridge Companion to Mill*. New York: Cambridge University Press, 1998. Important essayists update the scholarship on Mill's writings and the wide variety of themes that they contain.

Paul Marx, updated by John K. Roth

Michel Eyquem de Montaigne

In an age of violent religious and political struggles, Montaigne mediated for tolerance. He examined and interpreted the ideas of Greek Skeptics and developed a Renaissance version of skepticism.

Principal philosophical works: *Essais*, books 1-2, 1580, rev. ed. 1582; books 1-3, 1588, rev. ed. 1595 (*The Essays*, 1603); *Journal du voyage*, 1774 (*Travel Journal*, 1842).

Born: February 28, 1533; Château de Montaigne, Périgord, near Bordeaux, France

Died: September 13, 1592; Château de Montaigne, Périgord, near Bordeaux, France

Early Life

Michel Eyquem de Montaigne was born in his father's château in Périgord, a French county east and north of Bordeaux, which became a part of France in 1607. His father, Pierre Eyquem, held many important posts, including that of mayor of Bordeaux, and afforded an unusual model of religious tolerance by heading a Catholic family that included a Protestant wife of Spanish and Jewish blood and two Protestant children.

Montaigne dearly loved his father, who was responsible for his being positioned to enjoy a gentle and cultured life. At age six, he was sent to the finest school in Bordeaux, where he completed the twelve-year course in seven years. Sometime during the next eight years, he very likely studied law.

From 1557 to 1570, Montaigne was a councillor in the Bordeaux Parlement and took numerous trips to Paris. During this period, he made a close and erudite friend, Étienne de La Boétie, who in the remaining four years of his life came to be more important to Montaigne than anyone else and influenced Montaigne throughout his life. It was La Boétie's stoic acceptance of suffering and his courageous death, at which Montaigne was present despite the danger of contagion, that turned Montaigne toward Stoicism and probably inspired him to begin writing.

In 1565, Montaigne married Françoise de La Chassaigne. He seldom mentions her in his writing. Of his six children, only one, Léonor, survived childhood.

About 1567, Montaigne's father had him translate a work that was strongly opposed to Protestantism and atheism: *Theologia naturalis, sive Liber creaturarum* (1485; the book of creatures: or, natural theology), written in medieval Latin by a fifteenth century Spaniard, Raimond Sebond. His father, although terminally ill, arranged for the publication of the translation.

After his father's death, Michel became Lord of Montaigne, owner of the château and the estate, and at thirty-eight years of age retired to what he hoped would be a life of quiet study and composition. Much of his time was spent in the tower, which he asked to be added to his castle, and which even his wife was forbidden to enter. There he wrote his life's work, *The Essays*, which was placed on the Index of Prohibited Books in 1676 but was viewed favorably by the Vatican in Montaigne's day.

Life's Work

Over a period of thirty years, Montaigne dealt with every conceivable aspect of life by describing in detail his own thoughts, beliefs, experiences, and habits of living. Nothing was too abstruse to be tackled or too insignificant to be mentioned. His essay titles range from "Sur des vers de Virgile" ("On Certain Verses of Virgil") to "Des coches" ("Of Coaches"). His early essays were compilations of views followed by a brief

Michel Eyquem de Montaigne. *(Library of Congress)*

the Condé Museum at Chantilly depicts a handsome man with regular features, fine eyes, short-cropped hair, a small mustache, and a neat beard. Evidently he was not given to vanity. He enjoyed horseback riding, travel, and conversation with intelligent men. He also enjoyed the company of his "covenant daughter," Marie de Gournay, who became his literary executrix.

After Montaigne's retirement, all of his time was not spent in seclusion. Between 1572 and 1576, he attempted to mediate between his friend Henry of Navarre (later Henry IV) and the extremist Catholics of the Holy League. At the accession of Henry III in 1576, Montaigne was made a Gentleman of the Bedchamber, an office that gave access to the king without requiring residence at court. His disgust at the excesses of the Wars of Religion gave him a strong distaste for government, and although he loved the city of Paris, he avoided the royal court.

In 1580, Montaigne journeyed to take the waters at Lucca on the west coast of Italy. He hoped, but probably did not really believe, that the baths could cure his recurring misery caused by a kidney stone. Accompanied by his younger brother, two nobles, and a secretary, he left on horseback with no itinerary. En route to the baths, he visited Paris, Switzerland, and Germany. In Rome, he was declared a citizen of that city, an honor that he greatly coveted. During his second stay in Lucca, he learned to his dismay that he had been elected mayor of Bordeaux. He tried to refuse the responsibility but finally capitulated and arrived home after an absence of seventeen months.

Montaigne served two terms as mayor, from 1581 to 1585, and without showing undue zeal managed to initiate some reforms that included improving the lot of foundling children and imprisoned women and helping the poor by refusing to allow the rich to be exempt from taxation. He showed his concern for education by improving the Collège des Jésuites and his own old school, the Collège de Guyenne. He left office

moral, often showing the influence of Seneca the Younger or Plutarch, both of whom he admired immensely. These were followed by what is called his skeptical period, during which he coined his motto: "What do I know?" The years from 1578 onward are termed his Epicurean period, wherein he endeavored to find his own nature and to follow its dictates. His hero during this period was Socrates, and life was a great adventure to be lived as happily as possible, with due regard for the rights of others and guided by common sense. He counseled moderation in all things, freedom with self-control, and honesty and courage.

In the essay "De la proesumption" ("About Presumption"), Montaigne describes himself as below average height but strong and well-set, with a face not fat but full. A portrait of him in somewhat ignominiously, tendering his resignation outside the city, which was at that time stricken by the plague.

Although no longer mayor, Montaigne was unable to avoid involvement in the turbulent political situation. After a peaceful year at home working on *The Essays*, he found his unprotected estate overrun by soldiers and himself suspect to both the Catholics and the Protestants. In early 1588, he was sent to Paris on a secret mission to Henry III from Henry of Navarre. En route, he was detained by Protestants and a few months later found himself briefly imprisoned in the Bastille by the Catholics. After nearly a year spent in following the king from Paris to Chartres to Rouen and attending the Estates-General at Blois, Montaigne returned home and helped keep Bordeaux loyal to the king. In his remaining years, he continued to add passages to *The Essays*. There is no eyewitness account of his death, but numerous contemporaries claim that he died peacefully while hearing Mass in his room.

Influence

Montaigne's writing style is vivacious and strong, with unexpected images, picturesque details, and often ironic humor. He reaches his highest level when he discusses the interdependence of mind and matter; modern psychologists and even psychiatrists might well claim him as their forefather. It is said that Sigmund Freud was interested in *The Essays*. Perhaps it is the surprising intimacy that Montaigne creates that is the most novel characteristic of his work: The reader believes that he knows the author better than he knows his closest friends or his family and maybe better than he knows himself. This kind of writing was new to literature.

In politics and in religion, Montaigne was opposed to change; his aim was peace, and he worked toward that end. Despite personal reservations, he remained a loyal subject of the Crown and a practicing Catholic, proclaiming that one ought to accept the government of one's country and its religion.

In education, Montaigne was centuries ahead of his time: In his essay "De l'institution des enfants" ("Of the Education of Children"), he advocated training children to be efficient human beings by exposing them not to pedants but to people of all social stations. Children must be taught to observe and to judge for themselves.

In literature, Montaigne established the great principle of the seventeenth century: respect for and imitation of the classics. He insisted that the only subject suitable for study is humanity itself. There is no doubt that his essays influenced thinkers such as Francis Bacon, François de La Rochefoucauld, Blaise Pascal, Jean de La Bruyère, and Joseph Addison.

While Montaigne was describing himself in his writings, he was also depicting people in general; in fact, he was dealing with the human condition. In the twentieth century, Albert Camus, André Malraux, Jean-Paul Sartre, and a host of other eminent writers in Europe and the United States devoted their talents to examining the human condition. Whether they acknowledge it, directly or indirectly, they are all indebted to Montaigne.

Dorothy B. Aspinwall

"Apology for Raimond Sebond"

Type of philosophy: Epistemology, philosophy of religion

First published: "Apologie de Raimond Sebond," in *Essais*, book 2, 1580 (English translation in *The Essays*, 1603)

Principal ideas advanced:

◇ True religion must be based on faith; but given faith, reason can be used to strengthen faith.

◇ Rationality is a form of animal behavior; in many respects, animals surpass people, who seem vain, stupid, and immoral in comparison.

◇ The Greek Skeptics, the Pyrrhonists, were sensible in doubting everything, contesting all claims, and living according to nature and custom.

◇ Scientists, philosophers, and all others who seek knowledge—including those who seek knowledge of probabilities—fail in their efforts.

◇ People depend on sense experience for their knowledge of the world, but people do not know whether five senses are adequate, nor can they determine how accurately the senses represent the real world.

This essay, one of Michel Eyquem de Montaigne's longest, sets forth the reasons for the great French humanist's belief in skepticism. It is the work that was most influential in reviving and popularizing the Greek skeptical theory of Pyrrhonism during the Renaissance and in the seventeenth century. Montaigne's followers based their arguments on this essay, and many important philosophers, including René Descartes, Pierre Gassendi, Blaise Pascal, and Nicolas de Malebranche studied it and used some of Montaigne's ideas in developing their own philosophies. The essay is also one of the first writings that discuss philosophical issues in a modern language. It had a tremendous vogue in the seventeenth century. Late in the century it was put on the Roman Catholic Church's Index of Prohibited Books. It has remained one of the major classics of French literature and thought and is one of the richest examples of Renaissance humanism and skepticism.

The essay was apparently begun in 1575 when Montaigne was studying writings, recently translated into Latin, of the Greek Skeptic Sextus Empiricus, who wrote in the third century. These works so impressed Montaigne that they caused him to doubt all of his previous views and caused him to undergo his own personal skeptical crisis. During this crisis, he sought to show that the knowledge that people claimed to have gained through the use of their senses and their reasoning capacities was all open to doubt.

A Defense of Sebond's Views

The "Apology for Raimond Sebond" purports to be a defense of the views of the fifteenth century Spanish rationalist theologian Raimond Sebond. At the outset, Montaigne tells his reader that at the request of his father, he had translated Sebond's *Theologia naturalis, sive Liber creaturarum* (1485; the book of creatures: or, natural theology). His father had received the work much earlier from a French theologian who reported that he had been saved from Lutheranism by studying Sebond's rational arguments in favor of Christianity. After Montaigne's edition of Sebond appeared in 1569, shortly after his father's death, he found that many of the readers (especially, he says, women) required assistance in comprehending and accepting Sebond's message. Objec-

tions had been raised against Sebond's audacious contention that all the articles of the Christian faith can be proved by natural reason.

Because of the difficulties that readers were having with the work and because of the objections, Montaigne reports that he undertook the task of writing an apology (a defense) of Sebond's work. Because of the character of the "Apology for Raimond Sebond," scholars have debated and are still debating the question of Montaigne's real intent in publishing this essay. Was it to defend Sebond (which seems quite unlikely in view of the contents of the essay)? Was it to offer a different defense of Christianity through skepticism—or was it to employ skeptical thought to undermine all beliefs, including those of Christianity? The essay can be, and has been, read in the latter two ways, and it has greatly influenced the fideists (those who base their religious beliefs on faith alone) and those who are skeptical of all religious beliefs.

The "Apology for Raimond Sebond" is written in Montaigne's inimitable rambling style. It presents a series of waves of doubt, with occasional pauses to reflect. The various skeptical themes are interwoven with the recurring note that faith and revelation are the only unquestionable sources of any truth.

Montaigne begins his serious discussion by considering two kinds of objections that have been raised against Sebond's views, one that Christianity should be based on faith and not on reason, and the other that Sebond's reasoning is not sound. In discussing the first point, Montaigne develops his fideistic theme, and in discussing the second, his skepticism. He alleges to defend Sebond by contending first that Christianity is founded solely on faith, and then that, since all reasoning is unsound, Sebond should not be singled out for blame on this score.

Faith and Skepticism

Early in the essay, Montaigne excuses Sebond's theological rationalism by stating that there is nothing wrong with using reason to defend the faith, as long as one realizes that faith does not depend on reason and that one's rational capacities are unable to attain supernatural and divine wisdom. As far as Montaigne can see, true religion must be based on faith given to people by the grace of God. Purely human capacities are too weak to support divine knowledge. When one relies on human faculties to find and accept the true religion, one ends up accepting religions because of custom, habit, or geographical location. If, however, one has the real light of faith, then reasons such as those Sebond offers can be employed as aids to faith, although not as proofs of it.

To "defend" Sebond on the second charge—that his arguments are too weak—Montaigne begins a general attack on all human reasoning by arguing that no one can attain certainty by rational means. The first level of skepticism offered purports to show that human capacities are unimpressive when compared with those of animals. Humans, egotistically, believe that they, and they alone, can comprehend the world, which was created and operates for their benefit. However, they cannot tell that this is the case. When they compare their capacities with those of animals, they find that they possess no faculties or capacities that beasts lack; in fact, the beasts surpass humans in many respects. Montaigne introduces various examples from the writings of Sextus Empiricus to show that rationality is just a form of animal behavior. Montaigne insists that even religion is not a unique human possession, for even elephants seem to pray. When human behavior is carefully contrasted with that of animals, humans are seen as rather vain, stupid, and immoral. With all their alleged superior faculties, humans are not able to live as well or as happily as the animals. The illustrative material presented by Montaigne is supposed to have the cumulative effect of making people doubt their superior wisdom and knowledge. People think they know the truth, but their knowing is only a form of animal behavior, and it does not enable people to achieve even as much as the rest of the animals can and do. Hence, Montaigne insists, the human disease is the belief that people can know something. This is why religion recommends a state of ignorance as most proper for belief and obedience.

Montaigne continues this attack on intellectual pretensions by comparing the wisdom of the educated European of his day with the ignorance of the "noble savages," the recently discovered inhabitants of Brazil. The latter are portrayed as living a far superior life, because "they pass their lives in an admirable simplicity and ignorance, without any learning, laws, kings, or any religion whatsoever."

Christianity, according to Montaigne, teaches people to acquire a similar ignorance in order that they may believe by faith alone. Whatever truths one knows are gained not by one's own abilities, but by God's grace. Even one's religion is not acquired through reasoning and comprehension. Instead, one receives it only by God's revelation. One's ignorance is an asset in this regard, in that one's own inability to know anything leads one to be willing to submit oneself to God's will and to accept his teachings. To show that Christianity is based on an awareness of one's ignorance, rather than on any knowledge one might have, Montaigne quotes one of his favorite texts from the Bible, the attack on rational knowledge that appears at the beginning of Saint Paul's first letter to the Corinthians.

Pyrrhonism

Next, Montaigne presents a more philosophical basis for his complete skepticism in the form of a description and defense of the ancient Greek skeptical view, Pyrrhonism, as well as an explanation of the value of this theory for religion. The Pyrrhonists doubt and suspend judgment concerning any and all propositions whatsoever, even the claim that all is in doubt. They contest every assertion that is made. If they are successful, they exhibit their opponents' ignorance. If they are unsuccessful, they show their own ignorance. While they are doubting everything, the Pyrrhonists live according to nature and custom. Montaigne tells us that this attitude is both the finest of human achievements and that which is most compatible with religion. The Pyrrhonists show humanity naked and empty, a blank tablet, ready to receive any message that God wishes to write on it. The Pyrrhonists expose humanity as it really is, in total ignorance. This exposé should make people humble and obedient, ready to receive divine truth.

The ancient Pyrrhonists not only reached the summit of human wisdom in seeing that all is in doubt but also, Montaigne and his disciples insisted, provided the best defense of Catholicism against the Protestant Reformation. The complete skeptic would have no positive views and, consequently, no incorrect ones. He or she would accept only the laws and customs of his community. Hence, in sixteenth century France, he or she would accept Catholicism. Further, by being in doubt about everything, the Pyrrhonist would be in the perfect state to receive the revelation of the true religion. Thus, if God so willed, Montaigne tells us, the skeptic will be a Catholic by custom and tradition as well as by faith.

Montaigne next compares the achievements of the ancient Pyrrhonists with the failings of the more dogmatic philosophers. The latter have quarreled over every possible question without coming to any definite conclusion. In the end, the dogmatic philosophers have had to admit their failure to attain any indubitable knowledge in any field whatsoever. A survey of the attempts of philosophers throughout history to achieve any true knowledge leads one to the conclusion that "philosophy is only sophisticated poetry." All that philosophers ever offer us are theories that they have invented, not truths about the world. Some of these theories become accepted at various times and are regarded as authoritative and unquestionable. However, there is no more evidence that these theories are true than that they are false. The only true principles that people possess, Montaigne insists, are those that God has revealed to them. All other alleged truths are nothing but dreams and smoke.

The debacle of human intellectual undertakings is so complete that even the Pyrrhonist is unable to survive unscathed. If the Pyrrhonist declares, after looking at the sad history of humanity's intellectual achievements, that all is in doubt, then he or she has asserted something positive and is no longer in doubt about everything. The Pyrrhonist, Montaigne says, cannot state doubts without contradicting himself or herself. The fault lies with language, which is basically assertive. Only a negative language would allow for a genuine statement of the Pyrrhonian view.

Doubt and Understanding

After making all these points and digressing in many different directions, Montaigne, toward the end of the essay, finally states the evidence offered by the Pyrrhonists to show that all is in doubt. People do not seem able to gain any knowledge either from their experience or from their reasonings. People appear to be unable to tell what it is that they experience and whether they actually experience the things they think they experience. They cannot, for example, ascertain the true nature of heat or of any other experienced quality. Similarly, they cannot tell what their rational faculty is or even where it is. The experts disagree about everything, and when their various opinions are examined, they are revealed as quite uncertain. From these considerations, one concludes once more that people's only genuine understanding comes from God and not from any information or faculties.

Some philosophers, after seeing how everybody disagrees about everything, have come to the conclusion that nothing can be known, either about oneself or anything else, but that some opinions are more probable than others. This view, developed by the Academic skeptics in antiquity, Montaigne maintains, is more unsatisfactory than the complete doubt of the Pyrrhonists. If people could reach any agreement about probabilities, then they should be able to come to agreement concerning the probable characters of particular things. However, judgments change constantly with various bodily and emotional states; people do not find one view more probable than another, except at specific times and under specific conditions. As views change, people find that they disagree with what they formerly thought was probable and with what others think is probable. Thus, people cannot take probabilities as guides to truth, but can only fall back on the Pyrrhonian view that everything can be doubted and on the truths that God gives them.

When scientific achievements are examined, they are found to be as dubious as anything else because in every science, the experts disagree, and what is accepted as true at one time is rejected as false at another. For example, Montaigne points out, earlier astronomers said that the heavens moved around the earth, and now a new astronomer, Nicolaus Copernicus, says that the earth moves. Perhaps centuries from now, Montaigne says, another astronomer will disprove all of them. Prior to Aristotle, other theories seemed acceptable. Why should Aristotle's theory be accepted as the last word? Even in a science as apparently certain as geometry, there are difficulties that render it dubious. Paradoxes such as those developed by Zeno of Elea in the fifth century B.C.E. indicate that geometry is not completely certain. The recent discoveries in the New World indicate that the accepted beliefs about human nature are not so certain. (Montaigne was perhaps the first to realize the extent to which the information about the cultures in America indicated that the beliefs of Europeans about human nature were relative to their own experience and civilization.) Similarly, information about ancient Greece and Rome, as well as about the various cultures in Europe itself, shows that views about law, religion, social customs, and the like change all the time and that what has been accepted as true in one culture has been rejected by another.

Sense Knowledge

From here, Montaigne moves on to the theoretical basis of the Pyrrhonian position, the critique of sense knowledge, "the greatest foundation and proof of our ignorance." All knowledge appears to come from sense information, but there are certain basic difficulties with regard to this information that cast it in doubt. First of all, people do not know whether they possess all the necessary senses for obtaining true knowledge. People have five senses, but it may require ten to see nature correctly. Human sense information may be as far removed from the truth as a blind man's view of colors. Second, even if people possess all the needed senses, there is the possibility that they may be deceptive. The occurrence of illusions provides some grounds for distrusting the senses. Further, sense experience seems to vary according to people's emotional states. Besides the many reasons that Sextus Empiricus offered for distrusting the senses, there is also the problem that people cannot tell whether their sense experience is part of a dream or a genuine reflection of what the world is like. When all the Pyrrhonian arguments about sense knowledge are considered, one realizes that people can know only how things appear to them and not how they are in themselves.

Besides, Montaigne argues, the senses may distort what people perceive in the same way that certain kinds of lenses do. The qualities people perceive may be imposed on objects rather than actually being in them. What people experience differs with their condition, location, and so on. Unless they possess some standard by which to judge when they have the right experience, people have no way of distinguishing true information about the world from false information. However, this raises the classical skeptical problem of the criterion—how does one tell what standard is the true one? To answer this question, another standard is needed. If one tries to use reason to decide, one will need further reasons to justify the ones that were employed, and so on to infinity.

Hence, if senses are the sources of all ideas, people can be sure of nothing. They have no completely certain standard to use to judge when or if their ideas or sense impressions correspond to the real, external objects. People are forever in the position of the person who tries to determine whether a picture of Socrates is a good likeness without ever having seen Socrates.

These successive waves of skepticism leave one finally with the realization that trying to know reality is like trying to clutch water: It cannot be done. Until God decides to enlighten one, all of one's supposed knowledge will remain uncertain. It is only through the grace of God, Montaigne concludes, that one can ever achieve any contact with reality.

From Doubt to Faith

Montaigne's "Apology for Raimond Sebond" introduces, in an unsystematic way, many of the traditional arguments of the Greek skeptics. Throughout the essay, Montaigne couples the argument for complete skepticism with an appeal to faith as the way out of doubt. For some of his readers, his important message is that human beings cannot be certain of anything, including the truths asserted by traditional religions. For other readers, both his doubts and his fideistic solution were equally important. For them, Montaigne showed that human beings could not find any certain knowledge by their own devices; they could find it only through faith.

The "Apology for Raimond Sebond" is one of the works that was most important in setting the stage for the beginning of modern philosophy, for it provided a series of doubts about all previous theories. The new philosophers of the seventeenth century had either to find a way of answering the many skeptical arguments of Montaigne or to accept his skeptical conclusion. In the "Apology for Raimond Sebond," Montaigne provided the starting point for "the quest for certainty," as well as a skeptical resolution of the problems he considered.

Richard H. Popkin

Additional Reading

Burke, Peter. *Montaigne*. New York: Hill & Wang, 1981. Consists of ten articles devoted to different aspects of Michel Eyquem de Montaigne and his writings. Great resource for students. Each chapter includes its own bibliography, and the whole book is indexed.

Cottrell, Robert D. *Sexuality/Textuality: A Study of the Fabric of Montaigne's Essays*. Columbus: Ohio State University Press, 1981. An advanced study of Montaigne's writings.

Dikka, Berven, ed. *Montaigne: A Collection of Essays*. Vols. 1-5. New York: Garland, 1995. A five-part examination of Montaigne. Each volume concentrates on a different topic such as Montaigne's rhetoric, sources of his thought, and the relationship between Montaigne and the contemporary reader.

Frame, Donald M. *Montaigne: A Biography*. New York: Harcourt, Brace & World, 1965. A useful source of information about Montaigne's life and work.

_____. *Montaigne's Discovery of Man: The Humanization of a Humanist*. New York: Columbia University Press, 1955. The development of Montaigne's philosophy is examined against the background of his life experiences.

_____. *Montaigne's Essais: A Study*. Englewood Cliffs, N.J.: Prentice-Hall, 1969. This book examines Montaigne's influence on philosophy in the past four centuries. It also takes a detailed look at his life and development as a thinker. Includes a chronology, bibliography, and index.

Paulson, Michael G. *The Possible Influence of Montaigne's "Essais" on Descartes's Treatise on the Passions*. Lanham, Md.: University Press of America, 1988. This work examines Montaigne's influence on René Descartes's philosophy of the passions.

Quint, David. *Montaigne and the Quality of Mercy: Ethical and Political Themes in the "Essais."* Princeton, N.J.: Princeton University Press, 1998. This work examines Montaigne's concern with the ethical basis of society.

Sayce, Richard A. *The Essays of Montaigne: A Critical Exploration*. London: Weidenfeld & Nicolson, 1972. An important study on Montaigne's essays. Very readable.

Schaefer, David Lewis. *The Political Philosophy of Montaigne*. Ithaca, N.Y.: Cornell University Press, 1990. This book examines *The Essays* and argues that Montaigne is primarily concerned with political matters. Schaefer portrays Montaigne as a consistent and systematic thinker.

Sichel, Edith. *Michel de Montaigne*. London: Constable, 1911. An enjoyable biography that takes a personal view of Montaigne and his times based on quotations from *The Essays*. Contains facsimiles of portraits and manuscript and bibliographical notes.

Van Den Abbeele, Georges. *Travel as Metaphor: From Montaigne to Rousseau*. Minneapolis: University of Minnesota Press, 1992. This book studies the relation between critical thinking and the metaphor of travel in French Renaissance philosophy. The first chapter concentrates on Montaigne.

Dorothy B. Aspinwall,
updated by Tammy Nyden-Bullock

G. E. Moore

With his meticulous and uncompromising analytic technique, Moore helped lead the movement away from the dominance of idealism, establishing analytic philosophy as a major methodology in modern philosophical thought.

Principal philosophical works: *Principia Ethica*, 1903; *Ethics*, 1912; *Philosophical Studies*, 1922; *Some Main Problems of Philosophy*, 1953; *Philosophical Papers*, 1959; *Commonplace Book, 1919-1953*, 1962.

Born: November 4, 1873; London, England
Died: October 24, 1958; Cambridge, England

Early Life

George Edward Moore was born November 4, 1873, the fifth of eight children, in Upper Norwood, a suburb of London. His father, Daniel Moore, was a medical doctor; his mother, the former Henrietta Sturge, a member of a prominent Quaker family. The Moore home was situated down the hill from the Crystal Cathedral, a landmark of protomodern architecture and symbol of nineteenth century faith in progress through science, technology, and trade—an optimism characteristic of the nonaristocratic educated professional class to which Moore belonged and which was by then an important political and intellectual force in England.

The family had moved to Norwood so that Moore and his two older brothers could attend Dulwich College, a highly respected boys' school. When he was eight years old, Moore entered Dulwich and soon showed an aptitude and preference for the study of classics, excelling in both Greek and Latin. He also studied piano and voice. At that time, the study of classics was considered a primary avenue to literacy which, of itself, constituted a complete education for a gentleman, and consequently Moore studied very little mathematics or science. It is, therefore, remarkable that Moore's later work had the influence that it did on the development of philosophical movements that owed much of their inspiration and subject matter to science and mathematics.

A lonely boy, Moore seems to have been content to spend his time doing the prescribed translating of English verse into Latin and Greek, and, though he was exposed to some Greek philosophy, he showed no inkling of his later passion for philosophy or of his characteristic style of philosophical analysis with its demand for a rigorous accounting of the basis for one's beliefs.

Indeed, when Moore was twelve years old, he was converted by an evangelical sect that believed that an individual faced with a moral dilemma should ask what Jesus would do in that situation. For a time, the young Moore forced himself to act in a manner consistent with this view, and though it caused him great internal conflict and embarrassment, he stood on the promenade at a seaside resort and handed out pamphlets to passersby, among whom were some of his schoolmates. Before he left Dulwich, however, he had become, and remained for the rest of his life, an agnostic.

In 1892, Moore entered Trinity College, Cambridge, modestly expecting to put the finishing touches on his already thorough classical education, obtain a position at a boys' school as a master in his own right, and spend a comfortable life preparing other boys for the rigors of translating English verse into Latin and Greek. This was not to be: In his first year as an undergraduate, he was invited by an upperclassman named Bertrand Russell to a discussion given by a man who said that time was unreal.

The man was John McTaggert Ellis, a proponent of the then-fashionable Idealist philosophy of Georg Wilhelm Friedrich Hegel, which held that the picture of the world given by science and common sense of a multiplicity of objects that have an existence independent of the mind is false, and that, in fact, nothing has independent reality except the whole, or Absolute. Moore considered the idea that time is unreal monstrous and argued strenuously against it, earning the respect of Russell, who later encouraged him to pursue philosophy. McTaggert, too, was impressed enough to recommend Moore for membership in the Apostles, a kind of undergraduate debating society with a long and distinguished history of membership by some of the leading intellectuals in England.

G. E. Moore. *(Corbis/Bettmann)*

Moore's debut as an Apostle was said to have been electrifying. Unlike most newly elected members, he spoke without nervousness and with the greatest earnestness and enthusiasm. All were impressed with the passion and purity of his character, a feeling that did not fade—and, if anything, grew to the point where Moore's friendship with his contemporary Apostles became an important avenue, independent of his published work, for the wide dissemination of his ideas.

Taking Russell's advice, Moore began a formal study of philosophy at Cambridge, attending lectures given by Henry Sidgwick, James Ward, G. F. Stout, and McTaggert. For a time, Moore himself fell under the spell of Idealism. Yet even then his independence showed itself in his choice of the ethics of German philosopher Immanuel Kant for his dissertation topic. Although Kant was honored by the Idealists, who considered him the starting point for any study of their hero Hegel, Kant was not himself an Idealist. Though he believed that the individual's experience of the phenomenal world was a construction of the mind and that one could never know the "thing-in-itself," he rejected the view that reality was therefore mental.

Moore's dissertation was rejected, and it was only after he had worked another year and added a second part that it was accepted and he was elected to a six-year fellowship at Trinity College, Cambridge.

Life's Work

Moore's fellowship was unconditional, which meant that for a period of six years he would receive two hundred pounds per year no matter what he did or where he lived. Moore chose to live at Cambridge, where he would receive free room and board, and to work on philosophy. He had already reached the turning point in his philosophical thinking in his dissertation. The natural restraints on critical independence of the undergraduate were gone, and he had soon published the second half of his dissertation as a separate paper in the journal *Mind* under the title "The Nature of Judgment." The Idealists had held that there are no facts independent of one's experience of them. Moore argued against this view, holding that the objects of mental acts and perception have an existence wholly independent of a person's mind; thus, as Russell acknowledged, he took the lead in developing a new direction for philosophy that Russell himself soon followed.

As a new Fellow, Moore became involved in a number of projects. He contributed to James Mark Baldwin's *Dictionary of Philosophy and Psychology* (1901-1905), and he joined the Aristotelian Society of London, which, because of its frequent requests for papers, led to the production of many of Moore's published works. He also undertook to give a series of lectures on Kant's ethics, and on ethics in general. The notes from these lectures served as the basis for the elaboration of Moore's own ideas about ethics, which he developed slowly and painstakingly over the six years of his fellowship and which were finally published in 1903 as *Principia Ethica*.

The importance of this work was immediately recognized by both philosophers and educated laypersons. Biographer and critic (and fellow Apostle) Lytton Strachey hailed it as "the beginning of the Age of Reason," and Russell called it a "triumph of lucidity."

Again, turning against a long philosophical tradition, Moore argued that "good" is a simple and unanalyzable, nonnatural quality (a natural quality would be something such as a color or an emotion). Those who tried to say that good is identical with pleasure or with what one desires or approves of—or anything else in the world—were committing what Moore called the "naturalistic fallacy." Thus, one of the tasks of ethics is to determine the most important "goods" for humanity. Moore maintained that "personal affection and aesthetic enjoyments include all the greatest, and by far the greatest goods with which we are acquainted." Moral and ethical rules, as well as obligations and duties, are to be judged by whether they promote the greatest amount of good in the universe, a view called "ideal utilitarianism." The views expressed in *Principia Ethica* influenced an entire

generation of writers, artists, and intellectuals through their impact on the Bloomsbury Group, a literary coterie whose membership overlapped with that of the Apostles and included Strachey, Virginia Woolf, Leonard Woolf, E. M. Forster, Roger Fry, and Clive Bell.

Also in 1903, Moore's "The Refutation of Idealism," a paper in which his opposition to Idealism reached its most confident formulation, was published. He attacked what he considered to be the cornerstone of all Idealist systems, succinctly formulated by George Berkeley in the Latin phrase *esse es percipi* ("to be is to be perceived"), from which it was concluded that all reality was inescapably mental. Moore argued that this formula failed to distinguish the act of awareness in perception and the object of awareness. Once this distinction is recognized, the problem of the continued existence of unobserved objects disappears.

Moore later lost confidence in this argument, and he continued throughout the rest of his life to struggle with the problem of the relationship between perception and reality. He later confessed that he thought himself better at the precise formulation of philosophical questions than at answering them, and his work after 1903 became increasingly fragmented and inconclusive. With the publication of these works, Moore was at the height of his powers, his reputation established. Slender and handsome, he had achieved acceptance, even leadership, in one of the foremost intellectual debating societies in England.

Despite his achievements, however, when Moore's fellowship came to an end in 1904, he was unable to obtain a research fellowship to continue at Cambridge. He had, however, recently inherited enough money on which to live comfortably. He did not stay at Cambridge, though he could have. Instead, Moore moved to Edinburgh, where he lived with his friend Alfred Ainsworth. For six years, at Edinburgh, and later at London, he continued to work on philosophy, studying Russell's *The Principles of Mathematics* (1903) and writing reviews. During the period from 1903 to 1904, Moore and Russell had had frequent discussions on philosophy, and Russell in his introduction to his 1903 work credited Moore with a breakthrough that had cleared up many difficulties that had seemed insoluble. During that period away from Cambridge, Moore also wrote a small book titled *Ethics*, which he personally preferred to *Principia Ethica*, primarily because he believed that it was clearer and had fewer invalid arguments.

In 1911, largely because of the lobbying of economist John Maynard Keynes, Moore was offered a lectureship at Cambridge, which he gladly accepted. He remained at Cambridge for the next twenty-eight years. He first lectured in psychology, partly because there were no positions in philosophy proper available, but also because psychology was then still closely connected with philosophy, having only recently emerged as a separate discipline, and Moore was well qualified to teach all but its experimental aspects. Later, as a result of retirements and gracious adjustments by other faculty members, Moore was able to replace psychology with metaphysics and a course called Elements of Philosophy. Moore was a popular lecturer who made a point of leaving time for open discussion. When he lectured, he felt compelled to think his subject through again rather than rely on his lecture notes from the previous year. He believed this gave his lectures more life in that the lecture then centered on problems that currently interested him.

It was while he was lecturing on psychology that Moore met Ludwig Wittgenstein, the famous Austrian philosopher. Wittgenstein bluntly told Moore that his lectures were very bad because Moore did not express his own views. Like his relationship with Russell, Moore's relationship with Wittgenstein was a peculiar mixture of professional admiration and conflict. They experienced periods of frequent and fruitful discussions. Unfortunately, they also had a series of petty quarrels followed by long periods during which they would not even speak to each other. Despite their difficulties, however, Moore maintained that both Russell and Wittgenstein were more profound thinkers and had made more important contributions to philosophy than he. The people who knew Moore remarked on his total lack of professional vanity and on a kind of innocence or childlikeness in his personality. Wittgenstein, in a letter to Norman Malcolm, admitted this about Moore, but then went on to eviscerate the compliment by adding the following:

As to its being to his "credit" to be childlike—I can't understand that: unless it's also to a child's credit. For you aren't talking of the innocence a man has fought for, but of an innocence that comes from a natural absence of a temptation.

In 1916, at the age of forty-three, Moore was married to Dorothy M. Ely, a woman who had attended his lectures that year. They had two sons, Nicholas, who became a well-known poet, and Timothy. Moore continued to work in philosophy throughout his life, though he never again produced a full-length work such as *Principia Ethica*. His many papers were published in a series of anthologies under the titles *Philosophical Studies* and *Some Main Problems of Philosophy* and the posthumously published *Philosophical Papers* and *Commonplace Book, 1919-1953*. In these works, Moore continued to support common sense over the extravagantly metaphysical view of the world and insisted that the solution to philosophical problems required proper framing of the question and careful analysis of the meaning of the words and concepts involved.

From 1921 to 1947, he was the editor of the philosophical journal *Mind*, in which his own essay "The Nature of Judgment" had appeared. During his life, he received numerous honors, including the Litt.D. from Cambridge (1913), the honorary degree of LL.D. from the University of St. Andrews (1918), election as a Fellow of the British Academy (1918), and appointment to the Order of Merit (1951).

In 1939, Moore reached the mandatory retirement age for professors at Cambridge. He continued, however, to lecture and hold discussions with students at Oxford and later at universities in the United States. Until the end of his life, he continued writing and revising his earlier work. Moore died in Cambridge in 1958, shortly before his eighty-fifth birthday.

Influence

Moore was not a man of action in the conventional sense. His life was without significant outward conflict or change. He never suffered from financial worries or came up against serious obstacles to his goals, and he spent the major portion of his life doing exactly what he wanted to do, working in philosophy at Cambridge.

He has been called a "philosopher's philosopher," a characterization that is accurate both with respect to the esteem in which he is held by other philosophers and with respect to the difficulty that his writings present to the lay reader, based as they often are on the minute and critical examination of the positions of other philosophers. Yet Moore's writings account for only a part of his influence. His impact on his many students and contemporaries, his personal force in conversation both in and out of the classroom, and his pure and intense pursuit of the truth have caused him to be compared to Socrates. Moore's commitment to clear thinking affected not only the narrow technical confines of academia but also, through their influence on members of the Apostles and the Bloomsbury Group, such diverse fields as economics, politics, literature, and art criticism.

Scott Bouvier

Principia Ethica

Type of philosophy: Ethics
First published: 1903
Principal ideas advanced:

◇ The adjective "good" names an indefinable, unanalyzable, simple, unique property.

◇ The term "naturalistic fallacy" is applied to any theory that attempts a definition of good, for if good is simple, it has no parts to be distinguished by definition.

◇ Sometimes the value of a whole is not simply the sum of the values of its parts; this is the principle of organic unities.

◇ One's duty, in any particular situation, is to do that action that will cause more good than any possible alternative.

◇ The ideal good is a state of consciousness in which are combined the pleasures of aesthetic contemplation and the pleasures of admiring generous qualities in other persons.

That G. E. Moore's *Principia Ethica* has attained the status of a modern classic is amply attested

by the number of references made to its central concepts and arguments. Moore's central contention is that the adjective "good" refers to a simple, unique, and unanalyzable property. He claims that propositions containing value terms and ethical predicates are meaningful and can be found to be either true or false, even though the word "good" names an indefinable property knowable only by intuition or immediate insight. Moore also argues that the truth of propositions predicating intrinsic goodness—that is, that something is good on its own account, quite without reference to its value as a means—must likewise be seen immediately and without proof. The term "naturalistic fallacy" is proposed to name the error of mistaking some property other than goodness for goodness itself. Any definition of "good" would involve reference to something having distinguishable aspects or parts—hence, not simple; but since goodness is simple, any such definition would be false, an instance of the naturalistic fallacy.

The failure of previous systems of ethics, Moore alleges, is attributable to their imprecise formulations of the questions peculiar to ethics. His objective is to discover and lay down those basic principles according to which any scientific ethical investigation must proceed. Ethics should be concerned with two basic questions: "What kinds of things ought to exist for their own sakes?"—which presupposes knowledge of good—and "What kinds of actions ought we to perform?"

Defining Good

The first task of ethics, then, is to determine what "good" means. The only relevant type of definition is not a verbal definition but one that describes the real nature of what is denoted by stating the parts constituting the whole referent. However, in this sense of "definition," "good" cannot be defined. It is a simple notion, not complex. The word "good," like "yellow," refers to an object of thought that is indefinable because it is one of many similarly ultimate terms presupposed by those complex ones that can be defined. True, one can give verbal equivalents of these notions; for example, yellow can be described in terms of light vibrations of certain frequencies—as the physicist might describe it—but light waves are obviously not identical with yellow *as experienced*. One either knows yellow in one's experience or does not, for there is no substitute for the visual experience. Likewise, while there are other adjectives, such as "valuable," that can be substituted for "good," the property itself must be recognized in an act of direct insight.

With respect to the notion of good (as a *property* indicated by the adjective, not as a substantive, "a good" or "the good"), and to propositions predicating intrinsic goodness, Moore is an intuitionist. Such propositions are simply self-evident; proof is neither possible nor relevant. However, in other respects Moore rejects intuitionism; he denies that such propositions are true *because* they are known by intuition. Holding that this, like any other way of cognizing, may be mistaken, he also denies that propositions in answer to the second basic question—concerning what *ought* to be done—can be known intuitively, since it is a question of means involving intricate causal relations and variable conditions and circumstances. Judgments about intrinsic goodness are true universally if true at all, but in order to know what one ought to do, that is, to know that any given action is the best, one would have to know that the anticipated effects are always produced and that the totality of these reflect a balance of good superior to that of any alternatives. Such judgments can be only probable, never certain. Thus, both types of ethical judgment presuppose the notion of good but in ways not always clearly distinguished. The situation is complicated because various combinations of intrinsic and instrumental value and disvalue or indifference may occur. Obligatory acts may have no intrinsic value at all, and acts that are impossible and thus not obligatory may have great intrinsic goodness.

The Naturalistic Fallacy

Things having this simple, unique quality of goodness also have other properties, and this fact has misled philosophers into what Moore terms "the naturalistic fallacy." To take any other property, such as "pleasant" or "desired," no matter how uniformly associated with good, as *definitive* of "good," is to make this error. These other properties exist in space and time, and hence are in nature; on the other hand, good is nonnatural; it belongs to that class of objects and properties that are not included in the subject matter of the natural sciences. Thus, when someone insists that "good" *means* "pleasant," or in the substantive sense, "pleasure," the person is defining good in terms of a natural object or property; that this is fallacious may be seen by substituting for the meaningful question, "Is pleasure good?" the question implied by such a definition: "Is pleasure pleasant?" Clearly one does not mean the latter, Moore insists, or anything like it, and can by direct inspection see what one does mean—one is asking whether pleasure is qualified by an unanalyzable and unique property.

That one can have this notion of good before one's mind shows that "good" is not meaningless. The idea that it names a complex that might be analyzed variously must be rejected because one can always ask about any proposed definition of good as complex, "Is X good?" and see that the subject and predicate were not identical. For example, suppose "good" were defined as "that which we desire to desire." Although one might plausibly think that "Is A good?" means "Is A that which we desire to desire?," one can again ask the intelligible question, "Is it good to desire to desire A?" However, substituting the proposed definition yields the absurdly complicated question, "Is the desire to desire A one of the things that we desire to desire?" Again, obviously this is not what one means, and direct inspection reveals the difference between the notions of good and desiring to desire. The only remaining alternative is that "good" is indefinable; it must be clear, however, that this condition applies only to what is meant by the adjective "good," not to "*the* good"; were the latter incapable of definition and description, ethics would be pointless.

Organic Unities

Moore calls attention to another source of great confusion, the neglect of what he calls the "principle of organic unities." This is the paradoxical but most important truth that things good, bad, and indifferent in various degrees and relationships may constitute a whole in which the values of the whole and parts are not regularly proportionate. Thus, it is possible for a whole made up of indifferent or even bad parts to be good, or for one containing only good parts to be indifferent or bad, and in less extreme cases, for parts of only moderate worth to constitute wholes of great value.

Crime with punishment may make a whole better than one of these two evils without the other; awareness of something beautiful has great intrinsic goodness, but the beautiful object by itself has relatively little value, and consciousness may sometimes be indifferent or bad. The relationship of part to whole is not that of means to end, because the latter consists of separable terms, and on removal of a means, the same intrinsic value may remain in the end, which situation does not obtain for part and whole. Failure to understand the principle of organic unities causes erroneous estimation of the value of a whole as equal to that of the parts.

Hedonists

The foregoing principles and distinctions form the core of Moore's ethics and underlie both his criticism of other views and the final elaboration of his own. He argues that naturalistic theories that identify good with natural properties must either restrict the sense of "nature" if they define "good" in terms of the natural, because in other respects, the evil is just as "natural" as the good, or else must select some special feature of nature for this purpose. In any case, the naturalistic fallacy occurs. Hedonism, the view that "pleasure *alone* is good as an end," is by far the most common form of ethical naturalism, and it receives more detailed treatment. Hedonism is initially plausible, Moore concedes; it is difficult to distinguish being pleased by something from approving it, but we do sometimes disapprove the enjoyable, which shows that the predicate of a judgment of approbation is not synonymous with "pleasant." However, most hedonists have fallen into the naturalistic fallacy. John Stuart Mill furnishes a classic example when he asserts that nothing but pleasure or happiness and the avoidance of pain are desirable as ends, and then equates "desirable" with "desired." Actually Mill later describes other things as desired, such as virtue, money, or health; thus, he either contradicts his earlier statements or makes false ones in attempting to show that such things as virtue or money are parts of happiness. He thus obliterates

his own distinction—and one on which Moore insists—between means and ends.

Moore writes that of the hedonists, only Henry Sidgwick recognized that "good" is unanalyzable and that the hedonistic doctrine that pleasure is the sole good as an end must rest on intuition or be self-evident. Moore here freely admits what others might regard as a serious limitation in the intuitionist method—that Sidgwick's and his own intuitions conflict and that neither is able to prove hedonism true or false. However, this is disturbing primarily because of the disagreement rather than the lack of proof, Moore adds, since ultimate principles are necessarily incapable of demonstration. The best one can do is to be as clear as possible concerning what such intuited principles mean and how they relate to other beliefs already held; only thus can one convince an opponent of error. Mill rejected philosopher Jeremy Bentham's view that the only measures of value in pleasure are quantitative, and he suggested that there are differences in kind; one learns these by consulting competent judges and discovering their preferences. However, if pleasure is really the only desirable end, differences in quality are irrelevant; thus, Sidgwick reverted to the simpler form of hedonism but specified that the ultimate end is related essentially to human existence. Moore submits reasons for rejecting Sidgwick's intuitions. The first objection is that it is obvious that the most beautiful world imaginable would be preferable to the most ugly even if no human beings at all were there to contemplate either. It follows that things separable from human existence can be intrinsically good. However, pleasure cannot be good apart from human experience; it is clear that pleasure of which no one was conscious would not be an end for its own sake. Consciousness must be a *part* of the end, and the hedonistic principle is thus seen to be false: It is not pleasure alone but pleasure together with consciousness that is intrinsically good.

The importance of this conclusion lies in the method used to achieve it—that of completely isolating the proposed good and estimating its value apart from all related objects—for the same method shows that consciousness of pleasure is not the only good. Surely no one would think that a world consisting of nothing but consciousness of pleasure would be as good as one including other existents, and even if these were not intrinsically valuable, the latter world could be better as an organic unity. Similar methods of analysis refute other forms of hedonism—egoistic and utilitarian; Moore concludes that, at best, pleasure would be a criterion of good were pleasure and the good always concomitant, but he regards this as very doubtful and supposes that there is no criterion of good at all.

Metaphysical Ethics

The chief remaining type of ethics Moore criticizes is what he calls "metaphysical ethics," positing some proposition about a supersensible reality as the basis for ethical principles. He admits that the metaphysicians are right in thinking that some things that *are* are not natural objects, but wrong in concluding that therefore whatever does not exist in nature must exist elsewhere. Things such as truth, universals, numbers, and goodness do not exist at all. However, metaphysical ethicists such as the Stoics, Baruch Spinoza, and Immanuel Kant have tried to infer what is good from what is ultimately real and thus have committed a variant of the naturalistic fallacy, for whether the reality involved is natural or supernatural is irrelevant. To the second basic ethical question, "What kind of actions ought we to perform?" a supersensible reality might be relevant, but typical metaphysical systems have no bearing on practice. For example, if the sole good pertains to an eternal, perfect, Absolute Being, there is no way by which human action can enhance the goodness of this situation.

Perhaps the metaphysical ethicists have thus erred through failing to notice the ambiguity of the question, "What is good?," which may refer either to good things or to goodness itself; this ambiguity accounts for the inconsistency between such propositions as that the only true reality is eternal and that its future realization is good, when what is meant is that something like—but not identical with—such a reality would be good. However, in this case it becomes clear that it is fallacious to define good as constituted by this reality. Although "X is good" is verbally similar to other propositions in which both subject and predicate stand for existents, it is actually radically different; of any two existents so related one may still ask, "Is this whole good?," which again shows the uniqueness of the value predicate.

It is essential to remember that in answering the question as to what we ought to do once we know intuitively what things are good as ends, a different method must come into use. Because practical ethical judgments assert causal relations between actions and good or bad effects, the empirical method affording probability, never certainty, is indicated. Thus, Moore differs from traditional intuitionists both in his definition of "right" and in his account of how it is known. Right is not to be distinguished from the genuinely useful, and duty is "that action, which will cause more good to exist in the Universe than any possible alternative." In practice, knowledge of right and duty is most limited, so we must consider as duties those acts that will *usually* yield better results than any others. Such limitations do not excuse individuals from following the general rules, but when the latter are lacking or irrelevant, attention should be redirected to the much neglected intrinsic values of the foreseeable effects. It follows, of course, that virtue, like duty, is a means rather than an end, contrary to the views of some Christian writers and even of Kant, who hold inconsistently that either virtue or good will is the sole good, but that it can be rewarded by something better.

Good and Aesthetics

It remains to state Moore's conception of "*the good*," or the ideal. He notes that he will try to describe the ideal merely as that which is intrinsically good in a high degree, not the best conceivable or the best possible. Its general description follows: "The best ideal we can construct will be that state of things that contains the greatest number of things having positive value, and that contains nothing evil or indifferent—*provided* that the presence of none of these goods, or the absence of things evil or indifferent, seems to diminish the value of the whole." The method of discovering both the intrinsically valuable and its degrees of value is that previously mentioned: the method of isolation. It will show that "by far the most valuable things, which we know or can imagine, are certain states of consciousness, which may be roughly described as the pleasures of human intercourse and the enjoyment of beautiful objects." Moore stresses the point that it is these wholes, rather than any constituents, that are the ideal ends.

In aesthetic appreciation, there are cognition of the object's beautiful qualities and an appropriate emotion, but neither of these elements has great value in itself compared with that of the whole, and to have a positive emotion toward a really ugly object constitutes a whole that is evil. Beauty is thus not a matter of feeling: "The beautiful should be *defined* as that of which the admiring contemplation is good in itself." Whether an object has true beauty "depends upon the *objective* question whether the whole in question is or is not truly good, and does not depend upon the question whether it would or would not excite particular feelings in particular persons." Subjectivistic definitions of beauty commit the naturalistic fallacy, but it should be noted that beauty can be defined as it is above, thus leaving only one unanalyzable value term, "good." Consideration of the cognitive element in aesthetic appreciation shows that knowledge adds intrinsic value; aside from the value of true belief as a means or that of the actual existence of the object, it is simply and clearly better to know it truly rather than merely to imagine it. Thus appreciation of a real but inferior object is better than that of a superior but imaginary one.

The second and greater good consists of the pleasures of personal affection. All the elements of the best aesthetic enjoyments plus the great intrinsic good of the object are present here. Part of the object consists of the mental qualities of the person for whom affection is felt, though these must be appropriately expressed in the bodily features and behavior.

Admirable mental qualities . . . consist very largely in an emotional contemplation of beautiful objects . . . the appreciation of them will consist essentially in the contemplation of such contemplation. It is true that the most valuable appreciation of persons appears to be that which consists in the appreciation of their appreciation of other persons . . . therefore, we may admit that the appreciation of a person's attitude toward other persons . . . is far the most valuable good we know.

From these assertions it follows that the ideal, contrary to tradition, must include material properties, because appreciation both of beauty and of persons requires corporeal expression of the valuable qualities.

Because the emotions appropriate to both beautiful objects and to persons are so widely varied, the totality of intrinsic goods is most complex, but Moore is confident that "a reflective judgment will in the main decide correctly" both what things are positive goods and the major differences in relative values. However, this is possible only by exact distinction of the objects of value judgment, followed by direct intuition of the presence, absence, or degree of the unique property, good.

Modern-day students of ethics have benefited immeasurably from Moore's attempt to be clear and precise in the analysis of ethical principles and from his redirection of attention to the really basic questions. Some critics cannot accept certain major conclusions concerning the indefinability of "good," its presence to intuition, its objective status, and the consequent treatment of the "naturalistic fallacy," but even the nature and the extent of the disagreement he has aroused testify to Moore's stature as a philosopher of ethics.

Marvin Easterling

Additional Reading

Ayer, Alfred Jules. *Russell and Moore: The Analytical Heritage*. Cambridge, Mass.: Harvard University Press, 1971. Discusses G. E. Moore's early Platonism, his theory of truth, his conception of philosophical analysis and its aims, and his defense of "common sense," all in the clearest terms. Concludes by noting that, for Moore, philosophical problems are not only genuine but also capable of being solved.

Fratantaro, Sal. *The Methodology of G. E. Moore*. Brookfield, Vt.: Ashgate, 1998. This book aspires to see the range of Moore's methodology by exploring its intricacy and richness.

Levy, Paul. *G. E. Moore and the Cambridge Apostles*. London: Weidenfeld and Nicolson, 1979. Fascinating portrait of Moore as a philosopher and human being. Describes the "intellectual aristocracy" from which Moore descended, the milieu of the Apostles, Moore's student years at Cambridge, his rise to an academic career, and the genesis and reception of *Principia Ethica*. For the general reader.

O'Connor, David. *The Metaphysics of G. E. Moore.* Dordrecht, Holland: D. Reidel, 1982. This work sets aside specifically ethical topics but is otherwise a comprehensive interpretation of Moore's thought, suitable for undergraduates. Taking "Some Main Problems in Philosophy" as the centerpiece, O'Connor examines Moore's work on the central problems of metaphysics, his consistent antiskepticism, and his epistemology.

Regan, Tom. *Bloomsbury's Prophet: G. E. Moore and the Development of His Moral Philosophy.* Philadelphia: Temple University Press, 1986. Discusses Moore's development, as well as his role in the history of Bloomsbury and the powerful influence of *Principia Ethica*. Engaging for both the general reader and the specialist.

Shaw, William H. *Moore on Right and Wrong: The Normative Ethics of G. E. Moore.* Boston: Kluwer, 1995. An important reconstruction and examination of Moore's normative theory.

Stroll, Avrum. *Moore and Wittgenstein on Certainty.* Oxford: Oxford University Press, 1994. Wittgenstein's *On Certainty* (1969) is a commentary on three of Moore's greatest epistemological papers, though Moore had anticipated some of the issues as early as the 1930's. Stroll presents a penetrating analysis of differing approaches to a set of fundamental epistemological problems, extended to current issues in cognitive science and philosophy of mind. For the advanced undergraduate.

Sylvester, Robert Peter. *The Moral Philosophy of G. E. Moore.* Philadelphia: Temple University Press, 1990. Relates Moore's epistemology to his ethics and illuminates Moore's deep influence on twentieth century moral philosophy. Great scholarship, intelligible to undergraduates.

Scott Bouvier, updated by Grant A. Marler

Thomas More

Devoted to his faith and Renaissance learning, More served as the first lay Lord Chancellor of England, opposed Henry VIII's break with Rome, and forfeited his exalted position and his life rather than swear allegiance to the king as the supreme head of the Church of England.

Principal philosophical works: *The Life of John Picus, Earl of Myrandula*, 1510 (translation of Giovanni Pico della Mirandola); *De Optimo Reipublicae Statu, deque Nova Insula Utopia*, 1516 (*Utopia*, 1551); *A Dyaloge of Sir Thomas More*, 1529; *An Apologye of Syr Thomas More, Knight*, 1533; *History of King Richard III*, 1543; *A Dialoge of Comfort Against Tribulacion*, 1553.

Born: February 7, 1478; London, England
Died: July 6, 1535; London, England

Early Life

Thomas More was born February 7, 1478, in the Cripplegate neighborhood of London. He was the second of five children born to John More and Agnes Granger. Three siblings apparently died in childhood, and Thomas was the only surviving son. An ambitious and talented man, John More had succeeded his father as butler of Lincoln's Inn but aspired to be a barrister. The benchers of Lincoln's Inn liked the young fellow who managed their meals and approved him for membership; he subsequently was admitted to the bar. His marriage to Agnes Granger advanced his career, for she was the daughter of a prosperous merchant and sheriff of London. John More was appointed judge in the Court of Common Pleas, then promoted to the Court of King's Bench, and was even knighted by the king. Having risen from the working class himself, he had great expectations for his son.

Young More learned Latin at St. Anthony's School in London. He was much influenced by headmaster Nicholas Holt, who had taught John Colet and William Lattimer, both of whom became English humanists and friends of More. At thirteen, More was placed in the household of Thomas Morton, Archbishop of Canter-

bury and Lord Chancellor, who immediately took a liking to the intelligent boy. In 1492, at Morton's urging, More entered Canterbury Hall (later absorbed by Christ College), Oxford University, where he met and began lasting friendships with Thomas Linacre and William Grocyn, two scholars who had studied in Italy and drunk deeply of the Renaissance literature. Along with the classics, More studied mathematics and history and

Thomas More. *(Library of Congress)*

learned to play the flute and viol. His lifelong love of humanistic learning had been kindled.

Convinced that his son should pursue a legal career, John More recalled Thomas to London in 1494 and enrolled him as a law student at New Inn. Thomas moved to Lincoln's Inn in 1496, began lecturing on the law, and came to be known as an eloquent and insightful student of law. He did not, however, forsake literature. He wrote Latin and English verse, immersed himself in the humanistic writings of Giovanni Pico della Mirandola, and joined the intellectual circle that included Grocyn, Linacre, William Lily, and John Colet. He especially looked to Colet for direction in both life and learning. He and Lily published epigrams rendered from the Greek anthology into Latin prose. More met and began an enduring friendship with the remarkable Desiderius Erasmus of Rotterdam, undoubtedly the leading Christian humanist. As Erasmus later recounted, More seriously considered devoting his life to the Catholic Church. For almost four years, he lived near the Charterhouse in London and followed the discipline of the Carthusian order. Spending much of his time in prayer and fasting, he regularly scourged himself and began a lifelong habit of wearing a hair shirt. He came near to joining the Franciscan Order. During this time, he also lectured, at the request of his friend Grocyn, on Saint Augustine's *De civitate Dei*, 413-427 (*The City of God*, 1610).

After four years of living much like a monk, More apparently resolved his doubts about what he should do. Although he remained a pious Catholic, he threw himself into the practice of law. Various reasons have been suggested for this abrupt shift to the secular. The corruption of the Church, his own intellectual and material ambitions, and his unwillingness to remain celibate may all have contributed to his decision; he soon gained a reputation as a just and knowledgeable barrister. He also studied politics, adding to what he had learned from his father and Archbishop Morton. At twenty-six, he was elected to Parliament (apparently from the City of London) and quickly emerged as a primary critic of government inefficiency and heavy taxation.

More played a principal role in frustrating Henry VII's efforts to extract a hundred thousand pounds from Parliament upon the marriage of his daughter Margaret to the King of Scotland. Henry was so angry with young More that he trumped up charges against his father, John More, had him imprisoned in the Tower of London, and released him only after he had paid a large fine. This lesson on sovereign power was not lost upon Thomas, whose thoughts were concerned with much more than politics. In 1505, More married Jane Colte, the eldest daughter of a landed gentleman, and together they had four children. Upon her death in 1511, More wasted little time in marrying Alice Middleton, an affable but rather unattractive and unlettered woman who proved to be a fine mother for his children.

Life's Work

By the time of his second marriage, More was emerging as a leading London barrister. In 1509, the same year that Henry VIII ascended the throne, More was elected to Lincoln's Inn, where he became a reader in 1511. The year before, he was appointed undersheriff of London, a position of considerable responsibility in the sheriff's court. Especially well liked by London merchants, More was chosen by King Henry as a member of an English delegation sent to Flanders in 1514 to negotiate a commercial treaty. His contribution was minor, but during those six months abroad, he delighted in the company of Peter Giles, a renowned humanist and friend of Erasmus, and began work on his *Utopia*, published in 1516. His most significant work, *Utopia* was a skillful satire that condemned the poverty, intolerance, ignorance, and brutality of English society by juxtaposing it to the economic communism and political democracy that prevailed among the tolerant and peace-loving Utopians. Although surely attracted by the idealism of *Utopia*, More was always the realist, as his *History of King Richard III*, written about the same time although published much later, makes clear. Disturbed by the ineptitude and avarice in both church and state, he wanted change for the better, but not revolutionary change.

Over the next few years, More became a favorite of Henry VIII and his Lord Chancellor, Cardinal Thomas Wolsey. They sent him on several diplomatic missions dealing with commercial matters critical to the interests of London merchants. More's skill in arguing the law convinced

Henry that he should be an officer of the Crown. In 1517, he was appointed Master of Requests, the official through whom all petitions were passed to the king, and he was elevated to the Privy Council the next year. King Henry appreciated humanistic learning and found in More a delightful intellectual companion. He encouraged More to defend Greek studies against the obscurantist attacks of conservative critics. In turn, More joined Henry in denouncing the Lutheran heresy. On Wolsey's recommendation, More was appointed Speaker of the House of Commons in 1532 and generally worked smoothly with the powerful cardinal. More surely learned from Wolsey, as he had from Archbishop Morton, and proved to be a fair and effective official, respected by the people as well as his peers. Henry rewarded him with both sinecures and landed estates.

More bought more land in Chelsea in 1523 and built a mansion there with an orchard and spacious garden. It was a happy place, where More delighted in entertaining his many friends and relatives. Illuminati such as Desiderius Erasmus were frequent guests, and the king himself regularly visited More at Chelsea. As Erasmus portrayed him, More was the epitome of Christian humanism, a wonderfully enlightened public official who nurtured intellectual and scholarly pursuits. More's idyllic existence, however, was not to last. The king's "Great Matter"—his desire to divorce Queen Catherine and marry Anne Boleyn—threatened the kind of revolutionary change that was repugnant to More's conservative temperament. When Pope Clement VII denied Henry's request for an annulment, Wolsey was the first to feel his sovereign's wrath; he was deprived of his position as Lord Chancellor, dismissed from the court, and accused of treason. Although Henry knew that More disapproved of his plans for divorce, he nevertheless made him Lord Chancellor, the first layman to hold that august office. However, the real power in the Privy Council was exercised not by More but by the Duke of Norfolk, Anne Boleyn's uncle.

If Henry thought that the appointment to Lord Chancellor would make More more pliable, the king was mistaken. More performed his duties admirably enough, but he was increasingly on the fringes of the religious revolution that Henry and Parliament were undertaking. Even as Henry made overtures to leading English Protestants, More was trying his best to root out heresy. He even approved of torture for those who defied Catholic orthodoxy. Ironically, his own day of reckoning was coming. Between 1530 and 1532, Henry gradually extended royal authority over the Church of England, and More was at last compelled to resign as Lord Chancellor when Henry suggested relaxing the laws against heresy. More wanted to withdraw to his Chelsea estate and be left alone, but Henry demanded his assent to the laws taking England out of the Church of Rome. More resisted. He was motivated not by love for the Papacy but by reverence for the unity of the Church. Stripped of his office and stipends, he was confined to the Tower of London in 1534. After more than a year of increasingly harsh treatment, he still refused to yield. In July, 1535, More was convicted of defying the Supremacy Act of November, 1534, and executed. Instantly proclaimed a martyr to the cause of Catholicism, More was beatified in 1886 and canonized in 1935.

Influence

More was a man pulled in several directions at once. He was a talented royal official, a learned and intelligent humanist, and a devout Catholic. As a lawyer and a judge, he gained a reputation for fairness. As the first lay Lord Chancellor, he personified the growing secularization of both society and government in the sixteenth century. Yet like the prelates who had preceded him, More understood the practical limitations of politics, and as Lord Chancellor, he was not about to embrace the religious and political toleration so idealized in *Utopia*. Indeed, More was basically conservative when it came to religion and politics. He did not hesitate to prosecute religious heretics, regarding them as a threat to both the church and the state.

On the other hand, More found great satisfaction in intellectual and scholarly pursuits. Christian humanism shaped his writings and his relationship with friends and family alike. *Utopia* at once established his international reputation as a leading literary figure. Among his early works were poems, Latin epigrams, and an English translation and adaptation of the biography in

Latin of Giovanni Pico della Mirandola, the brilliant young Italian humanist whose writings More deeply admired. Like Pico, More prized the life of the mind. He carried on a prolific correspondence with fellow intellectuals, performed numerous tasks for friends such as Erasmus, and defended humanist literatures from obscurantist criticism. More was happiest when his family and friends were with him. The children of his household, whether male or female, were educated under More's personal supervision. Friends such as Erasmus celebrated the intellectual exchange and hospitality that they always enjoyed with More. He had a modern devotion to intellectual curiosity.

Yet for all of his reaching toward modernity, More remained tied to the religious faith of the Middle Ages. A part of him always yearned for the monastery. He was a pious man, and his piety was grounded in a fundamental distrust of the human animal. The spiritual realm was very real to him, and very difficult to reach, and in that quest for spiritual understanding, the Roman Catholic Church was crucial. It was not the pope, but the Church—its saints, its sacraments, and its history—that More loved and revered. Despite the sordidness of individual priests or even popes, he believed that the Church was pure and spiritual and must not be corrupted by either Martin Luther or Henry VIII. In the end, it was his spiritual side that prevailed. He defied his sovereign and paid for that defiance with his life. He cared more for his king than for any pope, but he truly loved his church best of all.

Ronald William Howard

Utopia

Type of philosophy: Ethics, political philosophy
First published: De Optimo Reipublicae Statu, deque Nova Insula Utopia, 1516 (English translation, 1551)
Principal ideas advanced:
◇ Philosophers ought not to advise princes, for rulers are not interested in advice, but would much prefer to have others assent to their fixed policies.

◇ An economic system that allows private property drives the poor from the land and thereby creates thieves whom the existing laws require to be hanged: Such a system and policy is neither just nor expedient.
◇ In opposition to the former ideas, which are defended by Raphael Hythloday, a world traveler, Thomas More (as a character in the conversation) argues that a nonspeculative, prudential philosopher might be useful in politics, but Hythloday is skeptical.
◇ More objects to Raphael Hythloday's call for the abolition of money and private property by arguing that unless people have the profit motive, they will not work.
◇ Hythloday describes Utopia, a carefully organized state in which the citizens engage in scientific farming according to assignments from magistrates and then return to the cities; they work a six-hour day and spend their leisure moments reading, attending lectures, and conversing on academic subjects.
◇ In Utopia, gold has no worth, marriages are regulated, work is cooperative, and pleasure in accordance with virtue is the aim of life.

Thomas More's *Utopia*, written during the turbulence of sixteenth century English political strife, presents an ideal map of the political countryside against which to measure existing states. The English word "utopia" derives its meaning from a Greek term that can be translated "nowhere." To call a scheme "utopian" is to suggest that it cannot actually be implemented. Thomas More invented the term and applied it to a mythical community, then used his account of this community as a means of criticizing certain European social and political practices that he considered unreasonable.

More's own life lends interest to the contents of his famous book, for More served Henry VIII, the strong-willed English king, in a number of important political capacities. In 1535, More died on the block for resistance to the monarch's policies in a power struggle between the English nation and the Roman Papacy. In spite of his humanistic leanings, More stood firm in refusing to recognize Henry's claim to the title that made him head of the Church in England. As an adviser to the monarch, More became a tragic figure caught between opposing institutional pressures that played a unique role in shaping modern English history.

More's *Utopia* is made up of two books. Book 2 (which contains an elaborate description of the Utopians) was written first, in 1515, a year before the completion of book 1 (which discusses several general political questions, including whether philosophers ought to advise princes). The latter portion of *Utopia* introduces the primary figures in the work, who include More himself, presented as having heard the ensuing account of social affairs while serving his monarch on state business in Antwerp (Belgium); a gentleman named Peter Giles, who is said to have introduced More to the leading participant in the written work; and a stranger named Raphael Hythloday, a world traveler widely acquainted with political matters who shows impatience with several customs then little questioned in European social and political life. Hythloday is a spokesperson for what must have been More's own critical opinions about contemporary practices.

Advising Princes

The early discussion centers on whether philosophers ought to advise rulers—a question provoked by Giles's and More's suggestion that Hythloday's extensive knowledge could be put to such use. Hythloday shows little interest in attempting to advise rulers. At the same time, he argues that the social arrangements of the Utopians (whom he discovered somewhere below the equator) would serve well as a basis for "correcting the errors of our own cities and kingdoms." He is nonetheless convinced that to serve a king in an advisory capacity would make him miserable. "Now I live as I will," Hythloday argues—illustrating the tension existing between private and public demands on a person—"and I believe very few courtiers can say that." Hythloday insists that princes do not want advice from philosophers, that what they seek is agreement with their fixed policies of waging constant, aggressive warfare. Princes ignore sound advice and refuse to tolerate any posture except that of absolute agreement among their counselors. "They are generally more set on acquiring new kingdoms rightly or wrongly, than on governing

well those that they already have." Hythloday illustrates his viewpoint by recounting an episode that had occurred at a dinner given by a famous Cardinal. At this affair, Hythloday became entangled in a discussion when another person present praised some judicial practices that Hythloday thought foolish.

What Hythloday advocates during the discussion resembles a reformist rather than a retributionist theory of punishment for wrongdoing. He also seeks a general theory that will explain why so many people (Englishmen, in this case) risk the death penalty by stealing. Hythloday wants to understand the causes of thieving. He presents a crude yet clear economic thesis, arguing that the land enclosures in sixteenth century England create economic conditions that increase the compulsion to steal. The existing practice of hanging culprits who steal deals only with the symptoms and not with the causes of that unfortunate practice. Unable to gain a fair hearing for their economic situation, the poor are finally driven from the land. "They would willingly work," Hythloday insists, "but can find no one who will hire them." Glaring social extremes tend to develop, such as abject poverty existing side by side with extreme luxury. Hythloday presents a bald and bold environmentalist theory about the origins of criminal activities. His views condemn the legal and judicial customs of the day. The economic situation inevitably produces the thieves whom the existing laws then require to be hanged. This policy is neither just nor rationally expedient.

Hythloday then proceeds to sketch a wiser policy respecting theft and its legal treatment. Citing the Roman practice of employing thieves to work quarries, he mentions the procedures of the mythical Polyerites (meaning "much nonsense") who require apprehended thieves to make full restitution. Thieves convicted of their crimes must work at public services, under state supervision, thus producing some social benefit. They are dressed in a common uniform and distributed in different regions of the country to prevent possible formation of rebellious political groups. Each year some are pardoned. This picture of penal procedures suggests the practices of a number of twentieth century states as opposed to the generally cruel systems prevalent in More's century.

Having heard Hythloday's account, the Cardinal admits that such procedures might well be tried. By this admission he introduces a note of experimentalism into the discussion. The Cardinal concludes that if, on trying such means, the thieves were not reformed, one could then still see them hanged.

More is described as wanting to hear even more from the interesting stranger, Hythloday. He reminds Hythloday that the Greek philosopher Plato thought that political wisdom could never prevail until philosophers became kings or kings became philosophers. Hythloday replies to this argument by setting up imagined cases in which a philosopher attempts to advise an actually existing ruler—say, the French king, in one instance. Hythloday attempts to show that if he asserts that the king, as shepherd of his people, ought to care more for the welfare of the sheep than for himself (an obvious borrowing from Plato), he will be ignored by the royal council. His conclusion is that the philosopher should never give advice when he knows it will fall on deaf ears. Hythloday also refers to the practices of mythical peoples such as the Achorians (a word that means "no place") and the Macarians (meaning "blessed"), the latter of whom permit their king to possess only a thousand pounds in his treasury at any time. The point of these cases is that Hythloday wants to convince the participants in the discussion that "there is no place for philosophy in the councils of princes."

To this somewhat cynical position, More makes a significant counterargument. More admits that speculative philosophy is unhelpful to practical princes. However, he argues that there exists another kind of philosophy. This practically useful philosophy "is more urbane" and "takes its proper cue and fits itself to the drama being played, acting its part aptly and well." Thus, More reveals himself as a believer in nonspeculative, prudential philosophizing able to adjust to changing circumstances. For this reason, he cautions Hythloday, "Don't give up the ship in a storm, because you cannot control the winds." The prudentially oriented philosopher must seek to guide policy formation in an indirect manner. Hythloday's response includes the argument that the prudential philosopher must "rave along with them" (meaning the ruling council). He in-

sists that even Christ's teachings run counter to many existing customs, even in England. Even Plato, Hythloday reminds his listeners, advised outstanding individuals to refuse to meddle in politics.

Private Property
Hythloday returns to his economic thesis—that the chief cause of evil customs is the existence of private property. Only among the Utopians has he found a social system that makes virtue the primary goal of living. Other nations seeking to create sane institutional arrangements undermine their own efforts by maintaining private property and a money economy. Their laws hopelessly try to protect for the individual what, by the nature of private property, must always stand under threat. Hythloday advocates the total abolition of money and privately held property.

More objects to this view, although he shows interest in a fuller description of the Utopians while insisting that absolute equality of possessions means that many will cease working. People need the incentive of the hope of gain, according to More. From a policy enforcing equal possessions in cases when all people experience extreme want, only warfare and constant factionalism can ensue. People require authority over themselves based on some distinction in abilities and worth. To More's objections, Giles adds his own view that other people are not better governed than the English. His reason for so thinking is that the abilities of English and European rulers are equal to those of other persons. European governmental practices also rest on long historical experience. Hythloday replies that the Utopians also possess a long history—that their peculiar success in managing their affairs results from their willingness to learn. His associates in the discussion ask Hythloday to provide more information about the Utopians.

Utopia
In book 2, three aspects of Utopian civilization receive consideration under a number of separate headings. Hythloday describes first the island where Utopia exists and the number, distribution, and geographical arrangements of its cities; second, the social and political institutions of

Utopia; and third, the ideas and moral norms by which the Utopians live.

Each city in Utopia is divided in a manner as to require several magistrates. From the body of the magistrates, three representatives are chosen to meet in the capital city once a year. Individual cities contain households fixed in number and built on a planned model, thirty households requiring one magistrate in a given district. Agricultural pursuits aiming at economic self-sufficiency require existence of country households containing forty men and women each. These households receive their members on a rotational basis from the cities. Each Utopian must take a turn at farming and related forms of labor, thus spreading the burden of physical work; but individuals particularly fond of country life and work may remain longer than the otherwise stipulated two-year period. Something very much like scientific farming operates in Utopia.

A wall surrounds each city. Its inhabitants work only six hours each day (an astounding suggestion in More's time). The remainder of a citizen's time is devoted to private pursuits. These pursuits indicate that Utopia is a society composed of professorial humanists or transcendentalist moral philosophers who enjoy academic talk. The citizens are well read. They also attend a wide variety of public lectures. Hythloday claims the Utopians undertake these surprising intellectual pastimes on a voluntary basis. The six-hour day in Utopia produces no idlers or maladjusted persons. Apparently, though a Christian, More could picture a human society in which evil does not exist. *Utopia* fails to discuss the problems associated with possible misuses of leisure time.

Living in a balanced, well-planned society, the Utopians wear casual, common dress (indicating that More's humanism reflects also some puritanical dislike of color and variety). Gambling, drinking, and related activities do not occur. Good teaching leads Utopians to ignore the usual allure of gold and precious stones. Gold is used for children's ornamentation and, in the adult world, for the making of chamber pots. The Utopians thus learn that gold has no intrinsic worth. Indeed, as Raphael points out, most of the genuinely valuable elements in nature, including air and water, exist in plentiful quantities. In Utopia,

marriages are also regulated. Children and parents dine in common halls (suggesting some of the practices of organized camp life). The Utopians live moderately, each doing his share of work—including cooperative building and repair of roads.

Social habits in Utopia remind one of aspects of Plato's ideal state, which also emphasized communal domestic life. The general picture reveals a society that trains people so as to minimize cupidity, channeling strenuous energies to productive community ends. However, each Utopian retains a large share of time for private pursuits. More's ideal society combines a moderate Puritanism with a humanistic stress on learning and moral development. Nowhere in More's *Utopia* is there a discussion concerning the realism or lack of realism of the humanistic social image presented.

More then considers the Utopians' moral philosophy, their marriage customs, the unique love of learning displayed by the citizens, their bondmen (who seem to do a large amount of bothersome menial labor), care of the sick, legal procedures and punishments, warfare, foreign relations, and religion. The Utopians seek knowledge without requiring irate schoolmasters or crass materialistic inducements. They are an admirably tolerant people, as consideration of a few of their beliefs will indicate.

Happiness (defined as pleasure in accordance with virtue) stands as the Utopian moral ideal. This shows the influence of Epicurean and Aristotelian ethical notions on More's humanism. In fact, the Utopians possess books given to them by Hythloday on a return voyage he made to their island—philosophical works by Plato and Aristotle; literary productions by Aristophanes, Homer, Sophocles, and Euripides; historical narratives by Herodotus and Thucydides. The Utopians are a rather philosophical people able to make fairly sophisticated ethical judgments based on reason. As More describes them, the Utopians "discriminate several kinds of true pleasure, some belonging to the mind, others to the body. Those of the mind are knowledge and the delight which comes from contemplation of the truth; also the pleasant recollection of a well-spent life and the assured hope of future well-being."

Bodily pleasures are classified in accordance with the way they produce some immediate sense effect or turn the senses inward (as in the case of the enjoyment produced by hearing music). The Utopians debate aesthetic issues and seek to find delight in "sound, sight and smell." They guard and nourish the mental and physical capacities.

Utopia does enforce some rigid sexual rules. Marriage occurs only when a man reaches twenty-two years and a woman, eighteen. Premarital sexual experience leads to severe punishment. Indeed, in the Utopian scheme, those who are caught in illicit affairs forfeit the right to marry for a lifetime unless pardoned by a prince. A few divorces are permitted, but only on the authorization of the senate.

More's account of the religious beliefs of the Utopians provides an interesting instance of tolerance. Different religious systems exist in Utopia. Dogmatic fights over doctrines and creeds are outlawed. Respect for views other than one's own prevails and is defended by the laws. Priests must be elected and are kept relatively few in number. All Utopians must accept belief in an afterlife as well as the view that God punishes in accordance with one's conduct in this life. No one may challenge these beliefs in public. The common element shared by all religions in Utopia affirms a providential order that reasoning about nature can discover. Some priests are celibate while others marry. The different religious worshipers call the object of their devotions Mithra. They pray for guidance in moral endeavors and ask for an easy death. Reason rather than revelation seems adequate to determine religious beliefs and practices.

Hythloday (as More's spokesperson) ends his account of Utopia with a criticism of humanity's essential weakness: pride. Only human pride keeps the world from adopting the sensible laws and customs of the Utopians. Reason shows that class distinctions, property rights, and human anxiety exist only in societies that fail to curb pride. More writes that Hythloday's picture of society fails fully to satisfy him, yet he concludes: "I must confess there are many things in the Utopian Commonwealth that I wish rather than expect to see followed among our citizens."

Whitaker T. Deininger, updated by John K. Roth

Additional Reading

Ackroyd, Peter. *The Life of Thomas More*. London: Chatto & Windus, 1998. A helpful biographical study of Sir Thomas More's life and times, which explores the ideas he developed and the difficult personal decisions that he faced.

Baker-Smith, Dominic. *More's Utopia*. New York: HarperCollins, 1991. An accessible study of the development and influence of More's reflections on the ideal human society.

Fox, Alistair. *Thomas More: History and Providence*. New Haven, Conn.: Yale University Press, 1983. This intellectual biography details the evolution of More's thought, delving deep into his views about God and humanity.

_____. *Utopia: An Elusive Vision*. New York: Twayne, 1993. A veteran More scholar offers an interpretation of More's aims in the writing and vision of his famous *Utopia*.

Marius, Richard. *Thomas More*. New York: Alfred A. Knopf, 1984. A well-crafted biography that analyzes a man torn between the medieval world of faith and the modern world of reason and who ultimately chose the spirit over the flesh.

Martz, Louis L. *Thomas More: The Search for the Inner Man*. New Haven, Conn.: Yale University Press, 1990. An effort to interpret the complexities of More's life, which involved politics, philosophy, and religion.

Monti, James. *The King's Good Servant but God's First: The Life and Writing of Saint Thomas More*. San Francisco: Ignatius Press, 1997. A biographical study that explores the clash of politics and religion in More's life.

Olin, John C., ed. *Interpreting Thomas More's "Utopia."* New York: Fordham University Press, 1989. Helpful essays by important More scholars explore and assess the meaning and significance of More's classic on the ideal human society.

Reynolds, E. E. *Thomas More and Erasmus*. New York: Fordham University Press, 1965. A careful study of the relationship between two dynamic thinkers who influenced the development of European humanism.

Ronald William Howard, updated by John K. Roth

Mozi

Mozi's doctrines of universal love, the need to follow the will of Heaven, and the condemnation of offensive warfare, as passed on by his devoted followers, formed the foundations of the first and best-organized alternative to the teachings of Confucius in China during the Warring States period (475-221 B.C.E.).

Principal philosophical works: *Mozi*, fifth century B.C.E. (*The Ethical and Political Works of Motse*, 1929; also known as *Mo Tzu: Basic Writings*, 1963; commonly known as *Mozi*)

Flourished: Fifth century B.C.E.; China

Early Life

Little is known with absolute certainty about any aspect of the life of Mo Di, usually known as Mozi; even his name has been called into question by scholars who point out that his family name, Mo ("dark" or possibly "branded"), seems more like a description than a surname. Considering Mozi's importance for early Chinese philosophical debate and the notable Chinese penchant for accurate dating and historical details, this lack of information seems remarkable.

One possible explanation lies in Mozi's probable class background. *Mozi*, the work traditionally attributed to the philosopher, is filled with examples drawn from the world of artisans. For instance, Mozi is quoted as saying that a single functional linchpin he has made is far more valuable than a fancy mechanical bird made by one of his rivals. The clumsy language of the work and the rough-hewn images Mozi employs further suggest humble origins. In the texts of rival schools, Mozi is always referred to as a commoner (*jian ren*) and belittled for his practical skills. The "Confucian" *Xunzi* (latter half of third century B.C.E.; partial translation, *The Works of Hsüntze*, 1928; complete translation, *Xunzi*, 1988-1994, 3 volumes) declares that "Doing it oneself is the way of a serf. [This is] Mo Tzu's theory."

Whether or not Mozi was from the lower classes, he was very well educated for his time. The eclectic Han Dynasty (207 B.C.E.-220 C.E.) text *Huainanzi* (late second century B.C.E.; *Tao, the Great Luminant: Essays from Huai Nan Tzu*, 1935; commonly known as *Huainanzi*) reports that "Mo Tzu studied the Confucian calling and received Confucius's arts, yet he considered their rituals bothersome and was not pleased [with them]." Passages in *Mozi* describe how Mozi always traveled with a great stack of books, evidently impressing his potential audiences with his learning. Based on the many passages of this sort recorded in early Chinese sources and the heavy reliance on quotations from ancient texts in Mozi's work, the philosopher had a good grounding in the works that were beginning to form the Chinese literary canon. Despite difficulties, Mozi must have found a way to spend a significant portion of his youth in study.

Life's Work

By the time Mozi appears in written sources, he is a mature adult, the leader of a tightly organized and well-regimented band of young unmarried men called *Mozhe*, or Mohists. It appears that Mozi and his disciples moved around a great deal; scholars disagree on the exact location of their home base. A careful reading of *Mozi* reveals that Mozi traveled "south to Ch'u [Chu]" or "northward going to Ch'i [Qi]." When these directions are laid out over a map of ancient China, it seems most likely that Mozi was based in Lu, the home state of Confucius perhaps a hundred years earlier.

Though the principles Mozi taught fall under the broad headings of philosophy and religion, his disciples were organized in a manner modern persons associate more with cults than with schools. *Zhuangzi* (c. 300 B.C.E., *The Divine Classic of Nan-hua*, 1881; also known as *The Complete Works of Chuang Tzu*, 1968; commonly known as *Zhuangzi*, 1991) describes Mozi's teaching as "very harsh" and claims that it "goes counter to the hearts of the people, and the people cannot endure it." *Huainanzi* emphasizes the control Mozi exercised over his followers, stating that "All could be commanded to rush into fire or tread on the edge of swords, and when faced with death they would not turn on their heels." In *Mozi*, Mozi is quoted as telling his disciples, "My ideas are sufficient for all uses. Discarding my ideas to think on your own is like discarding the harvest to pick up [individual] heads of grain."

It is clear that Mozi believed in and practiced a strict asceticism in his personal life and demanded the same austere self-denial from his followers. Both in the organization of his disciples and in his plans for an ideal society, Mozi was an advocate of absolute top-down intellectual conformity. In a section of *Mozi* dedicated to the principle of "Identification with the Superior," Mozi argues for the unquestioning submission of subordinates to their superiors' standards, from the level of peasants agreeing with the village head all the way up to the emperor, who is supposed to model his thought on the "will of Heaven." As the process of identification filters down from above, everyone ultimately identifies with the principles of Heaven, which Mozi explains as based on mutual love ("regarding others as one regards oneself"), nonaggression, and frugality. Mozi recognizes, of course, that this process works only if the persons in positions of authority are, in fact, morally superior to those below them. His most radical attack on the status quo lies in his insistence that society must be restructured so that the righteous and capable are given positions of real authority and rank.

The impression of Mozi left by his contemporaries, both critics and admirers, is that of a harsh, disciplined, uncompromising, and highly principled moralist. Mozi comes across as a man with absolute faith in the truth of his opinions, a philosopher willing to die for the sake of righteousness. His personality must have been powerful and commanding because his disciples

were willing to sacrifice everything—even life itself—to follow him on his quest to create an ideal world.

No armchair theorist, Mozi believed in action. His expectation, repeated throughout *Mozi*, is that once people have seen what is right, they will act on it, changing their ways immediately. Like Confucius before him, Mozi traveled widely through the warring feudal states of China, seeking a ruler wise enough to put his principles of statecraft into practice. Although in the *Shi-ji* (first century B.C.E.; *Records of the Grand Historian of China*, 1960; rev. ed. 1993), Sima Qian claims that Mozi was a "great official" in the state of Song, most modern scholars doubt the accuracy of this claim, coming roughly four hundred years after the fact. Other early sources show Mozi as an itinerant teacher his entire life. Again like Confucius, Mozi watched his students find employment where he consistently failed.

In the "Dialogues" section of *Mozi* (chapters 46 through 50), Mozi is depicted as a powerful debater, destroying his opponents with his impeccable logic and compelling moral force. Several of his basic assumptions are treated as novel ideas by the rulers of his day. Both his insistence on the absolute identity of means and ends and his claim that states must be held accountable to the same moral standards as individuals seem to have been ethical innovations. When he tells rulers that if murder is bad, then war is thousands of times worse, they seem genuinely surprised, saying that they had never thought of it that way. Mozi then polishes his opponents off with an apparently startling analogy: Calling murder bad but war good is like calling a bit of black black and a huge amount of black white. According to the "Dialogues," Mozi's opponents are left chastened and speechless.

Eventually, either Mozi or his first generation of disciples realized that logical reasoning suffered from severe limitations as a tool for reforming behavior, at least in the midst of the desperate wars of conquest that were transforming the political landscape of China. During the last years of Mozi's teaching career, or soon afterward, the Mohists became skilled in the military technology needed for the defense of the walled cities of the day. The final eleven surviving chapters of *Mozi* discuss defensive military strategies and technologies in great detail, demonstrating the deep commitment Mozi's followers made to the defense of unjustly attacked states. Some scholars think it likely that Mozi himself applied his practical skills as a carpenter and craftsperson to the design and manufacture of innovative defensive mechanisms. At the very least, they believe he initiated the process of study and invention that made the Mohists famous for their defensive skills.

One story in the "Dialogue" chapters recounts how Mozi walked for ten days and nights to the state of Chu to dissuade its ruler from attacking Song, a weak neighboring state. When his ethical arguments failed, Mozi made a model city wall, inviting the ruler's top advisers to mount an attack. Again and again, Mozi demonstrated how the invading forces could be repelled. Mozi's clinching argument was that he had already sent three hundred disciples, well trained in defensive warfare, to man the walls of Song. At this point, the ruler of Chu conceded defeat and called off the attack. If this is a true story, and not a later addition to the text, it demonstrates just how seriously committed Mozi must have been to his basic principles and shows how, in his own life at least, philosophical understanding necessarily leads directly to concrete action.

Influence

For at least two centuries after Mozi's death, his followers continued to survive in organized bands led by autocratic leaders known as *Zhu zi*. If their critics are to be believed, at their prime, the Mohists were powerful contenders for the ideological and political supremacy eventually attained by the followers of Confucius during the Han Dynasty.

Not content simply to propagate their master's teachings, the Mohists gained fame, or perhaps notoriety, as antiwar activists, rushing to the aid of beleaguered cites. Continuing Mozi's interest in effective persuasion, the later Mohists developed a system of logical and definitional propositions that appears to have heavily influenced the development of the *Bianshi*, or sophists.

Several scholars have suggested that Mozi's advocacy of society-wide ideological conformity, dictated by rulers to subjects, may have played a role in the development of the authoritarian Confucianism that became state orthodoxy for much of China's subsequent history. If true, this would certainly have upset Mozi because he saw fit to blame the followers of Confucius for much that was wrong with the society of his time.

By the first century B.C.E., the Mohist movement seems to have disappeared, its military skills no longer needed in a time of political unification and relative peace. As the followers of Confucius gained increasing control over the course of study engaged in by the young, interest in Mozi flagged. The text of *Mozi* quickly slipped into obscurity, preserved only through the efforts of isolated antiquarians and collectors. After the Manchu conquest of China and the formation of the Qing Dynasty in 1644, scholars sickened by war and political compromise were drawn to ancient texts such as *Mozi* that stood outside the orthodox mainstream. From this time on, interest in Mozi slowly grew, and he gained increasing recognition for his principled vision and the moral authenticity of his voice.

Scott Lowe

Mozi

Type of philosophy: Chinese philosophy, ethics, political philosophy

First transcribed: Mozi, fifth century B.C.E. (*The Ethical and Political Works of Motse*, 1929; also known as *Mo Tzu: Basic Writings*, 1963; commonly known as *Mozi*)

Principal ideas advanced:

◇ Universal love is the source of good, and by rewards and punishments, human beings can be encouraged to love universally.

◇ Uniformity of value standards is achieved by establishing the way of the most virtuous and capable "Son of Heaven" as the moral standard.

◇ Aggressive war should never be practiced because it is neither politically nor economically advantageous.

One of the most serious challengers of Confucian ideas in the fifth century B.C.E. was Mozi (originally Mo Di), whose obscure family background encouraged much speculation about his early life on the basis of his name. Some experts believe that his family name, Mo, which means "dark" or "branded," shows that he or an ancestor must have been at one time a lawbreaker because branding the convict with ink was a common practice in ancient China. His personal name, "Di," could mean a menial worker. Therefore, his name might have been a nickname, indicating his humble origins. Whatever the truth, a sharp contrast exists between the obscurity of the Mo clan and the aristocratic background of Confucius's family.

Like Confucius, Mozi studied the ancient texts. He followed the Confucian commentaries on these texts until he developed a system of his own. He promoted his system, competing with the Confucian commentaries for popular acceptance. Mozi traveled, much as Confucius did, and he talked even more persistently to rulers. Confucius refused to converse with anyone who was impolite to him, but Mozi forgot about ceremony as long as there was an audience.

Mozi traveled with his disciples, who numbered in the hundreds. These disciples were devoted to their master and were trained by him personally in the art of defensive warfare as well as in philosophy. They became a tightly knit and highly effective combat unit. After Mozi's death, the disciples elected a second master to continue the leadership of the confraternity, which lasted about a hundred years.

The Text

The original version of *Mozi* contained fifteen books divided into seventy-one chapters. Eighteen of these chapters are lost, and of the extant fifty-three chapters, only two are likely to have been written by Mozi himself. The others, including six chapters quite clearly written at a much later date, are records of Mozi's discourses, most likely transcribed by followers. Mozi probably said and wrote much more, for his influence was so great at one time that Mencius, the standard-bearer of Confucianism, bemoaned that "Under the sky everyone joined either the Yang Chu [Yang Zhu] or the Mozi school of thought." However, the remaining texts are quite sufficient in revealing the main tenets of Mohism.

Confucianism and Mohism

Throughout the book, Mozi maintains a hostile attitude toward Confucian views. His antagonism reaches its peak in chapters 38 (missing) and 39, which are entitled "Refutation of Confucianism." He dismisses the Confucian emphasis on rituals, acceptance of destiny, and lengthy observance of funerals. He virtually calls Confucius a hypocrite. Yet, in spite of his criticism of Confucianism, Mozi was in agreement with Confucius on the importance of the virtuous and the learned to the welfare of the state, as well as the importance of self-cultivation and self-discipline. Like Confucius, Mozi believed that no king can rule successfully without the assistance of capable and moral ministers. Also, like Confucius, Mozi holds the *junzi*, the perfect person who conducts himself above all reproach, as an exemplar for all people to emulate. Some Mohist and Confucian ethical views are quite similar. Mohists, for the most part, agree with their Confucian rivals on the ideal code of social conduct. However, Mohists, who practiced asceticism, stress self-denial far beyond what Confucians consider proper.

Universal Love

The philosophical system of Mozi has as its basis a concept of universal love. Mozi regarded the lack of love among people as the principal cause of all calamities, of which the worst is the aggression of the large state against the small state, the strong taking advantage of the weak, and the many imposing their will upon the few. Even among the equally situated, as Mozi points out, people indulge in mutual injury with weapons, poison, and other hateful means. Then Mozi asks, "Is it out of people's loving others and wanting to benefit others" that they behave this way? He objects to the Confucian doctrine that one must love one's own parents more dearly than the kin of others and one's own state more than other fatherlands. Mozi's concept of universal love goes beyond an ethical prescription to cure social ills; he actually regards universal love as a source of "goodness." In his argument, universal love is good because it brings untold and immeasurable benefit to humankind and because whatever benefits humankind must be right and good. In this argument, Mozi reveals a strong utilitarian element.

The Mohist concept of universal love is not only a perfect ideal but also a practical and easily practicable idea. First, Mozi tells us, universal love has been achieved by the Sage Kings of old. Mozi makes use of the past just as the Confucians do. Second, there is nothing that cannot be done if the rulers, or the people in power, encourage it. Mozi believes that if the ruler offers the lure of reward and displays the threat of punishment, then the people will go after love "like fire tending upward and water downward—nothing in the world could stop them." This is another parallel between Mohism and utilitarianism, both promoting the use of pain and pleasure to induce people to practice what is desirable.

The Will of Heaven

A more serious religious attitude is present in Mohism than in Confucianism. Mozi speaks of Heaven as an identifiable deity whose will is to uphold righteousness. It must be so because "if righteousness ceased to prevail, chaos would reign over the world." It is so also because any proper standard is always set by the superior for the inferior to observe, and because Heaven is the supreme authority, even above the sovereign on earth, it is Heaven who sets the universal standard of righteousness. Those adhering to this standard are rewarded; those violating this standard are punished. Furthermore, says Mozi, Heaven loves all people equally until and unless some people trespass the boundary of righteousness and forsake universal love.

The Mohist acknowledges the existence of spirits and their function as guardians of morality. He divides the spirits into three general categories: the most superior heavenly spirits, the secondary mountain and river spirits, and the spirits of dead human beings, which occupy the lowest stratum in this hierarchy. To prove the power of the spirits, particularly those of the dead, Mozi retells many ghost stories cited in the ancient texts and concludes with the admonition that the vengeance of the spirits is "sharp and fierce," especially when wrong is done to the innocent. Mozi, however, disapproves of any ritual practice to placate the spirits. He teaches his followers that they will continue to enjoy the blessing of the spirits as long as the living practice universal love and avoid harming one another.

Equality and the Son of Heaven

Mozi is emphatic in asserting the equal worth of all people. He insists that the sovereign ruler must honor the virtuous and the capable regardless of "their family connection, financial status, and their physical appearances." He reiterates his belief that the ruler can use punishment and reward to make all people strive for virtue in order that they all have an equal chance to prove their worth. The Mohist assumption is that everybody, following the ruler's instructions, has an equal chance to change his or her own destiny. This view is clearly opposed to the Confucian acceptance of fate, which is beyond humankind's powers.

Mozi's assumption that people are not born with a predestined pattern of development is fully explained in chapter 3, in which he metaphorically compares the environmental influence on people to the dyeing of silk. The one factor that influences people most, in Mozi's view, is their associations. People behave according to the company they keep; rulers in the past failed or succeeded according to the teachers and exemplars they followed.

A critical problem is evident in Mozi's system from an examination of the Mohist view on humankind. If people are basically equal, who then should rule and who should be ruled? Mozi offers two explanations of this point, one logical and the other historical. In his logical argument, Mozi starts from the premise that Heaven is the supreme authority that delegates its power to the sovereign king on earth. As the Son of Heaven, the king rules by observing Heaven's will. The people must obey their king because they must bow to Heaven. In his historical argument, Mozi recounts the evolution of society.

In the very beginning, says Mozi, the primeval society of humanity was full of strife and chaos because each individual had his or her own standard of behavior and no two people acted according to any common standard. As humanity improved and society formed, the most virtuous and capable person in the world was "selected" to serve as the Son of Heaven. The Son of Heaven then issued a mandate to the people, declaring that "what the superior [the king] thinks to be right, all shall think it right; what the king thinks to be wrong, all shall think it wrong." Consequently, a uniform standard was established, and strife ceased. Mozi goes on to urge his readers to observe this political precedence to ensure a peaceful and orderly society, but he does not make it clear how he thinks the "most virtuous and capable" were selected in the past or should be selected in the future.

Nonaggression

Nonaggression constitutes Mozi's most significant contribution to the ideas generated in the Warring States period (475-221 B.C.E.). Mozi talks about righteousness and universal virtue, but he does not appear to be a moralist when he deals with the question of war. He argues against aggressive war on the ground that it is not economically advantageous to attack others. He sounds extremely modern when he warns the aggressors that war creates wastelands that should be kept under productive activities. Even if a victory were won, Mozi says, "the costs of the expeditions would have exhausted the country." After a devastating war, neither the victorious nor the vanquished state is fit to take its place among the nations. His argument is made very persuasive by his practical skill in defensive warfare, which is described with technical detail in at least eleven chapters in the work. Only the conditions of the time—which often bordered on a free-for-all power struggle—prevented his views from being adopted by the chiefs of the states.

Once when Mozi heard that the ruler of one state was about to declare war against another, in hope of maintaining peace, he rushed to the aggressive state, walking for days and nights without stopping. When his feet became sore, he simply bandaged them with pieces of fabric torn from his garments and continued on his journey. Upon his arrival, he found that the ruler was too determined to carry out his war-waging plans to consider changing them. After futilely spending much time with this ruler, Mozi went to the attacked state and offered his services in defending it.

Frugality

Mozi's utilitarianism finds expression in his approach to economic problems. He encouraged only those economic endeavors that are useful and practical or that contribute to the wealth and populousness of the state. The sole criterion for his judgment of the success or failure of a state is the size of its granary and population. He is vehemently critical of any conspicuous consumption, and he believes that people should be and are actually happy if no more than the essential material supplies are abundant. An increase in the population means a rise in manpower, which at the time constituted the mainspring of the state's strength.

Mozi's insistence on frugality leads him to deny the usefulness of any niceties of life. He prefers to do away with music and rites and all other features of a cultured life. He even enjoins the artisans to cease producing carts and robes the moment the most essential needs of the people have been met and immediately to channel their energy into the production of staple foods.

The Mohist Legacy

Mozi is remembered as the first Chinese philosopher to be seriously concerned with the logical development of an argument. In *Mozi*, he devotes many passages to defining the term "dialectic." According to Mozi, dialectic is an effort to distinguish "the right from the wrong, the good from bad governments, similarity from difference, name from actuality, benefit from harm, and certainty from uncertainty." Using his own rules for the careful development of an argument, Mozi presents systematic expositions supported by evidence. Mozi introduces the "sorites formula" and makes a distinction between necessary and sufficient causes. In the latter connection, Mozi uses an illustration of the point and the line. The point, says Mozi, is a necessary cause but not a sufficient cause of the line. He is also the first Chinese philosopher to draw the distinction between class and species, pointing out to his students that the former includes the latter but not vice versa. He did much to promote the School of Names, which flourished during and after his time.

The most significant single contribution of Mozi to ancient Chinese thought is the consistent exposition of his materialistic view of humankind's nature and his persistent reference to the pain-and-pleasure approach to human problems. To be sure, his theory that people can and must be beaten into loving their fellows is at once paradoxical and repulsive to the idealistic Confucians, but the paradox may be more apparent than real when one realizes that both Mozi and Confucius assume a basically equal teachability of all people. In the development of Chinese thought, it was only a short step from Mozi's utilitarianism, which never completely loses sight of righteousness and virtue, to the Machiavellian realism expounded by the Legalists who rose to power at the end of the Warring States period. Mozi's materialism is not unqualified, but all the ingredients of a more thoroughgoing materialism are present in Mozi's system.

That Mohism as an organized body of doctrines ceased to exert appreciable influence by the first century B.C.E. must be blamed on the aridity of the mode of life advocated by the Mohists. Mozi himself, as far as we know, never married, and his close disciples all led a life of ascetic dedication to their confraternity. Some of them actually died for the leader of their group. In contrast, the Confucian doctrines offer a view of life that is much more reasonable and attractive to a wider range of people.

Kai-yu Hsu

Additional Reading

Graham, A. C. *Disputers of the Tao: Philosophical Argument in Ancient China*. La Salle, Ill.: Open Court, 1989. In this survey of early Chinese thought, Graham places Mozi in his intellectual context and gives a good feel for the kinds of reasoning being pioneered by the great teachers of this seminal period in Chinese history.

_____. *Later Mohist Logic, Ethics, and Science*. London: University of London, 1978. Graham's primary goal in this book is the reconstruction and translation of the jumbled, fragmentary texts attributed to late followers of Mozi, who wrote hundreds of years after the philosopher's death. His translations of later Mohist writings and his discussion of the Mohist tradition are essential reading for any student of Chinese philosophy.

Lowe, Scott. *Mo Tzu's Religious Blueprint for a Chinese Utopia: The Will and the Way*. Lewiston, N.Y.: Edwin Mellen Press, 1992. Lowe demonstrates the remarkable intellectual consistency and practical focus of Mozi's teaching. He shows that Mozi was the most systematic and comprehensive utopian thinker in early Chinese history.

Schwartz, Benjamin I. *The World of Thought in Ancient China*. Cambridge, Mass.: Harvard University Press, 1985. This book gives an excellent overview of the teachings of Mozi, though Schwartz writes from the perspective of a political scientist and historian, not a philosopher.

Scott Lowe

Iris Murdoch

Schooled in philosophy, Murdoch wrote more than twenty-five novels, many of them essentially philosophical, as well as several volumes that were overtly about philosophy.

Principal philosophical works: *Sartre: Romantic Rationalist*, 1953; *Under the Net*, 1954; The Sovereignty of Good, 1970; *The Fire and the Sun: Why Plato Banished the Artists*, 1977; *Acastos: Two Platonic Dialogues*, 1987; *Metaphysics as a Guide to Morals*, 1992.

Born: July 15, 1919; Dublin, Ireland
Died: February 8, 1999; Oxford, England

Early Life

Iris Murdoch, born Jean Iris Murdoch in Dublin, Ireland, in 1919, was the only child of John Wills Hughes Murdoch, a British civil service employee, and his wife, Irene Alice Richardson Murdoch, who abandoned her hopes of being an opera singer to marry at the age of eighteen. Although the family resettled in England during Iris's first year and she grew up outside London, in Hammersmith and Chiswick, she maintained a strong allegiance to Ireland and considered herself Anglo-Irish.

Murdoch spent holidays in Ireland with her Gaelic relations. An only child, she fantasized about having siblings, notably about having a brother, although as she matured, she realized that had she had a brother, the family's limited resources probably would have been spent to send him rather than her to the university.

Murdoch's early education was in the environs of London. At the age of thirteen, she qualified for a scholarship, one of two awarded, to the Badminton School in Bristol. After finishing Badminton, she received a scholarship to Oxford University's Somerset College, where she studied classical literature and philosophy. She also was quite involved in drama and the arts during her years at Oxford. She was granted a bachelor of arts degree with first class honors in 1942.

Only twenty years old when Britain was plunged into World War II, Murdoch completed her university studies but then worked for the British Treasury in London. She served as an assistant from 1942 until 1944, and she learned enough about the structure of Britain's civil service to write about it convincingly in some of her subsequent novels.

Later, she became an administrator for the United Nations National Relief and Rehabilitation Administration. She served in London and, at war's end, in Belgium, where she met Jean-Paul Sartre; she also served in Austria, where she worked at an encampment for displaced persons, an experience that helped her create the character of Nina, a displaced dressmaker facing deportation to Eastern Europe, in *The Flight from the Enchanter* (1956).

Upon her return to England, Murdoch spent a year doing little save for reading philosophical works and exploring London, whose byways she uses effectively in many of her novels. In 1947, she received a fellowship to study philosophy at Cambridge University's Newnham College. After completion of her studies, she was a tutor in philosophy at St. Anne's College, Oxford, until 1963.

In 1956, Murdoch married John Oliver Bayley, the Thomas Warton Professor of English Literature at Oxford and also a successful novelist and critic. In 1963, she became an honorary fellow of St. Anne's College. She served as a lecturer at the Royal College of Art in London from 1963 until 1967.

By 1962, Murdoch had published six novels. *Under the Net* (1954) was the first of these, followed by *The Flight from the Enchanter*, *The Sandcastle* (1957), *The Bell* (1958), *A Severed Head* (1961), and *An Unofficial Rose* (1962). She was soon to embark on a project with J. B. Priestley, who collaborated with her on turning *A Severed Head* into a play that opened in London in 1963, was produced in New York City the same year, and was released as a film by Columbia Pictures in 1971.

Life's Work

From the beginning of her professional career, Murdoch's consuming intellectual interest was moral philosophy. Well schooled in the history of philosophy and in ethics, she was as comfortable discussing Plato and Aristotle as she was in writing about Jean-Paul Sartre and existentialism, which she did in her landmark study *Sartre: Romantic Rationalist*, published by Yale University Press in 1953. Her novels consistently explore the moral questions with which she grappled as a

philosopher and as a university lecturer in philosophy.

During her university days, Murdoch, who leaned to the left politically, went so far as to join the Communist Party briefly, as many intellectuals did in the late 1930's and early 1940's. Her past membership in the Party resulted in her being denied a visa to study in the United States when she was granted a scholarship in the late 1940's.

Murdoch was intrigued by the theory, advanced by Austrian philosopher Ludwig Wittgenstein, that all people build their own nets, or structural protocols, in their lives. Murdoch had been exposed to the existentialism of Sartre and Albert Camus, with its emphasis on the meaninglessness of human existence. This approach is based on the notion that humans exercise free will and that the individual is all-important.

Although Murdoch denied that she was an existentialist, she imbibed a great deal from this

Iris Murdoch. *(Thomas Victor)*

school of thought, which, combined with Wittgenstein's notion of how people seek to structure their lives, emerges as a dominant theme in many of her novels. The title of her first novel, *Under the Net*, refers directly to Wittgenstein's theory that individuals create their own nets or structures. The protagonist, Jake Donaghue, seeks to find a structure for his life, but finally he rejects the net and accepts life as it is, acknowledging the significance of other people while denying the centrality of self. This first Murdoch novel, which reflected much of the hopelessness that Britain experienced following World War II, evoked considerable discussion and resulted in the author being widely recognized as a writer of note. The book was commended by most of the leading critics of the day and brought its creator considerable attention both within Britain and beyond its boundaries.

In *Under the Net*, which is dedicated to Raymond Queneau, Jake Donaghue displays two novels prominently on his bookshelf: Samuel Beckett's *Murphy* (1938) and Queneau's *Pierrot mon ami* (1943; *Pierrot*, 1950). Murdoch publicly acknowledged her considerable debt to both Queneau and Beckett, whose comic ironies are not unlike those in this first Murdoch novel.

Murdoch's use of language is carefully considered and self-conscious. She tends particularly to employ Germanic irony, writing something like "a not unattractive alternative" rather than merely "an attractive alternative." Her intimate and intelligent involvement with language began early and continued as she studied languages at the university level and later on her own. In her novels, this concern reaches its acme in *A Word Child* (1975).

In this novel, Hilary Burde, the protagonist, longs for the fixed routine that will bring order to his life. After becoming aware of his remarkable verbal skill during a rebellious adolescence, Hilary studied grammar extensively. He sought to find in the obdurate and absolutistic structure of grammar some refuge from the arbitrariness of life. Hilary attends Oxford on scholarship, then embarks on a university career that should prove satisfying and productive. He becomes involved, however, in a scandalous adulterous love affair that obliterates his chances of academic success. This experience leads to an increased rigidity in

Hilary's personality. He now tries to order the lives of those about him, imposing a structure comparable to that of grammar on them and on himself. Others, however, refuse to yield to this structure, completely upsetting Hilary's carefully orchestrated plans, often with comic results. In the end, Gunnar, the husband of the woman with whom Hilary committed his earlier adultery, returns after twenty years, accompanied by his second wife. Hilary again yields to temptation and has a disastrous adulterous affair with her. Hilary finally must accept the random order of life, the chance nature of human existence. A Sartrean nihilism pervades this novel as Hilary attempts to impose a structure on life only to be forced to recognize that the chaos against which he has reacted for most of his adulthood is life's only certainty.

As her work progressed, Murdoch explored in her novels as well as in her philosophical writing the question of Good versus God. Murdoch, who was raised in a Christian environment, viewed herself as a former Christian with strong leanings toward Zen Buddhism and other Eastern religions. She broached the question of Zen Buddhism particularly in *The Nice and the Good* (1968) and *An Accidental Man* (1971). The influences of her travels in Japan, which affected her thinking dramatically, are evident in *A Severed Head* and in her drama *The Three Arrows* (pr. 1972; pb. 1973).

Murdoch considered conventional Christianity to be incompatible with the technological age in which she lived, although she was not hostile toward that faith. She broke from Sartre's nihilism and solipsism, denying that the self is all-important. Instead, she contended, and in most of her novels demonstrates, that there can be no freedom unless one respects the sovereign being of other individuals. In *A Word Child*, for example, it is Hilary's failure to do this that leads to his downfall.

Murdoch was convinced that most people live in their own fantasy worlds, in worlds of illusion that bear little resemblance to reality, to those innate models (ideas) of which Plato spoke. She grappled with the question of whether people can repent and be given another chance or whether, given such a chance, they will merely repeat their earlier transgressions, as Hilary does.

In *The Message to the Planet* (1989), the protagonist, Marcus Vallar, is a mathematical genius whose philosophical quest in pursuit of pure thought is his undoing. When Vallar miraculously cures a dying man, that man becomes Vallar's follower. In the novel's subplot, Franca overlooks her infirm husband's adulteries and, in the name of perfect, selfless love, permits one of her husband's lovers to come and live with them. In Murdoch's view, love is the catalyst that enables people to overcome the obsession with self that stands in the way of goodness.

Influence

If one believes in the "great chain of being," all things bear a relationship to everything that has passed before them. Murdoch is a striking example of this. To her writing, both in her novels and in her philosophical and literary treatises, she brought the rich fabric that constitutes her literary and philosophical framework. Her early training in classical philosophy left its indelible mark on her thinking, particularly in her questions regarding what is real. Platonic idealism provides a strong undercurrent in most of her novels. Her quest was for that which is real, authentic, and true. She sought the Good as Plato sought it.

To her rich classical background, one must add her exposure to William Shakespeare, Britain's Victorian novelists, and much of the later philosophy that she absorbed in her extensive reading and in her personal contacts. She read extensively in the writings of Immanuel Kant, whose categorical imperative left its mark on her writing, as did Wittgenstein's theories regarding humankind's need to impose structure upon existence.

In *A Word Child*, Murdoch questions how far one can take Wittgenstein's theory. Although she refutes the nihilism of the leading existentialists, she cannot go so far as to accept Wittgenstein's solution to controlling the chaos in which life appears to be mired. Her solution to the conundrums that face modern humans is love; only love enables people to extend themselves outside the subjective bubbles in which they are prisoners.

If Sartre's *No Exit* (1944) portrays humans trapped in their own subjectivity, Murdoch comes to the rescue with the notion that love can mitigate subjectivity and can bring one into harmony with the subjective worlds of those around them. Love that is expansive and unconditional, as Murdoch portrays it through Franca in *The Message to the Planet* (1989), negates the isolation and the nihilism that characterize much existential thinking. Love, however, is not without its hazards, the chief one of which is the absolute necessity for humans to compromise.

Through her well-received novels, Murdoch influenced two or three generations of readers. Through her teaching and writing about philosophical topics, she evoked considerable interest among academics and those whom they teach.

R. Baird Shuman

Metaphysics as a Guide to Morals

Type of philosophy: Ethics, metaphysics
First published: 1992
Principal ideas advanced:

◇ In a modern technological society, Murdoch replaces God with Good.

◇ Earlier images of God are irrelevant in contemporary society.

◇ Christianity is being demythologized.

◇ Religion exists more completely if one eschews the idea of a personal, anthropomorphic God.

◇ Because people characteristically live with Self as the only reality, they must struggle to subdue their inherent egoism.

◇ In literary circles, deconstruction has separated meaning from truth and language from the world.

◇ Because she considers literature highly moral, she is skeptical of what contemporary critical theorists, in particular the deconstructionists, have done to dehumanize it.

Two major contemporary philosophical currents are apparent in Iris Murdoch's work, both in her novels and in her critical and philosophical writing. Early in her career, she met Jean-Paul Sartre; she wrote her first book, *Sartre: Romantic Rationalist* (1953), about him. At about the same time, she became engrossed in the philosophy of the Austrian philosopher Ludwig Wittgenstein. Sartre, the leading existentialist, was obsessed by the futility of human existence as well as by the loneliness of it. His nihilism as well as that of writers Albert Camus and Samuel Beckett defined a main current in continental philosophical thought that profoundly affected Murdoch.

Wittgenstein, on the other hand, espoused the notion that the major lifelong quest of humans is to establish their "net," his designation of the structure that helps people to define their existences. Wittgenstein's was not as pessimistic a philosophy as that of the existentialists. Murdoch publicly denied that she was an existentialist.

Her own thinking was tempered by that of the ancient philosophers she had studied at Oxford University, most notably Plato. His theory of innate ideas postulates ideal abstract forms toward which humans strive. Her extensive reading in other such philosophers as Immanuel Kant and Arthur Schopenhauer also helped to shape her philosophical thought, as did her early exposure to the plays of William Shakespeare and the writing of such Victorian novelists as Charles Dickens, Henry Thackeray, and Wilkie Collins.

Finally, Murdoch forsook conventional Christianity, finding in Zen Buddhism and Hinduism more appropriate religious approaches for her times. Never a shrill adversary of Christianity, Murdoch sought instead to redefine it for a technological age, something that its more conservative branches stand foursquare against.

A Wide-Ranging Philosophy

Metaphysics as a Guide to Morals, a volume of 520 pages, is a wide-ranging book that may strike some readers as disorganized or, at least, lacking in specific focus and interconnection of its parts. Its nineteen chapters deal with such disparate subjects as imagination, comedy and tragedy, morals and politics, morality and religion, will and duty, Arthur Schopenhauer, Martin Buber, Ludwig Wittgenstein, René Descartes, and Immanuel Kant.

That the various chapters are not arranged in chronological order and seem at times discursive and unrelated to the whole stems from the fact that the volume consists of the Gifford Lectures that Murdoch delivered at Oxford University in 1982. The tone and style are sometimes those of a

speaker rather than those of a writer, but this is not a disadvantage, nor is the nonchronological arrangement of the various chapters, most of which can be read in whatever order one prefers.

The unifying thread that pervades the book is Murdoch's unswerving belief that morality is a continuing part of all human activity rather than a separate small segment of philosophy studied in ethics classes. It is a quality to which all humans are continually subjected. This philosophy permeated Murdoch's novels from the beginning of her career and is central in most of her philosophical writing.

Good vs. God

To Murdoch, a knowledge of Good, with a capital "G," is inherent in all people. In contemporary technological society, the notion of a personal god is outmoded, as it was for such thinkers as Kant as early as the eighteenth century. Murdoch cited Buddhism, Hinduism, and Judaism as religions that function well and have a functional morality without belief in a personal god who presides over heaven and hell and who keeps people from sinning. In other words, Murdoch observed that religion in a scientific age, which has its roots in the Industrial Revolution of the eighteenth century, is, for better or worse, rapidly becoming demythologized.

The danger she saw in such demythologizing is that humans, their behavior no longer molded by their belief in a personal god that can wreak vengeance on them if they stray from the principles of basic morality, may deviate noticeably from the concept of the self as moral. Murdoch, however, was not pessimistic because she believed that a sense of what is good and moral lurks within all people and that, in the long run, they will strive for Good.

Every chapter in the book is infused with the Platonic theory of innate ideas. Murdoch molds Plato's allegory of the cave to her own purposes to show how humans, deceived into thinking that the shadows they see before them as they peer from their dank caves are reality, can gradually emerge from those caves into the sunlight of true understanding and goodness. She holds that of all the abstract elements with which Plato deals—Truth, Beauty, Justice—Goodness is the foremost, and it directly affects all the others.

In their quest for Goodness, humans, according to Murdoch, must first overcome their inherent subjectivity. Citing philosopher Edmund Husserl, she wrote, "Consciousness constitutes all objects and so all knowledge. Looked at in this way there is indeed nothing else but consciousness." This being the case, all people are the centers of their own small universes. Self-interest and self-absorption are inevitable, if, indeed, limiting and frequently destructive.

How, then, can humans move from this subjectivity as they seek the Good? This question is crucial to Murdoch's proposals regarding human behavior. For her, the quintessential move toward Goodness comes through love. Love enables people to move from one subjectivity to another, to combine two subjectivities and then, as their love becomes more encompassing, to understand and unite with other subjectivities.

Even as people move beyond their own subjectivities, however, they do not, in the name of Goodness, eschew those subjectivities. Murdoch acknowledges, "our conception of ourselves is, properly, far richer and more detailed, as well as of course more 'interesting,' than our conception of others!" Not given to overstatement, Murdoch here reveals the passion with which she believed in what she was saying by her use of the adverb "properly" and by the exclamation point with which she ends this crucial statement. She suggests not an annihilation of Self, which would be virtually impossible, but a broadening of one's subjective being to include other Selves, other subjectivities.

Views on Deconstruction and Structuralism

Perhaps the most strident of Murdoch's Gifford Lectures, reflecting much that both she and her husband, John Oliver Bayley, the Thomas Warton Professor of English Literature at Oxford University, believed ardently is found in chapter 7, "Derrida and Structuralism." In this passionately written chapter, Murdoch traces the origins of structuralism to its early bases in the anthropology of Claude Lévi-Strauss and the linguistics of Ferdinand de Saussure, two fields in which it is perhaps a more reasonable approach than it is in its applications to literary criticism.

Murdoch feared that structuralism, as appropriated by Jacques Derrida and his followers and set loose upon literary interpretation, would replace the writer-reader relationship upon which literature has depended through the ages with a dehumanized pseudo-scientific interpretation. Murdoch complained vigorously that Structuralist (deconstructionist) criticism does not see literature as a window opened upon an imagined world that is both like and unlike the "real" world, but that relates to it intimately. Literature instead is seen as a network of meanings esteemed for its liveliness, originality, and ability to disturb, and is judged in terms of a psychological-sociological analysis that also seeks out factors not consciously intended by the writer.

Throughout this essay, Murdoch objects to the disregard that critics like Derrida have for the history and the moral compass of literature, topics with which traditional critics long concerned themselves. She laments the ways in which structuralists and deconstructionists have reduced literature merely to language and language to trivial word play in which words relate not to the world but merely to other words. She chastises Saussure for having separated language from the people who use it and from its local settings, and she seems even more distressed by how the deconstructionists have divorced literature from the reader-writer relationship and from its historical backgrounds.

Although she does not say it in so many words, what Murdoch writes about the deconstructionists has to do with her entire concept of ego. These critics have worked toward creating an interpretive elite that is, in essence, a manifestation of their unbridled egos. In Murdoch's eyes, a person must struggle to control the ego as in moving toward the achievement of moral goodness and rectitude.

The Demythologization of Religion

Murdoch's contention that religion as the world has long known it is being demythologized whether people want it to be or not is cogent in the light of what she has to say about structuralism and deconstruction. By implication, one might regard recent pseudo-scientific approaches to literary interpretation as attempts to establish new, secular religions whose high priests have names and faces (Jacques Derrida, Jacques Lacan, Michel Foucault, Paul de Man) and faithful acolytes among beleaguered professors of literature and their graduate students.

Murdoch, who in her early years was attracted by Marxism, veered away from it because of its rejection of such concepts as moral responsibility, human transcendence, and religion. In the deconstructionists, she found a comparable philosophical posture, one that is anti-individual. Their denial of any reality outside language excludes the very morality that Murdoch was convinced is inherent in all things that affect human beings.

One of the more difficult chapters in this book, "The Ontological Proof," is, for all its difficulty, central to an understanding of how Murdoch progresses from a concept of God to a concept of Good. She demonstrates quite convincingly that the old ontological proofs of apologists such as Saint Anselm are essentially reductive in their arguments that begin with the deduction that the conception of God as a supreme perfection cannot be conceived not to exist. Anselm goes on to assert that if people can conceive of God, they must acknowledge, a priori, that He exists. The sophistry of this argument does little to convince contemporary thinkers, most of them skeptics, whose convictions must be based on more than medieval syllogistic reasoning. In short, Murdoch suggests that Anselm, in the eleventh century, was preaching to the choir, which modern apologists for the existence of God cannot credibly do.

Science vs. Religion

Murdoch found herself poised between two absolutes, that of conventional religion and that of the scientific revolution. She embraced parts of each while remaining steadfast in her beliefs that Goodness is the quality toward which humans must aspire and that morals transcend everything else in life. Without accepting a personal god, Murdoch demonstrated how humans can achieve high levels of morality through their own discovery of the attractiveness of Good as they broaden the bases of their own subjectivities.

A staunch devotee of Truth, with a capital "T," Murdoch pursued it as she perceived it throughout *Metaphysics as a Guide to Morals*. Never dogmatic, she assesses deeply and dispassionately the broad spectrum of ideas with which she grapples in this book and with which she

grappled throughout her career as both a novelist and a philosopher. Her readers in the philosophical community find her assessments thought-provoking, although modern critical theorists and people in conventional religious communities take umbrage at them.

Certainly her most passionate utterances in this, her most extensive philosophical treatise, are directed at those who would, in her view, distort Truth to their own purposes, notably the deconstructionists. What she writes about them has broad implications for her entire book: "The fundamental value which is lost, obscured, made not to be, by structuralist theory, is truth, language as truthful, where 'truthful' means faithful to, engaging intelligently and responsibly with, a reality which is beyond us."

R. Baird Shuman

Additional Reading

Baldanza, Frank. *Iris Murdoch*. New York: Twayne, 1974. Following Twayne's prescribed format, Baldanza writes about Murdoch's novels and about the plays made from *A Severed Head* (1961; drama written collaboratively with J. B. Priestley, 1963) and *The Italian Girl* (1964; drama written collaboratively with James Saunders, pr. 1967). Although dated, this critical biography offers significant details about Murdoch's life and writing before 1970.

Bloom, Harold, ed. *Iris Murdoch*. New York: Chelsea House, 1986. This contribution to the Modern Critical Views Series contains thirteen challenging essays on Murdoch's work. A number of the essays demonstrate how Murdoch's thinking moved toward the expression it reached in *Metaphysics as a Guide to Morals*. This volume and Lindsey Tucker's *Critical Essays on Iris Murdoch* combine to give readers solid overviews of critiques of Murdoch to the late 1980's.

Bove, Cheryl K. *Understanding Iris Murdoch*. Columbia: University of South Carolina Press, 1993. A slim volume, chronologically arranged, particularly valuable for its comments on Murdoch's aesthetics and moral philosophy as reflected in both her novels and her philosophical volumes. Bove's comprehension of Murdoch's complex moral aims is excellent. She communicates clearly and in appealing prose. A quintessential book for the beginner.

Conradi, Peter J. *Iris Murdoch: The Saint and the Artist*. New York: St. Martin's Press, 1986. Conradi offers comprehensive views of Murdoch's novels through *The Philosopher's Pupil* (1983). His writing is adroit and his reasoning apt. Conradi is uniquely sensitive to philosophical undercurrents in Murdoch's fiction.

Mettler, Darlene D. *Sound and Sense: Musical Allusion and Imagery in the Novels of Iris Murdoch*. New York: Peter Lang, 1991. Although specialized, this book presents a solid understanding of how Murdoch employed musical allusion and imagery in eight of her novels. Readers interested in cross-cultural approaches to literary criticism will appreciate this book. Less appropriate for general readers.

Murdoch, Iris. *Existentialists and Mystics: Writings on Philosophy and Literature*. Edited by Peter J. Conradi. New York: Allen Lane, 1998. Conradi's selections provide a serviceable sampling of Murdoch's nonfiction. His prefatory remarks reflect the progression of Murdoch's thinking about the moral necessity of Good as a replacement for God in technological times.

Todd, Richard. *Iris Murdoch*. London: Methuen, 1984. Todd focuses on Murdoch's novels from *Under the Net* (1954) to *The Philosopher's Pupil* (1983). His readings are incisive and occasionally profound. In this 112-page book, Todd shows how Murdoch's novels developed basic themes about which she wrote in her philosophical volumes.

_____. *Iris Murdoch: The Shakespearean Interest*. New York: Barnes & Noble, 1979. Todd detects in Murdoch's novels several themes that recurred in Shakespeare's dramas, notably those relating to the self, to enchanters, and to the romantic matching of pairs. Todd makes sound arguments for Shakespeare's thematic influence on Murdoch's writing.

Tucker, Lindsey, ed. *Critical Essays on Iris Murdoch*. New York: G. K. Hall, 1992. Four of twelve essays in this compact volume consider Murdoch's work generally; eight focus on individual works. A useful collection, especially valuable when used in conjunction with Bloom's aforementioned collection.

R. Baird Shuman

Arne Naess

Naess is Norway's most prominent philosopher. Before his retirement from the University of Oslo in 1969, his writings and personal influence shaped philosophy and social science in Norway. After 1969, Naess achieved international recognition as the founder of a style of environmentalism known as deep ecology.

Principal philosophical works: *Erkenntnis und wissenschaftliches Verhalten*, 1936; *"Truth" as Conceived by Those Who Are Not Professional Philosophers*, 1938; *Endel elementære logiske emner*, 1947; *Interpretation and Preciseness: A Contribution to the Theory of Communication*, 1953; *Filosofiens historie: En innføring i filosofiske problemer*, 1953; *Democracy, Ideology, and Objectivity: Studies in the Semantic and Cognitive Analysis of Ideological Controversy*, 1956 (with J. A. Christophersen and K. KvaIø); *Gandhi og atomalderen*, 1960 (*Gandhi and the Nuclear Age*, 1965); *Logikk og metodelære: En innføring*, 1963 (*Introduction to Logic and Scientific Method*, 1968); *Moderne filosofer*, 1965 (*Four Modern Philosophers: Carnap, Wittgenstein, Heidegger, Sartre*, 1969); *Scepticism*, 1968; *Hvilken verden er den virkelige?*, 1969; *Freedom, Emotion, and Self-Subsistence: The Structure of a Central Part of Spinoza's "Ethics,"* 1972, 1975; *The Possibilist and Pluralist Aspects of the Scientific Enterprise*, 1972; "The Shallow and the Deep, Long-Range Ecology Movements: A Summary," 1973; *Økologi, samfunn og livsstil: Utkast til en økosofi*, 1974 (*Ecology, Community, and Lifestyle: Outline of an Ecosophy*, 1989, revised and edited by translator David Rothenberg); *Gandhi and Group Conflict: An Exploration of Satyagraha—Theoretical Background*, 1974; "The World of Concrete Contents," 1985; "The Deep Ecology Movement: Some Philosophical Aspects," 1986; "Deepness of Questions and the Deep Ecology Movement," 1995; "Self-Realization: An Ecological Approach to Being in the World," 1995.

Born: January 27, 1912; Oslo, Norway

Early Life

Arne Naess was the youngest of four children in a wealthy Norwegian family. His father died less than a year after he was born. His mother, already in her forties at the time of his birth, had become pregnant unexpectedly, and Naess later reported that relations with his mother were strained. The mother hired a governess to take care of him as an infant, and the small boy formed a close emotional attachment to the governess. At the age of three, he lost this early caretaker when his mother fired her for spoiling him. As an older man, Naess attributed his lifelong concern with the use of language to his reaction against his mother and against what he saw as her exaggerated, emotional manner of expressing herself.

In high school, Naess developed an interest in philosophy after discovering the works of seventeenth century Dutch philosopher Baruch Spinoza. At the same time, the rugged terrain of his native country inspired him with a passion for mountain climbing, and he became an accomplished climber. In the early 1930's, he traveled to Vienna, Austria, an international center of philosophy in a mountain-climbing nation. He became the youngest member of the Vienna Circle, a philosophical school based on the early work of Ludwig Wittgenstein, and he underwent psychoanalysis under the care of a colleague of Sigmund Freud.

Naess married the first of his three wives, Else Hertzberg, in 1937. His intense working schedule and lifelong traveling strained his personal relations, and this marriage and a second one ended in divorce.

In 1938, Naess's interest in developing a scientific, empirical approach to psychology led to an invitation from behavioral psychologists at the University of California, Berkeley. He studied psychology at Berkeley with pioneering behavioral psychologist E. C. Tolman. The young Norwegian developed a fascination with Tolman's laboratory rats that grew out of a continuing appreciation for nonhuman life. The following year, at the age of twenty-seven, Naess was appointed to the chair of philosophy at the University of Oslo, a position he would hold for thirty years.

Life's Work

From the beginning of his academic career, Naess was an activist and a reformer as well as a philosopher. After taking his university position, Naess set about reforming university education in Norway. He persuaded the Norwegian university system to adopt a general examination in the history of ideas, known as the *examen philosophicum*, which all students had to pass before taking more specialized courses. Many observers believe that this changed the intellectual climate of Norwegian academic life, making it broader and more tolerant of varied perspectives.

Mountain climbing and nature continued to be important to the young philosopher. In interviews, he later remembered that he would often work long hours at the university and arrange that all his lectures be on Tuesdays and Wednesdays to make time to get away to the mountains.

Arne Naess, left, is presented with the award of Grand Officer of the Norwegian Order of Saint Olav by the Norwegian ambassador to England in 1986. *(AP/Wide World Photos)*

He built a small mountaintop cabin in 1937 and named it Tvergastein, meaning "crossed stones." There, Naess studied the classics of philosophy, scientific literature, and Sanskrit and other languages. At Tvergastein, he developed his ideas on semantics and, eventually, on ecology.

In April, 1940, the Nazis invaded Norway and occupied it, putting in place the Norwegian puppet government of Vidkun Quisling. Although Naess at first reacted by treating the occupation as unimportant and philosophically irrelevant, by 1942, he had made contact with the Norwegian resistance movement. Influenced by the ideas of Mohandas Gandhi, he advocated resisting the enemy by nonviolent means. When the Nazis closed the university in 1943 and tried to round up students to send to Germany for reeducation in concentration camps, Naess worked with the resistance to help students escape and go into hiding.

During the 1940's and 1950's, Naess became known for a radical approach to semantics known as empirical semantics, and he became recognized as the leader of a philosophical circle known as the Oslo group. His semantics were a reaction against the philosophers of the Vienna Circle, who maintained that only the most specific, strictly logical statements were meaningful. The members of the Vienna Circle concerned themselves with identifying what kinds of statements were logically meaningful and with how language could be used. Naess argued that one cannot find meaning in any words or sentences by themselves; instead, meaning is a matter of how people use language in particular situations. If a philosopher wants to find out what a given word or statement means, the philosopher must be empirical and investigate the use of the word or statement. The empirical approach led Naess to take a view of vague, general expressions that differed greatly from the view of the Vienna Circle and many other logicians. Instead of arguing that statements are made meaningful by rendering them specific and precise, Naess maintained that vague generalities can be starting points for reaching many parallel interpretations, making communication possible.

Naess pioneered an empirical approach to language with his 1938 work *"Truth" as Conceived by Those Who Are Not Professional Philosophers*. Researching the meaning of the word "truth," Naess constructed surveys and interviewed people about their use of this word. Naess and his colleagues refined the technique of using questionnaires to determine meanings through responses of ordinary users of language. Some philosophers claimed that this work was social science rather than philosophy.

It is sometimes suggested that the turn from academic philosophy to ecology was an abrupt life change for Naess. On the contrary, two essential characteristics of his semantic work were also fundamental to his ecological philosophy. First, Naess understood the world in relational terms. Words, he suggested, have meaning only in relation to other words in concrete situations. Later, he would maintain that human life can exist only in a web of relations with the nonhuman. Second, he maintained that goals, such as communication or protecting the environment, are achieved through an ongoing process of reaching an understanding on the basis of varied starting points.

Although best known for his work in semantics done before the 1960's, Naess also published widely in the philosophy of science, the history of philosophy, and other topics. He was an authority on Spinoza and clearly was influenced by Spinoza's concept of nature as an all-encompassing, interdependent system that could also be referred to as God. In 1958, Naess founded *Inquiry*, an interdisciplinary journal of philosophy and the social sciences, which he edited until 1975. He also served as visiting professor at universities around the world and gave frequent lectures in nonacademic settings.

By the late 1960's, after reading the books of American ecological writer Rachel Carson and observing worldwide environmental destruction, Naess became convinced that the world was facing an ecological crisis. In 1969, he resigned from his university chair to focus his thinking and action on the environment.

In the 1973 article "The Shallow and the Deep, Long-Range Ecology Movements: A Summary," Naess coined the term "deep ecology." Shallow ecology, according to Naess, aimed at specific goals, such as lowering pollution levels or struggling against the depletion of natural resources. Deep ecology, on the other hand, involved adoption of a new perspective. From this perspective, one would see human beings as existing in relation to an environment and would adopt the idea that all parts of the environment are, in principle, of equal value.

Naess refined the definition of deep ecology further in 1984, when he and ecologist George Sessions collaborated on the deep ecology platform in Death Valley in the United States. The eight points of this platform have been expressed in several versions, but the essential meaning of these points can be paraphrased as follows. First, Naess and Sessions asserted that all life, human and nonhuman, has intrinsic value; this means that all living things have value apart from their usefulness in achieving human goals. Second, they asserted that the diversity of living things also has intrinsic value. Third, Naess and Sessions stated that humans do not have the right to reduce biological diversity. Fourth, they maintained that human beings currently interfere too much with the nonhuman world and that human interference with the nonhuman world is getting worse. Fifth, the deep ecology platform insists on the possibility and necessity of reducing the human population to lessen human pressure on nonhuman life. Sixth, the platform maintains that major political, economic, and technological changes are needed to change current living conditions. Seventh, Naess and Sessions maintained that these political, economic, and technological changes will require an ideological change; this ideological change involves turning away from the goal of constantly raising standards of living and toward the goal of appreciating the quality of life. Finally, they proposed that all those who are in general agreement with the points of the platform are obligated to work to bring about change.

The deep ecology platform consists of intentionally broad statements, meant to establish a common basis of understanding and action for people coming from a variety of philosophical and religious backgrounds. Naess referred to the ecological philosophy expressed by deep ecology as "ecosophy." A key element in ecosophy is the idea of self-realization, which is realization of both the self and the Self. The self is the individual self, but the individual self can be fully realized only by identifying with the web of relations of which it is a part. This web of relations is the Self, the natural world in the broadest sense.

Living in his mountain cabin, Naess wrote prolifically on ecological issues. He also continued to act on his philosophical beliefs in nonviolent direct action. In January, 1981, Naess was one of about one thousand people who chained themselves together in an effort to stop the construction of a dam and power plant in northern Norway. This mass demonstration led to the largest police action in Norway's history, as thousands of police officers slowly cut the chains and carried away the demonstrators, including Naess.

Influence

Even before his involvement with the ecological movement, Naess was widely recognized as a major influence on Norwegian academic life. Although Naess credits Rachel Carson with founding deep ecology, he gave it the name and is generally considered deep ecology's central figure. Many of the ideas of the Green movement and of environmental counterculturalists have been drawn from Naess. The views of radical environmentalist activists, such as Dave Foreman of Earth First!, have been affected by Naess. Among philosophers, Naess has acquired an international following, including Warwick Fox of the University of Tasmania, David Rothenberg of Boston University, and Michael Zimmerman of Tulane University. The distinction that Naess drew between shallow and deep ecology was, for many of these thinkers, particularly influential. Deep ecology, a number of philosophers and social critics have argued, offers an alternative to Western civilization's traditional anthropocentric, or human-centered, view of the world.

Critics of deep ecology and Naess often accuse deep ecology of being unrealistic and excessively mystical. Murray Bookchin, the founder of the social ecology movement, has attacked deep ecology as a form of passive spiritualism without a clear program for political action. Bookchin and others have argued that attributing intrinsic value to nonhuman life is a weak basis for environmental action because applying the assumption of intrinsic value in argument and debate will convince only those who already believe in it. Ecological philosophy would be on much firmer ground, these critics claim, if it could demonstrate that it is in the interest of humans to maintain natural resources or diversity of species. Even when it has provoked debate, though, deep ecology has led proponents and opponents alike to carefully examine their own thoughts about the place of humans in the environment.

Carl L. Bankston III

Ecology, Community, and Lifestyle

Outline of an Ecosophy

Type of philosophy: Ethics, social philosophy

First published: Økologi, samfunn og livsstil: Utkast til en økosofi, 1974 (English translation, 1989, revised and edited by translator David Rothenberg)

Principal ideas advanced:

◊ The earth is threatened by an environmental crisis. Responding to this crisis requires that human beings live in equilibrium with other life-forms.

◊ Establishing this ecological equilibrium requires that human beings achieve self-realization. Self-realization means that people recognize their relationships to the world around them.

◊ All actions and beliefs should be derived from a recognition of the interconnected nature of the world.

◊ People can come to identify with nature by seeing that parts of nature are parts of themselves and that they cannot exist separate from the parts of nature.

◊ All parts of nature, both human and nonhuman, have intrinsic value.

Arne Naess was Norway's most prominent philosopher when he became convinced, in the late 1960's, that the earth was facing an imminent ecological crisis. Naess had been a mountain climber since his youth and had a profound appreciation for nature. He also was an admirer of seventeenth century Dutch philosopher Baruch Spinoza, who maintained that God and nature were identical and that nature was an intricate system of interrelated parts. Pessimistic about the future of the planet but inspired by his love of nature and by Spinozistic philosophy, Naess retired from his position as professor of philosophy at the University of Oslo in 1969 to concentrate on ecological problems.

A New Approach to Ecology

In his mountain cabin named Tvergastein, meaning "crossed stones," Naess developed an ecological philosophy that he called "deep ecology." Deep ecology, in his view, is a matter of seeing the complex web of relations that connect all life-forms, objects, and events. In 1973, Naess published an article titled "The Shallow and the Deep, Long-Range Ecology Movements: A Summary" in the journal _Inquiry,_ which he edited. In that article, Naess distinguished deep ecology from shallow ecology, an approach to ecological issues that concentrated only on specific issues, such as lowering levels of air pollution or saving particular species. Whereas shallow ecology seeks solutions to economic problems through technological fixes, deep ecology insists on fundamental economic, political, and cultural changes.

The Norwegian version of _Ecology, Community, and Lifestyle_ was an effort to present the ideas of deep ecology in a comprehensive fashion. Boston University philosopher David Rothenberg worked with Naess on an updated, revised English translation in a number of isolated retreats in Norway, including Tvergastein, whenever Naess was not on one of his frequent trips to distant countries.

Ecology, Community, and Lifestyle describes the character of the ecological crisis, introduces the ecological philosophy of "ecosophy," discusses the implications of this philosophy for human ways of life, and considers the economic and political implications of the philosophy. Naess identifies "ecophilosophy" as the linking of ecology and philosophy. This linkage gives rise to deep ecology, the perception of the connections among all elements of the ecological system, including human beings. It also gives rise to "ecosophy," a point of view concerning how humanity and nature are related. Naess refers to his own ecosophy as "Ecosophy T." Most commentators on the book have suggested that the "T" refers to Tvergastein, the cabin where Naess worked out many of his ideas.

Philosophical Pluralism

The distinction between deep ecology as a social movement guided by fundamental principles and Ecosophy T as the personal worldview of Naess is consistent with Naess's philosophical pluralism. Given a general basis of agreement, Naess maintains, there still can be a variety of approaches to shared goals. Naess presents his own ecosophy, his own worldview, as a guide rather than as a set of prescriptions. He wants readers to use his ecosophy to develop their own.

Establishing a set of general principles for deep ecology led Naess and ecologist George Sessions to write a deep ecology platform in 1984. A version of this platform is included in the English-language edition of *Ecology, Community, and Lifestyle*. The points of the platform maintain that nonhuman life and the diversity of nonhuman life have intrinsic value, that human beings are interfering excessively with the diversity of life, and that lessening this interference requires decreasing the human population and making extensive economic, technological, and ideological changes in human civilization.

Naess uses the ancient philosophical problem of qualities to illustrate his ideas of the "relational field" and of gestalt thinking. One of the classic questions of philosophy is whether qualities, such as size, color, or beauty, exist in things perceived in nature or in the mind of the person perceiving the things. The answer that became widely accepted during the seventeenth century was that primary qualities, such as size, exist in nature, but secondary qualities, such as color or warmth, are names for sensations produced in perceivers by objects. Tertiary qualities, such as beauty, exist in people and are projected onto objects. Naess maintains, however, that it makes no sense to talk about minds and objects as separate entities. They are parts of a single field of relations; therefore, qualities are types of relations in the field. Size, color, and beauty are relationships among objects, emotions, and people. Seeing how all parts fit together into a single whole, or gestalt (a term in psychology taken from a German word meaning "an overall form"), is gestalt thinking.

Naess argues that from the perspective of gestalt thinking, it is a mistake to criticize the ecological movement as an emotional reaction against scientific rationality. Emotion is a part of the relational field; it is a source of basic values that people use to evaluate a situation. Emotion therefore is related both to ethics, the area of philosophy that deals with what people ought to do, and to ontology, the area of philosophy that deals with the nature of what exists. An emotional objection to the severance of humanity from nature can lead to the recognition of nature as a set of relations that includes humans and to claims that people ought to act to restore the balance to the relations.

Norms

Statements about the character of the world, such as the statement that the world is best understood as a relational field, are hypotheses. Statements about the kinds of attitudes and behavior people should adopt based on these hypotheses are norms. Some norms are purely instrumental in character; they have no value in themselves and serve only to fulfill a more basic norm. Genuine norms are ultimate norms, norms that are independent of means/goals relations. Thus, the norm that nonhuman life-forms should be treated as having intrinsic value is a genuine norm, because it is an end in itself and not a means to an end.

The ultimate norm in Ecosophy T's normative system is that of self-realization. Naess acknowledges that "self-realization" is a vague and ambiguous term. It is a starting point, however, for becoming more specific, or for "precisation," as Naess calls the process. The norm of self-realization, at the first level of becoming more precise, refers to individualistic ego-realization, or norms of individual self-interest and self-expression. Taking a note from Spinoza, Naess argues that one's own self-preservation cannot be achieved without other people. There is, therefore, a self-realization beyond mere ego-realization, one that includes other people. Deep ecology takes this norm one step further and maintains that people's selves are not simply social selves but are embedded in the interconnection of all life-forms. The final level of Self-realization (for which Naess uses a capital "S"), then, is one of identification with all life-forms. This final type of self-realization is similar to what various philosophical and religious traditions have termed "the universal self" or "the absolute," or to what Hinduism refers to as the *atman*.

A Program for Change

Accepting the ultimate norm of Self-realization, according to Naess, implies changes in generally accepted lifestyles. In particular, the economic definition of happiness as continually improving standards of living should shift to a definition of happiness as quality of life. Meeting the basic needs of a population and promoting healthful lives should replace maximizing production and consumption as economic goals. In particular, the Gross National Product (GNP) should be abandoned as a measure of public welfare. GNP, from the point of view of deep ecology, emphasizes the quantity of production and consumption rather than popular well-being. Maximization of production and consumption favors meeting wants rather than needs, gives preference to environmentally destructive "hard" technologies rather than "soft" technologies, and encourages pollution and depletion of natural resources.

Changes consistent with the goals of deep ecology require political action as well as cultural transformation. According to Naess, those in the ecological movement should learn about the major sources of power in their countries so as to understand the forces that favor or oppose change. They also should try to keep conservation issues within the political arena. Naess suggests that ecologists, or "greens," should try to recognize and make use of their points of similarity with the two other major political poles of modern society, the "blues," or free-market capitalists, and the "reds," or welfare state proponents. The greens share with the blues an emphasis on personal responsibility and on opposition to bureaucracy. They share with the reds a commitment to social responsibility and an opposition to inequality. Recognizing these overlapping areas can help ecologically active groups move other political parties in a green direction.

Establishing societies that can live in balance with the nonhuman world, according to Naess, means achieving a large reduction in population and emphasizing small-scale, local communities. Green communities will tend to make decisions using direct democracy, show little inequality in wealth, and be highly self-reliant.

Following the teachings of Indian leader Mohandas Gandhi, Naess maintains that political action to bring ecologically viable communities and desirable policies into existence should base itself on norms of nonviolence. The political struggle should involve few illegal acts, and ecologists should act outside the law only when necessary. When it is necessary to break the law, activists should attempt to make personal contact with their opponents and to gently turn their opponents into supporters.

In international politics, Naess believes that the ability of poor countries to reverse environmental degradation is weakened by the exploitation of poor countries by richer ones. This exploitation is rooted in the rich countries' addiction to excessive production and consumption that uses up the raw materials of the poor and makes the poor countries dumping grounds for waste. Naess argues that transformation of the economies of the developed nations must be accompanied by shifting relations with the rest of the world from a basis of exploitation to one of mutual aid.

Naess sees green utopias, the ideal societies envisioned by radical ecologists, as statements of goals for the deep ecology movement. The alternative to moving toward these goals, in his view, is environmental devastation.

The Spread of Deep Ecology

Ecology, Community, and Lifestyle has provided the most complete statement available of the philosophical views of the deep ecology movement. The original Norwegian version of the book was widely read in Norway, going through five revisions during the 1970's. Outside Norway, Naess was well known to ecologically concerned individuals for his short articles on deep ecology. The English translation of this book provided international readers with the first major work on deep ecology by the movement's intellectual leader.

Some critics see the book as inconsistent, excessively mystical, and lacking in specific programs to address environmental problems. Others have objected to its utopian character, accusing Naess of being unrealistic. Admirers, however, believe that the book provides environmental activists with a sound philosophical basis for thinking about global problems in terms of the interrelations of humanity and nature. The book helped to establish Naess's reputation as the world's foremost visionary of ecological salvation.

Carl L. Bankston III

Additional Reading

Bookchin, Murray. *Remaking Society*. Boston: South End Press, 1990. Bookchin is the founder of the social ecology movement, an ecological movement that tends to be more human-centered than deep ecology. In addition to discussing his own philosophy, Bookchin criticizes deep ecology as excessively spiritualistic and mystical. He also maintains that deep ecology is misanthropic—that it promotes a low view of human beings and values only the nonhuman world. Bookchin also claims that deep ecology is a "wilderness cult" of the economically privileged and that it does not contribute to the struggle of oppressed people.

Devall, Bill, and George Sessions. *Deep Ecology: Living as If Nature Mattered*. Salt Lake City, Utah: Peregrine Smith Books, 1985. This book provides a description of deep ecology by two close collaborators of Naess.

Fox, Warwick. *Toward a Transpersonal Ecology*. Boston: Shambhala, 1990. Fox, an Australian proponent of deep ecology, examines the concept of ecosophy. He maintains that most deep ecologists share the worldview of Naess and claims that the norm of self-realization, as described by Naess, is the distinctive characteristic of deep ecology.

Milbrath, Lester. *Environmentalists: Vanguard for a New Society*. Albany: State University of New York Press, 1984. Milbrath provides an examination of the radical ecological movement and argues that it provides models for restructuring human society.

Reed, Peter, and David Rothenberg, eds. *Wisdom and the Open Air: The Norwegian Roots of Deep Ecology*. Minneapolis: University of Minnesota Press, 1992. This collection of writings by Norwegian environmentalists demonstrates the range of environmental thinking in Norway. It also shows the influence of Naess on contemporary Norwegian environmental thought.

Rothenberg, David. *Is It Painful to Think? Conversations with Arne Naess*. Minneapolis: University of Minnesota Press, 1993. A good introduction to the life and thought of Naess, this book consists of taped conversations between Naess and the author, many of them held in Naess's mountain cabin. Each conversation is prefaced with a short biographical essay; in combination, these essays provide a view of the development of the philosopher's thought over the course of his lifetime.

Tobias, Michael, ed. *Deep Ecology*. San Diego, Calif.: Avant Books, 1985. This collection of writings by some of the most important figures in the deep ecology movement includes an essay by Naess as well as essays inspired by him.

Zimmerman, Michael. *Contesting Earth's Future: Radical Ecology and Postmodernity*. Berkeley: University of California Press, 1994. Written by an American philosopher greatly influenced by deep ecology, this book provides a detailed consideration of deep ecology and of Naess's thinking. It compares deep ecology with other radical approaches to ecology, such as social ecology and ecofeminism, and attempts to find common ground among the different approaches.

Carl L. Bankston III

Thomas Nagel

Nagel explores the tension between the subjective and the objective standpoints in metaphysics, epistemology, the philosophy of mind, and ethics, arguing that, although these divergent points of view cannot always be comfortably fitted into a unified conception of the world, the solution is to find a way of living with the tension among them.

Principal philosophical works: *The Possibility of Altruism*, 1970; *Mortal Questions*, 1979; *Marx, Justice, and History*, 1980 (with Marshall Cohen and T. M. Scanlon); *The View from Nowhere*, 1986; *What Does It All Mean?*, 1987; *Equality and Partiality*, 1991; *Other Minds: Critical Essays, 1969-1994*, 1995; *The Last Word*, 1997.

Born: July 4, 1937; Belgrade, Yugoslavia

Early Life

Thomas Nagel began his academic career in 1954 as an undergraduate at Cornell University. His initial plan was to major in physics, but he soon discovered that his true interest lay in philosophy. At Cornell, he studied under Norman Malcolm, Rogers Albritton, and John Rawls, all of whom had a lasting effect on his conception of the practice of philosophy. In 1958, he went to Oxford University on a Fulbright scholarship. There he encountered philosophers such as J. L. Austin, Paul Grice, Peter Strawson, H. L. A. Hart, G. E. M. Anscombe, G. E. L. Owen, Philippa Foot, and James Thomson.

In 1960, Nagel began doing doctoral work at Harvard University. He met and worked with the renowned Harvard philosophers W. V. O. Quine and Noam Chomsky, but he wrote his dissertation—which was later to be published (after revisions) as *The Possibility of Altruism*—with John Rawls, who had moved from Cornell to Harvard. Rawls was then in the process of writing *A Theory of Justice* (1971); Nagel was fortunate enough to read and discuss various drafts of this seminal work. Thus, Rawls was probably the greatest formative influence on Nagel the philosopher. While at Harvard, Nagel also became friends with Gilbert Harman and Saul Kripke, the former a fellow graduate student and the latter an undergraduate.

Nagel taught at Berkeley for a few years (1963-1966) before moving on to a longer stretch at Princeton University and eventually, in 1980, to New York University, where he held a joint appointment in the Department of Philosophy and the School of Law.

Life's Work

In the late 1960's, together with Marshall Cohen and T. M. Scanlon, Nagel founded the journal *Philosophy and Public Affairs*, which has played a key role in applying work in moral philosophy to practical and political issues. Nagel himself contributed articles to the first two volumes in 1971 and 1972. Around the same time, he and Robert Nozick began the Society for Ethical and Legal Philosophy (SELF), a long-standing monthly discussion group that was also to include Ronald Dworkin, Judith Jarvis Thomson, Charles Fried, Michael Walzer, and other notable philosophers, many of whom later expressed their gratitude and their sense of indebtedness to SELF. Thus, Nagel was very much a part of the task of revitalizing substantive moral and political philosophy during the latter part of the twentieth century.

Given his involvement in such projects, it is no surprise that Nagel has always been philosophically engaged with current moral issues. In 1972, he published "War and Massacre," which concerned the morality of various military strategies that were then being played out in Vietnam.

Nagel rejects the "modern" view of war, in which the only relevant military moral principle is that the ends justify the means. He argues that in war, as in ordinary life, there are principles that govern how people may treat one another, and that these principles rule out the attack of civilians as well as the use of torture and certain horrific weapons. In 1973, he published "The Policy of Preference," which addressed the practice of giving preference to minority groups in decisions about who is to be given employment and education. In 1978, a few years after President Richard M. Nixon's resignation, he published "Ruthlessness in Public Life," a piece about power and public morality. These three articles, along with several other of Nagel's articles in ethics and the philosophy of mind, were gathered together in the important collection *Mortal Questions*. However, Nagel's interest in current events did not wane; for example, in 1998, amid the questions surrounding President Bill Clinton's sexual improprieties, he published "Concealment and Exposure," which took up the question of the limits of privacy in public (and private) life.

Nagel's first major publication was *The Possibility of Altruism*. His major argumentative strategy in this book is to show that the same basic considerations that justify a prudential concern for the interests of one's future self can be employed in a parallel fashion to justify a moral concern for the interests of other people. The rationality of altruism is defended not by showing how altruistic concern really serves some other purpose—for example, that it is in one's interest or satisfies one's desires—but rather by showing how altruistic considerations can themselves be basic rational requirements. This argument marks the beginning of Nagel's lifelong preoccupation with the relationship between the personal and the impersonal points of view.

Nagel's best-known and most influential piece of work is probably the article "What Is It Like to Be a Bat?" (1974; also reprinted in *Mortal Questions*). Nagel's argument is that even if we were to learn everything that science is capable of telling us about bat physiology, one fact about bats would inevitably escape the grasp of a scientific account: the fact of what it is like to be a bat. No amount of objective, third-person knowledge of bats can ever tell us what it is like to be a bat

"from the inside." This point could be made about any conscious creature, but a bat is an inspired choice because of its alien mode of perception. Nagel uses this example with dramatic effect to argue that there are facts about the world that are forever beyond the reach of science. These are facts about "what it is like" to be something, that is, facts about conscious experience. Critics such as Daniel Dennett, Paul M. Churchland, and Patricia Smith Churchland vehemently disagreed, arguing either that such "facts" are not genuine facts at all or that science can, in principle, discover them, and so a lengthy debate ensued in the literature on the philosophy of mind.

Nagel carried his work forward and presented it more systematically in a trio of very important books: *The View from Nowhere*, *Equality and Partiality*, and *The Last Word*. Running throughout these works are two main themes: First, Nagel believes that it is instructive to regard most of the central problems of philosophy as arising because of the conflict between the subjective and the objective points of view. Nagel explores such conflicts in ethics, the philosophy of mind, metaphysics, and epistemology in *The View from Nowhere*; he extends this discussion to political philosophy in *Equality and Partiality*. Second, Nagel is a realist, both about ethics and about metaphysics, and he is a rationalist, too: He thinks that it is reason's task to understand the basic principles of this physical, mental, and moral reality. Nagel is no friend of the various forms of idealism that are found in certain philosophical circles, whether it be of a Kantian or a positivist bent, but he is especially critical of the relativism that pervades much of popular culture.

Over the years, Nagel also worked on an account of the meaning and value of life and death. These are, of course, issues of great practical and philosophical importance, yet many philosophers have tended to avoid talking about such large and difficult questions. Many centuries ago, Epicurus and his followers argued that death cannot be bad because it involves no painful experiences. They believed this because they were committed to hedonism: Something can be good for me only if it brings me pleasure and bad for me only if it brings me pain. In "Death" (1970; reprinted in *Mortal Questions*), Nagel argues that this view is mistaken, for something can be bad for me even if it involves no painful experiences. If I am deceived or betrayed, for example, I am harmed even if I do not find out about it. Thus, hedonism is a flawed theory of value. Life is valuable because it contains a variety of good things, including but not limited to pleasure; death is bad primarily because it forever robs me of those goods. From the inside, then, my life is seen to have meaning because of the goods present in it: my projects and relationships, my health, simple pleasures, and so on. However, when I examine my life from the outside, such goods suddenly seem altogether insignificant. The thought that my little life has true meaning now appears absurd. Nagel is convinced that there is no way to reconcile the view of my life from the inside and the view from the outside. The result is absurd: My life is both meaningful and meaningless.

In addition to writing his own essays and books, Nagel has proven to be an astute critic of the philosophical writing of others. A number of his critical essays are gathered together in *Other Minds*. This volume also contains an illuminating account of Nagel's view of the contemporary philosophical culture and of his own relationship with that culture. Nagel's versatility is also witnessed in that he is one of the only well-respected academic philosophers to try his hand at a genuinely introductory-level book. As Nagel himself announces in the introduction to *What Does It All Mean?*, he really is writing for people who know nothing at all about philosophy. The book is clear and concise, and it acquaints readers with most of the major topics in philosophy. It is an excellent introduction to philosophy in general and to Nagel's thought in particular.

Influence

Nagel is one of the few philosophers working in the latter part of the twentieth century addressing nearly every area of philosophy, including ethics, political philosophy, the history of philosophy, the philosophy of mind, epistemology, and metaphysics. Furthermore, he does not shy away from asking about the really big and seemingly intractable issues, such as the nature of consciousness and the meaning of life. Nagel offers a systematic philosophical vision of the world, al-

though he would be the first to point out that this picture is incomplete and somewhat rough and sketchy in any number of places. His most distinctive contributions are probably his defense and development of a deontological account of our ordinary moral thinking and his rejection of a physicalist and reductionist conception of the human mind. However, in all his writings, a reader cannot but be struck both by the clarity and carefulness of his thought and by his intellectual modesty and restraint.

Randall M. Jensen

The View from Nowhere

Type of philosophy: Epistemology, ethics, metaphysics
First published: 1986
Principal ideas advanced:

◇ The subjective and the objective perspectives of the world cannot always be comfortably reconciled with each other, yet we must continue to embrace them both, for to do otherwise would be to neglect part of what is real.

◇ A pure physicalist account of the human mind cannot capture the subjective character of consciousness; that is, the physical sciences cannot explain what it is like to be a conscious subject of experiences. Nonetheless, the mind (the self) is identical to the brain; thus, the brain should be characterized as having "dual aspects"—both physical and mental aspects.

◇ Consequentialism does not provide a complete theory of value. There are agent-relative values, including some that are deontological. In fact, at present there seems to be no unified theory of value.

The View from Nowhere systematically develops a series of ideas that were first advanced in Thomas Nagel's earlier works—for example, the essays collected in *Mortal Questions* (1979), especially essays 5, 9, and 11-14. Three chapters of *The View from Nowhere* are descended from a series of lectures entitled "The Limits of Objectivity," which were earlier published in *The Tanner Lectures on Human Values* (volume 1, 1980).

Subjective vs. Objective Standpoints

Nagel's primary aim in this book is to explore the various philosophical puzzles that arise from the tension between the subjective standpoint and the objective standpoint. The subjective standpoint is the personal perspective of an individual person; it is her view of the world "from the inside," the world as she sees it; it is her own private window on the world, so to speak. The objective standpoint is the impersonal perspective a person adopts when she conceives of the world "from the outside," not as it appears to her but as it really is. From the subjective standpoint, a person is at the center of her world; from the objective standpoint, she is simply one of many people who all see the world as she does. Thus, Nagel also characterizes the objective standpoint as "centerless"; someone who looks at the world objectively strives to take in "the view from nowhere."

Nagel is convinced that the tension between the subjective and the objective standpoints surfaces in many of the enduring questions of philosophy. In this book, he focuses on questions about the nature of the self and the human mind, questions about the nature of reality and about our ability to have knowledge of reality, and questions about value and human freedom. In each of these areas, Nagel shows how the philosophical terrain appears quite different depending on which of the two divergent standpoints we occupy, and he then argues that each standpoint has a vital role to play. Some may react to this tension between subjectivity and objectivity by claiming that the subjective standpoint is of little significance, for why should we pay any heed to how the world appears to us? Others may react by asserting that the objective standpoint is unattainable; for whatever reason, we are inevitably confined to a merely subjective perspective. Nagel argues against each of these general reactions. He thinks that the conflict between these two perspectives is an essential part of our conception of ourselves and our world. In essence, Nagel finds the perplexity that arises from this tension more honest and illuminating than any tidy resolution of it.

As Nagel sees it, objectivity is a mode of understanding rather than a feature of the world. Thus, it is more appropriate to speak of an objective way of apprehending a truth rather than of a truth that is in itself objective; the latter is objective only in a derivative sense. Furthermore, objectivity comes in degrees: The more a person abstracts from the particularity of her own perspective, the more objective her point of view becomes (or, in Nagel's terms, the more she takes on "the objective self"). To move from her own perspective to the perspective of human beings in general and then to the perspective of conscious beings in general is to move, stepwise, toward greater objectivity. One of Nagel's aims is to acknowledge that there are two kinds of limits to this sort of objective understanding. First, an objective perspective can never completely subsume the subjective perspective; reality has an essentially subjective aspect: namely, consciousness itself. Second, given our limited perceptual and intellectual capacities, there is reason to think that our best objective portrait of the world will remain rough and incomplete, for there very well may be aspects of reality that are simply beyond our capacity to grasp.

The Human Mind

Nagel's first topic is the nature of the human mind. Here the tension between the two standpoints is very clear. From the outside, I appear to be simply another of the physical constituents of the universe, composed of the same basic parts as is everything else. Perhaps physics, that seemingly most objective of sciences, can give a complete account of everything, including me. However, from the inside, I simply cannot view myself in this way. From the inside, my connection to this hunk of matter that is my body (and brain) seems rather accidental. For some, such thoughts may inspire a Cartesian dualism of mind and body. However, Nagel argues that my concept of myself need not include all that is essential to me; while my concept of myself may be silent about my relationship to my brain, it may nonetheless turn out that I am essentially identical to my brain. Nagel is inclined to endorse this identity of self and brain; unlike René Descartes, he does not believe that the human mind is an immaterial entity that animates the body.

However, Nagel does not subscribe to any physicalist wholesale reduction of the mental to the physical. Instead, he subscribes to a "dual aspect" theory of the mind-brain, according to which a physical object, the brain, has mental features in addition to its physical features. Reality indeed has a mental aspect, but this aspect consists in a set of nonphysical features of physical objects rather than in a set of nonphysical objects. We can try to place these mental features within a more objective conception of the world, but such a conception will not be objective in a narrowly physicalist sense. For Nagel, the notion of objectivity is not exhausted by the objectivity of physics. It is an enduring theme in Nagel's work that even a fictionally completed physics cannot give a complete account of conscious experience—that is, what it is like, what it feels like from the inside, to be a subject of conscious experiences. However, we can try to think about consciousness from a more objective vantage point by thinking about what it is to be a conscious subject in general rather than about the contents of our own private consciousnesses; the result will be a kind of "mental objectivity."

Realist Metaphysics

Nagel's metaphysics is emphatically realist. The world exists independent of our thinking about it; in our quest for objective understanding, we are striving to grasp what is really "out there," rather than—as some idealists would have it—merely investigating the form and limits of human thought and language. This leaves Nagel the epistemologist facing a swarm of skeptical problems. How can we know what the world is really like when we cannot ever fully rid ourselves of our own perspective? Might I not be dreaming? Might I be a brain swimming in some scientist's jar? Nagel is refreshingly honest about our inability to rule out such possibilities. From within—that is, from the subjective standpoint—we cannot seriously entertain such skeptical doubts, but to advance toward objectivity is to make ourselves vulnerable to those doubts.

When we look at the world from the external (objective) standpoint, the actions of human beings appear as simply another sort of worldly event. Determinism—the view that human actions are causally determined just as much as are the movements of billiard balls—looms large. However, from the subjective standpoint, it

seems to me that I have a freedom that a billiard ball lacks. The supposition that I lack such freedom of the will threatens to undermine my very agency. That is what Nagel calls the problem of autonomy. How do we reconcile these opposing viewpoints? Here, Nagel is at his most modest; he says that the problem is not that it is unclear which of several promising solutions to choose, but rather that there seem to be no promising solutions at all. In particular, he rejects any "compatibilist" solution in which human freedom is somehow shown to be compatible with the truth of determinism. Thus, Nagel offers a diagnosis of the problem rather than a solution to it: It is our very capacity for objectivity that is the source of the difficulty. Here, just as in the quest for knowledge of reality, the pursuit of objectivity threatens to undermine itself.

Ethics

The conflict between the subjective and the objective is also found in ethics, in the guise of the personal and the impersonal practical points of view. Nagel argues that there are impersonal values, the most obvious cases being pleasure and pain. My pain is not just a bad thing for me; it is a bad thing objectively. Consequentialism is perhaps the clearest example of a purely impersonal moral theory: Always strive to bring about the best consequences, all things considered. Nagel finds the considerations that support consequentialism, which arise from the objective standpoint, compelling. However, he does not think consequentialism tells the whole story about ethics—for if we adopt the subjective standpoint, we just cannot regard ourselves, together with our projects, our commitments, and our relationships, as simply part of a universal ethical calculus. In fact, personal concerns may often seem to come into conflict with the demands of an impersonal morality, as when I can promote some great good or avert some great evil by doing something that I very much do not want to do. The consequentialist's typical response to this conflict is to characterize such personal concerns as biased and selfish; the nonconsequentialist's typical response is to argue that such a morality is unrealistic and excessively demanding and may even undermine the unity and integrity of moral agency.

Moral Considerations

Nagel spends most of his time articulating and defending a nonconsequentialist moral perspective, which involves showing that there are values that are personal (agent-relative) rather than impersonal (agent-neutral). One of his main theses in this regard is that in addition to consequentialist moral considerations—for example, preventing pain because it is objectively bad—we must also be concerned with deontological moral considerations—for example, refraining from intentionally bringing pain to others simply because it is wrong to do so. In Nagel's view, the wrongness of my assaulting you is not merely a matter of something bad (your pain) happening; it is also a matter of my doing something (assaulting you) that I should not do to you. The difference between these two sorts of negative value is brought out strongly in cases where we can prevent much bad from happening by doing something wrong. (Imagine that by torturing a prisoner we can find out information that will yield a swift end to the war.) Nagel thinks that such cases are genuine value conflicts; thus, both these (and other) kinds of value are real and have a place in moral theory. Does this mean that consequentialism is false? Not exactly. It rather seems to mean that in ethics, as elsewhere, the tension between the objective and the subjective standpoints simply cannot be resolved.

The Meaning of Life

The View from Nowhere closes with a discussion of the meaning of life. My life, which appears so serious and important from a personal point of view, may suddenly appear small and insignificant when I take on the objective standpoint. From the outside, what do I matter? We can try to harmonize these impulses toward self-transcendence and self-absorption, in part by recognizing that there are many others in the very same situation, but ultimately Nagel thinks we cannot avoid the absurdity of our predicament.

The View from Nowhere, and Nagel's work more generally, have probably been most influential in ethics and in the philosophy of mind. In ethics, he is one of the founding fathers of the contemporary deontological movement. In the philosophy of mind, he is one of the standard-bearers in the fight against those who believe that the mind can be completely characterized in purely physicalist terms. In each of these areas, it is his struggle with the tension between the subjective and the objective, between the personal and the impersonal, that is distinctive of his philosophy.

Randall M. Jensen

Additional Reading

Churchland, Paul M. *Matter and Consciousness.* Cambridge, Mass.: MIT Press, 1984. A short introductory text on the philosophy of mind. Unlike Nagel, Churchland believes that the physical sciences are capable of capturing every significant fact about the mind.

Dennett, Daniel C. *Consciousness Explained.* Boston: Little, Brown, 1991. Another of Nagel's major critics. Nagel presents a review of this book in *Other Minds.*

Hofstadter, Douglas C., and Daniel C. Dennett, eds. *The Mind's I.* New York: Basic Books, 1981. A popular collection of materials on the philosophy of mind. Includes Nagel's "What Is It Like to Be a Bat?" and several pages of critical remarks by the editors.

Jackson, Frank. "What Mary Didn't Know," *Journal of Philosophy* 83 (May, 1986): 291-295. Jackson employs a strategy similar to Nagel's in "What Is It Like to Be a Bat?" His argument turns on the case of Mary, a scientist who knows everything about the mechanics of vision but who has been confined to a black and white world since birth. This example, like Nagel's bat example, is supposed to show that physicalism cannot tell us the whole story about the world.

Kim, Jaegwon. *Philosophy of Mind.* Boulder, Colo.: Westview Press, 1996. A good intermediate introduction to the philosophy of mind, with a useful bibliography. Nagel's views are discussed in chapter 7.

Korsgaard, Christine. "The Reasons We Can Share: An Attack on the Distinction Between Agent-Relative and Agent-Neutral Values." In *Creating the Kingdom of Ends.* Cambridge, England: Cambridge University Press, 1996. This piece was inspired by Nagel's treatment of the two standpoints—subjective and objective—in ethics.

_____. *The Sources of Normativity.* Cambridge, England: Cambridge University Press, 1996.

Contains a very influential account of the normative status of ethical claims, including a discussion of Nagel's moral realism. Also contains comments by Nagel, Bernard Williams, and others, together with Korsgaard's replies.

McGinn, Colin. *The Character of Mind*. 2d ed. Oxford, England: Oxford University Press, 1997. A general introduction to the philosophy of mind, uncluttered by references to the secondary literature.

Parfit, Derek. *Reasons and Persons*. Oxford, England: Oxford University Press, 1984. Parfit covers some of the same ground as Nagel in this very influential work, notably concerning personal identity and its relation to the nature and source of moral reasons.

Scheffler, Samuel, ed. *Consequentialism and Its Critics*. Oxford, England: Oxford University Press, 1988. A much-used anthology of articles about the ethical debate between consequentialism and deontology (which is a more specific instance of Nagel's general tension between objectivity and subjectivity). Contains two pieces by Nagel and a helpful bibliography.

Randall M. Jensen

John Henry Newman

A leading figure in the Oxford Movement, which brought religious issues to the forefront of the Victorian consciousness, Newman, after his conversion to Catholicism, became the leading Catholic figure in Great Britain, writing eloquently about religion and education and influencing the course of theological and administrative practices within the Catholic Church in Great Britain and throughout the world.

Principal philosophical works: *Tract XXXVIII*, 1834; *Tract XLI*, 1834; *Tract XC*, 1841; *Lectures on the Prophetical Office of the Church*, 1837; *Lectures on Justification*, 1838; *An Essay on the Development of Christian Doctrine*, 1845; *Discourses on the Scope and Nature of University Education, Addressed to the Catholics of Dublin*, 1852; *Lectures and Essays on University Subjects*, 1859; *Apologia pro vita sua*, 1864 (*History of My Religious Opinions*, 1870); *An Essay in Aid of a Grammar of Assent*, 1870; *Causes of the Rise of Arianism*, 1872; *The Idea of a University Defined and Illustrated*, 1873; *Stray Essays on Controversial Points*, 1890.

Born: February 21, 1801; London, England
Died: August 11, 1890; Birmingham, England

Early Life

The eldest of six children, John Henry Newman grew up in a close-knit family and was educated at Dr. Nicolas's school at Ealing. At age fifteen, shortly before he matriculated at Oxford, Newman underwent a period of extreme mental crisis, which he later described as his conversion, and became deeply religious, convinced that God had destined him for a high calling. His reading during this period led him to appreciate the early church fathers and to fear the Roman Catholic Church's influence in the modern world.

In the fall of 1816, Newman's father took his son to Oxford and enrolled him at Trinity College. Newman did not actually move to the university until the following summer, when he began a period of intense study in the classics and mathematics. His performance during his first year earned for him a prestigious scholarship, but he was bitterly disappointed in 1820 when he failed to gain a coveted first in either classics or mathematics.

Believing that his performance at Trinity did not truly represent his abilities, Newman applied

for a fellowship at Oriel College. The examiners found him clearly the best applicant, and in April, 1822, he joined the college, where he was to achieve fame and then notoriety. At Oriel, he became acquainted first with Edward Pusey, Edward Copleston, Richard Whately, and Edward Hawkins, and later with Richard Hurrell Froude and John Keble. In 1825, Newman was ordained an Anglican priest. For the next several years, he combined duties as an educator at the college and at Alban Hall with priestly functions as vicar of St. Mary's Church, Oxford.

An extended trip through Sicily led to a serious illness, which forced Newman into a lengthy period of convalescence on the Continent. He returned to Oxford in time for his friend John Keble's famous sermon on national apostasy, which initiated what came to be known as the Oxford Movement.

Life's Work

Newman and his Oxford colleagues took advantage of the outcry generated by Keble's sermon to bring before the public their thoughts on the proper role of the Church. In September, 1833, Newman published his thoughts on Apostolic Succession in a small pamphlet, or tract, which

John Henry Newman *(Library of Congress)*

spent four years agonizing over his own religious future. Finally, he broke openly with the Church of England: On October 9, 1845, he was baptized into the Roman Catholic Church.

The Anglican Church hierarchy was shaken by this move; the Roman Catholic community was elated. Within two years, Newman completed his studies in Rome and was ordained a priest, receiving from the pope a commission to establish in Great Britain an Oratory like those of Saint Philip Neri. Newman established his community in 1848, in Birmingham, bringing into it several men who had converted at or about the same time.

The move into the bosom of Rome had ironic consequences. In the Anglican Church, Newman had been one of the chief spokespeople for conservative values; as a Roman Catholic, he found himself immediately cast as the champion of liberalism. Newman's belief in individual intellectual inquiry and in participation by the laity in the government of the Church set him at odds with numerous bishops and priests who viewed centralization of all authority as essential to the health of the "one true Church." These differences of opinion caused Newman considerable difficulty for almost two decades. Even within his own community in Birmingham he faced controversy. Several of the Oratorians, recent converts to Roman Catholicism, had found great solace in practicing the extreme forms of worship common in Italian churches. These men were disillusioned with Newman's moderate tone toward non-Catholics. Eventually, the community split, with a group establishing a separate Oratory in London under Frederick William Faber, one of Newman's most trusted friends and followers.

Newman was not anxious to challenge openly the Church of England; rather, he wanted to lead British Catholics to the Church of Rome through conciliatory measures. That plan was made especially difficult almost from the outset when, in 1850, the pope decided to reestablish bishops in residence in Great Britain; since the sixteenth cen-

he had delivered all over Great Britain. This first pamphlet was followed by dozens of others during the next eight years, written by various Tractarians, as Newman's group was called. Intended to establish the right of the Anglican Church to the title of "catholic," *Tracts for the Times* eventually led many to believe that the Church of Rome, not that of Canterbury, was the only body to preserve the true spirit of early Christianity. Newman's polemical *Tract XC*, in which he argued that even Roman Catholics could subscribe to the Thirty-nine Articles, caused such a stir that the tracts were terminated. Newman himself had grown to believe that the Anglican Church was not a "via media," as he had once argued so eloquently. In 1841, he left Oxford to reside at the parish house in nearby Littlemore, where he tury, the country had been a "mission" for the Catholic Church, without a designated diocesan headquarters. To make matters worse, Nicholas Wiseman, first archbishop of Westminster, inflamed public opinion by suggesting that the Catholic Church was "reclaiming" England. Protestants rallied against this "papal aggression," and Newman found himself explaining to both Catholics and Protestants that the Church had no temporal aims.

In the early 1850's, the Irish bishops, wanting to establish an independent university to provide Catholics with an education not influenced by the Protestant institutions of higher learning, sought out Newman to found a Catholic university in Dublin. Initial efforts were promising. In 1852, Newman delivered a series of lectures in Ireland, outlining his plans for the school, which were later collected, along with some other lectures, in *The Idea of a University Defined and Illustrated*. Newman wanted to build a university on the model of Oxford, where classical and scientific learning were the cornerstones of education. The bishops wanted little of such independent thinking; instead, they had hoped that the new colleges would indoctrinate students in Catholicism. Newman tried for several years to compromise and bring the school into existence; the effort eventually failed, and in 1858 he resigned.

During this period, Newman found himself embroiled in a lawsuit, brought against him by a former priest, Giacinto Achilli. Having fled to Great Britain, Achilli entertained Protestants by railing against the Church of Rome; in response, Newman, knowing Achilli to be a philanderer, castigated him in print. When Achilli sued, Newman was unable to obtain from Rome or from Archbishop Wiseman the documents he needed for a defense. Though a friend went to Rome and brought back witnesses against Achilli, Newman was still found guilty and ordered to pay a fine. Public outcry against what appeared to be Protestant injustice brought Newman considerable support, financial as well as moral; with the excess funds that were sent to him by well-wishers, Newman was able to build a church for the university in Dublin.

Almost immediately after he resigned from his position at the university in Dublin, Newman found himself at the center of another contro-versy over the *Rambler*, a monthly Catholic lay magazine that often questioned church authorities. To quell growing dissatisfaction, Newman agreed to become the editor, but his own practices were not acceptable to the bishops, who had originally objected. Newman was forced to resign almost immediately after he had assumed the editorship, but not before he published an influential article, "On Consulting the Faithful in Matters of Doctrine." His liberal ideas on the role of the laity—ideas based on his study of the Church and its early history—caused him to be accused of heresy and left him under a cloud with those in Rome.

Vindication for Newman came slowly and began not within the church he had adopted but rather within his country. The publication of an article by Charles Kingsley in 1864, in which Kingsley accused Newman of condoning lies as a means of promoting the Catholic faith, forced Newman to clear his reputation by explaining his conversion. The series of letters Newman published in the spring of 1864 were collected into a volume that became the most important religious autobiography of the century: *History of My Religious Opinions*. The work was praised by both Protestants and Catholics for its sincere presentation of a man's search for truth. After its publication, Newman became reconciled with several of the friends whom he had abandoned when he had converted two decades earlier. *History of My Religious Opinions* was followed in 1870 by *An Essay in Aid of a Grammar of Assent*, which explains how one can find assurances in faith that go beyond the merely intellectual.

In 1870, Newman was invited to the First Vatican Council to help determine an important and controversial issue: papal infallibility. He declined. He believed in the doctrine but feared that the council would declare the pope infallible in all of his pronouncements. He need not have been concerned. The council adopted a more circumscribed definition, that the pope spoke infallibly only on matters of faith and morals.

In 1878, Oxford honored Newman when officials of Trinity College elected him as the first honorary fellow. Not until Leo XIII became pope, however, did Newman gain the ecclesiastical recognition he deserved. One of the new pope's first acts was to make Newman a cardinal. After some initial concern, and an attempt by Henry, Cardinal Manning of Westminster to thwart the appointment, Newman eventually accepted the honor, and he was elevated to the cardinalate in May, 1879. The pope allowed Newman to retain his residence at the Oratory in Birmingham, where he died on August 11, 1890.

Influence

Newman's influence on the Catholic Church in England during the nineteenth century cannot be overestimated. His own conversion was the catalyst that led dozens of others to adopt the Roman rule. Within the Church, he served as a constant voice for liberalism, stressing the dignity of individuals and the importance of the laity. Many of his ideas about the role of the laity formed the basis for later decisions of the Second Vatican Council in 1965, seven decades after his death.

Similarly, Catholic education has accepted a number of Newman's ideas. His influence on Catholic colleges and universities both in Great Britain and in the United States has been significant. As Newman had urged, while most Catholic institutions of higher learning offer a liberal education that includes the study of theology, they also teach secular subjects and allow students to confront the evils of the world directly, offering guidance rather than trying to isolate students from life's challenges.

Though Newman was a poet of some merit, his major contributions to British letters are his volumes of prose, especially his spiritual autobiography, his analysis of the nature of belief, and his writings on education. In an eloquent yet accessible style, he explored his subjects with great erudition and sincerity. His works continue to be read as examples of the essay at its best.

Laurence W. Mazzeno

The Idea of a University Defined and Illustrated

Type of philosophy: Epistemology, philosophy of education, philosophy of religion
First published: Discourses on the Scope and Nature of University Education, Addressed to the Catho-

lics of Dublin, 1852; revised and enlarged as *The Idea of a University Defined and Illustrated*, 1873
Principal ideas advanced:

◇ Knowledge is to be taught for its own sake, not for its vocational or social usefulness.

◇ A university should teach the full spectrum of knowledge, which must include the science of theology, if it is to be considered as pursuing a truly liberal education.

◇ Theology, especially Catholic theology, must not trespass on the boundaries of other subjects, nor they on that of theology, but Catholic theology should act as a corrective to attempts by other disciplines to become greater than their natures permit.

◇ The goal of a university education is the cultivation of a "gentleman" who is prepared to take up roles of social leadership and responsibility through the use of a properly trained mind.

During the 1840's, Pope Pius IX had expressed a strong wish that a distinctly Catholic university be established in Ireland. In 1851, the Archbishop of Dublin acted on that desire by approaching John Henry Newman, who had recently converted to Catholicism and had been forced to resign his fellowship at Oxford. Newman accepted the position of rector of the new university, which ultimately opened in 1854.

In 1852, as part of the effort to convince Irish Catholics that they should send their children to an exclusively Catholic university rather than to Protestant Oxford, Cambridge, or the mixed-religion universities recently established in Ireland itself, Newman gave a series of lectures that later would form the foundation of his most famous written work, *The Idea of a University Defined and Illustrated*. Of the nine discourses eventually included, five were given publicly, while the other four were published as pamphlets. When the university finally opened, Newman presented additional lectures at the beginning of each school year, publishing ten in all in what was originally a separate volume. The original nine discourses from 1852 were revised for further publication in 1855, and in 1873 Newman published both volumes together as *The Idea of a University Defined and Illustrated*. This work was revised several more times until 1889, the year of

Newman's death. Ironically, Newman's ideas were more enduring than his administration of the university he wrote about. His strained relations with the Irish Catholic hierarchy led him to resign his post in 1858, and the university he helped to establish was later made part of the University of Ireland.

The Teaching of Theology

The "occasional" nature of Newman's original lectures makes it more efficient to group his ideas thematically. Most interpreters delineate three general themes, plus several minor ones taken mostly from Newman's later lectures. The first major theme surrounds Newman's conviction that there existed a need for a distinctly Catholic university that would teach Catholic doctrine alongside the full range of more secular academic subjects. Newman's experiences at Oxford, where the teaching of theology had fallen into increasing disrepute, led him to demand that theology take its place among the academic subjects taught at a university, though the relationship between theology and these other disciplines was the subject of some ambivalence for Newman, an ambivalence that is clearly present in his lectures. Yet Newman was consistent in his insistence that a university should pursue the teaching of the full range of knowledge, otherwise it could not presume to apply the word "liberal" to its definition of itself. Newman assumed that all discoverable knowledge had its source in the work of God, and therefore all physical knowledge should be categorized and shared within the context and framework of Catholic doctrine, which Newman the recent convert repeatedly affirmed as the fullest expression of divine truth.

Unlike more conservative Catholics in his day, Newman stressed that theology should not be permitted to trespass into the realms of other academic disciplines. All knowledge must be taught according to its own definitions and its own nature, each being allowed to remain absolutely free to follow its own course within its own boundaries. However, the presence of theology was necessary to ensure that no single discipline or group of disciplines become successful in an attempt to break out of their assigned boundaries and become absolutes in themselves. Theology was also necessary in and of itself because for

Newman, ignorance of the divine source of all physical nature was ultimately no different from ignorance of the physical world itself.

The Role of the University

The second general theme Newman elaborated was that knowledge was to be taught for its own sake and not for any social or vocational usefulness. Drawing more positively on his Oxford experience, Newman made a distinction between "liberal" knowledge and "professional" knowledge, and while not disparaging the latter, insisted that the former was the proper object of university teaching. Central to this theme was Newman's view that the ultimate goal of a university education was not to provide specific training in a professional or vocation specialty, but rather the cultivation of a "gentleman," one in whom could be found the proper habits of a disciplined mind and the capacity for social and civic interaction. There is no doubt here that the honing of English gentry as pursued at his beloved Oxford was the model he wished to apply to the Irish masses. Newman, however, went still further by claiming that the university was not the place for the discovery of new knowledge (arguably the main function of the modern research university) but was to emphasize the forming of young minds as its primary, if not exclusive, mission.

The third general theme identified by Newman's interpreters concerns what Newman himself believed a university could and should do, as opposed to what it could not and should not try. Put briefly, Newman believed that a university should concentrate on the education of the mind and leave off any attempt to save the soul. In defining the education of a gentleman, Newman insisted that the limit of what the university could cultivate was a person of broad knowledge, critical intelligence, moral decency, and social responsibility. However, it could not transform fallen sinners into saints, nor could it prepare the individuals under its charge for what Newman identified as genuine moral virtue. For this, what was needed was reference to the faith and doctrine of the Roman Catholic Church. However, even here, Newman was careful: While insisting that theology be accounted a "science" and therefore given a place alongside other forms of knowledge and while believing that Catholic doctrine specifically was a fit subject to include in any Catholic university curriculum, he nevertheless emphasized that the teaching of Catholic doctrine was only for the purpose of exposing the limits of the natural world and what could actually be known about it. At times, Newman also seemed to be saying that the teaching of doctrine was necessary to show the fallen state of the physical world, but at no time was the teaching of Catholic truth to be seen as the pursuit of the perfection of Christian souls. Education was for university professors, salvation the province of priests and bishops.

Other Themes

A number of other, more minor themes can be found in Newman's original nine lectures and also in the various occasional lectures given after his Irish university opened. In a speech given in 1854, for example, Newman defined "civilization" in a distinctly Western manner, as belonging to those cultures and traditions surrounding the Mediterranean Sea and resident in Europe. In particular, Jerusalem was defined as the fountainhead of religious knowledge, while Athens was the foundation of all secular knowledge, with Homer identified as the "first Apostle of Civilization." Rome was seen as the beneficiary of both traditions, which were then mediated to a Christianized Europe. Newman was certainly aware of other cultures lying outside the Mediterranean and European sphere but essentially dismissed them as irrelevant.

In a later lecture, Newman expressed the wish for a truly Catholic tradition of literature, but went on to douse his own hopes by saying that the English literary tradition was already essentially formed (almost exclusively by Protestants) and that the language such a tradition both presupposes and perfects was already set out as complete.

More important were several lectures given on the relationship between theology and the sciences, in which Newman essentially dismissed the growing tension between the two areas as artificially contrived. Central to his discussion was his distinction between science as an inductive pursuit and theology as a deductive pursuit: Science was engaged in the discovery of the pro-

cesses of the natural world and in the description and categorization of those processes, while theology concentrated on the understanding and characterization of divine revelation, which was complete in and of itself. This distinction allowed Newman to reiterate his belief that both science and theology could be taught side by side, without either one interfering with the proper work of the other.

Newman's Legacy

Any attempt to assess the impact of Newman's ideas must take both his immediate context and subsequent history into consideration. Within his own milieu, there is plenty of evidence to suggest that both Newman's work in Ireland and the ideas he presented in his lectures were somewhat of a failure. Newman's relations with the Irish Catholic hierarchy were never more than correct, and he could not seem to convince the larger Irish public that a distinctly Catholic university was either needed or even desirable, particularly in the face of the burgeoning Irish middle class and its attempts to raise its status by increased association with the British Protestant gentry. Indeed, there is some question as to the depth of Newman's understanding of the Irish situation, as there is also about what Newman himself thought he was doing: Was he attempting to establish a Catholic university specifically for the Irish or was he trying to replicate a "Catholic Oxford" for Catholics throughout the British empire? The preponderance of the evidence seems to point to the latter. Even so, Newman's emphasis on teaching as the proper activity of the university was a timely response to the abuses of the old fellowship system at his beloved Oxford and Cambridge, where precious little teaching was actually being done.

On the other hand, the publication of Newman's lectures, both the original nine and a varying number of his later speeches (depending on the edition), has had great impact on the definition of a liberal arts education as it evolved during the second half of the nineteenth century and throughout the twentieth, both in Europe and in the United States. Even here, the assessment will necessarily be a mixed one: Newman's demand that theology be taught as a science alongside other sciences has met with increased rejection at all but specifically religious and sectarian colleges as has his suggestion that the university is not the proper place for the pursuit of research. Nearly all modern interpreters of the tasks of higher education reject his "Eurocentric" view of civilization and the arts it produces, along with his limiting distinction between liberal and professional education.

Nevertheless, his advocacy of the teaching of the full range of what is currently known as a worthy end in itself, his insistence on the cultivation of a critical intellect and a sense of social responsibility, and his more "liberal" (for his time, at least) defense of the freedom of academic inquiry within the boundaries of a particular academic discipline continue to resonate throughout the world of the university. Modern interpreters of the tasks of higher education, even when they disagree with Newman, nevertheless find almost unanimously that they must continue to come to terms with him. Indeed, as one commentator put it, "No work in the English language has had more influence on the public ideals of higher education."

Robert C. Davis

Additional Reading

Bouyer, Louis. *Newman, His Life and Spirituality.* Translated by J. L. May. New York: Meridian Books, 1965. Detailed biography illuminating the complex psychology of its subject. Excellent analysis of John Henry Newman's motives for his conversion, his belief in the importance of the laity, and his insistence on the need for intellectual inquiry for all Catholics. Makes extensive use of Newman's diaries and letters.

Culler, A. Dwight. *The Imperial Intellect: A Study of Newman's Educational Ideal.* New Haven, Conn.: Yale University Press, 1955. Well-researched study of Newman's life, focusing primarily on his thinking, writing, and action concerning education. Excellent discussions of the *Idea of a University Defined and Illustrated* and of Newman's efforts to found such a university.

Dessain, Charles Stephen. *John Henry Newman.* 2d ed. Stanford, Calif.: Stanford University Press, 1971. Brief biography by the editor of Newman's letters. Concentrates on Newman's religious life and the controversies surrounding his conversion and his dealings with the hierarchy in Rome. Excellent analysis of Newman's lifelong quest to understand and propagate the notion of revealed religion.

Edgecombe, Rodney S. *Two Poets of the Oxford Movement: John Keble and John Henry Newman.* Madison, N.J.: Fairleigh Dickinson University Press, 1996. This book offers a history and criticism of Keble and Newman. Included are a bibliography and an index.

Hollis, Christopher. *Newman and the Modern World.* Garden City, N.Y.: Doubleday, 1968. Biographical sketch that examines Newman's ideas and contributions to religion as they affected his contemporaries and the subsequent actions and pronouncements of the Roman Catholic Church. Good source of information about both the major events of Newman's life and the impact his writings have had on changes brought about by the Second Vatican Council.

Ker, Ian. *The Achievement of John Henry Newman.* Notre Dame, Ind.: Notre Dame University Press, 1990. This brief study of Newman's major works is meant as an introduction to his thought. The author includes many quotations from Newman's work, looking at Newman as a writer, theologian, and philosopher.

_____, ed. *Newman the Theologian.* Notre Dame, Ind.: Notre Dame University Press, 1990. Though this work focuses on Newman's theological writings, it contains a valuable biographical study and a bibliography useful for anyone interested in Newman.

McGrath, Francis. *John Henry Newman: Universal Revelation.* Macon, Ga.: Mercer University Press, 1997. A good treatment of Newman's contributions to the theology of revelation.

Martin, Brian. *John Henry Newman: His Life and Work.* New York: Oxford University Press, 1982. Brief, highly readable biographical sketch, profusely illustrated. Provides short analyses of Newman's major works, including his novels. Stresses the difficulties Newman had in dealing with the conservative party within the Catholic Church.

Trevor, Meriol. *Newman.* 2 vols. Garden City, N.Y.: Doubleday, 1962. The standard biography. Provides well-documented sources, illustrations, and an extensive index.

Ward, Wilfrid. *The Life of John Henry Cardinal Newman*. 2 vols. London: Longmans, Green, 1912. First major biography of Newman. Makes extensive use of personal correspondence and private papers as well as anecdotes from those who knew him. Despite the title, deals almost exclusively with years Newman spent as a member of the Roman Catholic Church.

Yearley, Lee H. *The Ideas of Newman: Christianity and Human Religiosity*. University Park: Pennsylvania State University Press, 1978. Scholarly study that analyzes Newman's attitudes toward humanity's innate need for religion. Contains a good bibliography.

Laurence W. Mazzeno, updated by Patrick S. Roberts

Isaac Newton

Newton pioneered the science of physics, developing three laws of mechanics and a theoretical basis for the concept of gravity. He also established the idea that nature is a divinely created and operated system based on mathematical reason and order.

Principal philosophical works: *Philosophiae naturalis principia mathematica*, 1687 (*The Mathematical Principles of Natural Philosophy*, 1729, best known as the *Principia*, 1848); *Opticks*, 1704; *Arithmetica universalis*, 1707 (*Universal Arithmetick*, 1720); *Analysis per quantitatum series, fluxiones, ad differentias: Cum enumeratione linearum tertii ordinis*, 1711 (includes *De analysi per aquationes infinitas*; *Fragmenta epistolarum*; *De quadratura curvarum*; *Enumeratio linearum tertii ordinis*; and *Methodus differentialis*); *The Chronology of Ancient Kingdoms Amended*, 1728; *Observations upon the Prophecies of Daniel and the Apocalypse of St. John*, 1733; *The Method of Fluxions and Infinite Series*, 1736.

Born: December 25, 1642 (new style, January 4, 1643); Woolsthorpe, near Colsterworth, Lincolnshire, England
Died: March 20, 1727 (new style, March 31, 1727); London, England

Early Life

Isaac Newton was born on Christmas Day, 1642, to a farmer and his wife, at Woolsthorpe, just south of Grantham in Lincolnshire. His father died shortly before Newton's birth, and when his mother remarried three years later, Newton remained at Woolsthorpe to be reared by his grandparents. He attended the grammar school in Grantham. His scientific aptitude appeared early when he began to construct mechanical toys and models, and aside from a brief period when his mother tried to persuade him to follow in his father's footsteps and become a farmer (it is said that Newton tended to read books rather than watch sheep, with disastrous results), his education continued, and he was accepted as an undergraduate at Trinity College, Cambridge, in 1661. Although his mother provided a small allowance, Newton had to wait on tables at college to help finance his studies. Even at that time, his fellow students remarked that he was silent and withdrawn, and indeed, Newton was, through-out his life, something of a recluse, shunning society. He never married, and some historians believe that Newton had homosexual leanings. Whatever the case, it is certain that he preferred work, study, experimentation, and observation, sometimes to the detriment of his own health, to social activity.

After returning to Grantham for a short time, while Cambridge was threatened by plague, Newton returned to the university as a don in 1667 with an established reputation for mathematical brilliance. Two early discoveries demonstrated his genius. Shortly after his graduation, he developed differential calculus, a mathematical device for calculating rates of change (for example, that of acceleration) that had long evaded other scholars. As a result, in 1669, he was offered the Lucasian Chair of Mathematics at Cambridge, a position he held until 1701.

Newton's second major contribution during this period was in the field of optics. His experiments with light had led him to build a reflecting telescope, the first one of its kind that actually worked. After further refinements, he presented it to the Royal Society, where he was asked to present a paper on his theory of light and colors. Shortly afterward, he was made a fellow of this august body, which contained all the prominent intellectuals of the day. Newton's paper offered new insights into the nature of color. While experimenting with prisms, Newton had discovered that white light is a mixture of all the colors of the rainbow and that the prism separates white light into its component parts. Newton's theory was controversial, provoking strong feelings at the Royal Society and initiating a lengthy dispute with scientist Robert Hooke concerning the nature of light. Hooke criticized Newton with such vehemence that Newton presented no more theories on the nature of light until 1704, after Hooke's death.

Life's Work

For a scientist such as Newton, the seventeenth century was an interesting period in which to work. Scientific theories were still dominated by the Aristotelian worldview, which had held sway for more than two thousand years, but cracks in

that outlook were beginning to appear. Galileo had shown that, in fact, the planets traveled around the Sun, which was positioned at the center of the universe, while Johannes Kepler had observed that this motion was regular and elliptic in nature. The task confronting scientists, in keeping with the aim of explaining the universe mathematically from first principles, was to find some logical reason for this phenomenon. Newton, among others, recognized that there had to be a set of universal rules governing motion, equally applicable to planetary and earthbound activity. His researches finally led him to a mathematical proof that the inverse square law of attraction between bodies regulates all motion. From this beginning, he was able to explain why planets travel in ellipses around the Sun, why Earth's tides move as they do, and why tennis balls, for example, follow the trajectories that they do. It also led him toward a notion of gravity that neatly tied his mathematics together. When Newton published this work, it led to another major confrontation with Hooke, who claimed that he had reached the proof of the inverse square law before Newton; the argument between the two was lengthy and acrimonious.

In 1684, Edmond Halley, then a young astronomer, went to Cambridge to visit Newton, who was reputed to be working in a similar field. There Halley found that Newton claimed that he had proved the inverse square law but had temporarily mislaid it. (Throughout his life, Newton worked on scraps of paper, keeping everything from first drafts to final copies, so this assertion has the ring of truth to it.) Halley was astounded: Here was a man who claimed to have solved the problem that was bothering many leading scientists of the day and he had not yet made it public. When Halley returned, Newton had found the proof, and Halley persuaded him to

Isaac Newton. *(Library of Congress)*

publish his nine-page demonstration of the law. Still, Halley was not satisfied. Realizing that Newton had more to offer the world, he prodded him into publishing a book of his theories. In 1687, the first book of Newton's famous *Principia* was published at Halley's expense, and a year later, the second and third books reached the public.

The *Principia* was a highly technical and mathematical work that many of Newton's contemporaries had difficulty in following, but its effect on the scientific community was profound. In it Newton outlined his three laws of motion. The first states that every body continues in a state of rest or motion in a straight line until it is acted on by a force to do otherwise. The second law states that the acceleration of a body is proportional to the force applied to it and inversely proportional to its mass. The third law, perhaps the most widely quoted, states that for every action there is an equal and opposite reaction. From these three fundamental laws, Newton went on to construct his theory of gravity—a force that acts at a distance between two or more bodies, causing an attraction between them that is in inverse proportion to the distance between them.

Newton's theories were a major challenge to the dominant worldview, constructing the world, as they did, purely from mechanics. His theories seemed revolutionary and initiated a great debate that continued for the better part of a century after the *Principia* was first published. When they were eventually accepted as a correct description of nature, Newtonian science formed the basis of modern thinking until the twentieth century, when Albert Einstein's theories turned the world upside down again.

Writing the *Principia* dominated Newton's life; he became completely obsessed with the project, often forgetting to eat or even to sleep while he continued working. Despite his reclusive tendencies, in 1687 Newton entered the public arena. Cambridge University and James II, king of England, a Catholic, were in the middle of a battle over religion. The university had refused to grant a degree to a Benedictine monk and the officials of the university, including Newton, were summoned to appear before the infamous Judge George Jeffreys. Shortly after-

ward, Newton was elected the member of Parliament for Cambridge. Newton's entrance into politics was less than world-shattering; it is said that he spoke only once during his term of office and that was to ask an usher to open a window.

In 1693, he suffered a mental breakdown about which little is known, and he withdrew into his solitary state. Two years later, he returned to public office when he was asked to take over the wardenship of the Mint. There was to be a major reissue of coinage because of the increasingly pressing problem of clipped gold and silver coins. New coins needed to be minted with milled edges, and scientists were pressed into service to aid the process. Newton discovered a hitherto unrecognized penchant for administration and proved himself a highly able bureaucrat, being promoted to master of the Mint in 1699. In 1701, he was reelected to Parliament and continued in the public eye for the remainder of his life.

Until his death in 1727, honors were heaped on Newton, as befitted the most prominent scientist of his generation. In 1703, he was elected president of the Royal Society and was annually reelected to that post for the following twenty-five years. He moved to London and became more sociable but nevertheless earned a reputation for being cantankerous and ill-tempered. In 1704, Newton published a tract about the theories of light that he had earlier expounded to the Royal Society. It was more readable than the *Principia* and gained a wider audience. A year later, he was knighted by Queen Anne. Meanwhile, the *Principia* was proving to be a best-seller, as everyone wanted to read the theories that were pushing back the frontiers of contemporary science, and its second and third editions were published during Newton's lifetime.

Newton's work in the last years of his life, apart from another acrimonious dispute—this time with the German philosopher Gottfried Wilhelm Leibniz about who had first discovered differential calculus—was mainly religious. Newton spent hours attempting to understand the messages hidden in the Book of Revelation, seeing this task as simply another aspect of the search for truth as revealed in God's works, both written and created. Thus, in the end, Newton proved himself to be a medieval thinker despite his work laying the basis for contemporary scientific thought.

Influence

Newton made an outstanding contribution to the modernization of the scientific worldview. He followed in the footsteps of Nicolaus Copernicus, Galileo, Kepler, and others in asserting that the heavens and earth were part of one solar system (not separated as they are in Aristotelian philosophy), with the Sun at the center. Newton further developed the method of observation and experiment that had established itself in the seventeenth century by carefully checking and rechecking his work and by creating experimental verifications of his various theories. Most important, he demonstrated that a mechanical description of the world that seeks to explain matter and motion in terms of mathematics was possible. With the *Principia*, Newton effectively sounded the death knell of the old description of the universe and laid the basis for a modern approach. His was, perhaps, the greatest individual contribution to a rich and innovative period of scientific development.

Sally Hibbin

Principia

Type of philosophy: Metaphysics, philosophy of mathematics, philosophy of science

First published: Philosophiae naturalis principia mathematica, 1687 (*The Mathematical Principles of Natural Philosophy*, 1729; best known as the *Principia*, 1848)

Principal ideas advanced:

◇ The mechanical universe obeys a single set of laws that can be derived mathematically from experiment and observation.

◇ The laws of motion describe the influence of forces on objects.

◇ The law of gravitation describes the motion of the earth and all celestial bodies in the universe.

◇ Although the mechanical universe can be described in terms of mathematical laws, it

was created by and is controlled by divine influence.

In the summer of 1684, the astronomer Edmond Halley asked Isaac Newton for his thoughts on planetary motion. Newton's response, based on his early mathematical calculations, was that the planets would travel around the Sun in elliptical paths. Some months later, Newton provided Halley with a written mathematical proof of his prediction. At Halley's request, Newton then set about to further explain the forces of nature that governed the motion of objects, including the movement of celestial bodies. By July 5, 1687, the results of this work appeared as the first edition of Newton's *Principia*.

Newton was totally absorbed in the writing of the *Principia* for eighteen months. He would frequently forget to eat and slept only when overcome with exhaustion. Although it is not without errors, it has often been said that the *Principia* is the greatest work of science ever published. However, without considerable mathematical skills, it is difficult to follow and virtually impossible to comprehend. In addition to its complex mathematical language, the *Principia* was written in Latin (and not translated into English until two years after Newton's death). By writing for an elite audience, Newton hoped he would be spared the annoyance of debating his work with those of lesser education. Nevertheless, its influence on the scientific revolution of the seventeenth century was crucial in overturning the prevailing philosophers' view of the universe forever.

Newton divided the *Principia* into three books. In books 1 and 2, Newton describes the motions of bodies and outlines his mathematical treatments of both terrestrial and celestial mechanics. Book 1 contains almost one hundred propositions in which Newton develops a general theory of motion, including the motion of celestial bodies such as the planets. He describes how objects behave when subjected to forces. Book 2 examines resisted motions and the influence of fluids on a body's motion (for example, the effect of air resistance on a moving object). Newton's conclusion—that planetary motion is not impeded by any fluid object in space—was a departure from the long-held philosophical belief that a fluid substance, called ether, permeated space and affected the motion of heavenly bodies. In book 3, Newton uses his mathematical concepts from the first two books to describe his system of the world. He discusses the law of gravitation, tidal motion, and comet theory and calculates the speed of sound. Throughout the work, Newton relies on experiments and observations, both his and others' to derive his mathematical laws.

Motion and Forces

The *Principia* opens with a series of definitions and laws, which are followed by numerous explanatory notes and comments (scholia and corollaries). Included in these laws are Newton's three laws of motion: First, every body will continue in its state of rest or uniform motion in a straight line unless it is compelled to change its state by an external force impressed on it (law of inertia); second, a change of motion is always proportional to the force being applied to the body and the new motion will be in the straight line in which the force is impressed; and third, for every action there is always an equal and opposite reaction. From these laws, Newton developed his law of universal gravitation.

Mechanics is the branch of applied mathematics that deals with the motion of objects, and it had advanced considerably by the seventeenth century. However, the field of dynamics, which explains how forces influence motion, was not well understood until Newton introduced his laws of motion in the *Principia*. Of particular interest to Newton were forces that resulted in an object traveling in a circular (or near circular) motion because this represented the path traveled by the orbiting planets. Newton used the word "centripetal," meaning "seeking the center," to characterize forces involved in circular motion. He also recognized the significance of conic paths to describe the motion of a moving object with respect to a fixed point. The conic path is a curve obtained by cutting a plane through a right circular cone. Depending on where the cutting plane is located on the cone, the curved path may be a circle, ellipse, or hyperbola. His detailed account of conic properties enabled him to mathematically describe the orbits of celestial bodies. Planets, and moons around planets, had elliptical paths and would

never trace the exact orbit twice. Comets could have elliptical paths and therefore would reappear at regular intervals, whereas those with hyperbolic paths would not. Lack of experimental data prevented Newton from satisfactorily describing the motion of the Moon or of the moons of Saturn.

Newton's law of gravitation had important applications. The law describes the force between two objects and states that the force of gravity is always equal to the constant of acceleration times the product of the masses of the two attracting bodies divided by the square of the distance separating them. Therefore, the gravitational force between two objects increases as the mass of the objects increases and as the distance between objects decreases. Although the distance between Earth and the Moon is large, compared to terrestrial distances, their enormous masses generate strong gravitational forces. Therefore, Earth attracts the Moon, which causes it to maintain its orbit. At the same time, the Moon attracts Earth, a fact that Newton claimed was illustrated by the existence of tidal motion on Earth. Newton also explained that the gaseous atmosphere was held to the earth by the gravitational force, and he was able to show that air density decreased with elevation above sea level.

The *Principia* also contained Newton's mathematical treatment of hydraulics. Hydraulic machinery and hydraulic engineering rely on the motion of a fluid through a vessel (for example, water or air through a pipe or tube). Although there were errors in Newton's results, he did succeed in estimating the speed of sound in air, which was a remarkable achievement for seventeenth century science. He also described the ballistic curve (a path formed by a moving projectile such as a missile or ball traveling through air) as having the form of a distorted hyperbola.

A Perfect Universe and Mathematics

Despite his attempts to quantify the mechanical universe and his belief in the absolute nature of space and time, Newton was convinced that the perfection of nature was a reflection of its creation by a divine being: God being perfect would not create an imperfect universe. It was necessary, however, for God to intervene from time to time to maintain the stability and hence perfection of his creation. Natural philosophers attempted to deduce causes from their observed effects and, through reductionism, attempted to find the original cause that Newton believed would be divine rather than mechanical.

Although the *Principia* is a complex mathematical work, Newton's ideas transcended science. In philosophy, religion, and law, the results of the *Principia* contributed to the so-called Age of Enlightenment. It became a common, but erroneous, belief that new laws of mathematics would eventually be discovered and that these would permit anything to be calculated in the future. This was not an unreasonable assumption, because astronomers could use mathematics to predict even the future position of the Moon. Early twentieth century science discovered limitations to Newton's laws. The laws could not be applied accurately to interactions on the atomic scale or for the motion of objects traveling at near the speed of light. They also broke down between objects separated by large distances such as those that exist between galaxies.

The definitions, principles, and propositions contained in the *Principia* enabled scientists to take an entirely new approach to the study of nature and laid the foundations for modern physics and astronomy. The *Principia* began to be viewed as a work of modern science rather than as a work in philosophy soon after it was published. Newton's method of studying science, which was a combination of mathematical calculations, observation, and experimentation, came to be accepted as the standard approach for scientific investigation. From the *Principia* came an understanding of the science of mechanics, which in turn led to the development of practical and useful applications for commercial and industrial development. The motion of a baseball in flight, the movement of water through dams, and the paths of spacecraft and satellites launched from Earth are all examples illustrating the validity of Newton's laws.

Nicholas C. Thomas

Additional Reading

Brewster, Sir David. *Memoirs of the Life, Writings, and Discoveries of Sir Isaac Newton*. Edinburgh, Scotland: T. Constable, 1855. A classic two-volume biography pieced together from Sir Isaac Newton's private papers. A bit dated and ignores Newton's work on religion and alchemy.

Chappell, Vere, ed. *Seventeenth-Century Natural Scientists*. Vol. 7 in *Essays on Early Modern Philosophers*. New York: Garland, 1992. Part of a twelve-volume set of scholarly essays on seventeenth century philosophers in Europe. Contains six articles on Newton.

Christianson, Gale E. *In the Presence of the Creator: Isaac Newton and His Times*. New York: Free Press, 1984. This very readable biography places Newton's life in the context of the scientific revolution.

Cohen, I. B. *The Newtonian Revolution in Science and Its Intellectual Significance*. Norwalk, Conn.: Burndy Library, 1987. An important work by a leading Newton scholar.

De Gandt, Francois. *Force and Geometry in Newton's "Principia."* Translated by Curtis Wilson. Princeton, N.J.: Princeton University Press, 1995. An introduction to Newton's *Principia*.

Dobbs, Betty Jo Teeter. *The Janus Faces of Genius: The Role of Alchemy in Newton's Thought*. Cambridge, England: Cambridge University Press, 1992. Dobbs argues that Newton's primary goal was to establish a unified system that included both natural and divine principles. Special attention is given to alchemy.

Goldish, Matt. *Judaism in the Theology of Sir Isaac Newton*. Boston: Kluwer, 1998. An analysis of Newton's historical theology and how Newton's interest in Jewish studies greatly impacted all areas of his theology.

Hall, A. Rupert. *Isaac Newton: Eighteenth Century Perspectives*. New York: Oxford University Press, 1999. A compilation of five early eighteenth century biographies of Newton. Each biography is accompanied by a commentary. A bibliography of Newton's works is included.

Koyre, Alexandre. *Newtonian Studies*. Cambridge, Mass.: Harvard University Press, 1965. A collection of philosophical and historical essays on Newton.

Manuel, Frank E. *A Portrait of Isaac Newton*. Cambridge, Mass.: Harvard University Press, 1968. This work examines Newton's life and work in the context of Newton's papers and contemporary thinking about the methods and development of science.

Wallis, Peter, and Ruth Wallis. *Newton and Newtonia, 1672-1975*. Folkestone, England: Dawson, 1977. An exhaustive bibliography of works by and about Newton.

Westfall, Richard S. *Never at Rest: A Biography of Isaac Newton*. Cambridge, England: Cambridge University Press, 1980. This biography presents Newton's scientific discoveries in the context of his life. Includes a valuable bibliographical essay and an appendix. More than nine hundred pages.

_____. *The Life of Isaac Newton*. New York: Cambridge University Press, 1993. A condensed version of *Never at Rest*.

Sally Hibbin, updated by Tammy Nyden-Bullock

Nicholas of Cusa

Nicholas of Cusa contributed to preserving the hierarchical authority and unity of the Roman Catholic Church while advocating humanism and lay participation in both sacred and secular government during the early years of the Renaissance.

Principal philosophical works: *De concordantia catholica*, 1433; *De docta ignorantia*, 1440 (*Of Learned Ignorance*, 1954); *De coniecturis*, 1442.

Born: 1401; Kues, Upper Lorraine
Died: August 11, 1464; Todi, Papal States

Early Life

Nicholas Kryfts (Krebs) was born in the village of Kues, between Trier and Bernkastel, on the Mosel River in the German Rhineland. His moderately prosperous father operated a barge on the busy river, which served as a major commercial waterway in Northern Europe. Young Nicholas was first sent to a school administered by the Brothers of the Common Life at Deventer on the Lower Rhine. Nicholas was inspired by the new learning that the brothers emphasized, and they also encouraged him in a spirit of church reform centered on the idea of the Roman Church as a community of clergy and faithful.

In 1416, at the age of fifteen, Nicholas registered at the University of Heidelberg. Although Nicholas remained at Heidelberg for only one year, there, too, he was exposed to modern learning. Nominalistic philosophy—rejection of universals as myths and a turn toward philosophizing based on individualism—left its mark on young Nicholas. He began to question truths arrived at through pure deduction and based on traditional authority. The Scholasticism of the late Middle Ages was giving way to a humanistic thinking in both theology and philosophy.

Nicholas of Cusa (also known by his Latin name, Nicolaus Cusanus, and German name, Nikolaus von Cusa) next enrolled at the University of Padua in Italy. Padua was a major center for the study of canon law in Europe. In its lecture halls, scholars of science, mathematics, astronomy, and the humanities rigorously challenged established sacred and secular dogma. Yet the revival of Neoplatonism, which envisioned a hierarchy of knowledge extending from a perfect and infinite God to an imperfect and finite world, also played a crucial role in Nicholas's education. It was at Padua that young Nicholas had an opportunity to observe firsthand the government of Roman city-states, many of which inherited the idea of citizen participation from Greek antiquity. Nicholas studied at Padua for six years, earning a doctorate in canon law in 1423.

Nicholas's early education shaped his later life's work within the Roman Catholic Church; it reflected the change in worldview in the transition years from the late Middle Ages to the early Renaissance years. The medieval notion that God governed the world through unchallenged hierarchical authority was tempered by growing acknowledgment that the Creator provided all his creatures with freedom and responsibility, subject to divine judgment. The dialectic of God's transcendence and his immanence in the world dominated the thought and life of Nicholas of Cusa; he sought in his philosophy and in his daily life to reconcile these views of God and world.

Life's Work

Nicholas of Cusa returned to Germany in 1425 to embark on his life's work as papal diplomat, theologian, and philosopher. At first he enrolled at the University of Cologne to lecture and to continue his research. There he attracted the attention of Cardinal Giordano Orsini, who was impressed by a legal document prepared by Nicholas at his request. Cardinal Orsini was a noted humanist and progressive within the Roman Church; he played an important role in Nicholas's ordination as a priest in 1426. Orsini's influence was also instrumental in securing an appointment for Nicholas as a legal adviser to the Council of Basel in 1432.

Nicholas's career in church politics began in earnest at the Council of Basel. The debate centered on the issue of the pope's authority. Nicholas sided with those who believed that the Roman Church ought to be governed by a general council representing clergy and congregations. The council was to be superior to the pope, who would remain the Church's religious and administrative head but who could be discharged by the council. Nicholas's conviction was that it was through conciliar government that church unity would be best preserved. The congregation ought to be the source of church law, with pope and hierarchy serving the general council.

Nicholas expanded his thinking on church government in a philosophical treatise. This work, *De concordantia catholica* (on Catholic unity), sets forth what has been called the conciliar theory of government, based on Nicholas's belief that authority of the ruler must rest on

Nicholas of Cusa. *(Alinari/Art Resource, NY)*

consent granted by the ruled. His main thesis was that this governmental form would bring about unity within the Church.

The controversy over conciliar government continued after the Council of Basel. Subsequently, Nicholas of Cusa modified his antipapal stance. Three reasons have been offered to explain this turnabout. First, Nicholas was displeased with the turmoil between members of the council and the Holy See. Second, Nicholas's highest priority was church unity. Finally, Nicholas was motivated by the opportunities for his own career within the Church hierarchy.

Nicholas was rewarded with a papal appointment. In 1437, Nicholas was a delegate to a meeting between the Roman and Eastern Orthodox Christians in Constantinople. At the meeting, he invited Greek representatives to attend a scheduled council in Italy on reunification of the Greek and Roman churches. Although his efforts failed, Christian unity and reform continued to motivate Nicholas throughout his life, in his dealings with church politics as well as in his philosophical writings.

Nicholas continued to accept diplomatic posts from the Vatican. From 1438 to 1448, he was a papal delegate to Germany, where he worked for both reform and unity within the Church. As a reward, in 1449, Pope Nicholas V made Nicholas of Cusa a cardinal of the titular Church of Saint Peter in Chains in Rome. In 1450, he was named Bishop of Brixen, in Austria. During his tenure as bishop, Nicholas encountered the growing conflict between the Church and secular politics. It was a difficult phase in his life.

His later years were spent in a bitter struggle with the secular ruler of Austria, Archduke Sigismund. Nicholas set out to reform corrupt practices among the priests and monks of his diocese, but his efforts met with apathy and hostility among the clergy. At one point, he sought to reform a convent at Sonneburg, and there Bishop Nicholas ran into bitter opposition from secular authorities because many of the nuns had been recruited from noble families. Archduke Sigismund assumed the role of protector of the nuns.

Added to this controversy was one that concerned ecclesiastical appointments. Sigismund was unhappy over several of Nicholas's choices for church posts; the bishop had bypassed candidates supported by the duke. Open conflict between the bishop and the duke resulted in negotiations, appeals to the Vatican, and, ultimately, compromise. Nicholas was recalled in 1459 to Rome.

As a reward for his services to the Holy See, Nicholas was appointed to the high post of vicar-general for temporal affairs; he was Governor of Rome and the papal territories. It was Nicholas of Cusa's last and highest office. Unfortunately, Cardinal Cusa was not freed from conflict with the Austrian duke. Now the controversy turned into a dispute between Sigismund and the Church over certain property rights in Austria. Claims and counterclaims intensified.

On one occasion, the duke's soldiers surrounded and fired their guns on a castle in Austria in which Nicholas was temporarily residing as the pope's representative in the dispute. The cardinal surrendered and was put under house arrest. Pope Pius II, humiliated by this treatment of his representative, intervened directly and sought to punish the duke. Nicholas was extricated from the affair. He returned to Italy to live his final days in relative peace and contemplation.

During his many years of church diplomacy, Nicholas of Cusa continued his theological and philosophical research and writing. He wrote about forty-six books and manuscripts. In addition, he was an enthusiastic collector of literary and philosophical works. His two most influential works are *Of Learned Ignorance* and *De coniecturis* (on conjecture); together they make up a complete outline of his philosophy.

In *Of Learned Ignorance*, Nicholas sets forth the doctrine that humanity knows God only through whatever God chooses to reveal and through human experience. Human reason reaches its limitations in its knowledge of God, for humanity is finite and God is infinite. Reason is applicable to this finite world, but it is a stumbling block to knowing God. People will be the more learned the more they grasp their own ignorance of the unknown God. The infinite God is not accessible through reason, but his awareness is present in people's minds. Through humanity's recognition of reason's limits, a realization that is itself reached through reason, the wisdom of learned ignorance is achieved. For Nicholas's speculative metaphysics, humanity's highest stage of knowledge is the recognition that one cannot attain a comprehensive knowledge of God.

In *De coniecturis*, Nicholas expands his philosophy of learned ignorance. Here Nicholas argues that God is prior to the opposition of being and nonbeing. God is unity transcending the coincidence of all opposites; he transcends and confines in himself all distinctions and oppositions. God is thus the unity of opposites, of the finite and the infinite. He transcends humanity's understanding, and thus people cannot form a full and accurate concept of his nature. God transcends the world, but the world is his mirror. God is the unity of world and cosmos. These statements lead into Nicholas's theology, which concludes that because God is beyond human intellect, learned ignorance opens the way to Christian faith.

Nicholas of Cusa died in 1464. He is buried in the Church of Saint Peter in Chains in Rome. Inside the church is a statue of Nicholas kneeling before Saint Peter. His best monument, however, is the home and hospital for the poor that he and his family founded in his native Kues. The attached library contains many of Nicholas's original manuscripts and his collection of books. It remains in operation as a center for scholarly research.

Influence

Nicholas of Cusa is an outstanding example of a philosopher who was active in practical affairs; he combined a life of contemplation with one of action. Throughout his life, Nicholas attempted to resolve the conflict between old and new views of God and humankind while he remained an obedient member of the church hierarchy. His later writings and practical work reflected his moderation: He sought reform within the context of order and continuation. In philosophy and ecclesiastical politics, Nicholas advocated gradual development and progress, not rebellion and revolution. Nicholas lived his life according to the fundamental principles of his thought and remains an exemplar of the unity of thought and practice in a human being's life. As such, his life captured the spirit of the Golden Rule. Above all, Nicholas's life reflected his deep devotion to the ideal of the unity of all being in God, of harmony

between reason and faith, theology and philosophy, and church and state.

Scholars do not agree on whether Nicholas of Cusa was the first modern thinker or a transitional figure standing between the Middle Ages and the Renaissance. It is clear that he combined traditional elements of Neoplatonism and the Scholastic tradition with postmedieval nominalism and humanism. Evidence is inconclusive as to whether Nicholas contributed original ideas or dressed the thought of Plato, Saint Augustine, and others in the modes of his era. It is certain, however, that Nicholas of Cusa must be included in any list of the world's great philosophers. He forged a speculative metaphysics that influenced Gottfried Wilhelm Leibniz, Georg Wilhelm Friedrich Hegel, Martin Heidegger, and the existential philosophers. Nicholas's philosophical legacy remains his enduring contribution to Western civilization.

Gil L. Gunderson

Of Learned Ignorance

Type of philosophy: Metaphysics, philosophical theology

First transcribed: De docta ignorantia, 1440 (English translation, 1954)

Principal ideas advanced:

◇ God is the absolute maximum and the absolute minimum; he is in all things, and all things are in him.

◇ If people make their own ignorance the object of their desire for knowledge, they can acquire a learned ignorance; although God cannot be comprehended, some knowledge of him can be acquired by reflection on one's limitations.

◇ The absolute maximum (God) is absolute unity, for unity is the minimum (and God is the absolute minimum); God, as a unity excluding degrees of more or less, is infinite unity.

◇ The visible world is a reflection of the invisible; people mirror the eternal and the infinite by their conjectures.

◇ God is best studied through the use of mathematical symbols.

◇ In the Providence of God, contradictories are reconciled.

◇ The world is the absolute effect of the absolute maximum; it is a relative unity.

◇ Jesus is the maximum at once absolute and restricted; he is both God and humanity brought to perfection.

Nicholas of Cusa was both a man of action and a man of speculation. He spent his years in the Roman Catholic Church working for the cause of reform and ecclesiastical diplomacy; he was a Cardinal and Bishop of Brixen. As a metaphysical theologian, he synthesized the ideas of such predecessors as Johannes Scotus Erigena, Meister Eckhart, and pseudo-Dionysius the Areopagite. His work had a considerable influence on Giordano Bruno, particularly on the latter's *De la causa, principio e uno* (1584; *Concerning the Cause, Principle, and One*, 1950).

Of Learned Ignorance, Nicholas's most important treatise, is particularly interesting as an attempt to reconcile the Neoplatonic ideas prevalent in the Middle Ages with the growing confidence in empirical inquiry and the use of the intellect. The reconciliation is only partly successful from the logical point of view, and it involves an appeal to the revelatory power of mystical intuition. However, for those who sought to understand the possibility of unifying an infinite God and an apparently finite universe and who were disturbed by their learned ignorance, the efforts of Nicholas of Cusa were a godsend.

The work is divided into three books and is unified by a concern with the *maximum*, the greatest. The first book is a study of the "absolute maximum," or God, the being who is greatest in the sense that he is one and all—all things are in God, and God is in all things. Nicholas describes this study as one "above reason," and as one that "cannot be conducted on the lines of human comprehension." The second book is concerned with the maximum effect of the absolute maximum. The maximum effect is the universe, a plurality that is, nevertheless, a relative unity. The third book is devoted to the maximum that is both relative and absolute, the perfect realization of the finite plurality of the universe; this maximum is Jesus.

A Learned Ignorance

Nicholas begins his work by explaining that people have a natural desire for knowledge but are frustrated in their desire to know by the enduring fact of their own ignorance. People strive to understand what is not understandable—for example, the infinite as infinite, which is beyond comparison. The only solution, then, is for people to seek to know their own ignorance, even as Socrates advised. If people make their own ignorance the object of their desire for knowledge, they can acquire a learned ignorance. The suggestion is that from reflecting on their limitations people can, in knowledge, surmount their own ignorance, at least to some extent.

Finite intellects proceed by comparisons, according to Nicholas; and it is on that account that the Pythagoreans came close to the truth in saying that it is by numbers that all things are understood. However, if the effort is to understand the absolute infinite, the means of comparison will not work, for the absolute infinite is beyond comparison. To realize that the quiddity of things, the absolute "whatness" of them, is beyond our intellects—and that, in regard to the truth about ultimate being, one must be ignorant—is to draw closer to truth.

The Absolute Maximum

If one cannot comprehend the absolute maximum (which is God), then what is the point of working out the implications of the conception of the absolute maximum? Nicholas argues that although one cannot comprehend the absolute maximum, one can have some knowledge about it. One can know, for example, that the precise nature of the absolute maximum is beyond one's powers of understanding. However, there is more than that which one can know.

One can also know that the absolute maximum is also the absolute minimum. Nicholas proves this point in an engaging and simple argument: "By definition the minimum is that which cannot be less than it is; and since that is also true of the maximum, it is evident that the minimum is identified with the maximum." There is another good reason for supposing that the maximum and the minimum are synonymous: Because the absolute maximum is actually all that it can be, it is both as great as it can be and as small as it can be. Because it is the absolute, it can be absolutely minimum as well as absolutely maximum, and because it can be, it is. Furthermore, the maximum considered in itself, not as the maximum of a certain matter or quantity, is the infinite. However, so is the minimum. Because both the maximum and the minimum are the infinite, they are one. The maximum is absolute unity, for unity is the smallest number, or the minimum; God is a unity that "excludes degrees of 'more' or 'less,'" and is, consequently, an infinite unity.

Nicholas introduces his version of the cosmological argument: Finite beings are effects that could not have produced themselves; therefore, there must be an absolute maximum, not itself dependent on causes, without which nothing else could exist.

The conception of the Trinity is introduced by an elaboration of the Pythagorean idea that unity is a trinity. Diversity involves unity (two, for example, is two ones); inequality depends on equality (and, therefore, on unity); and connection depends on unity, for division is a duality or involves duality. Diversity, inequality, and division necessarily involve unity, equality, and connection; and the latter three are all unities, but unity is one. Unity is a trinity, since unity means nondivision, distinction, and connection.

The Line, the Triangle, and the Circle

According to Nicholas of Cusa, the visible world is a reflection of the invisible. By the use of conjectural images, people can, at least to some extent, mirror the eternal and infinite. The images most helpful to people are mathematical images, for, as Pythagoras pointed out, "the key to all truth [is] to be found in numbers."

The symbols that Nicholas found most useful in suggesting the nature of the absolute maximum are the line, the triangle, and the circle. An infinite line, according to Nicholas, would be at once a straight line, a triangle, a circle, and a sphere. He argues, for example, that as the circumference of a circle increases, the line becomes less curved; and he concludes that the circumference of the absolutely greatest possible circle would be absolutely straight, the smallest possible curve. (Although logically there is an essential difference between a curve, however slight,

and a straight line, Nicholas's figure, considered as a metaphor, achieves the purpose of suggesting that entities disparate in character are nevertheless such that, when taken to infinity, they are indistinguishable.)

A finite line can be used to form a triangle, he argues, by keeping one end fixed and moving the line to one side. (Actually, the figure so formed is not a triangle, but a segment of a circle, a pie-shaped segment.) If one continues the movement of the line (so that it functions as an infinite number of radii), the figure formed is a circle. Half a circle, if turned in three dimensions on its axis, forms a sphere.

An infinite triangle would have three infinitely long sides; infinitely extended, the triangle would finally be indistinguishable from a line. Such a triangle would have three lines in one and in that respect would resemble the infinite absolute maximum (God). Apparently Nicholas conceived of a triangle's sides as increasing and its base angles, say, as becoming more acute and the apex as becoming more and more obtuse, until finally there would be no triangle distinguishable from a straight line. However, he need not have conceived of it this way. He could have conceived of a triangle expanding while its angles remain constant. Part of Nicholas's argument, however, depends on the assumption that there cannot be more than one infinite. To maintain this point involves a peculiar use of the term "infinite."

Having demonstrated to his satisfaction that an infinite line is a triangle, a circle, and a sphere, Nicholas develops the image to suggest by analogy the relationship of the absolute maximum to all things: The infinite line is to lines what the absolute maximum is to things. The analogy is developed at great length, but the most important features are these: An infinite line is not divisible; it is immutable and eternal. Oddly, it shares its essential features with finite lines—for finite lines, for example, cannot be divided into anything other than lines and are, in that sense, indivisible. Just as the essence of an infinite line is the essence of all finite lines, so the essence of the absolute maximum is the essence of everything. This point is developed by reference to beings who have only a participation in being. Because the essence of such beings is the essence of the absolute maximum, once the feature of participation is eliminated, the distinction between beings that participate in being and the being in which they participate disappears.

Again, by mathematical analogy, Nicholas argues that there could not be four or more divine persons; there must be a trinity. A four-sided figure is not the smallest, simplest measure of things, as is the triangle. A circle, having neither beginning nor end, being perfect, possessing unity, and so forth, is an ideal figure of the divine. Nicholas thus comes to one of his characteristic contentions: "In the Providence of God contradictories are reconciled." God's providence includes all that shall be together with all that shall not be. God has foreknowledge of everything, for he foresees opposites. The absolute maximum is in all beings, and all beings are in it.

By the analogy of the infinite sphere, Nicholas argues that God is the "one infinitely simple, essential explanation of the entire universe." He is the final cause of everything, the determiner both of existence and of end. All names attributed to the infinite absolute maximum are anthropomorphic; none is adequate as a name, for God is beyond distinctions.

Infinity and Unity

Because God is ineffable, negative propositions are truer than affirmative ones. It is better to count on learned ignorance, as enlightened by God, than to count on positive knowledge. Nicholas proceeds, in the second book, to demonstrate the absolute effect of the absolute maximum. The unity and infinity of the universe are shown to be a consequence of that infinitude of matter that arises from its incapacity to be greater than it is. Because God is not jealous, because the essence of every created thing is his essence, and because he is essentially perfect, every thing is, in its way, perfect. The universe (and everything in it) is a principle and a maximum but in a restricted sense. The absolute maximum brings the universe into existence by emanation (a timeless outpouring of its essential nature).

Thus, everything is in everything, as the philosopher Anaxagoras said. Because God is in all things by medium of the universe, "all is in all, and each in each." Of course, the universe is in each thing only in a contracted or restricted manner; in fact, the universe is contracted, in each

thing, to whatever the thing is. The unity of the universe, which comes from the absolute unity of God, is a unity in plurality and is not an absolute but a relative unity. The universe is also a trinity as well as a unity, but just as it is a relative unity, so it is a relative or contracted trinity. The unity of the universe is a trinity in the sense that contraction involves a limitable object, a limiting principle, and a connection—or potency, act, and the nexus.

There are four modes of being: the absolute necessity, or God; the mode of being of things according to natural necessity or order; the mode of being of individuals; and the mode of being of that which is possible.

The soul of the world is a universal form that contains all forms, but it has only a contracted existence; forms are actual only in the word of God. However, it is possible to use the term "soul" in such a way that the soul and God are one. Every possibility is contained in the Absolute Possibility, God; every form (or act) in the Absolute Form, the Son of God; and every connecting harmony in the Absolute Connection of the Holy Spirit. The Father is potency; the Son, act; and the Holy Ghost, connecting movement. Thus, God, who is unity as well as trinity, is the efficient, formal, and final cause of all things; and the movements of the earth and stars are attributable to him, who is the center and circumference. In reflecting on the world and on the wonder of its arrangement, one cannot hope to understand God's reasons; but in the wonder of him and in one's learned ignorance one finds intimations of his light.

Jesus Christ is "the maximum at once absolute and restricted," and to the defense and clarification of this description, Nicholas devotes the third book. Human nature is peculiarly suited to provide God with the possibility of a maximum that reconciles the infinite and the finite by being at once absolute and contracted. As sensible and intellectual, human nature is a microcosm, a world in miniature. Unlike other things that, raised to perfection, could easily become greater because of the inferiority of their natures, humanity is such that, if perfected, reveals the nature of all things as perfected. By joining the nature of humanity to the divine nature, God made possible the union of the absolute maximum and the nature of all things. In Jesus, God is both God and humanity.

The remainder of Nicholas's work is a defense, in terms of his mystical metaphysics, of familiar dogmas: that Christ was conceived of the Holy Ghost and born of the Virgin Mary, that he was resurrected after the Crucifixion, that he ascended into heaven, that he is the judge of the living and the dead, that he redeemed all humankind. In this account, Jesus is God utilizing the nature of humanity and bringing it to perfection; Jesus is humanity made perfect in the image and essence of God. Because of Jesus, the Church comes into being, the fullest possible realization of the unity of the many "with the preservation of the personal reality of each, without confusion of natures or degrees." Additionally, by Jesus, the union of the subjects and the Church is resolved into the divine unity. Thus, for Nicholas of Cusa, as for Bruno, God is the cause, the principle, and the One.

Ian P. McGreal

Additional Reading

Bett, Henry. *Nicholas of Cusa*. London: Methuen, 1932. Standard biography, presenting a detailed account of Nicholas of Cusa's life coupled with a discussion of his writings and a critique of his philosophy. Stresses the consistency of Nicholas's thought throughout his political, philosophical, and theological writings; this thought culminates in the unity of all existence in the hidden God.

Cassirer, Ernst. *The Individual and the Cosmos in Renaissance Philosophy*. Translated with an introduction by Mario Domandi. Oxford: Basil Blackwell, 1963. Argues that Nicholas was a systematic thinker who presented a totally new philosophical orientation and that early modern philosophy cannot be understood without considering Nicholas's work. Nicholas offered the foundations for a new theory of knowledge and history; his greatness is enhanced because he achieved this major contribution to Renaissance philosophy from within the religious ideas of the Middle Ages. For the advanced reader.

Christianson, Gerald, and Thomas M. Izbicki, eds. *Nicholas of Cusa on Christ and the Church: Essays in Memory of Chandler McCuskey Brooks for the American Cusanus Society*. New York: Brill, 1996. These volumes include studies on Nicholas of Cusa and his times. A section is devoted to Nicholas' ideas on mystical experience and Christ.

Copleston, Frederick Charles. "Nicholas of Cusa." In *A History of Philosophy*, vol. 3. London: Burnes, Oates and Washbourne, 1946. 3d ed. Garden City, N.Y.: Doubleday, 1985. Chapter 15 is a concise treatment of Nicholas of Cusa's philosophy from the perspective of the contemporary Roman Catholic Church. Copleston's theme is that Nicholas's work and writings aimed at reconciliation, harmony, and unity in difference.

Hopkins, Jasper. *A Concise Introduction to the Philosophy of Nicholas of Cusa*. 3d ed. Minneapolis, Minn.: Arthur J. Banning Press, 1986. Includes Nicholas's "De possest" (1460; "On Actualized Possibility," 1978) in Latin and English. Hopkins contends that this short essay contains an excellent summation of Nicholas of Cusa's philosophy and recommends that students begin here. The long introductory interpretation and extensive bibliography serve as useful reader's guides.

Jaspers, Karl. "Nicholas of Cusa." In *The Great Philosophers*. Vol. 2, edited by Hannah Arendt and translated by Ralph Mannheim. New York: Harcourt, Brace and World, 1966. After a brief biography, Jaspers conducts a detailed analysis of key concepts in Nicholas's writings, considered from the perspective of Jaspers's own existentialist philosophy. He finds Nicholas's major contribution to have been keeping alive the idea of individual freedom in human relations and in relation to God. Accessible to undergraduates.

Nicholas of Cusa. *Unity and Reform: Selected Writings of Nicholas de Cusa*. Edited with an introduction by John P. Dolan. Notre Dame, Ind.: University of Notre Dame Press, 1962. Selected excerpts from Nicholas's major philosophical and theological writings. Text is supplemented by the editor's informative introduction, which serves as an excellent reader's guide.

Sigmund, Paul E. *Nicholas of Cusa and Medieval Political Thought*. Cambridge, Mass.: Harvard University Press, 1963. Concentrates on Nicholas's political theory, emphasizing the foundational principles of universal harmony and government by consent. Traces the philosophical and legal antecedents of Nicholas's political philosophy. Good bibliography of secondary sources in political philosophy.

Gil L. Gunderson, updated by Grant A. Marler

Reinhold Niebuhr

The leading American formulator of Neoorthodox theology, Niebuhr used the political and social arenas to place the Christian faith in the center of the cultural and political world of his day.

Principal philosophical works: *Leaves from the Notebook of a Tamed Cynic*, 1929; *Moral Man and Immoral Society: A Study in Ethics and Politics*, 1932; *An Interpretation of Christian Ethics*, 1935; *Beyond Tragedy: Essays on the Christian Interpretation of History*, 1937; *The Nature and Destiny of Man: A Christian Interpretation*, 1941-1943 (2 volumes); *The Children of Light and the Children of Darkness*, 1944; *Faith and History: A Comparison of Christian and Modern Views of History*, 1949; *The Irony of American History*, 1952; *The Self and the Dramas of History*, 1955; *Man's Nature and His Communities*, 1965.

Born: June 21, 1892; Wright City, Missouri
Died: June 1, 1971; Stockbridge, Massachusetts

Early Life

Reinhold Niebuhr was born June 21, 1892, in Wright City, Missouri, the fourth child of Lydia and Gustav Niebuhr. Lydia was the daughter of an Evangelical Synod missionary, and Gustav was a young minister for the denomination. Reinhold later said that his father was the first formative religious influence on his life, combining a vital personal piety with a complete freedom in his theological training. This combination reflected the stance of the German-originated Evangelical Synod with its "liberal" de-emphasis of doctrine and its stress on heartfelt religion. Although he never exerted pressure, Gustav began early to talk to his son about the ministry, and by the time Reinhold was ten, he had made the decision to be a preacher.

In 1902, the Niebuhr family moved to Lincoln, Illinois, where Gustav became pastor of St. John's Church. It was there that Reinhold experienced an incident that he was later to recount as a great influence on his thinking about the nature and destiny of humankind. During a recession, a local grocer for whom Reinhold worked, Adam Denger, had extended considerable credit to a number of unemployed miners. Embarrassed by his generosity and unable to pay him back, many of them moved away without even saying good-bye. Despite Denger's belief that God would protect him if he did what was right, he went bankrupt, and his young assistant, Reinhold, grew up to preach against sentimentality and reliance on special providence.

Niebuhr attended Elmhurst College in Elmhurst, Illinois, and Eden Theological Seminary in St. Louis, Missouri, both Evangelical Synod schools, but he found himself uninterested in any specific academic discipline. While Niebuhr was at Eden in April, 1913, his father, Gustav, suffered a diabetic attack and died. Niebuhr went on to Yale Divinity School and received his M.A. in 1915, but rather than continue his graduate studies, he chose to accept a parish of the Evangelical Synod.

Life's Work

The board of the Evangelical Synod chose for Niebuhr a newly organized parish in Detroit, Michigan, the location of the Ford Motor Company. That institution came to have a powerful impact on the thinking and actions of Niebuhr, taking on symbolic proportions and illustrating the tyranny of power.

Niebuhr experienced the problems common to all young ministers, many of which are told in his delightful *Leaves from the Notebook of a Tamed Cynic*, a kind of diary of his years as parish minis-

Reinhold Niebuhr. *(Archive Photos)*

ter. This book marked the beginning of a transition in Niebuhr's thought that eventually led to a rejection of all the liberal theological ideals with which he had ventured forth in 1915.

He said that the theological convictions he later came to hold began to dawn on him in Detroit "because the simple little moral homilies that were preached in that as in other cities, by myself and others, seemed completely irrelevant to the brutal facts of life in a great industrial center. Whether irrelevant or not, they were certainly futile. They did not change human actions or attitudes in any problem of collective behavior by a hair's breadth."

The problems of collective behavior to which he refers were the extreme working conditions and financial insecurity of the mass of industrial workers, especially employees of the Ford Motor Company, contrasted with the complacency and satisfaction of the middle and upper classes. People from all these groups were found among the membership of Niebuhr's church. He began to agonize about the validity and practicability of the optimistic liberal ideals that he was preaching each week.

Niebuhr's sermons began to contain more and more references to social and political issues, and he became more of a social activist, speaking on behalf of the industrial workers in Detroit and other cities and lobbying for the formation of labor unions. Although he was not directly involved in World War I, the tragedy of that event led him to join and ultimately to become the head of the pacifist Fellowship of Reconciliation. He was also instrumental in organizing the Fellowship of Socialist Christians in the late 1920's.

In 1928, Henry Sloane Coffin, then president of Union Theological Seminary, offered Niebuhr a teaching post at Union. Although he considered himself inadequately prepared for teaching, particularly theology, he accepted Coffin's offer to teach "just what you think," with his subject area labeled "Applied Christianity." The thin, eagle-eyed, balding minister soon became one of the most sought-after professors on the Union campus as he brought his experiences with world political and religious figures to the campus. He continued to preach, traveling every weekend to colleges and universities around the country, and he continued to take part in an ever-increasing number of religious and secular organizations besides his full-time teaching.

In 1931, Niebuhr married Ursula Keppel-Compton, daughter of a doctor and niece of an Anglican bishop, who was a student at Union. Ursula shared her husband's political interests and became a great help to him and a collaborator in his work. He later acknowledged that his wife was the more diligent student of biblical literature (she taught courses in biblical literature at Barnard College) and that she was responsible for many of his viewpoints.

Niebuhr's theology compelled him to become involved in an extraordinary range of activities. He was a pioneer in the movement for racial justice, strongly supporting the Tenant Farmers' Union and the Conference of Southern Churchmen. He was involved in the work of a cooperative farm in Mississippi, an effort to enable the sharecroppers in the South to improve their conditions. He participated in the World Conference on Church, Community, and State in Oxford in 1937. Later, he worked on the United States Federal Council of Churches. After World War II, he was a key member of the World Council of Churches' Commission on a Just and Durable Peace. He made hundreds of transatlantic trips, and his influence became strong in other countries, especially in Britain, where he had many ties.

Just before a worship service during the summer of 1934, Niebuhr casually jotted down a short prayer and used it in the worship. The prayer was "O God, give us serenity to accept what cannot be changed, courage to change what should be changed, and wisdom to distinguish the one from the other." After the service Niebuhr gave the notes to Chandler Robins, dean of the Cathedral of Saint John the Divine, and the "serenity prayer" gradually made its way into the religious folklore of the United States.

Because of his strenuous schedule in connection with war activities, Niebuhr was near nervous collapse at the end of each school year from 1938 to 1940. Contrary to his doctor's orders, he kept up the pace. His Neoorthodox theology, which he called Christian Realism, led him to conclude that because of humankind's freedom to sin, true sacrificial love could never triumph in history. Nevertheless, it was his belief that this sacrificial love was ultimately right and true and that this love might be approximated in history to divert or stop the abuse of power.

In February, 1952, Niebuhr suffered several small strokes. He was hospitalized for several weeks, being partially paralyzed on his left side. At last his rigorous schedule was curtailed; he was unable to do any work at all. He spent much of the rest of his nineteen years as an invalid or semi-invalid. Niebuhr continued his writing and made what appearances he could. He officially retired from teaching in 1960, becoming professor emeritus at Union and research associate at Columbia University's Institute for War and Peace Studies. He died June 1, 1971, one of the most influential thinkers of the twentieth century.

Influence

From the naïve liberalism of 1915, Niebuhr moved toward what he called Christian Realism. The events in which he had become involved not only forced him to recognize the effects of power in society, such as that of Ford Motor Company over its thousands of helpless workers, but also made him painfully aware of the corruption that had been imposed on the Christian norm. When confronted with the brutal realities of the industrialized city of Detroit, he came to realize the inadequacy of liberal thought with its naïve belief in the ultimate goodness of humankind to deal with evil in society. He first expressed his opposition to liberal viewpoints in terms of Marxist politics but came to the conclusion that Marxism essentially shared the same illusions in that it believed the ultimate goodness of human beings would prevail once capitalism was destroyed. Gradually, he articulated his search for an alternative to liberal and orthodox theologies and ethical views. In *Beyond Tragedy*, he focused on the symbol of the Cross of Christ as pivotal in understanding the human situation. While on the surface it appears that evil triumphed over the sacrificial love of Jesus, from the eschatological, or "beyond history," vantage point available to Christians, the Cross transcends tragedy.

Perhaps Niebuhr's clearest statement of Christian Realism is found in *The Nature and Destiny of Man*. In this work, he explains the paradox of selfless love, a divine attribute, coming into human society. Although the inherent evil of human society prevents the triumph of love in this world (that is, in historical existence), it will triumph in the end. Niebuhr's emphasis is not on a future vindication, although that is essential for his thought. Rather, he focuses on the acting out of sacrificial love by humans. Although that love can never be fully embodied in any human motive or action, it was the ultimate standard. Niebuhr saw the possibility of divine love having an impact on history only in a life that ends tragically, the ultimate example being that of Jesus Christ. He threw himself into the exercise of divine love, trying to rectify social and political evils, and in many ways, he ended his own life tragically in that pursuit. Theologically, no preexisting group fully agreed with him; his ideas were too orthodox for the liberals and too liberal for the orthodox.

Douglas A. Foster

The Nature and Destiny of Man

A Christian Interpretation

Type of philosophy: Ethics, philosophical theology
First published: 1941-1943 (2 volumes)
Principal ideas advanced:

◇ A person is both a child of nature and a spirit who stands outside nature.

◇ One has the capacity for self-transcendence; one can view oneself as an object, thereby making oneself a moral creature, subject to conscience.

◇ One's state of anxiety supplies one with the creative energy to transform the natural through the love of God.

◇ The alternative to faith, made possible by humanity's freedom, is sin; and sin is an act of will whereby the self, rather than God, becomes the center of human concern.

◇ God is *agapē*, self-giving love, and such love is not possible in this life; but by commitment to such love, humanity transcends itself and in the knowledge of God's forgiveness accepts judgment without despair.

As a young Protestant pastor, Reinhold Niebuhr entered a Detroit labor parish in 1915, prepared to establish social justice through the nurturing of human love. In the crucible of social conflict, Niebuhr discovered that the key problem was not one of personal ethics but of social structure and strategy. Detroit industrialists were no less moral in their personal relations than the average laborer, but in a system of competitive capitalism, operating by the impersonal laws of market,

profit, supply, and demand, direct application of the "simple teachings of Jesus" to the social sphere was impossible.

As a result of this practical conviction, Niebuhr wrote a book that strongly shook the American theological scene. Although tempered by liberal theology, Niebuhr's *Moral Man and Immoral Society: A Study in Ethics and Politics* (1932) marked the beginning of social realism in contemporary American Christianity. Gone was the idealism of the liberal period; the Kingdom of God was not humanity's to build, not simply in this generation but in any generation. The kingdom was the "impossible possibility" standing over against humanity eternally, the ideal perfect community of mutual love, judging all humanity's attempts to emulate it. The only possible possibilities were transient and imperfect forms of justice.

Accompanying these insights came Niebuhr's rejection of absolutism in ethics: There are no absolute goods and evils. The problem of ethics is the never-ending task of finding "proximate solutions for insoluble problems." Accompanying this position, classically formulated in Niebuhr's *An Interpretation of Christian Ethics* (1935), was a growing shift in emphasis from the liberal stress on society as the molder of humanity to the nature of humanity as the key to the nature and problems of society. The orthodox doctrine of Original Sin became increasingly relevant for Niebuhr in understanding the problems of culture. Humanity is essentially self-centered, seeking self-aggrandizement and domination over others. Although this tendency can be checked to a large degree on the personal level within the small confines of the interdependent family, in the larger dimensions of community, group, nation, and hemisphere, personal pride is compounded into impersonal, immoral, irresponsible pressure groups seeking their own untempered ends in hypocritical self-righteousness.

Democracy

This understanding led Niebuhr to sympathize with the Marxist analysis of social forces, but he saw that the Marxist realism about the present was naïvely undermined by an unfounded optimism about human capacity in the proletarian future. In 1944, these thoughts coalesced in a vindication of democracy, *The Children of Light and the Children of Darkness*. In this work, Niebuhr combined his political movement to the "left" with his theological movement toward the "right." All previous apologies for democracy, he declared, were wrongly grounded on an optimistic doctrine of humankind, defending it as the only form of government that respected human capacity. Such a defense, Niebuhr insisted, can lead only to catastrophe; the philosophy of John Locke must be tempered with that of Thomas Hobbes, as well as the reverse.

Humanity is capable of self-transcendence, but people are likewise motivated by an even stronger desire for domination. Socialism controls people, but in a manner that undercuts the creativity that emerges from self-transcendence; further, those tendencies that make control necessary undermine the integrity of those given the power to control. On the other hand, laissez-faire democracy so liberates people that their selfish propensities, compounded by monopoly, by cartels, and by simple numbers, destroy the integrity of the less organized and less privileged, using them as tools for maintaining their competitive place in society. The plight of the worker, exploited by the industrialist not out of vindictiveness but out of the necessity of competing in an uncontrolled business world, is Niebuhr's favorite case in point.

Niebuhr sees democracy as the only realistic answer for this dilemma. The only structure for social justice is that of competing pressure groups, deadlocked by their conflicting self-interests and thereby forced into self-transcendence for the mutual good. Because group power is never constant but changed by the circumstances of each new situation, democracy has two unique advantages. Its carefully designed system of internal checks and balances is alone in a position to prevent excessive governmental control, while its representative legislation can delegate power to the underprivileged and restrain the irresponsible. This system requires constant change and vigilance, for today's justice may be tomorrow's greatest injustice. To summarize with one of Niebuhr's most famous statements, "man's capacity for justice makes democracy possible; but man's inclination to injustice makes democracy necessary."

The Nature of Humanity

This is the basic understanding that runs throughout Niebuhr's prolific writings on economics, political theory, international relations, and the like. His writing career, however, climaxed in 1939 with his two Gifford Lecture series, combined in a large volume entitled *The Nature and Destiny of Man*. In this work, Niebuhr's lifetime of practical thinking is placed in a carefully created intellectual dialogue attempting to bring the various aspects of his thought into a systematic structure.

"Man has always been his own most vexing problem," begins Niebuhr, who proceeds to analyze rationalism, Romanticism, Marxism, Idealism, and naturalism as alternative attempts of Western thought to come to terms with the curious contradictions constituting the enigma that is humanity. For Niebuhr, anthropology is *the* problem from which all others follow, and theological anthropology alone is capable of dealing with the whole person. He systematically undermines every attempt to establish humans as simple, whether in terms of reason, animality, or the like.

For Niebuhr, every human contradiction points to two paradoxical facts about humanity. First, a person is "a child of nature, subject to its vicissitudes, compelled by its necessities, driven by its impulses." Second, a person is a "spirit who stands outside nature, life, himself, his reason and the world." It is only the Christian view that succeeds in holding these two aspects together. Not to do this is to overestimate or underestimate humanity, both of which could bring tragic practical consequences, whether they be the tyranny of totalitarianism or the exploitation by laissez-faire capitalism.

For the Christian, people are created in the "image of God" and in this rests their transcendence over nature. As Niebuhr understands this, the *imago* refers to people's capacity for self-transcendence, to make an object of themselves, to stand continually outside themselves in an indefinite regression. This is the root of "conscience," for it gives people a capacity for objectivity about themselves, viewing themselves as objects, appraising the degree to which these "objects" act as they would want to be acted toward. This ability and this inborn "golden rule," similar to German philosopher Immanuel Kant's ethic of rational consistency, is the source of morality for Niebuhr. People are not only "spirit" but also "natural"; they are finite creatures. Finitude does not mean evil, but dependency, creatureliness. This polarity means that humanity is at the intersection of time and eternity, or finitude and infinity, or nature and spirit.

The law of humanity's nature is love, pointed to by humanity's self-transcendence but clearly revealed in the Christian revelation. God's intent was that people should have faith and trust in the Creator, loving him for the gift of existence, and in gratitude loving their neighbors as they had been loved. Being at the intersection of nature (under the necessity of instinct, need, and drive) and spirit (under the freedom of infinite possibility), the inevitable condition of humanity is anxiety. If people trust in God, they know their anxious state to be God-intended, and anxiety therefore becomes the energy of creativity—infinite possibilities come as challenges, as leaven for humble achievement in service to God and humanity. The spirit transforms the natural by bringing it to fulfillment—this is to become a self. This was God's plan in creating the world.

Anxiety and the Way of Sin

Because of humanity's freedom, another option is open. This possibility Niebuhr finds classically portrayed in Genesis in terms of the Garden of Eden. This story, he insists, is not history but myth—myth, however, not in the sense of falsehood, but in the Platonic sense or the sense in which it is used in literature. Myth is the vehicle for communicating truths that are beyond the capacity of concept to communicate. Adam, then, is not simply "first man," but *every* man. What Adam did, all people do, not because Adam did it but because people are what they are. It is at this point that Niebuhr's difficult distinction arises—the fall of each person is "inevitable" but not "necessary." Reminiscent of philosopher Søren Kierkegaard, from whom Niebuhr drew much of his analysis, the fall is a personal affair, something that cannot be universally understood, but something that one does, for which one knows oneself to be responsible and which one understands in oneself. The feeling of guilt attending all actions is the guarantee of responsibility despite inevitability.

This alternative is the way of sin, as opposed to the way of faith. Anxiety is its psychological condition, but it is not the cause—the cause is the will. If one does not accept anxiety as God-given for creativity, one has no option but to try to eliminate it. This is sin, for it stems from disbelief, lack of trust—it is the substitution of the self and its own strength for God as center. This "elimination" of anxiety can be attempted in two ways, for anxiety, being the product of an intersection, can be denied by denying either dimension of the human polarity.

The first way, by far the most universal, is that of "pride." This is the denial of one's natural aspect, to reject one's limitations by deliberately mistaking one's self-transcendence for achievement. People, with the capacity to envisage the whole, are tempted to imagine themselves as the whole. This is not a matter of ignorance but of willed self-deception. There are four basic types of pride: pride of power (glorification in personal and group superiority, false or real), pride of knowledge (especially apparent in conflicting ideologies), pride of virtue (best exemplified by moral self-righteousness), and pride of spirit (religious fanaticism). These are all rooted in insecurity, tempting one to self-deception by deceiving others in a façade of word and deed. In effect, pride is the elevation of the relative to the absolute.

The second way is that of sensuality. Anxiety is "eliminated" by denying one's freedom, one's capacity for self-transcendence, and one's responsibility, affirming animality as humanity's essential nature. This may be done either to assert the self or to escape the self. In reality, sensuality is a result of pride, for one's own pleasure is made the only center. In whatever form it takes, sin is best understood as the attempt to hide contingency, to seek security at the expense of others. The continuity of sin rests in the fact that while anxiety tempts one to sin, the sin only compounds the insecurity in a vicious circle.

The fact that self-deception and rationalization are involved in all sin is the living refutation, for Niebuhr, of the doctrine of total depravity; unless the will is successful in disguising its actions, it cannot bring itself to do them. Thus, there are no personal acts that are purely evil, and yet it must be affirmed that pride infects every human action, to a lesser or greater degree. However, because the self, never deserving unconditional devotion, cannot ever fully convince itself, it craves allies to strengthen the deception. Herein lie the demonic proportions of group pride, formed by the attempt of individuals to escape insecurity in a blind, absolute devotion to race, religion, institution, nation, or party. Such idolatry is ruthless, for it possesses the instruments for power. No group escapes "sinful pride and idolatrous pretensions." This means that all judgments and distinctions are relative, and always a matter of degree; they cannot be made previous to the occasion. A "Christian" group or nation is characterized not in its achievement but in its willingness to hear judgment. Because a nation has no collective capacity for self-transcendence, its hope rests in a creative minority, heard because of the tension of competitive forces.

Christ's Self-Sacrifice

People, though "fallen," have a "vision of health," an awareness of the law of love as the "ought" of which they are incapable. This awareness is the "point of contact" for the Christian revelation. Although Niebuhr is willing to use much of the traditional terminology concerning Jesus Christ, he makes it clear that these terms have only symbolic meaning. Jesus is the fulfillment of prophetic religion, making vicarious suffering the final revelation of the meaning of history; for Niebuhr, this means that God takes the sins of the world on himself in the sense that divine forgiveness is the reverse side of divine judgment. This forgiveness cannot be effective until humanity takes sin seriously, knowing that sin causes God to suffer—this is the message of the Crucifixion that brings humanity to contrition. Without such contrition, divine forgiveness could not be appropriated. Anxiety can become creative to the degree that humanity has faith in the Crucifixion as the truth of history.

Niebuhr rejects the Chalcedonian and Nicene formulations of a two-nature Christology, declaring that although "it is possible for a character . . . to point symbolically beyond history and to become a source of disclosure of an eternal meaning, purpose and power which bears history," it is "not possible for any person to be historical and unconditioned at the same time." Through

Jesus, love is established as the center of life, but only in principle, not in fact. In this life, love is suffering, not triumphant. The Kingdom of God is not in history nor ever will be—it is the hope that keeps humanity from the despair of the moment through faith that the divine power cannot be overcome.

Through Jesus Christ, it becomes known that God is *agapē*, self-giving love, and that a life so lived can only end tragically, for it refuses "to participate in the claims and counterclaims of historical existence." Therefore, love as taught by Jesus is impossible, for to exist is to participate in the balance of competing wills that is the structure of earthly life. Such love transcends history. However, to the degree that humanity is capable of self-transcendence, to that same degree does this "impossibility" become "possible," not in the sense of being attainable but of being relevant—it judges every human attempt, revealing possibilities not realized or seen. Yet because this awareness of infinite possibility is that which tempts humanity to pride or sensuality, it is only in awareness of divine forgiveness that humanity can accept judgment without despair. This is the Christian answer for Niebuhr.

Such an understanding means that, for Niebuhr, there is no progress in history. This does not mean that there is no achievement, but since humanity's duality is never overcome, every greater possibility for good brings with it in direct proportion a greater possibility for evil. For example, nuclear research brings the possibility of unlimited industrial energy but also the possibility of total cosmic disaster. Humanity always walks the tightrope between antithetical possibilities, for each will walks the tightrope between the will to realization and the will to power.

What remains an enigma in Niebuhr's position is the combination of a negative doctrine of humanity with a liberal Christology. In liberal theology, the optimism concerning the former is the respective "weakness" of the latter. However, while Niebuhr's anthropology became more negative, his Christology and understanding of redemption did not change accordingly. Therefore, Niebuhr's ethic makes no fundamental distinction between the "redeemed" and "unredeemed." For him, social ethics and Christian ethics are identical, and what he calls "personal ethics" is very different from the former. Yet whatever other implications are involved, it cannot be denied that, on one hand, Niebuhr's doctrine of humanity has proved a powerful stimulus to theology and that, on the other, it has made ready contact with secular thinking in almost every area of group relations.

W. Paul Jones, updated by John K. Roth

Additional Reading

Beckley, Harlan. *Passion for Justice: Retrieving the Legacies of Walter Rauschenbusch, John A. Ryan, and Reinhold Niebuhr*. Louisville, Ky.: Westminster/John Knox Press, 1992. Explores the social ethics of three important religious thinkers and draws out the implications of their views for contemporary life.

Brown, Charles C. *Niebuhr and His Age: Reinhold Niebuhr's Prophetic Role in the Twentieth Century*. Philadelphia: Trinity Press International, 1992. Shows how Reinhold Niebuhr's political, philosophical, and theological views played an influential role in the public policy debates of his day.

Durkin, Kenneth. *Reinhold Niebuhr*. Harrisburg, Penn.: Morehouse, 1990. An introductory overview of Niebuhr's life and thought.

Fackre, Gabriel J. *The Promise of Reinhold Niebuhr*. Rev. ed. Lanham, Md.: University Press of America, 1994. An overview of Niebuhr's life and thought, synthesizing many of his views and concepts in a manageable and coherent way.

Fox, Richard Wightman. *Reinhold Niebuhr: A Biography*. New York: Pantheon, 1985. A well-written, meticulously documented study that offers a penetrating historical treatment of Niebuhr's life.

Kegley, Charles W., and Robert W. Bretall, eds. *Reinhold Niebuhr: His Religious, Social, and Political Thought*. New York: Macmillan, 1984. A collection of essays that interpret all phases of Niebuhr's work. The volume also contains an important intellectual autobiography by Niebuhr himself.

Lovin, Robin W. *Reinhold Niebuhr and Christian Realism*. Cambridge, England: Cambridge University Press, 1995. A leading Niebuhr scholar shows how Niebuhr's theology and religious philosophy both informed and reflected his political theory and practice.

McKeough, Colm. *The Political Realism of Reinhold Niebuhr: A Pragmatic Approach to Just War*. New York: St. Martin's Press, 1997. Explores how Niebuhr brought his theological insights to bear on twentieth century conflicts, especially those of World War II and the Cold War.

Niebuhr, Reinhold. *The Essential Reinhold Niebuhr: Selected Essays and Addresses*. New Haven, Conn.: Yale University Press, 1986. In addition to its excellent selection of Niebuhr's writings, this volume contains insightful and informative introductory material by editor Robert McAfee Brown about Niebuhr and his thought.

Rice, David F. *Reinhold Niebuhr and John Dewey: An American Odyssey*. Albany: State University of New York Press, 1993. A study of the relationship—personal and philosophical—between two of twentieth century America's most influential intellectual leaders.

Scott, Nathan A. *Reinhold Niebuhr*. Minneapolis: University of Minnesota Press, 1963. A survey of Niebuhr's thought that places special emphasis on the importance of *The Nature and Destiny of Man*.

Sims, John. *Missionaries to the Skeptics: Christian Apologists for the Twentieth Century, C. S. Lewis, Edward John Carnell, and Reinhold Niebuhr*. Macon, Ga.: Mercer University Press, 1995. A comparative study that shows how Niebuhr defended his version of Christian thinking during the middle decades of the twentieth century.

Stone, Ronald H. *Professor Reinhold Niebuhr: A Mentor to the Twentieth Century*. Louisville, Ky.: Westminster/John Knox Press, 1992. Tracing the implications of Niebuhr's thought, an eminently qualified interpreter shows how Niebuhr brought his religious and political ethics to bear on the important human needs and policy issues of his day.

Douglas A. Foster, updated by John K. Roth

Friedrich Nietzsche

Though mostly ignored during his lifetime, Nietzsche's writings became a bellwether in the twentieth century for radical philosophical, psychological, linguistic, and literary critiques of Western culture. Through a series of remarkable works of German prose, Nietzsche sought to smash the idol of Christian morality and liberate a few who might follow after him into a triumphant and tragic this-worldly life.

Principal philosophical works: *Die Geburt der Tragödie aus dem Geiste der Musik*, 1872 (*The Birth of Tragedy Out of the Spirit of Music*, 1909); *Unzeitgemässe Betrachtungen*, 1873-1876 (4 volumes; *Thoughts Out of Season*, 1909, 2 volumes); *Menschliches, Allzumenschliches: Ein Buch für freie Geister*, 1878 (*Human, All Too Human*, 1910, 1911); *Die fröhliche Wissenschaft*, 1882, 1887 (*The Joyful Wisdom*, 1910); *Also sprach Zarathustra: Ein Buch für Alle und Keinen*, 1883-1885 (*Thus Spake Zarathustra*, 1896); *Jenseits von Gut und Böse: Vorspiel einer Philosophie der Zukunft*, 1886 (*Beyond Good and Evil*, 1907); *Zur Genealogie der Moral*, 1887 (*On the Genealogy of Morals*, 1896); *Der Fall Wagner*, 1888 (*The Case of Wagner*, 1896); *Der Antichrist*, 1895 (*The Antichrist*, 1896); *Der Wille zur Macht*, 1901 (*The Will to Power*, 1910); *Ecce Homo*, 1908 (English translation, 1911); *The Complete Works of Friedrich Nietzsche*, 1909-1911 (18 volumes).

Born: October 15, 1844; Röcken, Saxony, Prussia (now in Germany)
Died: August 25, 1900; Weimar, Germany

Early Life

Friedrich Wilhelm Nietzsche—named for the reigning king of Prussia, Friedrich Wilhelm IV, whose birthday was also October 15—was born in a parsonage. His father, Karl Ludwig Nietzsche, was a Lutheran pastor; his mother, Franziska Nietzsche (née Oehler), was the daughter of a Lutheran pastor. The union produced two other children, Elisabeth in 1846 and Joseph in 1848, who died shortly before his second birthday.

After the death of his father in 1849, Friedrich Nietzsche spent most of his early life surrounded by women: his mother, his sister, his paternal grandmother, and two maiden aunts. The family moved in 1850 to Naumburg, in Thuringia, where the young Nietzsche attended elementary school and a private preparatory school. In 1858, he entered Germany's most renowned Protestant boarding school, the Schulpforta, on a scholarship. There he met Paul Deussen, also a student, who became one of his few lifelong friends;

Deussen found Nietzsche to be deeply serious, "inclined to corpulence and head congestions," and extremely myopic.

Nietzsche graduated from the school at Pforta in 1864 with a classical education; that same year, he entered the University of Bonn to study theology and philology, the latter under Friedrich Wilhelm Ritschl. Unable to fit into the rowdiness of student life at Bonn—despite entertaining students on the piano—Nietzsche abandoned any pretense of theological studies and transferred in 1865 to the University of Leipzig, where his friend Ritschl had gone. Writing to his sister Elisabeth about his abandonment of the Christian faith, Nietzsche told her that he had become a disciple of the truth, wherever it led; he could not be content with a religious happiness. That same year, the serious Nietzsche told Deussen that a recently published "life of Christ" by David Strauss was disingenuous in its removal of the miraculous Christ from the Gospels while holding on to his precepts. "That can have serious consequences," said Nietzsche; "if you give up Christ you will have to give up God as well."

The year 1865 was remarkable for two other reasons. As Deussen later wrote, Nietzsche had told him that a street porter, asked to take him to a restaurant in Cologne, instead had delivered him to a brothel. Speechless, Nietzsche soon left. Deussen speculated that his friend remained a lifelong virgin. There is much scholarly debate on the subject, but it seems likely that Deussen was wrong. Because there is no indication in Nietzsche's correspondence that he ever had sexual relations with a woman of his own class, it is probable that in 1865 or later Nietzsche acquired syphilis at a brothel. Early in 1889, he would collapse into insanity.

It was in 1865 that Nietzsche encountered the works of the pessimistic philosopher Arthur Schopenhauer, and though Nietzsche was later to renounce his allegiance to Schopenhauer's perspective and his anti-Semitism, by late 1865 he had announced that he had become a follower. The Leipzig years, from 1865 to 1869, saw Nietzsche taken under Ritschl's wing as his protégé, the development of his friendship with Erwin Rohde, and the entrance of composer Richard Wagner into Nietzsche's life. After hearing Wagner's music in 1868, Nietzsche became a convert; meeting with the composer that same year, Nietzsche found that Wagner, too, loved Schopenhauer. Nietzsche would one day reject Wagner as he would Schopenhauer.

Nietzsche entered into the cavalry company of an artillery regiment in October of 1867, but in March of the next year he suffered a serious chest injury while trying to mount a horse. On extended health leave from the military, Nietzsche resumed his studies in Leipzig; in 1869, the university (on Ritschl's recommendation) conferred a doctorate on Nietzsche on the strength of his published philological writings and without the customary examination and dissertation required for a German degree. That same year, Nietzsche was appointed to the chair of classical philology; he was twenty-four, a resident of Switzerland, and no longer a citizen of Prussia.

Friedrich Nietzsche. *(Library of Congress)*

Life's Work

In the two decades of sanity that remained to Nietzsche, he would often battle against long periods of ill health, especially after 1870, when he fell victim to dysentery and diphtheria while serving as a medical orderly with the Prussian army in the Franco-Prussian War (1870-1871). On his return to Basel to resume his teaching chores in philology (he was an unsuccessful applicant to the chair of philosophy), Nietzsche was plagued with frequent bouts of nausea and exhaustion.

For a time, his one surcease was his friendship with Wagner. From

1869 until Wagner moved to Bayreuth in 1872, Nietzsche visited the composer and his wife, Cosima, some twenty-three times at the Wagner residence at Tribschen, near Lucerne. The composer welcomed a disciple; yet his increasing use of Christian images, especially in his last opera, *Parsifal*, sickened Nietzsche, as did Wagner's anti-Semitism. By 1878, their friendship had been sundered.

Nietzsche's first book broke with tradition. *The Birth of Tragedy Out of the Spirit of Music* was far from a classical philological study burdened by arcane footnotes. Instead, Nietzsche had written a speculative treatment of what he found to be two competing forces in ancient Greek life: the Dionysian, representing potentially destructive passion, and the Apollonian, representing reason and restraint. Greek tragedy had fused the two, but with the triumph of Socrates, the Apollonian was in the ascendant. (Much later, Nietzsche would redefine the Dionysian impulse as a sublimated or perfected "will to power" and would ally himself with Dionysus.)

Nietzsche was granted a leave of absence from Basel in 1876 because of ill health, but his continued headaches, vomiting, and deteriorating eyesight led to his resignation in May, 1879, with a pension of three thousand Swiss francs a year for six years. From that time onward, Nietzsche increasingly became an enigma to his friends. His publication of the aphoristic *Human, All Too Human* was characterized by Wagner as the beginning of Nietzsche's slide into madness. Nietzsche cut his intellectual mooring to Schopenhauer as well, writing a friend that he no longer believed what the philosopher had said.

In the decade beginning in 1879, Nietzsche, moving from boardinghouse to boardinghouse, always seeking new curatives, lived in the French Riviera, Italy, and Switzerland, a virtual recluse. His letter writing was a substitute for most human contact. Suffering almost ceaseless pain, Nietzsche turned within—as if the pain itself were a spur to creativity, or as if, through his project of revaluing traditional Christian values, his literary genius would master his physiology.

There was much emotional pain as well. His friendship with philosopher Paul Rée (who was investigating the psychological basis of religious

belief), which had begun in 1873, was marred when in 1882 both men met Lou Salomé (later the wife of Orientalist F. C. Andreas, friend of Sigmund Freud, and mistress of the poet Rainer Maria Rilke) and both proposed—Nietzsche apparently through Rée. Declining both requests, Salomé counterproposed a platonic ménage à trois; Nietzsche's sister Elisabeth learned of the plan, took him to task for his immorality, and informed their mother of Nietzsche's behavior. The three continued in one another's company, but by November, with Salomé and Rée having departed, Nietzsche realized that he had been abandoned.

In January, 1883, in only ten days, Nietzsche penned the first part of what was to become his literary masterpiece, *Thus Spake Zarathustra*. The book (completed in 1885, the fourth and final part privately printed from Nietzsche's own funds) uses a biblical narrative style to parody the Socratic and Christian wisdom teachings and to bring to "everyone and no one" the teachings of the *Übermensch* (variously translated Superman or Overman). A more explicit elucidation of Nietzsche's philosophical orientation came in 1886 with *Beyond Good and Evil* and, in 1887, *On the Genealogy of Morals*. Books streamed from Nietzsche's pen. In the last year of his sanity, 1888, he wrote five of them, including *The Antichrist* and *Ecce Homo*, the last a semiautobiographical overview of Nietzsche's published works.

Several months of euphoria preceded Nietzsche's descent into madness, but following his collapse in the Piazza Carlo Alberto, in Turin, Italy, on January 3, 1889—he had seen a cab driver beating his horse and had flung himself around the horse's neck—the darkness was complete. For the next eleven years, Nietzsche was variously cared for in a Basel asylum, by his mother in Naumburg (until she died in 1897), and by his sister in Weimar.

Elisabeth, married in 1885 to anti-Semite Bernhard Förster (who committed suicide in 1889), managed to gain control of Nietzsche's literary estate and began zealously to refashion her brother's image into that of a proto-Nazi. She withheld *Ecce Homo* from publication for twenty years after Nietzsche had written it, established a Nietzsche archive, and compiled and published a series of notes Nietzsche had never intended for publication. She edited it and titled it *The Will to Power*.

Only in the last year of his sanity did Nietzsche begin to receive important public notice, a result primarily of the philosophy lectures given by Georg Brandes in Copenhagen. It seems ironic that the first commercial successes of the man who wanted to be understood came at the hands of his sister, who carefully crafted a mythical Nietzsche. Poignantly, it was the ever-prescient Nietzsche who had written in *Ecce Homo*, "I have a terrible fear I shall one day be pronounced holy." Nietzsche died in Weimar on August 25, 1900, not yet fifty-six, his mane of hair and his shaggy mustache still dark brown.

Influence

There is much scholarly dispute over the nature of Nietzsche's philosophy and even over whether he intended to have one. In his mature works, from *Thus Spake Zarathustra* on, many themes seem important to Nietzsche, from the concept of the Overman, the idea of eternal recurrence, of people being in love with their own fate and thus triumphant in it, to the psychological origins of traditional morality, the nature of the will to power in human affairs, and the death of God, the last announced by a madman in section 125 of *The Joyful Wisdom*. Yet in Nietzsche's modified aphoristic style, his themes receive no systematic exploration; therefore, scholarly interpretations are legion.

Nietzsche's analysis of the psychology of the priest and of Christian morality anticipated Freud. Traditional morality has quenched the instinct for life and has pronounced sexuality, nobility of self, and intellect to be evil; the afterlife is promised only to those who submit to the priest, to the slave morality. Nietzsche's message was that the sickness, the life-denying morality of the Church, must be replaced by the message of the Overman. Though perhaps an unachievable ideal, the Overman is able to fall in love with every aspect of his fate and, without self-deception, to will the eternal repetition of every part of his life. God is dead—the new learning killed him—but the late nineteenth century slumbered on in its nihilism, unaware of the consequences. Nietzsche's message of triumph and tragedy fell on deaf ears during his lifetime.

Yet his insights, often not fully developed, have been mined by twentieth century existentialists such as Albert Camus, deconstructionists such as Jacques Derrida and Michel Foucault, phenomenologists such as Martin Heidegger, religious thinkers such as Paul Tillich and Martin Buber, novelists such as Thomas Mann and Hermann Hesse, and playwright George Bernard Shaw. Psychoanalysis pioneers Sigmund Freud and Carl Jung also felt Nietzsche's influence. Nietzsche is a key to understanding some of the twentieth century's most influential and most deeply perplexing currents of thought.

Dan Barnett

Thus Spake Zarathustra

Type of philosophy: Ethics, metaphysics
First published: Also sprach Zarathustra: Ein Buch für Alle und Keinen, parts 1 and 2, 1883; part 3, 1884; part 4, 1885 (English translation, 1896)
Principal ideas advanced:

◇ Life is the will to power, and the individual who would truly live must overcome the beliefs and conventions of common people and become an Overman, or Superman (*Übermensch*).

◇ Those who teach the Christian virtues of pity and meekness seek to corrupt humanity, to destroy people's will to power, and to make them submit to those who prosper from the conventional way.

◇ Those who do not have the courage to live seek to escape by sleeping, by prizing the soul more than the body, and by seeking peace instead of war.

◇ The Overman is virtuous when freed from the belief in God and from the hope of an afterlife; this person is nauseated by the rabble, and joy comes from surpassing those who live by false hopes and beliefs.

◇ Worship of any sort is a return to childhood; if people must worship, let them worship donkeys if that suits them.

Friedrich Nietzsche belongs to the tradition of philosophers who wished to tell people how to live. His injunction is for one to become an individual and to follow one's own desires—if necessary, through the destruction of others. Nietzsche is often inconsistent, sometimes contradictory, but he is almost always provocative. His criticisms of nineteenth century institutions remind the reader of those of his contemporaries, philosopher Søren Kierkegaard and writer Fyodor Dostoevski.

There are three principal themes in *Thus Spake Zarathustra*: the will to power, the consequent revaluation of values, and the doctrine of eternal recurrence. Life is essentially a will to power, the feeling that one is in command of oneself and of the future. In controlling the future, one finds that the values that most people accept are inadequate and that one must adopt a new, in many cases opposite, set of values. However, neither power nor the new set of values is desirable for its consequences. If one were to use power to accomplish some final end, one would no longer need it; if one were to realize the new values, one would no longer need them. For Nietzsche, there are no final ends. Power and the revaluation of values are good in themselves; and consequently, there is no millennium, nothing but an eternal recurrence of people, things, and problems. These three themes are developed carefully in *Thus Spake Zarathustra*, in a manner of development that is both self-conscious and purposive.

Individuals and the Overman

The main theme in part 1 is that individuals stand alone with their fate in their own hands. They can expect no help from others either in this life or in some imagined future life. They must "make themselves," to use the phrase of the existentialists. As part 1 opens, Zarathustra is meditating on a mountain, where he has spent the last ten years. His companions have been his eagle, a symbol of pride, and his serpent, a symbol of wisdom. He has just decided to go into the world to teach some of the wisdom that he has acquired during his period of meditation.

On the way down the mountain, he meets a saint who tells him that the way to help people is to stay away from them and to save them through prayer. Here Nietzsche announces one of his important ideas, that the individual can expect no supernatural help because God is dead.

Zarathustra reaches a town where, finding a crowd engaged in watching a tightrope walker perform his act, he says to them, *"I teach you the Overman.* Man is something that shall be overcome." He explains that people have evolved from apes but that they are still apelike. People are poisoned by those who teach that salvation is found not in this world but in the next and by those who teach the Christian ethics of virtue, justice, and pity. However, the people in the crowd are not ready for Zarathustra's message. They think that he is announcing the tightrope walker's act. He reflects that they cannot be taught because they are not ready to take the first step toward learning by recognizing that their present beliefs are false. What Zarathustra must find is those "who do not know how to live except by going under, for they are those who cross over."

The tightrope walker falls and is killed. Zarathustra and the corpse are left alone in the marketplace. Zarathustra then realizes that one of his great problems will be to communicate his message to people too indifferent or too stupid to understand him. However, his purpose remains firm: "I will teach men the meaning of their existence—the Overman, the lightning out of the dark cloud of man." Because he cannot teach the multitude, he decides that he will have to select a few disciples who will follow him "because they want to follow themselves."

Throughout the rest of part 1, Nietzsche expresses a series of more or less disconnected criticisms of the people of his time. Most people are sleepers because sleep robs them of thought, makes them like inanimate objects, and imitates death. People use sleep as a means of escape, just as God created the world as a diversion, as an escape from himself. Another sort of escape is found by accepting the injunction to renounce the body and love the soul. However, the soul is only a part of the body, and one must love the whole more than one loves any part. Love of the soul to the exclusion of the body is a kind of renunciation of life. Another escape is the belief that life is full of suffering. So it is, but the Overman will see to it that he is not one of the sufferers. War brings out many of the best qualities in people, Nietzsche argues. "You should love peace as a means to new wars—and the short peace more than the long. . . . You say it is the good cause that hallows even war? I say unto you: it is the good war that hallows any cause." The state, another escape from reality, is one of the greatest enemies of individualism. It tells individual citizens what to do, how to live; it replaces their personalities with its own.

Another renunciation of life is dedication to the ideal of chastity. To deny the lust of the flesh is often to affirm the lust of the spirit. Why deny lust? Nietzsche asks. Women are only half human at best, more like cats or cows. What is great is the passion of love between men and women, for all creation is the result of passion. The solution to all of women's problems is childbearing; and this is the only interest women ever have in men. A man needs two things, danger and play. His interest in woman is that she is "the most dangerous plaything." She is "the recreation of the warrior." Her hope should be that she will bear the Overman. Men are merely evil, but women are bad. That is why they are dangerous. Men can overcome them only by subjugating them completely. An old crone agrees with Zarathustra and adds her advice, "You are going to women? Do not forget the whip!"

When should one die? Only when one has perfected one's life; but if one cannot live a perfect life, then it is best to die in battle. Death must come because one wants it.

Part 1 ends with the injunction that through Zarathustra's teaching one should not become merely a disciple and imitator of the prophet, but should learn through him to understand oneself. The section ends on a note that has become familiar: "*'Dead are all gods: now we want the Overman to live'*—on that great noon, let this be our last will."

The Will to Power

In part 2, Nietzsche develops the notion of the will to power. The first part is largely negative, but the second part provides the positive doctrine. It begins with the idea that the conjecture of God is meaningless because it defies the imagination. However, the conjecture of the Overman is within the scope of the human mind if one first eliminates error. One cause of error is pity; but the Overman is willing to sacrifice the self and, therefore, willing to sacrifice others. Priests cause error. They have taken death as their God's tri-

umph; they need to be redeemed from their Redeemer. They are virtuous because they expect a reward in the afterlife, but there is no reward. For the Overman, to be virtuous is to be true to the self and to follow where it leads. The mass of people want power and pleasure too, but they want the wrong kinds. The Overman must seek the higher powers and pleasures; he must be nauseated by the rabble that is around him.

Nietzsche's statement of his positive doctrine is often interrupted by criticisms. The contrast between the desires of the masses and those of the Overman reminds him of the belief that all people are equal. However, if people are equal, there could be no Overman. Those who have preached equality have told the people what they wanted to hear rather than the truth. The truth can be discovered only by the free spirit who wills, desires, and loves. Such a free spirit finds that not all things can be understood and that some must be felt. The will to truth is just one aspect of the will to power. Such a will carries the free spirit beyond truth and falsity and beyond good and evil as well. Slaves think that they can conquer their masters by their servility; they have the will to power but in its lowest form. The forerunner of the Overman has the will to be master, the will to command, the will to conquer. Because slaves are incapable of positive action, they can do neither good nor evil. Masters with their capacity for evil have a capability for good. If the good requires positive action, so does the beautiful. Zarathustra asks, "Where is beauty?" and answers, "Where I must will with all my will; where I want to love and perish that an image may not remain a mere image."

If one cannot find truth among those who tell the people what they want to hear, still less can one find it among the scholars, who have removed themselves from the possibility of action and who "knit the socks of the spirit." Neither can one turn to the poets. They know so little that they have to lie to fill the pages they write. They are the great mythmakers; they created God. Zarathustra's mission is to lead people away from myths toward an assertion of the will. People who accept the myths are like actors who play the parts assigned to them but who can never be themselves. Those who exercise the will to power can do so only by being themselves.

A Godless World and Eternal Recurrence

The third part of *Thus Spake Zarathustra* introduces the theme of eternal recurrence, but it is almost obscured by other themes. The main question is: What does one experience when one travels? Zarathustra decides that no matter where one travels one can experience only oneself. However, if this is the case, then the individual is beyond good and evil, both of which require some absolute standard or criterion of judgment. There is none. People live in a world not of purpose, knowledge, law, and design but of accident, innocence, chance, and prankishness. "In everything, one thing is impossible: rationality."

What of people who cannot accept this doctrine because they are weak in body and in mind? They cannot be expected to accept the truth; they talk but cannot think. They ask only for contentment and refuse to face life. They expect teachers of contentment, flatterers who will tell them they are right. They want those who will condemn as sins the acts that they never commit and who will praise their small sins as virtues. However, Nietzsche continues, "'Yes, I *am* Zarathustra the godless!' These teachers of resignation! Whatever is small and sick and scabby, they crawl to like lice, and only my nausea prevents me from squashing them."

Although much that Nietzsche says is negative and critical, he constantly warns the reader that criticism should be given only out of love and in preparation for a positive doctrine to follow. Condemnation for its own sake is evidence only of an interest in filth and dirt.

If God is dead, how did he die? Here Nietzsche cannot resist a criticism of the composer Richard Wagner, with whom he had been closely associated and with whom he had finally quarreled. Wagner had written an opera, *Götterdämmerung* (*The Twilight of the Gods*). It is a highly dramatic story of the destruction of the Norse gods. Nietzsche says that the gods did not die in the way that Wagner describes. On the contrary, they laughed themselves to death when one of their number announced that there was only one god. This jealous god had lost his godhead by saying the most godless word, and the other gods died laughing.

What are often considered evils turn out on close examination by Nietzsche to be goods. Sex, which is cursed by "all hair-shirted despisers of the body," is a virtue for the free and innocent. Lust to rule, which destroys civilizations, is a fit activity for the Overman. Selfishness, a vice only of masters as seen by their slaves, is a necessary virtue of great bodies and great souls. The first commandment is to love yourself; the great law is "*Do not spare your neighbor!* Man is something that must be overcome."

Nietzsche turns at last to the doctrine of eternal recurrence. The theory that history repeats itself in identical cycles is familiar to us through the Greek philosopher Plato, who derived it from the writings of Egyptian and Babylonian astronomers. It requires a concept of time that has not been congenial to Western thought ever since it was attacked by Saint Augustine. For Westerners, time seems to move in a straight line that has no turnings. Nietzsche, knowing that his doctrine would not be well received, stated it first as coming from Zarathustra's animals: "Everything goes, everything comes back; eternally rolls the wheel of being." Whatever is happening now will happen again and has happened before. The great things of the world recur, but so do the small. The recurrence of the small things, of the people farthest removed from the Overman, seems at first impossible for Zarathustra to accept. That the return is exactly the same—not that the best returns, not that the part returns, not that all except the worst returns, but that *all*, best and worst, returns—is difficult for him to acknowledge. However, at last he is willing to abandon the doctrine of progress for the truth of eternal recurrence.

Zarathustra and the Overman

The fourth part of *Thus Spake Zarathustra*, not intended by Nietzsche to be the last, is concerned with the consequences of accepting some portion of Zarathustra's teachings without accepting the whole. One must take all or none. Much of this part consists of parodies of Christian views—for example, that one must become like a little bovine to enter the Kingdom of Heaven.

Zarathustra, who is still concerned with the Overman, wonders what he will be like. As the philosopher goes from place to place in the world, he sees that people are fit only to be despised unless they are the prelude to the Overman. People are not to be preserved; they are to be overcome. People must be brave even though there is no God; people must be strong because they are evil; and they must hate their neighbors as a consequence of the will to power.

Once more, this doctrine is too strong for the people who listen to Zarathustra. Although God is dead, it is necessary for them to make a god of their own; and this time they choose a donkey. The animal fulfills all of the requirements for a god. He is a servant of humankind. He does not speak and therefore is never wrong. The world, created as stupidly as possible, is in his own image. Everyone is able to believe in the donkey's long ears. Zarathustra, after upbraiding the people for worshiping a donkey, is told by them that it is better to worship some god, even a donkey, than no god at all. At least here is something that the worshiper can see, touch, hear, and even smell and taste if he or she wants to. God seems more credible in this form. The first atheist was the person who said that God is spirit.

Zarathustra replies to this plea for the donkey by pointing out that worship of any sort is a return to childhood. The Overman has no wish to enter the Kingdom of Heaven; he wants the earth. However, if the people need to worship, let them worship donkeys if such a belief helps them.

No one except Zarathustra has seen the earth as it is. However, the Overman will come, and he will see it. He will command the earth and it will obey. With this vision in mind, Zarathustra turns again to the world to search for and bring into perfection the Overman.

John Collinson, updated by John K. Roth

Beyond Good and Evil

Type of philosophy: Ethics, philosophy of religion
First published: Jenseits von Gut und Böse: Vorspiel einer Philosophie der Zukunft, 1886 (English translation, 1907)
Principal ideas advanced:
◇ Ideas that preserve life and add to a person's power are more important than ideas sanctioned by logicians and seekers after the absolute.

◇ The metaphysical interest in the freedom of the will should give way to an interest in the strength of the will.
◇ People must turn conventional values upside down in order to live creatively; the established values of society were invented by the weak to enable them to triumph over the strong.
◇ Scientific minds are weak when they fail to pass judgment; whoever denies the will denies the power of life.
◇ Progress in life is possible only if there are people of action who have the courage to trust will and instinct; new values arise that go beyond conventional good and evil when the will to power asserts itself.

Friedrich Nietzsche holds a commanding historical significance in modern thought in spite of a continuing controversy about his stature as a philosophical mind. Many scholars refuse to judge Nietzsche's brilliant writings as serious philosophical contributions. They prefer to view him as a poet, as a critic of culture and religion, or even as a superb master of the German language. Yet some scholars insist on Nietzsche's importance as a genuine philosophical figure—a lonely, disturbed thinker who anticipated criticism of the classical ideal of a rigorously deductive model of philosophical knowledge and of the accompanying belief in the possibility of a completed metaphysics. Nietzsche felt keenly the impact of Darwinian evolutionary views that so stirred many nineteenth century thinkers in a number of intellectual fields. As a philosopher, he must be included in that group of thinkers for whom the philosopher's primary function is to lay bare the unexamined assumptions and buried cultural influences lurking behind supposedly disinterested moral and metaphysical constructions.

Symptomatically, *Beyond Good and Evil* begins with a chapter entitled "About Philosophers' Prejudices." Written during Nietzsche's intellectual maturity, hard on the heels of a lengthy literary development yet prior to the illness that ended his career, this book reflects the many important central tendencies of his thought. Its contents illustrate the surprisingly wide range of Nietzsche's intellectual interests: the origin and nature of moral valuations, the history and psychology of religion, the psychology of human motivation, and historical processes. Nietzsche often uses aphorisms that, though unsystematic from a logical point of view, manage to express a tolerably consistent philosophical viewpoint.

Nietzsche's writings contain numerous passages that suggest similar positions worked out in greater psychotherapeutic detail by Sigmund Freud. Frequently, he shows greater interest in the question, "What are the motives of philosophizing?" than in "What do philosophers say?" When he turns to an analysis of moral judgments, Nietzsche worries about what may hide submerged in such valuations—much as a student of icebergs wants to discover what exists beneath the surface. Perhaps the valuations produced by moralists always represent a perspective on things in the sense that there may exist no final metaphysical standpoint from which to render such valuations.

In a similar manner, the philosophical quest after truth may peculiarly express what Nietzsche terms the "will to power" rather than a disinterested description of things. Even assuming that genuine truth can be obtained in principle, Nietzsche points out that the value of an idea has greater significance than the truth of the idea. The value perspectives by which individuals live may be necessary and yet not objective. "Untruth" may carry greater value than "truth" in many situations. Such perspectives must be judged in terms of the degree to which they are life-furthering. Early in *Beyond Good and Evil*, Nietzsche suggests, "Even behind logic and its apparent sovereignty of development stand value judgments, or, to speak more plainly, physiological demands for preserving a certain type of life." On this supposition, a psychologist would ask of any belief whether it is conducive to sound health (a therapeutic matter) rather than whether it is true. "True" and "health-producing" become synonymous in Nietzsche's treatment of ideas.

Physiology and Philosophy
Nietzsche criticizes a philosopher such as Immanuel Kant for having assumed existence of an unknowable "thing-in-itself" behind the phenomenal universe available to science. Similarly,

he shows scorn for Georg Wilhelm Friedrich Hegel, who sought to find in the antithetical aspects of existence (passions, ideas, moral valuations) the expressions of a more fundamental rational reality. The tendency toward dualism, by which the "I" as subject stands independent of that which is perceived (as well as logically distinct as "subject" against "object"), receives criticism as a possible grammatical prejudice erected into a false and misleading metaphysical argument. Rather than philosophizing in "the grand manner," Nietzsche encourages piecemeal treatment of a host of specific, clearly stated problems. Physiology may hold the key to the solution of a number of old and baffling questions, including moral ones.

Philosophical investigators must forgo easy solutions happening to fit their prejudices—just as physiologists must cease thinking that the basic drive behind organic life is that toward self-preservation. The will to power may prove more fundamental than desire of self-preservation. The will to power expresses an expansive, assimilating, positive, value-creating tendency in existence, nonhuman as well as human. There may also be no immediate certainties like the philosopher's "I think" or "Schopenhauer's superstition, 'I will.'" The older superstition that thinking activity results from a human will requires sophisticated and subtle analysis, for "A thought comes when 'it' and not when 'I' will." Indeed, even to say "*It* is thought" instead of "I think" may cause another set of misleading metaphysical puzzles to arise. Nietzsche also argues that the metaphysical question about freedom of the will results from misuses of terms such as "cause" and "effect," which are simply concepts. These concepts are fictions useful for the facilitation of common understanding but not as explanations. People must stop creating myths about an objective reality based on pure concepts useful for other ends. There is neither "free" nor "nonfree" will, according to Nietzsche, but simply "strong will and weak will."

Psychological investigations done prior to Nietzsche's day are found suspect because of the subtle ways in which their conclusions reflect human prejudices and fears. This theme sounds constantly throughout Nietzsche's writings. Nietzsche wanted a new kind of psychologist able to resist the unconscious forces influencing one to accept conclusions dictated by one's "heart." The evidence is what must count in such investigations. He asks his readers to imagine an investigator in physiology-psychology who possesses the courage to believe that greed, hatred, envy, and such passions are "the passions on which life is conditioned, as things that must be present in the total household of life." So, too, the new philosophical breed will approach the study of the origins of morals with a ruthless honesty.

Values

In a later book, *Zur Genealogie der Moral* (1887; *On the Genealogy of Morals*, 1896), Nietzsche in practice attempted the kind of historical-genetic investigation his *Beyond Good and Evil* recommends in principle. In the former book, it is suggested that the concepts "good" and "bad," as well as "good" and "evil," arose out of a spiteful transvaluation of classical values by the meek and the lowly. "Evil" is the valuation placed on acts previously termed "good" in an aristocratic, healthy culture. Jewish and Christian priests, expressing their hatred of life, described as "evil" those biological functions fundamental to creation and healthful strength.

The central suggestion in *Beyond Good and Evil* is that another transvaluation of human values must now follow from the evolutionary notion of the will to power—that the cultural standpoint of Western Europe so influenced by Christian valuations must undergo a deep change to usher in gigantic, even sometimes cataclysmic, alterations in the table of values. Humanity must "get beyond" existing valuations in order to live creatively and even dangerously. A culture whose established values are foundering, in which the faith in metaphysical absolutes wobbles unsteadily on aging legs, throws up the question whether the belief in the possibility of an objectively justifiable morality is an illusion. Never does Nietzsche say that people can live without making valuations. Nor does he argue that moral valuations are unqualifiedly relative—one as good as another. His point is psychological and critical. Nietzsche believed that human nature, a product of evolution, demands the constant creation of new valuations even in the face of the absence of absolute standards. This aspect of his thought brings to mind existentialist thought that, however differently expressed by numerous existentialist writers, responds to the anguish of the human situation by making value judgments possible even though absolutes are lacking.

Nietzsche warns that the new philosopher must guard against some of the characteristics of the "intellectuals." Nietzsche cautions against bringing up a German generation so preoccupied with history that the *value* of those things whose history is studied could receive neither affirmation nor denial. Intellectualistic pursuit of objective knowledge tends to weaken the critical and evaluative capacities needed as a basis for living. Nietzsche never ridicules the scientific quest after objective knowledge as such. What he warns against is the production of scientific minds unable to make judgments about better and worse. Objective knowledge functions valuably only as a means to some other end or ends, such as those that actualize human potentiality in all its possible varieties. Scientific knowledge fails to show people what they should agree to or object to from a valuational standpoint. Judgment is a function of the will—something that the scientific person can never determine.

For many centuries, people decided on the value of actions by reference to their consequences. Nietzsche calls this the *premoral* period. Because he elsewhere caricatures English utilitarian thought, one must assume that Nietzsche thinks little of a value standard based on the tendency of acts to produce pleasure rather than pain. A second period, lasting for the past ten thousand years (according to Nietzsche, who made no anthropological survey of such an enormous space of historical time), is marked by a predominant tendency to judge the value or worthlessness of an act by its origins. "The origin of an action was interpreted to rest, in a very definite sense, on an *intent*." Such an intentional yardstick for judging actions reflected an aristocratic stance. In his own time, Nietzsche believed neither the intent nor the consequences of an act would play the crucial role. This would be the *amoral* period. In a famous passage, Nietzsche characterizes the nature of the philosophers who would conduct new amoral analyses of human valuations:

A new species of philosopher is coming up over the horizon. I risk baptizing them with a name that is not devoid of peril. As I read them (as they allow themselves to be read—for it is characteristic of their type that they wish to remain riddles in some sense), these philosophers of the future have a right (perhaps also a wrong!) to be called: *Experimenters*. This name itself is only an experiment, and, if you will, a temptation.

These thinkers will view pain and suffering as the necessary preconditions of any new valuations. They will also issue commands rather than simply describe or explain.

Religion

Nietzsche's treatment of what he calls "the peculiar nature of religion" bears a crucial relation to his prophesied transvaluation of existing values. According to Nietzsche, students of religious phenomena should develop that kind of malicious subtlety that moral investigators need in all times and places if they are to succeed in their work. Although he despised the moral values taught by traditional Christianity, Nietzsche nonetheless admired the psychological self-discipline of the Christian saints. Religious phenomena fascinated him. The faith demanded of early Christians, a rarely attained reality, provides an example possessing peculiarly tough and lasting appeal. Nietzsche writes that contemporary people lack the corresponding toughness to appreciate the paradoxical statement of faith: God died on a cross.

Early Christian faith demanded qualities found in the philosopher Blaise Pascal, according to Nietzsche. In Pascal, this faith "looks in a horrible way like a continuous suicide of the reason, a tough, long-lived, worm-like reason that cannot be killed at one time and with one blow." Nietzsche believed that such a faith would require careful study if the new experimenters were to learn how to succeed in their own transvaluation of Christian values. Especially intriguing are the three restrictions associated with what Nietzsche calls "the religious neurosis": solitude, fasting, and sexual abstinence. For students to understand the earlier historical transvaluation that occurred, they must answer the question, "How is the saint possible?" Genuinely to underst how from the "bad" person one gets, sudden saint, requires one to compare Christianity's v uations to the lavish gratitude characteristic earlier Greek religion before fear made Christian ity a possibility.

Moral Analysis

Nietzsche argues that the study of moral and religious phenomena can never be the work of a day or a brief season. Modern thinkers can hope only to assemble the necessary evidence, slowly and painstakingly. Their first concern is the statement of a morphology of morality rather than the former ambitious attempt to give a philosophical justification of the derivation of a morality. Only "the collection of the material, the conceptual formalization and arrangement of an enormous field of delicate value-feelings and value-differences that are living, growing, generating others, and perishing" is possible at the present time along with some observations about recurrent features of these value growths. Investigators must know where to look for the proper evidence. For this task, the scientific person lacks the capacities needed for directing the investigations. The scientific person functions best as an instrument—an enormously valuable one. Yet the instrument "belongs in the hands of one who has greater power"—one who commands what uses the instrument shall be put to. Most philosophers also fail to qualify for this kind of moral analysis. The reason is that they have reduced philosophizing to theory of knowledge, which produces a value skepticism when what is required is action—value commanding and value judging.

The whole problem of understanding moral valuations is reminiscent of the older faith-versus-reason controversy in theology. Does "instinct" (the tendency to act creatively without always knowing how to give reasons for one's actions) hold a more important place in the subject matter of moral analysis than reasoning (the capacity to give reasons for one's valuations)? This problem emerges early in the character of Socrates—a philosopher whom Nietzsche admires for his magnificent irony and dialectical skills even though Nietzsche denounces "Socratism," the dogma that beliefs are valuable only insofar as they are capable of logical justification.

Nietzsche considers Socrates a much greater figure than Plato. Socrates knew how to laugh at himself, realizing that his superior powers failed to discover the means by which to justify many beliefs he held important. Plato was more naïve than Socrates. Plato left a moral prejudice that Nietzsche simply rejects: the view that instinct and reason ultimately seek the same end—"God" or *the* Good." Plato, in thus dissolving all that Nietzsche finds fascinating in the faith-reason controversy, made possible a later Christian institutionalization of herd-morality.

Fundamentally, Nietzsche distrusts individuals who venerate reason and deny the value of instinct. He insists that people of action illustrate the gap that exists between those who merely know (intellectually) and those who act. Any existing morality needs a horizon provided by people of action who say: "It shall be thus!" This command source of any morality must itself go unjustified and unquestioned. Any existing morality is in this sense always "problematic." By this Nietzsche probably meant that after reasons for the existing valuations have been given, there must remain, at last, a self-justifying command for which no further reasons are possible. Indeed, all morality containing progressive aspects stems from an aristocratic type of commanding. Every command requires a commander, some individual who supplies the necessary value horizon that others must simply accept. There can be no objectively grounded perspective of all perspectives. Life as an expanding process requires the cutting off of deliberative procedures at some point.

Nietzsche was willing to accept some of the painful consequences of this view of the command origin of all moral valuations. One consequence is that any existing morality requires sacrifice of numerous individuals and of many nuances of feeling and human tendency. Morality requires the application of command in such a way that not all legitimately natural instincts can find total expression at any one time. It also rests on exploitation as a necessary element in the creation of values. Some instincts must give way to others—and the commanding ones ought to be domineering and aristocratic. There must occur "the forcing of one's own forms upon something else."

Nietzsche's analysis of morality led him to dislike equalitarian democracy and herd-utilitarianism ("the greatest happiness of the greatest number"). An order of rank must exist. Between commander and commanded must arise a social distance based on the former's greater value. The new philosopher seeking to transform valuations must stand "against his own time"—finding a value standpoint "beyond" the accepted valuations of his own era. To do so requires hardness and patient waiting. Philosophical success is thus partly a result of circumstances beyond any individual philosopher's control. *What* his creative response shall be is a function of what the situation is in which he finds himself. In this sense the philosopher must always be a lonely individual, "beyond" the good and evil of conventional morality. This loneliness will produce anguish.

In *Also sprach Zarathustra: Ein Buch für Alle und Keinen* (1883-1885; *Thus Spake Zarathustra*, 1896), Nietzsche describes the anguish that results from the discovery that no God is found beyond good and evil. Nor is there a higher, more ultimate Platonic harmony. The new philosopher must learn to embrace existence for its own sake. Nietzsche attempts to express the nature of this love of existence through a doctrine of "eternal recurrence." The philosopher of existence must say "yes" to reality while knowing that "God is dead." Any new values that arise in the evolutionary process do so as expressions of people's self-commanding capacity. Error and pain inevitably and necessarily are aspects of existence. "That everything recurs, is the very nearest approach of a world of Becoming to a world of Being: the height of contemplation," he wrote in the second volume of *Der Wille zur Macht* (1901; *The Will to Power*, 1910), which was published from remaining notes by Nietzsche's sister. The new philosopher of "beyondness" needs this doctrine of eternal recurrence because the new philosopher must command new values in an existence that expresses the will to power rather than a rational scheme of things.

In Nietzsche's style one finds a brilliance to match his intellectual daring—a wealth of suggestion, irony, maliciousness, a fine balancing of value antitheses, and playful criticism coupled with the most serious intention. Nietzsche was (as he says all people are) a philosopher who worked from an inner necessity to achieve self-understanding. Of philosophers he wrote: "But fundamentally, 'way down below' in us, there is something unteachable, a bedrock of intellectual destiny, of predestined decision, of answers to predestined selected questions."

Whitaker T. Deininger, updated by John K. Roth

Additional Reading

Berkowitz, Peter. *Nietzsche: The Ethics of an Immoralist.* Cambridge, Mass.: Harvard University Press, 1995. Shows how Friedrich Nietzsche's attacks on conventional and traditional morality entail a distinctive ethical outlook.

Conway, Daniel W. *Nietzsche and the Political.* New York: Routledge, 1997. A thoughtful discussion of the political implications of Nietzsche's philosophy.

Copleston, Frederick. *A History of Philosophy: Modern Philosophy.* Garden City, N.Y.: Doubleday, 1965. Copleston provides a good overview of Nietzsche's thought and situates him in his nineteenth century European context.

Hayman, Ronald. *Nietzsche.* New York: Routledge, 1999. An excellent biographical introduction to the thoughts of the philosopher, clearly presented and requiring no special background. Bibliography.

_____. *Nietzsche: A Critical Life.* New York: Oxford University Press, 1980. A chronological account of Nietzsche's life and work.

Heilke, Thomas. *Nietzsche's Tragic Regime: Culture, Aesthetics, and Political Education.* De Kalb: Northern Illinois University Press, 1998. A fascinating treatment of the theme of political education in Nietzsche's early work.

Higgins, Kathleen. *Nietzsche's Zarathustra.* Philadelphia: Temple University Press, 1987. Clearly written and accessible, this book explores in depth the themes and issues raised in Nietzsche's work *Thus Spake Zarathustra.*

Jones, W. T. *A History of Western Philosophy: Kant to Wittgenstein and Sartre.* New York: Harcourt, Brace, 1969. Provides a good introductory discussion of Nietzsche's main themes.

Kaufmann, Walter. *Nietzsche: Philosopher, Psychologist, Antichrist.* 4th ed. Princeton, N.J.: Princeton University Press, 1974. A standard and important account of Nietzsche's life and thought by one of his major translators.

Klein, Wayne. *Nietzsche and the Promise of Philosophy.* Albany: State University of New York Press, 1997. Discusses Nietzsche's vision of what philosophy should and should not be and traces the implications of his analysis.

Krell, David Farrell. *The Good European: Nietzsche's Work Sites in Word and Image.* Chicago: University of Chicago Press, 1997. Analyzes Nietzsche's philosophy in relation to the contexts and places in which he developed his distinctive vision.

_____. *Infectious Nietzsche.* Bloomington: Indiana University Press, 1996. Shows how Nietzsche's influence has been challenging, ongoing, and significant in ways that will continue to make him a thinker of immense importance.

Magnus, Bernd. *Nietzsche's Existential Imperative.* Bloomington: Indiana University Press, 1978. An interpretation of Nietzsche that focuses on his doctrine of eternal recurrence and takes *Thus Spake Zarathustra* as a principal source.

Magnus, Bernd, and Kathleen M. Higgins, eds. *The Cambridge Companion to Nietzsche.* Cambridge, England: Cambridge University Press, 1996. Nietzsche scholars contribute insightful articles about diverse aspects of his influential philosophy.

Nehamas, Alexander. *Nietzsche: Life as Literature.* Cambridge, Mass.: Harvard University Press, 1985. An instructive interpretation of Nietzsche's philosophy and his view that philosophy has close links to narrative.

Waite, Geoff. *Nietzsche's Corpse: Aesthetics, Politics, Prophecy, or, the Spectacular Technoculture of Everyday Life.* Durham, N.C.: Duke University Press, 1996. An assessment of Nietzsche's significance and impact on the development of culture, politics, and technology in the twentieth century and beyond.

Dan Barnett, updated by John K. Roth

Kitarō Nishida

Nishida created a highly original and distinctive philosophy, based upon his thorough assimilation of both Western philosophy and methodology and the Zen Buddhist tradition.

Principal philosophical works: *Zen no kenkyū*, 1911 (*A Study of the Good*, 1960; better known as *An Inquiry into the Good*, 1990); *Shisaku to taiken*, 1915; *Jikakku ni okeru chokkan to hansei*, 1917 (*Intuition and Reflection in Self-Consciousness*, 1987); *Ishiki no mondai*, 1920; *Geijutsu to dōtoku*, 1923 (*Art and Morality*, 1973); *Hataraku mono kara miru mono e*, 1927; *Ippansha no jikakuteki taikei*, 1930; *Mu no jikakuteki gentei*, 1932; *Tetsugaku no kompon mondai*, 1933-1944 (*Fundamental Problems of Philosophy*, 1970); *Tetsugaku ronbunshū I-VII*, 1935-1946; *Zoku shisaku to taiken*, 1940; *Nihon bunka no mondai*, 1940 (partial translation, "The Problem of Japanese Culture," 1958); *Zoku shisaku to taiken igo*, 1948.

Born: June 17, 1870; Unoke, near Kanazawa, Japan
Died: June 7, 1945; Kamakura, Japan

Early Life

Kitarō Nishida was born on June 17, 1870, in the Mori section of the village of Unoke in Ishikawa Prefecture, located near Kanazawa on the Sea of Japan. He was the eldest son, the middle child out of five. Nishida's family moved to Kanazawa in 1883. There Nishida entered the local school, the prefectural normal school, which boasted an enterprising Western-style school system. Typhus forced his withdrawal from the school one year later, and he studied privately with several teachers for the next two years. In July, 1886, Nishida entered the middle school attached to the Ishikawa Prefectural College. After completing his preparatory work there, Nishida entered the Fourth Higher School in July, 1889. While attending the Fourth Higher School, Nishida lived in the home of the mathematician Hōjō Tokiyoshi. His interest in Zen Buddhism, of which his mathematics teacher was an adept, dates to this period of his life.

Despite the urging of Hōjō that he become a mathematician, Nishida specialized in philosophy. He left the Fourth Higher School shortly before his graduation in 1890. The circumstances surrounding his departure remain mysterious. Lack of formal graduation from high school forced Nishida to enter the philosophy department of Tokyo Imperial University as a special student in September of 1891. There he was exposed to contemporary European thought. Nishida graduated from Tokyo Imperial University in 1894. He encountered difficulties in finding employment because of his irregular academic background and was unemployed for nearly a full year after graduation. He took a room in the house of a painter named Tokuda Kō; during this time he wrote a study of Thomas Hill Green, a British Hegelian. He then obtained a position with a meager salary at a prefectural middle school on remote Noto Peninsula.

Nishida married the daugher of Tokuda Kō, Tokuda Kotomi, in May of 1895. His first daughter, Yayoi, was born in March of 1896. Together, Nishida and Kotomi had eight children: six daughters and two sons. Shortly after his marriage, Nishida's religious interests deepened. Upon returning to Kanazawa in 1896 to take a teaching position at the Fourth Higher School, Nishida began Zen meditation. A diary begun in 1897 provides an account of his rigorous introspective regimen. This spiritual discipline intensified in 1897 to 1899, when Nishida was alone in Yamaguchi, separated from his wife as a result of a serious disagreement with his father.

Life's Work

After teaching as a part-time professor at Yamaguchi Higher School from 1897 to 1899, Nishida returned to teach again at the Fourth Higher School in Kanazawa. There he taught psychology, ethics, German, and logic for ten years, from 1899 to 1909; at this time, he developed the basic philosophical views that he would broaden and deepen for the rest of his life but never abandon. In addition to teaching, Nishida was active in establishing extracurricular literary groups. His most ambitious project was the establishment of a student residence and study center called San San Juku. San San Juku served as a meeting place for students to discuss problems of religion and literature with invited lecturers from various religious sects and denominations. This institution became a lasting part of the Fourth Higher School in Kanazawa.

In January of 1907, Nishida's daughter, Yūko, died of bronchitis. In June of that same year, another daughter, only one month old, died. Nishida himself fell sick. In the face of these tragedies, Nishida spurred himself toward greater self-reliance. He also disciplined himself to increase the level of his intellectual output. The fruit of this discipline was the publication of his first book, *An Inquiry into the Good*, in January of 1911. Nishida's lifelong concern was to provide a Western philosophical framework for Zen intuition. *An Inquiry into the Good* launched this project. It included a theory of reality, a study of ethics, and the skeleton of a philosophy of religion. One of Nishida's most central philosophical concepts, that of "pure experience," is introduced in this first major work. Nishida defines "pure experience" as direct experience without deliberative discrimination and without the least addition of one's own fabrications. Unlike many practitioners of Zen, Nishida does not give the impression of being anti-intellectual. "Pure experience" is not in opposition to thought and intellect but rather lies at the base of all the oppositions produced by the mind, such as those of subject and object, body and mind, and spirit and matter. Nishida was inspired by the American philosopher William James and found in French philosopher Henri Bergson a kindred spirit, but if he borrowed anything from either, it became thoroughly assimilated into his own philosophy. The publication of *An Inquiry into the Good* in 1911 was hailed as an epoch-making event in the introduction of Western philosophy into Japan. The

academic world perceived it to be the first truly original philosophic work by a Japanese thinker in the modern period (which began in 1868 with the Meiji Restoration). All prior attempts at combining traditional Japanese thought with Western philosophy had been patently eclectic.

Following one year at Gakushūin University in Tokyo, Nishida was appointed assistant professor of ethics at Kyoto Imperial University in 1910. In August of 1914, he was relieved from his chair of ethics in the Faculty of Letters and called to the first chair of the history of philosophy in the philosophy department of the University of Kyoto. There he taught until his retirement in 1928. Many brilliant students flocked to his classes. Together with Hajime Tanabe, he established what has come to be known as the Kyoto, or Nishida-Tanabe, School of philosophy. Around 1910, Nishida's philosophy was influenced by his study of Bergson and the German Neo-Kantians, especially Wilhelm Windelband, Heinrich Rickert, and Hermann Cohen. His thorough assimilation of the logical epistemology of Neo-Kantian transcendentalism and his own critique of its fundamental principles enabled Nishida to discover a deeper significance in Immanuel Kant's philosophy and the transcendental method of German idealism. This achievement enabled him to bring his earlier concept of "pure experience" to a higher level. In his second major work, *Intuition and Reflection in Self-Consciousness*, Nishida strove to eliminate psychologism from his thinking. In this work, he defined the ultimate character of self-consciousness as "absolute free will." "Absolute free will," when genuine, transcends reflection. It cannot be reflected upon, for it is that which causes reflection.

In August of 1918, Nishida's mother died; disaster struck again when his wife, Kotomi, suffered a brain hemorrhage in September of 1919. Kotomi was paralyzed for the remaining six years of her life. In June of 1920, Nishida's eldest son, Ken, died of peritonitis at the age of twenty-two. During the next several years, three more of his daughters fell ill with typhus. In January of 1925, Kotomi died after a prolonged period of suffering. She was fifty years old. Nishida's diary reveals that these personal tragedies affected him deeply. Nevertheless, he disciplined himself to maintain his philosophical activity. His next two works, *Ishiki no mondai* (the problem of consciousness) and *Art and Morality*, offered progressive refinements of the concepts of "pure experience" and "absolute free will."

The epoch-making *Hataraku mono kara miru mono e* (from that which acts to that which sees) formulates the concept of *basho no ronri* ("logic of place"). It is Nishida's notion of "place" and his "logic of place" that distinguish him in the history of philosophy. In this work, he discusses a realm of reality that corresponds to his own mystical experience. Indeed, with his concept of place, Nishida provided a conceptual and logical framework for a philosophical position that is usually categorized as mysticism in the West. According to Nishida, the "true self" is revealed in the "place" of "absolute nothingness." The concept of "absolute nothingness" has clear roots in Buddhist tradition. This "nothingness" is not relative nothingness, nothingness as contrasted with phenomenal existence; rather, it is absolute nothingness, wherein all phenomenal existences appear as determinations of it. "Absolute free will" emerges from creative nothingness and returns to creative nothingness.

Retirement from his teaching position at the University of Kyoto in 1928 did not slow Nishida's productive pace. His postretirement works include *Ippansha no jikakuteki taikei* (the self-conscious system of universals), *Mu no jikakuteki gentei* (the self-conscious determination of nothingness), *Fundamental Problems of Philosophy*, and *Tetsugaku ronbunshū I-VII* (philosophical essays). In the last stage of his philosophical development, Nishida was concerned with "the self-identity of absolute contradiction," or "the unity of opposites." This concept was discovered through his investigation of the relationship between the self and the world. Nishida used this concept to probe what he considered to be one of the fundamental problems of a philosophy of religion: the contradictions of an existence in which the satisfaction of desire means the extinction of desire and in which the will makes its own extinction its goal. These contradictions undergird religious experience, for it is only in the awareness of the absolute contradictoriness and nothingness of the self's existence that human beings are able to touch God and the absolute.

Nishida's first grandchild was born in October of 1928. He married again in December of 1931; his second wife's name was Koto. For perhaps the first time in his life, Nishida's family life became serene. The retired professor enjoyed the visits of his children and grandchildren immensely. There were no further deaths in the family until February of 1945, when his favorite daughter, Yayoi, died suddenly. Nishida found World War II to be a profoundly distressing event. He managed, however, to continue his philosophical writings at his home in Kamakura despite the destruction in Tokyo and other major Japanese cities. He died suddenly in early June of 1945, only two months before Japan's surrender.

Influence

Nishida is widely recognized as the first genuinely original Japanese philosopher of the modern period. He departed from the eclecticism of his predecessors and almost single-handedly created an indigenous Japanese philosophy. His true significance will probably not be determined until a comprehensive, global history of modern ideas is written: He is the only Japanese philosopher of recent times around whom a philosophical school has been formed. Most of the leading philosophers of twentieth century Japan were influenced by him, either as a result of being his students or through assimilation of his thought.

Since the late 1950's, Nishida's works have become known outside Japan. Although his thought has been severely criticized by Marxist and other antimetaphysical thinkers, on the whole Nishida's philosophy has been favorably received by the Western world. He is recognized as one of the first philosophers to offer a system that transcends the distinctions between Eastern and Western philosophy. He is further credited with having given Asian thought a logical foundation with his "logic of nothingness."

Ann Marie B. Bahr

An Inquiry into the Good

Type of philosophy: Buddhism, ethics, Japanese philosophy, metaphysics

First published: Zen no kenkyū, 1911 (A Study of the Good, 1960; better known as An Inquiry into the Good, 1990)

Principal ideas advanced:

◇ Pure or direct experience is the basis for all human thinking, judging, willing, emotional responses, and actions.

◇ Pure experience in itself is devoid of and is prior to all conceptualizations, emotions, and actions.

◇ All modes of thought based on dualistic assumptions are mere abstractions from and intellectual constructs of this pure experience.

◇ Pure experience is the sole, or ultimate, reality; it is equated with the Zen notion of absolute nothingness.

◇ Because pure experience functions as the "place" or "space" within which all distinctions, oppositions, thoughts, and actions reside, its realization is the only basis for ethical activity.

◇ Pure experience, or absolute nothingness, is equated with God and is both the unifier of the universe and the absolute "core" of all things.

Kitarō Nishida was born during the Meiji Restoration (1868-1912), a period in Japan's history marked by rapid industrialization and Westernization. Like many of the intellectuals of this time, Nishida was concerned about the pervasiveness of scientific and Western modes of thought; he believed that these fostered in the Japanese people an alienation from nature and traditional cultural values. The result of this alienation, Nishida believed, was a sense of personal meaninglessness and a view of the world as coldly rational and mechanical. This alienation seemingly became concretized in the suicide of an eighteen-year-old student named Fujimura Misao. Fujimura's suicide was seen, in part, as a protest against modernity's overrationalization of life and the loss of the mystery of the universe. As a response to this alienation and growing sense of meaninglessness, many Japanese thinkers became critical of the changes brought about by the Meiji Restoration, particularly its importation of Western modes of thought. Nishida, while realizing a return to pre-Meiji perspectives was impossible, sought to reassess these "foreign"

ideas in the context of traditional Buddhist thought, particularly in the Zen notion of "absolute nothingness." He found in absolute nothingness the critical "space" that could include Western thought and science and, more important, ground them in the prescientific insights of Buddhist thought.

A Concern for Unity

One of the major concerns in Nishida's work was to articulate a principle of unity underlying the manifold oppositions experienced by the modern individual. His philosophy was in part a response to the rapid industrialization of Japan during the Meiji period; he felt that Western thought and science were supplanting and uprooting long-held religious and cultural traditions. The individual's place in the world was also being transformed; no longer able to fully believe in traditional religious worldviews, humans were left alienated in a rationalized and scientifically explained universe.

Nishida saw the possibility of formulating a philosophical principle through which the various dichotomies in society and the individual could be "contained." Because Nishida believed that Western thought and science were inextricably bound to Japanese culture, he felt that the only way to overcome the fragmenting power of modernity was to critically rethink the dualistic assumptions underlying rational and scientific modes of thought. Appropriating various strands of Western metaphysics, critical philosophy, and psychology, Nishida took a synthetic approach in his attempts to construct a unifying principle. This unification of views under a single principle, however, was grounded in the Buddhist tradition, specifically the standpoint of Zen.

Pure Experience

Nishida took aim at the dualistic assumptions he believed plagued Western thinking. He maintained that the separation between, for example, the subject and object, mind and matter, the unconscious and conscious, were mere constructions abstracted from a unified experience. This experience, Nishida maintained, occurred prior to and formed the basis of these dualities. This unified experience he called "pure experience." Nishida defined pure experience as the direct perception of phenomena before the occurrence of thoughts, judgments, feelings, and other reactions. It is a state of mind devoid of conceptuality and emotionality. However, this pure experience does not come to an end the moment thoughts and emotions arise. Pure experience is always present as the ground and subtext of all activity.

One of the fundamental criticisms Nishida had of the scientific worldview was the assumption of the subject-object dichotomy: that the observing subject is separate from the material world. For the modern, rational mind, the scientist is viewed as an objective observer who, through the formation of hypotheses and experimentation, uncovers the underlying principles that control the cosmos. What the scientifically oriented society gains by rationalization and thus control of the world, it loses by concealing the mysterious nonrational character of existence.

Nishida's response to the scientific perspective included the insight that the perception of the world is a unitary phenomenon, that the objectification of nature into a thing to be analyzed presupposes the bare perception of the world. In Nishida's words, it is not that the individual has experiences, but that (pure) experience makes the individual possible. This bare perception, which is before the separation of experience into subjects and objects, makes science possible and is, therefore, the ground of all scientific and rational thought.

Although pure experience is prior to conceptualization and feeling, Nishida maintains that it is dynamic, not passive. This characterization of pure experience was, in part, a critical response to Western psychological theories. In general, perception was taken to be a passive mode of consciousness, a mere reception of perceived objects, while thinking, judging, and willing were considered the active modes of consciousness. For example, while a person watches a car go by, consciousness first passively receives the image of the car. Subsequent moments of consciousness include the thought, "that is a car," the judgment, "that car is going too fast," and the will to do something about it, for example, call the police. Nishida claims that this view assumes, like scientific perspectives, the split between the subject and object. What underlies this division is, again, the unitary phenomenon of pure experience in which the subject, objects, and the so-called events are not separated. The analysis of separate factors of experience is a result of intellectual constructions based on dualistic assumptions and does not accurately represent the way things are.

For Nishida, bare or pure experience, though not characterized by conceptual and emotional activities, is a dynamic process that provides the "space" or "locus" for the interactions of phenomena. Nishida can claim this because for him the irreducible ground of all existence is not some kind of atomic, "material" existence, but rather the "place" within which consciousness perceives phenomena. In other words, consciousness and phenomena are one in that they participate interdependently as different aspects of a singular activity. What is primary for Nishida is the interdependent relation between seemingly oppositional phenomena, not the particular things that interact with each other. To isolate particular phenomena is, for Nishida, an intellectual construct and an abstraction from the dynamic unitary reality he calls direct experience.

Nishida claims that the ultimate or sole reality is just this unified space that contains all oppositions and dualities. Furthermore, he avoids a second-level dichotomy between this "space" and interrelational activity by explaining the paradoxical nature of pure experience as a unity in differentiation and a differentiation in unity. Nishida's argument runs as follows: Phenomena that seem different—for instance, different colors—are in a logical sense interrelated, because if there were only a singular color (for example, red), there would in fact be no perception of the color red. Furthermore, there would also be no perception of color at all. Phenomena such as color occur, or are perceived, only in the context of opposition; that is to say, the color red is meaningful only in contrast with other colors. The same goes for the phenomenon of motion. Motion occurs only when there are at least three objects, because in the case of a singular object, there is no reference point from which one can judge movement. Even if there were two objects, there is no way to determine which object is moving and which one is not. There must be at least three objects to determine the relative motion or stasis of perceived objects.

Paradoxical Notions and Western Thought

These kinds of analyses are Nishida's way of rearticulating traditional East Asian Buddhist concepts in the context of modern modes of thought. Paradoxical notions found in Zen teachings—neither being nor nonbeing, form is emptiness and emptiness is form, and mind is no-mind—provided the foundation for Nishida's appropriation and overcoming of Western dualistic thinking. In other words, the Buddhistic notion of absolute nothingness provided Nishida with the "place" within which all contradictions and differences could merge and become one.

Nishida does not limit these insights into the paradoxical nature of reality to Eastern thought. He contends that the experiences of God in Christian mysticism are instances of pure experience. Nishida's discussion about God begins with the common notion that God is an all-powerful creator of the universe who stands outside of creation. He further notes that this notion of God as an external reality is necessary for common explanations of Christian ethics. To the latter notion of ethics Nishida responds by arguing why the necessity of postulating an external, all-powerful being for the establishment of ethics reduces God to a mere expediency. To postulate God in order to ground ethics is putting the cart before the horse. Against the notion of God being an external reality, Nishida asserts that these sorts of God-concepts are "childish" because they are founded on dualistic conceptual constructions. Like all of his criticisms against dualistic thought, Nishida maintains that direct experience is the sole reality, and a true understanding of God happens only on the basis of this direct experience. His interpretations of Christian mystical experience, therefore, point to an intimate and radically subjective experience of God, one that transcends all conceptual activity but is absolutely immanent. God, according to Nishida, is not an external reality but rather the ground of all existence; that is to say, God is absolute nothingness.

Reality and Absolute Nothingness

If there is no external authority, who demands that humans be moral, what is the basis for ethical activity? Nishida, again grounding his discourse in his notion of direct experience and ab-solute nothingness, maintains that ethics cannot be based on a dutiful obeying of formal laws of morality or on a morality based on the pleasure principle. The "good," according to Nishida, is in absolute conformity with ultimate reality, and in order to be truly moral, one must realize this ultimate reality. Another way of saying this is that when the self truly realizes ultimate reality, that is, by abandoning the self-centered standpoint, then *reality realizes itself*. Thus, ethics is grounded in the actualization of absolute nothingness. This actualization is the true manifestation of the true, the beautiful, and the good, and anything short of this cannot be deemed truly ethical.

The notion that in the realization of reality, reality realizes itself also underlies Nishida's view of religion. Nishida attacks two views of religion: one that sees religion as a means to benefit one's circumstances and the other that considers religion as a vehicle for inner peace. Examples of the former include what Nishida considered the childish practice of praying to God or some other higher being for the purpose of bettering one's lot. The latter includes various kinds of practices that cultivate a passive indifference to life. According to Nishida, both views are similar because they see the purpose of religion as something to benefit humans. Nishida claims the opposite, that the true purpose of the individual is religion. In other words, to be religious means to fully abandon oneself to the religious quest, which requires nothing more than the death of the small or relative self. And yet, in the death of the small self, one actualizes one's true self, which is none other than pure experience.

Although *An Inquiry into the Good* did not have the same impact in the West as the works of his student, Keiji Nishitani, Nishida is hailed as one of the most important philosophers of prewar Japan. Furthermore, most young philosophers at the time the book was published in the late Meiji period believed that *An Inquiry into the Good* accurately articulated the social and, more important, spiritual situation of the Japanese people. It was received enthusiastically as a work that succeeded in overcoming the alienating effects of modernization.

John Y. Cha

Additional Reading

Abe, Masao. Introduction to *An Inquiry into the Good*, by Kitarō Nishida. New Haven, Conn.: Yale University Press, 1990. Introduces Kitarō Nishida's 1911 work as a creative synthesis of Eastern and Western philosophy. Offers useful clarification of the book's relation to Zen and philosophy and locates it in the contexts of Nishida's career and Western thought.

_____. "Nishida's Philosophy of 'Place.'" *The International Philosophical Quarterly* 28 (December, 1988): 355-371. Abe's intended audience is composed of professional philosophers. Nishida's concept of "place" distinguishes him in the history of philosophy.

Carter, Robert E. *The Nothingness Beyond God: An Introduction to the Philosophy of Nishida Kitarō*. 2d ed. St. Paul, Minn.: Paragon House, 1997. A helpful introduction to Nishida's philosophy.

Knauth, Lothar. "Life Is Tragic—The Diary of Nishida Kitaro." *Monumenta Nipponica* 20 (1965): 335-358. A study of Nishida's life, based on his diary. Discussions of Nishida's personal and family life, his professional life, his reading interests, and the development of his philosophical ideas are included.

Merton, Thomas. *Zen and the Birds of Appetite*. New York: New Directions, 1968. Contains a chapter introducing Nishida's philosophy to Westerners. It would be helpful to know something about Western philosophy and have some knowledge of Zen before reading this article.

Nishitani, Keiji. *Nishida Kitaro*. Berkeley: University of California Press, 1991. Essays on Nishida's life and thought by a former student and a fellow member of the Kyoto School of Japanese philosophy.

Piovesana, Gino K. *Recent Japanese Philosophical Thought, 1862-1962: A Survey*. Tokyo: Enderle Bookstore, 1963. Contains an essay that introduces Nishida's thought, with some helpful comments that suggest how to approach the demanding aspects of Nishida's works. Includes an index and a bibliography.

Piper, Raymond Frank. "Nishida, Notable Japanese Personalist." *Personalist* 17 (1936): 21-31. The only English-language article on Nishida written while he was still alive, it is a study of Nishida's philosophy based on the author's acquaintance with *An Inquiry into the Good*.

Shibata, Masumi. "The Diary of a Zen Layman: The Philosopher Nishida Kitaro." *The Eastern Buddhist* 14 (1981): 121-131. A study of what can be learned about Nishida's Zen practice and his thoughts about Zen from the pages of his diary.

Shimomura, Torataro. Introduction to *A Study of the Good*, by Kitarō Nishida. Tokyo: Japanese Government Printing Bureau, 1960. Nishida's thought is related to the Japanese philosophy that preceded him. This article also contains brief overviews of Nishida's life and of his later philosophical development.

Viglielmo, Valdo Humbert. "Nishida Kitaro: The Early Years." In *Tradition and Modernization in Japanese Culture*, edited by Donald H. Shively. Princeton, N.J.: Princeton University Press, 1971. A detailed account of Nishida's early life, from birth to approximately thirty-three years of age. Viglielmo is a noted Nishida scholar, and this well-written work does nothing to detract from his reputation.

Ann Marie B. Bahr, updated by William Nelles

Keiji Nishitani

By synthesizing modern Western philosophy and Zen Buddhist thought, Nishitani sought to overcome the nihilism of the twentieth century and forge connections between Eastern and Western philosophy and religion.

Principal philosophical works: *Nihirizumu*, 1949 (*The Self-Overcoming of Nihilism*, 1990); *Shūkyō to wa nani ka*, 1961 (*Religion and Nothingness*, 1982); *Nishida Kitarō*, 1985.

Born: February 27, 1900; Ishikawa Prefecture, Japan
Died: November 24, 1990; Kyoto, Japan

Early Life

Keiji Nishitani was born in Ishikawa Prefecture, Japan. When he was seven years old, Nishitani's family moved to Tokyo, where Nishitani remained until he graduated from college. When he was sixteen, his father died of tuberculosis, and soon after, Nishitani also fell ill from a similar disease. This no doubt had a strong impact on the young Nishitani; it is reported that, from an early age, Nishitani was afflicted by profound feelings of despair. These experiences brought him face to face with the possibility of his own demise and gave him a general sense of life's impermanence and uncertainty. Nishitani would later call this condition of life "nihility." His personal sense of nihility, what the Zen Buddhist tradition terms the "Great Doubt," instilled in him during his boyhood, ultimately led him to a serious study of Buddhist philosophy, particularly Zen.

Nishitani was born during the years of the Meiji Restoration (1868-1912), a period marked by Japan's push to modernize. In the course of this modernization and industrialization, the country experienced drastic changes in its political system, social structures, military organization and agricultural technologies. These changes were implemented so that Japan could advance to the level of and compete with the industrialized countries, especially Europe. Along with this

drive toward modernization was an attempt to instill a sense of nationalism in the Japanese people. This took the form of an ideology of emperor worship and the adoption of Shintoism as a state religion. The term "restoration" was used to propagate the view that Japan was actually returning to its traditional heritage while undergoing the process of industrialization. However, these drastic changes brought untold suffering to many Japanese whose traditional ways of livelihood no longer had a place in this new era. A part of the impetus for the intellectual endeavors of the Kyoto School, a group of philosophers at Kyoto University, was the insight that a coherent and workable worldview had to include an understanding of the ways modernization affected culture; a people had to transcend the tendency toward simple ideology while in the process of industrialization.

The push toward modernization also meant a need to Westernize many aspects of Japanese culture. During this period, Japan modified its educational system according to Western models; this change, along with numerous required courses in Western culture and ideas, cultivated in many Japanese an appreciation for and understanding of Western philosophy, literature, and religion. This meant that students of Nishitani's generation were exposed to a wide range of literary, philosophical, and religious works from the West. Among the most influential for Nishitani were the writings of German philosopher Friedrich Nietzsche, American philosopher Ralph Waldo Emerson, and Russian author Fyodor Dostoevski; the works of Christian mystics such as Meister Eckhart and Saint Francis of Assisi; and the Bible.

Life's Work

The intellectual influences on the young Nishitani encompassed a wide range of Western philosophical, existential, and religious literature. Though highly influenced by the modernization in the Meiji period, Nishitani also found a deep appreciation for one of Japan's traditional religions, Zen Buddhism. Most important for Nishitani was Zen's direct confrontation with the uncertainty and impermanence of life; what seemed to resonate for him was the Zen notion of the Great Doubt. This Great Doubt challenged humans to face up to their finitude and death and thereby overcome the sense of meaninglessness that accompanied these facts of human existence.

Nishitani found both the push toward modernization and the return to a traditional religious outlook in one of his teachers at Kyoto University, Japanese philosopher Kitarō Nishida, considered Japan's first modern philosopher and the founder of the Kyoto School. Though Nishida was steeped in the traditions of Western (primarily German) philosophy, his thinking also reflected a confrontation with the sense of the loss of tradition brought by the Meiji period. He attempted to modernize Zen Buddhist thought while retaining the traditional concept of ultimate reality, "absolute nothingness." In his works, Nishida analyzed, developed, and communicated Japanese thought in the language of Western philosophy, so much so that he explicitly discussed very few Buddhist ideas. He worked in this way because of his belief in the universal applicability of the notion of absolute nothingness. Nishida's philosophy was motivated, in part, by a twofold agenda: restoring a Japanese rootedness (via Buddhism) and developing a transcultural philosophy that would assist humans in realizing their true nature.

Though explicitly Western in its style, analysis, and expressions, Nishida's philosophy always functioned in the context of a Buddhist, specifically Zen, outlook. He took seriously the Zen admonition of "directly seeing into one's true nature" and always directed his philosophizing toward expressing the "pure" or "direct" experi-ence of reality. This pure experience for Nishida was the nondualistic perception of absolute nothingness ("emptiness" in traditional Buddhist terminology). His notion of absolute nothingness was one of the central ideas underlying Nishitani's philosophy and became the ethos of the Kyoto School. In fact, one of the assumptions of the Kyoto School is that this emptiness is the only authentic ground where the philosophical, religious, and cultural foundations of both the East and West can become unified. As a student, Nishitani was surrounded by this spirit of synthesis and universality in the Kyoto School's philosophy.

Between the years of 1924, the date of his graduation from Kyoto University, and 1935, Nishitani began his academic career at a number of Japanese colleges and universities, teaching courses in ethics, German, Western philosophy, and Buddhist thought. These institutions included Buddhist Ōtani University and Kyoto Imperial College. In 1935, Nishitani took a professorship in the Department of Religion at Kyoto University. It was during his professorship in Kyoto that Nishitani had the opportunity to study philosophy in Freiburg with the German philosopher Martin Heidegger.

Nearly ten years after studying German philosopher Nietzsche with Heidegger, Nishitani gave a series of lectures on Nietzsche in Japan, portraying him as a radical thinker who overcame Western metaphysics and ushered in a new era of philosophizing. These lectures made up a large portion of one of Nishitani's early major works on Western nihilism, *The Self-Overcoming of Nihilism*.

It is important to note that Nishitani was, by studying in Germany with the important philosophers of the time, continuing a tradition of sorts of the Kyoto School. His mentor, Nishida, studied in Germany with the founder of phenomenology, Edmund Husserl. Nishitani was also not the first Japanese to study under Heidegger; Nishitani's senior contemporary and fellow Kyoto School philosopher, Hajime Tanabe, was the first to study with Heidegger in Freiburg during the 1920's.

Apart from his strictly philosophical works, Nishitani also attempted to think and write critically about the role of Japan during and after

World War II. The various articles and transcripts of Nishitani's thought and discussions during these periods have given rise to heated debate among scholars of Japanese intellectual history, specifically on the topics of the nationalism and military complicity of the Kyoto School philosophers. Although many of the conclusions suggest that philosophers such as Nishitani did not directly contribute to the militarism of Japan during the war, some have claimed that the Kyoto School is intrinsically nationalistic. It should be noted, however, that thus far on this topic, more questions than answers have been generated.

In 1949, the publication of Nishitani's *The Self-Overcoming of Nihilism* presented the first substantive treatment of Western nihilism in Japan, and for a long time, the work was widely read by those interested in Western philosophy, nihilism, and Nietzsche. According to the introduction of the English translation of *The Self-Overcoming of Nihilism*, this publication coincided with the rising interest in nihilism in Europe during the late 1940's and 1950's and is an example of the seriousness with which Japanese scholars have treated Western thought.

After the publication of *The Self-Overcoming of Nihilism*, Nishitani wrote a number of works (mostly articles) continuing his thoughts on nihilism and investigating themes in Christian mysticism and traditional Buddhist thought. It was the publication of *Religion and Nothingness* in 1961, however, that exposed audiences to Nishitani's mature thought on the Buddhist response to what he believed was the human situation of the twentieth century. The 1982 English translation of *Religion and Nothingness* was, for the most part, warmly received by American and European theologians and philosophers. The last two chapters, on time and history, were considered the most important because they provided a critique of Western views on these subjects.

In 1955, Nishitani left his post in the Department of Religion for the chair in modern philosophy at Kyoto University, retiring from this position in 1963. According to the introduction to the English translation of *Religion and Nothingness*, from his retirement until his death, Nishitani continued his philosophical work in various capacities, including professor of philosophy and religion at Ōtani University and president of both the

Eastern Buddhist Society and the Conference on Religion in Modern Society. Nishitani also continued his interreligious activities, in part by becoming president of the International Institute for Japan Studies at the Christian Kansei Gakuin University.

Influence

Nishitani found it necessary to confront the pervasive nihilism in society, not only in Japan but also in the world at large. The thoroughgoing criticism of modernism that he found in the philosophy of Martin Heidegger pointed to a way of thinking that sought to understand and finally overcome the problems of the meaninglessness and dehumanization of the twentieth century. This overcoming of nihilism marked for Nishitani the possibility of revitalizing human religiousness and articulating a new, more all-embracing worldview. These strands are reflected in all of Nishitani's work.

Nishitani is considered one of the foremost philosophers of Japan. His intellectual and religious commitment to the absolute nothingness of Zen thought coupled with his strong familiarity with Western philosophy and theology have made him one of the most influential comparative philosophers in the twentieth century. Furthermore, his works have laid the foundation for serious interfaith dialogue, in part by articulating the necessity to confront and finally overcome the nihilism of modernity.

John Y. Cha

Religion and Nothingness

Type of philosophy: Buddhism, Japanese philosophy, metaphysics, philosophy of religion
First published: Shūkyō to wa nani ka, 1961 (English translation, 1982)
Principal ideas advanced:
◇ Only a religious transformation can free humans from the pervasive nihilism of the twentieth century.
◇ Nihilism finds its roots not only in the scientific rationalism of the Enlightenment but also in Christianity itself; therefore, Christianity,

with the exception of mysticism, cannot successfully confront the problem of nihilism.

◇ The solution is a breakthrough beyond the field of consciousness to what the Zen Buddhists call "the field of emptiness."

The work of Keiji Nishitani bears a strong resemblance to the philosophical literature of twentieth century existentialism. His concerns include the problems of human meaning, uncertainty, death, finitude, and the possibility of transcendence. The resources he employs in his analysis, however, cover almost the entire range of Western thought, from early Greek thinking to existentialism, including Christian mysticism and theology. All these Western intellectual and spiritual currents form the context within which Nishitani formulates and argues his Buddhist standpoint. This is not surprising, given Nishitani's view that science and technology (whose roots lie in Western philosophy and, ironically, Christianity) have global ramifications, not only for practical concerns but also for human meaning and cultural and religious traditions.

Nihilism and Nothingness

Nishitani's primary concern is the impact that a scientific worldview, technological developments, and nihilism have on religion. According to Nishitani, nihilism, which he sees as an outgrowth of science and technology, is the major issue confronting humans in the mid-twentieth century. Unlike the antireligious currents during the Enlightenment, nihilism sees religion as irrelevant to humanity. Nishitani believes that this attitude underlies the crisis of the twentieth century (the sense of personal meaninglessness, the loss of traditional spiritual values, and rampant materialism) because it is only in the realm of religion that humans find ultimate meaning. He offers a standpoint from which humans can disclose and critique the foundations of nihilism and finally overcome it. This standpoint, according to Nishitani, is the Buddhist notion of emptiness.

Nishitani opens *Religion and Nothingness* with the question, "What is religion?" For him, religion encompasses not just a set of dogmas or various kinds of worship but also the question of human meaning and the nature of ultimate reality. Religion, then, is absolutely central for hu-

mans, whether they know it or not, because it provides the opportunity to realize what Nishitani calls the "elemental source" of all existence. Nishitani calls this elemental source "absolute nothingness," or, in traditional Buddhist terms, "emptiness." This emptiness, according to Nishitani, is not just negation but also includes the ultimate, nondual reality of all existence. Nishitani's conception of emptiness, therefore, contains both a negative and positive connotation: negative because emptiness discloses the nonsubstantial nature of existence and positive because beneath this insubstantiality lies the true reality of all existence. To reach this reality, however, humans must pass through the negative stage of meaninglessness, what Nishitani calls "nihility."

That the term "nothingness" figures in Nishitani's philosophy of religion is no accident; in both his personal life and the Zen Buddhist tradition to which he belongs, the problem of nihility takes central stage. For Nishitani, nihility is that which renders meaningless all that people hold as meaningful; some examples are the death of a loved one or the loss of everything due to a failed business venture. Death and uncertainty, therefore, are constant companions in human existence. Nishitani claims that an authentic religious orientation to life begins only when a person faces this ever-present nihility. The basis of religion, then, is the individual's search for ultimate reality, including the passage through nihility and the eventual breakthrough into what he calls "the field of emptiness." Nishitani stresses that the authentic religious quest is not an intellectual affair, although philosophical thinking is important. Religious meaning is found in what Nishitani terms the self-realization of reality, within which the entire person is transformed, body and mind.

Dehumanization

Nishitani believes that this personal sense of nihility reflects the nihilism of his own time; furthermore, nihilism has its roots in the scientific rationalism of the Enlightenment. This age is characterized by an abandoning of the traditional theocentric (Christian) view of a divine purpose and replacing it with an anthropocentric one, that is, the idea of *human progress*. According to Nishitani, the effect was that humans became free to inquire into truth on the basis of reason rather than religious authority and to work toward humanity's betterment without divine intervention; however, humans lost the sense of dwelling in God's world. In other words, the price for rationality's freedom from the divine was existence in an impersonal world indifferent to human beings. Furthermore, Nishitani claims that the scientific outlook eventually reduced humans to the level of those mechanical laws originally intended for nature; human beings could now be both explained away as a collection of chemical, biological, and psychical processes and controlled like the immaterial objects in the world. The result was that both human beings and nature became dehumanized and denaturalized.

For Nishitani, this eventual dehumanization brings to light an inherent contradiction in the Enlightenment ideal of human progress. It was thought that scientific investigations would uncover the laws governing nature, thus allowing humans to control nature for the benefit, or autonomy, of humankind. However, dehumanization undercut this autonomy, resulting in the loss of the very goal of human progress. Therefore, rather than acquiring more freedom through scientific discovery and technological development, humans actually lost the basis for their freedom, the sense of an autonomous self.

Christianity and Nihilism

Nishitani claims that despite the abandonment of divine revelation for human reason and the resulting rise of nihilism, the foundations of Enlightenment thought ironically lie in the Christian view of time and history. Both the Christian and Enlightenment perspectives include a search for origins (Genesis or the natural cause of the universe), as well as a view toward a future end (the Second Coming or the enlightened society). Both posit a linear structure of time and history that begins in the distant past, unfolds with historically significant events, and culminates in some future ideal. It is Nishitani's claim that traditional Christianity, by maintaining this historical worldview, not only is responsible for its own demise but also is unable to successfully confront nihilism.

However, Nishitani believes that *mystical* Christianity can overcome nihilism. He dis-

cusses, for example, the mystical theology of thirteenth century Dominican preacher and teacher Meister Eckhart, specifically Eckhart's view on the God-Godhead relationship. Briefly, "Godhead" signifies the essence of God, which transcends all forms and characteristics. "God," on the other hand, is the form that functions within the God/human, or Creator/created, relationship and is, therefore, secondary to the Godhead. Humans, because they have been "made in the image of God," also find their essence in the Godhead; during the event of mystical awakening, humans break through to their divine essence, the Godhead, realizing at once their own and God's essence. Eckhart characterizes this Godhead as "absolute nothingness." For Nishitani, it is only through this nothingness that Christianity can confront and transcend nihilism. It should be noted that Nishitani sees Eckhart's absolute nothingness as being similar to the Buddhist notion of emptiness.

It is important to emphasize that the breakthrough into absolute nothingness, either in its Christian or Buddhist form, signifies an awakening to the "eternal now," the nontemporal basis for the past, present, and future. This awakening renders meaningless the linear progression of time and also signifies the transcendence of the self. Therefore, Nishitani believes that, ironically, the phenomena of dehumanization and nihilism can mark an important opportunity for the realization of absolute nothingness. Dehumanization pushes a person to the brink of absolute nihility where no meaning, either internal or external, or in the past or future, can be grasped. It is precisely in this sense of complete meaninglessness that one finds the possibility of entering the field of emptiness, here and now.

The Paradox of Representation

Nishitani concedes that this realization is a difficult and subtle process because the various kinds of twentieth century nihilism are still rooted in the dualistic assumptions of the Enlightenment era, the subject/object dichotomy. In his analysis of the problem, Nishitani introduces us to his own concept of the "field of consciousness." In general terms, the field of consciousness is the locus for all ordinary experience, where anything that is perceived is seen as an object separate from a subject (the "self"). Nishitani claims that this dualistic standpoint is merely a process of mental construction that *represents* objects, events, and other people as things *out there* in opposition to the self *in here*. However, there is a paradox in this process of representation because the self (including all its moods and thoughts as well as its own existence) can also be represented as another object seen by a subject. Nishitani calls this "the paradox of representation." Even when the subject examines his or her own existence, it is still objectified as another object.

For example, according to Nishitani, the atheism of French philosopher Jean-Paul Sartre contains this paradox of representation. Sartre claimed that the essence of the human being is its existence and, furthermore, that this existence is founded on nothingness. Being founded on nothingness, human beings are free, autonomous subjects not bound by any authority. However, this freedom comes with a price; humans can rely on nothing, internal or external, to determine the right course of action. Moreover, humans bear the responsibility for their choices but have no criteria with which to judge these choices. People are, therefore, condemned to freedom.

Nishitani agrees with Sartre that the ground of existence is nothingness but questions the *field* on which Sartre makes this determination. According to Nishitani, Sartre conceives of this nothingness as a springboard from which humans launch into projects of their own making. This nothingness is taken to be the subject's ground and is *represented in an objectified way*. Sartre is, therefore, conceiving of nothingness on the field of consciousness and, as a consequence, is still caught in the subject/object dichotomy. The problem here, from Nishitani's perspective, is that the subject is not truly seeing itself simply because it is objectifying, or representing, itself to itself. The subject, therefore, only sees a mentally constructed representation of itself and never comes into contact with its own true ground. Sartre's concept of nothingness does not come close enough to solving the human problem of an alienated self caught up in its own self-centeredness because the very essence of the self is still objectified on the field of consciousness.

For Nishitani, the solution to the problem of representation is to break through the field of

consciousness and into the field of emptiness. In this field, all duality, including subject/object, existence/nonexistence, God/human, is transcended. Therefore, the field of emptiness is completely beyond the field of consciousness; however, emptiness also already exists as the reality underneath all things. This paradox signifies two aspects of emptiness: Emptiness is to be *realized* by going beyond the field of consciousness, and emptiness is originally *inherent* in all things. This twofold characteristic of emptiness, known in traditional Buddhist terminology as "actualized enlightenment" and "original enlightenment," is the reason Nishitani calls the breakthrough into reality a "transdescendence." That is to say, enlightenment means a transcendence of duality and, at the same time, a return to the original state of nonduality.

Philosophy, Theology, and Politics

The publication of the English translation of *Religion and Nothingness* marked the exposure to the West of a committed Buddhist thinker whose background included a broad and substantial understanding of Western philosophy and theology. Warmly received by theologians and philosophers in Europe and the United States, *Religion and Nothingness* provided many things at once: a Buddhist challenge to Western thought, a Buddhist interpretation of the religious and existential problems facing the mid-twentieth century, and a strong foundation for interfaith dialogue.

Until the 1990's, *Religion and Nothingness* was discussed and debated within the parameters of philosophy and theology. However, with the growing body of critical scholarship on Nishitani's Freiburg professor, Martin Heidegger, and Heidegger's involvement with Nazism, scholars of Japanese intellectual history have increasingly focused their attention on the connections between the Kyoto School philosophers and Japanese nationalism before and during World War II. However, no direct connections can be made between Nishitani's philosophy and the nationalistic fervor in Japan at the time.

John Y. Cha

Additional Reading

Bowers, Russell H. *Someone or Nothing? Nishitani's Religion and Nothingness as a Foundation for Christian-Buddhist Dialogue*. New York: Peter Lang, 1995. An important treatment of Nishitani's *Religion and Nothingness*, in which Bowers addresses a connection between Christianity and Buddhism.

Dallmayr, Fred. "Nothingness and Shūnyatā: A Comparison of Heidegger and Nishitani." *Philosophy East and West* 42, no. 1 (January, 1992): 37-48. This article presents a comparison of the basic philosophical ideas of Martin Heidegger and Keiji Nishitani. Dallmayr also develops a critique of Nishitani's understanding of Heidegger's thought.

Heine, Steven. "History, Transhistory, and Narrative." *Philosophy East and West* 44, no. 2 (April, 1994): 251-278. In this article, Heine discusses Nishitani's critique of Western understandings of history and provides a critique of Nishitani's view of history from the standpoint of literary and historical criticism.

Heisig, James W., and John C. Maraldo, eds. *Rude Awakenings: Zen, the Kyoto School, and the Question of Nationalism*. Honolulu: University of Hawaii Press, 1994. A collection of articles that addresses the issue of the relation between the leading intellectuals of the Kyoto School and Japanese nationalism. Although previous works on the Kyoto School have focused on theology and philosophy, this is the first book-length study in English on the political, social, and historical context of the Kyoto School.

Unno, Taitetsu, ed. *The Religious Philosophy of Nishitani Keiji*. Berkeley: Asian Humanities Press, 1989. A volume of a collection of papers presented at or connected to the symposium on *Religion and Nothingness* held at Smith and Amherst Colleges in 1984. The contributors, many of whom are well-known theologians, philosophers, and Buddhist scholars, explain, analyze, and debate the issues and implications set forth in *Religion and Nothingness*. The volume is divided into five parts: God, Science, Ethics, History, and Buddhism.

Waldenfels, Hans. *Absolute Nothingness: Foundations for a Buddhist-Christian Dialogue*. New York: Paulist Press, 1980. The first substantive and extended treatment in English of the philosophy of Nishitani, his work's context in the history of Buddhist thought, and its significance in the Buddhist-Christian dialogue.

John Y. Cha

Robert Nozick

Nozick's writings on political theory, decision theory, rationality, and metaphysics, among other areas, produced bold new insights. His attack on established doctrines catalyzed dynamic philosophical debate, adding new vitality to philosophy.

Principal philosophical works: "Newcomb's Problem and Two Principles of Choice," 1969; "Coercion," 1969; *Anarchy, State, and Utopia*, 1974; *Philosophical Explanations*, 1981; *The Examined Life*, 1989; *The Nature of Rationality*, 1993; *Socratic Puzzles*, 1997.

Born: November 16, 1938; Brooklyn, New York

Early Life

The only child of a manufacturer, Robert Nozick was raised in the Brooklyn working-class neighborhoods of Brownsville and East Flatbush. His early teenage memories include carrying a copy of Plato's *Republic* (*Politeia*, c. 388-366 B.C.E.; English translation, 1701) to impress others and to try to draw intelligent adult conversation. Later in life, he would reflect that the person he wanted most to attract was the person he would become. Nozick's parents encouraged him, as a brilliant student, to pursue a career in medicine. Instead, philosophy courses taught at Columbia College, particularly those taught by Sidney Morgenbesser, drew Nozick into continual fascination with philosophy and the intricacies of decision theory.

At Columbia, he became involved with campus socialist groups. Student activism took its toll; he failed five courses, three of them in philosophy. At Columbia, vigorous classroom debate caused Nozick to reexamine his socialist assumptions and to gravitate toward libertarian beliefs. After graduating in 1959, Nozick married and went on to Princeton University. He received his master's degree in 1961 and Ph.D. in 1963. Princeton's Carl Hempel, a leading decision theorist, became a seminal influence on Nozick, and under his influence, Nozick chose as his dissertation topic *The Normative Theory of Individual Choice* (published in 1990). Decision theory would be-come a major focus of Nozick's later works.

After receiving a Fulbright Fellowship to Oxford University (1963-1964), Nozick returned to Princeton (1964-1965) as an assistant professor. In 1965, he received an appointment at Harvard University, where he would remain, except for brief sojourns to such institutions as Stanford University and Rockefeller University. Early in his career, he published a variety of articles of a technical nature. In 1969, at the age of thirty, Nozick received tenure at Harvard. An article he published that year, "Coercion" (in *Philosophy, Science and Method*, edited by his former mentor, Morgenbesser), would become the basis for his famous *Anarchy, State, and Utopia*. At Harvard, over the next fifteen years, Nozick became legendary for refusing to teach the same course twice, preferring instead to use the classroom to refine thinking in diverse areas.

Life's Work

Although he was long recognized by his peers as a brilliant philosopher, it was *Anarchy, State, and Utopia* that catapulted Nozick into international fame. The study won the 1975 National Book Award for Philosophy and Religion, and it was embraced by the libertarian movement as a work of inspired revelation. Nozick's concept of a minimal state as a framework for a utopia came several years after *A Theory of Justice* (1971), the landmark work of another Harvard scholar, John Rawls. Rawls, in opposition to Nozick, argued for a distributive state, and these two books set in motion a vigorous debate reinvigorating interest in political theory. Uncomfortable with the entourage of libertarians he attracted, Nozick bemoaned that most people he knew and respected disagreed with him, and he supported positions they despised and detested.

Viewing his focus on political theory as accidental, in 1976 Nozick began, during a sabbatical year spent in Israel, his reflections on what is important and meaningful in life. The end result was *Philosophical Explanations*, which projected Nozick's vision of philosophy as both playing an important role in everyday life and serving as an art form. Nozick argued that philosophy should be noncoercive, attempting to offer explanations rather than absolute proofs about issues of central concern such as free will and the meaning of life. His major intent was to show how philosophy could add value to life and spur the reader on to further contemplation. Taking an indeterminist view of free will, Nozick admitted, "if we cannot solve the problem, at least we can surround it." *Philosophical Explanations* won the Ralph Waldo Emerson Award in 1982. Critics found it to be a brilliant book, but written at a level of abstraction far removed from the real world. Nozick himself, in the introduction, stated his love for unreadable books and his hope that he had written one that would inspire the reader to grapple with larger issues.

In 1981, Nozick's marriage to Barbara Fierer dissolved after having produced two children, Emily and David. Six years later, he married Gjertrud Schackenberg. Although Nozick was a libertarian, he joined the American Civil Liberties Union to fight against violations of individual rights. Also true to his belief that animals have basic rights, which were to be defined at some future date, he became a member of the Jewish Vegetarian Society.

Nozick continued his work on decision theory and free will in *The Examined Life*. In twenty-seven chapters

of widely varying length and quality, dealing with topics as varied as dying, sexuality, and the Holocaust, Nozick explored theories of rational decision and rational belief as they affect twentieth century life. For Nozick, the good life emerges as commitment to an ideal, not merely action directed toward satisfying desires or achieving goals. Knowledge and rational awareness are prerequisites to defining an ideal. Individuals with clearly defined ideals—such as Socrates, Buddha, Moses, Mohandas Gandhi, and Jesus—are capable of a more real existence than the rest of humanity. Critics pointed to Nozick's avoidance of addressing the evil side of rational belief.

Nozick furthered his study of rational belief in *The Nature of Rationality*, which contains concepts drawn from economics, social science, and com-

Robert Nozick. *(Princeton University Library)*

parative science. In this study, he attempts to show why rational behavior is important and how it is connected to rational belief and action. He defines the key concept of symbolic unity, the connection between action and its consequences. Nozick sees human rationality as evolving and not yet having reached the biological maturity to deal with many fundamental philosophical problems. Rationality nevertheless is the key that made civilization and human progress possible. In a somewhat ethnocentric manner, Nozick finds that the dominance of the West, in recent centuries, is the result of rational behavior. Truth itself, Nozick contends, can be discerned only through rational means. He goes on to discuss the rules to derive truth and avoid subjective bias, and the justifications for these rules. He offers practical advice to help people reason better but also floods the study with equations and formulas that make the content beyond the reach of anyone except a specialist in the field. Rationality is of utmost importance for Nozick, but by giving people control over their actions and emotions, he leaves the path open for creative imagination to introduce new meaningful insights to be explored rationally.

In 1994, at the height of his career, Nozick was diagnosed with stomach cancer. As he has related, when he came out of anesthesia following seven hours of surgery, his first words to his attending physicians were, "I hope we don't have to do this again. I don't have the stomach for it." He underwent months of chemotherapy and radiation treatment. He served as Guggenheim Fellow during the 1996-1997 academic year and was voted president-elect for the Eastern section of the American Philosophical Association. Also in 1997, he published *Socratic Puzzles*, in which he shows philosophy as constituting a way of life worth continuing until the end. The work, which Nozick admitted is only loosely related to Socrates, explores diverse topics such as animal rights, why intellectuals tend to oppose capitalism, extremism, and metaphysics. It also updates his thoughts on key concepts contained in *Anarchy, State, and Utopia*, such as his "invisible hand" explanation for the filtering and equilibrium process in causing protective associations to adjust to one another and the local environment. In the last section, titled "Philosophical Fictions,"

Nozick creatively explores the concept of God, the meaning of the Creation, and even his own existence.

Influence

Nozick is one of the foremost philosophers of the last quarter of the twentieth century, and he has few rivals in terms of originality, diversity, and controversy. Ironically, he is best known for his *Anarchy, State, and Utopia*, a work he viewed as an accident and one that he wanted to leave behind as an encumbrance to new ideas. The work reflects a strong early influence of philosopher John Locke's concept of the social contract and philosopher Immanuel Kant's categorical imperative. Nozick updates Locke (without accepting his deistic origins of rights given by nature) and joins Kant in viewing people as an end and not a means. Although not a traditional conservative, Nozick pushed the concept of private ownership of property further than would most conservatives. His end utopia, a minimal state composed of mutual protective associations entered into by voluntary agreements, fired the emotions of libertarians. By adding his intellectual stature to the libertarian movement, Nozick's study transferred legitimacy to libertarianism as a political theory. Although Nozick's interests changed and although he remained aloof from the fray, his delving into political theory caused a controversy within it that still raged at the close of the twentieth century.

Nozick is also a child of Enlightenment rationalism. His work on the nature of rationality, decision theory, and ethical behavior points to a future world that was envisioned in the eighteenth century but still seemed distant at the close of the twentieth. His emphasis on philosophy as a way of life would lead to a more rational world; however, the abstract vagueness inherent in much of Nozick's works acts counter to bringing his conclusions to any mass audience. He has stated the necessity for a kinder, gentler philosophy, one that rests on exploration and not coercive proofs of truths. Other philosophers may be wise, as Nozick has been, to share their uncertainties with their readers, draw intriguing eclectic connections, and seek not precise theory but stimulation of further thought by others. This is an age, however, as Nozick himself bemoans, in which students are more likely to discuss good films than be caught up in examining major issues or ideas.

It is striking that Nozick titled one of his later works *Socratic Puzzles*. Like his hero, Socrates, Nozick is a gadfly nihilistically stinging all those who mindlessly accept established philosophical truths, in his effort to move philosophy along the continued search for truth. Until the truths are obtained, according to Nozick, "there is room in philosophy for other than last words." The evolution of Nozick's own interests and the maturation of his thoughts will affect other philosophers for generations to come. He had the courage to reflect on the macro level at a time when scholars pursued smaller and smaller micro specialties that were of interest to only a handful of other microspecialists. Nozick also had the audacity to evolve new interests, stimulating debate whenever he wrote but refusing to be forced into the debate or into a track where he did not wish to remain. As a philosophical truth seeker, he readily admitted that his was not the definitive word, and like Socrates, he had the courage to ask questions for which he did not have easy answers. As a scholar, he never departed from his role as a teacher, teaching a wide variety of new courses to solidify his ideas, even if it meant learning from his students.

Irwin Halfond

Anarchy, State, and Utopia

Type of philosophy: Ethics, political philosophy
First published: 1974
Principal ideas advanced:

◇ Individuals have rights so strong and far-reaching that one must raise questions about what, if anything, the state and its officials may do.

◇ The minimal state in the role of "nightwatchman" is the only possible state that can safeguard private property and not violate individual rights.

◇ Within the minimal state, mutual protection associations will arise. Compensation would be paid by these associations for any "border crossings."

◇ Through a process of filtering and equilibrium, guided by an "invisible hand," the best-suited associations will survive and become models for others.

◇ Distributive justice (the right of the state to allocate resources such as in a welfare state) is wrong. State taxation results in continual interference with people's lives, and taxation of earnings is equivalent to forced labor.

◇ Entitlement justice should be employed in the acquisition and transfer of property, as well as in rectification for past injustices.

◇ Within the minimal state, utopia can be established, permitting people to live according to diverse and even opposed concepts of good. Individuals would be free to design and live in their own utopias.

Robert Nozick claims to have written *Anarchy, State, and Utopia* by accident, during a year spent at the Center for Advanced Study in Behavioral Sciences at Stanford University (1971-1972). He is almost boastful about the fact that the vast majority of his writings and attention focused on other subjects. Several years earlier, Harvard's John Rawls had published a landmark study, *A Theory of Justice* (1971), which set up the foundation for a distributive state, a type of welfare state antithetical to the type of minimal state Nozick conceptualized. Rawls's work became a handbook for liberalism and for advocates of the welfare state, and it was held up by humanitarians for making provisions for the least advantaged groups in society.

Rawls and Nozick published their studies at a time when the Vietnam War and the Watergate affair were producing serious disillusionment about the ends and means of the political system that had developed in the United States. The time was ripe for a raging debate in political philosophy. Nozick himself reminisced about the excitement produced in the 1950's by C. Wright Mills's *The Power Elite* (1956); the mid-1970's seemed similar. Nozick, however, refused to respond to the avalanche of critical literature about his work or to be bound to the specialty of political philosophy. He moved on to other areas of philosophy, but his first book-length work, his most controversial, remained central to the debate in political philosophy for the next quarter century.

Basic Human Rights

Nozick admits that his study does not reflect the slow process by which his earlier socialist views were slowly chipped away by libertarian beliefs. He begins the work with the dramatic assertion that individuals have rights upon which others, including the state, cannot infringe. Clearly, he is heavily influenced by John Locke's concept of the social contract; unlike Locke, however, he refuses to trace the origins of these rights to a divine power. Although he leaves the origins of human rights for some other study at some other time, he sees these moral rights as written in stone. Also in variance with Locke, Nozick wants a new social contract to stop at some level below that of the state. In this, Nozick is extremely radical; he is attacking a concept taken for granted in the United States for at least the past two centuries. Nozick also is heavily influenced by philosopher Immanuel Kant's idea of the categorical imperative and political view that the individual is an end, not a means to an end. Nozick also resurrects a basic eighteenth century notion of government, namely, that the government is best that governs least.

After examining why a state of anarchy would not be conducive to happiness, Nozick concludes that at least a minimal state is necessary to enforce basic moral prohibitions. Although he respects the utilitarian concept of happiness, he is diametrically opposed to the concept that such happiness can be computed mathematically within a mass society. He concludes that utilitarians would violate a great number of individual rights in service of the abstract notion of the greater happiness of the whole. In part 1 of his three-part study, titled "State of Nature Theory, or How to Back into a State Without Really Trying," he uses philosophical exposition to justify the minimal state and describe how it is to come about.

Mutual Protection Societies

For Nozick, the key to unobtrusive government is the formation of mutual protection societies, composed of individual clients, that would subsume many functions of the state. These associations would negotiate with one another in the event of a dispute, and they would provide compensation for disadvantaging individuals by their actions or for prohibiting individual activities that might involve risk.

The process by which the mutual protective associations would get permission for retaliation or pay full compensation for boundary crossings is detailed by Nozick in chapter 4, titled "Prohibition, Compensation, and Risk." The associations could not use unreliable or redistributive powers and would be limited to morally permissible means of enforcement to safeguard against violation of individual rights. The state thus would exist only as a "nightwatchman," taking on the limited functions of protection against force and fraud. Unlike anarchist concepts, Nozick's minimal state would have the right to punish and have a mandate for self-defense.

After many different groupings of associations had occurred, successful patterns would be copied. Individuals would always be free to join any of the associations or to remain outside them. Nozick refers to rugged individualists as "John Wayne types," but he tries to create a society that would accommodate their needs. Eventually, through the process of filtration and equilibrium, guided by an "invisible hand" (similar to eighteenth century economist Adam Smith's conception of an invisible hand guiding supply and demand in the marketplace, for the betterment of all), most areas would see the development of one dominant association, with a number of other agencies federally affiliated with it. The entire process would be formed and governed by a type of free market.

Justification for the State

In part 2, Nozick attempts to show that the minimal state, with the primary objective of safeguarding private property, is really the maximum type of state that can be justified. Anything more extensive, Nozick argues, would violate people's rights. He devotes particular attention to attacking distributive justice and Rawls's theory. Marxism and other egalitarian doctrines are analytically dissected and exposed as dysfunctional. He finds people's talents and abilities to be an asset in a free community; many people benefit from individual talents, not the least of whom should be the individual.

After leveling the other political philosophies, Nozick proceeds to establish his own entitlement theory for acquisitions (property). Holdings must be obtained and transferred according to the principle of justice, factoring in historical aspects, current time slice principles (who has what), and the increased value of the property caused by individual efforts. Nozick also qualifies that private ownership must not violate Lockean principles of life and liberty (using as an example ownership of the only watering hole in a populated desert) and that individual rights can be overridden to prevent a catastrophe. In some situations, he points out, past injustices can be so great as to necessitate, in the short run, a more extensive state to rectify them. Although Nozick has little regard for equality, he goes to considerable lengths to try to guarantee justice in acquisitions. He takes pride in working out a historical entitlement theory, something that Rawls had not done. He also congratulates himself for having probed the deep-lying inadequacies in Rawls's theory and in all other arguments for a state more extensive than a minimal state.

Utopia

Part 3 of Nozick's study, only thirty-three pages long, is titled "Utopia." As Nozick readily admits, he has created only a framework for a utopia. In Nozick's minimal state, people will have the freedom to choose among many different communities of extremely diverse character and to be treated with respect. People will be free to design and live in their own utopia. In this, Nozick almost reaches the existentialist conclusion that people all live separate lives, and he tries to accommodate a wide range of lifestyles.

Nozick raises problems that may exist between communities situated closely to one another but does not seek to resolve them. How the communities will turn out, Nozick does not know, and he is not tempted to guess. Critics charged, with a good deal of justification, that Nozick's utopia was skimpy and not very attractive. Others worried that Nozick's minimal state would wind up violating more individual rights than most maximal states.

Nozick ends his study with as much impact as he began it: "How dare any state or group of individuals do more. Or less." He chooses not to use exclamation or question marks, perhaps because he does not need to be more emphatic and believes that his study answers the question.

Fuel for Libertarianism and Conservatism

From the moment of its publication, *Anarchy, State, and Utopia* was controversial. It catapulted both its conclusions and the author into popular media such as *The New York Times* and *Time* magazine. The study was immediately heralded by the libertarian movement, which gained prestige. Conservatives also praised the study; though many neglected to read it, they used the conclusions to support trimming the welfare state and privatizing as widely as possible in the higher interests of producing a utopia.

Of particular interest to conservatives was Nozick's contention that the state had no business helping anybody in poverty. Such sentiments had not been expressed in such a broad public forum perhaps since English economist David Ricardo's statements two centuries earlier. Those who opposed government taxation took to heart Nozick's contention that state taxation was tantamount to forced labor.

The alliances claimed by conservatives appear to be why Nozick all but abandoned political philosophy and refused to answer his numerous critics. That Nozick chose not to confront his critics is either an act of cowardice or a statement of an individual who had other interests and refused to be shackled to a topic for which he had only a passing involvement and interest. Major reviewers found it difficult to fathom Nozick's complete study; as Roy A. Childs commented, "Nozick sometimes retreats into math and other modes of argument that are beyond me. I always skip this stuff and I've never had a sleepless night over it."

Nozick himself bemoaned the accumulation of unwanted company and the loss of respect among his peers caused by the study. Although he chose to clarify concepts and tie up loose ends in his *Socratic Puzzles* (1997), Nozick seemed to dismiss his major work as an accident. That recent critics have viewed his concept as almost medieval feudalism, or a United States under the Articles of Confederation, has done much to erase the meaningful conclusions of Nozick's work. Others would point to the fact that little, if anything, in Nozick's study relates to the real world or has more meaning than castles built in sand. Few pages were spent on sociological, psychological, or historical development questions, whereas the idealistic notion of individuals capable of making rational choices received great attention.

A Basis for Further Thought

Even Nozick's most severe critics could not help but compliment his deliberatively provocative style and brilliant examples interwoven throughout the study. Over the years, *Anarchy, State, and Utopia* became a work to which contemporary political philosophers had to refer, and it spawned many works seeking to refute its ideas.

Given a dearth of contemporary political philosophy, Nozick's study is bound to be a source of controversy well into the twenty-first century. That few social scientists can find any empirical validity to Nozick's key arguments seems to be beside the point. His study will remain important, if only as a point of reference and as a target that future students of political philosophy will readily attack.

Irwin Halfond

Additional Reading

Cohen, G. A. *Self-Ownership, Freedom, and Equality*. Cambridge, England: Cambridge University Press, 1995. The first chapter of this study, "Robert Nozick and Wilt Chamberlain: How Patterns Preserve Liberty," is an excellent Marxist critique of Nozick. Analysis of Nozick's libertarian political philosophy is made throughout the study. For Cohen, Nozick is one of the most extreme modern spokespersons for the capitalist view of the sanctity of private property.

Corlett, J. Angelo, ed. *Equality and Liberty: Analyzing Rawls and Nozick*. New York: St. Martin's Press, 1991. This book contains eighteen essays, divided between analyzing the political and moral concepts of John Rawls and Robert Nozick. Most of the essays are reprinted from major philosophical journals and represent continued scholarly interest in the famous Rawls-Nozick debate.

Hailwood, Simon A. *Exploring Nozick: Beyond Anarchy, State, and Utopia*. Hampshire, England: Avebury, 1996. Hailwood attempts to unify Nozick's earlier and later works by examining the theory of neutralism in the exercise of state power. He provides an in-depth critical analysis of the development of Nozick's moral and political theories. Nozick's evolution is also compared to that of other major political philosophers.

Luper-Foy, Steven, ed. *The Possibility of Knowledge: Nozick and His Critics*. Totowa, N.J.: Rowman & Littlefield, 1987. The first part of this book contains part 3 of Nozick's *Philosophical Explanations* (1981). This is followed by twelve critical essays about Nozick's work. Several essays find Nozick unsuccessful in rebutting skepticism; others criticize Nozick's externalist analysis of knowledge and evidence.

Paul, Jeffrey, ed. *Reading Nozick: Essays on Anarchy, State, and Utopia*. Totowa, N.J.: Rowman & Littlefield, 1981. A collection of essays on Nozick dealing with civil rights, anarchism, utopianism, and human rights. The majority are highly critical. Particularly illuminating is Paul's "The Withering of Nozick's Minimum State."

Wolf, Jonathan. *Robert Nozick: Property, Justice, and the Minimal State*. Stanford, Calif.: Stanford University Press, 1991. Wolf explains the attractions and limitations of Nozick's libertarian minimal state. He analytically dissects Nozick's core arguments while identifying digressions and vagueness in Nozick's ideas. Wolf argues that Nozick does not do justice to Locke's views and that Nozick, while exposing fallacies in competing political philosophies, fails to demonstrate the truth in his own views.

Irwin Halfond

Martha Craven Nussbaum

Nussbaum's writings and projects examine works of philosophy and literature to make a practical and compassionate inquiry into the deepest human concerns. Her philosophical approach, essentially Aristotelian in its breadth and scope, is directed toward solving problems that require international cooperation and recognizing universal moral obligations.

Principal philosophical works: *The Fragility of Goodness: Luck and Ethics in Greek Tragedy and Philosophy*, 1986; *Love's Knowledge: Essays on Philosophy and Literature*, 1990; *The Therapy of Desire: Theory and Practice in Hellenistic Ethics*, 1994; *Poetic Justice: The Literary Imagination and Public Life*, 1995; *For Love of Country: Debating the Limits of Patriotism*, 1996; *Cultivating Humanity: A Classical Defense of Reform in Liberal Education*, 1997; *The Feminist Critique of Liberalism*, 1997.

Born: May 6, 1947; New York, New York

Early Life

Martha Craven Nussbaum (born Martha Craven) was born in New York City on May 6, 1947. She attended Wellesley College from 1964 to 1966 and earned a B.A. from New York University in 1969. She received her M.A. and Ph.D. from Harvard University in 1971 and 1978, respectively. In graduate school, she encountered resistance to her intention to study ancient Greek literary works for their philosophical insight. At this time, academic tradition maintained that literary works studied philological and aesthetic issues, whereas philosophical works emphasized mainly positivist and metaethical concerns. Philosophical curricula also discouraged the study of substantive ethical theories.

Determined to examine certain philosophical concerns using literary and philosophical sources, Nussbaum created her own field of study, using ancient writers and their literature not simply as background or popular thought but as "thinkers-poets whose meanings and whose formal choices were closely linked." Her investigation into literature led her into a study of important questions about human beings and human life. Views of human life, she found, cannot be separated from the verbal expression of these views. She maintains that ideas arise out of

the style and language of a written work and cannot be separated from these elements. Nussbaum holds, therefore, that the same truths cannot be stated in abstract theoretical language and through narrative.

Life's Work

Nussbaum's journey into both literature and philosophy found a theme common to both: How should one live? The question led to an examination of philosophy not simply as a theoretical discourse but as one that is relevant to human lives. This inquiry, both empirical and practical, uses examples from life to find "a conception by which human beings can live, and live together." Her life's project, similar to that of the Greek philosopher Plato, is to employ literature and philosophy for practical purposes, particularly in education. Her project's methodology, however, is more like the Greek philosopher Aristotle's in its broad, open-ended approach of holding every domain of life approachable for enlightenment.

Her career reflects this open-ended approach. She taught philosophy and classics at Harvard (1980-1983), Wellesley College (1983-1984), and Brown University (1984-1995). In 1993, she moved into the domain of law as visiting lecturer at the University of Chicago, later becoming a professor of law and ethics there. This move into

1405

law channeled her writings into the public and political realms. She was pulled into international concerns in her position as a research adviser at the World Institute for Development of Economics Research in Helsinki, a research institute connected with the United Nations and charged with generating new interdisciplinary approaches to the economic problems of developing nations. As she acted in this capacity, she linked her philosophical classical training to recent work in economics as a means of producing new approaches to international issues. In this work, she moved closer to pursuing her goal of world citizenship and immersion in urgent ethical issues that, until resolved, prevent large numbers of people from flourishing.

Her diverse interests and methodologies find outlets in diverse venues: conferences on compassion, an Internet lecture, a book on education and the classics, televised interviews, and teaching ethics through literature to law students. As a writer seriously concerned with promoting philosophical discussion of political issues, Nussbaum would not shelter herself in the cloisters of academic work. She wrote reviews for *The New York Times Book Review*, *The New Republic*, and similar publications. She participated in the British Broadcasting Corporation series *The Great Philosophers* and in a segment of the television program *Bill Moyers' World of Ideas*. These activities reflected her wish to reach international audiences, particularly audiences in developing countries, through conferences and television.

In reaching out to an international audience, Nussbaum had to address questions of identity politics. In her work *Cultivating Humanity: A Classical Defense of Reform in Liberal Education*, she criticized relativistic beliefs that hold, for example, that only those who have experienced a problem can discuss that problem. (From this viewpoint, only female writers can understand the experience of women, only African American writers can understand the black experience, and so on.) Nussbaum counters this view with her understanding of world citizenship, wherein groups of people understand other groups of people through study and imagination.

She defends Aristotelian essentialism (a belief in common human concerns) and the possibility of basic universal values correlating with basic

functioning for human life. She broadens the definition of "culture," suggesting that diverse regions, classes, and ethnic and religious groups exist within each cultural group. Any discussion of culture, she maintains, should present not only dominant norms but also voices of resistance to those norms. She has argued against relativism and in favor of objectivity and validity in argumentation, and for clarity of definitions, in contrast to thinkers such as Stanley Fish, who find little distinction between rational persuasion and cultural manipulation. She has also stressed Aristotle's use of the general notion of the human being and the human form of life to provide a standard and a direction for ethical and political thinking. General notions of human functioning and human capability can, she says, be used to criticize local, subjective, or relativistic notions harmful to human functioning.

Nussbaum's teaching of ethics stresses a sense of urgency and the complexity of ethical problems. She wants students to see that philosophical positions are attempts to solve problems and that out of conflicts between rival positions will come understanding of complex philosophical problems. Her methodology is different from the approaches espoused by followers of German philosopher Immanuel Kant and those of utilitarians, which ask only "What is my duty?" or "How can one maximize utility?"

Nussbaum's practical and experiential methodology compares procedures, beliefs, and feelings of the participants. She uses literature to broaden experiences and viewpoints. Narrative art, she believes, involves readers and listeners in the lives of others, allowing them to imagine possibilities beyond their own immediate experience. She agrees with Aristotle that human experience, without fiction, is too parochial. She values novels as part of a philosophical investigation because of the interest novelists take in values. Novels also explore the noncommensurability of values; they explore emotions as sources of insight, and they explore particular circumstances for particular context-sensitive judgments.

Novels and tragic plays also involve audiences emotionally. For example, Nussbaum recognized that in choosing tragedy as the format for their thought, Greek tragic writers constructed their plots and used rhythm, music, and language to explore happenings beyond an agent's control that were ethically relevant to their characters and their audience. Responses of pity and fear evoked by the tragic format had ethical impact. Incidents found in these tragedies indicated that because human beings do not fully control their lives, their losses and their uncertain outcomes have moral implications. The emotions aroused in viewers indicate their involvement with their fate in this world and their lack of belief in a transcendent reality that would obliterate the meaning of their choices while in this world. Belief in a transcendent reality would lessen the reader's pity and concern for the plight of tragic heroes. Nussbaum shares this view of life, which explains why little about Christian or other religious transcendent beliefs is found in her works.

Throughout her writings, Nussbaum contends that the connection between forms of discourse and views of life was important to Greek writers and still is important to modern thinkers. She assumes that the styles in which matters of human choice are discussed indicate moral stances. She asks what shape and organization a work has and what kind of control over what happens in the work the author presents to readers. She wants to know what voices converse with readers and what status they claim for themselves. She asks whether these voices claim knowledge or belief, as well as the basis for any belief. Literature, unlike scientific writing, uses particular and concrete words, images, and incidents that lead readers to reflect not by general rules but by involvement with particular contexts of experience. Thus, the mode of explaining allowed in a literary text is different from that of other kinds of works and allows readers different kinds of understandings.

Nussbaum's philosophical project has moved steadily from her early investigations of academic issues found in Greek writings to her interest in international social and political issues. Her works written in the 1970's—such as *Aristotle's Motu Animalium: Text with Translation, Commentary, and Interpretive Essays* (1978)—converse mainly with other classical scholars. Her works written in the 1980's begin to address a wider audience. *The Fragility of Goodness* enthusiastically visits academic issues in a tone inviting to the interested lay reader. She does not lessen the rigor of her methodology or her allusions to scholarly works in *The Fragility of Goodness*, but she summarizes for the lay reader materials that would be familiar to classical scholars. In the 1990's, her concerns broadened to include law and international issues. Her interest in international and sociopolitical conditions of human flourishing can be seen in her works, including *Poetic Justice: The Literary Imagination and Public Life* and *For Love of Country: Debating the Limits of Patriotism*; in the latter, she advocates the Stoic ideal of cosmopolitanism.

Her interest in literary sources led Nussbaum to broaden the boundaries of ethical concerns. Kant and others have seen joke telling, hospitality, friendship, and even love as lying outside the discipline, but she would include them. Her stretching of the boundaries of moral concern evolved over several years. In her earlier writings, she believed that the Aristotelian ethical stance was inclusive enough to encompass "every constituent of the good human life, love included." In a later period, using her study of Henry James's *The Golden Bowl* (1904), she found that erotic love, in its demand for both exclusivity and privacy, was ethically problematic. She has examined several of Plato's dialogues for the philosophical importance of erotic love.

Nussbaum also has examined the role and function of the emotions in philosophical argumentation. Her concept of philosophy involves emotional as well as intellectual activity and gives priority to perceptions of people and situations, rather than to abstract rules. She suggests that this conception is not imprecise or irrational, but has its own rationality and precision. She argues, with Aristotle, that practical reasoning unaccompanied by emotion is not sufficient for practical wisdom. Emotions, she maintains, are not more unreliable than intellectual calculations; they frequently are more reliable and are less deceptively seductive than intellectual reasoning. She shares with Aristotle the concept that emotions are discriminating responses closely connected to understanding what is important. She says that belief is sufficient for emotion and that emotion is necessary for full belief. She does not, however, find emotions foundational or self-certifying sources of ethical truth.

Influence

Nussbaum favors the Greek philosopher Epicurus's definition of philosophy as "the activity that secures the flourishing life by means of reasoning and arguments." Certainly, if judged by her own writings, Nussbaum's life has flourished.

Her insistence on the active role of philosophy in solving problems facing individuals and cultures has permeated numerous disciplines and channels of information. Her belief that one's own reason and experience are authoritative in philosophical investigations has focused philosophic interest on the experiences of individuals. She has advanced the concerns of multiculturalism and world citizenship while still maintaining the importance of the ancient Greek philosophers in their approach to problems that most human lives share. Scholars such as Immanuel Wallerstein, Richard Falk, Benjamin Barber, Sissela Bok, Amy Gutmann, and Gertrude Himmelfarb have debated these concepts with her, as in *For Love of Country: Debating the Limits of Patriotism*. Nussbaum's views concerning the realism/antirealism debate can be heard at philosophical conferences and read about in professional journals. Her methods of ranging over many disciplines, developing themes from one work and applying them to others, have encouraged the broadening of disciplines. Her knowledge of ancient and modern philosophy allows for reciprocal insights into both, and her ability to combine epistemology, metaphysics, moral and political philosophy, and philosophy of literature in her methodology has allowed her to contribute new approaches and insights into current problems.

Barbara Kramer

The Fragility of Goodness

Luck and Ethics in Greek Tragedy and Philosophy

Type of philosophy: Ethics
First published: 1986
Principal ideas advanced:

◇ In looking for the good, moral agents often face conflicting requirements calling for reso-lutions that lessen control and that make their lives vulnerable to tragedy.

◇ In looking for the good and self-sufficiency, the role of the irrational—appetites, feelings, and emotions—must be examined. These elements lead to involvement with the world, to forming ties to the human community, and to opening opportunities for the moral agent to be betrayed.

◇ In trying to live well and in being involved with activities of the world and the lives of other people, a person is open to destruction. Human beings must recognize that goodness is fragile.

In her first chapter, "Luck and Ethics," Martha Nussbaum puts the reader on notice that her methodology in studying Greek ethical thought differs from the methods of other modern philosophers. She aligns herself with Aristotle's methodology of reflecting on the views of "the many and the wise." The writings that she subjects to scrutiny include some literature often not thought applicable to philosophic inquiry; in Nussbaum's opinion, it offers breadth to her exploration. Nussbaum also says in this chapter that she intends to study the ancient tragic writers as Plato studied them, that is, by studying their content and style as revealing their concept of human excellence.

Nussbaum favors the insights of tragic works because they explore such themes as human goodness and external circumstances. Tragic works focus particularly on the vulnerability of human lives to fortune, the mutability of circumstances, and the existence of conflicts among commitments. Tragedies also present alternative conceptions and evolving complex patterns of deliberation. Unlike practical experience, tragedies and literature in general present carefully thought out themes and situations designed to present those themes. There is, however, continuity between tragic and poetic works and Greek philosophical writings. Plato's philosophical search for a self-sufficient good life is motivated, Nussbaum says, by many of the same concerns seen in tragic works. She argues that in dialogues such as *Prōtagoras* (c. 399-390 B.C.E.; *Protagoras*, 1804) and *Symposion* (c. 388-368 B.C.E.; *Symposium*, 1701), Plato examines self-sufficiency, human ambition, and contingency. In this first chapter, Nussbaum prepares the reader for the rich tapestry of voices offered in *The Fragility of Goodness*.

Although the themes of this work are developed in chapters that could be read as separate and complete essays sharing common concerns, Nussbaum often poses questions in one chapter and replies to these questions in another chapter. In different chapters, she also finds separate answers to the overall, formidable question of this book: how the effects of chance and luck influence the goodness of humankind. Each literary work is examined for its philosophical import and its ways of transmitting its meaning. Throughout her work, Nussbaum supplies the relevant history of ideas, philosophical traditions, and literary devices. She takes care to examine works in their context to show how the ancient Greeks would have seen these issues.

Human Choice

In part 1, titled "Tragedy: Fragility and Ambition," Nussbaum begins her discussion of the conflict between human choice and uncontrollable circumstances using Aeschylus's *Agamemnōn* (458 B.C.E.; *Agamemnon*, 1777). Agamemnon must decide between sacrificing his daughter or having his expedition of ships remain becalmed, without wind to propel them. Agamemnon's options are, in Nussbaum's opinion, descriptive of the interaction between external constraints and personal choice that is found in ordinary situations. What solution can be found to this dilemma?

In the next chapter, Nussbaum wonders whether a rational person could plan a life to avoid this conflict. She then examines her answer in the context of Sophocles' *Antigonē* (441 B.C.E.; *Antigone*, 1729). In this work, the central characters attempt to ward off conflict and tension by restricting their commitments and love. Nussbaum examines the motivations of these attempts and their outcomes. Each character in the play is presented as molded to his or her decision, with attitudes of confidence and stability—supposedly safe from the damages of changes and chance.

In assessing each character's attitudes and perspective, Nussbaum guides her reader through original Greek passages to illustrate subtleties of choices and motives. She apprises readers of what audiences of this time would think about these conflicts. She selects lines of the play, allowing readers to see for themselves what she has described. She examines individual images and metaphors in the play for insight into themes. For example, the state, so important in *Antigone*, is like a ship—built by human beings to subdue nature and chance. It also can be an instrument of control, which is the way the character Creon sees it. In his opinion, any opponent of the city should be suppressed. He accuses Antigone of being rigid in her beliefs (that she must obey the gods and bury her brother), but he is as rigid in his belief that he must kill anyone who disobeys rules of the state. At the end of the play, Creon understands the complexity of the city, composed of individuals and families having conflicting concerns.

Plato

In part 2 of this book, "Plato: Goodness Without Fragility?," Nussbaum examines themes, presented in several dialogues of Plato, that appeared in the first section. She notes the distinctions between presentations of her themes in tragedy as compared to dialogue form; the dialogue gives opportunities for examining different views and choices. Plato's dialogue *Protagoras* is set in a time when Athenians thought that progress could eliminate ungoverned contingencies from social life. It was hoped that *tuchē* (translated as "luck" or "what happens") could be controlled by *technē* (translated as "human art or science") or *epistēmē* (usually translated as "knowledge," "understanding," or "science"). Socrates had confidence in *technē* because it stressed universal, teachable, and precise explanation. These features offered human control of unforeseen circumstances: universality and explanation order the past, teaching invites future progress, and precision yields accuracy. Both Socrates and Protagoras propose to teach *technē*. At the end of the dialogue, they agree that only a scientific *technē* of the type favored by Socrates can save the lives of human beings.

Plato's *Politeia* (middle period dialogue, 388-368 B.C.E.; *Republic*, 1701) is another opportunity for Plato to examine what is truly worthwhile in a human life; that is, what values will support self-sufficiency. After looking at several alternative lives, Socrates demonstrates that the life of the philosopher is the best human life. Plato finds that "true" pleasures are those chosen in harmony with true beliefs about value or worth, as opposed to those in which agents take part because they falsely believe them to have worth. In other words, only philosophic investigation will give truth. Philosophers alone can judge with the right criteria or from the appropriate standpoint; thus, the philosopher alone will know what values subject people to less risk and supply the most self-sufficiency: These are purity, stability, and truth. Correct beliefs remove the reason for fear. The good person attaches no importance to any external loss that is beyond the control of the rational soul.

Nussbaum questions Plato's limited, and therefore unrealistic, portrayal of human activity. She states that the *Republic* underestimates the complexity of human appetites and aesthetic activity. Plato's theory of values, she says, cannot use an ordinary human viewpoint but instead needs a transcendent viewpoint, from which no pressing human concerns can detract from clear reason.

Another example Nussbaum gives of Plato underestimating the complexity and importance of human activity (in this case, love) is found in the chapter on the *Symposium*. In analyzing Socrates' relationship with Alcibiades, Nussbaum wonders whether *eros* can have any place in a life that is governed by practical reason. Socrates maintains that despite their needy and mortal natures, people can transcend through desire itself to the good. Alcibiades' speech, however, shows the importance that passion has for human beings. Giving up the emotional component of love, Nussbaum says, is too much to ask. The safety from the contingencies of a love relationship sacrifices a quality of life that marks it as human.

Appearances and Human Experience

These defects found in Plato's project are not found in Aristotle's. Plato refuses to rely on human understanding of experience for truth; Aristotle says that the phenomena of human experience are all we have. In defiance of Plato's preference for the perfect god's-eye viewpoint as the only reliable one for finding truth, Aristotle finds truth inside what humans say, see, and believe. Aristotle does not attempt to describe or interpret except in the human context, using human language.

In part 3 of this work, "Aristotle: The Fragility of the Good Human Life," Nussbaum finds in Aristotle's methodology a "rich account of philosophical procedure and philosophical limits." His procedure first describes appearances relevant to the area under study. Next, he sets out any puzzles or dilemmas that arise from conflicting opinions about these appearances and asks for arguments for and against each side. After choosing a position, he analyzes the described phenomena to see if the position taken preserves them as true. Unlike for Plato, theory for Aristotle is integrated with the ways human beings live, act, and see. While discussing the truth of appearances as interpreted by humans, Nussbaum captures Aristotle at his most humorous and persuasive.

> To try to show that nature exists is comical; for it is obvious that there are many such [that is, changing] things. And to show the obvious through the obscure is what someone does who is unable to distinguish what is self-evident from what is not.

Thus, looking for a perspective outside appearances is, according to Nussbaum, both futile (because such a perspective is unavailable to humans) and destructive (because this perspective makes the human perspective seem unworthy). In seeking the good life, Aristotle, unlike Plato, is not looking for an intrinsic good severed from a particular human context. The values that constitute a good human life are plural and incommensurable—that is, one cannot measure freedom against wealth or height against musicianship. Each excellence is defined separately, as something that has its own value.

The human perspective is rich and complex. Although human beings reach out for understanding, as Aristotle says they do in *Metaphysica* (c. 335-323 B.C.E.; *Metaphysics*, 1801), Nussbaum agrees with Aristotle on the dangers of oversimplifying when theorizing. These dangers include hedonism, materialism, and mechanism. In wishing to control circumstances by *technē*, people may become estranged from that which they originally wished to control. People become strangers to some part of their lives.

Euripides' *Hecuba*

The epilogue concerns the tragedy *Hecuba* (*Heklabē*, 425 B.C.E.; English translation, 1782); it is titled "The Betrayal of Convention: A Reading of Euripides' *Hecuba*." Euripides' play concerns a mother's betrayal and loss. Hecuba, the former queen of Troy but now a Greek slave, entrusts her youngest child to the care of a Thracian king, Polymestor, thought to be her friend. After the child is killed by this king, Hecuba finds revenge by killing Polymestor's children and blinding him.

Hecuba is first seen as a strong woman, generous toward the needy and fair and loving toward her children. The deaths of many loved ones do not change her values; however, the murder of Polydorus brings about a reversal in her character. This crime is abhorrent because it is treason committed by a good friend, not the result of war. The crime is made real to Hecuba and the audience because she must see and handle the mangled dead child.

Noble Hecuba changes when she chooses revenge. Her revenge does not depend on any conventions of society; she frees herself from society's restraints. At the end of the play, Hecuba has created an isolated and secure world for herself where justice or piety do not enter. The events of the play show that loss of morality by one person can destroy another person, even a good person. It also can destroy human relatedness and human language.

Throughout her entire book, but particularly in the section discussing *Hecuba*, Nussbaum shows clearly the fragility of human goodness. German philosopher Friedrich Nietzsche had shown revenge as the project of base or deprived people, but Nussbaum claims that even the most noble of humans, when subject to the contingencies of nature or other people's actions, may turn into monsters. *Hecuba* shows that noble characters are, if anything, more open to corrosion than base characters because they have relied on others' goodness. Nussbaum's claim is that Greek literature, on the whole, shows that the fragility of goodness poses risks that cannot be suspended without impoverishment of human life. This view challenges many readers' beliefs about morality and goodness.

Barbara Kramer

Additional Reading

Cohen, Joshua, ed. *For Love of Country: Debating the Limits of Patriotism*. Boston: Beacon Press, 1996. This work juxtaposes Nussbaum's views concerning patriotism and cosmopolitanism with those of sixteen writers who respond to her views. Her call to regard all human beings as fellow citizens and neighbors is answered from various perspectives. Many of the contributors worry about trying to teach children the abstract concept of cosmopolitanism, which they cannot possibly experience. Some writers suggest that some terms, such as "patriotism" and "cosmopolitanism," are either unclear, not possible to define, or not opposites; they call for refinements in terms. This book is an excellent resource for readers searching for clear argumentation on this provocative topic.

Frum, David. "Teaching the Young." *Public Interest*, no. 131 (Spring, 1998): 105-109. Analyzes *Cultivating Humanity* and demonstrates that it reflects proof of a crisis in higher education. Frum notes and approves of the politicization of university curricula.

Hall, Ronald L. *The Human Embrace: The Love of Philosophy and the Philosophy of Love: Kierkegaard, Cavell, Nussbaum*. University Park: Pennsylvania State University Press, 1999. A comparative study of Søren Kierkegaard, Stanley Cavell, and Nussbaum.

McInerny, Daniel. "'Divinity Must Live Within Itself': Nussbaum and Aquinas on Transcending the Human." *International Philosophical Quarterly* 37, no. 1 (March, 1997): 65-82. Nussbaum fails in her attempt to defend transcendence as internal to human beings because she cannot justify a way of ordering the virtues in the absence of an extrinsic moral principle. According to McInerny, she does not appreciate the inherent relationships among virtues.

Melville, Stephen. "Just Between Us." *Philosophy Today* 36, no. 4 (Winter, 1992): 367-376. Notes that the works of Jean-François Lyotard and Nussbaum are concerned with relations between ethics and aesthetics, though Lyotard is a humanist and Nussbaum an antihumanist.

Pappas, Nickolas. "Fancy Justice: Martha Nussbaum on the Political Value of the Novel." *Pacific Philosophical Quarterly* 78, no. 3 (September, 1997): 278-296. Argues that Nussbaum's *Poetic Justice* attempts to show the political value of the novel as potentially promoting the development of sympathetic imagination. Pappas suggests that Nussbaum's attempt fails because she does not connect theoretical and practical imagination.

Barbara Kramer

Michael Oakeshott

Oakeshott was a philosopher of skeptical and conservative disposition, a student of the history of political thought, especially known for his work on Thomas Hobbes and on the idea of history. He expounded a distinctive theory of the rule of law, of civil government, and of the concept of authority.

Principal philosophical works: *Experience and Its Modes*, 1933; *The Social and Political Doctrines of Contemporary Europe*, 1942; *Rationalism in Politics, and Other Essays*, 1962, rev. ed. 1991; *Hobbes on Civil Association*, 1975; *On Human Contact*, 1975; *On History and Other Essays*, 1983; *The Voice of Liberal Learning*, 1989; *Morality and Politics in Modern Europe: The Harvard Lectures*, 1993; *Religion, Politics, and the Moral Life*, 1993; *The Politics of Faith and the Politics of Scepticism*, 1996.

Born: December 11, 1901; Chelsfield, Kent, England

Died: December 19, 1990; Acton, near Langton Matravers, Dorset, England

Early Life

Michael Joseph Oakeshott was educated at St. George's School, Harpenden, a coeducational school preferred by his parents to the typical schooling for bright English boys of his day. He loved the school and especially the headmaster, the Reverend Cecil Grant, with whom he maintained a close friendship until Grant's death in the 1960's. He entered Gonville and Caius College at Cambridge in 1920 as a history scholar. However, he was also intensely interested in philosophy, theology, the history of Christianity, and ultimately the history of political thought, the subject on which he later lectured regularly in Cambridge. He enjoyed friendships at Cambridge that reflected the influence of modernism in religious studies, and he wrote a number of compelling essays on how to think about religion in his early career. Some of these may now be found in *Religion, Politics, and the Moral Life*.

Oakeshott was taken by the idealist tradition in philosophy. His first major published statement within this tradition is *Experience and Its Modes*. In this work, he acknowledged as particularly important to his thought Georg Wilhelm Friedrich Hegel and F. H. Bradley. His numerous essays on history and the work of the historian, a subject of great interest to him throughout his career, show the influence of Bradley's work on this topic. The importance of Hegel must be traced more indirectly, for Oakeshott typically did not expound the work of those who interested him; rather, he adapted their thought to his own, recasting it in his own idiom. However, the notebooks he kept, beginning in his undergraduate days at Cambridge, show that he did detailed exegeses of major works of Plato, Aristotle, and Baruch Spinoza.

In the 1920's, Oakeshott spent some time in Germany at Marburg and Tübingen. He was interested in the work of the German theologians of the time, but it is not clear to what extent, if any, Martin Heidegger was of significance to him. In later writing, in his rare references to Heidegger, Oakeshott explicitly rejects what he understood to be Heidegger's view that the practical life is the basis of all the forms of knowing, and he had no sympathy for the quest for "authenticity." In fact, Oakeshott seems to have taken much more from the English essayists, especially David Hume and John Stuart Mill, and from French writers Michel Eyquem de Montaigne and Blaise Pascal in particular, whose style of writing he far preferred. Oakeshott thought of himself as an essayist, not a writer of books.

Life's Work

Oakeshott started his lifelong fellowship in Caius College in 1925. He began research and teaching, eventually becoming a university lecturer in history in 1933. It was during the 1930's that Oakeshott initiated his celebrated lectures in the history of political thought. His interests cut across historiography, philosophy, and political thought. The major work he produced at this time, _Experience and Its Modes_, contains an essay on history that R. G. Collingwood later was to praise as the high-water mark of English thought on history. There followed essays on legal philosophy and the book _The Social and Political Doctrines of Contemporary Europe_, which surveyed the current doctrines in Europe, providing readings with his commentary. In 1936, he published with his colleague Guy Griffiths _A Guide to the Classics or How to Pick a Derby Winner_, a serious book on horse racing, one of his passions at that time. Oakeshott served in the British army from 1940 to 1945 and then returned to Cambridge. He became editor of the _Cambridge Journal_ in which he published some of his most famous essays, later reprinted in _Rationalism in Politics, and Other Essays_. In 1946, he published his noted edition of Hobbes's _Leviathan_ (1651) in the Blackwell's Political Texts series, with an introduction that quickly became famous in Hobbes studies.

In 1949, Oakeshott moved from Cambridge to a research fellowship at Nuffield College, Oxford. However, he stayed there only briefly. In 1950, he was offered the chair of political science, recently vacated by Harold Laski, at the London School of Economics, and in 1951 he delivered his inaugural lecture, "Political Education," which became the subject of wide discussion and debate because its skepticism about the pretensions of political life were so markedly different from the views of his activist predecessor, Laski, and from the prevailing academic sentiments in political studies. The move to the London School of Economics meant resuming a substantial teaching load and also the administrative duties as head of the government department at the school. He continued in this post for fifteen years, building a large and notable department with many distinguished scholars. In 1964, he began a new master's degree program in the history of political thought, one of numerous one-year master's degree programs developed at the University of London at that time to substitute for the traditional two-year research degree. He continued to teach until his official retirement in 1969 and to participate in the history of political thought program he had founded until the 1980's.

In 1958, Oakeshott was a visiting professor at Harvard, where he gave a series of lectures published as _Morality and Politics of Modern Europe: The Harvard Lectures_. He published _The Voice of Poetry in the Conversation of Mankind_ (really a long essay) in 1959 and, in 1962, _Rationalism in Politics, and Other Essays_, a collection of essays previously published between 1947 and 1962. _Hobbes on Civil Association_ brought together his most important essays on Hobbes, including a significantly rewritten version of his celebrated introduction to the _Leviathan_ from 1946. _On History and Other Essays_ included three essays on history that are the final distillations of the papers he read in the history of political thought program at the London School of Economics. In 1991, a new and expanded edition of _Rationalism in Politics, and Other Essays_ was published, including all the essays from the 1962 edition and some additional ones, either out of print or never before printed. This was the last publication of his work in which he was involved before his death. In 1989, a volume of his essays on education was published, _The Voice of Liberal Learning_.

Influence

Oakeshott exerted a profound influence on debates in contemporary political philosophy, especially in the Anglo-American world. Since the 1960's, as the intellectual climate became more receptive to thinkers of a "conservative disposition," Oakeshott was more and more widely read and studied. However, his conservatism is not typical of what is understood by that term among political activists, for it presents no program and does not lend itself easily to practical, political activities. As a skeptic, Oakeshott did not easily identify with any political program, even though he had his preferences. His followers were typically students of politics who sought in detachment to understand what was going on in the political life and who typically sought the meaning of life apart from political engagement. Those most interested in his work were often not conservatives, but critics of the Enlightenment and Rationalist tradition who often espoused a liberal politics that Oakeshott would not have found congenial. As an essayist, Oakeshott is in the tradition running from Sir Francis Bacon to David Hume to John Stuart Mill and is the rightful twentieth century heir to that tradition of British writing. In this respect, his work on poetic experience has commanded attention. As a philosopher of education, Oakeshott remains a staunch defender of the idea of a university as a special place of learning set aside for the pursuit of learning for its own sake, where vocationalism and professionalism are secondary.

Timothy Fuller

On Human Conduct

Type of philosophy: Ethics, social philosophy
First published: 1975
Principal ideas advanced:

◇ A theory of "conduct" is not an analysis of "behavior" that reduces human action to explanation in terms of processes or causality.

◇ Conduct refers to the understanding of human beings as reflective, intelligent beings who choose to do one thing rather than another according to their understanding of the possibilities for them to achieve satisfaction.

◇ Human beings, as human, are individuals, "in themselves what they are for themselves," but they also must take into account that they act in the context of other individuals.

◇ Human beings thus associate themselves with one another according to chosen procedures and evolved practices, especially the rule of law, that specify moral restraints on how they set about to satisfy themselves.

◇ Their principal association, civil association, is association not in terms of a common end or goal that is the same for all, but in terms of agreed-upon conditions for constraining the manner in which they conduct themselves in one another's presence, finding a way to live together even if there are fundamental differences in terms of substantive wants.

◇ There is an alternative to civil association called "enterprise association," in which individuals understand themselves to be associated in terms of a substantive end held in common and see themselves as role players in a joint undertaking to which their individual wants and satisfactions are subordinate.

◇ The alternatives of civil association and enterprise association compete for determining how best to understand how we should be associated with one another; neither alternative has been able to defeat the other.

Michael Oakeshott thought of himself as an essayist, not a writer of books. Save for *Experience and Its Modes* (1933), his publications reflected this. Readers of *On Human Conduct* noted, however, that there is a systematic quality to that work that is somewhat at odds with Oakeshott's division of the book into what he thought of as three essays. This work appears in some respects to return to the form of *Experience and Its Modes*.

For many students of Oakeshott's work, *Rationalism in Politics, and Other Essays* (1962) is his most important and revealing achievement. It is the most reminiscent of Michel Eyquem de Montaigne. In this work, Oakeshott collected a number of essays in more or less chronological fashion with no introduction to guide the reader as to his intentions, claiming not to be arguing with others but rather to be disclosing his considered opinions, and asking that they be taken as invitations to a conversation. Taken together, these essays show Oakeshott at his most skeptical. They are conservative in the peculiar sense Oakeshott gave to the idea of being conservative: He rejects nostalgia and programmatic conservatism (for him an oxymoron), and he does not call for a social foundation in religion. What he does do is disclose his distrust of rationalism and ideology, his skepticism about the dominance over modern thinking of abstract ethical principles and technological preoccupations with progress in the Baconian sense, and his distaste for the increasing vocationalism and professionalism of the universities.

What he argues for is no program but rather the enjoyment of one's present possibilities. He encourages looking for meaning elsewhere than in politics—which he called a "necessary evil"—

and especially in pursuing the poetic intimations of life. Conversationality and poetry are the antidotes for the urge to politicize and systematize everything. However, with *On Human Conduct*, it becomes clear that Oakeshott, while not repudiating at all what he said in *Rationalism in Politics, and Other Essays*, was not satisfied that he had said all he meant to say. *On Human Conduct* is the most constructive work of political theory Oakeshott produced. There is no doubt he intended this to be the lens through which his readers should understand what he had previously said. His portrait at Caius College shows him seated at a table with a copy of *On Human Conduct* before him. In the preface, Oakeshott describes the book as "a well-considered intellectual adventure recollected in tranquillity," and he means to give a final, well-structured account of politics philosophically and historically understood.

Underlying Assumptions

The book contains three essays arranged in a manner recalling the structure of Thomas Hobbes's *De Cive* (1642, rev. ed. 1647; *Philosophical Rudiments Concerning Government and Society*, 1651) and *Leviathan* (1651). The first essay, "On the Theoretical Understanding of Human Conduct," sets out the assumptions underlying a theory of human conduct as opposed to a scientific or sociological explanation of human "behavior," reminiscent in form of Hobbes's account "of man" and of "the natural condition of mankind" in book 1 of *Leviathan*.

The assumptions are that human beings are free agents, capable of conditional transactions (transactions carried on according to certain background constraints such as learned practices and procedures) among themselves in the pursuit of satisfying their wants through deliberation, persuasion, and argument. These individuals conduct themselves not according to "human nature" or a form of "social being" but as reflective intelligences responding to their circumstances as they understand, or misunderstand, them. Oakeshott dismisses the idea that as humans we have a nature that is somehow independent of what we understand ourselves to be. We are "in ourselves what we are for ourselves." Every account of "human nature" involves deliberation and choice as to how we think about our-

selves, and thus every doctrine of human nature discloses a chosen self-understanding about which argument is always possible. We are associated as individuals among individuals, but there is no "society" that is an independent reality comprising us. Oakeshott demonstrates that we are radically individual and free in that we are beings who must interminably reflect, interpret, and choose one course of action as opposed to another in the context of others doing the same.

The Civil Association

In the second essay, "On the Civil Condition," Oakeshott explains what he understands to be the appropriate civil condition for beings of the sort examined in the first essay. His argument is that there is a set of arrangements particularly suited to free, individual agents who must live and act in regard to each other. In such a civil association, we are related to each other in terms of moral conditions that constrain our instrumental relationships, requiring civil law, the adjudication of disputes, a certain kind of authority, and obligation. "The conditions of civil association are moral conditions in not being instrumental to the satisfaction of substantive wants." Procedure takes precedence over outcomes in our interactions. The characteristic virtue is "civility," and this is understood to be an alternative to "rivalry" on the one hand or "tender concern" on the other.

Civil association requires establishing a proper distance among ourselves, neither too distant nor too close. There is no objective measure for striking this balance. It is to be understood as the implicit ideal of the inhabitants of the modern state (as opposed to those of the ancient city). The balance struck must always be struck again and adjusted as we respond to altered circumstances. In attending to the rules and procedures, someone must exercise authority. However, the exercise of authority is not the exercise of superior insight; it is, rather, the making of determinations to go one way rather than another by those whom we have acknowledged to be entrusted with this responsibility. The pronouncements of those in authority are to be followed because they proceed from those we have acknowledged to exercise authority, not because we are happy or unhappy with the implications for our substantive wants.

The civil association in and of itself has no special purpose or direction, no final end. Its purpose is to keep our ship afloat on a boundless and bottomless sea. Special purposes, directions, or ends are for individuals and their like-minded associates to pursue for themselves. A set of people associated amid the vast variety of their wants, interests, and aspirations as a civil association do not need to agree on their final ends. Insofar as existence in the civil order is coercive and unavoidable, it is of the highest importance to maintain the priority of procedural agreement over any suppositious agreement on ends, goals, or final purposes for the entire association. The law gives us "adverbial conditions" to which we subscribe. In other words, we must choose how to conduct ourselves for ourselves, but we do so in consideration of the agreed-upon background conditions that qualify how we choose what we shall do or not do. For instance, we shall not light fires "arsonically." Law does not strictly speaking tell us what to do, but it tells us what to take into account in doing what we do. Law and authority are thus complementary to our free agency, not a contradiction to it.

The Modern State

In the third essay, "On the Character of a Modern European State," Oakeshott gives us his account of the emergence from the medieval orders, over the past five centuries, of the modern European state, the place where the understanding of individual agency and civil association has reached its highest pitch as the animating spirit of the modern age. At the same time, Oakeshott detects an alternative understanding, also emergent after the medieval period, that contradicts the idea of civil association as he has set it out. The first he calls *societas* and the alternative he calls *universitas*. The latter involves association in terms of substantive satisfactions or outcomes, and would have us associated as contributors to an enterprise in which all the participants have roles to play in a division of labor pointing to a common final end. Here it is the role one plays rather than one's free agency to be "for oneself" that takes precedence. Corresponding to these alternatives, we find a difference between those who respond

to their individual freedom as a welcome opportunity, and those who respond to it as somehow a mistake from which they wish to rescue themselves in some collective identity or by fulfilling the quest for community. The ambiguity of the modern achievement appears in full force here. The fact that neither of these enjoys universal assent is salient.

These alternative ideals emergent in modern history constitute a dialectical tension that explains the characteristic terrain of modern political controversy. One cannot finally slay the other. Rather, the assertion of the one produces a heightened response from the other. The state as a formal apparatus cannot settle this conflict because it cannot treat these as alternative purposes or goals that it might adopt. The state must deal with the complexities arising from the conceptual and historical disputes that are the legacy of modern European history and the complex characters of modern human beings who have become used to understanding themselves in these terms. Oakeshott's conclusion is that of the historian and philosopher seeking to understand rather than to rule. He has sought to clarify for us what he finds to have been going on, but he does not offer to transport us to a simpler existence.

Timothy Fuller

Additional Reading

Coats, W. J. *The Activity of Politics and Related Essays.* Selinsgrove, Pa.: Susquehanna University Press, 1989. Coats is a Michael Oakeshott specialist and a student of modern political philosophy. In this volume, he provides several acute essays on Oakeshott's understanding of politics.

Farr, Anthony. *Sartre's Radicalism and Oakeshott's Conservatism: The Duplicity of Freedom.* New York: St. Martin's Press, 1998. Farr examines the opposing political philosophies of Sarte and Oakeshott. A section is devoted to the metaphysics influence on Oakeshott.

Franco, Paul. *The Political Philosophy of Michael Oakeshott.* New Haven, Conn.: Yale University Press, 1990. Provides the best exposition of Oakeshott's work as it was known up to the time of his death. He covers virtually all Oakeshott's major writing and places Oakeshott in the context of modern liberal thought.

Letwin, Shirley Robin. "On Conservative Individualism." In *Conservative Essays*, edited by Maurice Cowling. London: Cassell, 1978. Letwin was among the most powerful interpreters of Oakeshott's thought.

Norman, Jesse, ed. *The Achievement of Michael Oakeshott*. London: Duckworth, 1993. A collection of memorials on Oakeshott's life and work by people who knew him well and who cover a wide range of his ideas. Contains the most comprehensive bibliography of works by and about Oakeshott, compiled by John Liddington.

Political Science Reviewer 21 (1992). This special edition of the journal, edited by Timothy Fuller, is devoted to Oakeshott and contains essays by a number of students of his work.

Timothy Fuller